THE

WAR OF THE REBELLION:

A COMPILATION OF THE

OFFICIAL RECORDS

OF THE

UNION AND CONFEDERATE ARMIES.

E-70

PREPARED BY

The late Lieut. Col. **ROBERT N. SCOTT**, Third U. S. Artillery.

PUBLISHED UNDER THE DIRECTION OF

The Hon. **REDFIELD PROCTOR**, Secretary of War,

BY

Maj. GEORGE B. DAVIS, U. S. A.,
Mr. LESLIE J. PERRY,
Mr. JOSEPH W. KIRKLEY,

Board of Publication.

SERIES I—VOLUME XXXI—IN THREE PARTS.

PART I—REPORTS.

WASHINGTON:
GOVERNMENT PRINTING OFFICE.
1890.

PREFACE.

By an act approved June 23, 1874, Congress made an appropriation "to enable the Secretary of War to begin the publication of the Official Records of the War of the Rebellion, both of the Union and Confederate Armies," and directed him "to have copied for the Public Printer all reports, letters, telegrams, and general orders not heretofore copied or printed, and properly arranged in chronological order."

Appropriations for continuing such preparation have been made from time to time, and the act approved June 16, 1880, has provided "for the printing and binding, under direction of the Secretary of War, of 10,000 copies of a compilation of the Official Records (Union and Confederate) of the War of the Rebellion, so far as the same may be ready for publication, during the fiscal year"; and that "of said number 7,000 copies shall be for the use of the House of Representatives, 2,000 copies for the use of the Senate, and 1,000 copies for the use of the Executive Departments."*

---

*Volumes I to V distributed under act approved June 16, 1880. The act approved August 7, 1882, provides that—

"The volumes of the Official Records of the War of the Rebellion shall be distributed as follows: One thousand copies to the Executive Departments, as now provided by law. One thousand copies for distribution by the Secretary of War among officers of the Army and contributors to the work. Eight thousand three hundred copies shall be sent by the Secretary of War to such libraries, organizations, and individuals as may be designated by the Senators, Representatives, and Delegates of the Forty-seventh Congress. Each Senator shall designate not exceeding twenty-six, and each Representative and Delegate not exceeding twenty-one of such addresses, and the volumes shall be sent thereto from time to time as they are published, until the publication is completed. Senators, Representatives, and Delegates shall inform the Secretary of War in each case how many volumes of those heretofore published they have forwarded to such addresses. The remaining copies of the eleven thousand to be published, and all sets that may not be ordered to be distributed as provided herein, shall be sold by the Secretary of War for cost of publication with ten per cent. added thereto, and the proceeds of such sale shall be covered into the Treasury. If two or more sets of said volumes are ordered to the same address the Secretary of War shall inform the Senators, Representatives, or Delegates, who have designated the same, who thereupon may designate other libraries, organizations, or individuals. The Secretary of War shall report to the first session of the Forty-eighth Congress what volumes of the series heretofore published have not been furnished to such libraries, organizations, and individuals. He shall also inform distributees at whose instance the volumes are sent."

PREFACE.

This compilation will be the first general publication of the military records of the war, and will embrace all official documents that can be obtained by the compiler, and that appear to be of any historical value.

The publication will present the records in the following order of arrangement:

The **1st Series** will embrace the formal reports, both Union and Confederate, of the first seizures of United States property in the Southern States, and of all military operations in the field, with the correspondence, orders, and returns relating specially thereto, and, as proposed, is to be accompanied by an Atlas.

In this series the reports will be arranged according to the campaigns and several theaters of operations (in the chronological order of the events), and the Union reports of any event will, as a rule, be immediately followed by the Confederate accounts. The correspondence, &c., not embraced in the "reports" proper will follow (first Union and next Confederate) in chronological order.

The **2d Series** will contain the correspondence, orders, reports, and returns, Union and Confederate, relating to prisoners of war, and (so far as the military authorities were concerned) to State or political prisoners.

The **3d Series** will contain the correspondence, orders, reports, and returns of the Union authorities (embracing their correspondence with the Confederate officials) not relating specially to the subjects of the *first* and *second* series. It will set forth the annual and special reports of the Secretary of War, of the General-in-Chief, and of the chiefs of the several staff corps and departments; the calls for troops, and the correspondence between the national and the several State authorities.

The **4th Series** will exhibit the correspondence, orders, reports, and returns of the Confederate authorities, similar to that indicated for the Union officials, as of the *third* series, but excluding the correspondence between the Union and Confederate authorities given in that series.

ROBERT N. SCOTT,
Major Third Art., and Bvt. Lieut. Col.

WAR DEPARTMENT, *August 23,* 1880.

Approved:

ALEX. RAMSEY,
Secretary of War.

CONTENTS.

CHAPTER XLIII.

(v)

CONTENTS OF PRECEDING VOLUMES.

VOLUME I.

VOLUME II.

VOLUME III.

VOLUME IV.

VOLUME V.

VOLUME VI.

VOLUME VII.

VOLUME XXIII—IN TWO PARTS.

CHAPTER XXXV.

Operations in Kentucky, Middle and East Tennessee, North Alabama, and Southwest Virginia. January 21–August 10, 1863.

VOLUME XXIV—IN THREE PARTS.

CHAPTER XXXVI.

Operations in Mississippi and West Tennessee, including those in Arkansas and Louisiana connected with the Siege of Vicksburg. January 20–August 10, 1863.

VOLUME XXV—IN TWO PARTS.

CHAPTER XXXVII.

Operations in Northern Virginia, West Virginia, Maryland, and Pennsylvania. January 26–June 3, 1863.

VOLUME XXVI—IN TWO PARTS.

CHAPTER XXXVIII.

Operations in West Florida, Southern Alabama, Southern Mississippi, Louisiana, Texas, and New Mexico. May 14–December 31, 1863.

VOLUME XXVII—IN THREE PARTS.

CHAPTER XXXIX.

Operations in North Carolina, Virginia, West Virginia, Maryland, Pennsylvania, and Department of the East. June 3–August 3, 1863.

VOLUME XXVIII—IN TWO PARTS.

CHAPTER XL.

Operations on the coasts of South Carolina and Georgia, and in Middle and East Florida. June 12–December 31, 1863.

VOLUME XXIX—IN TWO PARTS.

CHAPTER XLI.

Operations in North Carolina, Virginia, West Virginia, Maryland, and Pennsylvania. August 4–December 31, 1863.

VOLUME XXX—IN FOUR PARTS.

CHAPTER XLII.

Operations in Kentucky, Southwest Virginia, Tennessee, Mississippi, North Alabama, and North Georgia. August 11–October 19, 1863.

1863.

	Sunday.	Monday.	Tuesday.	Wednesday.	Thursday.	Friday.	Saturday.		Sunday.	Monday.	Tuesday.	Wednesday.	Thursday.	Friday.	Saturday.
Jan...					1	2	3	July ...				1	2	3	4
	4	5	6	7	8	9	10		5	6	7	8	9	10	11
	11	12	13	14	15	16	17		12	13	14	15	16	17	18
	18	19	20	21	22	23	24		19	20	21	22	23	24	25
	25	26	27	28	29	30	31		26	27	28	29	30	31	....
								Aug ...							1
Feb...	1	2	3	4	5	6	7		2	3	4	5	6	7	8
	8	9	10	11	12	13	14		9	10	11	12	13	14	15
	15	16	17	18	19	20	21		16	17	18	19	20	21	22
	22	23	24	25	26	27	28		23	24	25	26	27	28	29
									30	31					
Mar ..	1	2	3	4	5	6	7	Sept ...			1	2	3	4	5
	8	9	10	11	12	13	14		6	7	8	9	10	11	12
	15	16	17	18	19	20	21		13	14	15	16	17	18	19
	22	23	24	25	26	27	28		20	21	22	23	24	25	26
	29	30	31						27	28	29	30			
Apr ..				1	2	3	4	Oct ...				1	2	3
	5	6	7	8	9	10	11		4	5	6	7	8	9	10
	12	13	14	15	16	17	18		11	12	13	14	15	16	17
	19	20	21	22	23	24	25		18	19	20	21	22	23	24
	26	27	28	29	30				25	26	27	28	29	30	31
May ..						1	2								
	3	4	5	6	7	8	9	Nov ..	1	2	3	4	5	6	7
	10	11	12	13	14	15	16		8	9	10	11	12	13	14
	17	18	19	20	21	22	23		15	16	17	18	19	20	21
	24	25	26	27	28	29	30		22	23	24	25	26	27	28
	31								29	30					
June..		1	2	3	4	5	6	Dec ..			1	2	3	4	5
	7	8	9	10	11	12	13		6	7	8	9	10	11	12
	14	15	16	17	18	19	20		13	14	15	16	17	18	19
	21	22	23	24	25	26	27		20	21	22	23	24	25	26
	28	29	30						27	28	29	30	31		

CHAPTER XLIII.

OPERATIONS IN KENTUCKY, SOUTHWEST VIRGINIA TENNESSEE, MISSISSIPPI, NORTH ALABAMA, AND NORTH GEORGIA.

October 20–December 31, 1863.

PART I.*

SUMMARY OF THE PRINCIPAL EVENTS.†

Oct.   20, 1863.—Maj. Gen. George H. Thomas, U. S. Army, supersedes Maj. Gen. William S. Rosecrans in command of the Army of the Cumberland.

Action at Philadelphia, Tenn.

Reconnaissance from Bridgeport toward Trenton, Ala.

Skirmish at Treadwell's Plantation, Miss.

Skirmish at Warm Springs, N. C.

20–29, 1863.—Operations on the Memphis and Charleston Railroad.

21, 1863.—Skirmish at Sulphur Springs, Tenn.

22, 1863.—Skirmish at New Madrid Bend, Tenn.

Skirmish at Brownsville, Miss.

Destruction of the steamer Mist on the Mississippi River.

Skirmish near Volney, Ky.

22–24, 1863.—Scout from Germantown, Tenn., to Chulahoma, Miss.

23, 1863.—Lieut. Gen. Leonidas Polk, C. S. Army, transferred from the Army of Tennessee to the Army of Mississippi, *vice* Lieut. Gen. William J. Hardee, reassigned to the Army of Tennessee.

Skirmish at Sweet Water, Tenn.

24, 1863.—Maj. Gen. William T. Sherman, U. S. Army, assumes command of the Army of the Tennessee, *vice* Maj. Gen. Ulysses S. Grant, commanding the Military Division of the Mississippi.

24–25, 1863.—Skirmishes at Tuscumbia, Ala.

24–Nov. 10, 1863.—Expedition from Goodrich's Landing, La., to Griffin's Landing and Catfish Point, Miss.

25–26, 1863.—Skirmishes at Philadelphia, Tenn.

26, 1863.—Skirmish at Jones' Hill, Tenn.

Skirmish at Warm Springs, N. C.

Skirmish at Vincent's Cross-Roads, near Bay Springs, Miss.

---

*Embraces the Union and Confederate reports of all operations October 20–December 31, 1863 (excepting the Chattanooga-Ringgold Campaign, November 23–27), and the Union Correspondence, etc., October 20–31, 1863.

†Of some of the minor conflicts noted in this Summary, no circumstantial reports are on file. All such are designated in the Index.

(1)

Oct. 26–27, 1863.—Skirmishes at and near Sweet Water, Tenn.

26–29, 1863.—Reopening of the Tennessee River, including skirmish (27th) at Brown's Ferry and engagement (28th and 29th) at Wauhatchie, Tenn.

27, 1863.—Skirmish in Cherokee County, N. C.

Skirmish at Clinch Mountain, Tenn.

Scout from Columbia toward Pulaski, Tenn., and skirmish.

28, 1863.—Maj. Gen. John M. Palmer, U. S. Army, assumes command of the Fourteenth Army Corps.

Skirmish at Clarksville, Tenn.

Skirmish at Leiper's Ferry, Tenn.

29, 1863.—Maj. Gen. Frank P. Blair, jr., U. S. Army, assumes command of the Fifteenth Army Corps.

Skirmish at Centreville, Tenn.

29–Nov. 2, 1863.—Scout from Winchester to Fayetteville, Tenn.

30, 1863.—Skirmish at Salyersville, Ky.

Skirmish at Leiper's Ferry, Holston River, Tenn.

31, 1863.—Skirmish at Barton's Station, Ala.

Skirmish at Yazoo City, Miss.

Nov. 1, 1863.—Skirmish at Fayetteville, Tenn.

Skirmish at Eastport, Tenn.

Skirmish at Quinn and Jackson's Mill, Miss.

Scout from Bovina Station to Baldwin's Ferry, Miss.

2, 1863.—Skirmish at Corinth, Miss.

Skirmish at Centreville, Tenn.

Skirmish at Piney Factory, Tenn.

3, 1863.—Skirmish at Lawrenceburg, Tenn.

3– 5, 1863.—Operations on the Memphis and Charleston Railroad.

4, 1863.—Skirmish at Maysville, Ala.

Skirmish at Motley's Ford, Little Tennessee River, Tenn.

4–Dec. 23, 1863.—The Knoxville (Tennessee) Campaign.

5, 1863.—Skirmish in Loudon County, Tenn.

Skirmish at Holly Springs, Miss.

6, 1863.—Action near Rogersville, Tenn.

8, 1863.—Maj. Gen. John C. Breckinridge, C. S. Army, supersedes Lieut. Gen. Daniel H. Hill in command of the Second Corps, Army of Tennessee.

10–13, 1863.—Expedition from Skipwith's Landing to Tallulah Court-House, Miss.

11, 1863.—Skirmish near Natchez, Miss.

12, 1863.—Skirmish near Cumberland Gap, Tenn.

Skirmish at Corinth, Miss.

13, 1863.—Skirmish at Blythe's Ferry, Tennessee River, Tenn.

Skirmish at Palmyra, Tenn.

14, 1863.—Brig. Gen. Nathan B. Forrest, C. S. Army, assigned to command of West Tennessee.

14–15, 1863.—Skirmishes at Danville, Miss.

14–17, 1863.—Expedition from Maysville to Whitesburg and Decatur, Ala.

15, 1863.—Skirmish at Pillowville, Tenn.

18, 1863.—Skirmish at Trenton, Ga.

18–22, 1863.—Expedition from Skipwith's Landing to Roebuck Lake, Miss.

19, 1863.—Skirmish at Meriwether's Ferry, near Union City, Tenn.

Nov.   19, 1863.—Skirmish at Mulberry Gap, Tenn.
              Skirmish at Colwell's Ford, Tenn.
              Scout from Memphis, Tenn., to Hernando, Miss.
     20, 1863.—Skirmish at Sparta, Tenn.
     21, 1863.—Expedition from Island No. 10 to Tiptonville, **Tenn.**
21–22, 1863.—Scout from Fort Pillow, Tenn.
     22, 1863.—Skirmish at Camp Davies, Miss.
              Skirmish at Fayette, Miss.
              Skirmish at Winchester, Tenn.
23–27, 1863.—The Chattanooga-Ringgold Campaign.*
24, 26, 1863.—Skirmishes at and near Sparta, Tenn.
     25, 1863.—Skirmish near Yankeetown, Tenn.
     26, 1863.—Scout from Columbia, Ky., to the south side of the Cumberland
              River.
     27, 1863.—Skirmish at Monticello, Ky.
              Skirmish at La Fayette, Ky.
28–Dec. 10, 1863.—Operations against the Memphis and Charleston Rail-
              road, in West Tennessee.
     29, 1863.—Skirmish near Jonesville, Va.
     —, 1863.—Skirmishes on the Cumberland River, Ky.
     30, 1863.—Skirmish at Salyersville, Ky.
              Skirmish at Yankeetown, Tenn.
30–Dec. 3, 1863.—Scouts to New Madrid Bend, Tenn.
Dec.   1, 1863.—Skirmish at Salyersville, Ky.
              Skirmish near Jonesville, Va.
              Scouts from Pulaski, Tenn., and skirmishes.
 1–10, 1863.—Operations about Natchez, Miss., and skirmish (7th).
              Affairs at Mount Sterling and Jackson, Ky.
     2, 1863.—Lieut. Gen. William J. Hardee, C. S. Army, supersedes General
              Braxton Bragg in command of the Army of Tennessee.
              Skirmish at Philadelphia, Tenn.
     3, 1863.—Skirmish at Greenville, Ky.
     5, 1863.—Skirmish at Crab Gap, Tenn.
              Reconnaissance from Rossville to Ringgold, Ga.
 5–10, 1863.—Scouts from Columbia, Ky.
     6, 1863.—Affair near Fayetteville, Tenn.
     7, 1863.—Skirmish at Eagleville, Tenn.
              Skirmish at Independence, Miss.
     8, 1863.—Skirmish near Scottsville, Ky.
     9, 1863.—Maj. Gen. John G. Foster, U. S. Army, supersedes Maj. Gen.
              Ambrose E. Burnside in command of the Department of the
              Ohio.
              Affair at Cumberland Mountain, on road to Crossville, Tenn.
              Skirmish at Okolona, Miss.
    10, 1863.—Scout from Memphis, Tenn.
    11, 1863.—Maj. Gen. John A. Logan, U. S. Army, supersedes Maj. Gen.
              Frank P. Blair, jr., in command of the Fifteenth Army Corps.
11–17, 1863.—Scout from Pulaski, Tenn., to Florence, Ala., and skirmish (12th)
              on Shoal Creek, near Wayland Springs, Tenn.
    12, 1863.—Skirmish at La Fayette, Ga.
    13, 1863.—Skirmish at La Grange, Tenn.
              Skirmish at Ringgold, Ga.

---

* For reports, field dispatches, etc., see Part II.

Dec.   13, 1863.—Skirmish at Powell's River, near Stickleyville, Va.
        14, 1863.—Capture of Union wagon train, near Clinch Mountain Gap, Tenn.
                Reconnaissance from Rossville to La Fayette, Ga.
        15, 1863.—Maj. Gen. Thomas C. Hindman, C. S. Army, supersedes Maj.
                Gen. John C. Breckinridge in command of the Second Corps,
                Army of Tennessee.
                Skirmish near Livingston, Tenn.
                Affair near Pulaski, Tenn.
        16, 1863.—General Joseph E. Johnston, C. S. Army, assigned to command
                of the Department of Tennessee, leaving Lieut. Gen. Leonidas
                Polk in command of the Army of Mississippi.
        17, 1863.—Skirmish at Rodney, Miss.
     18–31, 1863.—Operations in Northern Mississippi and West Tennessee.
        21, 1863.—Brig. Gen. Jacob D. Cox, U. S. Army, supersedes Brig. Gen.
                Mahlon D. Manson in command of the Twenty-third Army
                Corps.
                Skirmish at McMinnville, Tenn.
     21–23, 1863.—Scout from Rossville to La Fayette, Ga.
        22, 1863.—Lieut. Gen. Leonidas Polk, C. S. Army, assigned to command
                of the Department of Mississippi and East Louisiana (tempo-
                rarily in command of the Department of Tennessee).
                Skirmish at Cleveland, Tenn.
                Skirmish at Fayette, Miss.
        23, 1863.—Lieut. Gen. Leonidas Polk, C. S. Army, assumes command of
                the " Department of the Southwest" (Mississippi and East
                Louisiana).
                Skirmish near Corinth, Miss.
                Skirmish at Mulberry Village, Tenn.
                Reconnaissance from Blain's Cross-Roads to Powder Spring Gap,
                Tenn.
        24, 1863.—Skirmish in Lee County, Va.
                Skirmish at Rodney, Miss.
     24–28, 1863.—Operations near Mossy Creek and Dandridge, Tenn.
        26, 1863.—Skirmish at Sand Mountain, Ala.
                Skirmish at Port Gibson, Miss.
        27, 1863.—General Joseph E. Johnston, C. S. Army, assumes command of
                the Department of Tennessee.
                Skirmish at Huntingdon, Tenn.
        28, 1863.—Action at Calhoun and skirmish at Charleston, Tenn.
     28, 1863–Jan. 4, 1864.—Expedition from Nashville, Tenn., to Creelsbor-
                ough, Ky.
        29, 1863.—Action at Mossy Creek, Tenn.
                Skirmish at Talbott's Station, Tenn.
                Skirmish at Cleveland, Tenn.
                Skirmish at La Vergne, Tenn.
     29–30, 1863.—Scout to Bean's Station, Tenn.

OCTOBER 20, 1863.—Action at Philadelphia, Tenn.

REPORTS.

No. 1.—Maj. Gen. Ambrose E. Burnside, U. S. Army, commanding Department of the Ohio.

No. 2.—Brig. Gen. Julius White, U. S. Army, commanding Second Division, Twenty-third Army Corps.

No. 3.—Col. Frank Wolford, First Kentucky Cavalry, commanding Cavalry Brigade.

No. 4.—General Braxton Bragg, C. S. Army, commanding Army of Tennessee, with congratulatory orders.

No. 5.—Maj. Gen. Carter L. Stevenson, C. S. Army, commanding division, including skirmishes at and near Sweet Water, October 23, 26, and 27, and at Leiper's Ferry, October 28.

No. 6.—Col. George G. Dibrell, Eighth Tennessee Cavalry (Confederate), commanding Cavalry Brigade, including skirmishes at Sweet Water, October 23 and 26.

No. 7.—Col. J. J. Morrison, First Georgia Cavalry, commanding Cavalry Brigade.

No. 1.

Report of Maj. Gen. Ambrose E. Burnside, U. S. Army, commanding Department of the Ohio.

KNOXVILLE, TENN.,
October 23, 1863—9 a. m.

GENERAL : On the 20th instant, Colonel Wolford's cavalry brigade, at Philadelphia, was surprised by enemy's cavalry and driven back to Loudon, with a loss of six mountain howitzers and a considerable number of men. Colonel Wolford reports his loss at 100. The enemy has been driven back again beyond Philadelphia, and are said to be concentrating at Sweet Water a heavy force of infantry, cavalry, and artillery. The reports of the number of the enemy are indefinite, except as to the presence there of Stevenson's division of infantry and of some 3,000 or 4,000 cavalry. I have re-enforced the garrison of Loudon, and shall leave for there at once; from there I will endeavor to telegraph you more definitely. We have had a good deal of rain. Trains late, and I fear much of our supplies will be very badly delayed by high water and bad roads. It is reported from several sources that a considerable force, under Joe Johnston, has left Bragg's army.

A. E. BURNSIDE,
Major-General.

Major-General GRANT.

No. 2.

Reports of Brig. Gen. Julius White, U. S. Army, commanding Second Division, Twenty-third Army Corps.

LOUDON, *October 20, 1863.*

GENERAL : The skirmishing continued till dark, the infantry I sent out holding him in check. Lieutenant-Colonel Adams, of Colonel Wolford's command, brought in 50 prisoners. About 100 in all have been brought in.   My fighting will be done to-morrow, if any occurs, within the range of the cannon in our defenses.

I shall be able to use Wolford's men to-morrow.   They were a good deal confused and scattered to-day.

The enemy are reported within easy artillery range.

I shall take measures to know their position within the next three or four hours.

Colonel Wolford says he thinks there are about 200 prisoners.

Prisoners say Wheeler's cavalry are moving to our rear, on the north side of the river.   There is no other authority for statement.

Major Delfosse, of the Twelfth Kentucky Cavalry, is reported killed.

JULIUS WHITE,
General.

General BURNSIDE.

—

LOUDON, *October* 21, 1863.

We have driven the enemy through Philadelphia; they [the enemy] had destroyed his [Wolford's] camp equipage and furniture, and the wagons they captured.   It does not appear that many lives were lost yesterday.   We have lost none to-day.

Have captured a number of prisoners.   No report yet from the left flank.

JULIUS WHITE,
Brigadier-General.

General BURNSIDE.

———

No. 3.

Reports of Col. Frank Wolford, First Kentucky Cavalry, commanding Cavalry Brigade.

LOUDON, *October* 20, 1863.

About 10 o'clock this morning I got information that about 1,200 or 1,500 rebels had attacked my wagon train, 6 miles from camp. I sent Colonel Adams with the First and Eleventh Kentucky, who got into the rear of the enemy and were cut off by some 3,000 rebels.

I soon afterward got information that a large body of the rebels were coming up from Sweet Water.   I then mustered up the rest of my men, amounting to about 700, and attacked them and drove them back several times.   After driving them they re-enforced, and came upon us from every side.   Our artillery fired their last round. I rallied my men and charged through, saving most of my men and several of my prisoners.

We had several men killed and wounded, and several taken prisoners.   I am confident we killed more of them, and took more prisoners, than they did of us.   We have lost some of our wagons and baggage, and some of our artillery—perhaps all of it.   The enemy are in large force, both infantry and artillery, with several heavy pieces of the latter.

WOLFORD,
Colonel.

General BURNSIDE.

LOUDON, *October* 20, 1863.

The artillery officer, when I last saw him, reported to me that [we] had fired our last round. I ordered him to follow me, and if he could not bring in his pieces to abandon them. I do not think the guns will get in. Most of the cannoneers are killed, I think. The artillery officers are here, and will report in a few minutes.

About 50 of the prisoners have just come in; there will be more in soon. I am pretty sure we have from 300 to 400 of them prisoners.

WOLFORD,
Colonel.

General BURNSIDE.

ADDENDA.

Return of Casualties in the Union forces engaged at Philadelphia, Tenn., October 20, 1863.

[Compiled from nominal list of casualties, returns, &c.]

Command.	Killed.		Wounded.		Captured or missing.		Aggregate.
	Officers.	Enlisted men.	Officers.	Enlisted men.	Officers.	Enlisted men.	
1st Kentucky Cavalry............					3	124	127
11th Kentucky Cavalry...........		1		3	1	88	93
12th Kentucky Cavalry...........	1	1		13		97	112
45th Ohio (mounted) Infantry.....		4	1	8	3	131	147
Total	1	6	1	24	7	440	479

Officers killed or mortally wounded.—Maj. Julius N. Delfosse, Twelfth Kentucky Cavalry; Capt. Comfort E. Stanley, Forty-fifth Ohio (mounted) Infantry.

No. 4.

Report of General Braxton Bragg, C. S. Army, commanding Army of Tennessee, with congratulatory orders.

CHICKAMAUGA,
October 21, 1863.

The following dispatches received from Major-General Stevenson:

CHARLESTON, TENN.,
October 20, [1863.]

The cavalry under Morrison and Dibrell attacked the enemy's cavalry in force at Philadelphia to-day, capturing about 400 prisoners, their artillery, small-arms, camp equipage, &c. Our loss nothing. They are in pursuit of the enemy, who are completely routed.

CHARLESTON, TENN.,
October 21, [1863.]

The enemy were pursued to their defenses at Loudon. Arrived there after dark. The force there not known. Their loss is 700 prisoners, 50 wagons loaded with stores, 10 ambulances, 6 pieces of artillery, a lot of horses, mules, and other property.

BRAXTON BRAGG.

General S. COOPER.

GENERAL ORDERS, }   HEADQUARTERS ARMY OF TENNESSEE,
      No. 193.   }   *Missionary Ridge, October 22, 1863.*

I. The general commanding announces to the army with pride and satisfaction two brilliant exploits of our cavalry :

*   *   *   *   *   *   *

II. On the 20th instant, the cavalry under Colonels Dibrell and Morrison attacked the enemy in force at Philadelphia and captured 700 prisoners, 50 wagons loaded with stores, 6 pieces of artillery, 10 ambulances, and a lot of mules, horses, and other property. The enemy was driven to his defenses at Loudon, and is reported as completely routed. Too much praise cannot be given Colonels Dibrell and Morrison and the brave command under them for the dash and daring displayed in the expedition so completely successful. Such blows dealt the enemy in quick succession are no less honorable to our army than indicative of future success.

By command of General Bragg:

GEORGE WM. BRENT,
Adjutant-General.

No. 5.

Report of Maj. Gen. Carter L. Stevenson, C. S. Army, commanding division, including skirmishes at and near Sweet Water, October 23, 26, and 27, and at Leiper's Ferry, October 28.

HEADQUARTERS STEVENSON'S DIVISION,
Near Tyner's Station, November 12, 1863.

COLONEL : Agreeably to orders received from army headquarters on the 17th ultimo, I proceeded to Charleston, Tenn., arriving there with a portion of my command about 2 p. m. on the 19th ultimo. The failure of the railroad officials to carry out the arrangements and obey the orders relative to the transportation of the troops, and the delay caused thereby, have been made the subject of a special communication to the commanding general.

Immediately upon my arrival at Charleston I gave the following directions to Colonels Morrison and Dibrell, commanding brigades of cavalry :

Colonel Morrison with his whole effective force, re-enforced by Colonel McKenzie's and Major Jessee's commands, will move so as to reach the rear of Philadelphia by daylight to-morrow morning and be prepared to co-operate with Colonel Dibrell, who, with his effective command, will advance so as to attack the enemy, supposed to be at that point, at daylight. Should the enemy not be found at Philadelphia the commands will seek and capture, or drive him across the Tennessee. Having routed the cavalry they will move on Loudon, and should the force of the enemy's infantry there be small, will attack and carry that place. In that event Loudon will be held by a sufficient force, and suitable scouts be sent up the river for information with regard to the enemy in that direction. Colonel Morrison will send a select force of 150 men, in command of a suitable officer, to destroy the ferry at Kingston. He will also detail from his command two companies to picket the river on our left flank.

The movement directed was at once commenced, but owing to the difficulty in crossing the Hiwassee at the ford by which Colonel Morrison moved, the attack was not made until as late as 1 p. m. on the 20th ultimo. For a time the resistance was stubborn, the enemy making a gallant fight, but finally they broke and fled in the greatest confusion to their defenses at Loudon. The fact that they had there a fortified position, with an infantry support, the approach of darkness, and the exhaustion of our cavalry after their long march and severe fight, decided Colonels Morrison and Dibrell not to make an immediate attack upon Loudon.

Our loss amounted to 15 killed, 82 wounded, and 3 missing. That of the enemy was greater in killed and wounded, and by capture about 700 prisoners, 6 pieces of artillery, and all their wagons, ambulances, and camp equipage.

On the next morning the enemy advanced in force (infantry and cavalry) from Loudon, and Colonels Morrison and Dibrell withdrew their commands to Sweet Water, there to await the arrival of the infantry. The enemy fell back to Loudon that night.

I reached the front on the morning of the 22d ; moved the infantry to Mouse Creek that day, and soon afterward to Sweet Water.

On the evening of October 23, the enemy advanced in considerable force and engaged the cavalry for a short time, retiring at dusk. Their loss is not known ; ours was 5 wounded.

The same movement was again made by them on the evening of October 26.

In this affair our loss was 3 wounded and 5 missing. The enemy are known to have had 3 commissioned officers and several privates killed, and a number wounded.

On October 27, I was informed that the notorious bushwhacker and robber, Bryson, had been sent with his command by Burnside to get in my rear and obtain information as to our movements and intentions. I immediately gave Brigadier-General Vaughn a detachment of about 100 men, and directed him to intercept, and, if possible, destroy the party. He succeeded in dispersing them, killing several, and taking among the prisoners a captain. During the pursuit Bryson himself was killed.

On October 27, Cheatham's division, commanded during the expedition by Brigadier-General Jackson, reached Athens, and by this accession my force, before so weak as to be entirely inadequate for a decided movement against the enemy at Loudon, was strengthened to such an extent as would have enabled me to actively assume the offensive, but the enemy, informed doubtless by disloyal citizens of the arrival of these re-enforcements, evacuated Loudon on the night of the same day.

On October 28, I sent Brigadier-General Vaughn, with a force of cavalry, across the Little Tennessee River at Morganton, with orders to make a demonstration upon Knoxville, and gain all the information he could of the enemy's force, movements, and intentions. He found a force at Leiper's Ferry, attacked, and drove them across the river, after quite a sharp engagement, inflicting considerable loss upon them. He also went to Lenoir's Ferry. The sudden and heavy rain that fell at this time raised the Little Tennessee so rapidly that it became exceedingly hazardous for him to remain on that side, and he accordingly returned to Morganton.

On November 3, Colonel Dibrell crossed the Little Tennessee with about 700 men, but found the enemy in too great force in his front to permit him to make any decided move. The results of these scouts in eliciting information were promptly communicated to you by telegraph.

On November 4, I received orders by telegraph to send two of the brigades of Cheatham's division to Tyner's by railroad on the 5th, and the remaining two on the 6th, and immediately thereafter to send the two brigades of my own division.

On the 8th instant, I received orders from the commanding general to leave Brigadier-General Cumming to bring on my division, and report in person at army headquarters as soon as possible after the arrival of Lieutenant-General Longstreet at Sweet Water. He reached that point on the night of the 9th, and, as directed, I left Sweet Water on the morning of the 10th, arriving at Tyner's upon the same day.

I am, colonel, respectfully, your obedient servant,

C. L. STEVENSON,
Major-General, Commanding.

Col. GEORGE WILLIAM BRENT,
Assistant Adjutant-General, Army of Tennessee.

No. 6.

Reports of Col. George G. Dibrell, Eighth Tennessee Cavalry (Confederate), commanding Cavalry Brigade, including skirmishes at Sweet Water, October 23 and 26.

HEADQUARTERS SECOND CAVALRY BRIGADE,
Philadelphia, October 20, 1863—5 p. m.

DEAR SIR: The colonel commanding instructs me to say that he engaged the enemy in front of this place at 1 o'clock to-day.

After a sharp artillery duel of an hour or more the guns of Colonel Morrison's brigade were heard in the enemy's rear.

Colonel Dibrell immediately charged into the town. The enemy was completely routed. We captured all his wagons, ambulances, tents, and cooking utensils, all his artillery, about 400 prisoners, and at least that number of small-arms.

The colonel cannot speak too highly of the conduct of his officers and men. The rout is not yet over; prisoners, horses, and mules are hourly coming in. Our loss nothing.

By order of Col. G. G. Dibrell, commanding Second Cavalry Brigade:

DIXON A. ALLISON,
Acting Assistant Adjutant-General.

Major-General STEVENSON.

HEADQUARTERS SECOND CAVALRY BRIGADE,
Philadelphia, October 20, 1863—8 p. m.

DEAR SIR: Our forces pursued the enemy to within sight of their camps at Loudon, when darkness ended the pursuit. It is thought they have their infantry in rifle-pits. Our victory is much more complete and decisive than was thought when you were first dispatched.

The enemy's loss in killed and wounded was considerable, and the number of prisoners will not fall short of 700. We captured 50 wagons loaded with stores, 10 ambulances, 6 pieces of artillery, a large lot of commissary stores and beef cattle, together with a large lot of horses and mules. Colonel Wolford, who was in command here, told the gentleman with whom he boarded this morning that General Burnside, with his whole army, left Knoxville on yesterday for Loudon. The story is not credited. We are lying in line of battle to-night, and expect to advance early to-morrow. Prisoners, stock, &c., have been sent forward toward Charleston. It is confidently hoped you will move up your forces immediately.

By order of Col. G. G. Dibrell, commanding Second Cavalry Brigade :

DIXON A. ALLISON,
Acting Assistant Adjutant-General.

Major-General STEVENSON,
    Charleston.

HEADQUARTERS SECOND CAVALRY BRIGADE,
2½ Miles from Sweet Water, October 21, 1863—2 p. m.

The colonel commanding directs me to say the enemy is advancing on us with infantry and cavalry. Their cavalry is threatening our left and rear. We have a strong position here, and can hold it unless flanked. Colonel Morrison is protecting our left. We skirmished with them before retiring from Philadelphia, and sent one regiment toward their rear, near up to Loudon, which we suppose has checked the advance of their infantry, as it has not developed itself in our front here. All the captured property has already been sent forward. Two regiments are still holding Philadelphia, with instructions to fall back here if hard pressed.

By order of Col. G. G. Dibrell, commanding brigade :

DIXON A. ALLISON,
Acting Assistant Adjutant-General.

General STEVENSON.

HEADQUARTERS SECOND CAVALRY BRIGADE,
2½ Miles from Philadelphia, October 21, 1863—6 p. m.

The enemy failing to advance upon us this side of Philadelphia, I ordered forward our skirmishers, who drove them back through the town. Our advance vedettes stand just out this side of Philadelphia. I think their main force has fallen back to Loudon. In the Federal mail captured yesterday one letter states that there was a division of infantry at Loudon to fall back on when pressed too hard. Another, dated yesterday, that Burnside was advancing with his whole force to Loudon ; that it was impossible for them to subsist in East Tennessee unless they held the line of the railroad through this end of the State. Our best information is, there were only three regiments of Federal infantry out from Loudon to-day. We this evening forwarded to your commissary about 75 head fine Kentucky captured beef cattle. If possible, we will be obliged if a few can be reserved for us. I have just heard from Colonel Morrison that he is encamped to-night to my rear, between this and Sweet Water. All the roads are well picketed.

By order of Col. G. G. Dibrell, commanding brigade :

DIXON A. ALLISON,
Acting Assistant Adjutant-General.

Major-General STEVENSON.

Hdqrs. Second Cavalry Brigade, Armstrong's Div.,
Sunday, October 27, 1863.

Sir: According to previous orders received, I moved with my brigade and a detachment of General Morgan's command from Charleston on the 19th at 12 m.; crossed the Hiwassee River and traveled all night. By an agreement with Colonel Morrison, commanding brigade, I was to be in front of Philadelphia by 12 m. of the 20th. He was to cross the Hiwassee below me, and move to the rear of the enemy. Subsequently, Colonel M[orrison] notified me that he could not be at the appointed place before 2 p. m.

Meantime, I advanced my forces, drove in the enemy's pickets, kept up a skirmish at a respectable distance, keeping all of my command out of sight of the enemy except two regiments and one section of artillery until Colonel Morrison could get in position. As soon as this was known, I moved rapidly forward and opened upon the enemy with my artillery, and charged them with cavalry held in readiness for that purpose, completely routing the enemy and scattering them through the woods in every direction, capturing in all six pieces of artillery, all their wagons, ambulances, stores, &c., and a large number of horses, equipments, &c., 500 to 600 prisoners.

In this engagement I only claim for my brigade that they did their part most admirably, and are entitled to the reputation they had previously so richly merited, and I fully accord to Colonel Morrison's brigade an equal share of all the glories won for the gallant part acted by them in the engagements. Without their co-operation so brilliant a success would have proven a failure, as the enemy were but a few miles from a large infantry force to support them. My loss, 1 man killed and 3 captured. A few horses wounded.

Brigadier-General Vaughn had kindly volunteered his services, which were invaluable to me, and his gallantry and daring charge upon the enemy has endeared him to my brigade and caused them all to regard him as one of the bravest of the brave.

In the engagement of the 23d my loss was 5 wounded. The loss of the enemy not known.

In the engagement of yesterday my loss was 3 wounded and 5 missing; 2 horses wounded. The enemy left some 12 or 15 dead and wounded horses upon the field, and are known to have had 3 commissioned officers and several privates killed and a number wounded.

The conduct of the men and officers, both cavalry and artillery, was very fine during all the engagements.

I am, major, very respectfully, your obedient servant,

G. G. DIBRELL,
Colonel, Commanding Brigade.

Maj. J. J. Reeve, *Assistant Adjutant-General.*

No. 7.

Reports of Col. J. J. Morrison, First Georgia Cavalry, commanding Cavalry Brigade.

Headquarters Second Cavalry Brigade,
Lenoir's House, Philadelphia, October 20, 1863.

General: I have the honor to state that, agreeably to your instructions, I succeeded in getting between Loudon and Philadelphia, after making a march of 50 miles in fifteen hours. Found the enemy

(Colonel Wolford's brigade) in line of battle. Sent one regiment to Loudon to make a demonstration at that place to prevent Colonel Wolford's force being augmented by the forces at Loudon. I attacked him at once with the remainder of my force, numbering 1,200. After a very severe fight, with twice my number pitted against me, supported by six pieces of artillery, I succeeded in completely routing him, capturing all of his artillery (six pieces), entire wagon train, with many fire-arms and ammunition. Captured 400 prisoners.

My loss will foot up 10 killed, 68 wounded, and 70 missing.

The whole command acted very gallantly. I will report in full at the earliest opportunity.

I am, general, your obedient servant,

J. J. MORRISON,
Colonel, Commanding Second Cavalry Brigade.

P. S.—Colonel Wolford fell back in great confusion upon four regiments of infantry at Loudon. Night prevents me from pursuing him.

—

HEADQUARTERS MORRISON'S BRIGADE,
Ballard's, October 21, 1863.

GENERAL : I have the honor to acknowledge the reception of your dispatch. Have ordered the wagons, artillery, &c., back as directed. I have been skirmishing with the enemy's advance this morning. They have advanced their infantry, about 3,000 strong, this side of Loudon. The last I have heard of them, their cavalry have been trying to execute a flank movement. I think it very probable that we will have to fall back nearly to Sweet Water, where there are fine natural advantages, as it would not be prudent—so Colonel Dibrell, General Vaughn, and myself have concluded—if the enemy advances, to remain here, as he was re-enforced last night by the Ninth Army Corps, of Burnside's command ; so I have learned from a very reliable Southern man from Loudon this morning. I consider the information reliable. I do not think it possible to move them from Loudon without a stronger force than I have. When Mr. Ballard left Loudon the Ninth Corps was on the opposite side, but preparing to come to this side of the river. General White is in command. Loudon is not fortified yet by the enemy. I have thorough scouting parties in the neighborhood of Loudon and will push the enemy as far that way as possible. Will keep you constantly advised of their movements.

I am, colonel, your obedient servant,

J. J. MORRISON,
Commanding Second Cavalry Brigade.

Major-General STEVENSON,
Commanding Expedition, Athens or Charleston.

—

HEADQUARTERS CAVALRY FORCES,
Owen's, near Sweet Water, Tenn., October 27, 1863.

MAJOR : I have the honor to report that, agreeably to instructions from General Stevenson, I succeeded in getting my entire command, numbering about 1,800 men, across Hiwassee River at and above Kencannon's Ferry by 10 o'clock on the night of the 19th instant. I immediately took up the line of march for the rear of **Philadel-**

phia, the distance to the point where I expected to strike the Philadelphia and Loudon road being 50 miles. The weather was very disagreeable and the roads were in very bad condition, rendered worse and worse every hour by the incessant showers that had been falling since I left Harrison. Men and officers bore up astonishingly under the circumstances, having in crossing the river and making the march lost two nights' sleep in succession.

On arriving near Philadelphia, I communicated with Colonel Dibrell, suggesting that he had better move up and make a demonstration in the front, so that I could, without interruption and undiscovered, make the enemy's rear ; and reaching Pond Creek, a point to the left of and opposite Philadelphia, I intercepted and captured a forage train and 40 prisoners. From this point I sent a party on each of the roads leading into town, with instructions to drive in the enemy's pickets and hold their positions if possible, and thus prevent his learning the direction taken by the main part of my command. I finally reached the rear of Philadelphia, after a hard march of 50 miles in fifteen hours, unobserved. I caused the telegraph wire to be cut, and sent as rapidly as possible one regiment to Loudon, a distance of 4 miles, there to make a feint and prevent General White from re-enforcing Wolford at Philadelphia with his infantry from that point. The surprise was complete and the feint on Loudon a success.

I now hastened on to Philadelphia, a distance of 2 miles, and soon had a view of the enemy's line of battle, whereupon I dismounted my men and commenced the attack, Colonel Dibrell having opened an artillery duel in the front some time before. The enemy, on discovering me in their rear, at once turned their whole force, with six pieces of artillery, against my command, which was now reduced to about 1,000 men. Afterward ensued one of the hardest cavalry fights of the war, both sides struggling vigorously for the mastery. I was made to fall back twice, but with little effort each time rallied my men and soon had the enemy completely routed and fleeing in confusion toward Loudon, capturing their artillery (six pieces), wagon train, ambulances, stores, and between 500 and 700 prisoners. A portion of the latter was captured by Colonel Dibrell's command.

The officers and men of my command conducted themselves handsomely from the commencement of the march to the rout of the enemy at Philadelphia, but credit is especially due to Colonel Hart, of the Sixth Georgia ; Colonel Rice, of the Third Confederate, and Colonel Harper, of the First Georgia Cavalry, who lost a leg while leading his men in a gallant charge. Colonels Rice and Hart occupied the left, and nobly did each do his duty. From an intrepid charge on the enemy's rear, his artillery, wagons, and stores, with most of the prisoners, fell into their hands.

Lieut. George Yoe, Capt. Davidson Lamar, and Adjt. John W. Tench, acting on my staff, have my thanks for their assistance, efficiency, and gallantry on the field.

Although the victory was complete, the fruits of it fell short far of what they would have reached if I had had the prompt co-operation of the forces in front.

The casualties in my command are 14 killed, 82 wounded. Those of the enemy much larger.

J. J. MORRISON,
Colonel, Commanding Second Cavalry Brigade.
Maj. J. J. REEVE, *Assistant Adjutant-General.*

OCTOBER 20, 1863.—Skirmish at Warm Springs, N. C.

Report of Brig. Gen. Orlando B. Willcox, U. S. Army.

GREENEVILLE, TENN.,
October 20, 1863.

GENERAL : The rebels made a fresh attack on Warm Springs this morning at daylight, and were repulsed after a skirmish of two hours ; 1 killed and 5 wounded on our side. Adjutant Grace, Second North Carolina Infantry, supposed to be captured.

Last night our men captured a picket of 10 men on the Marshall road. Colonel Smith still calls for arms, and asks for re-enforcements.

The attack was made on Spring Creek road. Do you wish any more troops sent there ?

O. B. WILLCOX,
Brigadier-General.
General BURNSIDE.

OCTOBER 20, 1863.—Reconnaissance from Bridgeport toward Trenton, Ala.

Report of Lieut. Col. Edward S. Salomon, Eighty-second Illinois Infantry.

HDQRS. EIGHTY-SECOND REGT. ILLINOIS VOLUNTEERS,
October 20, 1863.

SIR : Pursuant to orders, I left Long Island at 12 o'clock to-day with 180 men of the Eighty-second Illinois, Forty-fifth New York, One hundred and forty-third New York, on a reconnaissance to ascertain the whereabouts of the enemy. We marched on the Moore Gap road toward Trenton. On the road I obtained the information from several citizens that two brigades rebel cavalry were stationed at Trenton, and that small squads of this cavalry were infesting the mountains.

At the top of the mountain my advance noticed a vedette of the enemy, who, after firing at my men, turned his horse and fled. I deployed some men as skirmishers, throwing them out to the right, left, and front, and captured 1. I then pushed forward as rapidly as the bad mountain road and heavy rain allowed, and after considerable skirmishing along the road we captured 2 more; we were then about 8 miles from Bridgeport and 9 miles from Trenton. After a careful and separate examination of the prisoners and a citizen named Potts, I found that the rest of the rebel cavalry company which had been out there had fallen back on Trenton, and as it was getting dark, and on account of the bad roads and weather it was impossible for me to push on any farther, I considered it best to return to camp, which I did. I also captured 3 horses and the arms of the prisoners.

I am, colonel, very respectfully, your obedient servant,
· EDWARD S. SALOMON,
Lieutenant-Colonel, Comdg. Eighty-second Ill. Vols.

Lieutenant-Colonel MEYSENBURG,
Assistant Adjutant-General.

OCTOBER 20–29, 1863.—Operations on the Memphis and Charleston Railroad.

SUMMARY OF THE PRINCIPAL EVENTS.

Oct. 20, 1863.—Skirmishes at Barton's and Dickson's Stations and Cane Creek, Ala.
    21, 1863.—Action at Cherokee Station, Ala.
    26, 1863.—Skirmishes near Cane Creek and at Barton's Station, Ala.
    27, 1863.—Skirmish at Little Bear Creek, Ala.
    29, 1863.—Skirmish at Cherokee Station, Ala.

REPORTS.

No. 1.—Maj. Gen. William T. Sherman, U. S. Army, commanding Fifteenth Army Corps, of skirmish at Barton's Station, October 20.

No. 2.—Brig. Gen. Peter J. Osterhaus, U. S. Army, commanding First Division, including operations October 20–November 4.

No. 3.—Brig. Gen. Charles R. Woods, U. S. Army, commanding First Brigade, of skirmishes near Cane Creek and at Barton's Station, October 26.

No. 4.—Lieut. Col. David J. Palmer, Twenty-fifth Iowa Infantry, Second Brigade, of action at Cherokee Station.

No. 5.—Col. George A. Stone, Twenty-fifth Iowa Infantry, of skirmishes October 26–27.

No. 6.—Maj. Gen. Stephen D. Lee, C. S. Army, commanding Confederate Cavalry in Mississippi.

No. 1.

Report of Maj. Gen. William T. Sherman, U. S. Army, commanding Fifteenth Army Corps, of skirmish at Barton's Station, October 20.

MEMPHIS, TENN., *October* 21, 1863.
(Received 8.40 p. m., 23d.)

Major-General HALLECK:

General Sherman telegraphs from Bear Creek:

IUKA, *October* 21, 1863.

My advance found Forrest's Cavalry, 400 strong, at Barton's Station, and whipped them handsomely yesterday, killing 2 and taking 9 prisoners. Our loss, 1 killed and 3 wounded slightly—all of the Fifth Ohio Cavalry, which acted most handsomely. The Tennessee River is up 8 feet on the shoals. I must cross over to communicate with Nashville and Chattanooga, and must have a steam ferry-boat. I will keep a regiment at Eastport. Wheeler, 10,000 strong, is near Decatur. I hope he will oppose my advance, but think he will swing up on my flank. My advance is at Cane Creek.

SHERMAN.

I send by this boat dispatch to Porter and Colonel Allen for a ferry-boat to be sent up, and hope it may be hurried forward; otherwise, after crossing, Sherman will be beyond reach of supplies, of which he has now fifteen days' on wagon train.

S. A. HURLBUT,
Major-General.

(Copy to General Grant.)

—————

No. 2.

Reports of Brig. Gen. Peter J. Osterhaus, U. S. Army, commanding First Division, including operations October 20–November 4.

HDQRS. FIRST DIV., FIFTEENTH ARMY CORPS,
Cherokee, Ala., October 20, 1863.

GENERAL : I have the honor to report that my advance to-day found the rebel pickets near Dickson's Station, and drove them for several miles, until they reached the open fields at Barton's Station, where Colonel Forrest's cavalry (about 400 men) had formed. The colonel was in command himself. On this intelligence, I immediately brought all the cavalry and one section horse artillery forward. Before I came up two companies of the Fifth Ohio Cavalry had made a brilliant saber charge, but could not cause the enemy to yield his very strong position.

After the re-enforcements were deployed, the Fifth Ohio advanced gallantly, driving the rebels from every inch of the first and a second position they had fallen back on on the east side of Cane Creek. Posting the artillery, supported by the Third Regulars, on a slight elevation commanding the road, I pushed the Fifth Ohio forward and succeeded in scattering the enemy completely. The cavalry and one section artillery is encamped in the rebel camp. Our loss is, 1 seriously wounded (since dead) and 3 slightly wounded, all of the Fifth Ohio. The names I will send in as soon as possible. Of the enemy, 2 dead, 4 wounded, and 5 prisoners fell into our hands.

The Fifth Ohio Cavalry, under command of Colonel Heath and Major Smith, did gloriously. I am sorry to be unable to give you the name of another officer, who, although shot through the left wrist, remained with the command during all the fight. I will send in the nominal list of casualties to-morrow.

I am, general, with great respect, your obedient servant,

P. JOS. OSTERHAUS,
Brigadier-General of Volunteers.

Maj. Gen. FRANK P. BLAIR, Jr.
Commanding Advance Fifteenth Army Corps.

—

HDQRS. FIRST DIVISION, FIFTEENTH ARMY CORPS,
Cherokee, Ala., October 21, 1863.

MAJOR : In consequence of your orders of last morning not to move forward, I deemed it prudent to withdraw the small force which I left after yesterday's engagement at Cane Creek, in the expectation to close up on them by this morning. I only left two companies of cavalry as picket at the creek. About noon the commanding officer of this picket sent me word that he was hard pressed by a large rebel mounted force. I ordered the division to fall in at once, and advanced a part of Second Brigade and one section of Missouri Horse Artillery to support the retreating picket. When I came up with these troops to the advance infantry picket, I met the retiring cavalry and the rebel mounted infantry hard on them. I ordered Col. J. A. Williamson, commanding Second Brigade, to deploy one battalion of infantry on each side of the main road and then advance; the remainder of Second Brigade was to follow in supporting distance.

The First Brigade, General Woods commanding, and batteries were placed so that they could be thrown forward on either flank. The two leading regiments of the Second Brigade advanced steadily and forced the rebels to fall back into an open field on the east side of the timber. I then brought the whole of the Second Brigade up; while I ordered them to deploy, the enemy made an impetuous charge, and for a short time succeeded in occupying the skirt of the timber again. Colonel Torrence, of the Thirtieth Iowa Infantry, was killed there at the head of the regiment.

This advantage lasted but a very short time, when the brave men of the Second Brigade drove them back across the open field I mentioned above.

Forced back in front, the enemy pushed his cavalry forward around my left, but the Twenty-ninth and Thirty-first Missouri Infantry, and a part of the Twelfth Missouri Infantry, of First Brigade, was soon brought into position and in readiness to repulse any attempt of the enemy. I now advanced the Fifth Ohio Cavalry and Third Regulars on the right, and a section of First Missouri Horse Artillery took position abreast of Second Brigade on the east skirt of the timber. The artillery dislodged, by very good practice, the enemy, who had formed again out of range of the artillery, and occupied several plantation houses, about 500 yards in my front. Seeing the effect of this section, the second section of First Missouri Horse Artillery was ordered forward and caused the rebels to yield their position again. The movement of the cavalry on the right and the advance of the whole line of infantry caused the enemy to abandon his attempts on my left. They withdrew rather promptly out of the [range of the] artillery and infantry and the flanking maneuver of the cavalry. Following them up by advancing both my lines of infantry and the artillery, preceded by the cavalry, I drove the rebels for about 5 miles, when night set in and I withdrew my command, leaving only very strong pickets on the ground we had taken from the enemy.

Only the Second Brigade, under Colonel Williamson, Landgraeber's battery, and the Fifth Ohio Cavalry, and Third U. S. Cavalry, participated in the fight, and they all did their whole duty.

The casualties are, since yesterday's report, 8 killed and 24 wounded. Some prisoners were made, and I learn that the enemy had quite a number of casualties.

The force attacking us was several thousand strong, mostly infantry and cavalry.

I inclose nominal list* of killed and wounded, as far as ascertained to-night.

I am, very respectfully, your obedient servant,

P. JOS. OSTERHAUS,
Brigadier-General of Volunteers.

Maj. W. D. GREEN,
Assistant Adjutant-General.

[Inclosure.]

List of killed and wounded in action at Cherokee, Ala., October 21, 1863.

Killed :
Officers.. 1
Non-commissioned officers.......................... 1
Enlisted men 5
                                                                   ——
    Total.. 7
                                                                   ══

Wounded :
Officers.. 7
Non-commissioned officers........................... 9
Enlisted men 12
                                                                   ——
    Total.. 28
                                                                   ══

    Total killed and wounded 35
                                                                   ——

* Omitted.

Many of the wounds are of very severe character; four capital operations of the lower extremities have already been performed.

M. W. ROBBINS,
Surg. Fourth Iowa Inf., Surg. in Chf., First Div., 15th A. C.

—

HDQRS. FIRST DIVISION, FIFTEENTH ARMY CORPS,
Bridgeport, Ala., December 15, 1863.

MAJOR : I have the honor to report on the operations of my division consequent on your order (received in camp, Cherokee Station, Ala.) to push the enemy's forces then in my front toward and into Tuscumbia, without, however, going beyond that place.

Before entering on the narrative, however, I beg leave to refer the general to my reports on previous engagements with the enemy on October 20 and 21, copies of which I now inclose.* The very signal repulse of the enemy's attack on our position at Cherokee, October 21 (see inclosure marked B), made him extremely careful, and all the information we could receive showed that he was receiving considerable re-enforcements, and occupied a very strong position on both sides of Cane Creek.

In compliance with your orders we left camp in the lightest possible marching order at 3 a. m., October 26, and arrived at the cemetery near Barton's Station (Memphis and Charleston Railroad) at 4.30 a. m.

The rebel pickets stationed there fled very hastily on our approach and gave the alarm in their camp.

As it was too dark to push my advance forward and endeavor to intercept them, I awaited daybreak, and then deployed the First Brigade (Brigadier-General Woods commanding) behind a slight elevation in the ground to the right and left of the graveyard mentioned above, and placed the First Missouri Horse Artillery (Captain Landgraeber) in the cemetery itself. The cavalry—Fifth Ohio, and Third Regulars—were formed on both wings of the First Brigade, while the Second Brigade (Col. J. A. Williamson commanding) was kept in reserve in column near Barton's Station.

The distance between my front line and the enemy's position was from 800 to 1,000 yards. (The cavalry engagement, reported on the inclosure marked A, was fought on the same ground.) The enemy's position was on a pretty steep ridge and well masked by timber, while my troops occupied the open fields, which extended, almost prairie-like, all the way from Cherokee Station to the hills in possession of the enemy. A "wet weather" branch of Cane Creek flows at the foot of the hills. The first rays of the rising sun gave us some light as to the enemy's forces.

He opened on us with artillery (rifle pieces) planted on the hill in my immediate front, and deployed a large column of cavalry on my right. The skirmishers of the First Brigade engaged those of the rebels in front and exchanged a brisk fire, while I dispatched Colonel Heath to the right with part of the Fifth Ohio Cavalry and two battalions of infantry of First Brigade. My instructions to the former were not only to check the advance of the enemy on that flank, but to attempt to gain his flank in turn ; to the latter, to support the movements of the cavalry.

---

*See pp. 16, 17.

The heavier metal of the enemy's artillery, against which the 12-pounder howitzers of Landgraeber's battery at about 1,000 yards were inadequate, caused me to order one section of 20-pounder Parrotts, of Fourth Ohio Battery, to relieve Landgraeber's pieces.

Under cover of the Parrotts, the whole line of General Woods was ordered to advance; I also brought forward the Second Brigade, and deployed it on the left of First Brigade.

The extreme left flank was guarded by the Third U. S. Cavalry. General M. L. Smith's division had, in the meantime, come up to Barton's Station, and acted as reserve. Landgraeber's battery followed the advancing infantry, and was brought into action on the right, exposing, with the Parrotts in the center, the enemy's artillery to a cross fire. The skirmishers on the right (Third and Twelfth Missouri) advanced gallantly over the undulations of the ground, and the Fifth Ohio Cavalry pressed the rebels back into the timber, bringing them under the fire of my artillery. The rebels, both artillery and cavalry, yielded after a weak resistance, and hastily retired to Cane Creek. Cane Creek is a pretty deep stream. A muddy, swampy bottom skirted the same on our side, while the opposite bank, which was occupied by the rebels, rises gently, and offered a splendid field for maneuvering his large cavalry forces. Our infantry pushed forward as fast as the very bad, rough, and muddy nature of the ground admitted. Dismounted rebel cavalry held on my right the skirt of timber along Cane Creek. Five of their pieces (mostly rifled) opened on my infantry as soon as it debouched, but their defense was by no means equal to the impetuous advance of my infantry, who hardly awaited the arrival of artillery and cavalry, but plunged into and forded Cane Creek, and, delivering a furious fire, made the enemy's artillery limber to the rear, and the dismounted cavalry look for their horses.

They retreated very rapidly, not, however, without showing, as a matter of form, a rear guard of about 200 cavalry, but at a very safe distance. Our cavalry, ordered forward again, drove these observing squads before them, and kept them at a very lively gait, the infantry skirmishers following in almost double-quick time. We came to Little Bear Creek without a halt of any consequence. This creek is only 4 miles from Tuscumbia, and, once in our possession, gave us control of that town. The creek runs in a narrow bed of rock, and the banks are very abrupt and high.

The Tuscumbia road, over which we were marching, crosses the creek and ascends the opposite cliffs through a very narrow gap. The defile thus formed is rendered, in a military point of view, more available by the semicircle formed by Bear Creek, which is bordered on the west bank by an open plateau, thus giving an opportunity to a defender on the eastern bank for a well-secured movement against the flank of any column attempting to cross by the main road.

When I reached this plateau on the west bank of the creek, I saw the enemy's entire force in line of battle on the high prairie on the opposite bank; he opened with his rifled guns at once, and his practice at a distance of at least 2,500 yards was perfect, but he had omitted to avail himself of the ground on my right and thus to threaten my flank. As soon as my infantry came up, I ordered skirmishers to be thrown across the creek on that exposed flank with instructions to guard it against an apprehended attack. My infantry was formed across the plateau and à cheval of the road. The skirmishers thrown across the creek were supported by the Third and Twenty-seventh Missouri Infantry, which regiments occupied the high bank along Little Bear Creek, forming an obtuse angle with the main line, and were covered by a narrow skirt of timber. All these preparations were completed while the enemy continued his artillery practice on my deploying infantry. I had to await the arrival of the Parrotts of the Fourth Ohio Battery (Captain Froehlich) to attend to them. When they arrived they participated in the artillery duel. Landgraeber's howitzers were unlimbered on the right in support of the skirmishers whom I had put across the creek.

The enemy, seeing too late his neglected opportunity on his left (my right), made a most vigorous effort to redeem this fatal mistake; a full brigade of cavalry (commanded, as I learned afterward, by Forrest) was formed, and, advancing against our skirmishers, drove them back to the timber skirting the creek.

Their leader, rendered sanguine by the retreat of the skirmishers, ordered them to charge; I could distinctly hear his command. They approached the creek at a furious gallop, when Lieutenant-Colonel Meumann, commanding Third Missouri Infantry, opened on them, delivering a fire by rank, volley after volley, with admirable regularity, into the gray cloud below. This fire scattered them in every direction.

They lost their leader in this fire, and Landgraeber's battery assisted handsomely in keeping them at a proper distance. It was now too late (5 p. m.) to undertake anything decisive, and, in compliance with Major-General Blair's orders, we bivouacked a little in rear of our position, a strong line of pickets holding the ground we had gained.

On the morning of the 27th of October, I received the general's order to delay my attack until a brigade of the Second Division, which was to cross the creek farther up, in order to get on the enemy's left flank, could co-operate with me; the Third Regular Cavalry was detailed to assist in this flank movement. We consequently took up our position of last night, excepting that the Parrott section of Fourth Ohio Battery (Captain Froehlich) was ordered to the right, with Landgraeber's battery of howitzers, while four 20-pounder Parrotts, of the Second Division, took the position occupied by Captain Froehlich's guns the day previous.

The enemy's line likewise appeared in the same order as yesterday. We, however, soon observed a commotion on their left, and it did not last long until I heard musketry fire in that direction. I immediately ordered my batteries to open and my whole line of infantry to advance. The practice of the Parrotts was brilliant, and the rebel sharpshooters along the creek in front gave way before the fire of my skirmishers. The fire on my right became very brisk and approached very steadily. The enemy, seeing his left flank exposed, repeated his maneuver of Cane Creek, that is, he retreated, pursued vigorously by the Fifth Ohio Cavalry (Colonel Heath), which I had ordered forward. A rebel force seemed inclined to make a stand on the west side of Tuscumbia, and formed in front of some high timber; the Fifth Ohio Cavalry formed and advanced through the open fields on both sides of the Tuscumbia road, supported by one section 6-pounder field pieces of Griffiths' (First Iowa) battery. The rebels, however, disappeared and we pushed on, Tuscumbia being in our possession by 11 o'clock. In all these engagements both officers and men behaved most gallantly. Our losses were very slight;

for the latter I refer to the nominal lists which I forwarded some time ago.

On the 28th of October, we left Tuscumbia for Cherokee, at 6 a. m., in compliance with orders received.

In order to facilitate this movement, I ordered Colonel Heath to advance toward the enemy, which he did, but finding no enemy, he remained in Tuscumbia until noon, when he followed the command.

The rebels, finding out that they were not pursued, turned round and made their appearance again near Cherokee Station, on October 29, exhibiting a very respectable strength, but at great distance. I made my arrangements to receive them, leaving my right on a very steep hill, thickly timbered, and protecting my camp *en échelon*. I was, however, unable to entice the rebels within range, and toward evening they fell back. Next morning we left for Chickasaw Landing (on Tennessee River), where we arrived, after a very tedious march over exceedingly bad roads, on 31st of October. Rebel cavalry followed us very closely, but without molesting us in any way. Colonel Heath's cavalry was sufficient to hold them in check. On the morning of November 4, the First Division (the last of your corps) crossed the Tennessee River.

I am, major, respectfully, your obedient servant,

P. JOS. OSTERHAUS,
Brig. Gen., U. S. Vols., Comdg. First Div., 15th A. C.

Maj. R. M. Sawyer,
Headquarters Fifteenth Army Corps.

No. 3.

Report of Brig. Gen. Charles R. Woods, U. S. Army, command-ing First Brigade, of skirmishes near Cane Creek and at Bar-ton's Station, October 26.

Hdqrs. First Brig., First Div., 15th Army Corps,
Cherokee Station, Ala., October 28, 1863.

Captain : I have the honor to report that at 3 a. m. of the 26th instant, I left camp at this place with my brigade, having the ad-vance of the division, and proceeded in the direction of Tuscumbia, Ala. The brigade is composed of the Twelfth Missouri Infantry, Col. Hugo Wangelin commanding; Thirteenth Illinois Infantry, Col. A. B. Gorgas commanding ; Twenty-seventh Missouri Infan-try, Col. Thomas Curly commanding ; Third Missouri Infantry, Lieut. Col. Theo. Meumann commanding ; Seventy-sixth Ohio In-fantry, Maj. W. Warner commanding ; Thirty-second and Twenty-ninth Missouri Infantry, forming one battalion, Lieut. Col. H. C. Warmoth (Thirty-second Missouri) commanding ; Seventeenth and Thirty-first Missouri Infantry, forming one battalion, Lieut. Col. S. P. Simpson (Thirty-first Missouri) commanding. It was accom-panied by the First Missouri Horse Artillery, Capt. C. Landgraeber commanding, and the Fourth Ohio Battery, Capt. George Froehlich commanding, and was followed by the Second Brigade of this division.

When I reached Barton's Station I found that the cavalry had driven the enemy to a strong position. I deployed two regiments—

the Thirteenth Illinois and Seventy-sixth Ohio—on the left of the railroad and the remainder of my brigade on the right, taking the two battalions, composed each of two regiments, to a position three-quarters of a mile to the right, and posting them in a piece of woods. Having completed these dispositions, and thrown skirmishers well to the front, I ordered the brigade to advance. The Second Brigade, with skirmishers in front, advanced at the same time on my left. The skirmishers moved forward in gallant style, driving the enemy from their position and pushing them back to Cane Creek, a distance of 1 mile. Here they reformed, having five pieces of artillery posted on high ground, with open fields intervening, and skirmishers strongly posted along the creek bottom. After reconnoitering, I pushed my right forward in the edge of the woods. The skirmishers soon reached the creek, and succeeded in crossing. At this point the firing was very heavy, but of short duration. The enemy, abandoning their positions, fell back to the Little Bear Creek, 3 miles from Tuscumbia. They made a stand upon a hill which commanded the valley between us I posted my brigade on the right of the road upon a hill. About the time the first two regiments were posted the enemy's cavalry made a charge across the open field on my right, with the evident intention of getting possession of the hill. They were checked and driven back by a volley from the Third and Twenty-seventh Missouri, by which Colonel Forrest was severely, if not mortally, wounded by a Minie ball through both thighs.

It being late, nothing further was done than to take a position and to hold it until dark. The troops, except three regiments, which were left on picket duty, were then withdrawn into a ravine. On the following morning, the 27th instant, I deployed the Seventeenth Missouri, Col. John F. Cramer commanding, as skirmishers, supported by the Third Missouri on the opposite side of the creek. At the same time the Second Brigade moved up on my left and the Second Division on my right. The movement was successful, and by 12 m. the troops were in Tuscumbia.

I append a list of killed and wounded.

I am, captain, very respectfully, your obedient servant,

CHAS. R. WOODS,
Brigadier-General, Commanding.

Capt. W. A. GORDON,
Asst. Adjt. Gen., First Div., 15th Army Corps.

No. 4.

Report of Lieut. Col. David J. Palmer, Twenty-fifth Iowa Infantry, Second Brigade, of action at Cherokee Station.

HEADQUARTERS TWENTY-FIFTH IOWA INFANTRY,
Cherokee, Ala., October 22, 1863.

CAPTAIN : I have the honor to transmit you the following report of the part taken by my regiment in the engagement of yesterday:

We formed in line of battle at the earliest intimation of the presence of the enemy, and, by order of General Osterhaus, we moved forward in line of battle, our left resting on the road near the open field, at the end of the woods. We engaged the enemy, and briskly returned their fire, holding the position for more than an hour, when we advanced across the fields, still occupying the right, but had no more engagements with the enemy.

The following is a full list of our casualties : John B. Fidlar, second lieutenant, D Company, gunshot wound in left forearm ; Lewis Hill-yard, private, D Company, contusion in left shoulder ; Charles L. Renz, private, E Company, flesh wound in left leg below the knee.

All of which is respectfully submitted.

By order of D. J. Palmer, lieutenant-colonel commanding:

SAM. W. SNOW,
Adjutant.

Capt. GEORGE E. FORD,
    A. A. A. G., Second Brig., First Div., 15th A. C.

No. 5.

Report of Col. George A. Stone, Twenty-fifth Iowa Infantry, of skirmishes October 26-27.

HEADQUARTERS TWENTY-FIFTH IOWA INFANTRY,
Bridgeport, Ala., December 19, 1863.

GENERAL : In consequence of our being constantly on the wing for the past sixty days, I have not been able to report you promptly the part taken by my regiment in the engagements of last month. On Sunday evening, October 25, at Cherokee, our division received marching orders for 4 a. m. next day, and accordingly the division moved at the hour indicated in the direction of Tuscumbia, in light marching order, and in fine fighting condition. The First Brigade, Brig. Gen. C. R. Woods commanding, had the advance; and ours, the Second Brigade, Col. James A. Williamson commanding, the rear. General Osterhaus' orders were very imperative and strict concerning the tactical arrangement of battalions, as the enemy, but some 3 miles in front of us, was composed entirely of cavalry, and equal fully in numerical strength.

About 2 miles from camp we met the enemy's skirmishers, and here formed our line of battle, the First Brigade on the right and the Second on the left, with one of the other divisions of our corps as reserve. My position was on the extreme left, and, in accordance with orders, I formed a square to repel cavalry, first, however, having covered my front properly with skirmishers. Our skirmishers pushed the enemy so vigorously and our lines followed so promptly that after a short resistance he fell back to another position some 4 miles to his rear, and made another stand. The same disposition was again made by our division, the same sharp, short fighting, with the same result—the hasty retreat of the enemy.

We continued this skirmishing during the entire day, and renewed it on the 27th, literally fighting them from Cherokee to Tuscumbia. We entered the town at 3 p. m. on the 27th.

Sergt. Nehemiah M. Redding, of Company D, was killed while skirmishing on the 26th. I have no other casualties to mention.

Officers and men behaved handsomely.

Very respectfully, general, your obedient servant,

GEO. A. STONE,
Colonel, Comdg. Twenty-fifth Iowa Volunteers.

Adjt. Gen. N. B. BAKER,
    Davenport, Iowa.

No. 6.

Reports of Maj. Gen. Stephen D. Lee, C. S. Army, commanding Confederate Cavalry in Mississippi.

HEADQUARTERS CAVALRY IN MISSISSIPPI,
Camp 19 *Miles East of Tuscumbia, October* 20, 1863.

COLONEL : For the information of General Johnston, I have the honor to report that up to the 19th instant General Wheeler declined to cross the Tennessee River with me, not deeming his command in condition to do so and feeling it incumbent on him to await instructions from General Bragg.

On the 17th, the inclosed copy of a communication from General Bragg was received, which indicates orders for a move in conjunction with my command will be sent. The communication was a reply to one from General Wheeler, written before the general was aware of my being near South Florence. No reply has yet been received to my communication to General Bragg, but it is expected at any moment.

I feel it incumbent on me to remain here some days longer till something more is heard from General Bragg, as General Wheeler feels confident the general intends an offensive move. The river is now too high for fording (since 17th), but is falling slowly, though I fear will not fall sufficient for fording for six or eight days, if at all this season.

The enemy are in the vicinity of Huntsville. General Roddey is over the river, and cannot cross to this side. I fear my expedition will be of no avail, as the enemy certainly are aware of the presence of so large a cavalry force in this vicinity by this time. General Wheeler's command was much demoralized by plunder, and officers and men behaved unbecomingly on the trip, thinking more of their plunder than of fighting the enemy. The enemy are certainly repairing the road from Corinth in this direction, and have repaired beyond Iuka. They have made several offensive moves across Bear Creek, but have been repulsed. I hope to report soon having crossed the river on my return to Mississippi.

Forage is scarce in this valley. General Wheeler's command is in the vicinity of Courtland. The last report from Huntsville gives a rumor that Rosecrans is sending troops back to Murfreesborough.

I am, colonel, yours, respectfully,

STEPHEN D. LEE,
Major-General.

Col. B. S. EWELL,
Asst. Adjt. Gen. to General Johnston, Meridian, Miss.

[Inclosure.]

HEADQUARTERS ARMY OF TENNESSEE,
October 14, 1863.

Major-General WHEELER,
Courtland:

GENERAL : In reply to your communication of the 9th, reporting your operations in Middle Tennessee, the general commanding desires me to say that he wishes you will without delay get your command in readiness for active movement in conjunction with Major-General Lee.

In the meantime, you will make inquiry as to the best means of crossing your command at some point between your present position and Bellefonte.   Should the enemy, previous to orders for your movement, lay himself open to attack, strike him at once.   His Excellency President Davis has been here and read your report.   He requested the general commanding to make known to you and your command his satisfaction and appreciation of your services.   Horseshoes can be had at Rome.

I am, general, very respectfully, your obedient servant,
GEORGE WM. BRENT,
Assistant Adjutant-General.

P. S.—The general directs that you order Col. J. E. Forrest, commanding North Alabama, to have the Memphis and Charleston Railroad effectually torn up from the nearest point to the enemy.

Respectfully,
KINLOCH FALCONER,
Assistant Adjutant-General.

—

HEADQUARTERS CAVALRY IN MISSISSIPPI,
Cane Creek, 10 Miles West of Tuscumbia,
October 21, 1863—5 p. m.

SIR : I received this morning your communication of the 17th instant.   On its receipt my command was then in motion to meet the enemy advancing from Big Bear Creek.   The enemy was attacked about 11 a. m. and his cavalry driven back to the vicinity of Cherokee Station, 14 miles from Tuscumbia.   Here we encountered a large cavalry force, which I find to be Osterhaus' and Blair's divisions, of Sherman's corps, which is advancing, repairing the road as they advance.   Sherman's headquarters are at Iuka.   From a prisoner taken I find that Sherman's corps has been increased, and the supposed destination is Chattanooga.   I will check the command as far as is in my power.   Their cavalry force is about two regiments, and they keep close to infantry supports.

I do not consider it prudent to go to Middle Tennessee with my command—at any rate until the cavalry which pursued General Wheeler has returned to its original position.   Scouts now report it in the vicinity of Shelbyville.   I will destroy the railroad as rapidly as possible.   General Roddey is across the river at Rogersville.   I will order his brigade to this side, as otherwise it will soon be cut off.   I do not think the river will be fordable again this season.   I had no time specified to be absent from Mississippi.   Was sent for a specific purpose, viz, to cut the road between Chattanooga and Nashville.   Will remain at least until I hear from General Johnston.

I am, major, yours, respectfully,
STEPHEN D. LEE,
Major-General.

Maj. GEORGE WILLIAM BRENT,
Asst. Adjt. Gen., Army of Tenn., near Chattanooga.

—

HEADQUARTERS CAVALRY IN MISSISSIPPI,
Ten Miles West of Tuscumbia, October 22, 1863.

COLONEL : I have the honor to inclose copies of communications from General Bragg to General Wheeler and myself.

On the night of the 20th, my command was put in motion to repel the enemy at this point. We attacked and drove the enemy to Cherokee Station, 4 miles west of this, where a large infantry force was encountered, and last evening I withdrew to this point. The force of the enemy consists of Osterhaus' division, and another, reported as Blair's, of Sherman's corps. Sherman's headquarters are said to be at Iuka by a prisoner captured. The enemy are gradually advancing, with an infantry force repairing the railroad. Their cavalry consists of about two regiments, and keeps close on their infantry. I do not anticipate a rapid advance of the enemy, as they are now in advance of their work. I am thoroughly destroying the railroad, and will impede their advance as much as possible.

General Roddey is over the Tennessee River. I have ordered him to cross at once, and so soon as he crosses will commence interfering more materially with the enemy's work. I do not consider it prudent at present to attempt to cross the Tennessee, as the cavalry of the enemy is in the vicinity of the railroad, and outnumbers my command. I shall remain in this valley until I hear from the general, and would suggest that General Chalmers be kept active on the Memphis and Charleston Railroad to impede the work of the enemy as much as possible. Have ordered an escort to be in readiness at Okolona to come with some ammunition I need and send for. It may be necessary for the train to come into the valley opposite Courtland, as the route by Russellville I do not consider safe. The enemy are without doubt rebuilding the railroad, and have the cars running to Bear Creek. Their force is nearly altogether infantry.

My loss yesterday was 3 killed and 12 or 15 wounded.

I am, colonel, yours, respectfully,

STEPHEN D. LEE,
Major-General.

Col. B. S. EWELL,
Assistant Adjutant-General, Meridian.

[Inclosure No. 1.]

HEADQUARTERS ARMY OF TENNESSEE,
Missionary Ridge, October 17, 1863.

Maj. Gen. S. D. LEE, *Commanding, &c.:*

GENERAL : The general commanding instructs me to say that he desires you will remain in this department as long as you can consistently with your instructions, and operate against the advancing columns of the enemy, checking and impeding him, breaking his communications, and, if possible, throwing a force north of the Tennessee, and to strike at the enemy's rear. Our cavalry in North Alabama will report to and act under you.

I am, general, very respectfully, your obedient servant,

GEORGE WM. BRENT,
Assistant Adjutant-General.

[Inclosure No. 2.]

HEADQUARTERS ARMY OF TENNESSEE,
Missionary Ridge, October 17, 1863.

Major-General WHEELER,
Commanding Cavalry Corps, Courtland, Ala.:

GENERAL : The general commanding instructs me to say that he wishes you to move with your command in that direction, and that you will receive orders at or near Guntersville. You may be required to cross the Tennessee at that point, and you should, therefore, provide yourself with the means of doing so if it be practicable. You will open communication, if possible, with General Roddey, from whom no report has been received. Major-General Lee has been requested to remain in this department as long as his instructions will permit, and to operate against the advancing columns of the enemy. Be good enough to have the letters for Generals Lee and Roddey delivered.

I am, general, very respectfully, your obedient servant,

GEORGE WM. BRENT,
Assistant Adjutant-General.

—

HEADQUARTERS CAVALRY IN MISSISSIPPI,
Six Miles East of Tuscumbia, October 28, 1863.

SIR: I have the honor to report that the enemy were held in check at Bear Creek, 3 miles west of Tuscumbia, till 9 a. m. yesterday morning, when my position was flanked, and I was compelled to withdraw. The enemy displayed about 6,000 infantry in line of battle. From prisoners captured I learn that Osterhaus' division is in front, Blair's next. The rest of Sherman's corps is still beyond Big Bear Creek. Grant now commands all west of the Alleghanies, Sherman commanding the Department of the Tennessee, Blair commanding Sherman's corps. The enemy have retired from opposite Decatur. I cannot account for the enemy allowing me to destroy so much of the railroad, as they have seen the work and are aware of it. General Ferguson has not been heard from yet. General Roddey returned in time to join me yesterday morning. I sent him in the rear of the enemy again last night. My scouts have captured the medical wagon attached to Osterhaus' headquarters full of valuable supplies. The enemy do not seem disposed to advance to-day. Their pickets are 2½ miles from Tuscumbia. I shall annoy them in every way, and break their communications.

I am, major, yours, respectfully,

STEPHEN D. LEE,
Major-General.

Lieut. Col. GEORGE WILLIAM BRENT,
Asst. Adjt. Gen., Dept. of Tennessee, near Chattanooga.

P. S.—I regret to state that the gallant Colonel Forrest was severely wounded while leading his regiment against the enemy on the 26th. He had to be left in Tuscumbia, as also some 15 or 20 men too severely wounded to be moved.

—

HEADQUARTERS CAVALRY IN MISSISSIPPI,
Tuscumbia, October 28, 1863.

COLONEL: I have the honor to report that yesterday morning, about 9 a. m., I was forced from my position on Little Bear Creek, the enemy attacking with several brigades. I retired to a point 6 miles east of Tuscumbia. Tuscumbia was occupied by the enemy at 12 m. yesterday.

About 1.30 p. m. to-day I discovered the enemy retiring. My command is following closely. Their rear guard left the town about 12 m., my advance arriving at 3 p. m. General Roddey left with 600 men at 3 a. m. this morning for their rear, and is now on their flank, I suppose, about Cherokee Station, 16 miles west of this point. The enemy's force consisted of two divisions, commanded by Osterhaus and Morgan L. Smith, Blair commanding all. They evacuated in consequence of finding the railroad so destroyed. Their intention was to rebuild the road or to cross at this point, but received orders to return last evening. The commanding officer of the provost guard stated to the gentleman at whose house he staid that they were returning to Eastport to take transports, and that the Tennessee and Cumberland were in good boating order—the latter to Nashville. The general impression among them was that they were going to Nashville and to re-enforce Thomas' army at Chattanooga.

The Memphis Bulletin of the 24th states that Grant has been assigned to the command of all departments west of the Alleghany with plenary powers. Thomas takes Rosecrans' place, who is ordered to Cincinnati to report to Washington by letter. It is supposed Grant will go to Chattanooga.

They acknowledge a loss of 100 killed and wounded on the 22d [21st] and put my force at 8,000. General Ferguson has not been heard from yet. I will report further as soon as their movements indicate their intentions clearly.

I regret to report that the gallant Colonel Forrest was severely wounded on the 26th. He had to be left in Tuscumbia and is now paroled.

I am, colonel, yours, respectfully,

STEPHEN D. LEE,
Major-General.

Lieut. Col. GEORGE WILLIAM BRENT,
Asst. Adjt. Gen.. Army of Tennessee, near Chattanooga.

—

HEADQUARTERS, CANE CREEK,
Ten Miles West of Tuscumbia, October 30, 1863—7.30 a. m.

COLONEL: I have the honor to report, for the information of the general, that my command attacked the enemy at daylight yesterday morning, and after a brisk skirmish I discovered that the enemy were in force at their camp near Cherokee Station. Their tents were standing, and my scouts could see no movement indicating breaking up of their camp. My scouts report (and I consider it perfectly reliable) that about a division of the enemy have crossed at Eastport, and last evening their advance was within a few miles of Florence. Two steamers and flat-boats were at Eastport crossing troops. There is but little doubt now that a column of the enemy will march north of the Tennessee, via Florence and Huntsville. I am in doubt whether the entire force will go by that route; will inform you as soon as reliable information is received. The force in my front is probably covering the crossing. Some of my scouts still report the enemy working on the railroad east of Bear Creek, and the cars have crossed the Bear Creek Bridge.

Brigadier-General Ferguson attacked and routed the Tory Alabama Regiment, and thoroughly scattered it over the country, capturing two pieces of artillery, some 40 prisoners, a number of horses;

small-arms, &c.* Brigadier-General Roddey is still on the flank and rear of the enemy between this point and Big Bear Creek. I am becoming short of ammunition; have sent for a supply at Okolona. My command is not in a condition to remain long from Mississippi, having left prepared only for a two weeks' scout against the Memphis and Charleston Railroad, when their destination was changed in this direction. They are much in need of clothing, shoes, &c. I will, however, remain as long as I can be of service, or until I receive orders from General Johnston. If I am to remain in this department, I should be informed as early as practicable, though I am of opinion that a large cavalry force will not be needed in this valley very long.

I am, colonel, yours, respectfully,
STEPHEN D. LEE,
Major-General.

Lieut. Col. George William Brent,
Assistant Adjutant-General, Army of Tennessee.

—

HEADQUARTERS,
Tuscumbia, Ala., October 31, 1863.

Colonel: I have the honor to report that on the 26th instant the enemy advanced in force, and after severe skirmishing on the 26th and 27th occupied Tuscumbia.

On 28th, the enemy evacuated Tuscumbia and moved back toward Big Bear Creek.

I attacked his rear guard 15 miles west of Tuscumbia on the morning of the 29th, and after a severe skirmish retired before his main force. The enemy's force consisted of two divisions of infantry, under Osterhaus and Morgan L. Smith, the whole commanded by General Blair, commanding Fifteenth Army Corps. The force of the enemy was about 8,000. They rebuilt the bridge over Big Bear Creek and run the cars to Cherokee Station, 8 miles east of that point. The thorough destruction of the railroad and the stubborn resistance made to their advance have deterred them from this route, and they are now crossing at Eastport and moving on the north side of the Tennessee River. They intended rebuilding this road to Decatur.

The enemy acknowledge a loss of 100 killed and wounded on the 22d [21st] instant. Their loss has been heavier since.

My loss so far is 6 killed and 40 wounded.

On the night of the 25th, I sent Brigadier-General Ferguson with two regiments after a raiding party from Corinth. He succeeded in meeting the enemy, routing him and scattering his entire force over the county, capturing 2 pieces of artillery, 4 guidons, 30 prisoners, a considerable quantity of small-arms, &c. Prisoners are still being caught over the country. The raiders were mostly composed of the Tory regiment from North Alabama. My scouts captured a valuable medical wagon attached to Osterhaus' headquarters, full of medicines, &c.

The enemy are marching through Florence, and I think toward Huntsville. There is little doubt that the enemy intend another flank movement on General Bragg via Will's Valley. There is lit-

_____
* See Skirmish at Vincent's Cross-Roads, October 26, 1863, p. 37.

tle further use for cavalry in this valley, and, unless I receive orders to the contrary, will leave for Mississippi in about a week. My horses need shoes and resting. Am having my command filled up as rapidly as possible. It would not be prudent for me to cross the Tennessee now with my present force and the dispositions of the enemy. Their main cavalry force from what I can learn is in the vicinity of Huntsville, and at last accounts the cars were running from Stevenson to Paint Rock, and the Nashville and Chattanooga Railroad was strongly guarded by troops from Meade's army.

I am, colonel, yours, respectfully,

STEPHEN D. LEE,

Major-General.

Col. B. S. EWELL,

Assistant Adjutant-General, Meridian, Miss.

OCTOBER 22, 1863.—Skirmish near Volney, Ky.

Report of Col. Cicero Maxwell, Twenty-sixth Kentucky Infantry, commanding District of Southwestern Kentucky.

HDQRS. U. S. FORCES, SOUTHWESTERN KENTUCKY,

Bowling Green, Ky., October 24, 1863.

CAPTAIN: On Thursday morning last I received information at Russellville, where I was, on my way to Hopkinsville, that 45 or 50 guerrillas were a few miles south of that place, robbing loyal people. I started immediately with a small squad of the Third Kentucky Cavalry, sent to accompany me to Hopkinsville, and some mounted men of the Twenty-sixth Kentucky Volunteers and Sixth New Hampshire Volunteers, numbering in all about 40, in search of the guerrillas. Shortly after leaving Russellville, we learned that they had gone to Gordonsville, a small village west of Russellville 6 miles, early in the morning, robbed several stores, shot and badly wounded an old citizen named Criswell, and had started back with their booty toward Tennessee by the same route they had come.

We soon got on their track, and came up with them a short distance southeast of Volney, in Logan County. Our men fired on them, but without waiting to return the fire, the guerrillas fled in great disorder, throwing away their booty, guns, &c., and many of them leaving their horses and escaping into the woods. We pursued them for 30 miles without stopping, our men overtaking and firing on them occasionally, until just below Mitchellsville, in Tennessee, all that then remained together scattered into the woods and eluded farther pursuit. They were completely routed and dispersed, several being killed and wounded. Our men also captured several prisoners, a number of horses, guns, pistols, &c. In their flight the thieves threw away their ill-gotten booty, and the road for miles was strewn with boots, shoes, hats, and various other articles of merchandise. They were under the command of one Captain Dyer.

One of our men, Jack Anderson, Twenty-sixth Kentucky, who behaved with great gallantry and bravery, was pretty severely wounded, but I hope not dangerously. Our men all behaved very well. Lieutenant Poindexter and [Corpl.] Thomas R. Blakey, formerly of the Eighth Kentucky Cavalry, though out of service, volunteered,

and acted with great gallantry.   I would respectfully commend
Lieut. J. Redfearn, Twenty-sixth Kentucky, especially, for his reck-
less daring and bravery.   He was in command of the squad of the
Twenty-sixth Kentucky, and for many miles led the pursuit, frequently with 1 or 2 men only charging upon a dozen of the flying
enemy.   They, however, scarcely ever returned the fire of our men,
relying on the fleetness of their horses for safety, and seemed to be
intent only on getting away.   I went from Mitchellsville to Franklin
on Thursday evening, and returned here yesterday.

        Very respectfully,

                        CICERO MAXWELL,
        Colonel 26th Ky. Vols., Comdg. U. S. Forces, S. W. Ky.
    Capt. A. C. SEMPLE,
        Assistant Adjutant-General.

P. S.—I sincerely regret to say that one of our men got into a difficulty with a citizen named Dinning, near the State line, and unfortunately killed him.   The men had been instructed to seize horses
when theirs gave out.   We were in hot pursuit of the robbers, and
the horse of one of our men gave out.   He undertook to seize Dinning's horse.   Dinning resisted and, the soldier says, drew a knife,
and he shot and killed him.   Dinning was a sympathizer with the
rebellion, but I understand, generally, a harmless man.   I will have
the matter investigated.   In our pursuit of the guerrillas, I was
more than ever convinced of the utter malignity and treachery of
the sympathizers with treason in the southern part of Logan County.
Some severe measures, in my humble judgment, will have to be
adopted with them before the daily and nightly robberies of their
friends can be stopped.

**OCTOBER 22, 1863.—Destruction of the Steamer Mist on the Mississippi
River.**

*Report of Brig. Gen. Napoleon B. Buford, U. S. Army, command-
ing District of Eastern Arkansas.*

            HDQRS. DISTRICT OF EASTERN ARKANSAS,
                    Helena, Ark., October 23, 1863.

    SIR : For the information of General Hurlbut, I report the steamer
Mist, Captain Calhoun, was burned by a party of 20 guerrillas, commanded by Dick Holland, at the foot of Ship Island, on the Mississippi
shore, yesterday at 3 p. m., the captain robbed of a large sum, which
he states to have been over $17,000, and the boat rifled.   The captain
and crew of 10 men were allowed to go free.   Captain Calhoun reports his engine was out of order.   He was anchored in the stream;
took a skiff and went ashore to get four bales of cotton ; the boat
was blown ashore.

    The cotton he said had been purchased from a man named Cole,
by McDonald, who had a permit to ship 50 bales.   Captain Calhoun states his pilot, E. Wood, was also robbed of $5,000 of Confed-
erate money, which was in the safe with the boat's funds.   The
guerrillas did not burn Cole's cotton.   The captain further states
that the steamer Evansville landed at the same place the day pre-

vious, and took on board about 20 bales of cotton without the protection of a gunboat.

There are inconsistencies in this story which are apparent. I am informed by Col. Silas Noble, who is here, that when he commanded at Paducah, Captain Calhoun was disloyal.

Your obedient servant,

N. B. BUFORD,
Brigadier-General, Commanding.

Capt. T. H. HARRIS,
Assistant Adjutant-General.

OCTOBER 22-24, 1863.—Scout from Germantown, Tenn., to Chulahoma, Miss.

Report of Lieut. Col. Reuben Loomis, Sixth Illinois Cavalry.

HEADQUARTERS SIXTH ILLINOIS CAVALRY,
Germantown, Tenn., October 24, 1863.

COLONEL : In compliance with your instructions, I started on the 22d with the effective force of my command and a part of Smith's battery, south, crossed the Coldwater at Quinn's Mill, took the road to Chulahoma, met teams going to Memphis with cotton from beyond and south of Holly Springs ; learned that some 25 of Richardson's command had passed through there going north on Tuesday. They report Chalmers at or near Water Valley ; no rebel force this side of Oxford ; contrabands report about the same. Before I got to Chulahoma I met Maj. S. Forbes, of the Seventh Illinois Cavalry, with 50 men. He had been within 4 or 5 miles of Wyatt; found no force except scouts. I scouted the country thoroughly in that vicinity. From all that I can learn, there is about a battalion scattered through the country in small squads this side of Tallahatchie. We charged through Byhalia and run out 8 rebels, but they were too well mounted to be caught ; that was the greatest number I saw together. The weather being inclement, the men's clothing, and in many cases ammunition, being thoroughly soaked with the rain of the night of the 22d and forenoon of the 23d, and no force of the enemy to be found this side of the Tallahatchie, I returned to camp.

Hoping what I have done may meet your approbation, I am, sir, very respectfully, your obedient servant,

R. LOOMIS,
Lieutenant-Colonel, Commanding Sixth Illinois Cavalry.

Col. EDWARD HATCH,
Commanding Cavalry Division.

OCTOBER 24–NOVEMBER 10, 1863.—Expedition from Goodrich's Landing, La., to Griffin's Landing and Catfish Point, Miss.

Report of Lieut. Col. George E. Currie, Mississippi Marine Brigade.

ON BOARD STEAMER B. J. ADAMS,
Napoleon, Ark., November 19, 1863.

GENERAL : Agreeably to your written instructions of the 23d ultimo, I left Goodrich's Landing, La., on the 24th ultimo, after being relieved from duty at that place by General Hawkins, and proceeded up the Mississippi River with four steamers, viz, Adams, Fairchild, Baltic, and Horner. A detachment of 125 cavalry, 160 infantry, and one section of Captain Walling's light battery arrived at Griffin's Landing, in Washington County, Miss., on the 26th ultimo.

On the 27th, I ordered Captain Brown with 100 cavalry to make a reconnaissance in the Deer Creek country, lying about 23 miles east of Griffin's Landing. The expedition left the boats at 6 a. m. and returned at 10 p. m., having marched over 45 miles in one day. They arrested and brought in 1 captain, G. C. Price, an agent of the Commissary Department for the purchase of stock in that country, with about $12,000 in Confederate money ; also 1 sergeant and 6 enlisted men belonging to the Sixth Texas Cavalry, detailed to drive stock.

From the prisoners I learned that a brigade of Jackson's cavalry was *en route* for that country to protect the stock drivers. Having but a small command mounted, I immediately impressed mules and horses to mount my infantry for the purpose of meeting the rebel brigade, and accordingly on the 1st day of November I landed all my available force, numbering about 200 cavalry and infantry, mounted, one piece of artillery, and two days' rations, and started at an early hour. About the time of starting the rain began to fall, which rendered the roads through the swamps almost impassable. At 3 p. m., however, I reached the plantation of Mrs. Buckner, on Deer Creek, where I was compelled to go into camp on account of the impassable condition of the roads for artillery, and having made a march of 23 miles, I posted my pickets and put the artillery into position, and made inquiry of the citizens concerning the rebel force, but was assured by them that there was none in that country.

Relying somewhat upon their information, and finding it out of my power to go farther with artillery, I resolved at once to send it back, guarded by the mounted infantry, leaving me a command of only 125 cavalry.

On the following morning, at 5.30 o'clock, I divided my force, one half returning, by way of Greenville, to Griffin's Landing, and with the cavalry I proceeded down the creek, intending to reach the river at Carolina Landing, a distance of 60 miles, where I had previously ordered the ram Horner to meet me on the 4th. We had gone but about 1 mile beyond my picket post, when the advance guard began skirmishing with rebel pickets. Here ensued a running fight for some miles until we came upon a portion of the enemy, supposed to be about 120 or 140 men, drawn up in line on the opposite side of the creek to prevent my command crossing on a bridge at that point, the only means of crossing in that vicinity. I instructed the advance to press them closely, intending to hold the enemy in position until the arrival of the artillery, which I ordered up immediately after encountering their pickets, but finding the enemy intended to fall back before the artillery could reach me, I directed a portion of the dismounted men to deploy and charge across the bridge at a double-quick, in order to clear the way for cavalry. The rebels gave way almost without resistance, and fled in great confusion, my cavalry close upon them. We followed them some 2 miles at a rapid rate, and, finding no other alternative, they took to the woods and canebrakes. By this time the artillery came up, and, after shelling the woods thoroughly, I started on my return to the boats, which I reached at 11 p. m., having marched over 40 miles in the afternoon, on my return to the boats.

I found 25 fat hogs at the plantation of Dr. L. L. Taylor, on Deer Creek, that had been purchased by Captain Price, for which he paid $1,250, but was arrested before getting them out of the pen. I also found a negro man with a large cotton wagon, drawn by six oxen, at this plantation, who had just returned from Catfish Point, having hauled a load of goods to that place for a rebel captain, for the purpose of having them taken across the river into Arkansas that night. I immediately took possession of the team and hogs, and brought them with me to the boats. At the same time sent a messenger to Captain Conner, of the ram Monarch, lying off Greenville, to run up the river as far as Catfish Point to look after the goods and ferry.

On the following day he reported the capture of a large quantity of salt and the destruction of two large ferry flats of sufficient capacity to cross artillery. These flats were entirely new, and were ingeniously hid from view by being sunk in about 4 feet water by means of barrels of sand, and never could have been discovered but for information received from a deserter from Price's army, who gave himself up.

On the 5th, landed the mounted infantry, Maj. D. S. Tallerday commanding, at Sunny Side, Ark., and directed him to proceed to Lake Village, county seat of Chicot County, where he arrested one Captain Gaines, Company G, Twenty-third Arkansas Infantry, and 5 enlisted men belonging to the same regiment, who were evidently engaged in burning cotton and enforcing the conscription. He also captured some valuable stock and met the fleet at Luna Landing the same night. I left the Monarch and Horner at Greenville to protect navigation.

On the 6th, landed the cavalry, Capt. O. F. Brown commanding, at Gaines' Landing, and he proceeded out in the direction of Monticello, Ark., about 15 miles, and thence up the river and met the fleet at Campbell's plantation at 5 p. m., having captured some mules. At 8 o'clock the same night I learned that a party of soldiers were in camp about 5 miles back from the river, waiting for an opportunity to cross over into Mississippi. I immediately sent out a party, in charge of Lieutenant Markle, Company E, First Infantry, and about 10 o'clock they returned with Lieutenant Brailsford (with a rebel mail) and 1 enlisted man belonging to Whitfield's Texas Legion.

On the 7th, landed the mounted infantry at the same place, with instructions to operate isolated (as companies) and effectually scout the country as far back from the river as possible. The parties returned soon after dark, bringing in several prisoners, among whom was a rebel mail-carrier making his way to the river to cross that night. They also brought in some stock.

On the 8th, landed the cavalry, Capt. O. F. Brown commanding, at Glencoe, Miss., and put off the mounted infantry, Major Tallerday commanding, on the Arkansas shore just opposite. The cavalry came in at Bolivar Landing late in the afternoon, having accomplished but little. The infantry, however, continued on up the river to Napoleon, where I met them with the fleet on the following day. They captured many prisoners and a rebel mail-carrier with over 200 pounds of mail, among which were a large quantity of official documents from Richmond, directed to some of the most prominent generals in the Trans-

Mississippi Department. They also captured and brought in 2 men, Barker and Keefe, cotton card manufacturers, with a cotton machine complete, which they had recently bought at Macon and Savannah, Ga., which cost them $8,000. They crossed the river but a short time prior to their capture, and were *en route* to Camden, Ark., where the machine was to be used in making cloth for the army.

On the 9th, learning that the guerrillas had burned the steamer Allen Collier that had landed opposite Laconia, Ark., a day or two previous, I immediately left Napoleon for that place, intending to ferret out the marauding party, landing at the mouth of White River for wood. I found a portion of the Allen Collier's crew that had been arrested and were subsequently released, who informed me the boat was burned by Montgomery's guerrilla band, and knowing that Montgomery and a portion of his company, numbering about 40 or 50 men, lived on Bayou Phalia, in Bolivar County, Miss., and owned plantations, I resolved to return at once with my command to Beulah Landing and break up the party. On the following morning, November 10, I left the boats at 7 o'clock with a small cavalry force and proceeded to the bayou, a distance of some 10 miles, when I arrested one of the party and learned from him that the company was still some distance from there in the canebrakes, and knowing the impossibility of overtaking them I went to Montgomery's plantation, where I found the family of General Charles Clark, C. S. Army, also the family of Montgomery, and after removing the furniture from the house, I set it on fire. I also burned the cotton gin and out-houses; in fact, everything but the negro quarters. I informed Mrs. Montgomery it was done by way of retaliation for her husband burning the steamer Collier a few days previous. She replied, "This is no more than I expected when I heard what my husband had done." I also obtained the names of some of his company who own plantations in that vicinity and notified them, through the present occupants of the plantations, that if another overt act should be committed by that company I would serve them as I had Montgomery, their captain.

We destroyed several yawls and flat-boats along the road that were being hauled to the river every night in a wagon and used in ferrying, then taken back in the woods, and came to their former hiding place before daylight in the morning.

We also arrested and brought in several prisoners, among whom were three citizens, mail-carriers, with each a small package of mail destined for Arkansas. We reached Bolivar Landing, Miss., about dark, where we met the fleet, having marched about 35 miles.

I also have the honor to inform you that large quantities of corn in cribs, of last year's growth, and hundreds of acres grown this year, and now standing in the field, can be procured within 5 miles of the river and in some places immediately on its banks. I also learn that parties with trading boats along the river are dealing in cotton and furnishing the citizens with supplies and other necessities.

I have the honor to be, general, your obedient servant,

GEO. E. CURRIE,
Lieutenant-Colonel, Commanding.

Brig. Gen. ALFRED W. ELLET,
Commanding Marine Brigade.

OCTOBER 26, 1863.—Skirmish at Vincent's Cross-Roads, near Bay Springs, Miss.

REPORTS.

No. 1.—Report of Capt. John W. Barnes, Acting Assistant Adjutant-General.
No. 2.—Report of Brig. Gen. Samuel W. Ferguson, C. S. Army.

No. 1.

Report of Capt. John W. Barnes, Acting Assistant Adjutant-General.

CORINTH, MISS.,
October 27, 1863.

Spencer yesterday, at 2 p. m., was attacked some 40 miles southeast of Glendale, in the direction of Jones' Cross-Roads. The messenger reports the rebel force, supposed to be Hanner's [?] and others, at 2,000 strong. Spencer had about 500.* He is said to be getting the worst of the fight. Shall I send the cavalry at Corinth to his aid?
Respectfully,

JOHN W. BARNES,
Acting Assistant Adjutant-General.

———

No. 2.

Report of Brig. Gen. Samuel W. Ferguson, C. S. Army.

HEADQUARTERS BRIGADE,
Near Courtland, Ala., October 31, 1863.

GENERAL: I have the honor to report that, pursuant to verbal orders from yourself, I left camp at Cane Creek shortly after dark on the evening of the 25th instant with two regiments of my brigade (the Second Tennessee, Lieutenant-Colonel Morton, and the Second Alabama, Colonel Earl), for the purpose of intercepting a raiding party of the enemy reported to be on their return from Walker County, Ala. Traveled all night, and at sunrise next morning halted and fed my horses at a ford of Bear Creek, about 2 miles above Mann's Mills. After a delay of two hours for this purpose, I pushed the command across Bear Creek and on to the Fulton and Iuka road. Here, as there was no sign of the enemy's having passed, I turned toward Fulton, and after reaching the intersection of this road with that to Bay Springs, I sent one squadron in the latter direction for the purpose of holding the enemy in check, should they move toward that point, and preventing their escape. With the remainder of my force (about 300 effective men) I moved toward the Bull Mountain country.

After pursuing this road about 3 miles I received the first positive information of the position of the enemy from a scout I had sent out, who reported them advancing on the same road. I immediately sent to recall the squadron previously ordered to Bay Springs,

———
* First Alabama Cavalry (Union).

and continued the march until the advance guards met and skirmishing began—about 1.30 p. m. The enemy were formed in thick woods across the road, with an open field in front, through which, swept as it was by two pieces of light artillery planted in the road, I had to advance to the attack. As rapidly as possible I formed my lines, had the men dismounted, and attacked the enemy, who were soon driven back by the Second Tennessee, under the able and gallant leadership of Lieutenant-Colonel Morton, and a portion of the Second Alabama. As soon as the horses could be brought up the fleeing enemy were hotly pursued and their retreat converted into a wild panic. The chase was kept up for some 10 miles through dense woods and over a mountainous country until dark. Their perfect knowledge and our ignorance of the country enabled most of them, however, to escape by separating into small squads and leaving the road.

It may be proper to remark that before the engagement began I had met Major Moreland, with his battalion, and ordered him to get in rear of the enemy on a road leading from their left flank to Bay Springs, of the existence of which he informed me, stating it was the only road by which they could escape, except directly back into Alabama. Had my instructions been strictly and energetically followed, few of the enemy would have escaped.

With a loss of 2 killed and 11 wounded, I have succeeded in effectually destroying the First Alabama Tory Regiment. Up to the time I left, the enemy's loss, as far as could be ascertained, was 20 killed, including 2 captains, the adjutant of the regiment, and 1 first lieutenant ; 9 wounded, including 1 first lieutenant mortally, and 29 prisoners. The woods was so dense and the fight kept up for so great a distance that many killed and wounded were not found. I do not think the number would fall short of 100 in all.

I captured 2 pieces of artillery, 5 stand of colors, 60 elegant breech-loading carbines, with an ample supply of ammunition for present purposes, 25 Colt hostler pistols, 10 pack-saddles, 52 horses and mules, and 56 saddles. I have received no report from Major Moreland, but understand he has collected a large number of prisoners, horses, mules, &c. My force scarcely equaled that of the enemy.

I am indebted to the officers and men of the command for gallant conduct and cheerful endurance of hardship and hunger on this scout ; but to Lieutenant-Colonel Morton and Maj. H. W. Bridges more than a passing tribute is due. The former led his gallant band with a cool skill and determination, admirable in the extreme, until knocked from his horse by a spent ball. The latter was, as usual, foremost in the fight, everywhere inspiring and encouraging the men and officers. With his own hand he killed 1 and wounded and captured several other Yankees. His horse was shot under him and his coat pierced by a bullet, an evidence of the close character of the fight.

To the officers of my staff who were present—Captain Nugent, assistant adjutant-general ; Captain Irwin, assistant inspector-general; Lieutenant Tomlinson, aide-de-camp, and Lieutenant Richardson, picket officer—I am indebted for zealous and efficient discharge of duty in gallant style.

S. W. FERGUSON,
Brigadier-General, Commanding.

Maj. Gen. S. D. LEE.

OCTOBER 26–29, 1863.—Reopening of the Tennessee River, including Skirmish (27th) at Brown's Ferry and Engagement (28th and 29th) at Wauhatchie, Tenn.

REPORTS.*

No. 1.—Maj. Gen. George H. Thomas, U. S. Army, commanding Department of the Cumberland, with field dispatches and congratulatory orders.

No. 2.—Charles A. Dana, Assistant Secretary of War.

No. 3.—Return of Casualties in the Union forces at Wauhatchie.

No. 4.—Brig. Gen. William F. Smith, U. S. Army, Chief Engineer, Department of the Cumberland.

No. 5.—Col. Timothy R. Stanley, Eighteenth Ohio Infantry.

No. 6.—Itinerary of the First Division, Fourth Army Corps.

No. 7.—Brig. Gen. William B. Hazen, U. S. Army, commanding Second Brigade, Third Division.

No. 8.—Lieut. Col. James C. Foy, Twenty-third Kentucky Infantry.

No. 9.—Lieut. Col. Bassett Langdon, First Ohio Infantry.

No. 10.—Col. Aquila Wiley, Forty-first Ohio Infantry.

No. 11.—Maj. William Birch, Ninety-third Ohio Infantry.

No. 12.—Maj. Gen. Joseph Hooker, U. S. Army, commanding Eleventh and Twelfth Army Corps, with congratulatory orders.

No. 13.—Maj. Gen. Oliver O. Howard, U. S. Army, commanding Eleventh Army Corps.

No. 14.—Surg. Daniel G. Brinton, U. S. Army, Medical Director.

No. 15.—Brig. Gen. Adolph von Steinwehr, U. S. Army, commanding Second Division.

No. 16.—Itinerary of the First Brigade, Col. Adolph Buschbeck commanding.

No. 17.—Itinerary of the Second Brigade, Col. Orland Smith commanding.

No. 18.—Lieut. Col. Godfrey Rider, jr., Thirty-third Massachusetts Infantry.

No. 19.—Col. James Wood, jr., One hundred and thirty-sixth New York Infantry.

No. 20.—Maj. Samuel H. Hurst, Seventy-third Ohio Infantry.

No. 21.—Maj. Gen. Carl Schurz, U. S. Army, commanding Third Division.

No. 22.—Itinerary of the First Brigade, Brig. Gen. Hector Tyndale commanding.

No. 23.—Itinerary of the Second Brigade, Col. Wladimir Krzyzanowski commanding.

No. 24.—Brig. Gen. John W. Geary, U. S. Army, commanding Second Division, Twelfth Army Corps.

No. 25.—Col. George A. Cobham, jr., One hundred and eleventh Pennsylvania Infantry, commanding Second Brigade.

No. 26.—Col. William Rickards, jr., Twenty-ninth Pennsylvania Infantry.

No. 27.—Capt. Frederick L. Gimber, One hundred and ninth Pennsylvania Infantry.

No. 28.—Lieut. Col. Thomas M. Walker, One hundred and eleventh Pennsylvania Infantry.

No. 29.—Brig. Gen. George S. Greene, U. S. Army, commanding Third Brigade.

No. 30.—Col. David Ireland, One hundred and thirty-seventh New York Infantry, commanding Third Brigade.

No. 31.—Itinerary of the Third Brigade.

No. 32.—Lieut. Col. Herbert von Hammerstein, Seventy-eighth New York Infantry.

No. 33.—Capt. Milo B. Eldridge, One hundred and thirty-seventh New York Infantry.

---

* See also General Grant's report, Part II, pp. —.

No. 34.—Lieut. Col. Charles B. Randall, One hundred and forty-ninth New York Infantry.

No. 35.—Maj. John A. Reynolds, First New York Light Artillery, commanding Artillery Brigade.

No. 36.—Brig. Gen. John B. Turchin, U. S. Army, commanding First Brigade, Third Division, Fourteenth Army Corps, with itinerary of brigade.

No. 37.—Record of a Court of Inquiry, and accompanying documents.

No. 38.—Lieut. Gen. James Longstreet, C. S. Army, commanding corps, with field dispatches, &c.

No. 39.—Organization of Hood's division.

No. 40.—Brig. Gen. E. McIver Law, C. S. Army, commanding brigade and Hood's division.

No. 41.—Col. James L. Sheffield, Forty-eighth Alabama Infantry, commanding Law's brigade.

No. 42.—Col. John Bratton, Sixth South Carolina Infantry, commanding Jenkins' brigade.

No. 43.—Brig. Gen. Jerome B. Robertson, C. S. Army, commanding brigade.

No. 1.

Reports of Maj. Gen. George H. Thomas, U. S. Army, commanding Department of the Cumberland, with field dispatches and congratulatory orders.

CHATTANOOGA, TENN., *October* 27, 1863—11.30 p. m.

(Received 9 p. m., 28th.)

General William F. Smith, commanding Hazen's brigade, Sheridan's division, Fourth Corps, and Turchin's brigade, Baird's division, Fourteenth Corps, floated boats of pontoon bridges down the river from Chattanooga to Brown's Ferry, 6 miles below; landed, surprised, and drove off the enemy's pickets and reserves; took possession of the hills commanding *débouché* of the ferry, on southwest side, and laid bridge and intrenched the command strongly enough to hold the bridge securely.

By the judicious precautions taken by General Smith before starting, and the intelligent co-operation of Generals Turchin and Hazen, commanding brigades, and Colonel Stanley, of the Eighteenth Ohio, commanding boat party, this was a complete success, and reflected great credit on all concerned.

Our loss, 4 killed, 15 wounded; enemy, 8 killed, 6 prisoners, and several wounded.

General Hooker, commanding troops composing Eleventh Corps and part of Twelfth, marched from Bridgeport at daylight to-day, to open road from Bridgeport to Chattanooga, and take some position protecting river. Two brigades of Palmer's division, Fourth Corps, should have reached Rankin's Ferry, to co-operate with General Hooker to-day. The Sixteenth Illinois reached Kelley's Ferry to co-operate with General Hooker. If General Hooker is as successful as General Smith has been, we shall in a few days have open communication with Bridgeport by water, as well as by a practicable road, running near the river on the northern bank.

GEO. H. THOMAS,
Major-General, Commanding Department.

Maj. Gen. H. W. HALLECK,
General-in-Chief.

CHATTANOOGA, TENN., *October* 28, 1863—11 p. m.
(Received 3 p. m., 29th.)

Hooker reached Brown's Ferry to-day about 3 p. m.   Met with no serious opposition.   The enemy still hold Lookout Mountain in considerable force.   The wagon road is now open to Bridgeport.   We have, besides, two steam-boats, one at Bridgeport and one here, which will be started to-morrow.   We have also another steam-boat here, undergoing repairs; will be ready for work as soon as portions of her machinery (sent for to Nashville) arrive.   By this operation we have gained two wagon roads and the river to get supplies by, and I hope in a few days to be pretty well supplied.   Intend to repair roads leading to Tracy City and McMinnville, two termini of branch railroads.   The importance of the position of Chattanooga is too great to neglect any means of supplying or re-enforcing it.

GEO. H. THOMAS,
Major-General, Commanding.

Maj. Gen. H. W. HALLECK,
General-in-Chief.

—

CHATTANOOGA, TENN., *October* 29, 1863—11.30 p. m.
(Received 6.50 a. m., November 1.)

In the fight of last night the enemy attacked Geary's division, posted at Wauhatchie, on three sides, and broke into his camp at one point, but was driven back in most gallant style by part of his force, the remainder being held in reserve.   Howard, while marching to Geary's relief, was attacked in the flank, the enemy occupying in force two commanding hills on the left of the road. He immediately threw forward two of his regiments and took both at the point of the bayonet, driving the enemy from his breast-works and across Lookout Creek.   In this brilliant success over their old adversary, the conduct of the officers and men of the Eleventh and Twelfth Corps is entitled to the highest praise.

GEO. H. THOMAS,
Major-General.

Maj. Gen. H. W. HALLECK,
General-in-Chief.

—

CHATTANOOGA, TENN., *October* 31, 1863—11.30 p. m.
(Received 10 p. m., November 7.)

Since the fight of the night of the 28th, the enemy has not disturbed us.   Hooker took prisoners 4 officers and 103 men, and captured nearly 1,000 Enfield rifles.   His loss, 350 officers and men, killed and wounded.   I have 2 steamboats now running between Bridgeport and Kelley's Ferry, from which point provisions are hauled to Chattanooga.   We can easily subsist ourselves now, and will soon be in good condition.

GEO. H. THOMAS,
Major-General.

Maj. Gen. H. W. HALLECK,
General-in-Chief.

HEADQUARTERS DEPARTMENT OF THE CUMBERLAND,
Chattanooga, November 7, 1863.

GENERAL: I have the honor to forward herewith the official reports of Major-General Hooker, commanding Eleventh and Twelfth Corps, and of Brig. Gen. W. F. Smith, chief engineer, Department of the Cumberland, commanding the expedition composed of Turchin's brigade, Baird's division, Fourteenth Army Corps, and Hazen's brigade, Wood's division, Fourth Army Corps, and detachments of the Eighteenth Ohio Infantry, under command of Col. T. R. Stanley, and of the First Michigan Engineers, under command of Capt. P. V. Fox, of the operations of their respective commands between the 26th and 28th ultimo, to gain possession of the south bank of the Tennessee River and to open the road for a depot of supplies at Bridgeport.

Preliminary steps had already been taken to execute this vitally important movement before the command of the department devolved on me. The bridge, which it was necessary to throw across the river at Brown's Ferry to gain possession of the northern end of Lookout Valley and open communication with Bridgeport by road and river, was nearly completed.

On the 23d, orders were sent to General Hooker to concentrate the Eleventh Corps and one division of the Twelfth at Bridgeport, informing him at the same time what his force was expected to accomplish, and that a force from this place would co-operate with him by establishing a bridge across the river at Brown's Ferry and seize the heights on the south, or Lookout Valley side, thus giving him an open road to Chattanooga when his forces should arrive in Lookout Valley. The force to throw the bridge was organized by Saturday, the 24th, and the boats and bridge completed, giving General Smith two days to examine the ground with the two brigade commanders, and to give all the necessary detailed instructions to insure success. General Hooker reported on the 26th that he would be ready to move on the 27th at daylight.

He was instructed to move at the appointed time, with full instructions how to provide for the defense of his flank, and to cover the approaches to the road from the direction of Trenton. The bridge was successfully thrown across the river on the night of the 26th, and General Hooker reached Lookout Valley and communicated with this place on the 28th. The enemy attempted to surprise him the night after reaching his position in Lookout Valley, and, after an obstinate contest of two hours' duration, was completely repulsed, with a loss of upward of 1,500 killed and wounded, over 100 prisoners, and several hundred stand of arms. I refer you to the reports of Generals Hooker and Smith for the details of the operations of their commands, commending to favorable consideration the names of those officers specially mentioned by them for gallant and meritorious conduct. The skillful execution by General Smith of the work assigned him, and the promptness with which General Hooker, with his troops, met and repulsed the enemy on the night of the 28th, reflects the greatest credit on both of those officers and their entire commands. I herewith annex consolidated returns of casualties.

I am, general, very respectfully, your obedient servant,

GEO. H. THOMAS,
Major-General, U. S. Volunteers, Commanding

Brig. Gen. LORENZO THOMAS,
Adjutant-General U. S. Army, Washington, D. C.

[Inclosure.]

Consolidated return of Casualties.

Troops.	Killed.			Wounded.			Missing.			Aggregate.
	Officers.	Men.	Total.	Officers.	Men.	Total.	Officers.	Men.	Total.	
Major-General Hooker's command, Eleventh Corps.	5	33	38	13	135	148	......	14	14	200
Second Division, Twelfth Corps*.......	4	30	34	15	159	174	......	8	8	216
Brigadier-General Smith's command ..	......	4	4	2	15	17	......	......	......	21
Total...........*..................	9	67	76	30	309	339	......	22	22	437

ADDENDA.

HEADQUARTERS DEPARTMENT OF THE CUMBERLAND,
Chattanooga, October 23, 1863.

Major-General HOOKER,
Stevenson :

The general commanding directs that one division of the Twelfth Corps will guard the railroad from Murfreesborough to Bridgeport, the remainder of the Twelfth Corps will concentrate at Stevenson to move with the Eleventh Corps on the south side of the Tennessee River. If transportation of the Eleventh Corps is at Stevenson, it will answer for that corps and the division of the Twelfth. If transportation of Eleventh Corps has not arrived, prepare to use flats and barges, which can be protected from the shore. General Howard has been telegraphed to prepare to move pontoon train by water.

J. J. REYNOLDS,
Major-General.

—

HEADQUARTERS DEPARTMENT OF THE CUMBERLAND,
Chattanooga, October 24, 1863—2.30 p. m.

Major-General HOOKER,
Stevenson :

You will leave General Slocum, with one division of the Twelfth Corps, to guard the railroad from Murfreesborough to Bridgeport. The Eleventh Corps and one division of the Twelfth will be concentrated at or in the vicinity of Bridgeport, preparatory to crossing the Tennessee River, and moving up the south side to take possession of Rankin's Ferry, between Shellmound and Running Water Creek. Look well to your right flank, which may be approached via Island Creek, the Moore road, McDaniel's Gap road, and the Nickajack road. Two brigades, under General Palmer, leave here this p. m. for Rankin's Ferry, which point they will probably reach on Monday evening. It is reported that the steam-boat at Bridgeport will be completed by Monday evening. The railroad may also be available. If you can do so, it is better not to move wagons to the south side of the river at present. You will, however, exercise your judgment on this point. Report by telegraph when you are ready. We will

* See revised statement, p. 76.

co-operate at Brown's Ferry, as well as Rankin's Ferry. Inform yourself with regard to the roads from Rankin's Ferry, via White-side's, to Brown's Ferry. The object of the movement is to hold the road and gain possession of the river as far as Brown's Ferry.

By command of Major-General Thomas:

J. J. REYNOLDS,
Major-General, and Chief of Staff.

—

STEVENSON,
October 24, 1863—6.10 p. m.

Colonel GODDARD,
  Assistant Adjutant-General:

Orders received for First Division, Twelfth Corps, to remain. The failure of the telegraph last evening caused delay in informing General Granger of the change. The rear of the division of the Twelfth Corps, ordered to concentrate at Bridgeport, passed Decherd this a. m. Distance, 30 miles marching, in consequence of the interruption of the railroad. One regiment of the Eleventh Corps will be ordered to remain at Battle Creek. The rear (100 wagons) of the train furnished the Eleventh Corps, leaving Nashville on the 12th instant, arrived here to-day. From this you can judge of the roads. I should like to have a small cavalry force attached to this command that crosses the river; have none now.

JOSEPH HOOKER,
Major-General.

—

STEVENSON,
October 24, 1863—7.15 p. m.

Major-General REYNOLDS:

I am informed by people familiar with country on south side of Tennessee River, that the direct route from Bridgeport to Brown's Ferry is not practicable for wagons, and in order to take artillery to that point it will be necessary to take the road to within two miles of Trenton, and from there turn down Lookout Creek Valley; that there are several bridle paths leading from the crest of Lookout Mountain into the valley between Trenton and the river, and that infantry can descend the north slope of Lookout at many points. My informants are men who have grazed their stock on Lookout Mountain. From the official map furnished me, there appears to be an ascent to the south of what is called Hotel Institute. If this is the case, from my present knowledge of the means at hand at Chattanooga to prevent enemy's infantry ascending the mountain from the south side, I can see no reason for his not detaching two-thirds of his force to thwart the execution of their purposed object. I may be incorrect in my views of this movement from the limited opportunity I have had in comparison with others to gain correct information, and only state the foregoing with the hope that I may be in error.

JOSEPH HOOKER,
Major-General.

STEVENSON,
October 24, 1863—8.30 p. m.

Major-General REYNOLDS,
            Chief of Staff:

The following just received from Bridgeport:

The steamer will probably be done next Sunday night.   One or two necessary parts of the engine are not here yet.   Every exertion will be made to have her fit to move Monday next.   She will be launched to-morrow.

O. O. HOWARD,
Major-General.

The roads being impassable, I have to depend on the cars for the movement of the Twelfth Corps.   If they don't fail me, I can have one division, as ordered, of the Twelfth Corps there.   The Eleventh Corps have one brigade at Battle Creek and an advance post at Sequatchie River.   From the order, I take it these are to be concentrated; also a portion of the pontoon bridge is in use at Battle Creek, crossing a portion at Sequatchie River.   How much there is not in use at these points I am not informed.   Detachments of the Pioneer Brigade, under the orders of chief engineer, I suppose have them in charge.   They have never been reported to me or put under my command.

JOSEPH HOOKER,
Major-General.

—

STEVENSON, *October* 24, 1863.

Major-General SLOCUM:

No change in the movement as ordered by telegraph.   Following copy of dispatch, from headquarters, is forwarded for your information and government:

CHATTANOOGA, *October* 24, 1863.

You will leave General Slocum, with one division of the Twelfth Corps, to guard the railroad from Murfreesborough to Bridgeport.

J. J. REYNOLDS,
Major-General, and Chief of Staff.

Acknowledge this and the dispatch of yesterday.   The general desires the division that can be quickest at Bridgeport be placed there.

DANL. BUTTERFIELD,
Major-General, and Chief of Staff.

—

STEVENSON,
October 25, 1863—10.45 a. m.

Major-General HOWARD:

The major-general commanding directs that you hold your command in readiness to move at 9 a. m. to-morrow, with three days' cooked rations, without wagons.   Those on south side of Tennessee can be picked up as you go along.   The balance of your command concentrate in readiness for the move, except the regiment ordered to Battle Creek and battery to Rankin's Ferry.

DANL. BUTTERFIELD,
Major-General, and Chief of Staff.

STEVENSON,
October 25, 1863—2.30 p. m.

Brigadier-General GEARY,
        Bridgeport:

Hold your command in readiness to march at 12 m. to-morrow. We march with three days' rations, without wagons. Will all your troops and batteries be up? If not, have word sent them not to lose a moment's time.

By looking at the map you will see that troops will save 10 miles' marching by taking a direct road to Bridgeport from Anderson, avoiding Stevenson.

JOSEPH HOOKER,
Major-General, Commanding.

—

STEVENSON,
October 25, 1863—3 p. m.

Major-General HOWARD,
        Bridgeport:

I am surprised to learn that you have but one reliable battery out of five. We will march to-morrow if we go without any. One battery will have to be sent, as ordered, and at once.

Rations are at Bridgeport. Your troops will be up. Have directions given for all your batteries to be put in condition for service without a moment's delay.

JOSEPH HOOKER,
Major-General, Commanding.

—

STEVENSON,
October 25, 1863—5 p. m.

Major-General HOWARD,
        Bridgeport:

It will not be possible to bring all the force together in season to march to-morrow. Let everything be in readiness for an early start the following morning.

JOSEPH HOOKER,
Major-General.

—

STEVENSON,
October 25, 1863—[10 p. m.]

Major-General REYNOLDS,
        Chief of Staff:

All but two batteries and two regiments of the force for operations on the south side of the river are now at Bridgeport. These should be up to-morrow. My headquarters will be here after 12 to-morrow. The command assigned me will be in readiness to commence the movement sunrise of 27th. The steamer is launched and waiting a necessary piece of pipe. General Howard reports a woman coming in our lines who states Bragg's forces fallen back 30 miles, but not confirmed by other reports.

JOSEPH HOOKER,
Major-General.

HEADQUARTERS DEPARTMENT OF THE CUMBERLAND,
Chattanooga, October 26, 1863.

Maj. Gen. JOSEPH HOOKER,
Stevenson:

Your telegram of 10 p. m. last night received. Commence the movement to-morrow morning, 27th, and open and secure the railroad and wagon road from Bridgeport to Rankin's Ferry, and thence as far toward Chattanooga as you can. General Palmer will co-operate with you at Rankin's Ferry. We will cross a co-operating force at Brown's Ferry, and take possession of the south bank there.

By command of Major-General Thomas:

J. J. REYNOLDS,
Major-General, and Chief of Staff.

—

OCTOBER 26, 1863—1.20 a. m.

General THOMAS:

Beat the enemy off Williams' Island twice to-night. Will hold it. Want no help.

WHITAKER,
General.

—

OCTOBER 26, 1863—11.40 a. m.

General WHITAKER:

Did the enemy attempt to get on Williams' Island in force?

THOMAS,
Major-General.

—

OCTOBER 26, 1863—12.20 p. m.

General THOMAS:

I do not know how much force. It was night. They made two strong efforts. I can beat them off.

WHITAKER,
Brigadier-General.

—

HEADQUARTERS DEPARTMENT OF THE CUMBERLAND,
Chattanooga, October 26, 1863—4.30 p. m.

Major-General HOOKER,
Stevenson:

The letter of General Wood forms no part of your instructions. It was simply sent as information from an officer who had passed over the road, and to be thrown with what other information you can gain from other sources.

Your instructions are contained in two telegrams from these headquarters—one of October 24, 2.30 p. m., and the other the telegram of this morning, directing the movement to commence to-morrow morning. Answer.

By command of Major-General Thomas:

J. J. REYNOLDS,
Major-General, Chief of Staff.

BRIDGEPORT, ALA.,
October 26, 1863—6.30 p. m.

Major-General REYNOLDS,
    Chief of Staff, Chattanooga:

Telegram of 2.30 p. m. received.* Movement will commence at sunrise to-morrow.

JOSEPH HOOKER.

—

OCTOBER 26, 1863—6.40 p. m.

General REYNOLDS,
    Chief of Staff:

The enemy's pickets have been doubled opposite Brown's Ferry. Lookout can be taken.

W. C. WHITAKER,
    Brigadier-General.

—

HDQRS. SECOND DIVISION, TWELFTH ARMY CORPS,
    Bridgeport, Ala., October 26, 1863—8.15 p. m.

Lieut. Col. H. C. RODGERS,
    Asst. Adjt. Gen., Twelfth Army Corps, Wartrace, Tenn.:

I move at sunrise. Have only three regiments here and four effective pieces of artillery. Please push my troops forward. Those who do not arrive in time are to follow my route.

JNO. W. GEARY,
    Brigadier-General, Commanding.

—

BRIDGEPORT, *October 26, 1863.*

Major-General REYNOLDS:

Two citizens from Lookout Mountain report that there is no enemy except near the foot of it, near Chattanooga. Some pioneers were repairing roads leading toward Nickajack Gap, about 3 miles south of Summertown. Stevens', and Cooper's Gaps held by small parties, not exceeding 200 in all, and a small force of cavalry. At Trenton, they say that 8,000 cavalry, under S. D. Lee, joined Wheeler at Muscle Shoals, with a view to strike our communications. If successful, Bragg intends to turn our right by roads below this point. If that expedition failed he should fall back nearer supplies. Bragg said to Jeff. Davis that it would take 10,000 lives to carry Chattanooga by storm. Davis objected to the sacrifice. There are rumors that a part of Longstreet's force have been withdrawn to La Fayette.

O. O. HOWARD,
    Major-General.

—

CIRCULAR.]   HDQRS. ELEVENTH AND TWELFTH CORPS,
    Bridgeport, Ala., October 26, 1863.

1. The movement on the south side of the Tennessee River will commence at sunrise October 27.

2. The mounted men from Alabama will precede the corps of Major-General Howard (the Eleventh), which will have the advance.

*See p. 43.

3. Brigadier-General Geary's division will follow immediately in rear of General Howard's corps. The commands will carry 60 rounds of small-arms ammunition, 40 in the boxes, 20 in the pockets; the artillery 200 rounds of ammunition. The commands will also carry their full complement of intrenching tools, three days' cooked provision, three days' forage for the animals. In the event of General Geary's wagons not being here, he will arrange for transportation with Major-General Howard.

4. The regiment from General Williams' division (Twelfth Corps) will remain, and after protecting the depots here by a proper guard, and furnishing the fatigue details, will hold the bridge head on the south side of the river. Brigadier-General Geary will promulgate this order to the regiments of the Twelfth Corps and cause them to take position at the time of his movement.

5. Brigadier-General Geary will move with such portions of his command as may arrive in time for the movement, leaving instructions for the balance of his command to follow immediately upon their arrival.

6. The column will proceed to Shellmound, and from thence to Rankin's Ferry. The commanding generals will look well to their right flanks, and guard against any injuries or annoyance from guerrillas.

By command of Major-General Hooker :

H. W. PERKINS,
Lieutenant, and Acting Assistant Adjutant-General.

—

DEPARTMENT HEADQUARTERS,
October 27, 1863—4.50 a. m.

General WHITAKER :

General Hazen's fleet has just left.

GEO. H. THOMAS,
Major-General, Commanding.

OCTOBER 27, 1863—5.30 a. m.

[Major-General THOMAS:]

We hold the crest, and the attack has just commenced. My troops are crossing more slowly than I expected. I should like a brigade in reserve here to hold this bank.

WM. F. SMITH,
Brigadier-General, Commanding.

[Indorsement.]

OCTOBER 27, 1863—6.30 a. m.

General Granger will send General Whitaker's brigade to Brown's Ferry immediately, to hold the crossing and be in reserve to General Smith.

GEO. H. THOMAS,
Major-General, Commanding.

OCTOBER 27, 1863—6.10 a. m.

Major-General THOMAS,
        Commanding:

A prisoner from the Fifteenth Alabama (Longstreet) states that his brigade is all there—is in this valley. Keep a close watch on the road over Lookout, and see that no troops get over there to-day. Send me some orderlies to communicate, as the smoke renders signals impossible.

WM. F. SMITH,
Brigadier-General, Commanding Expedition.

—

OCTOBER 27, 1863—7.02 a. m.

Major-General THOMAS:

Is the horse-boat where it can be sent to me? My men are not all across, and I am just going over. Look out for the mountain road, to keep off the rebels for a few hours. I should like a brigade to hold this bank until I get seated. Send me half a dozen orderlies.
        Yours, in good spirits and without breakfast,

WM. F. SMITH,
Brigadier-General, Commanding Expedition.

—

OCTOBER 27, 1863—7.20 a. m.

General WILLIAM F. SMITH:

The enemy are moving all their troops—infantry, cavalry, and artillery—out of the valley, toward Lookout Mountain.

W. B. HAZEN,
Brigadier-General.

—

HDQRS. FIRST BRIG., THIRD DIV., 14TH ARMY CORPS,
        October 27, 1863—8 a. m.

General WILLIAM F. SMITH:

The battery may be moved into the gorge or on the slope near the gorge.

J. B. TURCHIN,
Brigadier-General.

—

OCTOBER 27, 1863—8.40 a. m.

General REYNOLDS:

We are as busy at abatis and breastworks as our supply of tools will allow. I think, to make the line quite sure, we ought to have a couple more regiments to hold the gorge and road. I really think we are tolerably secure from all attempts to retake our position. Can Whitaker get in position to drive off this battery that is trying to get our bridge?

SMITH.

The fog has now cleared away, and communication will be much more rapid.

JESSE MERRILL,
Captain, and Chief Signal Officer.

BROWN'S FERRY, *October* 27, 1863.
(Received 10.30 a. m.)

General J. B. TURCHIN:

When your flanks are well protected by slashing, please let me know.

WM. F. SMITH,
Brigadier-General, Commanding.

—

CHATTANOOGA,
October 27, 1863—10.30 a. m.

General SMITH,
Brown's Ferry:

Whitaker has troops at Brown's Ferry. Call on them, if you want help. Have you ammunition enough? Will attend to the battery.

J. J. REYNOLDS,
Major-General.

—

OCTOBER 27, 1863—10.45 a. m.

General WHITAKER:

Keep a close watch on the road passing over Lookout, and see that the enemy passes no troops over there to-day. If the horse-boat can be brought to General Smith, I wish you to have it done.

THOMAS,
General.

—

CHATTANOOGA,
October 27, 1863—11 a. m.

General WILLIAM F. SMITH,
Brown's Ferry:

Report the appearance of the country in front, after you are seated. Cannot one brigade hold the place?

J. J. REYNOLDS,
Major-General.

—

OCTOBER 27, 1863—11 a. m.

General WHITAKER:

Go at once to Brown's Ferry with the most of your brigade to hold the bank of the river on your side, and support General Smith in establishing his men on the opposite hills.

THOMAS,
Major-General.

—

HEADQUARTERS ELEVENTH AND TWELFTH CORPS,
Shellmound, Tenn., October 27, 1863—11.10 a. m.

Brigadier-General GEARY,
Commanding Division:

The major-general commanding directs that you encamp your division at Shellmound to-night. A picket of 400 men is stationed at the forks of the road from Shellmound to Gordon's mines, with the road from Trenton via Warren's Mill; two companies at the fork near Warren's Mill. You will furnish a detail of 150 men to General Morton, of the Engineer Brigade, at Shellmound.

Very respectfully, &c.,
DANL. BUTTERFIELD,
Major-General, Chief of Staff.

—

HEADQUARTERS OF GENERAL HOOKER,
Shellmound, October 27, 1863—11.10 a. m.

Major-General HOWARD:

The major-general commanding directs that you occupy and hold Whiteside's with one brigade of your command, and encamp the balance of your corps, not otherwise ordered, at Running Waters to-night.

I am, very respectfully, your obedient servant,
DANL. BUTTERFIELD,
Major-General, and Chief of Staff.

—

OCTOBER 27, 1863—11.15 a. m.

General THOMAS:

No troops can pass in sight of these guns. They have a road diverging from the main road over the mountain, by which, after they leave the main road, they can pass unseen.

WHITAKER,
General.

—

OCTOBER 27, 1863—11.40 a. m.

General WHITAKER:

General Smith reports that the enemy is trying to hit his bridge with a battery. Can't you get in position to drive them off?

J. J. REYNOLDS,
Major-General.

—

HEADQUARTERS BROWN'S FERRY, *October 27, 1863.*
(Received 12 m.)

General TURCHIN:

Report to me the result of your scout sent out toward the mountain. My headquarters are where they were last night.

W. F. SMITH,
Brigadier-General, Commanding.

—

OCTOBER 27, 1863—12.40 p. m.

General THOMAS:

The bulk of the brigade is at Brown's Ferry; has been there for most three hours. The ferry-boat is probably filled with water; sunk at one end. If not under the enemy's sharpshooters she could be brought up ; she cannot now. A regiment and section of artillery went up the mountain toward the white house. This makes six or seven regiments that have passed where we could see them part of the way.

                    WHITAKER,
                        Brigadier-General.

Additional to General REYNOLDS :
    I will try and notify you when I can.
                    W. C. WHITAKER,
                        Brigadier-General.

--

                    · ON POINT OPPOSITE LOOKOUT,
                        October 27, 1863—1 p. m.
Captain LEONARD :
    A heavy column of infantry is moving across Chattanooga Valley toward our left.
                    S. A. THAYER,
                        Acting Signal Officer.

--

    HDQRS. FIRST BRIG., THIRD DIV., 14TH ARMY CORPS,
                        October 27, 1863—1.20 p. m.
General WILLIAM F. SMITH :
    The direction of the road is ascertained from the position. The breastworks were built and are manned by Hazen's brigade, and they would not change it at the suggestion of any officer of the day. Have found a road by which artillery may be brought to the top of the ridge ; will need some working.
                    J. B. TURCHIN,
                        Brigadier-General.

--

                    CHATTANOOGA,
                        October 27, 1863—1.30 p. m.
General SMITH,
    Brown's Ferry :
    Whitaker has troops at Brown's Ferry.   Call on them if you need help.   Have you ammunition enough?   Will attend to the battery.
                    J. J. REYNOLDS,
                        Major-General.

--

    HEADQUARTERS DEPARTMENT OF THE CUMBERLAND,
                Chattanooga, October 27, 1863—2 p. m.
Major-General HOOKER
    (Care Colonel Le Duc, Bridgeport):
    We have had possession of the south side of the river at Brown's Ferry since 5 o'clock this a. m.   Move forward with your force and take possession so as to command the road from Kelley's Ferry to

Brown's Ferry. Colonel Le Duc has been notified to see that you are supplied with forage and rations. Prisoners report that but two regiments of the enemy were in Lookout Valley this morning. Two brigades have been seen to pass over the point of Lookout and into the valley nearly out of range of our guns. So far as we now know, they have only six guns in the valley.

By command Major-General Thomas:

J. J. REYNOLDS,
Major-General, and Chief of Staff.

—

OCTOBER 27, 1863—2.20 p. m.

General THOMAS:

Two brigades, if not more, of mixed troops have passed over Lookout. They pass above the white house at the upper edge of the clearing. Shelling does not entirely prevent, though it greatly impeded their passage. There must be in Lookout Valley many more men of the enemy than General Smith has.

Respectfully,

WHITAKER,
Brigadier-General.

—

OCTOBER 27, 1863—2.30 p. m.

General WILLIAM F. SMITH:

Enemy have passed foot of mountain cliff on Lookout Mountain in heavy column in spite of my fire; coming this way.

W. C. WHITAKER,
Brigadier-General.

—

OCTOBER 27, [1863]—3.30 p. m.

General REYNOLDS:

This place cannot be carried now. I shall come into headquarters unless the general moves. A regiment has just gone up the mountain and all is quiet, so I suppose the sharpshooters have left the Suck.

SMITH,
Brigadier-General.

—

OCTOBER 27, 1863. (Received 4.40 p. m.)

General THOMAS and
General SMITH:

General Howard is here, and General Hooker is near in person. Howard had a slight skirmish, which detained them only a few moments. Had 5 or 6 wounded.

HAZEN,
Brigadier-General.

WHITESIDE'S,
October 27, 1863—4.40 p. m.

Major-General REYNOLDS,
    Chief of Staff:

Howard's advance encamps to-night at Whiteside's; the balance in rear along Running Water Creek. Geary's division, of Twelfth Army Corps, at Shellmound. No enemy, save one company, Ninth Kentucky (rebel) Cavalry, which retired at our approach. Pontoons left at Shellmound. We march at sunrise to-morrow.

JOSEPH HOOKER,
Major-General, Commanding.

—

WHITESIDE'S, TENN.,
October 27, 1863—7.30 p. m.

Brigadier-General GEARY,
    Shellmound :

The major-general commanding directs me to say that you will march your command at 5 a. m., instead of waiting until sunrise, as directed in previous order; that you will push on vigorously until you come up with the rear of the Eleventh Corps. Keep well closed up. Have your ammunition, artillery, &c., all up and in hand, ready for any emergency.
    Very respectfully,

DANL. BUTTERFIELD,
Major-General, Chief of Staff.

—

HEADQUARTERS ELEVENTH AND TWELFTH CORPS,
Whiteside's, Tenn., October 27, 1863.

Major-General HOWARD,
    Commanding Eleventh Corps :

Orders for October 28, 1863:

General Howard's command will march in the direction of Brown's Ferry, via Lookout Creek Valley. The detachment left at the forks of the Trenton and Gordon's Mines road will remain.

A force, to be hereafter designated from the Eleventh Corps, will remain at Whiteside's.

General Geary's division will march to come up with the rear of the Eleventh Corps, as early as practicable. All the commands will march at sunrise, prompt.

By command of Major-General Hooker :

DANL. BUTTERFIELD,
Major-General, Chief of Staff.

(Copy furnished Brigadier-General Geary.)

—

HEADQUARTERS ELEVENTH AND TWELFTH CORPS,
ARMY OF THE CUMBERLAND,
Shellmound, October 27, 1863.

Major-General HOWARD,
    Commanding Eleventh Corps :

GENERAL : I am directed by the major-general commanding to request that you will detach a regiment to take position at the junction of two roads leading from Trenton to Shellmound, and about 1 mile from last-named place on the branch railroad to Gordon's mines.

Direct the officer in command to detach two companies from this regiment to picket the forks of road leading to the right at the point [where] it intersects the direct road from Trenton to Bridgeport.

You will detach also a cavalry picket of 12 men to report to the officer in command of said regiment, and by him to be instructed to be thrown out at once in the direction of Trenton, extending their reconnaissance, if practicable, to that point. These men must be instructed to report all the information they can see and collect of the movements of the enemy. If they should discover a force at Trenton, they will endeavor to find out its strength, and report whether infantry or cavalry, or both, and, if important, to be communicated to headquarters (which will be at Running Waters to-night) without delay.

The officer intrusted with the command of this detached force will be instructed to hold the position at which his main force is posted at all hazards, and the two companies detached their position as long as it is practicable to do so, and if forced back it will be in the direction of their regiment.

By command of Major-General Hooker:

H. W. PERKINS,
Acting Assistant Adjutant-General.

—

SIGNAL STATION, BROWN'S FERRY, *October* 28, 1863.
(Received 6 a. m.)

General TURCHIN:

General Smith desires me to say that he wishes you to slash the isolated square piece of woods on your front center to-day. His headquarters are at this signal station.

P. C. F. WEST,
Aide-de-Camp.

—

CHATTANOOGA, *October* 28, 1863—8 p. m.
(Received 1.50 a. m., 29th.)

Maj. Gen. H. W. HALLECK,
Washington, D. C.:

General Thomas' plan for securing the river and south side road hence to Bridgeport has proven eminently successful. The question of supplies may now be regarded as settled. If the rebels give us one week more time I think all danger of losing territory now held by us will have passed away, and preparations may commence for offensive operations.

U. S. GRANT,
Major-General.

—

HDQRS. SECOND DIVISION, TWELFTH ARMY CORPS,
Within Three Miles of Whiteside's, October 28, 1863.

Maj. Gen. D. BUTTERFIELD,
Chief of Staff:

GENERAL: My command took up the line of march at the hour indicated, this morning, and I am progressing as rapidly as possible.

By placing strong working parties at labor we had the bridge at Shellmound completed at 1 o'clock this morning. Two regiments joined me this morning. I have detailed the Sixtieth New York, of Greene's brigade, to hold the pass leading to Trenton.

I have the honor to be, general, very respectfully, your obedient servant,

JNO. W. GEARY,
Brigadier-General, U. S. Volunteers, Commanding.

—

SHELLMOUND,
October 28, 1863.

Major-General REYNOLDS:

The advance arrived here at 10 o'clock. The gap leading toward Trenton is occupied, and troops have been moving toward Rankin's Ferry for half hour. Morton has the pontoon bridge here half laid. No news from Palmer. No signs of the enemy. It will be difficult— in fact, I should say impossible—to get the bridge higher up the river in season to be used by Palmer.

C. A. DANA.

—

OCTOBER 28, 1863—12 m.

Captain MERRILL:

The work I spoke of has four embrasures, and two guns have been fired from it. It is on this side of the ridge, about 200 yards from the point of rock. There is another gun just on the point toward opposite side, protected by high rock. Whitaker does not reach them.

PUTNAM.

—

DEPARTMENT HEADQUARTERS,
October 28, 1863—12.50 p. m.

General WHITAKER:

Hold yourself in readiness to re-enforce General Hooker if he calls upon you.

By command of General Thomas:

J. J. REYNOLDS,
Major-General, and Chief of Staff.

—

HEADQUARTERS ELEVENTH AND TWELFTH CORPS,
Near Whiteside's, Tenn., October 28, 1863.

Brigadier-General GEARY,
Commanding Division:

General Hooker directs that you encamp your division to-night at the point where you were directed to halt, viz., the intersection of the road to Kelley's Ferry and the one from Wauhatchie to Brown's Ferry. Headquarters to-night are about 1 mile south of Brown's Ferry.

Very respectfully,

H. W. PERKINS,
Lieutenant, Aide-de-Camp, and Actg. Asst. Adjt. Gen.

HEADQUARTERS ELEVENTH AND TWELFTH CORPS,
Rowden's House, Tenn., October 28, 1863—1.20 p. m.

Brigadier-General GEARY:

General Hooker directs that you halt your command and await orders at this place (Mr. Rowden's house, at the junction of Kelley's Ferry road and Brown's Ferry and Wauhatchie road).

Very respectfully,

H. W. PERKINS,
Lieutenant, Aide-de-Camp, and Actg. Asst. Adjt. Gen.

—

OCTOBER 28, 1863—2.45 p. m.

General THOMAS:

The enemy are shelling something up Lookout Valley, and have fired the bridge across Lookout Creek.

WHITAKER,
Brigadier-General.

—

HEADQUARTERS SIGNAL CORPS,
October 28, 1863—2.50 p. m.

Major-General REYNOLDS, *Chief of Staff:*

GENERAL: Officers report that the battery on Lookout Mountain is throwing shells up Lookout Valley in direction of Wauhatchie Junction. My own observations agree with this, as their guns can be seen pointed in that direction.

Respectfully submitted.

JESSE MERRILL,
Captain, and Chief Signal Officer.

—

(Received 3.25 p. m., October 28, 1863.)

General THOMAS:

The enemy are shelling down the road something upon Lookout Valley, and have fired the bridge across Lookout Creek.

WHITAKER,
Brigadier-General.

—

BROWN'S FERRY,
October 28, 1863—3.45 p. m.

Generals SMITH and THOMAS:

General Hooker's column is coming up from Lookout Valley within a quarter of a mile of our position.

W. B. HAZEN,
Brigadier-General.

—

SIGNAL STATION, CRANE'S HILL,
October 28, 1863—4.15 p. m.

Captain MERRILL:

The rebels have drawn their troops from their right for a mile. I cannot tell the effect of our shots from Fort Dunlap.

FITCH.

Hdqrs. Second Division, Twelfth Army Corps,
Rowden's House, October 28, 1863—4.30 p. m.

Maj. Gen. D. Butterfield, *Chief of Staff:*

General: I have the honor to report that my command has reached this point, where, pursuant to instructions, I will await orders.

Very respectfully, your obedient servant,
JNO. W. GEARY,
Brigadier-General, U. S. Volunteers, Commanding.

—

Fort Wood,
October 28, 1863—4.30 p. m.

Capt. W. Leonard:

Four regiments of infantry moved from crest of ridge to the enemy's extreme right, where they went into camp. Wagons have been going up to crest of ridge on almost every road all the afternoon.

Respectfully,
L. M. DE MOTTE,
Lieutenant, and Acting Signal Officer.

—

Station No. 2, Crane's Hill,
October 28, 1863—5.20 p. m.

Captain Merrill:

The rebels have drawn their troops from their right, for the effect of our shells from Fort Dunlap.

FORAKER,
Lieutenant, Acting Signal Officer.

—

Brown's Ferry,
October 28, 1863.

General Smith:

The rebels have this afternoon thrown up a line of works between Lookout Creek and the foot of Lookout Mountain.

W. B. HAZEN,
Brigadier-General.

—

Hdqrs. Signal Corps, Dept. of the Cumberland,
October 28, 1863.

Capt. J. P. Willard,
Aide-de-Camp:

Captain: The officers on the point opposite Lookout Mountain say the enemy's shells did no damage to us. I watched our own shells closely, and almost all of them fell short of the top of the mountain. One or two of them struck the crest, but not near their earth-works. The work has just been unmasked, and has three, or perhaps four, embrasures.

Very respectfully, yours,
JESSE MERRILL,
Captain, and Chief Signal Officer.

HEADQUARTERS ELEVENTH AND TWELFTH CORPS,
Whiteside's, Tenn., October 28, 1863—6.30 a. m.

Brigadier-General GEARY,
    Commanding Division:

The general directs that when your command reaches Whiteside's you detach one regiment to hold the branch road leading to Trenton, and direct the officer in command to examine the pass and select that position that will enable him to hold it against any force that may be sent against him. Press forward your own command, or we shall not be able to reach our destination to-night. Join the general with your command as soon as possible. Have your troops that are behind sent forward without delay.

    Very respectfully,

                    DANL. BUTTERFIELD,
                    Major-General, Chief of Staff.

—

                    CHATTANOOGA, *October* 28, 1863.

Maj. Gen. GEORGE H. THOMAS, *Chattanooga:*

It seems to me the steamer Paint Rock should by all means be got down to Brown's Ferry before morning, even if a house has to be torn down to provide the necessary fuel. There is every probability that the enemy will make every preparation possible before to-morrow night to prevent our accomplishing this.

                    U. S. GRANT,
                    Major-General.

—

HEADQUARTERS ELEVENTH AND TWELFTH CORPS,
    Lookout Valley, Tenn., October 29, 1863—1 a. m.

Major-General REYNOLDS,
    Chief of Staff, Chattanooga:

Major-General Hooker directs me to inform the major-general commanding that he has moved all his force to the assistance of General Geary, at Wauhatchie. No report has been received from General Geary, but heavy firing in that direction indicates that he has been attacked.

    Very respectfully,

                    DANL. BUTTERFIELD,
                    Major-General, Chief of Staff.

—

                    OCTOBER 29, 1863—1.15 a. m.

General THOMAS:

Heavy fire raging between this and Wauhatchie.

                    WHITAKER,
                    Brigadier-General.

—

                    OCTOBER 29, 1863—1.45 a. m.

General TURCHIN:

Leave one regiment of your eight regiments in position and move the rest of the regiments down to the gorge, and go down there in person and take command of all the troops there. I will be at General Hazen's headquarters. You can communicate with me by signal from this [point] or by sending up the mountain.

W. F. SMITH,
Brigadier-General.

—

OCTOBER 29, 1863—2.20 a. m.

General THOMAS:

A brisk engagement has been and is now going on in the vicinity of Wauhatchie, and General Hooker has moved part of his force down.

W. B. HAZEN,
Brigadier-General.

—

OCTOBER 29, 1863—2.30 a. m.

General THOMAS:

Fight still raging furiously. Think we are being driven a little.

W. C. WHITAKER,
Brigadier-General.

—

HEADQUARTERS ELEVENTH AND TWELFTH CORPS,
Lookout Valley, October 29, 1863—3 a. m.

General WHITAKER and Colonel MITCHELL,
Commanding Officers of Brigades, near Brown's Ferry Bridge:

Major-General Hooker directs me to say that, in accordance with instructions received from Major-General Thomas, you would be ready to move to his support. He desires that your commands move up and report to him.

Very respectfully,

DANL. BUTTERFIELD,
Major-General, Chief of Staff.

—

HEADQUARTERS ELEVENTH AND TWELFTH CORPS,
Lookout Valley, Tenn., October 29, 1863—3 a. m.

Major-General REYNOLDS,
Chief of Staff, Chattanooga:

General Hooker directs me to say that he has called up the brigades of General Whitaker and Colonel Mitchell; that the enemy has been foiled in his attempt thus far to break the line. We have prisoners from two brigades of Longstreet's corps. They state that two divisions, or all of Longstreet's corps that are here, have crossed, their aim being to prevent the opening of this line. Reports come in of sounds and commands as if massing and forming troops. The general anticipates from this and what the prisoners say a renewal of enemy's attack at daylight. He would like to have signal officers sent out.

Very respectfully,

DANL. BUTTERFIELD,
Major-General, Chief of Staff.

OCTOBER 29, 1863—3 a. m.

General TURCHIN :

You need not remove that regiment if you have not already done so.

W. F. SMITH,
Brigadier-General.

—

OCTOBER 29, 1863—3.30 a. m.

Colonel MITCHELL,
At General Whitaker's:

You will hold your command in readiness to proceed at a moment's notice to the support of General Hooker.

THOMAS,
General.

—

OCTOBER 29, 1863—3.30 a. m.

General WHITAKER :

The general commanding directs that you move to Brown's Ferry with your command, except your battery and proper support for it. Send this order also to Colonel Mitchell. Obey a call from General Hooker if one should come for aid.

J. J. REYNOLDS,
Major-General.

—

DEPARTMENT HEADQUARTERS,
October 29, 1863—3.50 a. m.

General WHITAKER :

Send a staff officer to Brown's Ferry to ascertain if you are needed, and if so move down at once.

By order of Maj. Gen. George H. Thomas :

J. J. REYNOLDS,
Major-General.

—

OCTOBER 29, 1863—4 a. m.

General THOMAS :

Fight abated. From sound enemy appear to hold Kelley's Gap, our troops having been apparently driven toward Wauhatchie. They have made an assault in direction of Smith's left, and have been repulsed. Do not know the troops. Judge from the sound.

W. C. WHITAKER,
Brigadier-General.

—

HEADQUARTERS ELEVENTH AND TWELFTH CORPS,
Lookout Valley, Tenn., October 29, 1863—4 a. m.

Brigadier-General GEARY,
Commanding Division:

General Hooker directs me to say that if you hear firing or fighting on your left, it will probably be General Schurz pushing out to join you. If you have to change position from the developments before or after daylight, aim to fight in this direction, but bear in mind if it should be necessary, which is not anticipated, that you have a line open via Kelley's Ferry to Brown's Ferry Bridge and Chattanooga. Schurz should be up with you by the time this reaches you.

Very respectfully,

DANL. BUTTERFIELD,
Major-General, Chief of Staff.

—

October 29, 1863—4.20 a. m.

General WHITAKER:

Send a staff officer to Brown's Ferry to ascertain if you are needed, and if so move down at once.

J. J. REYNOLDS,
Major-General.

—

HEADQUARTERS ELEVENTH AND TWELFTH CORPS,
Lookout Valley, Tenn., October 29, 1863—6.45 a. m.

Major-General REYNOLDS,
Chief of Staff, Chattanooga:

General Hooker directs me to say that the brigades of General Whitaker and Colonel Mitchell, ordered up at 3 a. m., have not yet reported.

Very respectfully,

DANL. BUTTERFIELD,
Major-General, Chief of Staff.

—

HDQRS. SECOND DIVISION, TWELFTH ARMY CORPS,
Rowden's House, October 29, 1863—7 a. m.

Maj. Gen. D. BUTTERFIELD,
Chief of Staff, Eleventh and Twelfth Army Corps:

GENERAL: My command is almost without ammunition. Please have some sent me, say 70,000 rounds. One brigade of General Schurz's has reported to me and been placed in position; the balance of his division is located in the mountain, and, I believe, is going to remain there.

I have the honor to be, general, very respectfully, your obedient servant,

JNO. W. GEARY,
Brigadier-General, U. S. Volunteers, Commanding.

—

HEADQUARTERS ELEVENTH AND TWELFTH CORPS,
Lookout Valley, Tenn., October 29, 1863—7.10 a. m.

Brigadier-General GEARY:

Yours of 7 a. m. received. Another brigade of General Schurz's has been sent you. With these you can relieve some of your regiments that are exhausted and out of ammunition.   Also another brigade from Chattanooga.   What ammunition we have has been sent forward, and is by this time up to the mountains where General Tyndale's brigade is posted, where you can get it.   When all these troops arrive detach a regiment to go and escort up the supply train 3 miles back toward Whiteside's.   Is your rear toward Whiteside's open? Can you send down in Lookout Creek Valley and find out anything for us concerning the enemy, with scouts or otherwise? .

Very respectfully,

DANL. BUTTERFIELD,
Major-General, Chief of Staff.

—

HEADQUARTERS ELEVENTH AND TWELFTH CORPS,
Lookout Valley, Tenn., October 29, 1863—7.45 a. m.

Major-General REYNOLDS,
Chief of Staff, Chattanooga:

The position now held and being intrenched by General Geary this side of Wauhatchie, at the forks of Kelley's Ferry and Chattanooga roads, should have the supervision of a competent engineer to locate lines and works in the most advantageous manner; the position is a very important one.   I have no engineer officer in the command. I have to request that one may be sent out here at once.

Very respectfully,

JOSEPH HOOKER,
Major-General, Commanding.

—

HEADQUARTERS ELEVENTH AND TWELFTH CORPS,
Lookout Valley, Tenn., October 29, 1863—8.20 a. m.

Major-General REYNOLDS,
Chief of Staff, Chattanooga:

General Schurz reports large columns of the enemy seen to march down along Lookout Creek, and then, turning to the right, marching up the mountain.   Is it not possible to injure them from the Moccasin Point or other batteries on the north side of the river? The prisoners captured last night on the ridge carried by Smith's brigade are sent in herewith.

Very respectfully,

JOSEPH HOOKER,
Major-General, Commanding.

—

HEADQUARTERS,
October 29, 1863—11 a. m.

General WHITAKER:

Report any change of pickets on Lookout Mountain.

J. J. REYNOLDS,
Major-General.

HEADQUARTERS ELEVENTH AND TWELFTH CORPS,
Lookout Valley, Tenn., October 29, 1863—2 p. m.

Brigadier-General CRUFT:

Major-General Hooker directs that you cross your command at Shellmound, if the bridge is still there, and move it up to this point.

Very respectfully, &c.,

DANL. BUTTERFIELD,
Major-General, Chief of Staff.

—

HEADQUARTERS ELEVENTH AND TWELFTH CORPS,
Lookout Valley, October 29, 1863—2.30 p. m.

Brigadier-General CRUFT,
Rankin's Ferry:

Please cross your command at Shellmound before bridge is removed, and march it to join General Hooker here, near Wauhatchie. A train of wagons will be to-morrow at Shellmound laden with supplies, for which you will please furnish an escort. If the bridge is removed at Shellmound before you can cross your force at Rankin's by it, march your command to Kelley's Ferry, where the bridge is to be sent, and cross it there, moving up to join here.

Very respectfully, &c.,

DANL. BUTTERFIELD,
Major-General, Chief of Staff.

—

HDQRS. SECOND DIVISION, TWELFTH ARMY CORPS,
Rowden's House, October 29, 1863—3.30 p.m.

Commanding Officer Advance Forces:

SIR: Bring your command to this point as rapidly as possible. We need re-enforcements. Guard well your right flank. Rowden's house is at the intersection of the Chattanooga and Brown's Ferry by the Kelley's Ferry road.

By command of Brig. Gen. John W. Geary:

THOS. H. ELLIOTT,
Captain, Assistant Adjutant-General.

—

OCTOBER 29, 1863—5 p. m.

General REYNOLDS:

See no change on the enemy's front or picket lines. As many are visible now as this time last evening. I have sent for the Ninety-ninth Ohio from the island to strengthen my pickets. Shall I stay here or go to the regiments re-enforcing General Hooker?

W. C. WHITAKER,
Brigadier-General.

HEADQUARTERS DEPARTMENT OF THE CUMBERLAND,
Chattanooga, October 29, 1863—6 p. m

Brig. Gen. CHARLES CRUFT,
Shellmound via Bridgeport
(Care Colonel Le Duc):

Leave one company at Rankin's Ferry to guard the supplies now there. Leave one brigade and your battery at Shellmound, where you will cross your whole command to the south side of river. Go with one brigade and Hooker's battery to Whiteside's and report to General Hooker.

By command of Major-General Thomas:

J. J. REYNOLDS,
Major-General, Chief of Staff.

—

DEPARTMENT HEADQUARTERS,
October 29, 1863.

General HOOKER:

General Cruft has been ordered to leave a battery and a brigade at Shellmound, and to move to Whiteside's with his other brigade and your battery, and report to you.

J. J. REYNOLDS,
Major-General.

—

OCTOBER 29, 1863—7.05 p. m.

General WHITAKER:

You can remain at your headquarters to-night, but be prepared to cross the river in case of an attack.

THOMAS,
General.

—

OCTOBER 29, 1863—7.25 p. m.

Signal Officer at General Whitaker's Headquarters:

In which direction did you see the rebel troops move this p. m.? Toward Missionary Ridge or Lookout Mountain? Answer immediately.

GEO. H. THOMAS,
Major-General.

—

HEADQUARTERS SIGNAL CORPS,
October 29, 1863.

Maj. Gen. J. J. REYNOLDS:

GENERAL: The officer on signal station opposite Lookout, at Fort Whitaker, reports the following:

Heavy columns of rebel troops have been passing across Chattanooga Valley from right (our right) to left. Were seen to pass front of General Baird's division. They occupied half an hour in passing one point. He estimates the number at about that of a division. No artillery with them. Battery No. 5 opened upon them. Could see them as they passed the different openings until they entered the woods at a point he judges to be opposite General Rousseau's command. This was at about 12 m.

Respectfully,

W. E. SHERIDAN,
Captain, and Acting Signal Officer.

—

Hdqrs. Second Division, Twelfth Army Corps,
Rowden's House, October 29, 1863—7.25 p. m.

Maj. Gen. D. Butterfield,
Chief of Staff, Eleventh and Twelfth Army Corps:

General : Two brigades of Schurz's division are now here, one having reported at 7 o'clock. I have placed it in position. Have received 11,000 rounds of ammunition from General Howard. Will send for more to the place where General Tyndale is located. My rear toward Whiteside's is open. I am looking for two of my regiments and the other section of my battery, which are reported near with the supply train. I will send out scouts down Lookout Creek Valley. Cavalry would be very useful.

I have the honor to be, general, very respecfully, your obedient servant,

JNO. W. GEARY,
Brigadier-General, U. S. Volunteers, Commanding.

—

OCTOBER 29, 1863—7.50 p. m.
General Thomas :

Rebel troops were moving about northeast. They were twenty-seven minutes in passing a given point.

WOOD,
Lieutenant, and Acting Signal Officer.

—

BRIDGEPORT, *October 30, 1863.*
Major-General Reynolds,
Chief of Staff:

The Paint Rock left Brown's Ferry at 6.30 o'clock this morning; arrived here at twenty minutes to 12. She came down nicely. In rounding Lookout Point last night she was fired into, doing no serious damage. A hole was made in one of the steam pipes, which will be repaired, calked. Also loaded with provisions and started back for Brown's Ferry. She will tow scows to Kelley's Ferry. The crabs at the Suck for hauling over are still there, and apparently in good order. They ought to be guarded at once, as the boat cannot get up without them, and one of the prisoners on the boat said the rebels were going to destroy [them.] A force should be in the vicinity of the Suck, the Pot and Pan, to prevent small boats of the enemy from keeping the boats back.

HENRY C. HODGES,
Lieutenant-Colonel, and Chief Quartermaster.

ORDERS.]   HDQRS. DEPARTMENT OF THE CUMBERLAND,
                              Chattanooga, November 1, 1863.

The general commanding tenders his thanks to Brig. Gen. W. F. Smith and the officers and men of the expedition under his command, consisting of the brigades of Brigadier-Generals Turchin and Hazen, the boat parties under Col. T. R. Stanley, Eighteenth Ohio Volunteers, and the pioneer bridge party, Captain Fox, Michigan Engineers, for the skill and cool gallantry displayed in securing a permanent lodgment on the south side of the river at Brown's Ferry, and in putting in position the pontoon bridge, on the night of the 26th instant. The successful execution of this duty was attended with the most important results in obtaining a safe and easy communication with Bridgeport and shortening our line of supplies.

By command of Major-General Thomas:
                                                    C. GODDARD,
                    Lieutenant-Colonel, and Assistant Adjutant-General.

—

GENERAL ORDERS,)   HDQRS. DEPT. OF THE CUMBERLAND,
          No. 265.   )   *Chattanooga, Tenn., November 7, 1863.*

The recent movements, resulting in the establishment of a new and short line of communication with Bridgeport, and the possession of the Tennessee River, were of so brilliant a character as to deserve special notice.

The skill and cool gallantry of the officers and men composing the expedition under Brig. Gen. William F. Smith, chief engineer, consisting of the brigades of Brigadier-Generals Turchin and Hazen, the boat parties under Colonel Stanley, Eighteenth Ohio Volunteers, and the pontoniers under Captain Fox, Michigan Engineers and Mechanics, in effecting a permanent lodgment on the south side of the river, at Brown's Ferry, deserve the highest praise.

The column under Major-General Hooker, which took possession of the line from Bridgeport to the foot of Lookout Mountain, deserve great credit for their brilliant success in driving the enemy from every position which they attacked. The bayonet charge, made by the troops of General Howard, up a steep and difficult hill, over 200 feet high, completely routing the enemy and driving him from his barricades on its top, and the repulse, by General Geary's command, of greatly superior numbers, who attempted to surprise him, will rank among the most distinguished feats of arms of this war.

By command of Maj. Gen. George H. Thomas:
                                                    C. GODDARD,
                                        Assistant Adjutant-General.

———

No. 2.

Dispatches of Charles A. Dana, Assistant Secretary of War.

                                        NASHVILLE, TENN.,
                                        October 21, 1863—9 a. m.

I arrived here at 10 last night, and return south with Grant this morning. Our train narrowly escaped destruction at a point about 8 miles from here. A tie had been inserted in a cattle guard to throw the train down an embankment, but it had been calculated for a train going south, and ours broke it off without damage. The purpose apparently was to destroy Grant on his way to Bridgeport.

[C. A. DANA.]

Hon. E. M. STANTON,
　　Secretary of War.

—

CHATTANOOGA, TENN.,
October 23, 1863.

No change in the situation here. Ten days' rations on hand. Thomas firmly resolved to hold at all events. Rain heavy since midnight and roads worse to-day than yesterday.

An immediate movement for the occupation of Raccoon Mountain and Lookout Valley is indispensable, but Hooker, though ordered ten days since to concentrate his forces for the purpose, has not done so, but waits on the ground that his wagons have not arrived from Nashville. The fact is, however, that about one hundred have arrived, and, besides, Thomas will not allow him to take any wagons at all in this movement. But Hooker seems to show no zeal in the enterprise. It will necessarily wait somewhat for the arrival of Grant, who was not able to make the whole distance of 55 miles on horseback yesterday, but will get in before night.

The interior line of fortifications is so far advanced that General Smith tells me only one day's work more is needed to make them tenable, and the place temporarily safe with a garrison of 10,000 men, though the works will still be far from finished. The pontoons are done for a bridge across to Lookout Valley as soon as Hooker has moved into that position.

The change in command is received with satisfaction by all intelligent officers so far as I can ascertain. The sentiment of the troops I do not yet know about. Of course Rosecrans has many friends who are unable to conceive why he is relieved, and these report he is to command the Army of the Potomac. The change at headquarters here is already strikingly perceptible. Order prevails instead of universal chaos. General Thomas thinks enemy are moving up against Burnside.

[C. A. DANA.]

Hon. E. M. STANTON,
　　Secretary of War.

—

CHATTANOOGA, TENN.,
October 23, 1863—3 p. m.

Among the officers who most resolutely required the relief of Crittenden and McCook was General Palmer. It appears that he expected to succeed Crittenden, for on the consolidation he resigned. Now that the Fourteenth Corps has to receive a new commander I would respectfully recommend that Palmer's resignation be accepted. This will leave Reynolds the ranking major-general in this army next to Rousseau, who is so unfit that he cannot be considered.

[C. A. DANA.]

Hon. E. M. STANTON,
　　Secretary of War.

CHATTANOOGA,
October 24, 1863—10 a. m.

Grant arrived last night, wet, dirty, and well. He is just going to reconnoiter an important position which General Smith has discovered at the mouth of Lookout Valley, and which will be occupied from here simultaneously with Hooker's occupation of Raccoon Mountain. This movement will probably take place within three days.

No demonstration from the enemy. Deserters report that Longstreet's men have all just received new clothing, and are going away, either up the river or to Virginia. Breckinridge's division goes with them.

[C. A. DANA.]

Hon. E. M. STANTON,
    Secretary of War.

—

CHATTANOOGA,
October 24, 1863—9 p. m.

There is good evidence that rebels are moving in large force toward Cleveland. Heavy railroad trains go up and light ones return. No doubt Longstreet is now going to Kingston.

This army is unable to act for want of animals, but the movement will facilitate the opening of the Tennessee.

[C. A. DANA.]

Hon. E. M. STANTON,
    Secretary of War.

—

CHATTANOOGA,
October 24, 1863—10 p. m.

The movement of the enemy to our left has obliged Grant to order Sherman up toward Stevenson, leaving Memphis and Charleston Railroad east of Bear Creek unfinished. It is indispensable to be able to hold McMinnville and have force ready to march north to cover Nashville.

[C. A. DANA.]

Hon. E. M. STANTON,
    Secretary of War.

—

CHATTANOOGA,
October 25, 1863—11 a. m.

Deserters who came in this morning report that Cheatham's old division, forming part of his present corps, is now at Charleston on the Hiwassee. It is also reported that 5,000 rebel mounted infantry have crossed the Tennessee above Washington, but this needs confirmation. I am going over to Bridgeport to observe General Hooker's movement to Raccoon Mountain, in which he has so far manifested a surprising unreadiness. The precise time for his advance is not yet fixed, but it will probably be to-morrow night.

Palmer's division moved from here last night on its way to Rankin's Ferry, where it will cross the Tennessee to co-operate with Hooker.

The force which will cross at Brown's Ferry to occupy the mamelon, at the mouth of Lookout Valley, will consist of three brigades, of which the first, under Hazen, will proceed to the spot in the pontoons, of which the bridge to be thrown across there will be composed. The other two march, the distance being about 4 miles, and all are to be on the ground before daylight Tuesday morning.

This expedition to Lookout Valley will probably be commanded by General Smith. Reconnaissance yesterday showed the rebels have only a cavalry picket at Brown's Ferry, and no force on the mamelon. Cold; cloudy; no rain.

[C. A. DANA.]

Hon. E. M. Stanton,
    Secretary of War.

—

CHATTANOOGA,
October 25, 1863—11 p. m.

Careful inquiry through the army discloses nothing but general satisfaction at recent changes. Officers generally feel that continuance of Rosecrans in command was the destruction of the army, and no men could be found in whom all would feel so much confidence as in Thomas and Grant.

Howard now occupies Shellmound, and has found one locomotive and three freight cars on the railroad there in working order. We have rebel papers to the 23d. Jeff. Davis was at Selma on the 18th. He unqualifiedly sustains Bragg. Returns from Georgia election show that in 105 counties only 25,800 votes were cast, including the army vote. All complain loudly of scarcity of provisions, and predict terrible suffering among the poor during the coming winter. Pleasant.

[C. A. DANA.]

Hon. E. M. Stanton,
    Secretary of War.

—

BRIDGEPORT,
October 26, 1863—2 p. m.

The movement for the occupation of Raccoon Mountain and Lookout Valley was to have begun this morning. Everything is ready at Chattanooga, and Palmer will be at Rankin's Ferry in season, but Hooker is behindhand and it is postponed till to-morrow. The forces sent from here are Howard's two divisions and Geary's, 10,000 men in all.

Our advices from Lookout indicate that the rebels have withdrawn from the valley and from the top of the mountain, keeping only a small force at Stevens' and Cooper's Gaps and Nickajack Trace. Their pickets were also much diminished last evening at the foot of the mountain on the Chattanooga side. They have gone up the railroad after Burnside on the west. The steam-boat building here will be ready to run within three days. Cloudy; rain threatened.

[C. A. DANA.]

Hon. E. M. Stanton,
    Secretary of War.

BRIDGEPORT,
October 27, 1863—6.30 a. m.

Troops are now just moving out for Shellmound and Raccoon Mountain. No evidence to show that the rebels will oppose the undertaking. Hooker came here from Stevenson last night. He is in an unfortunate state of mind for one who has to co-operate, fault finding, criticising, dissatisfied. No doubt the chaos of Rosecrans' administration is as bad as he describes, but he is quite as truculent toward the plan he is now to execute as toward the impotence and confusion of the old *régime.*

[C. A. DANA.]

Hon. E. M. STANTON,
Secretary of War.

—

WHITESIDE'S VALLEY,
October 27, 1863—4.30 p. m.

The advance of Hooker has just reached here. A rebel cavalry picket fled on our approach. Two captured report no considerable force in the valley. No reason to doubt that communication will be opened with Chattanooga to-morrow. Cloudy.

[C. A. DANA.]

Hon. E. M. STANTON,
Secretary of War.

—

CHATTANOOGA,
October 28, 1863—5 p. m.

Everything perfectly successful. The river is now open, and a short and good road in our possession along the south shore. We had an insignificant skirmish near Wauhatchie. The great success, however, is General Smith's operation at the mouth of Lookout Valley. Its brilliancy cannot be exaggerated.

[C. A. DANA.]

Hon. E. M. STANTON,
Secretary of War.

—

CHATTANOOGA,
October 29, 1863—9 a. m.

On reaching the mouth of Lookout Valley yesterday afternoon, Hooker encamped Howard's corps at the west base of the range of five mamelons or hills occupied and fortified by General Smith, while he encamped Geary's division at Wauhatchie, fully 2½ miles distant. These positions not only invited attack from the enemy, who could see everything from the top of Lookout Mountain, but were very bad for the defense of the valley, and General Hazen, commanding the forces on the mamelons, went to General Hooker and endeavored to get him to take up a compact line across the valley, and to bring all his forces together. But being confident the enemy would not disturb him, Hooker refused to change his dispositions. The consequence was that about 12 p. m. rebels fell upon Geary, seeking to crush and capture him before succor could be brought up. The moonlight was almost as bright as day, and Geary having strong pickets out got timely warning. The fight was very furious. Howard, marching to the relief of Geary, was heavily struck in the flank, but his corps behaved splendidly, and finally effected its junction with Geary. The enemy was successfully repulsed, and withdrew at 4 a. m. Our loss in killed is reported as small, but we had many wounded. No further details yet received. Two brigades from here have gone this morning to support Hooker, and Grant and Thomas are now there. The mamelons are also occupied by the brigades of Hazen and Turchin, temporarily under Smith.

No part of Palmer's division has yet got across the Tennessee, it having proved impossible to move the pontoon bridge above Shellmound, while Palmer had marched to Rankin's Ferry. This force will, however, join Hooker to-night, making in all 25,000 men in Lookout Valley. Prisoners report Longstreet's whole corps there. Hooker is hard at work intrenching. No news from enemy up river.

[C. A. DANA.]

Hon. E. M. STANTON,
    Secretary of War.

—

CHATTANOOGA,
October 29, 1863—1 p. m.

General Grant desires me to request for him that Lieut. Col. J. H. Wilson, of his staff, captain of Engineers, be appointed brigadier-general of volunteers. Grant wants him to command cavalry, for which he possesses uncommon qualifications. Knowing Wilson thoroughly, I heartily indorse the application.

Grant also wishes to have both Hooker and Slocum removed from his command, and the Eleventh and Twelfth Corps consolidated under Howard. He would himself order Hooker and Slocum away, but hesitates because they have just been sent here by the President. Besides, I think he would rather prefer that so serious a proceeding should come from headquarters. Hooker has behaved badly ever since his arrival, and Slocum has just sent in a very disorderly communication, stating that when he came here it was under promise that he should not have to serve under Hooker, whom he neither regards with confidence as an officer nor respects as a man. Altogether Grant feels that their presence here is replete with both trouble and danger ; besides, the smallness of the two corps requires their consolidation, and even after that it will be necessary to add troops to make the numbers of the new consolidated corps respectable.

[C. A. DANA.]

Hon. E. M. STANTON,
    Secretary of War.

—

CHATTANOOGA,
October 29, 1863—9.30 p. m.

Enemy have continued firing all day from four guns which they have placed on top of Lookout Mountain. The only effect of their shells has been the wounding of 3 men. They have also thrown up works at the west base of the mountain. We have also thrown up rifle-pits and epaulements in Lookout Valley. Precise number of casualties in last night's battle not yet reported, but as nearly as I can ascertain the killed are about 70; the wounded, 200. The new steam-boat Chattanooga, just finished at Bridgeport, landed her first cargo to-day at Rankin's Ferry, and will land another at Kelley's Ferry to-morrow. The distance from the last-named place to Chattanooga is 10 miles; road excellent. As soon as her powers are well ascertained she will try to come up through the Suck and other dangers of the river to Brown's Ferry, at the mouth of Lookout Valley.

[C. A. DANA.]

Hon. E. M. STANTON,
    Secretary of War.

—

CHATTANOOGA,
October 30, 1863—7 a. m.

The steamboat Paint Rock passed down from the landing here to Brown's Ferry shortly after midnight last night. In passing Lookout Mountain she was fired at by musketry, and the cannon on the summit gave her a few shots, but neither boat nor crew suffered injury. This boat can bring 200 tons of freight to Brown's Ferry landing daily. Rain this morning, but we have the river. As soon as the gaps in Raccoon Mountain are fortified, Chattanooga will be absolutely safe.

[C. A. DANA.]

Hon. E. M. STANTON,
    Secretary of War.

No. 3.

Return of Casualties in the Union forces engaged under Maj. Gen. Joseph Hooker, at Wauhatchie, Tenn., October 28–29, 1863.

[Compiled from nominal lists of casualties, returns, &c.]

Command.	Killed.		Wounded.		Captured or missing.		Aggregate.
	Officers.	Enlisted men.	Officers.	Enlisted men.	Officers.	Enlisted men.	
ELEVENTH ARMY CORPS.							
Maj. Gen. OLIVER O. HOWARD.							
SECOND DIVISION.							
Brig. Gen. ADOLPH VON STEINWEHR.							
First Brigade. *							
Col. ADOLPHUS BUSCHBECK.							
134th New York							
154th New York				1			1
27th Pennsylvania							
73d Pennsylvania				1			1
Total First Brigade				2			2

* In reserve.

Return of Casualties in the Union forces, &c.—Continued.

Command.	Killed.		Wounded.		Captured or missing.		Aggregate.
	Officers.	Enlisted men.	Officers.	Enlisted men.	Officers.	Enlisted men.	
Second Brigade.							
Col. ORLAND SMITH.							
33d Massachusetts..........................	3	23	5	56	......	1	88
136th New York..........................	......	2	......	4	......	......	6
55th Ohio *..........................							
73d Ohio..........................	1	11	5	50	......	1	68
Total Second Brigade.............	4	36	10	110	......	2	162
Total Second Division.............	4	36	10	112	......	2	164
THIRD DIVISION.							
Maj. Gen. CARL SCHURZ.							
First Brigade.							
Brig. Gen. HECTOR TYNDALE.							
101st Illinois...							
45th New York......							
143d New York......							
61st Ohio........							
82d Ohio.........							
Total First Brigade.............							
Second Brigade.							
Col. WLADIMIR KRZYZANOWSKI.							
58th New York....							
119th New York......							
141st New York......							
26th Wisconsin......							
Total Second Brigade.............							
Third Brigade.							
Col. FREDERICK HECKER.							
80th Illinois.......							
68th New York......							
75th Pennsylvania......							
Total Third Brigade.............							
Total Third Division †.............	1	2	3	24	......	7	37
CAVALRY.							
1st Alabama........							
5th Tennessee, Company G.............	......	2	......	1	......	......	3
Total Eleventh Army Corps.............	5	40	13	137	......	9	204
TWELFTH ARMY CORPS.							
SECOND DIVISION.							
Brig. Gen. JOHN W. GEARY.							
Staff........	......	......	2	......	......	......	2

* On picket.
† Losses by regiments not fully reported in detail.

Return of Casualties in the Union forces, &c.—Continued.

Command.	Killed.		Wounded.		Captured or missing.		Aggregate.
	Officers.	Enlisted men.	Officers.	Enlisted men.	Officers.	Enlisted men.	
Second Brigade.							
Col. George A. Cobham, Jr.							
Staff......			1				1
29th Pennsylvania		1		5		1	7
109th Pennsylvania	1	4	1	22		4	32
111th Pennsylvania	2	6	6	31		1	46
Total Second Brigade	3	11	8	58		6	86
Third Brigade.							
Brig. Gen. George S. Greene.							
Staff......			1				1
78th New York				2			2
137th New York		15	3	72			90
149th New York		1	1	11			13
Total Third Brigade		16	5	85			106
Artillery.							
Pennsylvania Light, Battery E (two sections)	1	2	1	18			22
Total Second Division	4	29	16	161		6	216
Total Eleventh and Twelfth Army Corps*	9	69	29	298		15	420

OFFICERS KILLED OR MORTALLY WOUNDED.

MASSACHUSETTS.

Lieut. Joseph P. Burrage, 33d Infantry.
Lieut. James Hill, 33d Infantry.
Lieut. Oswego Jones, 33d Infantry.
Lieut. William P. Mudge, 33d Infantry.

OHIO.

Capt. William H. McGroarty, 61st Infantry.
Capt. Luther M. Buchwalter, 73d Intantry.

PENNSYLVANIA.

Capt. Charles A. Atwell, Battery E, Light Artillery.
Lieut. Edward R. Geary, Battery E, Light Artillery.
Lieut. James Glendening, 109th Infantry.
Maj. John A. Boyle, 111th Infantry.
Lieut. Marvin D. Pettit, 111th Infantry.

---

* In addition to the casualties contained in this table, the command of General William F. Smith, in its operations at Brown's Ferry, suffered the loss of 4 killed and 17 wounded, a total of 21.   For detailed statement see Smith's report, p. 77.

No. 4.

Report of Brig. Gen. William F. Smith, U. S. Army, Chief Engineer, Department of the Cumberland.

HDQRS. DEPT. OF THE CUMBERLAND, OFFICE OF CHF. ENGR.,
Chattanooga, November 4, 1863.

GENERAL : I have the honor to submit the following report of the operations for making a lodgment on the south side of the river at Brown's Ferry :

On the 19th of October, I was instructed by General Rosecrans to reconnoiter the river in the vicinity of Williams' Island, with a view to making the island a cover for a steamboat landing and storehouses, and began the examination near the lower end of the island. Following the river up, I found on the opposite bank, above the head of the island, a sharp range of hills, whose base was washed by the river. This range extended up the river nearly to Lookout Creek, and was broken at Brown's Ferry by a narrow gorge, through which ran the road to the old ferry, and also flowed a small creek. The valley between this ridge of hills and Raccoon Mountain was narrow, and a lodgment effected there would give us the command of the Kelley's Ferry road, and seriously interrupt the communications of the enemy up Lookout Valley and down to the river on Raccoon Mountain. The ridge seemed thinly picketed, and the evidences were against the occupation of that part of the valley by a large force of the enemy, and it seemed quite possible to take by surprise what could not have been carried by assault, if heavily occupied by an opposing force.

The major-general commanding the geographical division, and the major-general commanding the department, visited with me the ferry a few days after this reconnaissance, and were agreed as to the importance of the position by itself, and especially in connection with the movements to be made from Bridgeport to open the river, and I was directed to make the necessary arrangements for the expedition to effect the lodgment. To do this, 50 pontoons, with oars, to carry a crew and 25 armed men, were prepared, and also 2 flat-boats, carrying 40 and 75 men. The force detailed for the expedition consisted of the brigades of Brigadier-General Turchin and Brigadier-General Hazen, with three batteries, to be posted under the direction of Major Mendenhall, assistant to General Brannan, chief of artillery.

Sunday, the 25th of October, I was assigned to the command of the expedition, and the troops were distributed as follows : Fifteen hundred men, under Brigadier-General Hazen, were to embark in the boats and pass down the river a distance of about 9 miles, seven of which would be under the fire of the pickets of the enemy. It was deemed better to take this risk than to attempt to launch the boats near the ferry, because they would move more rapidly than intelligence could be taken by infantry pickets, and, in addition, though the enemy might be alarmed, he would not know where the landing was to be attempted, and therefore could not concentrate with certainty against us. The boats were called off in sections, and the points at which each section was to land were carefully selected and pointed out to the officers in command and range fires kept burning, lest in the night the upper points should be mistaken. The remainder of General Turchin's brigade and General Hazen's brigade were marched across, and encamped in the woods out of sight, near the ferry, ready to move down and cover the landing of the boats, and also ready to embark so soon as the boats had landed the river force and crossed to the north side. The artillery was also halted in the woods during the night, and was to move down and go into position as soon as the boats had begun to land, to cover the retirement of our troops in case of disaster. The equipage for the pontoon bridge was also ready to be moved down to the river so soon as the troops were across. Axes were issued to the troops, to be used in cutting abatis for defense so soon as the ridge was gained. General Hazen was to take the gorge and the hills to the left, while General Turchin was to extend from the gorge down the river.

The boats moved from Chattanooga at 3 a. m. on the 27th, and, thanks to a slight fog and the silence observed, they were not discovered until about 5 a. m., when the first section had landed at the upper point, and the second section had arrived abreast of the picket stationed at the gorge. Here a portion of the second section of the flotilla failed to land at the proper place, and, alarming the pickets, received a volley. Some time was lost in effecting a landing below the gorge, and the troops had hardly carried it before the enemy began the attack. The boats by this time had recrossed the river, and Lieutenant-Colonel Langdon, First Ohio Volunteers, in command of the remnant of the brigade of General Hazen, was rapidly ferried across, and, forming his men quickly, pushed forward to the assistance of the troops under Lieutenant-Colonel Foy, Twenty-third Kentucky Volunteers, already hard pressed.

The skirmish was soon over, and General Turchin, who followed Lieutenant-Colonel Langdon, quietly took possession of the hills assigned to him. So soon as the skirmishers were thrown out from each command, the axes were set at work felling an abatis, and in two hours the command was sufficiently protected to withstand any attack which was likely to be made. So soon as the last of the troops were across, the bridge was commenced and continued under some shelling for an hour or so, and was completed at 4.30 p. m., under the vigorous and skillful superintendence of Capt. P. V. Fox, First Michigan Engineers, and Capt. G. W. Dresser, Fourth Artillery. Six prisoners were taken and 6 rebels buried by our command, and several wounded reported by citizens, and among the wounded the colonel of the Fifteenth Alabama Volunteers. Twenty beeves, 6 pontoons, a barge, and about 2,000 bushels of corn fell into our possession. Our loss was 6 killed, 23 wounded, and 9 missing.

The artillery placed in position was not used, but credit is due Major Mendenhall for his promptitude in placing his guns. To Brigadier-General Turchin, Brigadier-General Hazen, Colonel Stanley, Eighteenth Ohio Volunteers, who had the superintendence of the boats and was zealous in his duty, and to Captain Fox, First Michigan Engineers, all credit is due for their zeal, coolness, and intelligence. Captain Dresser, Fourth Artillery, and Capt. P C. F. West, U. S. Coast Survey, rendered every service on my staff. Lieutenants Klokke, Fuller, Hopkins, and Brent, of the signal corps, were zealous in the discharge of their duties, and soon succeeded in establishing a line of communication from the south side of the river.

I inclose the reports of the various commanders.*
Respectfully submitted.

                                WM. F. SMITH,
        Brigadier-General, Chief Engineer, Comdg. Expedition.

---

*A map of the country in vicinity of Brown's Ferry, made to accompany this report, will appear in Atlas.

[Inclosure.]

List of Casualties* during the action at Brown's Ferry, October 27, 1863.

Regiment.	Killed.	Wounded.	Missing.	Total.
33d Ohio Volunteer Infantry..	1	2	......	3
41st Ohio Volunteer Infantry..	1	2	......	3
124th Ohio Volunteer Infantry..	......	4	......	4
5th Kentucky Volunteer Infantry...	1	......	......	1
23d Kentucky Volunteer Infantry..	1	9	......	10
Total..	4	17	......	21

No. 5.

Report of Col. Timothy R. Stanley, Eighteenth Ohio Infantry.

HDQRS. EIGHTEENTH REGIMENT OHIO VOLUNTEERS,
Chattanooga, Tenn., October 28, 1863.

LIEUTENANT: I have the honor to report the part taken by the forces under my command during the recent expedition to Brown's Ferry, 9 miles by the river below this place.

On the 25th instant I was ordered by General Smith to have ready fifty pontoon boats and one ferry-flat to transport and ferry troops; to organize parties to man them; to superintend, and have all ready to move the following day. To do this required the building of some ten additional boats and the making of one hundred and fifty oars and row-locks, all which was being done under the direction of Captain Fox, of the Michigan Mechanics and Engineers. I detailed 100 men from my own regiment, under command of Captains Grosvenor and Cable, and requested details of river men from other regiments, which were furnished as follows: From the Thirty-third Ohio and Second Ohio, under command of Lieutenant McNeal, 88 men; from the Thirty-sixth Ohio, under command of Lieutenant Haddow, and from the Ninety-second Ohio, under command of Lieutenant Stephenson, each 44 men. I directed boats' crews to consist of 1 corporal and 4 men, and each two boats to be under command of a sergeant, each detail to be under command of a commissioned officer. I afterward added a large flat, in which I carried 60 men. The pontoons each carried 25 men besides the boats' crews, making in the whole fleet fifty-two boats and 1,600 men.

It was nearly night of the 26th before the boats were all ready, and far into the night before we were supplied with oars, and had it not been for the energy of the Michigan Mechanics and Engineers we would not have been supplied at all. The boats were, however, loaded, and at the appointed hour, 3 o'clock in the morning of the 27th, we left the shore and rowed to the other side of the river, passing through the opening made for us in the pontoon bridge. Keeping near the right bank, we floated down stream until the rear had well closed up, when we pulled steadily and silently under the shadow of the trees near the right bank, until opposite the point of Lookout Mountain, where the current, setting strongly toward the mountain, threw us some distance from shore, but we quickly, however, regained

---

* Nominal list omitted.

our place, and thus glided past the enemy's pickets on the left and part of our own on the right without being discovered by the enemy. We were seen by the enemy posted near Lookout Creek, but after some conversation among themselves they concluded it was only drift. I had provided one of the flats for General Hazen, and Captain McElroy, of the steamer, gave me a select crew to man her, and in that I took passage with General Hazen and staff, following the first boat. The moon was so obscured by clouds that we were favored in that respect, but the perfect order and stillness with which we moved prevented discovery.

I had divided the boats into two fleets, one half under direction of Lieutenant McNeal, to make the landing at Brown's Ferry, the other half under Captain Grosvenor to land at the gap above, our guide having pointed out to me the two gaps. I landed on the right shore above the upper one, and gave directions to each as they came down to make the proper landing, which was easily done without alarming the enemy, as the boats came down close to that shore. I was gratified to see how silently they came; how well they had obeyed my orders. The leading boat landing, the others quickly followed, all unloading the armed men, who quickly gained the top of the bank, surprising the enemy's pickets, the boats quickly, according to previous arrangements, crossing to the right shore, coming down and up to the Brown's Ferry landing, which point I had also at this time reached, where the remainder of the forces were in waiting, who, being properly counted off into boat loads, were quickly and regularly loaded, and thus the whole force were ferried, 5,000 men, in less than one hour. There was no confusion. Every officer and man did his whole duty, did it fearlessly, willingly, and well, although there was sharp firing by the enemy, and bullets were flying thick both on the river and the shore where we were loading into the boats.

Having thus crossed the whole infantry force, and daylight having come and my men being exhausted with their efforts, the boats were all tied up to shore in line ready. I ordered breakfast for most of the men, keeping, however, a sufficient number of boats running to carry officers' messages, and gave directions to Captain Cable to fit up the ferry-flat, and cross two pieces of artillery, which he did, taking command in person under fire of the enemy's artillery, which had in the meantime commenced throwing shells into our midst. While going over with the first piece of artillery, a shell passed a few feet over their heads; a little farther on another plowed the waters just above and passed under the boat, but neither the enemy's fire nor fatigue detained them from their work. After breakfast and a short rest, I was directed to make a road up the bank, on the south side, to be ready for the bridge, which was in process of construction by Captain Fox. After completing that work, thus relieving the armed men from other than their appropriate duty, I ordered my men to camp, remaining, however, in person until nearly night.

I am much indebted to Captain Grosvenor, to whom I had intrusted much of the details before starting, and the immediate command of the upper fleet, for the perfect manner in which he carried out my orders, and the system and coolness displayed in the crossing and landings. Captain Cable and Lieutenants McNeal, Haddow, and Stephenson were equally cool, ready, prompt, and active. These officers, without exception, obeyed my orders strictly and aided me throughout. Much of the success which characterizes the expedition is owing to their efforts. My thanks and commendation are

no less due to the brave men, the sergeants, corporals, and privates
under their command, who so gallantly disregarded danger and put
forth their utmost strength to such good purpose.   They did not
have arms in their hands to repay the enemy in kind, nor charge
upon the enemy to excite and nerve them, but stern duty was well
performed regardless of danger.

I regret to record the loss of 3 men of the Thirty-third Ohio.
Corpl. John W. Gillilin, Company I, was killed; Private Henry
Pierce, Company B, mortally wounded; Private Elijah Conklin,
Company C, slightly wounded.

Your obedient servant,

T. R. STANLEY,
Colonel.

Lieut. CAMPBELL TUCKER,
    A. D. C. and A. A. A. G. to Chief Engr. of Dept.

No. 6.

*Itinerary of the First Division, Fourth Army Corps.**

Until the 24th day of the month the division remained in camp at
Chattanooga, strengthening our defenses, making heavy details for
fatigue duty, and performing the ordinary routine of camp and
office work.

On the 24th, the general (Palmer) received orders to march with
two brigades—the First, General Cruft, and the Third, Col. P. S.
Post commanding (Colonel Grose being sick), and one battery, Fifth
Indiana—at 2 o'clock the next morning on the north side of the
river for Rankin's Ferry, at which point we should find a pontoon
bridge; to guard the bridge and co-operate with General Hooker,
who had been ordered to the same point by the south side of
the river. Our march was over Walden's Ridge. The road was
barely passable for loaded wagons. It was raining hard, and our
mules had no forage for three days. The march was tedious and
most difficult. With the assistance of the soldiers, the headquarters
and regimental wagons were all up the mountain before night
of the 25th. We encamped about 2 miles from the top of the hill
and 8 from Chattanooga. At this point we met a train going to
Chattanooga, and took from it a temporary supply of provisions and
forage. The artillery and ammunition did not succeed in getting
up the mountain until some time the next day.

After we got up the ridge we took the ridge road, leading from
Bennett's to Bob White's and coming into Sequatchie Valley at
Prigmore's. We found this quite a good road, with the simple exception of crossing the gorge made by Suck Creek. We made very
easy marches, waiting for the artillery and ammunition. Encamped
the evening of the 26th on the immediate brow of the hill overlooking the valley, and the 27th at Prigmore's, at the foot of the mountain. At this point General Palmer turned over the command of
the division to General Cruft, in consequence of the painful condition of his wound, which had greatly annoyed him during the march,

----

* From return for October.

and which now was so inflamed as to render it improper and dangerous to continue longer in the field.

On the morning of the 28th, we started at daylight, in a drenching rain, and arrived at Rankin's Ferry about 10 a. m., and immediately dispatched a courier to General Hooker to report our arrival and ask for orders. He had passed the evening before, and it was most difficult to reach him. At the forks of the road, 1½ miles from Rankin's Ferry, we met a courier from Brig. Gen. J. St. Clair Morton, informing the general (Cruft) that the pontoon bridge had been placed for him at Shellmound, but, the orders being positive to go to Rankin's Ferry, the general conceived it to be his duty to go to that point and report. This was immediately done, and the 28th we remained in camp waiting for orders.

On the 29th, a steam-tug came up the river with 2 barges, loaded with supplies for General Hooker. We hailed her arrival with joy, as it gave an assurance that the river was open, and all danger of any suffering in Chattanooga for supplies was at an end. About 12.30 orders were received from headquarters and from General Hooker to cross the river at Shellmound and join General Hooker. This we did, and encamped that night at Shellmound, on the south side of the river.

On the 30th, we waited until the boat came up from Bridgeport, from which we obtained supplies, broke up camp, and started in the most desperate rain I ever encountered. All our baggage had been left at Manchester two months before. Our soldiers are without tents and generally without blankets, and suffer dreadfully in such weather. Orders were received during the day to leave one brigade and the battery at Shellmound, and move the remainder of the command to Whiteside's. This was done on the 31st. The Third Brigade and headquarters there awaited orders.

No. 7.

Report of Brig. Gen. William B. Hazen, U. S. Army, commanding Second Brigade, Third Division.

HDQRS. SECOND BRIG., THIRD DIV., FOURTH ARMY CORPS,
    Brown's Ferry, near Chattanooga, Tenn., Oct. 30, 1863.

SIR: I have the honor to report as follows of the part taken by troops under my command in the occupation of the left bank of the Tennessee River at this point :

On the morning of the 25th instant, I reported, by order of the commanding officer of the Fourth Army Corps, to the chief engineer of this army for instructions, and was then briefly informed, for the first time, of the duty to be assigned me, and the method of performing it, which was to organize fifty squads of 1 officer and 24 men each, to embark in boats at Chattanooga and float down the river to this point, a distance, by the bends of the river, of 9 miles, and land upon its left bank, then occupied by the enemy, making, thereafter, immediate dispositions for holding it, while the remaining portions of my brigade, and another one, should be speedily sent over the river in the same boats to re-enforce me ; the movement was to be made just before daylight, on the morning of the 27th.

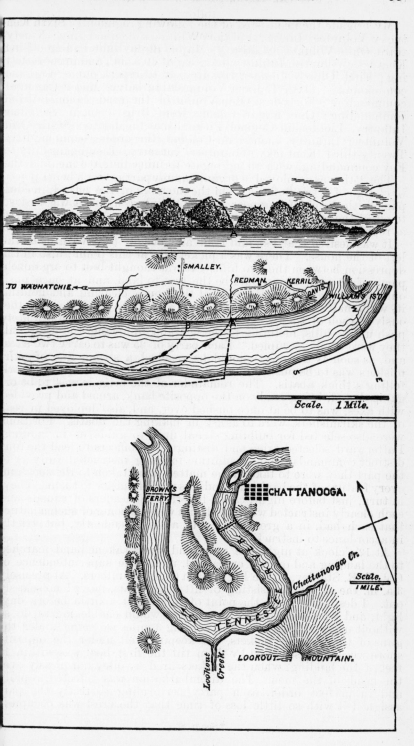

Scale. 1 Mile.

Scale. 1 MILE.

My brigade then consisted of the following regiments : Sixth Kentucky Volunteer Infantry, Major Whitaker commanding; Ninety-third Ohio Volunteer Infantry, Major Birch commanding ; Fifth Kentucky Volunteer Infantry, Lieutenant-Colonel Treanor commanding ; First Ohio Volunteer Infantry, Lieutenant-Colonel Langdon commanding ; Sixth Indiana Volunteer Infantry, Major Campbell commanding ; Forty-first Ohio Volunteer Infantry, Colonel Wiley commanding ; One hundred and twenty-fourth Ohio Volunteer Infantry, Lieutenant-Colonel Pickands commanding; Sixth Ohio Volunteer Infantry, Lieutenant-Colonel Christopher commanding ; Twenty-third Kentucky Volunteer Infantry, Lieutenant-Colonel Foy commanding, with an aggregate for duty of 2,166 men.

The 25th was employed in organizing my parties, each being placed in charge of a tried officer. On the morning of the 26th, I, in company with the chief engineer, visited the place where it was desired to effect the landing, and from the opposite bank found the position as represented below.*

It was desired that I should land and occupy the two hills to the left of the house. There was a picket post at this point; also in the depression between the two hills. It was thought best to organize a party of 75 men, who should be the first to land, and at once push out upon the road that comes in at the house, clearing and holding it, while half the first organized force should be landed simultaneously at each of the two gorges (A and B), who should immediately push up the hills, inclining to the left and following the crests till they were wholly occupied. Each party of 25 was to carry two axes, and, as soon as the crest should be reached, a strong line of skirmishers was to be pushed out and all the axes at once put at work felling a thick abatis. The remainder of the brigade was to be organized, and, being ready on the opposite bank, armed and provided with axes, was to be at once pushed over, and, also deployed in rear of the skirmishers, were to assist in making the abatis. Positions were also selected for building signal fires, to guide us in landing. I afterward selected tried and distinguished officers to lead the four distinct commands, who, in addition to being instructed fully as to the part they were to take in the matter, were taken to the spot, and every feature of the bank and landings made familiar to them. They in turn, just before night, called together the leaders of squads and each clearly instructed what his duties were, it being of such a nature that each had, in a great degree, to act independently, but strictly in accordance to instructions.

At 12 o'clock at night the command was awakened and marched to the landing and quietly embarked, under the superintendence of Col. T. R. Stanley, of the Eighteenth Ohio Volunteers. At precisely 3 a. m. the flotilla, consisting of fifty-two boats, moved noiselessly out. I desired to reach the point of landing at a little before daylight, and soon learned that the current would enable me to do so without using the oars. After moving 3 miles we came under the guns of the enemy's pickets, but keeping well under the opposite shore were not discovered by them till the first boat was within 10 feet of the landing, when the pickets fired a volley harmlessly over the heads of the men. The disembarkation was effected rapidly and in perfect order, each party performing correctly the part assigned it with so little loss of time that the crest was occupied

*See p. 83.

my skirmish line out, and the axes working before the re-enforcements of the enemy, a little over the hill, came forward to drive us back. At this time they came boldly up, along nearly our entire front, but particularly strong along the road, gaining the hill to the right of it, and would have caused harm to the party on the road had not Colonel Langdon, First Ohio Volunteers, commanding the remaining portion of the brigade, arrived at this moment, and, after a gallant but short engagement, driven the enemy well over into the valley, gaining the right-hand hill. They made a stubborn fight all along the hill, but were easily driven away with loss. General Turchin's command now came over, and taking position on the hills to the right, my troops were all brought to the left of the road. The enemy now moved off in full view up the valley.

The Fifty-first Ohio Volunteers, Eighth Kentucky, Thirty-fifth Indiana Volunteers, and two batteries of artillery were subsequently added to my command, and the three points farther to the left occupied. We knew nothing of the country previous to occupying it, excepting what could be seen from the opposite bank, nor of the forces there to oppose us. We found the hill facing the river precipitous, and the face opposite less steep but of difficult ascent; the top is sharp, having a level surface of from 2 to 6 feet in width, forming a natural parapet, capable of an easy defense by a single line against the strongest column. It is from 250 to 300 feet above the river. Beyond it is a narrow, productive valley, and the higher parallel range of Raccoon Mountain is about 1¼ miles distant; the entire opposite face of the hill now is covered with slashed timber. The enemy had at this point 1,000 infantry, three pieces of artillery, and a squadron of cavalry—ample force, properly disposed, to have successfully disputed our landing.

Our losses were 5 killed, 21 wounded, and 9 missing. We buried 5 of the enemy, and a large number were known to be wounded, including the colonel commanding. We captured a few prisoners; their camp, 20 beeves, 6 pontoons, a barge, and several thousand bushels of forage fell into our hands.

My thanks are especially due to Col. A. Wiley, Forty-first Ohio Volunteers, and Maj. William Birch, Ninety-third Ohio Volunteers, who commanded and led the parties that took the heights, and to Lieutenant-Colonel Foy, Twenty-third Kentucky, commanding party that swept the road, and Lieutenant-Colonel Langdon, First Ohio Volunteers, commanding the battalions formed of the residue of the brigade. Had either of these officers been less prompt in the execution of their duties, or less obedient to the letter of their instructions, many more lives might have been lost, or the expedition failed altogether.

The spirit of every one engaged in the enterprise is deserving of the highest commendation. My staff gave me the intelligent and timely assistance they have always done when needed, and to Lieutenant-Colonel Kimberly, Forty-first Ohio Volunteers, and Lieut. Ferdinand D. Cobb, same regiment, I am especially indebted for valuable services.

Very respectfully, your obedient servant,

W. B. HAZEN,
Brigadier-General.

Brig. Gen. WILLIAM F. SMITH,
Chief Engineer, Army of the Cumberland.

No. 8.

Report of Lieut. Col. James C. Foy, Twenty-third Kentucky Infantry.

HDQRS. TWENTY-THIRD REGT. KENTUCKY VOL. INFANTRY,
Camp Brown's Gap, Tenn., October 30, 1863.

SIR : According to instruction received from General W. B. Hazen, I proceeded on the morning of the 27th with my party of 75 men, under Captain Williams, Captain Boden, and Captain Tifft, to the point where we were to debark ; this was about 2 a. m. On arriving there, I found the boat with considerable water and some dozen or more pieces of heavy iron in, that had to be unloaded before we could start. After that was done we had to pull the boat up the river 300 yards, so that we would be able to make the gap in the bridge in crossing ; this accounts for our little delay in starting. I now saw that I would have to reduce my party to 50 men, that being the utmost number the boat would hold. I gave directions to each of my captains to take 16 men of their respective squads aboard, making an aggregate of 52 men including myself. The 27 men that were left I sent to the general to follow in his boat, and join us as soon as possible. We now shoved out and proceeded to cross the river, and float quietly down. I will say here that the men that were left to work the boat knew nothing about it, and Capt. T. J. Williams had to take the steering oar and pilot us down. I had the boat to proceed slowly and quietly, thinking it would be best not to get too far from the other boats. We arrived opposite the gap without any accident, except the knocking into the river of one man by the top of a tree, where we had run too close to shore. He was picked up by the first following boat.

On arriving opposite the gap we proceeded straight across the river; on nearing there we were fired into by the enemy's pickets. I do not know how much of a force was here; there were several shots fired, and I am sorry to say that some of our men returned the fire. I had them to cease immediately. I had given orders before starting that this would be only a small party, and we were to receive their fire and march on and take possession of the house. In a few minutes we struck the shore, landing a little below the point where the road strikes the river; at this point we had to scramble up a very steep bank, the men forming as soon as they gained a bench of land that runs along the river at this place. As soon as I had about 20 men up the bank we proceeded to the house. I directed Captain Williams with his squad of men to take possession of the house, while I remained outside awaiting the balance of my party. In a few moments Captain Boden, with the rear squad, arrived, when we all proceeded up the road, marching in one squad of 48 men by the front. After proceeding about 500 yards, and as far beyond the crest of the hill as I thought our skirmishers would come, I ordered halt, and gave the order for the rear rank to hold the guns of the men in the front rank, and to proceed to build breastworks, but the first thing I did was to throw out skirmishers to our front and well to our right. The men took hold of the work with a will, and we soon had a tolerable protection thrown up.

In a few minutes word was brought to me that our skirmishers could hear the enemy approaching. I proceeded to where our skirmishers were, and I could distinctly hear them giving orders, evidently coming down on our right. I now went back to the breastworks, disposed my force as far up the hill as possible, with my left resting on the road, and a little below. In as little time as it takes to write it, they were upon us, they adopting their usual plan of cheering and firing at the same time. We readily returned their fire, and soon had to fire nearly to our right. I knew by the report of their guns that they outnumbered us nearly four to one. Our surgeon, Dr. Hasbrouck, was standing a few steps to my rear. I told him to go to the river and tell any officer he should see that we would need assistance to enable us to hold our ground. He did not go, but some soldier carried word to Lieutenant-Colonel Langdon that we needed assistance, and he promptly came to our aid. But before this, and while we were fighting, Captain Williams, who commanded the right squad, informed me that the enemy had worked clear around our right, and in a minute or so would be able to cut us off. I now ordered the party to fall back, which was done in good order, meeting Colonel Langdon with part of his men. We did not go back quite to the house, but faced to the front and returned the enemy's fire, our little squad forming a nucleus for Colonel Langdon to form on our right, which I am proud to say he did with promptness and alacrity. The colonel's party soon cleared the hill to our right of the rebels, and we marched back and took possession of our breastworks, which we now commenced to make strong. We were joined at the river by Major Northup and part of his party, and soon our squad of 27 men that followed us down the river, began to come up. I now had the breastworks built strong, and about twice the length of my force, commencing on the creek and extending to the right across the road and up the hill. I now threw my skirmishers well to the front, knowing that I was protected on the right as well as on the left. I could now see the rebels moving off to our left, and after throwing a few shells toward us were seen no more that day. About 1 p. m. we were joined by the Eighth Kentucky Volunteers and the Thirty-fifth Indiana Volunteers, commanded by Colonel Barnes. At the request of Colonel Barnes, who preferred to have his two regiments together, we moved across the creek and extended the line to the left. We now built up good breastworks, and, being undisturbed by the rebels, have been very comfortable since.

In conclusion, I must thank the men and officers for the promptitude and bravery displayed by them.

The following is a list of casualties.* The casualties were all in the squad of 48 [men.]

Very respectfully,

JAS. C. FOY,
Lieutenant-Colonel, Comdg. Twenty-third Kentucky Vols.
Capt. JOHN CROWELL, Jr., *Assistant Adjutant-General.*

No. 9.

Report of Lieut. Col. Bassett Langdon, First Ohio Infantry.

HEADQUARTERS FIRST OHIO VOLUNTEER INFANTRY,
October 30, 1863.

SIR : I have the honor to submit the following report of my command, in the affair of the 27th instant, at Brown's Ferry :

On the afternoon of the 26th, I had been put in command of the

---

* Nominal list (omitted) shows 2 men killed and 8 men wounded.

remnants of the regiments composing the Second Brigade, and had proceeded to organize them into companies of one or two to a regiment, according to data obtained from the assistant adjutant-general of the brigade.   This organization was completed, but full reports from all the regiments had not been received at my head-quarters when I was notified to march with my command at once. Accordingly, the command, consisting of the Sixth Ohio Volunteer Infantry, under command of Major Erwin; Sixth Kentucky, under Captain Armstrong; Twenty-third Kentucky, under Major Northup; One hundred and twenty-fourth Ohio, under Major Hampson; Forty-first Ohio, under Captain Horner; First Ohio, under Captain Trapp; Ninety-third Ohio, under Captain Bowman; Fifth Kentucky, under Captain Huston, and Sixth Indiana, under Captain Prather, consisting of 750 men in the aggregate, as appears by the inclosed summary of reports, to which attention is respectfully invited, was at once assem-bled on regimental grounds, and, as soon as I could receive my in-structions from General Hazen, was formed on the road and moved to a point on the north bank of the river, near Brown's Ferry.

We found the road near this point completely blocked by the ambulance, guns, and caissons of the First Tennessee Battery, and the adjacent ground covered with sleeping men, reported to be-long to General Turchin's command.   Through and around these I attempted to move my command, until, arriving at the margin of the wood, I found and wakened Captain Abbott, of the battery, who in-formed me that the river was in our immediate front, and I could proceed no farther without exposure to the enemy.   Unable to find General Smith, who was expected to be awaiting my arrival, and under whose orders the enterprise was to be carried out, I directed regiments right and left of the road, as room could be found, and about 1 o'clock, on the morning of the 27th, officers and men lay down, without fires, to obtain such sleep as was practicable under the circumstances.   At 4.30 in the morning, Adjutant Homan, of the First Ohio, kindled the signal fires, as had been agreed upon, and left 6 men of the Twenty-third Kentucky, to keep them burning brightly; and a half hour later I succeeded in finding General Smith, who ordered my command forward at once, in the open ground, nearer the river, in three detachments, left in front, facing the river, and that seventy-four axes be distributed to the command.   These orders were speedily carried out, and we lay anxiously expecting the arrival of the boats which were to transfer us to the opposite bank of the river.

The boats from above seemed long in arriving, and I had just got orders from General Smith to move noiselessly to the water's edge with my command, when a sharp and rapid discharge of rifles told that the critical moment had arrived.   Reaching the river I saw for the first time the position assigned to my command, and was in-structed to embark it in the boats as soon as they should land, and push rapidly up the crest of the hill to the left of the gorge, as soon as we reached the opposite bank.   Our brigade was supposed to have already formed its squads on this crest, while at the same time I un-derstood that General Turchin had taken possession of the hill to the right of the gorge.   Lieutenant-Colonel Kimberly, of the Forty-first Ohio, having promised to see to the embarking of the troops, I my-self crossed in the first boat, to direct their formation and operations on the opposite shore.   The First Ohio was the first to land, and, with Captain Trapp at its head, crossed the ravine by a foot-log and pushed rapidly by the left flank up the narrow edge which forms the crest of the ridge. Adjutant Homan, my sole but very efficient aide, accompanied it as guide, and I remained at the landing to form and push on the others.

The last of this regiment had not crossed the log when a soldier of the Twenty-third Kentucky came hurriedly from the front, with a message from Colonel Foy that he had discovered a heavy force of cavalry in his front and must have re-enforcements at once. Knowing little of the situation, and having received explicit orders as to the disposal of my force, I told him to look for General Hazen, or some other officer in command of the squads, but that if the colonel should not get help before, I would send him the remnant of his own regiment when it arrived. Hardly had this messenger gone 20 paces on his return when a rattling fire opened down the gorge in front. The Sixth Indiana, which was the second regiment to cross, was at this time struggling up the bank and about to cross the log. I ordered them to form at once across the road, and move down to the assistance of Colonel Foy. The order was obeyed with alacrity by Lieutenants Siddall and Neal, who formed as many as could be got together speedily, and moved gallantly to the front, but meeting the command of Colonel Foy coming back under orders, and finding about the same time that the enemy held the hill to the right of the gorge, they came back and were closely followed up by the enemy to within 20 paces of the log crossing of the ravine.

As other squads came up from the boat (the Sixth Indiana and Sixth Kentucky first) they were pushed up the side crest on the right; except a part of the Sixth Indiana, which crossed the ravine, and received a severe fire in doing so, to occupy the side crest on the left, left vacant by the First Ohio, which had pushed on farther along the ridge. The Twenty-third Kentucky was ordered to report to Colonel Foy at once, and unite with the remainder of the regiment. Fragments of the One hundred and twenty-fourth Ohio and Sixth Ohio were also formed on the right crest, and the Fifth Kentucky, Ninety-third Ohio, and Forty-first Ohio, which landed last, pushed without orders straight to the very top of the hill, on the right, being led by that gallant officer, Captain Huston, of the first-named of these regiments. Before they reached position the enemy fled, and we were masters of the gap. I immediately directed an officer commanding a regiment near the road to send skirmishers to the front, and the advance of General Turchin's brigade (Thirty-first Ohio), under Colonel Lister, having arrived, I withdrew my command on the right and moved over and formed, under your direction, general, along the crest of the left ridge.

My command, as you know, was made up of odds and ends, after the best fighting men had been called out, and consisted of all who were able to march. Extra-duty men, unarmed men, company cooks, musicians, and cowards, huddled under the cover of the bank and log-house near the river. The hastily formed organization of the night before was not intended for fighting purposes, and had no reference to transportation in boats. It was completely broken in crossing the river, consequently it is almost unjust to refer to the troops engaged, who had landed after the fight opened, by name. The organizations broken up, the uncertain light of early morning rendering it difficult to distinguish the most familiar acquaintances, utterly ignorant of the country and the position of our other forces, or the strength of the enemy, troops who fight well under such circumstances deserve the highest praise. I shall not shrink from comparison of the valor displayed by my command with that of the squads selected for courage, &c. I regret that the circumstances above named, and want of familiarity with the command, prevent my doing justice in individual cases. The list of casualties has already been forwarded, and untoward circumstances compel me to give up the thought of accompanying this with a list of the names, which I had entertained.

I have the honor to be, &c., very respectfully,

BASSETT. LANGDON,
Lieut. Col. First O. V. I., Comdg. Remnant of Second Brig.
Capt. JOHN CROWELL, Jr.,
Assistant Adjutant-General.

No. 10.

Report of Col. Aquila Wiley, Forty-first Ohio Infantry.

HDQRS. FORTY-FIRST OHIO VOLUNTEER INFANTRY,
Brown's Ferry, October 30, 1863.

SIR: In compliance with your order, I have the honor to submit the following report of the part taken by the detachment under my command, in gaining possession of the ridge on the west side of the Tennessee River, at Brown's Ferry, on the morning of the 27th instant:

The detachment consisted of 150 officers and men, Forty-first Ohio Volunteers, Capt. W. W. Munn commanding; 175 officers and men, One hundred and twenty-fourth Ohio Volunteers, Lieut. Col. James Pickands commanding; 150 officers and men, Sixth Ohio Volunteers, Lieut. Col. A. C. Christopher commanding; 100 officers and men, Fifth Kentucky, Lieut. Col. J. L. Treanor commanding. The detachments from each regiment were organized into companies consisting of 24 enlisted men, and 1 commissioned officer each. The whole embarked on twenty-four pontoons. At 3 a. m. the fleet moved from the landing at Chattanooga in the following order: The Forty-first Ohio Volunteers, One hundred and twenty-fourth Ohio Volunteers, Sixth Ohio Volunteers, and Fifth Kentucky, and reached the landing at the ferry at 5 a. m. The fleet was preceded by a detachment under Lieutenant-Colonel Foy, Twenty-third Kentucky, on a barge which was not under my command. My orders were to land at the ferry, and carry and hold the height on the left of the gorge. The eminence to be gained is a ridge about 400 yards in length, parallel with the river, and about 300 feet above it, the face next the river being very precipitous; the ascent at the end next the gorge not so difficult:

The fleet proceeded without molestation until about 5 a. m., when as the first boat, which was almost abreast of the barge containing Lieutenant-Colonel Foy's detachment, was within about 10 yards of the landing, it was fired on by the enemy's pickets stationed at the landing. The crew of the first boat delivered a volley and leaped ashore, followed instantly by the second boat, in which I myself had embarked. The first company, deployed as skirmishers to cover the flanks of the column, were immediately pushed up the farther slope of the ridge; the second company, covering the head of the column, advanced along the crest toward the left.

The regiments effected their landing promptly in the order already indicated, and advanced in column by company up the height and along the crest, where the line was established, as previously indicated, in the following order: The Fifth Kentucky on the right, Forty-first Ohio on the left, Sixth Ohio on the right center, One hundred and twenty-fourth Ohio on the left center. Each regiment as soon as it gained its position, threw out two companies as skirmishers to cover its front, and commenced felling the timber and constructing a parapet, each company having carried two axes for that purpose. The enemy were encamped in the valley at the foot of the ridge, and at the first sound of the axes his skirmishers advanced up the hill and engaged ours vigorously for some time, when they were driven back to the road at the foot of the ridge; a section of artillery then opened on us, but without effect. No further effort was made to dislodge us. As soon as it became light, we discovered the enemy retreating to our left up the farther side of the valley. He left 5 dead and 1 wounded in front of our line of skirmishers.

The following is a list of casualties.*

I cannot commend too highly the gallantry and firmness of the troops engaged as skirmishers. The enemy's line attacked vigorously, encouraged by the shouts of their officers to "drive the Yankees into the river," and only gave way when within a few yards of our own line. I have also the pleasure of testifying to the promptness, skill, and efficiency of Lieutenant-Colonel Pickands, One hundred and twenty-fourth Ohio Volunteers; Lieutenant-Colonel Christopher, Sixth Ohio Volunteers; Lieutenant-Colonel Treanor, Fifth Kentucky, and Captain Munn, Forty-first Ohio Volunteers, commanding detachments from their respective regiments. The best evidence of the alacrity and skill with which they handled their troops consists in the fact of their effecting a landing, gaining the crest of the heights and the position assigned them, and making all their dispositions for defense before the enemy—who had doubtless been alarmed by the firing at the landing—who not only knew the country but could have gained it by a much less difficult slope.

I have the honor to be, very respectfully, your obedient servant,

AQUILA WILEY,
Colonel Forty-first Ohio Volunteers, Comdg. Detachment.

Capt. JOHN CROWELL, Jr.,
    Assistant Adjutant-General.

No. 11.

Report of Maj. William Birch, Ninety-third Ohio Infantry.

HDQRS. NINETY-THIRD OHIO VOLUNTEER INFANTRY,
    October 30, 1863.

SIR: I have the honor to submit the following report:

On the 26th, I received orders to take command of the following detachments: First Ohio Volunteers, seven companies, commanded

---

* Nominal list (omitted) shows: Killed, 1 man of Fifth Kentucky and 1 man of Forty-first Ohio; wounded, 1 officer and 1 man of Forty-first Ohio, and 1 officer and 3 men of One hundred and twenty-fourth Ohio.

by Major Stafford; Sixth Kentucky Volunteers, five companies, commanded by Major Whitaker; Twenty-third Kentucky Volunteers, two companies, commanded by Captain Hardiman; Sixth Ohio Volunteers, one company, commanded by Lieutenant Meline; Sixth Indiana Volunteers, six companies, commanded by Major Campbell, and Ninety-third Ohio Volunteers, five companies, commanded by Captain Lake—in all twenty-six companies. We were to make a night attack on a position held by the rebels, about 3 miles below Lookout Mountain, simultaneous with detachment commanded by Colonel Wiley, of the Forty-first Ohio.

The command numbered as follows : Field officers, 4; line officers, 26 ; non-commissioned officers, 104 ; privates, 520 ; total, 654.

We embarked on board twenty-six pontoon boats about 2 a. m. the 27th, and held the rebel position at daylight. The rebels were completely surprised and made but feeble resistance.

Killed, none ; wounded, 1 slightly in the Sixth Indiana ; missing, none. The rebels lost several killed and wounded. Every man seemed determined to succeed.

Very respectfully, your obedient servant,

WM. BIRCH,
Major Ninety-third Ohio Vol. Inf., Comdg. Detachment.

Capt. John Crowell, Jr.,
Assistant Adjutant-General.

No. 12.

Report of Maj. Gen. Joseph Hooker, U. S. Army, commanding Eleventh and Twelfth Army Corps, with congratulatory orders.

HEADQUARTERS ELEVENTH AND TWELFTH CORPS,
ARMY OF THE CUMBERLAND,
Lookout Valley, Tenn., November 6, 1863.

COLONEL : I desire to submit the following report of the battle of Wauhatchie, and the operations of my command preliminary to that engagement :

In conformity with orders from the headquarters of the department, I crossed the Tennessee by the pontoon bridge at Bridgeport, the morning of the 26th of October, with the greater portion of the Eleventh Corps, under Major-General Howard ; a part of the Second Division of the Twelfth Corps, under Brigadier-General Geary ; one company of the Fifth Tennessee Cavalry, and a part of a company of the First Alabama Cavalry, and at once took up my line of march along the line of railroad, to open and secure it in the direction of Brown's Ferry. A regiment was left to defend the bridge head when the column had crossed the river, and to take possession of and hold the passes leading to it through Raccoon Mountain. Our route lay along the base of this mountain until we reached Running Waters, when we followed the direction of that stream, and in the morning descended through the gorge into Lookout Valley. No event attended our first day's march deserving mention, unless it be that the enemy's pickets fell back as we advanced, and the leaving of two more of my regiments—one at Shellmound, with instructions to occupy a pass near Gordon's Mines, and another at Whiteside's, to protect the route over the mountains through which we had passed.

After entering Lookout Valley, our general course lay along a creek of that name, until within a mile or more of its mouth, where the Brown's Ferry road leaves it to the left.   This valley is, perhaps, 2 miles in width, and completely overlooked by the lofty crests of Lookout and Raccoon Mountains.   All the movements and dispositions of troops are easily descried from the heights of either, while the valley itself affords abundant opportunity for concealment from the observation of those within.   Another prominent feature in Lookout Valley requires mention to a clear perception of its topography and a correct understanding of our operations.   This is a succession of hills 200 or 300 feet high, with precipitous timbered slopes and narrow crests, which penetrate 3 miles up the valley and divide it as far as they go nearly in its center.   There are five or six of them in number, almost isolated, though in a direct line on the left bank of Lookout Creek, with the railroad passing between the two summits at the extreme of the range ; and still lower down the valley the road bears off to Chattanooga, about 2 miles distant, through these hills, while the road to Brown's Ferry continues along the west base to the Tennessee River.

The enemy held possession of these hills, as, indeed, of all the country through which we had passed after crossing at Bridgeport. They had also batteries planted on Lookout Mountain, overlooking them.   On the opposite side of the valley is Raccoon Range, and about 3 miles up is the gorge through it which leads to what is called Kelley's Ferry, 3 miles distant.   As it was proposed to make this our new line of communication with Chattanooga, my instructions required me, if practicable, to gain possession of and to hold it.   As the gorge debouches into Lookout Valley the road forks, one leading to Wauhatchie and up the valley, the other to Chattanooga and down the valley.   It was known that a portion of Longstreet's command was in the valley, it is presumed in part for convenience in supplying themselves with rations and forage, but mainly for his sharpshooters to annoy our communications on the north side of the Tennessee and compel our trains to make long *détours*, over execrable roads, in their transit from Chattanooga to our depots at Stevenson.   From its proximity to the enemy's line of investment around Chattanooga, and his facilities for detaching heavily from his masses, it was apprehended that the enemy would make unusual efforts to prevent the transfer of its possession, as a failure on our part to establish new communications involved a fact of no less magnitude than the necessity for the early evacuation of Chattanooga, with the abandonment of much of our artillery and trains.

To return to the column ; it pushed on down the valley until arrested by an irregular fire of musketry proceeding from the hill next the railroad as it passes through the central ridge before described. As it was densely covered with forest, we had no means of ascertaining the number of the enemy, except by feeling.   Howard's corps being in the advance, he was directed to throw a brigade to the right to turn the position, and a regiment, supported by the balance of another brigade, to the left for the same purpose.   No sooner had the brigade on the right deployed than the enemy took to his legs and fled across the creek, burning the railroad bridge in his flight.   We lost a few men here, as well as from the shelling we received from the batteries on Lookout Mountain, whenever our column was exposed to them.   The central ridge of hills afforded partial cover from the batteries; these, however, caused no serious interruption in the movement of the column, and about 5 p. m. halted for the night, and went into camp a mile or more up the valley from Brown's Ferry. Here we learned that a pontoon bridge had been thrown across the river, and that General Hazen's brigade held the heights on the south side of it.   Geary's division being in the rear, and being anxious to hold both roads leading to Kelley's Ferry, he was directed to encamp near Wauhatchie, 3 miles from the position held by Howard's corps.   Pickets were thrown out from both camps on all of the approaches, though no attempt was made to establish and preserve a communication between them.

The commands were too small to keep up a substantial communication that distance, and I deemed it more prudent to hold the men well in hand than to have a feeble one.   In my judgment, it was essential to retain possession of both approaches to Kelley's Ferry, if practicable, as it would cause us inconvenience to dispossess the enemy if he established himself on either.   Before night Howard threw out three companies in the direction of Kelley's Ferry to intercept and capture, if possible, the enemy's sharpshooters, who had been engaged in firing across the river into our trains, and had in fact compelled them to avoid that line entirely.   A regiment was also sent toward the point where the Chattanooga road crosses Lookout Creek, and about 12 o'clock had a little skirmishing with the enemy. An hour after, the mutterings of a heavy musketry fell upon our ears from the direction of Geary.   He was fiercely attacked, first his pickets, and soon after his main force, but not before he was in line of battle to receive it.   Howard was directed to double-quick his nearest division (Schurz's) to his relief, and before proceeding far a sheet of musketry was thrown on him from the central hills, but at long range, and inflicting no great injury.   This was the first intimation that the enemy were there at all.

Directions were immediately given for one of the brigades *en route* to Geary (Tyndale's) to be detached and assault the enemy in the hills on the left, and for the other brigade to push on as ordered. Meanwhile, Howard's First Division, under Steinwehr, came up, when it was discovered that the hill to the rear of Schurz's division was also occupied by the enemy in force, and Smith's brigade, of this division, was ordered to carry it with the bayonet.   This skeleton, but brave brigade, charged up the mountain, almost inaccessible by daylight, under a heavy fire, without returning it, and drove three times their number from behind hastily thrown up intrenchments, capturing prisoners, and scattering the enemy in all directions. No troops ever rendered more brilliant service.   The name of their valiant commander is Col. Orland Smith, of the Seventy-third Ohio Volunteers.   Tyndale, encountering less resistance, had also made himself master of the enemy's position in his front.

During these operations a heavy musketry fire, with occasional discharges of artillery, continued to reach us from Geary.   It was evident that a formidable adversary had gathered around him, and that he was battling him with all his might.   For almost three hours, without assistance, he repelled the repeated attacks of vastly superior numbers, and in the end drove them ingloriously from the field. At one time they had enveloped him on three sides, under circumstances that would have dismayed any officer except one endowed with an iron will and the most exalted courage.   Such is the character of General Geary.   With this ended the fight.   We had repelled every attack, carried every point assaulted, thrown the enemy headlong over the river, and, more than all, secured our new communications, for the time being, beyond peradventure. These several conflicts were attended with unusual interest and satisfaction, from the violence of the attack, the great alacrity displayed by the officers and men in springing to their arms on the first indication of the presence of the enemy, and the glorious manner in which they closed in on him for the struggle.

I regret that my duty constrains me to except any portion of my command in my commendation of their courage and valor. The brigade dispatched to the relief of Geary, by orders delivered in person to its division commander, never reached him until long after the fight had ended. It is alleged that it lost its way, when it had a terrific infantry fire to guide them all the way, and also that they became involved in a swamp, when there was no swamp or other obstacle between them and Geary, which should have delayed them a moment in marching to the relief of their imperiled companions.

For the instances of conspicuous individual daring and conduct, also of regiments and batteries, the most distinguished for brilliant services on this field, the attention of the commanding general is respectfully called to the reports of corps and division commanders herewith transmitted. I must confine myself to an expression of my appreciation of the zealous and devoted services of Major-General Howard, not only on the battle-field, but everywhere and at all times. Of General Geary I need say no more. To both of these officers I am profoundly grateful for the able assistance they have always given me. Our loss is 416, among them some of the bravest officers and men of my command.

General Greene was severely wounded while in the heroic performance of his duty. Colonel Underwood, of the Thirty-third Massachusetts Volunteers, was also desperately wounded, and for his recovery I am deeply concerned. If only in recognition of his meritorious services on this field, his many martial virtues, and great personal worth, it would be a great satisfaction to me to have this officer advanced to the grade of brigadier-general.

For the many whose deaths the country will deplore, I must refer you to the reports of subordinate commanders. Of the loss of the enemy, it cannot fall short of 1,500. Geary buried 153 rebel carcasses on his front alone. We took upward of 100 prisoners and several hundred stand of small-arms. With daylight to follow up our success, doubtless our trophies would have been much more abundant.

The force opposed to us consisted of two of Longstreet's divisions, and corresponded in number to our corps. From the prisoners we learn that they had watched the column as it descended the valley, and confidently counted on its annihilation.

To conclude, I must express my grateful acknowledgments to Major-General Butterfield, chief of my staff, for the valuable assistance rendered me on the field; also to Major Lawrence, Captain Hall, Lieutenants Perkins and Oliver, aides-de-camp, for the faithful, intelligent, and devoted performance of all the duties assigned them.[*]

Very respectfully, your obedient servant,

JOSEPH HOOKER,
Major-General, Commanding.

Lieut. Col. C. GODDARD, *Assistant Adjutant-General.*

---

[*]A map accompanying this report will appear in the Atlas.

GENERAL ORDERS, }   HDQRS. 11TH AND 12TH CORPS,
                                   ARMY OF THE CUMBERLAND,
    No. 5.   }   *Lookout Valley, November* 1, 1863.

It is with extreme pleasure that the major-general commanding communicates to the troops composing the Eleventh Corps, and to the Second Division of the Twelfth Corps, the subjoined letter from the major-general commanding the Army of the Cumberland, expressive of his appreciation of your distinguished services on the night of the 28th instant.

It is a noble tribute to your good conduct from a brave and devoted soldier.

The general hopes that it will inspire as much satisfaction in the breasts of his officers and men as it has in his own, and that we may all be stimulated by it to renewed efforts to secure the good opinion of our commander while we also emulate the courage and valor of our companions in arms.

HEADQUARTERS DEPARTMENT OF THE CUMBERLAND,
Chattanooga, October 30, 1863.

Major-General HOOKER,
    Commanding Eleventh and Twelfth Corps:

GENERAL: I most heartily congratulate you and the troops under your command at the brilliant success you gained over your old adversary (Longstreet) on the night of the 28th instant. The bayonet charge of Howard's troops, made up the sides of a steep and difficult hill over 200 feet high, completely routing and driving the enemy from his barricades on its top, and the repulse by Geary's division of greatly superior numbers, who attempted to surprise him, will rank among the most distinguished feats of arms of this war.

Very respectfully, your obedient servant,

GEO. H. THOMAS,
Major-General, U. S. Volunteers, Commanding.

By command of Major-General Hooker:
                                H. W. PERKINS,
                         Acting Assistant Adjutant-General.

———

No. 13.

Reports of Maj. Gen. Oliver O. Howard, U. S. Army, commanding Eleventh Army Corps.

HEADQUARTERS ELEVENTH ARMY CORPS,
October 29, 1863—7.30 a. m.   (Received 30th.)

GENERAL: My corps arrived at this point about 5 p. m. yesterday; went into camp, throwing out strong pickets and outposts. Between 12 and 1 a. m. there was considerable skirmishing not far from the wagon-road bridge over Lookout Creek. At 1 a. m., hearing General Geary's guns, by the commanding general's order the corps was got under arms. General Steinwehr, with Colonel Smith's brigade, carried the heights near the bridge, which had been previously intrenched by the enemy. General Schurz occupied the next succeeding knolls, and finally succeeded in pushing a brigade to the support of General Geary. The troops were more or less engaged until 4 a. m., when the firing ceased.

There is quite a large number wounded, but not many killed.

The enemy's attempt was to hold my corps in check while he destroyed Geary.   He did not succeed.

Respectfully,

O. O. HOWARD,
Major-General.

Major-General BUTTERFIELD, *Chief of Staff.*

—

HEADQUARTERS ELEVENTH CORPS,
Lookout Valley, November 1, 1863.

CAPTAIN: I have the honor to submit the following report of operations of this corps since the 27th ultimo:

In accordance with instructions of the major-general commanding, the Eleventh and Twelfth Corps left Bridgeport at sunrise on the 27th of October. One battery had been located at Rankin's Ferry, one full regiment at Battle Creek, and the transportation of the corps at Bridgeport. A portion of General Steinwehr's command already occupied Shellmound. A company of the Fifth Tennessee Cavalry and another of the First Alabama reported to me for the march. With this cavalry, supported by infantry, every approach from the right flank was carefully guarded during the passage of the column. The corps reached Whiteside's and was encamped by 8 p. m. A regiment, strengthened by a detachment from another from General Schurz's division, was detached at Shellmound and ordered to hold the pass toward Trenton, near Gordon's Mines. Small squads of the enemy's cavalry were driven before us and a few prisoners taken during the march.

At daylight on the 28th, the column moved in the same order as the day before, General Steinwehr's division leading. There was some little delay in crossing a mountain ridge just this side of Etna, battery wheels being broken by the roughness of the road, so that as soon as the head of the column debouched in the Lookout Valley a halt was called and the troops massed until the corps came up. The march was then continued with scarcely any interruption until we reached Wauhatchie. About a mile south of that point scouts and cavalry were met by a fire from the enemy concealed in the thick underbrush at the base of a spur from the ridge that extends along the southern bank of the Tennessee River. This point is at the fork of the Brown's Ferry and Chattanooga road. It was impossible at first to tell the strength of the enemy.

In accordance with instructions of the general commanding, I directed General Steinwehr to move forward cautiously with his leading brigade, covered by skirmishers, deploy a portion of his other brigade to the east of the railroad, threatening the enemy's left, and General Schurz to move a brigade toward the right of the position of the enemy. The movement had hardly begun when the enemy gave way and fled across Lookout Creek, burning the railroad bridge. Five or 6 men of Colonel Buschbeck's brigade were wounded.

The column again took up its line of march and effected a junction with the Chattanooga troops, already on the south and west shores. During the march from Wauhatchie to this point the enemy shelled the troops and train from the top of Lookout Mountain. One man was killed and 1 wounded. Here the corps was encamped with its left resting on the shore ridge of the Tennessee and its right at the foot of the Raccoon Mountain. A small portion of General Geary's division was halted at Wauhatchie. Strong outposts were posted, one toward Kelley's Ferry for the purpose of cutting off any sharpshooters of the enemy reported to be lurking in that direction, and another of a regiment toward the point where the Chattanooga road crosses Lookout Creek. Some skirmishing occurred with this regiment between 12 and 1 a. m. The regiment did not reach its destin tion, but halted near Ellis' house and drew up in line of battle, its skirmishers encountering those of the enemy on a height beyond.

At 1 a. m. heavy firing, infantry and artillery, was heard in the direction of General Geary. The corps was ordered under arms, and, in accordance with General Hooker's instructions, a brigade ordered to the position of the skirmish of the day before, and another to the assistance of General Geary. I instantly communicated the order to General Steinwehr.

At this time I joined General Hooker, who instructed me to fulfill the order just given with the troops nearest those points designated.

General Schurz's division, or a part of it, being already under arms, was moved out as quick as possible, and General Schurz directed to push his leading brigade as fast as possible to the relief of General Geary. Meanwhile, General Steinwehr's division was moved toward Ellis' house, and his second brigade, Colonel Smith commanding, was instructed to carry a height near that point, already occupied by the enemy in force. His other brigade and the batteries were held in reserve. Colonel Smith's brigade promptly executed the order given him, driving the enemy from his barricades, already established on the top of the heights. The troops charged up the heights under heavy fire, without returning it, until the enemy was completely routed. They took quite a number of arms and prisoners. General Schurz's division, after some delay, occasioned by losing the road and getting into a swamp, succeeded in carrying the next height occupied by the enemy. This was done by General Tyndale's brigade.

General Schurz, having been reinstructed by General Hooker in person, sent a brigade, Colonel Hecker's, to effect a junction with General Geary, which was accomplished about 5 a. m. These operations, and those of General Geary, repulsing the enemy's attack, had the effect of dislodging him from every position this side of Lookout Creek. This engagement, brief and, comparatively speaking, of small extent, has crowned our efforts to open the river. It has also cost us much in the lives of several valuable officers and in the disabling of others. For the mention of these I call attention to the reports of division commanders.

I shall make hereafter special recommendations on account of good conduct in this action. The conduct of the men, as well as their officers, was excellent. In the night, as it was, and uncertain as we were as to the enemy's position and strength, there was no giving way, and little or no straggling in the command. Several officers, endeared to us and invaluable to the country, have given their lives. Colonel Underwood, of the Thirty-third Massachusetts Volunteers, is seriously wounded. We cannot be too grateful to him and them for the noble part they have acted, and for the sacrifice they have made. I will frankly say that great encouragement and confidence was given us by the immediate presence of the commanding general.

Very respectfully,

O. O. HOWARD,
Major-General, Commanding.

Capt. H. W. PERKINS, *Assistant Adjutant-General.*

No. 14.

Report of Surg. Daniel G. Brinton, U. S. Army, Medical Director.

OFFICE OF MEDICAL DIRECTOR, ELEVENTH CORPS,
ARMY OF THE CUMBERLAND,
February 19, 1864.

SIR : I have the honor to submit the following report on the action of the medical department of the Eleventh Army Corps at the battle of Lookout Valley, or Wauhatchie :

On the morning of the 28th October, 1863, the Second and Third Divisions of the Eleventh Corps broke camp at Whiteside's Station, on the Chattanooga and Nashville Railroad, and followed slowly and cautiously the wagon road that leads over a spur of Raccoon Mountain into the Valley of Lookout Creek. At any moment the enemy might appear and an engagement commence. At any moment the medical officers might be called on to provide for the wounded. Accordingly, the acting medical director, Surg. Robert Hubbard, Seventeenth Connecticut Volunteers, was engaged with the surgeon-in-chief of the two divisions in looking for favorable locations for a field hospital, and in providing for the most economical employment of the medical and hospital stores on hand. There was urgent need of such economy. The command had left Bridgeport with no other transportation than the ambulances. No hospital tents were taken, and not only was there a very limited amount of medical stores, especially stimulants, on hand when they marched, but a portion of these, through an error of the ambulance officers, had been left behind.

No enemy was seen until well on in the afternoon, when the troops had passed the junction of the Trenton and Chattanooga Railroad, and entered a dense belt of woods that at this point stretched across Lookout Valley.

Here we came upon the enemy's outposts, and an irregular picket firing ensued. Our cavalry was withdrawn, the Second Brigade of the Second Division deployed in skirmish line and ordered to advance, while a portion of the First Brigade followed the railroad track on the right. The enemy made no resistance, but fired their guns toward the advancing line and hastened to make good their escape.

The casualties, from their irregular fire, amounted to 1 killed and 3 slightly wounded. A frame house, with spacious verandas, about 2 miles in the rear, had been chosen for a provisional field hospital, but only 1 of the wounded was sent there.

Before sunset the troops had reached their destined camping grounds, the Third Division being located in the valley, opposite what has since been called Tyndale's Hill, and the Second about half a mile nearer the river, on the main road. Near Wauhatchie Station, General Geary, with the Second Division of the Twelfth Corps, was encamped. The ambulances of the Eleventh Corps were parked with the ammunition train, near the Second Division. The night was clear and the moon almost full. Shortly after midnight our slumbers were disturbed by rapid musketry in the direction of Geary's command.

The Third Division of our corps was immediately ordered to move at double-quick to their assistance; but hardly were they fairly under way when a volley from the two hills which [are] on either side of the road leading over Lookout Mountain to Chattanooga, showed that the enemy were upon our flank. The Third Division was immediately ordered to stop, face toward the hills, and take the one on the south of the pass, while the Second Brigade of the Second Division was directed to take by assault the hill north of the road. These orders were at once executed, the enemy making but little resistance at the former, but so much the more determined and obstinate opposition at the latter point. Here was where we had our principal loss, and here the battle was decided, as the enemy was aware that this was the key to the position. This position lost, they at once retired and the firing ceased. This was 2.30. a. m.

In the meantime, a site had been chosen in a woods about a mile north of Tyndale's Hill, close to and on the right of the road to Brown's Ferry, convenient to wood and water, for a field hospital; fires built, candles procured, straw collected from a neighboring barn for beds, amputating tables knocked together, and all the stores of the different regiments deposited there, the whole under charge of Surg. W. H. Gunkle, Seventy-third Pennsylvania Volunteers. The moment the firing ceased the ambulances were put in motion for the scene of action, and plied to and fro until daylight.

At earliest dawn I rode over the field of the Second Division, and so well had the ambulance corps performed its duty that I found only 3 wounded still on the field. One of these was a Confederate, shot in the knee, in whom the collapse was so marked that the ambulance men had supposed him dying. A second had received a musket ball in the head, which entered posteriorly, carrying away a large fragment of the left parietal bone and much of the corresponding lobe of the brain. The man was senseless, but groaning piteously. He was laid in an adjacent cabin, and lived until toward evening.

At the hospital 109 wounded were received, and entered upon the list. Of these, 3 were Confederates. Four amputations were performed, two of the thigh, one of the upper third of humerus, and one of three fingers. Eight died at the hospital. The whole number of deaths are not received in this office. Those who died at the hospital were buried in the field across the road, while those who were killed outright were interred at the foot of Smith's Hill. All these were subsequently exhumed, and the remains transferred to the national cemetery at Chattanooga. At that time (February, 1864), there were 30 bodies found, but a number had been taken North by their friends.

As soon as it was clear that we should have a number of wounded, the acting medical director sent to Chattanooga for a barrel of whisky and other supplies. We had hardly received them ere orders came to send all the wounded at once to the general field hospital over the river. By the middle of the afternoon few were left on this bank. In consequence of this the statistics above given are not correct. Many of the wounded were never entered on the records of the hospital.

Some primary operations were not performed there. The results of all are unknown. I shall not offer guesses, but conclude with some observations of a general character.

All the wounds recorded were by small-arms, except some contusions, and one shell wound. The latter must have been from the battery on Point Lookout, as we used no artillery during the affair, while the artillerists on the mountain dropped their shells with the greatest impartiality over the field.

In such an action as this, if anywhere, we would look for bayonet wounds. Here was a charge—a hand-to-hand contest literally ; some of the contusions were given by clubbed muskets. Not a bayonet wound is recorded. I looked for them, but neither saw nor heard of any. There was none.

The case of Colonel (now Brigadier-General) Underwood, Thirty-third Massachusetts Volunteers, merits especial mention. A conical ball entered externally a few inches below the great trochanter, passed through the soft parts horizontally, fractured the upper third of the femur, passed out and into the dorsum of the penis, whence it, together with a piece of bone the size of a half pea, which it had carried with it, was extracted by Surgeon Hubbard. A few days after the affair he was taken to Nashville, and at the present writing, I am informed, the bone has united, the wound closed, and the general health good, though the injured leg is 4 inches shorter than before. The treatment was perfect rest, good diet, and an unmovable position of the wounded extremity.

I have the honor, sir, to remain, very respectfully, your obedient servant,

D. G. BRINTON,
Surgeon, U. S. Volunteers, Medical Director, Eleventh Corps.

Surg. GLOVER PERIN,
    U. S. Army, Medical Director.

No. 15.

Report of Brig. Gen. Adolph von Steinwehr, U. S. Army, commanding Second Division.

CHURCH OF JOHN THE BAPTIST,
October 30, 1863.

COLONEL: On the 27th instant, this division broke camp and left Bridgeport at 6 a. m., the First Brigade leading. At about 5 p. m. we arrived at Whiteside's and camped for the night. On the 28th, we marched at daybreak toward Brown's Ferry in the same order. At the Trenton road the first indications of the enemy were seen. At about 2 p. m. the advance guard of the First Brigade was fired upon. The Seventy-third Pennsylvania was deployed as skirmishers and advanced. The Second Brigade advanced, the Seventy-third Ohio in a deployed line to the right of the Seventy-third Pennsylvania, and the Thirty-third Massachusetts followed as a reserve, together with the artillery. When the advanced regiments reached the foot of the hill a skirmish ensued. After firing a few rounds, we charged upon the enemy, who fell back across the Lookout Creek. The command was then assembled upon the Chattanooga road and moved forward. Late in the afternoon we went into camp in Lookout Valley, about 4 miles from Chattanooga.

At about 12 midnight a firing was heard in our front and shortly afterward I received orders to advance with my division. I advanced with the Second Brigade, the First following. When we had advanced about one-quarter of a mile beyond the junction of the roads, I was ordered to take and hold a hill upon our left flank, which was occupied by the enemy. I ordered Col. O. Smith to advance upon the hill with the Seventy-third Ohio and Thirty-third Massachusetts in line of battle, and directed the One hundred and Thirty-sixth New York to ascend the hill on the left of the other two regiments. The troops were ordered not to fire, but to use the bayonet. They made a gallant charge and took the crest. The enemy fled, leaving some arms and intrenching tools in their rifle-pits. The tools were immediately made use of to strengthen their position by the men. We captured about 50 prisoners. The hill was occupied by Law's brigade, of Jenkins' division, Longstreet's corps, numbering five regiments, about 2,000 men. Our attacking force was not quite 700 muskets. The First Brigade was held as reserve immediately behind the Second Brigade, and advanced into the gaps right and left of the hill, to prevent a flanking movement of the enemy.

Respectfully,

A. VON STEINWEHR,
Brigadier-General, Commanding Second Division.

Lieutenant-Colonel MEYSENBURG,
Assistant Adjutant-General.

No. 16.

Itinerary of the First Brigade, Col. Adolphus Buschbeck commanding.

October 27, in the morning, this brigade, with the exception of the Thirty-third New Jersey Volunteers, which was stationed at Battle Creek, Tenn., marched in the advance of the corps from Bridgeport, Ala., and encamped at night near Whiteside's.

October 28, this brigade, still in the advance of the corps, marched in the direction of Brown's Ferry. Upon arriving at the Trenton road the Twenty-seventh Pennsylvania Volunteers was ordered to take position upon a hill commanding that road, and to hold the same. When the remainder of the brigade had arrived about 1 mile this side of the Wauhatchie road the advance guard was fired upon by the enemy, who was posted upon a steep hill. The Seventy-third Pennsylvania Volunteers were deployed as skirmishers. The reserve, consisting of the One hundred and thirty-fourth and One hundred and fifty-fourth New York Volunteers, was sent to the right and left of the hill, to outflank them. When the flanking parties had arrived at the hill a charge was made, and the enemy retreated in great disorder across Lookout Creek. The brigade then moved on and encamped at night in Lookout Valley. In this engagement 2 men were wounded. During the night the enemy attacked General Geary. The Eleventh Corps was ordered to his support. This brigade was held in reserve.

No. 17.

Itinerary of the Second Brigade, Col. Orland Smith commanding.

This command at date of last report was stationed at Bridgeport, Ala. It remained at that post until October 9, when it was ordered

---

* From return for October.

to Stevenson, Ala. The One hundred and thirty-sixth Regiment New York Volunteers was stationed at Anderson Station, on the Nashville and Chattanooga Railroad, and seven companies of other regiments at various bridges between that point and Bridgeport, Ala.

October 24, the entire command was ordered to Bridgeport, Ala., and on the day following crossed the Tennessee River, and moved to Shellmound Station.

October 27, it moved with the remainder of the Eleventh Corps to Whiteside's Station ; thence, on the 28th, to Brown's Ferry, near Lookout Mountain, having a slight skirmish with the enemy at the base of Lookout Mountain on the route thither.

October 29, at 1 a. m., the command was engaged with the enemy, suffering severely, but driving the foe (who were 2,000 strong) from a strong position, our force engaged being less than 700. Generals Thomas, Hooker, Howard, and Steinwehr, complimented the brigade on its good behavior. The command has remained on the ground where the engagement occurred since that date.

No. 18.

Report of Lieut. Col. Godfrey Rider, jr., Thirty-third Massachusetts Infantry.

HDQRS. THIRTY-THIRD REGT. MASS. VOLUNTEERS,
Near Lookout Mountain, Tenn., November 1, 1863.

COLONEL : I have the honor to submit the following report of the share taken by the Thirty-third Regiment Massachusetts Volunteers in the operations of the 28th and 29th ultimo :

On the afternoon of the 28th, this command was formed in line of battle behind the Seventy-third Ohio Volunteers, and advanced steadily, skirmishing through the woods and brush on the right of the railroad. Upon reaching an open space, where the line was ordered to halt, a brisk fire of solid shot and shell was opened upon it from a battery of heavy guns upon the top of Lookout Mountain. The men were ordered to lie down, and remained in this position about half an hour, when this command was ordered to follow the Seventy-third Ohio Volunteers which marched by the right flank back through the woods, recrossed the railroad, and took the main road on the other side. This movement was executed in good order and without hurry, the men marching steadily, regardless of the shot and shell which the enemy continued to shower upon the column, until it was beyond the reach of his guns. About sundown the regiment encamped with the brigade within our own lines. Our loss in this action was 1 man killed.

At half past 12 o'clock on the morning of the 29th, orders were received to march. This command immediately fell into line, and after a march of a little over a mile reached a steep hill covered with trees and underbrush, upon the crest of which the enemy were posted, behind breastworks and rifle-pits, with skirmishers thrown out in front. This regiment formed in line of battle upon the hill-side, its right resting upon the road, and with one company (H) deployed as skirmishers on the left, reaching almost to the crest of the hill, and was ordered to advance in line and connect with the Seventy-third Ohio in front.

The line advanced in good order, under fire of the enemy's skir-mishers, until it reached a crooked ravine some 20 feet deep running parallel with the hill-side, the sides of which were almost perpen-dicular, slippery with leaves and clay, and covered with brush, and its appearance rendered still more formidable by the deceptive moon-light. At this point it was impossible to preserve a perfect line, but the regiment gallantly plunged into it—the dead and living roll-ing down together—climbed the opposite side, and halted in some dis-order. Here the enemy opened a deadly fire from the whole length of their line upon our front flank and rear. Colonel Underwood fell dangerously wounded, and many other officers and file closers were either killed or wounded. Unfortunately, the exact position of the enemy was unknown, and the Seventy-third Ohio, with which we were ordered to connect, could not be found for that purpose, they having advanced farther on our right, while we supposed them to be in a position actually occupied by the enemy. In this emergency, the regiment believing itself without support, and fired into by its friends, some confusion naturally ensued, and the line fell back slowly into the road. Here it was quickly reformed and again advanced in line, with fixed bayonets and without firing, directly up the face of the hill until, within a few yards of the breastworks, it drew the enemy's fire, when, with a cheer, it turned by the right flank, gained the crest, crossed the rifle-pits, and charged upon the enemy's flank with the bayonet, at the same time pouring a volley into his retreat-ing ranks. The enemy, without waiting to reply, retreated precipi-tately over the hill, abandoning his killed and wounded, and leav-ing us in full possession of the hill. Here the regiment formed in line of battle, posted pickets, and commenced throwing up breast-works in case of an attack.

This command captured 2 commissioned officers (1 wounded) and 39 privates, together with a large number of muskets and all the enemy's intrenching tools. Three companies of this command were absent, having been sent on an expedition toward Kelley's Ford. The regiment, therefore, went into action with only seven companies, numbering about 230 men. Out of this small force the command lost: Killed, 3 commissioned officers and 22 enlisted men; wounded, 5 commissioned officers and 56 enlisted men; total, 8 commissioned officers and 78 enlisted men, one-third of the whole number engaged.

I have the honor to be, colonel, your obedient servant,

G. RIDER, JR.,
Lieutenant-Colonel, Comdg. Thirty-third Massachusetts Vols.

Col. ORLAND SMITH,
Comdg. Second Brig., Second Div., Eleventh Corps.

No. 19.

Report of Col. James Wood, jr., One hundred and thirty-sixth New York Infantry.

HDQRS. 136TH NEW YORK VOLUNTEER INFANTRY,
In the Field, Lookout Valley,
Near Chattanooga, Tenn., November 1, 1863.

CAPTAIN: I have the honor to submit the following report of the operations of the regiment under my command since and including the 26th day of October ultimo. On that day I was relieved from guarding that part of the Nashville and Chattanooga Railroad and the bridges and wooden structures thereon between Anderson and Tantalon, to which I had been assigned by orders from brigade headquarters, bearing date 11th October ultimo. The regiment marched from Anderson to Bridgeport to join the brigade from which it had been detached while guarding the railroad. The march was made over the Cumberland Mountains by a steep and declivitous road or bridle path inaccessible to wagons, under the guidance of L. Willis, esq., a firm and unconditional Union man, residing near Anderson. The regiment arrived at Bridgeport on the evening of the same day, having marched a distance of 16 miles. On arriving at Bridgeport I learned that the brigade had marched the evening before to Shellmound, on the south side of the Tennessee River. I thereupon reported, with my command, to Brig. Gen. A. von Steinwehr, division commander, and encamped for the night. During the evening I received orders to march with the Eleventh Corps at sunrise the next morning, and to join my brigade on the march.

In pursuance of the order, the regiment marched with the corps at the time designated, crossed the Tennessee River at Bridgeport on pontoon bridges, and took up the line of march on the Chattanooga road. At Shellmound the regiment came up with and joined the brigade. From this point the regiment, with the Eleventh Corps, of which it formed a part, marched to Brown's Ferry, on the Tennessee River, in Lookout Valley, about 3 miles from Chattanooga, at which point it arrived near sunset of 28th October ultimo. Although the troops were on two occasions during the march massed in column by division, preparatory to an engagement in case the enemy attempted to dispute our progress (of which it was reported there were indications), and some skirmish firing was heard on our front, this regiment did not see, nor was it in any way molested by, the enemy on this march, except that as soon as the marching column came within range of his artillery, posted on Lookout Mountain, he opened upon it with shot and shell, and kept up the fire until the whole had passed. But such was the elevation of the mountain, and necessary inaccuracy of aim, that the cannonade was entirely harmless. The shot and shell fell wide of the mark, and did not so much as create any sensible uneasiness among the men of my command. I may be allowed to mention that as I passed the point most exposed to the fire I found Major-General Hooker stationed beside the road notifying the men as they passed that there was no danger from the artillery firing, and testifying by his presence and position that he believed what he said. It is unnecessary for me to say that this conduct of our commanding general had the most inspiriting influence on the officers and men of my command.

On arriving at our place of destination this regiment, with the brigade, encamped for the night. About 1 o'clock of the morning of the 29th ultimo, I was awakened by skirmish firing, which seemed to be a short distance back on the road over which we had marched. The firing rapidly increased in intensity, and the roar of artillery soon mingling with it, admonished us that some part of our forces were engaged with the enemy. The regiment was immediately ordered to fall in under arms, and to march in direction of the conflict. It was soon ascertained that the firing was occasioned by an attack made by the enemy upon the command of Brigadier-General Geary, of the Twelfth Corps, who had been following us from Bridgeport, and was a few hours in our rear. His command, consisting of a part of his division, had encamped for the night at a place called Wauhatchie, about 3 miles from the position occupied by the Eleventh Corps. General Howard ordered his command to march at once to the aid of General Geary. This regiment, at a double-quick, took up the line of march in rear of the brigade, being preceded by the Seventy-third Ohio, Thirty-third Massachusetts, and Fifty-fifth Ohio. When about 1½ miles from camp it was ascertained that the enemy occupied the crest of a hill, at the foot of which the road on which we were marching passed, and it was regarded important to dislodge him. Col. O. Smith, commanding the brigade, was ordered to do it. Preparatory to executing the movement, the brigade was halted in the road. Colonel Smith sent forward the Seventy-third Ohio and Thirty-third Massachusetts, and directed them to charge the hill and drive the enemy therefrom.

In the meantime, I was ordered by Brigadier-General Steinwehr, division commander, to march my regiment by file to the left and form line of battle west of and perpendicular to the road on which we had been halted. This was at the foot of another hill, about 200 yards north of the one occupied by the enemy, and similar in appearance to it and from which it was separated by a gap or pass. When I had completed the movement ordered, I was directed to send two companies to skirmish up the hill at the foot of which our line of battle was formed, to ascertain if it was occupied by the enemy. I immediately detached Companies H and K from the left of my left wing to execute the movement, and placed the force in command of Captain Eldredge, Company K. The Seventy-third Ohio and Thirty-third Massachusetts being hard pressed by the enemy on the hill which they had been ordered to charge, my regiment was ordered to their support. I marched to the base of the same hill, halted, and formed line of battle facing it. My center was opposite the highest crest of the hill. Although it was a bright moonlight night, neither the height of the hill nor the obstacles to be encountered could be seen. I was ordered to charge in line of battle to the top of the hill, drive off the enemy, and form a junction with the Thirty-third Massachusetts on my right. It should be borne in mind that the two companies detached as skirmishers had not at this time rejoined the regiment.

I gave the command "forward," when the regiment advanced in line of battle at as quick a pace as the steep ascent of the hill would permit. Moved steadily and firmly forward under a brisk and constant fire from the enemy, reached and crowned the crest of the hill, drove off the enemy, and took possession. Not a shot was fired by my men until the crest was gained, when one volley was discharged at the retreating enemy. At the time the charge was made the enemy was engaged in throwing up a line of rifle-pits. We captured his intrenching tools. Having gained and occupied the crest of the hill, I deployed one company to the front as skirmishers, moved by the right flank, and formed a connection with the Thirty-third Massachusetts, which regiment had preceded me, charging up the hill on my right, and was vigorously engaged with the enemy when I reached the crest. The victory was complete. The crest of the hill is not more than 6 yards in width, from which there is a rapid descent into a valley on the other side. Down this declivity the enemy precipitately fled in the utmost confusion. He staggered under the intrepid charges and deadly blows delivered to him by the braves of the Seventy-third Ohio and Thirty-third Massachusetts. His discomfiture was made complete by the vigorous and splendid charge of the One hundred and thirty-sixth New York Volunteers. The ground over which he retreated was strewn with rifles, swords, hats, caps, and haversacks. As daylight opened upon us, we were all astonished at the audacity of our charge and astounded at our success. The hill is over 200 feet perpendicular height, and the distance from the road where I formed line of battle to the crest of the hill is 180 yards.

Prisoners report (and the report is confirmed by other information, and may be regarded as reliable) that the force of the enemy occupying the hill consisted of Law's brigade, Hood's division, Longstreet's corps. This brigade was composed of six regiments, five of which were posted on the crest of the hill, the sixth being held in reserve in the valley below. The face of the hill is covered by a forest and a thick coating of leaves, broken by gullies or ravines, and obstructed by brush and upturned trees. Over and through these obstructions, up an ascent of over 45 degrees, the men charged with a steadiness and precision that could not be excelled by the most experienced and veteran troops. At no time was there any confusion; at no time was there any wavering. From the commencement to the end of the charge the alignment of the line of battle was wonderfully preserved. My hearty commendation and profound thanks are especially due to the officers and men of my command for their brave and gallant conduct on this occasion, as I was deprived of the assistance of my able and energetic field officer, Lieutenant-Colonel Faulkner (being absent on detached service in State of New York) and Major Arnold (being detained at Bridgeport by an attack of illness which rendered him unable to take the field). There is no occasion to make special mention of any officer or man of my command, for every one engaged seemed to perform his whole duty. No one faltered; there were no stragglers. All are alike entitled to credit; all alike should receive the commendation of their superior officers, the gratitude of their country, and the friends of all may well feel proud of the bravery and gallantry which was exhibited.

Our casualties, it affords me much pleasure to say, are slight, our loss being only 2 killed and 4 wounded. This exemption from disaster is due to the steepness of the hill up which we charged, the bullets from the enemy's rifles passing harmlessly over our heads. The casualties happened after we reached the crest. We captured 5 prisoners and 40 rifles left on the field by the retreating enemy.

I have the honor to be, captain, respectfully,

JAMES WOOD, JR.,
Colonel, Commanding.

Capt. B. F. STONE, *Acting Assistant Adjutant-General.*

———

No. 20.

Report of Maj. Samuel H. Hurst, Seventy-third Ohio Infantry.

HDQRS. SEVENTY-THIRD REGT. OHIO VOLUNTEERS,
Near Chattanooga, November 2, 1863.

CAPTAIN : I have the honor to submit the following report of the part taken by this regiment in the actions of October 28 and 29 near Lookout Creek :

In the afternoon of October 28, shortly after leaving Wauhatchie, in our line of march toward Chattanooga, I was ordered to cross the Nashville and Chattanooga Railroad and move the regiment forward in line of battle, with its left touching the road, and ascertain whether the enemy were in force in the dense woods in that direction.   Having made the dispositions indicated, and massed our front and right flank with skirmishers, we moved forward until our line had passed that of the First Brigade, Colonel Buschbeck, with whom I was ordered to connect.   Here I halted the battalion while the skirmishers went forward to the banks of Lookout Creek, where they communicated with the skirmishers of the First Brigade, and assured themselves that the enemy was not in force in that immediate vicinity, yet a running fire of skirmishers and an attempt to burn the railroad bridge across the creek evidenced the intention of the enemy to dispute our advance in that direction.

In the meantime, the enemy's batteries on the mountain were vigorously engaged in shelling our position, which, however, resulted to us in no casualties, save the slight wounding of 1 man.   After remaining in this position about half an hour, I was ordered to withdraw the regiment and rejoin the brigade, which order I at once obeyed.   On the morning of the 29th, while the Second Brigade, with the Seventy-third Ohio in the advance, was moving to the support of General Geary, at about 2 o'clock in the morning, I was ordered to form line of battle on the left of the road and sweep through the woods on the west side of a range of hills that ran parallel with the road on which we had been advancing.   I immediately sent forward Captain Buchwalter, with instructions to deploy his company (A) as skirmishers and move in the direction indicated for the battalion. We then moved forward in line as rapidly as possible, considering the irregularities of the ground, the dense growth of underbrush, and the fallen timber.   We had advanced, however, only a few hundred yards when the enemy's skirmishers opened fire upon us from the hill-tops on our left and from our front.   I was ordered to wheel the battalion to the left and charge the hill, and was informed that the Thirty-third Massachusetts would connect with me on the left and move up the hill in the same line of battle.   I instructed Captain Buchwalter to move his skirmishers by the left into our new front and advance in that direction, in executing which order his line received a heavy volley from an unseen force of the enemy on our right, and the gallant captain fell mortally wounded.

We moved up the hill (steep and difficult though it was) for a hundred paces, receiving an irregular fire from the enemy in our front.   Then we lay down and rested for a minute.   The enemy's fire now indicated their position and the direction of their line of battle.   We had yet another hundred paces to climb before we could use our bayonets, and we rose up and moved forward again to the charge, cheering as we went, and driving in the enemy's skirmishers. The heavily increasing fire of the enemy provoked an occasional shot from our own lines in answer.   Our skirmishers had been constantly engaged, and now their line opened right and left, and we were confronted by the enemy's whole line of battle, sheltered behind formidable breastworks on the crest of the hill.   As we came in sight of them in the clear moonlight they lowered their guns and poured into our ranks a most deadly fire.   Our boys began to fall rapidly, but the ranks were instantly closed, and steadily, in the face of death, our little battalion kept shouting and charging forward. The firing in our front became so rapid and effective that I commanded the regiment to answer it, which they did handsomely, still, however, continuing to advance.

When we had approached within 2 or 3 rods of the enemy's breastworks there opened upon us a most murderous fire from a force on our right flank, completely enfilading our line. The appearance of this force on our flank seemed to forbid our farther advance. I knew we had no support on our right, and we had not held communication with the Thirty-third Massachusetts at any time during the engagement. Regarding the Seventy-third as the directing battalion, I had paid no attention to our support on the left, and it was impossible for me to learn whether Colonel Underwood was advancing or not, while heavy and irregular firing, with cries of "Don't fire upon your own men," coming from the left of our front, only increased the confusion. Under the circumstances I deemed it rash to advance farther until I knew that one, at least, of my flanks was protected. I ordered the regiment to retire a few rods, which they did in perfect order, and lay down again, while I sent Captain Higgins to ascertain the position and movements of the Thirty-third Massachusetts. Learning that, though they had fallen back, they were again advancing, I was preparing to go forward also, when information came that the Thirty-third had turned the enemy's flank, was gallantly charging him in his breastworks, and driving him from the left crest of the hill.

I immediately charged forward again, took and occupied the works and hill in our own front, from which the enemy rapidly fled. The taking of this hill had not been accomplished, however, without fearful cost. One-half of my line officers and one-third of my men were either killed or wounded in this brief but desperate struggle, and never had men shown higher courage than characterized the work of that morning. A full report of the casualties has already been forwarded. I cannot, however, neglect to mention specially the lamented Captain Buchwalter (wounded, and since dead), whose chivalrous spirit and high, manly, and soldierly qualities won all hearts, and gave promise of a brilliant and useful career.

Captain Barnes, Lieutenants McCommon, Hawkins, Talbott, and Martin were among the wounded, and deserve honorable mention. They behaved most gallantly in the fight, and their scars will be remembrancers of duty bravely done. But where all acted so nobly it were invidious not to award them a just meed of praise. Those who survived unscathed were no less courageous than their fallen comrades. Captain Higgins, acting major, behaved with his accustomed intrepidity, being always in the thickest of the fight, cheering the men forward. Lieutenants Hinson, Kinney, Downing, Stone, Peters, and Davis, all commanding companies, were constantly with their men, inspiring them with a sublime courage, and leading them with soldiery determination against that wall of fire. Lieutenant Hosler, acting adjutant, assisted me efficiently, and the non-commissioned officers and the men in the ranks did all that I could ask. With daring, dauntless spirits, they attacked an enemy vastly superior in numbers and holding a fortified and almost impregnable position, and drove them from that position by the most heroic and desperate effort. It was an achievement worthy the best men of a veteran army, and must add new luster to our already honorable names, and make it a consideration of just and honest pride to belong to the brave old Seventy-third.

I have the honor, captain, to subscribe myself, your obedient servant,

SAM'L H. HURST,
Major, Commanding Regiment.

Capt. B. F. STONE, *Acting Assistant Adjutant-General.*

No. 21.

Report of Maj. Gen. Carl Schurz, U. S. Army, commanding Third Division.

HDQRS. THIRD DIVISION, ELEVENTH ARMY CORPS,
Camp near Brown's Ferry, October 31, 1863.

GENERAL: About the part taken by my command in the night engagement of October 29, I have the honor to report as follows:

We arrived in camp near Brown's Ferry, north of the Kelley's Ferry road, about 4.30 p. m. on October 28. Part of my Third Brigade was left behind on detached service. The camp we occupied was flanked on the left by a row of steep hills; on the right by the Raccoon Mountain; front toward Wauhatchie. The road from Brown's Ferry to Wauhatchie runs along steep ridges, intersected by gaps and ravines, through one of which runs the Kelley's Ferry road, and through another the Chattanooga Railroad, the two being about 500 yards apart. On the right of the road is a valley about one-half mile wide, partly corn-fields and partly timber and brush. This valley is bordered on the right by the Raccoon Mountain. The hills are thickly wooded. My picket line ran along the Kelley's Ferry road, forming an angle where it touches the Raccoon Mountain, so as to cover our right. General Geary's command, which had followed mine on the march, encamped at Wauhatchie, about 3 miles from our camp. About midnight we were disturbed by a few shots on our picket line, which, however, indicated nothing serious.

About 1 a. m., October 29, lively firing was heard in the direction of Wauhatchie. Soon after, I was ordered to send one of my brigades to occupy the hill in the angle formed by the road to Wauhatchie and the Chattanooga Railroad. I ordered my First Brigade, under General Tyndale, to move at once, and as rapidly as possible, and placed myself at the head of the column. It was bright moonlight. About one-half mile from our camp, while moving through the fields, in order to cut off the angles of the road, according to your direction, the flankers on my left were attacked by a rebel force concealed in the woods on a hill on my left, and my leading regiment received a full volley, which wounded 1 of my staff officers, Captain Lender, and several men. This rebel force was, however, immediately afterward attacked by regiments of the Second Division, and we continued our march toward the hill General Tyndale was to occupy. Finding the ground on the open field boggy and impassable just before reaching the base of hill, the brigade had to march by the left flank to gain the road.

The hill being in possession of the enemy, orders were given to take it. A short engagement ensued. The enemy was speedily dislodged, the regiments of my First Brigade moving up rapidly. General Tyndale then established himself in the position assigned to him. I reported this to General Hooker, who ordered me to form a junction with General Geary's command. I directed Colonel Krzyzanowski, commanding my Second Brigade, to occupy the gap northeast of the hill held by General Tyndale, and Colonel Hecker, commanding my Third Brigade, to march to Wauhatchie with the Sixty-eighth New York, the One hundred and forty-first New York, and six companies of the Eightieth Illinois. He was ordered to open a passage, at whatever cost, if he found the enemy in force on his way. The Seventy-fifth Pennsylvania was directed to occupy the railroad gap.

We had no information of the enemy's movements, and could see but little in the darkness of the woods. Colonel Hecker, however, found no serious resistance, and, after a slight skirmish, effected his junction with General Geary's command. He arrived at Wauhatchie before daybreak, and reported himself to General Geary in person about 5 a. m.

At 6 a. m. I received the order to send another brigade to General Geary. Deeming it necessary to hold the important position occupied by General Tyndale, I ordered Colonel Krzyzanowski to leave a detachment in the position he then had, and to march with the remainder of his command to Wauhatchie. He reported there about 7 a. m.

My loss was 37 officers and men. We took a number of prisoners.

I am, general, most respectfully, yours,

C. SCHURZ,
Major-General, Commanding Third Division.

Major-General HOWARD,
Commanding Eleventh Corps.

No. 22.

Itinerary of the First Brigade, Brig. Gen. Hector Tyndale commanding. *

October 1, the brigade proceeded on the cars from Tullahoma, arriving at Bridgeport, Ala., on the evening of same day. Encamped on the west side of the river, doing picket duty, scouting, and building earth-works at the bridge head, across Tennessee River.

October 21, the Eighty-second Illinois Volunteers was attached to the Third Brigade, Third Division.

October 27, left Bridgeport, *en route* to Lookout Valley, arriving at Poison Hollow on the evening of the same day. The One hundred and first Illinois Infantry joined this brigade this day.

October 28, left Poison Hollow in the morning, arriving at the foot of Lookout Mountain on the afternoon of same day. Skirmished with the enemy, driving in their outposts, and arrived safely at the present camping ground; placed pickets on all suitable points, and joined the troops of this corps in successfully repulsing a night attack of the enemy on the 29th, at 1.30 a. m. Commenced building rifle-pits, &c., continuing the works without cessation during October 30 and 31.

No. 23.

Itinerary of the Second Brigade, Col. Wladimir Krzyzanowski commanding. *

October 1, the brigade arrived at Nashville, and established camp near Bridgeport, Ala., October 2.

October 19, the Seventy-fifth Pennsylvania Volunteers and Sixty-eighth New York Volunteers were transferred to the Third Brigade,

---

* From return for October.

Third Division, Eleventh Corps, Colonel Hecker commanding, in pursuance with Special Orders, No. 209, headquarters Eleventh Corps, dated October 19.

October 27, the brigade left Bridgeport, Ala., and reached Lookout Valley, opposite Lookout Point, October 28.

October 28 and 29, in the night an engagement took place with Longstreet's corps, which, however, the Second Brigade took little share in. A patrol of 150 men, under the command of Major Clanharty, of the One hundred and Forty-first New York Volunteers, discovered first the movements of the enemy, and much contributed to the favorable results.

No. 24.

Reports of Brig. Gen. John W. Geary, U. S. Army, commanding Second Division, Twelfth Army Corps.

HDQRS. SECOND DIVISION, TWELFTH ARMY CORPS,
Wauhatchie, Tenn., November 5, 1863.

GENERAL : I have the honor to submit the following report of the operations of my division from the morning of October 27 until November 1, 1863, embracing the engagement with the enemy at Wauhatchie on the night of October 28 :

When orders from Major-General Hooker reached me to concentrate my command at Bridgeport, it was extended from Tullahoma to Murfreesborough, Tenn., and three regiments were at Stevenson, all guarding the line of railroad. These orders were immediately acted upon, but, owing to the limited transportation and difficulty in procuring the same, combined with numerous interferences with the road and trains by hostile parties, much delay was occasioned. I reached Bridgeport with my advance regiment and two sections of Knap's (Pennsylvania) battery on the afternoon of the 25th ultimo, and, notwithstanding the strenuous efforts of myself and staff officers sent along the line, only four regiments, the Seventy-eighth and One hundred and forty-ninth New York Volunteers, under General Greene, and the Twenty-ninth and One hundred and ninth Pennsylvania, under Col. G. A. Cobham, jr., with the four pieces of artillery, had reported up to the hour indicated for the forward movement. With this fraction of my command I moved at 5 a. m. on the 27th, provided with three days' rations and 60 rounds of ammunition per man. I left several staff officers to use every exertion in accelerating the pushing forward of my troops. The speediness of the movement necessarily entailed some embarrassment upon us, as our trains and ambulances, just drawn, were not far from Nashville. Such necessary transportation as accompanied us was kindly furnished by Major-General Howard. We crossed the Tennessee River at 7 o'clock, and, pursuant to orders, camped at 2 p. m. at Shellmound, where the Sixtieth and One hundred and thirty-seventh New York and One hundred and eleventh Pennsylvania Volunteers joined us in the evening. I ordered heavy fatigue details to aid in constructing a pontoon bridge across the river at Shellmound, near Love's Ferry, which was completed at 1 a. m. of the following day.

We resumed the march at 5 o'clock on the morning of the 28th, and by way of Running Waters and Whiteside's, reached Wauhatchie at 4.30 p. m.   At Whiteside's the Sixtieth New York Volunteers, Col. A. Godard, was detached and ordered into the pass leading toward Trenton, with instructions to hold it at all hazards.   Owing to the heavy condition of the roads over a long extent of the route, the march was a trying one.   Our passage from the mountain gorge to our ordered destination, at the intersection of the Wauhatchie and Brown's Ferry, by the Kelley's Ferry road, was distinctly visible to the enemy's signal station on a table of the Lookout Mountain, upon which active signaling was plainly discernible to the naked eye. I ordered my command to bivouac upon their arms, with cartridge boxes on, and placed my guns on a knob about 30 yards to the left of the railroad and immediately to the left of Rowden's house, so that they could command either of the cardinal points.   Commanding officers were instructed to have their men spring to arms upon any alarm.   I selected Colonel Rickards for the duties of general officer of the day, and his regiment (the Twenty-ninth Pennsylvania Volunteers) for grand guard.   I ordered them to be posted according to Butterfield's Outpost Duty, which I always adopt in my command as a most efficient system, and which, well carried out, renders surprise from any force impossible.   The utmost vigilance was enjoined upon all.   I had not anticipated an attack from the direction it came, although I had provided for all contingencies, as the Eleventh Corps had passed that way, leading to a reasonable supposition that no enemy had position in that vicinity.   My anticipations were that we would be approached from the southward, and I accordingly made my strongest disposition that way.   During the night I learned from a citizen that Longstreet's command had been, and doubtless was, at the foot of Lookout Mountain, on the east side of the creek over which a bridge was said to be constructed.   I specially enjoined upon my pickets vigilance toward the reported locality of this bridge.

At about half past 10 o'clock picket-firing was heard to the left of the railroad and north of my position, which seemed to emanate from my outposts.   The entire command was put under arms at once, and I moved the One hundred and eleventh Pennsylvania Volunteers forward to the Kelley's Ferry road, so as to command the railroad and the approaches to the right and left of it.   The firing having ceased for over an hour, I returned the regiment, with a repetition of previous orders as to alertness.   Shortly after midnight our outposts gave the alarm, their challenge being distinctly heard, as well as the shots which struck them down at their posts, fully comprehensive, to a degree worthy of emulation, of the duty required of them in preservation of those they guarded.   The course of the enemy's advance was alone indicated by the opposition of my pickets.   The moon was fitful and did not afford light sufficient to see a body of men only 100 yards distant, and during the fight their whereabouts was mostly revealed by the flashes of the fire-arms.   I promptly formed my lines to receive their attack.   The One hundred and thirty-seventh New York was advanced about 50 yards west of the Kelley's Ferry road, forming my left, the One hundred and ninth and One hundred and eleventh Pennsylvania Volunteers, respectively, prolonged this line and constituted my front, which was perpendicular to the Nashville and Chattanooga Railroad.   The right of the One hundred and eleventh overreached the angle and faced the railroad.   My right was formed at right angles with the center, along the embankment of the railroad, held by the Seventy-eighth and One hundred and forty-ninth New York, who were advancing into position when the enemy assailed my left. The line of battle was, therefore, the corner of a square, one side parallel with the railroad. There were no desirable positions but those chosen, which covered, in advance, the intersection of the roads and the Kelley's Ferry road for some distance, together with the entire encampment. No protection was offered farther than about 30 yards of an ordinary fence, which was improved, under fire, into a rude breastwork. Skirmishers were immediately sent forward to support my gradually retiring pickets, but they were scarcely deployed before the enemy opened fire.

The enemy precipitately hurled his main body, without skirmishers, upon my left, where the One hundred and thirty-seventh New York and One hundred and ninth Pennsylvania and the two left companies of the One hundred and eleventh Pennsylvania met them with intense and well-directed fire. My men were cautioned to fire low, and expend their ammunition only with effect. The episode evidenced that they obeyed the injunctions ably. The first volley was fired at a half hour after midnight. The enemy pressed forward vigorously with a continuous line of fire, his first efforts being concentrated against the left, but not a point in our lines was swerved a foot.

The guns of Knap's battery, from their position about 50 yards in the rear and to the left of Rowden's house, were now served with admirable effect, being depressed as much as possible without doing injury to our own lines, but not interfering with efficacy of range; the projectile used was spherical case with short fuses. Charge after charge was made, each with redoubled effort upon our left, which they seemed determined to force, but each time the enemy's lines were hurled back under the unintermitting fire, both from infantry and artillery, that like a wall of flame opposed them. Prisoners began to come in, and we discovered we were opposing Hood's division of Longstreet's corps, commanded by General Jenkins.

After nearly half an hour's desperate fighting, being foiled in his attempt to pierce the redoubtable left, the enemy extended his attack without cessation of fire on the left, to the right of my center, front, and left flank, which he attacked simultaneously with great strength. The pickets of the Twenty-ninth Pennsylvania driven in were placed in support of the battery, and our utmost vigor was concentrated to meet this general combination of our adversary. Being so considerably outnumbered, the test point for our utmost capacity for resistance had now arrived ; these attacks were determinedly sustained along my line, which was actively engaged save on the extreme right, where, as yet, no demonstration had been made. The fire upon our right commenced from a piece of woods to the right of the railroad upon our skirmishers, covering the right, and advanced. One piece of Lieutenant Geary's section was turned to the right, and two companies of the One hundred and eleventh Pennsylvania, with the skirmishers, ordered hastily to take position behind the railroad embankment, where they checked the enemy's advance, who were much distressed and met with considerable loss by the combined efforts of the piece of artillery, with its excellent execution, and the indomitable behavior of my center, held by the One hundred and eleventh Pennsylvania, which faced, in portions, two directions to resist the enfilading fire. It was under this fire that my men fell rapidly and the battery suffered a most unparalleled loss.

The order, "Pick off the artillerists," was repeatedly heard along the rebel line. Lieutenant Geary fell, mortally wounded, while resisting this onslaught, which his piece contributed so effectually to repel Captain Atwell, of the battery, fell with a wound which since has caused his death. His men and horses fell so rapidly that only two guns could be manned after this attack. The command of the battery now devolved entirely upon the only artillery officer present, Maj. J. A. Reynolds, chief of artillery of Twelfth Corps. The infantry suffered considerably, but dealt destruction into the rebel ranks as correspondingly overwhelming as were their numbers to those of our own Spartan band.

The contest raged with vehemence along the whole line, while our artillery threw its missiles unsparingly into the opposing ranks. The One hundred and thirty-seventh New York, on the left, fought the over-reaching right of the enemy by part of them fighting back to back with the other part. After the lapse of an hour and a half the enemy evidenced an indisposition to continue the attack on the center, and, at the same moment, a redoubled attack on the entire left made manifest his strengthening of that portion of his line. Again they were met with that obstinate fire which kept them in abeyance by dealing death into their ranks with the fire of our men, whose unerring aim contrasted strongly with the want of precision and overflying shots of the enemy. While thus hotly engaged the enemy attempted to turn our left flank by uncovering it some distance to the left. The Hampton Legion, 1,600 strong, had penetrated to the Kelley's Ferry road, about 70 yards to the left, and, while marching by the flank, was attacked by two companies of the One hundred and thirty-seventh New York, under Adjutant Mix, moved around at right angles, and they were thrown into confusion by our sudden assault, and, the advantage on our side being followed up, they were hastily driven back, leaving a number of killed and wounded in the woods to the left and rear of our line.

Our ammunition was now, about 3 a. m., nearly exhausted, and a limited supply was gathered from the hospital and from the persons of the dead and wounded of both sides on the field. I had determined to depend upon the bayonet should our ammunition fail, and hold our position until relieved. A demonstration was now made on the right of the center angle, and also opposite the extreme right, while the firing on the left grew weaker. The enemy opened from a rising ground overlooking the railroad and from behind the railroad embankment. The two pieces of artillery still continued fire. One piece was dragged by two companies of the Twenty-ninth Pennsylvania to a pass over the railroad near the extreme right, and, under the supervision of Colonel Rickards, was ranged north, toward Chattanooga, sweeping the railroad, and, after several discharges, the rebels were driven from the embankment. The One hundred and forty-ninth New York now poured several volleys into them, punishing them severely, as was attested by the numbers left on the field in that locality.

A detachment was ordered to hold the woods farther to our right, which guarded against any attempt to turn that flank. At half past 3 o'clock they ceased firing on our left, their hostility manifestly having grown weaker during the last fifteen minutes, and, firing a few volleys at our center, which were promptly responded to, they retired, leaving the field in our possession, and our lines in the same position as when the battle opened. Our victory was complete— the disasters to the enemy palpably extensive. The veteran division of Hood had sought to surprise and capture us, or to annihilate us. Baffled in his every attempt to accomplish his mission, the enemy was driven from the field, after a most desperate struggle of three hours' duration, with such precipitation that he had not time to carry with him all his wounded, whether officers or privates. We had prisoners in our hands from the First, Second, Third, Fourth,* Fifth, Sixth, and Seventh South Carolina Regiments, Hampton Legion, and the Palmetto Sharpshooters, all of which were large regiments, reported by members of them to have been filled up. They informed us that General Longstreet directed their movements by signals from a point half way down the side of Lookout Mountain, which was perceptible to us during the engagement.

To the coolness and judgment of my officers in executing my orders, and in their promptness to appreciate emergencies, calling into use their discretionary actions, and to the men of my command, who evidenced only in repetition a prowess displayed on many well-contested fields in the Army of the Potomac, which fostered their soldierhood, and which has become a component of their military existence, is attributable the defeat of so large a force by such comparatively small numbers. All seemed to feel that the results of their first encounter would determine the nature of their introductory reception by their brothers in arms of the Army of the Cumberland. The officers were, without an exception known to me, collected and constantly engaged in inspiring and directing the men who, in turn, delivered their fire deliberately and with telling effect, as shown by the wounded and dead of the rebels, the majority of whom were struck in the chest or abdomen. No straggling, no confusion, was visible, except among the negro teamsters, who, under the first fire, deserted their teams, and the horses fled affrighted through different parts of the field, many of them falling from the shots of the enemy.

Brigadier-General Greene was wounded early in the engagement. With his proverbial bravery he was in the front, near the One hundred and thirty-seventh New York, prepared to contribute his valuable efforts to our success. During our movement he was ever zealous in seconding any measure productive of benefit to the service he so warmly espouses.

I beg to furnish the following statement as to the strength of my command engaged. Seven of my regiments had not yet come up. One was holding the pass between Whiteside's and Trenton. The Twenty-ninth Pennsylvania was engaged on grand guard duty. The actual fighting throughout the battle was sustained, in conjunction with the artillery, by the One hundred and thirty-seventh New York and One hundred and ninth and One hundred and eleventh Pennsylvania, with portions of the Twenty-ninth Pennsylvania, driven in from the picket front:

Command.	Officers.	Enlisted men.
General Greene's (Third) brigade : One hundred and thirty-seventh New York, Col. D. Ireland.	15	353
Colonel Cobham's (Second) brigade :		
109th Pennsylvania, Capt. F. L. Gimber	4	108
111th Pennsylvania, Lieut. Col. T. M. Walker	22	282
In line engaged	41	743

* This regiment was consolidated with the Hampton Legion November 11, 1862.

The following were present :

Command.	Officers.	Enlisted men.
Greene's brigade :		
78th New York, Lieut. Col. H. Hammerstein......................................	15	169
149th New York, Lieut. Col. C. B. Randall.................................	14	223
Cobham's brigade : Twenty-ninth Pennsylvania, Col. W. Rickards......................	23	364
Total infantry present.......	93	1,499

The Seventy-eighth and One hundred and forty-ninth New York
occupied an important position, but the latter only engaged for a few
minutes. The presence of these two regiments on the right had the
effect of retarding movements of the enemy in that direction. Of
the conduct of the One hundred and thirty-seventh New York and
One hundred and ninth and One hundred and eleventh Pennsylvania
in sustaining the brunt of the battle, I cannot speak too highly. They
acquitted themselves in a manner deserving all the commendation
that a commander can bestow upon them, and which I take pride in
mentioning officially, as well as the valuable services of all present.
Colonel Ireland is deserving of especial notice, not only in commanding his regiment in the heat of the battle, but also in his conduct
upon succeeding General Greene in command of his brigade. The
two sections of Knap's (Pennsylvania) battery contributed invaluably
to the successful result of the action. Nearly all its gunners were
killed or wounded, and about two-thirds of its horses, but, until the
last, all who were left did their duty at their posts. Among those
who, in this action, were numbered with the honored dead were the
only two officers attached to this battery present—Capt. C. A. Atwell and Lieut. E. R. Geary—who fell in the midst of their command, zealous in execution of their duty. Many regrets follow those
brave young hearts to their soldier graves, succumbing, in the hour
of youth's promising, brightest manhood, to the hostility of our
country's enemy. In the latter named, I may be permitted to remark, I experience, in conjunction with the keen regrets of a commanding officer for a worthy officer, the pangs of a father's grief for
a cherished son, whose budding worth in wealth of intellect and
courage was filling full the cup of paternal pride.

In the death of Major Boyle, of the One hundred and eleventh
Pennsylvania, the command is deprived of a valuable officer, society
of one of its choice gentlemen, and our country a noble martyr. To
Major Reynolds, chief of artillery of the Twelfth Corps, the highest
encomiums are due. From the opening of the fight he personally
contributed his knowledge and efforts to the action of the battery.
After its officers were killed he assumed exclusive command and retained it until November 4. To Colonel Cobham, commanding Second Brigade, I take pleasure in officially tendering my thanks for his
valuable co-operation, as well as to Colonel Rickards and Lieut. Col.
S. M. Zulich, of the grand guard, who were ever present where they
could contribute to the general good, which they did to an eminent
degree. The officers of my staff, present, Capt. Thomas H. Elliott,
assistant adjutant-general ; Capt. R. H. Wilbur, aide-de-camp ; Capt.
M. Veale, assistant commissary of musters, and Lieut. L. R. Davis,
aide-de-camp, manifested throughout the same coolness, zeal, judg-

ment, and courage which has marked their association with me upon many previous fields.   Captain Veale was lightly, and Lieutenant Davis severely, wounded early in the battle.   I am constrained to regret the loss of many brave and devoted men among the casualties.

The following is a return of the enemy's losses as far as ascertained: Killed, in our hands (from reports of burial parties), 153, including 6 commissioned officers; wounded, in our hands (3 commissioned officers), 52; prisoners taken with arms (3 commissioned officers), 50; arms captured (Springfield and Enfield rifles), 350.

From the statistics of most battle-fields, and judging of our own proportion of wounded (5½ to 1 killed), it is just to compute the loss of the enemy in wounded at a ratio of 5, which will render their loss in the engagement with my command about 1,000, a figure which, from all circumstances, is most reasonable.   Many arms and accouterments, as well as a number of guns thrown away by the enemy in flight, were found in the mountains, indicating that some of their troops had become disconnected from their commands and had wandered off.   Many of the arms captured were taken by the various commands to replace damaged ones; also by teamsters and others.

On the morning of the 29th, Colonel Hecker's brigade (Third), of the Third Division, Eleventh Corps, reported to me as re-enforcements, at half past 5 o'clock, two hours after the enemy had retired, and at 7.15 Colonel Krzyzanowski's (Second) brigade, of the same division and corps, reported.   The former I placed in position in single line, parallel with and overlooking the railroad.   The latter I formed on my extreme right, in prolongation of the line, in rear of the railroad junction.   I furnished them with intrenching tools and they worked industriously and cheerfully in constructing extensive breastworks with numerous traverses advantageously formed, to which I gave personal attention.   At shortly after 8 o'clock, Col. Jno. G. Mitchell reported with a detachment of Second Brigade, Second Division, Fourteenth Army Corps, which I placed in the intrenchments, partially constructed by our troops after the battle, relieving my own men, who were much fatigued and needed respite. Colonel Mitchell's command was directed to proceed in fortifying the position, which it did actively, while my men buried our own and the enemy's dead and gathered the wounded and arms from the field.   From 10 o'clock in the morning until late in the afternoon, the shells and shot of the enemy from Lookout Mountain penetrated every portion of our position, without any casualties or interference with the progress of the works.

At noon the Twenty-ninth Ohio and One hundred and forty-seventh Pennsylvania, with the remaining section of Knap's battery, reported.   The regiments were put in reserve, and, in the afternoon, my whole command was placed in line to the left and engaged in strengthening their position.   The Seventy-eighth and One hundred and forty-ninth New York regiments constituted the grand guards during the 29th and 30th.   The whole of the 30th was devoted to fortifying our lines, though the day was exceedingly inclement.   On the 31st, pursuant to orders, our line was changed to a range of hills 1½ miles to the rear of the railroad, in the direction of Kelley's Ferry, and our whole force at once engaged upon throwing up works in front of our lines, which constituted the right, resting on Raccoon Mountain.   Colonel Hecker's and Colonel Krzyzanowski's brigades were relieved at about 5 p. m. on the 31st, and Colonel Mitchell's at 9 a. m. on November 1.   The remaining four regiments of my First

(Candy's) Brigade reported late on the night of October 31, and were placed in position on the line.

Casualties in division : Killed, 36 ; wounded, 174 ; missing, 6 ; total, 216.

I have the honor to be, general, very respectfully, your obedient servant,

JNO. W. GEARY,

Brigadier-General, U. S. Volunteers, Commanding.

Maj. Gen. D. BUTTERFIELD,

Chief of Staff.

—

HDQRS. SECOND DIVISION, TWELFTH ARMY CORPS,
Wauhatchie, Tenn., October 30, 1863.

GENERAL : I have the honor to forward herewith a return of casualties in my command in the action at Wauhatchie on the morning of the 29th instant :

The regiments engaged were : Col. G. A. Cobham's (Second) brigade, Twenty-ninth Pennsylvania, Col. W. Rickards commanding, picketing (that portion of the pickets of this regiment in our front met the advance of the enemy) ; One hundred and ninth Pennsylvania, Capt. F. L. Gimber commanding, and One hundred and eleventh Pennsylvania, Lieut. Col. Thomas M. Walker commanding.   General G. S. Greene's (Third) brigade, One hundred and thirty-seventh New York, Col. D. Ireland commanding, and Seventy-eighth and One hundred and forty-ninth New York, in line on extreme right, but not much engaged with the enemy, not being assailed.   The actual fighting was done, therefore, by the One hundred and ninth and One hundred and eleventh Pennsylvania and One hundred and thirty-seventh New York.

My First Brigade has not reported from Bridgeport.   The Sixtieth New York, of Greene's brigade, was, and still is, guarding the pass between Whiteside's and Trenton.   The One hundred and second New York Volunteers, of the same brigade, is acting as escort to the division ambulance train, *en route* from Murfreesborough to Bridgeport.

Two sections of Knap's (Pennsylvania) battery, Capt. C. A. Atwell, under direction of Major Reynolds, chief of artillery, Twelfth Army Corps, were also engaged, and suffered severely.   One-third of the men present were killed or disabled, and more than half of the horses killed.   The loss of gunners rendered only two of the guns effective for nearly two hours of the engagement.   Ammunition expended, 224 rounds.

I forward an approximate return of the enemy's losses : Killed in our hands, from reports of burial parties, 90 ; wounded in our hands, about 50 ; wounded, carried off, and walked away, from reports of prisoners brought in some hours after the engagement, from 250 to 300 ; prisoners taken with arms, about 50 ; arms captured (Springfield and Enfield rifles), about 300.   Some of these have been taken by such of my command as had indifferent arms.   A portion of one rebel regiment threw down its arms and refused to advance under the fire we were pouring into them.

I append a list of casualties in commissioned officers :

Division staff : Capt. Moses Veale, assistant commissary of musters, slightly, in shoulder ; First Lieut. L. R. Davis, aide-de-camp, severely, in shoulder.

Second Brigade: General staff, Lieut. John J. Haight, acting assistant inspector-general, wounded severely; One hundred and ninth Pennsylvania Volunteers, Lieut. James Glendening, adjutant, killed, and Lieut. John McFarland, wounded severely in leg; One hundred and eleventh Pennsylvania Volunteers, Maj. John A. Boyle, killed; Lieut. Marvin D. Pettit, killed; Lieut. Albert Black, wounded severely; Lieut. Andrew W. Tracy, wounded slightly in foot; Lieut. Col. Thomas M. Walker, wounded slightly; Capt. James M. Wells, wounded slightly, and Capt. Wallace Warner, wounded slightly.

Third Brigade: Brig. Gen. George S. Greene, commanding, wounded severely in mouth and cheek; One hundred and thirty-seventh New York Volunteers, Lieut. Col. K. S. Van Voorhis, wounded slightly; Capt. Silas Pierson, wounded severely in foot; Lieut. Marshall J. Corbett, wounded severely, and One hundred and forty-ninth New York Volunteers, Capt. Ira B. Seymour, wounded in face.

Knap's (Pennsylvania) battery: First Lieut. Edward R. Geary, killed, and Capt. Charles A. Atwell, wounded seriously.

Killed, 4; wounded, 15; total, 19.

As soon as practicable a more statistical account of the engagement, together with my official report of the same, will be forwarded.

I have the honor to be, general, very respectfully, your obedient servant,

JNO. W. GEARY,
Brigadier-General, U. S. Volunteers, Commanding.

Maj. Gen. D. BUTTERFIELD,
Chief of Staff.

[Inclosure.]

Return of Casualties in the Second Division, Twelfth Army Corps, in action at Wauhatchie, Tenn., on morning of October 29, 1863.

Regiments.	Killed.			Wounded.			Missing.			Aggregate.
	Officers.	Enlisted men.	Total.	Officers.	Enlisted men.	Total.	Officers.	Enlisted men.	Total.	
Division staff				2		2				2
Third Brigade, Brig. Gen. G. S. Greene, staff.				1		1				1
78th New York Volunteers, Lieut. Col. H. Hammerstein.					2	2				2
137th New York Volunteers, Col. D. Ireland.		15	15	3	72	75				90
149th New York Volunteers, Lieut. Col. C. B. Randall.		1	1	1	10	11				12
Second Brigade, Col. G. A. Cobham, staff.				1		1				1
29th Pennsylvania Volunteers, Col. W. Rickards.		1	1		6	6		2	2	9
109th Pennsylvania Volunteers, Capt. F. L. Gimber.	1	4	5	1	22	23		4	4	32
111th Pennsylvania Volunteers, Lieut. Col. T. M. Walker.	2	7	9	5	29	34		2	2	45
Knap's (Pennsylvania) battery	1	2	3	1	18	19				22
Total	4	30	34	15	159	174		8	8	216

JNO. W. GEARY,
Brigadier-General of Volunteers, Commanding.

HEADQUARTERS SECOND DIVISION, TWELFTH ARMY CORPS,
Wauhatchie, Tenn., October 30, 1863.

No. 25.

Report of Col. George A. Cobham, jr., One hundred and eleventh Pennsylvania Infantry, commanding Second Brigade.

HDQRS. SECOND BRIG., SECOND DIV., 12TH ARMY CORPS,
Raccoon Mountain, Tenn., October 31, 1863.

CAPTAIN: I have the honor to submit the following report of the march of my brigade from Bridgeport to Wauhatchie, and of the part taken by it in the action of October 28 and 29 instant:

Having been supplied with three days' rations and 60 rounds of ammunition, we crossed the Tennessee at Bridgeport at 9 a. m. of the 27th instant and marched to Shellmound, arriving there at 2 p. m. Left Shellmound at 5 a. m. of the 28th, and marched to Wauhatchie, reaching that place at 5 p. m. Went into camp on the left of the railroad, about 2½ miles from the knob of Lookout Mountain. The Twenty-ninth Pennsylvania Volunteers was detailed for picket duty, and Colonel Rickards, commanding officer of the regiment, as division officer of the day. At 11 p. m. of the 28th instant, picket firing being heard in our front, under instructions from the general commanding division, I ordered the One hundred and eleventh Pennsylvania Volunteers under arms, and moved them forward, facing the railroad. The firing ceasing, the regiment returned to quarters, but on its renewal after a short interval, I placed that regiment and the One hundred and ninth Pennsylvania Volunteers in position on the Kelley's Ferry road, the right of the One hundred and eleventh Pennsylvania Volunteers resting on the railroad, and their left joining the right of the One hundred and ninth Pennsylvania Volunteers. Owing to the advantageous manner in which Colonel Rickards had posted his pickets, and to the obstinate resistance made by them, the enemy were held in check long enough to enable the line to be formed.

This was hardly accomplished, when the enemy opened a heavy fire on our front, and advanced to the attack. I ordered my men to lie down, to be careful of their ammunition, and to fire low. During the severe action that ensued, lasting until 3 a. m. of the 29th instant, the men never wavered, but conducted themselves with admirable coolness and courage. They had no other protection than that afforded by a few fence rails thrown hastily together under fire. The enemy failing to force our front, moved upon the flanks, and threw in a brisk fire, both from the wood upon our left and from a piece of ground overlooking the railroad on our right. I immediately dispatched orders for two companies of the One hundred and eleventh Pennsylvania Volunteers to move to the right flank and check their advance, but found that Lieutenant-Colonel Walker, commanding that regiment, had already made such a disposition of his troops. With the assistance of a piece of Atwell's battery, which was moved across the railroad, under the direction of Colonel Rickards, Twenty-ninth Pennsylvania Volunteers, and which opened finely upon the enemy, and of the two companies of the Twenty-ninth Pennsylvania Volunteers, which had been driven in from the picket line, the attack was repulsed. The left of the line was protected by a regiment of General Greene's brigade, the One hundred and thirty-seventh New York Volunteers.

During the greater part of the time the firing was exceedingly severe, and cost us the lives of some brave officers and men, besides severely wounding many others. Where all behaved so well, I cannot particularize without doing injustice. I have to regret the loss of Maj. John A. Boyle, One hundred and eleventh Pennsylvania; Lieut. Marvin D. Pettit, One hundred and eleventh Pennsylvania, and Lieut. James Glendening, One hundred and ninth Pennsylvania Volunteers, all of them excellent officers and gallant men. Lieutenant Pettit was killed by the premature explosion of one of our own shells. Lieut. John J. Haight, One hundred and eleventh Pennsylvania Volunteers, acting on my staff as acting assistant inspector-general, was very severely wounded. I would state that the Twenty-ninth Pennsylvania Volunteers, being on picket duty, the force under my command numbered less than 500 men.

I cannot omit paying a tribute to the gallant conduct of the officers and men of Atwell's battery; the deplorable loss sustained by them and their crippled condition sufficiently attest the gallantry with which their guns were worked, and the heavy fire to which they were exposed.

I thank the gentlemen of my staff for the manner in which they performed their duties. The loss sustained in the action was as follows:

Command.	Killed.		Wounded.		Missing.		Aggregate.
	Officers.	Enlisted men.	Officers.	Enlisted men.	Officers.	Enlisted men.	
General staff and pioneers	....	.....	1	4	....	.....	5
29th Pennsylvania Volunteers, Colonel Rickards...........	.....	1	.....	5	......	1	7
109th Pennsylvania Volunteers, Captain Gimber..........	1	3	1	23	......	4	32
111th Pennsylvania Volunteers, Lieutenant-Colonel Walker.	2	6	5	31	......	1	45
Total..	3	10	7	63	......	6	89

I am, very respectfully, your obedient servant,
GEO. A. COBHAM, Jr.,
Colonel, Commanding Brigade.
Capt. Thomas H. Elliott,
Assistant Adjutant-General.

No. 26.

Report of Col. William Rickards, jr., Twenty-ninth Pennsylvania Infantry.

Hdqrs. Twenty-ninth Regt. Pennsylvania Vols.,
Wauhatchie, Tenn., October 29, 1863.

Captain: The following report of the part taken by this regiment in the recent engagement with the enemy at this point is respectfully submitted:

Tuesday, October 27, cloudy, but cleared off in the middle of the day. Regiment was in line at sunrise, marched to depot in Bridgeport, where each man was supplied with 60 rounds of ammunition, crossed the Tennessee River on a pontoon bridge, and marched to Shellmound, where we arrived at 2 p. m.; distance about 10 miles. Lieutenant-Colonel Zulich was detailed to superintend the working parties building the pontoon bridge at Shellmound and making the roads leading to it.

Wednesday, October 28, cloudy, and heavy rain in morning; cleared at 12 m. Marched at 5 a. m., and reached Wauhatchie. Halted on the left of railroad and about 2½ miles from the knob of Lookout Mountain, on the road leading to Kelley's Ferry ; distance about 20 miles. The regiment was ordered on picket, and I officer of the day. I immediately made arrangements to post them to the best advantage. General Geary thought Wauhatchie Junction the most important point, and I sent three companies, K, E, and B, to that post with orders to throw up such defenses as would protect them from the enemy's shot. Captain Rickards, Company K, had command of the post. Companies I and H, under command of Captain Stork, I sent on the Kelley's Ferry road three-quarters of a mile. Companies A and F, under Lieutenant Coursault, I sent to cover the ground between the camp and Lookout Creek, and Companies C and G on the Brown's Ferry road one-half of a mile, and Company D to our left, between Stork and Rickards. From all these posts small posts and sentinels were sent out, making a continuous line around our camp.

I had made inquiries of men in the neighborhood and been informed there was no enemy between us and Lookout Mountain. General Geary also received the same information. The man most relied on for the correctness of this report was a Mr. Rowan [or Rowden], a magistrate who lived at the junction of the Kelley's Ford road and the railroad. After posting the pickets I went to his house, and, in conversation with a woman, learned that Longstreet's corps had been here yesterday, and were now lying just the other side of Lookout Creek, at the foot of the mountain. I took the man of the house to General Geary, and, after threats, succeeded in getting the information that there was a bridge across the creek, and that Longstreet's men lay just beyond it, not more than 1¼ miles from our camp. I hurried to the pickets, and found the road leading to the bridge and posted my men on it, near three-quarters of a mile from camp, with instructions to be very watchful, and directed Captain Millison, in charge of the reserve, to hold them in readiness to deploy as skirmishers on the least alarm.

I then proceeded on my rounds, and had visited the post at the junction, and was returning, when I heard firing which seemed to proceed from the picket on the bridge road. I rode as fast as I could, but found the firing was beyond my pickets. The firing having ceased, I returned to General Geary to report, and found the command under arms and in line. All remained quiet, and after half an hour the men were sent to quarters. They had just turned in when firing again commenced. I rode quietly to the outpost and met my men retiring, but in good order, contesting the ground with the enemy, who were advancing in line without skirmishers. We retreated slowly toward camp, and found our troops rapidly getting into line, the One hundred and thirty-seventh New York on the extreme left, next One hundred and ninth Pennsylvania Volunteers, One hundred and eleventh Pennsylvania Volunteers on right, and One hundred and forty-ninth on the railroad bank at right angles with the right of the One hundred and eleventh Pennsylvania Volunteers. Companies C and G, who had been driven in with me, I posted to support the battery, and afterward, when the enemy had made a strong demonstration on our right, I moved them to the railroad bank. The enemy were attacking us on our right, front, and left. Our men were falling rapidly, especially those of the battery.

The horses also suffered severely. Lieutenant Geary, of the battery, was killed by my side, being struck over the eye. Captain Atwell was badly wounded in the hip and spine. Most of the men were wounded or killed. They all acted nobly. We had started with 60 rounds of infantry ammunition and none in the train. This was nearly expended. The enemy now made a fresh demonstration on our right, and gained possession of the railroad bank, from which they delivered a very severe fire on us. Our efforts to dislodge them by firing from our present position proved fruitless. Being unable to find General Geary or Colonel Cobham at that time, and Major Reynolds, chief of artillery, having charge of the battery, I directed him to have one piece move to the outside of the railroad bank, at a crossing in our rear, and enfilade the bank. He objected, saying the enemy would take the piece, and also he had no horses to pull it. I told him I would take the responsibility and furnish the force. I brought Companies C and G and had the piece hauled outside of the railroad, carried ammunition, and did the labor of the piece, while those men who were left with the gun unwounded, loaded and fired. After two or three shots we got the range, and swept the enemy from the bank. This seemed to have a depressing effect upon the enemy, for their fire now ceased, and we remained masters of our position. Companies A and F, under charge of Lieutenant Coursault, of Company A, held the woods on the right of the railroad, and prevented the enemy from getting in our rear and right. They behaved with great bravery and discretion.

Too much praise cannot be bestowed on Companies C and G, under Captains Millison and Goldsmith, for their obstinate resistance to the enemy, checking his advance, and giving our troops time to get into line. The accident of my stopping at the house of Mr. Rowan [Rowden] when I did led to the information which showed the position of the enemy, and led to the advancing and strengthening of my pickets. The fact of the whole regiment being on picket, and many on posts away from fire, accounts for the small loss, viz, 1 man killed, 5 badly wounded, and 1 missing, who, being on the most exposed post, is no doubt a prisoner. The officers and men of Knap's battery acted nobly. Lieutenant Geary, son of our general, was killed at my side at the instant he commanded "fire," after aiming his gun. His death will be a serious loss to the service and country. The attack was made by Hood's division, of Longstreet's corps, and, having a knowledge of our numbers and position from their station on Lookout Mountain, they expected to surprise and capture our force with ease. None but White Stars were engaged, and they have shown they are capable of holding their ground against superior numbers of the best troops in the rebel army. The enemy having turned the left flank, captured our wagon train, which was recaptured by Lieutenant-Colonel Zulich, of this regiment, who, having collected and organized a number of loose men, drove off the enemy and brought it safely to the rear.*

Respectfully, your obedient servant,

WM. RICKARDS, Jr.,
Colonel, Commanding Regiment.

Capt. JOHN P. GREEN,
Assistant Adjutant-General.

---

* Nominal list of casualties (omitted) shows 1 man killed, 5 men wounded, and 1 man missing.

No. 27.

Report of Capt. Frederick L. Gimber, One hundred and ninth Pennsylvania Infantry.

HDQRS. 109TH REGIMENT PENNSYLVANIA VOLS.,
Raccoon Mountain, Tenn., October 31, 1863.

SIR : I have the honor to submit the following as my report of the march from Bridgeport, Ala., on October 27, and the part my regiment took in the engagement of Wauhatchie, Tenn., on the 29th instant :

Broke camp at Bridgeport, Ala., on the morning of the 27th, leaving that place at about 9 a. m., crossing the Tennessee River on pontoons, arriving at Shellmound Station on the railroad at about 3 o'clock, where the troops went into camp for the night. Reveille sounded at about 4 a. m. of the 28th, and the troops were again on the march by daylight, crossing the mountains and several streamlets, arriving at a point near Lookout Mountain. Firing occurring on our front, we were moved into a woods on the left of the railroad, where we formed into divisions, stacked arms, and the men allowed to rest. About midnight the troops were suddenly called to arms, firing occurring on the picket line. The regiment was then ordered to move by the left flank to a point in a field, the regiment taking a position behind a rail fence. Scarcely were the men in position before the enemy opened a cross and direct fire, which our men promptly replied to, and kept up a continuous fire for about two hours and a half, when the supply of ammunition fell short and the fire began to slacken, and though the enemy kept up a fire at intervals it failed to dislodge our men, who nobly stood their ground under the trying circumstances. The enemy having received a last volley from our boys, retreated from the field.

The regiment took into the engagement about 110, all told ; lost 5 killed and 21 wounded. Among the killed I regret to announce First Lieut. James Glendening, of Company A, and acting adjutant, a brave and efficient soldier, whose loss cannot well be replaced. Both officers and men behaved well, fully sustaining the reputation of the White Star division.

I have the honor to be, sir, very respectfully, your obedient servant,

FREDERICK L. GIMBER,
Captain, Commanding 109*th Pennsylvania.*

Capt. JOHN P. GREEN,
Assistant Adjutant-General.

No. 28.

Report of Lieut. Col. Thomas M. Walker, One hundred and Eleventh Pennsylvania Infantry.

HDQRS. 111TH REGIMENT PENNSYLVANIA VOLS.,
Lookout Valley, Tenn., October 31, 1863.

CAPTAIN : I have the honor to transmit the following report of the part taken by the One hundred and eleventh Regiment Pennsylvania Volunteers in the battle of Wauhatchie, October 28 and 29, 1863 :

The regiment marching from Stevenson, Ala., arrived in Bridgeport at 2 p. m. of the 27th instant, where we remained until 5 p. m.

(to be supplied with rations and ammunition), at which time we crossed the Tennessee River, following the route taken by our brigade for Shellmound, where we arrived at 8 p. m. and bivouacked. We broke camp at Shellmound at 4 a. m. of the 28th, and marched until 5 p. m., encamping at the junction of the roads to Kelley's and Brown's Ferries. The regiment was bivouacked by division, left in front. Soon after 11 p. m. we were aroused by picket firing in the direction of the point of Lookout Mountain, and immediately got under arms, forming line parallel with the railroad, fronting to the east.

We remained in line for about fifteen minutes, when we were again ordered to our bivouacs, but cautioned by the general commanding division to turn out and take the same ground should there be a repetition of the firing. We had scarcely remained in camp fifteen minutes when the picket firing was renewed, and we immediately took the line as directed and threw the two left companies forward as skirmishers. These were yet deploying when the advance of the enemy opened upon us from our left flank. I immediately changed front to the rear on the first company, facing nearly north, the right resting near the railroad and the line running nearly parallel with the road to Kelley's Ferry. The enemy were firing on our front and at the same time working around our left and right. By direction the two left companies opened on the advancing line, the rest of my regiment reserving fire until the advancing line should come to very close quarters. I now directed the right company to deploy as skirmishers on our right flank on the opposite side of the railroad, and soon received word from them that a line was advancing on our right. Two companies, under Captain Wells, were at once placed along the railroad embankment to check this advance; our skirmishers fell back to the same position. These three companies met the enemy and checked them at their first fire. We retained this position, the right facing to the east, the center to the north, and the left to northwest, until the enemy gave up the attack, soon after 3 o'clock. We were for a long time under a severe fire from three directions, fighting at a great disadvantage.

I mention with pleasure the steadiness and determination of my men. I was greatly indebted to the assistance given me by my major, John A. Boyle, who sealed his devotion with his life, and to Captains Wells and Warner, both of whom were struck slightly, also to Lieut. Albert Black, who was very severely wounded. I append herewith a list of casualties in the regiment.*

Very respectfully, your obedient servant,
THOS. M. WALKER,
Lieutenant-Colonel, Comdg. 111th Pennsylvania Vols.
Capt. JOHN P. GREEN,
A. A. G., Second Brig., Second Div., Twelfth Army Corps.

No. 29.

Report of Brig. Gen. George S. Greene, U. S. Army, commanding Third Brigade.

HOSPITAL AT BRIDGEPORT, *November* 1, 1863.

SIR: I have the honor to report of the battle on the 29th ultimo, near Lookout Mountain.

---

* Embodied in revised statement, p. 76.

Two regiments of my brigade having been placed in line of battle under the direction of the commanding general of the division, the action immediately commenced by an attack of the enemy, to which our fire promptly and efficiently replied.

I had been twice along the line sending in a few stragglers that were in the rear, when I was severely wounded in the mouth, and, from loss of blood and of voice, was unable to render efficient service in the field, and I retired to the hospital for attendance.

I can bear testimony to the good conduct of the brigade while on the field.

Most respectfully, your obedient servant,

GEO. S. GREENE,
Brig. Gen., Third Brig., Second Div., Twelfth Army Corps.

Capt. THOMAS H. ELLIOTT,
Assistant Adjutant-General.

No. 30.

Report of Col. David Ireland, One hundred and thirty-seventh New York Infantry, commanding Third Brigade.

HDQRS. THIRD BRIG., SECOND DIV., TWELFTH CORPS,
Camp near Lookout Valley, Tenn., November 5, 1863.

CAPTAIN : I have the honor most respectfully to submit the following report of that portion of the Third Brigade engaged in the action of the 29th ultimo, designated as the battle of Wauhatchie :

The following named regiments constituted the portion of the brigade alluded to above : The Seventy-eighth New York Volunteers, Lieutenant-Colonel Hammerstein commanding; the One hundred and thirty-seventh New York Volunteers, Col. David Ireland commanding, and the One hundred and forty-ninth New York Volunteers, Lieutenant-Colonel Randall commanding.

The command left Bridgeport on Monday, October 27, 1863, and marched to Shellmound, Tenn. We were there joined by the Sixtieth New York Volunteers, Col. A. Godard, and the One hundred and thirty-seventh New York Volunteers (which regiments left Bridgeport some two hours after the division had gone). A heavy detail was made from the Seventy-eighth New York Volunteers and the One hundred and forty-ninth New York Volunteers to assist in constructing a pontoon bridge over the Tennessee river at that point. We broke camp on the morning of the 28th ultimo and marched to Whiteside's, where the Sixtieth New York Volunteers were ordered to take position in a gap and remain there until further orders. The balance of the command marched to the Wauhatchie Valley and there camped for the night, in the following order : The One hundred and thirty-seventh New York Volunteers, in two lines, and at right angles with the railroad ; the One hundred and forty-ninth New York Volunteers, in two lines, and 20 paces in rear of the One hundred and thirty-seventh New York Volunteers ; the Seventy-eighth New York Volunteers, in two lines, and on the right of the One hundred and forty-ninth. At 11.15 p. m. the troops were summoned to arms by Lieutenant Davis, aide-de-camp to the general commanding the division, which summons was obeyed with great alacrity by officers and men, and after remaining some time under arms they were ordered to lie down behind their stacks with their accouterments on ; the slight firing of the pickets, in our front, which occasioned the alarm, having subsided, but a short time had elapsed when it became unmistakably apparent by the sudden and continuous firing that the enemy were in close proximity to us.

The reports of the musketry alone proved the soldierly qualities of the men ; they were up and in line and all empty muskets loaded, awaiting orders, when the general commanding division ordered them forward, the One hundred and thirty-seventh New York Volunteers in advance and moving by the left flank, followed by the One hundred and forty-ninth New York Volunteers. The One hundred and thirty-seventh New York Volunteers were ordered to take position on the right of the One hundred and ninth Pennsylvania Volunteers, and while they, the One hundred and thirty-seventh New York Volunteers, were executing the order, under the immediate supervision of the general commanding the division, the enemy opened on them a terrible musketry fire. They quickly formed and returned the fire with great effect, and maintained their position throughout the entire action. The One hundred and forty-ninth New York Volunteers were following in the rear and about 50 feet from the One hundred and thirty-seventh New York Volunteers, marching by the left flank, when the enemy opened, which, in connection with the retrograde movements of horses belonging to orderlies, ambulances, and wagons, passing through their lines, created momentary confusion, but Lieutenant-Colonel Randall, commanding One hundred and forty-ninth New York Volunteers, quickly reformed the regiment about 50 yards in the rear of the One hundred and thirty-seventh New York Volunteers, when he, Lieutenant-Colonel Randall, received orders from Lieutenant Davis, aide-de-camp to the general commanding division, to move the regiment out and take position by the side of the wagon road, at right angles to the line of battle and lying on the railroad embankment, thereby covering our right flank. The Seventy-eighth New York volunteers were deployed in the rear and along the line of the railroad to guard against an attack on our rear.

While this disposition of the troops was being made the enemy were firing on our front, and continued to do so for about half an hour. They then sent a body of troops (from prisoners captured we learned it was the Hampton Legion) around the left of the One hundred and thirty-seventh New York Volunteers, it being unprotected, and the left of our position, with the intention of turning our flank, but two companies, G and B, of the One hundred and thirty-seventh New York Volunteers, were thrown back at right angles with the line of battle, and succeeded in repulsing the enemy, firing on them as they marched by the flank, creating confusion in their lines, and driving them back. The enemy then moved around to our right, but our artillery, assisted by a few and effective shots from the One hundred and forty-ninth New York Volunteers, drove the enemy from the field. The action, which commenced about 12.30 a. m., was at this time, 2.45 a. m., about over.

The promptness with which the Seventy-eighth New York Volunteers fell into line and took position was commendable. Although not called into action, their position was one of importance. The conduct of the One hundred and forty-ninth New York Volunteers throughout the action was everything that could be desired. After they had reformed and taken position they held it in fine style. The conduct of the officers and men of the One hundred and thirty-seventh New York Volunteers during the action was truly heroic. They took position while under a heavy musketry fire and held that position throughout the engagement. When the enemy endeavored to turn their flank, not a man wavered, but, by a steady and well-directed fire, drove the enemy back every attempt they made to charge. Before the close of the action the cartridges were all expended, but by sending to the hospital and cutting the cartridge boxes from the dead and wounded they had a supply until the close of the action. When the firing ceased there were not 200 cartridges in the regiment. Of their bravery and good conduct during the engagement I need only mention that of the whole number killed and wounded in this command, viz, 105, 90 were of this regiment alone.

Brig. Gen. George S. Greene was wounded in the beginning of the action, and was obliged to leave the field. Previous to doing so he sent Lieutenant Knapp, commanding brigade pioneers, to inform me that I was in command of the brigade. I immediately endeavored to carry out the instructions of the general commanding division, which instructions not only saved our command from surprise and capture, but enabled us to drive the enemy from the field. When all did so well it would be wrong to individualize. Both officers and men had a full sense of their duty, and acted accordingly.

Loss in the brigade is as follows : Enlisted men killed, 16 ; officers wounded, 5 ; enlisted men wounded, 84 ; total loss, killed and wounded, 105. Missing, none.

Inclosed please find reports of the officers commanding the Seventy-eighth, One hundred and forty-ninth, and One hundred and thirty-seventh New York Volunteers; also a report from General G. S. Greene.

I am, very respectfully, your obedient servant,

DAVID IRELAND,
Colonel, Comdg. Third Brig., Second Div., Twelfth A. C.

Capt. THOMAS H. ELLIOTT,
Asst. Adjt. Gen., Second Div., Twelfth Army Corps.

No. 31.

*Itinerary of the Third Brigade.**

October 1, remained at Bellaire, Ohio, all day.

October 2, were transported in cars through Columbus, Dayton, Indianapolis, Louisville, and Nashville, to Murfreesborough, Tenn., arriving there October 6. The One hundred and thirty-seventh Regiment New York Volunteers were left at Nashville, and convoyed the Eleventh Corps trains and batteries to Decherd and returned to Fosterville.

October 22, the Seventy-eighth New York Regiment was sent to guard the bridge over Stone's River. The Sixtieth, One hundred and second, and One hundred and forty-ninth New York Volunteers remained at Murfreesborough to guard that place.

---

* From return for October.

October 23, the One hundred and forty-ninth New York Volun-teers were transported in cars, arriving at Bridgeport, Ala., October 25.   The rest of the brigade followed as fast as the cars could carry them, except the One hundred and second Regiment New York Vol-unteers, which went to Nashville to convoy the Second Division train.

October 27, the Seventy-eighth and One hundred and forty-ninth Regiments New York Volunteers left Bridgeport, Ala., at 9.30 a. m., and crossed the Tennessee River, and marched to Shellmound, Tenn., arriving there at 3 p. m.   During the afternoon the Sixtieth and One hundred and Thirty-seventh New York Volunteers joined us ; marched 7 miles.

October 28, left Shellmound at 5.45 a. m. and marched 15 miles, and encamped within 6 miles of Chattanooga, near Wauhatchie Station.   The Sixtieth New York Volunteers were left to guard a gap near Whiteside's Station.   At 11 o'clock at night we were awak-ened by picket firing, and the troops were put under arms ; but learning that it was not our pickets, the men were ordered to lie down behind their stacks.   Shortly afterward our pickets were driven in, and the One hundred and thirty-seventh New York Vol-unteers were ordered out by the left flank, and had barely got into line, with their right resting on the One hundred and ninth Penn-sylvania Volunteers, when the enemy opened fire.   The One hun-dred and forty-ninth Regiment New York Volunteers followed the One hundred and thirty-seventh New York Volunteers, and was put into position on the right of the line and against the railroad. The Seventy-eighth New York Volunteers was held in reserve. The fight commenced near midnight, and lasted about an hour and three-quarters.   The following are our losses in killed and wounded One hundred and thirty-seventh New York Volunteers, 90 ; One hun-dred and forty ninth New York Volunteers, 12 ; Seventy-eighth New York Volunteers, 2.

Brig. Gen. George S. Greene, commanding the brigade, was wounded in the face, the ball passing through the upper jaw.   The following officers were also wounded: Lieut. Col. K. S. Van Voor-his, Capt. Silas Pierson, and Lieut. Marshall J. Corbett, all of the One hundred and thirty-seventh New York Volunteers.

October 29 and 30, lay on the battle-field.

October 31, moved up to Raccoon Mountain and took position on the hills to the right of the Second Brigade, and commenced fortify-ing and slashing timber.

No. 32.

*Report of Lieut. Col. Herbert von Hammerstein, Seventy-eighth
New York Infantry.*

HDQRS. SEVENTY-EIGHTH NEW YORK VOLUNTEERS,
November 3, 1863.

CAPTAIN : I have the honor to submit the report of the part which my regiment has taken in the operations of the Third Brigade, Sec-ond Division, Twelfth Army Corps, from the morning of the 27th til the close of the engagement the morning of the 29th of October, 1863

The regiment arrived at Bridgeport at 3 o'clock on the morning of he 27th, after having been two days and two nights on the cars. At daylight, we continued our march on foot to Shellmound. After rriving there, my regiment was ordered to report to Brigadier-General Morton, chief engineer, to assist in building a pontoon bridge cross the Tennessee River, at which we worked till 9 o'clock that aight, fatiguing the men considerably. At daylight next morning he march was continued, my regiment marching as rear guard ehind the train of the division, and arrived at about 7 o'clock at a lace near the railroad called Wauhatchie.

I received orders from Brigadier-General Greene to go and bivouac n the right of the One hundred and forty-ninth New York Volunteers, the regiment in two lines, one behind the other. At about 0.30 o'clock I was startled by perhaps a dozen shots and a weak olley of musketry. I ordered my regiment under arms loaded, and he men lay down behind the stacks awaiting orders. The firing ad stopped about fifteen minutes, when it began again, this time vith great energy, from a force certainly superior to our own, the ullets flying in every direction through the camps. I then received rders, through Captain Greene, assistant adjutant-general, to deploy ay regiment and remain in reserve; then selected the embankment f the railroad as the best position to cover our right flank, and rom where to move to the assistance of others if called for. Not eing called for, the regiments in front succeeding in driving off he enemy alone, I remained in that position till about 2.30 a. m., vhen I was ordered by Colonel Ireland, commanding the brigade fter Brigadier-General Greene was wounded, to march to a position n our extreme left, which I did. The fight had then ceased. I lost men wounded, and did not fire a shot. When the alarm arrived he regiment was under arms in a minute; not a man left his post.

I have the honor to be, captain, very respectfully, your obedient ervant,

H. HAMMERSTEIN,
Lieutenant-Colonel, Comdg. Seventy-eighth New York Vols.

[Capt. C. T. GREENE,
Assistant Adjutant-General, Third Brigade.]

No. 33.

Report of Capt. Milo B. Eldredge, One hundred and thirty-seventh New York Infantry.

HDQRS. 137TH REGIMENT NEW YORK VOLUNTEERS,
Near Lookout Mountain, Tenn., October 31, 1863.

CAPTAIN: I have the honor to report that this regiment (the One aundred and thirty-seventh New York Volunteers) left Bridgeport, Ala., on the 27th day of October, 1863, about 12 m. We crossed the Tennessee River, and that afternoon we marched to Shellmound Station, and there joined the brigade and camped for the night. We resumed the march at daybreak on the morning of the 28th of October, 1863, and marched to the Wauhatchie Valley, near Lookout Mountain, in sight of the enemy, and there we encamped. We vere camped in two lines and at right angles with the Chattanooga oad. At 11.30 p. m. we were aroused and ordered under arms, occasioned by some picket firing on our front, but the firing ceased shortly afterward, so the men were ordered to lie down behind their stacks with their accouterments on, which they did. In about half an hour afterward we were again ordered to fall in and move out by the left flank, and take position on the left of the One hundred and ninth Pennsylvania Volunteers, which order we executed under the immediate supervision of General Geary, commanding Second Division, when the enemy opened on us. We formed as ordered, and then returned their fire with such effect that the enemy were driven back every time they attempted to advance.

The enemy, finding they could not drive us in front, sent a large force around on our left flank, which was entirely unprotected, and endeavored to turn our position, but Adjt. James E. Mix instantly threw two companies, G and B, back at right angles with our line of battle and drove them back handsomely, and when they retired he brought them forward into line. At this time our men were getting nearly out of ammunition, but, by sending to the hospital and cutting the cartridge boxes from the bodies of the dead, we were enabled to keep up a fire on the enemy until they retired; when they did so we did not have 200 cartridges in the regiment. Brigadier-General Greene having been wounded early in the fight, the command of the brigade devolved upon Col. David Ireland. Lieutenant-Colonel Van Voorhis immediately assumed command of the regiment, soon after which he (Lieutenant-Colonel Van Voorhis) was wounded near the right shoulder. He, notwithstanding, continued his duties until the close of the action, which lasted from about 12.30 until about 3 a. m.

The conduct of the officers and men of this regiment during the action was splendid; they fought like men, and when the enemy opened on their left the men fired back to back, but never yielded one inch of ground. At the close of the action they were in the exact line in which they were formed. The conduct of James E. Mix (adjutant) is worthy of special mention.

This regiment lost as follows: Enlisted men killed, 15; officers wounded, 3; enlisted men wounded, 72; total loss, killed and wounded, 90. Missing, none.

I am, very respectfully, your obedient servant,

MILO B. ELDREDGE,
Captain, Commanding Regiment.

Capt. C. T. GREENE,
A. A. G., Third Brig., Second Div., 12th Army Corps.

No. 34.

Report of Lieut. Col. Charles B. Randall, One hundred and forty-ninth New York Infantry.

HEADQUARTERS 149TH NEW YORK VOLUNTEERS,
Wauhatchie Valley, Tenn., November 1, 1863.

CAPTAIN: I have the honor to submit the following report of the operations of my command during the 27th, 28th, and 29th days of October last:

The regiment broke camp on the morning of the 27th and moved in the rear of the Seventy-eighth New York Volunteers, the men

arrying four days' rations and 60 rounds of ammunition. Arrived
t Shellmound Station about 3 p. m., and bivouacked. I furnished
or work on the pontoon bridge at that place a detail of 6 officers, 16
on-commissioned officers, and 110 men, who were on duty from 8
. m. until 1 a. m., the 28th.

At 4 o'clock, the regiment was called out, and at 5 took up line of
march, following the One hundred and thirty-seventh New York
Volunteers. We arrived at a point on Wauhatchie Valley, near the
unction, at about 5 p. m., and bivouacked in edge of a wood near
nd to the left of the railroad in two lines, the left wing being in
ear of the right, my position being at the right of the One hun-
red and thirty-seventh New York Volunteers. At 11 p. m. the
egiment was put under arms, but the men were allowed to lie down
ehind their arms with their belts on.

At 12 a. m. the 29th, I was directed by the general commanding
rigade to move by the left flank and follow the One hundred and
hirty-seventh New York Volunteers to form line of battle. In
ccordance with directions I moved directly forward until I came
o a road which ran to the right at an angle of about 45 degrees from
he direction I was pursuing, which road I was directed to follow.

The attack upon our position began at 12.30 a. m., October 29, and
t the moment of the attack the position of my regiment was as fol-
ows: Marching left in front, diagonally toward the enemy, with the
ear rank exposed to their fire, the leading company being about 25
ards in rear of the right company of the One hundred and thirty-
eventh New York Volunteers, which was just forming by "forward
nto line." The generals commanding division and brigade, both
nounted, and attended by their staffs and orderlies, were on the line
f battle directing its formation, when the enemy opened fire along
is whole line from a distance of about 100 yards. In an instant the
nounted men attending the generals, forming a cavalcade of some 20
orsemen, became very much scattered and broke to the rear, pass-
ng through my regiment in a dozen different places. In addition
o those, two or three ambulances and wagon teams, attached to
eadquarters, also passed through my lines. The regiment was thus
ntirely broken to pieces and disorganized, with no company forma-
ions whatever, and all exposed to a terrific fire. I immediately
hrew the left and leading company back to the rear, and commenced
eforming the line parallel with and about 50 yards in rear of the
ne hundred and thirty-seventh New York Volunteers, which was
t that time actively engaged. As the line was nearly formed, I re-
eived direction from Lieutenant Davis, of division staff, to place
he regiment by the side of the wagon road, perpendicular to the line
f battle, to guard against an attack upon our right flank. I imme-
iately changed "front forward," and took the position indicated.
'he enemy immediately attacked in my front, when, finding it pos-
ible to shelter the men, I moved the regiment forward some 20
ards to the railroad embankment and opened fire. After the regi-
nent had expended 3 or 4 rounds, the enemy, consisting of a force
f two regiments, withdrew from our front. I remained in that
osition until about 6 a. m. the 29th.

Too much credit cannot be given to the officers and men of the
ommand on this occasion. Entirely broken to pieces and disordered,
he line was rapidly reformed in a new direction, and a change of
ront executed, the men being all the time exposed to a murderous
re from a distance of about 150 yards, with a loss of but 3 strag-

glers. Owing to our sheltered position along the railroad, our los
was quite small compared to that of other regiments, being 1 ma
killed and an officer and 11 men wounded. About 6 a. m. my reg
ment was moved to a position in rear of the center of the line, an
held in reserve. By direction of Colonel Ireland, commanding th
brigade, I sent forward one company as skirmishers, which foun
large numbers of the enemy's killed and wounded, and arms in fron
and which captured and sent in quite a number of prisoners.

About 8.30 a. m., by direction of the general commanding divisio
I sent out a scouting party, consisting of the sergeant-major and 1
men, who examined the country along the banks of a creek runnin
along the base of Lookout Mountain for a distance of about 1½ mile
to a point opposite the point of the mountain, discovering the rou
taken by the enemy before and after the attack, and finding sever
of the enemy's dead in the woods opposite the position occupied b
my regiment during the action and several stand of arms, which the
brought in. About 11 a. m. the regiment was detailed for pick
duty, and was posted across the road leading to Kelley's Ferry, to th
left and rear of our position.

While the conduct of both officers and men was so nearly une
ceptionable, it would be almost impossible to discriminate betwee
them, but I cannot forbear calling particular attention to the galla
bearing of Orderly Sergeant Truair, of Company G, who was i
command of his company, none of its officers being present with i
I am greatly indebted to Capt. Robert E. Hopkins, acting field office
His coolness and judgment was worthy of special commendation
His assistance to me was invaluable. Annexed is the list of casua
ties.*

Very respectfully, your obedient servant,

C. B. RANDALL,
Lieutenant-Colonel, Comdg. 149th New York Volunteers.

Capt. C. T. GREENE,
Assistant Adjutant-General.

No. 35.

*Report of Maj. John A. Reynolds, First New York Light Artiller
commanding Artillery Brigade.*

Report of the movements of Battery E, Independent Pennsylv
nia Artillery, from Bridgeport, Ala., to Wauhatchie, and engag
ment of the night of October 28, 1863 :

Two sections of Battery E left Bridgeport with Second Divisio
Twelfth Army Corps, at 8 a. m. Tuesday, October 27, 1863; reach
Shellmound at 1 p. m., where they camped till next morning. At
a. m., 28th instant, broke camp and marched to Wauhatchie, cam
ing at 5 p. m., about one-half mile beyond the junction of the ra
road, on the right of Mr. Rowden's house, facing the railroad. Abo
11 p. m. musketry firing was heard, apparently by the pickets, on th
road toward Chattanooga. The troops were called out and placed
position to repel an attack, and the battery ordered to harness. Up
investigation it was found the firing was not from the pickets of th

---

* Embodied in revised statement, p. 76.

Twelfth Corps, and there being no appearance of an attack, the troops were dismissed with orders to resume their positions at once if any alarm took place.   At 12 p. m. firing was again heard, the troops were called out, and I directed the battery to harness at once.   By the firing, it was evident the enemy were advancing rapidly toward us, and I ordered the pieces to be run into position by hand, to cover the field to the left of the railroad.   The infantry were in line about 30 or 40 yards in the front of the battery, thus preventing the use of canister.   I directed the use of shrapnel, with short fuses.

The enemy at this time were apparently between 200 and 300 yards distant, and charged to the left of our front, at the same time opening their fire upon us.   Their line soon extended along our front and across the railroad.   On account of the darkness, their line could only be distinguished by their fire, upon which the gunners were directed to aim, depressing their pieces as much as they could with safety to our troops in front.   Some ten or fifteen minutes after the commencement of the engagement, the enemy opened on our right from the woods across the railroad.   Observing this, I directed one piece of Lieutenant Geary's section to be wheeled to the right in the rear of the house.   Their fire now was very destructive to the battery, having an enfilade from the woods, and being also on our front and left. Lieutenant Geary soon fell mortally wounded by a ball in the forehead.   Several cannoneers of this piece were also wounded.   A few moments later, Captain Atwell was severely wounded, and carried from the field.

So many men having been wounded that they could with difficulty work all the pieces, I directed one piece to be run to the rear, and the men to take positions on the others.   The battery kept up their fire as long as the enemy's firing made their line visible, they finally withdrawing from our left and front, and taking position behind the railroad to the left of our front, from where they continued their fire. I then directed one piece to be run to a crossing of the railroad, about 150 yards to our rear, and placed in position just across the track to fire along the north side of the railroad.   The fire of this piece was very effective, and soon compelled the enemy to fall back.   Their fire gradually slackened, and about 3 a. m. ceased entirely.   With regard to the effectiveness of the fire of the battery, the same defect that usually occurs with the paper fuses was very apparent on this occasion, not more than one in four of the projectiles exploding. The casualties of the battery, owing to the enemy concentrating their fire upon it, which they were enabled to do by the flashes of the guns, and also being at one time upon three sides of it, were very great.

The men behaved nobly ; too much credit cannot be given them. Although suffering the loss of both officers present, not a man, as far as I could learn, shirked his duty.   All remained nobly at their posts, ready and willing to perform not only their own duties, but in addition, those of their fallen comrades.

Sergeants Shaw, Hammann, and Nichol, and Corporal Jones are deserving of mention for their coolness and courage, but Corporals Volk and Kane are deserving of special notice for their conduct, being as cool during the whole engagement as on drill, thus inspiring their men by their example.   In the death of Lieutenant Geary the service has lost a brave and efficient officer, and a noble-hearted and courteous gentleman.   Though young in years he possessed rare natural qualifications as an officer, and while in his death the battery has suffered a loss which can with difficulty, if ever, be compensated, yet the bright example of his manly courage and devoted patriotism can never be extinguished.

The following is a list of casualties : Killed, 1 commissioned officer and 3 enlisted men; wounded, 1 commissioned officer and 17 enlisted men.

Horses killed and disabled, 35 ; mules, 2.

Number of rounds of ammunition expended, 224.

J. A. REYNOLDS,
Major First N. Y. Arty., Chief of Artillery, Twelfth A. C.

No. 36.

Report of Brig. Gen. John B. Turchin, U. S. Army, commanding First Brigade, Third Division, Fourteenth Army Corps, with itinerary of brigade.

HDQRS. FIRST BRIG., THIRD DIV., 14TH ARMY CORPS,
Brown's Ferry, Tenn., October 30, 1863.

SIR : I have the honor to submit a report of the part taken by my brigade in the expedition of the 26th instant :

The object of the expedition was to effect a landing on the left bank of the Tennessee River and to occupy the gorge at Brown's Ferry. According to instructions, my brigade was to support General Hazen's brigade, follow it across the river, and occupy the hills on the right side of the gorge.

On the morning of the 26th instant, a detail was made from the brigade of Second Lieut. James Haddow, Thirty-sixth Ohio Volunteer Infantry, and First Lieut. Joseph Stephenson, Ninety-second Ohio Volunteer Infantry, with 4 sergeants, 8 corporals, and 36 privates from each of the two regiments, all experienced boatmen, to work on the pontoons, take them to the ferry, and cross the troops. At 6.30 p. m. on the 26th instant the brigade moved from Chattanooga, crossed the Tennessee, and bivouacked in the woods near Brown's Ferry, leaving the tents and camp undisturbed. More than half of General Hazen's command was ordered to descend the river on the pontoons and effect a landing, while the remainder moved from Chattanooga and bivouacked near my brigade. The commander of the pontoons was instructed to ferry the remainder of General Hazen's brigade first, and then my brigade.

At 4.30 a. m. on the 27th, a few shots, and soon after several volleys, told us that the landing of our troops was effected. The Thirty-first Ohio, Seventeenth Ohio, and Eighty-second Indiana were the first of my brigade to cross, while the Eleventh Ohio was deployed to the right on the river bank to protect the passage. When my first regiment, the Thirty-first Ohio, reached the opposite shore they found portions of several regiments of General Hazen's command on the slope of the right hill, which was a necessary movement, because the enemy occupied both sides of the gorge. These regiments were relieved by the Thirty-first Ohio. Other regiments followed, and at 8 a. m. the whole brigade had crossed the river and occupied the position assigned to them. The expedition was successful. The portion of my command detached with Lieutenants

Haddow and Stephenson worked with skill and earnestness, and the success of the whole expedition depended considerably on their work.

I have no casualties to report.

I am, very respectfully, your obedient servant,

J. B. TURCHIN.
Brigadier-General, Commanding.

Capt. PRESTON C. F. WEST,
Aide-de-Camp.

ITINERARY.*

The regiments of which the brigade is now composed were in camp at Chattanooga from October 1 to 9.

October 9, by Paragraph XIV, Special Field Orders, No. 269, from headquarters Department of the Cumberland, the Eleventh, Thirty-sixth, Eighty-ninth, and Ninety-second Ohio Volunteer Infantry (being the Third Brigade, Fourth Division, Fourteenth Army Corps, old organization, excepting the Eighteenth Kentucky Volunteer Infantry and the Twenty-first Indiana Volunteer Battery), and the Seventeenth and Thirty-first Ohio and the Eighty-second Indiana Volunteer Infantry (being the First Brigade, Third Division, Fourteenth Army Corps, old organization, excepting the Thirty-eighth Ohio Volunteer Infantry and the Fourth Michigan Volunteer Battery), were announced as composing the First Brigade, Third Division, Fourteenth Army Corps, Brig. Gen. J. B. Turchin commanding. Brigade remained in camp at Chattanooga from October 9 to 26.

October 26, brigade was detailed, in conjunction with Hazen's brigade, of Palmer's division, to cross the Tennessee River at Brown's Ferry, construct a pontoon bridge. and build a *tête-de-pont*. Two officers and 88 men of the Thirty-sixth and Ninety-second Ohio Volunteer Infantry were detached to navigate the pontoons, which were to be floated from Chattanooga to Brown's Ferry during the night. The remainder of the brigade crossed the Tennessee at Chattanooga at 6.30 p. m., and bivouacked in the woods near Brown's Ferry. A landing was effected on the southern shore at 4.30 a. m. October 27, and the rebel force (two regiments) driven away. Hazen's brigade crossed first, occupying the ridge on the left of the ferry, this brigade following and occupying the ridge on the right of the ferry.

From October 27 to 31, brigade remained at Brown's Ferry, cutting timber, digging intrenchments, and building roads.

No. 37.

Record of a Court of Inquiry, and accompanying documents.

PROCEEDINGS OF A COURT OF INQUIRY WHICH CONVENED AT THE HEADQUARTERS ELEVENTH AND TWELFTH ARMY CORPS, LOOKOUT VALLEY, TENN., BY VIRTUE OF THE FOLLOWING SPECIAL ORDER :

SPECIAL FIELD ORDERS, } HDQRS. DEPT. OF THE CUMBERLAND,
No. 23.   } *Chattanooga, Tenn., January 23, 1864.*

*   *   *   *   *   *   *

XI. At the request of Maj. Gen. Carl Schurz, commanding Third Division, Eleventh Corps, and Col. F. Hecker, commanding Third

---

* From return for October.

Brigade of that division, a court of inquiry is hereby ordered to assemble at the headquarters of Maj. Gen. Joseph Hooker, commanding Eleventh and Twelfth Corps, at 11 a. m. on Monday, the 25th instant, or as soon thereafter as practicable, to investigate the circumstances which gave rise to the reflections on Maj. Gen. Carl Schurz and part of his command, contained in the following extract from General Hooker's official report of the night action of Wauhatchie, dated November 6, 1863:

> I regret that my duty constrains me to except any portion of my command in my commendation of their courage and valor. The brigade dispatched to the relief of Geary by orders delivered in person to its division commander, never reached him until long after the fight had ended. It is alleged that it lost its way, when it had a terrific infantry fire to guide it all the way, and also that it became involved in a swamp, where there was no swamp or other obstacle between it and Geary which should have delayed it a moment in marching to the relief of its imperiled companions;

and give an opinion as to whether the above strictures in General Hooker's report were deserved by the conduct of General Schurz, Colonel Hecker, or any part of their command during the said action.

DETAIL FOR THE COURT.

Col. A. Buschbeck, Twenty-seventh Pennsylvania Volunteers, commanding Second Division, Eleventh Army Corps.

Col. G. W. Mindil, Thirty-third New Jersey Volunteers, commanding First Brigade, Second Division, Eleventh Army Corps.

Col. James Wood, jr., One hundred and thirty-sixth New York Volunteers, commanding Second Brigade, Second Division, Eleventh Army Corps.

Capt. W. H. Lambert, Thirty-third New Jersey Volunteers, recorder.

   *   *   *   *   *   *

By command of Major-General Thomas:

WM. D. WHIPPLE,
Assistant Adjutant-General.

SPECIAL FIELD ORDERS, } HDQRS. DEPT. OF THE CUMBERLAND,
  No. 26.   }   *Chattanooga, January 26, 1864.*

  *   *   *   *   *   *   *

XXI. Col. G. W. Mindil, Thirty-third New Jersey Volunteers, commanding First Brigade, Second Division, Eleventh Army Corps, is relieved from duty as member of the Court of Inquiry instituted by Paragraph XI, Special Field Orders, No. 23, current series, from these headquarters.

Col. P. H. Jones, One hundred and fifty-fourth New York Infantry, is hereby detailed as member of the Court of Inquiry above named in place of Colonel Mindil, relieved, and will report to Col. A. Buschbeck, president of the same.

By command of Major-General Thomas:

WM. D. WHIPPLE,
Assistant Adjutant-General.

HDQRS. ELEVENTH AND TWELFTH ARMY CORPS,
January 29, 1864—11 a. m.

The Court met pursuant to the foregoing orders:

Present: Col. A. Buschbeck, Twenty-seventh Pennsylvania Volunteers, commanding Second Division, Eleventh Army Corps; Col. James Wood, jr., One hundred and thirty-sixth New York Volunteers, commanding Second Brigade, Second Division, Eleventh Army Corps; Col. P. H. Jones, One hundred and fifty-fourth New York Volunteers; Capt. W. H. Lambert, Thirty-third New Jersey Volunteers, recorder.

The orders instituting the Court having been read in the presence of Major-General Schurz and Colonel Hecker, the parties accused, they were asked whether either of them had any objection to any member of the Court as named in the order. Each of the accused answered they had no objections to any member of the Court.

The Court was duly sworn by the recorder, and the recorder was duly sworn by the president.

Col. F. Hecker, commanding Third Brigade, Third Division, Eleventh Army Corps, made objection to the Court making investigation into the command of Major-General Schurz, and of his own, in the same inquiry, and asked that the conduct of each be made the subject of separate investigation, stating that, as he had made a request for a court of inquiry, and had no legal knowledge of the application for such a court by Major-General Schurz, the cases were separate ones; the orders under which Major-General Schurz and he acted were different, and he therefore objected to the instructions of the foregoing order.

The court was cleared, and after due deliberation the doors were opened, and the decision of the Court announced: That the objection of Colonel Hecker is overruled, and the Court will proceed with the investigation as ordered; but if such proceeding was subsequently deemed necessary, the Court would consider the cases separately.

The recorder here asked time be allowed him for an interview with the witnesses, and a preparation for the conduct of the case, which was granted, and the Court adjourned to meet on Monday, February 1, 1864, at 10 a. m., at headquarters Eleventh and Twelfth Corps.

—

HDQRS. ELEVENTH AND TWELFTH ARMY CORPS,
February 1, 1864—10 a. m.

The Court met pursuant to adjournment.

Present: Col. A. Buschbeck, Twenty-seventh Pennsylvania Volunteers, commanding Second Division, Eleventh Army Corps; Col. James Wood, jr., One hundred and thirty-sixth New York Volunteers, commanding Second Brigade, Second Division, Eleventh Army Corps; Col. P. H. Jones, One hundred and fifty-fourth New York Volunteers, commanding First Brigade, Second Division, Eleventh Army Corps; Capt. W. H. Lambert, Thirty-third New Jersey Volunteers, recorder.

The proceedings of previous session were read.

The recorder asked leave to introduce as clerk Edward R. Wood, One hundred and fifty-fourth New York, to report the proceedings and testimony phonographically. Leave was granted and Private Wood was duly sworn to report impartially and correctly.

Major-General Schurz asked leave to introduce as counsel for himself, Maj. F. C. Winkler, Twenty-sixth Wisconsin Volunteers, which was granted.

The examination of witnesses was then commenced.

Maj. Gen. JOSEPH HOOKER, commanding Eleventh and Twelfth Army Corps, a witness for the prosecution, was duly sworn.

By the RECORDER:

Question. Are the words quoted in Paragraph XI, Special Field Orders, No. 23, headquarters Department of the Cumberland, as a part of your official report of the night action of Wauhatchie, the words used by you in that report?

Answer. I believe they are.

Question. What division is alluded to in the report?

Answer. The division of General Schurz.

Question. Was General Schurz then in command of the division?

Answer. He was.

Question. What orders were given by you to the division commander?

Answer. To double-quick his division to the relief of General Geary. I gave the order to General Schurz direct, and sent word to General Howard, for the attack was a sudden one, and no time was to be lost.

Question. Can you remember at what time these orders were given?

Answer. I can only approximate to the time. I think it was between 12 and 1 o'clock.

Question. What was the distance between the division of General Schurz and General Geary?

Answer. About 2 miles.

Question. What was the nature of the country between the division and General Geary?

Answer. There was some mud, but there was nothing that impeded our march as we came up.

Question. Were any other orders given to the commander of the division, or to the commanders of the brigades than those first alluded to?

Answer. I had nothing to do with brigades. I gave no other orders to brigades. Orders were given for one brigade of that division to be sent to the hill now known as the Tyndale Hill.

Question. Do you know how soon after you gave the first order to the division, the division started?

Answer. Soon after.

Question. What was the nature of the firing?

Answer. It was severe; it satisfied me that it was the determination of the rebels to whip Geary.

Question. Was any portion of the enemy between General Geary and General Schurz?

Answer. Some at the left of his (Schurz's) line of march.

Question. At what time did General Schurz's division reach General Geary ?

Answer. I think General Geary reports 5.30 o'clock.

Question. Were the enemy between General Geary and General Schurz in such position that they could detain or offer any obstacle to the progress of General Schurz ?

Answer. No other than the detention caused by the detachment of one brigade from the column.

By Major-General SCHURZ :

Question. Do you consider all the statements in your report relative to the Third Division correct in every particular ?

Answer. I do.

Question. You say in your report, "It is alleged that the brigade marching to the relief of Geary lost its way and became involved in a swamp." Where and by whom was that alleged ?

Answer. If I mistake not, in General Howard's report.

Question. You speak in your report of the brigade dispatched to the relief of General Geary; which of General Schurz's brigades was that ?

Answer. The whole division was under orders to go to General Geary ; afterward one brigade was detached to go to attack the enemy on the Tyndale Hill ; the remainder of the division was the brigade alluded to.

Question. You say in your report that the brigade dispatched to the relief of General Geary arrived there long after the fight had ceased ; which of General Schurz's brigades was that ?

Answer. Colonel Hecker's brigade reached there at 5.30; another brigade reached there at 7 o'clock.

Question. " Howard was directed to double-quick his nearest division (Schurz's) to his relief, and before proceeding far a sheet of musketry was thrown on him from the central hills. Directions were immediately given for one of the brigades *en route* to Geary (Tyndale's) to be detached and assault the enemy on the hills on the left, and the other brigade to push on as ordered." Is this a correct copy of the statement about the Third Division entered in your official report ?

Answer. It is correct.

Question. You speak in your report of only two brigades, Tyndale's, and the "other brigade." Was it known to you at the time that General Schurz had three brigades ?

Answer. I am not positive, but I think it must have been.

Question. Did you see Colonel Hecker on the field ?

Answer. Yes.

Question. What was your conversation with Colonel Hecker on the field ?

Answer. On returning from the column marching to the relief of Geary the first troops that I came to not on the march were troops commanded by Colonel Hecker. I inquired what his troops were doing there. He said he was there by order of General Howard. Some other conversation passed, but I do not think I can recall it, unless it is suggested to me. It is possible that I said to him to remain there until further orders from General Howard.

Question. At what particular stage of the battle was it when you saw Colonel Hecker?

Answer. It was immediately after riding back from the column at the head of which were General Howard and General Schurz after the fire had been thrown upon it. I had been on the left between the column and the hill from which the firing came.

Question. Do you recognize this letter (Appendix A) as a correct copy of a letter you addressed officially to Brigadier-General Whipple, assistant adjutant-general of the Army of the Cumberland?

Answer. This is my letter.

Question. Do you consider the statements contained in that letter correct in every particular?

Answer. I do. I made them under the impression that they were correct.

Question. You say in that letter that you were informed that Colonel Hecker's brigade was in its position by order of Major-General Howard. What had been your orders to General Howard?

Answer. General Howard was immediately advised of the orders given to General Schurz. After that, the order was given to General Howard to dispatch a brigade to the hill on the left.

Question. By whom [was the order] to take the hill on the left with Tyndale's brigade sent?

Answer. According to my recollection, by one of my staff officers.

Question. Did you see or hear anything of the Second Brigade of General Schurz's division being behind at the time you saw Colonel Hecker, or afterward?

Answer. I only saw what I took to be Colonel Hecker's brigade of that division. If I had supposed there were two brigades behind I should have ordered them, irrespective of General Howard's orders, to the relief of General Geary.

Question. When and where was it that you gave General Schurz the order relating to the movement to the relief of General Geary?

Answer. It was very near where General Schurz was encamped, and was after the attack on Geary.

By the COURT:

Question. What troops led the column advancing to the aid of General Geary?

Answer. General Tyndale's.

Capt. JOSEPH B. GREENHUT, acting assistant adjutant-general, Third Brigade, Third Division, Eleventh Army Corps, a witness for the accused, was duly sworn.

By General SCHURZ:

Question. State what you know of the movements of your brigade on the night of the 28th and 29th of October, 1863.

Answer. Captain Spraul, aide-de-camp on General Schurz's staff, ordered Colonel Hecker to form his brigade on the road. Colonel Hecker gave me instructions to form the brigade. I went down and as I came to the road Lieutenant-Colonel Otto, chief of staff, inquired of me what I was going to do there. I informed him that I had received instructions to form the brigade on the road. He then informed me that the brigade was not to be formed on the road, but was to move forward with the other brigade where the firing was heard. I informed Colonel Hecker of the fact, and he ordered the brigade forward. After marching for some time the column in front halted. We were marching very nearly parallel to the Second Brigade of the Third Division. When the column halted we were very near the ill up which the Thirty-third Massachusetts charged. After the column halted Colonel Hecker sent me forward to inquire the cause. As I came to the head of he Second Brigade I inquired of Captain Orlemann where Major-General Schurz vas. He told me that he went forward with the First Brigade. I inquired of him f he had received orders that the Second Brigade was to halt there. He told me hat he had. He did not inform me by whom he had received orders. I went back and informed Colonel Hecker of the fact that the Second Brigade had orders o halt, and that the First Brigade had moved forward with General Schurz. Colonel Hecker told me that he had received no orders to halt, and that he should push forward until he had. Accordingly we marched past the Second Brigade. After we had marched 100 yards beyond the Second Brigade, Major Howard came up and informed Colonel Hecker that he should march up to the cross-roads and halt there. As we came up to the cross-roads Major-General Hooker and staff were standing in the road. On seeing us approach General Hooker turned around and inquired what troops these were. Colonel Hecker replied that they were the Third Brigade, Third Division, Eleventh Corps. Upon which General Hooker inquired where General Schurz was. Colonel Hecker informed him that he must be somewhere in the front, as one of his aides who had been wounded had been carried to the rear a few minutes ago. He asked him what troops those were in the rear of him. Colonel Hecker replied they were the Second Brigade, Third Division. After standing on the road about fifteen minutes there was a volley fired down from the hill. General Hooker ordered Colonel Hecker to form his brigade in such a manner as to be able to form a line of battle either to the right or to the front, concluding with the words "stay here;" then rode off in the direction of the Second Brigade. We formed there as indicated by General Hooker, and remained somewhere in the neighborhood of an hour. During this time I saw General Hooker and staff standing in front of the Second Brigade. After we had been there very nearly an hour, I saw General Schurz and staff come from the front and proceed to where General Hooker was standing in front of the Second Brigade. In a short time General Schurz came back, and ordered Colonel Hecker to move forward. This was about 4 or 5 o'clock. It was long after Geary's firing had ceased; there was but little firing after we had taken the position indicated by General Hooker. We marched forward; General Schurz was at the head of our column till we reached the position which the First Brigade then occupied. General Schurz then ordered us to halt, and went to get another regiment for support. He said our brigade was too small; it was here that I heard General Schurz inform Colonel Hecker that we should have to move forward and form a junction with General Geary. After waiting a few moments the One hundred and nineteenth New York, Colonel Lockman, came up. He had but very few men, as he stated that the greater part of the regiment were on picket and could not be relieved. I then heard General Schurz order the One hundred and nineteenth to go back, and order one of his aides to go and order the One hundred and forty-first New York up, which came with little delay. During this time we made arrangements with the Seventy-fifth Pennsylvania Volunteers to move forward in the gap and cover it, that we might have our flanks protected. Immediately after the One hundred and forty-first came up we moved forward in the direction of Geary. The Seventy-fifth moved into the gap shortly before we started. We marched and did not stop on the road until we reached General Geary's position. As soon as we arrived there Colonel Hecker reported to General Geary, and we were ordered to relieve one or two of his regiments alongside the railroad and occupy their position.

Question. How long did the firing continue at Geary's?

Answer. It was at intervals when I heard it. I should think from half to three-quarters of an hour.

Question. Where did General Hooker go when he left you, after having given orders to the Third Brigade?

Answer. He went in front of the position that the Second Brigade occupied in the field, right in our front and our left.

Question. Did you see General Hooker remain with the Second Brigade any length of time?

Answer. Yes, sir; he was there the whole time that we occupied the position to which he ordered us.

Question. How much time did it take you to reach Geary after you had received the order to march?

Answer. Not more than twenty minutes.

Question. At what time did you reach Geary's position?

Answer. Just at daybreak.

Question. Did you see whether the Second Brigade, after you wer[e] halted, was formed from the column of a march into line of battle[?]

Answer. They were massed in a field to our front and left.

Question. When you first started did you see the First Brigade ?

Answer. I could not be positive. I saw troops marching. I did not know t[o] what commands they belonged.

By the RECORDER :

Question. About what time did the column commence moving ?

Answer. About 1 o'clock. I cannot positively recollect.

Question. Were any of General Hooker's staff present at the con[-] versation between General Hooker and Colonel Hecker ?

Answer. There were four or five of General Hooker's staff present.

Question. Did Major Howard or any other member of General[ ] Howard's staff give you any orders whilst you were waiting at the[ ] cross-roads ?

Answer. He did not.

Question. Between the time you first commenced moving and the[ ] time you reached General Geary did you receive any order from any[ ] commander other than General Hooker ?

Answer. I did not, except the order from Major Howard, which I supposed wa[s] from General Howard, which order was subsequently confirmed by an order from[ ] General Hooker.

By General SCHURZ :

Question. Did General Hooker give you any orders personally ?

Answer. "Tell Colonel Hecker to form his brigade in such a manner that he ca[n] form them to the right or to the front."

Question. When you halted was the Second Brigade moving ahead ?

Answer. I believe it was.

Question. Where did you see Colonel Otto ?

Answer. As soon as I got down on the road.

Question. When did the first volley come from the hill ?

Answer. After we were standing at the cross-roads.

Question. Did you know that that was the Second Brigade on your[ ] left ?

Answer. Yes ; I knew it before.

By the COURT :

Question. Where were you encamped that night ?

Answer. In the rear, and to the right of General Howard's headquarters.

Question. Before Captain Spraul came were the regiments in line ?

Answer. They were not under arms, but ready to take arms.

Question. After you received orders from Captain Spraul, which[ ] way did you march ?

Answer. We marched directly toward Wauhatchie road.

Question. Did any other troops move ahead with you?

Answer. The Second Brigade moved about the same time we did, the length of three regiments ahead.

Question. How long after you got on to the road before you were ordered to move forward?

Answer. Not more than two or three minutes.

Question. Were the roads blocked up by troops passing?

Answer. They were, but we marched in the fields and had no interruption until we got to where the Second Brigade was halted.

Question. Did you know whether the troops of General Steinwehr moved ahead of you?

Answer. I did not know.

Question. Did you hear that night that the Thirty-third Massachusetts Volunteers had stormed the hill?

Answer. Yes, sir; I heard it from one of General Hooker's aides.

Question. When you got up to the cross-roads, did you see General Steinwehr?

Answer. No, sir.

Question. Did you hear that night that troops trying to take the hill had been repulsed at first?

Answer. I did, but not officially.

The Court then adjourned to meet at headquarters Eleventh and Twelfth Corps, or, if permission were obtained, at headquarters Eleventh Corps, on Tuesday, February 2, 1864, at 9 a. m.

—

HEADQUARTERS ELEVENTH CORPS,
February 2, 1864—9 a. m.

The Court met pursuant to adjournment, permission having been obtained from headquarters Department of the Cumberland to assemble at headquarters Eleventh Corps.

Present: Col. A. Buschbeck, Twenty-seventh Pennsylvania Volunteers, commanding Second Division, Eleventh Corps; Col. James Wood, jr., One hundred and thirty-sixth New York Volunteers, commanding Second Brigade, Second Division, Eleventh Corps; Col. P. H. Jones, One hundred and fifty-fourth New York Volunteers, commanding First Brigade, Second Division, Eleventh Corps; Capt. W. H. Lambert, Thirty-third New Jersey Volunteers, recorder.

The proceedings of previous sessions were read.

Maj. CHARLES H. HOWARD, aide-de-camp, General Howard's staff, a witness for the accused, was duly sworn.

By General SCHURZ:

Question. Did you see Colonel Hecker on the field on the night of the battle of Wauhatchie?

Answer. I did.

Question. Where did you see him, and where did you come from when you met him?

Answer. I first saw Colonel Hecker between General Howard's headquarters, where they were that night, and the hill now known as Smith's Hill. I had come from carrying an order to General Steinwehr, and passed Colonel Hecker's column.

Question. Was Colonel Hecker's column then marching?

Answer. It was.

Question. State where you saw Colonel Hecker going.

Answer. I met Colonel Hecker and staff going, after I had joined General How-ard at the angle where the road makes a right angle toward the Smith Hill, at about, I think, rather less than a quarter of a mile back, and as I was returning with an order to Colonel Buschbeck from General Howard.

Question. Did you see Colonel Hecker going, and what was your conversation with him?

Answer. I saw Colonel Hecker going, on returning from carrying the order to Colonel Buschbeck, and had some conversation either with him personally or with his staff with regard to where General Howard was, and pointed out where I had left him. Either Colonel Hecker or some one of his staff said he had been unable to find General Howard where I had previously pointed him out. I think I ex-pressed some surprise that General Howard was not to be found there at the point previously mentioned, and immediately rode forward to that place and found there General Hooker and staff. Some member of General Hooker's staff informed me that General Howard had gone forward to join General Schurz.

Question. When did General Hooker arrive on the spot, and what was said then?

Answer. General Hooker was standing near where I had left General Howard. I went forward to General Hooker. Colonel Hecker joined us almost on the iden-tical spot which was just at the angle where the main road turns toward the Smith Hill. General Hooker spoke to Colonel Hecker, recognizing him, and to further conversation I did not listen.

Question. Did you refer Colonel Hecker to General Hooker in regard to the order to stop as soon as General Hooker and Colonel Hecker met?

Answer. It is my impression, very vivid, that I did mention to Colonel Hecker that "here is General Hooker" the third time meeting him.

Question. Did Colonel Hecker stop his column before you met him?

Answer. I think that I have stated, and I will repeat, that on meeting Colonel Hecker each time his column was in motion.

Question. Did you see General Schurz on the field?

Answer. I met General Schurz afterward, near the hill now known as the Tyn-dale Hill, after the meeting of Colonel Hecker and General Hooker.

Question. Did you report to General Schurz the fact that Colonel Hecker's brigade was stopped, and was under instructions from General Hooker?

Answer. It is my impression that I reported to General Schurz, on meeting him, that Colonel Hecker's brigade was stopped, and in the presence of General Hooker I might have said that he had received instructions from General Hooker.

Question. Do you remember the nature of the ground at that time between the place where General Hooker and Colonel Hecker met and the hill now known as the Tyndale Hill?

Answer. Considerable of the ground was wet and swampy at that time.

Question. Did you not, when riding over it, find considerable diffi-culty in passing on horseback?

Answer. I found some difficulty in several places.

By Colonel HECKER:

Question. Who said that General Howard was not to be found?

Answer. I cannot state with certainty whether it was Colonel Hecker or some one of his staff.

Question. When with General Hooker did you hear that orders were given?

Answer. As soon as I reached General Hooker I gave information that Colonel Hecker's brigade had arrived, and I understood, either from General Hooker himself, in person, or some one of his staff, that Colonel Hecker's brigade was authorized by him to halt there. At this moment Colonel Hecker himself came up, and I remember that General Hooker recognized him, speaking somewhat familiarly, as though he knew him well. I remember afterward that either General Hooker or General Butterfield gave the order directing Colonel Hecker as to the formation, in order to face, if need be, either to the Smith Hill or to the front, as he had been marching. I had received two orders from General Howard, and two only, and had communicated them, one to General Steinwehr, to which I have alluded, and one to Colonel Buschbeck.

Question. To whom had you pointed out the place where General Howard could be found?

Answer. It was on the second meeting with Colonel Hecker and staff that I pointed out the place where I had just left General Howard, either to Colonel Hecker in person or to some one of his staff, I cannot say which.

Question. Did you inform Colonel Hecker that he would have to stop his column at a certain place?

Answer. I have no recollection of giving him any such information.

Question. Did you not communicate to Colonel Hecker what you had heard when with General Hooker?

Answer. I think it possible, and even probable, that I communicated that information to Colonel Hecker relative to General Hooker's desiring him to halt, but I have not as distinct a recollection about that as I have about some other matters.

Question. Was my column not marching during the whole time and as often as you met me?

Answer. It was until this last meeting, which was almost simultaneous with Colonel Hecker's meeting General Hooker.

Question. Did you not, some distance from the cross-roads, give me the order to go there and halt?

Answer. I remember that either General Hooker or General Butterfield gave the order regulating Colonel Hecker's formation, so that he might face either to the hill or to the front as it might become necessary. I do not remember communicating this or any other order to Colonel Hecker at the distance he mentioned from the cross-roads.

Question. Was not my column marching when you brought me the order, and did I not stop in consequence of that order?

Answer. I believe I have stated that Colonel Hecker's column was marching each time on meeting it, and I believe that I stated further, that it is possible and even probable that I communicated the information that I received either from General Hooker in person or from some member of his staff, that Colonel Hecker was authorized by him to stop there. As to whether Colonel Hecker halted, in consequence of anything that I communicated to him, I cannot decide.

Question. Were you not all the time with me and saw me when for the first time I met General Hooker?

Answer. It was after my return from Colonel Buschbeck that Colonel Hecker met General Hooker in my presence, and I believe it was the first time of his meeting him, from the manner of General Hooker greeting him. I then went forward to look for General Howard.

Question. Did you not finish your previous conversation with me with the words, "There is General Hooker himself?"

Answer. It is my impression that I did say those words to Colonel Hecker. I will add as to the matters of conversation, I do not so distinctly remember the words as in the matter of orders.

Question. Was I not marching in the direction of the front to Wauhatchie, and did I not stop there when I had received your communication made to me ?

Answer. I think I have stated and I will repeat that each time on meeting Colonel Hecker I found him marching, and I will add, it was to the front and toward Wauhatchie.

Question. State the moment Colonel Hecker halted his column.

Answer. I do not think I can give the exact moment of Colonel Hecker's halting his column, but I think it was just before his meeting General Hooker.

Question. By whom did you report that Colonel Hecker's brigade was stopped ?

Answer. I cannot state positively that I reported by whom Colonel Hecker's brigade was stopped.

Question. Did you hear me mention at any time that I met swampy roads, or complaining about the roads over which I had passed?

Answer. I recollect no such complaints.

By the RECORDER :

Question. Was there anything either in the roads or in the ground adjoining the roads which would impede the passage of troops between where General Hooker and Colonel Hecker were, and where you met General Schurz?

Answer. The nature of the ground was such in several places, and a thicket in one place. I remember it was such in one place that it would impede troops in the night-time considerably.

Question. Where were these places which would have impeded troops in the night-time ?

Answer. There was a portion of the ground which was boggy and had a thicket upon it of several rods in width which was near to the Tyndale Hill.

Question. What do you think is the distance between the place where you left General Hooker and the place where you met General Schurz ?

Answer. I should think it somewhat more than a quarter of a mile.

By General SCHURZ :

Question. Did the two brigades march on the same road, namely, the Second Brigade, Second Division, and Colonel Hecker's brigade ?

Answer. I think they marched upon the same road until within a quarter of a mile of where I met General Hooker, at which point the Second Brigade, Second Division, turned to the left.

By the COURT :

Question. Do you know whether the Second Brigade, of General Steinwehr's division, preceded Colonel Hecker's brigade?

Answer. I am quite confident that it did, because it was pointed out to me at the time, somewhat in advance and considerably to the left flank of Colonel Hecker.

Question. At the time you met General Hooker with Colonel Hecker had the assault been made upon Smith's Hill by the Second Brigade, Second Division ?

Answer. It had certainly been commenced.

Question. Did you know that General Steinwehr formed line of battle fronting Wauhatchie ?

Answer. I remember that a portion of his troops held in reserve were fronting toward Wauhatchie.

Question. Was that before Colonel Hecker came up with his column?

Answer. I cannot say as to the exact time that formation was made, as I carried no orders relative to it.

Question. Did you know anything of the movements of Tyndale's brigade at that time—the time of the meeting of Colonel Hecker and General Hooker?

Answer. I understood at that time, I think from General Howard, that Tyndale's brigade had gone forward to join General Geary. General Howard stated to me that the order which I had carried to General Steinwehr had been modified by General Hooker so that General Schurz was to go to the relief of General Geary and not General Steinwehr.

Question. Where was the Second Brigade (Krzyzanowski's) at the time of the meeting of General Hooker and Colonel Hecker?

Answer. I am not certain that I know where that brigade was at that time.

First Lieut. PAUL A. OLIVER, aide-de-camp, Major-General Hooker's staff, a witness for the accused, was duly sworn.

By General SCHURZ:

Question. Did you see General Schurz on the field during the night engagement of Wauhatchie?

Answer. Yes; I did.

Question. Did you communicate any orders to General Schurz on the field?

Answer. Yes.

Question. What orders did you communicate to General Schurz?

Answer. I took the order to him to get his division or brigade—I am not certain which—under arms, and occupy the hill (Tyndale's Hill) where we had the skirmish with one brigade.

Question. Did you deliver the orders to get his division or brigade under arms, and the other orders to occupy the hill, afterward called Tyndale's Hill, at the same time or separately?

Answer. At the same time.

Question. From whom had you received your orders for General Schurz?

Answer. From General Hooker in person.

Question. Did you see General Schurz on the field afterward while on his march toward Wauhatchie?

Answer. I did.

Question. Where did you see General Schurz on the field?

Answer. I saw General Schurz in that field to the right of that hill, the Tyndale Hill. The troops had got off the road, and I had gone to find it. It was there I first met General Schurz.

Question. Did you communicate to General Schurz any orders at that time?

Answer. I did not; but immediately afterward when the troops had got on the road they were halted. There was some firing from the hill. I told General Schurz I thought that hill should be occupied. General Schurz said he had orders to join

General Geary, and I told him that I thought he had better join General Geary. He said there was a line of battle in front of him. The firing still continued. I told him to take the hill.

Question. Did you know what troops General Schurz had at that time with him?

Answer. I presumed he had another brigade immediately behind him, but General Schurz told me at the time that he had only one brigade there. I had heard an order issued previously—I think it was to General Howard—to move two brigades up there. I did not receive the order myself.

Question. Did you not ask General Schurz if he had no troops to push through to Geary; whether he could not send an orderly there?

Answer. Yes; I asked him if he could not communicate with Geary. I think he asked how. I said by an orderly. He replied that he had no orderly that he could trust.

Question. Was there firing in front at the time that conversation occurred?

Answer. There was firing from the hill; there was no firing in front; the firing was from the Wauhatchie side of the hill; it was in an oblique direction toward the railroad, as far as I could judge.

Question. Was there any firing at Geary's at that time?

Answer. The firing at Geary's at that time had almost ceased. So far as I can remember, there was not much firing at Geary's at that time.

Question. When did you inform General Hooker of General Schurz taking possession of Tyndale's Hill?

Answer. It was very shortly after my conversation with General Schurz. It was about the time Smith's Hill was taken; I do not know the exact hour.

Question. What did you tell General Hooker concerning the movements of the troops which were with General Schurz?

Answer. I told General Hooker that General Schurz occupied that hill, and that skirmishers had been thrown forward.

Question. Did you inform General Hooker that General Schurz had only one brigade with him?

Answer. No; I did not.

Question. Where was General Hooker when you rejoined him?

Answer. He was at the foot of Smith's Hill, near the house where his headquarters were afterward during the day.

Question. What did General Hooker say upon receiving that information?

Answer. I do not remember that he said anything.

Question. Did you carry any orders to brigade commanders that night?

Answer. I did not.

By the RECORDER:

Question. Where was it that the troops of General Schurz lost the road?

Answer. The troops were fired upon from Smith's Hill. They fronted, and returned the fire. I gave the order to cease firing, that we were firing upon our own men. Edging toward the right, the troops got off the road; they halted; the skirmishers found difficulty in going through the woods and thick underbrush. When the column halted I went to look for the road; found it, and reported to General Schurz and directed him to the road.

Question. How long did these troops halt there ?

Answer. I do not think over five or six minutes ; perhaps not so long.

Question. Do you know what particular troops of Schurz's division were with him then ?

Answer. I have heard the Forty-fifth Regiment mentioned. I think it was Tyndale's brigade.

Question. When you left General Schurz on the hill, what was the nature of the line of battle in his front ?

Answer. I do not know. I only heard General Schurz say there was a line of battle. I think it was at right angles to the road.

By General SCHURZ :

Question. Did I say there was a line of battle or that it was reported there was a line of battle ?

Answer. I am not certain whether General Schurz said there was a line of battle or that it was reported that there was a line of battle.

Question. To whom did you give that order to cease firing ?

Answer. I gave it generally in as loud a voice as I could command.

Question. Were many shots fired from the column in reply to shots from the hill ?

Answer. I think there were ; the whole line fronted.

Question. Did you see General Howard with General Schurz at the time ?

Answer. No ; I did not. He had gone forward. I had seen General Howard previously.

By the COURT :

Question. At the time you carried General Hooker's order to General Schurz, what was the order ?

Answer. It was to get his division or brigade under arms and occupy the hill, and put one brigade on the hill.

Question. Where was General Schurz at this time ?

Answer. He was close to General Howard's headquarters in an ambulance.

Question. Do you know that General Hooker at any time had an interview with General Schurz ?

Answer. I am not certain that he had.

Question. After you led the troops on to the road, did you meet with any impediment which hindered them from going to Tyndale's ?

Answer. There was only that firing which I have mentioned before, which was very slight.

After the examination of Lieutenant Oliver, the Court took a recess for an hour and a half.

2.30 p. m.

Court reassembled.

Report of testimony of Major Howard was read in his hearing.

Court adjourned to meet at same place at 9 a. m. Wednesday, 3d instant.

HEADQUARTERS ELEVENTH CORPS,
February 3, 1864—9 a. m.

COURT OF INQUIRY.

Court met pursuant to adjournment.

Present: Col. A. Buschbeck, Twenty-seventh Pennsylvania, commanding Second Division, Eleventh Army Corps; Col. James Wood, jr., One hundred and thirty-sixth New York, commanding Second Brigade, Second Division, Eleventh Army Corps; Col. P. H. Jones, One hundred and fifty-fourth New York, commanding First Brigade, Second Division, Eleventh Army Corps; Capt. W. H. Lambert, Thirty-third New Jersey Volunteers, recorder.

At the request of the recorder the court was cleared, those present retiring.

The doors being opened, the Court announced that it had decided, at the request of the recorder, to allow him counsel, whom he might introduce into court; that the questions to witnesses be all put into writing, and that one of the accused should finish his questions before the other commenced.

Proceedings of previous sessions read.

First Lieut. RUDOLPH MUELLER, acting aide-de-camp on Colonel Hecker's staff, a witness for the accused, was duly sworn.

By General SCHURZ:

Question. Did you accompany Colonel Hecker during the night of the engagement of Wauhatchie?

Answer. Yes, sir.

Question. Do you remember what way Colonel Hecker marched after moving camp, and what happened on his march?

Answer. When we heard the first shots fired we were aroused and had the men fall in; then Colonel Hecker sent me down to the road to headquarters for orders. I could not find it, where it was, and I rode back to the camping place and found the brigade gone, and went ahead after it and found it on the road. After marching on the road the column in front of us, the Second Brigade, halted. Colonel Hecker sent Captain Greenhut to ascertain the cause of the halt. Captain Greenhut returned and said the Second Brigade was ordered to halt there. Colonel Hecker said, "We have no orders to halt, and we will push ahead." We did so, leaving the Second Brigade on our left. We progressed farther, when Major Howard met our column and ordered us to march down to the cross-road and halt there. We did so, and having lost sight of the Second Brigade, Colonel Hecker sent me to find it. I found it on the road that forks off toward the hill. Going down I found the brigade in line of battle behind a fence in a corn-field, and fronted toward the hill taken by the Second Division (Smith's Hill). There we remained, and had a fence torn down by order of Colonel Hecker. We remained there until General Schurz came and ordered us to proceed on the road toward Wauhatchie. Then we advanced as far as the hill known as the Tyndale Hill, where we were ordered to halt again and form line. Then the Seventy-fifth Pennsylvania Volunteers were sent toward the railroad and toward the gap as skirmishers. Then we received orders to march to the relief of General Geary, which we did, after we were first re-enforced by a regiment from one of the other brigades. I think it was the One hundred and forty-first New York. Colonel Hecker pressed forward. We were detained there because a patrol had been sent out to see whether the enemy was ahead. The patrol was sent out toward Geary's position. We waited for the patrol to come back. Shortly after we marched on. I do not know whether the patrol had come back or not. The Sixty-eighth New York advanced as skirmishers and flankers. We then marched on until we came to Geary's position. We reached Geary's position in about twenty minutes, it may be twenty-five. We arrived at the opening of Geary's position about dawn. We did not know whether it was the enemy's position or not until we saw a soldier who told us it was the Twelfth Corps. We reported to General Geary, who seemed highly gratified at our arrival. We took position along the railroad to the right of his lines.

Question. How was the Second Brigade formed when you (after your having been ordered by Colonel Hecker to look for it) found it on your left?

Answer. I found it in column, halted by the right flank.

By Colonel HECKER:

Question. Did you hear much firing in the direction of Geary's at the time when you were stopped at the cross-roads near Smith's Hill?

Answer. No, sir.

Question. When and where did Colonel Hecker receive for the first time the order to march to join General Geary?

Answer. In front or opposite the Tyndale Hill after we had dispatched the Seventy-fifth Regiment that I heard it.

Question. By whom was Colonel Hecker detained to wait for the coming back of the patrol?

Answer. By Colonel Otto and by General Schurz himself.

Question. How long was Colonel Hecker detained?

Answer. Not very long; I should think about ten minutes.

Question. Had this brigade before halted by Major Howard received any orders on the march?

Answer. No, sir.

Question. Do you mean to say it was for the patrol that Colonel Hecker was kept waiting for about ten minutes?

Answer. Yes, sir.

Question. Did Colonel Hecker wait at all after the One hundred and forty-first New York joined you?

Answer. No; I do not think he did.

By the RECORDER:

Question. Did you hear Major Howard give the order to Colonel Hecker to go on to the cross-roads and halt there?

Answer. Yes, sir.

Question. Do you remember in what words these orders were given?

Answer. "March down to the cross-roads and halt there." These words I heard distinctly.

Question. From whom did your brigade receive the order to go to the relief of General Geary?

Answer. From General Schurz.

Question. Was there any firing going on when you were halted waiting for the patrol?

Answer. There was no firing.

Question. Was there any firing when you reported to General Geary?

Answer. No, sir.

Question. About what time did you report to General Geary?

Answer. It was about 5 or a little after; it was quite dusk.

Question. Did you see the Second Brigade, Third Division, after you found them halted?

Answer. I saw a line of battle in the opening in front of us, fronting toward Geary's position, forming a right angle with us when we fronted toward the hill.

Question. Was your brigade the only one that reported to General Geary at the time you did?

Answer. Yes, sir.

Question. Did you find any difficulty in marching over the road in the night?

Answer. No, sir; the only difficulty was when we started from the cross-roads. We marched on the right of the road. We found a run over which we could not pass in four ranks, so we passed in two.

Question. Did you see General Hooker that night?

Answer. No; I did not recognize him.

By the COURT:

Question. When did you leave your camp?

Answer. I think it was about midnight or after; immediately after the first firing; I could not say whether it was 12 or 1 o'clock; it was about that time.

Question. How long did you stop at the cross-roads?

Answer. About three-quarters of an hour or an hour.

Question. How long did the brigade stop at Tyndale's Hill?

Answer. About half an hour.

Question. How long were you on the march from camp to the cross-roads?

Answer. About three-quarters of an hour.

Question. How did you march?

Answer. In quick time.

Question. How long were you in marching from the cross-roads to Tyndale's Hill?

Answer. About half an hour.

Question. How long from Tyndale's Hill to General Geary?

Answer. About twenty-five minutes.

Question. Did you see Major Howard more than once?

Answer. No, sir.

Question. From what direction did he come when he delivered that order?

Answer. He came from the front and met us about 100 yards above the cross-roads.

Question. Where did you first see General Schurz when the brigade got on the march?

Answer. The brigade was standing near the cross-roads and General Schurz ordered us to proceed.

Testimony read in the hearing of the witness.
Court took a recess of one and a half hours.

1.30 p. m.

First Lieut. ALBERT KRAMER, acting aide-de-camp on Colonel Hecker's staff, a witness for the accused, was duly sworn.

By General SCHURZ:

Question. Did you accompany Colonel Hecker during the night of the engagement of Wauhatchie?

Answer. Yes, sir.

Question. Do you remember how Colonel Hecker's column was topped on its march to the front?

Answer. Yes, sir; when we were marching in the direction of Wauhatchie, Major Howard came and gave us the order to stop at the cross-roads. At the ame time General Hooker came up and had some conversation with Colonel Hecker.

Question. Do you remember the conversation between General Hooker and Colonel Hecker?

Answer. He asked, "What troops are these?" Colonel Hecker said the Third Brigade, Third Division. He then asked where General Schurz was. Colonel Hecker aid, "He is in the front, one of his aides is wounded." He then asked, "Where is he Second Brigade?" Colonel Hecker showed him the place in the field, and then, efore he went away, he said, "You stay here." Colonel Hecker said, "Certainly." eneral Hooker rode away at the same time that a volley came from the hill. eneral Hooker gave us instruction so that we might change our front, if neces- ary, toward Wauhatchie.

Question. Where did General Hooker ride to when he left you?

Answer. He rode to the Second Brigade, Third Division.

Question. Did you see where the Second Brigade, Third Division was?

Answer. Yes, sir; about 100 or 150 yards from us on the left in front of the bri- ade.

Question. Did you see General Hooker near the Second Brigade, Third Division, after he had left you?

Answer. Yes; I saw him there. I believe he was dismounted there in front of he Second Brigade.

Question. How long did your brigade stop at the cross-roads?

Answer. About twenty-five minutes or half an hour.

Question. How long did it take to throw down the fences and form the troops in line of battle?

Answer. It was very quick; about five minutes.

Question. By whom was the brigade ordered forward from the cross-roads?

Answer. When I came back General Schurz was there, and he took our brigade forward to Tyndale's brigade.

Question. Did you find General Schurz with Colonel Hecker, or with General Hooker?

Answer. I found General Schurz with Colonel Hecker.

Question. State what happened after General Schurz had ordered the brigade forward.

Answer. When we arrived at General Tyndale's brigade, General Schurz gave an order to send a regiment on that hill, and Colonel Hecker sent the Seventy-fifth Pennsylvania, and after awhile we received orders to march and connect with Gen- eral Geary.

Question. How long did you stop near the hill where General Tyndale was?

Answer. About fifteen minutes.

Question. Was the brigade interrupted in its march from there to General Geary, and when did it arrive at Wauhatchie?

Answer. It was not interrupted, and it arrived between 5 and 5.30 o'clock.

By the RECORDER:

Question. How long were you in marching from the camp to the cross-roads?

Answer. About fifteen minutes.

Question. About what time did you leave camp?

Answer. Between 12 and 1 o'clock.

Question. How often did your brigade halt after it left the cross-roads?

Answer. By General Tyndale's; that was the only time we halted.

Question. How long did it take you to march from where General Tyndale was to General Geary?

Answer. Fifteen or twenty minutes.

Question. How long did it take you to go from the cross-roads to where General Tyndale was?

Answer. Ten minutes.

Question. Did you hear what orders Major Howard gave to Colonel Hecker?

Answer. Major Howard gave him the order to go to the cross-road and stop there.

By the COURT:

Question. Who brought the first order to the brigade to march?

Answer. Captain Spraul.

Question. Did you hear what he said?

Answer. I saw him speaking to him (Colonel Hecker) but I did not hear what he said.

Question. Did the brigade halt on the road and form there.

Answer. No; we marched together; the Second Brigade marched in the road, and we marched to the right of the Second Brigade.

Question. Did Colonel Hecker receive any other orders until he received the order of Major Howard?

Answer. No, sir; that was all.

Question. Did Major Howard say from whom the order came to stop at the cross-road?

Answer. I do not know.

Question. Did the brigade take the double-quick any part of the way?

Answer. No, sir.

Question. Did you hear Major Howard give the order to Colonel Hecker?

Answer. Yes, sir.

Question. What words did he use?

Answer. He said "Go on to the cross-road and stop there and form line of battle."

Testimony read in his hearing.

Captain H. M. Stinson, aide-de-camp on General Howard's staff, a witness for the accused, was duly sworn.

By General Schurz:

Question. Did you see General Schurz on the field during the night of the engagement of Wauhatchie?

Answer. Yes, sir.

Question. Where did you meet General Schurz first, and under what circumstances?

Answer. I met him first as the troops were marching to the relief of General Geary, perhaps half a mile from where our headquarters were that night.

Question. Do you remember where the column received a volley from the hill on the left?

Answer. It was from the hill which was afterward taken by the Second Brigade, Second Division. We were in the field below on the right of the hill going down toward General Geary.

Question. Was the fire returned by the column of General Schurz?

Answer. Not many shots; mostly from the skirmish line.

Question. Did you see General Howard and General Schurz at the time?

Answer. I did; near the head of the column.

Question. State how the column moved, whether quickly or slowly.

Answer. It moved at the same rate that troops generally do; rather faster I think,

Question. What was the nature of the ground over which the troops passed?

Answer. It was a level field the greater part of the way; there were some brooks running through it. It was not particularly swampy until the advanced brigade halted. There it was swampy with thick woods which made it almost impassable for troops.

Question. By whom were you ordered to accompany General Schurz?

Answer. By General Howard. I was not ordered to accompany General Schurz particularly. I was ordered to keep with the advance.

Question. State what happened when the advance reached the boggy place near Tyndale's Hill.

Answer. There they halted for a few minutes; then they were ordered to march to the left to the road, which was done. They then marched forward on the road, and after advancing a few rods they encountered the enemy's fire, and the brigade was halted on the road.

Question. Did some regimens of the advance brigade march up the hill?

Answer. Yes, sir.

Question. Was there not firing from the enemy while the regiments took possession of the hill?

Answer. Yes, sir.

Question. Was there any firing at Geary's at the time when the advance brigade arrived at Tyndale's Hill?

Answer. I think the firing ended just about the time the brigade reached there.

Question. Do you think the troops could have marched much quicker over the ground from where you met them going to Tyndale's Hill, as it then was?

Answer. No, sir.

Question. Did you notice when General Schurz rode back from Tyndale's Hill?

Answer. I knew that he went back, but I do not particularly know when he left.

Question. Do you remember when General Schurz returned to Tyndale's Hill with Colonel Hecker, and what then happened?

Answer. I remember that Colonel Hecker and his brigade arrived there, but I do not remember about General Schurz.

Question. Did you accompany Colonel Hecker to Wauhatchie?

Answer. I did.

Question. How long a time elapsed from the moment when the advance brigade took Tyndale's Hill to the moment when Colonel Hecker arrived?

Answer. I could not say, sir; it was pretty long.

Question. State under what circumstances Colonel Hecker's brigade started from Tyndale's Hill, and whether it was detained on the march.

Answer. As near as I can remember, after the brigade arrived there some patrols were sent out in front, and after they returned, finding nothing in front of them the brigade moved forward to General Geary. There was no halt on the route there.

Question. Can you state with certainty whether the patrols were sent before or after Colonel Hecker's brigade arrived, and where the patrols went?

Answer. I cannot state where the patrols went; I think to the front. I think patrols were sent before Colonel Hecker arrived, and one or two afterward.

By Colonel HECKER:

Question. Who had sent out the patrol?

Answer. I do not know, sir.

Cross-examination of Captain Stinson postponed until next session.

—

HEADQUARTERS ELEVENTH CORPS,
February 4, 1864—10 a. m.

Court met pursuant to adjournment.

Present: Col. A. Buschbeck, Twenty-seventh Pennsylvania, commanding Second Division, Eleventh Army Corps; Col. J. Wood jr., One hundred and thirty-sixth New York, commanding Second Brigade, Second Division, Eleventh Army Corps; Col. P. H. Jones, One hundred and fifty-fourth New York, commanding First Brigade, Second Division, Eleventh Army Corps; Capt. W. H. Lambert, Thirty-third New Jersey Volunteers, recorder.

Proceedings of previous session read.

Testimony of Captain Stinson read in his hearing.

Cross-examination of Captain Stinson:

By the Recorder:

Question. Do you know about what time Colonel Hecker's column reached General Geary?

Answer. Just about dawn. I think it was about 5 o'clock.

Question. Did you see anything of the Second Brigade, Third Division, that night?

Answer. I don't remember having noticed it.

Question. Was Colonel Hecker's column detained by any swampy place in the grounds over which it marched?

Answer. It was not detained by any swampy place while I was with it.

Question. About how long was Colonel Hecker's column in marching from near Tyndale's to where it joined General Geary?

Answer. I cannot tell exactly; I think about twenty minutes.

Question. Was there any firing going on in the direction of Geary's position whilst you were marching toward him?

Answer. No, sir.

Question. Can you tell how long it was since the firing in the front had ceased?

Answer. I cannot.

By the Court:

Question. Were you charged by General Howard with the delivery of any orders to General Schurz?

Answer. When I left General Howard for the last time he told me to go and see that they moved forward rapidly toward General Geary. I gave the order to General Schurz in General Howard's name, that he should push forward as rapidly as possible toward General Geary, or words to that effect.

Question. Do you know whether that order was countermanded or modified in any way?

Answer. Only by what General Schurz told me that he had been ordered by General Hooker to take the hill on the left.

Question. Did you see Lieutenant Oliver, of General Hooker's staff, while on the march?

Answer. I did.

Question. Did he, to your knowledge, deliver any order from General Hooker to General Schurz?

Answer. I did not hear Lieutenant Oliver deliver any order from General Hooker to General Schurz.

Question. Where were you during the time that elapsed after General Schurz went back, until Colonel Hecker arrived with his brigade?

Answer. I was at the foot of Tyndale's Hill, with the exception of about fifteen minutes that I rode to the rear and back.

Question. Did you notice any movement of the enemy during that time?

Answer. There were a few shots from the front. I do not remember whether the hill was taken by Colonel Smith during that time or not.

Question. Did any body of troops pass that hill (Tyndale's Hill) during the absence of General Schurz?

Answer. No, sir.

Question. Did you see General Howard after you left with the orders that he gave you in charge?

Answer. Not until about daylight the next morning after returning from General Geary's.

Question. Did you see General Hooker at or near the Tyndale Hill?

Answer. I did not.

Question. Where did you join General Schurz when you delivered the order?

Answer. Near the swampy ground referred to before.

Capt. ROBERT H. HALL, acting aide-de-camp on General Hooker's staff, a witness for the accused, was duly sworn.

By General SCHURZ:

Question. Did you carry any orders during the night of the engagement of Wauhatchie?

Answer. I did.

Question. What orders did you carry and to whom?

Answer. First, the order to General Schurz to move his nearest brigade, the brigade nearest to General Geary, to his assistance; a similar order to General Howard, and an order to two different commanders on Moccasin Point; an order to the commanding officer of a brigade immediately in the rear of General Hooker's position to send some prisoners to Chattanooga. In reference to this order, I wish to explain that a number of prisoners came in and were questioned by General Butterfield. I was at some distance from the general. He turned to me and said : " Tell the commanding officer of that brigade to send them to Chattanooga." Believing he referred to the brigade itself, I gave the order to the commanding officer of the brigade to march to Chattanooga. Believing this to be an error, I reported what I had done to General Butterfield, and the mistake was corrected before the brigade had marched perhaps 50 yards. I gave another order on the field that night to the commanding officer of a regiment which had broken; and these are all that I remember now.

Question. What brigade was it to the commander of which you gave the order to march to Chattanooga?

Answer. I did not know who was the commanding officer at that time. I did not know whose brigade it was. I have since heard it was Colonel Krzyzanowski's; indeed, I learned that fact the next day.

Question. From whom did you learn the next day that the brigade commander referred to was Colonel Krzyzanowski?

Answer. From some officer on General Hooker's staff, I have forgotten whom. It may have been General Butterfield; I am not certain.

Question. What order did you carry to the commander of the brigade after the mistake was corrected?

Answer. To bring his brigade back to its original position, and to send the prisoners to Chattanooga.

Question. Did not the commander of the brigade go in person to General Hooker or General Butterfield in order to inquire about the correctness of the order?

Answer. Not that I am aware of.

Question. How long were General Hooker and staff near that brigade before the order was given?

Answer. I can form no accurate idea of the time; certainly fifteen minutes.

Question. In what position was the brigade when you delivered the order?

Answer. It was in line perpendicular to the line of hills facing up the valley.

Question. Did General Hooker know that the brigade was there?

Answer. I presume he did; it was a very short distance from us, in General Hooker's rear.

Question. Did you see the commander of the brigade at any time in the presence of General Hooker or General Butterfield?

Answer. I do not remember that I did, and I should have remembered it if I had seen him.

Question. Did you see General Hooker ride or walk about [with] the commanding officers of the troops in position there?

Answer. Indeed, I do not remember.

Question. Were you with General Hooker when he came to that place; and did he then make any inquiry as to what troops those in position there were?

Answer. I was with him, and I heard no inquiry from him of that kind.

Question. Where did you find the commander of the brigade when you delivered the order?

Answer. He was with his brigade, I think, and was in front, close by his men.

Question. Were those troops the nearest to the place where General Hooker stood?

Answer. They were.

By the RECORDER:

Question. About what time of the night was that that General Hooker and his staff were in position in front of that brigade?

Answer. Soon after 1 o'clock on the morning of the 29th.

Question. Did that brigade remain there during the whole time that General Hooker was in front of it?

Answer. General Hooker left his position, I know, before the brigade left its.

Question. Did you see the Second Brigade, Third Division, at any other period subsequently that morning?

Answer. I may have seen it; I do not remember; my attention was not called particularly to it.

Question. Was there any firing going on in the front during the time that General Hooker remained there—in the front toward Wauhatchie?

Answer. There was firing all along the lines, and toward Wauhatchie.

Question. Can you tell by whose orders that brigade was brought into position?

Answer. I cannot.

Question. Did you see General Schurz at any time after that during that morning?

Answer. No; not while the engagement was going on.

11 R R—VOL XXXI, PT I

Question. Did you know what brigade the regiment belonged to that broke?

Answer. I do not know; it was detached, marching singly.

By the COURT:

Question. Where was General Schurz when you delivered the order to him?

Answer. He was at his headquarters, near General Hooker's; it was immediately after the firing commenced.

Question. Did you accompany General Hooker all the time during the night of the engagement?

Answer. I did not.

Question. State where you left him, and where you found him on your return.

Answer. I left him first in camp, and found him about half way from his camp to the position I have mentioned; I left him again in that position, and found him again after the engagement had ceased at the house near that point.

Question. Where did you go when you left him the first time and when you left him the second time?

Answer. The first time, to General Howard's headquarters; second time, to Moccasin Point.

Question. How long were you with General Hooker after delivering the order to General Howard?

Answer. Until some time after the hill (Smith's Hill) had been charged. The firing had nearly ceased when I left him.

Question. Did you see Major Howard, of General Howard's staff, when you were with General Hooker?

Answer. I did.

Question. Did you know that the troops in the vicinity of General Hooker that you have referred to, were a part of General Schurz' command?

Answer. I did not.

Question. Did you see Colonel Hecker while with General Hooker?

Answer. I did.

Question. Can you state what passed between him and General Hooker, or between him and General Hooker's staff officers?

Answer. I cannot.

Question. Do you know of any orders being given by General Hooker to the troops then in his vicinity?

Answer. I do not.

Question. Or by any member of his staff other than you have stated?

Answer. Orders were carried by staff officers to troops in the vicinity; one to General Steinwehr and another to Smith's brigade.

Question. Any others?

Answer. No others the substance of which I remember.

Question. Did Major Howard carry any order from General Hooker, to your knowledge?

Answer. Not to my knowledge.

Question. The brigade to which you gave the order about the prisoners was drawn up in line of battle perpendicular to the line of hills. Do you know that a part of General Steinwehr's command was in that position also?

Answer. I knew that a portion of General Steinwehr's was in the field at some distance on the left of the brigade referred to, but of its formation I knew nothing.

Question. What kind of a night was it?

Answer. It was very clear; a bright moonlight night.

Question. How long did it continue moonlight?

Answer. It continued until morning.

First Lieut. DOMINICUS KLUTSCH, Eighty-second Illinois, a witness for the accused, was duly sworn.

By General SCHURZ:

Question. Were you at General Schurz's headquarters when the alarm took place in the night of the engagement of Wauhatchie?

Answer. Yes, sir.

Question. State what you observed about the orders that were given, and the marching of the troops.

Answer. General Schurz ordered me at night when he retired to call him whenever any alarm might be heard around the camp. It was about quarter to 1 o'clock when I heard the heavy firing and went down to the ambulance, after having called the other officers, to awaken General Schurz. When I was down at the ambulance, Lieutenant Oliver, of General Hooker's staff, in company with Lieutenant-Colonel Otto, came down to the ambulance and reported to General Schurz that he immediately ordered his troops under arms and marched one brigade to the front and have the others follow up the road. Major-General Schurz gave orders to Captain O'Dell to go down to General Tyndale and tell him to have his brigade fall in right away and march toward the picket line toward Wauhatchie. It was at five minutes past 1 o'clock when General Hooker himself passed our headquarters, and asked General Schurz if one brigade had been sent forward and the others ordered to follow up in the road? General Schurz answered, that the first brigade lying right in front of division headquarters was marching accordingly. It was ten minutes past 1 o'clock (I looked at my watch at the time) when the general, with all the troops, was marching toward Wauhatchie. I was to stay behind. Lieutenant-Colonel Otto was directed to communicate the orders given by General Schurz to the Second and Third Brigades.

Question. Did you see Lieutenant-Colonel Otto; where was he, and with whom did you see him?

Answer. I saw him at the division headquarters speaking to Colonel Krzyzanowski, who was asking for instructions. Afterward I saw him going down to the road toward Colonel Hecker's command.

Question. Did you see any of the troops of the Third Division afterward during the engagement?

Answer. Yes, sir. I went through the camps of the First Brigade lying in front of division headquarters, to order the stragglers ahead, and saw about three-fourths of a mile from division headquarters the troops halted. I saw nothing further.

By Colonel HECKER:

Question. Did you see the Third Brigade marching to the front, and that it was halted by Major Howard?

Answer. I heard it was halted by Major Howard, but did not see myself that the major stopped it.

By the RECORDER:

Question. Do you remember the language of the orders given by Lieutenant Oliver to General Schurz?

Answer. You will have your men under arms, and the brigade which is firs ready marched toward the firing.

Question. And do you remember what orders were given by Gen eral Hooker to General Schurz?

Answer. I remember that General Hooker asked General Schurz if he had sen one brigade already, and General Schurz answered that the First Brigade wa marching.

Question. Do you know what orders were given by Lieutenant Colonel Otto to the Second and Third Brigades?

Answer. Not to the Third Brigade, but to the Second Brigade it was said t follow up the road toward the firing.

Question. Did not General Hooker say, "Take the nearest brigad you have and throw it forward as fast as you can," or words to tha effect?

Answer. General Hooker repeated the order which Lieutenant Oliver brough and said that the nearest brigade, or the first one that should be ready, should b sent forward immediately.

Question. Did General Hooker give any other orders relative to th other brigades?

Answer. Not to my knowledge.

Question. Did General Hooker say anything to General Schur about taking the hill on which the skirmish had been on the after noon previous?

Answer. I do not remember.

Question. What troops of the Third Division were those that yo saw halted on the road?

Answer. They were the Second and Third Brigades when I came up wit tragglers.

Question. Do you know how long these brigades remained there

Answer. No, sir. I returned to the headquarters of the division.

The Court then took a recess of an hour and a half.

1.30 p. m.

First Lieut. EUGENE WEIGEL, acting aide-de-camp, Third Divis ion, Eleventh Army Corps, a witness for the accused, was dul sworn.

By General SCHURZ:

Question. Did you accompany General Schurz during the nigh of the engagement of Wauhatchie?

Answer. Yes, sir.

Question. State what came under your observation while you wer with General Schurz.

Answer. I joined General Schurz while he was coming back from Genera Hooker's headquarters, and I heard him give the order to get the First Brigad ready to march to the assistance of General Geary. I then accompanied the gen eral at the head of the brigade in the direction of the firing, and also after we ha taken position on what is now known as Tyndale's Hill. I accompanied the gen eral back to General Hooker's.

Question. Where was it that the brigade at the head of whic General Schurz found himself was first fired upon?

Answer. It was on first filing out of the corn-field opposite what is known Smith's Hill.

Question. Where was General Schurz at the time, and what was
[h]e doing?

Answer. At that time he had just moved to the head of the column and was
[ur]ging the men forward.

Question. State what happened afterward.

Answer. The brigade marched on to what is known as Tyndale's Hill, and just
[be]fore arriving there an aide of General Hooker came up and brought General
[Sc]hurz the order that it would be necessary to take that hill by all means.

Question. Did you see Captain Orlemann of Colonel Krzyza-
[n]owski's staff, on that field?

Answer. I saw him at the time that he brought the report to General Schurz
[th]at the Second Brigade had been stopped by orders from General Hooker, and had
[be]en ordered to Chattanooga.

Question. Did you accompany General Schurz from Tyndale's
[H]ill back, and where did you go with him?

Answer. I did; I accompanied him back to where we found General Hooker.

Question. Where did you find General Hooker?

Answer. We found General Hooker near the farm-house at the foot of Smith's
[H]ill.

Question. Do you remember anything of the conversation that
[to]ok place there?

Answer. I do. General Hooker asked General Schurz why he had not pushed
[th]rough with that brigade to General Geary, upon which General Schurz told him
[th]at one of General Hooker's aides had given him the order to take the Tyndale
[Hi]ll, and that he had no other troops with him. General Hooker told him he had
[gi]ven him the order in person to march through, and at the time did not seem to
[ac]knowledge this order of his aide's.

Question. Did you see Colonel Krzyzanowski at the time?

Answer. I did; Colonel Krzyzanowski was about 10 paces from General Hooker.

Question. State what then happened.

Answer. General Schurz then asked General Hooker if he could now have his
[tw]o brigades and then march the two brigades toward Tyndale's Hill.

Question. Do you remember what disposition was made of Colo-
[ne]l Krzyzanowski's brigade?

Answer. It was halted at the gap between Smith's and Tyndale's Hills, the whole
[of] it with the exception of one or two regiments which accompanied the Third Bri-
[ga]de.

Question. Do you remember what condition the brigade was in as
[to] strength?

Answer. I am not positive, but I think one-half the picket details had been
[th]rown upon it, amounting to about 150 men.

Question. Can you state about when and where Captain Orlemann
[re]ported to General Schurz that the Second Brigade was kept back?

Answer. I think it was a little after this aide of General Hooker had brought the
[or]der to take Tyndale's Hill.

By Colonel HECKER:

Question. Were you present when Colonel Hecker was ordered to
[jo]in General Geary, and when was this?

Answer. Yes, sir; I think it was at the foot of the Tyndale Hill. I cannot state
[th]e time exactly, but it was some time after the hill had been taken.

Question. Was the order executed immediately?

Answer. I think it was after some skirmishers had been thrown out to test the strength of the enemy.

Question. Were patrols sent out; by whom; of what regiment, and where?

Answer. Patrols had previously been sent out from the First Brigade, One hundred and forty-third New York, by order of General Schurz. They were first sent off to the left of the road, and, as it had been reported there was a column of the enemy to the right, they were afterward sent in that direction.

Question. Was there any firing in the direction of Geary's when the Third Brigade arrived at Tyndale's Hill?

Answer. It is my impression there was not.

By the RECORDER:

Question. Did you carry any orders to the Second Brigade before the First Brigade was fired upon from Tyndale's Hill?

Answer. I did not.

Question. After General Schurz had brought up the Second and Third Brigades, who gave an order for the Second Brigade to halt?

Answer. It was an order from General Schurz.

Question. How fast did the First Brigade march?

Answer. They marched a great part of the way at the double-quick until they became entangled in a marsh.

Question. How long were they detained by the marsh?

Answer. But a few minutes; they immediately filed out to the road.

Question. Was there any firing going on in the direction of General Geary's at the time that the First Brigade reached Tyndale's Hill?

Answer. It is my impression there was.

Question. How strong was the Second Brigade before the detachments were made?

Answer. I think it numbered about a thousand men.

Question. Which regiment was the largest of that brigade?

Answer. The One hundred and forty-first.

Question. What was its strength?

Answer. Some 350 men.

Question. Did you hear General Hooker give General Schurz any orders after he had returned from the head of his brigade?

Answer. I heard him give the order to push through now with all speed.

Question. After General Schurz had asked him if he could not have his two brigades, do you remember the language used by General Hooker in giving the order to General Schurz?

Answer. No, sir; I do not remember the words.

Question. How near each other were the Second and Third Brigades when you came up with General Schurz?

Answer. They were within 50 yards of each other, and drawn up, I think, line of battle, and the Second Brigade was facing perpendicularly to the Third.

Question. How near to the Second Brigade was General Hooker?

Answer. Some 30 or 40 yards.

By the COURT:

Question. What member of General Hooker's staff was it that brought the order to General Schurz to take Tyndale's Hill?

Answer. I cannot say. I was not acquainted with the members of General Hooker's staff, and, besides, it was somewhat dark, and I could not distinguish features.

Question. Do you know Lieutenant Oliver?

Answer. I know him now; I did not know him then.

Question. Do you now know that he was the staff officer that came here?

Answer. I know it from having heard that it was. I cannot identify him.

Question. State the whole conversation that occurred between General Hooker and General Schurz at the time they met as you have stated, in the order in which it occurred.

Answer. General Hooker asked General Schurz why he had not pushed through with the brigade with him to General Geary. General Schurz told him that one of General Hooker's aides had halted him at the foot of Tyndale's Hill, and brought him the order to take that hill. General Hooker then told him that he had given him the order in person to push through to General Geary. General Schurz then asked him whether he could now have his two brigades. General Hooker told him to take them and push through with all speed. That is all that I remember.

Question. What did General Hooker say, if anything, about the order carried to General Schurz by the staff officer to attack the Tyndale Hill?

Answer. From his conversation he seemed to ignore that order entirely.

Question. What did he say, if anything, about the two brigades being halted where they were?

Answer. I did not hear him say anything.

Question. At the time the First Brigade halted at the foot of Tyndale's Hill did you hear anything about a line of battle being in front of you?

Answer. I do not recollect.

Question. How long a space of time did it occupy in taking the Tyndale Hill by the First Brigade?

Answer. I think it was about an hour. The crest of the hill was gained in about fifteen minutes; there were still rebels on the other slope of the hill.

Question. Do you recollect the language used by Lieutenant Oliver when he ordered him to take the hill?

Answer. No, sir.

Question. Was it a direct order given by authority of General Hooker, or was it a suggestion of his own?

Answer. I think it was a direct order.

Question. You say that Lieutenant Oliver brought the order to General Schurz to take the Tyndale Hill with that brigade. What was the language used by Lieutenant Oliver in conveying that order to General Schurz?

Answer. I cannot give the exact words, but the spirit of it was that he should take the hill with that brigade.

Question. Was the order communicated by Lieutenant Oliver a

direct order purporting to come from General Hooker, or was it a suggestion of the lieutenant's own?

Answer. It was delivered as a direct order.

Question. Now, what were the words used by Lieutenant Oliver in giving that order?

Answer. That General Schurz should take the hill with that brigade.

Question. Do you remember any remarks that General Schurz made when that order was brought to him?

Answer. General Schurz expressed surprise, as he had before received positive orders to march to General Geary with his brigade.

Question. Did Lieutenant Oliver say anything in return?

Answer. Not that I recollect.

Court adjourned to meet at 10 a. m., February 5, 1864.

—

HEADQUARTERS ELEVENTH CORPS,
February 5, 1864—10 a. m.

Court met pursuant to adjournment.

Present : Col. A. Buschbeck, Twenty-seventh Pennsylvania, commanding Second Division, Eleventh Army Corps; Col. James Wood, jr., One hundred and thirty-sixth New York, commanding Second Brigade, Second Division, Eleventh Army Corps; Col. P. H. Jones, One hundred and fifty-fourth New York, commanding First Brigade, Second Division, Eleventh Army Corps; Capt. William H. Lambert, Thirty-third New Jersey Volunteers, recorder of the Court.

Proceedings of previous session read.

Lieut. Col. THEODORE A. MEYSENBURG, assistant adjutant-general, Eleventh Corps, a witness for the accused, was duly sworn.

By General SCHURZ :

Question. Did you carry any orders to General Schurz during the night of the engagement of Wauhatchie? •

Answer. Yes, sir ; I carried one order directing General Schurz to re-enforce Colonel Hecker's brigade with a part of Colonel Krzyzanowski's brigade, at least by a regiment.

Question. Where was that ; where was Colonel Hecker's brigade, and where was Colonel Krzyzanowski's brigade?

Answer. As near as I can remember, it was about 5 o'clock in the morning. Colonel Hecker's brigade, I believe, had passed what is called the Tyndale Hill, and as General Schurz told me at the time, Colonel Krzyzanowski's brigade was between the Tyndale and the Smith Hills.

Question. Was it not already daylight when you brought the order?

Answer. The day was just breaking.

Question. Did General Schurz ask you any questions as to whether the gap between Smith's Hill and Tyndale's Hill should be left uncovered?

Answer. I think he did. I think General Schurz said if Colonel Hecker were re-enforced by another regiment it would leave very little in the gap. My answer, as near as I can remember, was that the gap should be held, even if it were only by a small force.

By the RECORDER:

Question. Had General Howard previously, to your knowledge, given any orders to General Schurz or any part of his command?

Answer. I do not know of any order previous to that, as I was not with General Ioward until his return from General Geary.

Question. Was Colonel Hecker's column or brigade in motion at he time you carried the order to General Schurz?

Answer. I do not know.

Question. Where was General Schurz at the time you communi-ated the order, and what troops were with him?

Answer. General Schurz was at the foot and west of the Tyndale Hill, on the oad to Wauhatchie. I cannot say what troops were with him.

Question. Do you know how far Colonel Hecker's brigade had narched toward General Geary when you gave the order to General Schurz; whether it had reached him or not at the time?

Answer. To my knowledge, General Schurz had received no report from Colonel Iecker that he had arrived at General Geary's; but a few minutes after I returned o General Howard, who was at General Hooker's headquarters, an aide-de-camp f General Schurz, or of Colonel Hecker, reported that communication had been pened with General Geary.

Question. Do you know whether Colonel Hecker had been already e-enforced from the Second Brigade at the time of delivering the rder from General Howard to General Schurz?

Answer. General Schurz informed me that Colonel Hecker had been re-enforced y a part of Colonel Krzyzanowski's brigade, naming the troops, which I do not emember.

Question. Was there any firing going on in any quarter when you ave the order from General Howard to General Schurz?

Answer. None except stray shots.

By the COURT:

Question. After the firing commenced, and until you joined Gen-eral Howard, after his return from General Geary, where were you?

Answer. I was on nearly all parts of the field.

Question. At what time did General Howard leave the field here o go to General Geary?

Answer. He left Eleventh Corps headquarters at about 1 o'clock, leaving several taff officers, among them myself, at headquarters.

Question. Did you see General Hooker during the engagement; f so, where?

Answer. When the firing commenced near our troops, as I thought, I left head-quarters to join General Howard. I did not find General Howard, but found Gen-ral Hooker.

Question. Where?

Answer. In front of Colonel Krzyzanowski's brigade.

Question. Did you know that General Schurz's command was rdered to the re-enforcement of General Geary?

Answer. No, sir; I did not know that any such order had been given him.

Question. Do you know of any order directing Colonel Hecker or lirecting the Second or Third Brigade to take position where you saw them?

Answer. I do not.

Question. How long did you stay with General Hooker?

Answer. Only a few minutes.

Question. While you were with him, do you know of any orders being given by him?

Answer. I did not hear of any.

Col. F. Hecker, being summoned as a witness by Major-General Schurz, objection was raised by him to receiving his testimony, on the ground he was a party concerned in the subject of investigation before the Court.

Court was cleared, and after due deliberation the doors were opened and decision of Court announced, that the objection was overruled; that either General Schurz or Col. F. Hecker might be called as witness in the case on behalf of the other.

Col. F. HECKER, commanding Third Brigade, Third Division, Eleventh Corps, a witness for the accused, was duly sworn.

By General SCHURZ:

Question. Did you meet General Hooker on the field during the night of the engagement of Wauhatchie, and on what part of the field?

Answer. Yes, sir; near the tree which has now dry leaves upon it at the point where the road turns to the hill.

Question. Did any conversation occur between you and General Hooker concerning Colonel Krzyzanowski's brigade; and if so, what was it?

Answer. I can state as follows: I am not positive whether he asked where the Second Brigade was, or where the other brigade was, or where the other troops of the division were, but my impression is that he asked for the Second Brigade, because I was leaning forward on my horse and pointing with my finger to troops on my left perpendicular to my line of battle. I told him that the Second Brigade, Colonel Krzyzanowski's, was halted there. After some further conversation with me he rode over in the direction of the Second Brigade, and I did not pay any further attention to him, for I was looking toward Wauhatchie, and toward the hills from which there was still firing.

Question. Did you see an aide of General Schurz brought by the cross-road wounded, and about that time?

Answer. Yes, sir; it was Captain Lender, one of my captains in the Eighty-second. It was but a few moments after I had arrived at the cross-roads and before I saw General Hooker. I remember asking him where he was shot, and he said in the leg.

Question. Did you hear the first volley coming from the hills on the left, and where were you when you heard it?

Answer. My attention was most directed to the firing in the front toward Wauhatchie. I heard firing on the left, but I can only state about one volley which came from the hill when I halted and was in conversation with General Hooker; there had been firing previously as I was on the march. When the last shots were fired from the hill upon my troops, this was the moment that I was in conversation with General Hooker.

Question. Did you report to General Schurz your junction with General Geary immediately on your arrival there?

Answer. I am not certain when I had it reported to General Schurz. When I reached General Geary he ordered me to relieve some of his men and bring some of my regiments in their position, and I do not exactly remember when I reported to General Schurz. Captain Stinson, of General Howard's staff, had left me and returned when the junction with Geary was formed

Question. How long were you halted at Tyndale's Hill on your march to Geary, waiting for re-enforcements from the Second Brigade?

Answer. Not very long, but a few minutes, I think; not over eight or ten minutes elapsed from my arrival at Tyndale's Hill to my departure from it. When we arrived at Tyndale's Hill there was firing from it, and from the gap. I gave the order to halt and front, being directed to form line of battle. Then General Schurz ordered me to throw a regiment forward to the gap. I ordered the Seventy-fifth Pennsylvania forward, and went with it myself, and gave instructions to Major Lady [Ledig]. General Schurz, at about the same time, gave me the order, after posting the Seventy-fifth Regiment, to push forward to General Geary. When putting the Seventy-fifth Regiment in the gap, I gave my adjutant-general an order to deploy half of the Sixty-eighth New York as skirmishers and flankers on the railroad and flankers on the right and left of it as reserve. As I had only half of the Eightieth Illinois, General Schurz ordered first the One hundred and nineteenth New York, and as this regiment was small, afterward the One hundred and forty-first, and we marched as soon as I saw the One hundred and forty-first in motion. I did not take more than ten minutes.

Question. How long did you stop at the cross-roads?

Answer. It is difficult to state the length of time, as my attention was directed to an attack that I expected from the hill and from the front. It was quite a long time, three-quarters of an hour, more or less. I had asked some men in the meantime, who thought it was longer.

By the RECORDER:

Question. Can you state the conversation that occurred between General Hooker and yourself?

Answer. While marching on the main road from General Howard's headquarters, in the direction of Wauhatchie, Major Howard came up and asked, "Where is Colonel Hecker?" I answered him, and he gave me an order to halt at the cross-roads ahead of us, and bring my men into position, as there was firing from the hills on our left. I ordered two regiments, the Sixty-eighth New York and the Seventy-fifth Pennsylvania, to form line of battle toward the hill, and the Eightieth Illinois, in rear of the first line in column, doubled on the center. During the execution of this order Major-General Hooker arrived, as I was halting near the tree mentioned before. He asked me, "What troops are these?" I answered, "Third Brigade, Third Division, Eleventh Corps, sir." He asked me why I was halting there, or some words to that effect. I told him I had just received an order of that purport from Major Howard, and he then put to me the question mentioned before about the other troops. As the head of his horse was directed toward Wauhatchie and the head of my horse square toward the hills, I leaned forward and pointed out to him the place where the Second Brigade was. He then ordered me to be ready to form, if necessary, front to the right; that is, front toward Wauhatchie. I gave orders accordingly. I thought he directed me so because he expected an attack, not only from the hill on the left, but from the valley also, as pretty nearly at the same time shots were fired down on the troops and the bullets whistled around us. I thought some of the shots came from the gap. Then General Hooker told me, and I remember the tone of his voice as if he had spoken but a quarter of an hour since, "You stay here, colonel." He then rode over to the Second Brigade.

By the COURT:

Question. What orders did you receive before you left camp?

Answer. The first order that I received was brought by Captain Spraul, which was to march down to the road and form there. I put my column in motion, and, as this order seemed insufficient, I went around to find somebody who could tell me if the order meant only to form there. My adjutant-general informed me that we had to move forward, as I thought the order was to be understood; so we marched until halted by Major Howard. Then when General Schurz came up from the front he took us along, and at Tyndale's Hill the orders were received, as before stated. After General Hooker had asked what troops are these, he asked where is General Schurz? I answered, in front, sir; one of his aides has just been carried along wounded.

Maj. Gen. CARL SCHURZ, commanding Eleventh Army Corps, a witness for the accused, was duly sworn.

By Colonel HECKER:

Question. What orders were given by you to Colonel Hecker on the night of the engagement of Wauhatchie; when and where?

Answer. As soon as the first alarm was given, I sent aides around to the brigades with the order to have the troops under arms. Captain Spraul, one of my aides, went to the Second and Third Brigades with the order to have the troops march forward from the camps to the road, and halt there until further orders. Going to the front myself at the head of the First Brigade, I left my chief of staff, Lieutenant-Colonel Otto, behind with the order to put the two remaining brigades on the road and follow the First Brigade in the direction of Wauhatchie. While marching at the head of the First Brigade, before arriving at Tyndale's Hill, I received the report from Major Howard that the Third Brigade, Colonel Hecker's, was stopped, and under directions from General Hooker. I did not see Colonel Hecker again until after the taking of Tyndale's Hill, when I returned to the place where I found my troops and General Hooker. Upon my order Colonel Hecker marched forward to Tyndale's Hill, halted there a short time, until he was re-enforced by the One hundred and forty-first New York. There I gave him the order to march to Geary, which he executed immediately upon the arrival of re-enforcements. Patrols had been sent out from General Tyndale's command to ascertain whether the report previously received, that a column of the enemy was on our right in the valley, was true or not. Whether Colonel Hecker kept back until the return of the patrol I cannot now distinctly remember, but I do remember that he started off as soon as the One hundred and forty-first New York arrived. The halt made by the Third Brigade at Tyndale's Hill was made by my order. My impression is that the brigade did not halt over ten minutes.

The Court adjourned to meet Monday, February 8, at 10 a. m.

—

[HEADQUARTERS ELEVENTH CORPS,
February 8, 1864]—10 a. m.

Court met pursuant to adjournment.

Present: Col. A. Buschbeck, Twenty-seventh Pennsylvania, commanding Second Division, Eleventh Army Corps; Col. James Wood, jr., One hundred and thirty-sixth New York, commanding Second Brigade, Second Division, Eleventh Army Corps; Col. P. H. Jones, One hundred and fifty-fourth New York, commanding First Brigade, Second Division, Eleventh Army Corps; Capt. W. H. Lambert, Thirty-third New Jersey Volunteers, recorder.

Proceedings of previous session read.

Examination of Lieutenant-Colonel MEYSENBURG resumed.

By General SCHURZ:

Question. Did you see Colonel Hecker's brigade on its march from the cross-roads to Tyndale's Hill; and if so, where and when?

Answer. I met Colonel Hecker's brigade after it had passed the swamp, which is opposite the gap between Smith's and Tyndale's Hills, at about 4.30 a. m.

Question. Do you know exactly where the cross-roads are, and where the swampy place is, and what the distance is between the two places?

Answer. I never measured the distance between the place called the cross-roads and the swampy place.

Question. Did you deliver to General Schurz an order to send Colonel Krzyzanowski forward to Geary?

Answer. I did, I believe, at 7 o'clock in the morning.

Lieutenant WEIGEL, acting aide-de-camp on General Schurz's staff, a witness for the accused, was recalled.

By General SCHURZ:

Question. Do you remember about how many men were killed and wounded in the attack on the hill by Tyndale's brigade, on our side?

Answer. As near as I can recollect, we had 2 killed and some 10 wounded.

By the COURT:

Question. Where were they killed?

Answer. In the charge up the hill.

Question. In what capacity were you acting at that time?

Answer. As acting assistant adjutant-general to General Schurz, Third Division.

The testimony on behalf of the accused was here announced closed.

Major-General HOOKER, a witness for the prosecution, was re-called.

By the RECORDER:

Question. What inquiry, if any, did you make of General Schurz when you rode by his headquarters about 1 o'clock on the morning of the 29th of October?

Answer. I cannot positively state what inquiry, if any, I made at that time.

Question. Did you, at that time, give him the order to double-quick his division to the relief of General Geary?

Answer. I have already said that I took no note of time. I gave him the order, while on my way from my camp, to see that my troops were under arms. I will say there were those of my staff present who perhaps remember the conversation. I know the order was given while at the cross-roads at the foot of the Smith Hill.

Question. Did you see Major Howard, of General Howard's staff, while at the cross-road at the foot of the hill?

Answer. It is my impression that I did see him.

Question. Did he report to you that Colonel Hecker's brigade had arrived?

Answer. Why, it was near there that I saw Colonel Hecker's brigade. I do not know that he reported it. He may have reported to me. I knew it myself.

Question. Before you saw Colonel Hecker's brigade, did you give any orders directing that it should halt there at the cross-roads?

Answer. I did not.

Question. Where did you go after leaving Colonel Hecker at the cross-roads?

Answer. I was facing to the north and Colonel Hecker was facing to the south, and I think I passed off toward the hill.

Question. While at the foot of Smith's Hill, did you, at any period during the engagement, or during that night, see General Schurz?

Answer. I did, in that vicinity, near that time.

Question. Do you know about what time?

Answer. It seemed to me nearly two hours after I met Colonel Hecker. I was in a state of great anxiety at the time, and could not tell exactly, but it seemed to me about that time.

Question. Can you state what conversation took place between you and General Schurz?

Answer. I can state pretty nearly. General Schurz, I think, asked me a question of this kind: "Can I take my other two brigades?" at which I expressed great surprise, saying that I had ordered him to go to the relief of Geary two hours before, and repeated the order.

By General SCHURZ:

Question. Did you have more than one conversation with General Schurz about 1 o'clock?

Answer. Oh, yes; I saw him two or three times before the troops got under way, and something passed between us, I think, each time.

By the COURT:

Question. How near were you to Tyndale's Hill at the time General Tyndale took it?

Answer. I think when it was communicated to me that he had taken it I was close by the Smith Hill.

Question. Were you near enough during its progress to distinguish the nature of the action that occurred there?

Answer. I knew nothing of it; I could not see it.

Question. Was the opposition made by the enemy, judging from the nature of the firing, great or small?

Answer. I think it was a feeble resistance. I should call it a slight skirmish.

Question. Do you know how long it continued?

Answer. While there was firing; I do not know how long. From the time the fire was thrown from the hill on the troops marching to the relief of Geary up to the time that I heard of the taking of the hill, the firing was desultory.

Question. What kind of a night was it?

Answer. I would not call it a bright night or a dark night; it was a medium night. I could tell whether troops were marching in column or by the flank at a distance of 60 yards.

Court adjourned to meet on Tuesday, the 9th instant, at 10 a. m.

—

HEADQUARTERS ELEVENTH CORPS,
February 9, 1864—10 a. m.

The Court met pursuant to adjournment.

Present: Col. A. Buschbeck, Twenty-seventh Pennsylvania, commanding Second Division, Eleventh Army Corps; Col. James Wood, jr., One hundred and thirty-sixth New York, commanding Second Brigade, Second Division, Eleventh Army Corps; Col. P. H. Jones, One hundred and fifty-fourth New York, commanding First Brigade, Second Division, Eleventh Army Corps; Capt. W. H. Lambert, Thirty-third New Jersey Volunteers, recorder.

Proceedings of previous session read.

Maj. Gen. DANIEL BUTTERFIELD, a witness for the prosecution, was duly sworn.

By the RECORDER:

Question. Were you with General Hooker on the morning of the 29th of October?

Answer. I was.

Question. Do you know whether General Schurz met General Hooker after the taking of Smith's Hill?

Answer. He did.

Question. About what time was that?

Answer. I should think it was in the neighborhood of 2 o'clock; I could not state he time precisely.

Question. Do you remember what conversation took place between General Schurz and General Hooker?

Answer. I could not state exactly the words, only the tenor of the conversation. f my memory serves me correctly, General Schurz reported having possession of he Tyndale Hill, and th t he had posted his skirmishers in front. General Hooker sked why he had not moved, as directed, to General Geary, as he had given him he order over two hours before. I do not remember what reply General Schurz made, and he left soon after on that business.

Question. Did you hear the firing on the Tyndale Hill before General Schurz met General Hooker?

Answer. I cannot say. General Hooker's horse was saddled, and he got away efore my horse was saddled. I heard firing, but whether it was from the Tyndale Hill or from the Smith Hill I do not know.

Question. Can you state how long it continued?

Answer. I cannot. When I arrived on the ground all my attention was given to he Smith Hill, for a time.

Question. Can you tell about what time the Smith Hill was taken?

Answer. I should think it was about a quarter past 1 o'clock, but I took no note of the hour and only judge from my knowledge of the time when the firing first broke out.

Question. Was the firing at Tyndale's Hill over as soon as that at Smith's Hill?

Answer. My impression is that there was no firing on Tyndale's Hill after Smith's Hill was taken. Lieutenant Oliver was over at Tyndale's Hill, and he is better informed on that subject than I am.

Question. Was the firing at Tyndale's Hill over at the time of the meeting between General Hooker and General Schurz?

Answer. I think it was.

Question. Do you know whether any obstruction was offered by the enemy to General Schurz's advance to General Geary after leaving General Hooker at the time referred to, the time of the conversation?

Answer. None to my knowledge.

Question. Do you know whether there was at any time a line of battle between General Geary and the division of General Schurz?

Answer. Not to my knowledge; only from the report of staff officers. I was not on the ground.

By the COURT:

Question. Did you see Major Howard, of General Howard's staff, that night?

Answer. Yes, sir.

Question. Did you give directions to him, or to any one, to halt Colonel Hecker's brigade at the cross-roads?

Answer. No, sir; I had a conversation with him on the subject of Colonel Hecker's brigade being there. Major Howard rode up where General Hooker and

staff were, and at the same time Colonel Hecker's brigade was halted there.   I state
to him that there was a brigade that its commander said was halted by Genera
Howard's or General Schurz's order.   I told him he had better look into it and se
about it.

Question. Did you know that Colonel Krzyzanowski's brigade wa
in the same vicinity?

Answer. Well, I was entirely unacquainted with the brigade commanders of th
Eleventh Corps.   I knew only General Schurz and General Steinwehr as divisio
commanders.   I had not been in the immediate vicinity of the brigades until on th
march down, and the first knowledge I got of the several brigade commanders I go
on that night, with the exception of Colonel Buschbeck, who led on the march th
day before.

Question. Did you know that the troops commanded by Colone
Hecker, and the other troops there, were a part of General Schurz'
command?

Answer. No; I did not know it.   I supposed they were a part of General Stein
wehr's command, and did not know until I inquired.

Question. When did you inquire?

Answer. About five minutes before Major Howard rode up I inquired of Colone
Hecker to what division he belonged.   It was but a few minutes after this that w
rode off to a fire near Smith's Hill, where General Hooker saw General Schurz.

Question. Was that the first time that you saw Major Howard?

Answer. I think it was.

Question. At what place did you first see Major Howard?

Answer. Near the cross-roads, near where Colonel Hecker's brigade was.

Question. Did you give an order for a brigade or for any troops t
go to Chattanooga?

Answer. I did not.   I gave an order to Captain Hall to send some prisoners t
Chattanooga.   He misunderstood me, and gave the order to have the brigade go t
Chattanooga, but the mistake was rectified immediately.

Question. Did you know that General Hooker had given the orde
for General Schurz's division to move to the aid of General Geary

Answer. I did.

Question. How did you know it?

Answer. I heard General Hooker give the order to two different aides—one to g
to General Howard and one to go to General Schurz—and then heard him say h
was going to General Schurz himself.

Question. Who were the aides that he sent?

Answer. Captain Hall was one, and the other I do not know; the conversatio
occurred outside of the tent, as I was dressing, and I did not inquire.

Question. Do you know when the enemy crossed Lookout Cree
after their attack on Geary?

Answer. Not from my own knowledge.

First Lieut. PAUL A. OLIVER, aide-de-camp, General Hooker'
staff, was recalled as a witness for the prosecution.

By the RECORDER:

Question. Were you with General Hooker on the morning of the
29th of October, after the taking of Smith's Hill?

Answer. I was.

Question. Did General Hooker have an interview with General Schurz ?

Answer. Yes.

Question. Do you know about what time ?

Answer. It was not long after Smith's Hill was taken ; I do not know the exact time ; it was about 3 o'clock in the morning, not long after Tyndale's Hill was taken.

Question. Do you remember the conversation that occurred between General Hooker and General Schurz ?

Answer. General Schurz told General Hooker that he had taken the hill and had skirmishers in front. General Hooker seemed to be very angry, and asked him " What were your orders, General Schurz—to push through to General Geary immediately?"

Question. Were you present with General Hooker when it was reported to him that the troops of General Schurz had joined General Geary ?

Answer. I do not think I was.

Question. How long did the firing on Tyndale's Hill continue ?

Answer. I do not think it was hardly five minutes ; I should say there were hardly a dozen shots fired from the hill while I was there.

Question. Do you know what loss in killed and wounded there was on our side during the taking of Tyndale's Hill ?

Answer. While I was there I should think there was none.

By the COURT :

Question. In what position was Tyndale's brigade when you left ?

Answer. Part of the troops were still in the road. I think two regiments were marching up the hill. I know some troops were marching up the hill and the balance were in the road. I left there, as I have stated, soon after the conversation with General Schurz.

Question. Did you deliver from General Hooker to General Schurz an order to take that hill at that time ?

Answer. Yes, sir.

Question. What was that order, and where did General Hooker deliver it to you ?

Answer. General Hooker was near his headquarters when he delivered it to me, and the order was to take the hill where we had the skirmish the day before.

Question. And where did you deliver the order to General Schurz ?

Answer. Under the hill, as I have already stated.

Question. Did the order specify what forces were to take the hill ?

Answer. He said one brigade was to take the hill.

Question. In the conversation between General Hooker and General Schurz, testified to by you, when General Schurz said one of your aides directed me to take the hill, what reply did General Hooker make ?

Answer. General Hooker seemed to be very angry. He simply said "What were your orders?" His impression seemed to be that General Schurz had two brigades with him at that time, and one brigade was to go to Geary and one to take the hill.

Question. Did you hear General Hooker give the order to General Schurz to go to General Geary?

Answer. I heard him give an order; whether it was to General Schurz or to General Howard, I did not know. I am under the impression it was to General Howard for one brigade to take the hill and one to go to General Geary.

The recorder announced his case closed.

At the request of Major-General Schurz, the Court adjourned until Friday, 12th instant, to allow him time to prepare his defense.

HEADQUARTERS ELEVENTH CORPS,
February 12, 1864.

The Court met pursuant to adjournment.

Present: Col. A. Buschbeck, Twenty-seventh Pennsylvania Volunteers, commanding Second Division, Eleventh Army Corps; Col. James Wood, jr., One hundred and thirty-sixth New York, commanding Second Brigade, Second Division, Eleventh Army Corps; Col. P. H. Jones, One hundred and fifty-fourth New York, commanding First Brigade, Second Division, Eleventh Army Corps; Capt. W. H. Lambert, Thirty-third New Jersey Volunteers, recorder.

The proceedings of previous session read.

Maj. Gen. Carl Schurz presented his written address (appended and marked B), which was read by himself.

Col. Frederick Hecker, Eighty-second Illinois Volunteers, commanding Third Brigade, Third Division, Eleventh Corps, presented his written address (appended and marked C), which was read by himself.

The Court then adjourned to meet on Monday, the 15th instant, at 11 a. m., at headquarters Eleventh Corps.

HEADQUARTERS ELEVENTH CORPS,
February 15, 1864—11 a. m.

The Court met pursuant to adjournment.

Present: Col. A. Buschbeck, Twenty-seventh Pennsylvania Volunteers, commanding Second Division, Eleventh Army Corps; Col. James Wood, jr., One hundred and thirty-sixth New York Volunteers, commanding Second Brigade, Second Division, Eleventh Army Corps; Col. P. H. Jones, One hundred and fifty-fourth New York Volunteers, commanding First Brigade, Second Division, Eleventh Army Corps; Capt. W. H. Lambert, Thirty-third New Jersey Volunteers, recorder.

After a sitting of two sessions, the Court adjourned until Tuesday, 16th instant, at 9 a. m., headquarters Second Division, Eleventh Corps.

HDQRS. SECOND DIVISION, ELEVENTH ARMY CORPS,
[*February* 16, 1863—9 a. m.]

The Court met pursuant to adjournment.

Present: Col. A. Buschbeck, Twenty-seventh Pennsylvania Volunteers, commanding Second Division, Eleventh Army Corps; Col.

James Wood, jr., One hundred and thirty-sixth New York Volunteers, commanding Second Brigade, Second Division, Eleventh Army Corps; Col. P. H. Jones, One hundred and fifty-fourth New York Volunteers, commanding First Brigade, Second Division, Eleventh Army Corps; Capt. W. H. Lambert, Thirty-third New Jersey Volunteers, recorder.

It was agreed to present the statement of facts and the opinion (appended and marked D), as the statement of facts which the Court deemed established by the evidence brought before it, and as the opinion of the Court, rendered in accordance with the instructions of the order by which the Court was instituted.

The recorder was instructed to present the testimony and proceedings of the Court, with the accompanying papers, to Brigadier-General Whipple, assistant adjutant-general, Department of the Cumberland.

The Court then adjourned *sine die*.

A. BUSCHBECK,
Colonel Twenty-seventh Pennsylvania Volunteers, Comdg.
Second Div., Eleventh Army Corps, Pres. of the Court.
WILLIAM H. LAMBERT,
Captain, Thirty-third New Jersey Vols., Recorder of the Court.

[Appendix A.]

HEADQUARTERS ELEVENTH AND TWELFTH CORPS,
Lookout Valley, Tenn., January 12, 1864.

Brig. Gen. WILLIAM D. WHIPPLE,
Assistant Adjutant-General, Army of the Cumberland:

GENERAL: I have the honor to forward herewith an application of Col. F. Hecker for examination, or a court of inquiry, as it is called by Maj. Gen. Carl Schurz.*

The cause of complaint is based on exceptions to a part of my official report of the battle of Wauhatchie.

It is not known for what reason Colonel Hecker makes this application; or why he should connect his brigade with it.

The order I gave the division commander, was for him to double-quick his division to the relief of Geary, and afterward one brigade of it was ordered to assault the hill on the left. The latter was duly executed; the first order was not. Whether or not Major-General Schurz communicated this order to his brigade commanders, I am not advised. Probably a court of inquiry would be able to determine. It rests between the division commander and the commanders of the Second and Third Brigades, and in no way can other parties be concerned in the issue, unless it be supposed that the troops disobeyed orders, which I have not alleged, and do not believe.

With the application of Colonel Hecker, I also forward a communication from Major-General Schurz, on the same subject, in which he seems to lose sight of the fact that it was to him the order was communicated by me, to double-quick his division to the relief of Geary, and to place the issues between the commander of the Third Brigade, with the brigade itself, and myself. I remember very well the interview I had with Colonel Hecker, and of his informing me

---

*The inclosures following do not appear in the record of the Court, but were found with the original of General Hooker's letter in the files of the Department of the Cumberland.

that he was in his position by order of Major-General Howard. General Howard was advised of the orders General Schurz had received; hence I concluded that the Third Brigade was halted, awaiting orders in execution of the movement; even then I was under the impression that the balance of the division was in advance.

As the quickest and most satisfactory way of disposing of this issue, I would recommend the appointment of a court of inquiry, provided it should be the wish of those interested.

I have inclosed a copy of this letter to Major-General Schurz.

Very respectfully, your obedient servant,

JOSEPH HOOKER,
Major-General, Commanding.

[Inclosure No. 1.]

HDQRS. THIRD BRIG., THIRD DIV., ELEVENTH CORPS,
Raccoon Valley, Tenn., January 10, 1864.

Maj. Gen. CARL SCHURZ,
Commanding Third Division:

SIR: In the interest of the officers and men under my command, in the interest of justice and truth, and my own honor as a man and soldier, that has been during a long life without a stain, I address you these lines.

The official report of Major-General Hooker, of the battle at Wauhatchie, came to my hands to-day, and concludes as follows:

I regret that my duty constrains me to except any portion of my command in my commendation of their courage and valor. The brigade dispatched to the relief of Geary, by orders delivered in person to the division commander, never reached him until long after the fight had ended. It was alleged that it lost its way, when it had a terrific infantry fire to guide it all over the way; and that it became involved in a swamp, where there was no swamp or other obstacle between it and Geary which should have delayed it a moment in marching to the relief of its imperiled companions.

An official document, a historical document, must be based on truth, and render justice to all concerned.

I shall and must defend my honor with all means possible, and the present petition is one of them.

I therefore lay before you all that occurred during the night of 28th–29th October, 1863, so far as myself and my command were concerned.

Camping amongst the men of my brigade, I heard a heavy firing in the direction of Wauhatchie. Without waiting for orders, I ordered my men to fall in, and had the regiments in line of battle and ready to march, so that when Captain Spraul, aide-de-camp of Major-General Schurz, arrived with the order to march, and to guide us, I immediately started with my command from the hill, where I was encamped, down to the main road.

As all the brigades marched at the same time, there was some throng in the valley; and I marched forward to the front, immediately behind Tyndale's brigade, and would have marched till finding Major-General Schurz, who, as I ascertained, had gone to the front, if I had not been stopped by Major Howard, of Major-General Howard's staff, who ordered me to halt until further orders, and bring my men in position, front to the left, toward the hills. I placed the Sixty-eighth New York Volunteer Regiment and Seventy-fifth Pennsylvania Volunteers in line of battle, the Eightieth Illinois Volunteers in column, doubled on the center in second line and the interval between the two first named regiments.

During this operation arrives Major-General Hooker and staff. His question, addressed to me in person, was, "What troops are these?" "Third Brigade, Third Division, Eleventh Corps, sir," was my answer. "Where is Major-General Schurz?" he further asked. "In front, sir; one of his aides-de-camp was just carried along here wounded," was my reply. He asked then where the Second Brigade was, and as it had formed to my left at a short distance in an open field, I pointed it out to Major-General Hooker, showing him where the commander of the brigade had halted.

Major-General Hooker ended this conversation with the following words: "You stay here." "All right, sir," was my answer. Then he rode over to the Second Brigade (Krzyzanowski's), and I remained, according to orders, until, a considerable time afterward, called off by Major-General Schurz, who came back from the front. Marching up to the road, at the foot of the hill near the gap, the troops were halted a moment, where we met General Tyndale. I was ordered to bring one regiment, the Seventy-fifth Pennsylvania Volunteers, to the foot of the hill, at the entrance of the gap, and to march then to form, at all hazards, a junction with General Geary.

The Seventy-fifth Pennsylvania Volunteers was ordered in its position, and without losing a single moment I marched forward to Wauhatchie, the Sixty-eighth New York Volunteers, with advanced guards, flankers, and skirmishers in front, on the right and left, so that under all emergencies the enemy could not escape my attention, and I could meet him in all directions. I marched at the head of the troops [sic] the only regiment of my brigade, the Eightieth Illinois, and beside the One hundred and forty-first New York Volunteers, detached to me for that expedition by Major-General Schurz (the Eighty-second Illinois Volunteers being left at Russell's Mines to guard the gap). It did not take twenty-five minutes' marching, since I received the order to join General Geary, and I had formed the junction with him, reported to him, and he "was very glad to see me." At this time it was so dark that at 50 yards you could not easily distinguish the objects. I must observe that I was, during all this time, accompanied by Captain Stinson, aide-de-camp of Major-General Howard. As we marched on the main road no swamps were met, nor the road lost. From the moment I received the orders, I marched straight ahead, without interruption, to lose no time.

There was no terrific infantry fire at the time when I received the marching orders, and during the whole march to General Geary, from the moment I received the order, there was no firing at all in the direction we were marching to.

I never in my whole military life failed to do my duty, and so far as courage and valor are concerned, nobody has doubted it or shall doubt it. As I have been reproached without foundation, in a public document, all transactions in this case, of course, are of a public character; I therefore most respectfully pray,

Whereas, the official report of Major-General Hooker of the battle of Wauhatchie, just published, implies that my brigade was delaying in proceeding to the relief of General Geary, wanting courage and valor, unless he will publicly retract it, and fully exonerate me, I most respectfully demand a court of inquiry.

Your most obedient servant,

F. HECKER,
Colonel, Commanding Brigade.

[Inclosure No. 2.]

HEADQUARTERS THIRD DIVISION, ELEVENTH CORPS,
January 10, 1864.

Major-General HOOKER,
Commanding Eleventh and Twelfth Corps:

GENERAL : To-day I saw for the first time your official report on the engagement of Wauhatchie. It contains very strong reflections upon one of my brigades, which is stated to have been "dispatched to the relief of Geary, and never reached him until long after the fight had ended."

The wording of the paragraph referred to leaves it somewhat uncertain who was responsible for this delay, although it is stated that "the order was directed in person to its division commander."

Yet the expressions used are such as to throw the responsibility rather upon the brigade commander and the troops. Against this I would most respectfully remonstrate. The brigade commander in question, Colonel Hecker, is a man of more than ordinary spirit, activity, promptness, and gallantry, and his troops are as good as any in the service.

Believing that he and his command did on that occasion all they were ordered to do, and did it with conscientiousness and alacrity, I beg leave to assume the responsibility for their conduct, if any mistakes, or any violation of orders, were committed.

Some of the statements contained in your report concerning this matter, permit me to say, seem to rest upon a grave misapprehension. In recounting a few facts, I mean to furnish a supplement to my official report.

When we heard the firing in the direction of Geary's camp, you ordered me to take the troops nearest at hand, which was Tyndale's brigade, and to move forward as rapidly as possible.

The men were soon under arms, and after having sent one of my aides to my other brigade commanders, whose camps were farther back, with the order to move at once down to the road, I placed myself at the head of General Tyndale's brigade in order to direct its march. General Howard joined me there, and we remained together for a time, hurrying on the advance of the column under the fire of the enemy, until we arrived at a marshy place, covered with thick brush-wood (which your report states not to exist), where General Howard, after having ascertained the extreme difficulty of penetrating, left me in order to go to Geary by a *détour.* Tyndale's brigade had to march by the left flank up to the road, and then proceeded to accomplish the object for which, in the language of your report, it had been "detached." It attacked the enemy "in the hills on the left," and after a short engagement gained possession of the hill. I had been constantly at the head of the column until this brigade was properly placed in position.

Your report about this part of the transaction runs thus :

Directions were immediately given for one of the brigades *en route* (Tyndale's) to be detached and assault the enemy in the hills on the left, and the other brigade to push on as ordered.

By this it is acknowledged that the task assigned to Tyndale was the one he accomplished, but where was the other brigade which was to "push on as ordered ?"

To clear up this point, I must introduce the statements of those concerned.

Immediately upon the receipt of my order, the rest of my troops marched down from their camping places to the road. Colonel Hecker, who was at the head of the column, had not advanced very far, closely upon the heels of Tyndale, when he was stopped by an order to halt. This order was delivered by Major Howard, of General Howard's staff, and is said to have come from you. Major Howard had hardly left Colonel Hecker when you rode up in person. You stopped and asked the colonel "What troops are these?" "Third Brigade, Third Division, Eleventh Corps," was the reply. You asked, "Where is General Schurz?" "He is in front," answered Hecker, "and one of his aides was just brought by here wounded." After having made an inquiry about my Second Brigade, which Colonel Hecker pointed out to you, you left him, saying, "You stay here," and rode on to Colonel Krzyzanowski, with whom you halted.

What your conversation with him was, I do not know, and I have now no means of ascertaining, as Colonel Krzyzanowski is absent. But I do know that Colonel Krzyzanowski, upon what was said, although ready to march, continued to stand still, remaining continually in your presence until called off by me in person.

Thus the troops were halted there, and the brigade which was to "push on to Geary," as ordered, was kept back by your own order.

After this had happened, and after Tyndale's brigade was properly placed in the position assigned to it, I hurried back to the place where the rest of my troops were. Colonel Hecker was still where you had ordered him to stay, and Colonel Krzyzanowski I found in your immediate presence. If their troops were the column to be "pushed on to Geary," as ordered, I may respectfully ask why they had been ordered to stop, and why permitted to stand there so long a time under your very eyes and within the reach of your voice?

When coming up to you and reporting that Tyndale's brigade was in the position assigned to it, and asking for further instructions, you asked me "why I had not pushed a column to Geary?" I replied that only Tyndale's brigade had been at my disposal, and that brigade had been directed to occupy the hill near the railroad gap. You ordered me then to push on a column to Geary without delay, and to my question whether I could now have the rest of my troops, as I would have to give up the important position held by Tyndale, if I used his brigade for that purpose, you replied, I might take them all. I then ordered Colonel Hecker forward. He marched through to Geary without delay. Colonel Krzyzanowski, with one regiment and a fraction, was placed by my order in the gap, through which the main road runs. Colonel Hecker's movement was executed in as brief a space of time as it could be done. Your report speaks of its being alleged that "this brigade lost its way and became involved in a swamp, where there was no swamp or other obstacle." Nobody alleges any such thing with regard to this brigade, for it marched through to Geary on the road.

It was General Tyndale's brigade which was detained, although not long, by marshy and brushy ground in its front, to the existence of which General Howard, who was present, can testify, as well as myself. Yet General Tyndale's brigade is not blamed for it, as it accomplished its object in dislodging the enemy from the hill on the left. But the other brigade is blamed, although it was not so delayed at all.

That this column arrived at General Geary's camp after the

fighting had ceased, is very natural, for the fighting there cease
about the time when my first brigade took the hill assigned to i
In fact, if Tyndale, in disregard of the order to dislodge the enem
from the hill on the left, had moved on to Geary on a bee-line,
would have been impossible for him to reach Geary until after th
fighting had ceased. But Hecker, after having been halted by you
order, was moved forward from a position much farther back, som
time after this; and how he could be expected to reach Geary *befor*
the fighting had ceased, I cannot understand. Nor can he, or any
body else, be blamed for not having pushed on before the orde
stopping him was withdrawn.

I would respectfully submit that it is rather hard for an office
and a body of troops to be solemnly excepted from the commenda
tion for courage and valor bestowed upon other troops, after hav
ing done all they were told to do, and nothing less. If, indeed
somebody must be blamed, I would rather claim the blame entirel
for myself, than permit it to fall, even by construction, upon m
subordinate commanders and their men, who bear no responsibilit
in this matter, and always executed orders with promptness an
alacrity.

I may have erred in not sending to you for that part of my com
mand which was kept back, but I was obliged to suppose that yo
wanted it for some other purpose. And why was it not sent forwar
to me if it was not wanted where it was?

However this may be, I would most respectfully and earnestl
request you to exonerate my subordinate commanders and troop
from the grave accusation cast upon them, and to let the censur
fall where it belongs.

This letter accompanies a request by Colonel Hecker for a publi
exoneration from the censure inflicted on him and his brigade b
your report, or a court of inquiry. Colonel Hecker is a gallant
untiring, and conscientious officer, and a gentleman of a characte
and reputation which any man might be proud of. I sincerely trus
that in this case, where his conduct was strictly governed by orders
and he did his whole duty, justice be not withheld from him.

Very respectfully, your obedient servant,

C. SCHURZ,
Major-General.

[Appendix B.]

In submitting the case to this Court of Inquiry, I am obliged t
notice a circumstance which is of a delicate nature, but about whicl
I shall speak with entire frankness. I asked for this investigation
and it was granted. The manner in which it was granted deviate
in a remarkable degree from the recognized usages of military life
I think there never was a military court in the army of the Unitec
States, not one member of which held an equal rank with the ac
cused; and I doubt whether there ever was a court of inquiry in thi
army, all the members of which belonged to the command of the ac
cuser. I am far from intending any reflection upon the Court, as i
is now constituted; for there is probably no man in the army whe
has less of the pride of rank in him than I; nor do your official re
lations to the accuser in this case give me any uneasiness as to you
impartiality. But I wish to observe that in accepting the form i
which this investigation was offered to me, I had to waive a questior

of propriety.   In justice to you, I waived that question without hesitation; in justice to myself, I have to notice it.

In Major-General Hooker's report of the night engagement of Wauhatchie, we find the following paragraph:

> I regret that my duty constrains me to except any portion of my command in my commendation of their courage and valor.   The brigade dispatched to the relief of Geary, by orders delivered in person to its division commander, never reached him until long after the fight had ended.   It is alleged that it lost its way, when it had a terrific infantry fire to guide it all the way, and also that it became involved in a swamp, where there was no swamp or other obstacle between it and Geary which should have delayed it a moment in marching to the relief of its imperiled companions.

By this paragraph I considered myself and my command deeply wronged.   This censure has gone forth into the world, and I asked for a fair investigation of the charge, the result of which shall be as public as the charge itself.   You are ordered, after having investigated the circumstances connected with the case, to give an opinion whether the strictures contained in the above paragraph in General Hooker's report were deserved by the conduct of myself or Colonel Hecker, or any part of my command, during the engagement of Wauhatchie.   These strictures imply that a part of my command, directed to perform a certain task by orders delivered to me in person, rendered itself liable to be solemnly excepted in a commendation for courage and valor bestowed on other troops, or, in other words, to be stigmatized as lacking courage and valor.   To show the injustice of the reflection, I shall recount the occurrences of that night strictly according to the evidence before you.

On the evening of the 28th of October, the two divisions of the Eleventh Corps encamped near Brown's Ferry.   The command of General Geary lay at Wauhatchie.   The troops had arrived not long before dark.   The distance between the two encampments was about 3 miles, the country which separated them partly open, partly covered with woods and thickets, and here and there intersected by marshy water runs.   The road from Wauhatchie to Brown's Ferry was muddy, but not impassable; the ground alongside of the road in places wet and difficult of passage.   The night was pleasant; the light of the full moon from time to time obscured by streaks of clouds.

After midnight we were aroused by the sound of musketry, heard in the direction of Geary's camp.   The liveliness of the firing indicated an attack.   The troops were called under arms; orders were brought to me by two of General Hooker's aides and by General Hooker himself.   About the nature of these orders the testimony conflicts.   General Hooker says he ordered me to double-quick my whole division to the relief of Geary.   General Butterfield says the same, but he heard only the orders General Hooker gave two of his aides to transmit to me, one of whom was charged to communicate the same orders to General Howard.

The two aides referred to, Captain Hall and Lieutenant Oliver, testify that they delivered to me orders from General Hooker to throw forward the brigade nearest at hand.   General Butterfield is therefore mistaken.   One of my staff officers, who was present when General Hooker gave me his orders in person, states that I was ordered to throw forward my nearest brigade, Tyndale's, at once, and to follow up the movement with the rest of my command.   This has the weight of the testimony in its favor, and it agrees with my recollec-

tions. The difference, however, is not very material, as the manner
in which I executed the order, answered even General Hooker's
version of the story. The troops were soon in motion, and even
General Hooker admits that the turning out of the troops was
splendid. As soon as the alarm was given, and before the order to
march had reached me, I had sent one of my aides to my Second and
Third Brigades, to bring the columns from the camps down toward
the road. Then, leaving my chief of staff behind for the purpose of
superintending the movement of the Second and Third Brigades,
which were ordered to follow the First, I placed myself at the head
of Tyndale's column, and directed its march toward the firing. It is
proved that the orders I left to my chief of staff to transmit were
correctly given, first by Captain Greenhut, assistant adjutant-general of the Third Brigade, who received them, and then by Lieutenant Klutsch, who heard them communicated to the commander of
the Second Brigade.

These orders were not only correctly given, but also correctly executed, for it is proved that the troops marched without delay and
in the right direction, following the advance. No military man will
pretend that these orders were not answering the object and fitting
the circumstances. The ground over which I had to march was not
reconnoitered outside of the road. The only indication we had of
the intentions of the enemy was the firing at Wauhatchie. If the
attack on Geary was serious, it was not only possible but probable,
that the enemy occupied some position in the valley in order to protect their rear. This would have been correct, and was therefore probable. Whether we would meet them, where, and in what strength,
we had to find out ; and, in order to find it out, I placed myself at
the head of the advance. To give, in this state of absolute uncer-
tainty, special instructions to brigades marching in the rear to do
this or to do that, would have been absurd. Their part in the action
depended upon circumstances, and the circumstances had first to be
ascertained. My orders covered this case completely. According to
them, my brigades were to be at hand, to be used as circumstances
would demand, and the testimony shows clearly enough that they
would have been at hand had not other agencies interfered. Relying upon their following me, I pushed forward skirmishers in advance. The evidence shows that on the ground, as it then was,
troops could not be moved with more speed. When opposite the
hill, now known as Smith's Hill, the head of the column received a
volley from the left.

It was on this occasion that one of my aides, of whom the testimony
speaks, was wounded by my side. The head of the column stopped
a moment, fired a few shots in return, and upon the order to cease
firing, pushed on again toward Wauhatchie. Meanwhile, the firing
on Smith's Hill became lively ; it was evident that our troops were
engaged with the enemy on that spot. At the same time, the firing
near Geary's camp died gradually away.

General Howard, who had been with my column, and left it not
long before we reached the foot of the hill afterward known as Tyndale's, sent me word through Captain Stinson, one of his aides, that
he desired me to move forward as rapidly as possible. Soon afterward the skirmishers became entangled in a boggy thicket, which
was impenetrable for troops. We had left the road at a place a few
rods behind, where it makes a slight turn, and moved forward on a
bee-line. The skirmishers were recalled, and after a stoppage of a

few moments, the column regained the road by a movement to the left.

While this was going on, I received notice that my Third Brigade had been halted near Smith's Hill, and was under instructions from General Hooker himself, and also that the Second Brigade had been halted, by order of General Hooker, and was to go to Chattanooga. I received this notice, as the evidence shows, with regard to the Third Brigade, through Major Howard, of the corps staff, and with regard to the Second Brigade, through Captain Orlemann, a member of the Second Brigade staff.   Until then I had been firmly believing that the Second and Third Brigades were following me, according to orders, and the testimony proves this belief to have been very well founded until the brigades arrived near Smith's Hill.

About the same time, I received through Lieutenant Oliver, of General Hooker's staff, the order to take and occupy the hill now known as Tyndale's, with one brigade.   I replied to Lieutenant Oliver that I was ordered, by General Hooker himself, to push through to Geary.   I informed him expressly of the notice I had received about my other brigades, and that, if I placed the only brigade I had in hand on that hill, I would have no troops to send to Geary.   He observed that General Hooker wanted to have the hill occupied with a brigade, and repeated the order.   While this order struck me as contradictory to orders originally received, it struck me, also, that circumstances might have changed.   The firing at Geary's camp, as the testimony shows, had died out.   For some time the action had been far more lively in my rear than in my front.   The enemy had perhaps made a new movement.   The order delivered by Lieutenant Oliver was, indeed, not in keeping with General Hooker's original order, but General Hooker, as I was informed by two reliable staff officers, had kept back my two brigades, and that was likewise against the original understanding, and could hardly be without a sufficient cause.   The word General Howard had sent me through Captain Stinson could hardly come into consideration.   General Howard had been with my column and left it not long before; he would hardly be informed of what was going on in the rear; but, above all, the order brought by General Hooker's aide was positive. General Hooker was highest in command on the field.   This was his last order, and according to all military rules, it is the last order that counts.   I had no choice.

The testimony given by Lieutenant Oliver, when first on the stand, is remarkable in one respect.   While he expresses himself, with an air not uncommon among young staff officers, about other matters, how he ordered this and ordered that, he seems to leave it somewhat in doubt whether the order to take and occupy the hill was a suggestion of his own, or an order from General Hooker.   If it had been a suggestion of his own, if he really had given an order without due authority from his chief, his conduct would be open to grave charges; for that he delivered it as a positive order is proved by another witness, who heard him deliver it.   But to his justification it may be said, that his memory does not appear to be of the most faithful as to details.   He saw and heard my whole advance brigade halt and fire, when the other witnesses heard only a few scattered shots.   He heard of a line of battle in our front at Tyndale's Hill, a thing which would have been so important that every officer on the ground would have known or heard of it, but none of the other witnesses remember any such thing.

His conversation with me, as he reports it, must be taken with the same grain of allowance ; it is only the substance of it which can be accepted as reliable.   But there are three things which leave no doubt of the genuineness of this order ; all three of which show that I acted correctly in obeying it, and two of which bear out Lieutenant Oliver in giving it.   The first is, that Lieutenant Weigel, who heard Lieutenant Oliver deliver it, testifies that it was a direct and positive order ; the second is, that General Hooker, in his report, in his letter and in his testimony, states that the order was given by him and duly executed by me, and the third is, that Lieutenant Oliver reported the fact immediately to General Hooker, and General Hooker received the report with silent approbation.   General Hooker is very clear and positive about this matter, and it is perhaps the only point about which his testimony is not in conflict with that of other witnesses.   No doubt is admissible.

Let me continue my account of the occurrences which now took place.   Three regiments were sent up the acclivity and gained the crest with a loss of a few killed and wounded.   Lieutenant Oliver indeed heard but a very few shots, hardly any.   He heard perhaps not as many shots as we had men killed and wounded.   It is in keeping with his other statements about details.

But he testifies, also, that he left very soon after he had given me the order, and went back to General Hooker to report to him.   When he left, part of the brigade was still in the road.   If the firing had really been as he describes it, Generals Hooker and Butterfield, who were behind me at a considerable distance, would hardly have noticed it.   My situation was now as follows : Knowing that Lieutenant Oliver, General Hooker's aide, had gone back to General Hooker, and having informed him of the circumstance that after taking the hill I had no troops to send to Geary, as the balance of my command was kept back, I was justified in expecting that Lieutenant Oliver would give General Hooker a true and complete report of what had happened, for that is one of the duties of a staff officer.   If, then, anything was found to be wrong, or not in accordance with General Hooker's views, I had a right to expect that General Hooker would correct the mistake by sending me further orders, for Lieutenant Oliver, having just left me, he knew well where I was.

Meanwhile, being ordered to occupy the hill, the importance of which consisted in its commanding one of the few passes leading through that chain of ridges, we proceeded to do it as it ought to be done.   When we had obtained possession of the crest, the troops were properly put in position.   Such parts of the line as were loose and weak had to be strengthened, connections established, [and] a reserve placed in a suitable location.   The wounded were carried to the rear; patrols were dispatched to explore the ground in our front and [on] our flanks; the skirmishers were thrown forward.   It was reported by an officer that he had seen something like a column passing to our right.   Patrols were sent in that direction to ascertain the truth of the statement.   The completion of such arrangements will, under all circumstances, take some time, especially in the night, and on uneven and densely wooded ground, where nothing can be discerned with certainty, even at a moderate distance.   During that time Lieutenant Oliver might well have reported to General Hooker.   General Hooker might well have taken things into consideration, and sent me new orders if anything was not in accordance with his views.   I received no further orders.

The firing had, meanwhile, ceased at all points, except a few straggling shots here and there, such as skirmishers will fire at random
in or after a night engagement, and I was justified in supposing that
everything was as desired, so I went back in order to see what had
happened there. I found General Hooker in the midst of my two
brigades, which had been stopped on the way when following me.
Our conversation was of a singular nature. As the testimony indicates, he showed his dissatisfaction with my not pushing through to
Geary. I replied that I had received his positive order, through one
of his own staff officers, to occupy the hill near the railroad gap with
one brigade, and that the only brigade with me thus being disposed
of, I had no troops to push through to Geary. He observed that he
himself had given me the order to push through to Geary two hours
ago, and ordered me to do so now. I asked whether I might now
have the brigades which had been kept back, and upon his reply that
I might take them, I marched off.

This is the substance of the conversation according to the evidence. One of the witnesses who reports it gives it also as his impression that General Hooker, from what he said, seemed to disown
the order delivered to me by Lieutenant Oliver. Taking this as absolutely correct, we would be forced to one of two conclusions, either
General Hooker had really not given the order—but that is impossible, as he afterward so repeatedly and emphatically declared that he
did give it—or General Hooker had led me into a snare by first giv-
ng me an order and then disowning it, a supposition as unreasonable as it would be unworthy. Lieutenant Oliver, who also listened
to the conversation, gives it as his impression that General Hooker
supposed I had another brigade with me aside of Tyndale's. Accord-
ng to him, therefore, General Hooker must have thought that in some
manner some of my troops must be possessed of ubiquity.

But Lieutenant Oliver well knew this supposition to be erroneous.
According to his own testimony, I had informed him at the foot of
the Tyndale Hill that my other brigades were held back, and that if
I occupied the hill with one brigade I could not re-enforce Geary,
as I had nothing in hand to do it with. But he testifies, also, that,
when reporting to General Hooker the taking of Tyndale's Hill, he
said nothing to him of my having only that one brigade in hand. I
had been careful to give him all the information that was important.
There my duty ended and his commenced. That he did not communicate the whole of that information to his chief is a thing which I
have not to answer for. My responsibility does not extend to General Hooker's staff. But aside of all this, how it was possible for
General Hooker to suppose that I had more than one brigade with
me when taking the Tyndale Hill, you will find difficult to explain
when you hear and consider what meanwhile had happened.

Still, as the question whether I or somebody else bears the responsibility for the staying behind of the balance of my command seems
to be the point upon which this whole matter hinges, I shall return
to it in order to discuss it more fully after having sufficiently eluci-
dated the rest of my movements. The testimony shows that as soon
as I resumed command of my Second and Third Brigades I marched
forward. In passing I had the gap between Smith's and Tyndale's
Hills hastily reconnoitered, and ascertained that it was not held by
any troops. This is the gap through which the main Chattanooga
road runs, the road upon which a part of the enemy's force had come
into the valley. I ordered Colonel Krzyzanowski to take position on

this important thoroughfare with a portion of his brigade, which was decimated by picket and other details, while another portion was directed to join Colonel Hecker in marching to Geary. Arrived at Tyndale's Hill, Hecker's brigade was ordered to halt a little while, for the purpose of awaiting the re-enforcement, which arrived promptly. A regiment was thrown forward into the gorge through which the railroad runs, and as soon as the One hundred and forty-first New York, the strongest regiment of the Second Brigade, had closed up on Hecker's column, Hecker was ordered to march forward to Geary. He executed the order without delay. The ground between Tyndale's Hill and Wauhatchie was mostly covered with thick woods on both sides of the road. The column marched in a formation, which is proper in the presence of the enemy, front and flanks well covered with skirmishers. It arrived at Geary's position about 5 o'clock, and we are told that Geary met Hecker at 5.30. The day was just breaking.

Here I wish to say a word about the estimates of time occurring in the testimony. It must have struck you that these estimates, as given by the witnesses, are exceedingly uncertain and contradictory. Hardly anybody looked at his watch. An interval between two occurrences, which seemed to General Hooker nearly two hours, seemed to General Butterfield about five minutes. I abstain throughout from referring to the testimony of the latter because his recollection has evidently lost the thread of events. An interval of time appeared to an individual longer or shorter, as his attention was more or less engaged, or his mind possessed of greater or less anxiety. Thus the duration of the stay of the Second and Third Brigades at the cross-roads is evidently underestimated by most if not all our witnesses.

About the time occupied by the movement from the cross-roads to Geary we are fortunate enough to have very precise data. Lieutenant-Colonel Meysenburg met the column at the marshy run about 250 to 300 yards from the cross-roads. He looked at his watch; it was about 4.30. There the troops had to undouble files, which inevitably delays the march of a column a little. From that place to Wauhatchie the distance is not far from 2 miles. Taking into consideration that a little time may have elapsed between Colonel Hecker's arrival at Wauhatchie and his meeting with Geary, it may be concluded with reasonable certainty that his whole march from the cross-roads to Wauhatchie, a march with skirmishers and flankers through a wooded country and over muddy roads, occupied, inclusive of all delays, not over forty-five minutes, probably less. It is proved that this brigade never lost its way or became involved in a swamp, and nobody alleged so. This, I submit, was as quick a night march as anybody could desire; certainly as quick as anybody could execute. That Colonel Krzyzanowski reported to Geary much later is very natural. I had placed him with a fraction of his brigade into the gap, while a large portion of his command went to Geary with Colonel Hecker. That this measure was approved and adopted by my superiors in command is easily shown. Lieutenant-Colonel Meysenburg, assistant adjutant-general of the Eleventh Corps, testifies that I was ordered to send re-enforcements to Hecker, which I had already done, but not to evacuate the gap, even if I could leave only a small force in it. I had directed Colonel Krzyzanowski to stay there in person, because I considered the position important, and because it was held by fractions of several regiments. Lieuten-nt-Colonel Meysenburg testifies further that Colonel Krzyzanowski was ordered at 7 o'clock to join Geary with the rest of his command. Thus I acted under orders. This accounts sufficiently for the time of Colonel Krzyzanowski's arrival at Wauhatchie. With the manner in which these movements were executed, nobody that I know found fault, and I would not have dwelled upon these matters at such length had not the prosecution shown some disposition to shift from the censure contained in General Hooker's report upon a new ground, in order to detect by minute microscopic research perhaps a little flaw in those of my proceedings which had not yet been blamed.

In General Hooker's report the brigade dispatched to the relief of Geary is blamed for not having arrived there until long after the fight had ended. This cannot apply to the movements just described, for it is proved that when Hecker was ordered forward from the cross-roads, the fight at Wauhatchie had long been over. To blame him for not arriving there before the fight was over, when it was already over before he started, would have been an absurdity. The occurrence which called forth the censure, must have happened previous to the last movements. The report itself, together with General Hooker's letter and testimony, establishes the point beyond controversy. The report says:

Directions were immediately given for one of the brigades *en route* to Geary Tyndale's) to be detached and assault the enemy in the hills on the left, and the other brigade to push on as ordered.

A brigade was to push on to Geary, while Tyndale's brigade took possession of the hills on the left. Why did it not push on? He who is clear of the responsibility for this failure to push on ought to be clear of the censure. This is the point, and the only point to be decided.

I will state the circumstances which occasioned this failure strictly according to the testimony of five witnesses, all agreeing on the main points. Look back to the opening scenes of the action. The orders I had given before leaving our encampment at the head of the First Brigade were correctly carried out. The brigades marched forward on the road to Wauhatchie, the Second following the First, and Colonel Hecker, with the Third, following the Second, but, impatient to get on, pressing alongside where the ground would permit. After marching nearly three-quarters of a mile the Second Brigade suddenly stops. Hecker, still more impatient, sends one of his aides forward to ascertain the cause of the delay. The aide returns with the information that he had seen one of the staff officers of the Second Brigade, who had told him that the Second Brigade had just received orders to halt. Colonel Hecker replies, "I have received no orders to halt, and I shall march on." So he marches his column by the Second Brigade and continues on the road to Wauhatchie. He has hardly advanced beyond the Second Brigade when he meets Major Howard, of the Eleventh Corps staff, on the road. Major Howard tells him to halt his troops at the cross-road, one branch of which leads up to the hill on the left, now known as Smith's Hill. This is done. Major Howard perceives General Hooker near the spot, and referring the colonel to the general, says, "Here is General Hooker himself." General Hooker recognizes the colonel, with whom he is evidently acquainted. In reply to General Hooker's questions the colonel informs him that the troops halting there are the Third Brigade, Third

Division, and that he is halting in consequence of an order received through Major Howard. The general asks where General Schurz is, and Colonel Hecker replies: "In the front; one of his aides was just brought by here wounded."

The general inquires about the other troops or the other brigade, and Colonel Hecker points out to him the Second Brigade of my division standing immediately on his left, and mentions even the name of its commander, Colonel Krzyzanowski. General Hooker then instructs Colonel Hecker to form his brigade in such a manner as to be able to face toward the hill or toward the valley, as necessity might require. Then, saying to Colonel Hecker, "You stay here," General Hooker rides over to the Second Brigade, immediately in front of which he remains a considerable time. According to General Hooker's direction Hecker staid. For this we have the testimony of Major Howard, Captain Greenhut, assistant adjutant-general of the Third Brigade, Lieutenant Mueller, and Lieutenant Kramer, aides of Colonel Hecker, and Colonel Hecker himself. This conversation being an important matter, the testimony must be examined with greater care. Major Howard, when as a witness before you, must have made upon you the impression of a man who is careful and conscientious in his statements. He produces as facts only what he knows with absolute certainty; most of his recollections of what happened during a night of battle three months ago, he gives as impressions more or less distinct and reliable.

The testimony of a witness so conscientious can be taken at a valuation rather above than below that which he himself puts upon it. He states that he found Colonel Hecker marching, and admits it is not only possible, but probable, that he told Colonel Hecker to stop at the cross-roads. He tells us that before he did so he had been with General Hooker and staff, informing them of Colonel Hecker's arrival, and that he heard General Hooker or General Butterfield say that the troops might be halted at the cross-roads. He further gives it as his impression that he heard General Hooker or General Butterfield instruct Colonel Hecker to form his brigade so as to be able to make front toward the valley, as well as toward the hills. By the corroborative testimony of three other witnesses, Colonel Hecker, Captain Greenhut, and Lieutenant Kramer, this point is established as absolute certainty.

The testimony of Colonel Hecker himself is so clear, distinct, and positive that nobody who knows the man will breathe a doubt against it. That of Captain Greenhut and Lieutenant Kramer concurs with it in almost every particular. All three testify that Colonel Hecker was halted by Major Howard, and that General Hooker was informed by the colonel of the presence of my Second Brigade. All three testify to the instructions given by the general to Colonel Hecker, and all three testify to the words pronounced by General Hooker when he rode away, "You stay here."

This would seem sufficient to account for the Third Brigade. Colonel Hecker's case is as clear as sunlight. He acted under my orders when he marched toward Wauhatchie; he acted under General Hooker's orders when he staid at the cross-roads. As to the Second Brigade, it is to be regretted that its commander, as well as all its staff officers, without exception, are absent with the furloughed veteran regiments. I am, therefore, unable to produce them personally as witnesses. But if circumstantial evidence can prove anything, it proves in this case that an agency similar to that which stopped the Third Brigade on its march toward Wauhatchie stopped the Second also.

Recall to your minds the following facts, proved by the testimony before you : The Second and Third Brigades are pressing forward on their march toward Wauhatchie ; the Second Brigade suddenly stops, and, upon inquiry, Captain Greenhut is informed by a member of the Second Brigade staff that the Second Brigade has received orders to halt there. The Third Brigade still presses forward, but has hardly passed by the Second when it is halted also. It forms in line of battle, fronting toward the hills, and General Hooker instructs its commander to form his troops in such a manner as to be able to change front toward the valley. The Second Brigade is pointed out to General Hooker. He rides toward it and halts there, and immediately afterward it is noticed that the Second Brigade is formed front toward the valley. General Hooker remains in front of the Second Brigade a considerable time. That brigade is, of all troops, nearest to him. Orders are carried to that brigade by one of General Hooker's aides ; and when it is found out that the orders sending the Second Brigade to Chattanooga arose from a mistake, the brigade is directed to resume its old position.

While this is going on I am near Tyndale's Hill. Notice is brought to me, through a staff officer of the Eleventh Corps, that the Third Brigade is stopped near Smith's Hill, and under instructions from General Hooker. Almost at the same time notice is brought to me by a staff officer of the Second Brigade that the Second Brigade is also stopped near Smith's Hill and under orders to go to Chattanooga. Can these coincidences be accidental ? They speak for themselves. Nor is this at all strange. Consider the circumstances under which these things happened and you will find an easy explanation. At first there was no firing, except in the direction of Wauhatchie. The attention of everybody was fixed upon that point. My troops are hurried forward to the assistance of Geary. Suddenly, while my column is marching along, a volley is thrown upon it from the hills on the left. All at once it is discovered that this range of hills is occupied by the enemy. This changes the whole aspect of affairs. It is not foreseen in the original program. The effect of this discovery must be startling. General Hooker himself says in his testimony :

When the first fire was given, from the hills on the left, it suggested itself to me that the enemy was trying to get between me and Brown's Ferry.

And Captain Greenhut testifies it is his impression to have heard General Hooker say that he expected the enemy to break through between the hills. That would have completely altered the character of the action. The principal and most important fight would have been, not at Wauhatchie, but between the Chattanooga road and Brown's Ferry, for it was our main object to hold the road between Kelley's Ferry and Brown's Ferry open. Now, imagine General Hooker and staff on the very scene of action, with such apprehensions suddenly springing up in their minds. Is it not possible, nay, even probable, that at such a moment General Hooker, thinking of the new danger, and considering how to avert it, should have dropped the words, "These troops must be stopped here," or something to that effect ? Is it not equally probable that some zealous staff officer should have taken such words for an order, and hurried off to put the supposed order in execution ? Look at Major How-

13 R R—VOL XXXI, PT I

ard's case ; it is exactly in this way that he came to stop Hecke
and General Hooker confirmed his action by subsequent instru
tions of his own. It is not only probable, but almost certain (a
least it is my firm belief) that the Second Brigade, which precede
Hecker's, was stopped in a similar manner. General Hooker's ow
instructions to Colonel Hecker to be prepared for a change of fror
can be explained upon no other theory but that he was expecting a
attack. And the staff officers no doubt acted upon the inspiration
of their chief. All this was perfectly natural. There is nothin
surprising in it. But it was not natural that General Hooker shoul
have expected the same troops which were held at the cross-road
under his instructions, and with his knowledge, should at the sam
time march to the relief of Geary. And it is most unnatural that h
should in his report charge a lack of courage and valor upon con
manders and troops because they stood still where he, with his ow
instructions and under his own eyes, had held them.

It is true General Hooker's own testimony, although by some ur
guarded admissions supporting the theory upon which I explai
these occurrences, partly ignores, partly contradicts some of th
facts upon which this reasoning is founded. I would not subject hi
depositions on oath to a scrutiny were it not a duty I owe to mysel
and I owe to my companions. That duty I perform with regret an
reluctance, for when I look upon General Hooker's sworn testimon
as it stands there, unsupported by any other evidence, in conflic
with the testimony of almost every other witness, his own aide
included, in conflict even with itself, it is to me a subject of painfu
contemplation. As he informs us, Colonel Hecker told him that h
was in his position by order of General Howard. Colonel Hecke
asseverates that he said Major Howard, but General Hooker ma
have misunderstood him. This misunderstanding, however, is o
very little moment. General Hooker goes on to tell us that he ma
have said to Colonel Hecker to wait there for further orders fror
General Howard. General Hooker tells us also that he had advise
General Howard of the orders given to me to double-quick my d
vision to the relief of Geary. And then he supposed that Genera
Howard, after having been advised of that order, had stopped th
troops on the way. Indeed, does General Hooker not know tha
General Howard was my immediate commander, and that his order
were superior to mine ? If General Hooker really was under th
impression that General Howard had stopped the troops which, b
my orders, were marching toward Geary, and that these troops, afte
having been so stopped by General Howard, were left waiting fo
General Howard's further orders, and waiting in vain—if that wa
really General Hooker's impression, how in the name of commo
sense then could he blame me or my troops for a delay, which, i
his opinion, was owing to the orders, or to a neglect of Genera
Howard, my commander ?

Either General Hooker did not believe that General Howard ha
ordered these troops to stop, or, by blaming me and my command
he committed the most unaccountable injustice, an injustice fo
which even the cheap pretense of a misapprehension cannot serv
as an excuse. No ; this will not answer. It is well enough estab
lished that General Howard gave no orders to halt. He had, indeed
a far different idea of a double-quick movement. Instead of haltin
troops on the way, troops whose commanders were impatient to ge
on, he was with me and General Tyndale at the head of the colum

n march, making every exertion to accelerate its progress. It is
lso well enough established by the instructions given to Hecker
hat General Hooker thought very little of Howard or of Geary at
hat time. Such instructions are given only in expectation of an
ttack; they mean preparation for defense on the spot, and not
reparation for a double-quick movement. In this attitude the bri-
ades remained there for a considerable time, in General Hooker's
mmediate vicinity, under his very eyes, within the reach of his
oice, and he did not stir them. If he was under the impression
hat the troops were waiting for orders to march forward, why did
e not give the orders? If in his opinion there was a mistake, why
id he not correct the mistake? Is it not one of the principal priv-
leges and duties of a commander to correct the mistakes of his
ubordinates?

But, then, General Hooker indulges in statements still more seri-
us and still more untenable. He declares in his testimony, and
eclares with emphasis, that he gave no orders at all to brigades.
t is sworn to by four witnesses—by Colonel Hecker, Major Howard,
aptain Greenhut, and Lieutenant Kramer—that he gave the com-
nander of my Third Brigade, not only orders, but the very explicit
nstructions above mentioned. With due respect to General Hooker,
he concurring testimony of these four witnesses admits of no doubt.

Again, General Hooker declares that he knew nothing of the
resence of my Second Brigade on that part of the field. Is it pos-
ible? Three witnesses—Colonel Hecker, Captain Greenhut, and
Lieutenant Kramer—testify that he was not only informed of its
resence, but that Colonel Hecker, in his own emphatic and demon-
trative manner, which admits of no mistake, pointed it out to him
s standing immediately on their left. Even the name of its com-
nander, Colonel Krzyzanowski, was pronounced, and that is a name
vhich cannot well be mistaken for any other. It is further proved
hat General Hooker, as soon as their conversation was concluded,
ode over to the Second Brigade, and remained there. One of Gen-
ral Hooker's own aides testifies that he carried orders to that bri-
ade; that the brigade was of all troops nearest to the place where
eneral Hooker stood, and that he presumes General Hooker must
ave been aware of its being there, as it was so near him. Lastly,
Lieutenant Weigel states that when, after the taking of Tyndale's
Hill, he, with me, met General Hooker, the commander of the Secnd Brigade, Colonel Krzyzanowski, was in General Hooker's imme-
liate presence. And General Hooker was ignorant of all this!

Lastly, General Hooker declares, that had he known anything of
he presence of my Second Brigade, on that part of the field, or had
e known that I was forward with only one brigade, he would have
rdered Colonel Hecker instantly to march to Wauhatchie. This
ndeed he might have been expected to do, if he really wanted one of
ny brigades to occupy the Tyndale Hill, and another to push through
o Geary. Now mark what he did do. It is proved by three wit-
esses that immediately after the Second Brigade had been bodily
ointed out to him, he gave Colonel Hecker instructions how to form,
nd then left him with the words, "You stay here."

But to cap the climax, he says himself he was not positive whether
e knew that I had more than two brigades in all. He thinks he
nust have known it or ought to have known it, as he had marched
vith us from Bridgeport to Lookout Valley, but he was not positive.
Every candid mind will conclude from his report, that he did not

know it, for he speaks only of Tyndale's and "the other brigade."
And then, not being positive whether I had more than two brigades
in all, he tells us that he kept one of my brigades back, thinking
that two of my brigades were in advance.

Here my willingness to furnish an explanation is at a loss. There
is no theory upon which I can reconcile his acts with his declarations.
This testimony in its relation to the facts as proved by all the other
witnesses is to me a puzzle. It is almost impossible to suppose that
General Hooker did not know the brigades to be there, for if he had
eyes to see, ears to hear, and a mind to understand, he must have
been aware of their presence. But it is almost equally impossible to
suppose that he did know them to be there, for how strange is it,
how can it be explained, that he did not send them forward, if he
wanted to have Tyndale's Hill occupied and Geary re-enforced at the
same time, and above all, how can his report be accounted for? I am
irresistibly driven to the conclusion that either General Hooker did
not clearly fix his mind upon what he saw, heard, said, and did during
the night of the engagement, or that he did not clearly fix his mind
upon what he remembered and wrote at the time of composing his
report.

Now let me sum up the facts as they are established by the evidence.

It is proved that immediately upon receipt of orders, I hurried
forward at the head of my First Brigade, after having directed my
Second and Third Brigades to follow.

It is proved that my orders to the Second and Third Brigades were
correctly delivered and correctly executed. They did follow me.

It is proved that upon the arrival of the head of my column oppo-
site Tyndale's Hill I received official notice of the detention of my
Second and Third Brigades, by orders and instructions coming from
General Hooker.

It is proved that these notices were brought by staff officers whose
business it is to carry such information, and that, therefore, I was
justified in considering it as reliable, which, as the evidence shows,
it was.

It is proved that at the same time I received, through one of General Hooker's aides, an order to take and occupy the hill now known
as Tyndale's with one brigade.

It is proved by the aide who brought the order that I duly in
formed him of my having but one brigade in hand, and of the im
possibility of re-enforcing Geary if that one brigade was employed
in occupying the hill.

It is proved that the order was repeated, and that it was a positive
and direct order. That it was General Hooker's order is proved by
General Hooker himself in his report, in his letter, and in his testi
mony. It is proved by General Hooker, also, that I did right in exe
cuting it; in his own words, the order was "duly executed."

It is proved that all these movements were executed with all possible speed, and that the troops could not have moved quicker on
the ground as it then was.

So much for the first act of the drama. Now to the second. Gen
eral Hooker swears to his report. While Tyndale's brigade was
directed to take the hill on the left, "the other brigade was to push
on as ordered." This brigade is censured for not having arrived at
Geary's until long after the fight had ended, while, as the report
says, it had been "dispatched to the relief of Geary by orders de

vered in person to its division commander." Here is the censure,
ᴨd here is the question to be decided. Why did not the other
ʀigade push on, and why did it arrive long after the fight had ended?

It is proved that my Second and Third Brigades followed the First
ᴎ the direction of Wauhatchie according to my orders.

It is proved that after having marched a certain distance the Sec-
ᴎd Brigade was suddenly stopped on the road, and that the Third
ᴎarched by the Second in the direction of Wauhatchie, according
ᴏ my orders.

It is proved that immediately afterward the Third Brigade was
ᴀlted also, and received special instructions from General Hooker
ᴎimself.

It is proved that General Hooker's attention was directed to the
ᴇcond Brigade, and that it was pointed out to him, and that he re-
ᴍained with it a considerable time.

It is proved that both brigades remained under General Hooker's
ᴇyes and under his immediate control.

It is proved that I was officially notified of this by staff officers.

It is proved that General Hooker, while with my brigades, did not
ʀder them to march to Geary.

It is proved that when I came back from Tyndale's Hill, the com-
ᴍander of my Second Brigade was found in General Hooker's im-
ᴍediate presence.

It is proved that as soon as the control of my two brigades was
ᴇstored to me, Geary was re-enforced with all possible speed.

It is proved that when my First Brigade arrived near Tyndale's
ᴎill, the firing at Wauhatchie had already ceased, so that it would
ᴀve been impossible even for that column, in spite of all double-
ᴜick movements, to arrive there before the end of the fight.

It is proved that when Hecker was ordered forward from the cross-
ᴏads, the fight at Wauhatchie had long been over; it would have
ᴇen absurd, therefore, to expect him to arrive there before it was
ᴠer.

And now I ask you with all candor, what is there in all this that
ᴀm, or that my troops are, to blame for? Where is the non-com-
ᴏliance with orders, and where is the lack of courage and valor? No
ᴏubt mistakes were committed, but the question is whether they
ᴠere my mistakes. It may have been a mistake to take the Tyndale
ᴎill. But, if so, it was General Hooker's mistake, for he acknowl-
ᴇdges to have given the order.

It may have been a mistake that General Hooker was not imme-
ᴅiately advised of the impossibility to re-enforce Geary while this
ᴏrder was executed. But most certainly it was not my mistake, for
ᴉ informed General Hooker's aide explicitly of all the circumstances
ᴠhich produced that impossibility. What more had I to do? If
ᴎat aide, when he reported the facts to General Hooker, did not
ᴇport the facts fully, as his duty required, am I responsible for
ᴊeneral Hooker's aides?

It may have been a mistake that the troops were stopped at the
ᴄross-roads. But it was certainly not my mistake, for nobody, I
ᴊuppose, thinks that I ordered them to stop. The case of the Third
Brigade is clearly enough established, and as for the Second, how was
ᴉt possible, if such an order had come from me, that one of the bri-
ᴊade staff officers should report to me its detention by orders coming
ᴊrom General Hooker?

If the stopping of the troops was a mere mistake, it is to be re-

gretted that it was not at once rectified.   But that mistake happene
under General Hooker's very eyes; he, by giving instructions, pa
ticipated in it, and of all men in the world, he was the man to remed
it.   I did all I could to direct his attention to it by giving his aid
all the information that was necessary.   I will stretch self-criticisr
to the utmost limit, and say that I might have gone back when
heard that my troops were stopped at the cross-roads.   But, bein
informed by responsible staff officers that the two brigades were ur
der General Hooker's immediate control, had I not to suppose tha
General Hooker knew what he was doing and what he wanted ther
for?   Besides, I had communicated to General Hooker's aide a
that was important.   That aide went back to report to his chief.   I
anything was wrong, General Hooker, by his aide, knew where
was and could advise me.   Receiving no further orders I was just
fied in believing that all was right.   So I remained where I consid
ered my presence most desirable.   That General Hooker meanwhil
held my two brigades where he did not want them, is that my mi
take?

Whatever way you may turn and twist the occurrences of tha
night, you will always arrive at the conclusion that the mistake
committed were not my mistakes, and that of all persons that migl
be blamed, my troops and their commander were the very last.
think I could make even General Hooker feel the injustice of the cer
sure contained in his report.   What would he have thought if, a
the time of the battle of Chancellorsville, his corps commanders ha
received from Washington direct orders to remain in their positio
near United States Ford, and if then, in General Halleck's repor
the following paragraph occurred:

I regret that my duty constrains me to withhold the usual com
mendation of courage and valor from the commander of the Arm
of the Potomac, who, when he heard that General Sedgwick wa
engaged with the enemy near Fredericksburg, remained with th
whole army quiet and inactive in his intrenchments at Chancellor
ville, deaf to the stirring appeals of the terrific artillery and infantr
fire in the distance, which made known to him the desperate situa
tion of his imperiled companions.

Or, another case in point.   How would General Hooker feel if, o
the evening of our arrival at Lookout Valley, the commander of th
Eleventh Corps had received from General Thomas the direct orde
to camp his whole force near Brown's Ferry, and if then, in Ger
eral Thomas' official report, the following passage occurred:

I regret that my duty constrains me to except in my general con
mendation of good judgment the major-general commanding th
Eleventh and Twelfth Corps, who, after having marched his troo
into Lookout Valley, so far forgot all the rules of ordinary foresigl
and caution as to leave a weak detachment isolated at Wauhatchi
without even occupying with sufficient forces the gaps and fords an
bridges through and over which the enemy could penetrate into th
valley, place himself between the two camps, and overwhelm th
isolated detachment with superior numbers.

How would General Hooker relish that?   But if, under such ci
cumstances, such a censure would not be considered just, what mu
be your opinion of the censure in General Hooker's report?

Although the parallels are striking, I will confess that the circun
stances described are only made up for the sake of argument, for
do not know that General Halleck in the first, or General Thoma
in the second case, gave any direct orders to corps commanders.

Before closing, I deem it my duty to call your attention to one feature of this business which has an important bearing, not only upon my interests but upon yours and upon those of every subordinate commander in the army. We are bound by the iron chains of military discipline. The superior has it in his power to do all manner of things which may work serious injury to the honor and reputation of the subordinate, which the latter is but seldom at liberty to disprove and almost never able to resent. The greater, in this respect, the power of the superior, the more is he in honor and conscience bound to use his power with the utmost carefulness and discrimination, for the honor and reputation of every subordinate officer is a sacred trust in the hands of the superior commander. The most formidable weapon in the hands of the latter is his official report of campaigns and actions. It is universally received as documentary history, as the purest fountain from which the future historian can take his most reliable information. Praise and censure conveyed in such a report is generally looked upon as based upon irrefutable evidence. And it ought to be. Every conscientious commander will therefore consider it a sacred duty before making an official statement affecting the honor and reputation of a subordinate, to scrutinize with scrupulous care the least incident connected with the case, and when at last, after weighing every circumstance, he has arrived at the conclusion that his duty commands him to pronounce a censure, he will again well weigh every word he says so as to be perfectly sure that he does not say too much. For it must be considered that public opinion is generally swayed by first impressions, and an injury once done can but rarely be repaired by a subsequent modification of language.

And now I invite you to apply this criterion, which certainly is a just one, to the report of General Hooker. That it is severe in its reflections on a body of troops nobody will deny. By solemnly excepting them in a general commendation of courage and valor, it stigmatizes them as destitute of the first qualities which the soldier is proud of. That the report is a just one, who will after this investigation assert it? I am far from saying that General Hooker knowingly and willfully reported what was false; his position ought to exempt him from the suspicion of such an act. I have not entertained that suspicion a moment, but what excuse is there for his error?

There are two things which every conscientious man will be careful to guard against. The first is saying anything to the prejudice of another which he knows to be false, and the other is saying anything to the prejudice of another which he does not positively know to be true. And did General Hooker positively know his report to be true and just? He could not know to be just what is proved to be unjust. But would it have been impossible to ascertain the truth? I lived within five minutes' walk of his headquarters. My brigade commanders were all within call. I saw him almost every day, and a single question would have elicited a satisfactory explanation. The question was not asked. Five minutes' conversation with his own aides, Lieutenant Oliver and Captain Hall, would have removed the error. Was the error so dear to him that he shielded it with silence against the truth? But to me it is a mystery how that error could stand against the force of his own recollections. Were they, too, shut out when that paragraph was penned? They would, indeed, have ill-comported with the sensational dash with which the verbiage of the censure is flavored.

You will admit that this is not the way in which troops shoul. be declared destitute of courage and valor; troops belonging to a division which on three battle-fields lost far more killed an wounded than it counted men when I was put in command an than it counts men to-day; and this is not the way to treat an officer not one of whose subordinates will say that when he was in a plac of danger his general was not with him.   This is a levity whicl would not be admissible in the ordinary walks of life, much less in the military world, where every question of honor is weighed witl scrupulous nicety.   When looking at this most strange transaction every impartial observer will ask himself, "What can have been th motive of this?"   If the battle had been lost we might have foun the motive in the desire of the commander to throw the responsibil ity upon some subordinate whom he might select as the unfortunate victim of his embarrassments.   This, indeed, would not be noble no even excusable, yet we can find the springs of such actions among the ordinary weaknesses of human nature.   But we were victorious the results of the action were uncommonly gratifying, and that Gen eral Hooker should then sit down and coolly endeavor to consign a fellow-soldier and part of his command to shame, and affectingly ornament the scene with the fanciful pyrotechnics of a terrific in fantry fire flaming around imperiled companions—for that I seek th motive in vain.

Every candid mind will admit that such an act on such an occa sion can have been called forth by one of two things only: either the grossest misconduct on the part of the subordinate, or a morbid desire to blame on the part of the commander.   Public and official censures under such circumstances are so unusual that either the provocation must be enormous or the ill-will uncontrollable.   It may be asked why the censure in the report is so ambiguous as to admit of an application to some brigade of mine as well as to myself.   In my public life I have learned to understand the language of those who want to hurt.   It is never more insidious than when it merely suggests and insinuates.   By saying little that is positive, and say ing that little obscurely, it opens a wide field for a malevolent imag ination.   Just enough is said in that report to give a hold to back biting malignity, which now may point to an official document as proof, and suggestively add, no more was said in order not to ruin him.   I appreciate this tenderness as well as I fully appreciate the elaborate flourish of language with which the greatness of the dan ger is so artistically, so touchingly, and yet so gratuitously, contrasted with the tardiness of the relief.

Here I will stop.   I feel that I owe you an apology for the length and sweep of my remarks.   When I entered the army I left, without regret, a position of ease and splendor.   I might have led a life full of honor and enjoyment in other spheres of activity, but after hav ing co-operated in the development of the ideas governing this coun try, I desired to share all its fortunes to the last.   I entered upon this career with a heart full of enthusiasm and readiness for self-sacrifice.   I have been quietly endeavoring to do my duty, with zeal but without ostentation.   Knowing what material glory so frequently is made of, I did not crave for glory but for justice.   Everybody that knows me will tell you that here, as elsewhere, I have been and am the most forbearing and inoffensive of men.   And even in this case, I would have abstained from all sharpness of criticism had I not, by a series of occurrences, been tortured into the conviction that at last

I owed it to myself and to my companions to array on one occasion
the whole truth in its nakedness against official and private obloquy.

Since the battle of Chancellorsville, the first time that I had the
honor to participate in an engagement under General Hooker's command—since that time when, through newspaper articles, dated at
the headquarters of the Army of the Potomac, I was covered with
the most outrageous slanders, which, although easily disproved were
as easily repeated—since that time until the present day, I have had
to suffer so much from the busy tongue of open and secret malignity,
that even my well-tried patience was rather too severely tested.
Under the pressure of military discipline, I held out quietly and in
passive silence.   At last an official statement appears, intended to
throw disgrace upon me and part of my command.   Upon this official statement at last I can put my finger, and you will not blame
me if I put my finger upon it with firmness and energy.   But you
will bear me witness that, in discussing the facts in the case, I have
said nothing, absolutely nothing, that is not clearly substantiated by
the evidence before you.   If my language was severe, you must not
forget that the truth is still severer.

I said that the honor and reputation of a subordinate is a sacred
trust in the hands of his commander.   When this trust is violated
good fortune gives us, at least, sometimes an opportunity to right
ourselves before impartial men.   For this opportunity, furnished me
by the commander of the army, I am most profoundly thankful, for
if indeed a general could be found who, upon a knowledge of facts
so lamentably imperfect, upon impressions so vague and unaccountable, could launch into the world so odious and wanton an accusation, I doubt whether a court of inquiry can be found to sanction it.

Respectfully submitted.

C. SCHURZ,
Major-General.

[Appendix C.]

LOOKOUT VALLEY, *February* 12, 1864.

The report of Major-General Hooker concerning the engagement
of Wauhatchie on the night of 29th October, 1863, as far as it is an
object of the present inquiry, contains some facts and a conclusion
in the form of strictures of serious character, as drawn from those
facts.   It could be easily demonstrated that the conclusions drawn
from the premises could not stand a trial, even before the first prin-
ciples of logic; but we have to demonstrate further that the facts
are untrue in themselves, or are disfigured and misconstrued, and
by a confused mixture of time, place, circumstances, and undeserved
censure, were published and promulgated in newspapers of unofficial
character.   The solution of the following questions, in my humble
opinion, will exhaust the material before this honorable Court.   A
long and eventful life of fifty-three years lies behind me, and for
the first time I have to defend my honor against reproaches as contained in the said report; and, although my name and brigade is
not specified in the report; and, although Major-General Hooker's
letter to Brigadier-General Whipple expresses some surprise that I
connect my name and brigade with the censure in the report, I was
morally forced to apply for a court of inquiry in order to have my
conduct set in full light.

The questions are:

1. Was a brigade, and what brigade, detached to the relief of General Geary, and who detached it?

2. Was a brigade involved in a swamp, and had it lost its way, and what brigade was it?

3. Was the Third Brigade involved in a swamp and lost the road?

4. Did anybody allege that the Third Brigade was involved in a swamp and lost its way, and who did allege it?

5. Was there a terrific infantry fire that night?

6. How long did the fire at General Geary's last, and when was it over?

7. Could any brigade of the Third Division have reached General Geary before it was over?

8. Was there any brigade, purposely or by mistake, delayed or the march?

9. If so, whose duty was it to push it forward to the aid, as the report says, of the imperiled companions?

10. When did the Third Brigade receive for the first time the orders to join Geary, and how was the order executed?

The evidence before the honorable Court shows that in that night orders were carried by aides-de-camp; and of the same orders the commander, in whose name they were carried, ignores their origin and aides-de-camp are and must be regarded as representatives of the commanding officers, and orders carried by them must be executed promptly. Discussing their origin, authority, propriety, or end is a military impossibility. I return to the questions.

Answer 1. By the testimony of Major-General Hooker's aides-de camp, Captain Hall and Lieutenant Oliver, of Lieutenant Klutsch Lieutenant Weigel, [Captain] Stinson, and Major-General Schurz is left not the slightest doubt that the brigade nearest at hand, Tyn dale's brigade, was ordered to march to the relief of General Geary and was led by Major-General Schurz himself. The same witnesses state that the orders given to General Schurz by General Hooker were distinctly to detach one brigade to the relief of Geary, the other to follow up the road. In the execution of this order in the uncer tain light of the moon, over a terrain not known as it is now, in the ground soaked from former rains.

Answer 2. This First (Tyndale's) Brigade, on their march to the front and near the foot of the hill, now known as Tyndale's Hill, los the road, came in a swampy, brushy terrain, full of weeds and briar (as Lieutenant Oliver says); but a few minutes brought it out, and the positive order carried by Major-General Hooker's aide-de-camp Oliver, to take that hill, was executed. (See testimony of Lieuten ants Oliver, Weigel, and Captain Stinson; and Major Howard, with Lieutenant-Colonel Meysenburg, confirms the swampy nature of the ground.) But the clearest evidence is given that—

Answer 3. The Third (Colonel Hecker's) Brigade never was in volved in a swamp, never lost the road, neither from the camp to the cross-road, nor from there to Tyndale's Hill, nor from Tyndale's Hill to Wauhatchie. (See testimony of Captain Stinson, Lieuten ants Mueller, Kramer, and Captain Greenhut.) The full evidence is before you that the brigade which never marched to General Geary but was ordered to hold the hill taken by it, had for a short time los the road and got involved in a swamp, and that that brigade which marched to Geary and joined him never lost the road nor met a swamp; and—

Answer 4. General Hooker, when asked who alleged it, answered that in Major-General Howard's report was something of a swamp mentioned. Now, this report says not a single word, that [of] the brigade marching and reaching Geary; says not a word that Third

Brigade lost the road and was involved in a swamp. It mentions that the junction was executed. All that is mentioned there is expressly directed to the First Brigade, that never formed a junction with General Geary, and the report of Major-General Hooker labors under the misapprehension and misconstruction that the brigade involved in a swamp was identical with the brigade that marched through to Geary. We cannot understand how this misapprehension was possible, but it is certain that it could have been avoided. The censure in regard to courage and valor was principally based on the fact that an untrue and mean excuse had been preferred by the brigade that joined Geary to cover its unfortunate delay is received in the official report, and evidence before you shows that this is untrue and false; and with the structure crumbles the censure.

Answer 5. The terrific infantry fire is in the report introduced as a guide. Somebody who has lost no road, and has shown it by marching on that road without stopping, needs no guide to show him the road, and evidence is before you that Third Brigade found the road without meeting an obstacle or being lost. But if we can show that when the guide existed he was not of the promised quality, and that at the time he should show the road was a non-existence, another part of the report cannot stand the trial. Noah Webster's Dictionary consulted by us says that terrific means causing terror. We must confess we never had thought that the firing heard at Wauhatchie could create terror in any man's mind. Its intensity, duration, is in the memory of the honorable members of the Court, who all heard it; it is not necessary to compare it with Leipsic and Waterloo; and General Hooker himself declares in his testimony that it was only severe, an honest attack, an intention of the enemy to whip Geary, and the engagement at Tyndale's Hill he styles a slight skirmish. Should the enemy have had at Geary the masses of terror, and at the so important gap only a few skirmishers? Nothing is impossible, as General Hooker's aide heard only about a dozen shots fired, where we lost in killed and wounded that number. I need not enter into discussion about fires not severe, and attack without intention to whip; it seems to me that the evidence is given that the guide was not a terrific one.

But (Answers 6 and 7) I can show that at the time when my brigade was halted on the cross-road, if not all the firing at General Geary's was over it ended a few minutes afterward, and that at the time, when for the first time I received the orders to march to Geary, there was no firing at all in that direction. Captain Stinson states that the fire at Geary's had just ended when the advanced brigade (Tyndale's) arrived near the hill, although the troops could not have marched quicker—a statement in perfect harmony with Captain Greenhut [and] witnesses at that time posted at different and distant points. Let us compare with this the statement of Lieutenant Klutsch, who held his watch in hand and positively declares that it was ten minutes past 1 o'clock when the troops of the division did begin to march from their camps, and Lieutenant Mueller confirms the depositions of the other witnesses, and even where in other testimonies the time is fixed with less precision we find nothing to the contrary; and to our own observation from the place where Third Brigade was encamped, about 400 yards west west-northwest of General Howard's headquarters in a stump field at the foot of the Raccoon Mountain, to Wauhatchie it is not far from 3 miles, as General Hooker himself estimates the distance; and if we compare the time given by Lieutenant Klutsch and others with the time elapsed until the order to march had reached the troops, when we consider that in the night and on roads as they were at that time, when we do not forget that all the troops marched at the same time and a crowding of them causes always more or less delay, if we remember that the order to march was First Brigade, Second Brigade, Third Brigade, we can positively say that any brigade having started from the encampment of Third Division marching directly toward Geary could not have reached Geary at this distance of 3 miles, under the existing circumstances, before the firing had ceased there.

Answers 8 and 9. It is easy to show that all orders given to the commander of Third Brigade were executed immediately, and that all the acting of the brigade and its commander during that night was in consequence of orders, and nothing contrary to it. The first order given and executed in the night of the 29th was to march from camp down on the road and to form there. This order was carried by Captain Spraul, aide-de-camp of Major-General Schurz, and arriving at the road, the brigade was informed by Lieutenant-Colonel Otto to march forward on the road. Not a word was said of marching to the relief of General Geary, and it would be easy to show that great many commanding officers did not even know, or never were informed, that General Geary and his troops were encamped near Wauhatchie. Not a word was said because First Brigade was sent forward to [for] that purpose, and as it is confirmed by the testimony of the commander of the division that the only order given at that stage of the movement was to form and march on the road, we can pass to the time from this order to the first halting of the brigade. The Third Brigade executed the orders received, and marched forward and even passed forward when Second Brigade was halted, and Major Howard passing by the brigade at times found it always marching forward.

The distance from the camp of Third Brigade to the road is about 400 yards, and from Major-Generals Howard's and Schurz's headquarters to the cross-roads about 1,000 yards. So far, the Third Brigade had advanced, the Second Brigade having turned out to the left, when Major Howard brought the positive order to halt at the cross-roads, and bring my troops in position front to the hill. He himself states that he informed General Hooker that I was authorized to halt, and that shortly after Major-General Hooker saw me in person. This order was executed at once, and the reason why this order was given struck immediately my mind, as a firing from the hill on the left indicated an intention of the enemy to attack us there. Therefore I ordered to remove all hindrances in front; the fences on both sides of the road were thrown down to be ready to meet the enemy's attack with a counter attack, and Major-General Hooker himself stated before the Court, that seeing this firing from the hill he saw that the enemy's intention was to get between him and Brown's Ferry, and to stand prepared for any intention the enemy had. A short time after Major Howard had communicated that order, and Major-General Hooker presents himself in person and gives me the instruction to be ready to change front toward the right, if necessary. These instructions are not only heard by the officers surrounding me, but by Major Howard also, and Major-General Hooker leaves me with the words "You stay here." Those words from the lips of the commander-in-chief are positive. What his thoughts were, is not and was not in my reach. I had to obey.

General Hooker himself does not deny that he had told me to remain with my troops where I was.   It is confirmed by his letter to Brigadier-General Whipple.   I do not speak of impression, nor do the witnesses who accompanied me during that night.   Our minds were not troubled ; the events of that night are present at the mind as if it had been an hour ago.   There we halted, and the fire at Geary's was over shortly after we were halted, as above exposed. There we halted in the presence of Major-General Hooker.   Under all circumstances he was informed of the presence of my brigade, and under his instructions.   There we halted a long time under the very eyes of the commander-in-chief.   Why, if Geary was in peril, were not the troops nearest at hand pushed forward ?   Major-General Hooker halted in front of Second Brigade.   I had pointed it out to him ; this brigade had turned out from us to the left toward the hill, halting in an open field.   Somebody must have halted this brigade.   Why was not this brigade pushed forward ?   The commander-in-chief halting in front of it, is it possible that no inquiry should have been made, what troops there are halting at a short distance from the commander-in-chief at a time when there were other troops in peril ?   General Hooker knew during the time that Tyndale's (First) brigade took and occupied the hill in front; he had seen and spoken with the commander of Third Brigade.

Major-General Hooker says that I had informed him that it was halted by an order of Major-General Howard.   This is incorrect.   I informed him that I received the order from Major Howard.   All the persons surrounding us heard the same.   I did not even ask Major Howard who had issued the order.   I obeyed and executed it without delay.   During an attack of the enemy the battle-field is not the place for asking questions about the orders.   Major Howard was a well-known aide-de-camp.   He himself states, and it is proved, that he was with General Hooker, and that General Hooker himself, or Major-General Butterfield, caused the halting of the troops, and the evidence is before the Court that Major-General Schurz was informed of the halting of his two remaining brigades.   How could this, my brigade, have pushed forward to Geary, as I had not received any orders in that regard ?   How can I be blamed for not executing orders never given to me, or contrary to orders received ?

Let us suppose the brigade had halted by orders of Major-General Howard, or without orders, was it not the duty of the commander-in-chief, who had a long time for reflection, to push them forward and correct any fault or mistake committed by his subordinate commanders when a real danger existed, when another body of troops was in peril ?   The explanation of all the circumstances is near at hand.   A large terrain, a distance of over 2, nearly 3, miles, lay between the camp of the Eleventh Corps and the camp of General Geary, unoccupied by troops.   Three debouches from the enemy's camp at Lookout led to this terrain on the sides of Smith's and Tyndale's Hills.   When the night attack began it was clear that the enemy had passed out of those debouches.   The line to Brown's Ferry to the rear of Chattanooga was in danger.   It was necessary to stop the march of the troops to protect this line.   The fire from the hill and the gap indicated clearly the intention of the enemy. Words to that effect must have been uttered by the commander-in-chief.   Major Howard hears it ; communicates it to the troops. Major-General Hooker is informed of this, and he does not disapprove the movement.   On the contrary, he gives instructions for certain emergencies to the commander of Third Brigade.   How can any

censure fall, under those circumstances, on Third Brigade and its
commander? If in night attacks often reigns some confusion, if even
mistakes are made—and none of those things occurred with Third
Brigade—is there no other explanation possible but a lack of courage
and valor? Where is an evidence—a clear evidence—of facts justi-
fying so grave' an attack upon the honor of a body of men or its
commander? We stop here; we suppress our feelings; we will
not give them words, and suppress here and pass over to (answers
9 and 10) the time when Second and Third Brigades were led by
Major-General Schurz to Tyndale's Hill. There, for the first time,
I received the order to march forward to Geary, as Major-General
Schurz himself states. I need not refer to the testimony of Captains Greenhut, Stinson, Lieutenants Mueller, Kramer, and Weigel.
The short delay there was not caused by myself. I was halted by
the orders of my commander, and ordered to wait for the return of
the re-enforcements, and finds it full justification that the patrols
could have been easily mistaken for enemies, and a firing of our own
troops on each other could have resulted; and further, that as the
firing at Geary's had long ceased, no danger could be apprehended
in that regard. The re-enforcement of my brigade by Major-General Schurz finds its full justification in the following circumstances:
The brigade was composed of the Sixty-eighth New York Volunteers, 127 men; Seventy-fifth Pennsylvania Volunteers, 159; Eighty-
second Illinois Volunteers, 230, and Eightieth Illinois Volunteers,
358. Aggregate present for duty (deduction made of the sick and
those on special, extra, and daily duty) of this force were only present in the night of the engagement of Wauhatchie—the Seventy-
fifth Pennsylvania Volunteers, Sixty-eighth New York Volunteers,
and half of the Eightieth Illinois Volunteers. The other half of it
and the Eighty-second Illinois Volunteers were left near Shellmound
to guard the gap near the coal mines, and, as the Seventy-fifth Pennsylvania Volunteers was detached to the gap near Tyndale's Hill,
the commander of the division detached the One hundred and forty-
first New York Volunteers.

With this I submit, respectfully, to the sentence of the Court.

F. HECKER,
Colonel, Commanding Third Brigade.

[Appendix D.]

STATEMENT OF FACTS AS FOUND BY THE COURT FROM THE EVI-
DENCE ADDUCED BEFORE IT, AND THE OPINIONS OF THE COURT
THEREON.

On the evening of the 28th day of October, 1863, two divisions of
the Eleventh Army Corps, under command of Major-General Howard, arrived in Lookout Valley, Tenn., and encamped near Brown's
Ferry, having marched from Bridgeport, on the Chattanooga and
Bridgeport road. A part of the Second Division, of the Twelfth
Corps, under the command of Brigadier-General Geary, followed
and encamped the same evening at Wauhatchie, 2½ miles from the
camp of the Eleventh Corps, on the road over which it had passed.
The troops of the two corps were under the command of Major-General Hooker.

Between 12 and 1 a. m. of the 29th of October, the night being
pleasant and moonlight, the enemy made an unexpected and vigorous attack upon the troops commanded by Brigadier-General Geary.
General Hooker, being aroused by the firing, immediately and in
person ordered General Schurz to double-quick his division to the

id of General Geary and at the same time sent notice of the order
o General Howard.   General Hooker also sent orders to General
Schurz by one of his staff officers to push forward the brigade first
ready to march to the aid of Geary, and with another brigade to oc-
upy the hill known in this investigation as the Tyndale Hill.

The division commanded by General Schurz was the Third Divis-
on of the Eleventh Corps, consisting of three brigades, commanded,
respectively, by Brigadier-General Tyndale, and by Colonel Krzyzanowski and Colonel Hecker.   General Schurz, after receiving the
order, immediately got his troops under arms, put himself at the
head of General Tyndale's brigade, which was nearest the road and
first ready to march, and sent orders by Lieutenant-Colonel Otto, his
chief of staff, to the Second and Third Brigades to follow the First
Brigade on the road to Wauhatchie.   The Second Brigade, Colonel
Krzyzanowski, marched next after the First Brigade, and was fol-
owed by the Third Brigade, Colonel Hecker.   General Schurz con-
inued at the head of the marching column until the brigade arrived
at the foot of the Tyndale Hill, at which place Lieutenant Oliver,
one of General Hooker's staff officers, by orders from General Hooker,
directed General Schurz, with Tyndale's brigade, to take and occupy
he hill.

It seems that General Hooker started in the direction of Geary and
continued near the head of the column until it was fired upon from
Tyndale's Hill, when, apprehending that the enemy were trying to
cut him off from Brown's Ferry, after sending the order to General
Schurz to take the hill, he turned back and took what he regarded a
more appropriate position, near the foot of Smith's Hill.   It appears
that Tyndale's brigade, in marching from the foot of Smith's Hill to
he foot of Tyndale's Hill, got off the road and into a boggy thicket,
and was obliged to halt.   But the delay was short; the column by a
movement to the left recovered the road and proceeded on its way
vithout any considerable delay.   The march of this brigade from
ts camp to the Tyndale Hill was accomplished with commendable
promptitude.

The Second Brigade, Colonel Krzyzanowski, continued its march,
following the First Brigade until it got in the vicinity of Smith's Hill,
when it halted.   The Third Brigade, Colonel Hecker, not considering
himself authorized to halt, filed past the Second brigade and continued its march in the direction of Wauhatchie.   After passing the
Second Brigade, Colonel Hecker was directed by Major Howard, an
aide on the staff of the corps commander, to halt at the cross-roads,
then about 150 yards in advance.   On arriving at the point designated, Colonel Hecker halted his brigade and formed line of battle
facing the hill.   At this time General Hooker, returning from his
advance toward General Geary, rode up to Colonel Hecker and inquired what troops those were, and why they were halted there.   On
being answered by Colonel Hecker that it was the Third Brigade,
Third Division, Eleventh Army Corps, and that he halted there by
command of Major-General Howard, General Hooker, after giving
some directions in view of a contingency that might arise from a
change of front, rode off.

Major Howard, who continued with Colonel Hecker until the
meeting with General Hooker, rode forward to General Schurz, and
reported to him that Colonel Hecker's brigade had halted at the cross-
roads, and was under instructions from General Hooker.   Colonel
Krzyzanowski formed his brigade in line of battle to the left and
front of Colonel Hecker, and at right angles to his line of battle, not

far distant from the place selected by General Hooker for his head quarters, after the interview with Colonel Hecker. Some prisoners captured by the Second Division, were brought in, when Major-General Butterfield, chief of General Hooker's staff, directed them to be sent to Chattanooga. The staff officer to whom the direction was given understood that a brigade was to go, and ordered Colonel Krzyzanowski to march his brigade with the prisoners to Chattanooga. The brigade started, but the staff officer soon ascertained that he had committed an error. The order was countermanded before the brigade had marched 50 yards, and it was brought back to its late position.

As soon as Colonel Krzyzanowski received the order to march to Chattanooga, he dispatched an aide to General Schurz to advise him of the order. This aide, Captain Orlemann, rode forward to General Schurz and reported to him that the Second Brigade had marched to Chattanooga by orders of General Hooker. This report was made to General Schurz soon after Major Howard had reported the situation of the Third Brigade. The fact that the orders to Colonel Krzyzanowski was a mistake and had been countermanded and rectified was not communicated to General Schurz.

After driving the enemy from Tyndale's Hill and putting the First Brigade in position on its summit and establishing a line of skirmishers in front, General Schurz reported in person to General Hooker. When General Hooker learned that General Geary had not been reenforced, and that his orders in that respect had not been obeyed, he expressed his disapprobation and displeasure to General Schurz in emphatic and decided terms. He repeated the order, and directed General Schurz to carry it into effect immediately.

General Schurz then ordered forward the two brigades. The Second Brigade was placed in the gap between the Smith and Tyndale Hills to hold it, and to protect the flanks of the column in march. The Third Brigade was marched to the foot of Tyndale's Hill where it was halted to await the return of some patrols that had been sent out, and for some re-enforcements from the Second Brigade. After being re-enforced by a regiment from the Second Brigade, Colonel Hecker continued his march toward Wauhatchie and joined General Geary at 5.30 a. m. of the 29th of October. At 7 a. m. Colonel Krzyzanowski reached General Geary with the balance of his brigade. At the time the troops of the Eleventh Corps commenced to march toward Wauhatchie there was sharp and rapid firing of artillery and musketry in the direction of General Geary, which from its suddenness, proximity, severity, and being in the night-time, might well be termed "terrific." This continued until the head of the column had nearly reached Tyndale's Hill, when it gradually died away and finally entirely ceased.

The evidence shows, and it may be regarded as proved, that General Hooker, by orders delivered in person, directed General Schurz to march his division to the relief of General Geary, and that by orders sent by one or more of his staff officers he directed General Schurz to push one brigade rapidly forward to re-enforce Geary, and with another to take and occupy Tyndale's Hill. These orders were obeyed only in part.

It is also clear and well established that General Hooker did not after issuing these orders countermand or in any way modify them unless what was said by him to Colonel Hecker may be regarded a modification. It is evident that at the time he met Colonel Hecker General Hooker understood that the Third Brigade was halted by

rders from General Howard, and this would be so whether Colonel
Hecker said he was halted by orders from General Howard, as Gen-
ral Hooker recollects it, or that he was halted by orders received
rom Major Howard, as claimed and testified to by Colonel Hecker
nd his witnesses. It was to be presumed that Major Howard would
not deliver an order unless so directed by his chief, and Colonel
Hecker would be right in assuming that an order delivered by Major
Howard was issued by Major-General Howard. General Hooker
had communicated his orders to General Schurz, to General Howard,
nd General Howard is therefore to be regarded as under orders to
e-enforce Geary with General Schurz's division, and General Hooker
ssuming, as he had the right to do, that Colonel Hecker had been
halted by General Howard pending some movement to carry out the
riginal order, did not think it right and proper for him to interfere.
Hence, it may well be that he directed Colonel Hecker to stay where
e was until he got orders from General Howard. But it is appar-
nt that General Hooker did not intend to interfere with or change
his order to re-enforce General Geary.
    At the time he met Colonel Hecker he was under the impression
nd belief that all of General Schurz's command, except the Third
Brigade, had marched forward. He did not know, nor was he made
o understand, that another brigade of General Schurz's command
was still in the rear of Hecker, nor was he aware of the fact that
Colonel Krzyzanowski's brigade was a part of the Third Division
ntil the return of and the interview with General Schurz after the
ccupation of Tyndale's Hill. It is also apparent that the delay in
e-enforcing General Geary was not caused by the troops, or any of
hem, losing their way or becoming involved in a swamp. That
here was great and inexcusable delay must be conceded, but it was
aused by the halting of the brigades, as hereinbefore stated. Yet
he official report of Major-General Howard in reference to this mat-
er leaves it fairly to be inferred that whatever delay there was was
aused by the troops losing their way and becoming involved in a
wamp; and General Hooker's official report in this regard is
ounded on that of General Howard's.
    There is nothing in the evidence to authorize or justify the halt-
ng of the Second Brigade at the time and place it did. Orders
ad been given to and received by its commander to follow the First
rigade and march on the road to Wauhatchie. General Schurz
mmediately proceeded at the head of the First Brigade. He had
 right to suppose that the whole of his command would follow
nd continue marching until otherwise ordered by him. General
Howard accompanied him until near Tyndale's Hill, when he left,
nd pushed forward toward Geary more rapidly than the column in
arch, leaving orders with General Schurz to hurry forward his
ommand with all possible dispatch. The only evidence on this
ubject is the hearsay statement of a staff officer of Colonel Hecker,
ho testifies that he was told by a staff officer of Colonel Krzyza-
owski's that he (Colonel K[rzyzanowski]) had been ordered to halt.
He certainly received no such orders from General Schurz, his
mmediate commander. The last order given by General Howard
efore leaving the column to join General Geary was very different
om an order to halt. General Hooker testifies positively that he
ave no such order, or any other order directly to brigade com-
anders. The Court can come to no other conclusion from the
idence than that the Second Brigade of the Third Division was

halted without authority and against the orders of the division commander. To the neglect, then, of Colonel Krzyzanowski to obey the order of his commanding officer may be ascribed the delay in sending re-enforcements to General Geary. It was made to appear by the testimony that the troops of the Third Division could not have marched from their camp to the position of General Geary so as to arrive there before the firing ceased and the enemy withdrew or were repulsed. In the judgment of the Court it would require two hours to make the march in the then state of the roads, and in the night, and the weight of the testimony is that the firing at General Geary's did not continue more than one hour after the column started.

By the order by which this Court was assembled and organized the Court is called upon to give an opinion as to whether the strictures set forth in the order taken from General Hooker's official report of the night action of Wauhatchie were deserved by the conduct of General Schurz, Colonel Hecker, or any part of this command. From the evidence which has been adduced in this inquiry and investigation, the Court is of the opinion that General Hooker is justified in the censures and strictures contained in his official report. The attack on General Geary was a night attack, sudden and unexpected. The command of General Geary was comparatively small, and it was fair to presume that he was assaulted by a superior force. This command might well be said to be "imperiled." There was a necessity for prompt action and getting re-enforcements to him with all possible dispatch. To this end, General Hooker issued his orders and directed his attention. He supposed his orders would be obeyed and his plans carried into effect, and when, at the end of two hours, he learned that General Geary had not been re-enforced, it is not surprising that, in the language of one of the witnesses, he was very angry, and it was right and proper that he should give expression to his righteous indignation in his official report.

So far as the conduct of Colonel Hecker is concerned, it is not deserving of censure. It is apparent that the strictures contained in General Hooker's official report were not intended to apply to him or his command. In the opinion of the Court, these strictures were not deserved by the conduct of Colonel Hecker, or any part of his command.

Are the strictures contained in the report deserved by General Schurz? It is a well-settled principle of military law, that a subordinate commander is responsible for the execution and enforcement of all orders issued to him by his superior commander. General Hooker in this case had issued an order which was not obeyed. He had the right, and it was proper for him to hold responsible for the non-execution of the order the officer to whom he issued it. Hence, he says, as the ground-work of his censure:

The brigade dispatched to the relief of General Geary, by orders delivered in person to its division commander, never reached him until, &c.

It was in accordance with well-established military usage for General Hooker, in the first instance, to hold the division commander responsible for this apparent neglect. This calls upon General Schurz to show why he did not meet the exigencies of the order and fulfill the command. Has he done so? As soon as the orders were delivered by General Hooker to General Schurz, the latter promptly set about carrying them into execution. The troops were quickly under arms. They turned out splendidly. The necessary orders, "answering the object and fitting the circumstances," were given. The column was put in motion, and General Schurz took his proper place at its head. He had reason to assume and act upon the assumption that his entire command was following him; if any of his brigades failed to do so they acted in disregard of orders, or were stopped by orders which were regarded as superior to those of General Schurz.

When General Schurz found that his command had not followed him, as he directed, it was undoubtedly his duty to ascertain the cause of the delay, and proceed at once to rectify the omission, unless, indeed, he had received information, on which he would be authorized to rely, that a portion of his command had been halted, or its destination changed by orders superior to his. In this case it appears, as heretofore stated, that when the Third Brigade had arrived about 150 yards from the cross-roads, Major Howard informed Colonel Hecker that he was authorized to halt at the cross-roads; or, in the more emphatic language of Colonel Hecker and his staff officers, who testified in this case, Major Howard ordered him to halt at the cross-roads. Colonel Hecker properly acted in accordance with this order.

Major Howard accompanied Colonel Hecker to the cross-roads, saw him and General Hooker together, then immediately rode forward to General Schurz, and reported to him that Colonel Hecker's brigade had been halted at the cross-roads, and was under instructions from General Hooker. Soon after this, a staff officer from Colonel Krzyzanowski's brigade, rode up to General Schurz and reported to him that the Second Brigade had been ordered to Chattanooga, by General Hooker, and had gone. It is no fault of General Schurz that Major Howard was mistaken, both in the order he communicated to Colonel Hecker and in the statement he made to General Schurz, or that Colonel Krzyzanowski failed to advise him that the order to march to Chattanooga was countermanded immediately after it was given, and long before the staff officer sent to him could return to the brigade.

General Schurz had official information upon which, in the opinion of the Court, he was authorized to rely and act, that the Second and Third Brigades of his division had been detached from his command, and were acting under orders direct from General Hooker, which orders were in conflict with the orders issued by him. It is not denied that he was ordered to occupy the Tyndale Hill with Tyndale's brigade. If he did this, he had no troops with which to re-enforce General Geary. His orders were imperative. He occupied the hill and did not, for the reason stated, march to the relief of General Geary. This was what called forth the reprimand of General Hooker in the field, and gave rise to the reflections and strictures contained in his report.

In the opinion of the Court, General Schurz has fully explained his delay in going to the relief of Geary, and his apparent disobedience of orders in this regard, and fully justified his conduct in the premises, and consequently it follows that he has exonerated himself from the strictures contained in General Hooker's official report.

A. BUSCHBECK,
Colonel Twenty-seventh Pa. Vols., Comdg. Second Div.,
Eleventh Army Corps, Prest. of the Court.
WILLIAM H. LAMBERT,
Captain Thirty-third N. J. Vols., Recorder of the Court.

[Appendix E.]

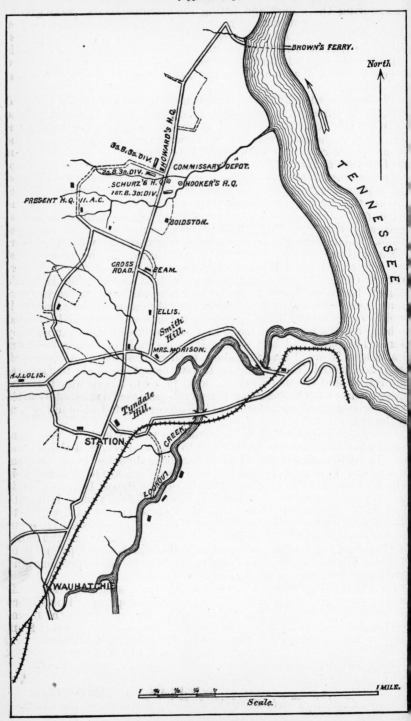

ADDENDA.

HEADQUARTERS THIRD DIVISION, ELEVENTH CORPS,
January 14, 1864.

Brig. Gen. WILLIAM D. WHIPPLE,
    A. A. G., and Chief of Staff, Army of the Cumberland:

GENERAL: In the official report of Major-General Hooker on the engagement of Wauhatchie, the following statements are made:

I regret that my duty constrains me to except any portion of my command in my commendation of their courage and valor. The brigade dispatched to the relief of Geary, by orders delivered in person to its division commander, never reached him until long after the fight had ended. It is alleged that it lost its way, when it had a terrific infantry fire to guide it all the way; and, also, that it became involved in a swamp, where there was no swamp or other obstacle between it and Geary which should have delayed it a moment in marching to the relief of its imperiled companions.

In a letter signed by Major-General Hooker, and addressed to you, an official copy of which was communicated to me by order of Major-General Hooker, the following passage occurs:

It is not known for what reason Colonel Hecker makes this application, or why he should connect his brigade with it. The order I gave the division commander, was for him to double-quick his division to the relief of Geary. And afterward one brigade of it was ordered to assault the hill on the left. The latter was duly executed. The first order was not. Whether or not Major-General Schurz communicated this order to his brigade commanders, I am not advised. Probably a court of inquiry would be able to determine. It rests between the division commander and the commanders of the Second and Third Brigades, and in no way can other parties be concerned in the issue, unless it be supposed that the troops disobeyed orders, which I have not alleged and do not believe.

This evidently throws the responsibility for the alleged non-execution of an order upon me. And I would respectfully pray that a court of inquiry be granted me, by Major-General Thomas, commanding Army of the Cumberland, for the purpose of investigating all the circumstances connected with the case, so as to determine whether the above strictures in General Hooker's report and letter were deserved by the conduct of myself and my command on that occasion.

I am, general, very respectfully, your obedient servant,
                                        C. SCHURZ,
        Major-General, Comdg. Third Division, Eleventh Corps.

—

HEADQUARTERS THIRD DIVISION,
                                    January 14, 1864.

Lieutenant-Colonel MEYSENBURG,
        Assistant Adjutant-General:

COLONEL: Have the kindness to send my letter accompanying Colonel Hecker's, for exoneration or a court of inquiry, along with that document to General Hooker.

Very respectfully,
                                    C. SCHURZ,
                                        Major-General.

[Indorsements.]

HEADQUARTERS ELEVENTH CORPS,
                                    January 14, 1864.

Respectfully forwarded.
A court of inquiry recommended.

                                    O. O. HOWARD,
                                        Major-General.

HEADQUARTERS ELEVENTH AND TWELFTH CORPS,
Lookout Valley, Tenn., January 15, 1864.

Respectfully forwarded. approved.

JOSEPH HOOKER,
Major-General, Commanding.

—

HEADQUARTERS ELEVENTH AND TWELFTH CORPS,
January 29, 1864.

Brig. Gen. WILLIAM D. WHIPPLE,
A. A. G., and Chief of Staff, Dept. of the Cumberland :

GENERAL : I have the honor herewith to transmit the original of the remonstrance shown you last evening, having in my possession an authenticated copy. I also send original copy, Paragraph XI, Special Field Orders, No. 23, current series.

I am, general, very respectfully, your obedient servant,
WILLIAM H. LAMBERT,
Captain Thirty-third New Jersey, Recorder.

[Inclosure.]

C SCHURZ'S REMONSTRANCE TO CERTAIN INSTRUCTIONS GIVEN TO COURT OF INQUIRY.

HEADQUARTERS ELEVENTH CORPS,
January 28, 1864.

The undersigned begs leave to enter a respectful remonstrance against the instructions to the Court, contained in Special Field Orders, No. 23, Department of the Cumberland.

I would respectfully call the attention of the Court to the Ninety-second Article of War, the spirit of which undoubtedly is, that as no court of inquiry can be ordered by any commander, except the President of the United States, unless demanded by the accused, so it can be ordered by a military commander upon such demand for no other purpose or for the investigation of no other matter than that specified by the accused in his application. The Ninety-second Article of War can be understood in no other way.

From my application, a copy of which is hereto annexed, it appears that I asked for a court of inquiry, "for the purpose of investigating the circumstances connected with the case (as specified in my application), so as to determine whether the above strictures in General Hooker's report and letter were deserved by the conduct of myself and my command on that occasion."

In Special Field Orders, No. 23, the object of the Court of Inquiry is defined as follows:

To investigate the circumstances attending all movements of troops ordered to the support of Brig. Gen. John W. Geary, commanding Second Division, Twelfth Corps, during the night action of Wauhatchie between the 28th and 29th of October, 1863, and give an opinion as to whether blame should attach to Major-General Schurz or Colonel Hecker.

It will be observed that there is a discrepancy between the object specified in my application and the object specified in Special Field Orders, No. 23. While I applied for an investigation of the circumstances connected with the case, such as would enable the Court to form and give an opinion as to whether I and my command deserved a certain censure pronounced in certain official documents, Special Field Orders, No. 23, orders an investigation of circumstances attending all movements of troops ordered to the support of Geary, a d an opinion as to whether blame attaches to myself or Colonel Hecker, irrespective of the censure contained in General Hooker's report and letter.

Although I have no reason to shrink from any such investigation, yet I would respectfully observe that I may be able to prove by witnesses now present and within reach that the circumstances of the case were such that the strictures contained in General Hooker's report and letter were not deserved by the conduct of myself and my command on that occasion, while it would require a number of witnesses now absent, some of whom will be out of reach for a long time and one of whom has meanwhile left the service, to enable the Court to investigate the circumstances attending all movements of troops ordered to the support of Geary. The investigation, as asked for in my application, therefore, might soon enable the Court to form an opinion on the point specified by me, while the investigation as ordered by Special Field Orders, No. 23, might indefinitely prolong the proceedings of the Court, and perhaps, other circumstances intervening, lead to no definite result at all.

I would also respectfully call the attention of the Court to the circumstance that the order to "give an opinion as to whether blame should attach to Major-General Schurz or Colonel Hecker," entirely ignores the fact that blame was already attached to Major-General Schurz or Colonel Hecker in official documents, and that it was the blame thus officially pronounced for the investigation of the justice of which I prayed. I asked for a court of inquiry for the purpose of investigating not whether some charges may be found against me and my command, but whether the charges already brought against me and my command are founded or not. I deem it essential that the specified grounds upon which I asked for a court of inquiry be taken official cognizance of in the instructions given to the Court.

I arrived at the inevitable conclusion that if there is a discrepancy between the objects of the investigation, as stated in the order convening and instructing the Court, and the object of the investigation as stated and specified in the application of the accused, the Court of Inquiry so ordered and instructed is not the court of inquiry asked for by the accused, but another, not asked for by the accused, and can, therefore, with its present instructions, not stand under the Ninety-second Article of War.

I would, therefore, most respectfully pray the Court to apply to Major-General Thomas, commanding Department of the Cumberland, for re-instruction concerning the objects of the investigation, in conformity with the specified issue stated in my application for a court of inquiry.

C. SCHURZ,
Major-General.

[NOTE IN PENCIL :] File the remonstrance ; destroy the order.

W.

SPECIAL ORDERS, }   HDQRS. DEPT. OF THE CUMBERLAND,
    No. 22.   }   *Chattanooga, Tenn., May* 26, 1864.

*   *   *   *   *   *

VII. The proceedings and findings of the Court of Inquiry in th
case of Maj. Gen. Carl Schurz, commanding Third Division, Eleventh
Army Corps, instituted by Paragraph XI, Special Field Orders, No
23, current series, from these headquarters, are approved.

The Court is hereby dissolved.

*   *   *   *   *   *   *

By command of Major-General Thomas:

WILLIAM McMICHAEL,
Assistant Adjutant-General.

No. 38.

*Report of Lieut. Gen. James Longstreet, C. S. Army, commanding
corps, with field dispatches, &c.*

GREENEVILLE, TENN.,
March 25, 1864.

COLONEL: Up to October 9, 1863, my forces were along the regular
line of investment, extending from Lookout Mountain, on the left,
to Lieut. Gen. D. H. Hill's corps, on the right. My left occupied the
base of the mountain, and sharpshooters extended the line to the
river on the west slope of the mountain. I had a small picket upon
the summit of the mountain, and a small cavalry force about Trenton reported to me from time to time.

On the 9th, I received orders to send my sharpshooters down the
river to occupy a point on the left bank between Raccoon Mountain
and Walden's Ridge for the purpose of preventing the use of the
road on the opposite bank by the enemy's wagon trains. As I had
but a small force of sharpshooters I thought it best to send a brigade
in addition, as a smaller force would be liable to be cut off and captured. A brigade was thought to be force enough to secure its retreat to the mountains, and finally to make its escape to our main
force should a movement be made against it.

General Law's brigade was selected for the service, and a sufficient
force was ordered to the point indicated as soon as practicable. Pits
were sunk and occupied by the troops, and they effectually put a stop
to the travel on the road on the opposite bank. We were advised in
a few days, however, that the enemy was using another road, a little
longer, which avoided this point, and he had several other roads of
communication that were entirely beyond our reach, particularly
the Poe and Anderson roads.

On the 25th, I was ordered to make a reconnaissance in the direction of Bridgeport. This reconnaissance was interrupted by the
enemy making a crossing of the river at Brown's Ferry, about 3
miles below the point of Lookout Mountain. As soon as the crossing was discovered, the troops near the point assembled and drove
back the enemy's advance, but the force was found to be crossing in
too much strength to be successfully opposed by a brigade. The
brigade was, therefore, concentrated and withdrawn to the foot of
the mountain on the west side. The force near the crossing was

mall, as the duty for which the brigade was ordered was to guard a
point some 6 miles below Brown's Ferry. The brigade could not be
re-enforced, as the enemy's Moccasin batteries commanded the only
road across the mountain. If it had been practicable to re-enforce,
I should not have thought myself authorized to do so by taking my
troops that were occupying their proper positions in the line of investment for that purpose, as my orders and the disposition of my
troops had no reference to any such move on the part of the enemy,
and to have done so would have broken our line and exposed the
whole army. Besides, the enemy's position was such that he could
re-enforce from any point of his lines in half an hour, while I could
only re-enforce from my nearest point in about 3 hours. He would
have the benefit of his artillery, and we could not cross the mountain
with ours.

On the 27th, I received orders to make arrangements and examinations for the purpose of dislodging the enemy from his new
position, and with that view was called to meet the commanding
general on the mountain on the following day.

On the afternoon of the 27th, I received a report from my signal
party near Trenton that the enemy was advancing in force from
Bridgeport. I sent this information up to the commanding general, but as it was not confirmed by the cavalry it was not
credited.

On the 28th, I met the commanding general on the mountain
in accordance with his appointment. While engaged in an examination of the enemy's new position, one of my signal party reported
to us that the enemy was advancing in force from Bridgeport.
He guided us to a projection on the mountain about a mile off,
where we saw the head of the enemy's column, and where we
saw his force (about 5,000) file past and unite with the force
already at Brown's Ferry. The rear guard of this command (about
1,500, with a battery of artillery) came up in about an hour and
halted about 3 miles from the main force. The road between the
two commands ran along the western base of a series of heights,
and parallel to them. The position that had been taken by General
Law's brigade was about a mile from this road, and opposite the
point of the road, about half way between the rear guard and the
main force.

As soon as the rear guard halted I sent orders to General Jenkins
to concentrate at the base of the mountain his three brigades that
were on the east side, and to be ready to cross it as soon as it was
dark enough to conceal our men from the fire of the enemy's batteries, and I directed that he should report to me upon the mountain
at once. I also ordered General Law to advance his brigade as soon
as it was dark and occupy the height in his immediate front, which
commanded the road between the enemy's forces.

General Jenkins reported in time to see the positions occupied by
the enemy. He was ordered to hold the point designated for General Law with a sufficient force, while a portion of his command
moved up the road and captured or dispersed the rear guard. He
was also directed, if time and circumstances favored it, to make a
demonstration against the main force, and if an attack at night
should give us such advantage as to warrant it, to endeavor to
drive the enemy across the river; but if the latter should appear
inexpedient, to recross the mountain before daylight.

As soon as it was dark his troops were put in motion, but the

route across the point of the mountain was so difficult that he wa
not able to get his troops into their positions until midnight. H
arranged two brigades under General Law to hold the position be
tween the enemy's forces, while his own brigade, under Colone
Bratton, was sent to make the attack upon the rear guard. Hi
fourth brigade (General Benning's) was held on the left of Genera
Law's two in readiness to re-enforce Colonel Bratton. The brigad
under Colonel Bratton claims to have had complete success up t
the moment that it was recalled. It was recalled in consequence o
General Law's abandoning his position, which was essential to th
safety of Colonel Bratton's command.

As soon as General Law yielded his position it became necessar
to recall Colonel Bratton and send the troops back to their positions
in order that they might pass the mountain before daylight. Th
loss sustained by the two brigades under General Law was probabl
one-tenth of the loss sustained by the single brigade which claims
victory. As General Law's troops were veterans, I can only attribut
the want of conduct with his troops to a strong feeling of jealous
among the brigadier-generals.

About 8 o'clock at night on the 28th, I received notice that th
commanding general had approved my plan, and information fron
him that another of my divisions had been relieved from the line
and could be used in this attack, but it was too late for it to cros
the mountain before daylight, and the success of the affair depende
entirely upon a night attack and a surprise. To have put two divis
ions on the west side of the mountain during daylight would hav
exposed them to an attack from the enemy's entire force withou
artillery, and in a position where they could not be re-enforced. M
object was merely to inflict such damage upon the enemy as migh
be accomplished by a surprise. That the point was not essential t
the enemy at Chattanooga is established by the fact that he supplie
his army at that place some six weeks without it.

About October 31, Lieutenant-General Hardee, Major-Genera
Breckinridge, and myself were ordered to examine this position wit
a view to a general battle. It was decided that an attack was im
practicable; that the only route by which our troops could reac
the field was a difficult mountain road, only practicable for infantr
and entirely exposed to the enemy's batteries on the other side of th
river. His positions were connected by a short and easy route, whil
ours would have been separated by a mountain, impassable to arti
lery except by a *détour* of some 50 miles, and hardly practicable fo
infantry. Our position was so faulty that we could not accomplis
that which was hoped for. We were trying to starve the enemy ou
by investing him on the only side from which he could not hav
gathered supplies.

Copies* of communications connected with this matter are ap
pended to this report. The reports of the subordinate officers hav
already been forwarded.

I am, colonel, very respectfully, your obedient servant,

JAMES LONGSTREET,
Lieutenant-General.

Col. GEORGE WILLIAM BRENT,
Assistant Adjutant-General.

---

* Not found.

* HEADQUARTERS,
December 25, 1863.

Respectfully forwarded.

The orders in this case were as stated by General Jenkins. The troops that he was to operate against were seen and carefully considered by General Bragg and myself. I put the force down at 5,000 at the outside. General Bragg without hesitation put it at a less figure. That is the force which marched down Lookout Valley toward Brown's Ferry. A force of about 1,500 men and a battery and a few wagons followed this force and encamped about 3 miles in rear of the main force. This was evidently the rear guard, and this was the force which I hoped to be able to cut off, surprise, and capture. The dispositions and movements of the forces, as mentioned by General Jenkins, were ordered by me. The division by its figures should have mustered 5,000 men (Hood's division). The force that we were to operate against was parts of the Eleventh and Twelfth Army Corps. These troops have more notoriety for their want of steadiness under fire than for anything else.

As they were marched down Lookout Valley a part of their force came under the fire of one of our batteries. About the third shot from a Parrott gun threw the line back in some confusion. Taking into consideration the condition of the enemy and the peculiar nature of the ground, I speedily arranged the plan mentioned by General Jenkins and ordered the movements. The ridge on his map marked A' B'', instead of being a continuous ridge as there represented, is a succession of what woodsmen call hogbacks, about 300 yards in length. The one at B was to be held by the brigades in position, while the enemy's rear guard was attacked and captured or dispersed. The officers do not seem to have appreciated a night attack. It should have been made with great vigor and promptness, and completed before the enemy could have time to know our purposes. When the order was given it was supposed by myself that it would be executed by 12 o'clock at latest. Had we succeeded in that time we should have been in good condition to follow up the first repulse of the enemy by General Law, and probably greatly discomfited the force at Brown's Ferry.

The reports of General Jenkins and General Law conflict, each apparently claiming that the other was at fault. Considerable stress seems to be placed upon the report of the prisoner who, after being captured, reported that part of the Twelfth Corps had encamped a little distance back just before night. This was the force seen by many officers, and estimated by all as already stated. I endeavored to impress upon the minds of the officers the fact that one musket at night would make more noise than fifty during the day. The only real weak point about us was the jealousy between the two brigades already mentioned. This I considered, and with a momentary doubt about the propriety of executing the plan, but concluded after a moment's hesitation that my troops were so steady that they would hardly require commanders after they were once in position. The plan was very simple and very strong. Had we been able to execute promptly, or had Law pressed his advantage after the first or second repulse of the enemy, we should have had a great success at a very light cost and trouble.

---

* Indorsement on the report of Brig. Gen. M. Jenkins, commanding Hood's division, of the affair at Lookout Mountain, October 28, 1863. Jenkins' report not found.

This is forwarded directly to the War Department, with the request that it may be sent to General Bragg for his indorsement.

JAMES LONGSTREET,
Lieutenant-General, Commanding.

ADDENDA.

HEADQUARTERS,
October 23, 1863.

Col. GEORGE WILLIAM BRENT,
Assistant Adjutant-General:

COLONEL: I have just received information from General Cheatham that General Buckner is to be withdrawn from my right in the morning, that he may re-enforce General Cheatham's right. I believe that my line is longer than all the balance of the army, and the enemy is threatening my left, which is the essential point with him.

I remain, sir, very respectfully, your obedient servant,

JAMES LONGSTREET,
Lieutenant-General.

—

SPECIAL ORDERS, } HDQRS. HILL'S CORPS, ARMY OF TENN.,
No. 7.   } *Missionary Ridge, October 24, 1863.*

*   *   *   *   *   *   *   *

II. Major-General Stewart will, from his reserve line, fill the gap made in the general line of the army by the withdrawal of Major-General Buckner's division. The movement of General Buckner's troops has commenced, and it is important that General Stewart should at once make his dispositions. It is suggested that one brigade will be sufficient to connect General Stewart's left with General McLaws' right, but if more troops are needed for that purpose they will be furnished by General Stewart.

By command of Major-General Breckinridge:

JAS. WILSON,
Assistant Adjutant-General.

—

HEADQUARTERS LONGSTREET'S CORPS,
October 26, 1863.

Col. GEORGE WILLIAM BRENT,
Assistant Adjutant-General:

COLONEL: Your note of yesterday in reference to reconnaissance in the direction of Bridgeport, &c., is received. General Jenkins was ordered to move a brigade down and endeavor to cut off a working party to-night, and all the cavalry was put under his command with directions that they should at the same time be pushed down to Bridgeport, Cameron's and Caperton's Ferries. This will give us a reconnaissance of all the points in the vicinity of Bridgeport at the same time. The infantry goes to Nickajack Cave, where the enemy is reported to have some 500 or 600 men at work.

I am, very respectfully, your obedient servant,

JAMES LONGSTREET,
Lieutenant-General.

P. S.—I have no doubt but the enemy will cross below and move against our rear. It is his easiest and safest move.

HEADQUARTERS,
October 27, 1863.

Col. GEORGE WILLIAM BRENT,
    Assistant Adjutant-General:

COLONEL: Your note of to-day is received. The enemy's designs seem to be to occupy this bank of the river for the purpose of shortening his line of communication and possibly for the purpose of creating a diversion near the point of Lookout Mountain, while he moves a heavier force up to occupy the mountain, via Johnson's Crook. The latter move and object seems to me to be more important, essential indeed, than any such partial move as his present one. The position just taken by the enemy is the ridge along the river bank, near Brown's Ferry. The position can be attacked on the flanks by about a company front, in front by a line covering the entire front. The ridge runs down close upon the water's edge, so much so, that troops cannot pass between it and the water.

Any force that may be designed to attack it will be obliged to pass under the batteries on the other side or up by Trenton. The only disposition that I have made is to draw the brigade that was on the other side of Lookout Mountain close into the foot of the mountain.

I remain, very respectfully, your obedient servant,
JAMES LONGSTREET,
Lieutenant-General.

—

HEADQUARTERS LONGSTREET'S CORPS,
October 27, 1863.

Col. GEORGE WILLIAM BRENT,
    Assistant Adjutant-General:

COLONEL: Your note of this afternoon is received. I have possession of Lookout Mountain, but may not have sufficient force there to hold it. My opinion is that it should be held by a division, and that a brigade of this should be at Johnson's Crook, so as to secure the mountain pass. Should I understand the order to take possession of the mountain to mean that I shall put such force there as I think necessary to hold it against everything that may come? To hold the mountain anywhere, short of Johnson's Crook, will only be to hold it until the enemy sees fit to take it away from us.

I shall order one of Walker's brigades up on the mountain to-morrow, his being the only troops that are not occupied. In the meantime, I would like the commanding general to give me the benefit of his views more in detail. I presume that he does not mean that I shall use forces in holding the mountain that may be necessary in holding our main line of investment. Yet I may need some of the troops upon this line that I ought to have upon the mountain.

I suggested to the commanding general some ten days ago that the mountain should be held by an infantry force, but he did not agree with me and I did not feel that I could detach any of my force for that purpose.

General Walker will be ordered to start one of his brigades to Johnson's Crook early in the morning.

I am, sir, very respectfully, your most obedient servant,
JAMES LONGSTREET,
Lieutenant-General.

HEADQUARTERS,
October 27, 1863.

Col. GEORGE WILLIAM BRENT,
         Assistant Adjutant-General:

COLONEL: Since answering your note in reference to taking possession of Lookout Mountain, I have received notice that the enemy is advancing in the direction of Trenton, and in force. Instead of trying to get Walker's troops up to-morrow, I have thought it better to send one of Jenkins' brigades to-night to get the mountain passes before the enemy reaches there. I have sent different orders to the cavalry to hold the mountain passes until the infantry arrives.

Jenkins' troops have such indifferent transportation that he will not be able to subsist his men so far off. In fact, he is now nearly half the time on half rations. The whole of Jenkins' division should be started down to Johnson's Crook by daylight, I think, to insure the entire possession of the mountain; but if it is moved, I should have another division on my left to hold that part of my line. Walker's division is not strong enough to occupy the line now held by Jenkins should the commanding general think it necessary to send Jenkins to hold the mountain at Johnson's Crook.

If the commanding general does not think it necessary to hold the mountain as far down as Johnson's Crook, I should be advised of it in time to recall the brigade that Jenkins has sent off, before morning. If, however, the division is to go down, we shall require much additional transportation, in order to supply our men and animals with food.

I remain, sir, very respectfully, your obedient servant,
                    JAMES LONGSTREET,
                              Lieutenant-General.

P. S.—The information about the enemy's advance upon Trenton comes from the signal corps. A report from Colonel Grigsby, dated 3.30 p. m., does not mention it. The signals are later, however.

—

SPECIAL ORDERS, }   HEADQUARTERS HILL'S CORPS,
     No. 10.   } *Missionary Ridge, October 28, 1863—1.30 a. m.*

I. The entire line of this corps will move immediately toward the left. Major-General Stewart will have his left to rest on Chattanooga Creek, and the divisions of Generals Stovall and Cleburne will move to such points as will keep the line entire. In case anything should occur to prevent the movement till after daybreak, the troops will move a short distance to the rear, so as not to attract the attention of the enemy.

By command of Major-General Breckinridge:
                    JAS. WILSON,
                    Assistant Adjutant-General.

—

HEADQUARTERS,
October 29, 1863.

Col. GEORGE WILLIAM BRENT,
         Assistant Adjutant-General:

COLONEL: Your note of last night is received. I did not contemplate any such move as your note would indicate. My intention was merely to seize a hill which commanded the enemy's road, and hold the hill against any force that might come up from his main body, send back on his track three brigades to pick up everything that was behind, and, if time and circumstances favored, make an attack with the entire division upon the main camp, and endeavor to crowd the enemy into the river.

The movement of even Jenkins' division was so much delayed that fear that nothing was accomplished. I left him about 1 o'clock, and we just got to the road. As there was nothing there, and it was too late to make any move against the main camp, I directed him to see if he could find any wagons behind, and stragglers, and return to his camp. As we had no artillery, nor any means of getting any over, I did not think it proper to put a force out where it could be exposed to that of the enemy during daylight, and to have moved in at that late hour to attack the enemy's main camp would have kept us till after daylight.

When I left the railroad, there seemed to be no prospect of doing anything.

About an hour and a half after I left, I got a message from General Jenkins, stating that a brigade was heavily engaging the Twelfth Army Corps.

I will send the report of General Jenkins as soon as it is made. I presume that little or nothing was accomplished.

I am, colonel, very respectfully, your obedient servant,

JAMES LONGSTREET,
Lieutenant-General.

No. 39.

Organization of Hood's division.

HOOD'S DIVISION.

Brig. Gen. MICAH JENKINS.
Brig. Gen. E. McIVER LAW.

Law's Brigade.

Brig. Gen. E. McIVER LAW.
Col. JAMES L. SHEFFIELD.

4th Alabama, Lieut. Col. L. H. Scruggs.
5th Alabama, Col. William C. Oates.
4th Alabama, Col. William F. Perry.
7th Alabama, [Col. M. J. Bulger.]
8th Alabama, Col. James L. Sheffield.

Robertson's Brigade.

Brig. Gen. JEROME B. ROBERTSON.

3d Arkansas, [Col. Van H. Manning.]
1st Texas, [Col. A. T. Rainey.]
4th Texas, [Col. J. C. G. Key.]
5th Texas, [Col. R. M. Powell.]

Jenkins' Brigade.

Col. JOHN BRATTON.

1st South Carolina, Col. Franklin W. Kilpatrick.
2d South Carolina Rifles, Col. Thomas Thomson.
5th South Carolina, Col. A. Coward.
6th South Carolina, Maj. John M. White.
Hampton Legion, Col. Martin W. Gary.
Palmetto Sharpshooters, Col. Joseph Walker.

Benning's Brigade.

Brig. Gen. HENRY L. BENNING.

2d Georgia, [Col. Edgar M. Butt.]
15th Georgia, [Col. Dudley M. Du Bose.]
17th Georgia, [Col. Wesley C. Hodges.]
20th Georgia, [Col. J. D. Waddell.]

No. 40.

Report of Brig. Gen. E. McIver Law, C. S. Army, commanding brigade and Hood's division.

HEADQUARTERS LAW'S BRIGADE,
Lookout Valley, November 3, 1863.

CAPTAIN : I have the honor to report that my brigade was detached, about October 8, for duty beyond Lookout Mountain. The object of keeping a force in that locality, as I understood it, was to blockade the road leading from Chattanooga to Bridgeport, which passed near the point of Raccoon Mountain and on the opposite or west side of the Tennessee. This object was accomplished by placing riflemen along this bank of the river, which at this point is about 300 yards wide, to fire upon the enemy's wagon trains as they passed. In order to secure the riflemen who were engaged in blockading the road it was necessary to picket the river from that point to the bend near the foot of Lookout Mountain, a distance of 5 miles. This would either prevent the enemy from crossing above and cutting them off, or give them sufficient warning to enable them to withdraw.

I employed two regiments in blockading the road and picketing the river, and held the remaining three, with a section of Barret's battery, in reserve at a convenient point for re-enforcing any part of the line. As the line was long and necessarily weak, my principal security for holding it was in having a sufficient reserve to foil the enemy, if he should attempt a crossing, by throwing it upon him before he could strengthen himself on this side.

On October 25, by orders from division headquarters, three of my regiments were withdrawn and brought to this side of Lookout, leaving the two on picket and the section of artillery. Being notified that Brigadier-General Jenkins would be absent for a few days from daylight on the 27th, and that I would be left in command of the division, I came to this side of the mountain, leaving Capt. L. R. Terrell, assistant adjutant-general, as my representative to superintend the operations in Lookout Valley.

On the morning of the 27th, just before daylight, the enemy, taking advantage of the fog which was very dense, commenced the passage of the river at Brown's Ferry. They crossed in two boats carrying about 40 men each. They were fired upon by the pickets at that point, and the landing was resisted as long as possible. Information of the movement was in the meantime conveyed to Captain Terrell, who at once brought forward the reserve, consisting of about 150 men, and attacked the first detachment of the enemy, which had landed and been placed so as to cover the passage of other troops. This detachment was driven almost to the river bank, where a second line was formed in position. This re-enforcement had crossed and been placed in position while the fighting with the first detachment was going on. Encountering this additional force, which could not be driven by the mere handful of our men engaged, our line was ordered to retire. This was accomplished in good order and a line of defense taken up across the valley, which was held until all the pickets on the river were withdrawn.

In about two hours and a half from the time the crossing began a brigade of the enemy moved out from the hills bordering the river (which they had been diligently engaged in fortifying) into the valey beyond. The section of howitzers commanded by Lieutenant Brown opened upon it, throwing it into confusion and compelling it temporarily to retire. The enemy was evidently much astonished at the presence of the artillery, and its fire was very effective. When a second advance in additional force was made, and upon information that the enemy was crossing at another point above them, the two regiments (Fourth and Fifteenth Alabama), which had now succeeded in collecting their pickets, with the artillery retired slowly toward Lookout Mountain. I met them with the remainder of the brigade at Lookout Creek, where I placed the command in line to await any farther advance. The enemy, however, did not advance as far as the creek, but continued to strengthen his position on the hill above Brown's Ferry, and commenced the construction of a pontoon bridge half a mile above the ferry, which was completed before noon.

In this affair we lost 6 men killed and 14 wounded. Among the latter was Col. W. C. Oates, the gallant and efficient commander of the Fifteenth Alabama Regiment. One of the wounded was left in the hands of the enemy too severely injured to be removed.

At 5 o'clock in the afternoon of the 27th, I learned from my scouts that a considerable force of the enemy was moving from Shellmound in the direction of Chattanooga, and that this force was then in 8 or 10 miles of my position on Lookout Creek. I ascertained further that a force of cavalry was advancing from Kelley's Ferry, where a bridge had been thrown across the river. This information was communicated to the brigadier-general commanding the division, with my views as to the object of the movement. My views, as thus communicated, were that it was probably not the intention of the enemy to attack Lookout Mountain at present, but to take possession of the railroad as far as the Trenton junction, 2 miles from the foot of Lookout Mountain, and by holding Lookout Valley to obtain supplies by running wagon trains from the junction across the bridge above Brown's Ferry to Chattanooga. This has since been done.

About noon on the 28th, I was notified by cavalry scouts and the signal post on Lookout that a heavy column of the enemy was approaching my position from the direction of Shellmound. Soon afterward his skirmishers appeared in front. They were checked for a time by my skirmishers, posted so as to command the intersection of the railroad with the wagon road leading from Chattanooga toward Bridgeport. My riflemen were soon forced, however, to abandon this position and take up the line of Lookout Creek. The enemy on crossing the railroad took the road leading to Brown's Ferry, [being] fired upon as he passed by my section of howitzers and the batteries on Lookout Point. During the afternoon 5,000 or 6,000 men must have passed toward my right.

Late in the afternoon I received a note from Lieutenant-General Longstreet directing me to cross the lower bridge over Lookout Creek, near its mouth, at dark, and advance cautiously until I commanded the Brown's Ferry road at its junction with the road leading across the lower bridge to Chattanooga; to blockade that road and capture any trains that might attempt to pass. This junction I should estimate to be about a mile from the bridge.

Just before night I met Brigadier-General Jenkins, commanding division. who informed me that three other brigades of the division were then moving across the mountain with the view of crossing Lookout Creek to cut off the enemy's trains and capture the rear guard and stragglers. He requested information regarding the roads, &c., as I was familiar with the locality. After giving all the information in my power, I ventured to remark to him that in my opinion the enemy had a large force at the point upon which we intended to move, and that one division was insufficient for the accomplishment of the end in view; that a failure would be the result, and that the troops engaged in it would be seriously injured. I was satisfied, from close and constant observation, that not less than 6,000 or 8,000 troops had been thrown across the river from Moccasin Bend; that one corps (6,000 or 7,000 more) had passed my position going toward Brown's Ferry, and that another of the same strength was following. General Jenkins replied that he had positive orders to proceed on the expedition. He desired me to send him two guides who knew the country beyond the creek. These were accordingly sent, and I immediately commenced the passage of the creek, having previously ordered my brigade under arms.

A few minutes after crossing, my advance guard captured a prisoner, who represented himself as belonging to Howard's corps. From him and others of the same corps, captured soon afterward at a picket post, I learned that this corps had passed the point toward which my advance was directed, viz, the junction of the Chattanooga and Brown's Ferry roads, and was encamped about a half mile to the right, and that a division and a half of Slocum's corps were following. These we afterward learned were encamped a mile higher up the valley to the left. Half a mile beyond the creek I formed two regiments in line, with skirmishers in front, the other regiments moving *en échelon* on the right, and advanced to the crest of the first wooded hill, where my line was adjusted and halted for a short time.

The hill on which I now rested was one of a range of similar hills running from Brown's Ferry close upon the river bank for about a mile, leaving the river as it bends toward the foot of Lookout Mountain and projecting into the valley beyond. The range at the point where my line was formed was three-fourths of a mile from the Tennessee, and the distance from the road along which my left advanced (and upon which it now rested) to the point at which the range ran immediately upon the river bank was about a mile. In the triangle formed by the range of hills, the river, and the Chattanooga road the ground was all cleared. My skirmishers had advanced as far as the Brown's Ferry road, driving off the picket, and now held the road. Another wooded knoll still intervened between my line of battle and the road.

At this time Brigadier-General Robertson reported to me with his brigade. By order of Brigadier-General Jenkins, commanding division, Robertson's brigade was at once placed in line with my own, with the exception of two regiments, one of which was placed in reserve on the road to my left, and the other was used to guard the bridge in my rear and to watch the space intervening between my right and the river, which was at least half a mile. With affairs in this position I recrossed the creek to see General Jenkins. I learned from him that Colonel Bratton, commanding Jenkins' brigade, was crossing or had just crossed the creek; that General Benning would follow with his brigade and take up a line on my left, uniting with me and commanding the Brown's Ferry road higher up the valley; that Colonel Bratton would push forward on the line of railroad until he came in contact with the enemy. If he encountered only a small force, he was to pick it up. If the enemy proved too strong for him, he was to retire across the creek under cover of the line held by General Benning. I was instructed to communicate with General Benning and to control the road, so as to prevent re-enforcements from moving up it toward the railroad, and in case Colonel Bratton's command had to retire to hold my position until he could withdraw his troops.

Sending a courier to remain with Bratton's command until it commenced moving, when he was to notify me, I returned to my own command. In a short time I received information that Bratton was in motion. My line was at once ordered forward and took position on the wooded slope overlooking the road, the left 30 or 40 and the right 150 or 200 yards from it. Here I remained nearly an hour. This time was employed in strengthening the position by the construction of rail and log breastworks before the firing began on the left.

In the meantime, General Benning had come up on my left in rear of Colonel Bratton, while the latter had moved on against the camp of the enemy. Soon after the fighting on the left began I was notified by Colonel Sheffield, of the Forty-eighth Alabama Regiment, commanding my brigade on the occasion, that a column of troops was moving from the camp on my right along the road in front. I directed the skirmishers to retire to the line of battle, and allowed the head of the column to get opposite to my left before firing. One volley scattered it in the fields beyond the road, where it attempted to reform and move on, but a second fire again dispersed it. While this was taking place other troops were coming up from the right, and, our position having now been disclosed, they turned to attack it.

Their line of attack was formed obliquely to our own, their left coming in contact with our line first and striking it near the right. This caused their left to be forced in upon our position by the other parts of their line as it advanced. The first attack was easily repulsed. The second was made in heavier force with a like result at all points of the line except one. This was at the junction of the Forty-fourth and Fifteenth Alabama Regiments. Here the enemy, forced in by the right of their line upon a vacant space in our own, caused by detaching a company for service as vedettes between my right and the river, broke through the line. Parts of both regiments gave way. By the exertions of Colonel Sheffield, and with the assistance of the Fourth Alabama, which had cleared its front of the enemy, the line was re-established and the enemy driven from it. Before this second attack took place the firing on the railroad had ceased, and a message was brought me by Captain Jamison, of General Jenkins' staff, to the effect that Colonel Bratton had encountered a heavy force of the enemy (a corps, I think, he said); that General Jenkins was withdrawing, and that he wished me to withhold my position until he could retire.

A few moments before this message came I had dispatched a courier to General Jenkins to report to him that the enemy was attacking me in front; that it was possible for him to pass troops in rear of those engaged in this attack to the point at which I supposed Colonel Bratton to be, and that if this should be done Bratton might be placed in a dangerous position. Very soon another messenger brought substantially the same message delivered by Captain Jamison, and informed me further that Colonel Bratton's command was at the creek, and either crossing or about to cross (I cannot now recall which). About the same time General Robertson, who was watching the extreme right, reported that a strong force of the enemy was moving over the adjoining hill on our right, the head of the column having made its appearance on the edge of the triangular opening in my rear, which I have already described, and near the river bank. My vedettes also reported the same thing.

In the meantime, the second attack had commenced. When the firing had almost ceased I gave orders for the whole line to retire to the hill on which it had first formed; thence into the hollow behind it, and thence by flanking to the left into the road and across the bridge. To cover this movement I held the road with a strong force of skirmishers, and directed General Robertson to place the First Texas Regiment, together with part of the Fifth Texas, already there, on an open hill between the bridge and the point from which the enemy was moving on our right. The movement was executed in a quiet and leisurely manner, the enemy in front making no effort to follow.

During the engagement of Colonel Bratton with the enemy no troops passed from the right along the road or in sight of it. It was possible, however, for them to pass near the foot of Raccoon Mountain while the attack on my position was progressing. When the order for my command to retire was given I had already received information that Colonel Bratton had been withdrawn; that he was actually at the bridge, and the firing on the left had ceased for nearly, if not quite, half an hour. Believing that the object for which my position was occupied had been accomplished, I withdrew. The movement of the enemy on my right would in a few minutes more have necessitated a change of position, and the intelligence of this movement had its influence in determining the precise moment of withdrawal. But independent of this, the order was based on my understanding of the plan of operations and the conviction that it was in accordance with that plan.

I would call attention to accompanying reports of General Robertson and Colonel Sheffield, commanding brigades.

For a statement of our loss, which was slight, I refer to the list of casualties.

Respectfully submitted.

E. M. LAW,
Brigadier-General.

[Capt. R. M. SIMMS,
Assistant Adjutant-General.]

No. 41.

Report of Col. James L. Sheffield, Forty-eighth Alabama Infantry, commanding Law's brigade.

HEADQUARTERS FORTY-EIGHTH ALABAMA REGIMENT,
November 3, 1863.

SIR: I have the honor to submit the following report of the part taken by Law's brigade in the engagement near Lookout Creek on the night of the 28th ultimo:

About 7 p. m. I received orders to put my regiment (Forty-eighth Alabama) under arms. In half an hour I received orders to move across the bridge across Lookout Creek. After crossing the creek we had not advanced very far before the pickets captured a prisoner, apparently very drunk, who reported he belonged to Howard's corps. After moving up the road a short distance I was ordered to file my regiment to the right in an open field at the base of a ridge in my front, and form line of battle in one rank. I then sent pickets in front under Captain Eubanks, who soon reported no enemy on the ridge. I then advanced rapidly, taking possession of the ridge.

The object in obtaining the ridge was, I suppose, to command the road leading down the valley from Trenton and Kelley's Ferry to Brown's Ferry, on the Tennessee River. It was very soon ascertained that there was another and higher ridge in our front, beyond which the road ran. The general commanding (Law) informed me of these facts, and ordered me to advance and obtain possession of the ridge in front at all hazards. I had sent Captain Eubanks forward with 5 men, who soon sent 1 of the men back; reported no enemy on the ridge, but a large encampment of Federal troops about half a mile from the point of the ridge where my left was to rest. He (Captain Eubanks) with 4 men crossed the ridge, came up the valley round to where the Chattanooga road intersected the same, and reported the above facts. While reporting to me the pickets near the forks of the road captured a prisoner. I had given orders to my lieutenant-colonel to move the regiment forward.

About this time I was informed that a line of 20 or 30 Yankee skirmishers was deployed on the right and left of the Chattanooga road, who had evidently come down the Kelley's Ferry road. I ordered Captain McDuffee, with his company, to the left, with instructions to get in the rear of the skirmishers if possible. The regiment had not advanced but a short distance till a fire was opened upon the left wing (from the skirmishers, I suppose). A few shots from Captain McDuffee's company soon scattered them, he capturing 8 prisoners. The regiment continued to advance, and soon had possession of the ridge, meeting with no resistance except a slight skirmish on the left. Here it was the brave and gallant Captain Eubanks fell mortally wounded and 3 privates severely wounded. I put my regiment in position with its left resting on the Chattanooga road, and some 30 or 40 paces from the valley road.

I was at this time notified to take command of the brigade. As each regiment arrived it was put in position—on the right, the Forty-seventh Alabama, the Fourth Alabama in the center, the Forty-fourth Alabama on its right, and the Fifteenth Alabama on the right of the brigade [?]. I immediately put out vedettes in front of each regiment along the valley road, and one company from the Fifteenth Alabama on the right across the ridge. I then ordered commanders of regiments to have their men put up breastworks of rails, logs, &c., which was promptly done.

Here we remained perfectly quiet about an hour, when the vedettes in front reported a column of Yankees advancing up the valley road from the direction of Brown's Ferry. Orders were given to let them advance till the head of the column was opposite the left of my line, which was done, when a well-directed fire drove them back in confusion.

In a short time he rallied, returned, and made an effort to charge the works on the [ridge.] He was handsomely repulsed and gave back in confusion. He must have suffered severely in this charge, from the cries and groans of the wounded in our front. Being driven back, he rallied and left the road, crossing a field in our front. The

left wing of the Forty-eighth Alabama and an Arkansas regiment on
my left opened fire upon him and caused some confusion in his ranks.
In a short time an attack was made on my right, which rested some
200 yards from the valley road, with thick undergrowth between our
works and the road, which was handsomely repulsed.

In a few minutes another and more vigorous attack was made upon
the right, meeting the same fate as the first attack. Being fearful
of a flank attack, I now strengthened the company on the right with
two other companies, one from the Fifteenth and one from the Forty-
fourth Alabama. Shortly afterward I was notified by one of the
pickets on the right that a column of Yankees had passed around
my right near the river. I notified General Law of the fact, and
he sent forward the Fourth Texas Regiment, which was promptly
placed in position on my right by Captain Terrell, assistant adjutant
general. In a few minutes after placing this regiment in position a
vigorous attack was made upon the front of the Fourth, Forty-fourth
and Fifteenth Alabama, some two or three columns deep. The enemy was repulsed, but returned in a short time more vigorously, and
strengthened by several columns, who broke through my lines over
our works, the left of the Forty-fourth Alabama having given way.

I here ordered Lieutenant-Colonel Scruggs, commanding the
Fourth Alabama, to swing his regiment across the ridge and to hold
his position at any sacrifice, which was promptly done, the men and
officers acting promptly. Here I ordered Colonel Perry, commanding the Forty-fourth Alabama, to rally his men and take his position
at all hazards. The Fourth Alabama co-operating with him soon
drove the enemy from and beyond the breastworks. He soon returned, but was driven back.

About this time I received orders from General Law to fall back
to the bald hill near the bridge. When I received this order the firing had ceased. I gave the order to fall back in order and in line of
battle. I fell back to the first ridge ; remained there a few minutes
and then fell back to where I first formed line of battle, when I received orders to recross the bridge. In leaving the ridge where I had
engaged the enemy I was notified of a column of the enemy advancing down the valley from the river between the two ridges. At the
same time I saw a heavy column marching by the flank on my left
which was evidently the column which passed through the field in
my front in the direction where General Jenkins' brigade was engaged. We had been in our position on the ridge, I suppose, one
hour or more before the firing commenced on our left by General
Jenkins' brigade.

I cannot close my report without expressing my thanks to Lieut.
Joseph B. Hardwick and Sergeant-Major Robbins, of the Forty-
eighth Alabama, who volunteered to assist me, in their promptness
to deliver every order ; also to the commanders and company officers
and men of the Fourth, Forty-seventh, and Forty-eighth Alabama
Regiments for promptness in driving back the enemy in the several
charges , also to Colonel Perry, of the Forty-fourth, for rallying his
men and driving the enemy from his position they had taken. These
regiments were under my immediate observation.

The casualties were : Fourth Alabama, 1 killed ; Fifteenth Alabama, 5 wounded, 2 officers and 9 men missing ; Forty-fourth Alabama, 1 killed, 10 wounded, 11 missing ; Forty-seventh Alabama,
none ; Forty-eighth Alabama, 1 mortally wounded (Captain Eubanks)
and 3 privates wounded.

The loss of the enemy was evidently very great; much more so than ours.

I am, captain, very respectfully, your obedient servant,
                                   J. L. SHEFFIELD,
                           Colonel, Commanding Law's Brigade.
Capt. L. R. TERRELL,
        Assistant Adjutant-General.

No. 42.

Report of Col. John Bratton, Sixth South Carolina Infantry, commanding Jenkins' brigade.

HEADQUARTERS JENKINS' BRIGADE,
                                   November 1, 1863.

CAPTAIN: I have the honor to make the following report of the action of General Jenkins' brigade on the night of October 28:

Having passed from our regular position on the line to the other side of Lookout Mountain, in accordance with orders crossed Lookout Creek near the railroad bridge and formed lines of battle. The Sixth Regiment (Major White) was sent to occupy a hill on the right of the road, and the Palmetto Sharpshooters one on the left. The rest of the brigade, except the Hampton Legion (Colonel Gary), which was left to guard a gap between me and General Law until relieved by General Benning, swept down the railroad between the hills mentioned to the Trenton road, capturing a few pickets or stragglers. I then changed direction to the left and advanced down the Trenton road with four regiments—the Palmetto Sharpshooters, Colonel Walker; Second Rifles, Colonel Thomson; First South Carolina Volunteers, Colonel Kilpatrick, and Fifth Regiment, Col. A. Coward. The Sixth (Major White) was ordered to advance to the Trenton road and throw its pickets out to watch the Selby Farm road as well as the Brown's Ferry road. The Legion was by this time relieved, and was following in our rear to be used as reserve.

The line thus formed advanced without opposition until near a branch, about half a mile from the point at which we entered the Trenton road. There, after some little picket firing, our skirmishers crossed the branch, and came in sight of the camp of the enemy. A hasty observation showed that there was considerable commotion in their camp. Whether it was of preparation to receive or leave us could not tell, but the hurrying hither and thither could be seen by the light of their camp fires, which they were then extinguishing. I immediately threw three regiments—Second Rifles, Colonel Thomson; First, Colonel Kilpatrick, and Fifth, Colonel Coward—upon them, with orders not to fire until they passed our skirmishers. The Palmetto Sharpshooters (Colonel Walker) were ordered to advance and take position on the railroad on what was supposed to be the enemy's flank. The three regiments had not advanced far before a very heavy fire was developed, so heavy on the Second Rifles as to cause it to halt and finally to fall back. This stopped the advance, leaving the other two *en échelon* on the field, the Fifth on the right and in advance. I at once ordered up the Sixth from its position in the rear to act as reserve, and put the Hampton Legion (Colonel Gary) in on the right of the Fifth (Colonel Coward). Colonel Gary

moved up and, passing over the line of skirmishers, who were fight
ing on the right and a little in the rear of the Fifth, drove the enemy
through their camp and entirely beyond their wagon camp.

By this time the Sixth, under Major White, had reported, and
was in position on the ground at first occupied by the Second Rifles
The position of things at this time was entirely favorable to a grand
charge.   Our line was, as it were, two sides of a wide-spread **V** (see
annexed sketch), the Fifth and Hampton Legion on the right, and

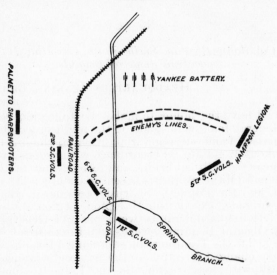

the Sixth and Palmetto Sharpshooters on the left, the First at the
point, Second Rifles on the left, behind the railroad.   The enemy
with his left driven, crowded and huddled upon his center, occupied
the base.   His line of fire at this time certainly was not more than
300 or 400 yards in length, and but from 50 to 150 yards in breadth
the sparkling fire making a splendid pyrotechnic display and en
couraging the hope that the balls intended for us were lodging on
themselves.

At this juncture I received orders to withdraw and move back in
good order, as the enemy were pressing in the rear.   While making
arrangements for the charge I had sent back to ask that Lieutenant
Colonel Logan, who followed us over the mountain with the pickets
of the brigade that were on post when we left, be sent up to me
The answer to this request was delivered just then, that Colonel
Logan was about engaging the enemy in the rear, and that I must
withdraw and move back at once.   I moved the Sixth Regiment to
the position behind the railroad and ordered it to pour its fire upon
the crowded mass of the enemy.   Under this fire the rest of the bri
gade was withdrawn.   Colonels Coward and Gary were first with
drawn and ordered to form line of battle about a quarter of a mile
in rear to cover the retreat of the others, which was done, and all
passed through, bringing away most of our wounded and many of
the guns left on the field.   I then moved on to the bridge over Look
out Creek, Colonel Coward bringing up the rear.   Here we formed
line of battle to cover the retreat and passage of General Benning's

rigade, and were the last to recross the creek.   I was ordered back
o camp, which I reached a little after sunrise on the morning of
)ctober 29.

Our loss, I regret to say, is most serious.   Colonel Kilpatrick, of
he First South Carolina Volunteers, distinguished not only for gal-
antry but for efficiency, was shot through the heart early in the
ngagement.   His bearing was such as those who knew [him] best
xpected, heroic.   His loss is irremediable to his regiment.

The inclosed list of casualties will display to you the character as
vell as amount of our loss.

To my fellow colonels and commanders of regiments I am deeply
ndebted for their gallantry, good management of their commands,
nd prompt and unhesitating obedience to orders.   The steady cour-
ge and cool bearing of officers and men under my command saved
is from any of the horrible accidents that can so easily attend night
ttacks.   To say that I am proud of their conduct would but feebly
xpress my feelings.   I refer you to accompanying reports* of com-
nanders of regiments for particulars as to the parts taken by them.

I have to regret the loss of the services of Capt. James L. Coker,
ixth Regiment South Carolina Volunteers, acting assistant adju-
ant-general on my staff.   He was seriously wounded while nobly
erforming his duty.

My couriers and a guide from General Law's brigade, whose name
did not learn, are entitled to my thanks for their conduct on the
ccasion.

I cannot close without special mention of Courier George Peitz,
vhose enthusiastic gallantry and intelligent conveyance of orders,
fter the fall of my acting assistant adjutant-general, contributed
greatly to the good order and success of the withdrawal.

Respectfully submitted.

J. BRATTON,
Colonel, Commanding.

Capt. R. M. SIMMS,
      Assistant Adjutant-General.

[Inclosure.]

*Casualties in Jenkins' brigade, Col. John Bratton commanding, in the action at
Lookout Mountain on the night of October 28, 1863*

Command.	Officers and men.			
	Killed.	Wounded.	Missing.	Total.
st South Carolina	2	38	5	45
d South Carolina Rifles	6	51	7	64
th South Carolina	9	84	9	102
th South Carolina		13	3	16
Hampton Legion	8	65	12	85
Palmetto Sharpshooters	6	35	3	44
Total	31	286	39	356

* Not found.

No. 43.

Report of Brig. Gen. Jerome B. Robertson, C. S. Army, command ing brigade.

HEADQUARTERS TEXAS BRIGADE,
Near Chattanooga, Tenn., November 5, 1863.

CAPTAIN: I herewith submit a report of the part taken by my brigade in the affair of the night of the 28th.

On arriving at the railroad I was ordered to report to Brigadier General Law, who had crossed at the lower bridge. On reporting to him I was ordered to form my brigade in line of battle in the open field at the foot of the first timbered hill, to act as a support to his brigade, which was in line of battle near the road. After remaining in this position a short time I was ordered to send forward to General Law two regiments. I sent my two left regiments (the Third Arkansas and the First Texas), which were placed on the left of General Law's line, the First supporting the Third. From where I first formed line I threw vedettes out to my right to watch the road running up the river from the direction of the enemy's camp near Brown's Ferry.

About the time the Third Arkansas and First Texas got into their positions one of these vedettes reported the enemy on or near the road above alluded to, and they were in the edge of the woods near the open field. I sent and notified General Law of it. I was then ordered to move one regiment to the bridge, and from it send a picket to the mouth of Lookout Creek and one up the Chattanooga road, and with the remainder to guard the bridge. The Fifth Texas was thus disposed of. This bridge guard was placed in the open field near the bridge and across the road leading down the river bank, with a strong picket thrown forward to the base of the hill in the field on the road, and from this picket vedettes were thrown forward to watch the approaches along the river bank.

The Fourth Texas, my remaining regiment, was ordered forward by General Law and placed on the right of his line. Finding that there was a considerable space between the right of General Law's line and the river, I sent forward two men, taken from the vedette post first established, to ascertain the movements of the enemy reported to be there. These men failed to return and were some of the missing. I regret that I did not in the hurry of the moment take their names, as they were very prompt in obeying the order to forward.

After giving orders to that portion of the Fifth guarding the approaches to the bridge to hold their position at every hazard, I hastened to General Law and reported this condition of affairs on his right. Very soon after this I received orders from General Law to form the First Texas Regiment, which he sent me, on the hill in the open field and to the rear of the place where I first formed line of battle, and cover the withdrawal of the command. This was promptly done, and the troops passed out across the bridge leisurely, in good order, without any confusion or excitement. I remained here with the First Texas until ordered by General Law to march this regiment out, which was done.

I herewith submit the reports* of the several regimental commanders.

My casualties are 1 wounded and 8 missing.

Respectfully submitted.

J. B. ROBERTSON,
Brigadier-General, Commanding.

Captain TERRELL,
Assistant Adjutant-General, Law's Brigade.

OCTOBER 27, 1863.—Skirmish in Cherokee County, N. C.

Report of Lieut. C. H. Taylor, Thomas' Legion, C. S. Army.

MURPHY, N. C.,
November 1, 1863.

SIR: On October 27, General Vaughn, with a detachment of his mounted men, overtook Goldman Bryson, with his company of mounted robbers, in Cherokee County, N. C., attacked him, killing and capturing 17 men and 30 horses.

On the 28th, I left Murphy with 19 men, taking Bryson's trail through the mountains; followed him 25 miles, when I came upon him and fired on him, killing him and capturing 1 man with him. I found in his possession his orders from General Burnside and his roll and other papers.

My men all acted nobly; marched two days, and without anything to eat.

Yours, respectfully,

C. H. TAYLOR,
Lieutenant, Comdg. Co. B, Infantry Regt., Thomas' Legion.

Lieutenant-Colonel WALKER,
Commanding Battalion, Thomas' Legion.

[Inclosure.]

SPECIAL FIELD ORDERS, }   HDQRS. ARMY OF THE OHIO,
   No. 56.   }   *Knoxville, East Tenn., October 22, 1863.*

*   *   *   *   *   *   *

VI. Capt. G. Bryson, First Tennessee National Guard, is hereby ordered to proceed with his command to North Carolina and vicinity, for the purpose of recruiting, and will return here within a fortnight, when he will report in person at these headquarters.

By order of Major-General Burnside:

EDWARD M. NEILL,
Major, and Assistant Adjutant-General.

[Indorsement.]

[General BRAGG:]

Permit me, general, to recommend to your notice C. H. Taylor, lieutenant, who commanded the Indians at the killing of Captain Bryson. You will pardon me, general, in not sending this through the proper channel, as we have no mails.

W. C. WALKER,
Lieutenant-Colonel, Comdg. Battalion, Thomas' Legion.

---

* Not found.

OCTOBER 29, 1863.—Skirmish at Centreville, Tenn.

Report of Maj. Gen. George H. Thomas, U. S. Army, commanding Department of the Cumberland.

CHATTANOOGA, TENN., *November 3, 1863—11.30 p. m.*
(Received 3.30 a. m., 4th.)

MAJOR: General R. S. Granger reports from Nashville that he sent a detachment of cavalry from that place, under Lieutenant-Colonel Shelley, to pursue Hawkins and other guerrilla chiefs. Overtook Hawkins near Piney Factory. Routed and pursued him to Centreville, where he made a stand. Routed him again and pursued him until his forces dispersed. Rebel loss, 15 or 20 killed and 66 prisoners. Our loss, 1 severely and several slightly wounded.

Rebels have fired 40 or 50 shells from top of Lookout to-day without doing any damage. We are getting supplies by steam-boat up the river as fast as they arrive by railroad at Bridgeport. We shall need more rolling stock on the railroad immediately to keep this army supplied. One of my scouts to-day reports that 20,000 or 30,000 rebels, under Buckner, have moved in direction of Knoxville to attack Burnside. The movement of troops in that direction is corroborated by other scouts, but they do not agree as to numbers.

My river guards, stationed as high up as Piney Creek, report all quiet in their front.

GEO. H. THOMAS,
Major-General.

Major-General HALLECK,
General-in-Chief.

OCTOBER 29–NOVEMBER 2, 1863.—Scout from Winchester to Fayetteville, Tenn.

Report of Maj. Joseph P. Lesslie, Fourth Indiana Cavalry.

NEAR WINCHESTER, TENN.,
November 3, 1863.

SIR: I have the honor to report to you that, according to instructions received at your headquarters October 29, under the instruction of Captain Greenwood, I proceeded to Fayetteville, by way of Lynchburg, where, on account of the inclemency of the weather, we lay over one-half of one day.

On the 31st of October, we arrived at Fayetteville about 12 m. where I established my quarters, allowing my men to occupy the vacant buildings of the town. I then stationed pickets on all the roads leading to town.

On the morning of the 1st November, I sent out two companies for the purpose of pressing stock, in charge of a commissioned officer, with instructions to receipt for all taken.

When the officer in charge returned in the evening he reported to me that he had been informed by good authority that there was a force of not less than 800 strong scattered through the vicinity, composed of three companies of guerrillas—one commanded by Captain Davis, another by Captain George; the other now I do not recollect. Also a detachment of Roddey's force. These were said to be in small detachments through the country. I also received the same information from citizens and negroes. I then ordered a lieutenant an

) men to take a report of the same to your headquarters, but imme-
iately after I received a report to me that the pickets were captured
n the Elkton road; also that the pickets were fired on from the
ridge across Elk River. Rockets were seen to be thrown up from
he opposite side of the river. I then deemed it unsafe for a small
orce to go through alone, so I countermanded the order, sending
he courier, but ordered two companies to proceed at once to take
he Elkton road and ascertain the nature of the attack. After an
bsence of about two hours they returned, bringing the body of
aptain Mason, who was in charge of the picket post, and 2 wounded
nen.

The account the wounded men gave was that at about 8 p. m. a
ody of about 20 men appeared to them from toward town. They
ere challenged at the proper distance. When asked, "Who comes
here?" the reply was, "Friends to relieve the pickets." Then, being
rdered by the deceased captain to advance, they advanced in mass
) where the captain stood in the road, shot him down, fired on the
alance of the pickets, and ordered them to surrender. They then
assed on to the vedettes, fired on them, wounded 1, and captured
nother. They did not take the arms or horses from any but the
edettes. They took but 1 prisoner.

I then—this being about 9 p. m.—ordered Major Lamson to take
companies and proceed with the led animals and cattle to Win-
hester, by way of Salem. I remained with the balance of the
ommand to prevent whatever force there might be from crossing
he river, as the force was reported to be on the Fayetteville side of
lk River.

I remained there until 7 a. m., when I proceeded to join my com-
nand at Winchester, bringing 1 prisoner, said to be a lieutenant
ately from Chattanooga at home on sick-leave.

The pressed stock consisted of 76 head of beef cattle, 76 horses,
nd 15 mules, which have been turned over to the quartermaster.
'here was no vedette in the rear of the captured picket post. The
eason of not having a medical officer along was this: We had but
ne in the regiment, and he was necessarily detained in camp. All
he sick were left with two-thirds the force of the regiment.

Your obedient servant,

J. P. LESSLIE,
Major Fourth Indiana Cavalry.

Maj. W. H. SINCLAIR,
Assistant Adjutant-General.

OVEMBER 1, 1863.—Scout from Bovina Station to Baldwin's Ferry, Miss.

Report of Lieut. Col. Newell W. Spicer, First Kansas Infantry.

HDQRS. FIRST KANSAS MOUNTED RIFLES,
Bovina Station, Miss., November 1, 1863.

GENERAL: I have the honor respectfully to report that, in obedi-
nce to your order, I started at daylight this morning with my
ommand, to reconnoiter the country and roads south of Black River
Bridge, between my position and the river, toward Baldwin's Ferry.
penetrated to the ferry, but during my scout discovered no signs
f the enemy other than the road-marks of the party, seen by our
ickets on yesterday afternoon.

The crossing at Baldwin's Ferry I judged not fordable, from the depth of water. It has evidently not been recently used as a crossing place from the absence of any marks or indications and the roads leading to it from this side being effectually blockaded by fallen trees. I attempted to go up the river bank for the purpose of discovering any crossing that might be in that direction, but on account of these obstructions I could not proceed. I discovered no roads leading to the right from the direct road to the ferry which converges with the Vicksburg road near the plantation of Mrs. Bachelor. Several roads diverge to the left, toward the Black between the position of our picket and the intersection of the roads and on one or two of which I sent patrolling parties, but to no great distance, desiring merely to pursue the Baldwin's Ferry road to the crossing. Upon the opposite bank at the ferry is a small earth-work for light artillery, but it had no appearance of having been recently occupied.

I have no accident whatever to report, and, so far as I could ascertain, the enemy has not been seen in the country since yesterday, and for several days previous.

I have the honor to be, general, very respectfully, your obedient servant,

N. W. SPICER,
Lieutenant-Colonel, Commanding Regiment.

Brig. Gen. JOSEPH A. MOWER.

NOVEMBER 3, 1863.—Skirmish at Lawrenceburg, Tenn.

Report of Maj. Thomas C. Fitz Gibbon, Fourteenth Michigan Infantry, and congratulatory orders.

HDQRS. FOURTEENTH MICH. VOL. MTD. INFTY.,
Columbia, Tenn., November 7, 1863.

CAPTAIN : Early on the morning of the 2d instant, deserters from the camp of Col. Albert Cooper informed me of the confinement in jail at Lawrenceburg of many Union citizens who refused to join the rebel army, as also some Federal soldiers captured from the various regiments that have been stationed and passed through here.

Cooper's force was represented as from 200 to 300 strong, partially and imperfectly armed, and as it was rumored that he intended leaving camp the day following, I resolved to surprise and capture him before daylight next morning. For that purpose I had 120 enlisted men, 6 lieutenants, and 2 captains detailed, and apportioning 20 to each lieutenant, and 3 lieutenants to each captain, at 3 p. m. on the evening of the 2d instant headed for Lawrenceburg. Believing that the oath-bound loyalty of the citizens of Columbia could not be relied upon, I gave out that I was going to Pulaski ; and to deceive those who might follow or watch my movements, I proceeded 1 miles on that pike, then turned southwest and went through Campbellsville. I purposed coming in rear (south) of Lawrenceburg, occupy all roads leading to it, at 4 o'clock a. m. dismount my force and walk into their camp. This could be done, for having no camp or picket guard out, as I had been reliably informed, they might have been taken in their quarters without firing a shot. But unfor

unately for the success of our movement, Lieutenant Miller, commanding rear guard, permitted the column to move too far ahead,
nd got lost in the woods. On being informed of this accident, or
blunder, my spirit sank within me, for with the three hours lost in
search of him and his command passed away the opportunity of
urprising the rebel camp.

It was now day, and being only 5 miles from Lawrenceburg, I de-
ermined to test the mettle of the "200 or 300 men," and refresh and
eed my men and horses from their stores. When within a mile of
he town the "intelligent contrabands" volunteered their fears of
my destruction, as Cooper had "over 500 men" ready to receive me.
He was told (they said) of my coming, and "got ready to lick me."
oon after my guide brought me word from a Union citizen, on
whose statement reliance could be placed, that there were over 500
men drawn up in line to welcome me; that Captains Kirk, Scott,
Birch, Payne, and Barnes, with their commands, under Col. Albert
Cooper, were determined to hold the town.

My advance guard, under Sergt. William Davis, had become hotly
engaged with a group of rebel mounted men who occupied the road
n my front, and to secure against defeat, which would be death and
destruction to my entire command, I dismounted all but 32 of my
men (who were armed with carbines and revolvers I captured a few
days previous), had them hitch their horses and form column of
companies in front of my position—and close to the rebel first line of
battle lay a piece of woods—and having ordered Sergeant Davis to
hold the road, surveyed their situation and movements. Masking
my movements from the enemy by taking possession of the woods, I
ordered Lieut. William Finn, with parts of Companies B and C, to
deploy his force as skirmishers, and giving Lieut. John M. Clarke
the "terrible 32," gave command of the reserve to Capt. J. J. Don-
elly, with directions to hold them well in hand and await orders.

The advance of the skirmishers brought on a brisk fire, but, in
spite of the efforts of the rebels to stay their march, on, on they went,
driving the enemy's vedettes and advance guard before them. Seeing now the material I had to deal with, I placed myself at the head
of the 32 and came on the left of, and in line with, my skirmishers.
Finn was driving them gallantly, and having come within close range
of their first line, which was protected by a long row of cotton bales
belonging to a Mr. Porter, pushed toward them at the double-quick,
and while Lieutenant Clarke threatened their right, Finn not only
occupied their front, but swung round his right and enfiladed them,
receiving the deliberate oblique fire of the skirmishers, by which 3
of them were wounded. The first line retired, or rather ran, in haste
upon the second. Deeming this the opportunity to strike, I ordered
up the reserve. Their right, I saw at a glance, was exposed, and as
their whole line ran along the Mount Pleasant road, hemmed in by
fences on either side, the center and left would be powerless in rendering the right any assistance. I resolved then to break through
their right, swing round their rear, and terrify the whole by badly
beating a part. Being vastly outnumbered, my enemy being nearly
500 strong, I dreaded to make known my numbers by an attack upon
their whole line.

The reserve, under Captain Donnelly, coming up, the skirmishers
advanced and engaged their whole front, receiving two volleys in
return. Under the smoke of their guns I ordered Clarke to "charge
and smash" their right, and bravely and gloriously did he obey my

words. The rebels fired by rank, but so nervous and unsteady as to pass closer in rear of my reserve than to my advance. Clarke crumbled their right, and, wheeling, aimed for their heart, but it was gone in all directions.

Occupying the court-house with two companies, the remainder pursued the flying force beyond the outskirts of the town. Fearing an ambuscade where there were so many, I ordered that the pursuit should be discontinued where opportunities for such would offer. Captain Walsh, however, could not restrain his fierceness, and taking Lieutenant Kirk and his company with him, drove Scott so close that he dropped him a first lieutenant and 3 men to stay his chase.

The jail and court-house had been emptied of prisoners an hour before our arrival, and, placing some loose cotton in the former, resigned it to the flames. The citizens begged that I would spare the court-house, as its destruction would disfigure and perhaps mutilate and destroy a monument close by, erected in memory of those of its former residents who died on the plains of Mexico defending the Republic.

Apprehending trouble on my return, and anxious to get into an open country before night set in, I gave the prisoners in charge of Lieutenant Kirk, left Lieutenants Clarke and Finn, under Captain Walsh, to guard the rear, while Lieuts. A. P. Sinclair and James Stewart, under Captain Donnelly, were to clear any hinderance to our advance. Lieutenant Miller I held to aid either front or rear when attacked.

The enemy, being informed as to my strength and numbers, fell chagrined at his discomfiture, and gathering his scattered force on the west side of the town, determined to take advantage of the hill and road through which I had to pass to annihilate my little band. I had scarcely gone 2 miles when a courier from the rear informed me that Clarke was hard pressed, and the fierce yells of my assailant gave warning of their near approach. I ordered Captain Walsh and Lieutenant Finn to form in the woods on the right, telling them that I would go back with Clarke's 32, feign an attack, give way, and run by them, when they should open on them and close in in their rear. I led Clarke's command to the rear, telling him my intention, but as I advanced to the brow of the hill the rebels were too close upon me to permit of my retiring with any chance of safety; they were about equal to my entire command, drawn up in the form of a crescent, their right resting on the road while the left lapped my rear.

Sending an orderly to the rear to bring up Captain Walsh, I determined to punish them on their own ground or perish in the attempt. I ordered a charge, telling my men to reserve their fire till we could strike them in the face with our revolvers. We were about 30 yards from the rebel semicircular line, and my men, deeming themselves close enough, hesitated for a moment. Putting spurs to my horse I dashed forward to show my contempt for the guerrillas that confronted me, and, beckoning to the noble and truly gallant Clarke, urged him to follow. Bravely, fearlessly, and heroically did he and his men obey the summons, and up to their very teeth we dashed. At this moment my horse was shot from under me, three of a volley of musket balls having penetrated his heart, brain, and side.

The struggle that now raged over me was fierce, terrific, and appalling, exceeding in stubbornness any hand-to-hand and face-to-face encounter that has marked any war of the present age. Completely encircled by a galling fire, the rebel commander twice essayed to capture us, but the undaunted Clarke still struggled bravely, and though one after another of our horses fell to earth, we converted their bodies into a barricade and cleared the field. Captain Walsh arrived in time to join in the pursuit. The rebels left (as Lieutenant Clarke, who counted the bodies, informed me) 8 of their men in the throes of death behind them, while Sergt. William Davis, who refused to go to the rear, though severely wounded, and Private Beebe L. Saxton, of Company I, and Private Heman Curliss, of Company E, wounded, besides 3 horses killed, was all the loss the "terrible 32" sustained.

Being extricated from my horse by the aid of my faithful orderly, O. B. Brombly, I formed both companies to resist another onslaught, telling them to retire alternately and join the column. Anticipating an immediate attack on the advance I hastened to the front to prepare for it, and scarce had I formed when one of the most terrific but wildest volleys that ever was hurled upon a column greeted Captain Donnelly's command from a frowning hill on his left. Coolly did that gallant officer receive it, and calmly did he deliberate upon his duty. Up that steep hill did he charge with his men, Stewart advancing direct upon their center, while Sinclair struck them on the right flank, both driving them in confused groups into a dense thicket, pouring volley after volley into the confused mass. Never before was such daring, dashing, cool, determined bravery exhibited by men, and, the cry of "no quarter to guerrillas" having been heard above the din and rattle of musketry, drove the enemy through briers and thickets to the mountains.

The force on this hill was little less than 150, half of whom were dismounted and contested Captain Donnelly's ascent. He himself blew the brains out of one, and, as I had ordered that no more prisoners should be taken, he says their loss must have been very great. Both these terrible reverses terrified the assailants, and, if I except one more desperate effort on the rear which Walsh, Clarke, and Finn gallantly met and repulsed, their firing was irregular and at long range. Providentially the only loss sustained by the onslaught upon the front was the killing and wounding of 7 horses, which I soon replaced from the stables of adjacent farm houses.

Finding themselves baffled and defeated at all points, Captain Barnes was dispatched to Mount Pleasant, 16 miles ahead, on my line of march, to notify Major Coffee to join and aid in a last attack at that place, he having about 50 guerrillas in the neighboring mountains, but he could not escape the watchful eye of Captain Donnelly, who sent two men on fresh horses in pursuit, and they, being unable to close on him, drove him off the road with their long-range rifles. Ignorant of this, about 100 of the enemy kept in my rear to Mount Pleasant, where the brave "32" were concealed to receive them. The rear of my column having passed out of town, these cowardly murderers galloped up, shouting as they came, when Lieutenant Clarke wheeled his men into line and, delivering one volley in their face, scattered them in all directions to trouble us no more.

I reached this post at 6 p. m., after an absence of twenty-seven hours, having traveled 82 miles, fought and defeated four times a superior force having advantage of ground and position, without food or rest. The prisoners, 26 in number, including 1 captain and 2 lieutenants, I turned over to Provost-Marshal Nixon, thus making in six days 107 prisoners captured by a single battalion.

It will doubtless seem strange to some that in such terrible and

close conflicts between armed forces, so few are killed and wounde
but to the intelligent officer or soldier who has witnessed the u
wieldy clumsiness of a Springfield rifle in the hands of a mounte
man, the wonder is easy of solution. Such men as compose the Fou
teenth Michigan, armed with breech-loading rifles or revolvers, wou
prove themselves a terror to any force with which they would con
in contact. No tremulous hesitation, no fear of danger or of deat
no retiring to load, or excuse to go to the rear, was visible in offic
or soldier. They fought coolly, bravely, nobly; repulsing every a
tack, and breaking every line and barrier that interposed betwee
them and success. The State of Michigan and the Republic [hav
just reason to be proud of such noble sons and gallant defenders.

Respectfully submitted.

Your obedient servant,

THOMAS C. FITZ GIBBON,
Major, Commanding Fourteenth Michigan Volunteers.

Capt. A. E. MAGILL,
Acting Assistant Adjutant-General.

—

GENERAL ORDERS,) HEADQUARTERS UNITED STATES FORCES,
No. 38. $ *Nashville, Tenn., November 8, 1863.*

The general commanding compliments the officers and men of t
Fourteenth Regiment of Michigan Volunteers. The late brillia
scouts through Lawrence, Giles, and Maury have done credit to o
arms and taught the people of that section that our flag is carri
by men who mean that it shall be respected. The general comman
ing feels assured that every portion of this command will emula
the energy, zeal, and gallantry of this regiment.

By order of Brig. Gen. R. S. Granger:

W. NEVIN,
Captain, and Assistant Adjutant-General.

**NOVEMBER 3–5, 1863.—Operations on the Memphis and Charleston Ra
road.**

SUMMARY OF THE PRINCIPAL EVENTS.

Nov. 3, 1863.—Skirmish at Quinn and Jackson's Mill, Coldwater River, Miss.
        Action at Collierville, Tenn.
  5, 1863.—Skirmish at Moscow, Tenn.
        Skirmish at La Fayette, Tenn.

REPORTS.*

No. 1.—Maj. Gen. Stephen A. Hurlbut, U. S. Army, commanding Sixteenth Arr
      Corps.
No. 2.—Col. Edward Hatch, Second Iowa Cavalry, commanding Third Cava
      Brigade.
No. 3.—Lieut. Col. George W. Trafton, Seventh Illinois Cavalry.
No. 4.—Brig. Gen. James R. Chalmers, C. S. Army.
No. 5.—Col. Robert McCulloch, Second Missouri Cavalry, commanding brigade.
No. 6.—Col. W. F. Slemons, Second Arkansas Cavalry, commanding brigade.
No. 7.—Col. R. V. Richardson, Twelfth Tennessee Cavalry.

---

* See Union Correspondence, etc., November 1, Stevenson to Hurlbut, and Hurl
to Dodge and Mizner; November 3, Hurlbut to Hatch, Mizner and Stevenson, a
replies, Part III.

No. 1.

eports of Maj. Gen. Stephen A. Hurlbut, U. S. Army, command-
ing Sixteenth Army Corps.

MEMPHIS, *November* 4, 1863.

Chalmers was handsomely repelled by Colonel Hatch with three
-giments of cavalry. General George captured. The railroad
ıd telegraph unhurt. The enemy are south of Coldwater, 3,000
rong, and Hatch is waiting for Mizner and McCrillis to come up
-om Corinth and La Grange on their rear and flank.

Dodge commences crossing the river to-day.

S. A. HURLBUT,
Major-General.

Major-General GRANT, *Chattanooga.*

—

HEADQUARTERS SIXTEENTH ARMY CORPS,
Memphis, Tenn., November 5, 1863.

GENERAL : Your orders contained in letter of 31st October, this
ay received, have been anticipated so far as it was practicable with
resent force.

No troops have as yet arrived from Arkansas, and therefore I
ave no movable column at Memphis.

I have ordered Stevenson, in the event of an attack in force, to
:aw in everything to Corinth as far as Moscow, and for that pur-
ıse directed him to keep a train and two engines.

Chalmers attacked Collierville day before yesterday, and was
·pulsed and pursued by Colonel Hatch with the Second Iowa, Sixth
ıd Seventh Illinois. I filled the Germantown and Collierville gar-
son with the Twenty-fifth Indiana Infantry.

The enemy's loss was serious in killed and wounded. Brigadier-
eneral George, of Mississippi Militia, and 8 officers captured at
ollierville. Hatch followed to Chulahoma. Mizner was ordered
·om La Grange to their flank and rear, but has not been heard from.
This morning at 3 a. m. the enemy, about 1,000 strong, pushed in
miles east of Saulsbury and commenced destroying track ; damage
ot ascertained. Hatch and Mizner are ordered to push in upon
ıem. I think the road is badly broken, but cannot yet tell. Cor-
ıth must take care of itself in that case until re-enforcements from
teele arrive. I fear McPherson will scarcely get Tuttle's division
p for want of fuel.

Your obedient servant,

S. A. HURLBUT,
Major-General.

Maj. Gen. WILLIAM T. SHERMAN.

No. 2.

Reports of Col. Edward Hatch, Second Iowa Cavalry, commanding
Third Cavalry Brigade.

COLLIERVILLE, TENN.,
November 3, 1863.

The enemy in force, under Chalmers, attacked this place about 12
'clock to-day and were badly whipped by 3 o'clock. They are in

full retreat, and my sabers are charging them. Brigadier-Genera
George is in our hands, and a number of other prisoners. Losses or
both sides not yet ascertained. There are no troops at Germantown
We are short of ammunition. Will report further soon. The lin
is all right east.

> EDWARD HATCH,
> *Colonel, Commanding.*

Major-General HURLBUT.

—

CObLIERVILLE, *November* 3, 1863—8.30 p. m.

The enemy have been driven across the Coldwater. The rou
is complete. At the Coldwater they made a stand with artillery
Firing has ceased. Colonel Mizner has assumed command of th
Second Brigade, and has issued orders to Colonel McCrillis whicl
conflict with my plans. Impossible to handle the First Brigade
owing to Colonel Mizner's rank. I think there is another columr
which passed through Salem; am not certain, though, and hardl
think it prudent to leave the road too far in pursuit with the forc
at my command. My advance is now near Quinn and Jackson'
Mill, and I leave here as soon as the infantry comes up.

> EDWARD HATCH,
> *Colonel, Commanding Division.*

Major-General HURLBUT.

—

CHULAHOMA, *November* 4, 1863.

The enemy's retreat, since leaving Coldwater, has been a rou
Retreating so rapidly, I have captured but few prisoners. Th
enemy have many killed and wounded lying along the line of retrea
Chalmers' force engaged, so far as ascertained, are McCulloch's Sec
ond Missouri Regiment, Jackson's old regiment (First [Seventh
Tennessee), George's Mississippi, McGuirk's Mississippi, Slemon
Second Arkansas, Bart's [?] Mississippi, Twelfth Tennessee, Cha
mers' Battalion, two 6-pounder guns, one rifle, three small calibe
I shall be on the road to-morrow.

> Respectfully, your obedient servant,
> EDWARD HATCH,
> *Colonel, Commanding.*

Major-General HURLBUT.

—

HEADQUARTERS THIRD BRIGADE CAVALRY,
Collierville, Tenn., November 9, 1863.

CAPTAIN: I have the honor to report the part taken by the Thii
Brigade Cavalry, Sixteenth Army Corps, in the attack on Collie
ville, November 3, 1863, by the Confederate General Chalmers, i
command of seven regiments and six pieces of artillery.

On the morning of the 3d of November, Collierville was occupie
by eight companies of the Seventh Illinois Cavalry, and two irc
howitzers, in command of Lieutenant-Colonel Trafton, with outpo
8 miles south on Coldwater. I was at Germantown with eight con
panies of the Sixth Illinois Cavalry, four mountain howitzers of tl
First Illinois Light Artillery, 450 men of the Second Iowa Cavalr
and a section of mountain howitzers, commanded by Lieutenai
Reed, Second Iowa Cavalry. Eight companies of this brigade we
guarding trestle-work and bridges from Memphis 40 miles east.

At 8 o'clock in the morning it was reported the pickets were fight-
g at Coldwater, and shortly afterward that the enemy were cross-
; at Quinn and Jackson's Mill. I immediately ordered Lieutenant-
lonel Trafton to throw the forces at Collierville into the stockade,
engthen the pickets, and dispute the ground as long as possible in
nt, and also ordered the Second Iowa to move rapidly toward Col-
rville; to halt in timber 1 mile from town; to make no show of
ce until the enemy were in town, or they heard the howitzers in the
t, then to move rapidly forward and come into position north of
e railroad, with the left of the Second Iowa resting on the stock-
e, the regiment dismounted.

When about 4 miles from Collierville, moving rapidly, a message
ched me that the enemy were close in on the town, and reports of
illery firing rapidly reached us. I immediately moved forward
a gallop, the Second Iowa going in at a run in columns of fours,
ved quickly by the right flank to the railroad, and prepared to
ht on foot, their howitzers in the center. The enemy moved a bri-
le to engage the Second Iowa Cavalry, one regiment dismounted
skirmishers on both flanks of a regiment mounted, led in person
General George. Mounted and dismounted men of the enemy
ne forward in fine style, the howitzers of the Second Iowa Cavalry
ng rapidly. The regiment, lying on the ground, waited until the
my's cavalry were within 50 yards, sprang to their feet, and, with
ers, poured in a severe fire from revolving rifles. A few men
ched the guns; among them General George and 2 officers. The
ulse was thorough. Nearly at the same moment a brigade charged
left and rear. In anticipation of this, I had ordered the Sixth
nois Cavalry to move rapidly in rear of our line, pass the stockade,
ne right into line, and charge, which was promptly done by Major
hitsit, commanding. The charge of the enemy was received,
ken, and repulsed.

he First Illinois Light Artillery coming into position at a gallop
a ridge east of town under heavy fire, losing one-half their horses
led and wounded, opened with canister, driving back the enemy's
ht. Our lines were then formed to resist what had the appear-
e of an assault directly in front; the Second Iowa and Seventh
nois on the right, and the Sixth Illinois Cavalry and First Illinois
ght Artillery on the left. The enemy advanced to within 500
rds firing; after waiting some time, and seeing the enemy declined
arther advance, I ordered the entire line forward, four companies
the Second Iowa Cavalry sabers charging, when the enemy made
veak resistance, falling back rapidly toward Coldwater. As soon
I could mount, the Second Iowa pursued them rapidly, making
8 miles to Coldwater in one hour and a quarter. Here the
my, having a position almost impregnable, kept up a severe fire
til an hour after dark, when the firing ceased. We were not able
force a crossing until the next morning, when I pushed after the
my as far as Chulahoma, 35 miles south, and finding no possi-
ity of engaging him north of the Tallahatchie, returned to camp
Collierville. After the resistance on Coldwater, the enemy's
reat became a perfect rout. During the attack at Collierville the
my attempted, in small parties, to burn trestle-work and cut the
egraph wires, but they were defeated in every instance. The
re was only cut from chance balls at Collierville and readily
paired.

We captured 50 prisoners, 7 commissioned officers, and have found

quite a number of small-arms. Our loss in killed, wounded, an
missing will not exceed 60 men. Our force engaged at Colliervil
was about 850 men. The enemy have left dead and wounded f
more than 30 miles on their line of retreat, also broken wagons an
ambulances. The Seventh Illinois was commanded by Lieutenan
Colonel Trafton, the Second Iowa by Lieutenant-Colonel Hepbur
Sixth Illinois by Major Whitsit, four guns First Illinois Lig
Artillery by Lieutenant Curtis, two howitzers by Lieutenant Ree
Second Iowa Cavalry. The guns in the stockade were ably serv
by Lieutenant Wainwright, Seventh Illinois Cavalry. All obey
my orders cheerfully and promptly, and fought their men wi
credit to themselves.

Very respectfully, your obedient servant,

EDWARD HATCH,
Colonel Second Iowa Cavalry, Comdg. Third Brigade.

Capt. T. H. HARRIS,
Asst. Adjt. Gen., Sixteenth Army Corps.

No. 3.

Report of Lieut. Col. George W. Trafton, Seventh Illinois Caval

HEADQUARTERS SEVENTH ILLINOIS CAVALRY,
Collierville, Tenn., November 5, 1863.

SIR : On Saturday, the 1st instant, I had two companies, viz.,
and B, in all about 50 men, on picket at Quinn and Jackson's Mi
Just before dark a courier came in stating that they were attack
from across Coldwater. In about three hours afterward anoth
courier reported that the enemy, about 150 in number, had retreate
and that all was quiet. The next morning I sent a scouting par
across Coldwater about 6 miles from the mill; they returned, havi
found no trace of the enemy. The next morning, the 3d, a couri
came stating the pickets were surrounded by a large force of rebe
another soon followed saying they were advancing in force to t
place. I immediately sent reconnoitering parties on all the roa
and Company L on the Quinn and Jackson's Mill road, with instr
tions to delay their approach as much as possible. They met th
about 4 miles out and skirmished, then falling back slowly towa
camp. A little before 11 o'clock they came in sight of our in
pickets and were fired on by them, which delayed them for a sh
time ; about this time the Second Iowa Cavalry came up and to
position on right and left flanks ; the action was now very wa
and lasted about three hours, the Sixth Illinois Cavalry and a b
talion of the Second Tennessee having meantime come up and joi
in the engagement. The enemy were repulsed with considerable l
to them.

The next morning, 4th, we started a little after 3 a. m. in pursu
followed them as far as Chulahoma; learned they had crossed
Tallahatchie at Berlin. To-day returned to camp.

Our loss in the engagement was as follows : At the picket post,
Quinn and Jackson's Mill, on the morning of the 3d, 2 men m
tally wounded, 2 severely, and 26 missing (among the latter was F
Lieut. Joseph O'Kane, of Company B); in camp 1 man wound
making, in all, a total of 31 killed, wounded, and missing. We
also 3 horses killed and 6 wounded.

I would mention with pleasure the services of Company L in de-
ying the approach of the enemy, as well as in killing and wound-
g several of their officers and men in their approach on the place.

GEO. W. TRAFTON,
Lieutenant-Colonel, Commanding Regiment.

Col. EDWARD HATCH,
    Commanding Brigade.

No. 4.

Report of Brig. Gen. James R. Chalmers, C. S. Army.

HEADQUARTERS CAVALRY IN NORTH MISSISSIPPI,
Oxford, November 16, 1863.

COLONEL: On October 26, I received a telegram from General
ohnston notifying me that Sherman was moving east, and ordering
e to harass his rear and break the railroad behind him.   I replied
y telegraph, that the road could be most seriously injured between
a Grange and Corinth, but that the enemy could concentrate there
ore troops and faster than I could, and suggested that I could
ake a demonstration on Germantown or Collierville, which would
raw the enemy's cavalry from the road between La Grange and
orinth, and that I would order Colonel Richardson with his bri-
ade to watch his opportunity and tear up the road as soon as it was
acated.   Major-General Gholson, of the Mississippi Militia, was
equested by me to co-operate with Colonel Richardson, and very
romptly agreed to do so.   My ammunition had not been replenished
ince my last forward movement, and the waters of the Tallahatchie
ere then up so high that I was compelled to build two floating
ridges to cross it.   This prevented me from moving earlier, but on
he morning of November 1 my whole command was put in motion.
olonel Slemons' brigade encamped that night at Looxahoma, Mc-
ulloch at Ingram's Mill, and Richardson at Cherry Creek.
On the night of the 2d, I concentrated Slemons' and McCulloch's
ommands at Anderson's house, between the fork of Pigeon Roost
nd Coldwater, 16 miles from Germantown and 19 from Collierville,
hreatening both places.   Major Mitchell, with two companies of
he Eighteenth Mississippi Battalion, had been sent forward on the
vening before, and drove in the enemy's pickets at Quinn's Mill,
xpecting that they would cross Coldwater in force the next day
fter him, and we were in a good position to cut them off had they
ttempted it, but they did not.   Before leaving camp I had ordered
aptain Henderson to keep scouts in Holly Springs and Hernando,
nd also on the railroad and State line road, with instructions to re-
ort instantly any movement of troops, and to cut the telegraph
ires.
The scouts from near Germantown and Collierville reported on
he night of the 2d that the enemy was evacuating the railroad;
hat the infantry had all been taken away, and that there was only
ne regiment of cavalry at Germantown and one at Collierville (the
ixth and Seventh Illinois Cavalry).   Supposing that the scouts were
n the State line road as ordered, and having heard nothing from
hem of any movement of troops from Memphis or La Grange, and
eeling able to encounter, even behind intrenchments, the two regi-

ments of cavalry, I changed my plan and determined to attack Collierville.

Starting before day on the morning of the 3d, we crossed Coldwater below Quinn's Mill; moved in rear of the pickets and cut them off, killing 2, wounding 4 too severely to move, and capturing a lieutenant and 26 men. This was about 10 o'clock, and we moved thence by two roads (Slemons on the western and McCulloch on the eastern road) to Collierville. The citizens up to within a mile of the place confirmed the statement of Henderson's scouts, that there was but one regiment at Collierville; and believing that if that were true the enemy would skirmish with me until re-enforcement could arrive, I ordered a charge to take the place by assault. Colonel Slemons moving on the left, and McCulloch on the left, charged up very gallantly. But we discovered at the first fire that the enemy were in position with infantry, artillery, and cavalry, and I determined at once to draw off as soon as we could do so successfully, and for this purpose ordered McCulloch's brigade to dismount and skirmish with the enemy until Slemons could be formed in his rear to cover his retreat. This was accomplished easily and in good order, each brigade forming alternately in rear of the other until we were out of reach of the enemy, when we moved slowly by the eastern road back to Quinn's Mill, and crossed Coldwater. The enemy pursued us with his artillery and a small force on the road, while his cavalry moved down the western road and endeavored to cut us off, but did not succeed. The Seventh Tennessee (Colonel Duckworth) was placed on that road to hold them in check until our column crossed. After Duckworth crossed the enemy came up to the river and opened a furious fire of small-arms, which was soon silenced by Captain Bledsoe with a few shots from his rifled gun, by which, it is said, he killed 7 men and 15 horses. We encamped within 3 miles of the mill. Started at 2 o'clock and crossed Tallahatchie that day before night.

Colonel McCrillis, with two regiments of cavalry and four pieces of artillery, taken from between La Grange and Corinth, moved through Holly Springs the same day to cut me off from the Tallahatchie; but, anticipating such a movement, we moved rapidly and eluded him.

My loss at Collierville was 6 killed, 63 wounded, and 26 prisoners. Among the last, Col. J. Z. George and my chief surgeon, Dr. William H. Beatty. Colonel George led the charge made by Slemons' brigade, and rode into the town followed by Captain Scales and Lieutenant Lamkin, of his regiment, and a few of his men. The main body of his regiment did not follow him, and, as we were mistaken about the force at Collierville, it is, perhaps, best that they did not.

The loss of the enemy at Collierville is not known, but believed to have been heavy. His loss at Quinn's Mill, including the skirmishes of the morning and evening, were 9 men and 15 horses killed, a lieutenant and 26 men taken prisoners.

We have learned since the fight that infantry came down from the east on the 2d, and that Colonel Hatch, with three regiments of cavalry, encamped on that night at Germantown, expecting me there, but holding himself ready to re-enforce Collierville, which was but 7 miles distant, and that he arrived there as we did. Colonel Richardson's command had been greatly reduced by details sent after clothing and by desertion, and Major-General Gholson, having heard

at the enemy were about to move against him, could only spare
Major Ham's battalion.

Colonel Richardson was unwell, and the force thus raised, which
mounted to only 270 men, were placed under command of Col. J. J.
Neely. He reached the railroad near Middleton on the morning of
the 4th, and found no enemy there. He destroyed three trestles,
about 800 yards of track and telegraph wire, burned the depot and
the stockade and the winter quarters of the troops.

It was a part of my plan to have made Major Blythe burn the water-
tank at White's Station, within 9 miles of Memphis, on the night
that I encamped at Anderson's, and for this purpose I ordered him
to meet me at Looxahoma with his command on the night of the 1st,
but he failed to do so, and, I am informed, says he will not obey my
orders, although notified that I have been placed by General Lee in
command of all the cavalry in North Mississippi. I have already
reported that this command, if allowed to continue its independent
action, would greatly demoralize my cavalry, and I now state that
he is keeping a large number of men out of the regular service who
are conscripts, and who would make good soldiers if properly organized.

If all the men were actuated by patriotism and a fixed determination to do a soldier's duty, these independent partisan organizations
might be very serviceable; but when such organizations are made
the receptacle of men seeking to avoid conscription merely, and who
serve only when it suits their convenience, and who boast of their
privileges in the presence of regular cavalry, they become essentially
hurtful, and, furthermore, they often degenerate into mere bands of
robbers, who steal indiscriminately from both friend and foe.

My thanks are due to Colonels Slemons and McCulloch for the
able manner in which they handled their brigades, and refer to their
reports for the action of their commands.

Inclosed please find a list of killed and wounded.

I am, colonel, very respectfully, your obedient servant,

JAMES R. CHALMERS,
Brigadier-General, Commanding.

Col. B. S. EWELL,
Assistant Adjutant-General.

[Inclosures.]

*Return of Casualties in Chalmers' command in the action at Collierville, Tenn.,
November 3, 1863.*

Command.	Killed.		Wounded.		Aggregate.
	Officers.	Men.	Officers.	Men.	
McCulloch's brigade:					
1st Mississippi Partisan Rangers.............................	....	......	1	12	13
18th Mississippi Battalion.................................	......	1	2	3	6
2d Missouri Cavalry	......	......	2	7	9
Slemons' brigade:					
3d Mississippi State Cavalry...............................	......	1	3	19	23
George's regiment [5th Mississippi Cavalry]...............	......	4	.....	14	18
Total killed and wounded	......	6	8	55	69
Missing	......	......	......	......	26
Grand total	......	......	......	......	95

No. 5.

Report of Col. Robert McCulloch, Second Missouri Cavalry, com manding brigade.

HEADQUARTERS MCCULLOCH'S CAVALRY BRIGADE,
Abbeville, Miss., November 8, 1863.

CAPTAIN : In compliance with instructions from the brigadier-gen eral commanding, I have the honor herewith to submit the follow ing official report of the actions at Collierville and Coldwater, so fa as my brigade is concerned :

On the morning of November 1, at daybreak, I moved with m brigade from my encampment at Abbeville, and the same evening about sunset, went into camp near Ingram's Mill, on Pigeon Roos Creek.

Major Mitchell, of the Eighteenth Mississippi Cavalry Battalion whom I had sent in advance with two companies of that battalio: with orders to drive in the enemy's pickets at Quinn's Mill, on Cold water, on the evening of the 1st, and to join the brigade at Ingram' Mill the same night, reported to me about 11 o'clock that night, hav ing driven in the pickets according to directions.

On the 2d instant, I moved to John Anderson's plantation, in th fork of Pigeon Roost and Coldwater, and formed a junction witl Colonel Slemons.

On the morning of the 3d instant, at daylight, I moved from thi place with a view of capturing the pickets at Quinn's Mill. Crosse the Coldwater about 3 miles below the mill, and on reaching the roa from Collierville to Quinn's Mill, I sent Lieutenant-Colonel McCul loch with his regiment (the Second Missouri) to another road to ou left, and leading also from Collierville to Quinn's Mill, to intercep the enemy should he attempt to escape by this way. I then move rapidly with the remainder of my command (the First Mississipp Partisans, Lieutenant-Colonel Hovis commanding, and the Eight eenth Mississippi Battalion, Lieutenant-Colonel Chalmers command ing) down the road to Quinn's Mill, and soon found the picket formed in line, when I ordered a charge. They fired one volley wheeled, and ran off, we pursuing them, and took a middle roa running between us and Lieutenant-Colonel McCulloch, who learne this fact on approaching the mill, and at once reversed his column and after a hard run of about 3 miles, intercepted a squad of 24 o the enemy commanded by a lieutenant, all of whom were capture and sent to Oxford, under guard of Captain Savery and company o the Second Missouri Cavalry, and also 2 or 3 others captured by th rest of the command.

About this time, having received orders from the brigadier-gen eral commanding, I moved my command rapidly up the road t Collierville, and on reaching that place was ordered to prepare fo action and to move forward and engage the enemy, which I did, dis mounting my men and forming them in line, and commenced brisk and simultaneous attack upon them from the south and east the Second Missouri, Lieutenant-Colonel McCulloch commanding on the right wing ; the First Mississippi Partisans, Lieutenant-Col onel Hovis, in the center, and the Eighteenth Mississippi Battalion Lieutenant-Colonel Chalmers commanding, on the left wing. Afte a sharp engagement of about one hour and ten minutes, in whicl both officers and men, with but few exceptions, behaved with th greatest coolness and gallantry, I was ordered to fall back, and retired slowly from the field, mounting my men, and directed Colonel Hovis to form in line of battle and hold the enemy in check, while with the rest of the brigade I moved off. After the entire column had passed near half an hour, Colonel Hovis retired slowly, expecting to find a support near.

After going about 3 miles the pursuing enemy fired on his rear guard, when he formed line of battle to repel their advance. The enemy halted and commenced shelling at long range, when he fell back according to orders, leaving Major Park with three companies to guard his rear. When in sight of the crossing on Coldwater, finding the command had not all crossed, Colonel Hovis again formed in line of battle and remained until the enemy opening a heavy fire, he crossed the river, dismounted his men, and returned to the ford and opened a brisk fire on the enemy, who soon retired.

Major Park and the companies under him are entitled to the highest praise for holding the enemy in check, thereby enabling the command to cross the river without confusion.

I may also mention that Captain Bledsoe, with his rifled gun, did good service at Coldwater in repelling the advance of the enemy.

You will find herewith inclosed a report* of the casualties in my command ; also of the horses, arms, equipments, and other property captured† and the disposition made of them.

All of which is respectfully submitted by your obedient servant,

R. McCULLOCH,
Colonel, Commanding.

[Capt. W. A. GOODMAN,
Assistant Adjutant-General.]

No. 6.

Report of Col. W. F. Slemons, Second Arkansas Cavalry, commanding brigade.

HEADQUARTERS SLEMONS' BRIGADE,
Burlingham, November 7, 1863.

CAPTAIN : In obedience to orders of this date, I have the honor to forward herewith the following report of the engagements at Collierville, Tenn., and Quinn's Mill, Miss.:

About 12 m. on November 3, I received orders from General Chalmers to move on Collierville, my command being at the [time] on the Quinn's Mill and Collierville [road.] Putting my force in motion—at that time consisting of George's cavalry, the Third Mississippi, and a detachment of the Second Arkansas, the Seventh Tennessee having been left south of Coldwater as an escort for the artillery—moving rapidly in the direction of Collierville, I encountered the enemy's skirmishers about 6 miles from town, and drove them back rapidly to a point known as the White House, where the enemy, re-enforced, made a stubborn resistance under cover of fences and farm houses, from which position a spirited dash upon their flank by Lieutenant Allen, Second Arkansas, forced them to retire. From this point, the country being open, I was enabled to bring my entire

---

* See inclosure to Chalmers' report, p. 249.
† Not found.

force against them, forming rapidly my line of battle—the right (Colonel George's regiment) resting on the Mount Pleasant road, my left (Colonel Barksdale, Third Mississippi) resting on the Collierville and Quinn's Mill road, the Second Arkansas acting as flankers.

My line of battle had scarcely been formed for the advance when the enemy opened on my right and center with light artillery. Believing it better to advance without waiting for further reconnaissance or re-enforcements than to risk the moral effect upon my troops (most of whom were new) of falling back out of range of the artillery, the order to advance was given, and the line moved steadily on to within 300 yards of the enemy's lines, which were partially concealed behind the crest of a ridge, when he opened upon me a heavy fire of artillery directly in front. I at once ordered the charge, which was responded to in gallant style. When within 60 yards of the brow of the hill the enemy opened upon us a most destructive fire of small-arms along our whole line. This fire was from rifle-pits, of the existence of which I was totally ignorant. At this shock the whole line wavered and showed signs of confusion.

About this time Colonel McCulloch appeared on the extreme left of the enemy's lines and attacked them vigorously, but for some time, say fifteen minutes, was unable to attract their attention from me. Having succeeded in drawing their attention, enabled me to withdraw my men in order, after having been under heavy fire for about one hour, the attack upon the place in front being a failure. Received an order from General Chalmers to move around to the support of Colonel McCulloch, who by this time had become closely engaged with the enemy's left. Moving rapidly to the right, I took position in rear of Colonel McCulloch, who withdrew upon the Mount Pleasant road; thence on the road to Quinn's Mill, on Coldwater, the enemy pursuing us closely with two pieces of artillery.

At Coldwater they made a dash upon the rear guard, under Lieutenant Allen, Second Arkansas, who being thrown from his horse fell into the hands of the enemy. My rear was attacked in its passage of the bridge, but no damage done. I formed on the south bank of the stream, and a brisk engagement sprang up for the possession of the bridge, which lasted until after dark, when the enemy withdrew. Leaving a force to guard the bridge and crossings in vicinity, I withdrew 3 miles and went into camp, from which point I moved to this place on the 4th.

My loss in these engagements was considerable, as you will see from list* of casualties forwarded herewith.

The conduct of the troops under my command, with a few exceptions, in the presence of the enemy was good.

Colonels George and Barksdale have a reputation too well established for gallantry to be benefited by any comment from me. Colonel George, with a gallantry discarding caution, dashed on ahead of his men and fell into the hands of the enemy.

It would be doing them injustice were I to omit speaking of the promptness and coolness with which Lieut. R. A. Sandford, my acting assistant adjutant-general, and Capt. P. H. Echols, Second Arkansas, my aide-de-camp, executed every order in the thickest of the fight.

I am, captain, very respectfully, your obedient servant,

W. F. SLEMONS,
Colonel, Commanding.

[Capt. W. A. GOODMAN, Assistant Adjutant-General.]

***

*See inclosure to Chalmers' report, p. 249.

No. 7.

Reports of Col. R. V. Richardson, Twelfth Tennessee Cavalry.

HEADQUARTERS,
Harris' House, [Chesterville,] Miss., November 7, 1863.

SIR : On the 3d instant, being too unwell to command in person myself, General Gholson and myself organized a force of 270 men, composed of detachments from Major Ham's battalion, State troops, Major Ham commanding ; from Twelfth Tennessee Cavalry, Lieutenant-Colonel Green commanding ; from Thirteenth Tennessee Cavalry, Major Thurmond commanding, the whole under the command of Colonel Neely.

This force left their camp at Knight's Mill at 1 p. m. ; ordered to so march as to strike the Memphis and Charleston Railroad by moonrise on the morning of the 5th instant, and to destroy road, telegraph, &c., as circumstances would warrant.   I have just received the following dispatch from Colonel Neely :

We succeeded in reaching the railroad about moonrise, as expected, after a ride of 62 miles that day, and burned three trestles and destroyed track, taking down the telegraph wire, 600 or 800 yards ; burned one hand-car just left by the Yankees, by daylight, and next morning burned the depot and the winter quarters and stockade the Federals were erecting at Middleton.   The Federals are evacuating the road, the infantry having left several places.   They say they are removing the old troops and bringing on conscripts to take their places.

As soon as Colonel Neely returns I will make a fuller report.
I have the honor to be, yours, &c.,
R. V. RICHARDSON,
Colonel, Commanding Northeast Mississippi.

Colonel EWELL,
Meridian.

—

HEADQUARTERS,
Chesterville, Miss., November 7, 1863.

SIR : Col. J. J. Neely has just returned from a scout on the Memphis and Charleston Railroad.

On the morning of the 5th instant, about moon-up, Colonel Neely— commanding detachments of his own (the Thirteenth Tennessee Cavalry), also detachment of the Twelfth Tennessee (Lieutenant-Colonel Green commanding), and also detachment of Ham's battalion (Major Ham commanding), in all 270 men—reached the railroad 2 miles above Saulsbury.   Learning that a force of 1,000 Federals were at Saulsbury that night, he directed his course up the State line road, and burned and destroyed three trestles, about 800 yards of telegraph wire, the depot, barracks, and stockade at Middleton, and a hand-car left there by the enemy.   He found Middleton evacuated by the enemy, and reports that the enemy was evacuating the road generally, for the purpose of running the Mobile and Ohio Railroad from Columbus, Ky., to Corinth.   Another report, derived from citizens near the road, was that the enemy was removing his old troops from the road, their places to be supplied with conscripts.   The citizens also report that the tories had left the neighborhood of Middleton, impressing wagons to carry off their chattels.   Colonel Neely left a company near the road to watch their movements, who will report daily. It is also rumored that the Yankees are fortifying and crossing the Tennessee River at Eastport. My headquarters will be Chesterville for a few days.

Very respectfully,

R. V. RICHARDSON,
Colonel, Commanding Northeast Mississippi.

Brig. Gen. JAMES R. CHALMERS,
Commanding North Mississippi.

NOVEMBER 4, 1863.—Skirmish at Motley's Ford, Little Tennessee River, Tenn.

Report of Brig. Gen. William P. Sanders, U. S. Army, commanding First Cavalry Division, Department of the Ohio, with complimentary letter from Maj. Gen. John G. Parke.

MARYVILLE, TENN., *November* 5, 1863.

GENERAL: Lieutenant-Colonel Adams has just returned from the Little Tennessee with 40 prisoners, 4 commissioned officers, all captured at Motley's Ford. Colonel Adams got near the river just as a regiment was crossing the river; charged them; drove them into the river, where he says at least 40 or 50 were killed or drowned in crossing, as his men were within a few yards of them while in the water. He describes the sight of the rebels in the river as most frightful; says the entire regiment of rebels lost their arms.

The prisoners and a citizen who escaped from them report Cheatham between Philadelphia and Loudon, with five brigades; Stevenson at Morganton with two brigades; Vaughn has 2,500 men on the other side of Little Tennessee, and a brigade at Sweet Water. Report says Forrest arrived at Sweet Water with 8,000 men; only rumor in the rebel camp. Report says the rebels are moving everything in the way of cattle and provisions south.

There are no rebels on this side the Little Tennessee River. Colonel Adams was at Niles' Ferry and Motley's Island. He saw quite a large force on the other side; estimates it at 2,000.

Respectfully,

W. P. SANDERS,
Brigadier-General, Commanding.

Maj. Gen. J. G. PARKE.

P. S.—Colonel Adams lost no men. He completely surprised the rebel camp.

—

KNOXVILLE,
November 5, 1863—7.30 p. m.

Brigadier-General SANDERS,
Commanding Cavalry Division:

GENERAL: Your dispatch of this evening, announcing Colonel Adams' forces on the Little Tennessee, just received. The general is much pleased with your report, and directs that you will please tender his thanks to Lieutenant-Colonel Adams and his regiment for the daring attack and fruitful results.

Very respectfully, yours, &c.,

JNO. G. PARKE,
Major-General.

OVEMBER 4–DECEMBER 23, 1863.—The Knoxville (Tennessee) Campaign.

SUMMARY OF THE PRINCIPAL EVENTS.

ov.   4, 1863.—Longstreet's corps detached from Army of Tennessee for operations against Burnside's forces in East Tennessee.

14, 1863.—Skirmishes at Maryville, Little River, Rockford, and Huff's Ferry.

15, 1863.—Skirmish near Loudon.
Skirmish at Lenoir's Station.
Skirmish at Stock Creek.

16, 1863.—Engagement at Campbell's Station.
Skirmish near Knoxville.

16–23, 1863.—Skirmishes at and about Kingston.

17–Dec. 4, 1863.—Siege of Knoxville.

23, 1863.—Assault on the Confederate lines about Knoxville.
Assault on the Union lines about Knoxville.

24, 1863.—Action at Kingston.

26, 1863.—Elliott ordered, with all available cavalry from Army of the Cumberland, into East Tennessee.

27, 1863.—Granger ordered, with Second and Third Divisions, Fourth Army Corps (Army of the Cumberland), to the relief of Knoxville.

28–Dec. 6, 1863.—Sherman's march to the relief of Knoxville, with Granger's command, the Eleventh Army Corps, the Second Division, Fourteenth Army Corps; part of the Fifteenth Army Corps, and the Second Brigade, Second Division, Cavalry Corps, Army of the Cumberland.

29, 1863.—Assault on Fort Sanders, Knoxville.

30, 1863.—Affair at Charleston.

ec.   1, 1863.—Skirmish near Maynardville.

2, 1863.—Action at Walker's Ford, Clinch River.

3, 1863.—Skirmish at Log Mountain.

4, 1863.—Skirmish near Kingston.

4–5, 1863.—Skirmishes at and near Loudon.

5, 1863.—Skirmish at Walker's Ford, Clinch River.

6, 1863.—Skirmish at Clinch Mountain.

7, 1863.—Skirmish at Rutledge.

9–13, 1863.—Skirmishes at and near Bean's Station.

10, 1863.—Skirmish at Gatlinsburg.
Skirmish at Long Ford.
Skirmish at Morristown.
Affair at Russellville.

11, 1863.—Maj. Gen. John G. Foster, U. S. Army, supersedes Major-General Burnside in command of the Department of the Ohio.

12, 1863.—Brig. Gen. Samuel D. Sturgis, U. S. Army, assigned to command of all cavalry serving in the Department of the Ohio.
Skirmish at Cheek's Cross-Roads.

12–13, 1863.—Skirmishes at Russellville.

13, 1863.—Skirmish near Dandridge's Mill.
Skirmish at Farley's Mill, Holston River.

14, 1863.—Engagement at Bean's Station.
Skirmish at Clinch Gap.
Skirmish at Granger's Mill.
Skirmish near Morristown.

15, 1863.—Skirmish at Bean's Station.

Dec.   16, 1863.—Skirmish at Rutledge.
    16-19, 1863.—Skirmishes at and near Blain's Cross-Roads.
      18, 1863.—Skirmish at Bean's Station.
        Skirmish at Rutledge.
      19, 1863.—Skirmish at Stone's Mill.
      21, 1863.—Brig. Gen. Jacob D. Cox, U. S. Army, supersedes Brig. Ge
        Mahlon D. Manson in command of the Twenty-third Arm
        Corps.
        Skirmish at Clinch River.
    22-23, 1863.—Scouts near Dandridge and skirmish.
        Confederate winter quarters established at and about Russe
        ville.

REPORTS, ETC.*

No. 1.—Charles A. Dana, Assistant Secretary of War.
No. 2.—Lieut. Col. James H. Wilson, Assistant Inspector-General, U. S. Army.
No. 3.—Abstract from returns of the troops in East Tennessee, under command
    Maj. Gen. Ambrose E. Burnside, U. S. Army, November 30.
No. 4.—Maj. Gen. Ambrose E. Burnside, U. S. Army, commanding Departme
    of the Ohio, with congratulatory orders, &c.
No. 5.—Maj. Gen. John G. Foster, U. S. Army, commanding Department of tl
    Ohio.
No. 6.—Return of Casualties in the Union forces.
No. 7.—Capt. Orlando M. Poe, U. S. Corps of Engineers, Chief Engineer D
    partment of the Ohio.
No. 8.—Capt. William H. Harris, U. S. Ordnance Corps, Senior Ordnance Office
No. 9.—Maj. Gen. John G. Parke, U. S. Army, commanding United States forc
    in the field.
No. 10.—Brig. Gen. Robert B. Potter, U. S. Army, commanding Ninth Army Corp
No. 11.—Itinerary of the Ninth Army Corps, October 20–December 31.
No. 12.—Lieut. Samuel N. Benjamin, Second U. S. Artillery, Chief of Artillery.
No. 13.—Capt. Jacob Roemer, Battery L, Second New York Light Artillery.
No. 14.—Capt. William W. Buckley, Battery D, First Rhode Island Light Artiller
No. 15.—Brig. Gen. Edward Ferrero, U. S. Army, commanding First Division.
No. 16.—Col. David Morrison, Seventy-ninth New York Infantry, commandir
    First Brigade.
No. 17.—Col. Benjamin C. Christ, Fiftieth Pennsylvania Infantry, commandir
    Second Brigade.
No. 18.—Col. William Humphrey, Second Michigan Infantry, commanding Thir
    Brigade.
No. 19.—Maj. Cornelius Byington, Second Michigan Infantry.
No. 20.—Capt. John V. Ruehle, Second Michigan Infantry.
No. 21.—Lieut. Col. Lorin L. Comstock, Seventeenth Michigan Infantry.
No. 22.—Maj. Byron M. Cutcheon, Twentieth Michigan Infantry.
No. 23.—Lieut. Col. Matthew M. Dawson, One hundredth Pennsylvania Infantr
No. 24.—Col. John F. Hartranft, Fifty-first Pennsylvania Infantry, commandir
    Second Division.
No. 25.—Brig. Gen. Mahlon D. Manson, U. S. Army, commanding Twenty-thi
    Army Corps.

---

*See also Chattanooga–Ringgold Campaign. Reports of Campbell, Cockerill, J.
Davis, Gambee, Grant, Holmes, O. O. Howard, Long, Miller, Morgan, Price, Reic
Rider, Schurz, William T. Sherman, Orland Smith, Van Tassell, Van Vleck, Wi
iam Wheeler, and James Wood, Part II of this volume ; also Samuel Jones' repo
of February 6, 1864, in Series I, Vol. XXX, Part II, p. 602.

o. 26.—Brig. Gen. Julius White. U. S. Army, commanding Second Division.

o. 27.—Itinerary of the Second Division.

o. 28.—Col. Samuel R. Mott, One hundred and eighteenth Ohio Infantry, commanding First Brigade.

o. 29.—Itinerary of the First Brigade.

o. 30.—Col. Marshal W. Chapin, Twenty-third Michigan Infantry, commanding Second Brigade.

o. 31.—Lieut. Col. Francis H. Lowry, One hundred and seventh Illinois Infantry.

o. 32.—Maj. William W. Wheeler, Twenty-third Michigan Infantry.

o. 33.—Maj. Isaac R. Sherwood, One hundred and eleventh Ohio Infantry.

o. 34.—Capt. Joseph A. Sims, Twenty-fourth Indiana Battery.

o. 35.—Itinerary of the Third Division, Brig. Gen. Milo S. Hascall commanding.

o. 36.—Itinerary of the First Brigade, Col. James W. Reilly commanding.

o. 37.—Itinerary of the Second Brigade, Col. Daniel Cameron commanding.

o. 38.—Brig. Gen. Orlando B. Willcox, U. S. Army, commanding Left Wing United States Forces in East Tennessee.

o. 39.—Brig. Gen. James M. Shackelford, U. S. Army, commanding Cavalry Corps, Department of the Ohio.

o. 40.—Brig. Gen. Samuel D. Sturgis, U. S. Army, commanding cavalry in East Tennessee.

o. 41.—Brig. Gen. William P. Sanders, U. S. Army, commanding First Cavalry Division.

o. 42.—Itinerary of the First Cavalry Division, Col. Frank Wolford commanding.

o. 43.—Col. Robert K. Byrd, First Tennessee Infantry, commanding Second Brigade.

o. 44.—Itinerary of the Third Brigade, Col. Charles D. Pennebaker commanding.

o. 45.—Col. John W. Foster, Sixty-fifth Indiana Infantry, commanding Second Cavalry Division.

o. 46.—Col. Felix W. Graham, Fifth Indiana Cavalry, commanding Second Brigade.

o. 47.—Col. Horace Capron, Fourteenth Illinois Cavalry.

o. 48.—Brig. Gen. James H. Wilson, U. S. Army, of engineer operations connected with Sherman's march to the relief of Knoxville.

o. 49.—Itinerary of the Second and Third Divisions, Fourth Army Corps (Army of the Cumberland), Maj. Gen. Gordon Granger commanding.

o. 50.—Itinerary of the Eleventh Army Corps (Army of the Cumberland), Maj. Gen. Oliver O. Howard commanding.

o. 51.—Itinerary of the Second Division, Fourteenth Army Corps (Army of the Cumberland), Brig. Gen. Jefferson C. Davis commanding.

o. 52.—Col. John M. Loomis, Twenty-sixth Michigan Infantry, commanding First Brigade, Fourth Division, Fifteenth Army Corps (Army of the Tennessee).

o. 53.—Itinerary of the Second Brigade, Second Cavalry Division (Army of the Cumberland), Col. Eli Long commanding.

o. 54.—Itinerary of the cavalry, Army of the Cumberland, Maj. Gen. David S. Stanley and Brig. Gen. Washington L. Elliott commanding.

o. 55.—Col. William J. Palmer, Fifteenth Pennsylvania Cavalry.

o. 56.—Brig. Gen James G. Spears, U. S. Army, commanding First East Tennessee Brigade.

o. 57.—Organization of the troops in East Tennessee under command of Lieut. Gen. James Longstreet, C. S. Army, November 30, 1863.

o. 58.—Lieut. Gen. James Longstreet, C. S. Army, commanding Confederate forces in East Tennessee, with charges against Brig. Gens. E. M. Law and J. B. Robertson, and resulting correspondence.

No. 59.—Return of Casualties in Longstreet's Corps, November 14–December 4.

No. 60.—Capt. Frank Potts, Assistant Quartermaster, C. S. Army.

No. 61.—Maj. R. J. Moses, Commissary of Subsistence, C. S. Army, Chief Commi sary.

No. 62.—Col. E. Porter Alexander, C. S. Artillery, Chief of Artillery:

No. 63.—Maj. Gen. Lafayette McLaws, C. S. Army, commanding division, wi findings of court-martial, &c.

No. 64.—Maj. William Wallace, Second South Carolina Infantry, Kershaw's b gade.

No. 65.—Col. James D. Nance, Third South Carolina Infantry.

No. 66.—Capt. E. J. Goggans, Seventh South Carolina Infantry.

No. 67.—Capt. Duncan McIntyre, Eighth South Carolina Infantry.

No. 68.—Capt. Stephen H. Sheldon, Fifteenth South Carolina Infantry.

No. 69.—Lieut. William C. Harris, Adjutant James' (South Carolina) Battalion.

No. 70.—Lieut. Col. N. L. Hutchins, jr., Third Georgia Battalion Sharpshooter commanding Wofford's brigade.

No. 71.—Brig. Gen. Benjamin G. Humphreys, C. S. Army, commanding brigade.

No. 72.—Col. Edward Ball, Fifty-first Georgia Infantry, commanding Bryan's b gade.

No. 73.—Brig. Gen. Micah Jenkins, C. S. Army, commanding Hood's division.

No. 74.—Brig. Gen. Bushrod R. Johnson, C. S. Army, commanding Buckner's c vision.

No. 75.—Col. John C. Carter, Thirty-eighth Tennessee Infantry, Hardee's corp Army of Tennessee.

No. 76.—Maj. Gen. Joseph Wheeler, C. S. Army, commanding Cavalry Corps.

No. 77.—Brig. Gen. William T. Martin, C. S. Army, commanding Longstreet's ca alry.

No. 78.—Thanks of the Confederate Congress to Lieut. Gen. James Longstreet a his command.

No. 1.

Dispatches of Charles A. Dana, Assistant Secretary of War.

KNOXVILLE, TENN.,
November 13, 1863—4 p. m.

After detailed conversation with General Burnside, I sum up h present situation, possibilities, and ideas as follows :

1. There is no reason to believe that any force has been sent fro Lee's army to attack him on the northeast.

2. It is certain that Longstreet is approaching from Chattanoog with from 20,000 to 40,000 troops. He already has all the fords the Little Tennessee strongly picketed, and is building pontoons o Pond Creek and elsewhere.

3. With Burnside's present forces he is unable to resist such a attack, and the question is how to obviate it, or in case that cann be done, what is the most advantageous line of retreat.

4. A successful demonstration by Thomas at the mouth of Chicl amauga Valley, by throwing a bridge across the Tennessee, fortif ing a bridge-head, and displaying a force to threaten the rebel li of communications between Dalton and Loudon, would compel Long street to return and allow Burnside not only to hold his present p sitions, but to advance and occupy the line of the Hiwassee.

5. In case this cannot be accomplished, the addition of 5,000 Thomas' cavalry to Burnside's present force would put the latter i

ondition to make an efficient diversion by destroying the enemy's
ine of railroad between Atlanta and Dalton, and at the same time
heck Longstreet's advance in this direction, or with this additional
avalry and 10,000 infantry from Sherman's command he could re-
ist Longstreet even if neither of the above-described diversions
hould prove successful.

6. In the event of an absolute necessity of leaving this country,
General Burnside is of the opinion that it would not be advisable
or him to march by way of Kingston, as General Grant has suggested, and this for the reasons that if he is going there he must
tart at once; that it will be impossible to collect there more than
our days' subsistence for troops, while no forage can be got there for
nimals; that by going there he will yield to the rebels the rich region south and east, whence he now draws the mass of his supplies;
nd that while he is about as far from junction with Thomas as here,
ie is of just as little use to East Tennessee as if he were at Chat-
anooga. Besides, if he is to retreat to Kingston, he must move
ow before the road is blocked, and this will uncover all the gaps in
he Cumberland Mountains and thus expose the trains and animals
ow coming through them to danger of loss.

7. By holding Knoxville as long as possible he can continue col-
ecting food and forage and living off the country to the latest moment. As to collecting these ahead he finds it impracticable, four
days' being the largest supply of meat and grain he has been able to
mass, even with the 100 miles of railroad on which he now runs un-
disturbedly 5 locomotives and 22 freight cars, all of which he gives
up by leaving Knoxville, as also all the mills and workshops which
ie is using.

8. If finally compelled he proposes to retreat on the line of Cumberland Gap, and hold Morristown and Bean's Station, which he
vould now fortify with a view to such a contingency. At these
points he will be secure against any force the enemy can bring against
iim; he will still be able to forage over a large extent of country on
he south and east; he can prevent the repair of the railroad by the
rebels, and he will still have an effective hold on East Tennessee.
At Morristown there are mills where he can grind a supply of flour
nd meal. His troops he reports as in first-rate fighting order, with
he exception of some raw regiments of East Tennesseeans and six-
months' men from Indiana. Present fine weather he regards as more
avorable to the enemy than to us; it lowers the rivers and enables
hem to move into new positions. Heavy rains would check Long-
treet, but would not stop our foraging, which is not only carried on
by the railroad but can also be kept up by flat-boats down the
numerous streams flowing hitherward.

                                              [C. A. DANA.]

Hon. E. M. STANTON,
        Secretary of War.

                                              KNOXVILLE,
                              November 14, 1863—6 a. m.

Enemy began at midnight building two bridges across Tennessee
near Loudon. Burnside has determined to retreat toward the gaps.
Ninth Corps at Lenoir's and White's division near Loudon ordered
o fall back on Knoxville, destroying cotton factory at Lenoir's

and delaying enemy as much as possible. All workshops and mill will be destroyed here and elsewhere on the line of retreat. Th force of the enemy reported as Longstreet's two divisions, Steven son's division, and Wheeler's cavalry entire. Burnside does not fee sure whether he will be compelled to pass the mountains. Possibl he may be able to stop this side, and not entirely abandon East Ten nessee. In the former event he may lose his trains and animals, bu can save artillery.

I leave immediately for Chattanooga, passing the Clinch some where north of Kingston.

[C. A. DANA.]

Hon. E. M. STANTON,
    Secretary of War.

—

LENOIR'S STATION,
November 14, 1863—11.30 a. m.

It is reported here enemy have not yet finished their bridges; hav no artillery or cavalry across. Burnside is resolved to attack then with one division of the Ninth Corps, about 3,000 strong. Distanc hence about 10 miles.

[C. A. DANA.]

Hon. E. M. STANTON,
    Secretary of War.

—

CHATTANOOGA, TENN.,
November 18, 1863—12 m.

Arrived here last evening. Had my departure from Burnsid been delayed a single day I could only have got out through Cun berland Gap or that of Big Creek.

Burnside's present position seems safe except for Longstreet's grea superiority in cavalry, the latter having Wheeler's whole force wit him, from 7,000 to 9,000 strong, while Burnside cannot concentrat more than 3,000 without abandoning the upper part of the valley t Sam. Jones, and endangering his communications on that side. Stil there is a reasonable probability that Burnside will be able to hol Knoxville until relieved by operations here. I found him possesse by the idea that he must expose his whole force to capture rathe than withdraw from the country, and so firmly was this notion fixe in his mind that when the report arrived at 1 a. m. on the 14th tha Longstreet had begun to build bridges at Loudon, he actually di tated the orders for throwing his whole army south of the Holsto into Blount County, where all his communications would be cut o at once, and where on his own estimate he could not subsist mo than three weeks, while General Parke thought ten days' subsistenc would be the utmost to be found there. Parke argued against th idea in vain, but finally General Wilson overcame it by representin that Grant did not wish him to include the capture of his entire arm among the elements of his plan of operations. Burnside's comman is in great want of first-rate general officers, both the Ninth an Twenty-third Corps being commanded by brigadiers who are con paratively inexperienced, General Hartsuff being incapacitated an General Parke employed as chief of staff.

I procured at Knoxville a dispatch from General Crittenden to urnside, dated Chattanooga, September 10, informing Burnside, by rder of Rosecrans, that Rosecrans' right was then at Rome and rittenden in full pursuit of Bragg. If General Halleck has not this ocument to use in preparing his annual report I can telegraph it. A dispatch of Rosecrans to Granger, after occupation of Chatta- ooga, informing Granger "our great flanking movement con- nues," General Halleck may also desire.   Pleasant.

[C. A. DANA.]

Hon. E. M. STANTON,
    Secretary of War.

—

CHATTANOOGA,
November 19, 1863.—12 m.*

I omitted to report in my dispatch of 12 m. yesterday that I had nversed with General Parke relative to Burnside's plan of holding orristown and Bean's Station, and that Parke pronounced the roject impracticable because the enemy could pass up behind Clinch ountain and cut off all possibilities of retreat.

[C. A. DANA.]

Hon. E. M. STANTON,
    Secretary of War.

—

CHATTANOOGA, *November* 21, 1863.

Following is letter of Crittenden to Burnside, mentioned in my spatch of the 18th :

HDQRS. TWENTY-FIRST ARMY CORPS, ADJUTANT-GENERAL'S OFFICE,
    Chattanooga, September 18 [10,] 1863—2 a. m.

aj. Gen. AMBROSE E. BURNSIDE,
    Commanding Department of the Ohio, Tennessee River:

SIR : I am directed by the general commanding the Department of the Cumber- nd to inform you that I am in full possession of this place, having entered it yes- rday at 12 m. without resistance. The enemy has retreated in the direction of ome, Ga., the last of his force (cavalry) having left a few hours before my arrival. t daylight I made a rapid pursuit with my corps, and hope that he will be inter- pted by the center and right, the latter of which was at Rome. The general mmanding the department requests that you move down your cavalry and occupy e country recently covered by Colonel Minty, who will report particulars to you, d who has been ordered to cross the river.

T. L. CRITTENDEN,
Major-General, Commanding.

This letter made Burnside believe Rosecrans perfectly successful, eding no assistance whatever.

On September 9, Rosecrans wrote to Granger, saying :

Chattanooga is ours. Our movement on the enemy's flank and rear goes on.

The rest of this letter is occupied with directions for the move- ent of various troops.

On September 9, Rosecrans ordered Crittenden to pursue Bragg.

The general commanding directs that you leave a light brigade to hold Chatta- oga, and with the balance of your command pursue the enemy with the utmost gor. Attack his rear whenever you can do so with a fair opportunity to inflict jury upon him. Order your train to follow your line of march under a sufficient

---

* For portion of dispatch here omitted, see Part II, p. —.

escort. Your march will probably lead you near Ringgold, and from thence to th
vicinity of Dalton. General Thomas marches on La Fayette, and General McCoo
on Alpine and Summerville.

On the same day Thomas was ordered :

> The general commanding directs you to move your command as rapidly as possi
> ble to La Fayette, and make every exertion to strike the enemy in flank, and, i
> possible, to cut off his escape.

While at Stevens' Gap Rosecrans told me that General Hallecl
had refused to allow him to advance beyond Dalton, saying tha
after Rosecrans had reached that point they would confer respectin;
further movements. Copies of all the above-cited documents ar
forwarded by mail. Weather dull and rainy.

[C. A. DANA.]

Hon. E. M. STANTON,
        Secretary of War.

—

CHARLESTON, TENN.,
December 1, 1863—7 a. m.

Sherman arrived here yesterday at 1 p. m. Howard leading o
one road and Davis on another. Small rebel force here fled towar
Loudon, destroying pontoon bridge and breaking out 36 feet of th
railroad bridge. The latter has been repaired and planked upo
the rails, and troops are now moving across. Granger not hear
from ; should have reached mouth of the Hiwassee yesterday. N
news from Knoxville. Cold.

[C. A. DANA.]

Hon. E. M. STANTON,
        Secretary of War.

—

MORGANTON, TENN.,
December 4, 1863—4 p. m.

The cavalry brigade under Colonel Long, which General Sherma
had kept out of sight on his right flank and rear till the afternoo
of the 2d instant (Wednesday), was sent to the front at Sweet Water
and pushed forward with all haste to Loudon, where it arrived a
3.30 p. m., with the design, if possible, of surprising Longstreet's rea
guard and seizing his bridge across the Tennessee. The advanc
from Sweet Water was made with such dash as to capture the ene
my's pickets, but he displayed a considerable force at his bridg
head, with two pieces of artillery, and Long judged it prudent nc
to attack.

Yesterday morning Howard's corps entered Loudon and found th
bridge destroyed, 3 locomotives and 48 cars run into the river, and a
the public stores burned. The main body of the army marched ye
terday to this place, where it was believed a practicable ford migl
be found, and Ewing's division reached here at 11 a. m. The forc
however, proved too deep for men, the river being 200 yards wide an
the water almost at freezing point. Horses and wagons can be forded
though not with perfect ease. General Wilson, of Grant's staff, wh
was with the advance, at once set about the construction of a trestl
bridge, and by working all last night has it now so far advanced tha
troops can begin to cross by dark this evening. Meanwhile an ol

erry-boat has been used to pass over the division of Ewing and its rtillery, and wagons have been forded. Sherman expects to get is whole army over by noon to-morrow, all its parts, including ;ranger's, being up. The distance hence to Knoxville is 34 miles.)ur advices from that place are to the 1st instant, and are derived rom a rebel mail captured last night.

Longstreet assaulted Burnside on the 29th ultimo, and was repulsed vith the loss of 1,000 men of McLaws' division. They reached the litch of the work they attacked, but were unable to cross it. Two egiments appear to have been captured by the garrison. Longstreet till remains at Knoxville, and very evidently supposes this army to)e only a small force. All the letter-writers speak of their condition n great despondency, and regard their chance of extrication as very)oor. Nights cold ; days beautiful.

[C. A. DANA.]

Hon. E. M. STANTON,
        Secretary of War.

—

KNOXVILLE,
December 6, 1863—3 p. m.

Sherman arrived at noon, leaving the Fifteenth Corps at Mary-ville with orders to halt there, and the Eleventh Corps at Louis-ville. Granger, with his two divisions, moves toward Sevierville to cut off any stray part of Longstreet's force that may endeavor to escape by way of the French Broad, direct pursuit of Longstreet from here being impracticable with infantry. Sherman will at once move back toward Chattanooga with all of his troops, except the command of Granger, taking the road by way of Columbus and Benton, not only because that country has not been eaten out by armies, but also that he may conveniently strike at Dalton if cir-cumstances favor and Grant so desires.

The only ill luck in this quarter so far is the failure of Elliott to get up with his cavalry, which was at Liberty on the 26th ultimo, got orders to move to Kingston on the 27th, and should have crossed the Clinch by the 30th at farthest. Nothing has yet been heard of him. No news here from Foster.

Yesterday morning, after Longstreet retreated, Burnside had fully twenty days' provisions, much more, in fact, than at the beginning of the siege. These supplies had been drawn from the French Broad by boats and by the Sevierville road. The people of the country did their utmost through the whole time to send in provis-ions and forage, and Longstreet left open the very avenues which Burnside most desired. Boats came down the Holston in open day without being fired upon, and the Sevierville road was never inter-rupted. The losses of our forces here from the first contact with Longstreet near Loudon until the evacuation will not exceed 1,000. Ammunition got very short before the siege was over, and project-iles for our rifle guns were made here. The utmost constancy and unanimity prevailed during the whole siege, from Burnside down to the last private; no man thought of retreat or surrender. I return to Chattanooga as soon as possible, probably leaving to-morrow; arrive there 12th or 13th.

[C. A. DANA.]

Hon. E. M. STANTON,
        Secretary of War.

CHATTANOOGA,
December 10, 1863—2 p. m.

Left Knoxville with General Sherman at 8 a. m. Monday, 7t
instant. He has gone to Tellico Plains with the Fifteenth Corp;
sending also a cavalry expedition about 1,000 strong to Murphy, N
C., to destroy a rebel wagon train, and, if practicable, make a rai
as far as Dahlonega. At the same time the division of Jeff. C
Davis occupies Columbus and Benton, on the Hiwassee, and th
Eleventh Corps is posted at Athens and Charleston. These force
will eat out the country and be here week hence. Granger grum
bled and complained so much about the destitution of his men tha
Burnside drew his two divisions into Knoxville, and, with all hi
own troops, moved out on Monday morning to pursue Longstreet.

Foster had not yet arrived, but Burnside expected to deliver th
command to him in a day or two and go north, via Cumberlan
Gap. Elliott's cavalry moved from Sparta for Kingston on the 5t
instant, eight days later than they should have moved; by whos
fault I have not yet learned. Longstreet was retreating in a
orderly manner with all his artillery. His rear guard was at Straw
berry Plains on afternoon of 6th.

No news here. Thomas and Grant have gone for the day to visi
Chickamauga battle-field. The campaign here being concluded,
ask leave to go north. If Grant is to make his proposed Alabam;
campaign, and you desire me to accompany him, I can join hin
from New York or Washington as well as from here. I am sur
that I can be more useful anywhere else than I can here, since al
has become safe, quiet, and regular. Weather sunny and beautiful

[C. A. DANA]

Hon. E. M. STANTON,
    Secretary of War.

—

CHATTANOOGA,
December 11, 1863—12 m.

I learn from General Thomas that the orders to Elliott to mov
his division against Longstreet reached him at Alexandria on the
26th ultimo, and on his answering that he did not understand them
were repeated and explained to him by telegraph the same day
upon which he replied that he now understood perfectly and woul
move at once. Alexandria is 80 miles from Kingston, and he shoul
have reached the latter place on the 1st instant at farthest. Bu
it now appears that he did not start till the 7th instant, for wha
reason is yet unknown. Grant has ordered him to report why i
writing. His division is not less than 3,500 strong, with fres
horses.

General F. P. Blair goes north this day on leave, with permissio
to apply for authority to visit Washington. He told me he woul
not resign if the Government would give him a command, whicl
General Grant says he is ready to do without his going to Washing
ton. But one of his staff informs me that he claims an army corps
on the ground that President Lincoln had promised him the Fif
teenth Corps, but that when A. L[incoln] went to the War Office t
have the assignment made he found E. M. S[tanton] had alread;
appointed J. A. Logan. Grant is very angry with Granger fo
misconduct in the Chattanooga battle, and now for unwillingness t

march after Longstreet. Granger will probably be removed and Sheridan assigned to succeed him, subject to approval of Government. Granger is certainly unfit to command.

[C. A. DANA.]

Hon. E. M. STANTON, *Secretary of War.*

—

CHATTANOOGA,
December 12, 1863—10.30 a. m.

Elliott was heard from yesterday. He was at Crossville on the 9th instant, moving with a forage train, though ordered to pursue Longstreet. Sherman was ordered back to Bellefonte yesterday with view to a demonstration against Rome, by one column starting from Bellefonte and one from Chattanooga, the object being destruction of railroad bridge over the Oostenaula and removing enemy farther south than Dalton, his present position. Winter rains, which now threaten to set in, may prevent this movement.

[C. A. DANA.]

Hon. E. M. STANTON, *Secretary of War.*

———

No. 2.

Report of Lieut. Col. James H. Wilson, Assistant Inspector-General, U. S. Army.

KNOXVILLE, *November* 13, 1863.
(Received 14th.)

GENERAL: Since the arrival of Mr. Dana and myself here, General Burnside, in a complete discussion of the situation in East Tennessee and its relation to the general campaign, has given us his views clearly and in detail, and requested me to communicate them to you without delay. He assumes that it is of the first importance to hold East Tennessee, because doing so he draws an ample supply of bread, meat, and forage from the rich country between the Clinch River, Rogersville, and the great Smoky Mountains, for his entire force protects and encourages a large population of loyal people, and deprives the enemy of a source of supplies of the greatest necessity to him. It simply becomes a question of how this can best be done, of how his forces can be most advantageously posted with that object in view, or in case he is compelled to give up the country entirely, to have for his selection such lines of retreat as will lead him in directions upon which he can reach supplies, and at the same time leave him most advantageously situated to assist the main body of your troops in future operations.

The instruction of the General-in-Chief seems to have no other object in view in furtherance of this; therefore he thinks Knoxville the point to be held and around which he must operate. For this point he has the use of the railroad from Lenoir's to Greeneville, and rolling stock sufficient to bring in such supplies as may be accumulated at various points along it. The Holston, French Broad, and tributary streams may be also used for flats when the road becomes too bad for wagons. Knoxville is in the region of supplies, and has mills in running order to turn out 150 barrels of flour per day, and can receive the product of other mills able to grind another hundred; contains shops capable of keeping the major part of the material in good order; is susceptible of vigorous defense, and when finally abandoned is so situated as to allow ready access to all the roads except the one leading through Kingston. In short, he can concentrate his forces here more rapidly, supply them more easily, defend himself quite as successfully, and finally, if it comes to the worst, he can carry off his command in better condition, and by routes which, although longer, would be safe, and ultimately enable him to move wherever you might direct.

In case he is compelled to relinquish Knoxville, after destroying everything that could help the enemy, he would prefer to go to Morristown and Bean's Station. He thinks he could maintain those positions against any force that could be sent against him; they being admirably situated with reference to the gaps, would enable him to keep up communication in that direction, to prevent the repair of railroad, and still allow him to forage much of the country to the south and eastward. There being plenty of mills, he could still be able to supply himself in a degree with bread from the country, and use his transportation for hauling sugar, coffee, and salt. In anticipation of this step he could at once set to work fortifying these places as strongly as possible from Knoxville.

If you should direct it, he could move when necessary by Clinton, Winter's Gap, and Morganton either to Carthage or McMinnville. But in this event his live stock, coming by way of the gaps, together with the main part of the cavalry should be turned back into Kentucky, to be disposed of afterward as necessity might demand.

The general's idea of Kingston is that, although a point of considerable natural strength, and, if well supplied, of strategic importance, it is almost entirely out of the question now either as a point of his line of retreat or as one from which he could exercise a controlling influence over East Tennessee. The country about it is poor, the Clinch and Emory River regions having been exhausted of supplies by his previous operations.

If his whole force were concentrated there, he could not possibly take with him more than seven days' supply. The railroad would at once fall into the enemy's hands, and could be repaired at leisure. They would also get Knoxville, all the mills, and nearly the entire productive region of East Tennessee. This would necessarily be the case, for, with a few more [days of] good weather, the Holston could be forded at any place south of Knoxville, and, in addition, bridges might be easily constructed so as to cross either it or the Tennessee. It is reported now that the rebels are building a pontoon bridge upon Pond Creek, and that they are watching every ford and ferry from the foot of the mountain to Kingston with the greatest care. It seems entirely practicable for the enemy to cross if he desires it, and that before Burnside's forces could be concentrated at any point; hence the general argues that if it becomes necessary to leave East Tennessee, and he were to be ordered to do it by way of Kingston, the enemy could precipitate that necessity, in spite of all activity, before our forces could possibly be disposed to prevent it or to effect their retreat. In this event his forces would either be beaten in detail or be compelled to go at once to Kingston, where they cannot feed themselves and are still far from a junction with Thomas.

This is the case considered defensively only, but if the good weather continues it will become desirable to concentrate a force sufficient to anticipate the enemy in offensive operations, and thereby prevent him from gaining even the temporary advantages to be derived from compelling Burnside to adopt either of the plans alluded to above.

Weather that will enable the enemy to operate will afford us the same opportunity, and any plan which may be adopted involving Sherman and Thomas can be co-operated with from here.

A bridge-head and bridge in the neighborhood of Dallas or Igou's Ferry, with a force threatening Cleveland, would probably bring the enemy either from the front of Burnside or Thomas. If from the former he could advance at least to the line of the Hiwassee, and if the whole plan was fortunately executed, would give us all the country as far south as Cleveland, and allow a complete junction of your entire army.

The general also says, should a plan of operations of this kind be put on foot, he could use four or five thousand of Thomas' cavalry to great advantage. Or, even if it is determined to do no more than try to hold the present line of the Little Tennessee, this additional cavalry force would be of great benefit to him. He thinks it would enable him to hold his line against any ordinary force that the enemy can send against him.

The general does not wish to be understood as requesting 10,000 infantry to be sent to him, but makes this suggestion in view of the possibility that no operation toward Cleveland on the part of Thomas may be deemed practicable, and that you may still desire and make his occupancy of this country certain.

> J. H. WILSON,
> *Lieutenant-Colonel, &c.*

Major-General GRANT, *Chattanooga*.

No. 3.

Abstract from returns of the troops in East Tennessee, under command of Maj. Gen. Ambrose E. Burnside, U. S. Army, November 30, 1863.

Command.	Present for duty.		Aggregate present.	Aggregate present and absent.	Pieces of field artillery.	Station.
	Officers.	Men.				
Ninth Army Corps:						
Headquarters	17	10	27	31	......	Knoxville.
First Division	194	2,720	3,490	6,774	10	Do.
Second Division	84	1,248	1,761	3,259	6	Do.
Unassigned	14	369	419	541	4	Do.
Total Ninth Army Corps	309	4,347	5,697	10,605	20	
Twenty-third Army Corps:						
Headquarters	12	95	144	178	......	Do.
Second Division	178	3,225	3,978	5,554	12	Do.
Third Division	149	3,379	4,200	5,607	16	Do.
Engineer troops	1	28	39	55	......	Do.
Reserve Artillery	9	220	239	265	(a)	Do.
Total Twenty-third Army Corps	349	6,947	8,600	11,659	28	
Left Wing forces in East Tennessee b	244	4,750	5,889	7,704	31	Cumberland Gap.
Cavalry Corps	428	8,245	10,166	14,755	32	
Grand total	1,330	24,289	30,352	44,723	111	

a Not reported in returns.
b Including garrison of Cumberland Gap.

No. 4.

Reports of Maj. Gen. Ambrose E. Burnside, U. S. Army, command-
ing Department of the Ohio, with congratulatory orders, &c.

Knoxville, Tenn.,
November 17, 1863—1.30 a. m.

Longstreet crossed the Tennessee River on Saturday (12th), at
Huff's Ferry, 6 miles below Loudon, with about 15,000 men. We
have resisted his advance steadily, repulsing every attack, holding on
till our position was turned by superior numbers, and then retiring
in good order.

He attacked us yesterday about 11 o'clock at Campbell's Station,
and heavy fighting has been going on all day, in which we have held
our own and inflicted serious loss on the enemy. No fighting since
dark. We commenced retiring, and the most of the command is
now within the lines of Knoxville. At the same time that Longstreet
crossed the river a heavy cavalry force crossed the Little Tennessee,
and advanced on this place by way of Maryville. Our cavalry force
at Rockford was slowly pressed back by superior numbers, and at
sundown Sunday (13th) night had fallen back to the infantry support
on the first ridge from the river.

They did not attack yesterday morning, but in the course of the
day disappeared from our front. I shall make every exertion to hold
this place, and trust we shall be able to do so. The men are in good
spirits and are behaving splendidly.

A. E. BURNSIDE,
Major-General.

His Excellency the PRESIDENT.

—

Knoxville, *November* 17, 1863—10 p. m.
(Received 6 p. m. 18th.)

Since I reported to you at 1 [1.30] this morning, troops, batteries,
and trains have all arrived. The enemy did not press us during the
night. The troops were placed in position, intrenchments thrown
up where none existed, and every exertion made to render the position secure. The enemy have made no serious demonstration during
the day.

Our cavalry on the Kingston road have been skirmishing all the
afternoon, and have been pressed slowly back, and the enemy's pickets
are now about 2 miles from town. His advance to-day has not been
vigorous, and he is evidently holding back for the arrival of his batteries or the development of some flank movement. If he should
assault our position here, I think we can give a good account of ourselves.

They still have a force on the other side of the river with pickets
in sight of ours, but have made no demonstration to-day.

A. E. BURNSIDE,
Major-General.

ABRAHAM LINCOLN,
      President.

(Copy sent General Grant.)

HEADQUARTERS,
Knoxville, November 21, 1863.

The enemy has not yet attempted an assault; he is, however, busily engaged throwing up batteries and making approaches.

We have the town completely surrounded by a continuous line of rifle-pits and batteries, and hold the heights on the opposite side of the river.

A desultory fire is kept up along our skirmish line, which is from 500 to 1,000 yards beyond our line of rifle-pits. The enemy thus far has not attempted a complete investment. His main body seems to occupy the ground extending from the river below town around to the Clinton road. There has been occasional cannonading since the 18th. Our loss has been trifling. The death of General Sanders is a serious loss, and keenly felt by us all. We have on hand eight days' bread, half rations; fifteen days' beef, and of fresh pork full rations, and an abundance of salt. Our forage trains cross the river daily, and have so far been successful. The cavalry force that threatened us on the opposite side of the river have retired from that immediate front and gone certainly beyond Little River, and there is but a small force between Little River and the Little Tennessee. The rains of last night and this morning will render the streams unfordable. We have a reasonable supply of ammunition, and the command is in good spirits. The officers and men have been indefatigable in their labors to make this place impregnable.

A. E. BURNSIDE,
Major-General.

General GRANT.

—

KNOXVILLE, *November* 23, 1863.
(Received Chattanooga, 25th.)

The enemy are still in our front. They have not yet molested the place, but hold all outlines here and other side of the river. Our defenses are comparatively strong, the men in good spirits; we have provisions for, say, ten or twelve days longer, and will hold out as long as we can. It is possible the enemy are strong enough to carry the place by assault. The enemy have last night attempted to break our pontoon bridge by floating rafts down against it, but did not succeed. We have taken precautions which we hope will defeat any future attempt.

A. E. BURNSIDE,
Major-General.

Major-General GRANT.

—

KNOXVILLE, TENN.,
November 28, 1863.

I dispatched you last on the 23d. During that night a body of the enemy crossed the river about 3 miles below our lines and established themselves on a high point just beyond our picket line and threw up a rifle-pit facing our position on that side. During next day and the forenoon of the 25th, continued skirmishing went on, and on that afternoon they assaulted our right on that side of the river with two brigades. Colonel Cameron, who held that position with his brigade, held his ground in the most gallant manner, and finally repulsed them and drove them half way up the opposite hill, inflicting severe loss upon them. Our loss was about 50 ; that of the enemy about 150.

Appearances indicating that the enemy were concentrating a heavy force there for another attack, our position was strengthened and reenforcements placed at the disposal of Brigadier-General Shackelford, who commanded the forces on the south side of the river. No further demonstration has been made on that side, and we still hold the same skirmish line as at the close of the fight. The enemy are still at work on the hill held by them. On this side of the river the situation is nearly the same as at last accounts. The enemy have thrown up some new works, but have not extended their lines, and no enemy is visible on our right except cavalry. Skirmishing is continual on our left, but we still hold the same line. By sending our trains on the roads still open to us, we have been enabled to keep up a fair supply of forage and subsistence.

                                A. E. BURNSIDE,
                                Major-General, Commanding.

Major-General GRANT,
    Chattanooga.

—

                        KNOXVILLE, *November* 30, 1863.
                        (Received Chattanooga, 3d.)

On the evening of the 28th, about 11 p. m., the enemy made an attack in force upon our picket line to the right of the Kingston road and forced us back some distance in front of Fort Sanders, the work commanding that road.

We afterward regained a portion of the distance. Sharp skirmishing continued nearly all night. About half past 6 yesterday morning they moved a column of assault of three brigades against Fort Sanders. In spite of our heavy fire, a portion of two brigades succeeded in gaining the ditch, but were unable to ascend the parapet. We swept the ditch with an enfilading fire with much slaughter. The rest of the attacking column retreated in confusion. We sent out a detachment, to whom the rebels in the ditch surrendered. About 300 men and 3 stand of colors were taken. Their killed and wounded amount to about 500. Our entire loss was about 20.

The morning being very cold and frosty, and the enemy's wounded in our ditch and in front of the fort crying for help, I sent out a flag of truce, offering the opportunity of caring for their wounded and burying their dead. General Longstreet gratefully accepted the offer, and a cessation of hostilities till 5 p. m. was agreed upon. Their slightly wounded were exchanged for our slightly wounded lost in previous affairs, and their dead sent to their lines. Ninety-eight dead passed through our hands, among them Colonel Ruff, commanding Wofford's brigade, which led the assault, Colonel McElroy, and Lieutenant-Colonel Thomas.

A simultaneous assault was made upon the right of our line, on the other side of the river, by a rebel brigade. They carried our first line of rifle-pits, but were soon after driven from them, and the whole line regained and held. Our loss on that side was about 40; that of the enemy is thought to be greater.

Our supply of provisions continues the same. The men are in the best of spirits. We have nothing definite of your movements, and are very anxious.

I have information that on the 27th the enemy received re-enforcements of one division, perhaps two—Bushrod Johnson's and Cheatham's. Some of Buckner's troops are certainly here, as some of our officers saw the rebel General Gracie during the flag yesterday. Let us hear from you soon.

A. E. BURNSIDE,
Major-General.

Major-General GRANT.

—

KNOXVILLE,
December 6, 1863—8 a. m.

General Wilson has arrived here, and has informed you in detail by telegraph of our present position. The siege was raised yesterday morning, and our cavalry is pursuing the enemy as rapidly as possible under the circumstances.

The horses are in bad condition and the men very much fagged by constant work in the trenches.

The infantry are not in a good condition for pursuit for the same reason, and the artillery can scarcely be moved for want of animals. The advance of Sherman's column is near and he will be here in person in a few hours, when we will try and organize a pursuing force large enough to either overtake the enemy and beat him or to drive him out of the State. The main body of his force is moving toward Morristown, and the indications are that he will try to reach the terminus of their railroad line at Bristol. We have saved all our rolling stock on the railroad, but will not be able to use it farther up than Strawberry Plains, as the bridge at that place has been destroyed. We have heard nothing from Foster or Elliott, but hope to this morning. Will telegraph you more fully after seeing Sherman. We thank you for the prompt aid rendered us. But for the approach of Sherman the siege would not have been raised.

A. E. BURNSIDE,
Major-General.

Major-General GRANT.

—

KNOXVILLE, *December* 7, 1863.

I have just written the following letter to General Sherman,* who at daylight this morning reversed all his troops with the exception of Granger, and started them back to you. Elliott has not yet reported; when he does I shall put him upon the right flank of the enemy. Our troops are in motion in pursuit of Longstreet, and I shall join them to-day unless Foster arrives. He was at Tazewell last night. I have been able to organize a column of pursuit of about 8,000 men. Granger is crossing Little River now, and will probably be here to-night. The rear guard of the enemy is at Blain's Cross-Roads. I can scarcely express to you my obligations for the prompt assistance rendered by you to my command.

A. E. BURNSIDE,
Major-General, Commanding.

Major-General GRANT.

---

* See Sherman's order, December 16, p. —.

KNOXVILLE, *December* 9, 1863.

The pursuing column has continued to press on the enemy's rear
Daily skirmishing between our cavalry and their rear guard. Ou
cavalry advance is now between Rutledge and Bean's Station. Th
main body of the enemy's infantry is undoubtedly going up th
main valley road toward Virginia. Indications are that the division
of Buckner's corps that joined Longstreet, and part of Wheeler'
cavalry, are endeavoring to rejoin Bragg by way of North Carolina
through the French Broad Gap. I have been ill for two days, con
fined to my room, and General Parke is at the front conducting th
pursuit ; he will take care not to involve himself in any disaster
General Foster was at Tazewell at last accounts, but my advices from
him are meager ; he will probably reach here within a day or two
Would it not be well for the forces in the east to make a serious and
desperate attempt to break the Virginia railroad in Longstreet'
rear ?

A. E. BURNSIDE,
Major-General.

Major-General GRANT.

—

NEW YORK, *November* 13, 1865.

SIR : I have the honor to submit the following report of the
operations of the Department of the Ohio during the time I was in
command.*

Nothing of importance occurred in this section until about the
1st of November, when the outposts at Kingsport and Blountsville
were driven in ; thus the road from Kingsport to Rogersville was
left unguarded. At the latter place there was a brigade of our cavalry under Colonel Garrard. A heavy force of the enemy, under
the rebel General Jones, moved down this unguarded road, surprising Colonel Garrard's force, which was completely routed. The
colonel with his shattered command fell back on Morristown. Not
knowing the strength of the enemy's force, I directed Genera
Willcox to fall back to Bull's Gap and hold that position. From
this time until the 17th of the month, operations were confined to
cavalry fighting, skirmishing, and foraging. In the meantime,
General Shackelford had been ordered to report to me at Knoxville
to take command of all the cavalry, and on the approach of Longstreet on Knoxville, Hoskins' brigade was ordered to that place.
This left General Willcox with his new division and with some
newly recruited North Carolinians, and Foster's division of cavalry,
composed of Graham's and Garrard's brigades. This command,
though composed of good men, was in bad condition for want of
almost every necessary supply. Upon the approach of Longstreet,
I directed General Willcox to make his arrangements to get his
command to Cumberland Gap, in case telegraphic communication with my headquarters was broken. On that night (the 16th)
communication was cut off. I beg to refer to General Willcox's report for a correct understanding of the very efficient work done by
him after that period. The enemy in the lower valley, on the south
side of the Holston, were very active during the early part of October.

---

* For part omitted, see Series I, Vol. XXIII, Part I, p. 11, and Vol. XXX, Part II
p. 547.

On the 19th of October, I received directions to report my operations to Maj. Gen. U. S. Grant, commanding Division of the Mississippi, and I accordingly reported to him a statement of the situation and condition of my forces.   On the 19th, I sent a flag of truce through Colonel Wolford's lines, whose headquarters were at Philadelphia, on the south side of the Holston.   The enemy's cavalry took advantage of this flag and made an attack upon him, capturing some 300 or 400 men and some mountain howitzers which he had with his command.

On the 28th, the force at Loudon was crossed to the north side of the river, and the pontoon bridge taken up and transported to Knoxville, at which point it was thrown across the Holston, and proved of immense service to us during the siege.   The indications at this time were that Bragg was sending a considerable force against us. I re-enforced Kingston with Colonel Mott's brigade of infantry, left General White with his command at Loudon, and posted General Potter, with the Ninth Corps, at Lenoir's.   All the available cavalry force was thrown on the south side of the Holston, with instructions to guard down to the Little Tennessee River, and General Potter was instructed to build a pontoon bridge over the Holston just above the mouth of the Little Tennessee, which bridge was constructed with great expedition, under superintendence of Col. O. E. Babcock.   The object of this bridge was to enable our force on either side of the river to communicate.   Some correspondence passed between Generals Grant, Halleck, and myself as to the proper points to be held in East Tennessee, which resulted in Mr. Dana, Assistant Secretary of War, and Colonel Wilson, of General Grant's staff, visiting my headquarters, by order of General Grant.   I gave them my reasons in full for desiring to hold Knoxville in preference to Kingston. They concurred with me in that view, and we all agreed that it would be proper to recommend the holding of both places, if possible, but certainly Knoxville.

At this time it was known definitely that Longstreet was moving against us.   Those gentlemen left my headquarters on the morning of the 14th.   On their return I accompanied them to Lenoir's, and soon after parting with them at that place, we were engaged with Longstreet's advance.   General Parke was left in command at Knoxville, with a portion of the Twenty-third Corps.   General Sanders, with the cavalry, was at the south side of the Holston.   The enemy endeavored to seize the heights on the south side of the river commanding the town, but was foiled in his attempts by the forces under General Parke.   Longstreet was building a bridge at Huff's Ferry, just below Loudon, and had thrown a force across in advance of the main body.   I directed Generals Potter and White to move in direction of Huff's Ferry and drive in the advance, Chapin's brigade, of General White's command, leading.   Skirmishing continued during the entire day, but our forces constantly advanced, and by night had driven the enemy back near to his bridge-head.   Knowing the purposes of General Grant as I did, I decided that he could be better served by driving Longstreet farther away from Bragg than by checking him at the river, and I accordingly decided to withdraw my forces and retreat leisurely toward Knoxville, and soon after daylight on the 15th the whole command was on the road.   Skirmishing continued during the day, the enemy following us as we retreated. That night (the 15th) we encamped at Lenoir's without serious molestation.   About 10 p. m. the enemy made a dash on our lines, but was easily repulsed. All of our trains and supplies had been started to Knoxville, except some wagons of General White's division, which were destroyed, and the teams taken to assist in moving the artillery, the horses of which were very much broken down.

Before daylight on the morning of the 16th, the command was started for Knoxville. General Hartranft's division, of the Ninth Corps, with Colonel Biddle's cavalry, was sent out in advance to seize the forks of the road at Campbell's Station, as I was satisfied the enemy would try to reach that point before us, in order to cut us off from Knoxville. They succeeded in reaching this point before the enemy, and at once took steps to hold the Kingston road, as well as the roads leading to Clinton and Concord. I sent Colonel Loring, of my staff, to Campbell's Station to reconnoiter the ground near that place, as I was satisfied that we would have to make dispositions there to check the enemy until night, so as to enable our trains to get into Knoxville. Before 11 a. m. all our forces had passed the junction of the roads held by Hartranft, and were being placed in position. Humphrey's brigade, which brought up the rear, was at one time severely pressed on the lower road, but he turned on the enemy and drove him back. General White's division had been placed in position on some rising ground on the south side of the main road, just east of Campbell's Station and about three-quarters of a mile from the junction of the roads. General Potter then proceeded to put his troops in position. General Ferrero's division was placed on the right of the road, General White's division was in the center, and General Hartranft on his left. The batteries were in rear of the first line of troops.

At about 12 o'clock the enemy commenced the attack, and at one time pressed the extreme right of Ferrero's division (Colonel Christ' brigade) so hard as to cause him to change front. He was, however, checked and driven back. He then passed round toward our left making demonstrations on different parts of the line, all of which were repulsed. There was some high ground on our left which entirely commanded the position we held, and I saw that the enemy was endeavoring to occupy that position, and, not having force sufficient to extend my line to meet these demonstrations, I determined to move to a ridge some three-quarters of a mile in rear, where I had dispatched Lieutenant-Colonel Bowen to reconnoiter for position. At 2 p. m. I gave the order to withdraw, and the new position was occupied under a heavy artillery fire without the slightest confusion. The movement was covered by Chapin's brigade of White's division. The new line was established about 4 p. m. We were hardly in position before the enemy made a fierce attack on Hartranft's division on the extreme left, but were handsomely repulsed.

He did not disturb us again that day. After nightfall I issued orders for Generals Potter and White to withdraw to Knoxville, the trains being secure. General White's command brought up the rear and arrived at Knoxville early the next morning. Great credit is due to the officers and men for the gallantry and coolness shown on this occasion. The entire command consisted of but little over 5,000 men, while the enemy's force was at least double that amount.

Our loss in killed and wounded and missing was about 300, and that of the enemy must have been very severe, as he was the attacking force. I arrived at Knoxville, with my staff, about midnight, and gave directions to Capt. O. M. Poe, chief engineer, to select positions for posting the troops as they arrived with a view to defend ng the place. I directed General Shackelford to dismount the cavalry command under General Sanders and send it out on the Kingston road a mile in advance of our proposed line of defense, for the purpose of holding the enemy in check until our men were able to take up their positions on the line and fortify. This work was most nobly accomplished. The troops worked all day and night of the 17th, and by noon of the 18th they were pretty well covered. During all this time the gallant Sanders, with his dismounted cavalry, held the enemy in check. Just as I sent out orders to withdraw within the lines I received information that he was mortally wounded. He was brought into the city, where he received all possible attention, but he died the next day. The service lost in the death of General Sanders one of the most noble spirits, and we, his comrades, a beloved and faithful friend.

Captain Poe had before leaving Kentucky organized an engineer battalion from the Twenty-third Corps, and had by great efforts succeeded in bringing over the mountains a quantity of intrenching and other engineer tools. These proved to be of the greatest possible value to us during the siege. The line of defense established commenced at a point on the river and ran at nearly right angles with the river to a fort which the enemy had commenced on the hill north of the Kingston road, and about 1,000 yards in front and to the right of the college; from this point it ran along and nearly parallel to the river across First Creek over Temperance Hill to Maybry's Hill, near Bell's house, thence to the Holston River at a point a little below the glass-works. An interior line was also decided upon, which ran from near the work on Temperance Hill to Flint Hill. The line on the south side was not continuous. We occupied four prominent hills, which commanded the city as well as the open country to the south of it. General Ferrero's division of the Ninth Corps, under General R. B. Potter, occupied the line from the Holston River to Second Creek, and General Hartranft's part of the line between First and Second Creeks. Chapin's brigade extended from Second Creek over Temperance Hill to near Bell's house, and the brigades of Colonels Hoskins and Casement extended from this point to the river. The interior line was occupied by some regiments of loyal Tennesseeans lately recruited. The positions on the south side of the river were occupied by Shackelford's cavalry and Cameron's brigade, of Hascall's division; Reilly's brigade was held in reserve, and used frequently during the siege to re-enforce the lines on both sides of the river.

Our force at this time in Knoxville was about 12,000 effective men, exclusive of the new recruits of loyal Tennesseeans. The enemy was estimated at 20,000 to 23,000, including cavalry.

I beg to refer to the full and able report of my chief engineer for a complete record of the positions of the different batteries. The line was rapidly brought into a defensible condition; many of the citizens and persons who had been driven in by the enemy volunteered to work in the trenches and did good service, while those who were not inclined, from disloyalty, to volunteer, were pressed into the service. The negroes were particularly efficient in their labors during the siege.

The beef cattle, hogs, &c., belonging to the commissary department, and many that belonged to the citizens, were driven into the city by the employés of Colonel Goodrich, chief commissary, where they were slaughtered and salted down. Orders were at once issued reducing the rations, and within three or four days the issuing of small rations to the command was entirely discontinued. The supply was so limited that it was found necessary to reserve them all for the hospitals. All useless animals were killed and thrown into the river in order to save forage.

Strenuous efforts were constantly used by the quartermasters of the different commands to collect forage and supplies along the French Broad River, and out on the Sevierville road, both of which we were able to keep open to our foraging parties during the principal part of the siege. By judicious management on the part of the quartermaster's and commissary departments we were kept from absolute want.

We were greatly indebted to the loyal citizens for a large amount of grain and meat, sent down the French Broad River in flats, during the dense fogs of the night, which prevailed at that period.

Captain Doughty, a most excellent officer, maintained a small force up that river during the whole siege, and directed the efforts of the people of that section in our behalf.

By the 20th of November, our line was in such condition as to inspire the entire command with confidence in our entire ability to hold the place against any rebel force that might be brought against it. But our men still continued to strengthen the lines by every possible means within their reach. First and Second Creeks were dammed, the backwater from them making most formidable wet ditches in front of a considerable portion of the line. Abatis, *chevaux-de-frise*, and wire entanglements were made wherever they were necessary.

Lieut. S. N. Benjamin, who commanded Fort Sanders, situated in the northwest angle of the line, was particularly conspicuous for his efforts to strengthen his position. I speak of this instance because this point was the only one assaulted by any formidable force of the enemy. This fort was commenced by the rebels before our troops entered East Tennessee, and had been considerably improved by the Engineer Battalion, under Captain Poe, before the commencement of the siege. It was named Fort Sanders in honor of the brave officer who fell on the second day of the siege.

The site occupied by the city of Knoxville, which we were to defend, was in front of a plateau of about one half a mile in width, running parallel to and close to the Holston River. This plateau was intersected by three creeks, First, Second, and Third, giving the position the appearance of separate hills. First Creek separated Knoxville from East Knoxville or Temperance Hill. Second Creek separated the town from College Hill, and Third Creek ran into the river beyond our lines. To the north and west of the town the plateau descended gradually to a valley or basin of about three quarters of a mile in width, beyond which was a second plateau similar to the one just described and of about the same height. On this ridge the enemy's forces were stationed with their batteries on prominent points.

He made great efforts to break our pontoon bridge by floating rafts down the Holston, but by the judicious efforts of Lieutenant-Colonel Babcock and Captain Poe, who constructed a boom across the river above the bridge, we were enabled to maintain it.

Nothing of great importance occurred until the 23d of November. Constant sharpshooting, skirmishing, and artillery firing was kept up without important results.

On the night of the 23d, a portion of General Hartranft's picket ine was driven in, but was re-established the next day with a loss of 22 killed and wounded. Houses that were occupied, or likely to be, by the enemy's sharpshooters, were destroyed, and some gallant sorties were made for that purpose.

On the 23d, an assault was made on the enemy's parallel by the Second Michigan, which, for a time, was successful, but they were finally driven back with loss of 6 killed, among whom was the commanding officer, and 44 wounded. Accompanying this are the reports of these engagements.

Longstreet's cavalry, under Wheeler, attacked Colonel Mott's command on the 24th of November, at Kingston, and was severely repulsed, our men behaving with the utmost gallantry.

About this time (the 24th) the enemy commenced crossing his forces to the south side of the river, and on the 25th he made a desperate attempt to seize the heights commanding the town, but was severely repulsed by General Shackelford's forces. Colonel Reilly's brigade was sent over as re-enforcements, and did most excellent service.

On the night of the 26th, I went over to the south side, accompanied by Captain Poe, and made a careful examination of our lines on that side of the river.

On the 27th, the enemy continued active on both sides of the river, indulging in considerable artillery firing, but our men were silent.

On the 28th, he opened a battery on the south side, which partially commanded College Hill and Fort Sanders. About 10 o'clock that night he drove in our pickets in the center of General Ferrero's line, capturing many of them and establishing his line on the crest of the ridge, about 80 yards in front of the fort.

It was now supposed that the enemy intended to make an attack at that point. Orders were issued for the whole command to be on the alert, and a brigade of General Hascall's division was sent during the night to re-enforce General Ferrero. I have before stated that the fort had been placed in most excellent condition for defense. Lieutenant Benjamin, who had bent all his energies to this work, was on the alert during the night, and roused the men at an early hour. They were placed in position, and strict silence enforced. At about 6.30 a. m. the enemy opened a furious fire upon the fort; our batteries remained silent, and the men quietly awaited the attack. The fort was so protected with traverses that only one man was injured during this heavy fire. In about twenty minutes the cannonading ceased and a fire of musketry was opened by the enemy. At the same time a heavy column that had been concentrated under the ridge, near the fort, during the night, charged on the bastions at a run. Great numbers of them fell in passing over the entanglements, but the weight of the column was such as to force the advance forward, and in two or three minutes they had reached the ditch and attempted to scale the parapet.

Our guns opened upon the men in the ditch with triple rounds of canister, and our infantry shot or knocked back all those whose heads appeared above the parapet. The forces placed on the flanks of the fort by General Ferrero had a cross-fire on the ground over which the enemy approached. The first column of attack was re-enforced by a second, which pushed up to the fort as desperately as the first, but were driven back with great slaughter. Most of those who reached the ditch were killed or mortally wounded. Such as could not retreat surrendered; in all, about 500. The ground between the

fort and the crest was strewed with the dead and wounded, who
were crying for help, and after the repulse was fully established
tendered to the enemy a flag of truce for the purpose of burying the
dead and caring for the wounded.   His loss was certainly over 1,000
men, while ours was but 13.

The gallantry of this defense has not been excelled during the war
and the division of General Ferrero may justly feel proud of this
great achievement, particularly Lieutenant Benjamin and the officers and men in the fort, who were so conspicuous in this service.

During the remainder of the siege, we were not seriously molested
by the enemy, and I again beg to refer to the accompanying report
of Captain Poe, for a more accurate and detailed account of the siege
than I have been able to give.

I omitted to mention that General M. D. Manson was in command
of the Twenty-third Corps at this time, General Hartsuff having applied for and received a leave of absence just before the commencement of the siege.

By the 2d of December, the indications were that the siege would
soon be raised.   On that day we received information from General
Grant of the approach of General Sherman with troops for our relief ; and on the night of the 3d, Captain Audenried, of General Sherman's staff, reached my headquarters.   The morning of the 5th, the
enemy raised the siege, and retreated in the direction of Strawberry
Plains.   The few cavalry we could mount were sent in pursuit ; but
they were in such bad condition as to be unable to make any great
impression on the enemy, who had moved off in remarkably good
order.

The same day (the 5th) I received from General Sherman the
following letter :

MARYVILLE, *December* 5, 1863.
General BURNSIDE :

DEAR GENERAL : I am here, and can bring 25,000 men into Knoxville to-morrow,
but Longstreet having retreated, I feel disposed to stop, for a stern chase is a long
one.   But I will do all that is possible.   Without you specify that you want troops
I will let mine rest to-morrow, and ride to see you.   Send my aide (Captain Audenried) out with your letters to-night.   We are all hearty, but tired.   Accept my con-
gratulations on your successful defense and your patient endurance.

Yours, in haste,

W. T. SHERMAN,
Major-General.

On the 6th, General Sherman came to my headquarters, leaving
the advance of his forces at Maryville.   After consultation, it was
decided that his forces would be of more service moving in another
direction, and he accordingly decided to return, leaving with me
General Granger's corps.   We thanked him and his command heartily for their assistance, and bade them God speed on their new
service.

On the morning of the 7th, the commands of Generals Potter and
Manson started in pursuit of Longstreet, the whole under command
of Maj. Gen. John G. Parke, who had during the siege rendered me
most efficient service as chief of staff.

Some days before this, I had received information that Maj. Gen.
John G. Foster was to relieve me of the command of the Department
of the Ohio.   This order was the result of a dispatch sent by me to
the President in October, when I was quite ill, stating that I might
be forced to ask to be relieved of the command of the department.

General Foster had arrived at Cumberland Gap, some days before the siege was raised, and had been directing the operations of the forces in that neighborhood in the meantime.

On the 10th, he arrived at my headquarters at Knoxville, and on the 11th assumed command of the department.

On the 12th instant, I left Knoxville for Cincinnati with best wishes for the success and happiness of General Foster and his command, both of whom had been so faithful, efficient, and brave while serving under me.

I shall ever remember with gratitude and pleasure the co-operation, devotion, courage, and patient endurance of the brave officers and men of the Ninth and Twenty-third Corps, who have served with me so faithfully and conspicuously in Kentucky and East Tennessee. During the whole siege and in the midst of the most arduous labor and greatest privations, I never heard a word of discontent or distrust from any one of them. Each man seemed anxious to do his whole duty, and to their perseverance and courage is due the ultimate success of the defense of Knoxville.

The loyal people of East Tennessee will always be gratefully remembered by me for their hearty co-operation, efficient aid, and liberal hospitality.

To the members of my personal staff who served with me in Cincinnati and East Tennessee, and who rendered most faithful and meritorious service, I beg to tender my hearty thanks.

Those who accompanied me to East Tennessee were as follows: Maj. Gen. John G. Parke, chief of staff; Lieut. Col. Lewis Richmond, assistant adjutant-general; Surg. W. H. Church, medical director; Lieut. Col. E. R. Goodrich, chief commissary; Lieut. Col. Charles G. Loring, jr., assistant inspector-general; Maj. J. L. Van Buren, aide-de-camp; Maj. William Cutting, aide-de-camp; Maj. Edward M. Neill, assistant adjutant-general; Capt. William H. Harris, chief of ordnance; Capt. O. M. Poe, chief engineer; Capt. George R. Fearing, aide-de-camp; Capt. D. A. Pell, aide-de-camp; Capt. R. H. I. Goddard, aide-de-camp; Capt. S. Sumner, aide-de-camp; Capt. John A. Morris, assistant quartermaster; Capt. D. R. Larned, assistant adjutant-general; Capt. W. H. French, commissary of subsistence.

The following were on duty at headquarters in Cincinnati: Capt. William P. Anderson, assistant adjutant-general; Capt. Robert Morrow, assistant adjutant-general; General N. H. McLean, provost-marshal-general; Brig. Gen. Tillson, chief of artillery; Col. J. H. Simpson, chief engineer; Maj. H. L. Burnett, judge-advocate; Capt. J. H. Dickerson, chief quartermaster; Lieutenant-Colonel Kilburn, commissary of subsistence.

Accompanying this please find the full and detailed reports of Generals Potter, Willcox, and Shackelford, also Capt. W. H. Harris, chief of ordnance, which gives a detailed account of his most efficient management of his department.

I cannot close this report without expressing my sincere obligations to the corps, division, and brigade commanders for their hearty co-operation and aid during the entire campaign.

I have the honor to be, very respectfully, your obedient servant,

A. E. BURNSIDE,
Late Major-General.

ADJUTANT-GENERAL U. S. ARMY,
Washington, D. C.

GENERAL FIELD ORDERS, }   HDQRS. ARMY OF THE OHIO,
    No. 33.   }   *In the Field, November* 30, 1863.

The brilliant events of the 29th instant, so successful to our arms, seem to present a fitting occasion for the commanding general to thank this army for their conduct through the severe experience of the past seventeen days, to assure them of the important bearing it has had on the campaign in the West, and to give them the news of the great victory gained by General Grant, toward which their fortitude and their bravery have in a high degree contributed.

In every fight in which they have been engaged, and recently in those near Knoxville, at Loudon, at Campbell's Station, and finally around the defenses on both sides of the river, while on the march, and in cold and in hunger, they have everywhere shown a spirit which has given to the Army of the Ohio a name second to none.

By holding in check a powerful body of the enemy, they have seriously weakened the rebel army under Bragg, which has been completely defeated by General Grant, and at the latest accounts was in full retreat for Dalton, closely pursued by him, with the loss of 6,000 prisoners, 52 pieces of artillery, and 12 stand of colors.

For this great and practical result, toward which the Army of the Ohio has done so much, the commanding general congratulates them, and with the fullest reliance on their patience and courage in the dangers they may yet have to meet, looks forward with confidence, under the blessing of Almighty God, to a successful close of the campaign.

By command of Major-General Burnside:

LEWIS RICHMOND,
Assistant Adjutant-General.

—

GENERAL FIELD ORDERS, }   HDQRS. ARMY OF THE OHIO,
    No. 34.   }   *In the Field, December* 5, 1863.

The commanding general congratulates the troops on the raising of the siege. With unsurpassed fortitude and patient watchfulness they have sustained the wearing duties of the defense, and, with unyielding courage, they have repulsed the most desperate assaults. The Army of the Ohio has nobly guarded the loyal region it redeemed from its oppressors, and has rendered the heroic defense of Knoxville memorable in the annals of the war. Strengthened by the experiences and the successes of the past, they now, with the powerful support of the gallant army which has come to their relief, and with undoubting faith in the divine protection, enter with the brightest prospects upon the closing scenes of a most brilliant campaign.

By command of Major-General Burnside:

LEWIS RICHMOND,
Assistant Adjutant-General.

—

HEADQUARTERS ARMY OF THE OHIO,
Knoxville, Tenn., December 11, 1863.

GENERAL: Before leaving Knoxville, permit me to express to you, and to the officers and men of the Fourth Army Corps, my sincere thanks and gratitude for the promptness and willingness with which

ou hastened to our assistance while we were menaced by a power-
l force of the enemy.   Although you, with your command, had
tely undergone the great hardships and exposure incident upon the
orious victory of Chattanooga, you cheerfully obeyed the order of
ur commanding general, and by a rapid and vigorous advance
on this place assisted in compelling the enemy to raise the siege
d retreat to Virginia.   Again I thank you.

I am, general, very respectfully, your obedient servant,
A. E. BURNSIDE,
Major-General, Commanding.

Maj. Gen. GORDON GRANGER,
Commanding Fourth Army Corps.

—

—PUBLIC RESOLUTION—No. 8.—A RESOLUTION of thanks to Maj. Gen. Ambrose E. Burnside, and the officers and men who fought under his command.

*Resolved by the Senate and House of Representatives of the United
ates of America in Congress assembled,* That the thanks of Con-
ess be, and they hereby are, presented to Maj. Gen. Ambrose E.
urnside, and through him to the officers and men who have fought
der his command, for their gallantry, good conduct, and soldier-
e endurance.

SEC. 2. *And be it further resolved,* That the President of the
nited States be requested to cause the foregoing resolution to be
mmunicated to Major-General Burnside in such terms as he may
em best calculated to give effect thereto.

Approved January 28, 1864.

No. 5.

*eports of Maj. Gen. John G. Foster, U. S. Army, commanding
Department of the Ohio.**

HEADQUARTERS DEPARTMENT OF THE OHIO,
Knoxville, Tenn., December 14, 1863.

GENERAL : I have the honor to report that I arrived here on the
ening of the 11th, and received the command from General Burn-
de on the 12th.   General Parke was at that time near Rutledge
ith about 10,000 infantry, being the number of the Ninth and
wenty-third Army Corps, capable of marching and fighting.   Gen-
al Granger was here with two divisions of his corps (the Fourth).
eneral Elliott, with 2,500 cavalry, was at Kingston.   The cavalry
this department were in front of Bean's Station, harassing the
emy near.   I ordered General Elliott here to join my cavalry, so
s to give us an equality of numbers of that arm with the enemy
d enable us to overcome the checks which they constantly gave
s.   But, owing to conflicting orders received from General Thomas,
eneral Elliott has not yet reported here.   I have to-day sent new
ders to General Elliott.

I find the commissariat of the department very destitute, there
ing only a few days' supplies of the most requisite parts of the

---

* See also Foster's correspondence with Burnside, Grant, and Halleck, November
–December 13, Part III.

rations, which are now, and have been for a long time, issued
half and quarter rations. Beef and pork only are issued in f
rations. Nearly all the breadstuffs have been drawn from the su
rounding country, and all the forage for the animals. This h
necessarily exhausted the country to a great extent, which exhau
tion has been increased largely by the depredations of Longstree
army.

The problem of supplying the army here this winter is very dif
cult, but I think it can be solved if I am allowed to draw from Ge
eral Grant's depots, at Chattanooga, by way of the river. To effe
this, two small steamers, the Chattanooga and Paint Rock, are no
available. The hull of another small steamer has been floated dow
to Chattanooga from Kingston to receive machinery. I have ordere
three more hulls to be built at once, and the machinery for them
be sent from Cincinnati. I have also ordered the railroad bridg
at Loudon and the Hiwassee to be rebuilt, but this work will occu
six weeks' time.

I have ordered the roads from Camp Nelson to Cumberland Ga
and from the former to Knoxville, via Somerset, Mouth of B
South Fork, Chitwood's, Wheeler's Gap, &c., to be made good mi
tary roads, and this work is now commenced, but as the season
late, it is doubtful whether they can be made good enough for t
passage of wagons after the winter rains set in. Anticipating thi
I have ordered Captain Dickerson to provide pack-saddles and pa
niers, so that as soon as the roads become impassable for wagons a
the draught animals may be employed in carrying packs, and th
keep up something like supply trains. I have also ordered the ro
to Carthage to be repaired, and a depot of provisions to be esta
lished at that place, and also at the mouth of the Big South Fork
the Cumberland.

The people of this country, from the presence of hostile armies
their midst since the opening of the war, are rendered nearly des
tute. These armies have rarely paid for what has been taken
foraging parties. Over $100,000 in claims are now here for settl
ment, and more than this is outstanding. To remedy this evil a
relieve the people, at the same time to insure the bringing in
what supplies are yet in the country, I have ordered the quarte
masters and commissaries to pay money for their purchases, and
make the necessary requisitions on their departments. I ha
ordered the broken telegraph lines to be restored, and a new li
direct from Somerset to this place to be put up. The railro
bridges at Strawberry Plains and Mossy Creek are also to be r
built. I trust my action in the above premises will meet with yo
approval.

With regard to the military situation I cannot speak definitely.
have known for several days that Longstreet had halted near Roger
ville, and to-day I am notified that an advance is made to drive ba
our pursuit. Should this be made in force I have directed Gener
Parke to fall back until I can join him with General Granger's d
visions. The rains of the past three days have made the roads
nearly impassable that it will be impossible to make a campaig
toward the northeastern part of the State in the present destitu
and weakened condition of the men and animals. I prefer, therefor
to wait until I can get them in effective condition. With regard
the kinds of troops here, I find that the mounted force is in th
broken and extended country the most in demand for all operatio

except a general engagement. This kind of arms is very much inferior in numbers to that of the enemy, and must be increased. I am satisfied that mounted infantry, for which service the Western troops are specially adapted, can be used to more advantage in this country than any other arm. I have, therefore, ordered all the troops, which General Burnside had enlisted for the purpose, to be organized and mounted, and have tendered inducements to the six-months' volunteers to re-enlist for the same purpose. All these are to be armed with the carbine or rifle. I also require one first-rate cavalry regiment, armed with the saber and revolver. The Third New York Cavalry or Eleventh Pennsylvania, if ordered to Lexington, will meet this want perfectly.

The infantry force is very much reduced in numbers by sickness arising from want of supplies, both in kind and quantity, of camp equipage, and of medicines. The vacant buildings of this town are full of sick. Of the Twenty-third and Ninth Corps, only 10,000 men are able to march and fight. I would, therefore, request that my old division, of the Ninth Corps, may be ordered from Virginia (Old Point Comfort) to Camp Nelson, whence I can order it where most needed.

Before closing I beg leave to call your attention to the matter of transportation to this point, and the necessity for some steps being taken to secure a sure line of travel which will be permanent and adequate to all wants. I mean a railroad connection between some railroad terminus in Kentucky and this place. Its importance, in a military point of view, cannot be overestimated. Its whole expense will not much exceed the annual outlay necessary to supply this army by wagon trains. I earnestly request that you will ask the Honorable Secretary of War and the President of the United States to urge upon Congress the necessity of providing for the building of this railroad as soon as possible, as a military measure. I believe the road can be built during this winter and spring. I regret that I am confined to my quarters from the effects of riding from Lexington to this place, the pain in my wounded leg having become very much increased. I hope, however, to be out again in a few days.

I have decided to make this place the headquarters of the department for the present, and to have an assistant adjutant-general at Lexington, a quartermaster and commissary at Cincinnati.

I have relieved Brigadier-General Boyle by Brigadier-General Cox in the command of the District of Kentucky; also relieved Brigadier-General Fry, and ordered him to the field. I have placed Brigadier-General Ammen in command of the troops to guard the depots at Point Isabella (mouth of Big South Fork) and Carthage, and to construct the two roads from those points to this place. Major-General Parke is in command of the Ninth Corps, and Brig. Gen. O. B. Willcox, temporarily, of the Twenty-third Corps. I have ordered Brig. Gen. S. D. Sturgis to take command of all the cavalry in a body, which I propose to keep together as the cavalry corps of the department. General Sturgis is now at the head of this force, rendering good service. I shall keep you fully advised by telegraph of all current operations, and report more fully by mail.

I have the honor to be, general, your obedient servant,

J. G. FOSTER,
Major-General, Commanding.

Maj. Gen. H. W. HALLECK,
General-in-Chief.

KNOXVILLE, *December* 17, 1863.

Longstreet has taken the offensive against General Parke, wh
has fallen back to Blain's Cross-Roads, where Granger is now con
centrating his corps.   I intend to fight there if Longstreet comes
It is reported that he is re-enforced by a portion of Ewell's corps
Elliott arrived yesterday, and I have ordered him toward Morris
town to meet Wheeler's cavalry and operate on Longstreet's flank.

This question of supplies is very serious, and cramps militar
operations, having to concentrate and call in the foraging parties
It is with great difficulty that I can get quarter rations of meal o
flour from day to day.   It is very important, therefore, to get boat
running on the Tennessee River so as to supply us this winter witl
bread, small stores, and ammunition.

Beef and hogs can be driven to us.   I have sent orders to Captair
Dickerson to this effect, but ask that you will also give such order
as will put the thing through.

The boat has just arrived at Loudon with timely supplies, whicl
have been brought up on the train.

Please order medicines and hospital stores to be brought up on th
next boat.

J. G. FOSTER,
Major-General.

Major-General GRANT,
   Chattanooga.

—

KNOXVILLE, *December* 19, 1863.
(Received Chattanooga, 21st.)

I have just returned from the front to find your telegrams of th
15th, 16th, and 18th.

Longstreet is near Rutledge with a force equal to my own, bu
shows no disposition to attack us in our position.   Had circumstance
been favorable, I intended to attack him, acting in accordance wit
what I understood to be the wishes of General Halleck, but I am nc
sure that it would prove a good operation ; at any rate, the freshe
in the river from the recent rains has delayed operations for som
days.   I would like to confer with you in order to understand mor
fully what operations will lead to the best results.

Can I do this by telegraphing from Tazewell, to which place I ca
go for the purpose, or will it be better to come to Chattanooga b
boat ?

J. G. FOSTER,
Major-General.

Major-General GRANT.

—

BLAIN'S CROSS-ROADS,
December 19, 1863.

I am here in force.   The high water from rains and the state o
the roads impeded operations very much.   The men are suffering
for want of shoes and clothing.   Ammunition is also becoming
scarce; of some arms entirely expended.   Please to send by steame
to Loudon, as soon as possible, 5,000 pairs of shoes, 10,000 pair
socks, 5,000 shirts, 5,000 blouses, 10,000 overcoats, 10,000 shelte

nts, 1,000,000 rifle cartridges caliber .58, 8,000 rounds for 3-inch
·dnance field pieces, 4,000 rounds for 12-pounder Napoleon guns,
500 rounds for 20-pounder Parrotts, 2,000 rounds for 10-pounder
arrotts, 3,000 Spencer rifle cartridges, 6,000 Sharps rifle cartridges,
000 Burnside rifle cartridges, 6,000 Colt revolver rifle cartridges.
'e need all the above as soon as they can be sent.   The appearances
·e that the enemy intend to try and hold a portion of East Ten-
ᴐssee.   If this proves true, we have sharp work before us.   The
ᴇn and animals are in poor condition, which must be improved
ᴣfore I can move with the necessary effect.   I desire that you will
ᴄnd up the camp and garrison equipage of General Granger's two
ᴌvisions, and also that you may give me the service of his third
ᴌvision for a little time.
I sent dispatch from Knoxville asking for medicines and hospital
ᴏres.
Skirmishing goes on almost constantly with little effect.   Long-
reet is near Rutledge.

J. G. FOSTER,
Major-General.

Major-General GRANT.

DECEMBER 20, 1863—4 p. m.

This dispatch has just been received, and a copy sent to General
rant.   I send this to you that you may see what General Foster
·quires.   Be good enough to return this as soon as you are done
ith it.
  Very respectfully, your obedient servant,

J. H. WILSON,
Brigadier-General.

—

STRAWBERRY PLAINS,
December 24, 1863—12.30 p. m.

Longstreet is moving his forces across the Holston in the direction
' Morristown, where, prisoners state, he intends to make a stand.
have crossed the cavalry under General Sturgis, and advanced
ᴉm to feel the enemy.   He engaged them this morning early, near
ᴌossy Creek, and drove in the force at that point.   I am pushing
·rward the railroad bridge at this place, and as soon as it is done
ᴌn advance.
We want ammunition, and cannot fight a general engagement
ᴎtil supplied.   We have more reports that re-enforcements have
·rived from Virginia, but as I have no proof of it, I discredit the
ᴣport.   Longstreet's force is 26,000 men—exactly what mine is.

J. G. FOSTER,
Major-General.

Maj. Gen. U. S. GRANT.

—

ONFIDENTIAL.]   BALTIMORE, MD.,
February 24, 1864.

ᴉaj. Gen. H. W. HALLECK,
  Washington, D. C.:
GENERAL : I send herewith a crude report of operations in East
ᴇnnessee, with reasons why offensive operations cannot be com-

menced before the 1st April with proper chances of success. I be
lieve General Grant is satisfied of this fact. I had a long interview
with him in Nashville as I came on. I like him very much. He i
a hard-working and excellent officer, and I think he will certainl
attain a great success in the South this season if he has good co-op
eration by the armies of the Potomac and of North Carolina an
Virginia. He is very anxious that a column of 50,000 or 60,00
should be put in motion in North Carolina and Virginia. If yo
would like, I will sketch the outline of his plan, and also give som
details from my knowledge of the situation, which will tend to mak
it a success. I will also propose a plan of operations for a smalle
force, if you desire.

I was much pleased with the Western troops and with the country
but the constant riding on horseback gave me great pain. As soo
as I am able, I shall report for duty, and I am so much encourage
that I hope it may be in four weeks.*

I shall be as able to do duty as before the last accident, and ar
willing to undertake anything. I would, however, prefer duty a
the East, which I can do better, as I shall have less riding than a
the West.

With kindest regards, ever yours, respectfully and truly,
J. G. FOSTER.

[Inclosure.]

BALTIMORE, MD.,
February 21, 1864.

GENERAL : I have the honor, in obedience to your direction, t
make the following report of the operations of the Army of th
Ohio, while I was in command, and of the general condition of a
fairs in East Tennessee :

I relieved General Burnside at Knoxville, East Tenn., on the 12t
of December, 1863. At that time the forces of the enemy under Gen
eral Longstreet, comprising his own force that had been engaged i
the siege of Knoxville, Ransom's division of infantry, and Jone
division of cavalry, with which he had formed a junction, were sup
posed to be in full retreat toward Virginia. They were at that tim
near Rogersville. General Parke with the Ninth and Twenty-thir
Corps (10,000 infantry and the cavalry, 4,000 men) was in pursui
having his advance at Bean's Station.

General Sherman was returning toward Chattanooga, leaving Gen
eral Granger with the Fourth Corps near Knoxville. As soon a
General Longstreet learned this latter fact and that the force pur
suing him was small, he turned on General Parke's advance an
repulsed it at Bean's Station. Advancing at once in his turn h
forced General Parke to fall back, first to Rutledge and afterward t
Blain's Cross-Roads. This being a good position I determined t
make it the standpoint, and accordingly hurried up the Fourth Corp
and every available fighting man. General Longstreet, howeve
did not attack, in consequence, probably, of the very inclemer
weather, which then set in with such severity as to paralyze for
time the efforts of both armies. Their numbers were equal, bein
26,000 effective men each.

At this time (the 23d of December, 1863,) my horse fell with me upo

_____

*Some personal matter here omitted.

ledge of rocks and contused my wounded leg, already very much inflamed by constant riding, to such an extent as to confine me to my quarters. General Parke retained the active command of the forces in the field. The condition of the army was bad. The troops were suffering for want of tents, clothing, food, and medicines. One-half the men were unfit for a march for want of shoes or clothing. The issue of bread or meal rarely came up to one-quarter of the ration, while the continual feeding upon fresh meat caused sickness among the soldiers, which we had no medicine to check. This state of things arose from the impossibility of getting supplies over the impassable roads from Kentucky, and the necessity for living on the country. The forage had become nearly exhausted, and had to be sought at distances varying from 10 to 40 miles. The stock of ammunition was also too limited. The enemy undoubtedly suffered privations similar to our own, for he soon retired to winter quarters at Morristown and Russellville.

Being anxious to follow and bring on a decisive engagement as soon as possible, I hurried the cavalry over the Holston as soon as it could be forded by that arm, and pushed it forward to Mossy Creek and beyond, and also to Dandridge. At the same time every effort was made to complete the bridge at Strawberry Plains, so as to cross infantry and artillery, as well as railroad cars. Earnest requisitions were, at the same time, made on Chattanooga for supplies of clothing, bread, and ammunition, to be sent up the Tennessee River in light-draught steamers.

These supplies commenced to arrive slowly, about the 28th of December. General Grant visited Knoxville on the 31st December. Seeing the suffering among the troops he decided to have me await the arrival of supplies and the completion of the Strawberry Plains Bridge before advancing. He left on the 7th January, to return by way of Cumberland Gap. The cavalry, under General Sturgis, was almost constantly engaged with the enemy's cavalry in the direction of Dandridge and Mossy Creek, after crossing the Holston. These fights culminated in a general cavalry engagement near Mossy Creek on the 29th, in which the enemy were driven from the field toward Morristown. General Elliott's division of cavalry, from the Army of the Cumberland, particularly distinguished itself for gallantry.*

I have the honor to be, very respectfully, your obedient servant,

J. G. FOSTER,
Major-General of Volunteers.

Maj. Gen. H. W. HALLECK,
General-in-Chief, U. S. Army.

---

* Portion here omitted, covering operations in East Tennessee, January 1–February 9, 1864, to appear in Series I, Vol. XXXII.

No. 6.

Return of Casualties in the Union forces, commanded by Maj Gen. Ambrose E. Burnside, U. S. Army, in the principal engagements of the Knoxville Campaign, November 4–December 2 1863.

[Compiled from nominal lists of casualties, returns, &c.]

ROGERSVILLE, TENN., NOVEMBER 6.

Command.	Killed.		Wounded.		Captured or missing.		Aggregate.
	Officers.	Enlisted men.	Officers.	Enlisted men.	Officers.	Enlisted men.	
2d Ohio Cavalry						1	
7th Ohio Cavalry				2	1	118	
2d Tennessee Infantry (mounted)........		5		1	20	474	
2d Illinois Light Artillery, Battery M........						33	
Total a..........		5		3	21	626	

a The wounded, of which there is no separate report, are probably included among the captured.

ROCKFORD, TENN., NOVEMBER 14.

Command.	Officers.	Enlisted men.	Officers.	Enlisted men.	Officers.	Enlisted men.	Aggregate.
1st Kentucky Cavalry..............		1	2	2	1	36	
45th Ohio Infantry (mounted)				2		5	
Total		1	2	4	1	41	

LENOIR'S STATION AND HUFF'S FERRY, TENN., NOVEMBER 14.

Command.	Officers.	Enlisted men.	Officers.	Enlisted men.	Officers.	Enlisted men.	Aggregate.
107th Illinois.......		1		1			
6th Indiana Cavalry..........							4
13th Kentucky............		4	3	36			
111th Ohio........		1		14	1	54	
45th Pennsylvania........				1			
Total		6	3	52	1	58	

HOLSTON RIVER, OPPOSITE KNOXVILLE, NOVEMBER 15–16.

Command.	Officers.	Enlisted men.	Officers.	Enlisted men.	Officers.	Enlisted men.	Aggregate.
11th Kentucky Infantry (mounted)............			1				3
27th Kentucky Infantry........		3					
45th Ohio Infantry (mounted)		3	1	7	4	79	
Total		6	2	7	4	82	

CAMPBELL'S STATION, TENN., NOVEMBER 16.

Command.	Officers.	Enlisted men.	Officers.	Enlisted men.	Officers.	Enlisted men.	Aggregate.
NINTH ARMY CORPS.							
Brig. Gen. ROBERT B. POTTER.							
HEADQUARTERS.							
6th Indiana Cavalry (four companies)............						2	
FIRST DIVISION.							
Brig. Gen. EDWARD FERRERO.							
First Brigade.							
Col. DAVID MORRISON.							
36th Massachusetts........	1	3	2	14		5	
8th Michigan........			1	13			
79th New York........							
45th Pennsylvania........				8		10	
Total First Brigade..........	1	3	3	35		15	

Return of Casualties in the Union forces, &c.—Continued.

Command	Killed.		Wounded.		Captured or missing.		Aggregate.
	Officers.	Enlisted men.	Officers.	Enlisted men.	Officers.	Enlisted men.	
Second Brigade. Col. BENJAMIN C. CHRIST.							
29th Massachusetts						1	1
27th Michigan		2		5		10	17
46th New York						3	3
50th Pennsylvania		1		5			6
Total Second Brigade		3		10		14	27
Third Brigade. Col. WILLIAM HUMPHREY.							
2d Michigan		3	1	26		2	32
17th Michigan		7	2	49	1	14	73
20th Michigan	1	2	1	29		4	37
100th Pennsylvania				3			3
Total Third Brigade	1	12	4	107	1	20	145
Artillery.							
2d New York Light, Battery L				2			2
1st Rhode Island Light, Battery D				1			1
Total artillery				3			3
Total First Division	2	18	7	155	1	49	232
SECOND DIVISION. Col. JOHN F. HARTRANFT. *First Brigade.* Col. JOSHUA K. SIGFRIED.							
2d Maryland						4	4
21st Massachusetts							
48th Pennsylvania		1		1		2	4
Total First Brigade		1		1		6	8
Second Brigade. Lieut. Col. EDWIN SCHALL.							
35th Massachusetts				3		1	4
11th New Hampshire							
51st Pennsylvania				3			3
Total Second Brigade				6		1	7
Total Second Division		1		7		7	15
ARTILLERY. 2d United States, Battery E							
Total Ninth Army Corps	2	19	7	162	1	58	249
TWENTY-THIRD ARMY CORPS. SECOND DIVISION. Brig. Gen. JULIUS WHITE. *Second Brigade.* Col. MARSHAL W. CHAPIN.							
107th Illinois				3			3
13th Kentucky				9		5	14
23d Michigan		8	1	22		8	39
11th Ohio			1	4			5
Illinois Light Artillery, Henshaw's Battery		2					2
Total Second Brigade		10	2	38		13	63
Total Second Division		10	2	38		13	63

Return of Casualties in the Union forces, &c.—Continued.

Command.	Killed.		Wounded.		Captured or missing.		Aggregate.
	Officers.	Enlisted men.	Officers.	Enlisted men.	Officers.	Enlisted men.	
RESERVE ARTILLERY.							
Indiana Light, 24th Battery.........................	......	......	......	1	......	......	......
Ohio Light, 19th Battery...........................	......	......	......	......	......	......	......
Total artillery.............................	......	......	......	1	......	......	......
Total Twenty-third Army Corps	......	10	2	39	......	18	6
FIRST CAVALRY DIVISION.							
Second Brigade.							
Lieut. Col. EMERY S. BOND.							
112th Illinois Infantry (mounted)...................	......	......	......	1	......	3	
8th Michigan Cavalry	......	......	......	......	......	1	
Total Second Brigade	......	......	......	1	......	4	
Total Cavalry	......	......	......	1	......	4	
Grand total.............................	2	29	9	202	1	75	31

Officers killed or mortally wounded.—Lieut. Marion P. Holmes, Thirty-sixth Massachusetts; Lieut. Alonzo P. Stevens, Seventeenth Michigan; Lieut. Col. W Huntington Smith, Twentieth Michigan.

SIEGE OF KNOXVILLE, TENN., NOVEMBER 17–DECEMBER 4.

Command.	Killed.		Wounded.		Captured or missing.		Aggregate.
	Officers.	Enlisted men.	Officers.	Enlisted men.	Officers.	Enlisted men.	
NINTH ARMY CORPS.							
Brig. Gen. ROBERT B. POTTER.							
HEADQUARTERS.							
6th Indiana Cavalry (four companies)...............	......	1	......	1	......	1	
FIRST DIVISION.							
Brig. Gen. EDWARD FERRERO.							
First Brigade.							
Col. DAVID MORRISON.							
36th Massachusetts..........................	......	......	1	2	......	2	
8th Michigan................................	......	......	......	2	......	4	
79th New York..............................	......	4	1	9	......	......	1
45th Pennsylvania...........................	......	......	......	4	......	......	
Total First Brigade......................	......	4	2	17	......	6	2
Second Brigade.							
Col. BENJAMIN C. CHRIST.							
29th Massachusetts..........................	......	4	......	4	......	20	
27th Michigan...............................	......	6	1	11	......	20	3
46th New York..............................	......	3	......	4	......	2	
50th Pennsylvania...........................	......	2	......	5	......	2	
Total Second Brigade	......	15	1	24	......	24	6
Third Brigade.							
Col. WILLIAM HUMPHREY.							
2d Michigan.................................	2	8	4	63	......	16	9
17th Michigan...............................	2	1	......	10	......	18	3
20th Michigan...............................	......	2	3	13	......	12	3
100th Pennsylvania...........................	......	3	1	8	......	......	1
Total Third Brigade	4	14	8	94	......	46	16

Return of Casualties in the Union forces, &c.—Continued.

Command.	Killed.		Wounded.		Captured or missing.		Aggregate.
	Officers.	Enlisted men.	Officers.	Enlisted men.	Officers.	Enlisted men.	
Artillery.							
ew York Light, 34th Battery				2			2
st Rhode Island Light, Battery D				2			2
Total artillery				2			2
Total First Division........	4	33	11	137		76	261
SECOND DIVISION.							
Col. JOHN F. HARTRANFT.							
First Brigade.							
Col. JOSHUA K. SIGFRIED.							
2d Maryland........		1	1	6		26	34
21st Massachusetts........		1	1	12		1	15
8th Pennsylvania........		3	2	5		5	15
Total First Brigade........		5	4	23		32	64
Second Brigade.							
Lieut. Col. EDWIN SCHALL.							
5th Massachusetts........		1	1	3		1	6
4th New Hampshire........		1	1	1		1	4
1st Pennsylvania........		2		1		1	4
Total Second Brigade		4	2	5		3	14
Total Second Division		9	6	28		35	78
UNATTACHED.							
d U. S. Artillery, Battery E........				1			1
Total Ninth Army Corps........	4	43	17	167		112	343
TWENTY-THIRD ARMY CORPS.							
SECOND DIVISION.							
Brig. Gen. JULIUS WHITE.							
taff........						2	2
Second Brigade.							
Col. MARSHAL W. CHAPIN.							
07th Illinois........							
13th Kentucky........							
23d Michigan........				8		2	10
11th Ohio........				5		2	7
llinois Light Artillery, Henshaw's Battery........							
Total Second Brigade				13		4	17
Total Second Division				13		6	19
THIRD DIVISION.							
Brig. Gen. MILO S. HASCALL.							
First Brigade.							
Col. JAMES W. REILLY.							
44th Ohio........		1	1	4			6
00th Ohio........							
04th Ohio........		1		10			11
1st Ohio Light Artillery, Battery D........						7	7
Total First Brigade........		2	1	14		7	24

Return of Casualties in the Union forces, &c.—Continued.

Command.	Killed.		Wounded.		Captured or missing.		Aggregate.
	Officers.	Enlisted men.	Officers.	Enlisted men.	Officers.	Enlisted men.	
Second Brigade. Col. DANIEL CAMERON.							
65th Illinois		3		20			
24th Kentucky		4	3	52			
103d Ohio		2		22		2	
8th Tennessee							
Indiana Light Artillery, Wilder Battery							
Total Second Brigade		9	3	94		2	1
Total Third Division		11	4	108		9	1
RESERVE ARTILLERY. Capt. ANDREW J. KONKLE.							
Indiana Light, 24th Battery							
Ohio Light, 19th Battery							
Total Twenty-third Army Corps		11	4	121		15	1
CAVALRY CORPS. Brig. Gen. JAMES M. SHACKELFORD.							
FIRST DIVISION. Brig. Gen. WILLIAM P. SANDERS.*a* Col. FRANK WOLFORD.							
Staff			1				
First Brigade. Col. FRANK WOLFORD. Lieut. Col. SILAS ADAMS.							
1st Kentucky		2	2	2			2
11th Kentucky							2
12th Kentucky	1	2		5			6
Law's Howitzer Battery *b*							
Total First Brigade	1	4	2	7			10
Second Brigade. Lieut. Col. EMERY S. BOND.							
112th Illinois Infantry (mounted)	1	17	2	36	1	11	
8th Michigan		3	1	13	1	27	
45th Ohio Infantry (mounted)		4	1	10	1	23	
Indiana Light Artillery, 15th Battery							
Total Second Brigade	1	24	4	59	3	61	1
Third Brigade. Col. CHARLES D. PENNEBAKER.							
11th Kentucky Infantry (mounted)				2			
27th Kentucky Infantry (mounted)		4	1	9		1	
Total Third Brigade		4	1	11		1	
Total First Division	2	32	8	77	3	72	2
SECOND DIVISION.							
2d Ohio							5
7th Ohio							
2d Tennessee Infantry (mounted)							
8th Tennessee							
Total cavalry	2	32	8	77	3	77	
Grand total	6	86	29	365	3	204	

a Mortally wounded November 18.   *b* Loss, if any, not of record

OFFICERS KILLED OR MORTALLY WOUNDED.

ILLINOIS.

Capt. Aza A. Lee, 112th Infantry.

KENTUCKY.

Capt. John W. Hill, 12th Cavalry. | Lieut. Matthias T. S. Lee, 24th Infantry.

MICHIGAN.

Maj. Cornelius Byington, 2d Infantry. | Lieut. Col. Lorin L. Comstock, 17th Infantry.
Lieut. Charles R. Galpin, 2d Infantry. | 　fantry.
Lieut William Noble, 2d Infantry. | Lieut. Josiah Billingsley, 17th Infantry.
Lieut. Frank Zoellner, 2d Infantry. | Capt. Wendell D. Wiltsie, 20th Infantry.

OHIO.

Lieut. Charles W. Fearns, 45th Infantry.

UNITED STATES VOLUNTEERS.

Brig. Gen. William P. Sanders.

WALKER'S FORD, TENN., DECEMBER 2.

Command.	Killed.		Wounded.		Captured or missing.		Aggregate.
	Officers.	Enlisted men.	Officers.	Enlisted men.	Officers.	Enlisted men.	
14th Illinois Cavalry				7			7
5th Indiana Cavalry		5	2	10		12	29
65th Indiana Infantry (mounted)		2		6			8
16th Indiana Infantry		1		4			5
18th Indiana Infantry		1		14			15
Total		9	2	41		12	64

BEAN'S STATION, TENN., DECEMBER 14–15.

Command.	Killed.		Wounded.		Captured or missing.		Aggregate.
	Officers.	Enlisted men.	Officers.	Enlisted men.	Officers.	Enlisted men.	
14th Illinois Cavalry		2		5		3	10
112th Illinois Infantry (mounted)		1		7		1	9
5th Indiana Cavalry		1				10	11
6th Indiana Cavalry				1		6	7
65th Indiana Infantry (mounted)		6		10	1	12	29
1st Kentucky Cavalry		1		4			5
11th Kentucky Infantry (mounted)				9		1	10
27th Kentucky Infantry (mounted)		3		9		4	16
8th Michigan Cavalry				1			1
9th Michigan Cavalry		1	1	1		4	7
2d Ohio Cavalry				1		1	2
7th Ohio Cavalry		1		2		2	5
45th Ohio Infantry (mounted)						3	3
Total		16	1	50	1	47	115

No. 7.

*Reports of Capt. Orlando M. Poe, U. S. Corps of Engineers,
Chief Engineer, Department of the Ohio.*

NAVARRE, STARK COUNTY, OHIO,
January 13, 1864.

GENERAL:* Meantime, I had dispatched Asst. J. H. Brooks to
Loudon, with instructions concerning defensive works at that point.
He had been directed to make a survey of the road from Knoxville
to Loudon, which road I had decided to adopt as the base of surveys on the peninsula included between the Clinch and Holston
Rivers, and extending as far to the eastward as Strawberry Plains.
The subsequent active military operations defeated this part of my
plan, though the data on hand will enable us to make a tolerably
good map of the territory alluded to.

On the 23d of October, I accompanied the general commanding to
Loudon, where the ground was thoroughly reconnoitered, and on
Tuesday, October 27, after two strong reconnaissances in the direction of the Sweet Water, it was decided to evacuate Loudon, not
because it was untenable but to adopt another line much more favorable. This was the line of the Tennessee, from Kingston to Lenoir's, where a pontoon bridge was to be thrown over the Holston,
thence by the right bank of the Little Tennessee River, sufficiently
near the mountains to render a movement in force by the enemy
around that flank impracticable. This line required a much smaller
force to hold, particularly as the autumn rains were coming on, when
the Little Tennessee would not be fordable. The wisdom of this
movement became apparent to those who had misunderstood it, when
Longstreet made his advance upon Knoxville, by two columns infantry, by way of the Kingston road, and a heavy cavalry force by
way of Maryville, having for its object to seize the heights on the
south side of the Holston, opposite Knoxville. We all have a lively
and grateful remembrance of the beautiful manner in which this
latter movement was thwarted by that very force which had been
guarding the right bank of the Little Tennessee. By direction of
the general commanding, I took up the pontoon bridge at Loudon
on the morning of the 28th of October, immediately after the troops
had crossed it, and transported it to the railroad track at the east
end of Loudon bridge, where the boats, some forty in number, the
chess, and a part of the anchorage were loaded upon cars and carried to Knoxville. This occupied the limited transportation of the
railroad for two days, so that it was not until 1 p. m. of Sunday,
November 1, that the bridge was finally in a condition to permit
Sanders' division of cavalry, with its baggage, to cross over it from
Knoxville to the south bank of the river. The bridge was thrown
across the river at the mouth of First Creek. The transportation
and reconstruction of this bridge, while it involved no great skill,
did require an immense amount of hard labor, but the usefulness of
the bridge has been so great that a hundred times as much would
have been well spent.

The bridge across the Holston at Lenoir's was successfully constructed out of the materials at hand by Lieutenant-Colonel Babcock,
assistant inspector-general, Ninth Army Corps. It was destroyed by

----

*For part (here omitted) covering operations August 12–October 10, in East Ten-
nessee, see Series I, Vol. XXX, Part II, p. 566.

ourselves in the subsequent operations. About this time I received orders to build a pontoon bridge, which could be transported upon the ordinary army wagons. There was absolutely nothing prepared in the way of materials; the lumber was standing in the woods, and the nails were lying around the railroad shops in the shape of scraps of old iron. Blacksmiths were at once set to work transforming these scraps into nails, and the saw-mills to sawing the lumber. Unfortunately the saw-mills under my control were sadly out of repair, and it was only after the most vexatious delays on account of broken machinery that we were able to get even a small portion of the lumber together. A part of the Engineer Battalion was at work upon this bridge when, on the morning of Friday, November 13, notice was received that the enemy had constructed a pontoon bridge at Huff's Ferry, near Loudon, and was crossing in force.

The major-general commanding, with a portion of his staff, left next morning for the scene of action. I was not one of those detailed to accompany him, hence am not able to report upon the well-fought battle of the 16th November—Campbell's Station. From Campbell's Station I was instructed to select, around Knoxville, lines of defense and have everything prepared to put the troops into position as they should arrive.

As I had been over the ground a great many times and had examined it in reference to this contingency, the examination directed was made very rapidly. I had made it a point to familiarize myself, as far as possible, with the organization of the Army of the Ohio, and was consequently able to designate, in writing, the positions to be occupied by the several subdivisions, as follows: Roemer's battery of four 3-inch rifle guns, at the University, to be supported by one brigade (Morrison's) of the First Division, Ninth Army Corps; Benjamin's battery of four 20-pounder Parrotts and Buckley's battery of six 12-pounder Napoleons (light twelves), at fort on hill northwest of the University—these batteries being supported by the remaining two brigades (Humphrey's and Christ's) of the First Division, Ninth Army Corps; the ground to be occupied by this division extending from the Holston River, near the mouth of Second Creek, around to the point where the East Tennessee and Georgia Railroad crosses Second Creek; this line was nearly at right-angles to the river to the position of Benjamin's battery, and thence parallel to the river. Gittings' battery of four 10-pounder Parrotts to occupy the small earth-works on Vine street near the depot. The Fifteenth Indiana Battery of 3-inch rifle guns to occupy the ridge between Gay street and First Creek; these two batteries to be supported by the Second Division, Ninth Army Corps, extending from Second Creek to First Creek, and parallel to the railroad. The Twenty-fourth Indiana Battery, Captain Sims, of six James rifle guns (3.8-inch caliber), and Henshaw's battery of two James rifle guns and four brass 6-pounders, to occupy the fort on Temperance Hill and the ridge adjacent, supported by Chapin's brigade, of White's division, and Reilly's brigade, of Hascall's division, of the Twenty-third Army Corps, extending from First Creek eastward to Bell's house. Shields' battery of six 12-pounder Napoleons and one section of Wilder's battery of 3-inch rifle guns on Mabry's Hill, supported by the brigades of Colonels Hoskins and Casement, the line of these brigades extending from Bell's house to the Holston River, at a point a little below the glass-works. Two sections of Wilder's battery of 3-inch rifle guns, and Konkle's battery of four 3-inch rifle guns, on the heights south of the river, supported by Cameron's brigade, of Hascall's division, Twenty-third Army Corps. One section of 12-pounder howitzers on Flint Hill, covering the bridge-head, and manned by soldiers detailed principally from the regiments of loyal Tennesseeans.

The troops began to arrive about daylight on the morning of November 17, and were placed in the positions respectively assigned to them, except Reilly's brigade, which was held in reserve in the streets of the town by the direction of the major-general commanding.

I may remark that during the whole siege the positions were scarcely changed, either of the artillery or infantry. As soon as any portion of the force arrived and was placed in position it was put at work to intrench itself, making use of the tools referred to in the first few lines of this report. There were no others in Knoxville except a few captured picks in the hands of the quartermaster, but he could not furnish either spades or shovels to accompany them.

The defenses thrown up at first were nothing but mere rifle-pits, having a profile of 4 feet wide by $2\frac{1}{2}$ feet in depth, with a parapet of 2 feet in height, making the height from the bottom of the trench to the interior crest of the parapet $4\frac{1}{2}$ feet. Two forts were in a defensible condition, viz, that occupied by Benjamin's battery and the one on Temperance Hill, the work upon them having been done by the Engineer Battalion. The troops worked all day and night, and by daylight on the morning of the 18th were tolerably well under cover; still the work was continued, the enemy being held at bay on the Kingston road by the cavalry under Sanders, and on the Clinton road by Colonel Pennebaker's mounted regiments. The hours in which to work that the gallant conduct of our cavalry secured us were worth to us a thousand men each. It is sad that they were bought at such a price as the life of that most gallant, chivalric soldier and noble gentleman, General Sanders. I hope I may be pardoned this allusion to the only classmate I had at the siege of Knoxville. General Sanders falling in front of the work occupied by Benjamin's battery, it seemed appropriate that the fort should be named after him, and, upon its being suggested to the major-general commanding, it was so ordered.

It was decided to dam First and Second Creeks; the dam across the former was made at the Vine street bridge and proved very successful, making an obstacle in front of and parallel to Temperance Hill for one-third of a mile, which could only be crossed by building a bridge. The dam across Second Creek was made at the tunnel by which the creek passes under the railroad. The character of the creek was not so favorable as in the first instance, still a very considerable obstacle was created.

At daylight on the morning of November 19 our position had been much strengthened, and we began to feel secure and confident; every man seemed conscious of the necessity for exertion and had made it, and with unflagging zeal the troops still continued the tasks imposed upon them. The citizens of the town and all the contrabands within reach were pressed into service and relieved the almost exhausted soldiers, who had no rest for more than a hundred hours. Many of the citizens were rebels and worked with a very poor grace, which blistered hands did not tend to improve. In anticipation of a necessity of giving up Mabry's Hill, an interior line of works was begun, running from Temperance Hill toward the river at Flint Hill. This line consisted of strong batteries at the two extremes, connected by a line of rifle-trenches of the character described above.

The enemy placed a battery on the Tazewell road, and from it hrew the first shells into the city. Up to this time the enemy did ot develop much strength east of the Tazewell road.

Friday, November 20.—The enemy erected lines of rifle-pits across he Kingston road, along the line which General Sanders had occu- ied, and commenced the construction of batteries on the ridge north f Fort Sanders, distant about 1 mile. We worked all day and night trengthening our defenses. The work on Temperance Hill was reatly strengthened by the enlargement of the face, which looked oward Mabry's Hill. A six-gun battery had been erected lower own on the eastern face of the hill, and is now in a defensible con- ition. On this day the lines of rifle-pits were made continuous, xcept the gorge between Temperance Hill and Mabry's Hill. Began vork on a third line of rifle-pits, between Temperance Hill and the iver, and commenced the construction of a battery on Flint Hill to nfilade the defile between our right and the river. The enemy from his time could not make an attack upon either of our flanks with- ut having his lines enfiladed by our fire from the south side of the iver. The enemy again fired a few shots at our center from their osition on the Tazewell road, but without doing any damage. The nemy having occupied a brick house, 500 yards in front of Fort anders, annoyed the troops of the fort by a fire of sharpshooters. he Seventeenth Regiment Michigan Volunteers made a sortie, rove them from the house, and burned it. While this was going n the enemy opened from all his guns on his right without damage o us.

Saturday, November 21.—Works were being steadily made tronger. Nothing remarkable occurred during this day.

Sunday, November 22.—Rather a quiet day. Received informa- ion that the enemy was constructing a raft at Boyd's Ferry, which hey intended to set adrift on the river with the hope that it would arry away our pontoon bridge and break our communication with he south side of the river. At 5 p. m. commenced the construction f a boom, made by stretching an iron cable across the river above he bridge. This cable was about 1,000 feet in length. I superin- ended in person the construction of this boom, and finished it at a. m. next morning. Meanwhile, all our tools were kept in use in he trenches.

Monday, November 23.—During the day everything was much as sual, with parties hard at work. In the evening the enemy ad- anced on our skirmish line, in front of the left of the Second Divis- on of the Ninth Army Corps, and our skirmishers fell back, setting ire to many buildings, which would have served as cover for the nemy's sharpshooters. Subsequent events proved that these houses vere unnecessarily burned.

Tuesday, November 24.—The Second Michigan Volunteers sallied, nd carried the most advanced rifle-pits of the enemy, but not being upported, were driven back, with considerable loss, by fresh troops f the enemy, which were brought up for the purpose of overwhelm- ng them. The picket line, from which our men had been driven he night before, was re-established. Laid out a work in front of Bell's house on Mabry's Hill, and the work on it progressed well. n the evening a second line of works was begun on our left, i. e., rom Fort Sanders via the College to the river, at the mouth of Sec- nd Creek. The enemy crossed some force and established himself n the hill on the south side of the river, 2 miles below the pon-

toon bridge. The absence of any signs of elation among the troops
of the enemy, indicated to us that General Grant's operations against
Bragg at Chattanooga had been attended with success.

Wednesday, November 25.—The enemy pressed forward on the
south side of the river, hoping to be more successful in his attempt
to occupy the heights opposite Knoxville than he had been in his effort
made ten days before; but again he was met and driven back with considerable loss. The hill occupied by the enemy was distant from
Fort Sanders about 2,800 yards, and it became necessary to defilade
the fort from the enemy's batteries upon it. This was soon done.
More reports about the raft came in, and I thought it prudent to begin the construction of a second boom, which I decided to make by
attaching long timbers together with chains, end to end, and allowing it to float on the water, being fastened on each side of the river.

Thursday, November 26.—Was quite ill this day, but managed to
be along the line. In the evening accompanied the general commanding to the south side of the river, where I laid out some rifle-
pits and an artillery epaulement for two guns, looking toward the
enemy's position on the hill and distant from it about 600 yards. The
enemy did not appear to do much this day. We finished the wooden
boom, 1,500 feet long. All our intrenching tools, as usual, were
kept busy adding to the strength of our works. After dark telegraph wires were stretched from stumps to stumps in front of our
most important positions in order to form an obstacle to the advance
of the enemy. Made a *cheval-de-frise* of pikes in front of Colonel
Hoskins' position, fastening the pikes in place with telegraph wire.

Friday, November 27.—The enemy still appeared to threaten us
on the south side of the river. I again carefully examined the
heights opposite Knoxville, this time accompanied by Lieutenant
Colonel Babcock. After consultation, it was decided that no change
should be made in the line I had previously selected, and that we
ought to begin at once the construction of works. Commenced a
battery for two guns and a line of rifle-pits on the first hill west of
the Maryville railroad; the enemy vigorously at work on the ridge
north of Fort Sanders. He appeared to be connecting his batteries
by lines of rifle-pits; the profile seemed too light for a first parallel.
The enemy was very active all day, and sharp firing was kept up
principally from the enemy, our troops reserving their fire.

Saturday, November 28.—Both armies hard at work. The enemy
displayed six guns at their position on south side of river, and
opened upon Roemer's battery, throwing an occasional shot at Fort
Sanders, but without doing any damage. Commenced the construction of a line of rifle-trenches on the Sevierville Hill (south side).
Sharp skirmishing in the evening. About 11 p. m. the enemy
attacked our picket lines, and, after a couple of hours of hot fighting, occupied them, thus turning their advanced line within about
120 yards of the northwestern salient of Fort Sanders. The skirmishing was continued all night, with a slow cannonade from all
the guns upon the enemy's right, principally directed upon Fort
Sanders. It now became evident that this was the real point of
attack.

Sunday, November 29.—At 6 a. m., under cover of a fog, the enemy
assaulted Fort Sanders, moving along the capital of the northwestern bastion. In spite of the gallantry and persistency of the attack
it was handsomely repulsed, with a loss to the enemy of almost the
entire brigade which led the assault. Our loss was 4 killed and 1

wounded.   I know of no instance in history where a storming party was so nearly annihilated.   It is even doubtful whether 100 men of this brigade returned unhurt to their lines.   The captures were 3 battle-flags, belonging, respectively, to the Thirteenth Mississippi Volunteers, the Seventeenth Mississippi Volunteers, and the Sixteenth Georgia Volunteers; between 200 and 300 prisoners, and some 500 stand of arms.   These are not given as strictly accurate, but I have endeavored to keep the number so small that more accurate reports would not diminish them.   The garrison of Fort Sanders was made up of Benjamin's battery, part of Buckley's, part of Seventy-ninth New York Infantry Volunteers, and a part of the Second Michigan Volunteer Infantry, making an aggregate of about 220 men.

A short description of Fort Sanders may be appropriate here.   It is a bastioned earth-work, built upon an irregular quadrilateral, the sides of which are, respectively, 125 yards southern front, 95 yards western front, 125 yards northern front, and 85 yards eastern front. The eastern front was entirely open, and is to be closed with a stockade; the southern front was about half done; the western front was finished, except cutting the embrasures, and the northern front was nearly finished.   Each bastion was intended to have a *pan coupé*. The bastion attacked was the only one that was completely finished. A light 12-pounder was mounted at the *pan coupé*, and did good service.   The ditch of the fort was 12 feet in width, and in many places as much as 8 feet in depth.   The irregularity of the site was such that the bastion angles were very heavy, the relief of the lightest one being 12 feet.   The relief of the one attacked was about 13 feet, and, together with the depth of the ditch, say 11 feet, made a height of 20 feet from the bottom of the ditch to the interior crest. This, owing to the nature of the soil, the dampness of the morning, and the steepness of the slopes, made the storming of the fort a very serious matter, and, when taken in connection with the neglect of the enemy to provide themselves with scaling-ladders, the confusion in their ranks, caused by passing through the obstacles of stumps, wire entanglements, and brush in front of the fort, the cool and steady fire to which they were exposed, coming from the very best troops in our service, sufficiently account for the repulse of one of the best divisions in the rebel army from that point of attack.   A short time after the repulse of the enemy a truce was offered him and accepted, during which he might take care of his wounded and bury his dead. The truce extended until 7 p. m.   During the assault on Fort Sanders, and for some time after that had been repulsed, sharp fighting took place on the south side of the river, but we were everywhere successful.

Monday, November 30.—Very quiet; our forces at work as usual; the line of rifle-trenches from the Sevierville road to the central hill was staked out.   The work on that part of the line from Sevierville Hill to the road was finished.   A two-gun battery was located just east of Second Creek, and good progress was made upon it.   The design of this battery was to enfilade the railroad out to the westward, and to flank the northern front of Fort Sanders, throwing fire upon ground which that fort could not reach.   The work upon the large fort on our right in front of Bell's house was so far advanced as to make it defensible.   During the day the enemy apparently did little or nothing, as though he were stunned by the severe punishment he had received the day before.

Tuesday, December 1.—The Engineer Battalion and contrabands at work. A line of rifle-trenches was located across the gorge between Temperance Hill and Mabry's Hill, and a portion of it completed. The troops on the south side of the river were hard at work with all the tools we had to spare from the north side. During the afternoon large trains belonging to the enemy were seen to move toward the eastward, and the belief began to grow upon us that the siege would be raised.

Wednesday, December 2.—The Engineer Battalion and contrabands were particularly engaged in the rifle-trenches between Temperance Hill and Mabry's Hill and an epaulement for two guns in the gorge. These were all finished by midnight. Still at work on large fort at Bell's house and on rifle-trenches on south side of the river. Everything unusually quiet for the fifteenth day of a siege.

Thursday, December 3.—Still hard at work on both sides of the river. A disposition apparent among the troops to consider their position strong enough to repel any assault the enemy might make, and a consequent indisposition to work. Evidently but a small force of the enemy east of the Tazewell road. The enemy's trains seen moving to the eastward.

Friday, December 4.—Still working a little, but the news of approaching re-enforcements and the movements of the enemy's trains lead us to believe that he will soon abandon the siege.

Saturday, December 5.—The siege of Knoxville terminated by the retreat of the enemy in the direction of Strawberry Plains (eastward). Heavy re-enforcements for us reached the south side of the river.

The enemy's infantry, or at least that part of it belonging to Longstreet's own corps, left in a solid body very deliberately, no signs of haste being apparent. The rear guard of his column passed the Tazewell road about 7 a. m.

A feeling of intense satisfaction pervaded the whole command, and many persons assured me of their conversion to a belief in "dirt-digging." It certainly proved efficient here. Examined the enemy's late position, and was surprised to find so little evidence of good engineering. I saw positions for only eighteen guns on the north side of the river, but could not discover that more than twelve of them had been used. Any other artillery he used was without cover.

The topography of the vicinity of Knoxville may be briefly described as follows : On the north bank of the river a narrow ridge is formed, extending from a point about 2½ miles east of Knoxville to Lenoir's. It has an average base of about 1½ miles in width. At Knoxville the width is about 1 mile. This ridge is cut through at short intervals by small streams, two of which, First and Second Creeks, run through the town of Knoxville at a distance from each other of about three-quarters of a mile. The main part of the town is built upon that portion of the ridge bounded on the northwest by the valley ; on the southwest by Second Creek ; on the southeast by the Holston River, and on the northeast by First Creek. It has the appearance of a table, elevated about 150 feet above the river and about 100 feet above the valley. Again, Third Creek is found about seven-eighths of a mile below Second Creek, forming a second similar table. A depression in the ridge about the same distance east of First Creek forms still another table, upon which is built East Knoxville. This elevated ground is called Temperance Hill. From this eastward the ridge is more broken until it disappears, and other ridges spring up. This last division is known as Mabry's Hill, and is the highest ground by some 20 feet to be found on the north side of the river within cannon range of Knoxville.

Commencing at Third Creek and going eastward, these tables may be numbered 1, 2, 3, and 4. A succession of ridges, all parallel to the one alluded to above, are found at short distances apart as one goes back from the river, the most important of which is at an average distance of 1 mile from the one Knoxville is situated upon, and is that which the enemy occupied. As near as can be ascertained by a pocket level, its elevation is exactly that of table No. 1 at its highest point. In selecting lines it was my opinion that tables Nos. 1, 2, 3, and 4 should be occupied. In this opinion the general commanding concurred, except regarding No. 4. It was a question whether it was most prudent, with our small force, to attempt to occupy No. 4 or to limit our occupation in force to Nos. 1, 2, and 3, simply holding No. 4 with a strong outpost. It seemed to me that we could (as we did) construct lines on No. 4 and also on No. 3, those on No. 4 to be thrown so far to the front that they could not be made available against us in event of their capture by the enemy and to be held by us with obstinacy, only leaving them when absolutely compelled to do so, in which case the lines on No. 3 would form our defense, and the enemy, after a stubborn fight, in which he would have suffered, would only have occupied a position, from which, in the former case, it would have been necessary to dislodge a mere outpost. In other words, after crippling him all we could in his successful assault upon No. 4, we would still have just as good a defense as if we had occupied No. 3 in the first place. But, on the other hand, by extending our lines to include No. 4, we made them weak in numbers at any one point, and we were consequently exposed to greater danger of being successfully assaulted along our whole position. This difficulty was partially obviated by the successful construction of a dam across First Creek, by which an impassable water obstacle of three-quarters of a mile in length was made immediately in front of and parallel to the crest of No. 3, which enabled us to greatly weaken our numbers (of infantry) on that part of the line. The general commanding yielded to my opinion, and all the foregoing positions were occupied as follows: On No. 1, Forts Sanders and Byington and Batteries Noble and Zoellner; on No. 2, Fort Comstock and Batteries Galpin, Wiltsie, and Billingsley; on No. 3, Fort Huntington Smith and Batteries Clifton Lee, Fearns, and Stearman; on No. 4, Fort Hill. All our works were connected by a continuous line of rifle-trenches. Between the ridge occupied by ourselves and that occupied by the enemy the valley varied in width, but its average breadth was in the neighborhood of 1 mile. It was almost entirely cleared of timber, and was at every point under the fire of our artillery. A direct advance over it would have been made only with serious loss. This would have been particularly the case in front of No. 4, where the valley widened to 1½ miles and was without timber or cover of any kind for troops. On the south side of the river the ground rises into a series of prominent points, the highest of which is about 350 feet, and is directly opposite Knoxville, the prolongation of Gay street passing directly over it. These knobs formed a range quite close to the river bank, with a wide valley beyond them. It was all important to us that at least three of these knobs should be held. We actually held four of them, commencing with the first hill east of the Louisville road and counting down the

river. As already stated, the enemy made several attempts to ge
possession of these heights, the first being made on Sunday, Novem
ber 15, by a heavy force of cavalry, under the command of Wheeler
which was repulsed by Sanders' division of cavalry, which had been
guarding the right bank of the Little Tennessee, and had gradually
fallen back before Wheeler's heavier force. Sanders was assisted by
Cameron's brigade of infantry. From these heights an artillery fire
can be delivered in front of each flank of the lines on the north side
of the river. Commencing with the most easterly hill (which we
called Sevierville Hill) and numbering them 1, 2, 3, and 4, our works
were as follows: On No. 1, only rifle-trenches; on No. 2, Fort Stan
ley; on No. 3, Fort Dickerson; on No. 4, Fort Higley. Nos. 1 and 2
were connected by rifle-trenches, while Nos. 3 and 4, though not con
nected, each was well provided with rifle-trenches to cover the in
fantry supports of the batteries. With sufficient time this disposi
tion could be very much improved by making the several forts of
such a character (building bomb-proofs for stores and cisterns for
water) that each would be self-reliant.

The siege of Knoxville passed into history. If mistakes were made
in the defense, they were covered by the cloak of success. That
many were made in the attack was apparent to us all. That the
rebels made a great error in besieging is as evident as it now is that
to accept siege at Knoxville was a great stroke of military policy.
The results of the successful defense are: the defeat of Bragg's army
and consequent permanent establishment of our forces at Chatta
nooga, with tolerably secure lines of communication; the confirma
tion of our hold upon East Tennessee; the discomfiture of and loss of
prestige by the choicest troops of the enemy's service.

There is no language sufficiently strong which I can use to express
admiration of the conduct of our troops. From the beginning of the
siege to the end every man did his whole duty. The cheerful looks
and confident bearing which met us at every turn made it seem as
though we were sure of victory from the first. It is doubtful whether
any man within our lines had at any time after the first forty-eigh
hours any fear of the result. All privations were borne, all hard
ships undergone with a spirit which indicated as plainly as if written
on the walls that success would attend our efforts. And is there
any man of that part of the Army of the Ohio which was in Knox
ville who would exchange his nineteen days of service there for any
other of the achievements of his life? Was there a regiment there
which will not put Knoxville as proudly on its banners as they now
bear Roanoke or New Berne, Williamsburg or Fair Oaks, Chan
tilly or South Mountain, Antietam or Vicksburg?

The troops of the Ninth Army Corps, and of the Twenty-third,
were chivalric rivals where duty was to be done. Never had an en
gineer officer less cause to complain of the manner in which his in
structions and directions were carried out. And here I feel it my
duty to refer to the great value of the services of the contrabands.
Tractable and willing (many of them came to me and volunteered to
work), they did an amount of work which was truly astonishing.
Day and night they worked without a murmur. For the first week
they labored regularly eighteen hours out of the twenty-four, and
during the whole siege, out of nearly 200 that we had at work, only
1 asked to be excused, and he for only one afternoon.

The question of supplies during the siege was second to none in
importance. The failure of the enemy to close the Sevierville road

and French Broad River enabled us even to accumulate a quantity of commissary stores. I was told that it was officially reported at the beginning of the siege that we had on hand full supplies for only one day and a half. Yet, after nineteen days' siege, we had accumulated to such an extent, over lines just referred to, that we had provisions enough to last ten days. The cavalry force was at once sent in pursuit of the retreating enemy, and during the day sent in quite a number of prisoners.

On Monday, December 7, all the available infantry force of the Army of the Ohio was put in motion toward the enemy, and followed him slowly until the 9th, when our forces halted—the cavalry at Bean's Station and the infantry at Rutledge. The enemy had halted at or near the Red Bridge, between Beans Station and Rogersville. No attack was made by us, as the enemy was still in vastly superior force.

On the 11th, Major-General Burnside, having been relieved by Major-General Foster, left for the North, and that properly fixes the close of this report.

To Lieut. Col. O. E. Babcock, assistant inspector-general of the Ninth Army Corps, and captain of Engineers, I am under very heavy obligations. Always ready with the most practicable advice, he cheerfully gave it, and it never passed unheeded. To Maj. S. S. Lyon, Fourth Kentucky Cavalry, and assistant engineer, I am under obligations for valuable reconnaissance. It is a matter of regret that the age and failing health of this officer impairs to a certain extent his usefulness as a topographer, for which branch of science he has such a wonderful talent. Capt. C. E. McAlester, Twenty-third Michigan Infantry, acting as chief engineer of the Twenty-third Army Corps; Capt. G. W. Gowan, Forty-eighth Pennsylvania Volunteers, assistant engineer of the Army of the Ohio; Capt. O. S. McClure, Fiftieth Ohio Volunteer Infantry, in command of the Engineer Battalion, rendered important assistance.

The Engineer Battalion proved almost invaluable. Its members were always ready to work, day or night, and did it with an intelligence which directed the labor toward a result. My thanks are due, and are freely given, to its officers and men.

All of which is respectfully submitted.

ORLANDO M. POE,
Captain, U. S. Engs., Chief Engineer, Army of the Ohio.

Maj. Gen. AMBROSE E. BURNSIDE,
Commanding Army of the Ohio.

—

HDQRS. MILITARY DIVISION OF THE MISSISSIPPI,
CHIEF ENGINEER'S OFFICE,
Nashville, Tenn., April 11, 1864.

SIR : * Meanwhile, I had dispatched Asst. J. H. Brooks to Loudon, with instructions concerning defensive works at that point. He had been directed to make a survey of the road from Knoxville to Loudon, which I had decided to adopt as the base of surveys on the peninsula included between the Clinch and Holston Rivers, and extending as far to the eastward as Strawberry Plains. The subse-

---

* For part (here omitted) covering operations in East Tennessee from August 12 to October 10, 1863, see Series I, Vol. XXX, Part II, p. 568.

quent active military operations defeated this part of my plans, though the data on hand will enable me to make a tolerably good map of the territory alluded to.

On the 23d October, I accompanied the general commanding to Loudon, where the ground was thoroughly reconnoitered, and on Tuesday, October 27, after two strong reconnaissances in the direction of the Sweet Water, it was decided to evacuate Loudon, not because it was untenable, but in order to adopt another line much more favorable.

This was the line of the Tennessee from Kingston to Lenoir's, where a pontoon bridge was to be thrown over the Holston, thence, by the right bank of the Little Tennessee River, to a point sufficiently near the mountains to render a movement by the enemy around that flank impracticable. This line required a much smaller force to hold particularly as the autumn rains were coming on, when the Little Tennessee would not be fordable.

The wisdom of this movement became apparent to those who had misunderstood it, when Longstreet made his advance upon Knoxville in two columns (infantry) by the way of the Kingston road and a heavy cavalry force via Maryville, having for its object to seize the heights on the south side of the Holston opposite Knoxville. We all have a lively and grateful remembrance of the beautiful manner in which this latter movement was thwarted, by that very force which had been guarding the right bank of the Little Tennessee.

By direction of the general commanding I took up the pontoon bridge at Loudon, on the morning of the 28th October, immediately after the troops had crossed it, and transported it to the railroad track at the east end of the Loudon bridge, whence the boats, forty in number, the chess, and a part of the anchorage, after being loaded upon the cars, were carried to Knoxville. This occupied the limited transportation of the railroad for two days, so that it was not until 1 o'clock p. m. of Sunday, November 1, that the bridge was finally in a condition to permit Sanders' division of cavalry with its baggage, to cross on it from Knoxville to the south bank of the river. The bridge was thrown across the river at the mouth of First Creek.

The transportation and reconstruction of this bridge, while it involved no great skill, did require an immense amount of hard labor, but the usefulness of the bridge has been so great that a hundred times as much would have been well spent.

The bridge across the Holston, at Lenoir's, was successfully constructed out of the material at hand, by Lieutenant-Colonel Babcock, assistant inspector-general, of the Ninth Army Corps. It was destroyed by ourselves in the subsequent operations.

About this time I received orders to build a pontoon bridge which could be transported upon the ordinary army wagons. There was absolutely nothing prepared in the way of material. The lumber was standing in the woods, and the nails were lying around the railroad shops in the shape of scraps of old iron. Blacksmiths were at once set at work transforming the scraps into nails ; and the saw-mills to sawing the lumber. Unfortunately, the saw-mills under my control were sadly out of repair, and it was only after the most vexatious delays, on account of broken machinery, that we were able to get even a small portion of the lumber together.

A part of the Engineer Battalion was at work upon the bridge when, on the morning of the 13th November, 1863, information was received at the headquarters of the Army of the Ohio that the enemy, under command of Longstreet, had succeeded in building a pontoon bridge over the Holston River at Huff's Ferry, near Loudon, and was crossing in force. The major-general commanding at once started for that point, taking with him a portion of his staff. I was directed to remain at Knoxville, in anticipation of instructions or the defense of that place.

From Campbell's Station, on the 16th of November, I was directed to select lines of defense around Knoxville, and to have everything prepared to put the troops in positions as fast as they should arrive. As I had been over the ground a great many times, and had examined it with reference to this contingency, the examination directed was made very rapidly. I had made it a point to familiarize myself, as far as possible, with the organization of the Army of the Ohio, and was consequently able to designate, in writing, the positions to be occupied by the several subdivisions, as follows :

Roemer's battery of four 3-inch rifle guns, at the University, to be supported by one brigade (Morrison's) of the First Division of the Ninth Army Corps.

Benjamin's battery of four 20-pounder Parrotts, and Buckley's battery of six 12-pounder Napoleons (light twelves), at the fort, afterward called Fort Sanders, on the hill northwest of the University—these batteries being supported by the remaining two brigades Humphrey's and Christ's) of the First Division, Ninth Army Corps, the ground to be occupied by this division extending from the Holston river, near the mouth of Second Creek, around to the point where the East Tennessee and Georgia Railroad crosses Second Creek. This line was nearly at right angles to the river, to the position of Benjamin's battery, and thence parallel to the river.

Gittings' battery of four 10-pounder Parrotts to occupy the small earth-work on Vine street, near the depot.

The Fifteenth Indiana Battery of three 3-inch rifle guns to occupy the ridge between Gay street and First Creek.

These two batteries to be supported by the Second Division of the Ninth Army Corps, extending from Second Creek to First Creek and parallel to the railroad.

The Twenty-fourth Indiana Battery (Captain Sims) of six James rifle guns (3.8-inch caliber), and Henshaw's battery of two James rifle guns and four brass 6-pounders, to occupy the fort on Temperance Hill and the ridge adjacent, supported by Chapin's brigade of White's Division, and Reilly's brigade of Hascall's division of Twenty-third Army Corps, extending from First Creek eastward to Bell's house.

Shields' battery of six 12-pounder Napoleons, and one section of Wilder's battery of 3-inch rifle guns, on Mabry's Hill, supported by the brigades of Colonels Hoskins and Casement, the line of these brigades extending from Bell's house to the Holston River, at a point a little below the glass-works.

Two sections of Wilder's battery of 3-inch rifle guns on the heights south of the river, supported by Cameron's brigade of Hascall's division, Twenty-third Army Corps.

One section of 12-pounder howitzers, on Flint Hill, covering the ridge, held and manned by soldiers detailed principally from the regiments of loyal Tennesseeans.

The troops began to arrive about daylight on the morning o
November 17, and were placed in the positions respectively assigne
to them, except Reilly's brigade, which was held in reserve in th
streets of the town, by direction of the major-general commanding
I may remark that, during the whole siege, the positions, either o
the artillery or the infantry, were scarcely changed.

As soon as any portion of the force arrived and was placed i
position it was put at work to intrench itself, making use of tool
brought from Kentucky by the Engineer Battalion. There were n
others in Knoxville, except a few captured picks in the hands o
the quartermaster, but he could not furnish either spades or shovel
to accompany them.

The defenses thrown up at first were nothing but mere rifle
trenches, having a profile 4 feet wide by $2\frac{1}{2}$ feet in depth, with
parapet of 2 feet in height, making the height from the bottom o
the trench to the interior crest of the parapet of $4\frac{1}{2}$ feet.

Two forts were in a defensible condition, viz, that occupied b
Benjamin's battery and the one on Temperance Hill, the work upo
them having been done by the Engineer Battalion.

The troops worked all day and night, and by daylight on th
morning of the 18th were tolerably well under cover. Still th
work was continued, the enemy being held at bay on the Kingsto
road by the cavalry under Sanders, and on the Clinton road by Co
onel Pennebaker's mounted regiments. The hours in which t
work that the gallant conduct of our cavalry secured us were wort
to us 1,000 men each. It is sad that they were bought at such
price as the life of that most gallant, chivalric soldier and nob
gentleman, General Sanders. (I hope I may be pardoned this allu
sion to the only classmate I had at the siege of Knoxville.)

General Sanders falling in front of the work occupied by Be
jamin's battery, it seemed appropriate that the fort should be name
after him, and upon its being suggested to the major-genera
commanding it was so ordered.

It was decided to dam First and Second Creeks. The dam acros
the former was made at the Vine street bridge, and proved ver
successful, making an obstacle in front of and parallel to Tempe
ance Hill for two-thirds of a mile, which could only be crossed b
building a bridge.

The dam across Second Creek was made at the culvert by whic
the creek passed under the railroad. The character of the creek wa
not so favorable as in the first instance, still a very considerab
obstacle was created.

At daylight on the morning of November 19, our position ha
been much strengthened, and we began to feel secure and confiden
Every man seemed conscious of the necessity for exertion and ha
made it, and with unflagging zeal the troops still continued the task
imposed upon them. The citizens of the town, and all the contra
bands within reach, were pressed into service, and relieved th
almost exhausted soldiers, who had seen no rest for more than on
hundred hours. Many of the citizens were rebels and worked wit
a very poor grace, which blistered hands did not tend to improve.

In anticipation of a necessity for giving up Mabry's Hill, an i
terior line of works was begun, running from Temperance Hi
toward the river at Flint Hill. This line consisted of strong ba
teries at the extremities, connected by a line of rifle-trenches, of th
character described above.

The enemy placed a battery on the Tazewell road, and from it hrew the first shells into the city. Up to this time the enemy did .ot develop much strength east of the Tazewell road.

Friday, November 20.—The enemy erected lines of rifle-trenches cross the Kingston road, along the line which General Sanders had ccupied, and commenced the construction of batteries on the ridge orth of Fort Sanders, distant about 1 mile. We worked all day nd night strengthening our defenses. The work on Temperance lill was greatly strengthened by the enlargement of the face which ooked toward Mabry's Hill. A six-gun battery had been erected ower down on the eastern face of this hill, and was now in a defensi- le condition. On this day the lines of rifle-trenches were made ontinuous, except the gorge between Temperance Hill and Mabry's lill, and the construction of a battery on Flint Hill commenced, to weep the defile between our right and the river. The enemy, from his time, could not make an attack upon either of our flanks with- ut having his lines enfiladed by our fire from the south side of the iver. The enemy again fired a few shots at our center from their osition on the Tazewell road, but without doing any damage. The nemy having occupied a brick house 500 yards in front of Fort anders, annoyed the troops in the fort by a fire of sharpshooters. he Seventeenth Regiment Michigan Volunteers made a sortie, lrove them from the house, and burned it. While this was going n the enemy opened from all his guns on his right without damage o us.

Saturday, November 21.—Works were being steadily made stronger. Nothing remarkable occurred during this day.

Sunday, November 22.—Rather a quiet day. Received informa- ion that the enemy was constructing a raft at Boyd's Ferry, which hey intended to set adrift on the river with the hope that it would arry away our pontoon bridge, and break our communication with he south side of the river. At 5 p. m. we commenced the construc- ion of a boom, made by stretching an iron cable across the river bove the bridge. This cable was about 1,000 feet in length. I uperintended in person the construction of this boom, and finished t at 9 a. m. next morning. Meanwhile, all our tools were kept in se in the trenches.

Monday, November 23.—During the day everything was much as .sual, both parties hard at work. In the evening the enemy advanced n our skirmish line in front of the left of the Second Division of he Ninth Army Corps, and our skirmishers fell back, setting fire to nany buildings which would have served as cover for the enemy's harpshooters. Subsequent events proved that these houses were nnecessarily burned.

Tuesday, November 24.—The Second Michigan Volunteer Infantry allied and carried the most advanced rifle-trenches of the enemy, ut, not being supported, were driven back, with considerable loss, y fresh troops of the enemy, which were brought up for the pur- ose of overwhelming them. The picket line from which our men ad been driven the night before was re-established. I laid out a ort in front of Bell's house on Mabry's Hill, and the work on it rogressed well. In the evening a second line of works was begun n the left, from Fort Sanders via the College to the river, at the nouth of Second Creek. The enemy crossed some force, and estab- ished himself on the hill on the south side of the river, 2 miles elow the pontoon bridge. The absence of any signs of elation among

the troops of the enemy, indicated to us that General Grant's oper‍-
tions against Bragg at Chattanooga had been attended with succes‍-

Wednesday, November 25.—The enemy pressed forward on th‍
south side of the river, hoping to be more successful in his attemp‍
to occupy the heights opposite Knoxville than he had been in h‍
effort made ten days before ; but again he was met and driven bac‍
with considerable loss. The hill occupied by the enemy was distan‍
from Fort Sanders about 2,300 yards, and it became necessary t‍
defilade the fort from the enemy's batteries upon it. This was soo‍
done. More reports about the raft came in, and I thought it pruden‍
to begin the construction of a second boom, which I decided to mak‍
by attaching long timbers together with chains, end to end, allowin‍
it to float on the top of the water, being fastened on each side of th‍
river.

Thursday, November 26.—Was quite ill this day, but managed t‍
be along the line. In the evening I accompanied the general com‍
manding to the south side of the river, where I laid out some rifl‍
trenches and an artillery epaulement for two guns, looking towar‍
the enemy's position on the hill and distant from it about 600 yard‍
The enemy did not appear to do much this day. We finished th‍
wooden boom, 1,500 feet long. All our intrenching tools, as usua‍
were kept busy, adding to the strength of our works. After dar‍
telegraph wires were stretched from stump to stump in front of ou‍
most important positions, in order to form an obstacle to the advanc‍
of the enemy. Made *cheval-de-frise* of pikes in front of Colon‍
Hoskins' position, fastening the pikes in place with telegraph wir‍

Friday, November 27.—The enemy still appeared to threaten us c‍
the south side of the river. I again examined carefully the heigh‍
opposite Knoxville, this time accompanied by Lieutenant-Colon‍
Babcock. After consultation, it was decided that no change shoul‍
be made in the line I had previously selected, and that we ought t‍
begin at once the construction of works. Whereupon we commence‍
a battery for two guns, and a line of rifle-trenches on the hill we‍
of the Maryville railroad. The enemy were vigorously at work c‍
the ridge north of Fort Sanders. He appeared to be connecting h‍
batteries by lines of rifle-trenches ; the profile seemed too light fc‍
a first parallel. The enemy was very active all day, and sharp firin‍
was kept up, principally from the enemy, our troops reserving the‍
fire.

Saturday, November 28.—Both armies hard at work. The enem‍
displayed six guns at their position on the south side of the rive‍
and opened upon Roemer's battery, throwing an occasional shot ‍
Fort Sanders, but without doing any damage. Commenced the co‍
struction of a line of rifle-trenches on the Sevierville Hill (sou‍
side). Sharp skirmishing in the evening. About 11 p. m. the enem‍
attacked our picket lines, and, after a couple of hours of hot figh‍
ing, occupied them, thus throwing their advanced line within abo‍
120 yards of the northwestern salient of Fort Sanders. Skirmishi‍
was continued all night, with a slow cannonade from all the gu‍
upon the enemy's right, principally directed upon Fort Sanders.‍
now became evident that this was the real point of attack.

Sunday, November 29.—At 6 a. m., under cover of a fog, the enem‍
assaulted Fort Sanders, moving along the capital of the northweste‍
bastion. In spite of the gallantry and persistency of the attack,‍
was handsomely repulsed, with a loss to the enemy of almost th‍
entire brigade which led the assault. Our loss was 4 killed and

ounded. I know of no instance in history where a storming party
as so nearly annihilated. It is very doubtful whether 100 men of
his brigade returned unhurt to their lines. The captures were:
three battle-flags, belonging, respectively, to the Thirteenth Missis-
ppi Volunteers, the Seventeenth Mississippi Volunteers, and the
ixteenth Georgia Volunteers, between 200 and 300 prisoners, and
ome 500 stand of arms. These are not given as strictly accurate,
ut I have endeavored to keep the numbers so small that more accu-
ate reports will not diminish them.

The garrison of Fort Sanders was made up of Benjamin's battery,
art of Buckley's, part of the Seventy-ninth New York Volunteer
nfantry, and part of the Second Michigan Volunteer Infantry,
making an aggregate of about 220 men.

A short description of Fort Sanders may be appropriate here. It
s a bastioned earth-work, built upon an irregular quadrilateral, the
ides of which are, respectively, 125 yards southern front, 95 yards
western front, 125 yards northern front, and 85 yards eastern front.
The eastern front was entirely open, and is to be closed with a stock-
de ; the southern front was about half done ; the western front was
nished, except cutting the embrasures, and the northern front was
early finished. Each bastion was intended to have a *pan coupé*.
The bastion attacked was the only one that was completely finished.
A light 12-pounder was mounted at the *pan coupé*, and did good
ervice. The ditch of the fort was 12 feet in width, and in many
laces as much as 8 feet in depth. The irregularity of the site was
uch that the bastion angles were very heavy, the relief of the light-
st one being 12 feet. The relief of the one attacked was about 13
eet, and together with the depth of the ditch, say 7 feet, made a
eight of 20 feet from the bottom of the ditch to the interior crest.
This, owing to the nature of the soil, the dampness of the morning,
nd the steepness of the slopes, made the storming of the fort a very
erious matter, and when taken in connection with the neglect of
he enemy to provide themselves with scaling ladders, the confusion
n their ranks, caused by passing through obstacles of stumps, wire
ntanglement, and brush in front of the fort, and the cool and steady
re to which they were exposed, coming from the very best troops
n our service, sufficiently account for the repulse of one of the best
ivisions in the rebel army, from that point of attack. A short time
fter the repulse of the enemy a truce was offered him, during which
e might bury his dead and take care of his wounded. It was ac-
epted, and extended until 7 p. m.

During the assault on Fort Sanders and for some time after that
ad been repulsed, sharp fighting took place on the south side of the
iver, but we were everywhere successful.

Monday, November 30.—Very quiet. Our forces at work as usual.
The line of rifle-trenches from the Sevierville road to the central hill
was staked out. The work on that part of the line, from Sevierville
Hill to the road, was finished.

A two-gun battery was located just east of Second Creek, and good
progress was made upon it.

The design of this battery was to enfilade the railroad cut to the
westward, and to flank the northern front of Fort Sanders, throw-
ng a fire upon ground which that fort could not reach. The work
upon the large fort on our right, in front of Bell's house, was so far
dvanced as to make it defensible. During the day the enemy apparently did little or nothing, as though he were stunned by the se-
ere punishment he had received the day before.

Tuesday, December 1.—The Engineer Battalion and contrabands a
work. A line of rifle-trenches was located across the gorge betwee
Temperance Hill and Mabry's Hill, and a portion of it completed
The troops on the south side of the river were hard at work with a
the tools we had to spare from the north side. During the afternoo
large trains belonging to the enemy were seen to move toward th
eastward, and the belief began to grow upon us that the siege woul
be raised.

Wednesday, December 2.—The Engineer Battalion and the cor
trabands were particularly engaged on the rifle-trenches betwee
Temperance Hill and Mabry's Hill, and an epaulement for two gun
in the gorge. These were all finished by midnight. Still at wor
on the large fort at Bell's house and on rifle-trenches on the sout
side of the river. Everything unusually quiet for the fifteenth da
of a siege.

Thursday, December 3.—Still hard at work on both sides of th
river. A disposition apparent among the troops to consider the pe
sition strong enough to repel any assault the enemy might make
and a consequent indisposition to work. Evidently but a small forc
of the enemy east of the Tazewell road. The enemy's trains see
moving to the eastward.

Friday, December 4.—Still working a little, but the news of th
approaching re-enforcements, and the movements of the enemy
trains led us to believe that he would soon abandon the siege.

Saturday, December 5.—The siege of Knoxville terminated by th
retreat of the enemy in the direction of Strawberry Plains (eas
ward). Heavy re-enforcements for us reached the south side of th
river. The enemy's infantry, or at least that part of it belonging t
Longstreet's own corps, left in a solid body, very deliberately, n
signs of haste being apparent. The rear of his column passed th
Tazewell road about 7 a. m.

A feeling of intense satisfaction pervaded the whole command
and many persons assured me of their conversion to a belief in "di
digging." It certainly proved efficient here. Examined the enemy
late position, and was surprised to find so little evidence of goo
engineering. I saw positions for only seventeen guns on the nort
side of the river, but could not discover that more than twelve c
them had been used. Any other artillery he used was without cove
The cavalry force available was at once sent in pursuit of the re
treating enemy, and during the day quite a number of prisoner
were brought in.

Monday, December 7.—All the available infantry force of th
Army of the Ohio was put in motion toward the enemy and followe
him slowly until the 9th, when our forces halted, the cavalry a
Bean's Station and the infantry at Rutledge. The enemy ha
halted at or near Red Bridge, between Bean's Station and Roger
ville. No attack was made by us, as the enemy was in vastly supe
rior force.

On the 11th, Major-General Burnside, having been relieved b
Major-General Foster, left for the North, and that properly fixes th
close of this report.

To Lieutenant-Colonel Babcock, assistant inspector-general of th
Ninth Army Corps, and captain of Engineers, I am under very heav
obligations. He was always ready with the most practical advice
he cheerfully gave it, and it was never passed unheeded.

To Maj. S. S. Lyon, of Fourth Kentucky Cavalry, and assistar

ngineer, Twenty-third Army Corps, I am under obligations for valu-
ble reconnaissances.   It is a matter of regret that the age and fail-
ng health of this officer impaired to a certain extent his usefulness
as a topographer, for which branch of science he has such a wonderful talent.

Capt. C. E. McAlester, of the Twenty-third Michigan Infantry,
acting as chief engineer of the Twenty-third Army Corps; Capt. G.
W. Gowan, of the Forty-eighth Pennsylvania Volunteers, as assistant engineer of the Army of the Ohio, and Capt. O. S. McClure, of
the Fiftieth Ohio Volunteer Infantry, in command of the Engineer
Battalion, rendered important assistance.

The Engineer Battalion proved almost invaluable.   Its members
were always ready to work day or night, and did it with an intelligence which directed the labor toward a result.   My thanks are due,
and are freely given, to its officers and men.

The siege of Knoxville passed into history.   If mistakes were
made in the defense, they were covered by the cloak of success.
That many were made in the attack was apparent to us all.   That
the rebels made a great error in besieging is as evident as it now is
that to accept siege at Knoxville was a great stroke of military
policy.

The results of the successful defense are, the defeat of Bragg's army
and the consequent permanent establishment of our forces at Chattanooga, with tolerably secure lines of communication; the confirmation of our hold upon East Tennessee; the discomfiture of and
loss of prestige by the choicest troops of the enemy's service.   There
is no language sufficiently strong which I can use to express my admiration for the conduct of our troops.   From the beginning of the
siege to the end every man did his whole duty.   The cheerful looks
and confident bearing which met us at every turn made it seem as
though we were sure of victory from the first.   It is doubtful whether
any man within our lines had at any time after the first forty-eight
hours the slightest fear of the result.   All privations were borne, all
hardships undergone with a spirit which indicated, as plainly as if
written on the walls, that success would attend our efforts.   And is
there a man of that part of the Army of the Ohio which was in
Knoxville who would exchange his nineteen days of service there for
any other of the achievements of his life?   Was there a regiment
there which will not bear Knoxville on its banner as proudly as it
now bears Roanoke or New Berne, Williamsburg or Fair Oaks,
Chantilly or South Mountain, Antietam or Vicksburg?

The troops of the Ninth Army Corps and the Twenty-third Army
Corps were chivalric rivals where duty was to be done.   Never before had an engineer officer less cause to complain of the manner in
which his instructions and directions were carried out.

And here I feel it my duty to refer to the great value of the services of the contrabands.   They were ever tractable and willing, and
many of them came to me and volunteered to work.   They did an
amount of labor which was truly astonishing.   Day and night they
worked without a murmur.   For the first week they labored regularly eighteen hours out of the twenty-four, and during the whole
siege, out of nearly 200 that we had at work, only 1 asked to be relieved, and he for only one afternoon.

The question of supplies during the siege was second to none in
importance.   The failure of the enemy to close the Sevierville road

and French Broad River enabled us to accumulate a quantity c
commissary stores. I was told that it was officially reported at th
beginning of the siege that we had full supplies for only one da
and a half, yet, after nineteen days' siege, we had accumulated t
such an extent, over the lines referred to, that we had provision
enough to last ten days.

The following order is here inserted. The several names wer
suggested by myself. Certainly none are so well entitled to what
ever of honor there may be in the names thus given to the forts an
batteries as those who shed their blood in defense of them.

GENERAL ORDERS, }   HEADQUARTERS ARMY OF THE OHIO,
    No. 37.   }   Knoxville, Tenn., December 11, 1863.

In order more clearly to designate the positions occupied by our troops during th
recent siege, and in token of respect to the gallant officers who fell in the defens
of Knoxville, the several forts and batteries are named, as follows :

Battery Noble.—At loop-holed house, south of the Kingston road, in memory c
Lieut. and Adjt. William Noble, Second Michigan Volunteers, who fell in th
charge upon the enemy's rifle-trenches in front of Fort Sanders, on the morning c
November 24.

Fort Byington.—At the College, after Maj. Cornelius Byington, Second Michiga
Volunteers, who fell mortally wounded while leading the assault upon the enemy
rifle-trenches in front of Fort Sanders, on the morning of November 24.

Battery Zoellner.—Between Fort Sanders and Second Creek, in memory of Lieut
Frank Zoellner, Second Michigan Volunteers, who fell mortally wounded in th
assault upon the enemy's rifle-trenches in front of Fort Sanders, on the morning c
November 24.

Battery Galpin.—East of Second Creek, in memory of Lieutenant Galpin, Secon
Michigan Volunteers, who fell in the assault upon the enemy's rifle-trenches i
front of Fort Sanders, on the morning of November 24.

Fort Comstock.—On Summit Hill, near the railroad depot, in memory of Lieu
tenant-Colonel Comstock, Seventeenth Michigan Volunteers, who fell in our line
during the siege.

Battery Wiltsie.—West of Gay street, in memory of Captain Wiltsie, Twentiet
Michigan Volunteers, who was mortally wounded in our lines during the siege.

Battery Billingsley.—Between Gay street and First Creek, in memory of Lieut
J. Billingsley, Seventeenth Michigan Volunteers, who fell in action in front of For
Sanders, November 20.

Fort Huntington Smith.—On Temperance Hill, in memory of Lieut. Col. [W.
Huntington Smith, Twentieth Michigan Volunteers, who fell at the battle of Camp
bell's Station.

Battery Clifton Lee.—East of Fort Huntington Smith, in memory of Capt
Clifton Lee, One hundred and twelfth Illinois Mounted Infantry, who fell in the
fight of November 18 in front of Fort Sanders.

Fort Hill.—At the extreme eastern point of our lines, in memory of Captain Hill
Twelfth Kentucky Cavalry, who fell during the siege.

Battery Fearns.—On Flint Hill, in memory of Lieut. and Adjt. Charles W
Fearns, Forty-fifth Ohio Volunteers (mounted infantry), who fell in the action o
November 18 in front of Fort Sanders.

Battery Stearman.— In the gorge between Temperance Hill and Mabry's Hill, i
memory of Lieut. William H. Stearman, Thirteenth Kentucky Volunteers, wh
fell near Loudon, Tenn.

Fort Stanley.—Including all the works upon the central hill, on the south side o
the river, in memory of Capt. C. E. Stanley, Forty-fifth Ohio Volunteers (mounte
infantry), who fell mortally wounded in the action near Philadelphia, Tenn.

Fort Higley.—Including all the works on the hill west of the railroad embank
ment, south side of the river, in memory of Capt. Joel P. Higley, Seventh Ohi
Cavalry, who fell in action at Blue Springs, Tenn., October 10, 1863.

Fort Dickerson.—Including all the works between Fort Stanley and Fort Higley
in memory of Capt. Jonathan [C.] Dickerson, One hundred and twelfth Illinois
Volunteers (mounted infantry), who fell in action near Cleveland, Tenn.

By command of Major-General Burnside :

                                        LEWIS RICHMOND,
                                    Assistant Adjutant-General.

The topography of the vicinity of Knoxville may be briefly de-
cribed as follows :

On the north bank of the river a narrow ridge is found, extending
rom a point about 2½ miles east of Knoxville to Lenoir's.   It has an
verage base of about 1½ miles in width.   At Knoxville the width is
bout 1 mile.   The ridge is cut through at short intervals by small
treams ; two of which, First and Second Creeks, run through the
own of Knoxville, at a distance from each other of about three-
ourths of a mile.   The main part of the town is built upon that por-
ion of the ridge bounded on the northwest by the valley, on the
outhwest by Second Creek, on the southeast by the Holston River,
nd on the northeast by First Creek.   It has the appearance of a
able, elevated about 150 feet above the river, and about 100 feet
bove the valley.   Again, Third Creek is found about seven-eighths
f a mile below Second Creek, forming a second similar table.   A
lepression in the ridge, about the same distance east of First Creek,
orms still another table, upon which is built East Knoxville.   This
levated ground is called Temperance Hill.   Eastward from this the
ridge is more broken, until it disappears and other ridges spring up.
This last division is known as Mabry's Hill, and is the highest
ground, by some 20 feet, to be found on the north side of the river,
within cannon range of Knoxville.   Commencing at Third Creek
nd going eastward, these tables may be numbered 1, 2, 3, and 4.   A
succession of ridges, all parallel to the one alluded to above, are
ound at short distances apart as one goes back from the river, the
nost important of which is at an average distance of 1 mile from the
ne upon which Knoxville is situated, and is that which the enemy
ccupied.   As near as can be ascertained by a pocket level, its eleva-
ion is about 15 feet more than that of table No. 1 at its highest
oint.

In selecting lines it was my opinion that tables Nos. 1, 2, 3, and 4
should be occupied.   In this opinion the general commanding concurred, except regarding No. 4.   It was a question whether it was
most prudent, with our small force, to attempt to occupy No. 4, or
to limit our occupation in force to Nos. 1, 2, and 3, simply holding
No. 4 with a strong out-post.   It seemed to me that we could (as we
lid) construct lines on No. 4, and also on No. 3 ; those on No. 4 to
be thrown so far to the front that they could not be made available
against us in the event of their capture by the enemy, and to be
held by us with obstinacy, only leaving them when absolutely compelled to do so ; in which case the lines on No. 3 would form a defense, and the enemy, after a stubborn fight, in which he would
have suffered, would only have occupied a position, from which, in
the former case, it would have been necessary to dislodge a mere
out-post.   In other words, after crippling him all we could in his
successful assault upon No. 4, we could still have just as good a defense as if we had occupied only No. 3 in the first place.

But, on the other hand, by extending our lines to include No. 4,
we made them weak in numbers at any one point, and we were consequently exposed to greater danger of being successfully assaulted
along our whole position.   This difficulty was partially obviated by
the successful construction of a dam across First Creek, by which
an impassable water obstacle of three-fourths of a mile in length
was made immediately in front of and parallel to the crest of No. 3,
which enabled us to greatly weaken our numbers (of infantry) in
that part of the line.

The general commanding yielded to my opinions, and all the fore
going positions were occupied as follows :

On No. 1, Forts Sanders and Byington, and Batteries Noble and
Zoellner.

On No. 2, Fort Comstock and Batteries Galpin, Wiltsie, and Bill
ingsley.

On No. 3, Fort Huntington Smith and Batteries Clifton Lee, Fearns
and Stearman.

On No. 4, Fort Hill.

All our works were connected by a continuous line of rifle
trenches. Between the ridge occupied by ourselves and that occu
pied by the enemy the valley varied in width, but its average breadth
was in the neighborhood of 1 mile. It was almost entirely cleared
of timber, and was at every point under the fire of our artillery.

A direct advance over it would have been made only with severe
loss. This would have been particularly the case in front of No. 4
where the valley increases in width to 1½ miles, and was without
timber or cover of any kind for troops.

On the south side of the river the ground rises into a series of
prominent points, the highest of which is about 360 feet, and is
directly opposite Knoxville; the prolongation of Gay street passes
directly over it. These knobs formed a range quite close to the river
bank, with a wide valley beyond them. It was all important to us
that at least three of these knobs should be held. We actually held
four of them, commencing with the first hill east of the Sevierville
road, and counting down the river.

As already stated, the enemy made several attempts to get posses
sion of these heights, the first being made on Sunday, November 15
by a heavy force of cavalry, under the command of Wheeler, which
was repulsed by Sanders' division of cavalry, which had been guard
ing the right bank of the Little Tennessee, and had gradually fallen
back before Wheeler's heavier force. Sanders was assisted by Cam
eron's brigade of infantry.

From these heights an artillery fire can be delivered in front of
each flank of the lines on the north side of the river.

Commencing with the most easterly hill (which we called "Sevier
ville Hill"), and numbering them 1, 2, 3, and 4, they were occupied
by us as follows :

On No. 1, only rifle-trenches.

On No. 2, Fort Stanley.

On No. 3, Fort Dickerson.

On No. 4, Fort Higley.

Nos. 1 and 2 were connected by rifle-trenches, while Nos. 3 and 4,
though not connected, each was well provided with rifle-trenches to
cover the infantry supports of the batteries.

With sufficient time, this disposition could be very much improved,
by making the several forts of such a character (building bomb-proofs
for stores and cisterns for water) that each would be self-reliant.

For the map* which accompanies this report, I am indebted to
Sub-Assistant Rockwell and Aide Talcott, of the U. S. Coast Survey.

The delay in the report was caused by my desire to await the com
pletion of the map, without which it would be crude enough.

The accompanying photographic views are intended to illustrate
still further the locality rendered historical by the siege of Knox-

---

* To appear in the Atlas.

ville. They are the work of Mr. George N. Barnard, photographer at the chief engineer's office, Military Division of the Mississippi.

All of which is respectfully submitted.

ORLANDO M. POE,
Captain of Engineers.

Lieut. Col. J. H. SIMPSON, U. S. Engineers,
Cincinnati, Ohio.

—

SIR: In accordance with your instructions, I have the honor of reporting as follows upon the engineer operations arising from the recent attempt of the enemy to gain possession of East Tennessee :

On the morning of November 13, 1863, information was received at the headquarters of the Army of the Ohio that the enemy, under the command of Longstreet, had succeeded in building a pontoon bridge over the Holston River at Huff's Ferry, near Loudon, and was crossing in force. The major-general commanding at once started for that point, taking with him a portion of his staff. I was directed to remain at Knoxville, in anticipation of instruction for the defense of that place.

From Campbell's Station, on the 16th November, I was directed to select lines of defense around Knoxville, and to have everything prepared to put the troops in position as fast as they should arrive.

As I had been over the ground a great many times, and had examined it with reference to this contingency, the examination directed was made very rapidly. I had made it a point to familiarize myself, as far as possible, with the organization of the Army of the Ohio, and was consequently able to designate, in writing, the positions to be occupied by the several subdivisions, as follows :

Roemer's battery of four 3-inch rifle guns, at the University, to be supported by one brigade (Morrison's) of the First Division, Ninth Army Corps ; Benjamin's battery of four 20-pounder Parrotts, and Buckley's battery of six 12-pounder Napoleons (light twelves), at fort on hill northwest of the University ; these batteries being supported by the remaining two brigades (Humphrey's and Christ's) of the First Division, Ninth Army Corps, the ground to be occupied by this division, extending from the Holston River, near the mouth of Second Creek, around to the point where the East Tennessee and Georgia Railroad crosses Second Creek. This line was nearly at right angles to the river, to the position of Benjamin's battery, and thence parallel to the river.

Gittings' battery of four 10-pounder Parrotts, to occupy the small earth-work on Vine street near the depot.

The Fifteenth Indiana Battery of three 3-inch rifle guns, to occupy the ridge between Gay street and First Creek ; these two batteries to be supported by the Second Division, Ninth Army Corps, extending from Second Creek to First Creek, and parallel to the railroad.

The Twenty-fourth Indiana battery (Captain Sims) of six James' rifle guns (3.8-inch caliber), and Henshaw's battery of two James' rifle guns and four brass 6-pounders, to occupy the fort on Temperance Hill and the ridge adjacent, supported by Chapin's brigade of White's division and Reilly's brigade of Hascall's division, of the Twenty-third Army Corps, extending from First Creek eastward to

Bell's house. Shields' battery of six 12-pounder Napoleons and one section of Wilder's battery of 3-inch rifle guns, on Mabry's Hill, supported by the brigades of Colonels Hoskins and Casement, the line of these brigades extending from Bell's house to the Holston River, at a point a little below the glass-works.

Two sections of Wilder's battery of 3-inch rifle guns, and Konkle's battery of four 3-inch rifle guns, on the heights south of the river, supported by Cameron's brigade of Hascall's division, Twenty-third Army Corps.

One section of 12-pounder howitzers on Flint Hill, covering the bridge-head, and manned by soldiers detailed principally from the regiments of loyal Tennesseeans.

The troops began to arrive about daylight on the morning of November 17, and were placed in the positions respectively assigned to them, except Reilly's brigade, which was held in reserve in the streets of the town by direction of the major-general commanding. I may remark, that during the whole siege the positions were scarcely changed, either of the artillery or of the infantry. As soon as any portion of the force arrived and was placed in position it was put at work to intrench itself, making use of tools brought from Kentucky by the Engineer Battalion. There were no others in Knoxville, except a few captured picks in the hands of the quartermaster, but he could not furnish either spades or shovels to accompany them. The defenses thrown up at first were nothing but mere rifle-pits, having a profile 4 feet wide by $2\frac{1}{2}$ feet in depth, with a parapet of 2 feet in height, making the height from the bottom of the trench to the interior crest of the parapet, $4\frac{1}{2}$ feet. Two forts were in a defensible condition, viz, that occupied by Benjamin's battery, and the one on Temperance Hill, the work upon them having been done by the Engineer Battalion.

The troops worked all day and night, and by daylight on the morning of the 18th were tolerably well under cover. Still the work was continued, the enemy being held at bay on the Kingston road by the cavalry under Sanders, and on the Clinton road by Colonel Pennebaker's mounted regiments. The hours in which to work, that the gallant conduct of our cavalry secured us, were worth to us 1,000 men each. It is sad that they were bought at such a price as the life of that most gallant, chivalric soldier and noble gentleman, General Sanders. (I hope I may be pardoned this allusion to the only classmate I had at the siege of Knoxville.)

General Sanders, falling in front of the work occupied by Benjamin's battery, it seemed appropriate that the fort should be named after him, and upon its being suggested to the major-general commanding, it was so ordered.

It was decided to dam First and Second Creeks. The dam across the former was made at the Vine street bridge, and proved very successful, making an obstacle in front of, and parallel to, Temperance Hill, for one-third of a mile, which could only be crossed by building a bridge. The dam across Second Creek was made at the tunnel by which the creek passes under the railroad. The character of the creek was not so favorable as in the first instance; still, a very considerable obstacle was created. At daylight on the morning of November 19, our position had been much strengthened, and we began to feel secure and confident. Every man seemed conscious of the necessity for exertion and had made it, and with unflagging zeal the troops still continued the tasks imposed upon them. Citizens of the own and all the contrabands within reach were pressed into service, and relieved the almost exhausted soldiers, who had had no rest for more than an hundred hours.   Many of the citizens were rebels and worked with a very poor grace, which blistered hands did not tend to improve.

In anticipation of a necessity for giving up Mabry's Hill, an inferior line of works was begun, running from Temperance Hill toward the river at Flint Hill. This line consisted of strong batteries at the two extremities, connected by a line of rifle-trenches of the character described above.

The enemy placed a battery on the Tazewell road, and from it threw the first shells into the city. Up to this time the enemy did not develop much strength east of the Tazewell road.

Friday, November 20.—The enemy erected lines of rifle-pits across the Kingston road, along the line which General Sanders had occupied, and commenced the construction of batteries on the ridge north of Fort Sanders, distant about 1 mile.

We worked all day and night strengthening our defenses. The work on Temperance Hill was greatly strengthened by the enlargement of the face which looked toward Mabry's Hill. A six-gun battery has been erected lower down on the eastern face of the hill, and is now in a defensible condition. On this day the lines of rifle-pits were made continuous, except the gorge between Temperance Hill and Mabry's Hill. Begun work on a third line of rifle-pits between Temperance Hill and the river, and commenced the construction of a battery on Flint Hill, to enfilade the defile between our right and the river. The enemy from this time could not make an attack upon either of our flanks, without having his lines enfiladed by our fire from the south side of the river. The enemy again fired a few shots at our center from three positions on the Tazewell road, but without doing any damage. The enemy having occupied a brick house, 500 yards in front of Fort Sanders, annoyed the troops of the fort by a fire of sharpshooters. The Seventeenth Michigan Volunteer Infantry made a sortie, drove them from the house, and burned it. While this was going on, the enemy opened from all his guns on his right without damage to us.

Saturday, November 21.—Works were being steadily made stronger. Nothing remarkable occurred during this day.

Sunday, November 22.—Rather a quiet day ; received information that the enemy was constructing a raft at Boyd's Ferry, which they intended to set adrift on the river, with the hope that it would carry away our pontoon bridge and break our communication with the south side of the river. . At 5 p. m. commenced the construction of a boom, made by stretching an iron cable across the river above the bridge. This cable was about 1,000 feet in length. I superintended in person the construction of this boom, and finished it at 9 a. m. next morning. Meanwhile, all our tools were kept in use in the trenches.

Monday, November 23.—During the day everything was much as usual, both parties hard at work. In the evening the enemy advanced on our skirmish line, in front of the left of the Second Division of the Ninth Army Corps, and our skirmishers fell back, setting fire to many buildings, which would have served as cover for the enemy's sharpshooters. Subsequent events proved that these houses were unnecessarily burned.

Tuesday, November 24.—The Second Michigan Volunteer Infan-

try sallied and carried the most advanced rifle-pits of the enemy
but not being supported, were driven back with considerable loss
by fresh troops of the enemy, which were brought up for the pur
pose of overwhelming them. The picket line from which our men
had been driven the night before was re-established. Laid out a
work in front of Bell's house, on Mabry's Hill, and the work on it
progressed well. In the evening a second line of works was begun
on our left, i. e., from Fort Sanders, via the college, to the river, at
the mouth of Second Creek. The enemy crossed some force, and
established himself on the hill on the south side of the river, 2 miles
below the pontoon bridge. The absence of any signs of elation
among the troops of the enemy indicated to us that General Grant's
operations against Bragg at Chattanooga had been attended with
success.

Wednesday, November 25.—The enemy pressed forward on the
south side of the river, hoping to be more successful in his attempt
to occupy the heights opposite Knoxville than he had been in his
efforts made ten days before, but again he was met and driven back
with considerable loss. The hill occupied by the enemy was distant
from Fort Sanders about 2,800 yards, and it became necessary to
defilade the fort from the enemy's batteries upon it. This was soon
done.

More reports about the raft came in, and thought it prudent to
begin the construction of a second boom, which I decided to make
by attaching long timbers together with chains, end to end, and
allowing it to float on top of the water, being fastened on each side
of the river.

Thursday, November 26.—Was quite ill this day, but managed to
be along the line. In the evening accompanied the general commanding to the south side of the river, where I laid out some rifle-
pits and an artillery epaulement for two guns, looking toward the
enemy's position on the hill, and distant from it about 600 yards.
The enemy did not appear to do much this day. We finished the
wooden boom, 1,500 feet long. All our intrenching tools, as usual,
were kept busy adding to the strength of our works. After dark
telegraph wires were stretched from stump to stump in front of our
most important positions, in order to form an obstacle to the advance
of the enemy. Made a *cheval-de-frise* of pikes in front of Colonel
Hoskins' position, fastening the pikes in place with telegraph wire.

Friday, November 27.—The enemy still appeared to threaten us
on the south side of the river. I again examined carefully the
heights opposite Knoxville, this time accompanied by Lieutenant-
Colonel Babcock. After consultation, it was decided that no change
should be made in the line I had previously selected, and that we
ought to begin at once the construction of works. Commenced a
battery for two guns and a line of rifle-pits on the first hill west of
the Maryville Railroad ; the enemy vigorously at work on the ridge
north of Fort Sanders. He appeared to be connecting his batteries
by lines of rifle-pits. The profile seemed too light for a "first parallel." The enemy was very active all day, and sharp firing was
kept up, principally from the enemy, our troops reserving their fire.

Saturday, November 28.—Both armies hard at work. The enemy
displayed six guns at their position on south side of river, and
opened upon Roemer's battery, throwing an occasional shot at Fort
Sanders, but without doing any damage. Commenced the construction of a line of rifle-trenches on the Sevierville Hill (south side).

harp skirmishing in the evening. About 11 p. m. the enemy attacked our picket lines, and after a couple of hours of hot fighting occupied them, thus throwing their advanced line within about 120 ards of the northwestern salient of Fort Sanders. The skirmishing was continued all night, with a slow cannonade, from all the guns upon the enemy's right, principally directed upon Fort Sanders. It now became evident that this was the real point of attack.

Sunday, November 29.—At 6 a. m., under cover of a fog, the nemy assaulted Fort Sanders, moving along the capital of the northwestern bastion. In spite of the gallantry and persistency of he attack, it was handsomely repulsed, with a loss to the enemy of almost the entire brigade which led the assault. Our loss was 4 killed and 11 wounded. I know of no instance in history where a storming party was so nearly annihilated. It is very doubtful whether 100 men of this brigade returned unhurt to their lines. The captures were 3 battle-flags, belonging, respectively, to the Thirteenth Mississippi Volunteers, the Seventeenth Mississippi Volunteers, and the Sixteenth Georgia Volunteers, between 200 and 300 prisoners, and some 500 stand of arms. (These are not given as strictly accurate, but I have endeavored to keep the number so small that more accurate reports would not diminish them.) The garrison of Fort Sanders was made up of Benjamin's battery, part of Buckley's, part of Seventy-ninth New York Volunteer Infantry, and part of the Second Michigan Volunteer Infantry, making an aggregate of about 220 men.

A short description of Fort Sanders may be appropriate here. It is a bastioned earth-work, built upon an irregular quadrilateral, the sides of which are, respectively, 125 yards southern front, 95 yards western front, 125 yards northern front, and 85 yards eastern front. The eastern front was entirely open, and is to be closed with a stockade. The southern front was about half done. The western front was finished, except cutting the embrasures, and the northern front was nearly finished. Each bastion was intended to have a *pan coupé*. The bastion attacked was the only one that was completely finished. A light 12-pounder was mounted at the *pan coupé*, and did good service. The ditch of the fort was 12 feet in width, and in many places as much as 8 feet in depth. The irregularity of the site was such that the bastion angles were very heavy, the relief of the lightest one being 12 feet. The relief of the one attacked was about 13 feet, and, together with the depth of the ditch, say 7 feet, made a height of 20 feet from the bottom of the ditch to the interior crest. This, owing to the nature of the soil, the dampness of the morning, and the steepness of the slopes, made the storming of the fort a very serious matter, and, when taken in connection with the neglect of the enemy to provide themselves with scaling-ladders, the confusion in their ranks, caused by passing through the obstacles of stumps, wire entanglement, and brush in front of the fort, the cool and steady fire to which they were exposed, coming from the very best troops in our service, sufficiently accounts for the repulse of one of the best divisions in the rebel army from that point of attack.

A short time after the repulse of the enemy a truce was offered him, and accepted, during which he might bury his dead and take care of his wounded. The truce extended until 7 p. m.

During the assault on Fort Sanders, and for some time after that had been repulsed, sharp fighting took place on the south side of the river, but we were everywhere successful.

Monday, November 30.—Very quiet. Our forces at work, as usual. The line of rifle-trenches from the Sevierville road to the central hill was staked out. The work on that part of the line from Sevierville Hill to the road was finished. A two-gun battery was located just east of Second Creek, and good progress was made upon it. The design of this battery was to enfilade the railroad cut to the westward, and to flank the northern front of Fort Sanders, throwing a fire upon ground which that fort could not reach. The work upon the large fort on our right, in front of Bell's house, was so far advanced as to make it defensible. During the day the enemy, apparently, did little or nothing, as though he were stunned by the severe punishment he had received the day before.

Tuesday, December 1.—The Engineer Battalion and contrabands at work. A line of rifle-trenches was located across the gorge between Temperance Hill and Mabry's Hill, and a portion of it completed. The troops on the south side of the river were hard at work, with all the tools we had to spare from the north side. During the afternoon, large trains belonging to the enemy were seen to move toward the eastward, and the belief began to grow upon us that the siege would be raised.

Wednesday, December 2.—The Engineer Battalion and contrabands were particularly engaged on the rifle-trenches between Temperance Hill and Mabry's Hill, and an epaulement for two guns in the gorge. These were all finished by midnight. Still at work on large fort at Bell's house and on rifle-trenches on south side of the river. Everything unusually quiet for the fifteenth day of a siege.

Thursday, December 3.—Still hard at work on both sides of the river. A disposition apparent among the troops to consider their position strong enough to repel any assault the enemy might make, and a consequent indisposition to work. Evidently but a small force of the enemy east of the Tazewell road. The enemy's trains seen moving to the eastward.

Friday, December 4, 1863.—Still working a little, but the news of approaching re-enforcements and the movements of the enemy's trains lead us to believe that he will soon abandon the siege.

Saturday, December 5.—The siege of Knoxville terminated by the retreat of the enemy in the direction of Strawberry Plains (eastward). Heavy re-enforcements for us reached the south side of the river. The enemy's infantry, or at least that part of it belonging to Longstreet's own corps, left in a solid body, very deliberately, no signs of haste being apparent. The rear guard of his column passed the Tazewell road about 7 a. m.

A feeling of intense satisfaction pervaded the whole command, and many persons assured me of their conversion to a belief in "dirt digging." It certainly proved efficient here. Examined the enemy's late position, and was surprised to find so little evidence of good engineering. I saw positions for only eighteen guns on the north side of the river, but could not discover that more than twelve of them had been used. Any other artillery he used was without cover. The cavalry force available was at once sent in pursuit of the retreating enemy, and during the day sent in quite a number of prisoners.

On Monday, December 7, all the available infantry force of the

Army of the Ohio was put in motion toward the enemy, and followed him slowly until the 9th, when our forces halted, the cavalry t Bean's Station and the infantry at Rutledge.

The enemy had halted at or near the Red Bridge, between Bean's tation and Rogersville. No attack was made by us, as the enemy vas still in vastly superior force.

On the 11th, Major-General Burnside, having been relieved by Major-General Foster, left for the North, and properly fixes the lose of this report.

To Lieut. Col. O. E. Babcock, assistant inspector-general of the Kinth Army Corps, and captain of engineers, I am under very eavy obligations. Always ready with the most practical advice, he heerfully gave it, and it never passed unheeded.

To Maj. S. S. Lyon, Fourth Kentucky Cavalry, and assistant engineer, I am under obligations for valuable reconnaissances. It is a latter of regret that the age and failing health of this officer impaired to a certain extent his usefulness as a topographer, for which ranch of science he has such a wonderful talent.

Capt. C. E. McAlester, Twenty-third Michigan Infantry, acting as hief engineer of the Twenty-third Army Corps; Capt. G. W. Gowan, 'orty-eighth Pennsylvania Volunteers, as assistant engineer of the Army of the Ohio, and Capt. O. S. McClure, Fiftieth Ohio Volunteer Infantry, in command of the Engineer Battalion, rendered important assistance.

The Engineer Battalion proved almost invaluable. Its members vere always ready to work, day or night, and did it with an intelligence which directed the labor toward a result. My thanks are ue and are freely given to its officers and men.

The siege of Knoxville passed into history. If mistakes were made a the defense they were covered by the cloak of success. That many vere made in the attack was apparent to us all. That the rebels lade a great error in besieging is as evident as it now is that to acept siege at Knoxville was a great stroke of military policy. The esults of the successful defense are, the defeat of Bragg's army and onsequent permanent establishment of our forces at Chattanooga, vith tolerably secure lines of communication; the confirmation of ur hold upon East Tennessee; the discomfiture of and loss of presge by the choicest troops of the enemy's service.

There is no language sufficiently strong which I can use to express dmiration for the conduct of our troops. From the beginning of le siege to the end every man did his whole duty. The cheerful ooks and confident bearing which met us at every turn made it seem s though we were sure of victory from the first. It is doubtful hether any man within our lines had at any time after the first orty-eight hours any fear of the result. All privations were borne, ll hardships undergone, with a spirit which indicated as plainly as written on the walls that success would attend our efforts.

And is there any man of that part of the Army of the Ohio which vas in Knoxville who would exchange his nineteen days of service here for any other of the achievements of his life? Was there a egiment there which will not put Knoxville as proudly on its banners as they now bear Roanoke or New Berne, Williamsburg or Fair aks, Chantilly or South Mountain, Antietam or Vicksburg? The roops of the Ninth Army Corps and of the Twenty-third were chivlric rivals where duty was to be done. Never before had an engineer officer less cause to complain of the manner in which his in structions and directions were carried out.

And here I feel it my duty to refer to the great value of the ser ices of the contrabands. Tractable and willing (many of the came to me and volunteered to work), they did an amount of wor which was truly astonishing. Day and night they worked withou a murmur. For the first week they labored regularly eighteen hou out of the twenty-four, and during the whole siege, out of nearly 20 that we had at work, only one asked to be excused, and he for onl one afternoon.

The question of supplies during the siege was second to none i importance. The failure of the enemy to close the Sevierville roa and French Broad River enabled us even to accumulate a quanti of commissary stores. I was told that it was officially reported the beginning of the siege that we had on hand full supplies for onl one day and a half, yet, after nineteen days' siege, we had accum lated to such an extent over the lines just referred to that we ha provisions enough to last ten days.

The topography of the vicinity of Knoxville may be briefly d scribed as follows:

On the north bank of the river a narrow ridge is formed, exten ing from a point about 2½ miles east of Knoxville to Lenoir's. has an average base of about 1½ miles in width. At Knoxville th width is about 1 mile. This ridge is cut through at short interva by small streams, two of which, First and Second Creeks, run throug the town of Knoxville, at a distance from each other of about thre fourths of a mile. The main part of the town is built upon th portion of the ridge bounded on the northwest by the valley; on th southwest by Second Creek; on the southeast by the Holston Rive and on the northeast by First Creek. It has the appearance of table elevated about 150 feet above the river and about 100 feet abo the valley. Again, Third Creek is found about seven-eighths of mile below Second Creek, forming a second similar table. A d pression in the ridge, about the same distance east of First Cree forms still another table, upon which is built East Knoxville. Th elevated ground is called Temperance Hill. From this eastward th ridge is more broken until it disappears, and other ridges spring u This last division is known as Mabry's Hill, and is the highe ground by some 20 feet to be found on the north side of the riv within cannon range of Knoxville. Commencing at Third Cree and going eastward these tables may be numbered 1, 2, 3, and 4. succession of ridges, all parallel to the one alluded to above, a found at short distances apart as one goes back from the river, th most important of which is at an average distance of 1 mile fro the one Knoxville is situated upon, and is that which the enem occupied. As near as can be ascertained by a pocket level, its elev tion is exactly that of table No. 1 at its highest point.

In selecting lines, it was my opinion that tables Nos. 1, 2, 3, and should be occupied.

In this opinion the general commanding concurred, except regar ing No. 4. It was a question whether it was most prudent with o small force to attempt to occupy No. 4, or to limit our occupation force to Nos. 1, 2, and 3, simply holding No. 4 with a strong outpos

It seemed to me that we could (as we did) construct lines No. 4, and also on No. 3, those on No. 4 to be thrown so far to t front that they could not be made available against us in event eir capture by the enemy, and to be held by us with obstinacy, ly leaving them when absolutely compelled to do so ; in which se the lines on No. 3 would form our defense, and the enemy, after stubborn fight in which he would have suffered, would only have cupied a position from which, in the former case, it would have en necessary to dislodge a mere outpost. In other words, after ippling him all we could in his successful assault upon No. 4, we ould still have just as good a defense as if we had occupied No. 3 the first place. But, on the other hand, by extending our lines to clude No. 4, we made them weak in numbers at any one point, and e were consequently exposed to greater danger of being successfully saulted along our whole position. This difficulty was partially viated by the successful construction of a dam across First Creek, y which an impassable water obstacle of three-quarters of a mile in ngth was made immediately in front of and parallel to the crest of o. 3, which enabled us to greatly weaken our numbers (of infantry) 1 that part of the line. The general commanding yielded to my inion, and all the foregoing positions were occupied as follows :

On No. 1, Forts Sanders and Byington, and Batteries Noble and oellner.

On No. 2, Fort Comstock, and Batteries Galpin, Wiltsie, and illingsley.

On No. 3, Fort Huntington Smith, and Batteries Clifton Lee, earns, and Stearman.

On No. 4, Fort Hill.

All our works were connected by a continuous line of rifle-trenches. etween the ridge occupied by ourselves and that occupied by the emy, the valley varied in width, but its average breadth was in e neighborhood of 1 mile. It was almost entirely cleared of timber, d was at every point under the fire of our artillery. A direct ad- nce over it would have been made only with serious loss. This ould have been particularly the case in front of No. 4, where the alley widened to 1½ miles, and was without timber or cover of any ind for troops.

On the south side of the river the ground rises into a series of rominent points, the highest of which is about 350 feet, and is irectly opposite Knoxville, the prolongation of Gay street passing irectly over it. These knobs formed a range quite close to the river ank, with a wide valley beyond them. It was all important to us at at least three of these knobs should be held. We actually held ur of them, commencing with the first hill, east of the Sevierville ad, and counting down the river. As already stated, the enemy ade several attempts to get possession of these heights, the first be- g made on Sunday, November 15, by a heavy force of cavalry, under e command of Wheeler, which was repulsed by Sanders' division f cavalry, which had been guarding the right bank of the Little ennessee, and had gradually fallen back before Wheeler's heavier rce. Sanders was assisted by Cameron's brigade of infantry.

From these heights an artillery fire can be delivered in front of ach flank of the lines on the north side of the river.

Commencing with the most easterly hill (which we call "Sevierville Iill") and numbering them 1, 2, 3, and 4, our works were as follows :

On No. 1, only rifle-trenches.

On No. 2, Fort Stanley.

On No. 3, Fort Dickerson.

On No. 4, Fort Higley.

Nos. 1 and 2 were connected by rifle-trenches, while Nos. 3 and 4, though not connected, each was well provided with rifle-trenches to cover the infantry supports of the batteries. With sufficient time this disposition could be very much improved by making the several forts of such a character (building bomb-proofs for stores and cisterns for water) that each would be self-reliant.

All of which is respectfully submitted.

ORLANDO M. POE,
Captain, U. S. Engrs., Chief Engr. Army of the Ohio.

Brig. Gen. WILLIAM F. SMITH,
  Chief Engineer, Military Division of the Mississippi.

No. 8.

Report of Capt. William H. Harris, U. S. Ordnance Corps, Senior Ordnance Officer.

ORDNANCE OFFICE,
Cincinnati, January 1, 1864.

SIR:[*] The ordnance and ordnance stores captured by the Army of the Ohio, in the twenty-one days' continuous fighting and skirmishing with the enemy, from the 14th of November, are as follows, viz: One 3-inch wrought-iron rifle gun, I. M. W., No. 410, P. I Co., 1862, 816 pounds; two 6-pounder brass guns, C. A. & Co., Boston, 1851, marked "Arkansas Military Institute;" one navy carronade, iron, caliber about 4.8 inch, no marks; two iron smooth-bore guns, caliber about 4 inch, marked T. M. Brennan, maker, Nashville, Tenn., 1861; carriages for each of the above unserviceable 500 stand of small-arms.

The arsenal, including storehouses and machine-shops, being without the line of intrenchments, was destroyed to prevent its falling into the hands of the enemy and becoming a shelter for sharpshooters. After its destruction, which was complete and total, a lathe was moved into the town, and, with the aid of water power, a small machine-shop was started, which was used in reducing the caliber of Hochkiss shells for James 3.8-inch rifle gun to 3.67-inch, after which they were fired from the 20-pounder battery commanded by Lieut. S N. Benjamin, of the Second U. S. Artillery. About 200 were thus prepared and found to answer satisfactorily. His own ammunition was partially exhausted during the series of battles in which he was engaged and partially abandoned to lighten his carriages on the retreat from Loudon to Knoxville. Communication was cut off, and no ammunition could be obtained elsewhere. Some of the shell thus prepared by the Ordnance Department were used with terrible effect as hand-grenades upon the rebels in the ditch of Fort Sander during the assault on the 29th of November.

The repeated assaults upon this fort, and the close proximity of the enemy's rifle-pits, made it very desirable to mount two or three mortars for the purpose of shelling out the enemy's trenches. As none were on hand, a wooden mortar was constructed, capable of throwing a 24-pounder howitzer shell. It was made of a live white oak, 2½ fe

---

[*] For portion (here omitted) covering operations in East Tennessee, August 15 October 10, 1863, see Series I, Vol. XXX, Part II, p. 571.

diameter, and, when finished, the thickness of the wood was 1 foot
..d in rear of the seat of the charge from 18 inches to 2 feet. It was
..oped with three iron bands shrunk on, and mounted on a bed of
..k. It was fired with a 24-pounder howitzer shell and 7 ounces
..powder, and withstood the test admirably; but, subsequently,
..ing fired with the same projectile and 16 ounces of good powder,
burst in two.

The 2,000 pikes captured from the enemy were turned to good ac-
..unt by constructing with them a kind of *cheval-de-frise* in front
..our rifle-pits. They have since been removed, and are at present
..the hands of Lieutenant Williams, commanding the Knoxville
..dnance depot.

In conclusion, I would respectfully submit that the regulations of
..e Ordnance Bureau at Washington, and the manner in which they
..ave been carried into effect from that office, have resulted in the
..rmy of the Ohio being at all times promptly and efficiently sup-
..ied with all necessary ordnance stores.

I have the honor to be, very respectfully, your obedient servant,

WILLIAM H. HARRIS,
Captain of Ordnance, Senior Ord. Officer Dept. of the Ohio.

Maj. Gen. AMBROSE E. BURNSIDE,
U. S. Volunteers.

No. 9.

*eports of Maj. Gen. John G. Parke, U. S. Army, commanding
United States forces in the field.*

FIFTEEN MILES FROM FLAT CREEK BRIDGE,
December 8, 1863—11.30 p. m.

GENERAL: I have ordered Manson and Potter to move on early in
..e morning. Have notified Shackelford of my position; told him
..move cautiously, and have also sent word to Foster of my move-
..ents. I have also directed officers to be sent to bring up further
..pplies by rail (to a point 2 miles short of Strawberry Plains) or by
..agon.

If wire is not disturbed, it would be well to send an operator to the
..int indicated.

Very respectfully, your obedient servant,

JNO. G. PARKE,
Major-General.

Major-General BURNSIDE,
Knoxville, Tenn.

—

RUTLEDGE,
December 9, [1863]—2.45 p. m.

GENERAL: I send copy of dispatch just received from Shackelford.*
..have halted the infantry here; they are fatigued, and I shall move
..farther unless ordered.

I have sent to Shackelford to open communication with General

---

*See dispatch of 12.30 p. m. same date, p. 411.

Foster, from whom I have heard nothing. Have sent a small force
to Strawberry Plains bridge, and picketed the roads to right and
rear.

Very respectfully, your obedient servant,

JNO. G. PARKE,
Major-General, Commanding.

Major-General BURNSIDE.

—

RUTLEDGE,
December 10, 1863—11.45 a. m.

GENERAL: Your dispatch of 3 p. m. yesterday only just received
I forwarded one to you at daylight this morning; since then have
heard from Shackelford that Colonel Ward had a severe skirmish
with enemy yesterday p. m. on Morristown road, and drove him
across river. This morning he (Shackelford) has sent a brigade on
each of the roads in his front to Morristown and Rogersville.
have directed him to hold Bean's Station in force, and make no
advance unless further orders or developments require it. Small
parties of the enemy are hovering on other side of river, even to
Strawberry Plains. Very glad to hear that you are better, and
trust that my later dispatches will have prevented your moving
out. Major Cutting has pressed on to communicate with General
Shackelford.

Very respectfully,

JNO. G. PARKE,
Major-General, Commanding.

Major-General BURNSIDE.

—

RUTLEDGE,
December 10, 1863—4.30 p. m.

GENERAL : Major Cutting reports from Bean's Station at 2 p. m.
that a portion of the brigade sent toward Morristown took the Russellville branch, and met the enemy at the river ; found them in too
great force to dislodge, and remains facing the enemy at Moore
Ferry, about 10 miles from Bean's Station, guarding wagon train.
Two strong divisions of their infantry had left there the morning previous. One hundred of the enemy's cavalry have attacked a company of ours on river 6 miles from here. A number of small parties
are reported on other side river. General Shackelford is in communication with Willcox, at Tazewell ; the road had not been obstructed
by the enemy. Willcox is about forwarding supplies and repairing
the telegraph.

Respectfully,

JNO. G. PARKE,
Major-General.

Major-General BURNSIDE.

—

RUTLEDGE, TENN.,
December 14 [or 15], 1863.

GENERAL : I send report from General Shackelford. The roads
are in bad condition, and moving now in any considerable distance
will be out of the question. Scouts have been sent out by General
Willcox and General Shackelford. As soon as these report I will for

ard copy.   General Shackelford is exceedingly anxious to take ad-
antage of his leave of absence on account of illness in his family.
would be very glad if General Sturgis would come up as soon as
ossible.

 Respectfully, yours,

JNO. G. PARKE,
Major-General.

Major-General FOSTER,
   Commanding Army.

—

RUTLEDGE, *December* 14 [or 15], 1863.
(Received 10.30 a. m.)

GENERAL : General Hascall has reported that the enemy at 9
'clock was advancing upon him at a point 4½ miles on the road to
Bean's Station.   I have ordered him, in case he is heavily pressed,
o fall back slowly.   It is very important that General Granger
hould move up to our support.

JNO. G. PARKE,
Major-General.

Major-General FOSTER.

—

RUTLEDGE, *December* 14, 1863—8.45 p. m.
(Received 15th.)

GENERAL : I have just returned from Bean's Station.   The enemy
ttacked Shackelford at 2 p. m.   At dark our advance has been
riven in so that the enemy occupied the road leading from Taze-
ell to Morristown.   Since dark the enemy has been pressing Shack-
lford so that he has been compelled to fall back a short distance.   I
ave ordered a division of infantry to move up to his support.   One
f the prisoners states that he belongs to Gracie's brigade of infantry ;
hat this brigade had the advance, and that Longstreet moved up to
vithin 2 miles of Bean's Station.   The fight will probably be re-
ewed to-morrow.   If this division of infantry cannot hold them in
heck, I will fall back on the road to Knoxville.

 Yours, respectfully,

·JNO. G. PARKE,
Major-General.

General FOSTER.

—

RUTLEDGE, *December* 14, 1863—11 p. m.
(Received 15th.)

GENERAL: General Shackelford's pickets, on the Poor Valley road,
eport cannonading in the direction of Tazewell.   This may be a force
f the enemy's cavalry trying to get in our rear.   I think it impor-
ant that Granger should occupy Blain's Cross-Roads as soon as
ossible.

JNO. G. PARKE,
Major-General.

General FOSTER.

BLAIN'S CROSS-ROADS,
December 16, 1863—12 m.

GENERAL: Have just arrived; have selected a position, and will post the troops that are here and the others as they arrive. I have no news from the front since morning.

JNO. G. PARKE,
Major-General.

Major-General FOSTER.

—

HEADQUARTERS,
Midway between Blain's Cross-Roads and Rutledge,
December 16, 1863—12.30 a. m.

GENERAL: I have just reached this place on my way back to Blain's Cross-Roads. The enemy attacked my advance to-day, consisting of one division of infantry and the cavalry. Our men held their own, but a large force of cavalry came from the direction of Morristown, crossed the river, and threatened our rear. I found that I had not sufficient cavalry to cope with the enemy; this determined me to fall back, in obedience to your order.

Your dispatch of 5.30 p. m. just received. I had received the report of Colonel Palmer in reference to Longstreet, but General Shackelford is equally confident that he is in our front. Whether or not this be so, I cannot at present determine. At any rate, we have prisoners from Johnson's and Gracie's commands. Elliott might move his command out this way, and, on a personal interview with Sturgis, the route for his command be determined. The question of rations is becoming a serious one. I will direct commissaries to make their requisitions, and draw from Strawberry Plains. Can a sub-depot be established there?

JNO. G. PARKE,
Major-General.

General J. G. FOSTER.

—

BLAIN'S CROSS-ROADS,
December 16, 1863—4.30 p. m.

GENERAL: I have a good position here. The enemy's cavalry has been skirmishing with our rear guard to within 2 or 3 miles of our line. Sturgis' last dispatch, at 4 p. m., says the enemy is not advancing so boldly as heretofore. If he undertakes to advance to-morrow, we will endeavor to check him, which I think we can do pretty well. Sheridan is up, and Wood protects his command at Flat Creek. I received the dispatches about rations, and we all feel easier on that score. I have just forwarded a dispatch from Willcox and Poe. We have, I think, a pretty strong position, and our flanks are now well watched. I fear that during the night some of our men straggled in advance. Should any of them reach Knoxville without proper authority, I hope they will be summarily dealt with.

Yours, respectfully,

JNO. G. PARKE,
Major-General.

Major-General FOSTER.

BLAIN'S CROSS-ROADS, *December* 16, 1863.
(Received 8 p. m.)

GENERAL: I transmit a report, just made by Captain Daniels, signal officer, of his observations yesterday. There was no infantry reported as engaged to-day with our rear guard. General Granger has arrived, and desires me to say that he has nothing new. The signal officer reports that the enemy withdrew their artillery this evening. I will keep you advised from time to time.

Yours, respectfully,

JNO. G. PARKE,
Major-General.

Major-General FOSTER.

—

BLAIN'S CROSS-ROADS,
December 17, 1863.

This morning the enemy advanced in small force on General Sturgis' pickets, but nothing serious since then; but few shots have been fired, and those at long range. There is no forage for Sturgis' horses in our front, and in conferring with him we have decided to move them to right and left and occupy the river roads and the Maynardville road, to observe and report any movement on our flanks. Will you please have Capt. George W. Gowan, in Captain Poe's office, ordered to report to me as an aide, if his place can be filled in the engineer office. The signal officer reports, "I cannot see any infantry, only a few scouts; a dense fog is rising where the flag was seen last."

JNO. G. PARKE,
Major-General.

Major-General FOSTER.

11.05 a. m.

P. S.—General Granger is here. He says he is of the same opinion still; he knows nothing more than when he left Knoxville. General Granger and I both think there is no necessity for your coming out at present.

—

BLAIN'S CROSS-ROADS,
December 17, 1863—4 p. m.

The enemy has not made any serious demonstration on the Rutledge road up to this time; since noon they have been pressing the brigade. Spears stationed at Stone's Mill, Richland Church, about miles on our right, where the river road crosses Richland Creek. They may be massing on the river road, but General Granger thinks it would be risky for them to attempt this move. Still, if this be so, we may be forced to fall back on the line of Flat Creek. General Sturgis will send a division of cavalry to occupy the line of Richland Creek. I regret that Elliott has been able to cross but one brigade. He is now at Strawberry Plains, and will get over as soon as he can. I am glad to hear you are coming up.

JNO. G. PARKE,
Major-General.

Major-General FOSTER.

BLAIN'S CROSS-ROADS,
December 17, 1863—11.30 p. m.

Yours of 8.25 just received. By the river road, I mean a road parallel to the Rutledge road, and on the north side of Holston—one of the many roads not indicated on our map.

The point where this road crosses Richland Creek (Stone's Mill) is still held by Spears' brigade. I have reason to believe that there was no infantry appeared against him this evening. The last report from there was all quiet. In fact, the enemy's advance had retired and were followed by our skirmishers. How far they pursued cannot say. No report yet made. I presume not far. My impression about Longstreet massing on the river road was not confirmed by the observations from our signal mountain. No large camp fires were visible, nor large smokes seen in our front on either road at sun down. In fact, I am now inclined to believe that there is nothing but cavalry in our immediate front. Shall I send an ambulance to Strawberry Plains for you? There is a very good one here that Colonel Babcock, of the Ninth Corps, has suggested to send.

JNO. G. PARKE,
Major-General.

Major-General FOSTER.

—

BLAIN'S CROSS-ROADS, *December* 21, 1863—8 p. m.
(Received 1.15 a. m., 22d.)

As soon as I had received the report of the raid to Graveston, had a brigade of cavalry moved, and Colonel Foster is of opinion that it is now so posted as to prevent a repetition. Colonel Capron, commanding the brigade, is directed to keep up communication with General Willcox.

JNO. G. PARKE,
Major-General.

General E. E. POTTER.

—

BLAIN'S CROSS-ROADS, *December* [21, 1863]—7 p. m.
(Received 1 a. m., 22d.)

We have now pretty reliable information that Longstreet's headquarters were last night at Shields' house, some 2 or 3 miles this side of Bean's Station. This information is given by 3 men, paroled Vicksburg prisoners, whom the rebel cavalry arrested near Buffalo Creek, on the river road. They were taken up to Rutledge and then had a pass given them to their command, Vaughn's, at Rogersville, a mile or two beyond Rutledge. They turned off the road, and during last night they returned to our lines. They saw no infantry in Rutledge or this side excepting a few stragglers beyond Rutledge. They saw extensive camp fires. This is confirmed by our signal officer's report of this evening. We have also reliable information that two brigades, rebel cavalry, are encamped on the river road near Buffalo Creek and Indian Ridge, some 6 or 8 miles in front of General Spears. The citizens report that Ewell has re-enforced Longstreet. This, I think, is the old report, and not entitled o credence. That also states that an infantry force has crossed Clinch. This also needs confirmation. I will send this to General Willcox. General Cox has arrived, and takes command of the Twenty-third Corps.

JNO. G. PARKE,
Major-General.

Major-General FOSTER.

—

BLAIN'S CROSS-ROADS,
December 22, 1863—8 p. m.

Nothing new has transpired to-day. The enemy's position remains about the [same.] The signal officer thinks the fires have somewhat increased in the direction of Buffalo Creek. The enemy picket Powder Spring Gap and other points on Clinch Mountain. Parties sent on the north side of the mountains to gain heights as lookouts returned unsuccessful, the enemy seeming to watch the position closely. In reference to General Manson, General Cox informed me this morning that he had gone to Knoxville to arrange some papers appertaining to corps headquarters. I was told last night he was going, but presumed he would get permission before leaving. I find it difficult to get any information in reference to action or movements of enemy beyond line of Bean's Station and Morristown. It is very important to know how far this side of Bristol the railroad is in running order. Cannot this information be acquired by parties sent from Knoxville?

JNO. G. PARKE,
Major-General.

Major-General FOSTER.

—

HEADQUARTERS,
Blain's Cross-Roads, December 23, 1863—2 p. m.
(Received 25th.)

About midnight last night I was informed by a scout that the cavalry on Buffalo Creek were saddled up and moving either across the river or up the river road. I sent this at once to General Sturgis, who had informed me of his move, and suggested a demonstration up the Rutledge road. I ordered Colonel Capron to send this morning a scouting party up Flat Creek to Powder Spring Gap, General Potter to make a reconnaissance up the Rutledge road, and General Spears up the river road. I have not heard from Capron or Spears. General Potter's advance is about 6 or 7 miles up the valley, and report no enemy in sight, and that citizens report Powder Spring Gap evacuated. Deserters report that the cavalry has crossed the river. A negro has just come in; says he left Bean's Station last night; that the cavalry was all moving; also that the infantry had gone; but on this point he was not clear. I have just received the accompanying dispatches* from General Willcox.

Our cavalry movements have evidently produced a commotion in the enemy's camp. I expect soon to hear from some of our own scouts in reference to the movements and position of the enemy's infantry.

_____

* Not identified.

A colonel of Tenth Tennessee (rebel) Cavalry told a citizen yesterday that our forces had crossed the river, and they feared we would get in their rear.

JNO. G. PARKE,
Major-General.

Major-General FOSTER, *Knoxville.*

No. 10.

Reports of Brig. Gen. Robert B. Potter, U. S. Army, commanding Ninth Army Corps.

HEADQUARTERS NINTH ARMY CORPS,
Knoxville, Tenn., November 18, 1863.

COLONEL: I have the honor to make the following report of the movements of my command since the 13th instant:

At an early hour on the morning of the 14th, my command being then at Lenoir's Station, I received notice that the enemy had crossed the river below Loudon, having thrown their bridge at Huff's Ferry. At the same time I received orders to hold myself ready to move. At a later hour, in accordance with orders, I disabled the mills and factories in my vicinity, destroyed a pontoon bridge over the Holston, and started my train from camp for Knoxville under a strong guard.

About 9 a. m. General White, with his command, arrived from Loudon.

After the arrival of the commanding general, about midday, I received an order to support Chapin's brigade, of White's command, in a movement against the enemy. I accordingly sent Ferrero with his division and a battery on that duty. About 4 p. m. we met the enemy's skirmishers; Chapin formed his line of skirmishers and moved forward rapidly, driving them handsomely for a mile and a half or more. Night setting in very thick and dark, and a dense wood, compelled us to halt, not, however, until the enemy had opened their artillery.

During the night I moved Sigfried's division, with Benjamin's battery and three guns of von Sehlen's battery, to a point upon the river opposite Loudon.

At or soon after daylight on the 15th, in accordance with my orders, we began moving back to Lenoir's. On the arrival of the column near the Loudon road, I ordered my artillery back to Lenoir's, sending Ferrero to the same point, with orders to cover the various approaches, and ordered Sigfried to replace Chapin, of White's command, who was covering the rear of the column. The enemy made no effort to push Sigfried, and he remained where he was until 2 p. m., when he fell back quietly to Lenoir's, the enemy having first moved a heavy column to his right. The enemy's skirmishers in strong force appeared before our position at Lenoir's about 4 p. m., and seemed disposed to push us in, but were checked by a shell or two from Roemer. About this time Colonel Biddle reported with 500 or 600 mounted men and Gittings' battery. I ordered him back to seize the junction of the Kingston and Loudon roads near Campbell's Station, and to station a small force on the roads to Clinton and Concord.

Hartranft having reported for duty, I ordered him to move to the same point with what force I had of the Second Division and the seven guns of Benjamin's and von Sehlen's batteries. Buckley's battery had already started for the same point. Hartranft started about dusk. I soon received a report from Biddle that the horses in his battery had given out; that he had dismounted some of his cavalry and put the horses to the guns, but owing to the fearful state of the roads he could make no progress. Hartranft soon after reported that he could not move his artillery, although he had a brigade of infantry assisting; had destroyed some ammunition and temporarily abandoned limbers and caissons. About 10 p. m. the enemy attempted to drive in our skirmishers, but were repulsed.

Between 4 and 5 a. m. I received a number of mule teams·from General White, which were given to the artillery, and it at once began to move.

At a quarter past 6 a. m. of the 16th, Ferrero's division began to move from Lenoir's after White, with Humphrey's brigade, of Ferrero's division, covering the rear. The enemy followed at once, but showed no force or disposition to press us until within 2 miles of Campbell's Station, when they began to press heavily on the rear, but were held in check by Humphrey. Meantime, Biddle and Hartranft had arrived, and Hartranft had placed Biddle and Sigfried, with a section of Gittings' [battery], in position on the Kingston road.

Hartranft's pickets along the river had joined him, and a company of cavalry at Low's Ferry moved to Knoxville.

Hartranft, after securing all the roads, sent a force of about 200 mounted men of Biddle's along the Kingston road with orders to move forward till they found the enemy and then attack. They found them about 2½ miles out and, deploying the whole force as skirmishers, attacked at once. The enemy's advance, evidently (as intended) supposing them the cover of a larger force, did not attempt to drive them until a considerable force came up. At 11 a. m. the enemy were pressing us heavily on both roads and turning Hartranft's right. Humphrey charged and drove them back on the Lenoir road, Hartranft's forces holding them back on the other. All the artillery and trains having passed the junction of the roads, and White being in position beyond the creek, at Campbell's Station, in accordance with orders, I prepared to withdraw, having first placed Morrison's brigade, of the First Division, below the junction of the two roads, with its right and left extending to them, and sending Biddle and Gittings' section of battery to the rear, followed by the troops of Ferrero and Hartranft not in position.

Having all the troops remaining now on the same line, I ordered them to retire, and they fell back slowly to their new positions; Humphrey first, on the left, followed by Morrison and Sigfried, which, in our new position, placed Christ's brigade, of Ferrero's division, on the extreme right, with Morrison next, and Humphrey in support of batteries, General White holding the center. Hartranft was placed next, holding the left, with one regiment in support of batteries and one in reserve, out of ammunition.

Benjamin's battery was placed on the right of the Knoxville road, with Gittings on his right and von Sehlen and Buckley in the rear, Roemer's battery being on the left of the road. The enemy attacked here at 12 m. Shortly after opening fire the rifled guns were moved to the left of the road, Benjamin being nearest the road, with Gittings on his left, the three guns of von Sehlen on his right and rear, and Roemer to the left and rear of Gittings, in reserve.

The enemy now annoyed Christ's right so much that he had to change his front in that direction. Buckley, executing the same movement, commenced shelling the wood on the right, with good effect, and the enemy's progress in that direction was checked.

At this time, by direction of General Burnside, I sent Captain Coddington, one of my aides, with two companies of mounted men to reconnoiter on the right. He passed along the skirt of the woods and over the hill to the right to a point where he could see the next valley. Finding nothing, he returned, leaving his men behind the edge of the woods to the right. I also sent two companies of the One·hundredth and twelfth Illinois Mounted Infantry down the Concord road, which, running beyond our left, entered the Knoxville road in our rear. The enemy having established his batteries, shelled us severely. General White's batteries being about out of ammunition, were withdrawn and placed in position on a hill to the rear by Lieutenant-Colonel Bowen, of my staff.

About 2.30 I received a report from the mounted force sent on the Concord road, that they had met the enemy's pickets, and that the enemy were crossing the road and moving through the woods to our left.

I shortly after received an order to prepare for withdrawing to a more favorable position on the hill in our rear. I first sent Buckley and von Sehlen, with his three guns, to the rear, followed by Benjamin and Gittings, who were placed on the right of the road, Roemer returning the fire of the enemy. The troops in reserve were also sent to the rear.

As soon as Benjamin and Gittings opened from their new position, I ordered Ferrero and Hartranft to retire on the right and left, while Chapin's command, relieving on the center, covered the movement. Roemer's guns were withdrawn at the same time.

These movements being executed at our leisure, although under a hot fire, occupied considerable time, and our new line was not established until about 4 p. m., Ferrero being on the right of the road, with Hartranft on our left, with Roemer's guns and a regiment of White's between his right and the road, the rest of White's command being in Hartranft's rear. Hartranft had scarcely formed his line and thrown out his skirmishers when he received a fire from the woods on his left in his flank and rear. He at once changed front with his left, throwing some skirmishers in the woods. At this moment the enemy were reported getting a battery in position on a high hill on our left, with which to enfilade our line. Simultaneously, a considerable force of the enemy came in sight, moving across some cleared ground about half way up the hill. Roemer, who was just getting into position, changed front to the left and opened a hot fire on them. They immediately fell back precipitately and in confusion, and were followed by their skirmishers, who ran out of the woods to our left. The enemy's infantry now seemed to have come to a halt, and made no further aggressive demonstration, their batteries, however, keeping up a hot fire until sundown.

Just before sunset General Burnside ordered me to retire to Knoxville, sending Ferrero forward, followed by the artillery and wagons, with Hartranft next, and I was also directed to send Biddle, with his mounted force and a section of artillery, under Lieutenant Bartlett, Third U. S. Artillery, to report to General White, who, it was under-ood, would bring up the rear. I accordingly withdrew leisurely, about 6, the enemy evincing not the least disposition to trouble us, and we heard no more of them.

It was understood that the forces in our front were the divisions of McLaws and Jenkins, of Longstreet's command.

Arriving near Knoxville at an early hour in the morning of the 17th, we waited until daylight enabled us to take up the positions designated for the command. My total strength, including Biddle, was about 3,500; my losses in the troops belonging to the Ninth Corps were 26 killed, 166 wounded, and 57 missing; total, 249. I have received no report of the loss in the mounted force, their report probably having been made to General Shackelford, to whose command they belong. Among the missing are included some few wounded, so badly hurt to move, and a few left at my first position beyond the Kingston road; the ambulances having got too far to the rear, we were unable to get enough up in time to move all. The rest are stragglers or a few detached pickets that the enemy succeeded in cutting off. I desire to call attention to the skill, energy, and bravery of all my officers and men, and particularly to General Ferrero and Colonel Hartranft, and Colonels Sigfried, Humphrey, and Biddle. To Hartranft's energy and prudence, we are in a great measure indebted for our success in getting off all our artillery, and in preventing the enemy from getting on our line of retreat at the junction of the Kingston road; it is to be hoped that he may speedily receive the promotion so long and so well deserved. Lieutenant Fletcher also rendered much valuable assistance.

My thanks are due to all the members of my staff for their gallantry and efficient and cheerful services, and particularly to Lieutenant-Colonels Bowen and Babcock, assistant adjutant-general and inspector-general of the corps, for important services on the march and in action. The whole command was almost continuously under arms, marching, maneuvering, and fighting for three days and nights, in bad weather, over the worst of roads, and in front of a largely superior force.

Very respectfully, your obedient servant,

ROBERT B. POTTER,
Brigadier-General, Commanding.

Lieut. Col. LEWIS RICHMOND, *Asst. Adjt. Gen.*

—

HEADQUARTERS NINTH ARMY CORPS,
Knoxville, Tenn., November 20, 1863.

COLONEL: I have the honor to report the effective strength of the Ninth Corps, as returned by division commanders November 19 and 20, as follows:

Command.	Officers.	Enlisted men.	Total.
FIRST DIVISION.			
First Brigade	45	601	......
Second Brigade	54	743	......
Third Brigade	78	803	......
Battery L, Second New York Artillery	3	192	......
Battery D, First Rhode Island Artillery	4	106	......
Total of First Division	184	2,445	2,629

Command.	Officers.	Enlisted men.	Total.
SECOND DIVISION.			
First Brigade	61	719	....
Second Brigade	34	706	....
Total of Second Division	95	1,425	1,5
UNATTACHED.			
Battery E, Second U. S. Artillery	2	87	....
Batteries L and M, Third U. S. Artillery	4	76	....
Seventy-ninth New York Volunteers	15	150	....
Total unattached	21	313	3
RECAPITULATION.			
First Division	184	2,445	....
Second Division	95	1,425	....
Unattached	21	313	....
Total of corps	300	4,183	4,4

The disposition of the command is as follows :

The First Brigade, First Division, holds the left of the line of de fense, commencing at the river at a point to the left of Powell' house and extending to Fort Sanders on the right of the Kingsto road.

The Third Brigade, First Division, holds the line from Fort San ders to a point to the right about midway between the fort and Sec ond Creek.

The Second Brigade, First Division, holds the line from the righ of the Third Brigade to where Second Creek passes under the rail road, connecting with the left of the Second Division.

The First Brigade, Second Division, with one regiment of the Sec ond Brigade, holds the crest of the bluff between Gay street an Second Creek, the left connecting with the Second Brigade, Firs Division, the right extending to Gay street.

The two remaining regiments of the Second Brigade, Second Di vision, occupy the field on the north side of Gay street, the right c the brigade resting near First Creek and connecting with Genera White's line.

Fort Sanders is garrisoned by Battery E, Second U. S. Artillery and Battery D, First Rhode Island Artillery, supported by the Sev enty-ninth Regiment New York Volunteer Infantry. Battery L Second New York Artillery, occupies the ground of the seminary supported by four companies of infantry of the First Division, num bering about 160 men.

Batteries L and M, Third U. S. Artillery, are posted on the blu overlooking the railroad depot about the center of the line held b the Second Division. The Fifteenth Indiana Battery is posted i the field to the right of Gay street, near the right of line of Secon Division.

Four companies of infantry from the Third Brigade, First Divi ion, with a portion of the First Brigade, occupy the rifle-pits fron the left of Fort Sanders to the Kingston road.

Powell's house to the left of the Kingston road has been barricade and loopholed for musketry, and the house of Mr. Barnes, on th extreme right of the line of the First Division, is occupied by a con pany of infantry.

In front of the Second Division, at the railroad depot, are several brick buildings, which have been loopholed and are occupied by small parties of infantry.

First and Second Creeks have been dammed, forming a barrier in front of fully two-thirds of the [ground] held by the Second Division.

Benjamin's and Buckley's batteries, as above stated, defend Fort Sanders. Roemer's, Edwards', and Von Sehlen's batteries are protected by earth-works, the two latter by cotton-bale embrasures.

The entire front held by the corps is a line of rifle-pits, in advance of which, at varying distance, is a line of skirmishers. In front of the Second Division the distance is some 800 yards, a strong position and well protected. The intrenched line held by the First Division is about 1¼ miles in length; that held by the Second Division about five-eighths of a mile. The skirmish line of the Second Division covers a front, in direct line from flank to flank, of 1⅛ miles.

Very respectfully, your obedient servant,

ROBERT B. POTTER,
Brigadier-General, Commanding.

Lieut. Col. LEWIS RICHMOND,
Assistant Adjutant-General.

HEADQUARTERS NINTH ARMY CORPS,
Knoxville, November 24, 1863.

COLONEL: I have the honor to offer the following report of the transactions on my front during the night of the 23d and morning of the 24th instant:

About half past 8 on the evening of the 23d, it being then quite dark and hazy, the enemy suddenly advanced in force on my front, near the Clinton road.

The enemy were not perceived until well up with the line of skirmishers, when they poured in a heavy fire, driving our men in and following them up closely. The firing parties barely had time to fire the buildings, and some of them were taken before they could make their escape. Many of the fires the enemy succeeded in getting under [control], but several houses were in flames, particularly the machine shops and round-house on the railroad occupied by the ordnance department, which last contained a good deal of explosive material and prevented any farther advance of the enemy, if such was meditated. The line of skirmishers on the right fell back just far enough to protect their flanks, but no farther. Colonel Hartranft, as soon as it was possible, from the subsidence of the fires, advanced his skirmishers through the burning ruins, but they were unable to recover all their ground, the enemy occupying it in considerable force, with men in all the buildings in which they had succeeded in extinguishing the fires. I ordered Colonel Hartranft to make his arrangements to recover all the lost ground at daylight in the morning. For this purpose he detailed the Forty-eighth Pennsylvania Volunteers and the Twenty-first Massachusetts Volunteers, the whole under command of Lieutenant-Colonel Hawkes. Reilly's brigade, Cascall's division, Twenty-third Corps, supplied their places in the rifle-pits, the rest of Reilly's brigade being held in reserve in the town. I also sent a note to General Ferrero to watch his opportunity, and if, on Hartranft's advance, a favorable opportunity should occur, to seize and occupy the enemy's advanced rifle-pits in front of his right, the fire of which was annoying us in our works.

The attacking force formed on the line of skirmishers at daylight and moved rapidly forward, taking the enemy somewhat by surprise recovering all the lost ground and re-establishing our line of skir mishers on the old ground. About the same time the Second Michi gan Volunteers, detailed by Ferrero for that duty, dashed at the rifle-pits before mentioned through a severe fire, drove the enemy and occupied them. Unfortunately, they afforded but little shelter The enemy's main line was right in front, strongly occupied, and our troops were exposed to a severe enfilading fire from their left They held this position for half an hour, but finding it untenable they retired after a loss of 50 killed, wounded, and missing, including the major and adjutant, who fell into the enemy's hands. Hartranft' loss amounted to 22, including 2 officers wounded and 5 men killed.

I have to congratulate myself on the gallant conduct of all the men engaged, expressing, at the same time, the regret I feel for the serious loss sustained by the gallant Second Michigan. I inclose copies of the reports of General Ferrero and Colonel Hartranft.

Very respectfully, your obedient servant,
ROBERT B. POTTER,
Brigdier-General, Commanding.

Lieut. Col. LEWIS RICHMOND,
Assistant Adjutant-General.

—

LEGG'S HOUSE, NEAR CHESTERFIELD,
December 8, 1863—2 a. m.

MAJOR : The enemy have their rear about 5 miles beyond this side of Blain's Cross-Roads. General Shackelford is up with them ; they won't move any faster than they are obliged to. I don't think they have any infantry this side of Rutledge. Foster (Colonel) was at Powder Mill Gap to-day, skirmishing with Jones. Chapin's brigad is here ; Hascall's division, I hear, crossed the river at Armstrong' Ferry, and went to Strawberry Plains. My command is under order to move at daylight, which will be countermanded, and we won' move till further orders. I think if we are going beyond this w ought to move on without delay; there are indications of a storm which, if it comes, is going to make marching bad on these roads and give us trouble with our artillery.

Your obedient servant,
ROBERT B. POTTER,
Brigadier-General.

Major VAN BUREN,
Aide-de-Camp.

—

MCKINNEY'S, ¼ MILE EAST OF BLAIN'S CROSS-ROADS,
December 8, 1863—3.45 p. m.

GENERAL : At noon to-day General Shackelford was at Powde Spring Gap road, 6 miles east of this. The last of the enemy cavalry left that point early in the morning. All of the infantr had passed here by Sunday morning. Early Sunday afternoo

Hood's division was at Rutledge, and McLaws' on the road this side, both moving east; all the cavalry in rear passed Sunday and Sunday night except one brigade (four regiments), which remained between this and Westfield (Chesterfield on the map), and left in a hurry yesterday afternoon. The last, a rear guard of 30 men, passed about sundown. The cavalry on the Powder Spring Gap road, over Copper Ridge, left last night, blockading the road behind them. Armstrong's division of cavalry passed through Rutledge on Sunday in advance of the infantry of McLaws' division, and probably some other. Most of their trains and artillery passed here Friday, and Saturday some cavalry and some wagons and probably a small force of infantry took the road below Westfield to Strawberry Plains.

Bushrod Johnson passed Saturday night at this point; Jones' command seems to have been on the road to Cumberland Gap, to cover the flank of the column. The enemy reported that they were going to Virginia and some to Georgia; seem to have moved in good order, and with no signs of demoralization or stragglers; some deserters among the Tennessee troops, but not many. They were marching their infantry at fair average rate.

The roads are sticky, and a little rain is going to make them bad. I am having some trouble now with artillery and teams and a good deal of straggling, partly because the men are so badly shod and are weak, and partly in search of food. All the enemy's infantry and artillery were more than two full days ahead of this point last night. If they moved on Monday as they did on Sunday, I don't think it possible for us to get near them unless they halt. General Shackelford is looking for Colonel Foster's division to come up; it was to have been here at 11 a. m., but I cannot learn that it has passed yet.

Your obedient servant,

ROBERT B. POTTER,
Brigadier-General.

Major-General PARKE,
       Chief of Staff.

P. S.—I am picketing the roads above here, but can't learn anything of any enemy. Citizens have a rumor that General Ransom had started from Virginia with 10,000 men to join Longstreet, but turned back.

No. 11.

Itinerary of the Ninth Army Corps, October 20–December 31, 1863. [*]

October 20 [corps at Knoxville, Tenn.], the First Division marched toward Loudon Bridge, a distance of about 30 miles.

October 22, the Second Division proceeded by cars to Loudon Bridge, arriving same day; the First Division also arrived at Loudon Bridge, and crossed the Tennessee River to Loudon.

October 28, the First Division, with part of Twenty-third Army Corps, evacuated Loudon, and marched back 6 miles to Lenoir's Station.

October 31, the headquarters of the corps and troops are stationed at Lenoir's Station, East Tenn., with the exception of the Third Brigade, Second Division, which is on detached service at Cumberland

---

[*] From returns for October, November, and December.

Gap, Ky., and Battery D, Independent Pennsylvania Voluntee
Artillery, on detached service at Covington, Ky.

November 1, headquarters of corps and troops were stationed a
Lenoir's Station, East Tenn., a distance of 25 miles from Knoxvill
on the East Tennessee and Virginia Railroad.

November 6, Batteries L and M, Third U. S. Artillery, proceede
to Knoxville and encamped there.

November 14, the corps broke camp (except the artillery) and pr
ceeded to Loudon, a distance of 6 miles, to meet the enemy, wh
were crossing at Huff's Ferry with two divisions, commanded b
Lieut. Gen. James Longstreet. The wagon trains were ordered t
Knoxville, arriving there safely on the 16th instant.

November 15, Batteries L and M, Third U. S. Artillery, arrived a
Lenoir's Station from Knoxville. At 9 a. m. the First Brigade, Se
ond Division, relieved General White's skirmishers that had bee
falling back slowly before the enemy. Our artillery arrived fro
Lenoir's Station, and the corps engaged the enemy, falling bac
slowly and in good order to Lenoir's Station, arriving there th
afternoon of the same day. The enemy appearing on our fro
again, the First Division was ordered in position to meet them o
the Kingston road. They remained in position until daybreak ne
morning. At 8 p. m. same day the Second Division, with Batter
E, Second U. S. Artillery, was ordered to fall back toward Kno
ville.

November 16, at daybreak, the First Division, with its artiller
was ordered to fall back to Campbell's Station, arriving there at
a. m. At 5 a. m. the First Brigade, Second Division, was move
quickly forward to Campbell's Station, to occupy the road betwee
that place and Kingston. At 9 a. m. the Second Brigade, Secor
Division, and Battery E, Second U. S. Artillery, arrived at Cam
bell's Station. The line of battle was then formed. The enem
attacked us in large force, but was repulsed with severe loss. A
dusk the corps fell back to Knoxville, the First Division arriving a
midnight, the Second Division at daybreak next morning.

November 17, our line was formed around Knoxville, and th
troops were immediately set to work constructing earth-works fo
the batteries and rifle-pits for themselves.

November 18, the enemy appeared on our front; skirmishing con
menced, and continued daily until the morning of Sunday, the 29t
when, at 5 a. m., our pickets were driven in and six regiments o
the enemy charged upon that portion of our works known as Fo
Sanders. It was occupied by Battery E, Second U. S. Artiller
and supported by the Seventy-ninth New York Volunteers, Secon
Michigan, and a detachment from the Twenty-ninth Massachuset
Volunteers, numbering, in all, about 300 men. They repulsed th
enemy, killing, wounding, and capturing about 750 of the enem
with 3 stand of colors. Nothing more of note transpired up to th
date of this return, except that the enemy is intrenching himse
and constructing breastworks for the batteries, and preparing
besiege the city. Both ours and the enemy's outposts have co
structed earth-works for themselves, and are continually skirmis
ing with each other, the distance from our outposts to those of t
enemy not being more than 150 yards.

November 30, remained in the same position as that taken on t
17th instant, awaiting the enemy to advance on our works. T
Third Brigade, Second Division, are still on detached service

umberland Gap, and Battery D, Independent Pennsylvania Volun-
er Artillery, at Covington, Ky.

December 1, headquarters of the corps were stationed at Knoxville,
ast Tenn.   The troops were in the rifle-pits around the city, closely
esieged by the enemy.

December 4, re-enforcements arrive for us from Chattanooga.

December 5, the enemy were compelled to raise the siege.   They
oved in the direction of Rutledge, East Tenn., a distance of 35
iles from Knoxville.

December 7, the corps started in pursuit of the enemy, except
attery E, Second U. S. Artillery, whose guns are too heavy to
ansport over the bad roads that are in this section of the country.

December 9, the corps arrived at Rutledge.

December 13, the Third Brigade, First Division, was ordered to
arley's Mills, about 7½ miles northeast of Rutledge, on the Holston
iver.   The enemy commenced to shell them from the opposite side
f the river, when they were ordered to fall back to within 3 miles
f Rutledge.

December 14, the First Division fell back to Blain's Cross-Roads.

December 15, the Second Division fell back toward Blain's Cross-
oads.

December 16, 12 m., the Second Division halted within 2 miles of
lain's Cross-Roads, formed line of battle, and remained in that
osition during the afternoon, our cavalry skirmishing with the
nemy half a mile in advance of our line during the whole after-
oon.

December 17, the cavalry was withdrawn from our front, the ene-
y's sharpshooters following them up to our infantry line, when
ight skirmishing commenced, without any loss.

December 18, drove back the enemy 4 miles, and posted our infantry
ickets and established the troops in camp.

December 22, the enemy, under cover of the night, retreated to the
outh side of Holston River.

December 31, the headquarters of the corps and troops are en-
amped near Blain's Cross-Roads, East Tenn., a distance of 18 miles
om Knoxville.   Battery D, Independent Pennsylvania Volunteer
rtillery, and Third Brigade, Second Division, still remain on
etached service, the first at Covington, Ky., and the latter at Cum-
erland Gap.

No. 12.

*Report of Lieut. Samuel N. Benjamin, Second U. S. Artillery,
Chief of Artillery.*

WEST POINT,
December 20, [1863.]

Major-General BURNSIDE,
          U. S. Army:

DEAR GENERAL : Inclosed you will find an account of the siege of
ort Sanders, giving the plan of the defense and a description of the
ssault.   It is miserably written, but I had to hurry it, as I am very
usy, and could hardly get time to write at all; so please excuse
istakes and all deficiencies.   The whole affair lasted full three-

quarters of an hour, and the actual fight at the ditch and on the parapet over twenty minutes. During the flag of truce I talked with many officers, among them Lieutenant-Colonel Alexander, chief of artillery on General Longstreet's staff, who spoke highly of our maneuvering at the battle of Campbell's Station.

I claim credit mainly for building up the work, getting it properly garrisoned, and, above all, for drawing the attack on the northwest salient. If the assault had been made anywhere else it would have succeeded. During the assault I handled the troops, giving all orders and seeing to their execution.

The greatest credit is of course due to the men, who fought splendidly. I saw one man use an ax.

I put my pistol within 6 inches of a rebel's face and pulled trigger three times. They were on the exterior crest of the parapet all the time.

Wishing you success and happiness, and hoping that you may have a command soon,

I remain, very respectfully, your friend,

SAMUEL N. BENJAMIN,
Captain, Second Artillery.

FORT SANDERS.

On the morning of November 17, 1863, in accordance with orders, I posted Gittings' battery near the depot; Roemer's at Seminary Hill; Buckley's and Benjamin's on the ridge to the northwest of the town, about 1 mile out and north of the main road to Campbell's Station. Here a bastion work (square) had been commenced, and was about one-fourth finished on three fronts—fourth front not commenced. It afforded no protection, nor could a gun be dragged into it until four hours' work with 200 negroes had made ways and cleared places for them. I assumed command by your order, and planned the defense.

The line held by our troops made a right angle here, with the fort at the angle. The northwest bastion being the salient of the angle, following its capital less than 80 yards from the fort, was an abrupt descent, running into a large thick wood; the descent covered with a thin growth of pines.

By dint of persuasion, and demonstrating the impossibility of holding this position otherwise, I prevailed on General Ferrero to occupy the hill due south from the fort, on the other side of the road to Campbell's Station. (Fire from that point would have taken much of our line in reverse.)

The northwest bastion was the point to attack, if the rebels could be induced to attack the earth-work instead of the low breastwork or rifle-pit thrown up by the men.

At the fort were four 20-pounder Parrotts, four light 12-pounders, and two 3-inch guns (Buckley's other two guns I placed on the hill to the south). I left the fort open in the rear, the rifle-pits running from the ends of the gorge south to the river and east up by the town. I procured the Seventy-ninth New York Volunteers for garrison (about 125 strong), and in case of attack on the fort four companies of the Seventeenth Michigan were to enter it and post themselves at the point assaulted. I placed the guns so as to sweep thoroughly all approach to the rifle-pits, leaving a large section without fire in front of the salient of the northwest bastion to induce them to assault there. Work went on night and day under my sole direction   The engineer officers of the corps being occupied on other parts of the line, no assistance or advice was asked or received, except I altered a portion of their rifle-pits so as to contract the line and not be forced to fire over our own men.   The first day of the siege, before the enemy had closed in, I dug two lines of pits for the pickets, about 80 and 30 yards from the fort—the second line to rally in if driven from the first.

On the 20th instant, at my request, the Seventeenth Michigan made a sortie in the night, driving the enemy's pickets and burning a house which they occupied.   The rebel sharpshooters were very annoying, causing casualties in the fort every day.   I stuck brush in the parapet, along the interior crest, so as to screen us from sight, and enable us to look out without being seen.   I also covered the embrasures with bags and barrels, so arranged as to see out without being seen.

On the 21st, the enemy had a parallel about 300 yards off, half enveloping the northwest bastion.   General Ferrero had now taken up quarters in the fort, in a small bomb-proof, built for telegraphic operations.

On the morning of the 23d, the attack on the enemy's parallel was made.   This attack I strongly opposed.

On the 25th, a battery was discovered on the other bank of the Holston, 150 feet above us (six guns), commanding and having a view of all in the fort.   They also had on west front an embrasure battery of six 12-pounders and one 20-pounder Parrott; on north front, embrasure battery of two 20-pounder Parrotts, same two 3-inch guns, two other two-gun batteries, caliber unknown (probably 3-inch).   These varied from 700 to 1,500 yards in distance from us—the one across the river 2,500 yards.   Every man in the fort had his place assigned him, and ate and slept at his place, so, on an alarm, they only rose and crouched by the parapet.   At night 1 man in 4 was awake, 2 officers and 2 non-commissioned officers, besides the regular guard on picket.   On an alarm, each man then up woke the three sleeping near him; thus the garrison was at once ready for an attack.   I made an embrasure in such manner that, by taking out a few shovels of earth, I could train a gun on the northwest bastion, sweeping its ditch and parapet.   The parapet there was strengthened.   The whole fort was well fitted with traverses to protect our men, as the enemy had a reverse and enfilading fire on each front. In front of the northwest bastion I made an abatis, concealed from the enemy by a small rise of ground, and inside of the abatis a little entanglement of telegraph wire.   We worked night and day, but still at many places we went out and in the fort over the parapet and through the shallow ditch.   The work was now known as Fort Sanders, and was very weak, and should have fallen by the ordinary chances of warfare; but the garrison were picked men.   We had many alarms and exchanged shots from time to time with the enemy.

About 10 p. m., November 28, the enemy captured most of the outer line of pickets, and drove the others into the fort.   Skirmishing and firing continued for two hours; at the end of which time we had not a picket 20 yards out from the fort, and the enemy had secured the crest of the ridge which the work was on, beneath which they could mass troops night or day, within 80 yards of the work, without our knowledge.   In spite of the opposite opinion held by most, I prepared for an attack at daybreak.

On the 29th, I rose early, roused and warned all the men, and had every one posted, watching for the attack. A little after 6.30 a. m. the enemy opened furiously on the fort, with over twenty guns, and also swept the parapets and rained through the embrasures a heavy fire of musketry from the crest of the ridge 80 to 100 yards off. I went about the fort enforcing strict silence, and seeing that the men were kept close against the parapet, ready to rise and fire. So well had I protected the fort with traverses, and also owing to the fog making it quite dusky, no one was hurt by this fire except one cannoneer. In about twenty minutes the cannonade slackened somewhat, and the musketry fire was directed on the northwest bastion ; at the same time a heavy column charged on a run from under the ridge upon the salient of bastion (five regiments formed the column— as near as I could judge, "Column by division closed in mass"). The guns were triple-shotted with canister, but only one got a shot at them, as they came up through the sector without fire. They burst through the abatis, and although great numbers fell flat in the entanglement, the weight of the column carried them promptly over it. They lost many at the entanglement, and in less than two minutes from their appearance, they were in the ditch, attempting to scale the parapet. As they endeavored to surround the fort, the two guns in the bastion poured triple rounds of canister in their faces (not 10 yards from them), and I soon had the flank gun firing through the ditch and across the salient. They climbed the parapet continually, but only to be shot as they gained the top, the men being ordered to fire at none except those on the parapet. I also threw shells with my own hand in the ditch, to explode among them. After a while they began to fall back, but another column coming up, the assault was pushed more savagely than ever, and three of their flags were planted in our parapet. At length they again fell back in great confusion to the ridge from which they charged, leaving the ground strewn with dead and dying and three colors in our possession.

We took over 250 prisoners unhurt, 17 of them commissioned officers (we were not 250 strong in the fort); over 200 dead and wounded lay in the ditch, among them 3 colonels. One-half in the ditch were dead; most of the others were mortally wounded. We also got over 1,000 stand of arms. The prisoners in the ditch represented eleven regiments, and estimated their regiments at about 400 strong, each.

From what I learned from their officers and from what I saw, I gathered the following plan of assault: Two brigades to watch and fire on our lines, one brigade to assault, and two more to support it. Two brigades came up to the ditch. The party actually engaged in the assault numbered about 4,000 men, not including reserves. Of these they lost from 1,300 to 1,500 killed, wounded, and prisoners; a very large proportion killed, and a large number mortally wounded.

In the fort we lost 13 men, 8 killed and 5 wounded.

General Ferrero was in the little bomb-proof, and I did not see him outside, nor know of his giving an order during the fight. The capture of the fort was to have been at once followed by a general assault on the town, their whole army being in readiness.

SAMUEL N. BENJAMIN,
Lieutenant, Second U. S. Artillery.

No. 13.

Report of Capt. Jacob Roemer, Battery L, Second New York Light Artillery.

HDQRS. BATTERY L, SECOND NEW YORK ARTILLERY,
East Tenn. College, Knoxville, Tenn., December 5, 1863.

SIR : The battery left Lenoir's Station November 14, at 11 a. m., narched to opposite Loudon ; bivouacked the night under heavy ain and storm in the woods.

The 15th, at 4 a. m., marched back to near Lenoir's Station and ook position on the left of the road at 11 a. m.   At 9 p. m. a charge vas made on the battery, but repulsed ; fired 5 rounds.

The 16th, fell back to Campbell's Station ; received a detail of 13 nen from the Twentieth Michigan Volunteers to assist the left sec-ion, which was ordered to cover the retreat ; lost 1 horse killed, 1 younded ; fired 12 rounds.   The other section took position at Campbell's Station, where the left section soon joined and a general ngagement ensued.   The battery was under fire from 11 a. m. till .30 p. m. ; fired 429 rounds.

The road from Lenoir's Station to Campbell's Station was very nuddy and interrupted with deep holes, and we had to hitch on ufficient mule teams to bring the pieces and caissons along.   One aggage wagon, disabled on the road, was burned by order of Gen-ral Burnside, with all its contents and 21 Enfield rifles.

One man, Private William Markland, was slightly wounded, ruised in the back by a piece of a shell.   One teamster of the Twenty-hird Army Corps (name not known), detailed to the battery with pair of mules, was severely wounded in the back by a piece of a hell.   One horse killed, 2 wounded.

During the night marched to Knoxville, distant 15 miles.   Ar-ived at Knoxville November 17, at 5 a. m., and took position in the reastworks at Tennessee College.   The cannoneers commenced to trengthen and widen the breastworks, and worked every day till)ecember 1, when they finished it.

November 18, fired 2 rounds.   The 19th, fired 11 rounds.   The 20th, ad 1 horse killed by the enemy's shell ; the left section took position n Fort Sanders.   The 23d, fired 3 rounds.   The 24th, fired 5 rounds. The 25th, fired 9 rounds ; the left section fired 5 rounds.   The 26th, ired 5 rounds.   The 27th, fired 5 rounds ; the left section fired 2 ounds.   The 28th, fired 12 rounds.   From 10.30 p. m. the 28th till 7 . m. the 29th, fired 169 rounds, both sections together, the left sec-ion in Fort Sanders.   Participated in repulsing the enemy's charge n the fort at 6 a. m.   The 29th, 1 horse killed, 1 wounded.   The letailed 13 men from the Twentieth Michigan Regiment returned o their regiment by order of General Ferrero.   The 30th, fired 5 ounds.   December 1, fired 4 rounds.   The 2d, fired 2 rounds ; the eft section fired 2 rounds.   The 3d, fired 3 rounds.   The 4th, fired 6 rounds ; the left section fired 7 rounds.   December 1 the axle of he first piece gave way ; repaired the 4th in the shop at Knoxville. The battery is in position as follows : The left section commanded y Lieut. Thomas Heasley in Fort Sanders.   The right section is in osition in the breastworks at Tennessee College, which we named]ybilla.

Officers and men behaved themselves in the fight, as well as on the very severe marches, alike good, and though they were all the time on short rations, had in day-time to work on the breastworks, and at night to be on guard by their guns, they endured every hardship cheerfully and enjoy a general good health.

JACOB ROEMER,
Captain, Comdg. Battery L, Second New York Artillery.

No. 14.

Reports of Capt. William W. Buckley, Battery D, First Rhode Island Light Artillery.

HDQRS. BATTY. D, FIRST RHODE ISLAND LT. ARTY.,
Fort Sanders, Knoxville, Tenn., December 5, 1863.

CAPTAIN : I have the honor to submit the following report of the operations of my battery since November 14:

November 14.—Lay in camp at Lenoir's Station ready to move.

November 15.—At 7.20 p. m. moved toward Campbell's Station. Arrived at 9.30 a. m. November 16, and moved into position on left of Loudon and Knoxville road. Engaged enemy at 11.30 a. m. Fired at intervals until 4 p. m., then withdrew and moved 1 mile on road toward Knoxville. At 5.30 p. m. moved toward Knoxville, arriving at 10.30 p. m.

November 17.—At 10 a. m. moved battery into Fort Sanders.

November 18.—Fired a few shots at enemy's skirmishers in brick house on Kingston road. Placed one gun in position in front of Powell's house.

November 19.—Changed position of guns in Fort Sanders and shelled woods on right of the fort.

November 20, 21, and 22.—Changed positions of one or two guns and fired shots at the enemy's skirmishers.

November 23.—Moved two guns to right of Second Division, Ninth Army Corps.

November 24.—No changes.

November 25.—Shelled woods to cover advance of Second Michigan on enemy's rifle-pits.

November 26 and 27.—No changes.

November 28.—Shelled enemy in the evening while they were driving in our skirmishers. Fired at intervals until 3 a. m of November 29.

November 29.—Engaged enemy at daylight until 7.30 a. m. Enemy charged on the fort. Fired canister.

November 30.—No changes.

December 1.—No changes.

December 2.—Fired a few shots at enemy's batteries to the right of the fort, and also at enemy's infantry.

December 3.—Shelled enemy's rifle-pits.

All the above movements and operations, in obedience to orders from headquarters First Division, Ninth Army Corps, and from Lieutenant Benjamin, commanding Battery E, Second U. S. Artillery.

On the march from Lenoir's Station to Knoxville I was obliged to abandon my battery wagon body and contents and one caisson-body, owing to my horses being unable to draw them. I also abandoned one caisson body which broke down on the road and could not be repaired. Most of the articles abandoned were destroyed and rendered useless.

I have expended the following ammunition since leaving Lenoir's Station : Twenty-five solid shot, 28 canister, 216 shell, and 239 case-shot. Have remaining on hand 71 solid shot, 92 canister, 172 shell, and 49 case-shot.

I wish to mention the name of Sergt. Charles C. Gray as having particularly distinguished himself by his behavior on the morning of November 29 during the assault on the fort.

I am, very respectfully, your obedient servant,

WM. W. BUCKLEY,
Captain, Comdg. Battery D, First Rhode Island Artillery.

Capt. GEORGE A. HICKS,
Asst. Adjt. Gen., First Division, Ninth Army Corps.

—

HDQRS. BATTY. D, FIRST RHODE ISLAND LT. ARTY.,
*Camp at Blain's Cross-Roads, Tenn., December 18,*1863.

GENERAL : I have the honor to forward the following report of the operations of my battery since leaving Cincinnati:*

October 20 to 22.—Marched to Loudon, 30 miles.

October 28.—Marched to Lenoir's Station, and camped.

November 15.—Longstreet's corps crossed river below Loudon and advanced toward our camps. At 7 p. m. ordered to march to Campbell's Station. It had been raining for two days, and the roads were in dreadful condition. It was almost an impossibility to move artillery. At 11.30 p. m. I had marched 3 miles and my horses were completely worn out. Lieutenant Benjamin, Second U. S. Artillery, and myself rode back to General Burnside's headquarters and represented the state of things to the general. He ordered ten mule teams turned over to each of us, burning the wagons for that purpose, and also ordered us to abandon the rear part of our caissons if we could not get along with the help of the mule teams. I got through to Campbell's Station at 9.30 a. m. of November 16. I was forced to abandon my battery wagon body and contents and the rear part of one of my caissons. They were destroyed and rendered useless. At 10.30 a. m. went into position. At 11 a. m. engaged enemy and continued in action until 4 p. m. At 5 p. m. ordered to Knoxville. Arrived at 11.30 p. m. One of my caisson axles broke on this march, and I was ordered to abandon the rear part of the caisson.

November 17.—Battery ordered into position at Fort Sanders.

November 18.—Threw shell at enemy's skirmishers. From the 18th to 29th remained in position in Fort Sanders. The enemy advanced their rifle-pits nearer each night, until their sharpshooters were within 125 yards of the fort, and forced our men to keep close under cover to avoid being picked off. I shelled their pits and batteries more or less every day. During the night of the 28th, they drove in our skirmishers the whole length of our line, and at daylight of the 29th, made an assault on the right bastion of the fort with nine picked regiments from Longstreet's corps. They charged desperately and succeeded in gaining the ditch of the fort and planting their colors

_____

*For portion (here omitted) relating to operations from August 15 to October 19, see Series I, Vol. XXX, Part II, p. 600,

on the parapet; at the same time a heavy fire was opened on the bastion from batteries on our front, right, and left. They fired from 20 and 10 pounder Parrotts, 3-inch and 12-pounder guns, and 24-pounder howitzers. The bastion was occupied by detachments from the Seventy-ninth New York and Twenty-ninth Massachusetts Infantry, numbering 80 men, one gun, 3-inch, of Roemer's (New York) battery, and one of my guns.

I fired 2 shots (canister) from my gun placed in barbette in the salient angle of the bastion, and then placed it in embrasure on the right face to allow infantry to occupy the angle. Roemer's gun was in embrasure on the left face, the most important point; but after firing 3 rounds, the horses of the limber became frightened and ran away with it, thereby depriving the gun of ammunition. My sergeant, Charles C. Gray, by my order, with his men, ran Roemer's gun back from the embrasure, and then carried their own gun over by hand, and occupied it. They worked the gun there until the engagement was over, firing double and triple rounds of canister. This movement was effected under a very heavy fire, both from artillery and musketry. The fight lasted about one hour. At the end of that time the enemy fell back, leaving 93 dead, over 100 wounded, 4 stand of colors, 500 stand of arms, and 300 prisoners in our hands. In addition to this the retreating enemy carried away a great many killed and wounded with them. The prisoners were captured in the ditch of the fort. They charged into it, and after getting in could neither get farther nor go back. Our loss in the fort was 2 killed and 8 wounded. The small loss was owing to the fact of our men being protected by the parapet, which was built up with cotton bales. Sergeant Gray and his detachment deserve great credit for their coolness and promptitude during the assault. Two of my guns, under Lieutenant Parker, were in position and enfiladed the enemy's line as it crossed the railroad from a point 700 to 800 yards on the right; also one gun in the left bastion of the fort, and one on the left of the Kingston road, under Lieutenant Rhodes, kept up a constant fire from their positions.

The night of December 4, the enemy evacuated their positions after having besieged us for eighteen days. A great many of my horses were burned as unserviceable, as I could not get forage for them. The men were reduced to 1¼ pounds of fresh beef and one-eighth of a loaf of bread per day for rations; no coffee, sugar, or small rations.

On the morning of December 7, I marched with four guns and two caissons (all I could hitch up for want of horses) to Rutledge, arriving the 9th, and remained there until the 14th; distance, 32 miles. The night of the 14th, we fell back to this point. We shall probably be engaged again soon, as the enemy is in force in our front.

The following is a list of casualties at Campbell's Station and Knoxville: Private Richard Lewis, leg shot off; Private William A. Oakes, wounded in face; Private Leonard G. Ellis, wounded in head (not badly); Private William T. Dinkins, wounded slightly.

I expended the following amount of ammunition at Campbell's Station and Knoxville: Twenty-five rounds solid shot, 43 rounds canister, 216 rounds of shell, and 239 rounds case-shot.

I had to be very saving, as there was no extra ammunition for 12-pounder guns in the corps, except a few shell and canister. This has probably been the hardest campaign of the war on troops. My men have drawn no clothing of any kind since leaving Cincinnati, and some of them are barefooted to-day. I have been unable to obtain any, as it has been impossible to get it over the mountains. Some of the men are quite ragged, and hardly any have stockings. The weather is getting quite cold, and they are in great need of all kinds of clothing. In addition to this, they have not drawn over one-half rations of coffee and sugar since the 28th day of August, and a great part of that time it has been but one-quarter rations, and sometimes none at all. They have had but very little hard bread; it has been flour and fresh beef, and the flour they can only cook to make it hardly eatable, as they have nothing to mix with it. Beans, rice, and vegetables, they have had none since leaving Cincinnati, and, only once in a great while, candles and soap.

I am, general, very respectfully, your obedient servant,

WM. W. BUCKLEY,
Captain, Comdg. Battery D, First Rhode Island Artillery.

Brig. Gen. E. C. MAURAN,
Adjutant-General, State of Rhode Island.

No. 15.

Reports of Brig. Gen. Edward Ferrero, U. S. Army, commanding First Division.

FORT SANDERS,
November 23, 1863.

COLONEL: I have the honor to report that, in accordance with instructions from the general commanding, I sent the Second Michigan forward to watch our opportunity to carry rifle-pits at the edge of the woods on the left of my northwest front; they charged and carried the pit gallantly, with severe loss, and held it half an hour, when their commanding officer was severely wounded. At the same moment the enemy opened a destructive flank fire on their left, compelling them to fall back, I regret to say, with severe loss, viz: Officers wounded, 5; men wounded, 40; officers killed, 1; men killed, 4; total, 50.

EDW. FERRERO.

Lieut. Col. N. BOWEN,
Assistant Adjutant-General.

HEADQUARTERS FIRST DIVISION, NINTH ARMY CORPS,
Erin's Station, East Tenn., February 5, 1864.

SIR: I have the honor to submit the following report of the operations of my command from the 14th of November to the 6th of December, 1863:

In accordance with instructions received from Major-General Burnside, I moved my command on the morning of the 14th of November from Lenoir's Station (at 11 a. m.) toward Loudon, for the purpose of ascertaining at what point on the Holston River Longstreet's forces were crossing.

On reaching the ruins of the Loudon bridge, I was informed that the enemy were laying a pontoon bridge at Huff's Ferry, a distance of 3½ miles from Loudon. I marched in the direction of said ferry and soon came upon the enemy's pickets. Halting my command and reporting the same to the general commanding, received instructions to support General White's command, who had been assigned to drive in the enemy's pickets, which he did. Following up his command until we were 1 mile from the ferry, I took position on his right, covering the main road leading from the ferry; it now became too dark and stormy for further operations, so I ordered the command to rest for the night on their arms. At 10 p. m. I received an order to report in person to Major-General Burnside's headquarters, where, after a council was held, it was determined to fall back slowly toward Lenoir's Station, so as to draw the enemy over the river and keep him engaged while other important movements were being carried out by the army in Middle Tennessee. In accordance with this plan, on the 15th, left Huff's Ferry at 4 a. m., having the advance. The roads were in a fearful condition, it having rained all night quite heavily. It became almost impossible to move the artillery, although some pieces had 16 horses, yet they were unable to get them up the hills without the assistance of the men. I thereupon detailed a regiment of infantry to each piece, and by this means reached Lenoir's Station, at 1 p. m., without sustaining any loss. I immediately placed my troops in position to cover the approach of the enemy from the Kingston road, Colonel Morrison's brigade in the advance, extending from the Kingston road on his right to the Loudon road on his left, forming a semicircle; Colonel Humphrey's brigade to the right of the Kingston road, connecting with General White's command; Colonel Christ's brigade and Buckley's battery in reserve; Roemer's battery in position on the right and left of the Kingston road. I had hardly completed the above disposition of my troops when the enemy attacked my line in force, but were repulsed by Colonel Morrison's brigade and Roemer's battery. Remained in this position during the night, the enemy making several attacks on my picket line with the intention of driving them in, but without avail.

I am indebted to Colonel Morrison, commanding First Brigade, for his valuable services, and to his command for their stubborn resistance of the enemy's advance, outnumbering them by thousands.

It having been decided, during the night of the 15th, to retreat and make a stand at Campbell's Station, I was assigned to bring up the rear with my command and destroy all property that could not be transported. A large number of wagons, utensils, ammunition, and baggage belonging to the Twenty-third Corps was destroyed, the mules having been taken to assist in drawing the artillery of the army, the roads being in such condition as to render it necessary to attach from 20 to 24 animals to each piece to enable us to move.

I ordered Colonel Humphrey, commanding Third Brigade, and a section of Roemer's battery, to cover the rear, drawing in our skirmishers, and retiring at daylight in the face of the enemy. On the 16th of November marched toward Campbell's Station, halting from time to time so as to check the enemy's advance while the troops were getting into position for battle at the station. Reached the forks of the Kingston road at 10 a. m., making a junction with Colonel Hartranft's command, when the enemy charged upon our lines and were met with a stubborn resistance and driven back, our forces gaining ground.

At this victorious moment received orders from the commanding general to fall back to a position at Campbell's Station, where the troops were formed in line prepared to give the enemy battle, retiring under fire, closely pursued by the enemy.

Colonel Humphrey is entitled to great praise for the able manner in which he covered the retreat, pursued by an overwhelming force, attacking him at every point, his command behaving with great gallantry, checking the enemy, thereby giving our forces time to select and get into position for a general engagement.

Position of my command at Campbell's Station was as follows: Colonel Christ, commanding Second Brigade, on the right of the road; Colonel Humphrey, commanding Third Brigade, on the right of Colonel Christ; Colonel Morrison, commanding First Brigade, supporting batteries; Captain Buckley's battery of light 12-pounders, in position commanding the right flank; Captain Roemer's battery the front; the enemy attacking our lines in force with infantry and artillery, but were repulsed at every point.

I have to state that never did troops maneuver so beautifully and with such precision as during the engagement; changing positions several times under a severe fire, it seemed more like a drill for field movements than otherwise; brigades moving forward to relieve each other, others retiring, having exhausted their ammunition; changes of front, passing of defiles, were executed by men and officers, so as to draw forth exclamation of the highest praise by those who were so fortunate as to behold their movements.

Colonel Christ, in command of the Second Brigade, executed movements with his command on the field which entitles him to the highest encomiums for ability and gallantry as a brigade commander.

The losses up to this time were quite heavy for my command, including the engagement at the forks of the road, but the enemy must have suffered very severely, as they advanced their lines against a murderous fire from our forces, compelling them to fall back, which must have told effectually upon their lines. They did not attempt to advance again, but devoted themselves to shelling our position with their batteries, and endeavoring to flank us with their infantry. At 5 p. m. was ordered to meet the general commanding, and after consultation it was decided to fall back to Knoxville. I was assigned the advance, and accordingly withdrew my command from the field and took up the line of march, reaching Knoxville at 12 o'clock the same night.

On the morning of the 17th of November, was assigned the following position for the defense of Knoxville: Right resting on creek to the western edge of town, extending in the form of a semicircle, to the Holston River, a distance of about $1\frac{1}{4}$ miles, including Fort Sanders and College Hill. Made the following distribution of my forces: Second Brigade, commanded by Colonel Christ, right resting on creek, connecting with Second Division, Ninth Army Corps, facing to the north; Third Brigade, commanded by Colonel Humphrey, connecting with Second Brigade on the right and extending to the Kingston road on the left; First Brigade, commanded by Colonel Morrison, from Kingston Road to the river. Lieutenant Benjamin's battery (Second U. S. Artillery), one section of Roemer's battery, two sections of Buckley's battery in Fort Sanders, supported by the Seventy-ninth New York Volunteer Infantry; one section of Roemer's battery in position on College Hill; one section of Buckley's battery in position near Powell's house on Colonel Morrison's line. Commenced digging

rifle-pits and other fortifications on my line; established advance
pickets and line of skirmishers; worked unceasingly all that day and
night.

November 18, our advance, consisting of cavalry, covering the
Kingston road and Clinton road, fell back to Knoxville, leaving the
skirmishers of my command to the front. At 4 p. m. the enemy
advanced on my pickets on the Clinton road, but were repulsed
Continued all that day and night strengthening my position.

November 19, the enemy commenced digging and fortifying their
position, from the river (Holston) to the Kingston road, near Mr
Armstrong's dwelling, at the same time moving a portion of their
forces to our right. Continued strengthening at points during all
day and night.

November 20, the enemy erected several batteries on my northwest
front, directly opposite Fort Sanders. The enemy occupying a dwell
ing on the Kingston road about 1,000 yards from the fort, doing
material damage to my line of skirmishers, I determined to obtain
possession and destroy the same. I accordingly directed Colonel
Humphrey, commanding Third Brigade, to detail a regiment to pro
ceed, under cover of the night, to dislodge the enemy from said house
and to destroy the same by fire.

The Seventeenth Michigan Volunteers, under command of Lieu
tenant-Colonel Comstock, was selected. They made the sortie at 8 p
m., and successfully accomplished their mission. On returning, the
enemy opened a severe artillery fire, with but slight injury to the
regiment. A number of buildings in front of the Second Brigade
were also destroyed.

November 21, heavy rain-storm all day; nothing of importance
occurred, with the exception of the usual picket firing.

November 22, enemy's batteries opened on our right without ma
terial damage; worked all day and night strengthening our fortifi
cations.

November 23, nothing of importance occurred, except the usual
picket firing; during the night stretched 2 miles of telegraph wire
in front of my line, forming an entanglement.

November 24, the enemy having dug rifle-pits within 500 yards of
Fort Sanders, received instructions to make a sortie with a regiment,
and drive the enemy's sharpshooters from the position.

I ordered Colonel Humphrey, commanding Third Brigade, to de
tail a regiment for the duty. He accordingly sent the Second Mich
igan Volunteers.

They gallantly charged the enemy's pits and drove them out, but
were compelled to fall back, after having held their newly gained
ground for an hour, which resulted in a severe loss of 4 killed, 60
wounded, and 24 missing.

The enemy were discovered on the heights on the opposite side of
the river (Holston), their position commanding Fort Sanders.
Erected traverses of cotton during the night to protect the gunners.

November 25, 26, and 27, nothing of importance occurred; usual
amount of skirmishing; repairing damages, and otherwise strengthen
ing our position. At 11.30 o'clock on the night of the 28th the en
emy commenced driving in my skirmishers, and by 12.30 had driven
them all in from the Kingston road, to the right of my line. An
attack evidently was near at hand, but owing to the darkness of
the night, the position and movements of the enemy could not be
seen. I posted vedettes as far as practicable in front of the rifle-

its, and during the balance of the night, at frequent periods, rdered the batteries to throw shells in different directions to do he enemy as much damage and to cause them as much annoyance s lay in my power.

On the morning of the 29th, at daylight, the expected attack took lace. The enemy poured out of the woods in front of the north-west salient of the fort, and with wild cheers advanced at a run for hat salient.

The telegraph wire caused many to fall, but the main body came n, while three guns of Benjamin's battery, one of Roemer's, and ne of Buckley's, were pouring in a destructive fire of grape, and the eventy-ninth New York Volunteers a deadly shower of musketry, pon the advancing column. Forcing their way through the abatis hey rushed up to the ditch of the fort, which at that point, being uit deep, caused a momentary hesitation.

In a moment, however, the ditch was filled with the enemy, and he outer slope of the parapet was covered with them, but the mus-ketry fire was so intense and steady that but few dared show their eads. One rebel with a flag endeavored to approach the embrasure, hen Serg. Frank Judge, Company D, Seventy-ninth New York Volunteers, rushed out of the embrasure under the hottest fire, eized him by the collar, and dragged him, with his flag, into the ort. Having no hand grenades Lieutenant Benjamin ignited some ime-fuse shells and threw them with his own hand over the parapet nto the ditch among the enemy, causing great destruction among hem.

I now ordered five companies of the Twenty-ninth Massachusetts Volunteers and two companies of the Twentieth Michigan Volun-eers into the fort to assist the Seventy-ninth New York Volunteers.

They obeyed the order with alacrity, and taking the positions as-igned them, rendered valuable aid in keeping the enemy out of the ort. Learning that the ditch was full of the enemy, I ordered one ompany of the Second Michigan Volunteers to advance into the litch from the right, and one company of the One hundredth Penn-ylvania Volunteers from the left of the fort. This was instantly arried out, and their advance was so determined that those in the litch at once surrendered, and being ordered into the fort, came ouring in through the embrasures and gave themselves up. Nearly 00 were captured in this manner, together with 2 other flags.

In the meantime, the column of the enemy in front of the fort, eing halted by the delay caused by their comrades in the ditch, were lischarging an incessant but harmless fire of musketry into the air, ill getting confused and demoralized by the terrible fire which was oured into them from the fort, they wavered, then broke, and ran n disorder back to the woods. Those nearest the fort being called n to surrender, came in through the embrasures.

Two hundred and fifty prisoners and 3 flags were captured from he enemy in this attack.

I at once ordered the skirmishers to advance, which they did, and ook position on the line which was occupied by their reserves the lay before. After this, up to the time the enemy retreated, nothing ut the usual skirmish firing took place, and that was not as annoy-ng as usual. In anticipation, however, of another night attack, I rdered balls of wick, soaked in turpentine, and fagots of hard pine,

coated with pitch, to be placed at different points on the skirmis
line, to be ignited in case of an alarm.

On the morning of the 5th of December, at 1 o'clock, I advance
vedettes from the skirmish line, and the pits of the enemy wer
found empty. When daylight appeared no rebels were to be see
from Fort Sanders.

I cannot speak too highly of the behavior of the officers and me
of my command during the past twenty-one days. In that time, a
the qualities embodied in the true soldier have been called int
action, and nobly have they stood the test.

On a scanty allowance of meat and coarse meal, without any othe
drink than cold water, they have performed these days and nigh
of incessant labor and watchfulness without a murmur.

In the officers that have been killed, I have lost brave and valu
able soldiers.

Col. W. H. Smith, Twentieth Michigan Volunteers, was sh
through the head and instantly killed, while leading his regime
into the fight at Campbell's Station.

Major Byington, Second Michigan Volunteers, was severe
wounded in the leg in the sortie made by that regiment, and led b
him, on the morning of November 24. He was left a prisoner i
the hands of the enemy, and his leg was amputated by their su
geons. He was exchanged on November 29, but died some da
afterward from the effects of the amputation.

Lieutenant-Colonel Comstock, of the Seventeenth Michigan Vo
unteers, after having passed safely through all the previous danger
was killed while standing in his tent by a stray bullet from th
enemy.

Captain Wiltsie, Twentieth Michigan Volunteers; Lieutenant Bi
lingsley, Seventeenth Michigan Volunteers; Lieutenants Nobl
Galpin, and Zoellner, Second Michigan Volunteers, and Lieutenar
Holmes, Thirty-sixth Massachusetts Volunteers, were all killed whi
in the performance of their duties.

Quite a number of officers were wounded, but for further detai
I refer you to reports of brigade and battery commanders inclose
herewith.

Capt. George A. Hicks, assistant adjutant-general; Capt. W. W
Tyson, assistant inspector-general; Capt. George E. Swinscoe, assis
ant commissary of musters; Capt. George B. Fuller, provost-marsha
and Lieut. H. H. Daniels, aide-de-camp, members of my staff, a
entitled to the highest praise for their gallantry and valuable ser
ices, rendered cheerfully, attending to their arduous duties wher
ever called upon.

Surg. E. J. Bonine, acting medical director of this division, wa
ever untiring in his efforts to administer to the comforts of th
wounded and dying.

The total number of killed, wounded, and missing, from Nover
ber 14 to December 6, was 482, a detailed report of which has alread
been forwarded.

I am, colonel, very respectfully, your obedient servant,

EDW. FERRERO,
Brigadier-General, Commanding.

Lieut. Col. N. Bowen,
Assistant Adjutant-General.

No. 16.

eport of Col. David Morrison, Seventy-ninth New York Infantry,
commanding First Brigade.

HDQRS. FIRST BRIG., FIRST DIV., NINTH ARMY CORPS,
Knoxville, Tenn., December 5, 1863.

CAPTAIN : I have the honor to forward you the following detailed
port of the operations of this brigade since leaving Lenoir's Station,
the 14th of November, to this date :

On the afternoon of Saturday, the 14th November, I moved from
enoir's Station in the direction of Loudon ; arrived there about 4
m. Halted about fifteen minutes, and took the road leading to
uff's Ferry, near which place we arrived between 6 and 7 p. m.,
rmed line of battle, and rested for the night.

On Sunday, the 15th, received orders to move back in the rear of
oemer's battery. Owing to the bad state of the roads our progress
as very slow. The troops were directed to bring off the batteries,
id, if necessary, to carry them over the hills, which were very
eep. This was accomplished without accident. We passed Loudon
our way back, and arrived at Lenoir's Station about 3 p. m. I
as then ordered to take up a position on the Kingston road, about
0 yards from Lenoir's Station, and support Roemer's battery, which
as in position at that place. About 4 p. m. I was ordered to picket
e Loudon road with 25 men, and the cross-roads leading to Huff's
erry with the same number. This party, in command of Lieuten-
t Jeffers, Forty-fifth Pennsylvania Volunteers, and under direc-
on of Lieutenant Daniels, of General Ferrero's staff, and Lieuten-
t Donaldson, of my own staff, proceeded about 2 miles on the
ingston road, when they were attacked by the enemy in force ad-
ncing toward Lenoir's Station. The picket party deployed in line
skirmishers and fought the enemy, retiring slowly. About this
me I arrived and found the enemy making a flank movement in
·der to cut them off. I ordered them to fall back at once, which
ey did just in time to clear their line of skirmishers. I was then
·dered to make a stand about 500 yards in front of Roemer's bat-
·ry, and deployed the Eighth Michigan Volunteers as skirmishers,
ith 25 men of the Forty-fifth, who were still in skirmish line on
e right. My right rested on the mill-dam ; my left extended toward
e Loudon road, forming a semicircle ; the Forty-fifth Pennsylvania
·olunteers and Thirty-sixth Massachusetts Volunteers in the center
s a reserve. About 9 p. m. my skirmish line was attacked by the
nemy in force on the right and was forced back about 25 yards,
here the line was maintained for the remainder of the night.

At 5.30 a. m. [16th], I was surprised by my line of skirmishers
lling back. I endeavored to stop them, but found I could not do so
ithout attracting the notice of the enemy, whom I distinctly heard
oving his forces at the same time. I fell slowly back toward Le-
oir's Station, sending word to the general commanding of the state
f matters in the front. The skirmishers on the right of the Kings-
on road, and in front of the enemy, under direction of Capt. John
Vindsor, acting assistant adjutant-general, held the original line.
Vhen I had withdrawn a sufficient distance to act without attract-
ig the notice of the enemy, I deployed two companies of the Thirty-
ixth Massachusetts Volunteers, advanced them slowly, and formed
unction with my line on the right. At this time orders came to

withdraw the whole line. I then inquired why the line of the Eighth
Michigan Volunteers had fallen back without orders from me, and
was told by Lieutenant-Colonel Ely, commanding that regiment,
that orders had come from the left to fall back, and that the line on
his left had fallen back some time previously. I told him he had
committed a very great error by falling back without orders from
me. I then formed the brigade on the railroad, when we fell back,
taking the road to Campbell's Station, and falling slowly back till
we reached the junction of the Kingston and Loudon roads, when
an officer of General Potter's staff asked me if I knew where General
Ferrero was, and said he could not find him, but that he had order
for Colonel Morrison's brigade to form in a field at that place and
await the enemy, who were driving the Third Brigade.

I immediately filed off the road, formed line of battle with skirmishers in front, joining the skirmishers of the Second Division
who were facing the Kingston road and expecting the enemy. This
line extended from the Loudon to the Kingston roads and forme
junction with the Second Michigan Volunteers, which was the left
of the Third Brigade. I fell back slowly with that brigade until
came to a good rail fence, where I determined to make a stand an
fight the enemy. They charged our lines several times, but were
handsomely repulsed. We held this position about thirty minutes
the men behaving in the most gallant manner. At this time a heavy
fire was opened in our rear, which I supposed was protected by
part of the Second Division, but found that they had fallen back
while I was engaging the enemy in front, thus exposing our rear t
attack from the enemy, on the road toward Kingston. Finding myself
between two fires, and not being hard pressed in front, I faced about
and opened a heavy fire on the forces in our rear, which broke the
line and threw them into confusion. At this juncture an aide arrive
and ordered me to fall back, which I did, taking the left of the road
and keeping well into the woods, the enemy from Loudon on the right
of the road and almost on a parallel line with me. He was first uncovered by coming upon a large open space, where he displayed three
different lines, each about 100 yards apart. I could have fought hi
at this point to advantage, but was ordered to fall back about a mi
farther and take up a position in support of Edwards' and Roemer
batteries, where I remained till between 3 and 4 p. m.

These batteries being ordered to fall back, I followed and took u
a position in support of Benjamin's battery, advancing two regimen
to the front about 200 yards, where I remained till dusk. I was the
ordered to move in rear of the Third Brigade, toward Knoxville
arriving at the fortifications near there on the morning of the 17th
from which time to this date I have occupied the defenses on the le
of the line from the Loudon road to the river. The Seventy-nint
New York Volunteers, garrisoning Fort Sanders, have been engage
daily, skirmishing with the enemy in front. On the 29th ultimo, t
enemy assaulted Fort Sanders, but were repulsed with great loss.*

On the afternoon of the 4th instant, I was ordered to feel the en
my's lines, and found them still there in force. At 2 o'clock on th
morning of the 5th, Capt. E. T. Raymond, acting assistant inspecto
general, of my staff, reported that the enemy's front had been e
ceedingly quiet for the last half hour. I immediately repaired

---

* A medal of honor was awarded to Sergt. Francis W. Judge, Seventy-ninth N
York Infantry, for capturing the flag of the Fifty-first Georgia Infantry in t
assault.

front, and after carefully reconnoitering the position became
ᶥvinced that the enemy had retired.   At fifteen minutes past 2 I
ᵥanced my vedettes, who reported the enemy's rifle-pits evacuated.
ᶦhen advanced my whole line of skirmishers, sending out vedettes
far as the Armstrong house.   Having reported to General Ferrero
ᵉ state of things in front, received orders to occupy and hold my
ˢt line of rifle-pits, and not to advance farther for the present.
daylight I ascertained that the enemy had entirely evacuated our
ᵒnt.   A number of deserters from the enemy have come into our
ᵉs, also Major Smith, of General Wheeler's staff, taken prisoner
one of the Eighth Michigan Volunteers, about 2 miles from the
ᵒnt.   This officer had been severely wounded in the leg, and was
ᶰt to hospital.   I still occupy the same position.
The conduct of the troops of this command was everything I
ᵤld desire, notwithstanding the heavy fire opened in their rear,
ᶦch is apt at all times to throw even the best-disciplined troops
ᵗo confusion.   They behaved with the utmost coolness and brav-
ᵧ.
I also transmit you a detailed list of casualties to this date.*
I have the honor to be, captain, very respectfully, your obedient
ᵛant,

DAVID MORRISON,
Colonel, Commanding Brigade.

Capt. GEORGE A. HICKS,
  Assistant Adjutant-General.

———

No. 17.

ᵖort of Col. Benjamin C. Christ, Fiftieth Pennsylvania Infantry, commanding Second Brigade.

HDQRS. SECOND BRIG., FIRST DIV., NINTH ARMY CORPS,
       Blain's Cross-Roads, Tenn., January 1, 1864.

SIR: In compliance with circular from ·division headquarters, I
ᵥe the honor to submit the following report of the operations of
ᵧ command from the time of breaking camp at Lenoir's Station
ᵗil its arrival at this point:
The brigade left their quarters about noon on Saturday, Novem-
ᵣ 14, and marched to Huff's Ferry, where it arrived after dark.
ᵂas ordered to the front with instructions, if possible, to push to
ᵉ river.   Arriving at the outer picket line of General White's
ᵛision of the Twenty-third Corps, I deployed a line of skirmishers,
ᶰder command of Capt. Samuel K. Schwenk, Fiftieth Pennsylva-
ᵃ Volunteers, and pushed them at first about 75 to 100 yards in
ᵈvance of General White's.   After forming in line of battle with
ᶦird Regiment (holding one in reserve), I sent a heavy support to
ᵃptain Schwenk, and ordered him to cautiously advance his line.
ᶦey did not, however, advance 50 yards before they were chal-
ᶰged by the enemy's picket.   Captain S[chwenk] halted his men;
ᵘght cover, and maintained that position during the night.   The
ᵒods were so dark and the enemy so constantly vigilant, that all
ᵉa of pushing to the river during the night had to be abandoned.
At 4 a. m. of the 15th, we left our position and marched to Lenoir's
ᵗation, where we arrived at 12 m. and remained, keeping the enemy

---

*Embodied in revised statement, pp. 288 *et seq.*

in check until daylight the next morning (16th), when we march
to Campbell's Station, where we arrived at 10 a m., and took up
position on the left of the road in support of some batteries.

About 12 o'clock I was ordered to take a position on the right
the road in rear of and as support of the Third Brigade (Colon
Humphrey's). A short time after taking this latter position I thre
forward the Twenty-ninth Massachusetts Volunteers (Colonel Peir
commanding) on Colonel Humphrey's right, to protect his fla
against a movement of the enemy in that direction. Subsequent
I relieved Colonel Humphrey altogether, and took a position on o
extreme right and in front. I held this position for about thr
hours under both artillery and infantry fire of the enemy.

At 3.30 p. m. I was ordered to retire, leaving my skirmishers
cover my line as much as possible. I moved to the rear about 2
yards under a severe fire of artillery in my front (now my rear) a
from the enemy's infantry and sharpshooters on our right (now n
left). I now halted my column, faced to the enemy, and called
my skirmishers, and then moved to the rear over an open plain f
near one-half mile under a heavy fire from one of the enemy's ba
teries. Arriving at our new position, I formed in rear of our ba
teries until 5 p. m., when, according to orders, I marched to Kno
ville, where I arrived at 3 o'clock on the morning of the 17th, a
was assigned a position in rear of Fort Sanders until 9 a. m., whe
was ordered to take a position near the railroad, with my right re
ing on Creek, and my left extending toward Fort Sanders and co
necting with Colonel Humphrey's right.

Although the men were worn down with fighting, marching, a
loss of sleep for the last three days and nights, yet they immediate
and under the circumstances with great alacrity, commenced di
ging rifle-pits, throwing up earth-works, constructing abatis, a
otherwise strengthening their position. At first this work was do
during the day, but after the advance of the enemy's lines it w
done under cover of the night.

From the 17th until the 5th of December my command, in comm
with the rest of the troops, were nearly surrounded by a superi
force of the enemy, by which all outward communication was near
.cut off.

On the evenings of the 18th, 19th, and 20th, a number of buildin
were by my order burned on my front, for the reason that th
afforded shelter to the enemy.

On the night of the 28th, from information received from divisi
headquarters and from indications and movements of the enemy
had every reason to expect an attack on my position, and con
quently had taken every precaution to render it unsuccessful. Abo
10 o'clock a charge was made, but by setting fire to some combus
ble materials previously prepared in the large round-house and oth
railroad buildings, as well as a number of private houses, maki
a complete wall of fire along my entire front, together with the
termined resistance of a strong line of skirmishers advantageous
posted in small pits and lunettes, the enemy were checked and so
after retired.

On the same evening, in compliance with orders from divisi
headquarters, I temporarily detached from the brigade and to
from their position in the rifle-pits the Twenty-ninth Regiment M
sachusetts Volunteers, and sent them to re-enforce that part of t
command occupying Fort Sanders and its immediate surroundin

About midnight five companies of this regiment were detached,
d, under the command of Capt. Thomas W. Clark, were ordered to
e support of Colonel Morrison, commanding First Brigade, in the
fle-pits on our left, the right wing of this regiment, under com-
and of Major Chipman, still occupying their position on the hill
. rear of the fort, but were subsequently ordered into the rifle-pits
1 the left and near the fort, and both detachments were thus
tuated when the attack on Fort Sanders on the morning of the 29th
egan. The detachment under command of Major Chipman were
rst ordered into the fort, and the one under Captain Clark, pursu-
1t to orders, soon followed, the first arriving during the hottest
' the fight, and the last before the battle was over, and both con-
·ibuting largely to the successful results on that occasion, each de-
chment capturing a battle-flag from the enemy * as a part of the
oils of the victory.

Detaching the Twenty-ninth Regiment Massachusetts Volunteers
om my command left me a long line of front to picket and protect
ith three small regiments. My men were obliged to go on picket
very other day, and when off such duty were obliged, from ne-
ssity, to be in a cramped position in the rifle-pits during the day to
void the balls of the enemy's sharpshooters, and at night, in pursu-
nce of orders, one-third of them were kept constantly awake to
uard against surprise. Add to this one-fourth rations of coffee and
ne-half rations of coarse, heavy corn bread, and the fact that they
ere poorly shod (some even barefooted) and poorly clothed, without
vercoats, and many of them without blankets, and it will be seen
iat their privations and sufferings were equal to, if not in excess of,
ny other portion of the Union forces since the commencement of
ie war. Yet, notwithstanding all these sufferings—and it should
e recorded to their credit—there was neither murmur nor complaint.
ll promptly and cheerfully performed their duty, and expressed
iemselves ready and willing to endure even greater hardships if it
ould contribute to the success of our arms and drive the enemy out
f East Tennessee.

As a further evidence of their patriotism and loyalty and their
etermination to assist to the last in crushing out this hell-born and
ell-bound rebellion, I would state that two of these regiments, the
'wenty-ninth Massachusetts and Fiftieth Pennsylvania, have already
e-enlisted as veteran volunteers. The Forty-sixth New York have
early if not quite the required number, while the Twenty-seventh
lichigan regret that they have not been in the service long enough
o avail themselves of the provisions of General Orders, No. —.

About 3 o'clock on the morning of the 5th of December, Cap-
ain Schwenk, of the Fiftieth Pennsylvania, in command of the
icket, brought in a prisoner, with the information that the enemy
ad raised the siege and under cover of the night had retreated.
'his prisoner I immediately sent to division headquarters.

At 10 a. m. (5th), in pursuance of orders, I proceeded with the
'wenty-seventh Michigan, Twenty-ninth Massachusetts, and Fif-
ieth Pennsylvania to a paper-mill about 4 miles below Knoxville,
etween the Loudon and Clinton roads, in search of a Georgia regi-
nent of rebels reported to have been cut off and unable to join their
ommand. I scoured the country from the river to the Clinton road

* Medals of honor awarded to Sergt. Jeremiah Mahoney and Private Joseph S.
Manning, Twenty-ninth Massachusetts Infantry, for the capture of Confederate
olors ; to Sergeant Mahoney for capture of the flag of the Seventeenth Mississippi.

and in the neighborhood and beyond the paper-mill, but from infor
mation received from citizens and from stragglers of the enemy I fel
satisfied that the regiment in question had left before daylight, and
that farther pursuit was useless. I returned to Knoxville at 4 p. m

During this march we took a number of prisoners, including sev
eral officers, one a major of General Wheeler's staff. I also found a
number of sick and wounded of the enemy in almost every house
I passed, many of them destitute of medicines, rations, and medica
attendance. At the paper-mill there were 130 sick and wounded
A mile below the mill, in a house abandoned by its former occupants
I found 12 entirely destitute ; Captain Fuller, of the division staff
was present and made arrangements to supply their wants.

On the 7th of December, we left Knoxville, and arrived at Rut
ledge, East Tenn., on the afternoon of the 9th. Left Rutledge on
the 15th, and arrived near Blain's Cross-Roads on 16th, where the
command is at present encamped.

From the time we broke camp at Lenoir's until we arrived at this
point—whether on the march to Huff's Ferry ; the night of duty in
front while there; during a severe storm, without fire or shelter
the rapid march to Lenoir's and Campbell's Station ; the six hours
fight at the latter place ; the night march that followed ; the eighteen days' siege at Knoxville, and the arduous duties since the rais
ing of the siege ; through all this on scant rations and scanter
clothing—both officers and men behaved with the accustomed cool
ness and bravery and strict discipline so characteristic of them in
previous campaigns and on numerous battle-fields.

To the members of my personal staff—Lieut. Charles D. Browne,
Twenty-ninth Massachusetts, and Lieut. E. N. Gilbert, Eighth Michigan Volunteers, as well as my orderly, Daniel K. Sell, Company E
Fiftieth Pennsylvania, and Corpl. Frank H. Barnhart, Company A,
Fiftieth Pennsylvania (clerk at these headquarters), who acted as
orderly—I am much indebted for their promptness and dispatch in
the execution of every order.

To Captain Schwenk, Company A, Fiftieth Pennsylvania Volunteers, I am much indebted for the manner in which he handled his
skirmishers on the evening we reached Huff's Ferry, and for the
effort he made to penetrate the enemy's line in order to ascertain
what he was doing. I am satisfied that in these attempts he failed
only because success was impossible.

Great credit is due to Lieutenants Truckey and Hadwick, of
Twenty-seventh Michigan Volunteers, for the gallant manner in
which they brought their skirmishers off the field at Campbell's Station after the regiment had left, and to the men for standing firmly
at their posts. after their support was taken away, until they were
called in.

Corp. William Johnson, of Company F, Twenty-seventh Michigan, went back alone under a heavy fire and succeeded in carrying
off a wounded comrade to a place of safety. In like manner Private
Francis Runciman, of Company H, returned and assisted a member
of the Thirteenth Kentucky (whose foot had been shattered by a
cannon-ball) off the field. I append a list of casualties.

All of which is respectfully submitted.

B. C. CHRIST,
Colonel, Comdg. Second Brig., First Div., Ninth Army Corps.
Capt. GEORGE A. HICKS,
Assistant Adjutant-General.

Command.	Killed.	Wounded.	Missing.	Aggregate.
h Michigan Volunteers...............................	4	20	30	54
h Pennsylvania Volunteers............................	4	9	2	15
h Massachusetts Volunteers..........................	4	4	1	9
h New York Volunteers...............................	2	4	5	11
Total..............................	14	37	38	89

apt. Edward S. Leadbeater, Company G, Twenty-seventh Michigan Volunteers, was the only cer wounded in the brigade.

No. 18.

eports of Col. William Humphrey, Second Michigan Infantry, commanding Third Brigade.

HDQRS. THIRD BRIG., FIRST DIV., NINTH ARMY CORPS,
Near Fort Sanders, November 30, 1863.

SIR : In accordance with instructions from division headquarters, have the honor of transmitting the following report of the condition of my front :

My pickets connect on the right with those of the brigade and on the left with those of the First Brigade, covering the front of the hird Brigade. The men are covered by light picket pits. In front of the western salient of Fort Sanders these pits are within about) yards of those occupied by the enemy's pickets. From this point both the right and left the lines diverge, till to the right of the ne they are 150 yards apart and to the left 200 yards apart.

During the past night an unusual quiet prevailed along the whole ne, scarcely a shot being exchanged, and no move was observed on ie part of the enemy beyond their line of pickets.

In regard to advancing the picket line to its old position, I am omewhat in doubt as to what would be best. To do it would probbly require a considerable force, well supported, and while a line iore advanced is desirable, the old one was very much exposed to ie enemy's whole line, and could receive no ready support from ur own line, and the enemy could approach very near to it entirely nder cover and unobserved. This applies to that part of the old ne to the left of the point where the railroad enters the wood.

Very respectfully, your obedient servant,
WM. HUMPHREY,
Colonel, Commanding Brigade.

Capt. GEORGE A. HICKS,
Assistant Adjutant-General.

—

HDQRS. THIRD BRIG., FIRST DIV., NINTH ARMY CORPS,
Near Knoxville, Tenn., December 6, 1863.

SIR : I have the honor to transmit the following report of the perations of my command from the morning of November 14 to he morning of December 5 :

November 14.—On the morning of November 14, I received orders rom division headquarters to have my command ready to move from its camp near Lenoir's at an early hour. The wagons were to b loaded and formed in train on the road and headed toward Knox ville, the train being under charge of Captain Curtin. The orde was promptly complied with, and at daylight the brigade was read to move.

At 9 a. m. I received orders to send one regiment to report t Captain Curtin, as a guard for the train. I sent the One hundredt Pennsylvania, Lieutenant-Colonel Dawson commanding.

At 12 m. I received orders to move the brigade on the road towar Loudon, following Roemer's battery. In this order we marched t Huff's Ferry, 5 miles below Loudon, where we bivouacked for th night.

November 15.—At 4 a. m. the 15th, I was ordered to follow in th rear of Roemer's battery back on the road toward Lenoir's Station We reached the station about 12 m., and halted between the rai road and river, awaiting orders.

At 2 p. m., by order from division headquarters, I sent th Twentieth Michigan, Lieutenant-Colonel Smith commanding, bac on the Loudon road to where the Kingston telegraph road leaves toward the right, with instructions to remain in that position unt the Second Division should pass through to the rear, then to repo back to the brigade. Colonel Smith reported to me with his reg ment at sunset, and was ordered at once to take position on the le of the First Brigade, connecting on the right with the Eighth Mich igan and his left resting on the railroad. Here the Twentiet Michigan remained until the line was withdrawn on the morning the 16th.

At 4 p. m. (November 15) I was ordered to move the two remain ing regiments of my command to the crest of the hill in front Lenoir's, on the Kingston road, to form in line on the right of th road, to throw out skirmishers to cover my front, and extend the to the right so as to connect at Lenoir's Dam with the skirmishe of General White's division, of the Twenty-third Corps. This di position was made, and in this position I remained until 2 a. m. the 16th, when I was ordered to withdraw my line, march back t the railroad, and halt.

November 16, at 4 a. m., General Ferrero notified me that m command would form the rear guard of the army in the march the day toward Knoxville, and one section of Roemer's battery w ordered to report to me for duty on the march. At daylight, th column having passed by far enough, I took up the line of marc moving leisurely along, halting and forming occasionally to allo the trains to get forward out of the way. The enemy did not get u with my rear—the Seventeenth Michigan, Lieutenant-Colonel Con stock commanding—until the brigade had nearly crossed——— Cree when a sharp fire was suddenly opened on the Seventeenth, on bot the rear and flank. The fire was promptly returned and the enem checked until the rest of the command could be formed in line, whe Colonel Comstock was ordered to withdraw and pass through to t rear of the line, and form on the left of the Twentieth Michigan, order to check the enemy in his attempt to turn my left. As soo as he was in the position designated, I commenced moving my lir to the rear, halting at every few rods, facing about, and checkin the enemy, who was now crowding on in strong force. Moving i this manner, I had succeeded in falling back to the rear of the woo beyond the large open field in front of Campbell's Station. Here was ordered to make a stand and hold the enemy in check until some move in my rear should be completed, when a smart fight of half an hour's duration occurred.

The enemy made a strong effort to get around my left, and at one time had nearly succeeded. He had thrown back the Seventeenth in considerable confusion, and was crowding on as if sure of accomplishing his object. To defeat his move I rode to the Seventeenth and ordered the regiment to charge at once, at the same time ordering the skirmishers from the Twentieth and Second Michigan to be thrown forward, with a yell, to aid the Seventeenth. The charge was finely made, driving the enemy through the wood into the field beyond and throwing his front line into considerable confusion. Before making this move on the enemy I had received orders to withdraw my line, and under [cover of the check], given the enemy by this repulse, I fell back unmolested to the position ordered, on the extreme right of the front line, at the battle of Campbell's Station. I held my position here, receiving and returning quite a smart fire, until half past 1, when I was relieved by Colonel Christ, with the Second Brigade, and moved back into the shallow ravine just in rear of town. Two hours later I moved back to the rear of the batteries then being put into position, on the right of the road. Thence at dark I fell into the column to the rear of Benjamin's battery and marched to this place, where we arrived between 4 and 5 a. m. of the 17th.

The men were allowed to rest until 9 a. m., when I was ordered to move to a position joining on the right the Second Brigade and my left covering the northern front of Fort Sanders. Just as I had established my line here, Lieutenant-Colonel Dawson reported to me with seven companies of his command (the other three companies having reported at Campbell's Station). During the afternoon I threw a rifle-pit along the whole front of my command, reaching from the western salient of the fort on the left to Colonel Christ's line on the right.

During the 18th, the men were kept at work strengthening our position by felling timber and spreading the loose brush that had been thrown into heaps over the ground along the front of the line.

At 12 m. on the 19th, the cavalry had all been withdrawn from the front, and I was ordered to form a strong picket line along the line of the railroad to the wood, thence across the Kingston road. The right of the line was afterward thrown forward so as to take a direction nearly perpendicular to the railroad. On the afternoon of the 20th, General Ferrero ordered me to send out a regiment in the night—coming at such an hour as I might choose—to burn a large brick house situated on the Kingston road and occupied by the enemy's picket reserve. I accordingly ordered the Seventeenth Michigan to burn the house at 9 p. m., which the regiment succeeded in doing with a loss of but 2 killed.

The 21st was a rainy day, and but little was done by the command except to watch the enemy.

November 22, moved the One hundredth Pennsylvania round to the left into a pit running from the fort to the Kingston road.

At daylight, on the morning of the 24th, General Ferrero ordered me to send out one regiment to take and hold, if possible, a line of light rifle-pits thrown up by the enemy on the night of the 22d. Major Byington was ordered by me to take the Second Michigan and carry out the instructions I had received from the general. He carried the pit and held it until just one-half the number that he had taken out with him were either killed or wounded, when a large force of the enemy charging the pit he ordered the regiment to fall back to its camp.

The 25th, 26th, and 27th were comparatively quiet days, and until the evening of the 28th, when, at 11 p. m., a general advance was made by the enemy's line, and the pickets in my front, together with those of the brigade on my right and left, were driven in nearly to the works.

At daylight of the 29th an assault was made by the enemy on the western salient of Fort Sanders. When the assault was made there was of my command two companies of the Twentieth Michigan and one of the One hundredth Pennsylvania within the fort, and four companies of the Second Michigan in the ditch across the southwestern front of the fort. These companies maintained their position in the ditch until the enemy's column reached it, then retired within the fort and aided in repelling the assault. A truce suspended for the remainder of the day any further operations.

The regiments were kept the 30th within their pits ready for an anticipated attack from the enemy, but none was made.

December 1, 2, 3, and 4.—With the exception of picket firing, these were very quiet days.

December 5.—This morning the enemy had disappeared from my front, and during the day the men passed beyond our lines and into the deserted camps of the enemy; found and brought in as prisoners some 70 or 80 who had failed to get away with their retreating commands.

Here ends the operations of my command, initiated by the advance of the army from Lenoir's, followed by the falling back of the army from Lenoir's, followed by the falling back of the army to Campbell's Station; a battle at this point, thence a severe night march to Knoxville, through the siege of the latter place, and closing with the raising of the siege during the nights of December 4 and 5. The service performed was extremely severe, and the loss in officers and men heavy, as shown by the following table:

Command.	Killed.	Wounded.	Missing.	Total.
2d Michigan:				
Officers	2	5		7
Enlisted men	25	78	21	124
100th Pennsylvania:				
Officers		1		1
Enlisted men	4	10		14
20th Michigan:				
Officers	1	4		5
Enlisted men	4	41	17	62
17th Michigan:				
Officers	2	2	1	5
Enlisted men	12	46	26	84
Aggregate				302

For details of the part taken by the several regiments of my command in the operations of the twenty-one days from November 14 to December 5, inclusive, I refer you to the reports of regimental commanders, copies of which are forwarded with this report.

In closing you will allow me to add that it was the fortune of the

Third Brigade to be in the thickest of all this conflict, as its long list of casualties attests, and whether in covering a retreat, in making a night attack, in meeting an assault, or in the charge, all, both officers and men, have performed their duties assigned them with the most determined bravery, and have proved themselves reliable in any emergency.

Very respectfully, your obedient servant,

WM. HUMPHREY,
Colonel, Commanding Brigade.

Capt. GEORGE A. HICKS,
Assistant Adjutant-General.

No. 19.

Report of Maj. Cornelius Byington, Second Michigan Infantry.

HEADQUARTERS SECOND MICHIGAN INFANTRY,
Knoxville, Tenn., November 22, 1863.

SIR : In accordance with orders from brigade headquarters, I have to make the following report of the part taken by my regiment in the operations of the 14th, 15th, 16th, and 17th of November :

About noon of the 14th November, the regiment left its quarters near Lenoir's Station, Tenn., and marched to Huff's Ferry, arriving early in the evening, and bivouacked near that place.

Early in the morning of 15th November, commenced our march back toward Lenoir's Station, where we arrived about noon of the same day and bivouacked in the fields between the river and station. Here we remained about four hours. At the end of that time this regiment, together with the Seventeenth Michigan, moved out the Kingston road to the high ground about 250 yards in front of the station and formed in line, right in front, on the right of the road and perpendicular to it, the right of the regiment being near to and in support of a section of Roemer's battery. On this ground we remained till about 2 o'clock in the morning of the 16th, when we fell back to our former position in rear of the railroad and parallel to it.

About daybreak this regiment, with the Twentieth Michigan, left the station, moving back on the road toward Knoxville, leaving the Seventeenth Michigan behind us, our brigade forming the rear guard in the retreat. About 9 o'clock in the morning we halted in our march and formed in line of battle, right in front, on the right of the road facing toward Lenoir's Station, in rear of ——— Creek, one company being thrown out to skirmish on our right flank, the Twentieth Michigan being formed in line of battle on our left, to the left of road, in support of the Seventeenth Michigan, which had commenced skirmishing with the enemy on the other side of the creek. Here we remained a short time without exchanging shots with the enemy and then moved off by the right flank on our line of retreat, the skirmishers moving along with us on our left flank.

About 1 mile from ——— Creek we halted, formed in line of battle in the same manner as before on the brow of an elevation, the right of the regiment being in the woods, the left in the fields, and threw out one company to skirmish in front of the regimental line, the left of the line being in support of one section of Roemer's battery. From this point we fell back slowly in line of battle through the woods, our skirmishers exchanging shots with the enemy, who followed closely our retreating line. But pressing too closely, the line halted, delivered a few volleys, then slowly retreated. Alternately halting and retreating, we arrived at length at an open field, on the edge of which the line halted and opened a hot fire upon the enemy, who was not slow to return the compliment. Up to this time our loss was about 10 killed, wounded, and missing, 1 officer, Captain Farrand, being among the wounded.

Falling back from this line toward Campbell's Station, the regiment formed in line in the open field, the Twentieth Michigan on our left. Here I threw out one company to skirmish between our right flank and the woods on our right. This company was relieved by skirmishers from Twenty-third Michigan. The enemy endeavoring to flank us by throwing troops from the woods against our right flank, was handsomely met and foiled in his attempt. It was while holding this line that the regiment lost the heaviest. The enemy having the cover of the woods, picked off our men who were exposed in the open fields. We were relieved at length by troops of the Second Brigade and fell back to a hollow, a short distance in rear of the line just spoken of. Toward evening we left this hollow, fell back about a quarter of a mile and again formed in line on the right of the road, facing the station, the Seventeenth Michigan on our right, the Twentieth Michigan on our left in support of artillery which was posted on high ground in front of us. Here we remained until dusk, when we moved off by the right flank on the Knoxville road, arriving at Knoxville about 4 o'clock in the morning of the 17th.

My losses in the engagement of the 16th were 3 killed, 27 wounded (1 officer and 26 enlisted men, 1 enlisted man having since died), and 2 missing, making a total of 32. I took into the engagement 13 officers and 201 muskets. Both officers and men behaved with their usual gallantry, and when all behaved more than well I cannot mention one without doing manifest injustice to his companions.

I am, sir, very respectfully, your obedient servant,

CORNELIUS BYINGTON,
Major, Commanding Second Michigan Infantry.

ACTING ASSISTANT ADJUTANT-GENERAL,
Third Brigade.

No. 20.

Report of Capt. John V. Ruehle, Second Michigan Infantry.

HDQRS. SECOND REGIMENT MICHIGAN VOL. INFANTRY,
In Rifle-pits, at Knoxville, Tenn., November 24, 1863.

SIR: I have the honor to report that, pursuant to orders, this regiment, except those on picket, was taken out the rifle-pits at 7 o'clock this morning by Major Byington, and made a charge on the enemy's intrenched pickets.

After the regiment had reached the line of our own pickets, it was ordered to charge on a double-quick, and, moving to the left oblique, reached and cleared the enemy's pickets intrenched, that is, opposite the right of Benjamin's battery. The regiment was then ordered halt, and under cover of the rebel pit, held it from the enemy for nearly a half hour, the regiment during this time subject to heavy musketry from their front and left, and from rebel sharpshooters on their right flank.

It was here that the adjutant was instantly killed, Lieutenant Halpin mortally wounded, and soon followed the report that the major was wounded. After he was wounded he gave the order to fall back, though he himself was not to be got off the field.

I, being next in rank, took command. The shortest way to the railroad was taken, and on reaching the reserve of our pickets, the regiment was halted and I ordered Captain Moores to report at brigade headquarters for further orders; whereupon the regiment was ordered to their rifle-pits, having been gone about two hours. The officers and men behaved as well as they always did. Men commenced falling from the time we left our own picket line until we got back to the railroad. Captain Stevenson, with 24 men, 10 of whom, besides the captain, wounded, were disconnected from the regiment, and were obliged to remain with our pickets until dark, when they could with safety rejoin the regiment.

Very respectfully, your obedient servant,

JOHN V. RUEHLE,
Captain, Comdg. Second Regiment Michigan Vol. Infantry.

Lieut. B. H. BERRY,
Acting Assistant Adjutant-General.

No. 21.

Reports of Lieut. Col. Lorin L. Comstock, Seventeenth Michigan Infantry.

HDQRS. SEVENTEENTH REGIMENT MICHIGAN INFANTRY,
Knoxville, Tenn., November 21, 1863.

LIEUTENANT: In compliance with orders, I have the honor to make the following report of my command from the 14th to the 17th of this month:

On the morning of the 14th instant, we received orders at 7 o'clock to pack all baggage and be ready to move at a moment's notice, leaving nothing behind. At 12 m. the assembly sounded, and we moved off toward Loudon, following the Second Michigan till near 7 or 8 p. m., and halted in the woods, resting in line of battle in front of the enemy.

Between 3 and 4 o'clock the next morning, the 15th instant, we marched quietly back, left in front, toward Lenoir's, where we arrived near 12 m. Here we stacked arms and the men made coffee. Moved again between 3 and 4 p. m., and took position with the brigade back of the village, on the Kingston road, threw out skirmishers, and lay in line of battle till near daylight, when we fell back to the railroad, stacked arms, and rested while the troops passed to the rear. Here we received notice that our regiment was to form the rear guard and cover the retreat toward Knoxville. Three companies, under Captains Tyler and Phillips, and Lieutenant Billingsley, were thrown out as skirmishers, under the general supervision of Capt. F. W. Swift (acting major).

We were overtaken and attacked by the enemy at 9.30 a. m.
—— Creek, near Campbell's Station. Col. W. Humphrey, co
manding brigade, sent me orders to hold the enemy at all hazar
until the brigade could find a better position and form line. T
enemy crowded upon us in overwhelming numbers, and here w
the most trying part of the day. The men fought well and he
their ground until flanked upon both right and left. We then f
back in line of battle to the open field in front of the brigade, whe
Colonel Humphrey ordered us to the rear. We had marched bu
few rods when we received orders to form on the left of the Twe
tieth Michigan and extend skirmishers farther to the left to preve
being flanked. The enemy pressed boldly forward, and the who
brigade was soon hotly engaged. Still they crowded us, but
fought them determinedly. They were flanking us on both rig
and left, our skirmishers were falling back in much confusion b
fore their strong lines, and everything looked gloomy ; but Colon
Humphrey came to us just in time, and ordered me to charge a
drive the enemy back out of the woods. The men sprang forwa
with cheer after cheer, and, the Twentieth coming gallantly to o
aid, we drove them back out of the woods and over the field
double-quick.

Colonel Humphrey at once ordered us to march in retreat, a
under cover of the shock given by the charge we marched slow
and in good order to the large brick house in the open field. He
we filed in by the flank and crossed to the right of the road. T
enemy soon came down upon us from the woods and high weeds
front. Colonel Humphrey commanded "Fire by file," and after o
round he ordered us to the right of the brigade. Here we found t
enemy coming out of the woods again, but one well-aimed voll
sent them reeling back under cover. Here we lay in line until t
brigade was relieved by colonel commanding Second Brigade, wh
we fell back to the creek, stacked arms, and rested until 3.30 p. m
when we marched back to the rear of the batteries, stacked arm
and rested till dark. We then fell in and marched toward Kno
ville, reaching it on the morning of the 17th instant near 4 o'cloc

I cannot speak in too high terms of all the officers and men of n
regiment, but will mention some who are especially deserving
notice. I am greatly indebted to Capt. F. W. Swift (acting major
Capt. John Tyler, and Adjt. R. A. Watts, for their brave, gallan
and efficient conduct during the entire day. Captain Tyler, aft
being severely wounded, used every effort to inspire courage a
steadiness among the men until, faint and exhausted, he was bor
from the field. Among the bravest of the men were Color Serg
Joseph E. Brandle, who being wounded severely, a ball entering h
head, passing through the right eye, still held to the colors until o
dered to the rear by myself ; and Charles Thompson, carrier of t
State colors, was equally gallant, and called upon the men to sta
firmly by the standard he bore ; also Corpl. A. P. Curtis, who to
the colors from the sergeant and bore them gallantly through t
remainder of the day.

Very respectfully, your obedient servant,

L. L. COMSTOCK,
Lieutenant-Colonel, Commanding Regiment.

Lieut. B. H. BERRY,
Acting Assistant Adjutant-General.

HEADQUARTERS SEVENTEENTH MICHIGAN INFANTRY,
Camp near Knoxville, East Tenn., November 21, 1863.

LIEUTENANT : I have the honor to report that, in obedience to orders from brigade headquarters, I started with my command at an early hour last evening to effect the destruction of the brick building which served as a safe cover for the enemy's sharpshooters in front of our fort batteries. On reaching our line of skirmishers I found the building was occupied by the enemy. Awaiting a favorable moment, Companies A and F, under command of Lieutenants Archibald and Billingsley, were deployed as skirmishers, and moved rapidly forward, followed by the burning party of 5 picked men, with orders to rally on the building. Pending this movement the regiment was drawn up in front of the skirmish line of Colonel Morrison's brigade. Skirmishers were thrown out on each flank, and the regiment was moved forward on the double-quick to support the detachment selected to clear and burn the building. The enemy in and around the building, after firing one volley and a few random shots, fled precipitately. After seeing the brick building and the out-buildings in its immediate vicinity well fired, the regiment moved back in good order to the skirmish line, where we remained a short time, to prevent any successful attempt of the enemy to save the building. Seeing no attempt made, we retired, coming up the road on the left of the fort, to avoid the glare of the fires and the fire of the enemy's pickets. Just before reaching the rifle-pits the enemy opened fire on us with artillery, killing 2 and wounding 4. Owing to a sharp cross-fire from the enemy's pickets on our right, and a fire in the rear of that part of our line which, from some misapprehension, came from the pickets of this brigade, it was not deemed advisable to make any persistent attempt to destroy the log barn on the hill to the right of the buildings burned. With this unimportant exception, the object of the expedition was successfully attained.

To Capt. F. W. Swift, acting major, and Adjt. R. A. Watts much credit is due for their gallant and efficient conduct on the occasion, and it affords me great pleasure to report that the conduct of the officers and men of the entire command was entirely satisfactory.

In the death of Lieutenant Billingsley the regiment and service have sustained the loss of a brave and efficient officer. All the wounded, owing to the very slight nature of the wounds, are still on duty with their companies.

Inclosed is a list of casualties.*

Respectfully, your obedient servant,

L. L. COMSTOCK,
Lieut. Col., Comdg. Seventeenth Michigan Volunteers.

Lieut. B. H. BERRY, *Acting Assistant Adjutant-General.*

No. 22.

Reports of Maj. Byron M. Cutcheon, Twentieth Michigan Infantry.

HEADQUARTERS TWENTIETH MICHIGAN INFANTRY,
Fortifications before Knoxville, Tenn., November 21, 1863.

SIR : In accordance with orders from brigade headquarters of this date I have the honor to forward the following report of operations

---

*Shows 1 officer and 1 man killed and 4 men wounded.

of this command from the time it left Lenoir's Station till it cam
within these fortifications :

On Saturday, November 14, we broke camp at Lenoir's at day
light, and about noon, in common with the remainder of the divis
ion, took up a line of march to Huff's Ferry, where we arrived a
about dark the same night, a distance of about 10 miles. Tha
night we slept upon our arms, and the men suffered considerabl
from the cold and rain.

Before daylight the next morning the regiment was again upo:
the road, and arrived again at Lenoir's at about noon, after a ver
tiresome march, on account of the bad· condition of the road fron
the recent rains.

At about 2 p. m. this regiment was ordered to return about 3 mile
upon the Loudon road to the point where the Telegraph road turn
off toward Kingston, and hold the forks of the roads until the Sec
ond Division should have passed us and then fall back coverin;
them.

The regiment had nearly reached the forks of the road when it wa
overtaken by an aide from Brigadier-General Potter, commandin;
Ninth Army Corps, who ordered it back to the point where the rail
road and highway separate, 1 mile from Lenoir's, where we took u:
a position on a slight eminence and formed in line of battle across th
highway and railroad.

The command remained here until the Second Division had passe(
and the stragglers had ceased to come in, when we moved to th
front and took a position in line with the remainder of the brigad
on the Kingston road. We had scarcely stacked arms when we wer
ordered again to the Loudon road to protect the left flank. By di
rection of Lieutenant-Colonel Smith, then commanding, I deploye·
four companies as skirmishers, their right connecting with th
Eighth Michigan Infantry on the crest of the hill and their lef
resting upon the railroad about three-fourths of a mile from the sta
tion. The remaining six companies were held in reserve, and all la:
upon their arms without sleeping or taking off their knapsacks.

Between the hours of 3 and 4 a. m. Monday, November 16, th·
regiment was ordered in, and after assembling the skirmishers i
rejoined the brigade near the station, where it lay until daylight
Meanwhile Company C was detailed to assist in destroying the train
of the Twenty-third Army Corps. It may be proper here to stat·
that most of the baggage of the officers of the regiment was destroyed
By whose order I am not aware.

The Third Brigade being the rear guard, the position of the regi
ment was next to the rear. We had scarcely left the station whe:
skirmishing commenced, and the enemy followed us closely, keepin;
most of the time in sight. No actual collision occurred until w·
reached a point about a mile from the junction of the Kingston witl
the Loudon road. Here a stand was made, the Twentieth being ii
line upon a hill to the left of the road, supporting a piece of artillery
Company B, Capt. C. T. Allen, which company had hitherto beer
acting as flankers, was now deployed as skirmishers to the right o:
the road in the woods. After a brief stand at this point the regi
ment was ordered back, and moved back by the left flank and agaiı
took position to the left of the road on a high hill, the Second
Michigan Infantry being on the right of the road, supporting a piec·
of artillery. At this point Company B retook its place in line, anc
Company D, Capt. C. B. Grant, was ordered to the front as skir

mishers, to cover the retreat of the Seventeenth Michigan Infantry, now falling back after a heavy skirmish.

When the Seventeenth Michigan Infantry had passed around our left flank and regained the road the regiment again fell back gradually, the skirmishers covering the movement, until it gained the edge of a piece of woods and formed, its right resting on the road and its left supported by the Seventeenth Michigan Infantry, which by this time had reformed on our left. The enemy advanced rapidly and attempted to outflank our left. The line had scarcely been formed when the regiment met its greatest loss in the death of Lieutenant-Colonel Smith, commanding. He fell pierced through the brain by a bullet, and expired instantly, without a word or a groan, while bravely encouraging the men and setting them an example of coolness and intrepidity. I cannot forbear here to testify to his efficiency as an officer, his faithfulness and courage as a soldier, and his worth as a man.

On the fall of Lieutenant-Colonel Smith the undersigned immediately assumed command. Notwithstanding the shock produced by the fall of their leader the regiment did not waver for a moment, but seemed to rally with new vigor and increased steadiness. The men were falling fast, when the regiment was again ordered back. We now fell back to near the junction of the Kingston and Loudon road, when the Seventeenth Michigan Infantry, being ordered to charge and drive back the enemy's skirmishers, the three left companies of the Twentieth, supposing the order to be general, charged with them, and did good service. We now fell back from the woods through a wide, open field, receiving a volley from the rebel lines at long range.

We next took position on the right of the road, a short distance in front of the village of Campbell's Station, and Company D retook its place in line, and a detail of 2 from each company, under Lieutenant Blood, Company D, was made to relieve them. Here we remained exposed to a galling flank fire until about 2 p. m., when we were relieved by the Second Brigade, after being constantly under fire for four hours.

After lying in reserve until near night we took a new position in rear of Campbell's Station, and at dark took up a line of march to this place, which we reached at about 5 a. m. on the morning of the 17th, exceedingly worn-out, weary, and yet ready for the labors before us, having marched 24 miles and been under fire eight hours out of the twenty-four.

Of the conduct and fate of Lieutenant-Colonel Smith I have already spoken, and it is only needful to say that every officer and man, so far as I observed, did his whole duty. The company commanders report that the conduct of their men was so uniformly good that they cannot specify instances. I will only speak of Capt. G. C. Barnes, who assisted me in command of the regiment, who was at all times prompt and efficient, and Captain Grant and Lieutenant Blood, who commanded the skirmishers, who exposed themselves freely and handled their men well.

I append hereto a list* of casualties, and may add that since our arrival in the fortifications we have lost 1 officer and 1 man wounded—Capt. F. Porter, Company E, and Private W. Filkins, Company B.

---

* Nominal list (omitted) shows 1 officer and 2 men killed; 1 officer and 29 men wounded, and 4 men missing.

Notwithstanding the hardships endured, the spirits and health o
the men are good, and they are still ready to undergo whatever may
be necessary to secure the success of our arms.

Very respectfully, your obedient servant,

BYRON M. CUTCHEON,
Major, Commanding Twentieth Michigan Infantry.

Lieut. B. H. BERRY,
Acting Assistant Adjutant-General.

—

HEADQUARTERS TWENTIETH MICHIGAN INFANTRY,
Fort Sanders, Knoxville, East Tenn., December 2, 1863.

LIEUTENANT: In accordance with circular of this date from brigade headquarters, I have the honor to forward the following report
of the part taken in the action of the night of the 28th and morning
of the 29th ultimo by my command:

At the time of the first attack, Lieut. C. S. Wortley, Company K,
of this regiment, was on picket with 35 men and 5 non-commissioned
officers in front of the southwest salient of the fort. When the attack was first made the men discharged their pieces, but were overpowered by numbers and obliged to fall back upon the reserve,
which in turn also was forced back. About half a dozen men came
back to the regiment, of whom 3 were slightly wounded; all but 1 I
sent back to their posts. When the picket line was re-established
Lieutenant Wortley succeeded in collecting 27 of his men, and established them upon the new line. Among the missing was a large
proportion of non-commissioned officers. Immediately after the
attack in front of the fort one was also made on that part of the line in
front of this regiment, which lies on the farther side of the railroad.
Though nothing could be seen, the command "Forward to the railroad" was distinctly heard from the rebel officers. Our men stood
their ground but a short time, and fell back across the railroad.
Immediately the firing ceased, I ordered several men at different
points along the line to make their way carefully to the railroad and
report the condition of affairs. They soon returned, and reported
that they had been to the railroad; that there was no enemy this side,
but that there seemed to be about a regiment on the other side,
intrenching along the bank of the railroad. This I reported to the
colonel commanding the brigade, who directed me to throw forward
vedettes to the railroad, with picks and spades, and there intrench
themselves.

Accordingly, I detailed 20 men, under charge of Lieutenant Lounsberry, Company I, who deployed his men in front of the works and
moved forward to the railroad. Within 3 rods of the latter they were
met by a heavy volley from a line of skirmishers which had crossed
the railroad. Lieutenant Lounsberry with his men returned the fire,
and fell back a few rods to the brow of the hill, with the loss of 1
man severely wounded, and 1 missing, supposed to be wounded and
captured. Lieutenant Lounsberry then intrenched himself on the
brow of the hill, which position he held the remainder of the night,
and during the fight of the morning.

At the time the pickets were driven in from beyond the railroad
one piece of the Second New York Artillery was taken from the
third redoubt and fired several times over the heads of the men in

the rifle-pits. One of the shells exploded at the muzzle of the gun, instantly killing Corporal Haight, of Company H, and wounding (probably mortally) Private Van Atter, Company K. We were also annoyed by shells from the enemy's battery on the south side of the river. One of these struck in the rifle-pit, killing 1 man and wounding another. Immediately after the first attack, by orders from brigade headquarters, Company C was sent into the fort and took position in the salient near General Ferrero's headquarters. There they remained, doing excellent service during the subsequent engagement. When the final attack was made at daylight, a part of the pickets, under Lieutenant Wortley, also took position in the fort, and fought bravely. In consequence of the lay of the ground it was impossible for any of our line to the right of the first redoubt to see the enemy, but Companies A and D, on the left, occupying the right wing of the fort, had an excellent position, commanding the whole of the west face of the fort. They kept up a rapid and effectual fire throughout the fight, firing nearly 40 rounds to the man.

Being myself at the center of the regiment, I did not witness the conduct of the men, but it is reported by the officers in charge to have been excellent ; every man stood to his post and behaved with the utmost activity and gallantry. I append hereto a list of our losses.

*   *   *   *   *   *   *

Recapitulation : Killed, 2 ; wounded, 8; missing, 13.   Total, 23.

It may be proper for me here to state that Capt. W. D. Wiltsie and Private Sevy, Company E, wounded in the pits on the 24th and 25th ultimo, died of their wounds on the 28th.

I have the honor to be, your most obedient servant,

BYRON M. CUTCHEON,
Major, Commanding Twentieth Michigan Infantry.

Lieut. B. H. BERRY,
Acting Assistant Adjutant-General.

No. 23.

Report of Lieut. Col. Mathew M. Dawson, One hundredth Pennsylvania Infantry.

HDQRS. ONE HUNDREDTH PENNSYLVANIA VOLUNTEERS,
Near Knoxville, Tenn., November 21, 1863.

SIR : I have the honor to report the operations of the One hundredth Pennsylvania Volunteers, from the 14th to the 21st of November, 1863:

Upon the breaking up of camp at Lenoir's Station, Tenn., the regiment was detailed as guard for the trains of the First Division, Ninth Army Corps. Subsequently a detail to load forage was called for, and Companies A, F, and D, under command of Capt. Thomas J. Hamilton, were detailed for that purpose. The remaining seven companies soon after moved with the train and arrived with it at Knoxville, Tenn., on the 16th November. The companies which had been detailed at Lenoir's remained at that place until 3 o'clock of the 16th November, when Captain Hamilton, having understood that he had been relieved, marched, via Concord and Campbell's Station, to rejoin the regiment, and at the latter place was halted by an aide of General Burnside, and upon reporting to Capt. George A.

Hicks, assistant adjutant-general, First Division, Ninth Army Corps, was assigned to duty with the Second Brigade of that division, Col. B. C. Christ commanding. He participated in the operations of tha brigade until the arrival of the Third Brigade, First Division, when he reported to Colonel Humphrey, its commander, and was under his command during the greater part of the action at Campbell's Station, Tenn. On the arrival of the brigade at Knoxville, Tenn. the regiment reported to Colonel Humphrey for duty.

I have the honor, lieutenant, to be, very respectfully, your obedient servant,

M. M. DAWSON,
Lieutenant-Colonel, Commanding Regiment.

Lieut. B. H. BERRY,
Acting Assistant Adjutant-General.

No. 24.

Report of Col. John F. Hartranft, Fifty-first Pennsylvania Infantry, commanding Second Division.

HEADQUARTERS SECOND DIVISION, NINTH ARMY CORPS,
Knoxville, Tenn., November 24, 1863.

COLONEL: I have to report that at about 9 p. m. on the 23d instant, the enemy advanced in force sufficient to compel the skirmishers on our front, at the intersection of their line with the Clinton road, to fall back. The enemy immediately occupied this point, and during the night constructed rifle-pits for the defense of their skirmishers.

On the morning of the 24th, at 7 o'clock, in obedience to the orders of the commanding general, I sent a force, consisting of the Twenty-first Massachusetts Volunteers and Forty-eighth Pennsylvania Volunteers, about 400 men, the whole under command of Lieutenant-Colonel Hawkes, with instructions to form in rear of the line of skirmishers (as existing at that time, forming almost a right angle with the original line), and to advance quietly and rapidly upon the enemy. They did so, and re-established the old line without much resistance.

The officers and men engaged behaved gallantly, taking 6 prisoners.

The following is a list of the casualties: Killed, 5 enlisted men; wounded, 2 officers and 11 enlisted men; missing, 4 enlisted men. Total, 22.

Very respectfully, your obedient servant,

J. F. HARTRANFT,
Colonel, Commanding.

Lieut. Col. N. BOWEN,
Assistant Adjutant-General:

No. 25.

Reports of Brig. Gen. Mahlon D. Manson, U. S. Army, commanding Twenty-third Army Corps.

HEADQUARTERS TWENTY-THIRD ARMY CORPS,
*13 Miles from Knoxville and 4 Miles from
Blain's Cross-Roads, December 8, 1863.*

COLONEL: I did not overtake the command last night until it had arrived, with the Ninth Army Corps, at Flat Creek, near this place.

I found General White here with his division. General Hascall, from some unknown cause, left the advancing column at the forks of the roads leading to Rutledge and Strawberry Plains, 4 miles this side of Knoxville, and took the right-hand road to Armstrong's Ferry, where, with his division, he crossed the river. He also took with him the supply train of my entire command, which had been directed to follow in his rear. I have ordered him to recross the river at Strawberry Plains.

I know nothing of the enemy. General Shackelford is about 2 miles in my front.

I am, colonel, very respectfully, your obedient servant,

MAHLON D. MANSON,
Brigadier-General, Commanding.

Lieutenant-Colonel RICHMOND,
Assistant Adjutant-General.

—

HEADQUARTERS TWENTY-THIRD ARMY CORPS,
Near Chesterfield, December 8, 1863—2.15 p. m.

COLONEL : General Hascall was this morning at Strawberry Plains. He notified me that he would cross the men on the railroad bridge and the wagons and artillery some little distance below. I learn from a contraband that the rebel force encamped last night at Powder Spring Gap, which is 12 miles beyond this. The infantry had all passed a day or two ago. General Shackelford moved early this morning. General Potter moved at 12 m. to Blain's Cross-Roads. Inclosed please find dispatch from General Shackelford. Hascall will certainly join me some time this afternoon.

Respectfully, yours,

MAHLON D. MANSON,
Brigadier-General, Commanding.

Lieutenant-Colonel RICHMOND,
Assistant Adjutant-General.

[Inclosure.]

BLAIN'S CROSS-ROADS,
December 8, 1863.

General MANSON,
Commanding Twenty-third Army Corps :

GENERAL : I learn from a reliable citizen that General Armstrong left this place at 11.30 o'clock on yesterday, and last night, with the infantry, was to encamp at the Powder Spring Gap road, 7 miles from here. The citizen heard General Armstrong direct a colonel to encamp his men on the river road about 4 miles to the right of this place.

Respectfully,

J. M. SHACKELFORD,
Brigadier-General.

P. S.—One regiment of the enemy's cavalry camped here last night. The citizen says the infantry left at 1 o'clock on Sunday. We are now 2 miles above the cross-roads.

HEADQUARTERS TWENTY-THIRD ARMY CORPS,
Haines' House, near Brice's Mill, December 8, 1863—5 p. m.

COLONEL : I have the honor to inform you that General Hascall's division has arrived and gone into camp at this place, and that my whole command is in readiness to move at a moment's notice. I shall, in accordance with instructions, await orders from the major-general commanding.

The Ninth Corps moved forward at 12 or 1 o'clock to-day, and will probably encamp to-night 8 or 10 miles from here, if their orders are to proceed that far and they meet with no opposition. General Shackelford is in front of the Ninth Corps some distance, and was, I am informed, joined this afternoon by the forces of Colonel Foster from above. My troops are in good condition for marching, and forage for the animals is abundant. General Shackelford arrived at Powder Spring Gap at 11.30 a. m. to-day.

I have the honor to be, very respectfully, your obedient servant,
MAHLON D. MANSON,
Brigadier-General, Commanding.

Lieutenant-Colonel RICHMOND, *Asst. Adjt. Gen.*

P. S.—The railroad bridge at Strawberry Plains, which was partially burned by the rebels, can be repaired in three days by a regiment of men.

Since writing the above have received the inclosed dispatch from General Shackelford.

[Inclosure.]

HEADQUARTERS CAVALRY CORPS,
Suburbs Rutledge, [*December* 8, 1863]—1.45 p. m.

Brigadier-General MANSON,
Commanding Twenty-third Army Corps:

GENERAL : We have just reached here. Captured 15 prisoners in the edge of the town. The enemy's cavalry are in line of battle, in plain view, in the other end of the town. General Longstreet, with his command, left here this morning. Of the truth of this there can be no question, as I learn from both prisoners and citizens. McLaws' headquarters were at the house I occupy, and he left here at 7 a. m. They left this point with the expectation of reaching Bean's Station to-night. I am waiting for my corps to get up before I make any further move.

. General Ransom's command also left here this morning.

Respectfully,

J. M. SHACKELFORD,
Brigadier-General.

No. 26.

*Report of Brig. Gen. Julius White, U. S. Army, commanding
Second Division.*

HDQRS. SECOND DIVISION, TWENTY-THIRD ARMY CORPS,
Knoxville, November 25, 1863.

CAPTAIN : I have the honor to submit the following report of the operations of a part of this command from the 13th to the 17th instant :

On the evening of the 13th, the Second Brigade, together with Comanies F and G, of the Eleventh Kentucky Volunteer Infantry, were ncamped on the north side of the Tennessee River, opposite Loudon, icketing the line from Blair's Ford to Huff's Ferry, about 6 miles elow Loudon, by the route on the north side of the river.

The First Brigade, under Colonel Mott, of the One hundred and ighteenth Ohio, had been marched to and stationed at Kingston ome days previously, by order of Major-General Burnside, comnanding the Army of the Ohio. At about 7 o'clock on the evening f the 13th it was reported that the enemy at Loudon exhibited nusual signs of activity, and soon afterward the picket at Huff's 'erry reported that the enemy had crossed in boats at that point in ufficient force to compel their retirement to avoid capture, and that bridge was in process of construction by the enemy.

The available men of the mounted infantry were at once disatched, under Capt. Henry Curtis, jr., assistant adjutant-general f the division, with orders to ascertain the truth of the report. He oon confirmed the previous statements, adding that a considerable orce had already crossed the river.

Colonel Chapin, commanding the brigade, was then directed to end a regiment (the Twenty-third Michigan Infantry) and a section f Henshaw's battery to oppose the crossing of the enemy and the onstruction of the bridge. This was about 11 p. m.

Shortly afterward I received an order by telegraph from Majoreneral Burnside to prepare my command to march toward Lenoir's tation at a moment's notice, and thereupon countermanded the rder to the detachment moving toward Huff's Ferry, and directed 'aptain Curtis to remain at the position held by him as long as ossible, observing the enemy's movements, and to cover the withrawal of the brigade, if ordered to march.

The exceeding darkness of the night prevented Captain Curtis rom obtaining a view of the bridge, and the presence of a heavier orce of the enemy prevented him from a close approach. He evertheless maintained his position, sending frequent reports, all onfirmatory of the previous statements.

Just before daylight I received an order from Major-General Burnside, directing the command to be marched to Lenoir's Station t once. General Burnside arrived at that point soon after my rrival, and subsequently directed the march of the command back o the vicinity of Huff's Ferry, supported by a division of the Ninth Army Corps, under Brigadier-General Ferrero.

On arriving at the meeting-house, about 3 miles from the ferry, he enemy's pickets were encountered and driven in. Colonel Chapin was directed to deploy two regiments, supported by a third, nd move forward on the enemy.

The Thirteenth Kentucky and One hundred and seventh Illinois nfantry were advanced, supported by the One hundred and eleventh Ohio, and moved briskly forward, driving the enemy from the voods in our immediate front. The nature of the ground over vhich the enemy retreated wholly precluded the use of artillery, nd it was therefore placed in position near the road, supported by he Twenty-third Michigan Infantry.

The enemy made repeated attempts to withstand the rapid advance f Colonel Chapin's command, but were as often routed and driven back. Their final stand was made about sunset, when they took osition on the crest of a wooded hill, in rear of an open field, which ronted the right of their line. From this position they opened a

severe fire, aided by their artillery, situated on the opposite side c
the river.

It became necessary, in order to dislodge the enemy, to charg
across this field or move by the flank around it. The latter move
ment would relinquish the protection which the river afforded t
my left flank, and greatly prolong the time the men would be unde
a fire, to which they could not respond.

The charge in line was therefore ordered. With a hearty chee
the men crossed the field at double-quick step in the face of a gallin
fire, dislodged the enemy, and drove him in disorder from the field.

The Thirteenth Kentucky was most exposed, and consequentl
suffered heavily in this gallant charge, the enemy's fire being chiefl
directed upon that regiment.

Night fell at this time, and the density of the woods and extrem
darkness of the night preventing farther pursuit of the enemy, th
command was halted on the hill from which he had been driven
The fighting had been almost continuous for 2 miles. Prisoner
were taken from different regiments of Longstreet's corps, fror
whom it was ascertained that the enemy's strength was equal if no
superior to ours, which was engaged.

The loss of the enemy was unknown, as night prevented an exam
ination of the field. It was known to be considerable, however.

At daylight on the morning of the 15th the command was ordere
to move back to Lenoir's, covering the rear of General Ferrero'
division. The One hundred and eleventh Ohio Infantry, with a sec
tion of Henshaw's battery, was detailed as rear guard, and wer
detained by a very heavy hill, where it became necessary to doubl
the teams and move all the guns and caissons of the artillery one a
a time to the summit. All had been so moved up except one caisson
when the enemy, who had approached covertly, attacked in heav
force. Colonel Chapin immediately prepared the One hundred an
eleventh Ohio to receive him, and soon repulsed the attack ; but th
numbers of the enemy increasing rapidly, his threatening move
ments on both flanks compelled the abandonment of the caisson a
the foot of the hill. The One hundred and eleventh Ohio, with th
artillery, was in position on the summit, where the progress of th
enemy was checked. Meanwhile, the Thirteenth Kentucky Infantr
and One hundred and seventh Illinois Infantry had been faced abou
and moved back to the support of the One hundred and eleventl
Ohio, but the manifest disadvantage of the ground did not warran
a general engagement for the recovery of the caisson, and which, i
successful, would have been at great loss of life.

The command then moved forward to a point opposite Loudon
where the duty of rear guard was assigned to Colonel Sigfried's di
vision, of the Ninth Army Corps. The march was continued to Le
noir's Station, where we bivouacked in line for the night.

On the morning of the 16th, in obedience to Field Orders, No. 81
from headquarters Army of the Ohio, a copy of which is herewitl
submitted, all the wagons of the division, brigade, and ammunitior
train, together with the camp furniture and equipage of the com
mand and the officers' baggage, was destroyed, in order that the
draught animals might be used in moving the artillery of both corps
the state of the roads rendering it impossible to move it otherwise.
The march was then continued toward Knoxville.

The picket line was ordered to remain in position until the with
drawal of the Ninth Corps, and the officer of the day, Major Brooks

f the One hundred and seventh Illinois Infantry, was directed to eport to Brigadier-General Ferrero for orders in the matter. Comany B, of the One hundred and eleventh Ohio, which, under command of Lieutenant Norris, had been detailed and posted at a point utside the line during the night, was, by some error, not notified of he withdrawal of the line, and were captured by the enemy. This ss will be made the subject of investigation by a competent tribu-al and a further report made thereon.

Arriving in the vicinity of Campbell's Station, where the junction f the Loudon and Kingston roads to Knoxville occurs, I was directed o place my command in position at a point beyond the junction by 1ajor-General Burnside.

The Second Brigade was accordingly ordered into line of battle, :s left and center resting on the Knoxville road at a point where it vas somewhat elevated above the country around. Henshaw's and he Twenty-first Indiana Batteries being placed in position at this oint, and the right wing, consisting of the Thirteenth Kentucky nd Twenty-third Michigan Infantry, advanced about 200 yards, ere deployed to the right of the road and skirmishers thrown to he front of the entire line.

The Ninth Corps, which had been skirmishing with the enemy on nd between the Loudon and Kingston roads, now formed in rear of ur line, and advanced a brigade to a position on our right and two egiments on our left flank. The enemy advanced in three lines; his dvance, being mostly clothed in United States uniform, deceived us ntil he had approached within easy musket range, when Colonel Cha-in was directed to open fire. The artillery and the right wing were oon engaged. The enemy was soon compelled to seek the cover of a avine in front and of the woods on either flank. A second attempt o drive our men from this position failed. Subsequently the enemy pened an artillery fire from several batteries of guns of heavier and onger range than those of the Second Brigade, when, finding that ur ammunition had been expended, with the exception of a few ounds, and that the batteries were suffering from a fire to which hey could not respond, they were directed to take position in rear f the heavier batteries of the Ninth Army Corps and await orders. 'he infantry held its position until ordered to cover the withdrawal f the Ninth Corps from the field to a new position about 1 mile to he rear, where the Second Brigade was ordered to form on the left f the line.

This movement was executed in the most perfect order. The Jinth Corps moved off the field at the ordinary quickstep, with its olumns well closed up and its front handsomely aligned.

Colonel Chapin's lines were formed, skirmishers deployed and 1oved forward, with each line in its proper position, frequently alting and facing about to the enemy, not a man hurrying his step r otherwise disfiguring the movement, although subjected to a evere fire from the enemy's artillery, which had been rapidly ad-anced to short range.

On reaching the new position, the line was formed on the left of he Ninth Corps, which was soon after withdrawn, and resumed the 1arch on Knoxville.

The Second Brigade was again intrusted with the duty of pro-ecting the rear, which position it held till the arrival of the entire orce at Knoxville, on the morning of the 17th.

Prior to resuming the march, however, the enemy charged on the

left flank, but Colonel Chapin promptly changed front with th
One hundred and seventh Illinois by a right wheel, and deliverin
its fire with such good effect as to cause the rapid retreat of th
enemy, who made no further attempt.

The losses of the Second Brigade during the three days were a
follows: Killed and mortally wounded, 19; wounded, 91; capture
(on picket duty), 53; missing, 13.   Total, 176.

For a detailed statement of the losses, I respectfully refer to th
report of Colonel Chapin and that of the chief surgeon of the br:
gade, which are herewith submitted.   Citizens state the loss of th
enemy at Campbell's Station to be 91 killed and over 300 wounded

I cannot close this report without bearing testimony to the ur
flinching steadiness and bravery of the officers and men of th
Second Brigade, as well as to their cheerful endurance of thre
days' almost unremitting toil.

The meager list of missing is of itself an eloquent testimonial t
the character of the brigade, considering the great hardships of th
march, and the fact that the list was composed almost entirely c
men weakened by sickness, for whom there was no transportatior
To furnish a list of those who distinguished themselves would be t
hand you the muster-rolls.   No instance of misconduct or neglect c
duty came under my observation, and but one has been reported
It would afford me great pleasure, would the limits of this repoi
permit me, to mention the names of all those who deserve honorabl
notice.   It is due to the several regiments and batteries that at leas
their commanding officers should be mentioned by name, and I ma
truthfully say that they are representatives of the merits of thei
respective commands, including officers of the line, non-commis
sioned officers, and privates.

Col. M. W. Chapin, commanding the brigade, executed all th
orders he received promptly and correctly, and when left to his ow:
discretion his acts were distinguished for ability.

Col. W. E. Hobson, Lieutenant-Colonel Estes, and Major Duncan
of the Thirteenth Kentucky; Colonel Kelly, late of the One hun
dred and seventh Illinois, who continued in command at the reques
of the officers of his regiment, notwithstanding his resignation ha(
been tendered and accepted; Lieutenant-Colonel Lowry and Majo
Brooks, of the same regiment; Major Sherwood, in command of th
One hundred and eleventh Ohio, and Captain Norris, acting major
and Maj. W. W. Wheeler, in command of the Twenty-third Michi
gan Infantry, all acquitted themselves honorably and with credit t
themselves and the several States from which they hail.   The officer
and men of Henshaw's battery and the Twenty-fourth Indiana Bat
tery, Captain Sims, exhibited all the qualities requisite to the effi
cient use of that important arm, and contributed largely to the suc
cessful resistance of the enemy's attack at Campbell's Station.

The officers of my personal staff—Capt. Henry Curtis, jr., assistan
adjutant-general; Capt. F. G. Hentig, commissary of subsistence
Capt. James A. Lee, assistant commissary of musters; Lieutenan
Lowrie, chief of ordnance, and Lieutenant Edmiston, aide-de-camp—
were always present, rendering valuable aid, and often greatly ex
posed.

Surg. J. G. Hatchitt, chief surgeon of the division, and Surg. L
A. Brewer, chief surgeon of the Second Brigade, devoted themselve:
assiduously to the treatment and care of the wounded, evincing a
warm interest in their welfare and a strong desire to perform thei
duty on the field, as well as in hospital.

Conspicuous acts of gallantry on the part of M. W. Chapin, commanding the brigade; Col. W. E. Hobson, commanding the Thirteenth Kentucky; Colonel Kelly, late of the One hundred and eventh Illinois; Maj. W. W. Wheeler, of the Twenty-third Michigan Infantry; Capt. Henry Curtis, jr., assistant adjutant-general of the division, and Lieutenant Price, of the Eleventh Kentucky Mounted Infantry, came under my personal observation, except in the case of Lieutenant Price, which was reported by a third person.

I have the honor to be, your obedient servant,

JULIUS WHITE,
Brigadier-General, Comdg. Second Div., 23d Army Corps.

No. 27.

*Itinerary of the Second Division.**

December 7, the Second Brigade marched from Knoxville and encamped near Flat Creek.

December 9, marched to within 7 miles of Rutledge and encamped.

December 17, in the night marched back to Blain's Cross-Roads and encamped.

December 18, the First Brigade arrived from Kingston and rejoined at Blain's Cross-Roads.

December 24, in the night marched to Strawberry Plains. [Brigadier-General White relieved in command by Brigadier-General Manson.]

December 25, marched to New Market.

December 26, marched to Mossy Creek, at which point an engagement took place on the 29th, resulting in the defeat of the enemy. Two regiments of the First Brigade participated in the action and behaved with gallantry.

December 25, in the night the Second Brigade marched from Blain's Cross-Roads to Strawberry Plains, where it has since been encamped.

No. 28.

Report of Col. Samuel R. Mott, One hundred and eighteenth Ohio Infantry, commanding First Brigade.

HDQRS. FIRST BRIG., SECOND DIV., 23D ARMY CORPS,
Kingston, Tenn., December 3, 1863.

COLONEL: I have the honor to report that this brigade was attacked on the 24th ultimo at this place by General Wheeler's force of cavalry and mounted infantry, numbering from 8,000 to 12,000 men, with eight pieces of artillery.

The attack was made at daylight, and after a brisk engagement of seven hours' duration the enemy was handsomely whipped and driven back with a loss of 250 killed, wounded, and prisoners. Among their killed was Colonel Russell, of the Third [Fourth] Alabama, and 2 other colonels were wounded. Wheeler retreated to Loudon, where he destroyed a large amount of quartermaster and commissary stores and ammunition, a large train of cars, three engines, and three bat-

---

* From return for December.

teries of artillery, alleging to citizens that he was pursued by Rosecrans' whole army.

Too much cannot be said in praise of the cool and determined
bravery of the officers and men under my command. Each one did
his whole duty. As an instance, I may mention the case of Captain
Murphey, of the Sixteenth Kentucky, who with a single company
charged a rebel regiment and demanded their surrender. Indeed,
there were many instances of both officers and men performing
prodigies of valor.

Our loss was 15 wounded, 1 of whom has since died.

I have the honor to be, colonel, with high consideration, your
obedient servant,

SAMUEL R. MOTT,
Colonel, Comdg. First Brig., Second Div., 23d Army Corps.

Col. LEWIS RICHMOND, *Assistant Adjutant-General.*

No. 29.

Itinerary of the First Brigade.*

December 4, we marched from Kingston, Tenn., to Lackey's plantation, a distance of 20 miles. Encamped for the night.

December 5, we were ordered to Loudon, Tenn., a distance of 8
miles.

December 8, we were ordered to Knoxville, Tenn. We marched
20 miles. Encamped on Rev. Mr. Parks' farm.

December 9, we marched 12 miles, encamping 1 mile east of Knoxville.

December 11, we marched 9 miles. Encamped 9 miles from Knoxville, on the Rutledge road.

December 16, we marched to Blain's Cross-Roads, which is 18 miles
from Knoxville.

December 25, we marched from Blain's Cross-Roads to New Market,
a distance of 16 miles; also marched to Mossy Creek, 4 miles from
New Market.

December 29, we were attacked by the combined forces of Martin, Armstrong, and Wheeler [Morgan.] The fight commenced at
9 a. m., ending at 7 p. m. The loss of the enemy was much heavier
than ours.

No. 30.

*Report of Col. Marshal W. Chapin, Twenty-third Michigan In-
fantry, commanding Second Brigade.*

HDQRS. SECOND BRIG., SECOND DIV., 23D ARMY CORPS,
Knoxville, Tenn., November 20, 1863.

SIR: I have the honor to report the conduct of the troops under
my command during three separate engagements with the enemy, and
also of their holding the enemy in check and covering the rear of the
army in the retreat from Huff's Ferry to Lenoir's Station, a distance
of 10 miles, and from Campbell's Station to Knoxville, a distance of
15 miles.

---

* From return for December.

On the night of the 13th of November, in accordance with an order
rom Brigadier-General White, I sent the Twenty-third Michigan
Volunteer Infantry, under Major Wheeler, and one section of Hen-
haw's battery, Illinois Light Artillery, under Lieutenant Putnam,
) make reconnaissance to Huff's Ferry, which they did, returning
) camp about daylight, bringing the information that the enemy,
nder Longstreet, were in force at Huff's Ferry, and throwing a pon-
)on across the river.

Soon after daylight General White ordered me to march my bri-
ade to Lenoir's. Here we rested a short time, and then, with the
inth Army Corps, marched back toward Loudon and on toward
Iuff's Ferry, my brigade taking the advance.

When within about 2½ miles of Huff's Ferry, General White or-
ered me to advance two regiments and attack the enemy. I ordered
p the Thirteenth Kentucky Infantry and the One hundred and sev-
nth Illinois Infantry, throwing out skirmishers ahead. The two
egiments were soon separated by the lay of the ground. Our skir-
ushers were soon engaged and driving the enemy. This continued
or about 2 miles, when the enemy came to a stand in the woods at the
op of a hill. Up to this time both regiments had been about equally
ngaged, but now the enemy seemed to concentrate in front of the
hirteenth Kentucky. The summit of the hill, being wooded, made
ood cover for the rebels, and the side of the hill toward the Thir-
enth Kentucky, being bare, afforded no cover for our men, who were
ill in the woods at the foot. This was the position of affairs when
eneral White came up, the firing being only moderate. He imme-
iately ordered me to move the regiment forward into the open field,
here they could get better sight of the enemy. This was immedi-
tely done, but we soon found that we were losing many men with-
ut being able to drive the enemy. The One hundred and seventh
linois having come up, General White ordered me to have the two
egiments charge up the hill and drive them out. This was done in
aost gallant style by both regiments, the One hundred and seventh
linois through the woods on the right and the Thirteenth Kentucky
p the bare hill in the face of a most galling fire, driving the enemy
ff the hill and taking possession ourselves, which position, it being
bout dark, we held till morning.

On the morning of the 15th, I was notified that the column would
etire toward Lenoir's, and was ordered to take three regiments of
nfantry and one section of artillery and cover the retreat. I took
he Thirteenth Kentucky, One hundred and seventh Illinois, and the
One hundred and eleventh Ohio Infantry, and one section of Hen-
haw's (Illinois) battery, the One hundred and eleventh Ohio bring-
ng up the rear, with skirmishers thrown out. We moved on slowly
ntil we came to a long, steep hill, about 2 miles from Loudon. Here
ve were obliged to double teams to get the section of artillery up,
nd I drew the One hundred and eleventh Ohio up in line on the
ill-side to cover the movement. I succeeded in getting the pieces
nd one caisson up, when the enemy attacked me in front in strong
orce. We checked them, but they soon got a force on our left flank
nd partially in our rear. I had sent for re-enforcements, but as
hey did not arrive, I came to the conclusion, as the enemy were in
ront and on my left flank and pressing on my right flank, that I
uust either lose the regiment or the caisson, so I ordered the One
undred and eleventh Ohio to fall back to the top of the hill through
he woods, which was done in good order, leaving the caisson be-

hind. Here I ordered Lieutenant Morrison to unlimber one of hi
guns, and as the enemy followed us through the woods, fired tw
rounds of grape and canister, thoroughly checking them for th
moment and giving us time to get our artillery off. We the
moved forward, our skirmishers holding the enemy sufficiently i
check until we reached Lenoir's, where we remained for the night

At Lenoir's, I ordered three regiments and Henshaw's battery i
line of battle on the north side of town, ordering the men to lie o
their arms and throwing out strong pickets.

In the morning we were ordered to move forward toward Camp
bell's Station, having our pickets to relieve afterward, which wa
done, all but one company of the One hundred and eleventh Ohio
that were never relieved and are supposed to have been captured
We reached Campbell's Station about 11 a. m., a portion of th
Ninth Army Corps bringing up the rear.

By order of General White, I drew up my brigade on this side o
Campbell's Station in line of battle, my right being advanced abou
150 yards and my left somewhat retired, owing to the lay of th
land, my two batteries, viz, Henshaw's Illinois and the Twenty
fourth Indiana, occupying the center on a small hill. At 12 m. w
opened fire from the batteries and drove back the enemy, who wer
advancing in three lines. My whole brigade was now engaged
Some demonstrations were made to flank us, but detachments of th
Ninth Army Corps were thrown on our right and left. After th
engagement had lasted some time and our batteries had about ex
hausted their ammunition, the enemy brought three heavy batterie
to bear on ours, and I was obliged to order the batteries to the rear
the infantry still remaining and holding the line, although th
enemy's fire from both artillery and infantry was very heavy.

About 3 o'clock I was ordered to cover the retreat of the Nint
Army Corps, which we did by stretching a line of skirmishers acros
the entire field and moving my brigade in line of battle slowly to th
rear, occasionally halting and checking the enemy. During thi
movement the fire from the enemy's artillery and infantry was ver
heavy, but the movement was performed deliberately and steadily
as though the regiments were on drill, falling slowly back until w
reached the ridge we were ordered to hold. Here we halted, took u
position, and again a portion of the Ninth Army Corps assisted us
We held this position until dark, when the Ninth Army Corps wa
withdrawn, and for a short time we were alone in the field.

As the Ninth Army Corps left the field the enemy charged on ou
left flank, but were handsomely repulsed by the One hundred an
seventh Illinois. Shortly after this we were ordered off the field t
bring up the rear, on the road to Knoxville, where we arrived abou
daybreak next morning.

I cannot, without extending this report, make such mention of th
gallant officers and men who took part in these engagements as
should. I might mention the gallant conduct of Colonel Hobson
Lieutenant-Colonel Estes, and Major Duncan, all of the Thirteent
Kentucky; of Lieutenant-Colonel Lowry and Major Brooks, of th
One hundred and seventh Illinois, in the charge made on the 14th o
November; also the conduct of our friend, ex-Colonel Kelly, formerl
of the One hundred and seventh Illinois, who, although his resigna
tion had been accepted some days before, declined to leave so long a
there was danger to be met, and remained with us during the engage
ments, encouraging the men of his former command.

On the second day Major Sherwood, commanding the One hundred and eleventh Ohio, proved himself a good soldier and a competent officer, and on the third day all did well, especially Major Wheeler, commanding the Twenty-third Michigan, who held his men firm to their work for over two hours, under a most galling fire from the enemy's infantry.

I could fill up much space by recounting exploits of both officers of the line and men, and also in speaking of the conduct of my staff. They all deserve notice, but time and room will not admit. However, I must not forget to mention the gallant conduct of Brigadier-General White, who, after giving the final orders for retirement of the troops, remained with me and personally aided in their execution, and at all times he showed a disposition to be where his presence was most needed and share the fate of the brigade, be that what it might.

Honorable notice should also be taken of the officers and men of Henshaw's (Illinois) battery and the Twenty-fourth Indiana Battery, who stood by their guns, working them well until ordered off.

The casualties of the brigade are as follows:

Command.	Date.	Killed.		Wounded.		Captured.		Missing.		Total.
		Officers.	Enlisted men.	Officers.	Enlisted men.	Officers.	Enlisted men.	Officers.	Enlisted men.	
7th Illinois Volunteer Infantry ..	Nov. 14		1		1					2
8th Kentucky Volunteer Infantry	Nov. 14		4	3	36					43
4th Ohio Volunteer Infantry.....	Nov. 14				2					2
1th Ohio Volunteer Infantry.....	Nov. 15		1		12	1	52		2	68
7th Illinois Volunteer Infantry...	Nov. 16				3					3
3d Michigan Volunteer Infantry.	Nov. 16		6	1	24				6	37
8th Kentucky Volunteer Infantry	Nov. 16				9				5	14
1th Ohio Volunteer Infantry.....	Nov. 16			1	4					5
enshaw's Battery, Illinois Volunteers.	Nov. 16		2							2
Total....................	..		14	5	91	1	52		13	176

I am, sir, very respectfully, your obedient servant,

M. W. CHAPIN,
Col. 23d Mich. Vol. Inf., Comdg. 2d Brig., 2d Div.. 23d A. C.
Captain CURTIS, *Assistant Adjutant-General.*

No. 31.

Report of Lieut. Col. Francis H. Lowry, One hundred and seventh Illinois Infantry.

HDQRS. 107TH REGIMENT ILLINOIS VOL. INFANTRY,
Knoxville, Tenn., November 30, 1863.

LIEUTENANT: I have the honor to submit the following report of my regiment in the three engagements, at Huff's Ferry, opposite Loudon, and Campbell's Station, on the 14th, 15th, and 16th instant:

In pursuance of orders from Colonel Chapin, commanding Second Brigade, received on the evening of the 13th November, I was ordered to have my command in readiness to move the next morning at 4 o'clock. The regiment all being on picket duty that night, it was near daylight before they were relieved and returned to camp.

About daylight, in connection with the rest of the brigade, took up the line of march for Lenoir's Station. Arriving at that point, I was ordered to halt and await further orders. After remaining there a short time we were ordered to return to Loudon, at which place we arrived about 2 p. m., the Thirteenth Kentucky being in advance. Here the command halted and was then ordered to march to Huff's Ferry, a distance of 6 miles below Loudon, at which place the enemy were reported to be crossing in force.

After marching a distance of about 2½ miles, the enemy were discovered stationed in a wood near a church. At this point the One hundred and seventh Illinois and Thirteenth Kentucky were ordered forward on the "double-quick" to dislodge the enemy. Arriving near the church, I ordered forward Companies K and F, under command of Major Brooks, as skirmishers. The Thirteenth Kentucky having formed on our left, we attacked the enemy in their position, and, after considerable skirmishing, drove him back a distance of 2 miles, where he chose his position on the crest of a hill heavily wooded, behind a fence. Arriving at the foot of the hill, I was ordered to form line of battle, in connection with Thirteenth Kentucky, and take the hill, the One hundred and seventh Illinois forming on the right, the Thirteenth Kentucky on the left, both supported by the One hundred and eleventh Ohio.

After forming at the foot of the hill, we received orders to charge and drive the enemy from his position, which order was handsomely executed by the two regiments. The Thirteenth Kentucky having to advance through an open field were much more exposed to the galling fire from the enemy than my regiment, we having cover of the timber on the right. Gaining the top of the hill after a severe contest, during which time, however, I lost 1 man killed and 1 wounded, we were ordered to hold our position until further orders. During this time the two companies, K and F, remained on our right, and prevented the enemy from flanking us. Here, also, I was ordered to send out one company as pickets to protect our front. I accordingly sent out company G, under Lieutenant Weedman, who advanced some distance to the front and held their position until about 5 o'clock the morning of the 15th, when I was ordered to fall back in the direction of Lenoir's Station, the Thirteenth Kentucky again taking the advance, and the One hundred and eleventh Ohio covering the rear and supporting Henshaw's (Illinois) battery. The retreat continued in good order until we again arrived at Lenoir's Station, where we were ordered to camp for the night.

On the morning of the 16th, at about 2 o'clock, I received orders to destroy all our transportation and turn over all the mules for the purpose of getting the artillery away, which was accordingly done. The wagons were all chopped down, our baggage, camp equipage, officers' valises, clothing, &c., were all destroyed, and at about 4 o'clock we started for Campbell's Station; arriving there, we were again ordered into line, supporting Henshaw's (Illinois) battery on the left, three companies, K, F, and B, under Captain Laurence, having been ordered to hold a position in front of the battery, which they did.

After remaining in this position a time under a severe fire, and during which time I had two men wounded, the brigade was ordered off the field, the One hundred and seventh Illinois forming the extreme right. During this retreat a heavy body of the enemy attempted to flank us on the right, when Colonel Chapin halted my egiment, faced us to the front, and ordered us to fire ; the volley completely checked the enemy's advance, and caused them to fall back. We remained in line until night came on, when we received orders to fall back to Knoxville, my regiment covering the rear of the Second Brigade, which point we reached on the morning of the 17th instant.

During these several engagements the officers and men of my regiment behaved gallantly, and evinced a determination to maintain the honor and fair name of our brigade. I cannot particularize all who thus did their duty, but must take this occasion to say that Major Brooks was efficient in the discharge of his duty at all times. So, too, were Captains Laurence, Ford, Turner, Waller, Wood, Milholland, Wismer, and Camp, and Lieutenants Moore and Weedman (who each commanded companies) ; they, as well as the other commissioned officers, non-commissioned officers, and privates, each and all did their duty faithfully and efficiently.

Colonel Kelly, late colonel of the regiment, was with us all the time, assisting me in commanding the regiment, from the time we left Loudon until we arrived at Knoxville, never leaving the regiment for a moment, and by his presence and coolness cheering and encouraging the men of the regiment. His conduct under the circumstances cannot be too highly spoken of. I must not omit also to mention Surgeon Wright and Assistant Surgeon Radmore, who were promptly at hand and took charge of the wounded and promptly cared for them, administering to their necessities, and it was not until long after nightfall, amid the storm of rain and wind, that they succeeded in getting the wounded to a place of safety and comparative ease and quiet. I must also on this occasion acknowledge the attention given this regiment by Colonel Chapin, our brigade commander, who ever was at his post of duty, encouraging us, by his presence and example, forward in the discharge of our duty, as well also as to carefully protect us from any unnecessary exposure to the fire of the enemy, and by which conduct he has endeared himself to the officers and men of this regiment.

Justice also to a brave and gallant officer requires me to make honorable mention of the conduct of Brig. Gen. Julius White, our division commander, who, by his constant personal attention since he assumed command at Columbia, Ky., has endeared himself to the officers and men of his command, and particularly in the late engagements in which this regiment has participated he was constantly present, ever at his post of duty, giving personal attention and directions, often in the most exposed positions, yet at all times cool and collected. By his efficiency and soldierly conduct, both in camp and on the field of battle, he has secured not only the confidence and esteem of his command, but has added new luster to the already bright fame of Illinois.

The casualties of this regiment were as follows :

At Huff's Ferry, November 14, killed, Dennis Leary, Company H ; slightly wounded in the foot, W. S. Throckmorton, Company B.

At Campbell's Station, November 16, Richard Watson, Company B, slightly wounded in leg ; William Williver, Company F, slightly wounded in hip; Franklin Coon, Company K, slightly wounded in leg.

I have the honor to be, respectfully, yours,

F. H. LOWRY,
Lieutenant-Colonel, Comdg. 107th Illinois Volunteers.

Lieut. C. MONTGOMERY, *Actg. Asst. Adjt. Gen.*

No. 32.

Report of Maj. William W. Wheeler, Twenty-third Michigan Infantry.

HEADQUARTERS TWENTY-THIRD MICHIGAN INFANTRY,
Knoxville, Tenn., November 30, 1863.

SIR: I have the honor to report that while the Twenty-third Michigan Infantry Volunteers (a part of the Second Brigade, Second Division, Twenty-third Army Corps, Army of the Ohio) was in camp opposite Loudon, Tenn. (after the evacuation of that place by our forces on the 28th October, ultimo), by order of Brig. Gen. Julius White, commanding said Second Division, I was directed, near midnight of the 13th and 14th instant, to proceed with the Twenty-third Michigan Volunteers and one section of Henshaw's (independent Illinois) battery toward Huff's Ferry (which is opposite the lower fortification at Loudon) for the purpose of verifying the information received of the passage of a portion of the enemy's forces on a pontoon bridge thrown across the river at that point.

About 2 o'clock on the morning of the 14th instant, I arrived with the forces above mentioned at a point distant about 1 mile from Huff's Ferry, having marched about 5 miles on the route, when I received an order from Brigadier-General White addressed to me, ordering me to return immediately to camp with the forces under my command. On reaching camp, in compliance with this order, I received instructions from your headquarters to send all baggage and transportation of the Twenty-third Michigan Volunteers to the rear toward Lenoir's and to march my regiment as escort of the division and brigade trains.

As directed, the Twenty-third Michigan Volunteers marched to Lenoir's, a distance of nearly 5 miles. At 12 m. of that day (Saturday, the 14th instant) I received orders from you to march my regiment (the Twenty-third Michigan Volunteers) toward Loudon, in rear of the other troops forming the Second Brigade aforesaid. Passing the site of our camp left that morning, the Twenty-third Michigan, with the brigade column, had reached a point distant about 2 miles from Huff's Ferry, when I received an order from Brigadier-General White to march the regiment in support of Captain Sims' (Twenty-fourth Indiana) battery, with which I proceeded in advance about half a mile, taking a position there assigned, and remained there during the night. Two sections of Henshaw's (independent Illinois) battery in the meanwhile came up and took position at the same point. At 5 a. m. Sunday, the 15th instant, I received orders from General White to proceed to the rear as rapidly as possible with the two batteries above mentioned.

For more than twenty-four hours the rain had fallen in torrents, and the roads, difficult at the best, were almost impassable for carriages. I therefore distributed the men of my command along the traces attached to the carriages, and by dint of the most arduous toil succeeded in reaching Lenoir's about 11 a. m., a distance of 9 miles. Here my command was again assigned to the support of the Twenty-fourth Indiana Battery, which was placed on a height commanding the river road from Loudon.

At 3 a. m., Monday, the 16th instant, I received an order from your headquarters to destroy my regimental wagons, and to proceed toward Knoxville, in escort of Henshaw's (Illinois) battery. The

Twenty-third Michigan Volunteer Infantry arrived *en route* at Campbell's Station, a distance of 9 miles, about 11 o'clock that morning. About noon the regiment was, by your direction, formed in line of battle behind a small branch (or creek) in a meadow to the left of the highway as one approaches Knoxville, and on the right of the Thirteenth Kentucky Infantry Volunteers Shortly after, as the rear guard of the army came in, I was ordered by you to take up a new position about 200 yards toward the enemy, just in advance of a barn. A brigade of the Ninth Corps occupied the position between the right of my regiment and the woods which skirted the open fields to our right, and which were distant about 60 perches. I had previously thrown forward Captain Buckingham's company (A) as skirmishers, who had orders from you to retire without engaging the enemy.

About 1.30 p. m. the enemy advanced a line of skirmishers on our front.   Captain Buckingham's company (A) retired in accordance with your instructions, leaving only the skirmishers of the Thirteenth Kentucky on the front of the right wing of your brigade.   At this juncture my regiment occupied the right center of our front, and was so placed that the right wing was on a slope looking toward the front and the woods before mentioned on our right, while the left wing occupied the crest and slope descending from our front.   Directly afterward the skirmishers of the Thirteenth Kentucky Volunteers came in, leaving my regiment exposed to a galling fire from the enemy's skirmishers on our front and on our right, which was replied to with considerable effect by Captain Raymond's company (F), which I had posted in the barn above mentioned.   Having received orders from you to hold this position at all hazards, I remained there with my regiment about two hours, suffering a loss of 6 enlisted men killed, 1 officer slightly wounded, and of enlisted men 2 mortally, 13 seriously, and 9 slightly wounded.   At the end of that time, perceiving the enemy making preparations to throw a light battery into position on our front, at a distance of about 700 yards (which I was unable to prevent), I sent an orderly to the rear to find you or some officer of your staff, in order that I might apprise you of the necessity of my forming a new line about 40 yards to the rear of my position, which could be sheltered by the crest of a ridge on the exposed front of which the regiment was then posted.   Presently Lieutenant Montgomery, your acting assistant adjutant-general, came up.   I explained the exigency to him, posted the markers and colors on the new line, and had just given orders for the new formation when the enemy opened his battery with a fire of spherical case, canister, and grape with great precision, but fortunately with little effect beyond dislodging Captain Raymond's company (F) from the barn already mentioned.

About half an hour after the formation of this new line I received orders from you through Captain Gallup, brigade inspector on your staff, to march in retreat.   This, therefore, I proceeded to do, unmasking our batteries, and exposed to the near and severe fire of the enemy's artillery crossing the highway leading toward Knoxville, and continuing beyond the range of the enemy's batteries, with no further loss and without confusion or trepidation in the ranks of the regiment.   We remained in this new position until nightfall, when the regiment took position in column of the brigade which formed the rear guard of the army, and about 7 p. m. proceeded toward Knoxville, which place we reached about 4 a. m., Tuesday, the 17th instant, having been under arms without rest four nights and three days with the slightest allowance of food, exposed to most inclement weather, and much of the time on fatiguing march in presence of the enemy.

On Tuesday morning, 17th instant, the regiment was assigned a position on Temperance Hill, Knoxville, and since that time has furnished heavy details for grand guard and fatigue parties, besides fortifying its own and adjacent front, but has not engaged the enemy.

Six enlisted men of this regiment, of a party left at Lenoir's Station to destroy ammunition, are still missing, and are supposed to have been killed or taken prisoners by the enemy. The list of casualties, therefore, of the past month in our engagements with the enemy is as follows: Six enlisted men killed, 1 officer and 24 enlisted men wounded, and 6 enlisted men missing. Total killed, wounded, and missing, 37.

In conclusion, sir, I am gratified to add my testimony of the gallant conduct of the officers of the line and of the enlisted men of the Twenty-third Michigan Volunteers, and of the untiring zeal and efficiency of the regimental and medical staff, during the engagement at Campbell's Station, which was the first in which it has been its fortune to take a part, and of the wonderful fortitude which has sustained them in all these trying circumstances without a murmur and without a doubt.

I have the honor to be, very respectfully, your obedient servant,

W. W. WHEELER,
Major, Comdg. Twenty-third Michigan Infantry Volunteers.

Col. M. W. CHAPIN,
Comdg. Second Brig., Second Div., 23d Army Corps.

No. 33.

Report of Maj. Isaac R. Sherwood, One hundred and eleventh Ohio Infantry.

HEADQUARTERS 111TH OHIO VOLUNTEER INFANTRY,
Knoxville, Tenn., November 28, 1863.

SIR: In obedience to an order of this date, asking for an official report of the casualties of this regiment of the 14th, 15th, and 16th instant, I have the honor to submit the following:

On the 14th instant, the regiment broke camp near Loudon and moved out at daylight to Lenoir's. At Lenoir's we were joined by a portion of the Ninth Army Corps and ordered back to Loudon. From there we proceeded to Huff's Ferry, on the Tennessee River, where a brief but sharp engagement took place. The One hundred and eleventh Regiment was ordered by General White, commanding division, to move to support of the Thirteenth Kentucky and One hundred and seventh Illinois. The regiment occupied a position about 50 yards to the rear of the advance line, and in the brilliant charge which drove the enemy from his position was but little exposed to the enemy's fire. Afterward I was ordered to the right of the advance, which position we occupied during the night. During the engagement the regiment lost but 2 men, both wounded.

On the 15th, at daybreak, in obedience to orders from your head-quarters, I moved the regiment in line of battle to the Kingston and Loudon road, when I was ordered to the rear to cover the retreat of the whole army. At a point nearly opposite Loudon the advance of the rebels appeared in sight. I immediately formed the regiment along the crest of a hill and awaited the approach of the enemy's skirmishers. They came in heavy line and in good order (the Sixth South Carolina Regiment Sharpshooters), supported, I afterward learned, by two regiments of infantry. When within 150 yards we delivered a well-directed fire from our Springfield muskets and con-tinued firing with considerable effect, holding them in check until our artillery was safely over the hill, when I was ordered by Colonel Chapin (commanding brigade) to fall back. This order we obeyed immediately and in good order. My loss in the engagement is 2 killed, 10 wounded, and 2 missing, supposed to be mortally wounded. The small loss in killed and wounded is accounted for from the fact that the men fought while lying on the ground, thus exposing but a small part of the body to the enemy. From this point we marched unmolested to Lenoir's.

On the 16th, at 2 a. m., I received orders to march, and at 3.30 a. m. moved out on the Knoxville road. We arrived at Campbell's Station at 11 a. m., and were ordered to support the Henshaw bat-tery, which had taken position on the left of the road. Scarcely had we got in position before skirmishing commenced in our front. The advance of the enemy was soon in sight, and the Henshaw battery opened on them immediately. They soon replied with a most terri-ble fire. The regiment changed position three times under fire, with great coolness and in good order. My loss in this engagement was 6 wounded, 1 supposed to be mortally.

I regret that I have to report a further loss in the capture of Lieu-tenant Norris and 52 enlisted men (Company B). They were de-tailed on the night of the 15th, at Lenoir's, as pickets, and, through the negligence of the officer in charge of the pickets, were not re-lieved. They were captured on the railroad, near Campbell's Sta-tion, just previous to the engagement of the 16th.

While I regret that so many of the officers and enlisted men of this regiment were unavoidably absent during these engagements, I most heartily acknowledge that great credit is due those who were present for the prompt manner in which they performed their duty.

Recapitulation.

Date.	Killed.	Wounded.	Missing.	Total.
November 14, 1863		2		2
November 15, 1863	2	10	2	14
November 16, 1863		6	52	58
Total	2	18	54	74

Respectfully submitted.

I. R. SHERWOOD,
Major, Commanding.

Lieut. C. Montgomery,
Acting Assistant Adjutant-General.

No. 34.

Report of Capt. Joseph A. Sims, Twenty-fourth Indiana Battery

HDQRS. TWENTY-FOURTH BATTERY INDIANA VOLS.,
Near Knoxville, Tenn., November 28, 1863.

COLONEL : I have the honor to submit the following report of my
command, and the part taken by it in the several engagements since
our departure from the front at Loudon :

Information having been received on the 14th that the enemy had
succeeded in crossing the Tennessee River in force at some point below Loudon, my command, temporarily attached to the Second Brigade, was ordered, at an early hour, to move to Lenoir's. at which
place the column was reversed and moved back to the Tennessee
River, to a point near Huff's Ferry, where our advance, composed of
the Thirteenth Kentucky, commanded by Col. William E. Hobson,
and the One hundred and seventh Illinois, commanded by Lieutenant-Colonel Lowry, encountered the enemy, and, after a sharp engagement, gallantly drove the enemy from the cover under which
they had been fighting, and held the ground at nightfall. My command, being held in reserve, was not engaged. On the following
morning the brigade, with the battery, was moved back to Lenoir's,
where we encamped for the night.

At 4 o'clock on the morning of the 16th, my command, with the
brigade, moved in the direction of Knoxville, arriving at Campbell's
Station, an intermediate point, at about 10 a. m., where the brigade
was drawn up in line of battle to check the progress of the enemy,
who were closely pursuing us. The battery was ordered to take
position on a rising piece of ground immediately on the left of the
Knoxville road in front of Swann's house. The Thirteenth Kentucky and Twenty-third Michigan were thrown upon our right, the
Henshaw battery, the One hundred and eleventh Ohio, and the
One hundred and seventh Illinois occupying the left. At 11 a. m.
the enemy, in line of battle, came within range of our guns, when
we immediately opened fire upon his advancing lines, which was
continued with effect for some time, the enemy meanwhile slowly
but steadily advancing until his skirmishers were within easy rifle
range of the battery and his lines had gained the bank of the creek
on our front. At this point our guns, charged with canister, poured
upon the enemy a destructive fire, which for the time effectually
checked his progress.

The enemy in the meantime had advanced his artillery, placing one
battery upon our right and one upon our left, which, from the natural advantage of the ground, enabled him to concentrate upon us
a heavy fire, to which, from the peculiar inclination of the position
occupied by us, we could not reply. We, however, maintained our
ground until our ammunition was nearly exhausted, two of our guns
disabled, 1 man wounded, and 6 of our horses killed, when we were
ordered, with our four remaining guns, to occupy an elevated position on the right of the Knoxville road, about a half mile in the rear
of the one first taken, where we again awaited the approach of the
enemy.

His long lines, stretching to the woods on either side of the valley, again came forward, and we again opened fire upon his left,
which effectually scattered his ranks and compelled him to seek

helter in the woods. Our fire was continued until nearly dark, and, all our ammunition being exhausted and the enemy apparently checked, my command was ordered to move at once to Knoxville. All of which is respectfully submitted.

With respect, I remain, your obedient servant,

J. A. SIMS,
Captain Twenty-fourth Battery Indiana Volunteers.

Colonel CHAPIN,
Commanding Second Brigade.

No. 35.

Itinerary of the Third Division, Brig. Gen. Milo S. Hascall commanding. *

December 7, in the morning the division broke camp at Knoxville and marched in pursuit of the rebels, under Longstreet, to a point within 3 miles of Rutledge, where the division lay until the evening of the 14th, at which time it marched to the support of the Cavalry Corps, at or near Bean's Station.

December 15, in the morning, at daylight, the division was deployed in line of battle to throw up such works as could be made of rails, &c., and to receive the enemy. During the day they occupied this line, skirmishing constantly with the enemy until dark, when, agreeably to orders, the division fell back to the bivouac, from whence it marched on the evening of the 14th.

December 16, the division fell back to Blain's Cross-Roads, where it remained until the 28th, when it marched to Strawberry Plains, where it has since been encamped.

No. 36.

Itinerary of the First Brigade, Col. James W. Reilly commanding. †

Portions of the brigade were engaged in all the series of operations in vicinity of Knoxville, beginning on the 12th instant. Battery D, First Ohio Artillery, temporarily detached from the brigade, participated in all the engagements on the south side of the Holston River. One section of the Nineteenth Ohio Battery was stationed in Fort Sanders, the remainder on the right of the defensive works on the north side of the river. The infantry of the brigade was held in reserve, though frequently engaged in throwing up earth-works.

November 25, the Forty-fourth, One hundredth, and One hundred and fourth Regiments Ohio Volunteer Infantry crossed the river, and from that time until the 29th instant were engaged in digging rifle-pits and doing picket duty. Four companies of the One hundred and fourth Regiment were engaged in the skirmish of the 29th instant, with slight loss. On the evening of the same day the One hundredth and One hundred and fourth Regiments recrossed the river and were stationed on the second line of pits, on the left of our defensive works, which position they have since occupied. The Forty-fourth Ohio remained on the south side of the river, and has been doing picket duty since the 29th instant.

---

* From return for December.
† From returns for November and December.

December 7, the One hundred and fourth and Forty-fourth Reg
ments, and Battery D, First Ohio Volunteer Artillery, left Knoxvil
Tenn. Forded the Holston River at Armstrong's Ferry, and
crossed at Strawberry Plains.

December 8, marched to Blain's Cross-Roads, a distance of 9 mil

December 9, marched 15 miles and bivouacked within 2 miles
Rutledge, Tenn., where they remained until December 14. Duri
the evening marched to the front ; 9 miles.

December 20, moved forward in the morning and came in sight
the enemy. The brigade participated in all the skirmishes un
ordered back to Blain's Cross-Roads.

December 27, left Blain's Cross-Roads and marched to withir
miles of Strawberry Plains.

December 28, in the morning went into camp at Strawberry Plai
and have remained there since, the One hundredth Regiment Oh
Volunteer Infantry and Nineteenth Ohio Battery being left
Knoxville during the month.

No. 37.

Itinerary of the Second Brigade, Col. Daniel Cameron commanding

November 1, the Second Brigade, Third Division, Twenty-thi
Army Corps, occupied heights on the south side of Holston Rive
opposite Knoxville.

November 15 and *16*, engaged in skirmish with and assisted
repulsing enemy's cavalry, under Wheeler. From that time
November 24 employed in fortifying the heights.

November 24, engaged in skirmish with enemy's infantry, 1½ mil
southwest of Knoxville.

November 25, repulsed an assault made by Hood's division, Lon
street's corps, after a severe engagement, lasting two hours and
quarter. From that time to the 29th instant daily skirmishing co
tinued with the enemy.

November 29, the enemy again advanced, but after four hou
heavy skirmishing was driven back by the Twenty-fourth Kentuck
and six companies of the Sixty-fifth Illinois. The Eighth Tennes
Infantry did not serve with the brigade during November.

No. 38.

*Reports of Brig. Gen. Orlando B. Willcox, U. S. Army, comman
ing Left Wing United States Forces in East Tennessee.*

ON ROAD TO WALKER'S FORD,
December 2, 1863—1 p. m.

Colonel Graham reports that he thinks Wheeler is present wi
his full force, 6,000 men ; they are pressing his left wing—the ca
alry. He is falling back under cover of two regiments of infantr
It is possible they may move up to the left with a view of crossir
at one of the upper fords.

O. B. WILLCOX,
Brigadier-General.

Maj. Gen. JOHN G. FOSTER, *Tazewell.*

---

*From return for November.

INTERSECTION IRWIN'S AND WALKER'S FORD ROADS,
December 2, 1863—1 p. m.

A messenger who left Walker's Ford 12 o'clock brings word from
ne of my staff officers at the ford that Colonel Graham is skirmish-
ıg with enemy about 2 miles from the ford and is falling back
radually. Colonel Jackson is at the ford. This point is 5 miles
rom the ford, and I have sent word to Jackson to see if he needs
e-enforcements. Part of the brigade of reserves with the battery
ook the middle road instead of the Irwin Ford road, and I am
vaiting to hear from Jackson before concentrating at this point.

It may be that the troops on the other road will be needed at the
ord ; if so, they will have a better road than from here. If you
lecide to send a regiment of cavalry to re-enforce Graham, Colonel
'oster is at Tazewell, and you can communicate directly with him.

O. B. WILLCOX,
Brigadier-General.

Major-General FOSTER.

—

INTERSECTION WALKER'S AND IRWIN'S FORD ROADS,
December 2, 1863—1.30 p. m.

Understanding that Jackson is crossing part of his infantry over
he river, I have ordered Colonel Curtin to the ford, with two regi-
nents and the remaining battery, leaving one regiment here with
Colonel Mahan. I shall now proceed at once to Walker's Ford. I
understand that Colonel Graham feels no uneasiness about his abil-
ty to withdraw, that he is falling back slowly, and that the main
oody of the enemy is on other side of the mountain.

O. B. WILLCOX,
Brigadier-General.

Maj. Gen. JOHN G. FOSTER, *Tazewell.*

—

WALKER'S FORD,
December 2, 1863—5 p. m.

After quite a struggle to-day, our troops remain in possession of
Walker's Ford. A regiment of infantry held the road on the opposite side of the river until toward dusk. The enemy withdrew after
in vain having attempted to force our infantry line. They seemed
to draw off both to their left and right. There are only two companies picketing Needham's Ford.

Colonel Graham's brigade expended all their ammunition, and
will require to be replenished by morning. Colonel Jackson lost
about 10 killed and 20 wounded, and Colonel Graham's loss will not
exceed 25 or 30.

O. B. WILLCOX,
Brigadier-General.

Maj. Gen. JOHN G. FOSTER, *Tazewell.*

—

ONE AND A HALF MILES FROM WALKER'S FORD,
December 2, [1863]—9.30 p. m.

GENERAL : The following dispatch has just been received from
Colonel Jackson, commanding forces at ford :

I sent 80 men with a commissioned officer 2 miles in advance ; found the enemy
in camp, and thought they were preparing to move. I have sent parties to watch

their movements. All is quiet at the ford above; One hundred and twenty-nin
in good position. While the One hundred and twenty-ninth Ohio were taking the
position, the enemy opened on them from opposite side of the river. They we
answered by the One hundred and twenty-ninth and silenced. The enemy ha
one regiment and two pieces of artillery. The foregoing is from good authority.

Colonel Lemert, commanding Cumberland Gap, reports a hand
some success by the Sixteenth Illinois Cavalry at Jonesville. Th
rebels were commanded by Colonel Slemp, 350 strong. The Si:
teenth Illinois, with about 250, charged them at once; killed :
and wounded a large number. Captured 26 prisoners and 100 stan
of arms. Major Beeres pursued them 3 miles beyond Jonesville
completely whipped and scattered them in every direction, and d
stroyed their train.

Very respectfully,

O. B. WILLCOX,
Brigadier-General.

Maj. Gen. JOHN G. FOSTER.

—

ONE AND A HALF MILES FROM WALKER'S FORD,
December 3, 1863—8 a. m.

The North Carolina regiment that remained across the river las
night, sent out scouts during the night who reported that the enem
were retiring toward Knoxville ; none are visible in our front thi
morning. I hear nothing from them at the lower fords, and hav
ordered a regiment of cavalry across the river and will try an
find out what has become of them. Patterson's battery of Napo
leon guns, that did such good work yesterday, is reported immova
ble on account of the condition of the horses for want of forage
Two of the horses died yesterday. I don't know what we can do ur
less you order down ten spans of horses from the First Tennesse
Battery at the gap, which would give Patterson's battery 8 horses t
a team. The harness must accompany the horses.

Very respectfully,

O. B. WILLCOX,
Brigadier-General.

Major-General FOSTER,
Tazewell.

—

ONE AND A HALF MILES FROM WALKER'S FORD,
December 3, 1863—1 p. m.

GENERAL : I have just received the following dispatch from Col
onel Graham :

Colonel Capron, 5 miles from the river, reports the enemy 5 miles in the advance
still retreating.

He does not state the direction, but I suppose toward Knoxville

Very respectfully, yours,

O. B. WILLCOX,
Brigadier-General.

Maj. Gen. JOHN G. FOSTER,
Tazewell.

ONE-HALF MILE FROM WALKER'S FORD,
December 3, 1863—1.45 p. m.

GENERAL: Your dispatch just received. The ammunition came
own in due time. After waiting till something had to be done for
ꞁrage, I sent the remainder of Graham's brigade across the river,
ꞌhere it will go into camp about a mile and a half from the river.
I send you a prisoner, taken yesterday, from whom I learn that
ꞁe enemy had two brigades and a battery in the fight, and one in
ꞁserve. Armstrong was present with Harrison's and Dibrell's bri-
ꞁdes, of Wheeler's cavalry. Carter's brigade was back toward
ꞁaynardville. Our officers estimate the enemy's loss at least 100
ꞁilled. They endeavored to gain Graham's rear by a flank move-
ꞁent through one of the side gaps near the river, but were severely
ꞁunished. They made several bold charges in the road, exposing
ꞁemselves, and suffered accordingly. Citizens report that our ar-
ꞁlery damaged them considerably. On the whole it was a pretty
ꞁttle repulse.

  Respectfully, yours,

        O. B. WILLCOX,
          Brigadier-General.

Maj. Gen. JOHN G. FOSTER,
    Tazewell.

—

FOUR MILES FROM WALKER'S FORD,
December 3, 1863—6 p. m.

GENERAL: I forward dispatches received from scouts. Prisoners
ꞁill be forwarded in the morning. One of them by the name of
ꞁmith, First Tennessee, was attached to General Jones' headquarters;
ꞁis company was on duty as scouts and guides. He says that Jones
ꞁld him the night before the fight that he was going to Blain's
ꞁross-Roads. It is possible that while Wheeler's brigade started
ꞁward Kingston, Jones' command will move up toward Virginia to
ꞁover Longstreet's left flank. There is no doubt that Colonel Dib-
ꞁell was wounded and Assistant Adjutant-General Allison killed in
ꞁhe affair of yesterday.

        O. B. WILLCOX,
          Brigadier-General.

Major-General FOSTER.

—

IRWIN'S FORD ROAD,
December 3, 1863—7.30 p. m.

GENERAL: I have sent your dispatch for General Granger* to Col-
ꞁnel Graham, with orders to send an officer and 2 or 3 intelligent
ꞁen, all of whom shall be fully posted. I would advise, in addition,
ꞁhat you send from Tazewell to Colonel Davis, who is at Fincastle or
ꞁear Clinton, and has already opened communication with Colonel
ꞁyrd. Colonel Harney, who is at Tazewell, will forward the com-
ꞁunication. The prisoner who was at Jones' headquarters said that
ꞁeneral Jones told him that he was going to Bean's Station. I don't
ꞁlace much reliance in this, except upon the theory that Longstreet

---

 * See Foster to Granger, same date, Part III, p. —

has commenced his retreat, of which there is no evidence. I a
satisfied that Longstreet was re-enforced by Buckner and perhaj
Cheatham. I have ordered Colonel Graham to have the enemy fo
lowed and watched closely, and to support the advance regimer
with any force required.

Very respectfully,

O. B. WILLCOX,
Brigadier-General.

Major-General FOSTER,
        Tazewell.

—

DECEMBER 4, 1863.

GENERAL: Will you do me the favor to address the inclosed lette
to my wife, Detroit? I have no pen and ink. As the report tha
the rebel cavalry had gone toward Kingston pressing axes to bloc
up the roads is not confirmed, but went on toward Knoxville,
seems to me that Longstreet will soon be put in a fix, for he canno
afford to cross the river and fight Sherman, nor to leave the river a
open to Sherman and fight Granger; hence, unless his force is greate
than we suppose, he must retreat. The move of Ransom to Bean
Station may be intended merely for our benefit, or to keep us from
moving down through Clinch Mountain. Since my Indiana boy
have done so well, I think we could whip Ransom if we could con
centrate upon him; but I think the present disposition of our force
is all that can be desired in the present attitude of affairs.

A citizen here thought he heard cannon firing in direction of Clin
ton yesterday morning, but did not seem confident of it.

Please send my letter home by the most speedy means, and oblig

Yours, respectfully,

O. B. WILLCOX,
Brigadier-General.

Major-General FOSTER,
        Tazewell.

—

DECEMBER 4, 1863—4 p. m.

GENERAL: Captain Hutchins has made a mistake. I sent him u
to ask you to give Garrard his orders, if you had not done so alread
through Colonel Foster; but it seems that Captain Hutchins con
founded Garrard with Graham. I have sent copies of both you
instructions to Colonel Graham already, myself adding that h
might be delayed by the presence of the enemy on the roads, an
must act according to circumstances. His last dispatch mentione
a force, and he had sent to re-enforce his scouting party so as t
observe it more closely. As there is some fear of further mistake
will you please send me as definite orders as possible to send Colone
Graham to-night?

Very respectfully,

O. B. WILCOX,
Brigadier-General.

Major-General FOSTER.

HEADQUARTERS,
In the Field, 4 Miles from Walker's Ford, Dec. 4, 1863.

GENERAL : I have received a telegram from Mrs. Burnside for the *general*, which I have taken the liberty to forward to Knoxville, having sent two couriers. I also communicated the intelligence that *our* forces had met with a success at Walker's Ford, that General *Sherman* would reach him to-day, and that Granger was close at *hand*. We are suffering for the want of axes, horse and mule shoes, *and* nails. Would it not be well to telegraph Captain Hall, assistant quartermaster at Camp Nelson, to send on immediately in light *loads* the above-mentioned articles ; also trenching tools.

Very respectfully, your obedient servant,
O. B. WILLCOX,
Brigadier-General, Commanding, &c.

Major-General FOSTER.

P. S.—There is a train at Cumberland Gap loaded with hard bread *for* First Division, Ninth Army Corps. As it will be impossible for *the* infantry to move without rations, will you please have the bread *ordered* on to us ?

—

FOUR MILES FROM WALKER'S FORD,
December 5, 1863—9.15 a. m.

GENERAL : Immediately upon the receipt of your first instructions yesterday I sent the necessary orders to Colonel Graham, *who* ordered out the blockading party at once to Bean's Station road *via* Powder Horn Gap ; found Ransom's whole command between *Rutledge* and Blain's Cross-Roads, one regiment on top of the *mountain*. This, of course, rendered the blockading expedition impracticable. Some of Colonel Graham's scouts yesterday were pursued, and by mistake of the guides were conducted into the enemy's *lines* toward Knoxville, and finally made their escape by taking to *the* mountains. Enemy's force from "Haversower's" road to Rutledge estimated at 10,000 ; Ransom's force estimated from 5,000 to *8,000*. There is a large force at Ball's Bridge, 7 miles north of Knoxville. Scouts in the direction of Clinton report the enemy's picket *at* Lay's Cross-Roads.

Among the wounded reported in the fight of December 2 is Major-*General* Martin.

Yours, respectfully,

O. B. WILLCOX,
Brigadier-General.

Major-General FOSTER.

—

FOUR MILES FROM WALKER'S FORD,
December 5, 1863—12.15 p. m.

GENERAL : Colonel Graham is threatened with an immediate attack, and is probably now engaged. I have therefore ordered back *another* regiment to Walker's Ford, making two regiments and two *guns* to cover the ford. I shall wait here until I hear from Colonel *Graham* again.

Yours, respectfully,

O. B. WILLCOX,
Brigadier-General.

Major-General FOSTER.

TAZEWELL,
December 9, 1863—6.40 p. m.

GENERAL : General Longstreet and staff passed Bean's Station yesterday morning about 10 o'clock. Some of his infantry is with the teams on the Morristown and Greeneville road, but most of the infantry passed on the Bean's Station and Rogersville road. They say they are going to make a stand at Bristol. The cavalry brigade retired from Clinch Mountain late last evening and this morning, leaving two pieces of artillery and one regiment of cavalry ; picket of the enemy are still in the gap. I have no doubt this information is substantially correct.

Very respectfully,

O. B. WILLCOX,
Brigadier-General.

Maj. Gen. JOHN G. FOSTER,
Commanding Department of the Ohio.

—

TAZEWELL, *December 11, 1863.*

Your dispatch of the 8th (8 p. m.) received yesterday. I have telegraphed to all commanding officers, quartermasters, and commissaries, from here to Camp Nelson, to hurry forward provisions, shoes, and stockings. I have just received a dispatch from Major Conover, Mulberry Gap, who reports 300 rebels near the Black Water salt-works ; and he also learns by scouts sent beyond Sneedville and by deserters who came in this morning that there is a large force at Flat Gap, 10 miles from Sneedville. This, of course, has prevented his scouting force, as I advised you in my last dispatch. The force at that gap is variously estimated from 1,000 to 10,000 men. I suppose it is a brigade guarding Longstreet's flank from an attack in this quarter, but possibly they may have in view a raid across our line of communication.

The block-house at Mulberry Gap is progressing well.

O. B. WILLCOX,
Brigadier-General.

Major-General FOSTER.

—

TAZEWELL, *December 14, 1863.*

GENERAL : Nothing further from the enemy on my left, except that yesterday a force of about 400 cavalry were this side Clinch River, on the Sneedville road, committing depredations ; probably scouting and foraging. Nothing from them to-day. I sent your order to Captain Gross, who is coming on. I have sent to Barboursville for wire ; also sent to Cumberland Gap for axes, and they will leave there for Knoxville to-morrow. No cross-cut saws, and have telegraphed Hall for one hundred.

The Sixth Indiana Cavalry are used up, and there is not sufficient cavalry force to scout the Sneedville road.

Very respectfully,

O. B. WILLCOX,
Brigadier-General.

Major-General FOSTER.

TAZEWELL, *December* 20, 1863.

GENERAL : A citizen came into Evans' Ford this morning and re-
orted to the officer in command there that a brigade of rebel cav-
lry were crossing the Clinch, 8 miles above Evans' Ford, and were
oving in this direction. I have halted the regiments that were
tarting from here until the truth can be ascertained.
                                        O. B. WILLCOX,
                                            Brigadier-General.

Major-General FOSTER.

—

TAZEWELL, *December* 20, 1863.
                                        (Received 21st.)

GENERAL : Major Conover scouted from Mulberry Gap up Sneed-
ille road, and across the Clinch to Sneedville, within 6 miles from
lat Gap.   Except a few guerrillas in the mountains, he has driven
ut what rebels there were this side of Clinch River.   He reports
hat the rebels are throwing up works in Flat Gap and Union Gap,
nd posted artillery.
Now would be a grand opportunity for a descent on the salt-works
rom Berlin.   If we had the cavalry it would be a good thing also to
urn the New River railroad bridge.   I have authorized Major Con-
ver to promise $5,000 to Union men who might do the work.   I am
vaiting orders with regard to the Twenty-third Corps.
                                        O. B. WILLCOX,
                                            Brigadier-General.

Major-General FOSTER.

—

NEAR WALKER'S FORD,
                                        December 21, 1863.

GENERAL : I arrived here last evening with the available force of
ny command.   Part was detained above till this noon by reports of
he enemy's crossing Clinch River, the truth of which is not known
et.   After leaving a sufficient force at Tazewell, of course I am far
rom strong.   Wagons are out for subsistence, and I expect them in
his evening.   I have started an ammunition train to Knoxville, 18
vagons loaded with Enfield rifle ammunition, caliber .58, which I
nade up on seeing your dispatch to General Grant.   Your dispatches
vith regard to the Twenty-third Corps, dated 17th and 19th instant,
vere received yesterday.   Please relieve me as soon as possible from
he unpleasant state of suspense in which I have been placed for nearly
hree months about my command.   I have been without a positive
:ommand, and tied to six-months' troops and recruits, while my
uniors have been commanding corps.   If this continues I must resign or cease to be a man.   You will appreciate my feeling, and I
nave every confidence in your justice.
I remain, general, very respectfully, your obedient servant,
                                        O. B. WILLCOX,
                                            Brigadier-General.

Major-General FOSTER.

NEAR WALKER'S FORD,
December 22, 1863—8.30 a. m.

GENERAL: Your dispatches of 20th to concentrate at Tazewell, an 21st to remain there, &c., were received last night. I shall keep sharp lookout for the trains, but should feel safer with more cavalr on this side the river to scout in strength on my left flank, as m leaving here will make the enemy bolder along your courier line.

I would recommend frequent cavalry patrols between Blain Cross-Roads and the Clinch. There were numerous small parties i the valley, which, however, I hope Foster's brigade will clean ou Just above Walker's Ford there is a band of them across the rivel

Very respectfully,

O. B. WILLCOX,
Brigadier-General.

Major-General FOSTER.

—

HEADQUARTERS FIRST DIVISION, NINTH ARMY CORPS,
January 23, 1865.

SIR: I have the honor to submit a report of the operations of th Left Wing forces of East Tennessee prior to and during the sieg of Knoxville.

I joined General Burnside at Bull's Gap, October 8, 1863, with division of re-enforcements from Camp Nelson, Ky., consisting c the One hundred and fifteenth, One hundred and sixteenth, On hundred and seventeenth, and One hundred and eighteenth Indian (six-months') Volunteer Regiments, Twelfth Michigan, Twenty-firs Ohio, and Twenty-third Indiana Batteries. Next morning, on th advance to Blue Springs, Hoskins' brigade, of the Twenty-thir Corps, reported to me. I had also two companies of Third Indian Cavalry.

In the fight at Blue Springs my command was partly on dut supporting batteries engaged, and partly in reserve and guardin cross-roads. After that action I took post at Greeneville, with Ho: kins' brigade advanced as far as Rheatown, supporting Shacke. ford's cavalry operations.

About the 1st of November, owing to reports of a large rebel forc concentrating at Zollicoffer and Abingdon, and about to advanc Shackelford drew in his outposts from Kingsport, Blountsville, an Carter's Station and fell back as far as Rheatown, reporting to you headquarters by telegraph, and then reporting to me, by directio of the major-general commanding. I halted him at Rheatown an ordered him to advance his pickets as far, at least, as Jonesborougl The road by Kingsport toward Rogersville was thus left unguardec and on the morning of November 6 firing of artillery was heard a Rogersville. The enemy had marched down through Kingspor and suddenly attacking Garrard's cavalry, completely routed i Garrard fell back with his shattered command to Morristown, anc supposing that the enemy intended an attack on Morristown, th major-general commanding telegraphed me to fall back to tha point and defend it. Accordingly, I withdrew from Greeneville an the neighborhood. On the night of the 6th, Shackelford reache Russellville with his cavalry, and I halted with the infantry an artillery at Bull's Gap on finding that the enemy had not advance farther than Rogersville. I then seized the passes of the Bull Moun ains, from the Holston, opposite Rogersville, to Chucky Bend, an

ommenced fortifying Bull's Gap. The enemy were reported by
oyal Tennesseans to be in force at and below Kingsport, Greene-
ille, and Newport; and from the 6th to the 17th my operations
vere confined to scouting in those directions, cavalry skirmishes,
nd foraging, on which we were, men and animals, mainly depend-
nt for food.

On Longstreet's appearance opposite Loudon, Hoskins' brigade
vas ordered to Knoxville. Shackelford had previously been de-
ached to the same point to assume command of the Cavalry Corps.
My command now consisted of the Indiana six-months' regiments,
he batteries already mentioned, a skeleton regiment of North Caro-
ina recruits, and Graham's and Garrard's brigades of cavalry,
orming a division, under Colonel Foster. At Morristown was the
Thirty-second Kentucky Infantry, the Eleventh Michigan Battery,
nd a battalion of mounted Tennesseeans, under Lieutenant-Colonel
Davis. At Mossy Creek was a battalion of Tennessee recruits, under
Colonel Patton. It will be observed that my infantry was all raw.
The cavalry was good, but half mounted; no horseshoes, and forage
carce. My artillery was out of all proportion, and a perfect encum-
orance; horses scarcely able to drag the pieces. I had an immense
vagon train, being the transportation of the command proper and
of other troops now gone to Knoxville or otherwise left with me. On
Longstreet's crossing at Loudon I received a dispatch from your
ieadquarters to make arrangements for getting my command up to
he vicinity of Cumberland Gap.

November 16, received an order from General Parke, chief of staff,
hat, in event of telegraphic communication being cut off, I should
ecure my retreat to Cumberland Gap, where it was expected that
00,000 rations were accumulated, and which point was to be held
n every event. The same night telegraphic communication with
Knoxville ceased.

I had now to retreat 52 miles in the face of superior numbers;
ross the Holston and the Clinch, two rocky, deep, and rapid rivers;
arry an immense train of wagons and cumbersome artillery; the
oads broken up with mud and blocked up with thousands of refugees,
vith their families, ox-teams, furniture, tables, and feather-beds.

On the morning of the 18th, I made a demonstration as if to advance against the enemy, started cavalry parties on every road lead-
ng toward Greeneville, and threw Garrard's brigade (not the same
roops formerly defeated) across the Holston at Rogersville, with
orders to advance straight up the road toward Kingsport. Mean-
ime, my infantry, artillery, and trains were marching in retreat
oward Bean's Station, under the cover of this cavalry movement.
The troops at Morristown, including those from Mossy Creek, were
ordered to the same point by a different ford. Everything, except
oarts of the cavalry division, was concentrated at Bean's Station that
hight without a single accident.

I was rather in hopes the enemy would attack me, and halted
here through the next day. We had stolen a march on the enemy,
nd the men felt as well as if they had gained a victory.

On the morning of the 19th, I sent a cavalry detachment down the
elegraph line as far as Morristown, and succeeded for a short time
n reopening communication. A party had been sent out from Knoxille, and repaired the wires at that end of the line. The orders of
he major-general commanding were here renewed, viz, to push on
o Cumberland Gap and make that point secure.

On the afternoon of the 19th, I began getting the artillery ove
the steep and rocky pass of the Clinch Mountain above Bean's Sta
tion, and on the morning of the 20th renewed the march. Cavalr
detachments were sent in advance to seize the passes and cross-road
leading toward Rogersville and Jonesville. A detachment was als
sent toward Knoxville, with orders to return by way of Walker'
Ford and Tazewell with information.

One party, Captain Hammond, scouted as far as Mulberry Ga
toward Jonesville and surprised Slemp's Sixty-fourth or Sixty-fift
Virginia* in their camp, charged in, and drove them 3 miles, captur
ing and destroying a considerable portion of their arms and cam
equipage. By these enterprises the slow-moving train arrived with
out molestation at Tazewell on the 19th, and at Cumberland Gap o
the 20th. Beyond a day or two's half rations of bread and sma
stores for my men, I found no more stores at the gap than were re
quired for the garrison, under Colonel Lemert, for thirty days, an
the road to Camp Nelson had become impassable for wagons by th
rise of the river. I was therefore compelled to scatter my comman
for forage and subsistence.

In order to watch and threaten Ransom, who was on the Kings
port and Rogersville road, Garrard's brigade was ordered to cam
near Evans' Ford, with scouts near Bean's Station and headquarter
at Big Springs. Graham's brigade occupied the Walker's For
route to Knoxville. The camp of dismounted cavalry and Foster'
division headquarters were at Tazewell; the infantry at Cumberlan
Gap, Powell's Bridge, and on the Jacksborough road. I communi
cated with Captain Hall, quartermaster at Camp Nelson, who starte
1,000 horses for me to remount the cavalry. I was also able to ge
some ammunition from a train at Barboursville by means of a foot
bridge which we built at Cumberland Ford. But the men were su
fering for food; corn was scarce; the hogs we had got by foraging o
the Chucky and French Broad were dying with the cholera, and th
weather was very severe. There was some wheat in the Powe
River Valley, but the enemy controlled it with their force at Jones
ville, and Colonel Lemert had abandoned to them all the mills o
the river. I communicated the situation of affairs to Major-Genera
Halleck, commander-in-chief, and to Major-General Grant, com
manding the Western Grand Division, and transmitted the intelli
gence received through my scouts of the siege of Knoxville an
General Burnside's situation. They both directed that I shoul
render General Burnside every assistance in my power, but left i
discretionary with me as to what course to pursue.

General Grant suggested that I should move upon Abingdon an
attack the salt-works, in order to draw off Ransom and Jones an
keep them from uniting their forces with Longstreet. I had alread
ordered Lemert, who had some good cavalry of an Illinois regiment
to send an expedition to Jonesville, which lies on the road to Abing
don. He sent Major Beeres, with 300 men, who attacked the rebel
at Jonesville, and drove them across Powell River, killing and captur
ing quite a number. I now made strenuous efforts to fit out the com
mand for an advance to Abingdon. Five hundred of Foster's cav
alry were remounted with the horses from Camp Nelson, and som
horseshoes were obtained. The mills on Powell River were set t
grinding corn and wheat, and some beef was found. Colonel Davi
mounted force was sent toward Jacksborough, and drove off th

---

* The Sixty-fourth was Slemp's regiment.

bel cavalry which had come to that neighborhood, and commenced izing a large drove of hogs, which was on its way from Kentucky Knoxville, when the siege stopped them. I also sent a cavalry arty from Foster's division to Clinton, with orders to communicate ith Granger's cavalry, which it did, at some point toward Kingston. he movement upon Abingdon, however, was abandoned in consequence of orders received from General Burnside, through my scouts vho got into Knoxville), for me to send my cavalry toward Knoxille and advance the infantry to supporting distance. Graham's rigade was at once ordered to proceed as far as Blain's Cross-Roads, possible, and harass the enemy, and draw off as much of Wheeler's bel cavalry corps as possible, falling back toward Tazewell, if ompelled by superior force. I did not deem it wise to take Garrard's rigade from the Bean's Station road, where it was usefully employed, reatening Ransom's flank. On November 30, Major-General Foster rrived at Cumberland Gap. My plans were fully approved; and n December 1, by his orders, we set forward with the infantry to azewell, leaving a minimum garrison at Cumberland Gap.

On the night of December 1, a courier from Graham reported that e enemy in large force were pressing him back toward Maynardille, and on the morning of the 2d, I moved with the infantry ivision, now commanded by Colonel Curtin, Forty-fifth Pennsylania Volunteers, toward the Clinch, with orders from General ostei to march as far as Walker's Ford. I sent Jackson's brigade y the direct road to the ford, with Patterson's (Twenty-first Ohio) attery, with orders to put his artillery in position at the ford, and ither cross over to the assistance of Graham or cover his retreat cross the river, according to circumstances. The rest of the division took another road, which enabled us to check any attempt of the nemy to cross above Walker's Ford. Graham lit his camp-fires at Iaynardville, and withdrew during the night of the 1st, leaving ne company to observe the enemy. Wheeler's cavalry, re-enforced y a brigade of Jones' (or Williams'), which latter had come down y the south side of the Holston, appeared at Maynardville at dayight, drove out Graham's rear guard, and soon came upon Graham's nain body. Graham fell back slowly, fighting at every advantaeous point. My staff officers found him about 3 miles from the ford, n the Clinch Mountain, and apprised him that supports were at and. He also communicated directly with Colonel Jackson, who rossed over two regiments of infantry, and relieved a portion of the avalry, whose ammunition was exhausted.

The enemy sent a brigade to turn our left flank and cross the river y a ford just above Walker's. This movement was detected by Graham, who detached a part of Capron's (Illinois) regiment, armed vith Henry rifles, by whom the enemy was met and repulsed, losing heavily under the rapid firing of a much inferior force. The main body came upon our two infantry regiments, which, although new troops, stood up bravely and repulsed the enemy in about twenty minutes. The enemy had a battery of light artillery, which our artillery, under Captain Patterson, silenced, firing over the heads of our own men.

The enemy fell back half a mile before dark, and then 3 miles; finally, at midnight, they were in full retreat toward Knoxville. We captured some prisoners that night and the next day or two—about 125. Our loss was about 50 killed, wounded, and missing. The enemy outnumbered us two to one, and were commanded by General

Martin in person, in Wheeler's absence from his command.   Colon
Graham, having replenished his exhausted ammunition in the nigh
started at daylight in pursuit, and picked up quite a number of stra
glers, which were sent to Tazewell.   All the prisoners were sent i
Camp Nelson.   This action terminated my operations under Majo
General Burnside, who was relieved a few days afterward by Ger
eral Foster.

I beg leave to mention for good conduct throughout the campaig
Capt. Robert A. Hutchins, assistant adjutant-general, U. S. Volu
teers; First Lieut. L. C. Brackett, Twenty-eighth Massachuset
Volunteers, aide-de-camp; First Lieut. William V. Richards, Se
enteenth Michigan Volunteers, aide-de-camp; Capt. P. Heistanc
assistant quartermaster, U. S. Volunteers, and Surg. P. A. O'Cor
nell, U. S. Volunteers.   And, for great energy at Cumberland Gaj
in supplying the troops from the country, First Lieut. R. M. Cros
Thirty-sixth Massachusetts Volunteers, acting commissary of sul
sistence.   Also, for bravery and skill in action, Colonel Jackson, Or
hundred and eighteenth Indiana Volunteers, commanding brigade
Colonel Graham, Indiana Cavalry, commanding brigade, and Captai
Patterson, Twenty-first Ohio Battery.

I have the honor to be, colonel, very respectfully, your obedier
servant,

O. B. WILLCOX,
Brevet Major-General.

Lieut. Col. Lewis Richmond, *Asst. Adjt. Gen.*

No. 39.

Reports of Brig. Gen. James M. Shackelford, U. S. Army, con
manding Cavalry Corps, Department of the Ohio.

Knoxville, Tenn., *November* 15, 1863.
General Burnside:

The following just from General Shackelford.   I wrote him tha
in case he had to fall back upon Colonel Cameron's brigade he mus
co-operate with General Hascall to hold the enemy in check.

1 p. m.

We are still at the same place as when last wrote you; still fighting.   The enem
firing from four guns, showing considerable force.

J. M. SHACKELFORD.

P. S.—Since writing the within I learn the enemy is moving in heavy force upc
our left.

I have ordered my advance to fall back to within 4 miles of town.

JNO. G. PARKE,
Major-General.

Headquarters Cavalry Corps,
In the Field, 4½ *Miles from Knoxville, Nov.* 15, 1863—2 p. m.

The enemy is still advancing in very heavy column.   The fightin
is heavy.

I am, general, truly, yours,

J. M. SHACKELFORD,
Brigadier-General, Commanding.

Major-General Parke.

HEADQUARTERS CAVALRY CORPS,
In the Field, December 5, 1863—midnight.

GENERAL : I have just met Mr. Summers, a very reliable man, who lives on the south side of the river, and was captured by the enemy yesterday and taken to the Plains. He says the whole of the force went this road ; he met 500 cavalry this morning at Lay's Station, 60 miles above Knoxville. He thinks their force 25,000. They said they were going to Morristown. I send Summers to you.

SHACKELFORD,
Brigadier-General.

Major-General BURNSIDE.

P. S.—Part of the cavalry crossed 3 miles below Strawberry Plains, and part, if not all, the trains did also.

I send 4 more prisoners, and we are still picking them up.

—

FIVE MILES FROM KNOXVILLE, ON MORRISTOWN ROAD,
December 5, 1863—2 a. m.

GENERAL : I received your order to move slowly, and have just reached this point. This point is near the junction of the main road on which the rebels traveled on yesterday and last night. Three rebels left here about one hour and a half ago, who had been here for some time, who said they were remaining here to show a brigade of cavalry the right road. The citizens report that the enemy's cavalry is now in line of battle on the road that the enemy traveled— I mean the road that forms a junction with this just above this point. I have ordered a party out to ascertain the facts. I also ordered scout down to Armstrong's Ferry. I think, from the best information I can get, that the main body of the enemy came into this road just above here and went directly up the road to Morristown.

I send back 2 prisoners.

Yours, truly,

SHACKELFORD,
Brigadier-General.

Major-General BURNSIDE,
Commanding Army of the Ohio.

—

CAMPBELL'S, SEVEN MILES FROM KNOXVILLE,
December 5, 1863—5 a. m.

GENERAL : My advance is 3 miles beyond this place. I would have gone farther, but for your order that I should travel slowly and that I might be ordered on the Jacksborough road, and the further reason of having the rebels reported in line of battle on my left, which I had investigated and proved to be a mistake. About 1,500 cavalry crossed at Armstrong's Ford. The infantry and trains and part of the cavalry passed on parallel road about 2 miles from this point, and part of the cavalry passed up this road, the last passing about 9 o'clock this morning. I am satisfied, from all that I can learn from prisoners and citizens, that the rebels are moving for Bristol direct. It will be very difficult to get forage for the regiments.

We will do the best we can.

I am, general, yours, truly,

J. M. SHACKELFORD,
Brigadier-General.

Major-General BURNSIDE.

TEN MILES FROM KNOXVILLE, TENN.,
December 6, 1863.

GENERAL : We have been skirmishing with rebel cavalry for ov
an hour. Two thousand of the enemy encamped 2 miles from th
point last night. A brigade of rebel cavalry was in line of battle
sundown last evening a mile from here, on the Rutledge road ;
stated by citizens. My advance is at the junction of the Rutledg
and Strawberry Plains roads. We found forage for our horses la
night.

I am, general, yours, truly,

J. M. SHACKELFORD,
Brigadier-General.

Major-General BURNSIDE, *Knoxville.*

—

CAMPBELL'S,
December 6, 1863—8.10 a. m.

GENERAL : We had some skirmishing with the enemy's cavalr
last evening about dark. After the skirmish the enemy built larg
camp fires in our front. I will have some 15 or 20 prisoners to sen
back this morning. The rebel officers have at least made the im
pression upon their men that they were going to Morristown. Fron
the best information I can get the enemy forded the river som
place near the Plains. I shall move forward and communicate wit
[you] as often as possible.

I am, general, yours, truly,

SHACKELFORD,
Brigadier-General.

Major-General BURNSIDE.

—

HEADQUARTERS CAVALRY CORPS,
Junction of S. and P. Roads, December 6, 1863—noon.

GENERAL : I have just been out a short distance on the Rutledge
road. The enemy's cavalry is in line of battle out about 1 mile from
the junction, on the Rutledge road. A citizen reports that a considerable column of rebel cavalry passed up the Jacksborough road
on yesterday. I do not think that the rebel infantry succeeded in
crossing the river on yesterday. Their men are in bad condition
for traveling, judging from the prisoners I have taken. We have
captured several that were unable to march back to Knoxville.
Some rebels (a squad) have just shown themselves on the opposite
side of the river. I have a good position, and I think we could hold
it against a large force. The cavalry of the enemy at this point is
evidently covering the movement of the enemy across the river,
near the Plains.

I am, general, yours, truly,

SHACKELFORD,
Brigadier-General.

Major-General BURNSIDE.

—

HEADQUARTERS CAVALRY CORPS,
December 6, 1863—2 p. m.

GENERAL : The enemy has fallen back from his position, and my
advance now occupy the ground on which he had his line. I could

ove forward, but I can get forage here, and I occupy the position
ou ordered me to. I have sent scout out on the Plains road, and
ill order another on the Rutledge road.

> SHACKELFORD,
> *Brigadier-General.*

Major-General BURNSIDE,
    Commanding Army of the Ohio, Knoxville.

—

> HEADQUARTERS CAVALRY CORPS,
> *Near Junction R. and S. Roads, Dec. 6, 1863—4.30 p. m.*

MAJOR: Yours of 1.30 p. m. is at hand. The enemy fell back
rom his position on Rutledge road, and I have ordered scout out
pon that road, which has not reported. The scout on the Straw-
erry Plains road reported when 4 miles out and within 1 mile of the
Plains. The report was that the rear guard left there at 9 a. m.,
ut that the main force of the enemy had gone on the road north of
hat.

I suppose the officer of the scout means the Rutledge road. We
ave captured between 50 and 70 prisoners since we left, and also
3 horses and mules. If the weather should change and become bad
ve would doubtless get several hundred of the enemy.

I will be upon the alert, and will not leave anything undone that
he command can do to annoy and injure the enemy to the greatest
ossible extent.

I am, major, yours, truly,

> SHACKELFORD,
> *Brigadier-General.*

Major VAN BUREN, *Aide-de-Camp, Knoxville.*

—

> HEADQUARTERS CAVALRY CORPS,
> *In the Field, December 6, 1863—7.30 p. m.*

GENERAL: The scout sent on the Strawberry Plains road has just
eturned. He stated that he went to the Plains, saw 1,000 or 1,500
avalry encamped above the Plains, on this side of the river. The
nfantry all went the Rutledge road. The rear guard of the infantry
re encamped 10 miles above the Plains. The scout upon the Rut-
edge road has not returned.

I am, general, truly, yours,

> J. M. SHACKELFORD,
> *Brigadier-General.*

Major-General BURNSIDE,
    Commanding Army of the Ohio, Knoxville.

—

> HEADQUARTERS CAVALRY CORPS,
> *In the Field, December 7, 1863—7 p. m.*

GENERAL: The enemy has fallen back. My advance is encamped
1 mile from Blain's Cross-Roads. I will move forward early to-morrow morning.

I am, truly, yours,

> J. M. SHACKELFORD,
> *Brigadier-General.*

Major-General BURNSIDE,
    Commanding Army of the Ohio, Knoxville.

HDQRS. CAVALRY CORPS, FORKS OF SCOTT'S MILL ROAD,
December 7, 1863—10.30 p. m.

GENERAL : The enemy's infantry all came up the Scott's Mill road
passed up the Rutledge road. His cavalry is just in our front. Som
little skirmishing this morning. We are moving forward. I hav
not heard from Colonel Foster.

I am, general, very truly, your obedient servant,

J. M. SHACKELFORD,
Brigadier-General.

Major-General BURNSIDE, *Knoxville.*

—

HEADQUARTERS CAVALRY CORPS,
2 *Miles from Blain's Cross-Roads, Dec.* 8, 1863—6 a. m.

MAJOR : Your dispatch was received at a quarter to 5 this morn
ing. Since dispatching the general at that hour, I have had Genera
Foster's dispatch translated, and I am satisfied that he is mistake
as to the position of Colonel Foster. After giving copy of telegran
from General Grant to General Foster, which I presume the genera
has already received, he adds :

I sent you a dispatch last night informing you of the exact position of the tw
brigades of my division and the position of the enemy (I did not get that dispatch
The officer bearing this dispatch will inform you of our position this morning.
am anxious to know the position of our cavalry below, and its operations, in orde
that I may know how to operate against the enemy. I found Jones' division yes
terday in the Flat Creek and Bull Run Valley, this side of Powder Spring Gap. W
attacked and drove them beyond Copper Ridge Gap, capturing 1 captain and
number of prisoners and about 7 horses. I will try to-day to force the passage c
Powder Spring Gap, or some of the gaps over Clinch Mountain above there.

JOHN W. FOSTER,
Colonel, Commanding.

The enemy had a heavy force of cavalry in my front and on m
right on yesterday. I had not sufficient force to attack him, and th
general had ordered me not to attack with the force I came out with
As soon as General Ferrero reached me I made a forward movement
the enemy had just fallen back to Blain's Cross-Roads, and was i
my immediate front at dark. The estimate placed upon the enemy'
cavalry by citizens is from 6,000 to 10,000. The citizens represen
the infantry in bad condition for marching, and very much demoral
ized. No citizen was permitted to go within their lines on yesterday
and therefore we could not get any information of his movement
above this point. I am satisfied, however, that the infantry is mov
ing on for Rogersville, or some point above that.

A part of their train went by Morristown. I am now in the ac
of moving forward.

I am, major, yours, truly,

SHACKELFORD,
Brigadier-General.

Major VAN BUREN, *Aide-de-Camp.*

—

HEADQUARTERS CAVALRY CORPS,
Junction of Rutledge and Powder Spring Road,
December 8, 1863—11 a. m.

GENERAL : I have just reached this place. Generals Martin an
Armstrong were between this and Blain's Cross-Roads, and on th
river road last night. They commenced leaving last night abou

midnight, the last of them leaving at 8 o'clock this morning. Jones' command was out on the Powder Spring road and came in to the Rutledge road this morning at this point, and went on up the road. I heard from Colonel Foster this morning. Graham's brigade was to have been at Blain's Cross-Roads by 10 or 11 o'clock. Garrard's brigade was to cross the mountain at one of the gaps to-day. I think when I get the corps together, with the artillery, I will be enabled to do the enemy some damage. The enemy's infantry finished passing here late Sunday evening, since which time I have heard nothing of them.

I am, general, very truly, yours,

J. M. SHACKELFORD,
Brigadier-General.

Major-General BURNSIDE, *Knoxville.*

—

HEADQUARTERS CAVALRY CORPS,
Bean's Station, December 9, 1863—12.30 p. m.

GENERAL: I have just reached this place with my advance. We drove the rebel cavalry for 4 or 5 miles. We found them in position, with artillery planted, at this place, but they left in considerable haste at our approach. A large body of cavalry went down the mountain road. The infantry was passing this point on yesterday until 4 p. m., and from the best information I can get, Longstreet encamped last night near Rock Spring, 4 miles on the Rogersville road.

I have sent scouts out on all the roads, and will feed before moving any farther.

I am, general, yours, truly,

SHACKELFORD,
Brigadier-General.

Maj. Gen. J. G. PARKE, *Commanding Forces.*

—

HEADQUARTERS CAVALRY CORPS,
Bean's Station, December 9, 1863—5 p. m.

GENERAL: I occupied this place with my command at 12.30 o'clock instant. I am directed by General Parke, commanding forces in pursuit of the enemy, to remain here with my command and open communication with you across the mountain. The rebel infantry finished passing this point, going up the Rogersville road late last evening.

Citizens report that some infantry under Jones went out on the Morristown road. A large body of rebel cavalry, with artillery, went down the Morristown road this morning. I have had considerable skirmishing with the enemy's cavalry to-day. We have captured over 100 prisoners since we left Knoxville.

The greater part of Colonel Foster's division is greatly in want of ammunition, both small-arms and artillery. I sent a messenger to Tazewell this morning with dispatch for you, and also to try and obtain rations for my command. I directed him to give you full particulars of our condition.

I am, general, very respectfully, your obedient servant,

J. M. SHACKELFORD,
Brigadier-General, Commanding.

Major-General FOSTER, *Tazewell.*

N. B.—General Parke is at Rutledge, 9½ miles from this place.

[Indorsement.]

TAZEWELL, *December* 10, 1863.

Respectfully forwarded.

Colonel Foster ordered his train to Blain's Cross-Roads; it probably contains ammunition. A train of rations is expected here at 9 o'clock this morning, and will be sent to Bean's Station without delay.

O. B. WILLCOX,
Brigadier-General.

—

HEADQUARTERS CAVALRY CORPS,
Bean's Station, December 10, 1863—8.15 a. m.

GENERAL: I would have reported to you again last night, after receiving your orders, but for the fact that I had nothing of importance to communicate. I immediately forwarded, on the reception of your order, a messenger with communication for General Foster across the mountain. After my report of 12.30 o'clock yesterday, Colonel Ward had some skirmishing with the enemy on the Morristown road and drove him across the river. I have ordered this morning a brigade out upon the Rogersville road, and also one upon the Morristown road, and I will report immediately upon hearing from either. I regret that I did not send you a report last night, but I supposed that you did not expect one before this morning.

I am, general, yours, truly,

SHACKELFORD,
Brigadier-General.

Major-General PARKE,
Commanding Forces.

—

HEADQUARTERS CAVALRY CORPS,
Bean's Station, December 10, 1863—3 p. m.

GENERAL: I have just received report from Colonel Adams, commanding reconnaissance on Rogersville road. He had gone as far as Mooresburg, 3 miles this side of Red Bridge, when he came up with the enemy in considerable force guarding wagon train. He was then skirmishing with them. He represents that the enemy was dismounted and in a gorge, and that he would withdraw soon, as he could not dislodge him. Colonel Adams says that the last of the infantry left Mooresburg yesterday morning; that his cavalry encamped within 1½ miles of the point at which they were skirmishing. His dispatch was sent at 2 p. m. No further news from reconnaissance on Morristown road since Major Cutting left.

I am, general, yours, &c.,

SHACKELFORD,
Brigadier-General.

Major-General PARKE,
Commanding Forces.

—

HEADQUARTERS CAVALRY CORPS,
Bean's Station, December 10, 1863—8.10 p. m.

GENERAL: Your dispatch just received. Colonel Adams, commanding reconnaissance on Rogersville road, has returned. Not a word from Colonel Garrard, commanding reconnaissance on Morristown road, since Major Cutting left. Artillery firing reported in the direction of Morristown late this evening. I have just ordered 100 men to go out to forks of road, one-half mile of ford on Morristown road, and to send patrol to the ford to learn something from the reconnaissance. Colonel Adams reports that the enemy in considerable force, after he withdrew, came out and occupied the ground he held during the skirmishing. A prisoner from this command, Fourteenth Illinois, who escaped from the enemy last night, says that he marched 21 miles day before yesterday and 9 miles yesterday; that he left the rear of the enemy's infantry last night 3 miles this side of Rogersville; that their train was in front and their cavalry in the rear; that their encampment extended 8 miles. Immediately on hearing from reconnaissance on Morristown road I will report.

I am, general, yours, &c.,

SHACKELFORD,
Brigadier-General.

Major-General PARKE,
Commanding Forces.

—

HEADQUARTERS CAVALRY CORPS,
Bean's Station, December 10, 1863.

GENERAL : I have just received a report from the brigade sent out on the Morristown road under Colonel Garrard. He found rebel brigade, under General William E. Jones, at Morristown, occupying the fortifications built by our forces, engaged him, and drove him out of the works and out of the town. The brigade will come back and encamp at the river to-night. We lost several men, but the enemy's loss is reputed much heavier than ours.

I am, general, yours, truly,

SHACKELFORD,
Brigadier-General.

Major-General PARKE,
Commanding Forces.

—

HEADQUARTERS CAVALRY CORPS,
Bean's Station, December 11, 1863—9.25 a. m.

GENERAL : The engagement of Colonel Garrard's brigade with Jones at Morristown on last evening was a gallant affair. The enemy held every advantage in the ground, yet our men dashed into their midst and drove them from the fortifications and the town. Between 40 and 50 rebels are reported killed and wounded. Our loss, 6 wounded, none killed. It is thought that the rebels who went via Morristown will move on across the mountains into North Carolina. Colonel Garrard had the pleasure of defeating the same or a part of the same command that defeated him at Rogersville. Nothing heard from the enemy this morning.

Yours, &c.,

SHACKELFORD,
Brigadier-General.

Major-General PARKE,
Commanding Forces.

HEADQUARTERS CAVALRY CORPS,
Bean's Station, December 12, 1863—6.30 p. m.

GENERAL : The reconnaissance under Colonel Graham upon the Rogersville road came upon the enemy at Mooresburg, drove them back about 1 mile into a position from which he could not dislodge them without bringing on a general engagement. He withdrew his troops this side of Mooresburg. A prisoner from Fifty-first Virginia Regiment states that he left the rebel infantry 8 miles beyond Rogersville last night; they had stopped and were foraging. He states that the principal part of the rebel cavalry were at Russellville.

The reconnaissance to Morristown, under Colonel Pennebaker, found no enemy at that place, but found their pickets beyond town, on the Russellville road, and drove them in ; came upon line of battle, and they retreated up the road.

I am, general, yours,

J. M. SHACKELFORD,
Brigadier-General.

Major-General PARKE.

—

HEADQUARTERS CAVALRY CORPS,
Bean's Station, December 13, 1863—6 p. m.

GENERAL : I would have communicated with you before this to-day, but did not know where the communication would reach you.

In pursuance with your orders, I ordered 200 men to proceed to Morristown this morning, for the purpose of examining telegraph wire. They met enemy's pickets on this side of Morristown, and from statements of citizens in relation to there being rebels in the town and a heavy force at Cheek's Cross-Roads, the officer in command did not attempt to go to the town. Colonel Garrard, with his brigade, was sent to Morristown on yesterday, with orders to make reconnaissance upon the Russellville road. He found no enemy at Morristown, but found the enemy in considerable force at Cheek's Cross-Roads. He says he saw in line 2,000 or 2,500 rebels ; he had heavy skirmishing with them. Our loss 4 killed and a number wounded. Colonel Garrard says the enemy had 5,000 men at that point. It was Wheeler's command, under Martin. A prisoner captured from Third Alabama states that Wheeler's force was at that point. He gives their number at 5,000 or 6,000. I ordered a reconnaissance of 200 men up the Rogersville road this morning. They were attacked and driven in by the enemy, the enemy following up to our picket stand. Colonel Wolford's command lost three or four wagons that were on that road foraging. We met them at the picket stand, and drove them back 4½ miles.

Prisoners captured from the Fourth Kentucky (rebel) Cavalry stated that there were two rebel regiments, the Fourth and Tenth Kentucky. One of the prisoners stated that the Fourth Kentucky and one battalion of the Tenth were out there, making 600 men. One of the prisoners, who seemed to speak the truth, stated that Longstreet's command was at Red Bridge ; that Longstreet's headquarters were 5 miles above Mooresburg ; that Ransom's command had gone across the river at Rogersville, but that all of Longstreet's command was on this side of Rogersville. He also stated that all the cavalry, except that we were fighting this evening had gone this morning over to Cheek's Cross-Roads ; that they were sent down to feel our orces while that movement was being made. The statement in relation to Longstreet's headquarters is corroborated by a citizen who got through this evening, who lives 13 miles above this. General Willcox states that 3 prisoners were brought into his headquarters on last night who belonged to a Georgia regiment—Hood's division. All 3 had written passes up to 2 o'clock yesterday. They stated that their command was 7 miles below Rogersville, and that Bushrod Johnson's command was in the rear. It may be that the enemy is concentrating his cavalry at Cheek's Cross-Roads with the view of attacking me at this point, as he could much more easily attack from that direction than from the road leading to Rogersville. His movements this evening in both directions seem to indicate some such purpose.

I have ordered the troops to stand at arms at 6 a. m. to-morrow. I would suggest that if the enemy was to throw a considerable force of his cavalry over Clinch Mountain, he could seriously damage the trains from Cumberland Gap. If you have leisure, I would ask for you to ride up early in the morning.

I am, general, yours, truly,

J. M. SHACKELFORD,
Brigadier-General.

Major-General PARKE.

P. S.—I have been quite sick for two or three days.

Since writing the above Colonel Bond, who was in command of my advance, this evening reports that citizens who have come through since dark report that the cavalry on the Rogersville road was supported by infantry and artillery at Rock Spring, 5½ miles from here.

Since writing the above, Colonel Capron reports the rebels on the other bank of the river up and down; that his commissary and 6 of his men were at a mill on the other side of the river this evening; his men, except the commissary, were captured. I would suggest the propriety of an infantry force being moved up to-night to cover the road leading off to Turley's Ford, about 1 mile this side of Rutledge.

[Indorsement.]

RUTLEDGE,
December 13, 1863—10 p. m.

General FOSTER, *Knoxville:*

GENERAL: I have just arrived, and met the following* dispatch. I have ordered a force of infantry to march in the morning to the road indicated by General Shackelford. General Potter has pickets at Turley's Ford, at Turley's Mill, and on the road this side of there. The indications are that Longstreet has halted, and probably turned back a portion of his command, possibly all. To-morrow will probably develop his plans.

Yours, &c.,

JNO. G. PARKE.

———

HEADQUARTERS,
Bean's Station, December 14, 1863.

GENERAL: Since my report on last night, there has been no demonstrations on the part of the enemy. Reconnaissance on Rogersville made before daylight this morning ascertained that the

—————————
* Preceding.

enemy had fallen back from the position he occupied where the skirmishing closed at dark last night.   The glare of the enemy's camp fires could be seen 2 or 3 miles from the position he occupied at dark last evening.   The patrols on the roads to the river saw nor heard nothing of the enemy.

Respectfully, yours,

SHACKELFORD,
Brigadier-General.

Major-General PARKE.

No. 40.

Reports of Brig. Gen. Samuel D. Sturgis, U. S. Army, commanding Cavalry in East Tennessee. *

MILLIKEN'S HOUSE,
December 16, 1863.

GENERAL : The detachment sent by me to-day to examine the valley south of the hills on my right has returned, and the major reports that just before night he saw a regiment of rebel cavalry in line just beyond Eldridge's Mill ; that is, about 5½ miles from Blain's Cross-Roads.   I have already sent, according to your request, a small brigade of cavalry to Stone's Mill, and have five companies of infantry picketing a road leading in the general direction of Stone's Mill from this place.

I am, general, very respectfully, your obedient servant,
S. D. STURGIS,
Brigadier-General, Commanding Cavalry.

Maj. Gen. J. G. PARKE,
Commanding U. S. Troops.

HEADQUARTERS,
Milliken's, December 17, 1863—8.45 a. m.

GENERAL : Our pickets are now engaged, and the enemy (cavalry) appears to be advancing in column.   He has not developed his intentions yet.   Yesterday it seems that Colonel Graham sent a party in search of provisions through Powder Spring Gap, beyond the Clinch Mountain, and were fired upon, as reported by one of the members who returned.   We have heard nothing from the party since.   This probably was the firing heard by Lieutenant-Colonel Ward's party, as reported by him last night.

Respectfully,

S. D. STURGIS,
Brigadier-General, Commanding Cavalry.

Maj. Gen. J. G. PARKE.

[Indorsement.]

GENERAL : The within note has just been received.   If convenient, I would be much obliged if you would come up to my headquarters.

JNO. G. PARKE,
Major-General.

---

* See also Sturgis' correspondence with W. L. Elliott.

MILLIKEN'S HOUSE, *December* 17, 1863.

GENERAL: Our rear is getting up all right. The enemy is not advancing so boldly as heretofore. If he undertakes to advance to-morrow we will endeavor to check him, which I think we can pretty well. The question of forage, however, is very embarrassing, and I do not know what we shall be able to do on that score yet, nor do I suppose it is in your power to throw much light on the subject.

Respectfully,

S. D. STURGIS,
Brigadier-General, Commanding.

Major-General PARKE.

—

HEADQUARTERS,
Godwin's House, Four Miles from Rutledge,
December 17, 1863—4 p. m.

GENERAL: The enemy are now using a four-gun howitzer battery they have in position on the high ridge to our right, and can observe all our movements from that point. I would therefore suggest that you stop any movement of your troops at Rutledge until I can get under way, of which I will speedily inform you.

I think that if it is discovered that your troops and those here are falling back simultaneously we shall be too heavily pressed.

It is this moment reported by citizens (no doubt exaggerated) that a rebel force of 10,000 cavalry are coming down our right and rear.

I am, general,

S. D. STURGIS,
Brigadier-General, Commanding.

Maj. Gen. J. G. PARKE.

—

HEADQUARTERS,
Minett's House, Maynardville Road,
December 18, 1863.

GENERAL: Your note is just received. A brigade was sent last evening to occupy the gap on General Spears' left and to examine the country from Stone's Mill to the Holston. I will send an officer at once to see that there is no mistake in this matter. Your request in regard to a chain of couriers to Tazewell will be complied with at once.

I have just received a note from General Elliott, at Richland Creek bridge. He reports one of his brigades crossing at McKinney's Ford. General Spears represents to him that the enemy is in possession of Nance's Ford, or commands it. I think he should satisfy himself of this by a reconnaissance, and I will direct him to do so, which you will have time to countermand should you deem necessary. I would respectfully suggest that as General Spears has a brigade of cavalry at Stone's Mill, he might order such reconnaissances as are necessary from that, in the event of any misunderstanding by the other troops I have sent.

Respectfully, your obedient servant,

S. D. STURGIS,
Brigadier-General, Commanding Cavalry.

Major-General PARKE,
Blain's Cross-Roads.

27 R R—VOL XXXI, PT I

HEADQUARTERS CAVALRY CORPS,
Near McKinney's Ford, December 18, 1863—8 p. m.

GENERAL : I arrived here this moment with Wolford's division (three brigades) and one brigade of Foster's division, and find that but one brigade of General Elliott's division has crossed. He expects to complete the crossing by 9 a. m., commencing by daybreak to-morrow. General Elliott has sent out scouts, whom he expects to return during the night, and will be able to inform us what movements, if any, are going on in our front and below. The commanding officer at Strawberry Plains has been informed of the reported crossing of the enemy at Buffalo Ford. There is a force watching the ford about 2 miles below the Plains. This ford can hardly be used by cavalry at the present time.

I am, general, very respectfully, your most obedient servant,

S. D. STURGIS,
Brigadier-General, Commanding Cavalry.

Major-General FOSTER.

———

HEADQUARTERS CHIEF OF CAVALRY,
McKinney's Ford, December 19, 1863—7 a. m.

GENERAL : After General Elliott had crossed one brigade of his command the river rose, and is now from 3 to 4 feet deeper than it was at dark. There is no danger from the cavalry of the enemy crossing the river below.

I would suggest that a pontoon bridge be sent by rail to Strawberry Plains and thrown across the river at that place. In the meantime, I will let the brigade now on the other side move down to that place, and move the rest of General Elliott's command to Strawberry Plains to cover the collection of supplies by the brigade while awaiting your instructions. The rest of my command will go where it can be foraged.

I am, general, very respectfully, your obedient servant,

S. D. STURGIS,
Brigadier-General, and Chief of Cavalry.

Major-General FOSTER.

———

HEADQUARTERS CAVALRY CORPS,
Near Strawberry Plains, December 20, 1863—10 p. m.

GENERAL : Major Thornburgh, First Tennessee Cavalry, who was sent last night by General Elliott with two companies to the mills in the vicinity of New Market, has returned, and reports a large force of cavalry on the north (this) side the Holston, below Mossy Creek and at the mouth of Buffalo Creek.

Respectfully, your obedient servant,

S. D. STURGIS,
Brigadier-General, Commanding Cavalry Corps.

Maj. Gen. J. G. PARKE,
Commanding Army in Field, Blain's Cross-Roads.

(Same to Foster.)

HEADQUARTERS CAVALRY CORPS,
December 21, 1863.

Colonel Wolford reports that 3 of his men have just returned who were cut off while foraging near Bean's Station the 14th instant. They report having passed through the enemy's camp three days ago. That Longstreet's army, or the main body of his infantry, was at Bean's Station, between that place and Rutledge—reaching to Rutledge; his cavalry was at May's Mill, 4½ miles from Bean's Station, at Morristown, and at Mossy Creek. They think Longstreet has about 25,000 men.

S. D. STURGIS,
Brigadier-General.

Brigadier-General POTTER, *Chief of Staff.*

—

HEADQUARTERS CAVALRY CORPS,
Strawberry Plains, December 22, 1863.

Brigadier-General Elliott sends me the following information, which he received from Major Dyer, commanding force on the road from Rutledge to Dandridge. Major Dyer reports all quiet on the south side of the river. His citizen scout has seen a deserter, whom he knows to be a reliable man, and this man stated that he knew of but two divisions of infantry, though another was reported, all on the north side of the river, and that they are stationed 4 miles above Rutledge. The deserter also reported that he heard his brigade commander say they were going to move to the mouth of the Chucky and establish a line from Bean's Station to that point via Morristown. It is reported to Major Dyer that there is a cavalry force 10,000 strong in his immediate front, but that there is no infantry force on the south side of the river.

The enemy is guarding one of the fords on the Holston by infantry and artillery. I am endeavoring to find out what ford. Major-General Parke has been informed of this.

S. D. STURGIS,
Brigadier-General.

Major-General FOSTER, *Commanding.*

—

HEADQUARTERS CAVALRY CORPS,
Cobb's House, near Strawberry Plains,
December 22, 1863—9.30 p. m.

GENERAL: Elliott will cross his remaining brigade at the ford below the Plains by daylight to-morrow, ferrying over his artillery. He will march on New Market, which place he will reach by noon. Wolford, with two brigades, and Garrard, with one brigade, will cross at McKinney's Ford at daylight also, and march on the main road to New Market. Immediately upon crossing, a force will be sent to the upper fords to watch them.

I would suggest that you send Capron's brigade, now on the Maynardville road, up the Rutledge Valley early in the morning to make a demonstration there.

I am, general, very respectfully, your obedient servant,
S. D. STURGIS,
Brigadier-General, Commanding Cavalry Corps.

Maj. Gen. J. G. PARKE.

HEADQUARTERS CAVALRY CORPS,
December 22, 1863.

Five prisoners have just been brought in by General Elliott's troops, representing Armstrong's, Morgan's, and Martin's divisions. They say the enemy has two corps of cavalry, 10,000 in all; that Longstreet has been re-enforced from Virginia, and has 40,000 men. McKinney's Ford is still 2 feet higher than when crossed by General Elliott's brigade.

S. D. STURGIS,
Brigadier-General.

Major-General FOSTER.

—

HEADQUARTERS CAVALRY CORPS,
Near Strawberry Plains, Tenn., December 22, 1863.
(Received 23d.)

GENERAL: General Elliott will cross his remaining brigade over the Holston early to-morrow, and I have ordered Colonel Wolford to cross his division at McKinney's Ford at daylight. Colonel Garrard will cross his brigade at the same time and place.

I have requested Major-General Parke to order a demonstration on his front by means of the brigade of Colonel Foster's division, now (temporarily) under his control. You will perceive I leave two brigades behind—the one just referred to, of Colonel Foster's division, and the one sent from Colonel Wolford's division to the vicinity of Tazewell.

In view of the sudden rise the Holston and French Broad Rivers are subject to at this season, I would respectfully urge upon the general commanding the great importance of a pontoon bridge at Strawberry Plains, in order to keep open our line of retreat; for should these rivers rise suddenly, and Longstreet be able by the railroad to throw a column of infantry against us, our safety might be placed in great jeopardy in the absence of such a bridge. Of his power to use the railroad in any event I know nothing; of this the commanding general is probably better posted than myself.

I am, general, very respectfully, your obedient servant,

S. D. STURGIS,
Brigadier-General, Commanding Cavalry Corps.

Brig. Gen. E. E. POTTER,
Chief of Staff.

———

No. 41.

Reports of Brig. Gen. William P. Sanders, U. S. Army, commanding First Cavalry Division.

HEADQUARTERS FIRST DIVISION CAVALRY CORPS,
November 14, 1863.

GENERAL: Major Graham was attacked early this morning at Maryville; he had two companies as scouts. The rebels rode into his camp, and he reports that most of his men are captured. I hope a number of them will get in. I moved out with two regiments,

First Kentucky and Forty-fifth Ohio, to assist him ; met the enemy about 2 miles beyond here.   The First Kentucky was in the advance and driven back in confusion.   I succeeded in rallying a portion of them, and was driving them slowly when I got your letter.   They are now formed about 2½ miles from here.   I fear Captain Drye, First Kentucky, was killed.   Our loss, besides Major Graham's, is small. I can fall back without further trouble.

Respectfully,

W. P. SANDERS,
Brigadier-General.

Major-General BURNSIDE.

—

NOVEMBER 17, 1863—9.20 a. m.

GENERAL : Have met the advance of the enemy about 2 miles beyond the railroad crossing.   I can't say yet whether their force is advancing or not.   Only a few shots have been fired.

Respectfully,

W. P. SANDERS,
Brigadier-General.

Major-General BURNSIDE.

—

RAILROAD CROSSING,
November 17, 1863—11.50 a. m.

GENERAL : I have fallen back to this place, and will make another stand here.   I have just been pretty well shelled, though so far have had but slight loss ; 3 or 4 wounded, none killed.

Respectfully,

W. P. SANDERS,
Brigadier-General.

Major-General BURNSIDE.

———

No. 42.

*Itinerary of the First Cavalry Division, Col. Frank Wolford commanding.**

The division occupied position in the rifle-pits on the south side of Holston River, at Knoxville, until the morning of the 5th, when, the enemy having withdrawn his force of the investment, the division started in pursuit.

December 6, came up with the enemy and skirmished.

December 7, 8, and 9, skirmished when the division reached Bean's Station, where we went into camp.

December 10 and 11, scouting parties skirmished with the enemy on the Morristown and Virginia road.

December 11, the Third Brigade made a reconnaissance to Morristown and returned December 12.

December 13, quiet.

———

* From return for December.

December 14, heavy skirmishing with the enemy on the Virginia road; about 2 p. m. enemy drove in our pickets on the Virginia road. Soon the whole division was engaged, and fought until dark, when we fell back 4 miles. Lost about 130 killed and wounded.

December 15, took position and skirmished until dark, when we fell back to Blain's Cross-Roads and encamped.

December 21, sent the Third Brigade on reconnaissance toward Tazewell.

December 23, the First and Second Brigades (Third still at Tazewell) moved to New Market, crossing the Holston River at McKinney's Ford.

December 24, moved on the Dandridge road 1 mile from town and remained in line of battle all day, and then encamped.

December 25 and 26, all quiet.

December 27, moved to Mossy Creek and encamped.

December 28, all quiet; division doing heavy picketing and scouting.

December 29, moved to Dandridge, 12 miles, and returned to old camp.

December 30 and 31, all quiet; Third Brigade still across the Holston, near Buffalo Creek. Have found great scarcity of forage this month. Stock is much reduced and in poor condition from lack of forage, shoeing, and heavy service in picketing, scouting, &c. Some 1,200 of the command are dismounted.

No. 43.

Report of Col. Robert K. Byrd, First Tennessee Infantry, commanding Second Brigade.

HEADQUARTERS,
Kingston, Tenn., November 24, 1863—4.30 p. m.

A rebel force attacked us this morning about daylight, and we drove them back, taking 12 prisoners, killing 8 of them. The force is said to be from 5,000 to 6,000 strong; we saw a large number. Wheeler is in command. I sent the hull of a steam-boat last night. I hope it will arrive safe. I hear of 20 mules below here; all safe. General Burnside is still in Knoxville; said to be surrounded. We have no communication with him.

Your obedient servant,

R. K. BYRD,
Colonel, Commanding Post.

General GRANT.

No. 44.

Itinerary of the Third Brigade, Col. Charles D. Pennebaker commanding. *

November 1, the brigade crossed to the south side of the Holston River. From Knoxville marched to Rockford, 10 miles. Encamped near Rockford.

---

* From returns for November and December.

November 2, marched to Maryville, 5 miles. Went into camp. Scouting parties sent out daily. Skirmishing with the enemy until the 10th. Moved back to Rockford and remained until the 14th, when the enemy attacked and moved back to Knoxville, and returned as far as Mount Olive (4 miles) same day.

November 15, skirmished all day. Fell back to Knoxville.

November 16, recrossed the river at dark.

November 18, in the morning, met the enemy on the Kingston road, 3½ miles out from Knoxville. Fought him on the 18th, 19th, and 20th. At 3 o'clock was ordered inside the fortifications.

November 22, recrossed to the south side of the river. From that time until the 30th the brigade was engaged in building fortifications and occupying the rifle-pits on the south side of the river, with continued skirmishing during the siege.

December 1, this brigade occupied its place in the rifle-pits on the south side of the Holston River, opposite the city of Knoxville, until the morning of the 5th, when, the enemy having withdrawn his forces from the investment, the mounted forces started in pursuit. The Forty-fifth Ohio Mounted Infantry, forming a part of the Third Brigade, moved 8 miles; came up with rear of the enemy.

December 6, skirmished with him.

December 7, same.

December 8, came up with enemy at Rutledge.

December 9, arrived at Bean's Station, and with one regiment skirmished the enemy at the Holston, on the Morristown road.

December 10, lay in camp.

December 11, made a reconnaissance to Morristown.

December 12, lay in camp.

December 13, skirmished with enemy on the Virginia road and moved camp a half mile back.

December 14, enemy attacked; fought until dark, when we moved back 4 miles.

December 15, took position; skirmished the enemy all day. At night fell back to Rutledge and encamped.

December 16, fell back to Blain's Cross-Roads; skirmished with the enemy all day.

December 17, sent out a reconnaissance 10 miles in the direction of Tazewell; returned in the evening.

December 18, remained in camp at Blain's Cross-Roads.

December 19, remained in camp until night, when the brigade moved 5 miles in the direction of McKinney's Ford.

December 20, moved back to Blain's Cross-Roads and remained in camp all day.

December 21, at 2 p. m. started on a reconnaissance in the direction of Tazewell, and encamped for the night near Maynardville.

December 22, marched to Tazewell and went into camp.

December 23, remained in camp at Tazewell.

December 24, started back in the direction of Blain's Cross-Roads and encamped at Walker's Ford, on Clinch River.

December 25, returned to Blain's Cross-Roads and went into camp.

December 26, remained in camp.

December 27, in the evening moved 10 miles to the front and encamped near the mouth of Buffalo Creek, on the Holston.

December 28, went into camp and remained until December 31, performing picket duty, scouting, guarding ferries, &c.

ADDENDA.

Report of Casualties in Third Brigade, First Division, Cavalry Corps, from th
24th day of September, 1863 (the time of leaving Kentucky for East Tennessee), t
December 20, 1863:

Regiments.	Field and staff.			Company officers.			Enlisted men.			Total.	Aggregate.
	Killed.	Wounded.	Missing.	Killed.	Wounded.	Missing.	Killed.	Wounded.	Missing.		
27th Kentucky Mounted Infantry		1					9	22	6	37	3
11th Kentucky Mounted Infantry					2			16	18	34	3
45th Ohio Mounted Infantry	1			3		4	11	42	259	a322	a32
Total	1	1		3	2	4	20	80	283	393	40

a Error.

Respectfully submitted.

C. D. PENNEBAKER,
Colonel, Commanding.

No. 45.

*Report of Col. John W. Foster, Sixty-fifth Indiana Infantry, com
manding Second Cavalry Division.*

DECEMBER 6, 1863.

One brigade of my division is at Mr. Fetridge's, 4 miles southeast of Maynardville; the other is 2 miles from it, between Log
Mountain and Copper Ridge, on Bull Run Creek. Jones' cavalry division is just beyond Copper Ridge within sight of my pickets.
Heavy skirmishing with him to-day, capturing a number of prisoners,
including 1 captain and 70 fine horses.

Wheeler's cavalry corps is protecting Longstreet's rear. A part
of his force is protecting Blain's Cross-Roads. His retreat is quite
leisurely. My force is not large, and in bad condition. I will push
the enemy as much as I can. Have the cavalry below communicate
with me. Generals Foster and Willcox are at Tazewell.

God bless you.

JOHN W. FOSTER,
Colonel, Commanding Cavalry Division.

Brigadier-General SHACKELFORD.

No. 46.

*Reports of Col. Felix W. Graham, Fifth Indiana Cavalry, com-
manding Second Brigade.*

MAYNARDVILLE,
December 1, 1863—11.30 a. m.

A party which I sent on the Knoxville road has come up with
rebels about 3 miles out; they are skirmishing now. A scout
which I sent toward Blain's Cross-Roads reports half a regiment at
the cross-roads, and a party of about a hundred 4 miles this side;

y scout is within a mile of the latter.   A citizen just in reports the
nemy as having evacuated Knoxville, and retreating in direction
f Morristown.   A rebel woman of this place, who left here a few
ays ago for the purpose of visiting her husband in the rebel serv-
:e, returned last night, and says she did not see her husband, as
ongstreet had been ordered to fall back to Georgia, and is gone,
nd that none but cavalry remained around Knoxville.

F. W. GRAHAM,
Colonel, Commanding Brigade.

Lieut. J. S. BUTLER,
   Acting Assistant Adjutant-General.

—

MAYNARDVILLE,
December 1, 1863.

SIR : Skirmishing has been kept up all day on the main Knoxville
oad about 4 miles from town, without any detriment to either side.
'he enemy had a position on the mountains, and kept it.   Our scouts
'ent out on the road to Blain's Cross-Roads; came up with the enmy about 8 miles out; skirmished with them nearly all day without
ny loss on our side.   Late this evening Carter was reported within
 miles of town.   I have decided on holding this place until the enmy's intentions are more fully known.   Firing commenced at Knoxille about 3 o'clock this afternoon, and still continues.

F. W. GRAHAM,
Colonel, Commanding Brigade.

Lieut. J. S. BUTLER,
   Acting Assistant Adjutant-General.

—

HDQRS. SECOND BRIG., SECOND DIV., CAVALRY CORPS,
December 3, 1863.

GENERAL : A prisoner taken below here a few miles states that the
ebel forces had orders to fall back to Maynardville last night.   He
lso reports that they had orders to move on Kingston ; also states
hat the forces yesterday were four brigades, commanded by Generals
Iorgan, Jones, and Armstrong, and Colonel Dibrell, commanding
rigade.   Colonel Dibrell was badly wounded.   The assistant adju-
ant-general was killed in the charge.   From all information their
oss was not as large as first expected; will not exceed 50.   Perhaps
 will be able to get forage for the brigade.
   Respectfully, yours, &c.,

F. W. GRAHAM,
Colonel, Commanding.

Brigadier-General WILLCOX,
   Commanding Forces.

—

FOUR MILES FROM WALKER'S FORD,
December 4, [1863]—1.20 p. m.

GENERAL : The following has just been received from Colonel
Iraham :

My scouts have been down on Knoxville road 18 miles, and have been in direction
f Blain's Cross-Roads ; within 5 miles of the cross-roads learned that one brigade,
nder General Jones, went off in the direction of Blain's Cross-Roads.   Major-Gen-

eral Martin, with his division, moved to Knoxville. One brigade went off on ?
Clinton road in the direction of Kingston. I think their object is to get forage.
will have information from Rutledge and Clinton by 12 o'clock to-day. I will st?
General Foster's dispatch at once. Fighting has been going on at Knoxville
day.

Yours, respectfully,

HENRY BOWMAN,
Colonel, and Chief of Staff.

Maj. Gen. John G. Foster.

—

HEADQUARTERS SECOND BRIGADE,
December 5, 1863.

Colonel : The scouting party that went to Powder Spring G?
report a large amount of camp fires on the road leading from Blai?
Cross-Roads to Rutledge. The soldier that I started with dispat?
to Knoxville did not get through, but returned this morning, a?
reported a column of rebels passing on the road leading from Kno?
ville to Blain's Cross-Roads; that the column continued all nigh?
that they remarked, on the road, that they were going to Virgin?
They expected the Yankees had them surrounded, and that th?
expected to fight their way out. From all information, it appea?
that they are moving in the direction of Virginia. Whether the
object is to move in our rear or not, I cannot tell, as their mov?
ments are mysterious, and hard to understand. My headquarte?
will be, this morning, 8 miles from the river.

Respectfully, yours, &c.,

F. W. GRAHAM,
Colonel, Commanding.

Col. Jno. W. Foster, *Commanding Division.*

P. S.—My patrol just returned reports, as far as can be relied o?
no rebels in the direction of Clinch, except small scouting partie?
that they expected to leave here, and would take everything of a?
value.

—

Sir : I have the honor to report that, in accordance with orders,
marched from camp, near the bridge over Powell River, on ma?
Cumberland Gap road, on 27th November, 1863.

My brigade consisted of the Fourteenth Illinois Cavalry, Colon
Capron commanding; Fifth Indiana Cavalry, Lieutenant-Colon
Butler commanding; Sixty-fifth Indiana Mounted Infantry, Capta?
Hodge commanding, and Colvin's (Illinois) battery, Captain Colv?
commanding. Beside the four guns of Colvin's battery, there we?
four mountain howitzers, attached to Fourteenth Illinois Cavalr?
and two 8-inch rifled guns, attached to Fifth Indiana Cavalry. ?
entire force numbered 10 field and staff officers, 47 company officer?
and 1,031 non-commissioned officers and enlisted men, making ?
aggregate of 1,088.

I moved, via Tazewell, taking the Straight Creek road at th?
point to within 4 miles of Walker's Ford, where I encamped for t?
night.

On the morning of the 28th, I crossed Clinch River and bivo?
acked at Brock's, 4 miles from Walker's Ford, where my commar?
fed. Toward night, moved down the right-hand road, recrossi?
Clinch River at Headham's Ford, and camped for the night ne?
Headham's Mill.

On the morning of the 29th, I moved down Clinch River to Ons-ly's Ford, where I crossed and took the direct road to Maynard-ille, where I camped for the night.

On the morning of the 30th, I marched with all of my available orce on the main road leading from Maynardville to Knoxville, aving previous to starting sent a detachment of Fifth Indiana avalry in advance with orders to go to the enemy's pickets and eport back as soon as they were found. I had proceeded 15 miles, hen a courier reported a small rebel patrolling party on the road, bout 4 miles in advance of my main force, and which my advance ad driven in. I halted my command at this point, and remained here some time, awaiting further information. On learning there as a force of rebels at or near Blain's Cross-Roads, I moved back o Maynardville and camped for the night, throwing out strong icket force and small patrol parties on all the roads on the front nd left.

On morning of December 1, my pickets were attacked at the gap, miles below Maynardville, on Knoxville road. They were speedily e-enforced by detachments from each regiment and two of the Four-eenth's howitzers. More or less firing took place during the day, oth parties holding their ground. Scouting parties were also sent ut in considerable force during the day. The one on the road lead-ng to Blain's Cross-Roads was driven back, and during the after-oon I had such information as led me to believe that a considerable avalry force of the enemy was approaching, and by 9 p. m. I be-ame convinced that an attempt would be made to surround and apture my command.

I decided at once to move, but several of my scouting parties be-ng several miles out I could not get my force concentrated till near nidnight, when, all being in, I moved quietly on the road to Walk-r's Ford, leaving Company M, Fifth Indiana Cavalry, at the point vhere the road from Blain's Cross-Roads comes in, with instructions or a part of it to patrol the road back to Maynardville; proceeding n to Brock's, I halted that the men and horses might be fed. This vas about 5 a. m., December 2.

Forage parties were sent out, and rations were being issued as laylight appeared, and my pickets in rear of camp were vigorously ttacked. Although my command was tired, men sleepy and hun-gry, and the natural condition of my camp, after a night's march, omewhat irregular, yet all were under arms and in shape to repel he attack in the very shortest possible time.

I immediately sent the Fourteenth Illinois Cavalry to the river nd down the road leading from Walker's Ford to Rutledge, feeling onfident that I could, with the remainder of my force, keep the nemy in check and make good my retreat to and across the river. Two guns of Colvin's battery were sent to Walker's Ford, with rders to cross and take position on the bank of the river, so as to ommand all the approaches to the fords. By half past seven o'clock ny pickets had fallen back to Brock's house, the enemy advancing n such numbers as to compel them to give way at this time. My nain force was in position, the Sixty-fifth Indiana on the left of the ine, a portion of the Second and Third Battalions, Fifth Indiana Cavalry in center, and one company of the Sixty-fifth Indiana, and ne from the Fifth Indiana Cavalry on right. The guns of the Fifth Indiana Cavalry were put in position in rear of center, on a rise of ground, from which they did good service in keeping the enemy in check. Three companies of Fifth Indiana Cavalry, under comman of Major Woolley, and one section of Colvin's battery, under Ca tain Colvin, were placed in reserve.

The firing had now become somewhat brisk, and the enemy n only showed his force, but made attempts to flank my position. could only prevent him from doing so by gradually falling bacl which I did, to the point near Yeadon's house, where I brought m command into close order, and under cover of a fence and a lc house or barn. The enemy here made a charge in column, whic was splendidly met by a portion of each regiment, and which prove decidedly disastrous to the enemy.

My artillery had now been retired, the formation of the groun on which it had to pass being unsuited to its use. The enemy bein exhausted [exasperated] at their repulse pushed on furiously, bu the gallant officers and men of my command were not to be drive back so easily; on the contrary, they manfully contested every foo of ground, falling back slowly to a point about 1 mile from the rive where they were re-enforced by the One hundred and sixteent and One hundred and eighteenth Indiana Infantry, Colonel Jacksc commanding brigade.

These regiments being in position and my men being out of an munition, I retired my force across the river, thus ending the figh so far as the Fifth Indiana Cavalry and Sixty-fifth Indiana Mounte Infantry were concerned. Colvin's battery was engaged for som time after in shelling the enemy, and the Fourteenth Illinois Ca alry was also engaged for a short time after on the road leading t Rutledge. I respectfully refer you to the report of Colonel Capro herewith attached, for an account of the part the Fourteenth Illinoi Cavalry took in repelling the attack and advance of the enemy.

I now come to speak of the enemy, his designs and expectation After hearing reports of prisoners and the citizens along the line c the enemy's march, I am confident that there were five brigades c cavalry and mounted infantry brought against my little force, th whole under command of Major-General Martin. The design wa to keep my force engaged at the gap, 4 miles below Maynardville until a portion of their forces could be moved from Blain's Cross Roads into the road between me and Walker's Ferry, and at th same time a sufficient force had been sent around my front (Onsley' Ford) to blockade the road to that point. At daylight, on mornin of 2d instant, my entire command was to have been surrounded The enemy moved on to a consummation of the object he so devoutl wished for, only to find he had surrounded a camp barren of every thing save the fires which my [men] had left in good order.

In surrounding my camp he did, however, capture a portion of N Company, Fifth Indiana Cavalry, which had been left to patrol th road back to Maynardville, and were not able to cut their way out Finding themselves foiled in their first attempts, they next tried t cut my command off at Walker's Ford, and that, too, proved a fail ure, and at the same time cost them a considerable loss in killed wounded, and prisoners.

From all the information I can get, and having made every effor to get at their loss, I am satisfied they lost 25 killed, about 5 wounded, and 28 prisoners.

Major-General Martin was wounded in the wrist. Colonel Dibrel commanding brigade, was seriously, if not mortally, wounded. Hi adjutant-general was killed. Captain ———, who led in the charge was also killed.

Of the officers and men of my command I cannot speak too highly; ghting as they did, at the least calculation, five times their number, nd standing unflinchingly as they did for eight hours before such a ıperior force, and only retiring from the field for want of ammu- ition, certainly indicates the highest order of bravery. It is hard) make special mention of any single one when all did so well. I ust, however, speak of those who came under my special notice. ieut. John O'Neil, Company I, Fifth Indiana Cavalry, my acting ssistant adjutant-general, rendered me great assistance in conduct- ιg the engagement, was constantly under fire, and was finally ounded and taken from the field. Lieut. R. P. Finney, Company I, Fifth Indiana Cavalry, my aide-de-camp, proved himself a brave nd efficient officer. Captain Hodge, commanding Sixty-fifth Indi- na Mounted Infantry, displayed the highest order of bravery, as ell as decided good judgment in commanding his force, and I take leasure in recommending [him] for speedy promotion to the posi- .on of a field officer. Lieutenant-Colonel Butler, Fifth Indiana 'avalry, was, as on all previous occasions, cool and determined, and t all times kept control of his men. Adjutant Roberts, Fifth Indi- na Cavalry, had his horse shot under him.

I am glad to state that the officers and men of the Fourteenth Illi- ois Cavalry all acted nobly their part. On their efforts depended uch of the success of the day.

In conclusion, I have to append a list of casualties, which, under ll the circumstances, I am happy to record as small, considering the ırgely superior force opposed to mine and the closeness of the two uring certain portions of the engagement:

Sixty-fifth Indiana Mounted Infantry, 2 men killed and 6 wounded; 'ifth Indiana Cavalry, 2 officers wounded and 5 men killed, 10 men ounded and 10 men missing; Fourteenth Illinois Cavalry, 7 men ounded. Total, 2 officers wounded and 7 men killed, 23 men ounded and 21 men missing.

Very respectfully,

F. W. GRAHAM,
Colonel, Commanding Brigade.

Lieut. J. S. BUTLER,
Acting Assistant Adjutant-General.

No. 47.

Report of Col. Horace Capron, Fourteenth Illinois Cavalry.

HEADQUARTERS FOURTEENTH ILLINOIS CAVALRY,
In Camp, near Clinch River, Tenn., December 4, 1863.

SIR: I would respectfully report that on the morning of the 2d nstant, being ordered to move down the right bank of Clinch River o the forks of the road, 5 miles from Walker's Ford, I moved my ommand, the Fourteenth Illinois Cavalry, down the river 2 miles ıntil I came to a ford and road leading to Maynardville, intersecting he main road from Maynardville to Walker's Ford, in the rear of he enemy, at that time engaging the remainder of your brigade. Iesitating to proceed farther, I halted my regiment and awaited our orders, sending scouting parties on the Maynardville and river oads. I had hardly received your orders to hold the Maynardville oad and river crossing before our advance on the Maynardville road

was attacked by the rebels 2 miles from the main body. My regime
was then posted at the river crossing. I immediately sent the Thi
Battalion to re-enforce the advance, which, after advancing one-ha
mile, engaged the enemy, our forces taking position in the center
the road running through a narrow gorge, the rebel cavalry advan
ing in column down the road and charging our center, but were 1
pulsed. The rebels then moved a column on our right and charge
our right and center, and were again repulsed at both points. Th
then deployed skirmishers on both our flanks on the hills and aga
charged our right. The remainder of my regiment having bee
placed in position, the Third Battalion was ordered to the rear a1
reform, which they did, the rebels advancing on our rear line, a
tacking the whole line with skirmishers. Two companies were se1
to the hills to dislodge their sharpshooters, who were annoying o1
lines, and a rapid and heavy firing was continued through our who
lines.

At 1 p. m. the Third Battalion, with howitzers, were withdraw
to the left bank of the river, the First and Second Battalions sti
fighting the rebels, but compelled to gradually fall back, overpov
ered by superior numbers and flanked by sharpshooters. The Thi
Battalion was immediately deployed on the left bank of the rive
and the howitzer battery placed in position. At this moment o1
position became critical, as their sharpshooters occupied the heigh
in good range of our position, but were fortunately held in check k
our howitzers until, the fire of the rebels gradually slackening a1
our ammunition nearly exhausted, the main part of my regime1
was withdrawn to your command at Walker's Ford, leaving tw
companies with the small amount of ammunition necessary to ho1
the ford, which they did until relieved by a regiment of infantry.

The whole command fought with coolness and bravery, and o1
loss must have been much greater had not the natural position of t1
ground been greatly advantageous to us—twenty-four officers a1
300 men, with the following casualties: Wounded, 7; missing, 11.

The engagement commenced at 10 a. m., continuing until 3 p. n
From information obtained of prisoners, the force attacking us w;
General Jones' cavalry division, consisting of two brigades.

I would also report the capture of 18 prisoners on the 2d and 3
instant.

Respectfully, your obedient servant,
HORACE CAPRON,
Colonel, Commanding.

Lieut. R. P. FINNEY, *Acting Assistant Adjutant-General.*

No. 48.

Report of Brig. Gen. James H. Wilson, U. S. Army, of enginee
operations connected with Sherman's march to the relief of Kno;
ville.

HDQRS. MIL. DIV. OF THE MISSISSIPPI,
Nashville, Tenn., January 14, 1864.

SIR: I have the honor to submit the following report of enginee
operations during the march of Major-General Sherman's comman
to the relief of Knoxville, East Tenn. :

Having been directed by General Grant to join the expedition,

eported in person to General Sherman at Charleston on the evening of November 30.   The troops of the Eleventh Corps were at that
time engaged in repairing the bridge across the Hiwassee at that
place.   At the suggestion of General Sherman, I examined it and
found that the injury done could soon be repaired.   The rebels had
sawed the string-pieces of only one span in two, so that the trestle
upon which they rested had fallen against the one adjacent, leaving
a breach of about 30 feet to be repaired.   New string-pieces were
soon obtained and put in their place; the entire bridge was then
planked over with materials which the enemy had sawed for the
purpose of rebuilding a truss bridge in the place of the old one.   By
morning it was ready for the passage of troops.   This work was
done by Colonel Asmussen and Major Hoffmann, of General Howard's staff.

General Granger's command crossed the Hiwassee at Kincannon's
Ferry, using a steam-boat and several flats.

On the 3d of December, at 11 a. m., the advance of Sherman's column reached the Little Tennessee River, 15 miles from its junction
with the Holston at a point opposite the village of Morganton.
That place was selected under the expectation that our troops might
be crossed through the ford said to be there.   The ford, however,
was found to be 3½ feet deep, with a hard gravel bottom, but full of
uneven spots.   In addition to this, the stream is 240 yards wide and
quite swift.   The temperature of the water at the time was 37° Fah-
renheit.   These facts rendered it difficult and unsafe to undertake
to use the ford.   Having no pontoon train and but two poor flat-
boats capable of carrying 40 or 50 men each, we were compelled to
devise means of building a bridge.   The enemy not having shown
himself, troops were gradually ferried across by the boats till a sufficient force was on the northern side of the river to furnish working parties and establish pickets

Under the direction of Captain Cassell, of General Ewing's staff,
a number of unoccupied frame and hewed log-houses were selected
and torn down.   The timber thus obtained was hauled to the river
by the troops and wagons obtained in the town; the square stuff was
framed into trestles by the pioneer company of Ewing's division,
and the planks got ready for decking.   The site selected for the
bridge was along the axis of the ford, to avoid the deep water above
and below and secure good approaches.

The working parties, detailed by chance from infantry regiments,
were divided into four sections, each under reliable officers.   The
first, on the south side of the river, was directed to get out green
logs for abutments and crib-piers; the second was directed to prepare the approach and build the abutment; the third, on the north
side, was to prepare the abutment and the road up the bank, and
the fourth was ordered to assist the pioneers in building the bridge
itself.

The work was commenced at dark and continued till the part up
accidentally fell.   This was occasioned by neglecting to counteract the
shore thrust against the trestles by bracing or tieing.   The work was
fairly begun again by daylight, and completed by 8 p. m. the same
day.

The bridge was 240 yards long; two bays in the shallowest water
next the bank on the south side were of split timber, resting on oak-
log cribs 15 feet apart; the balance was of trestles.

The trestles were composed of cap and ground sills, 10 feet long

and from 6 to 10 inches square, with uprights of the same sized tim
ber, but only 4½ and 5 feet long. They were framed or bunte
together with square joints, and secured by nailing to the uprigh
pieces of plank sufficiently long to extend from the top of the ca
sill to the bottom of the ground sill, and the whole strengthened b
diagonal braces of plank nailed on in the same way.

The balks were hewed house logs and rafters from 14 to 20 fee
long. From three to five were used in each span. The deck wa
made of planks taken from the fences and houses, but having a ver
limited supply of nails and no rope for rack lashings it could not b
firmly secured. Side rails were laid on, and in most cases were kej
in place only by their own weight.

To give further stability to the bridge, and particularly to guar
against the shore thrust, where it was practicable, braces extendin
from the top of one trestle to the bottom of the one adjacent wer
set in. As the pioneers could raise only three saws, six axes, a ver
limited supply of nails, no rope, and but three augers, almost er
tirely useless, the means of firmly assembling all parts were ver
limited.

The trestles were set by using one of the flat-boats in the manne
prescribed by the pontoon or bridge manual.

With slight repairs, the bridge just described was used by all th
troops of Sherman's command in crossing or recrossing except How
ard's corps.

I have no official account of the means used by General Howard
but understand that he constructed a foot-bridge for his infantry b
using a number of wagons abandoned by the rebels at Loudon. Th
wagons and artillery went through the ford.

His crossing was made at Davis' Ford, 3 miles above the junctio
of the Little Tennessee and the Holston.

I am, general, very respectfully, your obedient servant,

J. H. WILSON,
Brigadier-General, U. S. Vols., Captain of Engineers.

Brig. Gen. WILLIAM F. SMITH,
Chief Engineer.

No. 49.

Itinerary of the Second and Third Divisions, Fourth Army Corp
(Army of the Cumberland), Maj. Gen. Gordon Granger com
manding.*

November 28, ordered to make a forced march to the relief o
Knoxville, and moved at once [from Chattanooga], leaving thei
records, books, papers, and baggage stored at Chattanooga.

December 1, on the march to Knoxville; crossed the Hiwasse
River in boats at Kincannon's Ferry, working day and night.

December 3, head of column encamped near Morganton.

December 5, crossed Little Tennessee River at Morganton.

December 6, went into camp, awaiting orders, between Maryvill
and the Little Tennessee River, and within 12 miles of Knoxville
ordered to Knoxville to hold the place, and reached there the 7th.

---

* From returns for November and December.

December 15, ordered to the front of Knoxville, toward Blain's
ross-Roads, holding a defensive position near the latter place until
e close of the month.

No. 50.

inerary of the Eleventh Army Corps (Army of the Cumberland),
Maj. Gen. Oliver O. Howard commanding. *

November 29, corps marches [from Red Clay] to Cleveland ; reached
at place at 5 p. m.
November 30, 8 a. m., marches to Charleston ; went into camp at 1
, m.
December 1, corps marches to Athens.
December 2, corps marches to Philadelphia.
December 3, corps marches to Loudon, capturing some supplies of
e enemy.
December 4, the Eighty-second Illinois Volunteers, sent over the
ver, takes four guns and a flag abandoned by the rebels.
December 5, 1 a. m., corps marches to Davis' Ford ; crossed on a
agon bridge ; encamped at night between Unitia and Louisville.
December 6, corps stationary.
December 7, marches to Davis' Ford ; crosses the Little Tennessee ;
nd encamps.
December 8, corps marched to Sweet Water ; Hecker's brigade to
thens.
December 9, corps marched to Athens ; Hecker's brigade to
harleston.
December 10 and 11, corps stationary.
December 12, corps marched to Charleston.
December 13, Second Division marches to Cleveland.
December 14, First Brigade, Third Division, marches to Cleve-
nd.
December 15, Third Division marches to Cleveland.
December 16, corps marches to Tyner's Station.
December 17, marches to Lookout Valley, the former encampment.

No. 51.

inerary of the Second Division, Fourteenth Army Corps (Army
of the Cumberland), Brig. Gen. Jefferson C. Davis command-
ing. *

November 29, marched [from Parker's Gap] through McDonald's
ap, and encamped.
November 30, near Cleveland, Tenn., under orders, with General
herman's command, to move to the assistance of General Burnside
t Knoxville.
December 1, division in the vicinity of Charleston, Tenn., moving
oward Knoxville, with the command of General Sherman, to the

---

* From returns for November and December.

relief of General Burnside. After crossing the Tennessee Riv
received orders to countermarch by way of Columbus, on the I
wassee River, to Chattanooga.

December 7 to 14, stationed at Columbus, gathering supplies fr
that vicinity and using the several mills for grinding.

December 15, marched for Chattanooga, where it arrived on
afternoon, on the 19th, and went into its former camp.

December 26, broke up camp at Chattanooga; marched out a
went into camp near Rossville, Ga., where it now remains, doi
picket duty, &c. During the campaign in East Tennessee the
vision marched 240 miles, with but six days' provisions drawn fr
the Government.

No. 52.

Report of Col. John M. Loomis, Twenty-sixth Michigan Infant
  commanding First Brigade, Fourth Division, Fifteenth Ar
  Corps (Army of the Tennessee).

SIR: I have the honor respectfully to report that, pursuant
orders from headquarters Fourth Division, Fifteenth Army Corps
marched from Graysville, Ga., November 29, 1863, on the Clevela
road, following the advance of Colonel Cockerill, and, after a sev
march of 25 miles over difficult roads, I bivouacked late at nig
near Cleveland, on the line of the East Tennessee and Georgia R
road.

On the following day, after having destroyed a portion of t
road above mentioned, I marched with my brigade in advance of t
division from Cleveland to Charleston, and from thence on the f
lowing day to Athens, Tenn.

December 2, the march was resumed, going from Athens, Ten
to Philadelphia, and on the 3d of December, from Philadelphia
the Little Tennessee River, opposite Morganton. Here it was fou
necessary to build a bridge over the river, and while this was bei
done Colonel Cockerill and myself ferried our respective brigac
across the stream and held the opposite bank until the bridge w
completed.

December 5, marched from Morganton to Maryville, Tenn.,
present location of the command. This command has been alm
entirely subsisted during the march by foraging upon the count
yet it has been done so regular and systematic that no scarcity
provisions has existed nor has straggling, private foraging, or pl
dering been tolerated, but, on the contrary, men caught at it ha
been most severely punished. Each day a detail of 4 commissior
officers and 40 men has been sent out with instructions to collect s
sistence for the brigade, but in no case to allow pillaging or for
ing for the benefit of private individuals. The subsistence th
obtained I have had brought to my headquarters and distributed
the command. In this way I have been able to supply the demar
of my men and maintain proper discipline, at the same time I ha
endeavored, so far as possible, to obtain my supplies from rebels a
their sympathizers, and where I have found it absolutely necess
to take the property of loyal citizens I have caused the proper
ceipts to be given.

No particular incidents have marked the march from Graysville, ., to this place except the heroic endurance of the troops, which s been beyond all praise. They have made long and forced arches on short rations and with insufficient clothing, too many of e men marching barefooted over the frozen ground, yet all has been eerfully borne, officers and men being animated by the desire of lieving Major-General Burnside and his troops from their im- isonment and of capturing the famed General Longstreet and his my.

I have the honor to transmit herewith the accompanying reports regimental commanders.

I have the honor to be, captain, very respectfully, your obedient rvant,

JOHN MASON LOOMIS,
Colonel 26th Ill. Infty., Comdg. 1st Brig., 4th Div., 15th A. C.

Capt. J. D. McFARLAND,
Assistant Adjutant-General.

No. 53.

inerary of the Second Brigade, Second Cavalry Division (Army of the Cumberland), Col. Eli Long commanding.*

December 1, brigade marched from Benton, Tenn., to Columbia, enn., and thence to Athens via Charleston. From Athens the bri- de marched in advance of General Sherman's command to Loudon, ear which place the advance regiment met a force of rebel cavalry. outed them and took 30 prisoners, losing 1 man killed and 2 wounded.

December 3, Colonel Long being ordered to move forward to noxville and open communication with General Burnside, crossed ittle Tennessee River and marched via Maryville, reaching Knox- lle early next morning.

On the night of the 6th, pursuant to orders from General Sherman, rigade marched to Maryville, and from here started in pursuit of a bel wagon train, and followed it across the mountains into North arolina, encountering no resistance, except from a small force of bel cavalry at Murphy, N. C.

December 11, started back, and arrived at Calhoun, Tenn., De- ember 15. On the 1st, a detachment of the Third U. S. Cavalry as added to the command and relieved on arrival at Calhoun. The ifth Ohio Volunteer Cavalry being temporarily attached, a line of uriers was established to Loudon and Kingston, and communica- on opened with Chattanooga in same manner. The Third Ohio olunteer Cavalry was sent to Columbus, Tenn., on the Hiwassee iver, to guard that point and the adjacent fords.

December 22, the courier post at Cleveland was attacked by 60 bel cavalry and had 1 man wounded. Rebel casualties, 2 wounded.

December 28, General Wheeler, with 1,500 rebel cavalry and some rtillery, attacked a wagon train, moving to Knoxville from Chatta- ooga, and escorted by infantry, convalescents, &c. Colonel Long t once mounted the small portion of his command not on duty (less han 150 men) and charged the enemy, whose ranks had been broken

---

*From return for December. The Ninety-eighth Illinois, Seventeenth Indiana, nd detachments of the Fourth Michigan and Third U. S. Cavalry Regiments were ttached to this command.

by the infantry escort, scattering them in every direction. Pur sued one column of 400 or 500 men several miles and captured 1 prisoners, including 5 officers and many stand of arms. Wheele lost several killed and many wounded; among the latter, 2 colonel

December 30, the Fifth Ohio Volunteer Cavalry was relieved, b order, from duty with the brigade.

No. 54.

*Itinerary of the Cavalry, Army of the Cumberland, Maj. Gen David S. Stanley and Brig. Gen. Washington L. Elliott con manding.**

Headquarters of cavalry command and First Division remained camp at Winchester, Tenn., until November 16. Detachments wer sent out various times to drive away guerrillas infesting the neigl borhood.

November 1, in an encounter with them at Fayetteville, Tenn Capt. C. C. Mason, Fourth Indiana Cavalry, was killed.

The Second Division headquarters, with those of the First ar Third Brigades, remained at Huntsville, Ala., at the close of tl month.

November 18, Col. Eli Long, Fourth Ohio Cavalry, commandir Second Brigade, with detachments of his own and First and Thir Brigades, Second Division, 1,500 men in all, under orders from de partment headquarters, was sent in rear of General Bragg's arm on a raid to Cleveland, where he destroyed 12 miles of railroad b tween Cleveland and Chattanooga and Cleveland and Dalton. F burned a large rolling-mill, captured 233 prisoners, and brought o his command with but little loss. While returning to Chattanoog Colonel Long burned the baggage and headquarters train of tl rebel General Wright's division.

November 16, Maj. Gen. D. S. Stanley, U. S. Volunteers, was r lieved from duty as chief of cavalry, per Special Field Orders, N 303, November 12, 1863, headquarters Department of the Cumbe land, and on the 19th, at Murfreesborough, turned over the con mand of the cavalry in the Department of the Cumberland to Bri Gen. W. L. Elliott, U. S. Volunteers. Col. E. M. McCook, Secor Indiana Cavalry, succeeded General Elliott to the command of tl First Division.

Headquarters of the cavalry command and the First Cavali Division, with First and Second Brigades thereof, marched fro Winchester, via Shelbyville and Murfreesborough, to Alexandri Tenn., arriving at the latter place November 21. The First Briga took post at the forks of Auburn and Liberty turnpikes. The Se ond Brigade was posted at Alexandria, Tenn.

November 25, detachments from the First East Tennessee ar Ninth Pennsylvania Cavalry were sent to Sparta, Tenn., under con mand of Lieut. Col. J. P. Brownlow, First East Tennessee Cavalr and had frequent skirmishes with a band of guerrillas under tl rebel Colonels Hughs and Murray. The detachments invariabl routed the rebels, inflicting more severe losses than they suffered, ar driving them from their haunts around Sparta. In one of the affairs, Capt. Thomas S. McCahan, Ninth Pennsylvania Cavalr was severely wounded.

---

* From returns for November and December.

November 27, telegraphic orders were received from headquar-
s Department of the Cumberland, directing Brigadier-General
lliott to march, with the First and Second Brigades, First Division,
Kingston, Tenn., harass Longstreet's rebel force, and, if unable
find him, to report to Major-General Burnside, commanding De-
rtment of the Ohio.

November 28, at daylight, the two brigades marched, and at the
d of the month the First Brigade had reached Sparta, Tenn., and
e Second Brigade was ferrying the train of the division over Caney
rk (unfordable), the passage of which retarded the march of the
mmand several days. The weather being exceedingly cold, and
e covering the rope used in ferrying, caused the drowning of 7
en of the Second Indiana Cavalry, through the foundering of a
ry boat. The Third Brigade of the First Division, Col. L. D.
atkins, Sixth Kentucky Cavalry, commanding, remained in camp
ring the month at Caperton's Ferry, on the Tennessee River, near
evenson, Ala.

December 1–7, the headquarters of the cavalry command, with the
rst and Second Brigades of the First Division, remained at Sparta,
nn., waiting for the closing up of the column by the arrival of the
agon train from Nashville, loaded with clothing and stores, much
eded by the command. Frequent successful skirmishes occurred
ith the guerrilla bands infesting the vicinity, invariably routing
em.

December 7, the column moved across the Cumberland Mountains,
ssing through Crossville and Post Oak Springs, reaching Kingston
the 11th.

December 14, orders were received from General Foster, command-
g Department of the Ohio, for General Elliott to march with his
mmand to Knoxville, re-enforce the cavalry of the Army of the
hio, and harass Longstreet's army in their retreat toward Virginia.

December 16, moving as ordered, the command reached Armstrong's
ord, on the Holston River, 7 miles above Knoxville, where it had
en intended they should cross to the west side of the river, push
toward Morristown, and engage Martin's rebel cavalry ; but the
ream proved unfordable there for artillery and wagons, so the
irst Brigade was pushed over to meet the rest of the column at
trawberry Plains, having secured forage for it, if possible. On
riving at that place a ford could not be found, so the brigade on
e west side recrossed at McKinney's Ford December 18, and leav-
g the train at Strawberry Plains the command marched to Nance's
ord, 8 miles above, and reported in possession of the enemy. No
emy was found nor any fording, so the two brigades counter-
arched to McKinney's Ford ; the First Brigade again crossed
ere.

December 18, during the night the river rose 4 feet, rendering it
ecessary to wait its fall, when the Second Brigade and train re-
rned to Strawberry Plains.

December 23, the river falling, the Second Brigade and Lilly's bat-
ry crossed, joined the First Brigade, and pushed on to New Market.

December 24, Brigadier-General Sturgis, chief of cavalry of the
rmy of the Ohio, and by seniority commanding the cavalry of the
epartments of the Ohio and Cumberland, detached the First Bri-
ade of the First Division, Col. A. P. Campbell commanding, to
arch to Dandridge, in conjunction with some of his own cavalry,
nd cut off a rebel brigade supposed to be there. At Hay's Ferry

Campbell briskly attacked the enemy, who, being heavily re-e
forced, compelled him to retreat.   On the retreat one gun of Lilly
(Eighteenth Indiana) battery was spiked and abandoned on accou
of an axle breaking.   In this affair our loss was 7 killed, 47 wounde
and 7 missing.   We captured 30 prisoners, besides killing Maj
Bale, of the Sixth Georgia Cavalry, and killing and wounding ov
100 of the enemy.

    December 25, 26, 27, and 28, almost constant skirmishing wi
Martin's cavalry, during which we advanced to Talbott's Statio
within 9 miles of Morristown.   In these affairs the loss was slig
on both sides.

    December 29, General Sturgis again detached La Grange's Seco
Brigade with his own cavalry to Dandridge, having ordered the
maining brigade (Campbell's) to cover the front and fall back, wit
out much resistance, if attacked, to Mossy Creek.   At about 10 a.
Martin, with Armstrong's and Morgan's divisions, about 5,000 stron
advanced in overwhelming force.   The First Brigade fell back,
ordered, to Mossy Creek, and there held the enemy at bay till
p. m., when he commenced falling back.   We then advanced, a
La Grange's brigade, arriving from Dandridge, struck the enemy
the flank and signally routed them, driving them beyond Talbot
Station and pushing the pursuit until after dark.   The casualties
this affair were 4 commissioned officers wounded, 12 enlisted m
killed, and 36 men wounded severely.   The enemy being much mo
exposed in his attacks doubtless lost more.

    A small battalion, composed of detachments of the Fifteenth Pen
sylvania and Tenth Ohio Cavalry, from the Department of the Cu
berland, under command of Col. William J. Palmer, Fifteen
Pennsylvania Cavalry, were under the orders of General Ellio
and participated in the engagement, as did Mott's brigade of t
Twenty-third Army Corps.   The cavalry of the Army of the Oh
took no part in the battle.

    The line from Talbott's Station was held after the Mossy Cre
battle through the rest of the month.   The Third Brigade, Col.
D. Watkins commanding, was detached from the division during t
month, and, after Bragg's defeat at Missionary Ridge, march
from Caperton's Ferry, Ala., to Rossville, Ga., where it remain
in camp at the close of the month.

No. 55.

Reports of Col. William J. Palmer, Fifteenth Pennsylvania Caval

HEADQUARTERS ANDERSON CAVALRY,
    Trotter's Bridge, December 11, 1863.

    GENERAL: I have the honor to report that on yesterday morni
a little after daybreak I reached Gatlinburg, 15 miles from Sevi
ville, on the Smoky Mountain road, with 150 men, having approach
from a point on the same road 3 miles in the rear of Gatlinbur
which point I reached by a circuitous and almost impassable tr
from Wear's Cove.

    At the same time Lieut. Col. C. B. Lamborn, with about 50 me
reached Gatlinburg from the north by the Sevierville road, whi
he intersected at Trotter's Bridge, 7 miles north of Gatlinburg, b
road leading from Wear's Cove, where our forces divided.

Capt. H. McAllester, with the remainder of our force, consisting chiefly of men whose horses were unshod or unfit to travel over the rough mountain trails, had been sent the previous afternoon to Sevierville from Chandler's, 18 miles from Knoxville, where I turned off to go to Wear's Cove. His instructions were to picket the roads out of Sevierville, preventing any one from leaving the place, in order that information of our movements might not reach the enemy.

Lieutenant-Colonel Lamborn and myself reached Gatlinburg from opposite directions at about the same moment, both finding pickets posted, who immediately fired, thereby alarming the enemy's camp, which we found situated on a steep wooded ridge, commanding both roads and intercepting communication between us.

It being impossible to make a dash upon them, we were obliged to dismount our men and deploy them as skirmishers. We drove them from their position, which was a strong one, in about an hour, but, unfortunately, the steep wooded ridge on which they had their camp butted on to the mountain on the east, and it was impracticable to prevent the rebels on retreating from taking up this mountain where we could not reach them, and where they continued firing from behind the thick cover for several hours. They finally retreated, scattering over the ridges to the Great Smoky Mountain.

From all the information I could get, I estimate their force at about 00, of which 150 were Indians and the remainder white men, the whole under the command of Colonel Thomas, an old Indian agent.

We captured their camp with 1 prisoner, 16 horses, 18 muskets, 2 boxes of ammunition, several bushels of salt, meal, dried fruit, &c., and a large quantity of blankets, old clothing, &c. A number of squaws had reached them the previous evening, and they had evidently intended remaining at Gatlinburg for the winter, as their declarations to the citizens in the vicinity proved.

We destroyed the log huts and frame buildings composing their camp, and have returned most of the horses to their loyal owners. Colonel Thomas was evidently taken by surprise, as he had not time to get his hat from his quarters at the foot of the ridge, which one of our men captured.

I regret to report that two of my officers and a sergeant were wounded in the skirmish, Captain Clark seriously in the knee. Captain Betts received a painful flesh wound in the arm. The sergeant's wound was trivial. The loss of the enemy is not known. If any were killed they carried them off when they retreated.

Colonel Thomas has most probably taken his men back to Quallatown, in North Carolina, but I have sent a scouting party out this morning to ascertain.

I very much regret that we were not more successful. We rode all night over a foot path that many of the citizens considered impracticable; and while I cannot see that we could have done better under the circumstances than we did, yet I can now see from my knowledge of the ground (which was entirely unknown to us before) how I might have captured most of the party by making certain dispositions before reaching Gatlinburg.

I start this morning for Evans' Ford, on French Broad, 9 miles from Sevierville, and between that place and Dandridge, where I learn 100 rebel cavalry crossed last night.

I am, general, yours, respectfully,

WM. J. PALMER,
Colonel.

HEADQUARTERS ANDERSON CAVALRY,
Dandridge, December 13, 1863—6 p. m.

GENERAL : I have just received the order to move with my command to Morristown to protect a telegraph party sent out from Strawberry Plains.

My pickets were attacked at 10 o'clock this morning by a small scouting party of the enemy sent out (as prisoners assert) from Bull' Gap. I happened to be near the picket post at the time and immediately pursued them with the reserve, on the Bull's Gap road, and succeeded in capturing 6 of them belonging to the —— Arkansas cavalry, after a chase of 6 miles. We got their horses, arms, and saddles. I send the 6 prisoners to you herewith, together with other belonging to Wheeler's cavalry, whom we captured in a recent skirmish with a battalion of Indians, under Colonel Thomas, at Gatlinburg. Also a rebel soldier named Hightower, belonging to Buckner's command, reported to me since writing the last sentence.

I have sent three companies under Lieutenant Mather at once to Mossy Creek, which they will reach before midnight, and will start with the balance of my command at about daybreak on the direct road to Morristown. I hope, however, it will not be necessary to remain very long at Morristown as I am better able to watch operations of the enemy by being farther to the east. I have sent scouting parties out to Newport and the mouth of Chucky, who will report by morning.

I am, general, very respectfully,

WM. J. PALMER,
Colonel.

Brigadier-General SPEARS,
Commanding U. S. Forces at Strawberry Plains.

—

HEADQUARTERS ANDERSON CAVALRY,
Dandridge, December 13, 1863—8 p. m.
(Received 15th.)

GENERAL: From interrogation of the prisoners I send you, who left their camp at about 4 p. m. yesterday, 12th instant, at 5 miles this side of Bull's Gap, I feel satisfied that Armstrong's division of rebel cavalry is encamped at that point (5 miles this side of Bull's Gap), and that the other division, formerly Martin's, now Morgan's, of Alabama, was encamped not far from Armstrong's, toward Rogersville.

The prisoners belong to a party who were sent out on a scout. They say their instructions were to find out whether or not there were any Federals in this direction, and that they think the expectation of their cavalry was to come down this way and attempt to join Bragg either this side or the other of Great Smoky Mountain.

Martin now commands all their cavalry, which they say consists only of Armstrong's and Morgan's divisions, and of Jones' command from Virginia.

The point referred to is 23 miles from here.

I am, general, yours, respectfully,

WM. J. PALMER,
Colonel, Commanding.

Brigadier-General SPEARS,
Commanding U. S. Forces, Strawberry Plains.

HEADQUARTERS ANDERSON CAVALRY,
Dandridge, December 14, 1863—7 a. m.

GENERAL: A scouting party of citizens of this neighborhood sent ut by me yesterday evening have returned. They went out a istance of 13 miles from Dandridge, where the road from here to ull's Gap intersects the road leading from Morristown to Warm prings, via mouth of Chucky ; at that point they were within half mile of the rebel cavalry pickets. The information they got from Union citizens was that a train of about one thousand wagons left Morristown, on last Thursday morning before day on the road to Warm Springs ; that they went as far as the mouth of Chucky with-ut crossing, and on Friday morning returned to the intersection of he road from Dandridge to Bull's Gap, and took up the road to Bull's Gap, the last of them passing that intersection late on Friday ight. They also learned that the enemy's cavalry was stationed esterday evening at Russellville, and on the road from Dandridge Bull's Gap, 7 miles this side of the gap and at McClester's, close the Chucky River, on the road leading from Russellville to Chucky Bend—five brigades in all. Rebel scouts had informed citizens of a skirmish at Russellville on Saturday last with our cavalry.

A scouting party of 42 of the enemy came yesterday afternoon at o'clock to the intersection of the road leading from Morristown ith the road to Bull's Gap at Widow Kimbrough's.

They appeared to be very much excited, made only a slight halt, nd returned immediately toward Bull's Gap. I start at once for Morristown, to protect the telegraph party's operations, having sent hree companies yesterday evening to Mossy Creek, which they eached about midnight.

My pickets were attacked here yesterday morning at 11 o'clock by small scouting party of rebels sent out from their camp near Bull's Gap. We pursued them with the picket reserve, and captured 6, elonging to Armstrong's division, with their horses and arms.

I am, general, yours, respectfully,
WM. J. PALMER,
Colonel, Commanding.

Major-General PARKE. *Chief of Staff.*

—

HEADQUARTERS ANDERSON CAVALRY,
2 *Miles E. of Mossy Creek, Monday, Dec.* 14, 1863—10 p. m.

GENERAL : I started from Dandridge this morning, on the direct oad to Morristown, expecting there to meet the three companies of avalry that I sent from Dandridge to Mossy Creek last night. When ithin 4 miles of Morristown, a little beyond McFarland's place, I eard firing on my left, on the cross-road to Panther Springs, a point n the Knoxville and Morristown road 5 miles this side of Morris-own.

I found that the firing was at the rear of my three companies, who ad gone on this morning to within a half mile of Morristown, where hey drove in the rebel cavalry pickets, but being pursued by a force hey considered too large for them, and learning that there was a eavy body of the enemy's cavalry in Morristown, they had retired y the cross-road referred to to make the junction with me.

I then crossed, with a portion of my command, by the Panther Springs road, to the Knoxville and Morristown road, pursued the scouting party sent out from Morristown, and captured 7 of them with their arms and 8 horses.

I heard cannonading from about 2 o'clock until dark in the direction of Noyes' Ferry, or between there and Bean's Station.

From the prisoners captured I learned, in entire confirmation o the report previously given to me at McFarland's house by a bo who had left Russellville at daybreak this morning and had com through Morristown, that General Martin, commanding the rebe cavalry (*vice* Wheeler), had left Russellville at daybreak this morn ing, and had reached Morristown at about 9 a. m., with five regiment of cavalry—the First, Second, Third, Fourth, and Sixth Georgia— composing Colonel Crews' brigade, of Morgan's division, and tha they were drawn up in line of battle at Morristown at the time th scouting party was sent out.

The rest of this division the prisoners understood to be over to ward the Chucky ; Jones' cavalry, they thought, was near Bean' Station, and they believed the fighting to-day to be with him. Whil I was pursuing the scouting party, the pickets I had left on the Dan dridge and Morristown road beyond McFarland's house saw, abou a mile beyond them on the road leading from mouth of Chucky t Morristown, a heavy rebel column of cavalry, supposed to be a di vision, passing toward Morristown, which is 2 miles from that inter section. This was at about 3.30 p. m. ; they did not perceive m pickets.

Our prisoners also assert that Longstreet's infantry had crosse over from Rogersville to the Bull's Gap and Greeneville road, an were now encamped on that road 8 miles east of Bull's Gap, and tha the wagon trains were on the same road. I brought my comman over to this road where I found that the telegraph party had no got up to Panther Springs ; returning, I found it at Colonel Tal bott's, 18 miles from Strawberry Plains.

There being no forage convenient, I brought the party and escor back to this point, 15 miles from Strawberry Plains, with my com mand.

The force of rebel cavalry in Morristown this evening was so larg that I cannot consider myself very safe here, as yours is, I believe the nearest supporting command, and I cannot see that it is ver prudent to continue putting up a telegraph line toward Morristow while there is a division or more of rebel cavalry there, who hav the facility to return to the place without interruption, even if the now retire.

Until a large force is thrown on the south side of the river ther is nothing to prevent the enemy's cavalry from cutting the wire whenever they please, even down to Strawberry Plains.

It is possible that a body of rebel cavalry may be thrown dow this road in the morning from Morristown. I await orders at thi point. Please telegraph them. One of the prisoners we capture was an orderly sergeant, sent out by General Martin from Morris town this afternoon to recall the scouting party. I shall endeavo to ascertain in the morning the condition of affairs at Morristow and vicinity.

Yours, respectfully,

WM. J. PALMER,
Colonel, Commanding.

Brigadier-General SPEARS,
Comdg. United States Forces at Strawberry Plains.

HEADQUARTERS ANDERSON CAVALRY,
Evans' Ford, December 17, 1863—5 p. m.

CAPTAIN: I have the honor to report that a scout, who went within sight of their fires last evening, has reported to me this afternoon that he saw what he considered to be one brigade of rebel cavalry at a point on the Morristown and Strawberry Plains road 2 miles beyond New Market at about dark yesterday evening (December 16); that their pickets, 30 in number, were at New Market, and that another picket was stationed at James Brazilton's, where the road from New Market intersects the Rocky Valley road (leading from Dandridge to Strawberry Plains); that these pickets were posted at those points at about dark. He also understood that there was another brigade of cavalry back near Mossy Creek.

Finding that the French Broad at my back was rising rapidly, I re-crossed it this afternoon at this point, 3 miles from Shady Grove, where I camped last night.

I got across with difficulty, and the river is now past fording, in my opinion, at any point between the mouth of Chucky and the Holston.

A small party of 11 rebels entered my camp at Shady Grove a few hours after we left it, and 6 were seen about dark on the opposite side of the river a mile above this. Whether the 11 rebels were a small scouting party, or the advance of a larger force sent to attack us, I do not know; but incline to the latter opinion, from the fact 2 rebel citizens living near Shady Grove, whom we had under arrest last night, escaped during the night.

I sent out two scouting parties this morning, one to Newport, up this side of the French Broad, and another, of Lieutenant Gregg and 26 men, toward Panther Springs. Neither have yet returned, and I have same apprehensions that the last-mentioned party will find a force of rebels in their rear. I have two boats ready to cross them here, and have sent word by a citizen to Dandridge to have them cross there if they pass through that place.

Please inform me where General Elliott's cavalry is, of the Army of the Cumberland.

WM. J. PALMER,
Colonel, Commanding.

Captain GOURLAND,
Acting Assistant Adjutant-General.

—

HEADQUARTERS CAVALRY DIVISION,
On Dumpling Creek, December 23, 1863—3 p. m.

GENERAL: I have the honor to inform you that I scouted with my command yesterday evening on the Bend of Chucky road from Dandridge to within 4 miles of Mosier's Mills, 14 miles from Dandridge, and close to the intersection of the Dandridge and Bend of Chucky road with the road running from Morristown to Warm Springs via mouth of Chucky and Newport. At said point I was about 4 miles below and to the west of mouth of Chucky. I reached that point at about 7 p. m. and found a small detail of rebel cavalry, who had been sent from Bean's Station on Sunday last, with directions to gather cattle and report with them to Morristown as soon as possible. We captured 5 of these men, together with 30 head of cattle, which they were guarding; also 18 horses. I wish to retain 6 head of these cattle, and will send the remainder, with the prisoners, to you by first opportunity. As my force is rather small, I would be glad if some small scouting party from your command, coming in this direction, could take them back, in case you require them; they are small cattle. One of these prisoners states that at the time they left all the rebel cavalry was on the other side of Holston, but that they expected to meet their command at Morristown about Wednesday (to-day).

Learning from Union citizens that a brigade of rebel cavalry had entered Mosier's Mills at about dark yesterday, and that a regiment was posted at Franklin's, near mouth of Chucky—the first part of which information I have had reason since to doubt—I deemed it best to move my command to this point, which I reached at 1 a. m.

This morning I have sent a lady to Mosier's Mills, whose report I shall expect this evening. I have also sent a scouting party of 10 men toward Morristown. From these I have heard that they fell on the track of a rebel scouting party of 40 coming from the direction of Morristown, on the Dandridge road. The 10 men are following them, and I have sent a company to near Dandridge to intercept them.

I have also sent a single scout to Mossy Creek. He reports at 2 p. m. that no rebels are there, but that Union citizens informed him there was a considerable force—one said lying in ambush—about 3 miles above Mossy Creek, near Talbott's Station, on the Knoxville road. This is also corroborated by citizens who have come in to me here. If this is so, and you have a brigade at New Market, I would like to have it led by the Panther Springs road to Panther Springs, 4 miles in rear of Talbott's Station. I have been over this by-road and know it. If this could be done, I believe the enemy could be damaged considerably.

3.20 p. m.

My scouting party sent toward Dandridge reports that they are within 3 miles of that place, and that 30 rebel cavalry are in Dandridge. He also reports a rumor that a brigade was approaching Dandridge from a road running from mouth of Chucky to Dandridge, which I do not credit.

From Newport my scout reports 100 rebel cavalry in that vicinity. Forty staid at Gorman's Church, 1½ miles south of Newport, on night of 21st. They have arrested 4 conscripts at Wilsonville. My scout from Greeneville has not yet returned.

I am, general, yours, respectfully,

WM. J. PALMER,
Colonel, Commanding.

Brigadier-General ELLIOTT.

P. S.—Shall I report to you or to General Sturgis direct?

[Indorsement.]

HEADQUARTERS CHIEF OF CAVALRY,
New Market, December 23, 1863—7.30 p. m.

Respectfully forwarded.

From 150 to 200 rebel cavalry drove back a scouting party from my command. Colonel McCook did not get the order in time to send out the brigade to-night. I will send it out at daylight to-morrow. Colonel Wolford has crossed, and is in camp near my command.

W. L. ELLIOTT,
Brigadier-General.

HEADQUARTERS ANDERSON CAVALRY,
Hale's, at the Foot of Flat Gap, December 23, 1863—7 p. m.

COLONEL: I have just moved here from Dumpling Valley. I as. certained this afternoon from my scouting parties that a large force of the enemy's cavalry was advancing toward Dandridge on the Morristown and Dandridge road. One of my companies attacked their advance guard of one company at Dandridge, scattering them, when it was in turn attacked by the enemy's reserve. We took 4 prisoners, losing nothing.

My rear has skirmished with the rebel advance in retiring on the road from Dandridge to this place, but the rear is now up and there is no pursuit. The prisoners confirm the statements of my scouts and of citizens who came to me to-day on Dumpling Creek, that John T. Morgan's division, composed of Colonel Crews' and Colonel Russell's brigades (the latter with six pieces of artillery), left Panther Springs, 13 miles from New Market, on the Morristown road, and crossed over to the Dandridge and Bull's Gap road, on which they advanced toward Dandridge; the advanced company having been sent ahead at about noon from Widow Kimbrough's, 8 miles from Dandridge. It was from this company we got the prisoners. General Martin, chief of the enemy's cavalry, is along with Morgan's division. There are five regiments in Russell's brigade and four reported in Crews' brigade. The prisoners belong to the Fourth Alabama, whose adjutant informed them this morning there were 250 men in their regiment. There are only two brigades in this division.

The prisoners say that Armstrong's division went up the Holston on the other side—they think to Noyes' Ferry, opposite Morristown. I send you also 5 prisoners we captured yesterday near mouth of Chucky; also 24 head of cattle (of 30 we captured with a rebel guard near mouth of Chucky yesterday). Morgan's division forded the Holston River near Panther Springs. Some action should be taken immediately, as both brigades are probably in Dandridge, although Crews' brigade may have kept on from Widow Kimbrough's to the mouth of Chucky. I should like to consult with you in regard to the course to be pursued, as I have become tolerably familiar with the roads hereabouts. Is General Elliott with you? Where is the rest of our cavalry?

I am, colonel, yours, respectfully,
WM. J. PALMER,
Colonel, Commanding.

Col. E. M. McCOOK.

No. 56.

Reports of Brig. Gen. James G. Spears, U. S. Army, commanding First East Tennessee Brigade.

HEADQUARTERS UNITED STATES FORCES,
Near Loudon, Tenn., December 6, 1863.

GENERAL: In obedience to orders from Major-General Granger, I arrived with my command at Kingston on the evening of the 3d instant. A dispatch from you was handed me in an hour or so after my arrival, in which the senior officer at Kingston was directed to collect the forces at Kingston, and on the appearance of the steamer Paint Rock, then coming up the river, to move forward with the forces, the right flank to rest on the river, a small force to be left at Kingston as a garrison.

I, being the senior officer commanding First Tennessee Brigade, assumed command of all the forces there, consisting, in addition to the Tennessee Brigade, of the First Brigade, Second Division, Twenty-third Army Corps, Colonel Mott (four regiments), and the First Tennessee Mounted Infantry, Colonel Byrd, together with battalion Third Indiana Cavalry, Lieutenant-Colonel Klein, and eight pieces of artillery attached to my brigade, and nine pieces artillery attached to Colonel Mott's brigade, in all, eight regiments of infantry (one mounted), battalion cavalry, and seventeen pieces artillery.

I moved forward with all of the above forces, excepting Colonel Byrd and his regiment, then on picket duty on the river, whom I left at Kingston with orders to draw in his force and to aid and assist in getting the steamer up from off White Creek Shoals, where I was informed by Lieutenant-Colonel Remick, chief commissary subsistence, that she was aground. I sent two experienced pilots, well acquainted with the river and channel, to assist the steamer in getting through, and supposed she would get to Kingston by the next morning, December 4. Colonel Byrd was further instructed that should it be necessary he would press every wagon in the country and unload the supplies from the steamer and bring them up, especially the ammunition, or at least lighten the steamer so as to get her off the shoals.

I was informed that quite a large cavalry force of the enemy were in my front, and that their pickets were within 4 miles of Kingston. I deemed it most prudent (expecting the boat to arrive every moment on the morning of the 4th) to move forward with my force, which I did, accordingly, by three different routes, throwing a force around on the river bank. In about 4 miles from Kingston we drove in the rebel pickets and proceeded on to a point 10 miles from Kingston, having skirmished with and drove the enemy before us, occupying their camps on the night of the 4th, with headquarters at Mrs. Beazeal's. We captured 26 prisoners, some horses and equipments.

On the morning of the 5th, I learned by dispatch from Colonel Byrd that he had ordered the steamer to return to Chattanooga, and to get a lighter boat, the Paint Rock being too heavy for the purpose, and unable to get over the shoals. I had instructed Colonel Byrd to unload the boat and lighten her up, so as to get her over the shoals. I arrived here yesterday, and am at a loss what to do—whether to remain and wait for a boat or to proceed on to Knoxville.

The enemy that we routed is reported by citizens and prisoners to be 2,000. I am certain that there are 1,000, and perhaps 1,500, and will not exceed 2,000. They went on the main Knoxville road toward Knoxville, a small number going in the direction of Loudon.

On arriving here I found six pieces of cannon, abandoned by the enemy. The retreating rebels had eight pieces with them. They are Wheeler's command, under Colonel Hart.

I shall remain here until further orders. I have sent several dispatches to both Major-General Granger and to you, but have not heard a word from either up to this morning. All is quiet. I am foraging for subsistence and forage here in the country. I think we can do very well here as for meat, but the bread question is what troubles us, but I believe we can subsist for a while, both as to the animals and men.

I remain, general, yours, &c., waiting for instructions,

JAMES G. SPEARS,
Brigadier-General, &c.

Major-General SHERMAN.

HEADQUARTERS UNITED STATES FORCES,
Near Loudon, Tenn., December 6, 1863.

GENERAL : By an order received from Major-General Sherman to the senior officer at Kingston, Tenn., I assumed command of all the forces at that place, being directed by said order to collect all the forces there, and, with the exception of a small force to be left at Kingston as a garrison, to proceed, on the appearance of the steamer Paint Rock (then coming up the river to Knoxville), toward Knoxville, with my right flank resting on the river.

I assumed the command, which consists of my brigade, First East Tennessee Brigade, Colonel Shelley, with battalion Third Indiana Cavalry, Lieutenant-Colonel Klein, and eight pieces artillery, the First Brigade, Second Division, Twenty-third Army Corps, Colonel Mott, and nine pieces artillery, and the First Tennessee Mounted Infantry, Colonel Byrd.

I left Colonel Byrd with his regiment to garrison Kingston, and proceeded to move forward with the remaining forces, having learned that a large cavalry force (rebel) were in my front with their pickets within 4 miles of Kingston. Expecting the steamer to arrive every moment on the morning of the 4th, I deemed it most prudent to move forward and drive them before me. I had been informed that the steamer was unable to get over the shoals at White Creek, and directed Colonel Byrd to aid and assist with his command in getting her through. I advanced by three routes toward Knoxville, and when about 4 miles from Kingston we drove in the enemy's pickets and pushed forward, skirmishing as we advanced. I halted on the night of the 4th, and encamped 10 miles from Kingston, with my command occupying the vacated camps of the enemy, who fled before us. They are reported to be 2,000 cavalry. I am certain that there are 1,000, and perhaps 1,500, but will not exceed 2,000. They took the main Knoxville road, with eight pieces of cannon, and a few took the Loudon road. I arrived at this point yesterday and found six pieces of cannon which were abandoned by them, three of which are spiked.

In the rout we captured 26 prisoners, and the balance scattered in wild confusion. They are Wheeler's command, under Colonel Hart. I am now encamped here, owing to the non-arrival of the steamer, which Colonel Byrd informs me he has ordered back to Chattanooga.

In consequence of the orders under which I am acting, I shall wait here at this point for further orders, having dispatched to Major-General Sherman all of the particulars, as also to Major-General Granger, both of whom, with their forces, are perhaps in your vicinity, as they passed up the river three days since.

I am, general, very respectfully, your obedient servant,

JAMES G. SPEARS,
Brigadier-General, Commanding U. S. Forces.

Maj. Gen. AMBROSE E. BURNSIDE.

P. S.—Our supplies are limited ; we have a small supply of cattle, hogs, and sheep, and can, I think, get along for meat, but the bread question troubles us, inasmuch as there is none on hand. I am foraging for subsistence and forage both, and feel hopeful that we will subsist both men and animals for a short while, until stores can reach us.

HEADQUARTERS,
Strawberry Plains, December 15, 1863—8 a. m.

GENERAL : I have just received a lengthy dispatch from Colon*
Palmer, commanding Anderson Cavalry, which will reach you t*
day by courier. The substance is that he with his command a*
vanced to near Morristown, and found a division of cavalry the*
and in that vicinity, and that it is unsafe to go into Morristown, an*
thinks likely a rebel raid will be made down the river and perha*
to this place.

Colonel Palmer had, with the telegraph party and escort, falle*
back to a point 15 miles above this place and awaits further order*
Colonel Palmer dispatches also that he heard cannonading betwee*
Morristown and Bean's Station.

I have thought it advisable to telegraph to you the substance of th*
dispatch in advance of the dispatch, that you may give such instru*
tions by telegraph as you may see proper.

Respectfully,

JAMES G. SPEARS,
Brigadier-General.

Major-General FOSTER.

—

NEAR NANCY'S FERRY,
December 16, 1863.

GENERAL : I arrived here and proceeded at once to station th*
proper pickets, both infantry and cavalry. The cavalry pickets*
have supported by infantry. All is quiet. It is reported that th*
enemy are 15 miles from here, and some say 8 miles ; the same is mer*
rumor.

I am, general, very respectfully, your obedient servant,

JAMES G. SPEARS,
Brigadier-General, Commanding.

Major-General PARKE.

—

UNITED STATES FORCES,
River Road, near Nance's Ferry, December 17, 1863.

GENERAL : I have reliable information that a rebel force crosse*
the river above here last night at Stone's Ferry, 4 miles from her*
I hear firing this morning in the direction of Strawberry Plains, r*
sembling the skirmishing of pickets, and I think it more than likel*
that they have gone down the river on the south side and attacke*
the pickets there. There was 1 man killed on outpost last nigh*
but all is quiet now.

I remain, general, very respectfully, your obedient servant,

JAMES G. SPEARS,
Brigadier-General, Commanding, &c.

Major-General PARKE.

—

UNITED STATES FORCES,
Richland Creek, December 17, 1863.

GENERAL : The enemy have attacked and driven in both my cav*
alry and infantry pickets, and are in force, both mounted and di*

ᴌounted forces. I am momentarily expecting the attack on me in
ᴅrce; the firing has commenced. I have about 900 men that will do
ꜱ much as any other 900 can.

Yours, respectfully,

JAMES G. SPEARS,
Brigadier-General.

General PARKE.

—

NEAR NANCE'S FERRY,
December 17, 1863.

GENERAL: Yours is at hand. I have my whole force on the south-
ᴀst side of Richland Creek, and maintain my position as yet. The
ᴀttery, however, is on the northwest side and has a good position.
'he enemy is still advancing and has driven my pickets pretty well
ᴌl in. Their line of battle is within 600 yards of my position.
'hey are on foot and horseback, with artillery. We have had heavy
ᴋirmishing, the enemy evidently intending to make feints both on
ᴌy right and left flanks. They have been promptly met and re-
ᴇlled. We will endeavor to do our whole duty as well as we can.

Yours, with respect,

JAMES G. SPEARS,
Brigadier-General.

Major-General PARKE.

—

UNITED STATES FORCES,
Southeast Side Richland Creek, December 17, 1863.

GENERAL: Yours of to-day is at hand, in obedience to which I
ᴌmediately forward to you ——— ———, who is well acquainted
ᴡith the fords from Strawberry Plains up. I can also inform you
ᴌat Mills' Ford and Nance's Ford are both fordable, having been
ᴅrded to-day. Both of these fords are above the mouth of Richland
'reek. I have held my ground and have advanced my forces some;
ᴌe enemy make bold demonstrations, but do not seem to take hold.
'hey have withdrawn from sight and I have thrown forward three
ᴅmpanies as skirmishers to feel of them. They have been gone
ᴅout fifteen minutes, and no report yet.

I am, general, very respectfully, your obedient servant,

JAMES G. SPEARS,
Brigadier-General, Commanding, &c.

Major-General PARKE.

—

HEADQUARTERS FIRST EAST TENNESSEE BRIGADE,
Richland Creek December 18, 1863.

GENERAL: Your dispatch just received. All is quiet in my front,
ᴀnd nothing demonstrated by the enemy since last night. I dis-
ᴀtched you yesterday evening of the position I occupied. My skir-
ᴌishers advanced about one-half mile and drew the fire of the
ᴌemy's artillery, and then fell back to the former position first
ᴅcupied by me on arriving, where they now are. On my left, and
ᴄross the creek, is stationed Colonel Bond, with one brigade of cav-
ᴌry, dismounted, in support of my artillery, which has a fine posi-
ᴌon on the other side, on a hill. My line extends on the right to a
ᴅint some 400 yards from Richland Creek, there connecting with
ᴌr forces, whom, I am informed, are a part of the Ninth Army

Corps. I have just been shown a dispatch by General Elliott speak
ing of line of couriers extending from the right of your line of batt
to my left. I have no information of there being any courier there
it has not been reported to me. General Elliott, with a part of h
division, has arrived; of this you have been notified by dispatch.

Very respectfully,

JAMES G. SPEARS,
Brigadier-General, &c.

Major-General PARKE.

—

HEADQUARTERS FIRST EAST TENN. BRIGADE,
Richland Creek, December 18, 1863—3 p. m.

GENERAL: There has nothing transpired in my immediate fro
to-day. I have ordered skirmishers to be thrown forward, whic
was done. They returned; report large smoke, indicating a larg
force some 2 miles up the river, extending from the river to the roa
and beyond the road. Three mounted pickets approached my lin
this morning, and, upon being fired on, withdrew. The road fro
here to Nance's Ferry is clear of any rebel force, they not havir
returned since being driven back yesterday evening by my ski
mishers. The river at Nance's Ford is not fordable. Gener
Elliott's cavalry arrived here and returned in a few hours to-da
the same way that it came. I maintain my position *statu quo.*

I remain, your obedient servant,

JAMES G. SPEARS,
Brigadier-General, Commanding.

3.10 p. m.

Two women, said to be Union ladies, have just come through th
rebel lines in my immediate front, and report a heavy force of ca
alry and infantry (rebel) about 4 miles up the road.

JAMES G. SPEARS,
Brigadier-General, &c.

Major-General PARKE.

—

HEADQUARTERS FIRST EAST TENN. BRIGADE,
Richland Creek, December 19, 1863.

GENERAL: All is quiet in my front to-day. I made a reconnai
sance this morning some 3½ miles up the road to where the enem
had his outposts last night; they fled, but were visible upon th
Indian Ridge, about three-quarters of a mile from where we we
to. I do not believe that they are in very strong force; all caval
and mounted infantry; they perhaps have a battery. When the
made the attack, the citizens who live up the country say that thr
regiments dismounted; two of them formed a line of battle and o
held in reserve. There was a considerable number of cavalry al
held in reserve, as well as cavalry on each flank. They are encampe
from 4 miles above here, extending up to Masengale's Mill, 8 mile
which mill and a distillery they are running. The Holston has rise
from 4 to 6 feet. Richland Creek is not fordable for 2 miles up fro
its mouth, the first mile being too deep in consequence of backwat
from the river—which is now up to the mill-dam—the second mile
consequence of backwater from the dam. The bridge is the on
means of crossing Richland for 2 miles from its mouth up, and th
can be destroyed in a very few minutes, if it becomes necessary.

I have reliable information from the south side of the river, and that is, there are a few rebels in New Market and some at Dandridge. I further understand that Colonel Palmer, Fifteenth Pennsylvania Cavalry, is now on the south side of French Broad River. There is some forage north of here, between me and where the rebels are encamped on this side, but near their picket lines. If you desire, and will send a section of artillery and two regiments, I will take one of my regiments and go up there and gather it for you.

I am, general, very respectfully, your obedient servant,

JAMES G. SPEARS,
Brigadier-General, &c.

Major-General PARKE.

———

HDQRS. FIRST EAST TENN. BRIGADE, U. S. FORCES,
Richland Creek, December 22, 1863.

GENERAL : I have just been informed by Captain Haworth, Third Tennessee Infantry, who is returned from a reconnaissance from my front, that the enemy are advancing on my line. A Union lady reports to me the same information, and says the whole force are coming this way. Their pickets are this side of the position I occupied while out yesterday morning with my command. They occupy the hill where I had the section of artillery posted, and at the point where you found me yesterday. They are in force. I am on the alert with my command and shall not permit them to come farther than is possible.

Yours, &c.,

JAMES G. SPEARS,
Brigadier-General, &c.

Maj. Gen. J. G. PARKE, *Blain's Cross-Roads, Tenn.*

———

No. 57.

*Organization of the Troops in East Tennessee under command of Lieut. Gen. James Longstreet, C. S. Army, November 30, 1863.**

LONGSTREET'S CORPS.

M'LAWS' DIVISION.

Maj. Gen. LAFAYETTE McLAWS,

Kershaw's Brigade.

2d South Carolina, Col. John D. Kennedy.
3d South Carolina, Col. James D. Nance.
7th South Carolina, Col. D. Wyatt Aiken.
8th South Carolina, Col. John W. Henagan.
15th South Carolina, Col. Joseph F. Gist.
3d South Carolina Battalion, Lieut. Col. William G. Rice.

Humphreys' Brigade.

13th Mississippi, Col. Kennon McElroy.
17th Mississippi, Col. William D. Holder.
18th Mississippi, Col. Thomas M. Griffin.
21st Mississippi, Col. William L. Brandon.

Wofford's Brigade.

16th Georgia, Col. Henry P. Thomas.
18th Georgia, Col. S. Z. Ruff.
24th Georgia, Col. Robert McMillan.
Cobb's Legion, Lieut. Col. Luther J. Glenn.
Phillips Legion, Lieut. Col. E. S. Barclay.
3d Georgia Battalion Sharpshooters, Lieut. Col. N. L. Hutchins, jr.

Bryan's Brigade.

10th Georgia, Col. John B. Weems.
50th Georgia, Col. Peter McGlashan.
51st Georgia, Col. Edward Ball.
53d Georgia, Col. James P. Simms.

———

* Including Ransom's division of the Department of Western Virginia and East Tennessee. The commanders, except in Ransom's division, are given as reported for November 20.

Artillery.

Maj. A. LEYDEN.

Peeples' (Georgia) Battery, Capt. Tyler M. Peeples.
Wolihin's (Georgia) Battery, Capt. Andrew M. Wolihin.
York's (Georgia) Battery, Capt. Billington W. York.

HOOD'S DIVISION.

Brig. Gen. MICAH JENKINS.

Jenkins' Brigade.

1st South Carolina, Col. Franklin W. Kilpatrick.
2d South Carolina Rifles, Col. Thomas Thomson.
5th South Carolina, Col. A. Coward.
6th South Carolina, Col. John Bratton.
Hampton Legion, Col. Martin W. Gary.
Palmetto Sharpshooters, Col. Joseph Walker.

Robertson's Brigade.

3d Arkansas, Col. Van H. Manning.
1st Texas, Col. A. T. Rainey.
4th Texas, Col. J. C. G. Key.
5th Texas, Col. R. M. Powell.

Law's Brigade.

4th Alabama, Col. Pinckney D. Bowle
15th Alabama, Col. William C. Oates.
44th Alabama, Col. William F. Perry.
47th Alabama, Col. M. J. Bulger.
48th Alabama, Col. James L. Sheffiel

Anderson's Brigade.

7th Georgia, Col. W. W. White.
8th Georgia, Col. John R. Towers.
9th Georgia, Col. Benjamin Beck.
11th Georgia, Col. F. H. Little.
59th Georgia, Col. Jack Brown.

Benning's Brigade.

2d Georgia, Col. Edgar M. Butt.
15th Georgia, Col. Dudley M. Du Bose.
17th Georgia, Col. Wesley C. Hodges.
20th Georgia, Col. J. D. Waddell.

Artillery.

Col. E. PORTER ALEXANDER.

Fickling's (South Carolina) Battery, Capt. William W. Fickling.
Jordan's (Virginia) Battery, Capt. Tyler C. Jordan.
Moody's (Louisiana) Battery, Capt. George V. Moody.
Parker's (Virginia) Battery, Capt. William W. Parker.
Taylor's (Virginia) Battery, Capt. Osmond B. Taylor.
Woolfolk's (Virginia) Battery, Capt. Pichegru Woolfolk, jr.

BUCKNER'S DIVISION.*

Brig. Gen. BUSHROD R. JOHNSON.

Johnson's Brigade.

17th and 23d Tennessee, Lieut. Col. Watt W. Floyd.
25th and 44th Tennessee, Lieut. Col. John L. McEwen, jr.
63d Tennessee, Maj. John A. Aiken.

Gracie's Brigade.

41st Alabama, Lieut. Col. Theodore C Trimmier.
43d Alabama, Col. Young M. Moody.
1st Battalion, Hilliard's Alabama Le gion, Maj. Daniel S. Troy.
2d Battalion, Hilliard's Alabama Le gion, Capt. John H. Dillard.
3d Battalion, Hilliard's Alabama Le gion, Lieut. Col. John W. A Sanford.
4th Battalion, Hilliard's Alabama Le gion, Maj. John D. McLennan.

*Attached to Longstreet's corps.

CAVALRY CORPS.

Maj. Gen. WILLIAM T. MARTIN.

MARTIN'S DIVISION.

First Brigade.

Brig. Gen. JOHN T. MORGAN.

1st Alabama, Lieut. Col. D. T. Blakey.
3d   Alabama, Lieut. Col. T. H. Mauldin.
4th Alabama, Lieut. Col. J. M. Hambrick.
7th Alabama, Col. James C. Malone, jr.
51st Alabama, Capt. M. L. Kirkpatrick.

Second Brigade.

Col. J. J. MORRISON.

1st Georgia, Lieut. Col. S. W. Davitte.
2d   Georgia, Lieut. Col. F. M. Ison.
3d   Georgia, Lieut. Col. R. Thompson.
4th Georgia, Col. Isaac W. Avery.
6th Georgia, Col. John R. Hart.

ARMSTRONG'S DIVISION.

Brig. Gen. FRANK C. ARMSTRONG.

First Brigade.

Brig. Gen. WILLIAM Y. C. HUMES.

4th Tennessee, Lieut. Col. Paul F. Anderson.
8th Tennessee, Lieut. Col. Ferdinand H. Daugherty.
9th Tennessee, Col. Jacob B. Biffle.
10th Tennessee, Col. Nicholas N. Cox.

Second Brigade.

Col. C. H. TYLER.

Clay's (Kentucky) Battalion, Lieut. Col. Ezekiel F. Clay.
Edmundson's (Virginia) Battalion, Maj. Sylvester P. McConnell.
Jessee's (Kentucky) Battalion, Maj. A. L. McAfee.
Johnson's (Kentucky) Battalion, Maj. O. S. Tenney.

WHARTON'S DIVISION.

First Brigade.

Col. THOMAS HARRISON.

3d Arkansas, Lieut. Col. M. J. Henderson.
65th North Carolina (Sixth Cavalry), Col. George N. Folk.
8th Texas, Lieut. Col. Gustave Cook.
11th Texas, Lieut. Col. J. M. Bounds.

Artillery.

Freeman's (Tennessee) Battery, Capt. A. L. Huggins.
White's (Tennessee) Battery, Capt. B. F. White, jr.
Wiggins' (Arkansas) Battery, Capt. J. H. Wiggins.

RANSOM'S DIVISION.

Maj. Gen. ROBERT RANSOM, Jr.

Corse's Brigade.

Brig. Gen. MONTGOMERY D. CORSE.

15th Virginia, Lieut. Col. E. M. Morrison.
29th Virginia, Col. James Giles.
30th Virginia, Lieut. Col. Robert S. Chew.

Jackson's Brigade.

Brig. Gen. ALFRED E. JACKSON.

Thomas' (North Carolina) Regimen Lieut. Col. James R. Love.
Walker's Battalion, Maj. James A. M Kamy.

Wharton's Brigade Sharpshooters.

Brig. Gen. GABRIEL C. WHARTON.

30th Virginia Battalion, Lieut. Col. J. Lyle Clarke.
45th Virginia, Col. William H. Browne.
51st Virginia, Col. Augustus Forsberg.

Jones' Cavalry Brigade.

Brig. Gen. WILLIAM E. JONES.

8th Virginia, Col. James M. Corns.
21st Virginia, Col. William E. Peters.
27th Virginia Battalion, Lieut. C Henry A. Edmundson.*
34th Virginia Battalion, Lieut. Col. V. Witcher.
36th Virginia Battalion, Capt. C. Smith.
37th Virginia Battalion, Maj. James Claiborne.

Williams' Cavalry Brigade.

Col. H. L. GILTNER.

16th Georgia Battalion, Maj. Edward Y. Clarke.
4th Kentucky, Maj. Nathan Parker.
May's (Kentucky) Regiment, Lieut. Col. Edwin Trimble.
1st Tennessee, Lieut. Col. Onslow Bean.
64th Virginia, Col. Campbell Slemp.

Jenkins' Cavalry Brigade.

Col. MILTON J. FERGUSON.

14th Virginia, Col. James Cochran.
16th Virginia, Col. Milton J. Ferguson
17th Virginia, Maj. Frederick F. Smit

Artillery.

Otey (Virginia) Battery, Capt. David N. Walker.
Rhett (Tennessee) Battery, Capt. William H. Burroughs.
Ringgold (Virginia) Battery, Capt. Crispin Dickenson.
Tennessee Battery, Capt. Hugh L. W. McClung.
Virginia Battery, Capt. George S. Davidson.
Virginia Battery, Capt. William M. Lowry.

No. 58.

Report of Lieut. Gen. James Longstreet, C. S. Army, commandir
Confederate Forces in East Tennessee,† with charges against Bri
Genls. E. M. Law and J. B. Robertson, and resulting correspon
ence.

HEADQUARTERS DEPARTMENT OF EAST TENNESSEE,
Russellville, January 10, 1864.

GENERAL : I have the honor to forward my report of the oper
tions of my troops in the late campaign in East Tennessee.   As I

---

*See also Tyler's brigade, Armstrong's division.
† See also, in Part III, Longstreet's orders and miscellaneous correspondence wi
Bragg, Carter, Cooper, Davis, Jenkins, B. R. Johnson, Jos. E. Johnston, Sam
Jones, William E. Jones, Leadbetter, McLaws, Martin, Ransom, Seddon, Van
Vaughn, and Wheeler.

ot know where General Bragg is, I must ask you to send him the
eport for his remarks. I have not been able to have a map of the
opography of the country. I shall endeavor to send you one as soon
s it can be obtained.

I remain, sir, very respectfully, your most obedient servant,
JAMES LONGSTREET,
Lieutenant-General, Commanding.

HEADQUARTERS,
Russellville, East Tenn., January 1, 1864.

GENERAL: About November 1, a camp rumor reached me to the
ffect that I was to be ordered into East Tennessee, to operate against
he enemy's forces at and near Knoxville. Such a move had not oc-
urred to me previously as practicable. I therefore set to work to
ix upon some plan by which it might be executed. After two days'
eflection I concluded the move might be made with safety by with-
rawing our army behind the Chickamauga to some strong position,
t the same time withdrawing our forces then at Sweetwater, so as to
ive out the impression that we were concentrating behind the Chick-
mauga, but at the same time to make a rapid movement by the most
etired route into East Tennessee with a force of 20,000, and to strike
he enemy so suddenly and so severely that his force should be
rushed before he could know anything of our purposes; then to
etire to meet the enemy at Chattanooga, or, better, to operate rap-
dly against his rear and flank. The reason for retiring behind the
Chickamauga with our main force was, that our extended line being
o near the enemy would enable him to concentrate and march against
ny point of it in twenty minutes after leaving his works.

The day after arriving at this conclusion (November 3) I was called
o council by the commanding general, with Lieutenant-General
Iardee and Major-General Breckinridge. The subject of the move-
nents of our army being called, campaigns were proposed and dis-
ussed, and pronounced by those familiar with the country as im-
racticable, owing to the scarcity of supplies in the country. The
ampaign in East Tennessee was then discussed, and I proposed the
lan that I have already mentioned.

A campaign was settled upon. Two divisions (McLaws' and
Iood's), under my command, were spoken of as the force from Chat-
anooga to execute it. I repeated my apprehensions about our lines
hus weakened remaining so near the enemy's works, but failed to
nake any impression upon the minds of the other officers, and en-
leavored to explain that the force that I would have would be too
veak to operate with that promptness which the occasion seemed to
equire. At the end of the consultation I was ordered verbally to
egin my preparations for the campaign.

After reaching my headquarters I gave orders for the withdrawal
f Alexander's battalion of artillery at once, and ordered General
McLaws to withdraw his division after night; these commands to
narch the following day to Tyner's Station, to take the cars for Sweet
Water. Leyden's artillery was withdrawn the next day, and Hood's
livision the following night. Leyden's artillery and Hood's division
vere ordered to meet the cars at the tunnel through Missionary Ridge.
I applied at general headquarters for maps and information about
he country that I was to operate in; also for a quartermaster and
ommissary of subsistence who knew the resources of the country,

and an engineer officer who had been serving on Major-General
Buckner's staff at Knoxville. None of the staff officers asked for
were sent me, nor were any of the maps, except one of the country
between the Hiwassee and Tennessee Rivers. Major-General Buck
ner was kind enough to give me some inaccurate maps of the country
along the Holston—all that he had. The best one a map of roads
and rivers only.

There was much delay in getting the troops up to Sweet Water by
rail. As I had no control over this transportation I could. apply no
remedy further than to make details from my command to assist
wherever aid was needed. Letters from the commanding general's
headquarters seemed to urge upon me the importance of prompt
movements in a spirit which appeared to intimate that the delays
which had occurred were due to some neglect of mine, or some want
of appreciation on my part, of the importance of prompt and energetic action. As I had urged from the moment the campaign was
proposed the importance of such action, I thought that I ought not
to have been urged on in such a tone, particularly as all of the delays that had occurred were upon the railroad over which I had no
control. Hence my letter of the 11th, in answer to Lieutenant Ellis'
of the 9th. I mention this not as an excuse for the letter, but in
palliation of it.

Major-General Stevenson, who had been in command of our forces
at Sweet Water, told me with entire confidence in his information that
the enemy's forces were 23,000. This information he had also sent
to General Bragg. This I now believe to be a correct statement of
the enemy's force under General Burnside upon his entrance into
East Tennessee. He also informed me that he had not been advised
of my move, and so far from being ordered to have rations or supplies for us, he was ordered to send everything of the kind to the
army of Chattanooga.

As my orders were to drive the enemy out of East Tennessee, or,
if possible, capture him, I determined that the only possible chance
of succeeding in either or both was to move and act as though I had
a sufficient force to do either. I endeavored, therefore, to do as I
should have done had the 20,000 men that I asked for been given me.
Had the means been at hand for making the proper moves I should
have marched for the rear of Knoxville via Morganton and Maryville, and gained possession of the heights there by forced marches.
My transportation was so limited, however, that I could not spare a
wagon to haul the pontoons for our bridge. The only move that I
could make under the circumstances was by crossing the river where
the cars delivered the bridge—Loudon.

On the night of November 13, Major-General Wheeler was detached with three of his brigades of cavalry, with orders to surprise
a cavalry force of the enemy at Maryville (reported to be a brigade),
capture it, and move on to the rear of Knoxville and endeavor to get
possession of some of the heights on the south side, and to hold them
until our arrival, or failing in this, to threaten the enemy at Knoxville, so as to prevent his concentrating his forces against us before
we reached Knoxville. He surprised the force at Maryville (only
about 400 strong), captured a part, and dispersed the balance of it.
He moved on to Knoxville and failed to get possession of any of the
heights which commanded the town, but created the diversion in my
favor.

His other brigade, under Colonel Hart, was sent down to Kingston as soon as we crossed the river, with orders to break up any force that the enemy might have there, and to leave a regiment there on picket. The balance of the brigade was ordered to return to our column and advance to Campbell's station, in front of General McLaws' division. After making the diversion at Knoxville, General Wheeler was ordered to retire and rejoin us by crossing the Holston on our right flank.

Colonel Alexander, chief of artillery, and Major Clarke, chief engineer, were sent to select a point where we could make a crossing in front of the enemy, that being the only place to which we could transport the bridge. Fortunately a very good point was found near Loudon at Huff's Ferry the day before the troops got up. Most of the troops being up on the 12th, the order to advance on the 13th at daylight was issued. The troops then in rear came up during the night of the 12th, and these moved forward to join us as soon as they could cook their rations. The head of the column was halted near Loudon beyond the enemy's view during the day, and the cars with the pontoons were stopped out of sight till after night. A select detail was made to throw across the river in advance, and details were made to roll the cars up to the nearest point of the river as soon as dark came on. At dark the cars were pushed up and the boats were taken down to the river as quietly as possible, with the hope that we might surprise and capture the enemy's pickets on the opposite bank. The information that we got from our cavalry pickets not being accurate, we failed in the effort. The picket escaped and gave the alarm, but the enemy did not attempt to molest us.

The night of the 13th and 14th was occupied in laying the bridge and in crossing.

In the afternoon of the 14th a considerable infantry force advanced and skirmished with us for some time, driving in our line of sharpshooters and deploying along our front as if to give battle.

Upon moving out on the morning of the 15th the enemy was found to be retiring. The sharpshooters of Hood's division, under Lieutenant-Colonel Logan, after a brisk skirmish drove in the enemy's rear in some confusion, he taking up his line of retreat along the road which follows the railroad. Not having a map of the topography of the country, I was of necessity dependent upon such information as I could get from the guides and from my own observation. I found that the enemy in retiring to his line of retreat had crossed a considerable ridge, which runs parallel with the railroad, and is impassable to vehicles except at certain gaps. Putting a small force at the pass over which the enemy retired, I advanced along the west side of the ridge on a road running parallel with the ridge and to the road by which the enemy must retire.

Arriving opposite Lenoir's Station I found a picket guard of the enemy at a gap in the ridge. After a little examination I found the enemy at Lenoir's in considerable force and taken completely by surprise, thinking that our force immediately in his rear was the only force that was advancing. With confident hope of reaping the full benefit of this surprise I moved down upon him. The ground was so muddy and the hills so high (almost mountains) that we were not able to get one division up and in position till after night. Some of the troops were sent under guides after night to get possession of the roads in the enemy's rear, and about midnight General Jenkins advanced his brigade and got possession of the only ground that the enemy could expect to occupy to give battle.

When daylight came it was found that the guides had failed to put the troops upon the right road, and that the enemy had during the night abandoned part of his wagon train and made a hurried retreat. Hood's division was put in pursuit, and McLaws' division, being on the road to Campbell's Station, was ordered to move forward as rapidly as possible and endeavor to intercept the enemy (in full retreat) at Campbell's Station. Jenkins' sharpshooters pursued rapidly, skirmishing nearly all of the time and making every effort to force the enemy to make a stand, but did not succeed in doing so until after he had passed Campbell's Station. He escaped General McLaws also and took a strong position east of Campbell's Station. As soon as General McLaws got up he was ordered to deploy three of his brigades in front of the enemy, and to put his other brigade upon a ridge on our left, so as to threaten the enemy's right.

At the same time Colonel Alexander put his artillery in position, and General Jenkins was ordered with Hood's division around the enemy's left, and upon arriving opposite the enemy's position to make an attack upon that flank, while General McLaws was advancing against the enemy's front to follow Jenkins' attack. The flank movement and fire of our batteries caused the enemy to retreat in some haste. McLaws' division advanced promptly and brought the enemy to a stand about a mile farther toward his rear in a more commanding position. If General Jenkins could have made his attack during this movement, or if he could have made it after the enemy had taken his second position, we must have destroyed this force, recovered East Tennessee, and in all probability captured the greater portion of the enemy's forces. He attributes his failure to do so to some mismanagement of General Law. Before I could get a staff officer to him to ascertain the occasion of the delay night came on and our efforts ceased. The enemy drew off as soon as it was dark and retired to Knoxville.

We advanced again at daylight, but only came up with the enemy's rear guard of cavalry. There was more or less skirmishing with this force until our line of skirmishers and our advanced battery came under the fire from the enemy's fort at the northwest angle of his lines at Knoxville. His line of skirmishers was about 1,000 yards in front of his works. General McLaws' skirmishers engaging them, Hart's brigade of cavalry was ordered over to the Clinton road to drive in the skirmishers of the enemy, and as soon as Hood's division came up it was ordered over to that road, and Hart's cavalry was sent on to the Tazewell road, so as to prevent as far as possible the escape of the enemy. I rode over to the Clinton road to make an examination of the country and select some position for Hood's division before night.

The next day, on riding to General McLaws' front, I found that the enemy's pickets occupied the same ground that they held the day before, and that his line had been strengthened during the night by making a defense of rails. Colonel Alexander was ordered to use his guns against this defense, and succeeded once or twice in driving the enemy off from some points of it; but our skirmishers did not move up to occupy it, and the enemy returned to it. I finally ordered General McLaws to order his troops up to take the position. Part of the troops moved up handsomely and got partial possession others faltered and sought shelter under a rise of the ground, when Captain Winthrop, of Colonel Alexander's staff, appreciating the danger of delay at such a moment, mounted his horse and dashing up to the front of our line led the troops over the work. He had the misfortune to receive a severe wound in this affair. Our force was not strong enough to risk an assault from so great a distance from the enemy's works. He had as many as we in a strong position fortified. We went to work, therefore, to make our way forward by gradual and less hazardous measures, at the same time making examinations of the enemy's entire positions.

General Wheeler retired from Knoxville and crossed the Holston near Louisville and joined us on the 18th. His three brigades were stationed on the Tazewell road, and Hart's brigade was sent back to Kingston, where a brigade of the enemy's cavalry was reported to be. Our transportation being limited we had brought no tools for intrenching or other work, except those that our small pioneer parties had. We were so fortunate, however, as to capture a large number of picks and spades in the abandoned wagons of the enemy at Lenoir's Station; also a pontoon bridge in the river near that place. We had the tools brought up by our cavalry upon their horses, and set to work to strengthen our position and make advances by throwing our picket lines forward at night. The enemy's line along General Jenkins' front seemed very weak and his entire line very long.

Upon an examination of his line on the 20th, on the Clinton road, General Jenkins thought that he might push in his skirmishers and find the means of breaking the enemy's line. He was ordered to advance his skirmishers a little before night, and to have his command ready, and if the opportunity proved favorable to throw his entire force upon the enemy and break his line. A little after dark he reported the matter impracticable. Our line was then about 700 yards from the enemy's. After careful examination I became convinced that the true key to the enemy's position was by the heights on the south side of the Holston, and crossed a small force (Law's and Robertson's brigades) in flat-boats and obtained possession of one of the heights near and opposite the lower end of the enemy's line. This position gave us command of the fort and line in front of General McLaws, but the range from the hill to the fort was too great for our limited supply of ammunition. With a view to operations on a more extensive scale on the south side, the pontoon bridge that we had captured was ordered up. Our first effort was to get it up by the river, but that was reported impracticable, as there were rapids that the boats could not be hauled over. We were, therefore, obliged to send wagons to haul the bridge.

On the 22d, General McLaws seemed to think his line near enough for an assault, and he was ordered to make it at dark on that night. General Jenkins was ordered to be prepared to co-operate. After night General McLaws reported against the assault, saying that his officers would prefer to attack by daylight.

On the 23d instant [?], Major-General Wheeler, in conformity with instructions, moved upon Kingston with three brigades of cavalry.

A portion of the next day was passed in skirmishing with the enemy at that place, General Wheeler finally desisting and withdrawing a short distance on account of the strong position occupied by the enemy, and the superior numbers which he reports him to have had. Colonel Hart, who was left at Kingston with a brigade of cavalry, reported that the enemy's force in front of General Wheeler there consisted of but three regiments of cavalry and a battery of artillery.

On the 24th, General Wheeler received orders from General Bragg to rejoin him in person, and in accordance with those orders the command of the cavalry was turned over to Major-General Martin. The official report of General Wheeler will explain fully his operations before Kingston. The cavalry, with the exception of one brigade, returned from Kingston on the 26th, and resumed its operations about Knoxville.

On the 23d, I received a telegram from the commanding general informing me that the enemy had moved out and attacked him at Chattanooga. Later on the same day I received another dispatch announcing that the enemy was still in front of him, but the firing had ceased. On the night of the same day his letter of the 22d was received.

On the 25th, I received a telegram from Brig. Gen. B. R. Johnson, at Loudon, informing me that the enemy's cavalry was advancing upon Charleston. As I had received nothing from the commanding general on the 24th, I concluded that the enemy had moved out on the 23d for the purpose of threatening him, while he passed his cavalry out for the purpose of making a raid on Charleston and thus cut off the re-enforcements then on their way to me.

On the night of the 25th, General Leadbetter joined me. We made a hasty reconnaissance of the enemy's entire position on the 26th. From the heights on the south side he pronounced the enemy's fort in front of General McLaws assailable. After riding around the enemy's lines, however, he expressed his preference for an attack against Mabry's Hill, at the northeast of the position.

On the 27th, a more careful examination of Mabry's Hill was made by Generals Leadbetter, Jenkins, Colonel Alexander, and myself. The opinion of all on this day was that the ground over which the troops would have to pass was too much exposed and the distance to be overcome under fire was too great. General Leadbetter was urgent that something should be done quickly, but admitted that the way to the enemy's position was by the heights on the south side.

On the 27th, Colonel Giltner's brigade of cavalry, of Major-General Ransom's command, arrived near Knoxville for co-operation with me, and on the 28th Brig. Gen. W. E. Jones reported with his brigade of cavalry of the same command.

On the 26th and 27th, we had various rumors of a battle having been fought at Chattanooga, the most authentic being from telegraph operators. There seemed to be so many reports leading to the same conclusion that I determined that I must attack, and, if possible, get possession of Knoxville.

The attack upon the fort was ordered for the 28th, but in order to get our troops nearer the works the assault was postponed until daylight of the 29th. The line of sharpshooters along our entire front was ordered to be advanced at dark to within good rifle-range of the enemy's lines, and to sink rifle-pits during the night in its advanced position, so that the sharpshooters along our whole line might engage the enemy upon an equal footing, while our columns made the assault upon the fort.

Our advance at night was very successful, capturing 60 or 70 prisoners without any loss. The assault was ordered to be made by three of General McLaws' brigades, his fourth being held in readiness for further operations. General Jenkins was ordered to advance a brigade a little later than the assaulting columns and to pass the enemy's lines east of the fort, and to continue the attack along the enemy's rear and flank. Two brigades of Major-General Buckner's division, under Brig. Gen. B. R. Johnson, having arrived the day before, were ordered to move in rear of General McLaws, and at a convenient distance, to be thrown in as circumstances might require.

On the night of the 28th, General McLaws' letter of that date was received. General McLaws' letter was shown to General Leadbetter, and my answer was read to him. General Leadbetter then suggested the postscript which I added to the answer. The assault was made at the appointed time by Generals Wofford's, Humphreys', and Bryan's brigades. The troops were not formed as well to the front as they should have been. Their lines should have been formed close up on our line of rifle-pits, which would have given them but about 200 yards to advance under fire. Instead of this the lines were formed several hundred yards in rear of the pits.

My orders were that the advance should be made quietly until they entered the works, which was to be announced by a shout. The troops moved up in gallant style and formed handsomely at the outside of the ditch. As I approached the troops seemed to be in good order at the edge of the ditch, and some of the colors appeared to be on the works. When within about 500 yards of the fort I saw some of the men straggling back, and heard that the troops could not pass the ditch for want of ladders or other means. Almost at the same moment I saw that the men were beginning to retire in considerable numbers, and very soon the column broke up entirely and fell back in confusion. I ordered Buckner's brigade halted and retired, and sent the order for Anderson's brigade, of Hood's division, to be halted and retired, but the troops of the latter brigade had become excited and rushed up to the same point from which the others had been repulsed, and were soon driven back. Officers were set to work to rally the men, and good order was soon restored.

About half an hour after the repulse Major Branch, of Major-General Ransom's staff, arrived with a telegram from the President through General Ransom, informing me that General Bragg had retired before superior numbers, and directing that I should proceed to co-operate with him. Orders were issued at once for our trains to move back to Loudon in order that we might follow as soon as possible to rejoin General Bragg.

On the afternoon of the same day I received a note from General Wheeler, by General Bragg's authority, directing that I should rejoin him at Ringgold, if practicable. Reports began to come in at the same time that the enemy were in force at Cleveland. As the note of General Wheeler seemed to indicate that it was doubtful whether I could effect a junction with General Bragg, I ordered my trains to return to me at Knoxville. It appeared to me that the best thing for us was to hold the enemy at Knoxville until the army at Chattanooga should be obliged to make heavy detachments to succor the garrison at Knoxville, and that in that way we would be able to relieve General Bragg's army, and give him time to rally and to receive re-enforcements. The principal officers of the command were called to advise, and the general opinion expressed was, that it would be imprudent to attempt to rejoin General Bragg with the lights then before us. About this time two messengers came from General Bragg to state that he had retired to Dalton, and that I must depend on "my own resources." Upon this I determined to remain at Knoxville until seriously threatened by a succoring army from Chattanooga, and wrote to General Ransom, then at Rogersville, to move down and join me and aid me in reducing the enemy, or to aid me in the event that a small succoring force should attempt to relieve Knoxville.

On December 1, Colonel Giltner, commanding one of General Ransom's brigades of cavalry, reported to me that he had received orders from General Ransom that he (Colonel Giltner), with his brigade, should rejoin General Ransom.

On the same day a courier from General Grant was captured, bearing an autograph letter to General Burnside with the information that three columns were advancing to his relief—one by the south side, under General Sherman ; one by Decherd, under General Elliott, and one by Cumberland Gap, under General Foster. The enemy were then reported as pressing our forces below Loudon with superior numbers. General Vaughn, in command at Loudon, had been ordered to move all stores that he could haul to the north side of the river, and to be prepared, in case the enemy marched against him with superior forces, to destroy such property as he could not remove, and to cross the river with his troops and join me at Knoxville. General Leadbetter, who was at Loudon before this, had been requested by me to order General Vaughn to rejoin General Bragg's army by passing through the mountains, if he thought it practicable.

Major-General Wheeler wrote about the same time for the cavalry of General Bragg's army serving with me to be returned to that army. As I was cut off from all communication and entirely dependent upon the surrounding country for supplies, and threatened from all sides, I did not think it prudent to dispense with the cavalry and declined to send it. As General Vaughn was not sent to General Bragg, as suggested, and was seriously threatened by the enemy in his rear (the enemy's force at Kingston also being reported as increasing), he was ordered to destroy everything that he could not remove that would be of value to the enemy, and to proceed to join me at Knoxville. As our position at Knoxville was somewhat complicated, I determined to abandon the siege and to draw off in the direction of Virginia, with an idea that we might find an opportunity to strike that column of the enemy's forces reported to be advancing by Cumberland Gap.

The orders to move, in accordance with this view, were issued on December 2.

Our trains were put in motion on the 3d to cross the Holston at Strawberry Plains, escorted by Generals Law's and Robertson's brigades, of Hood's division, and one of Alexander's batteries.

On the night of the 4th, the troops were withdrawn from the west side of Knoxville and marched around to the east side, when they took up a line of march along the north bank of the Holston River. General Martin, with his own and General Ransom's cavalry, was left at Knoxville to cover the movement. As our march was not interrupted by the enemy, we were enabled to reach Blain's Cross-Roads on the afternoon of the 5th, where we met General Ransom with the infantry and artillery of his command.

On the 6th, we marched to Rutledge, where we remained until the 8th. As there was no indication of a force moving from Cumberland Gap, I did not feel that I should keep General Bragg's cavalry any longer ; and as the enemy's cavalry had moved out, and seemed disposed to annoy us—I could not remain so near him and depend upon our small cavalry force to protect our foraging trains—I concluded to retire to Rogersville and to order General Bragg's cavalry back to Georgia.

We accordingly marched for Rogersville on the 8th, ordering all of our cavalry except Giltner's brigade across the Holston, near Bean's Station. Martin's cavalry, belonging to General Bragg's army, was ordered to return to that army through the mountains of North Carolina and Georgia, and Jones' brigade, of General Ransom's command, to cover the movements of our troops and trains on the south side of the Holston.

The column reached Rogersville on the 9th. The accounts that we got of the resources of the country were favorable, and we halted and put our trains out getting provisions, &c. As there were not enough mills to grind more than flour to feed the command from day to day, we were obliged to reduce the bread ration one-half in order to accumulate a few days' rations.

On the 10th, I received a telegram from the President which seemed to give me discretionary power with regard to the troops and their movement. The order for General Martin's cavalry to return to General Bragg was countermanded at once, and it was held in position between our main force and the enemy.

On the 12th, I received information that I thought reliable that a part of the enemy's re-enforcements from Chattanooga had returned to that place, and that the enemy had a force consisting of three brigades of cavalry and one of infantry at Bean's Station, his main force being between Rutledge and Blain's Cross-Roads.

Orders were issued for the troops to be in readiness to march on the 14th, with the hope of being able to surprise and capture the enemy's force at Bean's Station, our main force to move directly down from Rogersville to Bean's Station. General Martin, with four brigades of cavalry, was to move down on the south side and cross the Holston opposite Bean's Station, or below, and General W. E. Jones, with two brigades of cavalry, was to pass down on the north side of Clinch Mountain and prevent the enemy's escape by Bean's Station Gap.

On the 13th and that night we had heavy rains, which retarded our march and made a slight rise in the Holston. The infantry column, however, reached Bean's Station in good time and surprised the enemy completely. General W. E. Jones also got his position in good time and captured a number of the enemy's wagons. His information with regard to our movements, however, was not correct, and he retired from the gap after securing his captured wagons. General Martin was not heard at his crossing till about night. He then only crossed a part of his command, and afterward withdrew it. As our column was composed of infantry and artillery only, we could only drive the enemy back. Brig. Gen. B. R. Johnson, commanding Buckner's division, advanced directly against the enemy and drove him steadily to the buildings at Bean's Station, where he met with a strong resistance.

General Kershaw, at the head of General McLaws' division, was ordered in upon the right of Johnson to push forward and cut off the force that was occupying the gap, and then to pass down upon the left flank of the force in the valley. General Kershaw executed his orders literally and most promptly; but we could not catch the enemy's cavalry. The night was dark and General Kershaw halted after he had executed his orders. Our cavalry was not up, and the enemy escaped to a strong position 3 miles from us. During the night he strengthened his position by rail defenses and some re-enforcements. He was found in this position in the morning.

Upon ordering Major-General McLaws to send a part of his command up in the gap on the morning of the 15th to capture the force that had been cut off there, he informed me that his troops had had no bread rations for two days. I directed him to send a brigade up, and to hurry his rations up and have them issued and cooked at once.

General Jenkins, commanding Hood's division, was ordered to pursue at daylight, which he did, and found the enemy in the position above mentioned, 3 miles below Bean's Station. Upon a casual examination the force appeared to be the cavalry that we had engaged the day before. I directed General Jenkins to examine the force and position, and to attack if he found an opportunity. I rode back to secure the force in the gap, reported by the citizens at the station to be stronger than I had supposed. Humphreys' brigade had been ordered into the gap, and upon reaching it he found that the enemy had abandoned everything except his arms, and escaped during the night by passing along the top of the mountain.

Brigadier-General Law, with his own and Brigadier-General Robertson's brigade, had been on detached service guarding our trains, and was some 8 miles behind his division on the night of the 14th. He had been ordered to join it on the 13th, but did not succeed in doing so.

On the night of the 14th, he was ordered to march early on the following day and join the division as soon as he possibly could. He reported to General Jenkins, the division commander, between 3 and 4 o'clock in the afternoon. If he started at the hour that he should have done (6 o'clock) he must have been about 11 hours marching as many miles. General Jenkins reports that the enemy re-enforced with infantry before General Law joined him.

A little before sunset General Jenkins reported that he thought the enemy was preparing to advance against him. I ordered General McLaws to send him one of his brigades to re-enforce him. General McLaws sent me in reply that his men had not yet had any bread rations. He, however, sent the brigade ordered up. The enemy's move, which created the impression of his advance, was probably caused by the appearance of General Martin's cavalry on his flank.

A little after night the enemy retreated and our skirmishers occupied their defenses. The pursuit was ordered by daylight by Hood's division of infantry and Martin's cavalry. As I rode to the front General Law preferred a complaint of hardships, &c. General McLaws was not yet fed, and there seemed so strong a desire for rest rather than to destroy the enemy, that I was obliged to abandon the pursuit, although the enemy were greatly demoralized and in some confusion. This was the second time during the campaign when the enemy was completely in our power, and we allowed him to escape us. General Martin was ordered to pursue with his cavalry.

General Armstrong, who followed immediately behind the enemy, reported his retreat so rapid that he could not bring him to a stand until he reached Blain's Cross-Roads. There he made a successful stand against our cavalry. After exhausting the supply of forage between Blain's Cross-Roads and Rogersville, the command was moved to its present position on the south side of the Holston and ordered to make shelters for the winter.

As we did not succeed in bringing the enemy to battle, there was but little opportunity for personal distinction on the part of subordinate officers. I should mention, however, Brig. Gen. B. R. Johnson for his fine march from Cloud's Creek to Bean's Station (about 6 miles over very bad roads), and for his handsome attack upon the enemy's cavalry, driving him steadily back. Brigadier-General Gracie (who was severely wounded) and Brigadier-General Kershaw for their very creditable parts in the same affair. Brigadier-General Jenkins for his vigorous pursuit from Lenoir's Station. Brigadier-Generals Anderson, Humphreys, and Bryan for their gallant assault on the enemy's fort at Knoxville on November 29.

Colonel Ruff, of the Eighteenth Georgia Regiment, had command of Wofford's brigade in the same assault. He was killed at the ditch. He was a very promising officer, and is a great loss to the service and his country.

In this assault Colonel McElroy, Thirteenth Mississippi Volunteers, and Colonel Thomas, Sixteenth Georgia Volunteers, also fell. Their bodies were afterward found in the ditch of the fort foremost in the attack.

Lieutenant-Colonel Fiser, Seventeenth Mississippi, lost an arm after having mounted the parapet.

Lieutenant Cumming, adjutant of the Sixteenth Georgia Volunteers, with great gallantry rushed up to the fort with 10 or 12 of his men, and made his way through an embrasure to the interior, where the party was finally captured.

The conduct of Captain Foster, of Jenkins' brigade, who had charge of the select party thrown across the Tennessee on the night of November 13, was highly creditable, both as to the coolness of the officer and the skill with which his party was handled.

Lieutenant-Colonel Logan had at various times through the campaign control of the line of skirmishers of Hood's division, and always managed it with courage and skill.

The conduct of Captain Winthrop has already been noticed. The gallantry of this officer on the occasion referred to was most conspicuous, and had the happiest effect in leading the troops over the enemy's cover, at which they had faltered.

Colonel Alexander, chief of artillery, is entitled to great credit for his untiring efforts and zeal throughout the campaign and during the siege.

I desire to express my obligations to the officers of my staff—Lieutenant-Colonel Sorrel, Major Latrobe, Major Fairfax, Major Walton, Lieutenant Goree, Lieutenant Dunn, Lieutenant-Colonel Manning, and Captain Manning (signal officer)—for their usual assistance and attention.

My aide-de-camp, Lieutenant Dunn, was severely wounded in the leg during the siege of Knoxville.

In the absence of Lieutenant-Colonel Manning, chief of ordnance, during the greater portion of the campaign, the affairs of his department were well conducted by his assistant, Lieutenant Dawson.

Major Moses, chief commissary; Major Taylor, chief quartermaster; Captain Potts, assistant quartermaster, and Surgeons Cullen and Barksdale displayed their usual intelligence and energy in the administration of their respective departments.

I refer to the reports of the chief commissary of subsistence and chief quartermaster for information in regard to the condition of their departments upon our arrival at Sweet Water; also to the accompanying copies of letters in explanation of our affairs at the beginning and during the progress of the campaign.

As the case of Brigadier-General Robertson has more or less important bearing upon the campaign, it should be mentioned in this report. As his division commander had made several complaints of his incompetency, it was suggested to me by higher authority that I should ask for a board of officers to examine and report upon his case. It was suggested at the same time that when he was relieved to attend the board another brigadier could be sent to the brigade. The board of officers was asked for by me and ordered by the commanding general; but the brigadier was left in command of the brigade. He seemed to exercise an injurious influence over the troops, and I was induced again to ask that he be relieved. An order was issued relieving the officer at my request. When the troops were started upon the campaign I found to my surprise that Brigadier-General Robertson had been ordered back to the command of his brigade. The letters and orders in the case are a part of this report. Brigadier-General Robertson is now in arrest under charge of a serious character.

Respectfully submitted.

JAMES LONGSTREET,
Lieutenant-General, Commanding.

General S. COOPER,
Adjutant and Inspector General.

—

HEADQUARTERS,
Russellville, East Tenn., January 19, 1864.

General S. COOPER,
Adjutant and Inspector General:

GENERAL: In my report of the campaign in East Tennessee I neglected to state that Brigadier-General Law, with his own and Brigadier-General Robertson's brigade, was ordered to make a diversion on the south side of the Holston at the same time that the attack was made on the enemy's fort by Major-General McLaws, and that he succeeded in turning the enemy's position and got possession of his trenches at the point of his attack. This diversion on the south side I have learned since had the effect to prevent the reserve intended for the enemy's fort re-enforcing there, and that there was but 150 men in the fort, and that at one time it was virtually surrendered, but that our troops did not enter, and the enemy recovered courage and again opened fire. May I ask the favor to have this attached as part of my report of the campaign?

I remain, very respectfully, your obedient servant,

JAMES LONGSTREET,
Lieutenant-General, Commanding.

ADDENDA.

HEADQUARTERS CORPS,
November 1, 1863.

Col. GEORGE WILLIAM BRENT,
Assistant Adjutant-General:

COLONEL: I have the honor to ask that Brig. Gen. J. B. Robertson be relieved from the command of his brigade pending the proceedings of the board now examining his case. This officer has been complained of so frequently for want of conduct in time of battle that I apprehend that the abandonment by his brigade of its position of the night of the 28th may have been due to his want of hearty co-operation.

I remain, sir, very respectfully, your most obedient servant,

JAMES LONGSTREET,
Lieutenant-General.

———

SPECIAL ORDERS, }   HEADQUARTERS ARMY OF TENNESSEE,
No. 284.   }   *Missionary Ridge, November 2, 1863.*

*   *   *   *   *   *   *

VI. At the request of Lieutenant-General Longstreet, Brigadier-General Robertson will be relieved from duty while the proceedings and actions of the examining board in his case are pending.

*   *   *   *   *   *   *

By command of General Bragg:

GEORGE WM. BRENT,
Assistant Adjutant-General.

———

SPECIAL ORDERS, }   HEADQUARTERS ARMY OF TENNESSEE,
No. 290.   }   *Missionary Ridge, November 8, 1863.*

*   *   *   *   *   *   *

VII. The proceedings of the examining board in the case of Brigadier-General Robertson having been suspended by the movement of troops, Brigadier-General Robertson will rejoin his command until the board can renew its session.

*   *   *   *   *   *   *

By command of General Bragg:

GEORGE WM. BRENT,
Assistant Adjutant-General.

———

SPECIAL ORDERS, }   HEADQUARTERS,
No. 33.   }   *Russellville, Tenn., December 23, 1863.*

*   *   *   *   *   *   *

II. Brig. Gen. J. B. Robertson will proceed to Bristol, and there await the assembling of the court for the trial of his case.

*   *   *   *   *   *   *

By command of Lieutenant-General Longstreet:

G. MOXLEY SORREL,
Assistant Adjutant-General.

———

HEADQUARTERS,
Russellville, East Tenn., December 30, 1863.

General S. COOPER,
Adjutant and Inspector General:

GENERAL: I am here without authority to order courts-martial or any other authority which is necessary to a separate command. I am entirely cut off from communication with General Bragg's army, and cannot get from those headquarters orders for courts, boards of examination, or anything else. I desire to be assigned as part of some other officer's command, whom I may reach with less trouble and in less time. A part of General S. Jones' command is with me, and should remain here if the Department intends that this should be a field for future operations. If the command is to remain, it should be so understood from the Department.

If this field is to be held with a view to future operations, I earnestly desire that some other officer be sent to the command. If a senior officer can be sent, I can cheerfully give him all the aid in my power. If none but a junior can be spared, it will give me much pleasure to relinquish in his favor, and aid him by any suggestions that my experience may enable me to give.

I regret to say that a combination of circumstances has so operated during the campaign in East Tennessee as to prevent the complete destruction of the enemy's forces in this part of the State. It is fair to infer that the fault is entirely with me, and I desire, therefore, that some other commander be tried.

I thought it necessary a few days ago to relieve Major-General McLaws from duty with this command and to order him to Augusta, Ga. Charges will be forwarded in the case in a few days. Since his removal I find other plans in operation, some which seem to be with a view to the promotion of individuals, and others probably for the purpose of avoiding the arduous service which my troops are exposed to. These are my excuses. But, as I have already stated, the fair and proper inference is that the fault is entirely with me. I am therefore exceedingly anxious that the country should have the services of some officer who may be better suited to such a position. I believe that this is the only personal favor that I have asked of the Government, and I hope that I may have reason to expect that it may be granted.

I remain, sir, very respectfully, your most obedient servant,
JAMES LONGSTREET,
Lieutenant-General, Commanding.

[Indorsement.]

JANUARY 5, 1864.

Respectfully submitted to the Secretary of War.

I have telegraphed General Longstreet that no authority exists with a commanding general to relieve officers of his command from duty and send them beyond the limits of his command; that he might have arrested General McLaws on his charges and held him to await the action of the Department, and that he had better now recall him for that purpose. He was also told that as senior officer in the Department East Tennessee he was, by military rule and usage, the commander of that department, with all the rights and privileges pertaining to such command. He has therefore the right to order courts-martial, except in cases where he himself prefers the charges.

S. COOPER,
Adjutant and Inspector General.

—

HEADQUARTERS,
Russellville, Tenn., December 30, 1863.

General S. COOPER,
Adjutant and Inspector General, Richmond:

GENERAL: I have the honor to inclose herewith charges and specifications against Maj. Gen. L. McLaws* and against Brig. Gen. J. B. Robertson.

*See p. 503.

I have no authority to order courts, and have therefore to ask that a court be ordered for the trial of Brig. Gen. J. B. Robertson. General McLaws was not arrested when he was relieved from duty here, for the reason that it was supposed that his services might be important to the Government in some other position. If such is the case, I have no desire that he should be kept from that service, or that his usefulness should be impaired in any way by a trial.

I remain, general, very respectfully, your most obedient servant,

JAMES LONGSTREET,
Lieutenant-General, Commanding.

[Indorsements.]

JANUARY 5, 1864.

Respectfully submitted to the Secretary of War.

S. COOPER,
Adjutant and Inspector General.

JANUARY 6, 1864.

Respectfully submitted to the consideration of the President.

Shall General Longstreet's earnest request to be relieved be granted? Shall the court to try the charges against General McLaws and General Robertson be ordered?

J. A. SEDDON,
Secretary of War.

It will be proper to consider the question of a successor before deciding that of relieving the present commander.

The charges against Major-General McLaws seem to imply that Lieutenant-General Longstreet, commanding, had ordered those things to be done the failure to do which are charged, and in that event the fault was very grave.

When the interests of the service will permit (the charges requiring investigation) let the court be assembled.

J. D[AVIS.]

JANUARY 11, 1864.

ADJUTANT-GENERAL:

Might not a court be assembled at Bristol or Abingdon during the present pause in operations, or, if General Longstreet be relieved, in this city?

J. A. SEDDON,
Secretary.

JANUARY 14, 1864.

I think the court had better be assembled at Russellville, where, I presume, all the witnesses are, or in that vicinity, and especially as General Longstreet himself may be required as a witness.

Respectfully submitted.

S. COOPER,
Adjutant and Inspector General.

JANUARY 16, 1864.

ADJUTANT-GENERAL:

Your suggestion approved. Can you recommend a court?

J. A. S[EDDON,]
Secretary.

ADJUTANT AND INSPECTOR GENERAL'S OFFICE,
Richmond, January 26, 1864.

Respectfully referred to Maj. Garnett Andrews, assistant-adjutant general, judge-advocate of the general court-martial convened by Paragraph XXVI, Special Orders, No. 21, Adjutant and Inspector General's Office, January 26, 1864, for his information.

By command of the Secretary of War:

JNO. WITHERS,
Assistant Adjutant-General.

[Inclosure.]

CHARGE AND SPECIFICATION AGAINST BRIG. GEN. J. B. ROBERTSON.

CHARGE.—Conduct highly prejudicial to good order and military discipline.

Specification.—In this, that he, the said Brig. Gen. J. B. Robertson, his command being under orders to advance, the enemy being immediately in front and in retreat, did call together his regimental commanders, Lieutenant-Colonel Bryan, Fifth Texas Regiment; Major Winkler, Fourth Texas Regiment, and Capt. D. K. Rice, First Texas Regiment, and did use language to them (his said regimental commanders), in substance, as follows: That there are but three days' rations on hand, and God knows where more are to come from; that he (meaning himself, the said Brig. Gen. J. B. Robertson) had no confidence in the campaign; that whether we whipped the enemy in the immediate battle or not we would be compelled to retreat, the enemy being believed by citizens and most others to be moving around us, and that we were in danger of losing a considerable part of our army; that our men were in no condition for campaigning; that General Longstreet had promised shoes, but how could they be furnished; that we only had communication with Richmond, and could not even get a mail from there in less than three weeks; that he (meaning himself, the said Brig. Gen. J. B. Robertson) was opposed to the movement, and that he would require written orders, and would obey them under protest; and other language of similar character, all of which language was calculated to discourage them (the said regimental commanders) and weaken their confidence in the movement then in progress for the development of the campaign, to create a distrust in regard to the safety of the troops, to prejudice them in regard to the management of the campaign, and tending to prevent that hearty and hopeful co-operation necessary to success. All this near Bean's Station, Tenn., on or about the 16th day of December, A. D. 1863.

M. JENKINS,
Brigadier-General, Commanding Division.

Witnesses:

Lieut. Col. K. BRYAN, Fifth Texas Regiment; Maj. C. M. WINKLER, Fourth Texas Regiment; Capt. D. K. RICE, First Texas Regiment.

[Indorsement.]

Respectfully forwarded, asking that a general court-martial be ordered to try the case.

JAMES LONGSTREET,
Lieutenant-General, Commanding.

HEADQUARTERS,
Greeneville, East Tenn., March 22, 1864.

General S. COOPER,
        Adjutant-General, Richmond, Va.:

GENERAL: I have the honor to inclose herewith charge and specification prepared against Brig. Gen. E. M. Law. I desire that a court-martial may be convened for his trial as soon as exigencies of the service may permit.

I remain, sir, very respectfully, your most obedient servant,

JAMES LONGSTREET,
Lieutenant-General, Commanding.

[Indorsement.]

The resignation within referred to never came to the office. It appears, from inquiry at the War Department, that it was presented by a friend of General Law unofficially to the Secretary of War, and never came through the regular channel as an official paper.

S. C[OOPER.]

[Inclosure.]

CHARGE AND SPECIFICATION PREPARED AGAINST BRIG. GEN. E. M. LAW, OF THE CONFEDERATE STATES SERVICE.

CHARGE.—Conduct highly prejudicial to good order and military discipline.

Specification.—In this, that Brig. Gen. E. M. Law, aforesaid, did tender the resignation of his office as brigadier-general in the service aforesaid, and did obtain a leave of absence of his commanding general, Lieut. Gen. J. Longstreet, in consequence thereof, under the pretext that it was his (Brigadier-General Law's) design and desire to give up his commission for service in the cavalry, he having arranged at the same time with officers of his brigade to petition the War Department for service for the brigade in Alabama or elsewhere, with the expressed purpose of aiding the petition and returning to the brigade as its commander, thus obtaining a leave of absence under false pretenses, and thus deceiving his commanding general as to his real intentions, and thus using the influence of his high official position to create discontent amongst his troops, by encouraging them to hope for more pleasant service in some field other than that to which they properly belong.

This near Bean's Station, East Tenn., on or about the 19th of December, 1863.

JAMES LONGSTREET,
Lieutenant-General, Commanding.

Witnesses:

Lieut. Gen. J. LONGSTREET, C. S. Army; Lieut. Col. G. M. SORREL, assistant adjutant-general; Lieutenant-Colonel JONES, Forty-fourth Alabama Volunteers; Lieutenant-Colonel HARDWICK, Forty-eighth Alabama Volunteers; Maj. W. MACK ROBBINS, Fourth Alabama Volunteers; Major LOWTHER, Fifteenth Alabama Volunteers; Col. W. F. PERRY, Forty-fourth Alabama Volunteers; Captain CLOWER, Forty-seventh Alabama Volunteers; Captain LINDSEY, Forty-seventh Alabama Volunteers.

HEADQUARTERS DEPARTMENT OF EAST TENNESSEE,
Bristol, April 8, 1864.

General S. COOPER,
Adjutant and Inspector General, Richmond, Va.:

GENERAL: I have the honor to transmit herewith additional charge and specification against Brig. Gen. E. M. Law, C. S. Army. Th additional matter has been more recently ascertained.

I remain, sir, very respectfully, your obedient servant,

JAMES LONGSTREET,
Lieutenant-General, Commanding.

[Indorsement.]

These charges are not entertained, and General Law has been o dered to assume his command. See dispatch to General Buckner, o April 18.

S. C[OOPER.]

[Inclosure.]

ADDITIONAL CHARGE AND SPECIFICATION PREFERRED AGAINST BRIG GEN. E. M. LAW, OF THE CONFEDERATE STATES ARMY.

CHARGE.—Conduct unbecoming an officer and a gentleman.

Specification.—In this, that Brig. Gen. E. M. Law aforesaid, having obtained a leave of absence from his commanding general (Lieut Gen. J. Longstreet) upon the tender of his resignation as a brigadier general in the army aforesaid, did ask for and obtain permission o his commanding general aforesaid to take with him the tender o his resignation from the headquarters of the Department of Eas Tennessee, to the War Department, for the purpose of delivering the said official communication in person, and did take said communication from the headquarters aforesaid, and did purloin o clandestinely do away with said communication, thereby abusing th confidence of his commanding general aforesaid, and robbing the War Department of its true and proper official record.

This commencing at or near Bean's Station, East Tenn., on o about the 19th day of December, 1863.

JAMES LONGSTREET,
Lieutenant-General, Commanding.

Witnesses:

Hon. J. A. SEDDON, Secretary of War; Lieut. Gen. J. LONGSTREET C. S. Army; Lieut. Col. G. M. SORREL, assistant adjutant-general Capt. J. W. RIELY, assistant adjutant-general.

—

ADJT. AND INSP. GENERAL'S OFFICE, WAR DEPT., C. S.,
Richmond, Va., April 18, 1864.

Maj. Gen. S. B. BUCKNER,
Bristol, Tenn.:

Send Law's brigade to Charlottesville to report to General Field. General Law will be relieved from arrest and put in command of it. The charges against him will not be further entertained.

S. COOPER,
Adjutant and Inspector General.

GORDONSVILLE, *April* 26, 1864.
General S. COOPER:

Have the additional charge and specification preferred against General Law been received at your office?
JAMES LONGSTREET,
Lieutenant-General.

—

RICHMOND, VA., *April* 27, 1864.
Lieut. Gen. JAMES LONGSTREET:

All the charges against General Law have been received. They are not entertained, and he has been ordered to resume his command.

S. COOPER,
Adjutant and Inspector General.

—

HEADQUARTERS, *April* 30, 1864.
General S. COOPER,
Adjutant and Inspector General, Richmond, Va.:

GENERAL: I have the honor to transmit herewith copies of charges preferred by Lieutenant-General Longstreet against Brigadier-General Law.*

They were sent to me when the originals were forwarded by General Longstreet to Richmond for attention. Not supposing that any action on my part would be necessary, I did not consider them when I notified General Longstreet that Brigadier-General Law's brigade had been ordered to join him. I informed him that I had been advised that the charges had not been entertained, and that Brigadier-General Law had been restored to duty. Upon the reception of General Longstreet's reply, which I inclose, I examined the charges against General Law, and find them of a very grave character. I think it due to General Law, as well as to the interests of the service, that they should be investigated, and that his innocence or guilt should be declared by a court-martial. There have been instances of officers obtaining indulgences on not the true grounds, which I think discreditable and prejudicial to military discipline, and should be stopped. The only doubt in my mind in this case, is as to the expediency of convening a court at this time. If it is thought unadvisable to do so, I would recommend that General Law be relieved from duty until an investigation can be had.

I am, most respectfully, your obedient servant,
R. E. LEE,
General.

[Indorsements.]
MAY 5, 1864.

Respectfully submitted to the President, with the original charges against General Law, being the same as the copies herewith.
S. COOPER,
Adjutant and Inspector General.

MAY 18, 1864.

The Secretary of War, being fully informed of the facts in relation to the conduct of General Law in the matter of resignation,

---

*See pp. 471, 472.

will communicate them to General'Lee as the reason for declinin
to entertain the charges on that point.   If General Law has misbe
haved at Lookout Mountain or elsewhere in the face of the enemy
charges should have been preferred, not injurious statements mad
in a letter to prejudice his case in a different transaction.   Genera
Longstreet has seriously offended against good order and militar
discipline, in rearresting an officer who had been released by th
War Department, without any new offense having been alleged.

JEFFERSON DAVIS.

—

HEADQUARTERS HARDEE'S CORPS,
Dalton, Ga., April 8, 1864.

Lieut. Gen. JAMES LONGSTREET,
Greeneville, East Tenn.:

MY DEAR GENERAL: I am in receipt of your letter of the 24t]
ultimo, in which you ask me to give you my recollections of th
views expressed by you in the council at Missionary Ridge in No
vember last in regard to any campaign for our army, and particu
larly your views in regard to the campaign in East Tennessee.

Your first proposition in that council was to turn the position o
Chattanooga by crossing the Tennessee River with our army below
Bridgeport, to march on Stevenson, destroy the depot at that place
and move into Middle Tennessee.   This was opposed, on the ground
that our horses would starve before we could get forage for their
subsistence; that the country over which we should have to pass
was a barren wilderness, and that we could not rely on any supplie
for man or beast before reaching Duck River.   You replied, if tha
was the case and our horses would be five days without forage, tha
the plan was impracticable.   You then proposed a movement int
East Tennessee, and expressed the opinion that 15,000 men would
be a force sufficient to destroy Burnside.   Bragg stated that Sher
man, with large re-enforcements, was on his way to join Grant, bu
he and others were of opinion that the army sent to East Tennesse
could whip Burnside, and, if need be, return before Sherman coul
reach Chattanooga.   It was agreed, also, that the movement in Eas
Tennessee would compel Grant to send re-enforcements to that quar
ter.   The movement was decided on, and Bragg stated that he would
send your corps, and would make such additions as would increase
it to 15,000 men.   I do not remember that anything was said by yo
touching the necessity, in view of this movement, of retiring the
army behind the Chickamauga.   It is but just to say, however, that
if a proposition of that character had been made, it would not, in
my opinion, have been approved by General Bragg.

With best wishes, very respectfully and truly, yours,
W. J. HARDEE,
Lieutenant-General.

—

HDQRS. FIRST CORPS, ARMY OF NORTHERN VIRGINIA,
April 27, 1864.

General R. E. LEE,
Commanding Army of Northern Virginia:

GENERAL: I have the honor to acknowledge the receipt of your
letter of yesterday, informing me that "the President had declined

entertain the charges, and ordered General Law to be restored to uty."

The "authorities at Richmond" are aware that it is my opinion at our failures at Lookout Mountain on the 29th of October, and ; Campbell's Station on the 16th of November last, were due to a ant of conduct upon the part of Brigadier-General Law. In addi-on to this, charges of a very grave character have been preferred gainst General Law, which, if established, must dismiss him from e service. If my efforts to maintain discipline, spirit, and zeal in e discharge of official duty are to be set aside by the return of eneral Law and his restoration to duty without trial, it cannot be ell for me to remain in command. I cannot yield the authority of y position so long as I am responsible for the proper discharge of s functions. It is necessary, therefore, that General Law should e brought to trial upon the charges that have been preferred gainst him, or that I be relieved from duty in the Confederate tates service. I have ordered the rearrest of General Law upon is return.

I remain, general, very respectfully, your most obedient servant,

JAMES LONGSTREET,
Lieutenant-General, Commanding.

No. 58.

eturn of Casualties in Longstreet's Corps, November 14–December 4.

Command.	Officers and men killed.	Officers and men wounded.	Officers and men missing.	Officers and men, total.	Date.
HOOD'S DIVISION.					
nkins' brigade..........................	22	109	5	136	} November 14 to December 5.
nning's brigade..........................	1	5	....	6	
bertson's brigade......	8	17	6	31	November 25.
bertson's brigade..........................	1	1	....	2	November 29.
w's brigade..........................	14	64	7	85	November 25.
w's brigade..........................	1	5	1	7	November 29.
derson's brigade..........................	3	57	....	60	November 17 and 18.
derson's brigade........	33	129	25	187	November 29.
Total	83	387	44	514	
M'LAWS' DIVISION.					
offord's brigade.	48	121	81	250	} November 29.
yan's brigade..........	27	121	64	212	
mphreys' brigade	....	18	....	18	
mphreys' brigade	21	87	56	164	November 29.
rshaw's brigade	19	116	3	138	November 17 and 18.
Total	115	463	204	782	
Grand total..........................	198	850	248	1,296	

Loss in the assault on Fort Loudon, November 29 : Killed, 129 ; ounded, 458 ; missing, 226 ; aggregate, 813, included in the above.

G. MOXLEY SORREL,
Lieutenant-Colonel, Assistant Adjutant-General.

NEAR ROGERSVILLE,
December 12, 1863.

No. 60.

Report of Capt. Frank Potts, Assistant Quartermaster, C. S. Arm

OFFICE CHIEF QUARTERMASTER, LONGSTREET'S COMMAND,
                                       Russellville, Tenn., December 26, 1863.

COLONEL : I have the honor to acknowledge receipt of your con
munication of this date, conveying to me the desire of the lieutenan
general commanding that I should report the condition of the tran
portation of the command at the time of its arrival at Sweet Wate
Tenn.

This command reached the Army of Tennessee without transpo
tation, but received from various sources enough to give us, c
October 14, within 143 wagons of the quantity allowed by Genera
Orders, No. 182, Army Headquarters. Subsequent to that time an
previous to our leaving Chickamauga we received more transporta
tion, reducing our deficiency to 30 wagons. I would remark tha
while before Chattanooga we drew forage and subsistence store
altogether from the railroad station, thus relieving us of the pressin
necessity for a supply train ; the want of which, however, becan
apparent soon as we moved from a line of railroad. We reache
Sweet Water 30 wagons short of the transportation allowed us, whi
all our supplies were delivered at the railroad terminus 8 miles of
and opportunities given to make every wagon available by unloadin
baggage. While at Sweet Water our supplies for men and horse
had to be collected and many wagons had to be repaired, which r
duced the number available. We had no supply trains for eithe
division, and were 25 wagons short of the artillery ordnance tran
portation required by General Orders, No. 182.

Maj. M. B. McMicken, chief quartermaster, Army of Tennesse
informed me that 70 wagons for a supply train would report to me a
Sweet Water. Thirty-nine wagons reported, 4 of which were forge c
baggage wagons, leaving 35 for distribution to the two divisions. On
day after the troops marched to Loudon 25 more arrived, which I ha
loaded with artillery ammunition and sent to the front. While w
were numerically short of transportation, the condition of what w
had was beyond all question the worst I ever saw; wagons fre
quently breaking down, mules just able in a large proportion c
cases to carry their harness, harness much worn, and many team
without collars or saddles.

I have the honor to be, colonel, with much respect, your obedier
servant,

FRANK POTTS,
    Captain, and Assistant Quartermaster, Longstreet's Corps.

Lieut. Col. G. MOXLEY SORREL, *Asst. Adjt. Gen.*

No. 61.

*Report of Maj. R. J. Moses, Commissary of Subsistence, C. S
                    Army, Chief Commissary.*

OFFICE CHIEF COMMISSARY, ETC.,
                                       Russellville, January 1, 1864.

SIR : I have the honor to report that when we left Tyner's Statio
for Sweet Water we were without meat rations. I applied to Genera

ragg's chief commissary, and received two days' rations. When we rrived in Sweet Water, four days afterward, our troops had been wo days without meat, and no provision whatever had been made or their supplies. The country within our lines was completely exausted of beef cattle, and the few hogs collected by Major Gillespie, ommissary of Stevenson's division, had been ordered to the rear. f 90,000 pounds flour at Charleston, 40,000 pounds had been sent ack to Chickamauga. I applied to General Longstreet, and obtained n order upon Major Gillespie for the hogs and flour in his control. ut for this order the army must have suffered intensely. Under he order I obtained from three to four days' rations of fresh pork, nd an order on Charleston for two days' rations of flour.

The flour from Charleston, a distance of 14 miles by railroad, could ot be got to Sweet Water for forty-eight hours. At Sweet Water the ngineer refused to remove it farther. Our troops were then near oudon, and out of flour rations, except such as could be collected rom wheat hauled to the mills, for which purpose no supply train ad yet been furnished. In order to get the flour to the troops I had o take forcible possession of the road and run the engine with an fficer detailed from one of the Tennessee regiments.

A few days later a supply train of 35 wagons reached me. It hould have consisted of at least 70. We commenced hauling wheat nd used every possible exertion to ration the troops, but as they vere then moving on the enemy toward Knoxville it was impossible o collect supplies and keep the trains up with the troops.

In consequence of these difficulties the army was two or three days vithout flour rations, and some portions of it more than double that ength of time. With every energy in the power of this department he troops were a day or two in front of Knoxville before they could e regularly rationed, and it was only a day or two before we moved rom Knoxville that as much as three days' rations could be accumuated. The department, on our arrival at Sweet Water, was utterly nprovided for, and its condition as bad as it could be in a country ot utterly exhausted,

Respectfully, your obedient servant,

R. J. MOSES,
Major, and Chief Commissary.

Lieut. Col. G. MOXLEY SORREL,
Assistant Adjutant-General, &c.

No. 62.

Report of Col. E. Porter Alexander, C. S. Artillery, Chief of Artillery.

WASHINGTON, GA.,
January 15, 1864.

COLONEL: I have the honor to submit the following report of the operations of the artillery of General Longstreet's corps in the recent ampaign against Knoxville:

It consisted of my own and Leyden's battalion, the former numbering twenty-three and the latter twelve guns. Leyden's battalion vas very deficient in horses, and the three 20-pounder Parrott rifles of my battalion were furnished with but about 75 rounds of ammu-

nition each, all efforts to supply these deficiencies having prov
unavailing.

The artillery rendezvoused at Tyner's Station on November 4, 18(
The horses and wagons were the next day dispatched to march
Sweet Water Station, the men and guns to follow by rail after t
infantry. Owing to the inefficiency of the railroad transportati
the last of the artillery only reached Sweet Water Station on t
morning of November 13, when the whole of it marched imme(
ately, accompanying the infantry, to the vicinity of Loudon. Th
night a pontoon bridge was commenced, and my battalion was post
to cover the crossing should the enemy oppose it.

On the evening of the 14th, the infantry having commenced
cross, a force of the enemy approached from above and engaged o
advance skirmishers. Captain Parker immediately moved his ba
tery to their support and contributed to the repulse of the enemy.

On the 15th, the corps marched to Lenoir's Station, the batteri
being distributed along the column. On arriving near the stati
the enemy were found in line of battle awaiting us, and althou$
the sun was already setting, an attack was ordered by General Lon
street, and the dispositions for it commenced. Darkness, howeve
fell before one-half of the column could be deployed into line, a1
the night being rainy and the ground rough, wooded, and unknow
the attack was necessarily postponed until dawn. Our lines advan
ing at this hour found the enemy in retreat.

The pursuit was immediately ordered on two roads, General Je
kins on the right, General McLaws on the left (the two roads unitir
at Campbell's Station), half the artillery accompanying each colum
The right column arrived at about 12 m. at Campbell's Station, t}
left about 2 p. m., and the enemy was found in line in a strong po
tion. General Jenkins being sent around his right flank, I w.
ordered to attack him in front with the artillery, which I did wi1
seventeen pieces of my battalion and Major Leyden's. After a sha1
fight of a half hour the enemy fell back so rapidly as to avoid tl
flank attack of General Jenkins.

During this engagement, one of my 20-pounder Parrott rifles bur
in front of the trunnions, and the efficiency of all our rifles was mu(
impaired by the tumbling of the shell and their frequent expl
sions in the guns, or failure to explode at all. And I may say he
that the same trouble preceded this campaign and followed
through it to a greater degree than ever before. The ammunitio
was procured from the depots of the Army of Tennessee.

I should have stated above also that one battery of Major Le
den's battalion was left at Loudon on the 15th for lack of horse
thus reducing that battalion to eight guns and our entire strengt
to thirty. On the retreat of the enemy, we followed, skirmishir
until dark, during which time Major Leyden gallantly engaged
heavy 6-gun battery of the enemy's with but three of his own, a1
inflicted on them a severer loss than he suffered.

At dawn the next morning (November 17), the pursuit was r
newed with Parker's battery, of my battalion, in front, and tl
enemy in front was driven under cover of the works surroundir
Knoxville by 11 a. m., and our lines were at once formed, investir
the city on the north side, the artillery being divided among the tw
divisions of infantry.

On the 18th, an attack was made on the enemy's advanced lin
which was gallantly carried. Captain Taylor's battery, of my ba

talion, deserves much credit for their share in this assault, and my adjutant (Capt. S. Winthrop, assistant adjutant-general) was severely wounded, leading on horseback the charge of our infantry within a few feet of the enemy's breastworks. Reconnaissances of the ground and the enemy's works (all totally unknown to us) and strengthening the long line to be held by our small force, occupied the next few days, when, a favorable position having been discovered on the south side of the river to assist in it, it was decided to assault Fort Loudon, the ground being very favorable for an approach on its southwest bastion, and the ditch in front of it being of small dimensions, as was seen by the enemy's soldiers frequently passing in and out of this bastion by crossing the parapet and ditch with great apparent ease.

This assault was determined on on the 23d, and a ferry prepared, troops and guns crossed, and everything in readiness for the 25th. Owing to the approach of a re-enforcement of two brigades, under Brig. Gen. Bushrod R. Johnson, whose assistance would be most valuable in the assault, the attack was postponed to the 26th to allow it to come up.

On the evening of the 25th, Brigadier-General Leadbetter, chief engineer Army of Tennessee, arrived at headquarters, and favoring an attack upon another quarter of the town, it was postponed another day to allow a reconnaissance. This developing no such favorable ground, the attack on Fort Loudon was again ordered for the 27th. It was intended that the attack should be preceded and covered by a heavy bombardment of the fort by every one of our thirty guns, some of them being arranged also to fire as mortars.

The 27th was such a rainy and foggy day that the artillery could not be used, and there being little prospect of the weather improving soon, the attack was ordered by the infantry at daylight on the 29th, the artillery being ordered to open just before day on the fort as a signal, and to fire on it for a few minutes, and then over the enemy's approaches to it as long as the fort resisted. The attack was accordingly made in this manner, the artillery fire being directed by the flashes of the enemy's guns in the darkness until the flashes of our own muskets were seen under the parapet, and after that a slow random fire was kept up to the rear of the fort until daylight. This showed our men retreating, unsuccessful in the assault, and our fire was again turned on the fort to keep down its fire upon the retreat, which was fully accomplished.

From this date, until December 4, my guns remained in position along the line, occasionally firing upon the enemy's camps, or exchanging shots with their forts. Had we not been cut off from all sources of supply, and compelled to husband our scanty supply of ammunition for emergencies, we might have accomplished important results by persistent shelling of camps, wagon-yards, and cattle-pens within our range, but the necessary kinds of ammunition were almost entirely exhausted.

On December 4, the artillery all marched during the afternoon, withdrawing unobserved from its positions, and commencing the retreat.

Encamping at Blain's Cross-Roads on the 5th, at Rutledge on the 6th and 7th, and Mooresburg on the 8th, we stopped near Rogersville, Tenn., on the 9th. Here Major Leyden, with his battalion, was ordered to proceed on to Bristol to winter and recuperate his horses, no longer fit for field service.

On the 14th, my battalion accompanied the infantry in the march and attack upon the enemy at Bean's Station, Parker's and Taylor's batteries in front, the others in the middle of the column. The intense cold and high wind unfortunately delayed the march, nearly freezing the ragged and shoeless drivers. Parker's and Taylor's batteries were engaged, and advanced with the foremost infantry, and sustained the fight alone until sundown, when, the other batteries arriving (all had marched 16 miles that day), I advanced Moody's, Parker's, and Taylor's batteries within 400 yards of the enemy's line of battle. Darkness, and the advance of Kershaw's brigade upon the enemy's left flank coming near our line of fire, alone prevented our making a heavy slaughter of the enemy. During the night they retreated, and have avoided all subsequent efforts to engage them.

We encamped near Bean's Station until December 22, when we crossed the Holston River at Cobb's Ford, and on the 23d established winter quarters near Russellville. The battery of Leyden's battalion left at Loudon was thrown into the river there by General Vaughn on the evacuation of that place for lack of animals to remove it. The guns were brass 6-pounders (2) and iron 12-pounder howitzers (2). No other loss of material was suffered in the campaign except a limber in Major Leyden's battalion destroyed by the enemy's shot. But 2 men were killed and 2 wounded in the artillery, and a very few horses killed or disabled. Major Huger commanded my own battalion, I being assigned as chief of artillery of the corps.

The highest praise is due to officers and men of both battalions for gallantry on the field, and the patience and fortitude with which they endured their labors and exposure to the inclement weather, with only the summer allowance of blankets and tents, and in great need of clothing and shoes.

One of my most gallant officers (Capt. G. V. Moody) was compelled to be left dangerously ill at a private house near Knoxville, and must have fallen into the hands of the enemy.

The artillery horses suffered severely and some were lost for lack of horseshoes. Our only source of supply for over a month was what could be collected from dead horses on the roadside and those thrown in the river opposite Knoxville by the enemy and floating down to our lines, where they were picked up and their shoes taken off.

I am, colonel, very respectfully, your obedient servant,

E. P. ALEXANDER,
Colonel, and Chief of Artillery, Longstreet's Corps.

Lieut. Col. G. MOXLEY SORREL,
Assistant Adjutant-General, Longstreet's Corps.

No. 63.

Report of Maj. Gen. Lafayette McLaws, C. S. Army, commanding division, with findings of court-martial, &c.

SPARTA, GA., *April* 19, 1864.

General S. COOPER,
Adjt. and Insp. Gen., C. S. Army, Richmond, Va.:

GENERAL: I have the honor to forward herewith a report of the operations of my command from November 4 to December 17, 1863, including the siege of Knoxville:

My report has been necessarily delayed because I was suddenly rdered away from the army in East Tennessee on December 17 last, nd on my return to it to attend the court-martial, and the court djourned, by request of General Longstreet I was ordered by Genral Longstreet to Abingdon, Va., and upon the reassembling of the ourt I had no opportunity to write, as I was attending the court, nd when the final adjournment took place I was ordered here. The eports from two brigades sent to me are not made by the officers vho were in command during the campaign, and that of General Humphreys, the only brigade commander who has made a report, s so defective as regards descriptions and dates, and that of the ther brigade (Wofford's), made by an officer who was not in command of the brigade because the brigade commander (Colonel Ruff) vas killed, is so incomplete that I have sent them back for correction.

Very respectfully, your obedient servant,

L. McLAWS,
Major-General.

My division was withdrawn from the lines around Chattanooga vest of Chattanooga Creek during the night of November 4, and rrived at the railroad near the tunnel through Missionary Ridge he next morning. The brigades in turn were thence taken on the ars and arrived at Sweet Water, the first brigade on the 6th and the ast on November 8.

The division remained in camp at Sweet Water until the 12th, when it was ordered to take position on the road leading from Morganton to Loudon, so as to cover the ferry crossings from that place nd below leading towards Loudon.

Arrived in place about 12 m. on the 13th, and on that night received an order to move on Loudon, so as to arrive there, if possible, before daylight on the 14th. The division was accordingly put in motion, and arrived at Loudon about 5 a. m. on the 14th, and bivouacked about 1½ miles from the town ; weather very bad.

On the 15th, the division was ordered to cross the Holston and follow the division of General Hood, which was done ; roads very bad. About 4 p. m. arrived at Burns' house, at the forks of the road, the left-hand leading into the Knoxville and Kingston road and to Campbell's Station (an old Indian station), the right-hand leading to Lenoir's, a station on the railroad. General Hood's division, under Brigadier-General Jenkins, had here turned to the right and marched toward Lenoir's Station, distant from 3 to 5 miles.

I received orders on my arrival to halt at the forks of the road and relieve the picket of General Benning on the Campbell's Station road, which was done at once. I then rode toward Lenoir's Station, and finding General Longstreet on a hill overlooking the station, which was about 1½ miles distant, I reported myself and asked for orders. He told me to encamp my command for the night at the forks of the road. While with him I took his glass and could see railroad trains and batteries of artillery in motion, moving, as I supposed, toward Knoxville. General Hood's division was being formed in line of battle and artillery was being put in position. I was not informed of the object of this arrangement, and returning to my command ordered it to encamp in the places the troops then were, or in the immediate vicinity. After dark I received orders to have my division in readiness to move at daylight the next morning.

On the 15th, my command was in readiness to move at an early hour, as directed, but no orders were received until 8 o'clock, when the following communication was brought me by courier from General Longstreet's assistant adjutant-general, Lieutenant-Colonel Sorrel:

HEADQUARTERS,
November 16, 1863.

General McLAWS,
Commanding Division:

GENERAL : The enemy appears in full retreat, leaving in confusion and abandon ing many of their wagons.   The commanding general desires you to push on a once by the Campbell's Station road, communicating with us from time to tim Col. J. R. Hart has some cavalry on the Knoxville road opposite Lenoir's, which yo can use as you wish.   You should move as quickly as possible.
Respectfully,
G. MOXLEY SORREL,
Assistant Adjutant-General.

P. S.—You are to move on to Campbell's Station.   I will send you a good guid as soon as I can find one.
G. M. S.

No intimation was given me as to the movements of the other di vision, now separated from my command from 3 to 5 miles.   As m command was all ready it was put in motion at once and marche rapidly toward Campbell's Station, the cavalry, under Colonel Har in advance, driving a line of skirmishers of the enemy very rapidl and gallantly.   There was but one halt made on the way, and tha was but for a few minutes to enable the division to close up.
The following communications were received when on the march

HEADQUARTERS,
November 16, 1863.

General L. McLAWS,
Commanding Division:

GENERAL : When you get to Campbell's Station the general wishes you to commu nicate with him across the country to Concord Station (a railroad station), whe we will probably be.
Very respectfully,
G. MOXLEY SORREL,
Assistant Adjutant-General.

P. S.—The enemy have left in haste, leaving behind 80 wagons, and colors and good deal of plunder.

And afterward the following :

HEADQUARTERS,
November 16, 1863.

Major-General McLAWS,
Commanding Division:

GENERAL : General Longstreet wishes you to push on on the road on which yo are until you intersect the road on which we are, about 16 miles short of Knoxvill
Respectfully,
OSMAN LATROBE,
Assistant Adjutant-General.

As Campbell's Station is 15 miles from Knoxville, the intersectio spoken of was, I suppose, 1 mile from the former and on the Loudo side between me and Campbell's Station.   Arriving in the vicinit of Campbell's Station, I was informed that General Longstreet wa but 100 or 200 yards to my right, and reporting to him, was ordere and deployed my line to the front, but not to show it beyond th oods skirting the plain toward Campbell's Station, Humphreys' rigade on the left occupying a hill, the enemy in lines beyond Campell's Station across the valley.

After waiting several hours for the purpose, as I have understood, allow the command of General Jenkins (Hood's division) to get to position, so as to make a flank attack upon the enemy's left, I as ordered to form the brigades of Kershaw, Wofford, and Bryan line of battle across the valley and move to the front toward the nemy. One of the brigades (Bryan's) being held in reserve or secnd line, the deployment was made, and the line advanced in excelnt style until directed to halt by General Longstreet's order, the nemy having changed his position to another more commanding in he rear. General Humphreys' brigade continued on the left flank, nd marched along the heights during this movement. The enemy's rtillery (one or two batteries) fired upon my line when advancing nd upon General Humphreys' brigade, but no engagement resulted vith small-arms, excepting that the skirmishers of General Humhreys exchanged shots with those of the enemy. The loss was but rifling, 4 or 5 men having been wounded by shells. The plain intent f the enemy was to retreat only. My division encamped that night in he neighborhood of Campbell's Station, Kershaw a mile in advance.

On the 17th, about 7.30 a. m., my division was put in motion, leadng the advance, and marched rapidly toward Knoxville, halting once r twice, as the enemy showed a disposition to dispute the advance, ut no engagement beyond skirmishing ensued. Kershaw's brigade as in advance and drove the enemy easily from every point. Ariving in sight of Knoxville and Fort Loudon, my division was deloyed to the left and right, the right resting on the Holston River, nd one brigade (Bryan's) held in reserve on the right near the main oad by which we came.

On the 18th, Wofford's brigade, which had been extended to the left s far as Crawford's house, having the battalion of sharpshooters on icket, was relieved by a brigade of General Jenkins' command Hood's division) and took its place in the line on the left of General Iumphreys' brigade. On that day about 3 p. m. an order was given or General Kershaw's brigade to assault the advance line of the enmy. They occupied a breastwork of rails about $1\frac{3}{4}$ miles from the own, constructed upon a hill, and the houses of a Mr. Armstrong, ear the bank of the river, consisting of brick dwelling, outhouses, citchen, stables, &c. The advance was made under cover of the fire f two pieces of artillery, and the enemy were driven in confusion o their works nearer the town.

My loss in this affair was about 140 in killed, wounded, &c.

The brigade remained in the position from which the enemy were driven and fortified it. My line was then definitely formed from right o left, as follows : General Kershaw's brigade with his right on the river ; General Humphreys' next, and then General Wofford's, comnanded by Colonel Ruff, of the Eighteenth Georgia. Rifle-pits, or, ather, a continuous line of trench, was dug, extending, with a few broken intervals, from the Holston River to a point beyond the northwest bastion of Fort Loudon, and the enemy were employed in adding o and strengthening their defenses. My sharpshooters occupying oits in advance of the main bodies on both sides were constantly exchanging shots whenever the slightest opportunity was offered by either party for even a chance hit, as they were in easy rifle range f each other.

On the 21st, I received from General Longstreet a communication of which the following is a copy :

HEADQUARTERS,
November 21, 1863.

Maj. Gen. L. McLaws,
        Commanding Division :

GENERAL : General Bragg telegraphs me that the enemy is threatening his left and wants to know if it is not possible to bring the enemy here to battle. The only chance that I see of doing anything in time to do good is an assault upon the re doubt. This made in the moonlight by three of your brigades, I think, would re sult in a great success ; yet I am loath to put the troops at it when there is a disin clination to it. Suppose you organize an assault to-morrow and have a talk with the officers, and see if you cannot impress the importance of it upon them. The loss, I feel assured, will not be great compared with the importance of the move. will be up to see you in the morning. The officers and men must understand that once they start they must move rapidly on till the work is over.
        Very respectfully,

JAMES LONGSTREET,
Lieutenant-General, Commanding.

I consulted with some of my best officers, and finding that they were adverse to the assault, especially if made at night, as they could not hold themselves responsible for their men unless they could see them, I so reported to General Longstreet. In discussion with Gen eral Longstreet I informed him that two regimental commanders. viz, Lieutenant Colonel Fiser, of the Seventeenth Mississippi (Hum phreys' brigade), and Lieutenant-Colonel Holt, of the Tenth Georgia (Bryans' brigade), were of the opinion that they could take the work and I would put them at it if an assault should be made. And as the works of the enemy had not at that time been reconnoitered to an extent sufficient to give any positive knowledge of its strength or of the depth of the ditch around it, I proposed to take bundles of straw, each man to carry a bundle, and fill up the ditch, if there was any.

There was a doubt about there being any ditch, because citizens had told us, and also some officers of artillery who had been in Knox ville when the works were constructed, so far as we constructed them, that the dirt to make the parapet had been taken principally from the inside of the work (Fort Loudon) ; that the fort was around the apex of a hill which had been smoothed off and the earth thrown to make a parapet, and if there was any digging on the outside it was in holes here and there with intervening high places, and that there was no regular ditch ; but this assault, as I have said, was aban doned.

The picket line of Wofford's brigade and the left of my division having been advanced to cover it, with that of my right, was no supported by a proper advance of General Jenkins' line on my left This want of support was reported to General Longstreet, but wa not corrected up to the 24th, when the enemy, taking advantage of it, made a sortie with the Second Michigan Regiment and attacked the left flank and rear of Wofford's skirmishers, gaining a temporary advantage ; but the picket reserves coming up the enemy were driven back with the loss of 50 or 60 in killed, wounded, and prisoners The sharpshooters of Wofford's brigade had 5 men wounded, 2 mor tally. The Third Georgia Battalion Sharpshooters (Lieutenant-Col onel Hutchins) distinguished itself in this encounter.

After dark on the 26th, I received a communication from General Longstreet, of which the following is a copy :

HEADQUARTERS,
November 26, 1863.

Major-General McLaws,
    Commanding Division :

GENERAL : The result of an examination to-day leads to the hope that Mabry's Hill may be partially turned and taken with but slight loss. A further examination will be made to-morrow, and if the ground is found to be such as we hope that it may be, the attack will be made then at dawn on the 28th with Hood's and the part of Buckner's division. Your division will have to hold the ground that it now occupies, and you will have to put Bryan's brigade on picket along the front now occupied by General Jenkins. A cavalry brigade will be sent across the river for the protection of the two guns which will be left there. You will have to make a diversion upon the Loudon fort by bombardment and such other indications of an assault as you can at earliest dawn, while we attempt to get the hill on the other side. We shall push on down toward the fort in your front as rapidly as possible after getting the hill. I shall send a cavalry brigade to-morrow to report to you. It is to cross, as I have said, and relieve the troops under General Law, and he will return to his division. As I shall be out looking at the ground, I shall have to get you to see that the troops are crossed and recrossed, and marched over ground that cannot be seen by the enemy. You must relieve General Jenkins' line of pickets by sunset to-morrow.

    Very respectfully,

JAMES LONGSTREET,
Lieutenant-General, Commanding.

And early on the 27th the following was received :

HEADQUARTERS,
November 27, 1863.

Major-General McLaws,
    Commanding Division :

GENERAL : I wish you would start the brigade which is to occupy General Jenkins' picket line right away. Send them by a route which will be entirely concealed. Do have all the movements under your eye so conducted that they may not be seen.

    With respect,

JAMES LONGSTREET,
Lieutenant-General, Commanding.

Accordingly General Bryan's brigade was put in readiness, and I went with my staff officer, Major Goggin, and after a long search found a way about 2 miles to the rear by which the brigade could be marched to occupy General Jenkins' picket line without being seen from the enemy's works. I then conducted the brigade myself until it had reached the rear of General Jenkins' line, when, receiving notice from Major Goggin, who had been sent for that purpose, that the cavalry could not cross the river at the ferry without being seen by the enemy, I left General Bryan, with instructions to relieve General Jenkins' pickets, and joined Major Goggin at the river. This was about 3 o'clock in the afternoon. Shortly after my arrival I received notice that the contemplated attack on Mabry's Hill had been abandoned, and that Bryan's brigade and all the other troops and the artillery, which had been moved in contemplation of that attack, must resume their original positions.

During the night of the 27th, I received notice that my division would assault the redoubt the next morning at daylight, but before daylight an order was received suspending the assault until the weather cleared up. The night had been very stormy, and it had

turned very cold and misty. After daylight—several hours after
I received the following communication from General Longstreet:

HEADQUARTERS,
November 28, 1863.

Major-General McLAWS:

GENERAL : I wish you would double your pickets and reserves and advance a
occupy the line now occupied by the enemy's pickets, and at the same time ma
your arrangements to assault as soon as the weather lights up enough for our art
lery to play upon the enemy's position. The assault will be made after ten minut
brisk play of our batteries.

With respect,

JAMES LONGSTREET,
Lieutenant-General.

P. S.—General Jenkins is ordered to advanc his picket line in the same way, a
advance to the assault following your movement. General Johnson's two brigad
will be ready to support you and General Jenkins.

There was such a fog or mist over the country that the enemy
works could not be seen from my lines. The assault was therefo
delayed, waiting for the fog to clear away, as shown by Gener
Longstreet's order. The time was so short from the reception of tl
order to its contemplated execution that I had no time or oppo
tunity to give definite or detailed instructions upon any point.
had, therefore, but to give general orders only, and to rely up
those which I had suggested to the brigade commanders on the 22
when I discussed with them the probabilities or chances of succe
in making an assault in compliance with General Longstree
wishes, as expressed in his letter to me of the 21st, hereinbefore r
corded.

General Longstreet came to my headquarters, at Armstrong
house, on the morning of the 28th, before his written order abo
quoted could be carried out, and on account of the dense fog, whi
still enveloped the enemy's works and our own lines, ordered th
the assault be delayed until, I think, 2 p. m. of that same da
General (then Col.) E. P. Alexander, in consultation with m
then arranged the following programme for the part his artille
was to take in the assault and how I should regard its fire
signals for the skirmishers or sharpshooters and columns of atta
to move, viz :

Colonel Alexander will commence with his mortars, and then his batteries w
fire slowly all along the line, which will be kept up for twenty minutes, and th
will fire rapidly for ten minutes. When the mortars open it will be a signal
the pickets to be doubled and to get ready for an advance, and when the sl
firing of the batteries all along the line commences the rifle-pits will be tak
and occupied by our pickets and sharpshooters and the main line will take positi
for the assault, and when the rapid firing commences all along the line the assa
will be made.

I gave or sent these instructions to the brigade commanders, a
having assembled those who were to engage in the assault, discuss
the subject with them.

The following orders were given for the assault :

1. A regiment from Humphreys' (Mississippi) brigade and one from Woffor
(Georgia) brigade should be selected to lead in the assault. Wofford's regiment
lead the column composed of Wofford's brigade assaulting from the left, an
Humphreys' regiment the column assaulting from the right, composed of two re
ments of Humphreys' brigade and three of Bryan's following close on Humphr
as a reserve.

2. The brigades to be formed for the assault in columns of regiments.

3. The assault to be made with fixed bayonets and without firing a gun.

4. Should be made against the northwest angle of Fort Loudon.

5. The men should be urged to the assault with a determination to succeed, and should rush to it without halting, and, mounting the parapet, take possession of the work and hold it against all attempts to recover it.

6. That the sharpshooters should keep up a continuous fire into the embrasures of the enemy's works and along the fort, so as to prevent the use of their cannon, and distract, if not prevent, the fire from all arms.

7. General Kershaw to advance to the assault on the right of the fort so soon as the fort was taken.

After this I proposed to General Longstreet that if he would delay the assault until daylight the next morning (the 29th) I would drive in the enemy's pickets that night and occupy a line with my sharpshooters which would command the enemy's works going beyond the line occupied by the enemy's sharpshooters, if such was found necessary in order to obtain eligible positions. He assented, and the assault was put off until daylight of the 29th. I then addressed the following circular to my brigade commanders :

Circular.]

GENERAL : The operations discussed to-day will take place to-morrow morning. I wish you to make the necessary preparations and advance your skirmishers to-night, so as to occupy the line of rifle-pits now held by the enemy and make them tenable for your men, so that your sharpshooters can open fire on the main rifle-pits of the enemy, and, firing into the embrasures of the main work, prevent them from using their cannon with effect when the main assault is made; and if an opportunity is offered, which may happen, we may dash at the main works. Further instructions will be sent, if any are thought necessary. If any brigade commander is not fully informed, he is requested to make proper inquiries at once.

Copies of this circular were delivered to each brigade commander by my division inspector (Major Costin). I then reassembled my brigade commanders, and in discussion with them it was ordered that the sharpshooters should advance at moonrise, which took place at that date about 10 p. m.; and that they should choose and intrench a line so far beyond the rifle-pits of the enemy as was necessary to give command of their main works, and thus give more complete protection to the assaulting columns. The signal agreed upon for the assault was the opening of fire from Major Leyden's battery, which had been sunk in pits on the advance line of General Kershaw, near Armstrong's house. It was also ordered that the sharpshooters should open fire in the morning so soon as it was light enough for them to see. I ordered the assault in two columns, because there was considerable felled timber and much broken ground between the positions of Humphreys' brigade and that of Wofford's, and besides, I thought that the spirit of rivalry between the two brigades leading the assault (one being from Georgia and the other from Mississippi), united to their previous well-tried gallantry, would urge them to their work with accelerating dash and vigor.

I had been previously impressed by General Alexander, chief of artillery, of General Longstreet's staff (then colonel), that there was no ditch at the northwest angle of the work that offered any obstacle to the assault, and by General Longstreet himself that there would be no difficulty in taking the work so far as the ditch was concerned; that he had seen a man walk down the parapet across the ditch and up and on the outside without jumping and without apparent difficulty; and, as there could be no difficulty contemplated in running up the exterior slope of an earth-work, I was confident that there would be no difficulty in getting into the work, and that the obstructions offered by the work itself would not be the obstacles to be overcome. But, to quote the words of Colonel Alexander before the general court-martial assembled in East Tennessee, and before which I was tried, in reply to the following question :

Question 8. Did you not state, after your reconnaissance, that there was no ditch opposite the bastion at northwest angle ; that there was some fresh dirt at that point, and that there had been a little scratching there? Did you communicate this to Generals Longstreet and McLaws?

Answer. I never stated that there was no ditch at that point, but I stated that the ditch was of such small dimensions as to be no obstacle to an assault, and of such shape (see figure 3) as to be no obstacle in the way of an assault. I communicated it to both repeatedly, and advised the attack on this point. On one occasion I took General Longstreet to a point where he could see it, and showed him a man crossing the ditch.

General Longstreet, in his testimony before the same court, says :

I made several very careful examinations of the fort myself before it was attacked on all sides, as near as I could get to it. I think I got within 400 yards of it on the north side.

* * * * * * *

I remember particularly to have seen a soldier march out the fort, down the ditch, and up to the other side, outside of the ditch on the west side, from the north side. The cut in the ditch on the west side seemed to have been made more for the purpose of getting dirt than for obstructions. In passing over the ditch more than half of the person of the soldier could be seen on the west side. In passing down the ditch he seemed to walk and not jump; he seemed to find no difficulty in getting out of the ditch on the outside. I was told by some officers that dogs were seen to pass over the same ditch. These circumstances led me to believe that the ditch on the west side was a slight obstacle. In all of my conversations about the ditch I stated very much what I stated in the previous part of this answer. I think that I stated it frequently to Generals McLaws and Jenkins, and that I stated it in the presence of many others, staff and line officers.

Again, in reply to the question—

Question 11. Did you furnish the accused with any officer of engineers or of artillery to assist him in preparing his attack, or of obtaining information by reconnaissance or otherwise to the same end?

Answer. I did not. I furnished him with no officer of engineers ; I had none to use myself for that service. Colonel Alexander, chief of artillery, and a professional military engineer, was ordered to confer with General McLaws, and did confer with him in regard to his operations, and he used all his artillery that could be used in co-operation with the assault made by General McLaws. * * *

Thus at the point where the assault was made, viz, about the northwest angle of Fort Loudon, I had been informed by the officer charged with conferring with me in regard to my operations, and who was a professional military engineer, and by the commander-in-chief himself, that the ditch was of such small dimensions that it offered no obstacle to an assault, and was of such a shape as to be no obstacle in the way of an assault, and that it was a slight obstacle, and General Alexander (then colonel) stated that his information was gained from reconnaissances made two days before the assault.

And the reply to question 9th—

Question. Did you advise ladders for the attack ?

Answer. I did not. I did not consider them essential. Something was said about fascines, and I said they might be useful to protect the men from bullets in their approach, but I did not consider them essential in crossing the ditch.

All these points were discussed at my headquarters, which was so situated as to be a place of general resort, and the impression was made general that there was no ditch at the northwest angle and its vicinity which would offer any obstacle to an assault. I endeavored to convey this idea to all concerned, and, in connection with it, urged the officers and men to rush to their work with a determination to

cceed.   I did not consider that ladders or fascines or any other ap-
iances were necessary to enable the men to get into the work—
ne certainly to cross the ditch, which had been declared to be no
stacle in the way of an assault, and none certainly to ascend par-
ets sloping at an angle of 45 degrees.   And even if I had thought
, I had no time or materials, or tools, or any means of any kind
herewith to make anything.   The commands were without tools of
ny kind, without axes even, and their wagons and quartermasters
ere at Loudon; left there by orders from General Longstreet's
eadquarters.   And, in addition, no such aids to get into the work
ere for a moment thought essential or were ever mentioned, except
be scouted at by the officer acting as chief engineer, whose duty
was to have advised them, at least, if he thought them necessary.
did think of them myself; but when I considered that nothing could
be made at the time allowed me before the assault, I thought that to
ention them even and not to have them would create hesitation
nd detract from the dash and determined purpose so necessary to
ucceed, although I did not consider them essential.
The following certificate (copy of) will explain itself in connection
ith the above:

I, the undersigned, J. J. Middleton, captain and acting quartermaster Fifteenth
uth Carolina Regiment, do hereby depose and certify that I was acting division
uartermaster McLaws' division from the time we left Loudon, on November 15,
63, until some days after the assault on November 29.   During this period we
ere without trains, carpenters, tools, blacksmiths, &c.; had no appliances for the
anufacture of ladders, and had no lumber out of which they could have been made
operly.   Had an order for such articles been issued, it would have been necessary
call for large details, and for said details to have found their own tools.   Com-
unication with Loudon was very uncertain, owing to the miserable condition of
e roads, and the division to which I was attached might almost have been termed
lf-supporting, so entirely was it dependent on its own exertions for almost every-
ing that was effected.

J. J. MIDDLETON,
Captain, and A. Q. M., 15th South Carolina Regiment.

Sworn to and subscribed before me this December 17, 1864.

JAMES M. GOGGIN,
Assistant Adjutant-General.

After dark on the 28th, before moonrise, I sent my inspector (Major
ostin) and my aide-de-camp (Captain Lamar) to superintend the
dvance of my sharpshooters all along my line, and they reported to
e during the night that the enemy had been driven from their pits,
number of prisoners taken, and that my sharpshooters had ad-
anced beyond the enemy's pits and within easy range of the enemy's
orks, and were intrenching themselves.   I reported this fact to
eneral Longstreet, and communicated also that General Humhreys' advance had found an abatis in front of their line.   In reply,
olonel Sorrel wrote: "The point (or front) of attack is not the
me to make discouraging reports."   My report was of a fact which
ad come to my knowledge, and was for the information of the com-
ander-in-chief only.   I did not intend any discouragement, cer-
inly.
Before 4 o'clock on the morning of the 29th I went around with
y staff to superintend the execution of my orders for the assault.
was evident to me that the enemy were aware that one was in-
nded, and I think it probable they knew where it was to be made,
r while I was talking to Colonel Ruff on the railroad the enemy
rew a shell, which burst over the woods just in rear of us through

which Colonel Ruff's command (Wofford's brigade) was passing
assembling by regiments for the assault. I have since heard tha
the enemy were informed, and that during the night of the 28th the
had been employed in pouring buckets of water over the parapets t
render it difficult to ascend, the night being very cold. The con
mands being in position and in readiness, and the sharpshooter
having been directed to open fire all along their lines as soon as it wa
light enough to aim, I distributed my staff officers along the line, an
rode over to Major Leyden's battery and to General Kershaw's lin
and found Major Leyden awaiting until it was light enough to se
his elevators, and Kershaw's line ready, I gave Major Leyden orde
to open fire while I was there and rode toward the assaulting co
umns. As I went they could be seen advancing in fine style. I roc
straight to Wofford's brigade, on the left, and as I approached th
work found the men falling back, the officers reporting it was in
possible to mount the parapet, and that the brigade commande
(Colonel Ruff) and his next in command (Colonel Thomas) had bee
killed and the next in command wounded. I rallied the brigac
about 400 yards from the work, reformed the regiments in the orde
they went to the assault, notified them who was their brigade con
mander, and the regiments who commanded them, and then consul
ing with Generals Humphreys and Bryan ; and finding it was uselei
to attempt to take the work, I reported to General Longstreet, an
asked authority to withdraw my command. Permission was give
and the main body was withdrawn, but the advanced line of pi
was still held by sharpshooters. When it was seen that Wofford
brigade could not mount the parapet, General G. T. Anderson's br
gade, of Hood's division, came rushing to the assault in the sam
place where my command had attempted it, but was repulsed at one
and retired.

I will remark here that I saw no panic among either officers o
men, and I am assured by the different commanders that there wa
none ; but, on the contrary, there was evidence of mortification onl
at their failure to take the work. The companies and regimen
reformed readily within a short distance of the work and awaite
orders. Concerning the assault, I am satisfied—

1. That my line of sharpshooters was advanced to within eas
range of the enemy's works, and tnat their fire was most efficiei
along the entire line ; that they prevented the enemy from usin
their cannon upon the assaulting columns, and that but few me
were shot by musketry even in front of my line, and many of tho
by the enemy holding their guns over their heads and firing witho
aim ; that most of the men were killed by a fire from the left of n
line, over which I had no control, and that if I had had straw wher
with to fill up the ditch, as General Longstreet testified he expect
me to have, it would have been set on fire by the hand grenad
thrown over the parapet by the enemy, and my wounded in the dit
would have been burned to death.

2. That the heads of my assaulting columns did all that men cou
do to enter the work, showing that, in selecting bodies of men to lea
in the assault who were already organized and distinguished for the
gallantry and dash, I had acted more prudently than would ha
been the case had I called for volunteers and organized them in
companies and battalions and appointed officers for the occasion ov
men with whom they were not acquainted and to whom they wou
not perhaps be known.

3. That the only possible place to enter the work was at and about the northwest angle, where the assault was made, and that if I had assaulted the fort on the west side from shoulder to shoulder of that front, which I am charged with "not informing my officers offered but a slight obstacle to infantry in entering the work," I would have ordered them to a place where the ditch was from 12 to 13 feet deep, which, with a corresponding parapet, would have required ladders 30 feet long to surmount.

4. That the assault failed because of the state of the weather the night previous to the assault and on the night of the assault; it having rained on the night of the 27th and then turning very cold, the parapet was hard frozen and a heavy ice crop was formed by the moisture from the bank, which prevented the men from obtaining a foothold, and the absence of a berme upon which the men could mount and start from. The main cause of failure was, however, the slipperiness of the parapet, upon which it was impossible for any large body of men to gain a foothold, and the severe fire from the north side of the fort, which drove the men from the most accessible point of ascent. And I may add that it is the opinion of distinguished officers who were engaged in the assault that if the skirmishers on the railroad side of the work had silenced the enemy's fire coming from that side, as it was silenced by my line of sharpshooters, the work would have been carried in spite of all the other obstacles. I do not think that ladders would have been of material assistance, unless they had been furnished in great numbers and had been 20 feet long. The reconnaissances were also defective, giving false notions of the character of the work and of the ditch.

Surgeon Cullen, of General Longstreet's staff, who was in the ditch (sent there under a flag of truce to attend the wounded), testified before the court that the ditch on the west side of the work from shoulder to shoulder was from 12 to 13 feet deep and on the north front it was on an average of 10 feet deep, and that it was about 10 feet wide all around the work; but from shoulder to shoulder of the northwest bastion it was but from 4 to 4½ deep, and here it was the assault was made. From the bottom of the ditch along the west front from shoulder to the top of the parapet must have been. over 20 feet perpendicular, and the same in the north front from the shoulder of the northwest bastion.

The evening of November 28, hearing from various sources, which I believed were entitled to consideration, that a serious engagement had occurred between General Bragg and General Grant at Chattanooga, I addressed a communication to General Longstreet, of which the following is a copy, as furnished from the adjutant-general's office of General Longstreet:

HEADQUARTERS DIVISION,
November 28, 1863.

GENERAL : It seems to be a conceded fact that there has been a serious engagement between General Bragg's forces and those of the enemy; with what result is not known so far as I have heard. General Bragg may have maintained his position, may have repulsed the enemy, or may have been driven back. If the enemy has been beaten at Chattanooga, do we not gain by delay at this point? If we have been defeated at Chattanooga, do we not risk our entire force by an assault here? If we have been defeated at Chattanooga, our communications must be made with Virginia. We cannot combine again with General Bragg, even if we should be successful in our assault on Knoxville. If we should be defeated or unsuccessful here, and at the same time General Bragg should have been forced to retire, would we be in condition to force our way to the army in Virginia? I present these con-

siderations, and with the force they have on my mind I beg leave to say that I think
we had better delay the assault until we hear the result of the battle of Chattanooga.
The enemy may have cut our communication to prevent this army re-enforcing
General Bragg, as well as for the opposite reason, viz, to prevent General Bragg
from re-enforcing us, and the attack at Chattanooga favors the first proposition.

Very respectfully,

L. McLAWS,
Major-General.

The letter of which the foregoing is a copy, with no address beyond that on the
envelope, was received by Lieutenant-General Longstreet on the night of November
28, 1863.

G. MOXLEY SORREL,
Assistant Adjutant-General.

The fortifications of the city of Knoxville are upon a series of
heights circling the town, comprising Mabry's Hill, Temperance
Hill, Loudon Fort Hill, and College Hill. These heights were connected by rifle-pits and defended by redoubts and rifle-pits, and
besides these there were intermediate redoubts, loop-holed houses,
and other kinds of defenses, abatis, &c.; also a series of heights on
the opposite or south side of the river, which are superior in elevation to those on the north side, and which were fortified and commanded the town completely. A pontoon bridge across the river at
the southeast corner of the town connected the two sets of defenses.
A creek called Second Creek, which flowed between Fort Loudon
and Summit Fort, on Summit Hill, had been dammed up, so as to
make a pond between the two heights (so I am informed), thus dis-
connecting Fort Loudon from the line of defenses to the east, viz:
Summit Fort, Temperance Hill Fort, Mabry's Hill, &c.

The accompanying sketch,* with a profile of heights along the
dotted lines A B, will give an idea of the heights and the relative
position of the enemy's works. The forts are merely indicated; it
is not attempted to give their character or shape, nor the line of rifle-
pits, or other than the main fortifications.

If an assault was made upon Knoxville which did not contemplate
the immediate occupation or destruction of the bridge across the
Holston connecting the town with the south side of the river, the
enemy would undoubtedly cross to that side if the town should be
seriously threatened, and occupying the heights there prevent our
occupation of the town, and bidding us defiance remain there until
their re-enforcements arriving (should Grant have forced General
Bragg to retire), they would then have assumed the offensive, and by
crossing the French Broad and moving on our rear toward Virginia
force us to a precipitate retreat in that direction; for we would have
no other way to go, leaving our sick and wounded—and the number
of the latter must have been very large to have forced the enemy
from Knoxville—and we would have retired with but a very limited
amount of ammunition, and with no chances of a resupply within the
borders of Tennessee.

On the other hand, if General Bragg had defeated General Grant
Knoxville was ours without the necessity of an assault. I was not
informed of any plan of assault beyond what was communicated to
me in General Longstreet's letter to me of November 28, herein recorded, wherein he directed me to prepare for the assault, and informed me that General Jenkins would advance to the assault, "following my movement," and General Johnson would support General
Jenkins and myself; but I supposed his intentions, after taking Fort

*See p. 493.

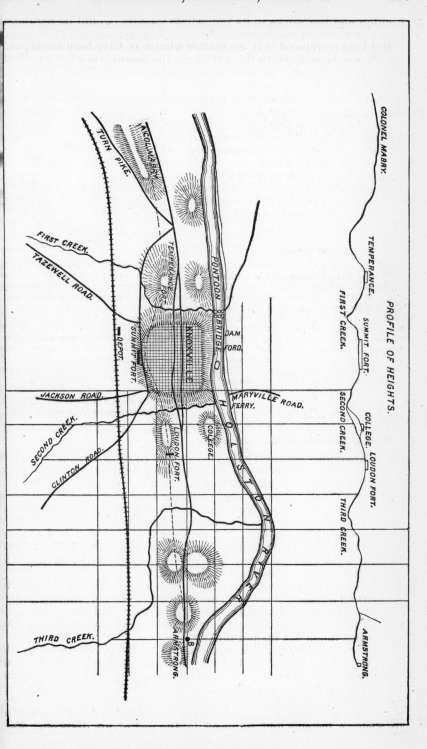

Loudon and the works in its immediate vicinity, would be regulated by what he could judge of the then existing state of affairs.

But I am convinced that, no matter what may have been attempted whether to bear down to the left along the enemy's works or to dash at the bridge, would have been attended with a very heavy loss and with very doubtful results.

Under these circumstances I addressed the foregoing letter to General Longstreet, supposing that if he had considered the existing state of affairs as I did it would be gratifying for him to have the written opinion of the officer next in rank to himself if he thought proper to delay the assault until we could hear definitely of the result of the battle, which was said to have taken place near Chattanooga. I had already shown my desire to co-operate cordially with him in making the assault, and wished to inform him that my hearty co-operation would still be with him if he should desire to delay it.

The following is a copy of his reply:

> HEADQUARTERS,
> *November* 28, 1863.

Major-General McLaws:

GENERAL: Your letter is received. I am not at all confident that General Bragg has had a serious battle at Chattanooga, but there is a report that he has, and has fallen back to Tunnel Hill. Under this report I am entirely convinced that our only safety is in making the assault upon the enemy's position to-morrow at daylight, and it is the more important that I should have the entire support and co-operation of the officers in this connection, and I do hope and trust that I may have your entire support and all of the force you may be possessed of in the execution of my views. It is a great mistake to suppose that there is any safety for us in going to Virginia if General Bragg has been defeated, for we leave him at the mercy of his victors, and with his army destroyed our own had better be also, for we will be not only destroyed, but disgraced. There is neither safety nor honor in any other course than the one I have chosen and ordered.

Very respectfully, your obedient servant,

> JAMES LONGSTREET,
> *Lieutenant-General, Commanding.*

P. S.—The assault must be made at the time appointed, and must be made with a determination which will insure success.

On November 20, the Tenth Georgia, of Bryan's brigade, was sent across the Holston River and occupied the heights there, which were immediately opposite my position on the north side, driving the enemy from them. Bryan's whole brigade after this crossed and took post on the heights. It occupied them on December 3, after the assault, and rejoined the division after dark on the 4th, when the whole army was withdrawn from before Knoxville and marched toward Rogersville, passing Rutledge, Bean's Station, and Mooresburg, and halting near Blevins' farm, 6 miles from Rogersville, on the 9th, where the division encamped until December 14.

On the 13th, General Humphreys was sent with his brigade to support an advance of cavalry, under Colonel Giltner, toward Bean's Station. He went within 3 miles of that place, and returned to his camp that night, having marched 24 miles. The weather very bad and roads much cut up and muddy.

On the 14th, the division was ordered to Bean's Station (an old Indian station), following the two brigades of Buckner's division, under General Johnson. The enemy's cavalry and mounted infantry were found in position there, and, after a sharp engagement, were driven off by General Johnson's command attacking on the right and Kershaw's brigade moving on their left flank, supported by Bryan's brigade and followed by the rest of my division. Ker-

aw's men obtained enough bacon to give one day's supply to most
' the brigade, and a number of saddles and accouterments and
orses were captured by the division.

On the 15th, I was ordered to send one of my brigades toward
utledge to give support to General Jenkins, who was threatened by
a advance of the enemy; to send two brigades, if they had been
applied with rations.   As Kershaw's brigade was the only one
hich had any, having obtained them from the battle-field, as before
entioned, I ordered his brigade only, and directed it to move at
nce.   It was so late at the time the order was received that it was
'ter dark before his brigade reached the vicinity of General Jenkins'
ommand, and the enemy retiring that night no engagement ensued,
nd the brigade rejoined the division on the next morning.

On the 16th, General Humphreys was ordered to move his brigade
o the gap in Clinch Mountain and attack the enemy reported to be
a that position, but, on reaching the gap, it was found that the One
undred and seventeenth Indiana Regiment, which was there on the
ay before, had retreated during the night along the crest of the
dge by torch-light, leaving their baggage, all their tents, cooking
tensils, and commissary stores, 12 mules, and five wagons.   A
giment was at once sent in pursuit, but failed to overtake them.
welve prisoners were brought in and a considerable number of
rms.   On my return from the gap I was ordered to select a line
nd encamp my division.

I cannot too highly praise the conduct of both officers and men for
eir admirable conduct during the campaign and for their patient
adurance of hardships of all kinds.   Their want of food, of cloth-
ng, of shoes and blankets, and of tents did not dampen their ardor
or take away from that cheerfulness and alacrity in the perform-
nce of all duties which is so inspiring to behold, and which gives
uch assurance to commanders that their courage and zeal and devo-
on can always be relied on.

I call particular attention to the conduct of General Kershaw,
ho, in command of his brigade, was distinguished at the storming
f the enemy's outworks on November 18, and in flanking the enemy
t Bean's Station on December 14.

The conduct of Colonel Nance, of the Third South Carolina, on
ovember 18; of Colonel Kennedy, of the Second South Carolina,
ho was wounded on the 18th, and Colonel Henagan, of the Eighth
outh Carolina; Lieutenant-Colonel Gaillard, who succeeded Col-
nel Kennedy in command of the Second Regiment, and also Maj.
Villiam Wallace, of the same regiment, who was conspicuous for
is gallantry on this as on all other occasions, deserve special notice,
s also Captain Dwight and Lieutenant Doby, of General Kershaw's
taff.

The conduct of General Bryan during the siege and afterward,
nd especially at the assault, is worthy of all praise.   He led his
rigade to the work, and, after seeing that all was done that could
e done, was the very last to retire.

Col. E. Ball, of the Fifty-first Georgia, and Colonel Simms, of the
ifty-third Georgia, who was wounded in the assault; Lieut. Col.
V. C. Holt, of the Tenth Georgia, and Major McBride and Adju-
ant Strickland, and Lieut. J. T. Stovall, Company F, all of the
enth Georgia, were distinguished for gallantry and good conduct
uring the siege.

Captain Ellis, adjutant-general of the brigade, who was wounded

during the assault, is a gallant soldier and an accomplished gent
man, and I recommend him for his good conduct during this ca
paign and elsewhere for promotion.

Major Hartsfield, of the Fifty-third Georgia, and Captain Van
griff, Fifty-third Georgia, were also distinguished for gallantry.

My special thanks are due to Brig. Gen. B. G. Humphreys, w
commanded the assaulting column, composed of parts of his ov
and Bryan's brigade, for his zeal, courage, and coolness in condu
ing that assault, and for his activity, energy, and earnestness in t
performance of all his duties on every occasion. I take pleasure
recommending him for promotion.

Lieut. Col. J. C. Fiser, of the Seventeenth Mississippi Regimer
who lost an arm while endeavoring to scale the parapet of Fc
Loudon, was conspicuous on this occasion, as on all others, for l
daring and brilliant courage.

Captain Cherry, of the same regiment, was wounded in the assau
and was also greatly distinguished for his gallantry.

Major Donald, of the Thirteenth, and Captain Brown, of the san
regiment, Captain Wright and Lieutenant Gunn, of the Seventeent
exhibited the brightest qualities of soldiers in rallying and refor
ing their shattered regiments.

Captain Barksdale and Lieutenant Hobart, of General Humphrey
staff, deserve particular notice for their zeal and courage and se
vices during the campaign.

Captain Dortch, of the Twenty-fourth Georgia, who drove in t
enemy's pickets with his regiment on the night of the 28th; Lie
tenant-Colonel Hutchins, who commanded the sharpshooters on th
occasion and afterward the brigade; Major Hamilton, who cor
manded Phillips Legion and led the assault on the left of the li
against the northwest bastion of Fort Loudon, and who was wound
in his efforts to get his men into the work, is an officer of great ga
lantry, fine intelligence, and a good disciplinarian.

Captain Norris, of Phillips Legion, a good soldier, good discipl
narian, and gallant officer, deserves especial mention.

There are many others whose names are not before me who we
distinguished for the brightest qualities, of whom mention will b
made hereafter.

I am especially indebted to Maj. James M. Goggin, my adjutar
general, for his devotedness and zeal in the performance of all h
duties. I know of no officer more deserving promotion to the rar
of brigadier than himself, or who possesses higher qualities to illu
trate the position. His experience in military affairs, his calm, co
courage, his strict integrity and impartiality, and straightforwa
manner would soon give him the confidence of any community
any body of men, and his services entitle him to high preferment.

Surg. John T. Gilmore, chief surgeon of my division, who has n
a superior in his profession, added to his previous distinction by h
prompt and efficient arrangements for the sick and wounded, an
for the most faithful discharge of all the duties pertaining to h
office.

To Major Peck, chief quartermaster of division, and Maj
Edwards, chief commissary, and Lieut. Alfred Edwards, ordnan
officer, I am indebted for their faithful and efficient discharge
their several duties during the campaign.

To Maj. E. L. Costin, inspector, and Captain Lamar, my aide-d
camp, I return many thanks for their efficiency and cordial co-op

tion with me, and I call particular attention to these officers for their gallantry and good conduct.

The country has to mourn the loss of many of its best and bravest men, who were killed while fighting bravely during this campaign. Among them I will mention Colonel McElroy, of the Thirteenth Mississippi Regiment, who was killed in the assault on Fort Loudon on November 29. He was shot at the angle of the wall at the head of his regiment, which led in the assault on the right. He was a man of very fine courage, united to a self-possession on all occasions, with a knowledge of his duties and a natural capacity for command which inspired confidence and made him always conspicuous. His death is much to be regretted.

Colonel Ruff, of the Eighteenth Georgia, who commanded Wofford's brigade and led it to the assault, was shot while cheering on his men. He was a gallant and accomplished officer, whose merit was concealed by his modest and unobtrusive manner, but who was fast becoming known as occasions forced a display of his zeal and worth. I knew of no one whose career promised to be more useful.

Colonel Thomas, of the Sixteenth Georgia, a brave and determined officer, was also killed while leading his regiment and attempting to scale the work. He was found dead sitting in the corner of the ditch facing the enemy.

There are many other officers and men whose gallantry and deeds of daring deserve that their names should be especially recorded, but the number is so great it cannot be done in this report.

On December 17, I received an order from General Longstreet's headquarters, of which the following is a copy:

SPECIAL ORDERS, }   HEADQUARTERS,
    No. 27.   }   *Near Bean's Station, December* 17, 1863.

Maj. Gen. L. McLaws is relieved from further duty with this army, and will proceed to Augusta, Ga., from which place he will report by letter to the Adjutant and Inspector General. He will turn over the command of his division to the senior brigadier present.

By command of Lieutenant-General Longstreet:
                                         G. MOXLEY SORREL,
        Lieutenant-Colonel, and Assistant Adjutant-General.

Major-General McLAWS,
        C. S. Army.

Being totally uninformed of any reasons for such an order, I addressed the following communication to Colonel Sorrel:

                     CAMP ON BEAN'S STATION GAP ROAD,
                                         December 17, 1863.

Lieutenant-Colonel SORREL,
    Assistant Adjutant-General:

I have the honor to acknowledge the receipt of Special Orders, No. 27, from your headquarters, of this date, relieving me from further duty with this army. If there is no impropriety in making inquiry, and I cannot imagine there is, I respectfully request to be informed of the particular reason for the order.

    Very respectfully,
                                         L. McLAWS,
                                             Major-General.

In reply to which I received the following:

                                         HEADQUARTERS,
                             Near Bean's Station, December 17, 1863.

Major-General McLAWS,
        C. S. Army:

GENERAL: I have the honor to acknowledge the receipt of your note of to-day asking for the particular reason for the issue of the order relieving you from duty with this army.   In reply, I am directed to say that throughout the campaign on which we are engaged you have exhibited a want of confidence in the efforts and plans which the commanding general has thought proper to adopt, and he is apprehensive that this feeling will extend more or less to the troops under your command. Under these circumstances the commanding general has felt that the interest of the public service would be advanced by your separation from him, and as he could not himself leave he decided upon the issue of the order which you have received.

I have the honor to be, general, with great respect, your obedient servant,

G. MOXLEY SORREL,
Lieutenant-Colonel, and Assistant Adjutant-General.

As I was not informed of any instance wherein I had exhibited any want of confidence in the plans and efforts of the commanding general, and am still ignorant that I have ever done so, I can but close with the regret that my conduct has been misunderstood or misrepresented.   If I have failed ever in any duty it was because I was ignorant of the plans or efforts which the commanding general wished me to carry out or to make.

As I left my division on the next day after receiving the orders above quoted and went across the country to Augusta, Ga., I am not informed personally of its movements thereafter.

On reviewing the campaign I cannot but remark—with no spirit of fault-finding, however, as I was totally unacquainted with General Longstreet's plans and therefore not informed whether or not he desired to bring the enemy to an engagement or to force them to retire only toward Knoxville—that if the leading division (Hood's), commanded by Brigadier-General Jenkins, had marched on instead of turning to the right and forming line of battle toward Lenoir's Station on November 15 the enemy could have been intercepted in his retreat either at Campbell's Station or at a point 7 miles from the forks of the road, where my division was halted and brought to a decisive engagement, which, in the existing demoralized state of the enemy, as shown by his hasty retreat from Lenoir's Station, would have rendered the siege of Knoxville unnecessary and its fall a sequence of the battle.   Our army could then have either returned to Chattanooga or have threatened the enemy's rear in the direction of Kingston, and the battle of Missionary Ridge would never have occurred, or the final result would have been more favorable to our cause.

I was informed on the evening of the 15th, after dark, by one of my couriers, who was acquainted with the country, and by citizens of standing who lived in the vicinity, that there was a road which, turning off from the Campbell's Station road 4 miles from the forks where I was, led into the road upon which the enemy were, 6 or 7 miles from my position, and that if we could gain the junction a small force could hold the place against great odds, as the position was a very strong one.   I wrote to General Longstreet informing him of this road after dark on the 15th, but whether or not he received my note I am not aware, as no answer was returned.   The leading division could, however, have easily marched to Campbell's Station the evening previous, and a demonstration of my division upon Lenoir's Station would have covered the movement until after dark, when I could have joined the leading division, or have remained in position to act as the movements of the enemy demanded.

Again, I believe that if Knoxville had been assaulted on the evening of our arrival there, or the evening after (the 18th), when Kershaw's brigade assaulted and carried the outworks of the enemy,

hat we could have either forced an evacuation on the night of the
7th or have gained a position which would have rendered the town
ntenable ; but our troops were never assembled for an assault un-
il the 29th, but, on the contrary, they were deployed in enveloping
he town.

When the assault was made on the 29th, if Hood's division, on my
eft, had assaulted the enemy's works to the left (my left) of Fort
Loudon, and at the same time my assault was made, both points
would probably have been carried, and without the loss of as many
men as I suffered in attempting the fort alone, as my loss was in-
licted chiefly by a deliberate fire from the left of the fort, which
was not kept down by the sharpshooters there, but which would
iave been diverted and rendered less accurate if the point had been
ssaulted.   But if the assault had not been made at all we could have
hanged our base upon the receipt of the news of General Bragg
aaving been compelled to fall back from Missionary Ridge, selected
, position in the rear of Knoxville toward Virginia, and retired at
ur leisure, for I do not believe that the enemy would have ventured
o have followed us to an engagement, even if he had been re-
nforced, for the country, by reason of its narrow valleys between
naccessible mountains, offered strong defensible positions to enable
, small force to successfully resist one much superior, and we thus
ould have made use of a vast amount of grain and hay and sub-
istence which was afterward wasted by the enemy.   As it was, the
nemy made no pursuit of us, but following at a distance retreated
s we turned on them.

On the night of the 8th, after my arrival at Mooresburg, I sent
or my chief quartermaster and commissary, who had been there in
dvance of the command, and they informed me that in the section
f country which could be foraged from that place subsistence stores
nd forage were more abundant than in any section north of it, and
he commissary (Major Edwards) gave me a list of mills around the
ountry which could be used in making flour and corn-meal for the
roops.   I informed General Longstreet by letter to his adjutant-
;eneral (Lieutenant-Colonel Sorrel) of these facts, but no reply was
;iven.   The troops were marched on, however, and the enemy came
ip in the rear, destroying and wasting everything not absolutely
aeeded for themselves, and then our army returned on the 14th and
aad to fight to get back the country which they could have had un-
nolested by remaining there.

After the assault (the day after, I believe, or it may have been two
r three days after), at a council of war called by General Long-
treet, consisting of Lieutenant-General Longstreet, Maj. Gen. L.
McLaws, Brig. Gen. B. R. Johnson, Brigadier-General Jenkins,
Brigadier-General Kershaw, and Col. E. P. Alexander, the question
was submitted as to the best course to be pursued—whether to join
General Bragg or to change our base looking toward Virginia.   The
ouncil was informed by General Longstreet that he had received a
elegram from President Davis directing him to join General Bragg,
f possible, with his forces.   Several telegrams, or one at least, from
General B., was shown, wherein it stated that General Bragg's
rmy had retired toward Dalton, Ga., the exact point I do not recol-
ect, and intimating that if he (General L.) could join him it would
e desirable, but he could not expect any assistance from General
3. in making the effort.   Such is my recollection.   Telegrams from

the officers in command at Loudon and below, showing that the en emy were advancing toward Loudon, were also submitted.

To the question, then, whether we should attempt to join Genera Bragg, or change our base toward Virginia, I was called on for m opinion, being next in rank to General L. I submitted that our firs duty was to endeavor to join General Bragg, as the President di rected, and General Bragg intimated as being his desire, and in dis cussing that question I argued against making the attempt, for th reason that we could not go by the route we came, but would hav to choose one farther to the east, and there was none in that direc tion that did not lead through a rough, mountainous, and desolat country, where neither forage nor subsistence could be obtained fo the men and animals. That snow, as we could perceive, had falle over that country, which would add to the difficulties of the march as many of our men were without shoes, and our sick would be un able to keep with us. That in all probability the command woul have to be divided in order to obtain subsistence, in which event i would be a long time before we could be united again, so as to b of efficient service, and that the mere fact of retiring in that direc tion would have a very bad moral effect upon our troops, as w would thus abandon East Tennessee to the enemy, and the fain hearted would despond and perhaps leave us, especially those o that class in the regiments from Tennessee, and at the same tim the enemy, having nothing to oppose them in East Tennessee, coul re-enforce General Grant at Chattanooga with nearly their entir force from Knoxville, and thus enable him to push on before ou forces could possibly join General Bragg, even in the unserviceabl condition they would be in after the long and tedious march ove the desolate country we would be compelled to travel.

On the other hand, if we remained in East Tennessee, with ou base changed toward Virginia, our force would act as a constan menace upon General Grant's flank and rear, and compel him t keep one equally as large in and about Knoxville to watch our move ments. That we owed it to the people of East Tennessee, who ha been loyal to us, to afford them some protection and not abando them suddenly to the enemy. That the effect upon our troops woul be beneficial, and that we would by remaining relieve Georgia an the whole South, excepting East Tennessee, from the burden of sul sisting our forces, at a time, too, when the relief would be very sel sibly felt; and that if we did have to draw heavily upon the re sources of East Tennessee we would be drawing from a populatio the large majority of which were inimical to our cause, and whic would be much better than necessitating us to oppress those farthe south who were entirely loyal.

There was no dissent from these views and the army was witl drawn toward Virginia. I do not claim that my views were th cause of that course being adopted, but I merely place my opinio upon record. I have no doubt but any other member of the counc would have given the same opinion and have more forcibly ex pressed it.*

L. McLAWS,
Major-General.

---

* Casualties in McLaws' division at Bean's Station : Kershaw's brigade—killed, wounded, 52 ; missing, 5 ; total, 62. Bryan's brigade—killed, 1 ; wounded, 1 ; t tal, 2.

AUGUSTA, GA.,
January 17, 1864.

General S. COOPER,
Adjt. and Insp. Gen., C. S. Army, Richmond, Va.:

On the 15th instant I received from General Longstreet's headquarters a copy of a charge preferred against myself, with an accompanying letter, being a copy of one which he had forwarded to you, referring to the charges. To prevent any misunderstanding, I herewith inclose copies of both the charges and letter. I beg leave to remark concerning the charge and specifications:

The assault against Fort Loudon, which was made by three brigades of my division, on the morning of November 29 last, had been ordered to be made on the 28th, the day previous, at, I think, 2 p. m., perhaps earlier; but at my request and on my suggestion it was delayed until the morning of the 29th, to enable me to advance my line of sharpshooters so as to fire along the enemy's works and thus facilitate the advance of the assaulting columns by distracting and preventing the enemy's fire. The enemy's pits were taken all along my line, and my sharpshooters advancing beyond them established a new line for themselves within easy musket range of the main work. This was done, excepting with the sharpshooters from Bryan's brigade, and the exception was made for the following reasons: The sharpshooters of the brigades were arranged from left to right, as follows: Wofford's, Humphreys', Bryan's, Kershaw's. Kershaw's line was so far advanced on the right that the connection could not be established with Bryan's, and Colonel Holt, of the Tenth Georgia, who commanded Bryan's sharpshooters, came to me some time late in the night of the 28th, and informing me of the circumstance, requested authority to throw the right of his line back, so as to protect his right flank, which I authorized him to do, deeming it essential for the safety of his line.

The enemy had not long previous assaulted my line of sharpshooters by coming down on their flank, which had not been properly supported on the left by the advance of Hood's division, and had taken their pits temporarily, but were finally driven back with considerable loss by the reserves coming up. I did not wish the experiment to be repeated, and therefore had the right of Bryan's line thrown back, or, rather, authorized it to be done; but that it had any effect upon the final result I deny, because my loss was but about 50 or 60 before reaching the ditch, and the enemy fired but one gun, as some say, and others but two, upon the advancing columns, being kept down by the sharpshooters.

To the second specification I merely assert that the Seventeenth Mississippi, of Humphreys' brigade, and Phillips (Georgia) Legion, of Wofford's brigade, two as fine bodies of men and as well commanded as can be found anywhere, were selected to lead, and did lead, the assaulting columns, and they, as well as all others, were ordered to take the work and hold it against all comers until I arrived to direct otherwise. My orders were to take the works; that was all for the assaulting column to do, and I was notified that General Jenkins, commanding Hood's division, would follow my column and lead division to the left. I am at a loss to conceive as to what definite instructions further than those I gave could have been given, as the inside of the work was an unknown quantity. What was to be done after it was taken was to be found out. If there was no ditch on the left (the west side) that offered any obstacle, or but

little, to the entrance to the work, I have been most egregiously mis-
informed, for I have in my possession a paper, of which the accompanying one, marked B, is a copy from the column of my division
which assaulted on the left, showing a very different state of affairs.

In regard to the men not being supplied with ladders or other
means of crossing the ditch, I was assured by General Longstreet
himself, and by members of his staff who made observations of the
work from the heights around on both sides of the river by means of
powerful glasses, that there was no ditch that offered any great obstacle. I was pertinaciously pressed with the fact that there would
be but little difficulty, so far as the ditch was concerned, in entering
the work, and I endeavored to impress the fact upon the men, and
in connection with it urged them to rush to the assault with impetu-
osity and without halting. How well my instructions were obeyed
the history of the contest will show. I, however, contemplated getting bundles of wheat for the men to carry, and therewith fill up the
ditch if one was found offering a serious impediment to our advance
but there was not a sufficient quantity available for the purpose
where I expected to find it. As for ladders, I had no means, or
time, or material to make any. The idea of obtaining them was
entertained, but as I had nothing to make them with I said nothing
about them, deeming it unadvisable to broach the subject. No one
ever mentioned the probability of any necessity for them, as it was
regarded as a work requiring dash and daring only. If General
Longstreet, after reconnoitering the works, had considered that ladders, or other means for crossing the ditch, were necessary, I suppose
he would have made some mention of them at least on some occasion.
I should think it was his place to order them. His omission to do
either looks very strange, when he charges me with being criminally
negligent in not getting them.

It is an easy matter after the assault is over to see where errors
have been committed; but of those I am charged with, where there
was any in fact, I do not consider myself responsible, and hold myself unjustly charged; and I object to being put forward as a blind
to draw attention away from the main issue, which is the conduct of
the campaign in East Tennessee under General Longstreet.

I assert that the enemy could have been brought to an engagement
before reaching Knoxville; that the town, if assaulted at all, should
have been on the first day we arrived, or on the next at farthest
that when the assault was made on Fort Loudon it was not called for
by any line of policy whatever; but, on the contrary, no good results
could possibly have been attained.

You will recollect that on December 29, ultimo, I forwarded to
you a copy of an order relieving me from duty with General Longstreet's command. Before leaving I addressed a note to his head
quarters inquiring the reason why the order was issued, and the
reply was that, having exhibited a want of confidence in the plans
and efforts of General Longstreet throughout the campaign on which
he was then engaged, he (General Longstreet) was apprehensive i
might be extended to the troops under my command, and as he could
not leave himself, I was ordered to do so. This was the sole reason
assigned at that time, and yet after my departure a charge of neglect of duty, with three specifications, was forwarded to your office
against me, and in the letter accompanying the charges he writes I
was not arrested for the reason he thought I might be of service
elsewhere. I inquired why I was relieved from duty for the reason

that, if there was any part of my conduct needing investigation, I might before leaving be informed, so that I might make the necessary preparations to defend myself. But as it is now you can perceive the disadvantages I am laboring under. I must therefore demand that the charges be investigated at an early day by a court of inquiry or court-martial, or they be withdrawn and I restored to duty at once.

Very respectfully, your most obedient servant,

L. McLAWS,
Major-General.

[Inclosure.]

HEADQUARTERS,
Russellville, Tenn., December 30, 1863.

General S. COOPER,
Adjutant and Inspector General, Richmond:

GENERAL : I have the honor to inclose herewith charges and specifications against Maj. Gen. L. McLaws and against Brig. Gen. J. B. Robertson.* I have no authority to order courts, and have therefore to ask that a court be ordered for the trial of Brigadier-General Robertson. General McLaws was not arrested when he was relieved from duty, for the reason that it was supposed that his services might be important to the Government in some other position. If such is the case, I have no desire that he should be kept from that service or that his usefulness should be impaired in any way by a trial.†

I remain, general, very respectfully, your most obedient servant,

JAMES LONGSTREET,
Lieutenant-General, Commanding.

[Sub-inclosure.]

CHARGE AND SPECIFICATIONS PREFERRED AGAINST MAJ. GEN. L. M'LAWS.

CHARGE.—Neglect of duty.

Specification 1.—In this, that Maj. Gen. L. McLaws, being in command of a division of the Confederate forces near Knoxville, Tenn., and being ordered by his commanding officer (Lieut. Gen. J. Longstreet) to advance his line of sharpshooters at dark on the night of November 28 to within good rifle range of the enemy's works, so as to give his sharpshooters play upon the enemy behind his works (it being part of a plan of attack that the sharpshooters should engage the enemy behind his works along our entire line while an assault was made upon one of the enemy's forts), did fail to arrange his line of sharpshooters so as to meet this view, and did allow a portion of the rifle-pits to be sunk about 200 yards from the point to be attacked under a hill entirely out of view of the fort aforesaid, thus failing to give his assaulting columns the protection of the fire of his sharpshooters at this point during their advance and attack.

Specification 2.—In this, that the aforesaid Maj. Gen. L. McLaws,

---

* See p. 470.
† See Confederate Correspondence, etc., McLaws to Cooper, December 29, 1863, and Cooper to Longstreet, January 5, 1864, Part III, pp. 881, 893.

being ordered by his commanding officer (Lieutenant-General Long
street) to arrange an assaulting column of three of his brigades, and
to attack the enemy's fort at the northwest angle of his works at
dawn of day on November 29, did fail to organize a select body of
men to lead in the assault as is customary in such attacks, and did
allow his three brigades to advance to the assault without definite
and specific instructions for the leading columns, and for the troops
that were to enter the fort first, which are essential to success in such
attacks.

Specification 3.—In this, that the aforesaid Maj. Gen. L. McLaws
being ordered to assault the enemy's position at the northwest angle
of his works at daylight on November 29, did make his attack upon
a point where the ditch was impassable, and did fail to provide any
of his assaulting columns with ladders or other means of crossing
the ditch and entering the enemy's works, and did fail to inform his
officers that the ditch on the west side of the fort was but a slight
obstacle to his infantry, and that the fort could be entered from that
side with but little delay, thus failing in the details of his attack to
make the arrangements essential to success. All this near Knox
ville, Tenn., on or about November 28 and 29, 1863.

Witnesses: Brig. Gen. B. G. Humphreys, Brig. Gen. Goode Bryan,
Brig. Gen. M. Jenkins, Col. E. P. Alexander, Maj. J. M. Goggin,
Lieut. Col. W. C. Holt, Surg. J. S. D. Cullen, Surg. R. Barksdale,
Lieut. A. D'Antignac.

JAMES LONGSTREET,
Lieutenant-General.

[Inclosure B.]

HEADQUARTERS WOFFORD'S BRIGADE,
December 1, 1863.

Maj. JAMES M. GOGGIN,
    Assistant Adjutant-General:

I herewith forward a brief of the evidence of officers and men who
were present and participated in the assault on the enemy's work
on the 29th ultimo relative to the points inquired of in General
McLaws' note of this instant, together with the names of those who
are ready to verify the statements. There are hundreds, perhaps, in
the brigade whose testimony would corroborate it.

Very respectfully,

N. L. HUTCHINS, JR.,
Lieutenant-Colonel, Commanding Brigade.

The following is the substance of the evidence of officers and men
of Wofford's brigade, who were present at and in the ditch and on
the enemy's works when the assault was made on the morning of the
29th ultimo, relating to the construction of the fort, to wit:

The ditch is from 8 to 10 feet wide, and its depth from 4 to 6 feet,
and its sides are almost perpendicular. There was no berme noticed
by most of them, while others say there is, perhaps, one of not
exceeding 6 inches in width, now filled by the crumbling dirt. The
slope of the exterior slope of the parapet is at an angle of 60° or 70°
with the base line, and the height of the work from the bottom of
the ditch about 18 feet on a perpendicular line. The earth (clay) of
the slope is hard and slippery, and it was difficult to obtain a foot

old upon it. There was a ditch along the whole length of the fort
n both sides of the angle as far as they could see, and that on the
eft was flanked by rifle-pits. Wire was tied from stump to stump,
n order to impede the advance upon the work. Those who suc-
eeded in getting on the slope of the parapet did so by the assistance
f others.

Names of those who testify to these facts: Capt. John S. Norris,
Capt. F. C. Fuller, Capt. S. Y. Harris, Capt. John L. Dodds, Phil-
ips' Legion; Lieut. C. W. Baldwin, Lieut. G. F. Pierce, Private W.
R. Head, Cobb's Legion; Lieutenant Dyer, Lieutenant Brannon,
Sergt. E. W. Strickland (Company I), Private Sanders (Company
C), Private Cleghorn (Company D), Sixteenth Georgia; Captain
Crawford, Captain Calahan, Lieutenant Hardin, Lieutenant Mad-
lox, Private J. Kennedy, Eighteenth Georgia.

GENERAL ORDERS, }   ADJT. AND INSP. GENERAL'S OFFICE,
    No. 46.   }   *Richmond, May* 4, 1864.

I. At a general court-martial, convened by Special Orders, No.
1, current series, Adjutant and Inspector General's Office, was ar-
raigned and tried Maj. Gen. L. McLaws, Provisional Army Confed-
rate States, on the following charge and specifications:

CHARGE.—Neglect of duty, to the prejudice of good order and military discipline.

Specification 1.—In this, that Maj. Gen. L. McLaws, being in command of a divis-
on of the Confederate forces near Knoxville, Tenn., and being ordered by his commanding officer, Lieut. Gen. J. Longstreet, to advance his line of sharpshooters at
lark on the night of November 29 [28], to within good rifle range of the enemy's
works, so as to give his sharpshooters play upon the enemy behind his works, it being
part of a plan of attack that the sharpshooters should engage the enemy behind
his works along our line, while an assault was made upon one of the enemy's forts,
did fail to arrange his line of sharpshooters so as to meet this view, and did allow a
portion of the rifle-pits to be sunk under a hill entirely out of view of the fort
aforesaid, thus failing to give his assaulting columns the protection of the fire of
his sharpshooters at this point during their advance and attack.

Specification 2.—In this, that the aforesaid Maj. Gen. L. McLaws, being ordered
by his commanding officer, Lieutenant-General Longstreet, to arrange assaulting
columns of three of his brigades and to attack the enemy's fort at the northwest
angle of his works at dawn of day on November 29, did fail to organize a select
body of men to lead in the assault, as is customary in such attacks, and did allow
his three brigades to advance to the attack without definite and specific instruc-
ions for the leading columns and for the troops to enter the fort, which are essen-
ial to success in such attacks.

Specification 3.—In this, that the aforesaid Maj. Gen. L. McLaws, being ordered
o assault the enemy's position at the northwest angle of his works at daylight on
November 29, did make his attack upon a point where the ditch was impassable,
and did fail to provide any of his assaulting columns with ladders or means of en-
ering the enemy's works, and [did] fail to inform his officers that the ditch on the
west side of the fort was but a slight obstacle to his infantry, and that the fort could
be entered from that side with but little delay, thus failing in the details of his attack
o make the arrangements essential to success. All this near Knoxville, Tenn., on
or about November 28 and 29, 1863.

FINDING AND SENTENCE OF THE COURT.

After mature deliberation the court find the accused, Maj. Gen. L. McLaws, Provisional Army, Confederate States, as follows:

Of the first specification not guilty, as, though one part of the line of rifle-pits was
out of view of the fort, yet the order requiring the line of sharpshooters to be advanced, so as to give the assaulting columns the protection of their fire, was substantially complied with.

Of the second specification not guilty, though no select bodies of men were organized to lead in the assault, yet organizations already existing were selected for
that purpose.

Of the third specification guilty, of so much of the third specification as relate to his not providing means of crossing the ditch, and in this of failing in the detail of his attack to make the arrangements essential to his success.

Of the charge guilty ; and the court do therefore sentence the accused, the said Maj. Gen. L. McLaws, to be suspended from rank and command for sixty days.

It is the opinion of the court that there are many circumstances shown by the evidence which exonerate Maj. Gen. L. McLaws from any high degree of crimi nality in his failure to provide the ordinary means of crossing the ditch. He had many reasons for considering it a slight one, and was encouraged in this belief by the opinion of those officers in the army whose opinions should have had the most weight with him. The court acquit Major-General McLaws of any deliberate pur pose to fail in any duty devolved upon him, but it is their opinion that his only fault was in failing to appreciate the full weight, and they may say the almost fearful extent, of the responsibility resting upon him as the director of an assault ing column.

II. The court was convened by order of the War Department From the record it appears that the court adjourned on Februar 13, 1864, at Morristown, to meet at New Market on the 15th of th same month, and on the same day, in accordance with the sugges tion of Lieutenant-General Longstreet, reassembled, and, in the ab sence of two members of the court who had voted at the previou session and of the accused, adjourned indefinitely. The record fur ther shows that after the court had been organized a leave of ab sence was granted for thirty days, by Lieutenant-General Longstreet to Brigadier-General Humphreys, a member of the court, under th direct orders of the War Department, and an important witness Without reference to the merits of the case, these irregularities ar fatal to the record.

III. The finding of the court upon the third specification is no sustained by the evidence. The witnesses attest the fact that th ditch at the northwest angle of the fort, where the attack was made was not more than $4\frac{1}{2}$ feet deep by 8 to 10 feet wide, and that ther was no necessity for artificial means to cross it. There could not therefore, be guilt in having failed to provide such means. More over, the finding is defective in not responding to the material allega tion in the specification that the accused " failed to inform his offi cers that the ditch on the west side of the fort was but little obstacl to his infantry, and that the fort could be easily entered from tha side with but little delay." The court should have taken cognizanc of this allegation, and found upon it either for or against the ac cused. The finding was easy to be determined, since it appears from the evidence that the ditch on the west side was " 12 to 13 feet deep There cannot be guilt in having omitted to make statements which would not have been true. The allegation in the third specification that the accused " failed, in the details of attack, to make arrange ments essential to success," was evidently introduced as a conclusio to previous allegations, and was not issuable in itself. The cour erred in finding upon it, and moreover the finding is not sustaine by the evidence.

IV. The proceedings, finding, and sentence of the court are disap proved. Major-General McLaws will at once return to duty with his command.

V. The court-martial of which Maj. Gen. S. B. Buckner is presi dent is hereby dissolved.

By order:

S. COOPER,
Adjutant and Inspector General.

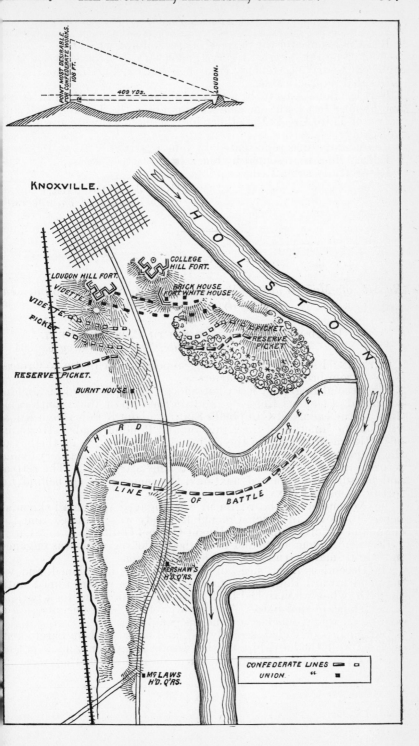

ADDENDA.

Reconnaissance for the purpose of ascertaining whether a point can be found suitable to erect reserve picket—a work for sharpshooters sufficient to drive the enemy from their guns at Fort Loudon.

Decided impracticable.

Fort Loudon seems to be a two-sided bastion, with ditch in front, and about 8 feet high, one side commanding the Loudon road and valley of Third Creek, the other side facing northward toward the railroad.*

Confederate lines represented by blue [☐ ☐].

Enemy lines represented by black [■].

Respectfully submitted.

THOS. J. MONCURE,
Lieutenant of Engineers.

No. 64.

Report of Maj. William Wallace, Second South Carolina Infantry, Kershaw's brigade.

HEADQUARTERS SECOND SOUTH CAROLINA REGT.,
Russellville, Tenn., January 6, 1864.

CAPTAIN: I submit the following report, in obedience to Orders No. —, from brigade headquarters:

The Second Regiment left Chattanooga on November 4 last, under command of Colonel Kennedy, and on the 16th of that month came up with the enemy at Campbell's Station, about 15 miles from Knoxville, at the junction of the Kingston and Loudon roads. Here line of battle was formed, and the regiment in its position on the left of the brigade advanced. The enemy, after some little artillery firing retired, and were pursued until some time after dark. The retreat and pursuit were renewed next day, the enemy retiring behind his fortifications at Knoxville.

On November 18, the regiment was engaged in a small skirmish before the town, in which Colonel Kennedy was wounded, and the command devolved upon Lieutenant-Colonel Gaillard.

Between November 18 and December 4, the regiment was engaged in several small skirmishes, and lost a few men.

On December 4, the siege of Knoxville was abandoned, and we marched toward Rogersville, near which place we encamped until the 14th, when we marched back to Bean's Station and took part in the skirmish at that place. The enemy retired before us, and night coming on we bivouacked around his camp fires.

Our men, poorly clad, scantily fed, and many of them barefooted, endured well the hardships of this winter campaign, and acquitted themselves creditably in all the skirmishes in which they were engaged.

---

* See map, p. 507.

Below is a list of casualties during the period called for:

	Killed.	Wounded.	Missing.	Total.
around Knoxville	3	13	......	16
Bean's Station	2	19	1	22
Total	5	32	1	38

Respectfully submitted.

WM. WALLACE,
Major, Commanding Second South Carolina Regiment.

Capt. C. R. HOLMES,
Assistant Adjutant-General, Kershaw's Brigade.

I omitted to include Colonel Kennedy in the list of wounded around Knoxville; the number should be 14 instead of 13.

No. 65.

Report of Col. James D. Nance, Third South Carolina Infantry.

HDQRS. THIRD SOUTH CAROLINA REGIMENT,
Near Russellville, Tenn., January 6, 1864.

CAPTAIN : In obedience to instructions from brigade headquarters, I have the honor to submit the following report of the operations of this command from the time it left Chattanooga to its arrival at this camp :

Nothing of special interest occurred to the regiment from November 4, the date it left Chattanooga, to November 8. when we arrived at Sweet Water; to November 14, when we arrived at Loudon ; nor until the 17th, when we reached Knoxville, although after the 15th we were constantly in the presence of the enemy, who were retiring upon that town.

On the evening of the 17th, when within 3 miles of Knoxville, I was ordered by Brigadier-General Kershaw to cross the railroad on my left and flank the enemy's advanced line of skirmishers, which crossed the railroad perpendicularly about 2 miles from town and extended at least to the woods on the west side. I immediately sent scouts in advance and followed with the regiment, crossing Second Creek and the railroad and making into the woods beyond, when I turned to the right and marched parallel to the railroad. After going in this direction about a third of a mile I discovered, from my own observations as well as from the reports of my scouts, that the enemy's skirmishers had withdrawn to the east side of the railroad, but they were plainly visible in a line perpendicular to the railroad and running over the hill which was carried by assault the following evening. I was then on their flank, but too far off to deliver an effective fire.

Upon a reconnaissance made by myself and scouts, I found that I could not push farther to the north, so as to come more in the enemy's rear, without disclosing the movement to their vedettes, who

were still on the west side of the railroad and in an open field to th
north of the wood.   I therefore concluded to work my way as quietl
as possible to the edge of the wood next to the railroad, and the
make a dash upon their flank.   Accordingly, after throwing Captai
Nance's company on my left, deployed as skirmishers, to report an
movement of the enemy and to guard against any flank attack fron
that direction, I moved out of the woods unperceived by the enemy
and simultaneously opened fire and charged on their right flank
They immediately broke and retired beyond the hill on which the
were posted, but just before we reached the railroad I discovered fo
the first time a considerable body of troops, who were unmasked b'
our passing from behind a thicket of small pines, posted on the rai¹
road and about 500 yards to our left, some of whom were mounte
and others dismounted.

Under these circumstances I halted at the railroad, where I foun
protection for my men behind the embankment, and engaged th
enemy, who changed front and returned my fire from behind th
brow of the hill, intending to act as circumstances might dictate
Just beyond the railroad was an open meadow, which it was unad
visable to enter while the enemy's cavalry was on my flank.   Ther
was no sign of an advance of our line of skirmishers (whose lef
rested on the railroad) to connect with my right.

Captain Nance reported a large body of cavalry passing aroun
my left and to my rear, toward the woods from which I had jus
emerged, and a fire at the same time being opened on my left fron
up the railroad, I determined, upon consultation with my field offi
cers, to retire by the same route by which I approached.   I did so
and some time after having reached the woods I received an ordei
from General Kershaw, through Lieutenant Dwight, assistant in
spector-general, to rejoin the brigade on the Loudon road.   I did s
immediately.   Not knowing the exact purpose of my orders, I can
not say how far the design was executed, but if not fully carried ou
it was as much so as circumstances would allow.

A list* of casualties in this affair is herewith submitted.   Among
the wounded was Lieut. Wade Allen, who was struck while bearin
a message from me to Captain Nance.   I regret to state that he fel
into the hands of the enemy when we retired from Knoxville.

On the morning of the 18th, by order, I took my position in lin
of battle, and after marching near to Mr. Armstrong's house I wa
halted in a ravine to the left of the road, where I remained until lat
in the afternoon.   During the whole day there was heavy skirmish
ing in front and considerable cannonading from our batteries, th
effort being to carry a high hill on the left of the road and just to
the south of Mr. M. M. Armstrong's house.

I received an order about 4 p. m. from General Kershaw, throug
Lieutenant Doby, aide-de-camp, to carry the enemy's rail defense
situated on this hill, but not to advance beyond them.   I was tol
that the line of these works was indicated by two cedar trees on th
top of the hill, and I directed my men not to stop short of thes
trees, but not to go beyond them.   We then advanced in excellen
condition under heavy fire until we reached the cedars, but perceiv
ing that the trees were short of the works, I urged my men forward
by every means in my power, but perhaps because of the genera
direction "not to go beyond the cedars," and on account of having
once halted, and the difficulty of renewing the advance under such

---

*Not found.

, terrible fire, there was some hesitation, which was further in-
reased by the regiments on my right failing to come up in time on
ccount of natural obstacles encountered in their advance. At
ength the left of the regiment reached the breastworks, when cries
f "we surrender" issued from their ranks. I ceased firing and
vent forward to receive the surrender, but upon being fired on im-
nediately renewed the firing and soon took possession of their works,
fter killing about 17 of their men and taking several prisoners, a
ew of whom were wounded.

It is but truth to state that this was the most desperate encounter
n which my command was ever engaged, and as it was perhaps one
f the most brilliant charges of the war, I cannot speak too highly
f the conduct of my comrades. In reference to the alleged bad
aith of the enemy in pretending to surrender, it is a charitable con-
truction, and perhaps not an unreasonable one, to suppose that they
lid not understand each other, rather than that they intended to
leceive us.

A list* of casualties from this assault is herewith submitted.
Among the mortally wounded was First Lieut. D. S. Maffett. Cir-
umstances had often thrown him in command of his company for
ong periods, and his competency as an officer was well tried and
vell established. He was efficient and gallant, and his loss is a
evere one to his company and regiment. Among the killed and
vounded were many of the best spirits in the command. As we ad-
anced to the charge that memorable evening, we overtook at the
oot of the hill the skirmishers, commanded by Maj. William Wal-
ace, Second South Carolina Regiment, who, with his command,
oined us and contributed their share to the brilliant success. Major
Wallace was conspicuous for gallantry and coolness, and it is with
leasure that I make this honorable mention of him.

We intrenched ourselves that night in that position, where we re-
nained for several days. Besides picketing and lying in the trenches
1othing occupied us until the night of December 3, when we retired
rom Knoxville. We marched in the direction of Rogersville, the
1eighborhood of which we reached on December 9.

On the 14th, we returned as far as Bean's Station, where in the
fternoon the brigade, as well as other portions of the corps, became
ngaged with the enemy's mounted infantry. Although my com-
nand was on the field and in proper position, it did not become very
ctively engaged. After nightfall I was ordered by General Ker-
haw to march across the fields on the left of the valley until I came
o the road, and there to halt and report. I came into the road just
t Mr. Gill's house, where I halted and reported as ordered, and soon
fterward was directed to connect my picket line with that on my
ight and go into camp with the rest of the brigade. Near the
10use of Mr. Gill I captured several inferior horses, saddles, and
ridles, enough bacon and crackers to ration my command for about
wo or three days, besides other articles of inconsiderable value.

On the morning of the 18th, by order, I assumed command of the
rigade, but as nothing special occurred after that date I may com-
lete the report of the operations of the command by saying that it
emained at Bean's Station until December 20, when we took up the
ine of march for this point, which we reached on December 22,
863.

---

* Not found.

Besides lists of casualties already referred to, you will observe a list* of men left behind in front of Knoxville, who have fallen into the hands of the enemy.

I am, very respectfully,

JAMES D. NANCE,

Colonel, Commanding.

Capt. C. R. HOLMES, *Assistant Adjutant-General.*

No. 66.

Report of Capt. E. J. Goggans, Seventh South Carolina Infantry

HDQRS. SEVENTH SOUTH CAROLINA REGIMENT,

January 8, 1864.

CAPTAIN : In obedience to orders, the following report of the operations of the Seventh South Carolina Regiment since it left Chattanooga is respectfully submitted :

The regiment left Lookout Mountain on the night of November 4, 1863, marching via Rossville and McFarland's Spring over Missionary Ridge.

About noon on the 5th arrived at the artificial tunnel, a few miles from Tyner's Station, where it remained until the 7th, when it took the cars.

After a most miserable trip arrived at Sweet Water Station on the evening of the 8th, where it was encamped until 10 a. m. on the 12th, when it was moved off ; encamped that night at Philadelphia.

Morning of 13th, moved off in a direction to the right ; struck up camp on the river near Morganton ; remained there until midnight, took up line of march, and daylight of the 14th found it at Loudon, where it remained until morning of 15th, when it crossed the river on pontoon bridge and moved off in the direction of Campbell's Station, expecting and hoping to make the place before halting ; but to the evident chagrin of many who needed and hoped to get blankets from the captured or slain of the enemy, it was halted and encamped for the night long before reaching the place.

At early dawn of the 16th it was moving on, and toward the middle of the day came near the enemy, when it was thrown in line of battle with other regiments of the brigade to support another brigade that was confronting the enemy in advance of it. Soon, however, it moved with the brigade to the right and fronted the enemy in an open field. Jenkins' brigade, commanded by Colonel Bratton, moved out, and the Seventh, with the others of the brigade, moved to its position and advanced upon the enemy's position, under a sharp artillery fire, without any loss. Night closing in, it moved with the brigade by a flank, and it was said the object was to entrap Yankee cavalry, but we found them not. Moving on a mile or so encamped for the night.

Morning of 17th, were moving soon. Soon came up with the enemy's rear guard. The skirmishers were engaged and the Seventh was moved in line of battle on the right of the Third South Carolina (Colonel Nance's) to support them. Moving on rapidly, it was soon in sight of the Yankees, and under a sharp fire of Yankee cavalry. The enemy being routed by our skirmishers and artillery, it moved by a flank up the railroad. Crossed a creek and was again thrown in line of battle on the right of the road to support our skir-

---

* Not found.

ishers.   The enemy being driven back near to Knoxville, it was alted and built a line of breastworks, which, in obedience to orders, occupied by daylight on the 18th.

Morning of 18th, skirmishing opening briskly, the regiment, with the brigade, moved up to support.   Ours lay for most of the day in ne to the rear and right of first Armstrong house.   In the evening moved by a flank up the river in rear of Fifteenth South Carolina, and took position in line at second Armstrong house and built breast-works.   That night went on picket in front of third or last Armstrong ouse ; relieved the skirmishers from our brigade.   Captured that ight 2 Yankee cavalrymen on horseback, who inadvertently rode into our lines.

In the skirmishes of the 17th and 18th lost 2 men killed and 8 seri-usly wounded, this loss being from Companies D, F, and L, who were engaged in or as skirmishers.   In the regular line of battle a few slight bruises were received, which may not be officially noted.

While at Knoxville, or while engaged in the siege of Knoxville, the regiment did a full share of the multifarious and severe duties that the circumstances necessarily imposed upon all, and the men were often exposed to shell, yet not a man was lost upon any occa-ion or by any cause.

Night of December 4, 1863, left Knoxville ; moved slowly, delib-rately, toward Rogersville, via Blain's Cross-Roads, Rutledge, and Bean's Station.

Encamped near Rogersville on the 9th.   There remained until aylight on the morning of 14th, when it again moved toward Bean's Station.   Arriving that evening at a small mountain by a creek 2 miles from the station, it was once more in range of the enemy's hell.   Crossing the creek by a flank and moving that way across the road, following the brigade (it being that day in rear by the rule of alternation in marching), advanced a considerable distance under over of the hills, making a *détour* to gain the rear of the enemy. At or near the church on our right the enemy appeared.   The Sev-nth, being in rear, was not engaged.   Moving on, it was thrown ut in line in rear of the Second South Carolina Regiment to sup-port it.   Advancing some distance, the nature of the ground made t necessary to move by a flank.   Gaining the top of the hill, the vork was over.   Went into camp around the bright fires built by he routed and retreating foe.

Lost 2 men wounded ; 1 severely, if not mortally.

Remained in camp with but little interruption until 19th, then moved near Long's Ferry.   Crossed on 20th.

On 21st, came to this place.

On 23d, the regiment went back to the ferry to do picket duty.   It was relieved on 27th.   The regiment is now as comfortable as their slender means will admit of.

Thanks are due Capts. Benjamin Roper and T. A. Hudgens for heir skill and bravery during the campaign.

To both officers and men of the command all praise is due for heir bravery and patient endurance of hardships seldom equaled in war.

Very respectfully,

E. J. GOGGANS,
Captain, Commanding.

Capt. C. R. HOLMES, *Assistant Adjutant-General.*

No. 67.

Report of Capt. Duncan McIntyre, Eighth South Carolina Infantry.

HDQRS. EIGHTH SOUTH CAROLINA REGIMENT,
January 8, 1864.

COLONEL : In obedience to orders, I beg leave to submit the following report of the operations of the Eighth South Carolina Regiment during the campaign of East Tennessee :

Colonel Henagan being in command, the regiment, with the brigade, left Chattanooga on the night of November 5, 1863, and arrived at Sweet Water on November 8.

Remained here until the 12th, when we marched, via Philadelphia, to Morganton, and crossing the Tennessee River at Loudon on the morning of the 16th and going in the direction of Knoxville, came up with the skirmishers of the enemy during the evening.

We skirmished with them all day of the 11th, driving them near to Knoxville.

On the morning of the 18th, the Eighth Regiment was ordered in front to support the line of skirmishers on the right, resting on the river. Here we sustained a heavy fire for five or six hours, holding in check a strong line of the enemy until about 3 p. m., about which time, the Third Regiment becoming engaged on our left and the Fifteenth Regiment coming up on the line, we were ordered to advance and charged the strong position of the enemy, driving them in confusion behind their fortifications around Knoxville. We then remained in the position, with no incident of importance, until November 29.

I was placed in command of the regiment on November 27.

On the night of the 29th, I was ordered to report to Lieutenant Colonel Gaillard with the regiment, and at 10 p. m. my regiment being on the right of the battalion and Second Regiment along the line of breastworks near the river and on the extreme right, I was ordered to advance on the enemy's outposts and capture or drive them in and occupy the rifle-pits. After crossing the creek in front of our position, and advancing cautiously to the open field beyond without being discovered, halted and rectified my line.

In crossing the creek and ascending the hill the regiment became separated from the battalion about 200 yards, and I received orders from Colonel Gaillard to advance alone on the fire of the enemy in the rifle-pits, which I did immediately, the regiment preserving good line, and coming within a few paces of the pits, I ordered charge, which was executed in good order, the enemy discharging their pieces and running precipitately. Soon after, the battalion and Second occupying the pits in front of their position, I was ordered to establish outposts in front, and a working party, detailed for the purpose, constructed a line of rifle-pits in advance of the position already occupied, which was done under a heavy fire, of grape and canister from the forts on our left. The pits being finished, we held them until 10 or 11 a. m. next day, when we were ordered to fall back to our original position. Here we remained until the night of December 4, when, with the brigade, we marched to camp near Rogersville, where we remained until December 14.

On the morning of December 14, with the brigade, we came back to near Bean's Station, and coming up with the enemy the brigade was formed in line of battle, the Eighth occupying second position

1e Fifteenth being on the right to the right of the main road and in
ear of Captain Parker's battery.   After remaining here a few min-
tes the brigade was moved by the right flank about three-fourths
f a mile.   Here we were opposite the extreme left of the enemy.
'he Fifteenth, being fronted, was ordered to move forward.   The
lighth was fronted and moved forward.   Here I received orders
rom General Kershaw to advance on an eminence occupied by the
1emy about 700 yards in front.   In consequence of the right of the
egiment having to move through a thick woods and diagonally over
fence we moved slowly for about 300 yards, and the regiment
oming into the open field we advanced rapidly on the enemy, driv-
1g him from the position near the church.   Here we halted and
djusted the line, and the Second and Fifteenth coming up, General
.ershaw ordered me to join onto the Fifteenth, and after moving
y the right flank about 300 yards were fronted and moved forward,
nd after advancing about 200 yards came upon the enemy under a
eavy fire, driving them from the position.   Darkness preventing
arther advance, we encamped here for the night.

In this engagement the regiment lost 2 men killed and 20 wounded;
1ost of the wounds were severe.

The regiment and brigade remained here until December 20, when
e marched in the direction of the Holston River.

On the 21st we crossed the river, and on the 23d came to our pres-
nt camp.

D. McINTYRE,

Captain, Commanding Eighth South Carolina Regiment.

Col. J. D. NANCE, *Commanding Brigade.*

———

No. 68.

Report of Capt. Stephen H. Sheldon, Fifteenth South Carolina
Infantry.

HDQRS. FIFTEENTH SOUTH CAROLINA REGIMENT,
Russellville, Tenn., January 9, 1864.

SIR : I have the honor to submit the following report of the oper-
1tions of this command from the time of its leaving Chattanooga
1ntil the arrival at this camp :

On the evening of November 4, 1863, pursuant to orders from bri-
3ade headquarters, the regiment took up the line of march with the
1rigade for Tyner's Station, on the East Tennessee and Georgia Rail-
·oad.

We arrived within the vicinity of the station on November 5, and
1n the 7th took the cars for Sweet Water, at which place we arrived
1n the 8th, and went into camp in the vicinity of the village.

On the 12th instant, moved with the brigade to Philadelphia, and
1n the 13th to the vicinity of Morganton, and on the night of the
ame day marched to Loudon.

On the 15th, crossed the Tennessee on the pontoon bridge and pur-
ued after the enemy, who had retreated that morning some 7 miles,
when we halted and remained until morning.

Next day came up with the enemy at Campbell's Station, when the
1rigade formed in line of battle.   The regiment occupied its proper
position in the line, and with one company thrown forward as skirmishers advanced with it.   The enemy meantime fell back, and the

command after advancing 800 or 900 yards was ordered to halt. W were then marched by flank some half mile or farther in the direc tion the enemy had taken, when we were again formed in line of bat tle and ordered to advance on the position the enemy occupied whe last seen before night came on, and which was distinguishable by the camp-fires they lighted and left burning. Upon reaching this poin it was found the enemy had retreated. The troops were ordered t halt for the night, and Major Gist was also ordered to send six com panies forward to picket the Knoxville road. Companies A, C, B K, E, and H, under Capt. J. B. Davis, were ordered to perform thi duty.

Resumed the pursuit early next morning, coming up with the en emy's rear guard some 5 miles from Knoxville. General Kershaw or dered Major Gist to move with his regiment, along with Colonel Hen agan, who was ordered to make a *détour* to the right, and if possibl get in the enemy's rear and attack him, while the rest of the brigad pressed him in front. Owing to the distance we had to go to get i the rear of the enemy, they were driven off by the troops that as sailed them in front before we had arrived in the position desired t be occupied, and which would have cut off the enemy's retreat ha we succeeded. The regiment then marched to rejoin the brigade which it succeeded in doing shortly before the column was halted i sight of Fort Loudon.

On the 19th instant, when the brigade advanced on the enemy' position at Armstrong's house, the regiment occupied the extrem right next the Holston River. Owing to the nature of the groun in our front, when near our picket lines the regiment was marche by a flank along the river bank until the right reached the positio occupied by Colonel Henagan on the picket line. Major Gist halte the regiment here and ordered the men to close up, and moving dow the line to see that the order was promptly obeyed, he was shot b one of the enemy's sharpshooters concealed behind their breast works in front, and instantly expired. The command then devolve upon Capt. J. B. Davis, the senior officer present. Just at this mo ment Lieutenant Doby, of General Kershaw's staff, gave Captai Davis orders to charge the hill in his front. The order was give and the hill carried with a rush, and with but little resistance fron the enemy, who were posted behind the trees and in the houses abou Armstrong's premises. The regiment continued to press on rapidl until ordered to halt and fall back to Armstrong's house, where w threw up a sort of breastwork of rails, to be used in case the enem should attempt to regain the position.

The regiment lost in that affair its brave and intrepid commander Maj. William M. Gist. Company K, of the regiment, which was o picket duty during the day, had 2 men killed and 4 wounded.

During the siege there were no other casualties in the command and nothing occurred in which the regiment was engaged worthy o mention until the afternoon of December 4. The regiment was o picket that day.

Late in the afternoon the enemy advanced three companies agains our right, where the line was weakest and least protected, evidentl with a view to discover our number and strength. The companie on the right gave them good information by several well-directe volleys, which seemed to check their curiosity rather suddenly, an sent them back to their intrenchments with more haste than is pre scribed by tactics for movements of the kind.

That night, at 11 o'clock, the regiment was withdrawn, under the
rection of Lieutenant-Colonel Rutherford, of the Third South Caro-
na Regiment, in a most successful manner, and without arousing
e suspicions of the enemy as to the nature of our movement. We
en followed on after the brigade, which had preceded us several
urs, and caught up with it next morning about 9 miles northeast
Knoxville. The regiment continued the marches along with the
igade until we arrived within 8 miles of Rogersville, where we
lted and rested for several days.

On December 14, accompanied by the rest of the brigade, the com-
and marched in the direction of Bean's Station. Finding the
emy at this place, measures were taken to attack, and, if possible,
pture him. We occupied the extreme right, and after the brigade
d been put in position along the slope of the Clinch Mountains we
lvanced upon the enemy at a charge and drove him back from his
sition. We were then moved farther to the right and again ad-
nced, capturing a few prisoners and killing and wounding some
w. Night coming on soon after, we were ordered by the general
mmanding brigade to halt, stack arms, and rest for the night.

The regiment had only 7 men wounded and none killed.

Remained in the vicinity of Bean's Station until the 20th, when we
ceived orders to march with the brigade to Long's Ferry.

On the 21st, crossed the Holston, and on the 22d marched to this
mp.

During six weeks of severe campaigning, with many hardships and
privations, this command has been particularly fortunate.

Our whole losses since we left Chattanooga are as follows:

	Killed.	Wounded.	Total.
ficers	1	......	1
n	2	11	13
Aggregate	3	11	14

The command suffered during the marches for want of shoes and
roper clothing, and oftentimes scarcity of rations. However, these
fferings were all borne with becoming fortitude by the brave and
llant men, of which this command is a part, composing this army.

S. H. SHELDON,
Captain, Commanding Fifteenth South Carolina Regiment.

Capt. C. R. HOLMES, *Assistant Adjutant-General.*

No. 69.

*eport of Lieut. William C. Harris, Adjutant James' (South Car-
olina) battalion.*

HEADQUARTERS JAMES' BATTALION,
Camp near Russellville, East Tenn., January 7, 1864.

CAPTAIN: Synopsis of this command since leaving Chattanooga,
enn.:

This battalion left Chattanooga, Tenn., on the night of November
1863, and arrived at the railroad—East Tennessee and Atlanta,
yner's Station—and there remained until the 5th instant, when it

took the train for Sweet Water on the 8th, and arrived at that place on the 9th and encamped until the 12th instant, when it again took up line of march for Philadelphia, encamping at the latter place for the night, resuming the march on the following day to Little Tennessee River.

On the night of the 13th, marched to Loudon, and there encamped until the 15th, and crossed the river at that place on pontoons, and marched again for Campbell's Station, where it arrived on the 16th driving the enemy toward Knoxville.

On the 17th instant, we came in sight of the city of Knoxville found the enemy well posted and strongly fortified.

On the 18th we had a skirmish fight with the enemy, driving him from his outposts, losing 1 man killed and 26 wounded.   On the 18th we encamped or bivouacked near Armstrong's house, remaining comparatively quiet, with exception of intrenching ourselves from the fire of the enemy's Loudon fort.

On the night of the 28th, charged the enemy's rifle-pits, driving them from them, losing 3 men wounded ; enemy's loss not known Hearing the news of the discomfiture of our forces at Chattanooga we left Knoxville on the night of December 4. We marched a night and resumed the march next morning, and continued the march toward Rutledge, where we arrived on the 6th, and encamped until the 8th, when we resumed the march in direction of Rogersville, passing Bean's Station and taking up camp 8 miles this side Rogersville, where we remained until the 14th, and retraced our steps toward Bean's Station, and there coming up with the enemy, made an attack upon him and drove him from his position, losing 3 men Enemy's loss not known.

On the 20th, we left Bean's Station and crossed the Holston River at [Long's] Ferry on the 21st, and marched to Russellville on December 22, 1863, and at this place took up winter quarters.

W. C. HARRIS,
Adjutant.

Capt. C. R. HOLMES, *Assistant Adjutant-General.*

No. 70.

Report of Lieut. Col. N. L. Hutchins, jr., Third Battalion Georgia Sharpshooters, commanding Wofford's brigade.

CAMP NEAR RUSSELLVILLE, TENN.,
January 1, 1864.

MAJOR : I have the honor to submit the following report of the operations of Wofford's brigade during the late campaign.   In consequence of the changes that have occurred in brigade and regiment commanders it is necessarily imperfect :

The brigade was withdrawn from our lines at Chattanooga on the night of November 4 last, and on the 6th was transported by railroad from Tyner's Station to Sweet Water, where it remained in camp some days.

On the 12th it took up the line of march and moved by way of Philadelphia to a point on the Tennessee River about 6 miles above Loudon, where it arrived at 2 p. m. the 13th.

At 12 o'clock on the night of the 13th the march was resumed and the command arrived at Loudon at daybreak on the morning of the 14th.   Here it remained until the 15th, when it crossed the Tennessee

iver and pursued the line of march to a point near Lenoir's Station
id bivouacked for the night.

On the 16th the march was continued to Campbell's Station, where
ie enemy had halted and made a stand. Disposition for battle was
ade and the line advanced, but the brigade did not become engaged,
or did the enemy's artillery, which kept up a sharp fire on the line
it advanced, do any serious injury.

That night the enemy retreated and next morning (the 17th) the
ursuit was continued until we arrived in sight of the enemy's posi-
on and fortifications at Knoxville, when the brigade was moved to
ie left and took position near Crawford's house, where it remained
ith one battalion on picket until the 18th, when it was relieved by
eneral Anderson's brigade, and then moved back and took its proper
osition in the line of the division.

Having advanced the picket line to the railroad, 600 to 800 yards
om Fort Loudon, a rifle-pit was dug, by direction and under the
iperintendence of Colonel Ruff, 100 yards in front of the picket
osts on the left, thus leaving its left partially exposed and unpro-
ected ; it was, therefore, used only for vedettes and sharpshooters.

A sortie was made on this work on the morning of the 24th by a
egiment of the enemy (the Second Michigan). Crossing the rail-
oad far to the left it moved down, its right flank perpendicular to
ur picket line, thereby getting completely on the flank and in rear
f the rifle-pit, and there being but few men on post made an easy
apture of it. A portion of the Third Georgia Battalion Sharp-
hooters being on duty at this position, the remaining portion was
ioved up to its support and soon succeeded in driving the enemy
rom the works with a loss, as nearly as could be ascertained, of 50
r 60 killed, wounded, and prisoners, while the battalion's loss was
men wounded, 2 of them mortally. The pickets of General Law's
rigade took a part in this affair.

During the night of the 28th of that month the Twenty-fourth
ieorgia Regiment, in co-operation with the pickets of other brigades,
dvanced the line to a position about 250 yards from the fort, cap-
uring a few pickets.

On the morning of the 29th the brigade moved out under orders
o assault the works. The battalion of sharpshooters having re-
ieved the Twenty-fourth Georgia on picket, immediately the artil-
ery opened fire on the fort. In accordance with orders advanced
kirmishers to easy rifle range and kept up a rapid fire into the port
ioles, which effectually prevented the working of their guns by the
nemy until the column of attack had advanced to the summit of
he hill near to the fort.

The disposition for assault was column of regiments, and in the fol-
owing order: First, Phillips Legion; second, Eighteenth Georgia Reg-
ment; third, Sixteenth Georgia Regiment, and fourth, Cobb's Legion.

The advance was obstructed by fallen timber, tangled bushes,
&c., but so soon as this was passed the column formed in good order
ind moved forward with a cheerfulness, confidence, and enthusiasm
that promised success ; but arrived at the fort the column encountered a ditch 4 to 6 feet deep, 8 to 10 feet wide, and extending along
the length of the work to the rifle-pits on either side. The height
of the parapet, estimating from the bottom of the ditch, was about
18 feet, and its exterior slope at an angle of 65 to 70 degrees, with a
base line. The berme, very narrow, soon wore away, and it was with
difficulty that a foothold could be obtained upon it ; yet by assistance

of their comrades some men succeeded in getting on the slope, but not in sufficient force to venture over the parapet into the fort. After remaining at the fort for twenty or twenty-five minutes and failing of success, the brigade withdrew and returned to its camp.

In this assault Phillips Legion was commanded by Maj. Joseph Hamilton, wounded; the Eighteenth Georgia Regiment, by Capt. John A. Crawford; the Sixteenth Georgia Regiment, by Lieut. Col. Henry P. Thomas, killed; Cobb's Legion, by Maj. William D. Conyers, and the brigade by Col. S. Z. Ruff, of the Eighteenth Georgia Regiment, who was also killed.

The conduct of both officers and men in this assault was admirable. The loss of the brigade on that occasion was 246 killed, wounded and missing.

From the time of the assault on Fort Loudon to the night of December 4 last the brigade continued to perform picket duty on the line in front of the enemy's works. The siege was then raised and the brigade withdrew from its position and moved off with the division along the road leading by way of Rutledge, Bean's Station, and Mooresburg, and on the 9th or 10th arrived at a position 6 miles from Rogersville, and there went into camp and remained until the 14th. On that day it returned to Bean's Station, and the enemy having been driven back by other brigades, this, not being engaged, went into camp in the valley near Kentucky Gap.

On the 20th, it moved to Long's Ferry, where, on the night of the 21st, it crossed the Holston River by flat-boat, and on the 22d marched to its present encampment.

The number, with a list of casualties during these operations, has been heretofore forwarded.

During the campaign, particularly while at Sweet Water and on the march from Knoxville and in camp in Hawkins County, the supply of rations was scanty, and some bad men would straggle and commit depredations on private people. Many were without shoes and much in need of clothing and blankets, and experienced severe and disagreeable weather; but notwithstanding these privations, hardships, and sufferings, they continued cheerful, and their general conduct was exemplary.

Since halting at its present position the men of the brigade have been engaged in the construction of huts, chimneys to tents, &c., and are now quite comfortable.

Respectfully submitted.

N. L. HUTCHINS, Jr.,
Lieutenant-Colonel, Commanding Brigade.

Maj. JAMES M. GOGGIN, *Assistant Adjutant-General.*

No. 71.

Report of Brig. Gen. Benjamin G. Humphreys, C. S. Army, commanding brigade.

HEADQUARTERS BRIGADE,
Near Russellville, Tenn., January 2, 1864.

MAJOR : In obedience to orders from division headquarters, I have the honor to make the following report of the operations of the brigade from the time we left Chattanooga to the present time :

The brigade left the foot of Lookout Mountain on November 4

fter dark ; took the cars at the tunnel in Missionary Ridge the next ay, and arrived at Loudon on the 14th ; crossed the Tennessee River on the 15th.

On the 16th, the corps overtook the enemy at Campbell's Station n line of battle, when skirmishing and a heavy artillery duel en-ued.   My brigade being on the extreme left of our line, my pickets ecame engaged with the enemy for a short time only.   At dark the nemy retired toward Knoxville, where we found them next day.

On the 18th, General Kershaw's brigade drove the enemy into their vorks and our army settled around the town of Knoxville for a reg-lar siege.

On the 28th, General Longstreet ordered an assault on the enemy's vorks be made the next morning.   In accordance with the arrange-ient and understanding of the plan of attack the enemy's pickets vere driven in at moonrise, about 10 o'clock that night, and our ickets intrenched within short range of their works by daylight.

At daylight my pickets and General Bryan's, on my right, com-ienced firing on the southwest salient and south curtain of the fort, ollowed immediately by our artillery from Armstrong Hill.   The pening of the artillery was the signal for the infantry to make the ssault.   I immediately put the Thirteenth Mississippi Regiment, nder the command of Colonel McElroy, and the Seventeenth Mis-issippi Regiment, under the command of Lieutenant-Colonel Fiser, i motion, the Eighteenth and Twenty-first Mississippi Regiments eing on picket, and was followed by three regiments of General Bryan's brigade, all in column of regiments, and directed against he southwest salient of the fort.   Moving slowly, but with zeal, ope, and enthusiasm, through a tangled abatis for about 150 yards, e came to comparatively open ground, where a rushing charge was iade upon the fort.   The column was arrested in its progress by a itch from 4½ to 6 feet deep and from 8 to 12 feet wide, fringed with network of wire, with a parapet about 10 or 12 feet high, the earth et from previous rains and freezing.

In the meantime, the enemy firing artillery and musketry from all oints of their works, throwing hand grenades, billets of wood, axes, c., over the parapet into the ditch, killing and mangling our men. ur pickets soon silenced the artillery and sharpshooters on the outh side of the fort, but a raking fire continued from the west side, ronting the railroad.   The intrepidity and dauntless efforts of the nemy, the absence of ladders, fascines, &c., and the strength of the orks rendered every effort to escalade them unavailing.   Those iat succeeded in climbing up the parapet to the crest were shot own, and rolling back dragged all below them back into the ditch. olonel McElroy and 5 other officers were killed; Lieutenant-Colonel iser and 8 other officers wounded.   The whole column was thrown ito confusion and compelled to retire.   The Thirteenth and Sev-nteenth Regiments rallied behind the pickets and formed, losing i the assault 140 men killed, wounded, and missing.

That evening I received orders to hold the brigade in readiness to eave Knoxville.

On December 4, the whole army moved after dark, and passing hrough Rutledge and Bean's Station, halted at Cloud Creek on he 8th.

On the 16th [15th], the whole army retraced its steps and drove he enemy from Bean's Station toward Rutledge.

On the 17th [16th], I was ordered to move my brigade to the gap

in Clinch Mountain and attack the enemy in that position.   Arriv
ing at the gap about 10 o'clock, I found the One hundred and seven
teenth Regiment Indiana (six-months' men) had retreated on th
crest of the mountain toward Notchey Gap, leaving all their baggag
and transportation behind them.   I immediately dispatched Majo
Donald, in command of Thirteenth Regiment, in pursuit, who fol
lowed them to Notchey Gap, and finding they had succeeded i
making their escape toward Rutledge, returned with 6 prisoners
We captured in all 12 prisoners, 6 wagons, 12 mules, all their tents
cooking utensils, clothing, and commissaries.

On the 20th, we were ordered to cross the Holston River and en
camp near Russellville, where we are now encamped in winte
quarters.

In reviewing the operations of this brigade, I am called upon t
notice the patience, fortitude, and constancy with which the troop
endured the privations and hardships of the campaign ; the ardo
zeal, and courage with which they discharged every duty ; and espe
cially the valor and heroic daring of the Thirteenth and Seventeent
Mississippi Regiments in the assault upon Fort Loudon, at Knoxvill

The loss of the heroic McElroy is irreparable.   A grateful countr
will mourn his untimely end, and embalm his memory among he
brightest ornaments.

Lieutenant-Colonel Fiser and Captain Cherry, of the Seventeent
Regiment, were greatly distinguished for their gallantry and intre
pidity, and their temporary loss to the service is deeply deplored.

Major Donald, of the Thirteenth, and Captain Brown, of the sam
regiment ; Captain Wright and Lieutenant Greene, of the Sever
teenth Regiment, exhibited the highest qualities of a soldier in rally
ing and forming their shattered regiments.

I am greatly indebted to Capt. J. A. Barksdale, adjutant-genera
and Captain Hobart, inspector, for their invaluable services throug
out the campaign.

Very respectfully,

BENJ. G. HUMPHREYS,
Brigadier-General, Commanding.

Maj. JAMES M. GOGGIN,
Assistant Adjutant-General.

No. 72.

*Report of Col. Edward Ball, Fifty-first Georgia Infantry, comman
ing Bryan's brigade.*

HEADQUARTERS BRYAN'S BRIGADE,
Near Russellville, Tenn., January 13, 1864.

MAJOR : In obedience to circular from division headquarters, I ha
the honor to make the following report of operations of this briga
since it left Chattanooga :

On the evening of November 4, 1863, left camp in Lookout Vall
en route for Sweet Water, East Tenn., and arrived at Tyner's Stati
on the evening of the 5th.   The troops were ordered on board t
cars and remained at this place until the morning of the 6th, wh
the brigade started for Sweet Water and arrived at that place on t

evening of the same day. Went into camp at this place and remained until the 12th, when, in obedience to orders, this brigade, with the balance of the division, moved in the direction of Loudon, Tenn., arriving at Philadelphia, on the East Tennessee and Georgia Railroad, on the evening of the same day. Bivouacked here until the morning of the 13th, when we moved in the direction of Morganton, which is 6 miles northeast of Loudon. Reached it the same evening and bivouacked for the night.

At about 12 p. m. on the 13th, the march was again resumed in the direction of Loudon, arriving at that place about 6 a. m. on the 14th.

Here the brigade remained until the 15th, when it crossed the pontoon bridge across the Tennessee River below Loudon and took up the line of march in the direction of Knoxville, and bivouacked for the night about 7 miles from Loudon.

On the morning of the 16th, the march was again resumed, and about 12 m. we came up with the enemy at Campbell's Station. Here, although exposed to a severe fire from the enemy's artillery for several hours, our loss was very slight.

On the morning of the 17th, the brigade again moved in the direction of Knoxville, and arrived in front of Fort Loudon, south of and defending the place, by the Knoxville and Loudon road, about 10 p. m.

The brigade was here formed in line of battle and so remained until November 20, when one regiment (the Tenth Georgia Volunteers, under command of Lieutenant-Colonel Holt), was detached and sent to the south side of Holston River.

Capt. A. J. McBride, commanding Tenth Georgia Volunteers, remarks in his report that—

On November 23, a detachment of 17 men from Companies F and H, of my regiment, were attacked by about 100 of the enemy. They drove him back, inflicting a severe loss in killed and wounded. The participants in this little affair distinguished themselves by their coolness and courage, and I would particularly mention Lieut. J. T. Stovall, Company F, of my regiment, who led the charge which resulted in routing the attacking force.

The brigade crossed and recrossed the Holston on several occasions in flat-boats, and finally rejoined the balance of the division on the north side of the Holston on November 27.

On the night of the 28th, the Tenth Georgia Volunteers, under command of Lieut. Col. W. C. Holt, was detached to drive the enemy from his rifle-pits in front of Fort Loudon. The rifle-pits having been carried, the regiment remained all night and until the evening of the 29th, without participating in the assault on Fort Loudon.

On the night of the 28th, the three remaining regiments of the brigade, viz, Fifty-third, Fifty-first, and Fiftieth Georgia Volunteers, were formed into columns of regiments immediately in rear of and supporting General Humphreys' brigade. The assaulting column moved forward about daybreak, and though our advance was obstinately contested by the enemy, we gained the summit of the hill and reached the work with a comparatively small loss; but, owing to the obstructions with which the work was surrounded, it was found impossible with appliances in our possession to carry it, and the troops were therefore withdrawn. A great many men and officers having fallen into the moat in attempting to scale the walls of the work, and being unable to get out again when we retired, were consequently taken by the enemy.

The loss in this brigade on that occasion was 8 officers and 19 men killed, 15 officers and 106 men wounded, and 5 officers and 59 men missing, making a total of 28 officers and 184 men, and an aggregate loss of 212 men and officers killed, wounded, and missing.

The brigade having returned to camp, remained there until December 3, when it again crossed to the south side of the Holston and remained there until the evening of the 4th, when it again recrossed the Holston and rejoined the division.

Withdrew from Knoxville on the night of the 4th, marching in the direction of Rogersville, and arrived at Blevins' farm on the 9th.

The brigade remained in camp at this place until the 14th, when it marched to Bean's Station, and supported General Kershaw in passing the enemy's left flank.

Left Bean's Station on the 20th; crossed the Holston at Long's Ferry on the 21st, and arrived at this place on December 23, 1863.

I have the honor to be, major, very respectfully, your obedient servant,

E. BALL,
Colonel, Commanding Brigade.

Maj. JAMES M. GOGGIN,
Assistant Adjutant-General.

No. 73.

Report of Brig. Gen. Micah Jenkins, C. S. Army, commanding Hood's division.

HEADQUARTERS HOOD'S DIVISION,
Morristown, Tenn., January 13, 1864.

COLONEL: In obedience to orders from headquarters forces East Tennessee, I have the honor to submit the following report of the operations of this division during the campaign commencing at the time of our leaving Lookout Mountain to our reaching Morristown, inclusive:

Leaving our camp near Lookout Mountain on the night of November 5, 1863, to prevent being observed by the enemy, with severe marching on account of the weather, we reached the railroad station the next morning, and after some delay, on account of the inefficient working of the railroad, arrived at Sweet Water, Tenn., with part of the command. Collecting with difficulty a few days' rations, and before the railroad had brought up Law's brigade, we commenced our march to Knoxville via Loudon. Before reaching Loudon I was joined by Law's brigade. Arrangements having been perfected by the lieutenant-general commanding for effecting a crossing of the Tennessee at Loudon, a detachment of Jenkins' brigade, under Captain Foster, of the Palmetto Sharpshooters, was sent across to seize the enemy's picket, and the rest of that regiment was afterward crossed to cover the laying of the pontoon bridge.

As soon as the bridge was completed this division, on the morning of November 14, marched over, and in accordance with the directions of the lieutenant-general commanding proceeded to construct breast-works for the protection of the bridge. Scouting parties having been sent out, reported during the afternoon the enemy advancing, and just before dusk a brisk skirmish ensued, which was hand-

somely sustained by our skirmishers.   The enemy advanced in line
of battle again t the right of my line of pickets, composed of skirmishers of General Jenkins' brigade, and after a sharp skirmish retired with a loss of some 40-odd killed and wounded, our loss being
very slight.

The next morning, placing the skirmishers of the entire division
under command of Lieutenant-Colonel Logan, of the Hampton
Legion, Jenkins' brigade, and giving them strong support, I ordered
an advance, following with the division, such being the orders of the
lieutenant-general.   The skirmishers soon became hotly engaged,
and charging handsomely drove back the enemy from a stony hill,
capturing a caisson and a quantity of baggage and inflicting upon
them severe loss.

We lost in this engagement some 8 or 10 killed and wounded.

Leaving Robertson's brigade to watch the enemy, who had retired
toward the railroad, I advanced the division in column on a converg-
ing road toward Lenoir's Station.   Arriving in the vicinity late in
the day, I sent forward Colonel Walker's regiment (Palmetto Sharpshooters, South Carolina Volunteers), and Colonel Coward's Fifth
South Carolina Volunteers, to seize commanding hills, and then
placed the brigades in position as they came up.

Brig. Gen. G. T. Anderson was directed to take possession of an
advanced hill, and from thence to feel his way to the railroad if possible; this was about dark.   He gained the hill without opposition.
Colonel Bratton, commanding Jenkins' brigade, was directed to occupy a hill in his front, which was thought to command the station,
but owing to the darkness a nearer hill was occupied by mistake.
The troops were ordered to repose in line and frequent scouting parties ordered to be kept up during the night by the advanced brigades
to give news of any movements of the enemy.

Early the next morning an advance was made, but the enemy had,
by keeping up a vigilant line of skirmishers, prevented our getting
information and had decamped during the night.   Pressing vigorously forward I engaged the enemy's rear with a strong line of skirmishers from the division under charge of Lieutenant-Colonel Logan
and Lieutenant-Colonel Wylie, Fifth South Carolina Volunteers.
Supporting this line closely and effectively with Jenkins' brigade;
the other brigades of the division were ordered to follow without
delay, my instructions being to press upon the enemy's rear, and if
possible to bring him to bay, and give an opportunity for McLaws'
division, as I understood it, by moving on a different road, to strike
the enemy in flank or rear.   I engaged the enemy sharply, so as to
compel him several times to make stands to save his guns, and thus
gained great delay on his part.   We soon in our advance captured a
company of the enemy, and a large number of wagons loaded with
commissary, ordnance, and other stores.

The enemy were driven from point to point by heavy attacks of
the skirmishers, strongly re-enforced from Jenkins' brigade, till I
had forced their rear so close upon their trains and main body that
they were obliged to offer battle with their whole force.   Starting at
about 7 a. m., we had forced upon the enemy at Campbell's Station,
distant 10 or 11 miles, by 11 a. m., and succeeded from all indications
in greatly harassing and demoralizing the enemy.   At this place the
road upon which McLaws' division was in march joined the road by
which we had marched, but that division had not as yet arrived.
Hoping to throw the enemy, who had not formed line, into sufficient

confusion to warrant an attack on my part with the brigades under
my command, two of which (Jenkins' and Anderson's) were up, I
ordered forward a battery to open upon the dense columns of the
enemy, and having already Jenkins' brigade in line upon their front
went to place Anderson on their left flank. Not understanding, I
presume, the importance of the movement, which could only succeed if done at the right moment, and fearing that the battery ordered would be destroyed by the superior artillery force of the enemy, Colonel Alexander, chief of artillery, countermanded during
my absence the order for the battery to advance and open, and about
this time the lieutenant-general commanding arrived upon the field.

The enemy had now formed his line to receive our attack. My
command was disposed as follows : Jenkins' brigade fronting the
enemy, Anderson's in line to the right. Law was ordered on Anderson's right, with his right advanced and threatening the enemy's
flank. Benning's brigade (small) in reserve. Maintaining our position for a long time under very severe shelling, with considerable
loss in Jenkins' brigade and slight loss in Anderson's, at about 3 p.
m. no movement upon the enemy's right flank having been made as
I expected by McLaws' division, I reported to the lieutenant-general
that the enemy had been, I thought, retiring his forces, and received
instructions to proceed along the hills on the enemy's left and make
an attack on their flank.

Every indication being that the enemy was *in transitu*, and the
shortness of the time before it would be too dark for movements impressing upon me the necessity of speed, I gave such orders as would
institute most prompt and vigorous movements. Brigadier-General
Law, being on the right, was ordered to move, followed by Anderson's
brigade, far enough along the hills upon the enemy's left to bring
the next to the last of Anderson's regiments opposite the enemy's
guns, so that not only the guns but their supporting lines might
be struck in flank and rear by an attack in line by the two brigades.
Benning was ordered to cover the right flank of the attacking line
with his brigade. Withdrawing Jenkins' brigade by a flank movement from the open field in the front of the enemy into the woods, I
directed the primary movements of the other brigades to be made
with the utmost promptitude.

The hills and ground over which our column was required to pass
was very difficult, being covered with a close undergrowth of scraggy
oaks, and the distance having been increased by the enemy's front
lines going back under the fire of our artillery, it required considerable time to attain the desired position upon their flank, their lines
having open ground to retire upon, being able to move at least as
rapidly as our column. Hastening the movements, however, about
the time Jenkins' brigade reported, General Law reported himself in
the directed position, and I ordered Anderson's immediately to the
attack. Upon reaching Law's brigade I found that he had not gone
far enough to the right to put Anderson in position, but his own
brigade by advancing would strike the battery and enemy's flank.
Sending to stop Anderson, I directed in person General Law to make
the attack with his brigade independently of Anderson.

Having received my assurance of support and protection to his
flanks, he commenced his advance, and the other brigades were
promptly placed to support and follow up his attack. In a few
minutes, greatly to my surprise, I received a message from General
Law that in advancing his brigade had obliqued so much to the left

s to have gotten out of its line of attack. This causeless and inex-
usable movement lost us the few moments in which success from
nis point could be attained. Although it was getting dark, I de-
ided to try and repeat the intended move on the enemy's next posi-
.on, or to cut the road upon which they were retiring, and ordered
Benning, who was on the right, forward, directing General Law to
rolong Benning's line by a flank movement.

Brigadier-General Law on seeing me stated that his brigade had
een misled by the mistake of his regiment of direction in closing
he interval between it and Anderson's brigade on its left. I do
ot conceive that a regiment of direction should have been so in-
tructed as to leave such a change of direction discretionary, and
he immediate directing presence of the brigade commander, by
whom the position of the enemy to be attacked had been seen and
xamined, should have corrected the mistake in its inception. Gen-
ral Anderson states that his brigade was partially lapped when the
wo came together, and I had distinctly and emphatically told
eneral Law, when he spoke of the relative movements of Ander-
on's brigade, that he would attack independently of Anderson.

Movements by Benning's, Law's, and Anderson's brigades to cut
he enemy's line of retreat, though promptly and vigorously made,
vere defeated by the darkness, the difficulties of the ground, and
he enemy's movements in retreat, and no other opportunity was
resented for attack. The gallantry and dash of our skirmishers
uring this day has never been surpassed. Attacking fearlessly lines
f battle and artillery, Lieutenant-Colonel Logan, Lieutenant-Colonel
Vylie, and Capt. S. D. Cockrell (the latter of the Ninth Georgia)
istinguished themselves among many others. We captured about
00 prisoners, and drove the enemy with heavy loss from every stand
hey made. The movements of the brigades were prompt and will-
ig.

Our loss during the day was as follows :

Command.	Killed.	Wounded.	Total.
nderson's brigade...........	3	34	37
enkins' brigade	18	106	124
aw's brigade..	1	12	13
Total	22	152	174

Moving the next morning to Knoxville, nothing of special or mo-
nentous interest took place till the attack on the enemy's works on
he morning of November 29, the intermediate time being occupied
n gaining positions and strengthening them. Handsome skirmish-
ng was done by Anderson's brigade in gaining the hill we occupied
.s a permanent line. Two brigades (Law's and Robertson's) having
een detached for duty across the river, my command was reduced
o three brigades (one very small), and being called on to maintain
he old line with the reduced force, my picket duty was heavy, and
till further reduced the disposable force. The part assigned this
ommand being to follow up the attack by which McLaws' division
vas expected to carry Fort Loudon by an attack on the enemy's
reastworks, and after carrying them to sweep down their lines and
ain as much ground as I could advantageously, I directed Ander-

son's brigade to lead the movement of the division. Being com
pelled by a deep railroad cut running along my front to cross th
railroad on the right of my line, I massed my troops near the righ
to support and continue the attack when begun.

By previous arrangements with the lieutenant-general comman
ing, I directed Lieutenant-Colonel Logan, in charge of my picke
line, to advance during the night previous and drive in or captur
the enemy's picket line, and to place his skirmishers in rifle-pits a
close range to the enemy's breastworks, so as fully to comman
them. This was successfully done, capturing some 60 of the enemy
driving the rest into their works, and occupying such a positio
with the sharpshooters as greatly to embarrass the enemy durin
the attack of the next day.

Expecting the attack to be begun at first dawn, I placed Ande
son's brigade in position during the night, and at 4 a. m. massed th
other two brigades on my right.

Having explained the plan of operations to my brigade comman
ers and taken every precaution to follow up the attack successfully
I awaited the concerted signal. General Anderson, in accordanc
with the part assigned my command, was ordered to subordinat
his move as to time to the attacking column of McLaws. I i
structed him to break over the enemy's breastworks at a poin
which I designated to him personally about 100 yards to the left c
the fort, and then to wheel to the left and sweep down the breas
works. If, however, McLaws' attack upon the fort was unsucces
ful, he was instructed, after passing over the enemy's breastwork
instead of wheeling to the left to wheel to the right and take th
fort by an attack in reverse.

Just before the time for the expected attack, I received orders t
meet any demonstration the enemy might make on my line, whic
was an extended one, with my left brigade. In accordance wit
this order, I was compelled to send Jenkins' brigade some distanc
toward the left to be in position to meet such a demonstration, an
my effective force in hand for immediate use was thus reduced t
the brigade of Anderson, diminished by picket details to some 9(
or 1,000 rifles, and Benning's brigade, with about 500 rifles. Upo
a given signal the sharpshooters along the whole line opened a co
tinuous fire, and the attack was begun by McLaws' column. Givin
due time, as directed, Anderson's brigade advanced in two lines i
gallant style, and I then moved Benning's brigade forward to pres
any advantage that might be gained. The columns of McLaw
instead of directing their attack against the salient indicated to n
by the lieutenant-general commanding as the point for their attac
advanced to the right of the designated point, and after a vain effo
failed to carry the work and were compelled to retire.

Anderson's brigade—as stated by General Anderson, through son
misunderstanding of his instructions by the colonel commanding h
front line, who was misled by the movements of McLaws' column s
far to the right—instead of directing its attack, as I had ordere
against the breastworks to the left of the fort, and then, in case c
the failure of McLaws' column taking it in reverse, also moved tc
far to the right, and before the staff officer and courier, dispatche
the moment I perceived their misdirection to order them to th
point already designated, could reach them, the distance being sho
from their starting point to the fort, became involved in the dire
attack upon the side of the fort.

After gallant efforts on the part of officers and men to overcome the physical difficulties and storm the work, the brigade fell back to its previous position, and then formed for further action in good spirits and undemoralized.

I beg to refer to the report* of this affair by General Anderson for causes of mistake in carrying out instructions and for a fuller view of the performance of his brigade.

Upon seeing the attacking column falling back, I sent orders to Jenkins' brigade to return to the right, and held it and Benning's brigade in hand for further movements, but soon received orders to reoccupy our old line.

The loss sustained by Anderson's brigade in its gallant attack was 4 killed, 33 wounded, —— missing.

Upon the withdrawal of our army from the siege of Knoxville my command covered the rear. The withdrawal from the immediate presence of the enemy (our advance line being within 250 yards of their works) was effected without loss, and we marched leisurely, with convenient stops for collecting commissary supplies, to the vicinity of Rogersville.

Notwithstanding a great want of shoes in the command, a very handsome forced march was made on December 14 to Bean's Station. Being, unfortunately for us, in rear of the column, it was nearly dark before we reached the scene of the spirited conflict with the enemy of Johnson's and part of McLaws' divisions. After considerable delay by the slowness with which the preceding division (McLaws') crossed a small creek, being ordered to support the left of the line, I placed my leading brigade (Anderson's) on the left of Johnson's line, and had it advanced in concert with Johnson's line, but found no enemy in front, and it being now dark no further move on the part of my command was required.

The next morning I received orders to advance my command, numbering some 2,500 rifles, to Rutledge and assist Major-General Martin, who, with his cavalry, was to cross the Holston River in the enemy's rear. Advancing as directed, my skirmishers engaged those of the enemy about 3 miles from Bean's Station, and I found the Yankees, some 6,000 in number, drawn up in line of battle behind a formidable breastwork of rails, with each flank upon neighboring heights. Sending back a report of the facts to the lieutenant-general commanding, he soon appeared in the front, and I was informed that General Martin had failed to cross as expected.

The condition of the enemy's line as reported by Maj. W. H. Sellers, assistant adjutant-general of this division, after a reconnaissance, promising a chance for a successful flank attack if made in sufficient force, with the concurrence of the lieutenant-general commanding I rode to make a personal reconnaissance. It being then between 10 and 11 a. m., the lieutenant-general informed me that before I returned Brigadier-General Law would have arrived with the two brigades which had remained detached. After careful reconnaissance, I concluded that I could make a successful flank attack by using the entire division, and ordered Jenkins' brigade immediately forward to the enemy's right flank to make the attack, intending to support it with Law's brigade, and to use the other three brigades (two very small, together not exceeding 800 rifles) in pressing concertedly the enemy's front and left flank. On my re-

*Not found.

turn, however, General Law not having arrived, I was compelled to stop the movements of Jenkins' brigade.

Some time after this, and before the arrival of General Law, which took place about 2.30 p. m., the enemy, who had previously shown only dismounted cavalry, advanced an infantry force to the front Reports being brought me from General Benning, who was on my right, of the movement of long columns in view, and information from the lieutenant-general commanding that the enemy was reported to have both of their corps, I was induced to believe that they had brought their full force to the field, and no other troops being within supporting distance, was reluctantly obliged to recall Jenkins' brigade and give up my intention of attacking with this division alone, and so reported to the lieutenant-general commanding.

Late in the afternoon General Martin, having effected a crossing appeared upon the hills upon the enemy's right and opened a few guns, but when I became aware of his position it was too late.

The enemy withdrew during the night, and I was ordered in the morning to pursue, and, if possible, bring them to bay. Moving on as far as Rutledge, I received orders to cease the pursuit and return to camp.

On the morning of December 23, I proceeded with the division to Long's Ferry, on the Holston, and being delayed in beginning my passage till 1 p. m. by the preceding division, I worked into the night and succeeded with a single boat in crossing the entire division in eleven and one-half hours. Proceeding as soon as it was day to Morristown, the division rested from its fatigues in comfortable camps.

The campaign was rendered severe by want of shoes and clothing and failure of regular supplies of rations, but owing to the judicious arrangements of the marches there was much less suffering than might have been expected, and all was borne with commendable cheerfulness and high spirit by the men. There was exhibited, however, on the part of some, a tendency to straggle and a most disgraceful spirit of plunder, which by stringent measures has been restrained and corrected.

I fear that difficulties were increased and the full benefit of well aimed strategy prevented in this campaign by the absence of high and cordial sustaining support to loyal authority on the part of some high officers, and that the spirit of the army, instead of being encouraged and sustained against sufferings and necessary hardships by some from whom the country had a right to expect it, was, on the contrary depressed and recognition of dangers and hardships cultivated. Of this I have been able to find evidence for charges in but one case.

My humble efforts were during the greater part of the campaign greatly aided by the intelligence and activity of Maj. W. H. Sellers assistant adjutant-general of this division (whose aptitude for high military affairs I desire to call attention to), and by Maj. E. H. Cunningham, assistant adjutant and inspector-general; Capt. W. H. Whitner, assistant adjutant and inspector-general, and Lieut. J. W. Jamison, aide-de-camp. Surg. F. L. Parker, acting chief surgeon was also very efficient.

I take pleasure in mentioning the ability displayed by Brigadier Generals Anderson and Benning.

I had every satisfaction in the general conduct of the officers and men. Their boldness in danger, their patience under want and hardships, and their promptitude in obedience, entitle them to the confidence and thanks of their country.

The loss in the campaign was :

Command.	Killed.	Wounded.	Missing.	Total.
enkins' brigade	22	109	5	136
nderson's brigade	36	186	25	247
enning's brigade	1	5	......	6
aw's brigade	18	56	4	78
obertson's brigade	7	20	7	34
Total	84	376	41	501

I have the honor to be, colonel, most respectfully, your obedient ervant,

M. JENKINS,
Brigadier-General, Commanding.

Lieut. Col. G. MOXLEY SORREL,
Assistant Adjutant-General.

No. 74.

Report of Brig. Gen. Bushrod R. Johnson, C. S. Army, command-ing Buckner's division.

HEADQUARTERS BUCKNER'S DIVISION,
Morristown, January —, 1864.

SIR : In response to your communication dated headquarters forces n East Tennessee, Russellville, December 31, 1863, calling for a report of the operations of this division from the time of its coming within the command of Lieutenant-General Longstreet until the late at which it went into encampment at this place, I have the honor to submit the following summary :

On November 22 last, this division moved from Rossville, Tenn., t the foot of Missionary Ridge, under written orders and additional oral instructions from headquarters Army of Tennessee, for the pur-pose of being attached to Lieutenant-General Longstreet's command, t that time operating before Knoxville, where the Federal forces nder Burnside, routed in the open field, had found shelter.

The division consisted of :

Command.	Effective total.	Aggregate.
Brigadier-general commanding and staff	......	7
Escort	20	26
Gracie's brigade	1,541	1,953
Johnson's brigade	1,084	1,572
Reynolds' brigade	995	1,581
Williams' battalion artillery	246	a267
Total	3,886	5,406

a Or twelve guns.

This force was badly shod and poorly clad. The infantry, the artillery carriages, and baggage were ordered to be transported by rail, and the empty trains and the horses to move on the common road to Loudon.   At Chickamauga Station Maj. Gen. P. R. Cleburne whose division was moving under orders in conjunction with thi division, assumed command of the column.

With the approbation of General Cleburne, I left Chickamaug. Station on the evening of November 22, to proceed at the head of m command, in order to expedite the transfer of the troops to the Eas Tennessee railroad at Dalton, and the passage of the rivers a Charleston and Loudon.   At Charleston the transportation by rai to Loudon was only sufficient for the baggage, and the troops wer consequently put upon the march at that point.   They were, how ever, subsequently picked up and brought in by the train runnin, out to meet them.

On November 23, just as Gracie's brigade had with its baggage ammunition, &c., effected the crossing of the Hiwassee River a Charleston, I received a telegram from Major-General Cleburne ordering me to return with my command to Missionary Ridge.   Thi brigade immediately recrossed the river, and I then received a dis patch from Colonel Brent, of General Bragg's staff, to the effect tha the order for the return of troops to Missionary Ridge only applie to such of my troops as had not left Chickamauga, and that I woul proceed as previously ordered.

On November 24, I arrived at Loudon with a portion of Gracie' brigade, and communicated with Lieutenant-General Longstreet who directed me, by telegram, to move forward my command as fas as possible to Knoxville.   A pontoon bridge was then in process o construction at Huff's Ferry, below Loudon.   The ferry across th Tennessee at Loudon was being employed in crossing trains loadec with supplies to meet the pressing wants of the troops before Knox ville, as I was informed by Brigadier-General Vaughn, command ing at Loudon.   It was not, therefore, until afternoon of Novembe 25 that I was enabled to commence crossing my command, whicl was mainly effected by the ferry.

Johnson's brigade reached Loudon on the 25th, and I learned fron Colonel Fulton, commanding, that after a part of Reynolds' brigad was placed on the cars at Chickamauga Station, and when the trai was all ready to start, the cars containing the part of Reynolds' bri gade were detached, and all the troops which had not left Chicka mauga Depot, including the artillery of Buckner's division, wer ordered back to Missionary Ridge.   Two brigades (Johnson's anc Gracie's)—effective strength 2,625, aggregate 3,525—comprised th forces remaining under my command.

On November 27, I reported in person to Lieutenant-Genera Longstreet, Gracie's brigade having preceded me and joined hi command, and Colonel Fulton, in command of Johnson's brigade arrived in front of Knoxville on the 28th.

On Sunday, November 29, having previously received orders fron the lieutenant-general commanding to that effect, my comman moved at daylight at the signal for the attack from the rifle-pits i front of Fort Loudon, to support the assaulting column under Brig adier-General Humphreys.   Gracie's brigade advanced on the righ or south of the East Tennessee and Virginia Railroad, and Fulton' command moved from a position on the north of this road, distan some 800 or 1,000 yards from the fort.   In the advance the latte command crossed the railroad, which curved to the north in fron of the rifle-pits, and approached to within about 250 yards of the for on the left or north of the salient, on which the assault was made

t here came under the enemy's fire, especially from the rifle-pits on
the north of the fort. At this time Gracie's brigade, which was
moving up in rear and on the right, was ordered by the lieutenant-
general commanding, who was in its front, to be withdrawn, and
seeing it move to the rear, Johnson's brigade was halted, and the
men covered themselves from the enemy's fire by lying flat on the
ground. The attack was now abandoned, and my two brigades were
ordered to relieve Humphreys', Benning's, and Wofford's, and to
occupy with skirmishers our advanced rifle-pits within some 250
yards of the fort.

During the assault on Fort Loudon Johnson's brigade lost First
Lieut. S. M. Ross, of the Forty-fourth, and Private J. P. Hicks, of
the Seventeenth and Twenty-third Tennessee Regiments, killed, and
2 lieutenants and 17 privates wounded. A list of the killed and
wounded of this division at the assault on Fort Loudon was forwarded to you on December 3.

While the pickets were being relieved on November 29, Private
John T. Dodson, of Company C, Forty-third Alabama Regiment,
Gracie's brigade, was killed, and Private A. M. McMillan, of Com-
pany B, of the same regiment, was wounded.

On December 3, by order of the lieutenant-general commanding,
my train left its camp near Knoxville preparatory to retiring our
forces from that vicinity, to move via Strawberry Plains to Russellville, and the pickets from Gracie's brigade were relieved from duty
in the rifle-pits.

On December 4, at dark, my command withdrew from the line of
investment in front of Knoxville and moved in front of Longstreet's
corps on the old stage road, which passes via Blain's Cross-Roads to
Bean's Station and Rogersville. We marched all night over muddy
roads and reached Blain's Cross-Roads about 4 p. m. on December 5.

The pickets of Johnson's brigade were withdrawn from the rifle-
pits in front of Fort Loudon at 11 p. m. by Major Lowe, of the
Twenty-third Tennessee, and brought up to the column. Many of
my men were barefooted and poorly clad, and the weather was chilly
and damp. I regret to state that during this and the subsequent
march, as well as during the operations before Knoxville and the
march to that place, many desertions occurred in this division,
especially among the Tennessee troops.

On December 6th, we reached Rutledge, where we remained until
the 8th endeavoring ineffectually to gather full rations for our farther march.

On December 9th, we encamped at Cloud's Creek, 5 miles west of
Rogersville, and remained on half rations of flour and full rations of
meat until the 13th, when my command moved back some 4 miles
preparatory to a movement on the enemy at Bean's Station.

During this period (from December 9 to the 13th) several tan-
yards and shoe-shops were taken possession of by my order, and a
number of tanners and shoemakers from my command were placed
on extra duty preparing leather and shoes for the men.

On Monday, December 14, this division moved on Bean's Station at the head of the infantry, preceded by 100 cavalry, under
Captain Moore, of Colonel Giltner's regiment. The roads were very
wet and muddy and the weather was cold and inclement. Many of
our men were barefooted, and of these numbers failed to keep up
with their regiments. Others more enduring and persistent pressed
nobly on, and were seen among the foremost and most active in the

subsequent engagement. About 3 miles east of Bean's Station at ? p. m. the cavalry encountered and drove back the enemy's picket and sharply engaged the reserve. My leading brigade (Gracie's) was moved up, and seven companies of the Fifty-ninth Alabama Regiment, commanded by Lieut. Col. J. D. McLennan, was advanced as skirmishers, the center moving along the road. The cavalry under Captain Moore closed in to the left and uncovered its front. The enemy continued to fall back skirmishing with this regiment of infantry for about 2 miles, and twice endeavored to make a stand. We then crossed the creek about half a mile east of Bean's Station, and the Forty-third Alabama Regiment, commanded by Col. Y. M. Moody, was deployed in rear of the Fifty-ninth and moved to the right, extending in the woods on the slope of the mountain on the north side of the valley. As the skirmishers ascended to the top of the hill east of the station, the enemy's artillery opened from three points on the elevations west of the station. Two of these points are on the north side and one on the south side of the Knoxville road. Our skirmishers were now ordered to lie down until our artillery could be brought up.

About this time Brig. Gen. A. Gracie was wounded by a rifle ball in the arm. That I was deprived of his valuable services I was not aware until later in the day, as I had seen him return to the field after having had his wound examined.

Taylor's battery of four Napoleon guns was placed in position on the north side of the road and supported by the Forty-first Alabama Regiment, commanded by Lieutenant-Colonel Trimmier, and Parker's battery was placed on the left of the road, with the right piece resting in the road. These batteries opened mainly on the two batteries of the enemy beyond Bean's Station and to the north of the road.

Johnson's brigade was now advanced in line of battle with skirmishers in front to the top of the hill, east of the station and on the left of the Knoxville road, and became exposed to the fire of the Federal battery on an elevation on the south side of the valley while skirmishing with the enemy's cavalry on an elevation just in its front.

In the meantime, Major-General McLaws' division, after crossing the stream in our rear, was moved by the flank on to the ascent of the mountain on the north side of the valley, and two companies of the Forty-third Alabama Regiment, under Colonel Moody, by order of General Longstreet, were moved as skirmishers by the right flank along the edge of the woods on the slope of the mountain to cover the movement of McLaws' division, intended to turn the enemy's left flank.

After our two batteries had fired some thirty rounds each from their first positions, I ordered a section of Parker's battery to move to the left and front to a commanding position on the right of Johnson's brigade, where it opened on a well-formed line of the enemy's cavalry in its front and on the battery on the south side of the valley.

While this section of Parker's battery was moving to its position on the right of that occupied by Johnson's brigade, I received an order from the lieutenant-general commanding to press my line forward. The line of Gracie's brigade had, however, been somewhat advanced, and was exposed to the fire of the Federals occupying the large hotel building at Bean's Station and firing through loop-holes cut in the wall of the second and third stories.

A large frame house east of the hotel was about this time set on fire, it is believed, by the enemy to prevent us from using it as a shelter. I accordingly sent two of my staff officers with the necessary orders to move forward Gracie's brigade, while Colonel Fulton advanced Johnson's brigade under my eye, and the two batteries of our artillery still continued to play upon the enemy's lines in our front.

The advance in Gracie's brigade was made mainly by the Sixtieth Alabama Regiment, under Colonel Sanford, the Fifty-ninth and eight companies of the Forty third Alabama Regiments moving up as skirmishers on its right and rear. Captain Blakemore, my aide-de-camp, first conveyed to Colonel Sanford the order to advance about the time Johnson's brigade commenced moving. This regiment rushed forward gallantly, and with a shout passed the line of the Fifty-ninth and eight companies of the Forty-third Alabama Regiments deployed as skirmishers. In this movement the Sixtieth Alabama Regiment was exposed to the heavy fire of the enemy, concealed in the hotel, and of a line of Federals in the plain west of the hotel, and it consequently halted, and the men attempted to cover themselves by lying on the ground. The deliberate fire delivered with accuracy from the loop-holes of the hotel continually struck the men of the Sixtieth Alabama Regiment as they lay immovably on the ground, and when that regiment subsequently arose to advance again on the hotel, under orders conveyed to Colonel Sanford by Lieutenant Moorhead, Gracie's brigade inspector, it left its line marked out by the dead and wounded.

Johnson's brigade was now moving in a handsome line down the western slope of the hill east of the station and south of the Knoxville road. In this movement it was exposed to the fire of the enemy's cavalry in line of battle and to a battery of artillery in its front, and on passing the creek at the foot of the slope its line was enfiladed from the loop-holes of the hotel on its prolongation to the right. This brigade sought by lying down to secure the shelter afforded by the undulations of the ground, while the companies on the right fired on the hotel. The enemy's battery in front of Johnson's brigade retired as soon as that brigade descended below its range. The cavalry retired a little from the brow of the hill, but maintained their line. The Sixtieth Alabama Regiment, of Gracie's brigade, now arose and advanced on the right of the Knoxville road directly upon the hotel in the face of the fire from that building, and from a line of the enemy extending across the valley south of the hotel, which caused the regiment to take to the shelter of a large stable some 50 yards east of the hotel building, where it continued to return the enemy's fire. In this advance Colonel Sanford was knocked down by a shot, but afterward joined the regiment at the stable, where it had moved under command of Lieut. Col. D. S. Troy.

The Fifty-ninth and eight companies of the Forty-third Alabama Regiment, deployed as skirmishers, stretched from a point some distance to the right of the Sixtieth Alabama Regiment, and advanced somewhat later than that regiment on to the slope of the hollow north of the hotel. About this time Taylor's and Parker's batteries were directed to fire a few shots at the hotel, which was done. Some two shots were unfortunately fired by mistake into the stable occupied by the Sixtieth Alabama Regiment, by which 2 men are said to have been killed and 2 or 3 wounded.

In the above attitude of affairs I was advised that I could call on Brigadier-General Jenkins for support from his command (Hood's division) if I should need it. I immediately requested General Jenkins to move one or two brigades by the flank through the woods on the slope of the mountains on the south side of the valley with a view to turn the enemy's right flank. This was about sunset. About dusk I directed Colonel Fulton to push his brigade to the top of the hill in his front, which was done without resistance. About this time McLaws' division opened fire on the enemy's left flank on the north side of the valley. I now learned that General Jenkins had decided that it was too late to make the proposed movement on the enemy's right flank, and I consequently concluded to press no farther my left brigade, which was very weak.

It being reported to me indirectly from Colonel Sanford that the enemy were still occupying the hotel building, I ordered the left section of Parker's battery to move up to within 350 yards and fire into it. Some two balls were fired into the building, when the battery ceased to allow the infantry to advance and take possession of it. It was now found that the Yankees, all but 3 captured in the cellar, had made their escape from the west end of the hotel. Buckner's division was now in complete possession of Bean's Station, from which, with the aid of the artillery and the movement on the flank by McLaws' division, it had driven the enemy. The Federal forces had resisted our attack persistently and gallantly, no doubt with a view to save their little camp equipage, trains, &c., and in the darkness of the night their cavalry, once fairly in motion, could not be successfully pursued by our shoeless infantry. We therefore rested on our line at Bean's Station during the night.

During the fight Parker's battery fired 375 rounds of shell and Taylor's battery perhaps as many.

The following is the report of the strength of Buckner's division in the affair of Bean's Station, December 14, 1863:

Command.	Effective total.	Aggregate.
Johnson's brigade	370	434
Gracie's brigade	765	852
Total	1,135	1,286

The report of casualties in Buckner's division in the affair at Bean's Station December 14, 1863, is as follows:

Command.	Killed.		Wounded.		Missing.		Total.	Aggregate.
	Officers.	Men.	Officers.	Men.	Officers.	Men.		
Johnson's brigade	1	5	5	47		2	54	60
Gracie's brigade	2	22	9	119		10	151	162
Total	3	27	14	166		12	205	222

The enemy's forces are represented to have been three brigades of avalry. We have had no means of determining the number of heir killed and wounded. Common reports, which seem to come rom the enemy, place their killed at 100. The officers and men of ny command behaved handsomely in this affair.

On December 16, my command moved, by order of the lieutenant-eneral commanding, to Judge Mayse's, on the Holston River.

On December 19, it moved up the river to Long's Ferry and com-nenced crossing its train in the afternoon. By working day and ight the division, with all its wagons and ambulances and Parker's attery of artillery, was crossed on a ferry-boat to the south bank of he Holston by sunrise on the morning of December 21.

Having heard from various sources, and especially from an officer vho represented that he was the brigade inspector of Brig. Gen. ohn H. Morgan's brigade of cavalry, that the enemy were advanc-ng from Strawberry Plains in the direction of Morristown, 4 miles listant from my command, with a view to a raid on that place, vhere there is a valuable flouring mill, I moved early on the morn-ng of December 21 to this town, reporting my movement to the ieutenant-general commanding. The information proved to be in-orrect and unfounded. Some two days later I was ordered to make emporary shelters for my command, with a view to protection from he inclemency of the weather during the winter.

The highest meed of praise is due to the men of this command, vho have toiled faithfully on amid privations and discouragements, nd who have, half clad, braved alike the winter's rains and the ullets of the invading foe, while they have been abandoned by less letermined comrades, who have hitherto honorably borne their part n this cruel, iniquitous war, and who have bravely fought at their ide on the most bloody fields of battle. In view of the services of hese faithful men I feel that there are no other instances of courage r valor necessary to be specified. These have all nobly performed heir duty to their suffering country and to the cause of liberty. Vay God give them what man may never be able to bestow upon hem—an adequate reward. They enjoy at least the proud conscious-ess of arduous duties nobly performed.

Very respectfully, your obedient servant,

B. R. JOHNSON,
Brigadier-General, Commanding Division.

Col. G. MOXLEY SORREL,
Assistant Adjutant-General.

No. 75.

Report of Col. John C. Carter, Thirty-eighth Tennessee Infantry, Hardee's corps, Army of Tennessee.

HDQRS. THIRTY-EIGHTH TENNESSEE REGIMENT,
December 5, 1863.

CAPTAIN: I have the honor to report that on November 24, I was eft in command at Charleston, Tenn. The Thirty-eighth Tennessee Regiment, Lieutenant-Colonel Gwynne commanding, having an effective total of 215; portions of four companies of engineer troops, Captain McCalla commanding, having an effective total of 112; 17

effective cavalrymen, commanded by Major Shaw, and 44 effectiv
men belonging to Captain Van Dyke's cavalry company, constitute
the force under my command.

On the morning of November 26, Colonel Long's cavalry brigad
of Federal troops were moved from Cleveland, Tenn., against ou
position. Our troops were formed on the north side of the Hiwas
see River, for the purpose of protecting the bridges across th
stream. After a struggle of more than an hour, the enemy wer
driven back, with slight loss. We did not suffer. The bridges wer
saved.

On November 29, I received from General Bragg an order to Lieu
tenant-General Longstreet. I forwarded this order immediately b
telegraph and by courier to Lieutenant-General Longstreet. B
this order Lieutenant-General Longstreet was ordered to fall bac
immediately upon Dalton, Ga., or to retire to Virginia. I immedi
ately telegraphed to General Longstreet, stating that unless h
intended to fall back upon Dalton, there was no necessity to hol
my position longer. The dispatch was sent at 3 p. m. Had I bee
informed by General Longstreet that he did not intend to use th
bridges at Charleston, I should have left for Dalton on the night o
the 29th. I could have reached the place with safety. The enem
were at Cleveland in heavy force, yet by moving on the old Federa
road, I should have left them far to the right. General Longstree
replied to my telegram, asking for information, and led me to sup
pose he might retire from Knoxville by way of Charleston. I imme
diately replied, giving him what information I could, and agai
stated that my position was becoming very critical, and that unles
he intended to use the bridges it was entirely unnecessary for me t
remain longer at Charleston.

I received instructions from General Longstreet when the enem
was on all the roads between me and Dalton. I was ordered by hin
to destroy the bridges when I retired. I waited on the north side o
the Hiwassee River until the enemy came up. Four thousan
infantry, distinctly seen and counted, in two lines of battle, wit
cavalry on the flanks, were moved against us. Six pieces of artiller
opened upon us a heavy fire, and I was informed that about 800 cav
alry were crossing the river below. I immediately ordered the wag
ons and troops, preceded by a small cavalry force, to move rapidl
on the Riceville road. I and my staff remained in Calhoun, on th
north side of the river, until the skirmishers of the enemy reache
the bridges. They found the bridges destroyed. The troops of th
enemy were still passing through a defile in a range of hills on th
opposite side of the river. I waited until I had seen about 6,000 sol
diers debouch upon the plain before us. I then, with the remainde
of the cavalry, followed our wagons and troops, leaving 3 me
behind to watch the movements of the enemy. These men subse
quently reported that the enemy were at least 15,000 strong, and tha
they had with them more than fifteen pieces of artillery. Our me
reached Riceville a very short time before the enemy's cavalry did
having marched more than 7 miles within an hour and a half.

We continued our march, moving as rapidly as possible, and a
Sweet Water took the cars for Loudon. I reported to Brigadier
General Vaughn, commanding at that place.

I am glad to say that during the march we lost nothing. I started
from Charleston with 50 barefooted men, yet only 12 of them wer
left behind.

The supplies in the hands of the post commissary were loaded in a car, which was placed on the north side of the river.   Knowing as I did that we might be compelled to retire at any hour, I kept an engine for the purpose of taking a car off when necessary.   Mr. Wallace, the president of the East Tennessee and Georgia Railroad, repeatedly ordered the engine to Loudon; but conceiving that it would be much more useful to the Government where it was, I took the liberty of keeping it.   On the night of November 29, 1863, he informed me by telegraph that the engine at Charleston was unserviceable and that if I would send it to Loudon he would send me by 8 o'clock next morning a serviceable one in its stead.   I had the engine thoroughly inspected by those who should have been familiar with the machinery, and their opinion was that its power of locomotion might be at any time entirely destroyed.   Under such circumstances, I sent Captain Day, post assistant quartermaster, on the engine to Loudon, with instructions to bring back by 8 o'clock next morning (this was 8 o'clock at night) a serviceable engine from Loudon.

I left Charleston at 3 p. m., on November 30, 1863.   Up to that time no engine reached us, and I subsequently learned that none was ever sent to us.   Knowing that the supplies must necessarily fall into the hands of the enemy, I ordered them to be distributed among the citizens.   Though I regretted very much the loss of the supplies, yet I am certain had they been taken to Loudon they would have been lost there, for a quantity of quartermaster's and commissary stores were destroyed at that place because there was no transportation for them.   I took in my wagons as large a quantity of the supplies as I could.

I take great pleasure in acknowledging the service performed by Captain Van Dyke and his company.   With 40 men he covered our entire front, and executed with promptness and efficiency every duty assigned him.   There were eight roads leading from the south side of the river to our position.   Under such circumstances it was unsafe to have the picket posts stationary.   It was necessary that the whole cavalry force should be a constant patrol.

I placed the cavalrymen of Major Shaw's battalion under command of a captain, and ordered him to establish communication with Dalton, Ga., via Spring Place, by couriers.   I sent a number of dispatches to Colonel Brent, assistant adjutant-general, Army of Tennessee, and to yourself, by this courier line, but I had no intelligence at all from the Army of Tennessee, except what I received (the order previously mentioned) sent by General Bragg to Lieutenant-General Longstreet.

I must be permitted to return my thanks for the valuable assistance rendered by Lieut. Col. A. D. Gwynne and Maj. H. W. Cotter, Thirty-eighth Tennessee Regiment; Maj. J. P. Trezevant and Major Maney, commissaries at the post; Captains McCalla and Ramsey, engineer troops; Captains Neely and Nevill, Lieut. and Adjt. R. L. Caruthers, Thirty-eighth Tennessee Regiment, and Mr. J. A. Gardenhire, acting post adjutant.

To the soldiers I give all the praise.   They manifested, as they have always done, unflinching courage and devoted patriotism.

I am, captain, very respectfully, your obedient servant,

JNO. C. CARTER,
Colonel, Commanding.

Capt. LEON TROUSDALE,
Assistant Adjutant-General, Wright's Brigade.

No. 76.

Report of Maj. Gen. Joseph Wheeler, C. S. Army, commanding Cavalry Corps.

HEADQUARTERS CAVALRY CORPS,
Dalton, Ga., December 31, 1863.

COLONEL : I have the honor to submit the following as my official report of the operations of the cavalry under my command, while under the orders of Lieutenant-General Longstreet, in the campaign against the enemy's forces in East Tennessee up to the 24th ultimo, at which time I was recalled to headquarters of the department at Missionary Ridge :

On the evening of the 11th ultimo, I arrived at Sweet Water, Tenn., with portions of four brigades of cavalry, much worn and depleted by the arduous service they had undergone during the preceding two months, and reported to the lieutenant-general commanding. The next day I received the following order :

GENERAL ORDERS, }   HEADQUARTERS,
    No. —. }   *Sweet Water, Tenn., November* 12, 1863.

I. The command will march to-morrow morning at daylight.

II. Major-General Wheeler, with his cavalry, will move by the most practicable route to Maryville, and endeavor to capture the enemy's force at that point, and otherwise make a diversion upon the enemy's flank.

*   *   *   *   *   *   *

By command of Lieutenant-General Longstreet :

G. MOXLEY SORREL,
Lieutenant-Colonel, Assistant Adjutant-General.

In addition to this order the lieutenant-general commanding instructed me to leave sufficient cavalry to guard the Tennessee River from mouth of Hiwassee to Loudon. He also gave me verbally much valuable information regarding the country into which I was moving, and also instructed me how to protect my rear and flank should the enemy attempt a movement across the Holston at Lenoir's Station. The force of the enemy at Maryville had been variously estimated from 500 to 4,000 strong.

At this time I received some captured papers, which were transmitted to the lieutenant-general commanding, and which showed the organization of Burnside's cavalry, and to some extent the organization of his infantry. These papers showed that he had twenty-nine mounted regiments connected with his army.

In obedience to the preceding order I crossed the Tennessee at Motley's Ford with the balance of the four brigades (two under General Martin and two under General Armstrong) at dark on the 13th ultimo, and made a night's march to strike between the enemy at Maryville and their line of retreat. On approaching Maryville I found that but one regiment (the Eleventh Kentucky Cavalry) was at that place. I accordingly pushed on rapidly to attack. My guides having deceived me in reference to its exact location, and being a short distance in advance with my escort and a squadron of Dibrell's brigade, I came suddenly upon it while passing through a wood, drawn up in line of battle. We immediately charged the enemy, Lieutenant Pointer, my aide, being in advance. We made a few captures and scattered the remainder. The country was an open wood without fences, which enabled the enemy to flee in all directions. Dibrell's brigade, which was but a few rods behind, was immediately upon them, and scattering into small parties charged after the fugitives, who, in their anxiety to escape, had separated in small groups of 2 to 6 men. In this manner we ran down and captured 151 men, the remainder of the regiment being dispersed over the country. While Dibrell's brigade was thus engaged the Federal Colonel Wolford, with his brigade, came to the assistance of the Eleventh Kentucky and attacked my command. He was met and repulsed by the Eighth and Eleventh Texas and Third Arkansas Regiments, and they, assisted by Col. J. T. Morgan's brigade, charged the enemy and drove him over Little River in the wildest confusion, capturing 85 prisoners. In both of these fights we killed and wounded several of the enemy.

During the night I received a dispatch from General Longstreet stating that he desired me to cross Little River, provided I had a decided success at Maryville, or if I thought a decided success could be secured by crossing.

Pursuant to these instructions I moved over Little River on the following morning, the condition of the ford making it nearly noon before the entire command was crossed. We pressed upon the enemy, which consisted, as I learned from prisoners and citizens, of Sanders', Shackelford's, Wolford's, and Pennebaker's brigades, with one battery of rifled guns, all being commanded by General Sanders. After driving them for 3 miles we came to Stock Creek, which was not fordable for horses, and the enemy had partly torn up the bridge. Just beyond the enemy had taken a strong and elevated position behind a fence inclosing a thick wood, with large fields intervening between the enemy and my position, the ground descending rapidly toward the line occupied by my troops. The flanks of the enemy from Little River to Knoxville were protected by a high ridge on their left and the Holston River on their right, thus preventing my turning their position and compelling me to fight superior forces in positions chosen by themselves.

To accomplish the desired object I determined to overcome these advantages of the enemy by the vigor of our attack. The enemy kept up a warm fire of artillery and musketry, during which Major Burford, of my staff, was slightly wounded. I dismounted nearly half of my command, crossed the creek under cover of a fire from my battery, and drove the left wing of the enemy from its strong position. This enabled a detail to repair the bridge while I pressed on with the dismounted men, compelling the entire line of the enemy to retreat. Immediately after crossing the creek I sent orders to General Armstrong to move rapidly up the road with his entire command, which up to this time had been held in reserve.

In the meantime we continued to push the enemy with the dismounted men, driving him from several strong positions. After a delay of more than an hour General Armstrong overtook us, and as soon as his command could be prepared we charged the enemy with his command in the following order: The Eighth Texas Regiment in advance, followed by the Eleventh Texas, the Third Arkansas on the flanks, the whole supported by Dibrell's (Tennessee) brigade. The lines of the enemy were broken and the entire mass of the enemy swept on toward Knoxville in the wildest confusion. The charge was continued successfully for 3 miles to within less than half a mile of the river opposite the city. The bulk of the enemy dashed over their pontoon in their fright into the city, creating the greatest consternation. Great numbers scattered over the country and many plunged into the river, some of whom were drowned. One hundred and forty prisoners were taken in the charge and a considerable number killed and wounded. The Federal commander of cavalry was reported in their papers as having received wounds from which he died. We were only prevented from following the fugitives into the city by a strong force of the enemy's infantry and artillery in the fortifications on a high hill on the south bank of the river, who opened a heavy fire upon us as we approached. It being now dusk and the balance of the command being 4 miles to the rear, after some warm skirmishing I withdrew to Stock Creek, which was the nearest point at which forage could be obtained. The enemy did not come out of their fortifications to follow us.

As I had some reason to believe the enemy might withdraw their forces to the other bank of the river, I returned at daylight and found instead of withdrawing they had strengthened their position during the night, from which they opened warmly upon us as we advanced.

Here I received a communication from the lieutenant-general commanding, of which the following is an extract:

Unless you are doing better service by moving along on the enemy's flank than you could do here, I would rather you should join us and co-operate.

As there was little prospect of accomplishing any further good in that vicinity, I determined to march without delay to join the main body of the command. After commencing the march I received a note from Colonel Sorrel, which read as follows:

If you can get across the Holston River the lieutenant-general would like you to cross your whole command and operate with us.

With considerable difficulty we crossed the Holston near Louisville and reported to the lieutenant-general commanding about 3 p. m. on 17th ultimo. The investment of the city commenced the following morning, and I was directed to continue the line from the left of the infantry to the Holston River, upon which my left flank rested, while my right rested upon the Knoxville and Clinton Railroad, giving me a line of about 4 miles. This line was kept almost continually skirmishing with the enemy, and, notwithstanding its extensions, the enemy made no serious demonstration against us. Detachments of my command sent out in our rear succeeded in capturing 12 prisoners and 10 Government and 2 sutler wagons loaded with a large steam cracker-baking machine and some clothing and shoes.

The next six days were spent in closely besieging this portion of the line, and engaging the enemy with both artillery and small-arms on several occasions, pursuant to orders from the lieutenant-general commanding.

On the evening of the 20th, I engaged the enemy warmly all along the line, pursuant to the following instructions:

HEADQUARTERS,
November 20, 1863.

General JOSEPH WHEELER,
    Commanding, &c.:

GENERAL: General Jenkins is going to feel the enemy sharply at the railroad depot about sunset. I wish you would open your batteries about that hour and advance your line of skirmishers as far as you can, threatening along your front.
    Yours, respectfully,

JAMES LONGSTREET,
Lieutenant-General, Commanding.

On the evening of the 22d, I received the following dispatch from he lieutenant-general commanding and disposed my forces for the ttack :

HEADQUARTERS,
November 22, 1863.

Maj. Gen. JOSEPH WHEELER,
        Commanding Cavalry :

GENERAL : General McLaws is trying to arrange for an assault upon the redoubt in is front to-night. It will be made by an advance of our entire line of skirmishers fter dark. The skirmishers must advance as near as possible to the enemy's trenches, ay 100 yards. They are to get shelter there and continue to engage the enemy in is trenches until the work is accomplished. Advance your skirmishers as you hear he firing of the pickets on your right and hold the enemy in his trenches along our front. If he quits them, take the hills in front of you, or at least one of them. f your skirmishers will get up tolerably close they can see if the enemy quits his renches. If the artillery in front of you is opened upon our right put your batteries n position and engage the enemy's batteries, so as to relieve our columns as much s possible.

        Most respectfully,

JAMES LONGSTREET,
Lieutenant-General, Commanding.

P. S.—The battery on General Jenkins' left is ordered to open upon the Temper-nce Hill a little before night to get the range, and it will play upon the same hill fter night, so as to try and create the impression that the attack will be made there. ry and favor that diversion as much as you can. Keep the matter perfectly uiet.

On the 21st, I had received a communication from the lieutenant-general commanding, of which the following is an extract :

Colonel Lyon, in command near Kingston, reports two regiments of cavalry nd two pieces of artillery at Kingston. It appears to me this party might be aptured.

About 10 o'clock on the night of the 22d, I received a dispatch rom the lieutenant-general commanding, saying that the contem-lated attack would be postponed, and continued by saying :

You will have to march, therefore, early to-morrow for Kingston, leaving a bri-ade to picket and scout upon our left. You will please give particular and minute nstructions to the brigade commander whom you leave. Try and reach Kingston efore day on the 24th ; drive in the pickets there, and you will then ascertain vhether the enemy has been re-enforced. If he has not, capture or disperse the orce that is there.

Pursuant to these instructions I issued orders for the march and lirected the command to fall back and feed. To accomplish this it vas necessary for half the command to fall back 7 miles, and there-ore it did not get into camp until nearly daylight, shortly after vhich time I was obliged to commence the march. The roads were o bad that the most strenuous exertions enabled me to make but 26 niles before dark. Being still 20 miles from Kingston, I left orders or the command to follow, and proceeded with my escort rapidly on he road toward that place. On arriving in the vicinity I learned hat the enemy had re-enforced with infantry, but could not learn he extent.

About 3 a. m. the command came up much worn and exhausted, ialf of the men having lost two nights' sleep, and during the march of the preceding day had necessarily received short allowance of ra-ions. Five of our best regiments had been left at Knoxville, and, is I afterward learned, many of our men had been left at various ooints along the road, they from exhaustion being absolutely unable o keep up with the command. After an hour's rest I proceeded on vith the command and encountered the enemy's pickets 3 miles from

Kingston about one hour before day. A party was sent to cut off the pickets but failed. We pressed on toward the town against a warm resistance of the enemy. It was my hope to reach the town before they could form. In this I was disappointed. Notwithstanding the rapidity of our movements, on arriving at the foot of a hill near the town, we found it covered with long lines of infantry and dismounted cavalry. I immediately dismounted the entire command except one regiment to guard my flanks, and pressed upon the enemy who had by this time opened a warm fire of infantry and artillery two of their guns throwing 24-pound shot. The enemy's line extended along the crest of the ridge, the concavity being toward us. Their flanks were thrown forward so as nearly to envelop our lines which enabled him to fire upon our flanks, and even the rear of our right.

I hoped from their extended position that I might charge their center, but after a careful personal reconnaissance I found that they were very strong at every point. To approach the enemy it was necessary to advance up a gentle slope through open fields which the enemy swept by both direct and cross fire. Finding that I could gain nothing by continuing in my present position, I determined to withdraw, Generals Martin and Armstrong recommending it. At this moment the enemy charged our right, but were most gallantly repulsed with considerable loss by a counter-charge by our troops. We then withdrew quietly without being followed by the enemy.

Having received orders from General Bragg through the lieutenant-general commanding to report to department headquarters, turned the command over to General Martin, and started in compliance with said order.

My thanks are due Generals Martin and Armstrong for their gallant and good conduct during the campaign. I must leave it fo them to do justice to the many brave officers and men in their commands whose gallant bearing fully sustains their former reputation.

General Vaughn, who was with me until I reached Knoxville rendered valuable service by his gallantry and knowledge of the country.

Lieutenant-Colonel Rogers, assistant inspector-general; Major Jenkins, assistant inspector-general; Major Burford, assistant adjutant-general; Major Humes, chief of artillery; Captain Steele, engineer, and my aides, Lieutenants Pointer and Hudson, were gallant and efficient at all times.

Col. H. B. Lyon reported to me on the 20th and was assigned to the command of the troops stationed near Kingston, where he did efficient service.

I am, colonel, with much respect, your obedient servant,

JOS. WHEELER,
Major-General.

Col. G. MOXLEY SORREL, *Assistant Adjutant-General.*

[Indorsement.]

HEADQUARTERS,
February 16, 1864.

Respectfully forwarded.

Later information of the force near Kingston at the time General Wheeler advanced against it indicates that it was not re-enforced as it was thought at the time.

JAMES LONGSTREET,
Lieutenant-General, Commanding.

No. 77.

Report of Maj. Gen. William T. Martin, C. S. Army, commanding Longstreet's cavalry.

HEADQUARTERS CAVALRY IN EAST TENNESSEE,
January 8, 1864.

COLONEL : I have the honor to submit the following report of the ervices rendered by the cavalry divisions of Brigadier-Generals Armstrong and Morgan, under my command. That the condition f the command when it devolved upon me may be understood, I eg leave to call attention briefly to services rendered by it immedi-tely preceding its moving to East Tennessee :

In August last, having had for the first time in twelve months a hort period of rest, the command moved to the front and took an ctive part in the skirmishes and battle at and near Chickamauga, ighting dismounted, with or on the flanks of the infantry during he battles. Soon after, with the exception of the First and Sixth Georgia Regiments, it moved up the Tennessee River and crossed ear Washington, fighting or marching with short intervals of rest or six days. After the destruction of several railroad bridges and tockades, and of 800 of the enemy's wagons and 2,000 mules and a arge amount of stores, and the capture of 1,200 prisoners and many nules, horses, and stores, it recrossed the river at Courtland, Ala., and rom thence through a desolated country marched to Kingston, Ga., nd thence to Parker's Ford, on the Little Tennessee River. With rders to take two days' rations and no wagons, the command crossed he river, and making a night march attacked Maryville at daylight, apturing 200 prisoners and routing a brigade of cavalry.

The next day it was moved toward Knoxville, and after fighting ill after dark ran the entire cavalry of the enemy (four strong bri-ades with artillery, outnumbering us two to one) into the intrench-ents opposite Knoxville.

The second day afterward the command was marched to a point elow Louisville, and crossing the river marched to Knoxville, when t reported to Lieutenant-General Longstreet.

A few days afterward, the First and Sixth Georgia having reported o me for duty, the command moved upon Kingston by a forced narch and made an ineffective attempt to take that place. The trength of the position, the weight of metal of their artillery, and he steadiness of the enemy's force there foiled our efforts. Major-General Wheeler, under whose immediate orders the foregoing move-nents were made, placed me in command and left to report to Gen-ral Bragg on November 24 last.

On the 24th, I moved the command to Knoxville, and it was en-aged in picketing and skirmishing with the enemy in front of that lace, suffering greatly for forage.

On the 26th, I moved Harrison's brigade, of Armstrong's division, nd Russell's brigade, of Morgan's division, under command of Brigadier-General Morgan, across the Holston below Knoxville to articipate in a demonstration upon the enemy's lines there. The nen were dismounted and moved with the infantry on its left flank. Russell's brigade was warmly engaged, and drove the enemy from is rifle-pits upon the side of a difficult ridge. Col. Thomas Harri-on, on the extreme left, found no enemy in his front.

35 R R—VOL XXXI, PT I

On November 29, these two brigades recrossed the river, and by forced march, made by order of Lieutenant-General Longstreet, moved with part of my force toward Tazewell to meet a suppos advance of the enemy from that direction.

Reaching the vicinity of Maynardville in the afternoon of t 30th, I found General Jones' division skirmishing with the enem It was too late to attack. General Armstrong, with his divisic was sent around to the right to reach the rear of the enemy befo daylight. The remainder of my force moved at daylight on Ma nardville, but the enemy had rapidly retreated soon after dayligh leaving a small picket, which was captured, Being joined by Ge eral Armstrong, his division was pushed toward Clinch River, whi General Jones' command was sent to the right to endeavor to effe a lodgment between the enemy and the river. A force of the enem prevented his success. General Armstrong pushed the enemy front, and finally he was driven across the river, after being pu sued for some miles through difficult gorges, made more difficult a frozen stream.

I returned to Knoxville in obedience to orders, reaching there D cember 2. The army on the second night afterward, the siege Knoxville being raised, commenced its retreat toward Rogersvill General Morgan's division followed, covering the rear of Gener McLaws' division on the south side of the Holston. General Arm strong's division performed the same service on the Knoxville an river roads. The infantry and artillery having passed Bean's St tion, I was ordered to move to the south side of the Holston an cover the railroad and left flank.

On December 10, a brigade of the enemy's cavalry attacked Ge eral Morgan's division at Russellville, while the greater portion it was foraging. The enemy was handsomely repulsed by one-thi of its number, leaving dead, wounded, and prisoners in our hands.

In this affair the First and Sixth Georgia and Third Alaban Regiments were conspicuous for gallantry. Colonel Crews deserv mention for his skill and bravery on this occasion.

Lieutenant-General Longstreet having turned upon the enem and attacked him at Bean's Station, I was ordered to cross the riv and operate in his rear. While engaged in this movement, in ord to cross the river it became necessary to dislodge the brigade of ca alry guarding May's Ford. This was done by a rapid fire of artille from White's and Wiggins' batteries, of Morgan's division. T enemy lost 60 killed and wounded here.

Early next morning the enemy's pickets were driven in, and fore I had entirely effected a crossing I was ordered to move up the enemy's flank on the Knoxville road, 4 miles from Bean's S tion. This was done immediately, and a high hill gained, fro which my artillery could enfilade the enemy's breastworks. Wi great labor the guns were placed in position and rapidly and effe ively served.

In the meantime, Morgan's division was dismounted and mov upon the enemy's flank. My guns were in sight of, and only 400 500 yards from, our infantry skirmishers, who it was expected wou attack in front. My fire was continued for 1½ hours, and the enem began to retire, but was able to detach a large force to hold my m in check, as he was not pressed in front. With concert of acti great damage could have been done the enemy on this day. Colo Giltner, with his cavalry brigade, was on the side of Clinch Mou

n, on the enemy's left flank, and prepared to second any move-
ent of our infantry. As no movement was made, I held my posi-
on..

The next day I moved down the Knoxville and river roads in
ont of the enemy, who had retired in the night, and after sev-
ral unimportant skirmishes we found him in a strong position, on
ichland Creek, holding both roads with a force too great for
y cavalry to cope with in a country not at all suited for cavalry
perations.

On December 22, the command returned across the Holston and
stablished a picket line from near New Market to Dandridge. Col-
nel Russell's brigade was posted 4 miles east of Dandridge. Col-
nel Crews' half way from Morristown to Dandridge. General
rmstrong's division was concentrated at Talbott's Depot, on the
oad leading from Morristown to New Market. Commanders of di-
isions were instructed to attack the enemy in flank or rear if he
ade an attack upon any of these positions.

On the morning of the 24th, simultaneous attacks were made upon
eneral Armstrong and upon Colonel Russell. After spirited skir-
ishing the former, being flanked and outnumbered, was compelled
o withdraw his pickets from near New Market to the eastern side
f Mossy Creek. An unexpected attack upon Colonel Russell was
ade by 2,000 cavalry under Colonel Campbell. Russell's brigade
as for a moment in confusion, but rallied and repulsed the enemy,
ho fell back 2 miles toward Dandridge.

In the meantime, four regiments of Crews' brigade (in all 600 men)
oved in the rear of the enemy. Two of the regiments being in ad-
ance made a spirited charge on the enemy and captured his battery of
rtillery. Support being too far off, the brave men who made the
harge were driven from the guns, and Major Bale, commanding
ixth Georgia, was left dead in the midst of the battery. Two pieces
f artillery and the two remaining regiments of the brigade coming up,
nd the whole command being dismounted, the enemy was pushed
om one position to another, until finally routed he abandoned one
un and caisson, his dead and wounded, and under cover of night
scaped capture. Colonel Russell's brigade should have moved up,
ut the courier sent with orders failed to reach him. He was watch-
g the movements of 500 of the enemy, who were moving on Crews'
ght, trying to escape.

I have never witnessed greater gallantry than was displayed by
olonel Crews and the officers and men of the First, Second, Third,
nd Sixth Georgia Cavalry. The Fourth Georgia Cavalry was on
etached service from this engagement at Kingston till December 30.

The enemy, mounted, three times charged our dismounted men in
pen field and were as often repulsed, but not until, mingling in our
anks, some of his men were brought to the ground by clubbed guns.
he enemy was pursued without effect by Colonel Russell in the
ight to New Market.

On the 27th, I made an effort to dislodge the enemy from Mossy
reek, but desisted, as couriers with orders to General Morgan did
ot find him, and he without orders moved his command, dismounted,
rom the position I had assigned to him, and made it thus impossible
o effect my object.

On the 29th, I engaged the enemy at 9 a. m. with all my guns and
,000 men. The fighting occurred on both sides of the railroad lead-
ng from Mossy Creek to Morristown, and commenced one-quarter

of a mile west of Talbott's Station and ended near the same place
dark. General Morgan's division was dismounted and formed
the left of railroad, General Armstrong on the right. The count
from this station to Mossy Creek is composed of open, rolling fiel
that had been tilled during the past year, flanked by high woodla
on each side. I could not maneuver the artillery, except near t
railroad. Armstrong's division, with the artillery, was moved ra
idly upon the enemy to engage his attention, while I hoped to fla
him with Morgan's division on his right. His rapid retreat enabl
him to avoid this, and both divisions finally were moved at doub
quick and drove the enemy rapidly and in confusion back to Mos
Creek. Up to this time the force opposing us was not greater th
4,000 men, with two batteries. Owing to the nature of the grou
Crews' brigade had been thrown to the right of the railroad, a
General Armstrong, with Crews' brigade, was ordered to move
his artillery to within canister range and to charge some woods
his front and that of Colonel Crews.

Colonel Russell's brigade had its right resting on the railroad a
his left on the woods. Immediately in his front the enemy h
occupied some barns and outhouses. I ordered him to dislodge hi
The whole line moved forward. The enemy was driven from l
position on our left, but by a charge of cavalry upon our right a
of a brigade of infantry upon Crews' brigade and Armstrong's le
we were compelled to yield the ground. The enemy fixed bayone
and moved into the open field to charge the Georgians and two ho
itzers some 200 yards in his front. Perceiving this I wheeled t
Seventh Alabama Regiment to the right and moved it into a cut
the railroad, securing a good position within 50 yards of the flank
the advancing infantry. The fire from this regiment and a count
charge by the Georgians soon drove the enemy into and throu
the woods, with heavy loss in killed and wounded.

At this time the enemy made three cavalry charges upon Russel
left and produced some confusion for a moment. Assisted by t
officers I was enabled to rally the men under a heavy fire from t
cavalry and the enemy's artillery. For a short time all firing cease
except from the artillery. Upon reconnoitering the enemy's positi
preparatory to another attack, I found him strongly posted in m
front and overlapping my line on both flanks with three brigades
cavalry, six regiments of infantry, and three batteries of artillery
position to sweep the open fields in my front. On the opposite side
the creek in full view, was a reserve of cavalry and infantry.
fresh brigade of cavalry was coming in from the Dandridge road
full view.

My artillery had exhausted the supply of ammunition, except ca
ister. The division commanders reported an average of only fi
rounds of ammunition for small-arms. The Third Arkansas, a g
lant little regiment, had fired the last round in its cartridge box
and had been ordered to the rear. The men had been fighting stead
without relief for seven hours. To advance was impossible, and
mount and retire on the open fields in daylight before so large a fo
with such a preponderance of mounted men would, I knew, be di
cult. It could only be accomplished by the utmost steadiness. T
retreat, under a heavy fire of artillery and small-arms, was effect
in perfect order, the regiments falling back in succession to adva
tageous points, and then fighting until, having checked the ene
sufficiently, they could gain another point of vantage.

Vhile officers and men deserve great credit for their gallantry in advance, their conduct during this difficult and hazardous move-nt to the rear entitles them to the highest praise. The enemy's les often sounded the charge. At first the charge was made, but a second one. At dusk, after nine hours of severe fighting and rching, the command was halted and formed, and the enemy lly repulsed. There was not then an average of 1 round of munition to the man.

o action has taken place since the 29th; only slight skirmishes e occurred.

would mention Brigadier-Generals Armstrong and Morgan, and onels Crews and Harrison, commanding brigades, and Colonel mpson, Third Georgia, and Colonel Malone for gallantry on the h.

aptain Huggins, Lieutenants Pue and Blake, all of the artillery, erve special mention. It is difficult, however, to distinguish. officers and men vied with each other in the discharge of their ies.

cannot omit to mention a most gallant charge made by the hth Texas Regiment (the Rangers).

would call attention to remarks of the division and brigade com-nders upon the destitute condition of their men. Their repre-tations are not colored. A very large proportion of my men, and n officers, are ragged and barefooted, without blankets or over-ts. Owing to the want of attention to the duties of his office, the rtermaster of General Wheeler's corps left my command in great d of clothing. We have drawn none for fall or winter. A very ge number of my horses are unshod. The men have received no for six months. The extremely cold weather has made it almost possible for me to move. I refer to the reports* of Generals Arm-ng and Morgan and Colonels Harrison, Biffle, and Crews for ther particulars.

A tabular statement* of casualties is hereto appended.

The activity of the cavalry and multiplicity of its marches since ok command of it will furnish an excuse for the length of this ort.

Respectfully submitted.

WILL. T. MARTIN,
Major-General, Commanding.

Lieut. Col. G. MOXLEY SORREL,
   Assistant Adjutant-General, Longstreet's Corps.

No. 78.

*anks of the Confederate Congress to Lieut. Gen. James Long-
street and his command.*

42.—JOINT RESOLUTIONS of thanks to Lieutenant-General Longstreet and
the officers and men of his command.

Resolved by the Congress of the Confederate States of America,
at the thanks of Congress are due, and hereby cordially tendered,
Lieut. Gen. James Longstreet and the officers and men of his
mmand, for their patriotic services and brilliant achievements in
present war, sharing as they have the arduous fatigues and

---

* Not found.

privations of many campaigns in Virginia, Maryland, Pennsylvan
Georgia, and Tennessee, and participating in nearly every gr
battle fought in those States, the commanding general ever displa
ing great ability, skill, and prudence in command, and the offic
and men the most heroic bravery, fortitude, and energy, in eve
duty they have been called upon to perform.

Resolved, That the President be requested to transmit a copy
the foregoing resolution to Lieutenant-General Longstreet for pu
lication to his command.

Approved February 17, 1864.

NOVEMBER 5, 1863.—Skirmish in Loudon County, Tenn.

*Report of Col. George G. Dibrell, Eighth Tennessee Cavalry, co
manding brigade.*

HEADQUARTERS,
McGee's, November 5, [1863]—1.15 a. m

DEAR SIR : I started Colonel Biffle, with about 350 men, across t
river on a scout this a. m. When his advance was about a quar
of a mile from the river, the balance in the river crossing, they w
met by a large cavalry force of the enemy, pouring a heavy f
into my men, charging them. Colonel Biffle attempted to recr
the river, but quite a number of his men were cut off, and went
and down the river, and I fear are captured. Several are known to
killed and wounded. We rallied to the river on foot with the bala
of the command and drew them off, and firing had ceased. Thirty
40 are yet missing. There may some get across below and above.
have sent additional pickets to all the fords near. Will advise y
if attacked again. I think they are moving up to hold the no
bank.

Very respectfully, &c.,

G. G. DIBRELL,
Colonel

Maj. J. J. REEVE.

NOVEMBER 6, 1863.—Action near Rogersville, Tenn.

REPORTS.*

No. 1.—Col. Israel Garrard, Seventh Ohio Cavalry, commanding United St
forces.
No. 2.—Maj. Daniel A. Carpenter, Second Tennessee (mounted) Infantry.
No. 3.—Brig. Gen. James M. Shackelford, U. S. Army.
No. 4.—Col. Selby Harney, Thirty-fourth Kentucky Infantry.
No. 5.—Maj. Gen. Samuel Jones, C. S. Army, commanding Department of Wes
Virginia and East Tennessee.
No. 6.—Maj. Gen. Robert Ransom, jr., C. S. Army, commanding District of So
western Virginia and East Tennessee.
No. 7.—Brig. Gen. William E. Jones, C. S. Army, commanding Cavalry Briga
No. 8.—Col. James M. Corns, Eighth Virginia Cavalry.
No. 9.—Col. H. L. Giltner, Fourth Kentucky Cavalry (Confederate), comman
Second Cavalry Brigade.

* See also Burnside to Grant, November 6 and 7, Part III.

No. 1.

Report of Col. Israel Garrard, Seventh Ohio Cavalry, commanding United States forces.

MORRISTOWN,
November 6, 1863.

GENERAL : I was attacked this a. m. and totally defeated. I lost my guns and two-thirds of my command; rebel force not known, as they were continually sending their troops forward. I think the whole of the Second Tennessee is lost. About one-half of the Seventh [Ohio] Cavalry is lost.

The rebel cavalry was following us this side of Bull's Gap.

Very respectfully, your obedient servant,

I. GARRARD,
Colonel, Commanding.

General BURNSIDE.

No. 2.

Report of Maj. Daniel A. Carpenter, Second Tennessee (mounted) Infantry.

KNOXVILLE, TENN.,
September 14, 1864.

SIR : Having but recently been released from a rebel prison, I have the honor to embrace the earliest opportunity to submit the following report of the affair which led to the capture of a large part of the Second East Tennessee Mounted Infantry on the 6th of November last :

On the 5th of November, 1863, the Seventh Ohio Volunteer Cavalry, Second East Tennessee Mounted Infantry Volunteers, and four guns of Captain Phillips' (Second Illinois) battery were encamped 4 miles east of Rogersville, Tenn., Major McIntire commanding the Seventh Ohio Volunteer Cavalry, myself commanding the Second East Tennessee Mounted Infantry, and a lieutenant, name unknown, commanding the artillery; the whole under command of Colonel Garrard, of the Seventh Ohio Volunteer Cavalry. Late in the afternoon Colonel Garrard informed me that the rebels were crossing Holston River at Kingsport, Tenn., 18 miles east of our encampment. About 12 o'clock that night he (Colonel Garrard) ordered me to detail 50 men, under a good officer, and have them to report to him at 2 o'clock the following a. m., for the purpose of going out on a scout. Accordingly Captain Marney, Company A, and Lieutenant Jones, Company E, were detailed, with 50 enlisted men, and ordered to report to Colonel Garrard at the appointed hour, which they did, and were ordered by him to proceed to the Carter Valley road and up said road to where Captain Rogers, with a company of home guards doing picket duty, was posted.

Captain Marney arrived at Captain Rogers' quarters at the specified time. Colonel Garrard had ordered Captain Marney to take Captain Rogers' company, together with his 50 men, and proceed up Carter Valley about 9 miles and establish a line of pickets from the Carter Valley road to the Kingsport road, informing him (Colonel

Garrard) of everything they could learn concerning the movement of the enemy.

While Captain Marney and his men were waiting on Captain Roger to get ready to start, Captain Marney discovered a body of mounted men moving rapidly toward them from the direction of Kingsport Captain Marney asked Captain Rogers if he had pickets out, to which Captain Rogers replied he had. Just at that moment a brigade o rebels with drawn sabers charged upon Captain Marney and his men The road being narrow, the rebels ran over Captain Marney and hi men, making a large portion of them prisoners. The rebels tarried but a few moments, left a small squad with the prisoners, and pro ceeded toward Rogersville. Very near all of the men captured es caped and returned to our camp in advance of the rebels, and in formed Colonel Garrard of what had happened; this was about sun rise. Previous to this time Colonel Garrard had ordered me to strik tents, load my wagons, saddle my horses, and be ready to move o: fight at any moment. Colonel Garrard came very soon to my quar ters. I had everything ready, and was just finishing my breakfast He informed me the rebels were at that time in Rogersville; re quested me to have my train to move out on the Rogersville road : short distance and halt.

Near this time the train of the Seventh Ohio Volunteer Cavalry came up. I ordered my train to fall in behind said train; they did so and then halted. Colonel Garrard informed me he would take the Seventh Ohio Volunteer Cavalry and move down toward Rogers ville and see if he could ascertain anything from the rebels, at the same time ordering me to send out two companies east of our camp to meet the enemy if they should come from the direction of Carter's Valley; also ordered me to detail 50 men and send them east of ou camp to hold a hill and prevent the enemy from occupying it. This was promptly done. Colonel Garrard moved with the Seventh Ohio Volunteer Cavalry toward Rogersville, but had not gone far when I heard a volley of musketry, and very soon the Seventh Ohio Volun teer Cavalry returned at full speed; a number of them had thrown their guns down and were in a perfect state of confusion.

Major McIntire, of the Seventh Ohio Volunteer Cavalry, came to me and stated that Colonel Garrard was killed and I would have to take command of the forces. I requested Major McIntire to try and collect his men, they being completely demoralized. He said the panic and confusion in his regiment resulted from the death of Colonel Garrard. At this time two guns of Phillips' battery were nearly a half mile east of our position without support. I im mediately dispatched Lieutenant Shaw, of the Seventh Ohio Volun teer Cavalry, to order the two guns to fall back across the creek and take position near where I was with the remainder of my regiment. Lieutenant Shaw delivered the order, and the lieutenant command ing the guns remarked that the rebels were within 100 yards of his position in a ditch, and would certainly capture them if he attempted to move, though he thought he could keep them at bay for a while with grape and canister. Lieutenant Shaw directed him to do so and returned. By this time Colonel Garrard arrived; he had lost his hat and was, seemingly, very much excited. He stated the rebels were coming from Rogersville, and ordered me to move with my regiment in that direction, to the edge of the woods, and advance two companies as skirmishers. Colonel Garrard accompanied me. pointing out the position he wished my regiment to occupy. He

equested me to tie my horses and put as many men in the fight as
could; that we would not try to escape, but whip the rebels if pos-
ble, ordering me to hold the position assigned me at all hazards
ntil further orders from him. I ordered Captain Carns to move
rward with companies C, G, and B as skirmishers. He did so, and
on met the enemy and commenced a brisk skirmish, driving them
ack some 300 yards. I then ordered Captain Carns to return to
e.

At or near this time the rebels charged and captured the two guns
ast of —— Creek near the house of Mr. Russell. They then moved
ward our camp. The Seventh Ohio Volunteer Cavalry was formed
ear the camp and supporting the two guns yet remaining in our
ossession. Colonel Garrard sent me orders to send three companies
 support the two guns. I started three companies under command
f Captain Carns; when he got in sight of the point ordered to, he
iscovered the rebels had taken the guns. They (the rebels) raised
he yell and commenced advancing from every direction on my posi-
ion. I sent an orderly to inform Colonel Garrard if he did not
ssist me I would soon be completely surrounded. By this time
'aptain Carns returned; he had been cut off from me by the rebels,
nd very nearly the whole of the three companies captured. Cap-
ain Carns informed me that Colonel Garrard and the whole of the
eventh Ohio Volunteer Cavalry had left the field, and were across
he Holston River.

The 50 men detailed to hold the hill east of our camp, also the two
ompanies sent east of our camp, had been skirmishing some time.
When the Seventh Ohio Volunteer Cavalry left the field they, the
wo companies and 50 detailed men, were compelled to fall back to
y position. A number of them were captured in returning. At
his time I did not have more than 200 men who had ammunition,
nd was completely surrounded by at least 4,000 rebels, who were
ithin 75 yards of us, demanding a surrender. They had already
ossession of my horses, and were killing and wounding my men at
 fearful rate. I summoned the officers of my regiment and con-
ulted with them as to what measures best to adopt. All instantly
greed that a surrender was the only thing possible, so I at once sur-
endered myself and command. William Russell, of Company A,
as shot and killed after we had grounded arms.

The officers and men of Captain Phillips' (Second Illinois) battery
ischarged their duty nobly.

We were marched the whole of the night following our capture.
uring that night a number of the men effected their escape.

The officers and men of the Second East Tennessee Mounted In-
antry performed their duty with the most gratifying coolness and
ourage, and were only induced to surrender to greatly superior
umbers after all hope of further successful resistance was gone.
he position in which we were placed by Colonel Garrard I was
rdered to hold until he should give me directions to abandon it,
nd it was in carrying out my instructions that the regiment was
aptured.

Colonel, I some time since made application for a court of inquiry
 investigate the circumstances of our capture, and as statements
ave been made prejudicial to the good name of my regiment, I re-
pectfully reiterate my request for a court of inquiry, in order that
he blame may be placed where it properly belongs. I feel fully
atisfied that when the facts of the case are known, the officers and

men of the Second East Tennessee Mounted Infantry will be found to have done their whole duty.

As the time of service of my regiment will soon expire, I respectfully urge that the court may be ordered at as early a day as practicable.

Very respectfully, your obedient servant,

D. A. CARPENTER,
Major Second East Tennessee Mounted Infantry.

Lieut. Col. G. M. BASCOM,
Assistant Adjutant-General.

No. 3.

Reports of Brig. Gen. James M. Shackelford, U. S. Army.

MORRISTOWN, *November* 7, 1863.

I have as yet been unable to learn definitely of more than 60 or 70 of the Second Tennessee that escaped, but they are still coming in small squads of 2 and 3, and as they were familiar with the country I take it for granted that many are still unreported who were not captured. The horses that were not killed in the race were ruined. Many [men] lost their arms; the rest of them, I understand, left for Knoxville this a. m. There are 360 of the Seventh Ohio who have arrived. I will send scouts as directed. If I am not more deceived than I think possible, you may rest perfectly easy in relation to an attack on the force up here by the enemy; he has not exceeding 3,500 mounted men, all told. His infantry will not cross the rivers. They are not doing one thing by way of rebuilding bridges, &c.

J. M. SHACKELFORD,
Brigadier-General.

General BURNSIDE.

MORRISTOWN, *November* 7, 1863.

GENERAL: Since sending you dispatch in relation to numbers of Second Tennessee and Seventh Ohio that escaped, Colonel Garrard reports that Captain Rankin and his company, who had been sent to Jonesborough on scout, had come in, making 430 of the Seventh Ohio. Captain Jones, of the Second Tennessee, has just reported that he understands that 56 of the Second Tennessee were at Bean's Station this a. m.

J. M. SHACKELFORD,
Brigadier-General.

General BURNSIDE.

No. 4.

Report of Col. Selby Harney, Thirty-fourth Kentucky Infantry.

HEADQUARTERS UNITED STATES FORCES,
Morristown, Tenn., November 7, 1863.

COLONEL: I have the honor to make the following report:

About 3 o'clock yesterday afternoon, information was brought to me that the rebels were coming in force on the Greeneville road, driv ing Colonel Garrard's command from Rogersville before them. Pretty shortly after, squads of them (Garrard's command) could be seen galloping bare-headed into town, and to all appearances perfectly demoralized. I had in the meanwhile moved my regiment upon the hill, directing Lieutenant-Colonel Dillard to support the battery. The greater part of the Eleventh Tennessee I ordered out on the Greeneville road, if possible to get some information of the enemy. The other portion I sent on the Bean's Station road.

After being directed by you to hold this place at all hazards, I received a dispatch from General Willcox (copy inclosed), directing me, in case I could do no better, to fall back. I telegraphed him what your orders were, and that I should wait for him.

At 6 o'clock, after showing Colonel Garrard what I had done and the men I had for defense, I turned over the command to him, he being senior officer. I, however, continued to throw up rifle-pits all night.

I cannot close without expressing surprise that Colonel Garrard did not send word in advance to me that he was coming, and I am doubly thankful to the officers and men of my command for the promptness and alacrity with which they took their position in line, notwithstanding the reports from the panic-stricken and demoralized men seen galloping around the base of the hill on which we were posted.

I am, colonel, respectfully yours,

S. HARNEY,
Colonel Thirty-fourth Kentucky Infantry, Comdg. Post.

Lieut. Col. LEWIS RICHMOND,
Assistant Adjutant-General.

[Inclosure.]

GREENEVILLE, *November* 6, 1863.

Colonel HARNEY:
I shall move to Bull's Gap. If you cannot do better, fall back in as good order as possible.

O. B. WILLCOX,
Brigadier-General.

No. 5.

Reports of Maj. Gen. Samuel Jones, C. S. Army, commanding Department of Western Virginia and East Tennessee.

NARROWS, *November* 7, 1863.

GENERAL : The following just received from Blountsville:

Our cavalry, under Brig. Gen. W. E. Jones and Colonel Giltner, yesterday captured at Rogersville 850 prisoners, 4 pieces of artillery, 2 stand of colors, 60 wagons, and about 1,000 animals. Our loss, 2 killed and 6 or 8 wounded.

R. RANSOM, JR.,
Major-General.

General Echols has reached Union. Extent of his loss not reported. I will join him to-morrow.

SAM. JONES,
Major-General.

General S. COOPER.

(Same to General Bragg.)

[Indorsements.]

NOVEMBER 8, 1863.

Respectfully submitted to the President.

I am happy to relieve in some measure the anguish inspired by the news I was constrained to communicate this morning* by the more cheering intelligence of the within just received by me.

J. A. SEDDON.

This success may affect the movements of the enemy in front of General Jones.

J. D[AVIS].

—

HDQRS. DEPT. OF WESTERN VIRGINIA AND EAST TENN.,
Dublin, December 11, 1863.

GENERAL : I have the honor to forward with this the reports of Maj. Gen. R. Ransom, jr., and his subordinate commanders of the attack on the enemy near Rogersville, Tenn., and the reports of Brig. Gen. John Echols and subordinate commanders of the battle of Droop Mountain, in Pocahontas County, W. Va. Both these affairs occurred on the same day (6th ultimo).

The affair at Rogersville was a complete success and reflects great credit on the officers and men concerned.†

With great respect, your obedient servant,

SAM. JONES,
Major-General, Commanding.

General S. COOPER,
Adjt. and Insp. Gen., C. S. Army, Richmond, Va.

———

No. 6.

Report of Maj. Gen. Robert Ransom, jr., C. S. Army, commanding District of Southwestern Virginia and East Tennessee.

HDQRS. DIST. SOUTHWESTERN VIRGINIA AND EAST TENN.,
Camp near Blountsville, Tenn., November 14, 1863.

MAJOR : I have the honor to inclose reports of Brigadier-General Jones and Colonel Giltner relative to late attack upon the enemy at Rogersville. General Jones has supplied copies of my letters to him, and they accompany his report. Colonel Giltner's report was sent to General Jones for indorsement. I inclose both the note of my adjutant-general to General Jones and his reply thereto; also my letter of instructions to Colonel Giltner. I regret there should be any discrepancies in the two reports, but I am satisfied they are not irreconcilable. It was intended for the attacks by both brigades to be independent, but simultaneous, and of course when the two forces came together the senior officer was to take command of the

———

*Report of Echols' defeat at Droop Mountain, W. Va. See Series I, Vol. XXIX, Part I, p. 525.

†Portion here omitted is printed with reports of engagement at Droop Mountain, W. Va. See also Jones' report of February 6, 1864, in Series I, Vol. XXX, Part II, p. 602.

whole. I did not intend to unite the brigades as my instructions show.

The result of the expedition is the best proof that it was conducted well, and I am unwilling to create or sustain bickering or jealousy when there should be mutual good feeling. General Jones was verbally instructed to change the point of crossing the river, if from fuller information it should become advisable. The first report gave as captured 850 prisoners, 4 pieces of artillery, 60 wagons, and 1,000 animals. About 775 prisoners arrived, the artillery as at first reported, 32 wagons, and 3 ambulances. The regimental colors and our garrison flag are in my hands. One regimental flag was captured, but in some way lost. I regret that up to this time I have been unable to have accounted for more than about 300 animals, all told. I much fear they were appropriated by the men and have been sent off and sold. There is no other reasonable conclusion. The affair was a decided success, and I have thanked the officers and soldiers engaged in it.

Very respectfully, your obedient servant,
                                    R. RANSOM, Jr.,
                                              Major-General.
Maj. C. S. STRINGFELLOW,
    Assistant Adjutant-General, Dublin, Va.

[Inclosures.]

HDQRS. DIST. SOUTHWESTERN VIRGINIA AND EAST TENN.,
        Near Blountsville, Tenn., November 12, 1863.

Brig. Gen. W. E. JONES,
              Commanding, &c.:

GENERAL: The major-general commanding directs me to inclose the report of Colonel Giltner for your indorsement, inasmuch as the two brigades were united in the latter part of the affair of the 6th instant. He requests that you forward your report of the same affair as soon as possible.

Very respectfully, your obedient servant,
                                    T. ROWLAND,
                                Assistant Adjutant-General.

HEADQUARTERS JONES' BRIGADE,
            November 13, 1863.

Maj. THOMAS ROWLAND,
    Asst. Adjt. Gen., Dist. of S. W. Va. and East Tenn.:

MAJOR: In reply to yours, inclosing a report of Colonel Giltner relative to the attack on the enemy near Rogersville, the 6th instant, I can say if by indorsement you wish me to confirm his statements, such is not in my power. My report will show you the affair appears to me in a different light from what it does to Colonel Giltner. As the report is not addressed to me, and is not sent through me, I presume it was not intended I should correct errors in it. I was under the impression I commanded in this affair, and the statement of Mr. Watterson will show Colonel Giltner was of the same opinion before the fight.

Very respectfully, your obedient servant,
                                    W. E. JONES,
                                        Brigadier-General.

HEADQUARTERS DIVISION,
Camp near Blountsville, November 3, 1863.

Brig. Gen. JOHN S. WILLIAMS,
  Commanding Cavalry Brigade:

GENERAL: It is represented that there is at Rogersville a body of two or three regiments of the enemy, and it is desired to capture that force. You will drop down the river with your brigade, having pickets at the fords, cross the North Fork of Holston, and attack at Rogersville at daylight in the morning of Friday, the 6th instant. Brig. Gen. W. E. Jones will proceed by the Horse Creek and Beach Creek Valley roads and attack simultaneously with you. Your march after getting across the North Fork should be rapid and in the night. You can go a few miles below Kingsport, so as to reach Rogersville easily in the night of Thursday, and make the attack as directed. No wagons except for ammunition will be taken. You can carry the battery now with you if you desire it. Have prepared enough cooked rations for the movement. After executing the movement and the attack you will return rapidly to your present position. Concert between you and Brigadier-General Jones will be necessary. General Jones has been directed after the attack to return to his present position.

  Very respectfully, your obedient servant,
            R. RANSOM, JR.,
              Major-General.

[Indorsement.]

HDQRS. DIST. SOUTHWESTERN VIRGINIA AND EAST TENN.,
  Blountsville, Tenn., November 4, 1863.

Brig. Gen. John S. Williams having been relieved of his command, and Colonel Giltner assigned to the command of his brigade, the latter officer will execute the order herein conveyed.

            R. RANSOM, JR.,
              Major-General.

No. 7.

*Report of Brig. Gen. William E. Jones, C. S. Army, commanding
Cavalry Brigade.*

HEADQUARTERS JONES' BRIGADE,
  Near Carter's Station, Tenn., November 13, 1863.

MAJOR: In accordance with inclosed instructions from headquarters District Southwestern Virginia and East Tennessee, my command rendezvoused at Banchman's Ford on the 4th instant. On inquiry finding if it crossed here there would be danger of alarming the enemy, I deemed it best to cross near Spurgeon's Mill, and encamped for the night a few miles below.

Moving early next morning the command halted at Easly's, on Horse Creek, 5 miles from Kingsport, and fed the horses. From this point I communicated with Colonel Giltner near noon my intention to execute the original plan of attack. Arriving 17 miles from Rogersville on the Beach Creek road near dark, we halted to eed and cook rations. Here it was ascertained the road leading to Smith's and Dodson's Fords ran within 6 miles of the camps of the enemy. It was also ascertained both fords were difficult and dangerous, and the night was dark and rainy.

To reach the point assigned me by the hour designated required me to cross the Holston before daylight. By intricate mountain paths, exacting the utmost care on the part of all, we reached the Long Shoals, 12 miles above Rogersville, and crossed in safety. Reaching the old stage road, nothing could be heard of Colonel Giltner's command, but I determined to turn the position of the enemy at the mouth of Big Creek by way of the Carter's Valley road, my brigade crossing the old stage road for this purpose. Soon a messenger overtook me with tidings of Colonel Giltner, also reporting about 100 Federal Tennessee home guards at Kincade's. Pushing ahead part of the Eighth Virginia Cavalry to surround and capture this force, they encountered near where the home guards were expected a scout of 50 men from the Second Tennessee Federal Regiment. The attack was made with such vigor that but 17 men of this force escaped this onset. Moving on briskly to the junction of the roads, the Eighth Regiment turned east on the old stage road and took position on the first eminence.

As it was now long after Colonel Giltner should have made his attack and no engagement could be heard, I felt assured the enemy must have made his escape, but moved the Eighth across to the river road from Big Creek to Dodson's Ford in hopes of intercepting fugitives. The men of the Twenty-seventh Battalion Virginia Cavalry, under Capt. J. B. Thompson, were ordered to charge into Rogersville, and in so doing captured upward of 100 prisoners and some army supplies. For the same reason the Eighth was ordered to the river road. Colonel Witcher was ordered with his own and the Thirty-seventh Battalion Virginia Cavalry to Smith's Ford. The Thirty-sixth Battalion Virginia Cavalry was held in reserve near town, and the Twenty-first Regiment Virginia Cavalry in the position first held by the Eighth Regiment. The Twenty-seventh Battalion Virginia Cavalry was ordered, after the captures in Rogersville, by the railroad to the river. After these dispositions had been made a party of 55 home guards (Federal) attacked the town from the west, but were easily dispersed by a small party under Lieut. W. M. Hopkins, aide-de-camp.

After all the prisoners had been collected and marched out east of the town, the wagons loaded, hitched to, and driven to the forks of the main roads, was heard the first firing in the direction of Big Creek. The Twenty-first Regiment was immediately ordered up the old stage road with directions to be guided by the firing and to join in the battle. The Thirty-sixth Battalion was ordered up from town and all the other commands were recalled in haste. The old stage road being open, the Twenty-first having moved across toward the river, a party of 125 of the enemy attempted to escape toward Rogersville, but were intercepted and all captured by the timely arrival of Witcher's, Claiborne's, and Smith's commands. By this time firing had ceased in front and I felt assured of the surrender of the enemy, as proved to be the case.

Two hundred and ninety-four prisoners were taken by my brigade, acting alone. The Eighth Virginia took 9 wagons and teams, 7 of which were secured. The remainder of the command took 3 wagons and 2 ambulances, all of which were secured.

From Colonel Corns' report it will be seen the roads west of th
position of the enemy were held by the Eighth Virginia Cavalry
and a large part of the 556 prisoners taken here were taken by th
Eighth and sent in charge of an officer to Colonel Giltner. Had Co
onel Giltner made a prompt and bold attack that would have di
covered the position of the enemy before my dispositions were made
under the impression of his having abandoned his position, it is be
lieved none would have escaped. The unaccountable delay, doub
less, has proved very detrimental to our interests. ·

To Captain McKinney, of General Jackson's staff; to Mr. W. F
Watterson, clerk of my brigade quartermaster, and to Mr. Fipps an
other guides my thanks are especially due for their activity, energy
and judgment on this occasion.

To Lieut. W. M. Hopkins, of my personal staff, I am under grea
obligations for the efficient discharge of his official duties.

Very respectfully, your obedient servant,

W. E. JONES,
Brigadier-General.

Maj. THOMAS ROWLAND,
Asst. Adjt. Gen., Dist. S. W. Va.; and E. Tenn.

[Inclosure No. 1.]

HEADQUARTERS DIVISION,
Camp Near Blountsville, Tenn., November 3, 1863.

Brig. Gen. W. E. JONES,
Commanding Cavalry Brigade:

GENERAL : I inclose a letter of instruction and a map* for you
guidance. I find the Horse Creek Valley too much to your righ
You must take the most direct road, or the one you think bes
Dodson's Ford is represented to me as the best. I will send to yo
Captain McKinney, of General Jackson's staff, who knows the cour
try thoroughly about Rogersville. It looks as though it would rair
and we may be prevented from making the movement. William
will be relieved to-morrow, and I shall have to send the letter of ir
struction to Colonel Giltner. You had best have the battery com
to this side of the Holston, and let me know where you have it.
shall move up toward the junction of the two rivers to-morrow o
the Jonesborough road. It may rain and cause the river to rise afte
you get to Rogersville. In that event you may make your way ou
by Kingsport. Reports from Kingsport and Rogersville represen
the enemy encamped on Big Creek 4 miles above Rogersville. Giv
directions so that your wagons may not get into any difficulty. I
you can do so it would be well for you to come here to-night.

*   *   *   *   *   *   *

Giltner will have orders to attack at the same hour you do, that i
at daylight on Friday morning. Neither should wait for the othe
as both have the same orders.

Yours, truly,

R. RANSOM, JR.,
Major-General.

---

* Not found.

HEADQUARTERS DIVISION,
Camp near Blountsville, November 3, 1863.

Brig. Gen. W. E. JONES,
Commanding Cavalry Brigade:

GENERAL: It is represented that there is at Rogersville a force of two or three regiments of the enemy, and it is desired to capture that force. You will please collect your brigade, throwing a force in the direction of Jonesborough, and with greater part proceed to Rogersville by a route leading up Horse Creek and down Beach Creek Valleys, cross the Holston at one of the fords near Rogersville, and attack at daylight on Friday morning, the 6th instant. You will cover the road leading to my rear by small pickets, so as to carry information both to yourself and to the infantry on the north side of the Holston east of Kingsport. Brigadier-General Williams, commanding cavalry brigade, will move by way of Kingsport across the North Fork of Holston and join in the attack at the same time as yourself.

After starting directly for Rogersville rapidity will be required both in the execution of the march and attack, and in your return to your present position. I need hardly caution you as to your left flank. The force sent toward Jonesborough should cover it, as well as check a direct advance in that direction. You will have enough cooked rations prepared, and take nothing else except ammunition. No wagons except for ammunition will be taken. I leave it to your discretion to take the battery of artillery now with you or not, as you may deem best. If not carried have it properly posted, so as to do good service if needed and not to be subject to capture.

Very respectfully, your obedient servant,

R. RANSOM, JR.,
Major-General.

[Inclosure No. 2.]

HDQRS. JONES' CAVALRY BRIGADE, Q. M. DEPT.,
November 13, 1863.

Being called upon by Brig. Gen. W. E. Jones to give a statement of my connection with the affair at Big Creek, Hawkins County, Tenn., I most respectfully submit the following:

Left by General Jones at the house of Mr. William Lyons, where the road from Long's Ford crosses the old stage road, in order to see that the brigade under his (General Jones') command took the right road, when I saw that Colonel Giltner's column had arrived I went to the head of it, and while there understood from him that he was going to halt his brigade at Surgoinsville until he heard from General Jones. This was concluded upon, I supposed, since General Jones had crossed the river at least 14 miles from and above the ford at which it was intended when the expedition begun, and to have an understanding as to the plan of attack. When the rear of Jones' brigade had passed the crossing of the roads I hastened on to inform General Jones of Colonel Giltner's intention. I overtook General Jones about 3 miles from where he came into Carter's Valley road going very rapidly at the head of his column. When I told him that Colonel Giltner was awaiting at Surgoinsville to hear from him he seemed surprised, and ordered me to go immediately and tell Colonel Giltner to move on and attack the enemy in front.

I started back to the first cross-road, and had got about 1½ mile when I met a courier from Colonel Giltner who said that his whole brigade had passed down the old stage road in a great hurry, having routed the Yankee pickets at Surgoinsville. I then turned to follow on after General Jones, and had gone on the Carter's Valley road to within 5 miles of Rogersville, when I learned that Colonel Giltner had not gone on down farther than C. C. Miller's, 8 miles east of Rogersville. I immediately about faced and went back to the road leading from the Carter's Valley road to the old stage road, coming out at Mr. C. C. Miller's, where Colonel Giltner was understood to be. When I turned back I was about 4 miles from C. C. Miller' (or Yellow Store), but when I got there all of the brigade under Giltner had passed along, except the artillery (Lowry's battery) and the rear guard.

I went on after Colonel Giltner, passing about half of his column (the rear half) in motion, and overtook him only a few hundred yard east of Dr. John Shields', 6 miles east of Rogersville. Colonel Giltner was at the time, with a portion of two companies of Colonel Carter's (First Tennessee). cavalry, together with Major Goforth and Captain Fulkerson, in a field on the right-hand side of the road. The squadron was under the command of Major Goforth, as I soon after learned. I delivered General Jones' order to Colonel Giltner to attack as soon as possible. The squadron under Goforth went on the right to flank the movement of the main column in its advance to attack the enemy, who were understood to be about a mile distant on an elevation in the woods to the left of the road. think the attack was made about 9 a. m., nearly thirty minutes after I delivered General Jones' order to Colonel Giltner.

Respectfully, your obedient servant,

W. H. WATTERSON.

No. 8.

Report of Col. James M. Corns, Eighth Virginia Cavalry.

HDQRS. EIGHTH VIRGINIA CAVALRY,
November 13, 1863.

GENERAL: At your request I make the following report of the part taken by the Eighth Virginia Cavalry at Rogersville, on the 6th instant:

After a forced march of twenty-four hours my regiment arrived at and crossed the Holston River, near Rogersville. At this point was ordered across the country on a by-road to the Carter's Valley road, at a point some 8 miles above the town, and there await the arrival of Colonel Giltner. I had not waited but a few minutes when I was informed by you that Colonel Giltner was moving on the road between me and the river. At this juncture, being informed by you that there was a company of cavalry on picket some 4 miles in advance of me, I threw forward Company E, of this regiment, with instructions when they arrived at the enemy's picket to charge down upon them, and not to permit any of them to reach Rogersville to give the alarm. This order was carried out to the letter, not one of

the enemy being permitted to enter the town. Company E, led by
Capt. H. C. Everett, having captured some 40 of them, dispersed
the remainder of them in the woods.

Meeting with no further obstruction, my command was moved,
by your direction, immediately in rear of the enemy, on road leading to a ferry below Rogersville. While moving my command
through the woods (the undergrowth is very dense at this point) I
found myself within 20 yards of the wagon train of the enemy,
which had been sent to the rear, their pickets being already driven
in from the front by Colonel Giltner. Finding the enemy's wagon
train about to move, I ordered my command to charge the guard,
composed of about 75 or 80 men, which they did, capturing the
whole of the wagon train and nearly all of the guard. I then immediately moved on with my regiment, and soon found myself closely
engaged with the main force of the enemy. I immediately posted
my command behind a fence and on a wooded hill-side, in easy range
of the enemy's camp, where we remained under a heavy fire about
fifteen minutes.

The enemy were about to charge my position when Colonel Giltner commenced the action in front, which appeared to disconcert
the enemy so much that, although they made an effort in considerable force to dislodge me, they were quickly repulsed and driven
back on their former position. Colonel Giltner attacking vigorously about this time, the enemy threw down their arms and fled in
every direction, large numbers of them surrendering on the field.
Others were captured in squads through the neighborhood; a few of
them, however, made their escape across the river.

My command succeeded in capturing in this affair upwards of 300
prisoners, 9 wagons and teams loaded with quartermaster's stores, 7
of which we succeeded in bringing with us. We also captured a
large number of small-arms, saddles, and about 90 horses and mules,
in addition to the mules that were attached to the wagons.

The command was moved, by your direction, on the Carter's Valley road back to Blountsville, where we arrived safely on the 8th
instant, bringing with us, besides captured property above mentioned, some 800 prisoners.

Our loss in this affair is 1 killed and 2 or 3 slightly wounded.

I am, general, with the highest respect, your obedient servant,

J. M. CORNS,
Colonel, Commanding Eighth Virginia Cavalry.

Brig. Gen. W. E. JONES,
Commanding Cavalry Brigade.

No. 9.

*Report of Col. H. L. Giltner, Fourth Kentucky Cavalry (Confeder-
ate), commanding Second Cavalry Brigade.*

HEADQUARTERS SECOND CAVALRY BRIGADE,
Near Kingsport, Tenn., November 10, 1863.

SIR: I have the honor to submit the following report of the operations of the troops under my command during the recent expedition
into the enemy's lines:

In obedience to orders from district headquarters I moved out of

Kingsport at 6 p. m. on 5th instant. You are already furnished with the general order containing the different corps of the command and their order of march. The whole force did not exceed 1,200, as the return of my adjutant-general for that day exhibits. Such was the secrecy with which the movement was conducted that not only the citizens, but the officers had no idea of its contemplation until it had progressed considerably toward its execution.

Some delay occurred in crossing the river on account of the darkness of the night and the difficult passage of the horses and artillery over a bad ford. All was, however, soon in order, and the march continued in a cold, chilling rain, without further obstacle until we were unexpectedly halted by the passage of Brigadier-General Jones' brigade across our road to the Carter's Valley road, upon our right. I did not see General Jones, but learned from his staff officer that this change in the original plan was rendered necessary by the impracticability of the road to and across the river at the ford he proposed at first to cross.

As soon as General Jones' brigade had crossed I moved on slowly, intending to halt a short time at Surgoinsville in order to give General Jones time to reach the enemy's flank and rear before attacking him in front. But just as my advance reached Surgoinsville it was fired upon by a scouting party of the enemy which had reached there that morning (now 4.30 a. m.), as I afterward learned. I communicated this fact to General Jones. The enemy, about 30 in number, retired precipitately on being pressed by a squadron of the First Tennessee, which constituted my advance.

On arriving within 2 miles of Big Creek, where the enemy were understood to be encamped, we came upon a body of the enemy in a strong position, and though not discovering more than 25 or 30, furnished reason for the suspicion of a larger force masked behind the ridge and under cover of dense pine thickets. Some time was consumed in revealing their intention and force by throwing forward flanking and skirmishing parties, before which they again retired. We moved forward without delay, and on approaching Big Creek discovered that the enemy were in the act of crossing at Russell's Ford. Colonel Carter (First Tennessee) was sent at double-quick to cut them off, which he did in most gallant style.

Being cut off from the ford the enemy took a strong position on the opposite side of Big Creek, where they had been encamped, leaving one section of Phillips' battery, supported by three companies Second East Tennessee Mounted Infantry, at Russell's house, 300 yards in front of their position and on this side of Big Creek. Lieutenant-Colonel Trimble, Tenth Kentucky, and Major Parker, Fourth Kentucky, were brought forward and dismounted in 350 yards of this section and moved up. The men all went forward with the greatest enthusiasm, making no halt for balls, shells, or bullets. Colonel Carter, after intercepting their retreat by the ford, turned upon these two guns, and advancing by a shorter route was the first to reach them, capturing at the same time a large number of wagons which had moved out to cross the river. Without halting, a simultaneous advance was made by the three regiments (Tenth Kentucky, First Tennessee, and Fourth Kentucky) across Big Creek, which, though deep and rapid, proved no obstacle, and up the hill on which was posted their other section of artillery, supported by their main force.

At this time Captain Lowry's battery, detained by difficult roads, arrived upon the field and engaged the battery of the enemy, delivering its fire most effectually. Immediately on crossing the creek our forces encountered the enemy in a chosen position, where, after an hour's sharp conflict, they succeeded in capturing the other section of Phillips' battery and about 450 of the enemy. The remainder endeavored to effect their escape by precipitate flight. Here I ordered forward Major Clarke, Sixteenth Georgia Battalion, and Colonel Slemp, Sixty-fourth Virginia, whom I had held in reserve mounted, and sent them at double-quick to pursue and overhaul the fugitives, which was done in the most praiseworthy manner, the Sixteenth Georgia Battalion following them across the river and the Sixty-fourth to Rogersville. A party of these, endeavoring to escape by a lower ford, was met by the Eighth Virginia, of General Jones' command, and most of them captured.

In all about 550 prisoners were taken by the forces under my command; four brass 6-pounder James guns (Company M, Second Illinois Light Artillery), some 30 wagons loaded with all manner of quartermaster's and commissary, medical, and ordnance stores, together with all their camp and garrison equipage, the horses and arms of the prisoners, all the papers appertaining to the adjutant-general's department, containing most valuable information, &c.

As already mentioned, our forces did not exceed 1,200, of which not more than 600 were engaged actively. The forces of the enemy, commanded by Col. Israel Garrard, Seventh Ohio Cavalry, consisted of Second East Tennessee Mounted Infantry, about full; Seventh Ohio Cavalry, 580 strong, and Phillips' battery, all composing half of Col. James P. T. Carter's brigade (Third Brigade Cavalry, Fourth Division, Twenty-third Army Corps). Colonel Garrard, commanding, escaped with the first who crossed the river. One major, several captains, and one acting adjutant-general were among the prisoners.

Our loss will not exceed 10 killed and wounded. The enemy's about 25 or 30. Seven wounded were paroled and left in charge of a surgeon.

Every exertion was used to secure all the captures and the artillery, and about 30 wagons were brought off safely, but, owing to a want of harness for the teams, two caissons and some 20 wagons were disabled and abandoned.

It was my intention to retire to where I could find a good position and obtain forage and remain until everything valuable was secured and sent to the rear, but, General Jones coming up, ordered me to fall back that night beyond the river, which was accomplished by 9 o'clock the next morning.

Two stand of colors captured by the Fourth Kentucky Cavalry were sent up this morning. One captured by the Tenth Kentucky was delivered to you by Brigadier-General Jones, and another taken by First Tennessee was afterward stolen from the regimental wagon.*

No discrimination can be made in the gallantry of troops where every corps commanded the admiration of its officers and the gratitude of their country. Their soldierly bearing in the presence of the enemy furnishes a just cause for pride and receives the unqualified approbation of their commander. Those actively engaged and those held in check manifested alike an equal willingness, even

---

* The regimental flag of the Second East Tennessee Infantry is reported as having been captured by Company B, Fourth Kentucky, and the national flag of same regiment as captured by Lieutenant-Colonel Trimble, Tenth Kentucky Battalion.

anxiety, to discharge their full duty as soldiers, even the most dangerous. Any discrimination among individuals would be invidious, and no one is slighted when it is asserted that all, with a trifling exception, may remember their actions that day with a just pride.

I am especially indebted to Colonel Heiskell, volunteer aide ; Captain Flusser, acting aide, and Captain Guerrant, assistant adjutant-general, for invaluable services on the field and throughout the expedition.

I am, most respectfully, your obedient servant,

H. L. GILTNER,
Colonel, Commanding Brigade.

Maj. THOMAS ROWLAND, *Assistant Adjutant-General.*

NOVEMBER 10–13, 1863.—Expedition from Skipwith's Landing to Tallulah Court-House, Miss.

Report of Col. Embury D. Osband, Third U. S. Colored Cavalry.

HEADQUARTERS POST,
Skipwith's Landing, Miss., November 15, 1863.

COLONEL : I have the honor to report that my command, consisting of the First Battalion, Fourth Illinois Cavalry, and three companies of the First Mississippi Cavalry (African Descent), 300 strong, in pursuance of instructions from major-general commanding, left Vicksburg at 11 a. m. the 10th instant, arriving at and crossing the Yazoo River at Anthony's Ferry in the afternoon, camping for the night at the ferry, on the north side of the river. Marched at daylight on the 11th, crossing Deer Creek at Black Fork, and moving up on the east side of it to within 7 miles of Rolling Fork, and camping for the night on Clark's plantation, a march of 37 miles.

Learning that Barksdale's (Mississippi) cavalry and the Seventh [?] Texas Cavalry, about 700 strong, had been at Rolling Fork four days previously, and had disabled the bridges across that stream and Deer Creek, at daylight on the 12th I recrossed Deer Creek, and arrived at the Mississippi River near Tallulah Court-House, and camped at the landing opposite Lake Providence.

Marched at 6 a. m., 13th instant, and arrived at this place at 12 m. I met no enemy and obtained no recruits, the route of march being through a deserted and abandoned country, and am now satisfied, from information which I regard reliable, that the two regiments of Confederate cavalry came from Yazoo City to intercept my march here. Failing to find us, they returned in the same direction, with what conscripts, horses, mules, hogs, and negroes they could obtain. About 50 men of the same class remain across Deer Creek, engaged in the same business.

I leave to-morrow morning with 170 men of my command, accompanied by Lieutenant Lee, Thirty-second Ohio Volunteers, and shall proceed beyond the Sunflower, if practicable, to assist Lieutenant Lee and to recruit.

I am, colonel, very respectfully, your obedient servant,

E. D. OSBAND,
Colonel, Commanding.

Lieut. Col. W. T. CLARK, *Assistant Adjutant-General.*

NOVEMBER 12, 1863.—Skirmish near Cumberland Gap, Tenn.

Report of Col. Wilson C. Lemert, Eighty-sixth Ohio Infantry.

CUMBERLAND GAP,
November 13, 1863—7 a. m.

Yesterday, at 5 a. m., I sent a train of 21 wagons 12 miles out the Virginia road for forage, with a guard of 31 men. At 10 a. m., learning that the rebels meditated an attack upon it, I went out with 100 cavalry, arriving just in time to witness the capture of the entire train and guard by a Confederate force under Captains Hurd and Dove, 71 strong. We charged them at once with the saber, completely routing them, recapturing the whole train in good order; recovered all the prisoners. We killed 3, wounded 7, captured 9 prisoners, nearly all their small-arms, and several horses. Captain Dove, commanding Confederates, was mortally wounded. We pursued them 10 miles, scattering them in every direction. I lost a fine horse ; was the only damage suffered. The Fourth Battalion, Ohio Volunteer Cavalry, behaved very gallantly, charging finely under a brisk fire, using the saber exclusively. No other news.

W. C. LEMERT,
Colonel, Commanding.

General BURNSIDE.

NOVEMBER 14–17, 1863.—Expedition from Maysville to Whitesburg and Decatur, Ala.

Report of Maj. J. Morris Young, Fifth Iowa Cavalry, commanding expedition.

CAMP NEAR MAYSVILLE, ALA.,
November 18, 1863.

CAPTAIN : I have the honor to report that, under orders from Col. W. W. Lowe, temporarily commanding Second Cavalry Division, dated November 13, 1863, instructing me to thoroughly scour the country situated between the Memphis and Charleston Railroad and the Tennessee River from Whitesburg to opposite Decatur, and drive out or capture the marauding rebel bands known to be roving over that country, pressing horses, mules, cattle, sheep, hogs, wheat, &c., and running them across the river for Confederate use ; to capture and destroy all boats and ferries on the river from Whitesburg to Decatur ; to break up or capture a band of rebels, supposed to be encamped near the Tennessee River, about the mouth of Limestone Creek, and to destroy or render unserviceable a grist and saw-mill in that vicinity and in the service of the rebels, I left camp early on the morning of November 14, with detachments from the Fifth Iowa, Fourth United States, Seventy-second and Seventeenth Indiana—in all, 400 men, and moving by a circuitous route across the mountains, leaving Huntsville to the right, reached Whitesburg at 5 p. m., capturing 2 Confederate soldiers after a lively chase of some 4 miles, a drove of 29 young, fat hogs, and the ferry-boat which had just come over for them. Learning that the island above was used as a rendezvous for captured stock, I detached Lieutenant McCamant, Fifth Iowa Cavalry, and 24 men to proceed with the ferry-boat and search it thoroughly. He returned about midnight with 25 head of horses and mules. The ferry-boat was then destroyed.

November 15, broke camp at daybreak and moved down the river some 3 or 4 miles below. Captain Bowman, Fourth United States, was detached with 150 men to make a *détour* northward, by way of Madison Station, down the Memphis and Charleston Railroad, and to secure a position in the rear of Limestone Creek, guarding the roads leading out by way of Mooresville and the point opposite Decatur, on this side the river; while I, with the remaining command, moved on down by way of Triana to the mouth of Limestone Creek.

At Triana, captured a sergeant (Confederate States Army), but found the ferry-boats (two of them) on the opposite side of the river, and saw rebels apparently guarding them; also learned that all boats below were, by Confederate authority, kept on the opposite side of the river and sent to this side only on certain preconcerted signals.

Patrolling the banks of the river, a skiff and two canoes were found. The detachment of the Fifth Iowa Cavalry was called on for volunteers to cross in these and bring off the ferry-boats. The call was almost unanimously responded to. Quartermaster Sergt. A. T. Phelps, Company G, and 11 men were selected, who, under cover of 25 sharpshooters selected from the Seventy-second Indiana, dashed across and brought off both the large boats without loss or accident. The information that all the boats below were on the opposite side of the river and also that a number were collected for some purpose over there and secreted up a creek some miles below, necessitated the idea of organizing a regular boat expedition. Lieutenant Cassell, Company I, Seventy-second Indiana, and 30 men were selected, and with instructions to capture all boats where it was practicable and join me with them at the mouth of Limestone Creek, where, should we be fortunate enough to find the enemy, they could co-operate in the attack from the river side. The boat party moved out into the stream, just beyond Triana. The advance chased a party of 15 rebels several miles, but their horses were too fleet for ours. Arriving at the mouth of Limestone [Creek] I found no enemy there; communicated with Captain Bowman, who was already in position. Learned from him that he had chased a squad of rebels and been fired on in the rear by a small party, but in both cases the enemy's horses were too fleet. He (Captain Bowman) also informed me that the day before a squad of 20 and another of 60 rebels had passed down the road and crossed over the river to Decatur. Shortly after our arrival Lieutenant Cassell and party arrived with eight boats, some of them being 60 feet long. Having learned that Major Falconnet, with four companies of rebels, was commanding the post at Decatur, I thought that with the eight boats now in my possession we could attack the post and bring off the ferry-boat without incurring too much risk; accordingly, organized an expedition to start from the mouth of Limestone, which is 5 miles above Decatur, two hours before daybreak the next morning. About 12 midnight the enemy commenced throwing up rockets, and continued some time.

November 16, deeming it advisable to be cautious and reconnoiter before dispatching the boat party, parties were sent out in all directions. At dawn the rebels opened on us a brisk fire of small-arms from across the river. A party returning from opposite Decatur brought information that two pieces of artillery could be seen across

he river in position and covering the landing. A prisoner cap-
ured by the same party reported he had been sent over that morn-
ng with a small party; that General Roddey had been sent for,
and was to be at Decatur by sunrise; that a portion of General Lee's
command had already arrived, and that they had been intrenching
on the upper and river side of Decatur since midnight. Another
party reported seeing the enemy throwing up earth-works.

Rather amused than otherwise at so unexpectedly stirring up so
much trouble for the rebels, I deemed it not advisable to attempt
just at that time capturing that only remaining boat mentioned in
my instructions, and had the boats moved around from under fire of
he enemy and up Limestone Creek, where they were chopped up
and burned.

Having destroyed certain portions of the machinery of the mill
referred to in my instructions, and which I found to be in the service
of the rebels, grinding corn and sawing lumber to build boats, the
command was divided into three separate detachments, and, with
instructions to concentrate at Huntsville, moved out by different
routes, leaving the rebels across the river still shoveling dirt, accord-
ng to last accounts.

We had 1 man slightly wounded. No means of ascertaining the
oss, if any, of the enemy. Arriving at Huntsville, the Fourth
United States reported having captured on the way 5 Confederate
soldiers, 1 of them the notorious Captain Robison.

November 17, arrived in camp here about noon. The country
from Whitesburg to Decatur is bottom lands, exceedingly rich, and
n a high state of cultivation; the plantations very large, generally
from 2,000 to 4,000 acres each. The crop of corn is enormous, and
horses, mules, cattle, hogs, and sheep were in abundance as I passed
through. Many who had their stock hid out or run across the river,
had just had it returned or brought out, thinking the Yankees all
out of the country. As the result of the expedition, we captured
and destroyed 9 ferry-boats, 9 Confederate States soldiers, one (supposed to be) a captain, and one a sergeant, and remounted the command with from 150 to 200 fine mules and horses, with a loss of 1
man slightly wounded.

Respectfully, your most obedient servant,

J. MORRIS YOUNG,
Major, Commanding Expedition.

Capt. R. P. KENNEDY,
Asst. Adjt. Gen., Second Cavalry Division.

ADDENDA.

CHATTANOOGA, TENN., *November* 30, 1863.

Brig. Gen. GEORGE CROOK,
Commanding, &c.:

GENERAL: I have the honor to acknowledge the receipt of the
report of Maj. J. M. Young, Fifth Iowa Cavalry, of his expedition
through the country situated between the Memphis and Charleston
Railroad and the Tennessee River, between the 14th and 17th instant.
The major-general commanding directs that you tender his thanks
to Major Young for the brave, energetic, and prudent manner in
which the expedition was conducted.

Very respectfully, your obedient servant,

WM. D. WHIPPLE,
Brigadier-General, and Assistant Adjutant-General.

NOVEMBER 15, 1863.—Skirmish at Pillowville, Tenn.

Report of Col. George E. Waring, jr., Fourth Missouri Cavalry

HDQRS. FIRST BRIG., SIXTH DIV., 16TH ARMY CORPS,
Union City, Tenn., November 18, 1863.

On Sunday, the 15th instant, I sent out Captain Hencke, Company B, Fourth Missouri Cavalry, in command of 100 cavalry to attack a conscripting party which I was informed would be at Pillowville 33 miles southeast of here, on the morning of the 15th instant He arrived there at about 10 a. m., and came upon the party, numbering 34 men. They fled and he pursued them for 3 miles, killing 5 of the enemy and capturing 3 prisoners, including a lieutenant o Faulkner's command. No loss on our side.

Very respectfully, your obedient servant,
GEO. E. WARING, JR.,
Colonel Fourth Missouri Cavalry, Commanding Brigade.

Capt. J. HOUGH,
Assistant Adjutant-General, Columbus, Ky.

NOVEMBER 19, 1863.—Skirmish at Meriwether's Ferry, near Union City Tenn.

Report of Capt. Franklin Moore, Second Illinois Cavalry.

UNION CITY, *November* 20, 1863.

I have just received the following from Capt. F. Moore, whom sent after the rebels, who went to Hickman. "We came, we saw we conquered."

NOVEMBER 20, 1863.

Colonel WARING,
Commanding, Union City:

I attacked the devils at Meriwether's Ferry, at noon, yesterday. I whipped them and killed 11 men, and took Colonel Sol. G. Street and 55 men ; also one wagon-load of arms and some horses. My loss none, except 1 man wounded.

Yours, truly,
F. MOORE,
Captain, Commanding Battalion.

The cavalry to guard working party is ordered.
GEORGE E. WARING, JR.,
Colonel, Commanding.

Captain HOUGH,
Assistant Adjutant-General, Columbus, Ky.

NOVEMBER 19, 1863.—Skirmish at Mulberry Gap, Tenn.

Report of Brig. Gen. Orlando B. Willcox, U. S. Army.

TAZEWELL, TENN.,
November 20, 1863.

I have the honor to report everything comes through in good order. The rebel force that was at Kingsport seems to have been concentrating several days toward Cumberland Gap. At Mulberry tap and Sneedville it is reported that a considerable force was rossing Clinch River at Walker's Ford to-day, 7 miles above Sneed-ille. That is probably the force that moved down toward Rogers-ille. A small scouting party, under command of Captain Ham-nond, Sixty-fifth Indiana, mounted, charged through the camp f a rebel regiment (Sixty-fourth Virginia), and scattered it at Mul-erry Gap last night, killing 3, wounding 1, capturing 1 prisoner, ome horses, and arms. We now hold Mulberry Gap, with small orce. There are two rebel regiments at Sneedville. I expect to nove to Cumberland Gap to-morrow.

O. B. WILLCOX,
Brigadier-General.

Major-General GRANT.

NOVEMBER 19, 1863.—Scout from Memphis, Tenn., to Hernando, Miss.

Report of Brig. Gen. Benjamin H. Grierson, U. S. Army.

HDQRS. CAVALRY DIVISION, SIXTEENTH ARMY CORPS,
Memphis, Tenn., November 19, 1863.

CAPTAIN: Colonel Hawkins, commanding the Seventh Tennessee Cavalry, has just returned from an expedition south and reports hav-ng met no force until he arrived at Hernando, where he found a icket of about 20 men, who fled upon his approach. He succeeded n killing 1 and capturing another. The prisoner has been sent to rving prison. From the best information obtained he thinks there re about three small companies, probably 100 men in all, encamped t the ford on Coldwater, 6 miles south of Hernando. He could earn nothing of any other force this side of the Tallahatchie, except uch information as was brought by the old men and ladies from frenada, whom the general commanding saw this morning. Colo-nel Hawkins reports a great many people upon the roads, especially adies.

Respectfully, your obedient servant,
B. H. GRIERSON,
Brigadier-General.

Capt. T. H. HARRIS,
Assistant Adjutant-General.

NOVEMBER 21, 1863.—Expedition from Island No. 10 to Tiptonville, Tenn.

Report of Capt. Rufus S. Benson, Thirty-second Iowa Infantry.

HEADQUARTERS UNITED STATES FORCES,
Island No. 10, *Tenn., November* 22, 1863.

SIR: I have the honor to report that in obedience to Special Orders, No. 284, extract 2, on the morning of the 21st November, 1863, I roceeded with 30 men of my command on the steamer O'Brien to New Madrid, Mo., and reported to Colonel Harding, commanding hat post.

Colonel Harding furnished 50 additional men, and the expeditio now under the command of Captain Schmitz, Company B, Twenty fifth Missouri Infantry, started for Tiptonville. On our way to tha place we destroyed two boats, and at Beckham's Landing, Tenn seized 5 barrels of salt. We approached the town as quietly as po sible, and had it not been for a man who, standing on the river bank discovered our approach and gave the alarm, we should have suc ceeded either in killing or capturing a party of guerrillas. As it wa landing and making our way into town as soon as possible, we ha the mortification of seeing the party, all on horseback, disappearin round a bend in the road about 200 yards distant. A volley of bu lets was sent after them, with the effect of killing 1 horse and wound ing 1 man.

There were in the place two stores which, having been in th habit of dealing in contraband of war, Captain Schmitz determine to confiscate their contents, which was accordingly done, and th articles they contained placed on the steamer O'Brien, which w then sent to New Madrid, having determined to proceed to Islan No. 10 by land through New Madrid Bend. We remained all nigh in Tiptonville without being disturbed, and next morning marche unopposed to the landing opposite Island No. 10. We saw not single armed man on our march. The O'Brien having arrived a the island early in the morning, went immediately on board, anc landing myself and men on the island, proceeded to New Madri with Captain Schmitz and his party. The salt and articles take from the stores in Tiptonville were left at New Madrid. I seized on mule in the bend and brought it to the island to make out the num ber I had been ordered to seize heretofore.

At the time I made my former report, I supposed 12 mules ha been seized, but I was mistaken; there were 11. The man who noti fied the guerrillas of our approach is in our hands, and will be sen to Columbus. Colonel Harding expressed a willingness to furnis us all the assistance in his power whenever called upon.

I remain, very respectfully, your obedient servant,

R. S. BENSON,
Captain Company H, Thirty-second Iowa Infantry.

Capt. J. HOUGH,
Assistant Adjutant-General.

NOVEMBER 21-22, 1863.—Scout from Fort Pillow, Tenn.

Report of Col. Edward H. Wolfe, Fifty-second Indiana Infantry

HEADQUARTERS POST,
Fort Pillow, Tenn., November 22, 1863.

CAPTAIN: Having received information that a body of rebels, unde the command of General [Colonel] Faulkner, were in the vicinity o Ripley, some 25 miles from this post, I accordingly ordered out a scou in that direction, consisting of 125 men (all my effective mounte force). The force left at 7 p. m. yesterday evening, and have jus now returned (4 p. m.). Capt. J. W. McCowick, commanding, re ports that the enemy are encamped near Woodville, and are fron 700 to 800 strong ; mostly well armed.

Five prisoners, belonging to Faulkner's command, were brought n, 3 of whom were captured while on picket duty, and finding the nemy in too large force, Captain McCowick returned without naking any further demonstration. Faulkner is conscripting and illing up his command rapidly, and by the end of the present week vill have collected together probably 2,000 or more men.

I take occasion again to respectfully ask that the cavalry force at his post be increased.

I have the honor to be, captain, very respectfully, your obedient ervant,

E. H. WOLFE,
Colonel Fifty-second Indiana Infty. Vols., Comdg. Post.

Capt. JOHN HOUGH,
  Assistant Adjutant-General.

NOVEMBER 22, 1863.—Skirmish at Camp Davies, Miss.

Report of Brig. Gen. John D. Stevenson, U. S. Army.

CORINTH, MISS.,
November 22, 1863.

A force of enemy, 150 strong, under Ham, appearing on Ripley oad, 5 miles from Camp Davies, were attacked by Major Cramer, 'irst Alabama Cavalry, with 70 men, and after a sharp fight were riven in confusion in direction of Rienzi. Enemy's loss, 4 known) be killed. Our loss, 2 severely wounded.

JOHN D. STEVENSON,
Brigadier-General.

Major-General HURLBUT.

NOVEMBER 24, 26, 1863.—Skirmishes at and near Sparta, Tenn.

Reports of Lieut. Col. James P. Brownlow, First Tennessee Cavalry.

HEADQUARTERS FIRST TENNESSEE CAVALRY,
Sparta, November 25, 1863.

COLONEL: I entered this place yesterday on three different roads, nd had a skirmish on each road. I whipped Colonel Murray's force, illing 1, wounding 2, and capturing 10 men, with them 1 of Champ erguson's lieutenants. I have also captured several horses and rms, and destroyed some ammunition. I have sent dispatches to Vashington and Pikeville. It will be impossible to hear from Vashington before Saturday.

Colonel Murray has sent for the forces under Hughs, Hamilton, 'augherty, Ferguson, and others, who will probably attack me to-iorrow night. I will give them hell if they come, although their 'rce is largely superior to my own.

I would like if you would send me 20 men of the Second Michi-an, with their six-shooters, and the remainder of my own regiment. can then hold my own against any force. Have Major Dyer to nd me the ammunition of the dismounted men in camp, as I proba-ly will need it.

If you send me more men have them start early, and not stop unt
they reach this place, as it will be dangerous for a small force t
camp on the road.

Very respectfully, your obedient servant,

JAS. P. BROWNLOW,
Lieutenant-Colonel, Commanding.

Col. A. P. Campbell,
Commanding First Brigade.

I have just learned that Farley is collecting a force of soldiers an
citizens, to join Hughs.

[Indorsements.]

They forded with their horses by swimming 15 feet.

A. P. CAMPBELL,
Colonel, Commanding First Brigade.

Respectfully forwarded to General Elliott.

The man at the ferry says he is afraid the enemy will cut his ferr
loose to-night. I sent 100 men from the Second Michigan Cavalr
to-night before dark. They will be at the ferry in the morning
Advise me what to do further by my orderly, and I will await fur
ther orders.

A. P. CAMPBELL,
Colonel, Commanding.

HEADQUARTERS CHIEF OF CAVALRY,
Alexandria, Tenn., November 26, 1863.

Respectfully referred for the information of Colonel McCook, com
manding First Division.

The general commanding directed the detachment to be sent to th
ferry, and a re-enforcement of 100 men, in addition, to be sent t
Colonel Brownlow. This communication to be returned.

By command of Brigadier-General Elliott:

J. E. JACOBS,
Assistant Adjutant-General.

—

HEADQUARTERS FIRST TENNESSEE CAVALRY,
Sparta, Tenn., November 27, 1863.

COLONEL: I received your dispatch at 2 a. m. My scouts had
skirmish with the rebels yesterday within 2 miles of their camj
capturing 4 and killing 2. I have had 2 men slightly wounded.
also destroyed their salt-works, which were very extensive. Withi
4 miles of this place there are six fine merchant mills, and withi
10 miles there are fourteen. The rebels are threatening to bur
them, but I can easily prevent it. The road is in very fine cond
tion.

Very respectfully, your obedient servant,

JAS. P. BROWNLOW,
Lieutenant-Colonel, Commanding.

Col. A. P. Campbell,
Commanding First Brigade.

NOVEMBER 27, 1863.—Skirmish at Monticello, Ky.

Report of Col. John M. Hughs, Twenty-fifth Tennessee Infantry (Confederate), including skirmishes near Sparta, Tenn., November 30; at Scottsville, Ky., December 8, and near Livingston, Tenn., December 15.

DALTON, GA., *April 28, 1864.*

SIR: I have the honor herewith to submit the following report of my operations in Middle Tennessee.*

On the 27th November I attacked Monticello, Ky., with 149 men, and captured the town with its entire garrison, numbering 153 officers and men, with but little stores of any kind. The prisoners were paroled on the spot. In this affair Major Bledsoe, of the Fourth Tennessee Cavalry, was severely wounded by accident.

On the 30th November, a fight occurred between the rear guard of my command, under Capt. R. H. Bledsoe, and a party of Colonel Brownlow's (Tennessee) regiment. For the numbers engaged the fighting was very severe. The enemy lost 13 killed, 8 wounded, and 7 captured. My loss, 5 killed.

On the 8th December I attacked, with about 200 men, Scottsville, Ky., capturing the place with its garrison, composed of Captain Gilliam's company of the Fifty-second Kentucky Regiment, numbering 86 men, and a considerable quantity of quartermaster and commissary stores, together with about 500 stand of small-arms and several hundred saddles, bridles, &c. The prisoners were paroled. My loss, 1 killed.

On the 15th December, near Livingston, Tenn., I attacked, with a portion of my command, numbering less than 100, a detachment of the Thirteenth Kentucky Mounted Infantry [Cavalry], numbering 250 men, under Major Hurt, and succeeded in whipping and driving them out of the State, a distance of 18 miles, killing and wounding several and capturing 6. My loss, 2 wounded.†

Very respectfully, your obedient servant,

JOHN M. HUGHS.

NOVEMBER 27, 1863.—Skirmish at La Fayette, Ky.

Report of Col. Cicero Maxwell, Twenty-sixth Kentucky Infantry.

HEADQUARTERS U. S. FORCES, SOUTHWEST KENTUCKY,
Bowling Green, Ky., December 2, 1863.

CAPTAIN: Yesterday I received report from Colonel Murray, Third Kentucky Cavalry, commanding at Hopkinsville, that a few days since Lieutenant Brunner and 17 men of the Third, in a stockade at La Fayette, Christian County, were attacked by the rebel Hawkins with largely over 100 men, and after an obstinate contest and after robbing several stores, which Brunner could not protect from his stockade, the rebels retired, losing 3 killed and 7 wounded, 4 mortally, Brunner losing none.

Hawkins, after leaving La Fayette, went in the direction of Canon, stealing all the horses he could find, pursued by Colonel Mur-

---

*Portion here omitted is printed in Series I, Vol. XXX, Part II, p. 646.

†Portion here omitted relates to operations in Middle and East Tennessee from January to April, 1864, and will appear in Series I, Vol. XXXII.

ray; and the colonel says but for the treachery of one Captain Cox, of the steam-boat Duke, who used his boat to ferry the rebels over the Cumberland River, he (Colonel Murray) would have overtaken Hawkins at the river, as he was only an hour or so behind him.

Lieutenant Brunner and his little band deserve great credit for their gallant and successful defense against such great odds.

Very respectfully,

CICERO MAXWELL,
Colonel 26th Ky. Vols., Comdg. Southwestern Kentucky.

Capt. A. C. SEMPLE,
    Assistant Adjutant-General.

NOVEMBER 28–DECEMBER 10, 1863.—Operations against the Memphis and Charleston Railroad, in West Tennessee.

SUMMARY OF THE PRINCIPAL EVENTS.

Nov. 28, 1863.—Skirmish near Molino, Miss.
Dec. 1, 1863.—Skirmish at Ripley, Miss.
      2, 1863.—Descent on Saulsbury, Tenn.
    3-4, 1863.—Action at Wolf River Bridge, near Moscow, Tenn.
      4, 1863.—Skirmish at La Fayette, Tenn.
          Affair at Ripley, Miss.

REPORTS.

No. 1.—Maj. Gen. Stephen A. Hurlbut, U. S. Army, commanding Sixteenth Army Corps, with complimentary orders.
No. 2.—Brig. Gen. Benjamin H. Grierson, U. S. Army, commanding Cavalry Division.
No. 3.—Col. John K. Mizner, Third Michigan Cavalry, commanding First Brigade.
No. 4.—Col. Edward Hatch, Second Iowa Cavalry, commanding Second Brigade.
No. 5.—Col. Frank A. Kendrick, Second West Tennessee Infantry, African Descent.
No. 6.—Lieut. Col. George W. Trafton, Seventh Illinois Cavalry.
No. 7.—Col. Fielding Hurst, Sixth Tennessee Cavalry.
No. 8.—General Joseph E. Johnston, C. S. Army.
No. 9.—Brig. Gen. James R. Chalmers, C. S. Army.

No. 1.

Reports of Maj. Gen. Stephen A. Hurlbut, U. S. Army, command ing Sixteenth Army Corps, with complimentary orders.

MEMPHIS, *December 3, 1863.*
(Received Chattanooga, 5th.)

The enemy, under Lee, Forrest, and Ferguson, broke into Saulsbury yesterday. We had no troops there. They destroyed track and bent rails. It will take twenty-four hours to repair. Mizner fell back to Pocahontas against orders, and left this gap open Hatch is following their main body, which is retreating south by Holly Springs. Forrest escaped north with about 500 men. We have lost no men nor trains, and have, so far, 40 prisoners. I can not learn with certainty of any infantry below this cavalry movement.

S. A. HURLBUT,
Major-General.

Major-General SHERMAN.

MEMPHIS, TENN., *December* 5, 1863.

The enemy, about 3,000 strong, with three pieces of artillery, under Lee and Chalmers, struck La Fayette and Moscow yesterday at 1 p. m. They were met at Moscow by Col. E. Hatch, who, after a sharp conflict, drove them 4 miles, and again engaged them. They retreated to Mount Pleasant, and have gone this morning. We lost 4 killed and 11 wounded and 25 captured. The Sixth Illinois Cavalry lost 125 horses and equipments. Full particulars not received. Colonel Hatch severely wounded. The line is open to-day. Loring's division of infantry is at Okolona, so reported. Roddey, at Courtland. Two regiments north of the river. Bell, at Trenton, with 2,500 men, looking toward Paducah.

Tuttle's division is lying east of La Grange ready to concentrate in Corinth, if required, and I shall keep them until my rolling-stock can be worked in.

If Dodge is not much wanted at Pulaski, he would do great service by moving on Okolona and Columbus, via Tuscumbia.

S. A. HURLBUT.

Major-General SHERMAN.

—

MEMPHIS,
December 7, 1863.

The affair at Moscow the other day was more spirited than thought. The negro regiment behaved splendidly. Our loss is 7 killed and about 40 horses—10 captured. We have captured in the movement 54 prisoners; buried 30. The entire loss of the enemy cannot be less than 150. Forrest is gathering the guerrillas together at Jackson. I shall move on him from Columbus and Moscow simultaneously.

S. A. HURLBUT,
Major-General.

Major-General SHERMAN, through
Major-General GRANT.

—

GENERAL ORDERS,)   HDQRS. SIXTEENTH ARMY CORPS,
    No. 173.   }   *Memphis, Tenn., December* 17, 1863.

The recent affair at Moscow, Tenn., has demonstrated the fact that colored troops, properly disciplined and commanded, can and will fight well, and the general commanding corps deems it to be due to the officers and men of the Second Regiment West Tennessee Infantry, of African descent, thus publicly to return his personal thanks for their gallant and successful defense of the important position to which they had been assigned, and for the manner in which they have vindicated the wisdom of the Government in elevating the rank and file of these regiments to the position of freedmen and soldiers.

By order of Maj. Gen. S. A. Hurlbut:

T. H. HARRIS,
Assistant Adjutant-General.

No. 2.

Reports of Brig. Gen. Benjamin H. Grierson, U. S. Army, co
*manding Cavalry Division.**

HDQRS. CAVALRY DIVISION, SIXTEENTH ARMY CORPS,
Memphis, Tenn., January 24, 1864.

CAPTAIN: I have the honor to report that, in obedience to Speci
Orders, No. 296, from headquarters Sixteenth Army Corps, date
November 24, 1863, I ordered the brigade commanded by Color
Hatch to move on the morning of the 26th of November by separa
columns north of the railroad, sweeping round and assembling (
Somerville, for the purpose of covering the taking up of the mat
rial on the Somerville Branch Railroad. At the same time I order
the brigade of Colonel Mizner to move south from Corinth as far
was safe without risking his command.

Colonel Mizner moved south about 40 miles, when he captured
number of the enemy, and ascertained that they were moving nor
in large force, evidently with the intention of attacking the ra
road. Having received this information, agreeable to instructio
from the major-general commanding, I immediately sent couriers
Colonel Hatch with orders to move as quickly as possible with h
brigade to La Grange. The enemy's advance were met by Color
Mizner and several times repulsed. They, however, overpower
and drove him back to Pocahontas, when they moved south, prob
bly as a feint, and taking another road moved upon Saulsbur
Colonel Hatch arrived at La Grange, and was immediately order
to move east along the railroad, scouting south toward Ripley. I
met the enemy at Saulsbury, after they had succeeded in destroyi
the railroad at that point; and starting a portion of their commar
north, Colonel Hatch fought and drove the remainder of the enen
some distance south and returned with his command to La Grang

The next morning I sent scouts south, and information was so
obtained that the enemy were moving west, evidently with the inte
tion of again attacking the railroad. I immediately ordered Color
Hatch to move west with his command. He arrived at Mosc
simultaneously with the enemy. Here a brief, but severe, engag
ment ensued, in which Colonel Hatch was severely wounded. T
enemy were, however, repulsed, and moved south. Their loss w
probably over 100 in killed, wounded, and prisoners, they havi
left 26 dead upon the field. Our loss was 4 killed and 19 wounde
I beg leave, in connection with this engagement, to bear witness
the bravery displayed by the colored regiment under Col. Fran
Kendrick, stationed at this point.

The enemy having moved south of the Tallahatchie, my comma
renewed their former status upon the line of the railroad. T
force of the enemy, which had moved north from Saulsbury, prov
to be about 1,500 strong, under General Forrest, who had con
north of the road for the purpose of conscripting in West Tenn
see.†

Respectfully, your obedient servant,
B. H. GRIERSON,
Brigadier-General, Commanding Cavalry Division.

Capt. T. H. HARRIS, *Assistant Adjutant-General.*

---

*See also Grierson's dispatches in Part III.
† For portion of report here omitted, see p. 607.

No. 3.

Reports of Col. John K. Mizner, Third Michigan Cavalry, commanding First Brigade.

RUCKERSVILLE, *December* 1, 1863—4 p. m.
(Received 10.30 p. m.)

The enemy in full force, not less than 6,000, is making for Pocahontas. He has pressed me very hard to this point, where I have
finally checked their advance. One of my columns has been falling
back on the Middleton road and find the enemy pursuing with a much
smaller force, showing the main column making for Pocahontas.
I will hold every inch possible, but they must be prepared for heavy
work at Pocahontas to-morrow.

J. K. MIZNER,
Colonel, Commanding Cavalry.

Major-General HURLBUT,
Memphis.

—

HDQRS. FIRST BRIG., CAV. DIV., 16TH ARMY CORPS,
Corinth, Miss., December 15, 1863.

CAPTAIN: I herewith submit a report of the operations of the First
Cavalry Brigade, in obedience to Special Orders, No. 296, from headquarters Sixteenth Army Corps, of November 24, 1863:

I left Corinth at daylight, on the morning of the 26th ultimo, with
about 900 men, consisting of 400 from Third Michigan, 300 from
Seventh Kansas, and 200 from First Alabama. Marched 31 miles
and encamped 3 miles south of Blackland. Believing that no force
of the enemy were nearer than Okolona, except a regiment at Chesterville, I moved through Carrollville to Ellistown. This gave me a
position from which I could scout a greater number of roads leading
toward points which the enemy might occupy, and securing a better
line of retreat if encountering a superior force, which I had reason
to expect, as the enemy were reported from 8,000 to 12,000 strong at
Okolona and vicinity, preparing to move north. At Ellistown I
captured a rebel officer and 10 men engaged in conscripting. I moved
3 miles south on Chesterville road and halted to feed. Here several
rebel officers and men rode unsuspectingly into my camp and were
made prisoners, expressing their surprise at finding us there and reporting much of their cavalry north of us.

At this point I also learned that Lee had moved with a heavy force
from Okolona to Pontotoc, on his way north. Also, capturing one of
Lee's command who left him 8 miles north of Pontotoc at noon,
moving toward New Albany. I therefore moved to a safer position
near Molino, from which I could better watch the movements of the
enemy, and remained until the morning of the 28th, when, it being
necessary for me to change my position, both to keep the enemy in
ignorance of my whereabouts and to obtain forage, I moved toward
Dumas post-office. Soon after leaving camp, I was attacked in rear
by a regiment of the enemy's cavalry, which I dispersed with a loss
to them of 8 killed and 17 wounded, and no casualties in my command. Scouted the roads toward New Albany and camped for the
night 5 miles south of Ripley, which place, I was satisfied, would

be a point on their line of march, and also, being a central point i
front of our lines, made it an excellent position for observatio
Having up to this time captured 35 prisoners, which were becomin
a burden, the First Alabama Cavalry, being miserably mounte
and wholly unequal to expected marches, were ordered to Corint
with the prisoners.

No enemy being encountered by my scouts, I moved south on Ne
Albany road as far as Orizaba, where I sent scouts south, southeas
and southwest, one of which captured at about noon a lieutenant an
private with a pass from New Albany dated the same morning. Fro
these prisoners and other sources I learned that the rebel Genera
Forrest, Lee, Ferguson, Chalmers, and Richardson were at Ne
Albany, with a force of 6,000, preparing six days' cooked rations f
a raid north. I also learned that, on receipt of information by th
enemy at New Albany of my moving north from Ellistown on Rij
ley road, Ferguson's brigade broke camp at midnight of the 27th an
moved toward Ripley to intercept my retreat, but on reachin
Orizaba he learned that I had moved from Molino east toward Blac
land, and consequently returned to New Albany.

On the 28th, about 3 p. m., I moved north again to within 3 mil
of Ripley, where, finding forage, I camped at Parmer's until 3 a. n
of the 30th, then moved into Ripley, taking position on the nort
side of town, scouting southward, so as to intersect all roads leadin
north from New Albany. No enemy appearing during the day,
moved north a short distance to procure forage, and encamped for tl
night, leaving a small force in Ripley.

December 1, moved to Ripley, continued scouting, and, havin
pushed the Third Illinois Cavalry (which had joined me the evenin
previous) well south on the New Albany road, they struck the a
vance of the enemy, at about 10 a. m., 5 miles south of Riple
While the Third Illinois were falling back before the enemy, I di
posed my command as follows to receive him: The Third Michiga
on the Pocahontas road, the Seventh Kansas on the Middleton roa
and sent instructions to the Third Illinois to fall back on the Saul
bury road to the intersection of the Middleton, where they wou
join the Seventh Kansas, communication to be kept up betwee
these forces by cross-roads in rear, and so soon as the enemy reli
quished the pursuit on either road this force should re-enforce tl
party sustaining the main attack.

The enemy struck my first position with overwhelming force, a
vancing in three columns, one in the road dismounted and one c
either flank mounted, rendering it almost impossible for my di
mounted men to regain their horses. The enemy soon gave up h
pursuit on all roads save the Pocahontas, on which he massed h
columns and pushed irresistibly forward, driving the Third Micl
gan before him, then only about 350 strong, at a rapid walk, co
stantly forming from one to two squadrons on selected positions, wi
intervals usually not to exceed 200 yards, to check him. Every avai
able position was taken and determinedly held to the last possib
moment, and a constant and scathing fire poured in upon the a
vancing enemy and continued, occasionally checking his advance f
a moment, until within about a mile of Ruckersville, where, takin
a very favorable position, his farther advance was finally checked
sunset, when the enemy retired. In consequence of the numbers
parallel and cross-roads, I thought it prudent to fall back, und
cover of the night, to the vicinity of Jonesborough, and camped f

e night.   The enemy relinquishing the pursuit on other roads west
id pursuing me so far on this one, it was believed that he designed
 attack Pocahontas.   At an early hour on the following morning I
cordingly moved back and took up position near Ruckersville,
nding a patrol forward to feel the enemy.
After waiting a reasonable time and the enemy not appearing on
.e main road, and hearing of him on my right flank, I moved back
ward Pocahontas, near which place I received the report of my
itrol informing me that the enemy had returned to the neighbor-
)od of Ripley and moved west.   The movements, advance, and all
formation gained of the enemy were reported from time to time to
.e major-general commanding Sixteenth Army Corps and to com-
anders along the line.
The Seventh Kansas and Third Illinois joined me at Pocahontas,
here I received orders from the major-general commanding to refit
y command and open communication with Colonel Hatch, sup-
)sed to be moving from La Grange to Ruckersville.   Colonel Hatch
ith his brigade, and General Tuttle with a force of infantry, were
und to be at Middleton, where I communicated to them all infor-
ation I had of the enemy.   On the following morning I was in-
ructed by General Tuttle to hold Pocahontas during the temporary
)sence of Colonel Geddes' command, who was ordered west by rail
 join General Tuttle near Saulsbury.   Colonel Geddes returned at
i early hour of the afternoon bringing information that the enemy
id been dispersed near Saulsbury and his main force was retreating
uth.   Upon this information coming direct from the front, I moved
uth to intercept him; reached the vicinity of Ripley at 11 p. m.;
ent the night in examining roads, and found that no enemy had
treated in that direction.   I remained until near noon to rest and
ed, when, being fully satisfied that the enemy were all still north
 me, moved out on Saulsbury road, camped 8 miles south of that
ace, and moved into La Grange on the 6th instant.
From this time I was employed in scouting along the line of the
ilroad, returning to camp on the 10th instant, after an absence of
teen days.
The general result of this expedition was a thorough scouting of
.e entire front from Corinth to La Grange, discovering and report-
g the movements and strength of the enemy, engaging him twice,
lling 8 and wounding 17, capturing 50 prisoners, with a loss of 2
illed and Major Jenkins and 5 or 6 enlisted men wounded slightly.
But few horses were found in the country, which were taken to
ount prisoners and were turned over to the quartermaster at Cor-
ath; most of them were unfit for cavalry service.   A triplicate list
 prisoners of war has been forwarded, and I inclose herewith a list
 casualties.*
All of which is respectfully submitted.
      Very respectfully, your obedient servant,
                                      J. K. MIZNER,
                      Colonel, Commanding First Cavalry Brigade.

Capt. SAMUEL L. WOODWARD,
          Assistant Adjutant-General.

---

* Nominal list (omitted) shows: Third Michigan Cavalry: Killed, 2; wounded, 3;
isoner, 1; total, 6.   Seventh Kansas Cavalry: Wounded, 1.   Grand total, 7.

SAULSBURY ROAD, NINE MILES NORTH OF RIPLEY,
December 4, 1863—3 p. m.

SIR: Your dispatch of the 3d instant just received. I left Poca hontas at 3.30 p. m. yesterday, moving south to intercept rebels sai to be retreating. I arrived 4 miles north of Ripley at 11 p. m., an after a careful examination of roads found that no rebels had passe south. Camped at 3 this morning. Sent cavalry into Ripley a daylight, capturing 9 prisoners and a wagon-load of ammunitior which they were guarding.

At Ripley I learned that Ferguson and Chalmers, after the figh on the 1st instant, returned to neighborhood of Ripley, camped fo the night, and moved on the 2d north, on Saulsbury road, thei strength about 3,000 men and eight pieces of artillery. Forrest an Lee, with a force of about 4,000, moved north from New Albany leaving Ripley to the right. Information derived from all prisoners citizens, and every other source, agree that the rebel generals Fo: rest, Lee, Ferguson, and Chalmers, with a force in all about 7,00(moved north from New Albany *en route* for West Tennessee. Nor have returned on this road or by any route east of this.

I have been absent nine days from Corinth, have been 7 mile south of Ellistown, have had two engagements with the enemy, th first on the 28th ultimo with Richardson, a little north of Ellistow: in which the enemy lost 8 killed and 17 wounded ; the other occurre on the 2d instant on the Ripley and Ruckersville road, in which, wit 350 of the Third Michigan, I fought Ferguson's and Chalmers' con mands for three hours, though compelled to fall back finall: Checked the rebel advance a mile south of Ruckersville. Enemy loss variously stated, but unknown to me. I have taken 54 prisoner Lost 2 killed, and Major Jenkins and a few enlisted men slightl wounded. My whole strength present is 42 commissioned officer 540 enlisted men, and 3 howitzers.

From sickness, after long exposure and loss of horses, I have ser about 60 men to Corinth, also 30 men sent as escort to prisoner The horses of the First Alabama, only 200 in all, were so poor tha I was obliged to order them back to Corinth. The Sixth Tennesse(has but 350 horses, and I understand are at Grand Junction. N one of my command has been captured by the enemy. At least 8 horses will be required to mount my brigade as shown by my la tri-monthly. As my men and animals are greatly exhausted, I w: camp at Pegram's, 10 miles north of this point.

Very respectfully, your obedient servant,

J. K. MIZNER,
Colonel, Commanding First Cavalry Brigade.

Brig. Gen. B. H. GRIERSON.

No. 4.

Report of Col. Edward Hatch, Second Iowa Cavalry, commandi Second Brigade.

HDQRS. SECOND BRIG., CAV. DIV., 16TH ARMY CORPS,
Collierville, Tenn., December 10, 1863.

GENERAL : I have the honor to report that, in obedience to yo orders, I moved with my brigade, with the exception of the Seven Illinois Cavalry, on the morning of the 26th of November ultimo, ylight.   Crossing Wolf River near Germantown we moved in the rection of Covington, which place we reached on the 28th without eeting any obstacle.

Upon receiving information that Quinn and Sherrar's flouring ill on the Loosahatchie was keeping guerrillas, I burned it.

From Covington we marched to Stanton's Depot, about 12 miles orth of Somerville, thence to the latter place, which we reached on e 2d instant.

During the entire expedition, which occupied six days, we saw no iemy, except small squads, which fled at our approach.

The result of the expedition was about 300 head of horses and ules, and 12 or 15 prisoners.

I am, general, very respectfully, your obedient servant,
EDWARD HATCH,
Colonel Second Iowa Cavalry, Commanding Brigade.

Brig. Gen. B. H. GRIERSON.

No. 5.

eport of Col. Frank A. Kendrick, Second West Tennessee Infantry (African Descent).

HEADQUARTERS LEFT WING, SIXTEENTH ARMY CORPS,
Corinth, Miss., December 12, 1863.
apt. T. H. HARRIS,
Actg. Asst. Adjt. Gen., Sixteenth Army Corps:

CAPTAIN : I herewith inclose the official report of Col. Frank A. endrick, Second Regiment West Tennessee Infantry (African De-ent), of the part taken by himself and command in the engagement ith the rebel forces commanded by Maj. Gen. S. D. Lee, at Wolf River ridge, near Moscow, Tenn., on the 3d and 4th instant.   I specially ommend to the notice of the commanding general Colonel Ken-rick and the several officers mentioned in his report, and also the ldierly qualities evinced by the Second West Tennessee Infantry, African Descent) in this their first encounter with the enemy.

I am, respectfully,
JNO. D. STEVENSON,
Brigadier-General, Commanding.

HDQRS. SECOND REGT. WEST TENN. INFANTRY, A. D.,
Moscow, Tenn., December 7, 1863.

SIR : I have the honor to submit the following report of the opera-ons of my regiment on the 3d and 4th of December, 1863 :

Since it became known to me that the road was threatened by a onsiderable force of the enemy, I have taken every precaution to uard my position against surprise.   To this end the wagon bridge cross Wolf River, on the main Collierville road, about 300 yards outhwest from my camp, being the most practicable approach to his position, has been the object of especial vigilance.   The planks f the bridge are put down only when the bridge is in use for legiti-iate and authorized crossing.

At 3 p. m., December 3, a small cavalry force made a demonstra-ion on this bridge, dashing up on the gallop even to the bridge, and ring on the pickets stationed there.   I immediately re-enforced

the pickets with two companies, and after a few rounds had bee
exchanged the enemy retired. My loss in this affair was two guns
and 1 man severely wounded. That of the enemy is not known, hi
dead and wounded, if any, being carried away.

During the succeeding night and the next day I kept my regimen
in constant readiness for attack, and reconnoitered all the approache
to as great a distance as it could be safely done without the assist
ance of cavalry. Early in the afternoon of the 4th, observing
dense smoke in the direction of Grisson's Bridge and La Fayette,
concluded that the enemy had passed here and gone in that direc
tion. This was likewise the opinion of the officers of the Sixth Illi
nois Cavalry, which arrived here at 1.30 p. m., in the advance o
Colonel Hatch's cavalry brigade, and accordingly such of the cav
alry as had arrived were proceeding on the road toward Colliervlle
The Sixth Illinois and a portion of another regiment had crosse
the bridge—the same upon which the demonstration of the preced
ing day had been made—when they fell into an ambuscade of th
enemy a short distance beyond the bridge.

At the sound of the first scattering shots I supported my picket a
the bridge with Companies A and D of my regiment, deploying thes
companies across the road behind rifle-pits, and in position to swee
the bridge with their fire. The picket guard, about 50 strong, unde
Captain Harris, of my regiment, I posted on the left of the road, i
the bottom next the river, in such position as to secure a cross-fir
on the bridge. I ordered Lieutenant-Colonel Foley, of my regiment
with Companies B and G and portions of two others, to take posi
tion on the right of our line and hold the railroad bridge over Wol
River, a structure of much importance. The remainder of my regi
ment I posted in an unfinished fortification, situated on the railroad
350 yards distant from the wagon bridge, with Major Wiley in com
mand.

Although I was the senior officer present at this time, I did no
take command of the cavalry, being in momentary expectation o
the arrival of Colonel Hatch, who was reported to be a short dis
tance in rear with the remainder of his brigade.

Very shortly after the firing began the cavalry, which had crosse
the bridge, retreated in much disorder. The bridge soon becam
obstructed with artillery, caissons, and wagons from the train which
had got over, and great numbers of the retreating cavalry plunge
headlong into the river, which, though narrow, is deep and rapid
and many men and horses were thus lost. The enemy now made
desperate attempt to force a passage of the bridge, but his im
petuous charges were met by the steady and effective fire of th
companies posted as I have described.

About half an hour after the fight commenced Colonel Hatch ar
rived, and almost immediately fell severely wounded. I thereupo
assumed command of all the forces engaged, which I continued t
exercise throughout the engagement. I now withdrew Company D
of my regiment, and the picket guard from their station at the bridg
and ordered them to the fort, supplying their places with two com
panies of the Second Iowa Cavalry, who were armed with revolving
rifles. The efforts of the enemy to gain possession of the wagon
road bridge still continued, and, indeed, did not cease throughout the
fight.

Meanwhile, Lieutenant-Colonel Foley, with his detachment, wa
vigorously attacked by vastly superior numbers of the enemy, who

ade desperate efforts to gain the railroad bridge, probably with the
esign of destroying it, but all their attempts were bravely and suc-
essfully resisted.   By my order the artillery in the fort, manned by
etails from my regiment, under the command of Lieutenant Fullen,
f the same, was worked throughout the action, and its firing was
ery effective, several shells striking the wagon bridge where the
aemy were charging, and, I am informed by a soldier of the Sixth
linois Cavalry, who was taken prisoner (but effected his escape
aring the engagement), that several shells fired from the fort ex-
loded among the led horses of the enemy, producing a panic.   The
aemy made a precipitate retreat at ten minutes past 4 p. m., leav-
ag many of his dead and wounded on the field.

The casualties in my regiment are 3 killed and 12 wounded.   My
aen fought in most instances under cover.   The enemy's losses are
ot known, but must have been very heavy, as he left 22 killed and
wounded on the field, and citizens report that he carried many
agon-loads of dead or wounded with him on his retreat.   In this
agagement we took 8 prisoners, 5 of whom were wounded.   Three
f the latter died, and the other 2 were sent to Dr. Irwin, chief of
ospitals, at Memphis.   The 3 unwounded prisoners were sent to Gen-
ral Tuttle, at La Grange, as I had no secure place to keep them.

The officers of my regiment, without exception, acquitted them-
elves with great credit.   The majority of the men were for the first
me under fire, but their conduct did not disappoint my most san-
uine anticipations, as, after the first few rounds, they received and
eturned the enemy's fire with the steadiness and deliberation of
eterans.   Among the officers of other regiments who were distin-
uished for gallantry were Captain Moore, commanding Rifle Bat-
alion, Second Iowa Cavalry, and Captain Perkins, of the Ninth Illi-
ois Cavalry, and in command of the howitzers attached to that regi-
aent, who, by their determined resistance, contributed much to the
uccess of our arms.

I inclose herewith a sketch* exhibiting the principal points referred
o in this report.

I have the honor to be, sir very respectfully, your obedient serv-
nt,

FRANK A. KENDRICK,
Colonel Second Regt. West Tenn. Infty., A. D., Comdg.

Capt. F. F. WHITEHEAD,
     Assistant Adjutant-General.

No. 6.

Reports of Lieut. Col. George W. Trafton, Seventh Illinois Cavalry.

HDQRS. SEVENTH REGIMENT ILLINOIS CAVALRY,
La Grange, Tenn., December 8, 1863.

SIR: I have the honor to report that on the morning of the 2d of
his month the Seventh Illinois Cavalry started from near Middle-
on (where we had bivouacked for the night) about 1 o'clock in the
norning.   Our force consisted of Second Iowa, Sixth, Seventh, and
Ninth Illinois Cavalry Regiments, under command of Colonel Hatch.
The Second Iowa led the advance, the Ninth Illinois next to them,

---

* Not found.

the Seventh and Sixth in the rear. We moved toward La Grange
About 5 o'clock I heard two or three shots in direction of the ad
vance; shortly afterward a volley, and from that time till 7 a. m
frequent volleys. About 7 a. m. I heard sharp firing, and soon th
report of artillery followed. At this time I was ordered by Colone
Hatch to the front. I ordered the regiment forward at a gallop, an
on reaching the front was ordered by Colonel Hatch to support som
companies which he had sent to the left flank. I at once moved t
the left and advanced to a position on the left flank of the enemy
where I could command the road leading from Saulsbury to Ripley
on which I thought probable the enemy might attempt to retreat.

I received orders to remain in this position, till the center advanced
I accordingly sent a squad of men to a position where they coul
observe both flanks and the center, with instructions to report to m
any movement of the center. Shortly afterward they reported th
center moving forward. I immediately moved my regiment dow
the road to rejoin the brigade at the cross-roads just south of Sauls
bury, which we did, meeting only a few stragglers in range of ou
carbines. We sustained no loss in the engagement.

GEO. W. TRAFTON,
Lieutenant-Colonel Seventh Illinois Cavalry.

Colonel Prince,
Commanding Seventh Regiment Illinois Cavalry.

Headquarters Seventh Illinois Cavalry,
La Grange, Tenn., December 9, 1863.

Colonel: I have the honor to make the following report of th
part taken by the Seventh Illinois Cavalry in the action with th
enemy at Moscow on the 3d instant:

In accordance with orders from Colonel Hatch, I left La Grange
with the regiment about 10 a. m. of the 3d instant, following th
Ninth Illinois Cavalry toward Moscow, where we arrived soon afte
12 m. We halted about half an hour there, then started again on
the road leading toward La Fayette. The Sixth Illinois Cavalry wa
in advance, the Ninth Illinois Cavalry next, and the Seventh in rea
of the Ninth. We had proceeded but a short distance when I hear
firing in the direction of the advance, which soon became quite heavy
The artillery also opened fire. The Sixth Illinois Cavalry and part o
the Ninth had crossed Wolf River Bridge. I started forward to repor
to Colonel Hatch for orders, but learned before I got to the advance
that he had not come up yet. I immediately rode back to the regi
ment and ordered them to "prepare to fight on foot with all possible
celerity." As soon as they were dismounted, I ordered them for
ward on double-quick. When we got to the bridge it was so clogged
with horses, ambulances, wagons, and artillery that it was almos
impossible to get a man across it. Several of the horses had broker
through the bridge and were fast, and the bridge was so torn up
that it was impossible to clear it. I ordered my men across, and suc
ceeded by jumping our horses, crawling under wagons and ambu
lances, &c., in getting about 50 men across. About 25 men swan
across. Several were knocked off the bridge into the river in trying
to cross. I found it impossible to get any more men across withou
their swimming, which so injured their ammunition as to nearly ren
der it useless. At this time the artillery of the Sixth was in a critica

position. It had very little support and was entirely exposed to the enemy, who were coming upon it with a charge. The artillery was stationed at the west end of the bridge, and my object in rushing my men over there was to save it. Consequently, when I saw the enemy coming upon it, I ordered my men to fire and charge, which they did with a hearty good will.

I will venture to say there was never a braver charge made by a handful of men than was made by the few men I had with me against the overwhelming odds; the enemy could not stand it; they gave way, but soon rallied again and came pressing down on us from both flank and the front. Still my men stood by the artillery, resolved to die by it rather than see it captured. The artillery itself had all this time been dealing out grape and canister to them by mouthfuls. The artillerymen of the Sixth deserve great credit for the way they fought there. The contest over the battery lasted nearly an hour, and was sometimes almost hand to hand; in fact, some of our men were knocked over by the butts of the enemy's guns. The bridge had during this time become cleared, and the artillerymen ran their pieces back across the river, and what men I had there followed them. All our regiment, except what got across the river, were deployed on the right. I immediately, after recrossing, ordered them to the left to try and secure the led horses of the Sixth, which were still across the river. They succeeded in securing part of them; many of these were already killed or captured. About this time the Second Iowa Cavalry came up and engaged in the action.

Colonel Hatch had come up soon after the action commenced, but was severely wounded soon after his arrival.

Our line was now formed on the east side of the river, and pressed down to the river. The enemy gave way and fell back. About this time Morgan's brigade of infantry came up and crossed the bridge. I ordered our brigade of cavalry "to horse," and the cavalry, with the howitzers, followed them. The infantry drew up in line about half a mile from the bridge, but our brigade passed on after the retreating rebels. About 3 miles from Moscow we found the enemy had taken the Mount Pleasant road. I ordered the Seventh Illinois Cavalry to reconnoiter that road for a mile or two, and then rejoined the column, which moved on toward Collierville, where we were instructed by Colonel Hatch to go that night. The regiment had gone but a short distance when I heard sharp skirmishing in that direction, and ordered the Second Iowa to move to their support, which they did. But the Seventh Illinois routed and was pursuing what proved to be a strong rear guard of the enemy left on the road. I immediately ordered both regiments to their places in the column, and proceeded to Collierville, where we arrived about 10 o'clock at night.

I would mention G Company, of the Seventh Illinois Cavalry, as displaying great courage and determination in the contest over the artillery at the bridge, where a few of them defended and held their position against an odd tenfold. Captain Stiles, of said company, was severely wounded there, and 1 of his men killed and 6 wounded.

Our casualties in the fight were 1 man killed and 10 wounded, including Captain Stiles, above mentioned.

GEO. W. TRAFTON,
Lieutenant-Colonel Seventh Illinois Cavalry.

Colonel PRINCE, Seventh Illinois Cavalry.

No. 7.

Reports of Col. Fielding Hurst, Sixth Tennessee Cavalry.

HDQRS. SIXTH REGIMENT TENNESSEE CAVALRY,
La Grange, December 2, 1863.

Major-General HURLBUT:

Have just received the following dispatch:

My scouts came in from 9 miles of Ripley. Captured 4 prisoners. They state
that 600 left Ripley in direction of Salem. My other scouts came in from Saulsbury,
and report they had a skirmish with the enemy, and negroes report the enemy in
Saulsbury. The negroes also state that Saulsbury is burned.

FIELDING HURST,
Colonel, Commanding Grand Junction.

Respectfully,

WILLIAM H. MORGAN,
Colonel, Commanding.

—

HDQRS. SIXTH REGIMENT TENNESSEE CAVALRY,
Grand Junction, December 5, 1863.

My couriers have returned. They went 5 miles past Saulsbury;
could find nothing of Colonel Mizner. They saw some soldiers who
say Colonel Mizner left Ripley at 3 p. m. yesterday evening. Send
me all news of the fight yesterday.

FIELDING HURST,
Colonel, Commanding.

General B. H. GRIERSON,
La Grange, Tenn.

I have sent scouts to Bolivar.

H.

———

No. 8.

Reports of General Joseph E. Johnston, C. S. Army.

MERIDIAN,
November 26, 1863.

Mr. PRESIDENT: As soon as Major-General Lee returned from his
expedition in aid of General Bragg he was instructed to take his
whole available force within reach, including that of Brigadier-General Forrest, and break up as much as possible of the Memphis and
Charleston Railroad. He has not moved yet, but will do so, I hope,
before the end of the week. After this expedition Brigadier-General
Forrest will go into West Tennessee. The extent of frontier upon
which our cavalry operates is too great, I respectfully submit, for
the control of one officer. Major-General Lee has found occupation
for the last two months on the northern frontier. With another
such officer in the west our cavalry would be far more efficient.
Major-General Hampton is intimately acquainted with much of that

country; I, therefore, respectfully suggest his transfer to this department.

I have just had the honor to receive Your Excellency's letter of the 18th instant. I believe the name appended to the notices inclosed to you to be that of Colonel Logan's quartermaster, and, therefore, directed Brig. Gen. Wirt Adams to have that person arrested for trial.

Most respectfully, your obedient servant,

J. E. JOHNSTON,
General.

His Excellency JEFFERSON DAVIS.

—

MERIDIAN,
December 7, 1863.

Major-General Lee reports of the expedition mentioned in my letter of the 26th:

Chased 800 enemy's cavalry from Ripley into Pocahontas on 1st. On 2d destroyed 2 miles of railroad at Saulsbury, and Forrest passed into Tennessee at Macon. Routed and drove into Wolf River two regiments of Federal cavalry, killing, wounding, and drowning 175, taking 40 prisoners, killing 100 and taking 40 horses. One hundred yards of trestling destroyed between La Fayette and Moscow.

J. E. JOHNSTON.

His Excellency the PRESIDENT,
Richmond.

————

No. 9.

Report of Brig. Gen. James R. Chalmers, C. S. Army.

HEADQUARTERS CHALMERS' CAVALRY,
Near Como, January 16, 1864.

MAJOR: I was ordered by Major-General Lee to move on the 28th of November against some point on the Memphis and Charleston Railroad, between La Grange and Memphis, to cover a movement which he expected to make with the brigades of General Ferguson and Colonel Ross, between La Grange and Corinth, the main object of which was to escort General Forrest safely into West Tennessee. A very great and unexpected rise in the Tallahatchee River prevented the movement. A pontoon bridge had been built across the river by Colonel McCulloch, under many difficulties and with great dispatch, but the slough on the south side of the river was swimming and we could not get to the bridge with ammunition wagons and artillery.

About noon on the 28th, I received a dispatch from General Lee, then at New Albany, countermanding the order to move. At 12 m., on the 30th, I received a dispatch from General Lee ordering me to move forward as before directed, and notifying me that he would move on the morning of the 30th from New Albany. The river was still swollen and rising, and it was impossible to cross except at Panola, 30 miles west of me, or at Rocky Ford, 20 miles east. There was but one ferry-boat at each place, in which I could not cross my command in less time than one day. If I had gone to Panola I would have gone 75 miles from the railroad, and after losing a day in going to Panola and a day in crossing the river, I could not have reached the road in time.

On the other route General Lee had one day and 35 miles the start of me, but supposing that I could be of service in case he had to fall back, I determined to move. Colonel Slemons, with his brigade from Panola, to strike the railroad at Grisson's Creek, and to move with McCulloch's brigade by way of Rocky Ford in rear of General Lee. Orders were telegraphed to Colonel Slemons, and he commenced crossing that night and had his entire command over by 10 o'clock the next morning. McCulloch's brigade moved to Rocky Ford, 20 miles, that night, and commenced crossing; one regiment got over by daylight the next morning and the rear of the column did not get over until 4 p. m. We crossed on a very small ferry-boat, and had to get out in water nearly waist deep on the opposite side, and both officers and men deserve commendation for the energy and promptness displayed in crossing.

We camped the night of the 1st December from 10 to 17 miles north of the river. General Lee did not get off from New Albany until the morning of the 1st, and encamped the same night near Ripley. Under orders from him we made a forced march the next day and joined him about midnight on the 2d December. We moved westward at daylight on the 3d; on the 4th we moved to Moscow, where Colonel Ross was ordered to burn the railroad bridge, and I was ordered to move McCulloch's brigade upon his right flank, and keep out of sight, ready to support Colonel Ross if necessary.

Colonel Hatch's brigade of Federal cavalry was at the time crossing Wolf River on the bridge over the State Line road, and two regiments had crossed.

Before McCulloch's brigade could get into the position where we were ordered to remain hid, the enemy's pickets commenced firing. I was ordered to send forward my front regiment, the First Mississippi Partisans, which I did, and along with it, my escort and a squadron composed of one company of Second Arkansas and one company of George's regiment; they were led by Col. Robert McCulloch in person in the most gallant style, and for particulars of the fight I refer to his report.

Colonel Slemons had been ordered by me to burn the railroad trestle over Grisson's Creek, between Moscow and La Fayette, and do any damage to the road that he could. He accomplished the work assigned to him with promptness and skill. For particulars I refer to his report.*

My loss was 4 killed, 37 wounded, and 5 missing.

My most severe loss was in the damage sustained by the horses from hard marching.

I am, major, &c.,

JAMES R. CHALMERS,
Brigadier-General.

Maj. J. P. STRANGE,
Assistant Adjutant-General.

----

* Not found.

NOVEMBER —, 1863.—Skirmishes on the Cumberland River, Ky.

Report of Brig. Gen. Edward H. Hobson, U. S. Army.

MUNFORDVILLE, KY.,
December 4, 1863.

My scouting parties on Cumberland have captured 15 rebels, and killed the notorious thief and rebel, Captain Belbo. My scouting parties are in all the border counties, doing good execution. Will send force to Clinton County to-morrow.

E. H. HOBSON,
Brigadier-General.

Captain SEMPLE,
Assistant Adjutant-General, Louisville.

NOVEMBER 30, 1863.—Skirmish at Yankeetown, Tenn.

*Report of Lieut. Col. James P. Brownlow, First Tennessee Cavalry.**

HEADQUARTERS FIRST TENNESSEE CAVALRY,
Sparta, Tenn., December 1, 1863.

COLONEL: Colonel Hughs' command, consisting of Murray's, Hampton's, [Hamilton's?] Bledsoe's, Ferguson's, Daugherty's, and other bands, attacked Lieutenant Bowman while scouting, on yesterday, and after skirmishing for some time, drove him across the river within 2 miles of this place, killing 4, wounding 1, and capturing 5. I went immediately to his assistance, and drove the enemy numbering 500) 8 miles, killing 9, and wounding between 15 and 20.

I would take no prisoners. One of the Ninth Pennsylvania was mortally wounded (died this morning), and Captain McCahan wounded in the ankle.

Eighteen scouts, of the Second Michigan, got leave last evening. Send Doctor Green to this place. On account of the heavy picket duty, I would like to have one more company, unless the brigade is coming soon.

Very respectfully,

JAS. P. BROWNLOW,
Lieutenant-Colonel, Commanding.

Col. A. P. CAMPBELL,
Commanding First Brigade.

NOVEMBER 30–DECEMBER 3, 1863.—Scouts to New Madrid Bend, Tenn.

Report of Capt. Rufus S. Benson, Thirty-second Iowa Infantry.

HEADQUARTERS UNITED STATES FORCES,
Island No. 10, Tenn., December 4, 1863.

SIR: I have the honor to report that, on the morning of November 30, 1863, I sent into New Madrid Bend a party of 40 men, under the command of O. A. Lesh, first lieutenant Company H, Thirty-second Iowa Infantry, with instructions to conscript all able-bodied men

* See also Hughs' report of skirmish at Monticello, Ky., p. 575, and itinerary of the Cavalry, Army of the Cumberland, p. 436.

subject to military duty, in accordance with General Orders, N. 68, headquarters Sixth Division, Sixteenth Army Corps, November 26, 1863. The party made quite an extensive scout through the bend and returned in the evening to the island, with 29 conscript. That night the guerrillas conscripted quite a number of men, and seized many horses and mules.

On the 2d and 3d of December, I proceeded again into the bend and procured 6 more conscripts, 50 horses and mules, 4 wagons, and 16 harnesses, somewhat worn; also several old saddles and bridles and 15 blacks.

The conscripted white men, numbering, altogether, 35, were examined by the post surgeon, and 28 of them were pronounced able for duty. Those rejected by him I have permitted to return home. Ten have already volunteered and joined the two companies posted here.

There is a large quantity of corn in the bend, which ought to be taken possession of for the benefit of the Government. The bend is pretty effectually cleared of male inhabitants, as the guerrillas have taken all we left, so that this grain is wholly uncared for and will probably be destroyed by the secesh, unless soon seized by the Government. If we had any means to get it across the river, I should commence bringing it to the island at once, and save what I could of it, but as the O'Brien has been ordered to Cape Girardeau, I expect to obtain but little, if any.

I remain, very respectfully, your obedient servant,

R. S. BENSON,
Captain Co. H., 32d Iowa Infantry, Comdg. Post.

Capt. J. Hough,
Assistant Adjutant-General.

DECEMBER 1, 1863.—Skirmish at Salyersville, Ky.

Report of Col. George W. Gallup, Fourteenth Kentucky Infantry.

Louisa, Ky,
December 1, 1863.

General : My outpost was attacked at Salyersville this morning and badly scattered. Dispatches to me very indefinite. I have sent forward re-enforcements. Enemy's strength reported 800 cavalry. May move in direction of Mount Sterling.

Respectfully, your obedient servant,

GEO. W. GALLUP,
Colonel, Commanding.

[General J. C. Boyle.]

DECEMBER 1, 1863.—Skirmish near Jonesville, Va.

Report of Maj. Gen. John G. Foster, U. S. Army.

Tazewell, Tenn., *December 3, 1863—11.20 a. m.*
(Received 4.25 p. m.)

A battalion of the Sixteenth Illinois Cavalry, sent out from Cumberland Gap, attacked Slemp's regiment of rebel cavalry ᴸear Jonesville, Va., on Tuesday, December 1. The rebels were ᵈriven beyond Jonesville in great confusion, losing 20 killed and 30 ᴾrisoners, and a quantity of horses and arms. The rebel cavalry ᵒrce that drove in Graham's brigade yesterday consisted, according ᵗᵒ the statement of prisoners, of Wheeler's and Jones' cavalry united. ᴬ lieutenant-colonel and 125 men and officers have just arrived from ᴷnoxville. They left on Tuesday at 10 a. m. They report every-ᵗhing favorable. Nothing new.

> J. G. FOSTER,
> *Major-General.*

Maj. Gen. H. W. HALLECK,
>   *General-in-Chief.*

DECEMBER 1, 1863.—Scouts from Pulaski, Tenn., and Skirmishes.

REPORTS.

ᴺo. 1.—Brig. Gen. Grenville M. Dodge, U. S. Army.
ᴺo. 2.—Lieut. John W. Barnes, Acting Assistant Adjutant-General.

No. 1.

Reports of Brig. Gen. Grenville M. Dodge, U. S. Army.

> PULASKI, *December* 2, 1863.

Lieutenant-Colonel Phillips, Ninth Illinois Mounted Infantry, ᵃttacked the rebel cavalry on this side of river, near Flor-ⁿce, drove them across; captured 5 officers, one General Bragg's ⁱⁿspector-general of cavalry, and 35 enlisted men. Colonel Phillips ˢays that an extensive raid is being fitted out under Forrest at Oko-ⁿa, and that all scattering troops are ordered and going to him.

> G. M. DODGE,
> *Brigadier-General.*

Major-General SHERMAN.

> PULASKI, *December* 3, 1863.

Colonel Rowett, Seventh Illinois Infantry (mounted) on his trip ᵗᵒ Eastport, encountered Johnson's regiment, Fourth Alabama, of ᴿoddey's brigade, and routed them, taking 25 prisoners. No force ⁿow of any account north of Tennessee. Colonel Cypert, of loyal ᵀennessee cavalry, some 300, are now stationed at or near Waynes-ᵇorough, Wayne County.

> G. M. DODGE,
> *Brigadier-General.*

Major-General SHERMAN.

No. 2.

Report of Lieut. John W. Barnes, Acting Assistant Adjutant-General.

> PULASKI, TENN., *December* 10, 1863.

Lieutenant Roberts has returned from Eastport. Had a fight ʷith some guerrillas at Rawhide. Brought in 20 prisoners.
Colonel Rinaker left on 6th for Hamburg. Johnson is in neigh-

borhood of Florence with his regiment. Major Murphy, Fift
Tennessee Cavalry, has sent you request to send him 4,000 ration
to Waynesborough. Can you spare them? I refused.

If Rowett goes to Lexington after the two Union families, ha
not some other regiment better be sent out and instructed to cc
operate with him against Johnson.

J. W. BARNES,
Lieutenant, and Acting Assistant Adjutant-General.

General GRENVILLE M. DODGE,
Athens, Ala.

DECEMBER 1–10, 1863.—Operations about Natchez, Miss., and Skirmis (7th).

REPORTS.

No. 1.—Maj. Gen. James B. McPherson, U. S. Army, commanding Seventeent
    Army Corps.
No. 2.—Col. Bernard G. Farrar, Thirtieth Missouri Infantry.
No. 3.—Brig. Gen. Alfred W. Ellet, commanding Mississippi Marine Brigade.
No. 4.—Brig. Gen. Wirt Adams, C. S. Army.

No. 1.

*Reports of Maj. Gen. James B. McPherson, U. S. Army, command
ing Seventeenth Army Corps.*

*HEADQUARTERS SEVENTEENTH ARMY CORPS,
Vicksburg, Miss., December 9, 1863.

GENERAL: Shortly after the transfer of Crocker's division from
Natchez to this vicinity, and in fact before T. Kilby Smith's br
gade—the last to come up—had reached here, I received informatic
from scouts and citizens that there was a movement of rebel cavalr
in a southerly direction, not in masses, but in companies and squac
chiefly, Brig. Gen. Wirt Adams, late Colonel Logan's command, an
that they were concentrating at Gallatin, Liberty, and near Fa}
ette, and had at least one battery of artillery with them.

A portion of Harrison's command, under Colonel McNeill, wit
six pieces of artillery, had moved down from Monroe, and were ope
ating between the Tensas and Mississippi, below Lake Saint Josepl
They had made their appearance on the river at Water Proof, abou
30 miles above Natchez, and had fired into two or three transport
only one, however, the Welcome, with artillery.

On learning this, I ordered the [Mississippi] Marine Brigade, whic
had been cruising in the vicinity of Greenville, to come down an
cruise between Rodney and Natchez. When General Gresham can
up with his brigade, about two weeks ago, he landed a couple c
regiments below Water Proof, moved rapidly across the point, an
appeared unexpectedly before the place, and captured some 18 pri
oners, the remainder of the force escaping back into the country.

As he had no mounted men he could not pursue them, but it ha
the effect of making them keep their artillery back from the river.

---

*A similar letter of same date addressed to Sherman.

On the evening of the 3d, I became satisfied that Adams contemplated an attack on Natchez, with a force variously estimated at from ,000 to 3,000 men and six pieces of artillery. I immediately ordered Gresham to embark on board of transports, with two regiments of infantry, two of cavalry, and a section of artillery, and proceed down the river to Natchez, take command of the U. S. forces, and disperse the enemy, if the place was threatened. If it was not threatened, he was to disembark at Rodney and move out through Fayette, coming in to the rear of Natchez, then re-embark, and come up to the vicinity of Water Proof, and disembark and clean out McNeill, or drive him across the Tensas.

He embarked his command on the afternoon and evening of the 4th, and started at daylight the next morning, in company with the [Mississippi] Marine Brigade, which arrived most opportunely and took on board a portion of his cavalry, and reached Natchez the same night about 10 o'clock, just in time to frustrate the plans of the enemy and prevent an attack on the place. During the night the enemy fell back, and were pursued the next day by General Gresham, but without getting into a fight, though some slight skirmishing ensued.

Gresham reports that Adams has from 2,500 to 4,000 men and ten pieces of artillery—two 10-pounder rifled, two 6-pounder rifled, and six 12-pounder howitzers.

Cosby's and Whitfield's brigades are still out here in our front, in the vicinity of Brownsville and Clinton, and Loring's division is at Canton, three brigades, and about 4,000 infantry at Brandon, Meridian, and Enterprise, which can be moved to Canton rapidly.

It is reported through a deserter, this evening, that Harrison's force has fallen back and gone to join Taylor. Rumors come up from below that the force which has been annoying steam-boats below the mouth of Red River is crossing Red River and coming north, but it needs confirmation.

I shall leave Gresham in command at Natchez, for a while, at last, as I consider him one of the best officers in my corps.

My kindest regards to all the staff.

    Sincerely, your friend,

JAS. B. McPHERSON,
Major-General.

Maj. Gen. U. S. GRANT.

—

HDQRS. 17TH ARMY CORPS, DEPT. OF THE TENNESSEE,
Vicksburg, December 16, 1863.

GENERAL: I inclose herewith a report from Colonel Farrar, and also a report from Brigadier-General Ellet, showing the movements of the [Mississippi] Marine Brigade in connection with our forces under General Gresham:

Colonel Farrar has shown himself a bold, adventurous, and skillful partisan, and in his recent operations about Natchez has rendered most efficient service. His forte lies in commanding a small body of resolute, daring men.

From the best information I can obtain, Loring's division is still at Canton, Whitfield's and Cosby's brigades of cavalry from Brownsville, via Clinton, around to Raymond; Wirt Adams' (late Logan's) somewhere in rear of Natchez, and last week French's

division (infantry) was moved from the vicinity of Meridian t
Brandon, in consequence of a report that I was about to make a
expedition to Canton. Strenuous efforts are being made by th
rebels to stop the navigation of the Mississippi, or, at least, make i
so insecure as to practically close it for commercial purposes.

There has been some firing on boats in the vicinity of Rodney
nothing very serious, however. But with the force of cavalry no
at Natchez and the [Mississippi] Marine Brigade, I think I will be abl
to keep the river clear within my jurisdiction. The most seriou
affairs have occurred in the vicinity of Morganza, and several boat
have been quite seriously injured. It is reported that General Dic
Taylor is fortifying on Red River, below Alexandria, and that he i
preparing a raft somewhere between the mouth of Black River an
Alexandria to obstruct navigation.

As soon as the waters rise so that gunboats can run up Red Rive
and down the Atchafalaya, I think the "rebs" will be getting ou
from Morganza. I send this letter and reports direct, becaus
Major-General Sherman seems to be out of the line of direct com
munication.

Very respectfully, your obedient servant,
JAS. B. McPHERSON,
Major-General, Commanding.

Major-General GRANT,
Comdg. Military Division of the Mississippi.

No. 2.

Report of Col. Bernard G. Farrar, Thirtieth Missouri Infantry

HEADQUARTERS POST,
Vidalia, December 12, 1863.

CAPTAIN : I have the honor to report that, in accordance with i
structions from the general commanding the District of Natchez,
moved from this post with 206 mounted men, consisting of 100 c
the Tenth Missouri Cavalry, Capt. F. R. Neet ; 50 mounted men c
the Twenty-ninth Illinois Infantry, Captain Call ; 50 mounted me
of the Thirtieth Missouri Infantry, Captain Wilkinson, and 6 pi
neers of the Second Mississippi Artillery, A. D., Lieutenant Orgar
The object of the expedition was the capture of Camp Cotton, c
the south side of Little River, 7 miles above Trinity, La., and th
picket stations at Trinity and Garrett's plantation.

At 10 a. m., December 10, Captain Wilkinson with his commar
moved down the Mississippi River to a point 12 miles below Vidali
with instructions to remain until the main body, which was embarke
on a steamer at Natchez, could unite with him.

At 3 p. m. I moved with the entire command in the direction c
Johnson's plantation, on the Black River, 19 miles below Trinit
The road, being through a swamp, and very miry, precluded a rap
advance, so that we did not reach the Black River Ferry, until 7 p. n
The boat was on the opposite side of the river, the ferryman being ir
structed not to cross at that hour, but, on the order of Mr. Johnson
which I compelled him to give, he came over. At Mr. Johnson's plant
tion Capt. E. J. Hall, assistant quartermaster in the Confedera

ervice, and one private were surprised and captured. Taking all ossible precaution against my movements being discovered, I ommenced the crossing of my forces. The boat being small, but 6 orses could be taken over at a trip, and it was 12 o'clock before I ould cross the two detachments of mounted infantry, 100 men. eaving the cavalry, under Captain Neet, to cross as rapidly as pos- ible, with instructions to move on the Trinity road, on the west bank f the Black, and if possible capture the picket station on Garrett's lantation, taking the mounted infantry I struck off through the wamps and plantations direct for "Camp Cotton." A drizzling rain endered the darkness so intense that it was with great difficulty my uides could follow the route indicated. For several miles the road d direct through the swamp. Several deep bayous were crossed, and t one part of the road, for over half a mile, our horses waded belly- eep in water. Owing to the fall of one of my men, about 50 of the ear guard became detached from me. Fearing that we would arrive o late to accomplish a surprise, I left a competent guide to bring em up as soon as possible and pushed on to the camp.

Arriving within a quarter of a mile of the camp, I dismounted my en and moved cautiously to within 100 yards of the quarters.

Ordering a charge, we rushed upon the enemy, surrounded their uarters, and captured every man but Major Wyche, who rushed rom his bed at the first alarm, plunged boldly into Little River, and scaped. We here captured 1 officer and 15 men.

Here our lost detachment rejoined us, and, seeing that the enemy ere routed, made a bold charge into the camp. A large amount f quartermaster and commissary stores were captured and destroyed, onsisting of shoes, hats, cloth, sugar, flour, &c., and also about 20 uskets.

Not wishing to alarm the picket at Trinity, which I was anxious capture, along with the ferry-boat at that place, I refrained from ring the quarters. Mounting my prisoners at once, I dispatched aptain Call across Little River, with orders to proceed with all haste the Harrisonburg road, and then on that to move down on Trinity. Vith the remaining force and prisoners, I followed the road on the uth bank leading to Trinity.

My advance, being discovered by vedettes 4 miles above, and fear- g that the boat would be destroyed, I divided my command and ushed on with all speed, deploying a portion of my command along e river bank opposite the town. I threw the remainder of my men cross the ferry and into the town as quickly as possible. Here a risk firing took place between my men on the bank and the retreat- g rebels, who, mounting their horses, fled in wild confusion to the vamps.

Owing to the heaviness of the roads and the jaded condition of the orses and my own rapid advance, Captain Call failed to arrive in me to surprise the enemy at Trinity.

Captain Neet succeeded in bringing his men across by 5 a. m. oving rapidly on the road indicated, he skillfully surrounded the icket on Garrett's plantation, capturing all of it, consisting of 1 fficer and 10 men. He rejoining me at 10 a. m.

The object of the expedition being accomplished, I commenced e crossing of my men to the east bank of the Black. At 4 p. m. I oved on the direct road to Vidalia, reached Black Bayou at 7 p. m., t which place we were delayed two hours in crossing. The prison- rs, under a strong escort, in charge of Captain Organ, moved

through to Vidalia, camping on York's plantation, 8 miles out.
arrived at Vidalia at 10 a. m. this morning.

Both officers and men heartily co-operated with me in our long an
tedious expedition. A part of the force marched within thirty-three
hours a distance of 82 miles, through a country almost entirely
swamp, and over roads when the horses sunk knee-deep in mud
Many of the horses failed on the march, but their places were immedi
ately and easily supplied by fresh ones from the nearest plantations

Lieutenant Organ, whom I sent back with dispatches to you, cap
tured 2 men, with arms in their hands, who claimed to be citizens
but are known to be soldiers.

Altogether we captured 3 officers, 28 privates, and 30 horses, als
1 battalion flag.

Inclosed find list of prisoners.*

I have the honor to be, very respectfully, your obedient servant,
BERNARD G. FARRAR,
Colonel, Commanding.

Capt. GEORGE S. BABBITT,
Acting Assistant Adjutant-General.

No. 3.

*Report of Brig. Gen. Alfred W. Ellet, commanding Mississippi
Marine Brigade.*

HEADQUARTERS MISSISSIPPI MARINE BRIGADE,
Flag-ship Autocrat, Natchez, Miss., December 8, 1863.

GENERAL : I proceeded with all possible dispatch to join m
command. Not finding the fleet at Rodney, I followed to Natchez
where I arrived in time to see and confer with General Greshan
previous to his leaving for the front. The enemy was said to be i
considerable force but a few miles from town. It had been decide
before my arrival to march out and meet him by two roads. M
command, under Lieutenant-Colonel Currie, had already left on th
Pine Ridge road, General Gresham commanding in person by th
Washington road, the two commands to meet about 5 miles beyon
Washington and proceed together to Fayette, &c. I immediatel
followed my little force and assumed command upon coming u
with it. Arriving at the junction of the two roads I could lear
nothing from General Gresham nor the enemy, and consequentl
returned to Natchez through Washington, the way the genera
should have gone out.

Upon reaching Natchez, after night I learned for the first time tha
the enemy had retreated south and the general was in pursuit, an
that his couriers to me had miscarried. Captain Clark, of his staf
soon after arrived with a request from the general for me to dro
down to Ellis' Cliff, that the enemy was marching for that poin
which I accordingly did, arriving soon in the morning. I ha
scarcely landed at Ellis' Cliff and disembarked my forces and r
ceived information that the enemy had been in camp on the cli
during the night, but had marched about 3 o'clock toward Natches

---

* Omitted.

hen I received a dispatch from General Gresham, forwarded by ver by Colonel Johnson, to the effect that his cavalry had obtained position in the enemy's rear, and wishing me to return to Natchez nd march down to his assistance by the Woodville road, and thus ntercept and cut off his retreat. I at once returned to Natchez and narched out as requested on the Woodville road; met the general returning, after his arduous chase, the enemy having eluded him and scaped by the Washington road. You will readily observe that although all hands have been pretty actively employed we have not accomplished much except to give Mr. Adams something of a bad care. He was at last account in full retreat, not having fulfilled his purpose of taking Natchez, much to the disappointment of his entirely loyal friends of this vicinity.

I shall proceed to-morrow to Water Proof, and propose to feel the country through to Lake Saint Joseph. Any communication will nd me somewhere between Natchez and your city during the next three or four days.

    Very respectfully, your obedient servant,

ALFRED W. ELLET,
Brigadier-General, Commanding.

Maj. Gen. J. B. McPHERSON.

———

No. 4.

Report of Brig. Gen. Wirt Adams, C. S. Army.

HEADQUARTERS BRIGADE,
Near Kingston, December 7, 1863.

CAPTAIN : I have the honor to present the following brief report the movements and operations of this command since leaving Gallatin up to the present date :

In obedience to orders from the commanding general of division, I marched from Gallatin on the 1st instant in the direction of the Mississippi River, and took the shortest road from that point to Natchez, by way of Union Church, at which place Colonel Wood joined me with his regiment on the 2d instant, raising my total effective strength to 1,059 men. From that point I moved rapidly to the vicinity of Natchez, halting east of and near Washington on the afternoon of the 4th instant, and threw out active scouts and spies in and around the city, with the view of attack if the strength of the garrison and the state of its defensive works afforded reasonable prospect of success.

Reliable information, obtained during the afternoon and night of that day, was procured to the effect that the garrison consisted of 200 white and 1,500 negro troops, all inside the fortifications, which were completed, or nearly so, and mounting six heavy guns, commanding all the practicable approaches. These works were perfectly protected on the river side by a precipitous bluff of 100 feet running their whole length, thus preventing ingress of a dismounted force from that side, which I deemed the place of attack most promising success.

A dash into the city by either a part or the whole of the force promised no compensating result. I therefore determined to move my command by the nearest practicable route to Ellis' Cliff, 10 miles below Natchez in a direct line and 21 by the river, and take position there with my battery to obstruct navigation. I reached that point on the evening of the 5th and found a gunboat stationed there ; but selecting a favorable position for the battery I awaited on the evening of the 5th and the entire day of the 6th instant the passage of transports.   None passed, however, during daylight, and but two at night, which, owing to the elevation of the cliff and the slender prospect of inflicting injury by the fire of the battery in the dark, I did not open on.

About 7 p. m. of the 6th instant, I received reliable information that the enemy had been re-enforced at Natchez by a brigade of infantry and one of cavalry from Vicksburg, and that, relying upon the difficulties of my position between Natchez and the Homochitto River, which is impassable owing to the destruction of its bridges, he meditated a movement to occupy the only two routes of egress and attack me with his infantry and cavalry forces.   It is proper to state, however, that previous to marching to that point I fully considered these probable difficulties.   When, therefore, I learned last evening that he had posted his cavalry force of 1,000 to 1,200 on the Kingston road within 4 miles of my encampment, and was to move an infantry and artillery force this morning directly against me, I at once got my command in readiness to attack and force my way through his cavalry at daylight this morning before the remainder of his forces could be brought up.   With this view I kept the two roads from Kingston and Natchez strongly picketed during the night, and moved my whole force and trains by a plantation road to within a mile of his position.   Obtaining as accurate information of this as the darkness permitted, I made my dispositions for attack and moved forward as soon as the dawn permitted me to distinguish objects.

The enemy occupied a very strong position along the crest of a ridge east of the creek, with a broad slope and open field toward the direction of our approach, thus completely commanding the road along which I was moving.   But after a slight skirmish with the Eleventh Arkansas Regiment, dismounted and deployed, under the gallant Colonel Griffith, and a few artillery shots, the enemy gave way and fled with great precipitation in the direction of Natchez. I ordered the Fourteenth Confederate and Stockdale's battalion in pursuit.   These commands followed at a gallop for 6 or 8 miles, but such was the rapidity of his flight that they killed and captured but few. Guns, haversacks, shoes, poultry, &c., were picked up along the road by which they escaped.

I moved my command to Kingston, 16 miles from Natchez, and shall move from here to-morrow morning in the direction of the Mississippi River above Natchez, endeavoring in passing the latter place to draw out and engage the enemy's cavalry force.

I have been burning all buildings, cotton, &c., upon the plantations of certain traitors about Natchez, and removing negroes, stock, &c., for the use of the Government.

I am, captain, very respectfully, your obedient servant,

WIRT ADAMS,
Brigadier-General.

[Capt. GEORGE MOORMAN,
Assistant Adjutant-General.]

DECEMBER 1-10, 1863.—Affairs at Mount Sterling and Jackson, Ky.

REPORTS.

No. 1.—Brig. Gen. Jeremiah T. Boyle, U. S. Army.
No. 2.—Maj. Gen. Samuel Jones, C. S. Army.

No. 1.

Report of Brig. Gen. Jeremiah T. Boyle, U. S. Army.

HEADQUARTERS,
Louisville, Ky., December 4, 1863.

Colonel True notified me his pickets were driven in last night at Mount Sterling, on the Perryville road; that the enemy [numbered] 300. He had taken to the houses. I ordered him out of the houses to fight; that enemy could burn town. Enemy not exceeding 200, and that he could and must whip them. Don't believe there are 200.

He telegraphed General Fry that it was reported that 3,000 of Longstreet's had come in.

Colonel Gallup is at Paintsville. The whole story a rebel lie to scare Colonel True.

I leave for Lebanon and Camp Nelson. Will you send Major Simpson to meet me there in regard to roads and place for working negroes?

J. T. BOYLE,
Brigadier-General.

Capt. W. P. ANDERSON,
Assistant Adjutant-General.

No. 2.

Report of Maj. Gen. Samuel Jones, C. S. Army.

HDQRS. DEPT. WESTERN VIRGINIA AND EAST TENN.,
Dublin, December 8, 1863.

GENERAL: Capt. P. M. Everett, whom I sent into Kentucky with a detachment of about 200 Kentucky cavalry, informs me to-day from Gladesville, Va., that he had burned $700,000 worth of stores at Mount Sterling and Jackson, captured 250 horses, and killed, wounded, and captured 100 of the enemy without losing a man of his detachment. He has his prisoners with him. The enemy, about 1,200 strong, followed him through Pound Gap.

Very respectfully, your obedient servant,

SAM. JONES,
Major-General.

General S. COOPER,
Adjt. and Insp. Gen., C. S. Army, Richmond, Va.

DECEMBER 5-10, 1863.—Scouts from Columbia, Ky.

Report of Brig. Gen. Edward H. Hobson, U. S. Army.

MUNFORDVILLE, KY., *December* 12, 1863.

Scouting parties sent across Cumberland into Clinton and other counties returned to Columbia. Had four fights; killed 10 (Fer-

guson's) men ; captured 18 men and 15 horses. What shall I d●
with prisoners ? They are the meanest of Ferguson's guerrillas
Would it not be well to have them shot ?

E. H. HOBSON,
Brigadier-General.

Captain SEMPLE,
>   *Assistant Adjutant-General, Louisville.*

DECEMBER 6, 1863.—Affair near Fayetteville, Tenn.

*Report of Brig. Gen. Joseph F. Knipe, U. S. Army, commanding
First Brigade, First Division, Twelfth Army Corps.*

DECHERD, TENN.,
December 9, 1863.

COLONEL : I have the honor to submit the following report :
The detail furnished from this post, in obedience to orders from
headquarters Army of the Cumberland, as guard to working party
taking up railroad iron on Fayetteville railroad, was attacked on the
6th instant, in the neighborhood of Fayetteville, and 1 man wounded
and 4 taken prisoners. A small bridge beyond Salem was destroyed
on the night of the 6th instant. I have sent forward hands to rebuild this structure ; will have it completed by this time, I think. I
apprehend some difficulty in the removal of these rails with the force
employed.
I have just learned that the contractor uses the troops furnished
as guard to secure contrabands in the neighborhood to do the work,
and that while so employed the 4 men were captured by a party
calling themselves First Tennessee Battalion. The men captured
have returned to this post with inclosed parole paper. I have returned the men to duty, regarding the parole as of no account.
I would respectfully suggest that the company of mounted infantry under command of Captain Brixey, stationed at Tracy City, could
be advantageously used on this work, and would ask permission to
so use them.

JOS. F. KNIPE,
Brigadier-General, Commanding Post.

Lieut. Col. H. C. RODGERS,
>   *Assistant Adjutant-General, Twelfth Corps.*

DECEMBER 10, 1863.—Scout from Memphis, Tenn.

Report of Capt. Lucius B. Skinner, Sixth Illinois Cavalry.

HDQRS. THIRD BATT., SIXTH ILLINOIS CAVALRY,
Memphis, Tenn., December 10, 1863.

CAPTAIN : In pursuance with orders from General Grierson, received this morning, I sent Lieutenant Cover, of Company M, with
25 men, out east of the city to Mrs. Governor Jones', where they
learned that 2 guerrillas had been in that neighborhood, and between
there and White's Station, for several days. About 1½ miles east of
Buntyn Station, found 2 men just getting on their horses after cut-

ting the telegraph wires. They immediately gave chase and, after a ride of 5 miles, pursued them across Nonconnah. They were obliged to give it up, losing their track in the bottom. They gave them a very close chase, capturing the old musket I send you, also a pair saddle bags, but did not get near enough to shoot with any accuracy. They could hear of no others in that vicinity.

Hoping the above will be satisfactory, I remain, your obedient servant,

L. B. SKINNER,
Captain, Commanding Battalion.

Capt. SAMUEL L. WOODWARD,
 Asst. Adjt. Gen., Cav. Div., Sixteenth Army Corps.

DECEMBER 11–17, 1863.—Scout from Pulaski, Tenn., to Florence, Ala., and Skirmish (12th) on Shoal Creek, near Wayland Springs, Tenn.

Report of Col. Richard Rowett, Seventh Illinois (mounted) Infantry.

HDQRS. SEVENTH ILLINOIS MOUNTED INFANTRY,
Pulaski, Tenn., December 18, 1863.

SIR : I have the honor to report that, in accordance with orders from headquarters Second Division, Sixteenth Army Corps, dated Pulaski, December 10, 1863, I started on the morning of the 11th with eight squadrons of my regiment in the direction of Lamb's Ferry, Ala., passed through Lawrenceburg, Tenn.; sent one squadron with train of wagons to Waynesborough, Tenn.; moved with the remaining seven squadrons again in the direction of Lamb's Ferry; encamped near Rogersville, Ala., where Major Murphy, with 100 home guards, reported to me. Moved next morning to Bainbridge Ferry, capturing 2 prisoners, Martindale and Taylor; thence to Florence, Ala. Heard that the enemy was near Wayland Springs. Moved after him and sent Major Murphy on the Waynesborough road to cut off his retreat; had some skirmishing and took 4 prisoners. Fell in with Moreland's battalion, and 100 of the Fourth Alabama Cavalry (in all, 350 strong, and under command of Major Moreland), on Shoal Creek, 3 miles from Wayland Springs. Through a mistake of the guide we passed by their camp, when the enemy attacked us in the rear. The rear guard held the enemy in check until the regiment was dismounted and moved to the rear of our horses. I fought the enemy about three-fourths of an hour, when he was driven from the field, leaving 8 dead and 22 prisoners in our hands. Our loss 1 man slightly wounded and 3 horses killed. Major Murphy heard the firing but was not able to take part in the fight; he reported to me the next morning. I followed the enemy 1½ miles, when darkness prevented farther pursuit.

Arrived at camp yesterday, December 17, with 35 prisoners (3 commissioned officers and 30 enlisted men, and 2 murderers of Union soldiers, Taylor and Martindale). The prisoners were turned over to the provost-marshal at this post. Captain Burnham not being there, they were given in charge of Captain Armstrong.

I have the honor to be, very respectfully, your obedient servant,

R. ROWETT,
Colonel Seventh Illinois Infantry Mounted Volunteers.

Capt. L. H. EVERTS, Assistant Adjutant-General.

DECEMBER 12, 1863.—Skirmish at La Fayette, Ga.

Report of Col. Louis D. Watkins, Sixth Kentucky Cavalry.

HDQRS. THIRD BRIGADE, FIRST DIVISION CAVALRY,
Rossville, Ga., December 14, 1863.

GENERAL: I have the honor to report that on Saturday morning, December 12, at 8 a. m., with a force of 200 men from the Fourth and Sixth Kentucky Cavalry, I left this post on a scout in the direction of Dalton. At 4 p. m., 12th instant, I charged into the town of La Fayette, capturing 18 prisoners, 6 of whom were officers of the rebel signal corps, and some 30 animals. Two hours before we arrived at La Fayette the Second Kentucky (rebel) Cavalry had left the town, greatly to the regret of myself and all my command.

After camping for the night on Pigeon Ridge, 5 miles from La Fayette, we crossed the Chickamauga at a bridge 3 miles above Crawfish Spring, and scouting through McLemore's Cove without discovering any enemy we retured to camp.

We found on the route forage only sufficient for the use of the command while out.

I am, sir, very respectfully, your obedient servant,

LOUIS D. WATKINS,
Colonel, Commanding Brigade.

Brig. Gen. W. D. WHIPPLE,
Chief of Staff.

DECEMBER 13, 1863.—Skirmish at Powell's River, near Stickleyville, Va.

Report of Col. Wilson C. Lemert, Eighty-sixth Ohio Infantry.

CUMBERLAND GAP, TENN.,
December 18, 1863.

GENERAL: My cavalry is just in from Jonesville. They drove the rebel pickets from Jonesville and came upon the encampment of the Sixty-fourth Virginia at Hickory Flat, 7 miles beyond. The enemy fired one volley, and fled to Powell's River, 5 miles this side of Stickleyville, where they were re-enforced by part of the Twenty-seventh Virginia, and a brisk skirmish ensued. A few shell drove them from the ford, when the cavalry dashed over and drove them in confusion to Stickleyville, killing 5 and taking 26 prisoners (2 officers) and quite a number of small-arms. The enemy during the night left Stickleyville in the direction of Abingdon. They number about 500. No other force in that direction. Major Beeres, who commanded the expedition, says there is no force at Abingdon, and but a small number at the salt-works.

Your obedient servant,

W. C. LEMERT,
Colonel.

Brig. Gen. O. B. WILLCOX.

DECEMBER 14, 1863.—Capture of Union Wagon Train, near Clinch Mountain Gap, Tenn.

Report of Col. Thomas J. Brady, One hundred and Seventeenth Indiana Infantry.

BLAIN'S CROSS-ROADS,
December 21, 1863.

LIEUTENANT: I would respectfully report to you that, the 14th December, while carrying out Colonel Mahan's instructions respecting the improvement of the road through Clinch Mountain Gap, I was alarmed just at sundown by the repeated report of musketry, and information was brought me that the train just corraled at the opposite foot of the mountain was attacked. I immediately dispatched Captain Braxton with three companies to its defense. Shortly after I learned that the force attacking was larger than first supposed, and immediately led five other companies to its relief. Half way down the mountain the firing ceased, and knowing from the cheers that followed that the train was captured, I entertained the idea of attempting its recapture. At this time Captain Braxton returned, the train having surrendered before he could reach it. Making what dispositions I thought necessary for the attack, I had barely given the orders to advance, when informed the enemy was marching up the eastern hill and upon my right flank, seemingly regardless of my presence, and a few shots fired not causing him to pay us equal attention, I withdrew to the gap and dispatched a company (Captain Woodmansee's) to the summit of the aforesaid hill. The captain most gallantly repulsed his four several attempts to possess it.

Night had already set in, and my attempt to communicate with General Shackelford at Bean's Station proving futile, and learning from scouts sent out that the enemy in my rear was in force, and perceiving the fact from his numerous camp fires, I adopted the only alternative left me—to retreat. Accordingly at 9 p. m. camp was abandoned, and we took up our line of march over the crest of the mountains toward Rutledge. The night was dark and cold and our route pathless and very rough, while the enemy was on either side of us, his pickets extending far upon the sides of the mountain, but all were impressed with the danger attending the movement and marched in silence. All night and the next morning until 10 o'clock we kept the mountains. At that hour the sound of battle below us drew our attention to the south valley, where we could easily discern the contending forces. Glad to leave our elevation, I marched below and reported to General Hascall for duty, and was quickly placed in position to avenge upon rebel heads our night's hurried march. From him I received orders to report to Colonel Graham, and was put in position upon the ground occupied by Fifth Indiana Cavalry (which moved farther to the right), near the right center. In front and to our right was a heavy wood. By order I dispatched a company (B, Captain King) as skirmishers, with instructions to gain a fence skirting the woods immediately to our front.

The position was gained with scarcely any opposition, but upon the first appearance of the enemy's skirmishers the company withdrew in disorder. I immediately called upon Captain Braxton, Company H, to regain the fence at any cost. Most gallantly was the order obeyed and under a heavy fire, while the captain held the position until withdrawn. In the meantime, the enemy had succeeded in planting batteries upon our right flank, and shot and shell flew thick and fast over us, but the position assigned us by Colonel Graham was held until night set in. In the meanwhile, I had been ordered to report to Colonel Gilbert, and by him to Colonel Reilly, from whom I received instructions to withdraw in silence when night had fairly set in. This I did without creating alarm and without loss, and marched 3 or 4 miles south of Rutledge, where we bivouacked for the night. Starting the following morning at 7 a. m., we came to these cross-roads, where we, for the first time since leaving the gap, received something to eat.

Our transportation, camp equipage, and the greater portion of regiment and camp property, and books and papers were lost.

To Captain Woodmansee, for his gallant conduct in repulsing the enemy, to Captain Braxton, who led the advance over the mountain and who distinguished himself as commander of skirmishers, to Lieutenant-Colonel Sayles and Major Bryant for hearty co-operation, and to the regiment for good conduct, I am under obligation.

Commissary Sergeant Kesler and Private Lawton, Company B, were indefatigable and fearless in their efforts to trace the enemy's line below in the valley.

Sergeant McGinnis, Corporal Rawlins, and Private Carlton, Company I, discovered the forces and positions of the enemy at the foot of the mountain and to rear of us; and while doing this Carlton was captured, but finally overpowered his guard, escaped, and rejoined us.

First Sergeant O'Haver, Company B, acting lieutenant, commanded pickets during the night, and only withdrew at dawn, when the enemy prepared to assault.

I am, with respect,

THOS. J. BRADY,
Colonel, Commanding 117th Indiana Infantry.

Lieut. BENJ. F. OLDEN,
Acting Assistant Adjutant-General.

DECEMBER 18–31, 1863.—Operations in Northern Mississippi and West Tennessee.

SUMMARY OF THE PRINCIPAL EVENTS.

Dec. 24, 1863.—Skirmish at Estenaula, Tenn.
        Skirmish at Jack's Creek, Tenn.
    26, 1863.—Skirmish at Somerville, Tenn.
        Skirmish near New Castle, Tenn.
    27, 1863.—Skirmish at La Fayette, Tenn.
        Skirmish at Collierville, Tenn.
        Skirmish at Grisson's Bridge, Tenn.
        Skirmish near Moscow, Tenn.
    28, 1863.—Skirmish at Mount Pleasant, Miss.
    29, 1863.—Skirmish at Coldwater, Miss.

REPORTS.

No. 1.—Brig. Gen. Benjamin H. Grierson, U. S. Army, commanding Cavalry Division, Sixteenth Army Corps.

No. 2.—Col. Edward Hatch, Second Iowa Cavalry, commanding Second Brigade, of skirmishes at La Fayette and Collierville, Tenn. (27th).

No. 3.—Lieut. W. Scott Belden, Sixth Iowa Cavalry, Acting Assistant Adjutant-General.

No. 4.—Col. Edward Prince, Seventh Illinois Cavalry, of skirmishes at Estenaula (24th) and near New Castle, Tenn. (26th).

No. 5.—Lieut. Col. Jefferson Brumback, Ninety-fifth Ohio Infantry, of skirmishes at La Fayette and Collierville, Tenn. (27th).

No. 6.—Col. William H. Morgan, Twenty-fifth Indiana Infantry, commanding Third Brigade.

No. 7.—Maj. Gen. Nathan B. Forrest, C. S. Army.

No. 1.

Report of Brig. Gen. Benjamin H. Grierson, U. S. Army, commanding Cavalry Division, Sixteenth Army Corps.

HDQRS. CAVALRY DIVISION, SIXTEENTH ARMY CORPS,
Memphis, Tenn., January 24, 1864.

CAPTAIN:* In pursuance of Special Orders, No. 324, dated headquarters Sixteenth Army Corps, December 18, 1863, Colonel Mizner was ordered to move his command (except the Sixth Tennessee), in connection with a brigade of infantry and battery, under General Mower, from Corinth north toward Purdy. At the same time I prepared to concentrate the rest of my command at La Grange, for the purpose of moving north and operating in conjunction with General Mower from Purdy, and General A. J. Smith, [who was to move south] from Union City, toward the position of the enemy at Jackson, Tenn. Information arrived, however, that General Smith was not yet prepared to leave; accordingly my movements were postponed, with the exception of Colonel Mizner, who, in connection with General Mower, was ordered north to Purdy, there to await further developments.

On the 22d of December, however, I concentrated the rest of my command at La Grange, for the purpose of moving north to Bolivar. Upon arriving at La Grange, I was informed by General Tuttle that a considerable force of the enemy under General Chalmers was posted near Salem. This information having been telegraphed to the major-general commanding, it was thought best to remain at La Grange for the present. Accordingly, at daylight on the following morning, I started Colonel Prince with about 500 men of the Seventh Illinois north, with instructions to cover all the crossings of the Hatchie, and, if pressed by the enemy, to fall back toward Grand Junction. At the same time I sent 200 men south to feel Chalmers. Colonel Prince proceeded to Bolivar, thence northwest along the Hatchie, destroying all the boats as he proceeded. When near Estenaula, he came upon a considerable force of the enemy under Richardson, who were crossing the Hatchie at that point.

He attacked and drove them back until night compelled him to suspend operations, and he fell back to secure a safe position in which to encamp. Upon reception of this news I immediately dispatched Major Burgh, with the Ninth Illinois Cavalry, to re-enforce Colonel Prince, and, it being the belief that the enemy would attempt to

---

* For portion here omitted, see p. 578.

cross the railroad between La Grange and Pocahontas, I disposed
my command as well as possible to intercept him. That night Forrest succeeded in crossing his whole command at Estenaula.

To prevent being flanked, Colonel Prince was compelled to fall
back to Somerville; here he remained all day on the 25th, and communicated with me at La Grange. I immediately ordered him to
move east to New Castle, where Major Burgh had by this time arrived. He started on the morning of the 26th on the road to New
Castle. About 4 miles from Somerville, he met the enemy in force
and engaged them, but being attacked vigorously in the rear, his
command was thrown into disorder and compelled to retreat. They
arrived in La Grange, as did also Major Burgh, the same afternoon.

On the morning of the 27th, I learned that the enemy had moved
west. I telegraphed this information to the general commanding,
and suggested the propriety of starting a regiment of cavalry west.
This was approved, and Major Burgh was immediately ordered to
Collierville, with his regiment, and instructions to report by telegraph to the general commanding immediately upon his arrival at
that point. Scarcely had he started when the operator at La Fayette
stated that the enemy were coming, and a few moments afterward
the wires were cut. The bridge at this point had been repeatedly
ordered destroyed, and when passing there upon the railroad on the
22d instant I sent a staff officer to inquire if it had been done. He
was told by Lieutenant Roberts, of the Ninth Illinois Cavalry, who
was in command there, that it was entirely destroyed.

The information of their approach was received about fifteen minutes after 1 p. m. on the 27th. I immediately telegraphed Colonel
Morgan, who was at Grand Junction with his brigade and a train of
cars, which he had been ordered to keep in readiness to move at a
moment's notice, to embark his command and run to La Fayette as
speedily as possible, as the enemy had attacked that place. Considerable delay occurred before Colonel Morgan left La Grange, at least
two hours being consumed in embarking his command and running
2½ miles. At this point I gave him written instructions to attack
the enemy vigorously wherever he might be found, and sent with
him Major Starr, one of my staff, for the purpose of sending me information.

In the meantime I suggested to Brigadier-General Tuttle that the
force of white troops under Major Henry, stationed at Moscow, be
sent to Grisson's Bridge until the arrival of Colonel Morgan. The
suggestion was approved and acted upon. When Colonel Morgan
arrived at Grisson's Bridge he found Major Henry stationed there
and his advance already skirmishing with the enemy. He (Major
Henry) received orders to advance with his command, which he did
with alacrity, and engaged the enemy sharply; and I beg leave here
to make mention of the bravery displayed by Major Henry and his
troops upon this occasion. He drove them back, and Colonel Morgan
advanced with his train to within 1½ miles of La Fayette, where he
disembarked and formed in line of battle, although Major Henry
was still in his advance for some distance with skirmishers and reserves engaging the enemy.

Finding it impossible to get through the swamp in line, he formed
column and deployed again into line three or four times. In this
way at least one hour was consumed, during which time the enemy
was fast crossing Wolf River, and succeeded in crossing his entire
force before Colonel Morgan had fired a shot. In the meantime

Major Burgh, with the Ninth Illinois Cavalry, about 300 strong, marched by wagon road from La Grange and met the enemy about ½ miles west of Moscow. He skirmished with and drove them, in connection with Major Henry, until he arrived at La Fayette. Here the enemy divided, part going west along the railroad and the rest going south.

Major Burgh pushed west, and again came up with them near Collerville before midnight. He immediately dispatched Colonel Morgan, who had gone into bivouac at La Fayette. At 3 a. m. on the 8th, Colonel Morgan moved upon them, but before he arrived at ollierville they had gone. From this point he communicated with the major-general commanding, stating that his command were worn out, when they had marched but 8½ miles in two days and had not yet succeeded in coming within shooting distance of the enemy. He was ordered both by the major-general commanding and myself to start immediately in pursuit of the enemy. The last order he received at 6 p. m. on the 28th, but did not move until 3 o'clock the next morning. In the meantime, Colonel Mizner's brigade had returned from Purdy to Corinth and was brought by rail to La Grange.

On the morning of the 28th, I started the Second Brigade, under Major Coon, southwest to Mount Pleasant, thence to Hudsonville. As soon as Mizner arrived at La Grange I proceeded with his brigade to Hudsonville. At midnight on the 28th, I started scouts to ascertain the whereabouts of the enemy, who had passed southwest from Hudsonville the morning before.

At daylight on the 29th, I started the Second Brigade in pursuit. I soon received information from Major Coon that Forrest had been joined by Chalmers, and that another movement on the road was contemplated by the combined forces. Taking this information, in connection with a dispatch which about this time I received from the major-general commanding, with information that a considerable force of the enemy had crossed Coldwater north to re-enforce Forrest, I deemed it best to move to Mount Pleasant with the rest of my command, and sent detachments to Olive Branch and farther west, in order to completely cover the line of the railroad, and sent expeditions to all the fords and crossings on Coldwater, and one to proceed, if possible, as far as Byhalia.

The next morning (30th) I received information from all the scouts that the enemy had passed rapidly southward, and a cold rain, accompanied by snow, setting in, I ordered Colonel Mizner to proceed with his command, via Mount Pleasant, to La Grange, sent the Sixth Illinois, via Olive Branch, to Germantown, and with the rest of the command fell back to Collierville.

I herewith transmit report by Colonel Morgan of the part taken by his command in the late pursuit ; also, extract from the report of Maj. M. H. Starr, acting assistant inspector-general of the Cavalry Division, who was present during the movements of Colonel Morgan's brigade from La Grange at La Fayette.

If Colonel Morgan had evinced as much enterprise in pursuing and attacking the enemy as he has in making excuses for his tardy movements, success would undoubtedly have attended our efforts.

Respectfully, your obedient servant,

B. H. GRIERSON,
Brigadier-General, Commanding Cavalry Division.

Capt. T. H. HARRIS, *Assistant Adjutant-General.*

[Inclosure.]

HDQRS. CAVALRY DIVISION, SIXTEENTH ARMY CORPS,
Memphis, Tenn., January 1, 1864.

Lieut. Col. W. H. THURSTON,
Assistant Inspector-General, Sixteenth Army Corps:

*   *   *   *   *   *   *

Touching the destruction of the railroad at La Fayette, on the 27th day of December, and the escape of the rebel forces under Forrest, I would report that the Third Brigade of this division received orders to move to La Fayette and attack the enemy wherever found; that ample time was given in which to move to La Fayette before the enemy could have crossed his whole force; and, further, that no disposition was shown by the brigade commander to press the enemy while there was a probability of preventing the crossing and escape of his whole force.

I would report Col. W. H. Morgan, Twenty-fifth Indiana Infantry Volunteers, commanding Third Brigade, Cavalry Division, Sixteenth Army Corps, as inefficient.

*   *   *   *   *   *   *

Respectfully submitted.

M. H. STARR,
Major 6th Ill. Cav., A. A. I. G., Cav. Div., 16th A. C.

No. 2.

Report of Col. Edward Hatch, Second Iowa Cavalry, commanding Second Brigade, of skirmishes at La Fayette and Collierville, Tenn. (27th).

HEADQUARTERS SECOND BRIGADE, CAVALRY DIVISION,
Collierville, January 1, 1864.

CAPTAIN: I have the honor to submit the following report of the part taken by the detachments of this brigade which were left in camp when the command was ordered out during the recent advance of the enemy:

At 3 p. m. on the 24th of December, 1863, in compliance with orders received from your headquarters by telegraph, I ordered a detachment of 30 men, under Lieutenant Dunham, mounted on the wagon mules, to Macon, Tenn. They swam Wolf River about miles northeast of this place, and proceeded to Macon, reaching there about daylight on the morning of the 25th, found no enemy in the vicinity, and returned to camp, arriving about 3 p. m., 25th December.

On the 25th December, received orders from General Hurlbut to destroy all the crossings of Wolf River immediately. Telegraphed the orders to Germantown and La Fayette, and sent details from Collierville to perform the duty. On the 26th and on the morning of the 27th December, repeated the orders, and supposed that they were obeyed, but have since learned that the destruction of the bridge at La Fayette was only partial.

About half past 1 p. m., on the 27th December, received information that the enemy in large force was crossing the Wolf River at a Fayette; that they had driven Lieutenant Roberts, Ninth Illinois avalry, with his command of two companies of the Ninth Illinois avalry, from the town, and were pushing him west on the State Line ad. This information came by mounted courier. I immediately ounted every man that was available in camp, using the transportion mules for the purpose, and sent Captain Foster, Second Iowa avalry, in command of the detachment, amounting to about 100 en, on the State Line road toward La Fayette. They met Lieunant Roberts, Ninth Illinois Cavalry, with his command, about men, 2 miles west of La Fayette, and immediately joined with m and engaged the enemy; checked their advance. Drove it back alf a mile, but heavy re-enforcements of the rebels coming up they gain drove our men slowly but steadily back, pursuing them until ithin range of our guns in the fort at Collierville, which were pened. Our little detachment fought so stubbornly that it was ter dark when our artillery opened.

The enemy, 2,000 strong, under General Forrest, formed a line of attle three-fourths of a mile east of the fort, sending 400 west and 0 south of the town. The night was intensely dark, and it was ining.

Before daylight on the morning of the 28th December, General orrest moved his whole command south on the Chulahoma road. on after daylight the Ninth Illinois Cavalry came into camp from e east; about 9 a. m. Colonel Morgan's brigade arrived.

At 12 m. the Ninth Illinois Cavalry started in pursuit of the emy, and at 3 a. m. on the 29th, Colonel Morgan's brigade followed. The pursuit was continued a few miles south of the Coldater, but the enemy having twenty-four hours the start of any nsiderable portion of our forces, of course the pursuit was fruitless. The command returned to camp on the morning of the 31st December.

The conduct of Captain Foster, Second Iowa Cavalry, and of rgeant Pullman, Ninth Illinois Cavalry, and most of the men of eir commands, is highly commendable.

Our casualties are as follows: Two men wounded and 8 men cap-red. The losses of the enemy much greater than ours, and as far known were 1 man killed and 7 men wounded.

I am, captain, your most obedient servant,

EDWARD HATCH,
Colonel Second Iowa Cavalry, Commanding Brigade.

Capt. SAMUEL L. WOODWARD,
Asst. Adjt. Gen., Cav. Div., 16th A. C., Memphis, Tenn.

No. 3.

eport of Lieut. W. Scott Belden, Sixth Iowa Cavalry, Acting Assistant Adjutant-General, of the destruction of bridges at La Fayette.

HDQRS. SECOND BRIG., CAV. DIV., 16TH ARMY CORPS,
Collierville, Tenn., January 2, 1864.

CAPTAIN: I have the honor to submit the following report in gard to the destruction of the bridges at La Fayette:

In compliance with orders received by telegraph from your head-

quarters, December 25, 1863, ordering the destruction of all crossing
on Wolf River, I telegraphed to Lieut. S. O. Roberts, Ninth Illinoi
Cavalry, commanding at La Fayette, to destroy all crossings on th
Wolf, in the vicinity of La Fayette. This order was repeated on
the 26th and 27th days of December, 1863, and was received by Lieu
tenant Roberts (see certificate of telegraph operator at Colliervill
and La Fayette), but the destruction of the bridge was not com
plete, a foot-path being left, whereby the enemy crossed on the 27tl
December, and from thence south.

I am, very respectfully, your most obedient servant,

W. SCOTT BELDEN,
Lieutenant, and Acting Assistant Adjutant-General.

Capt. T. H. HARRIS,
Assistant Adjutant-General.

[Inclosures.]

COLLIERVILLE, TENN.,
December 29, 1863.

I certify, and am willing to testify under oath, that on the 25th
26th, and 27th, one or all of these days, in December, 1863, I sent a
least three messages to Lieutenant Roberts, Ninth Illinois Cavalry
in command at La Fayette, ordering him in positive and unmistaka
ble terms to destroy all crossings of Wolf River, to prevent th
enemy getting over.

The same orders were also sent to commanding officer at German
town, and all bearing the signature of W. Scott Belden, lieutenant
and acting assistant adjutant-general, Second Brigade Cavalry, Six
teenth Army Corps.

E. F. BUTLER,
Operator.

LA FAYETTE,
December 29, 1863.

Lieutenant BELDEN,
Acting Assistant Adjutant-General:

All the messages are destroyed that were in my office. I received
several messages for Lieut. S. O. Roberts from you to destroy al
crossings, and he received them all, for I delivered them in person

Respectfully,

W. A. THAYER.

No. 4.

*Report of Col. Edward Prince, Seventh Illinois Cavalry, of skir
mishes at Estenaula (24th) and near New Castle, Tenn. (26th).*

HDQRS. SEVENTH ILLINOIS VOLUNTEER CAVALRY,
La Grange, Tenn., December 27, 1863.

SIR: I have the honor to report that, in pursuance of orders from
General Grierson, commanding division, I marched on the morning
of the 23d instant at 6 a. m. The orders above alluded to directed
me to proceed with my regiment, with five days' rations and 10
rounds of ammunition, to Bolivar. From that point to send patrol

as far as practicable up and down the Hatchie, to watch all the crossings and destroy all the means of crossing that stream. I was further advised that the general commanding division would hold his command near La Grange for the present, in view of information relative to an attack from below. I was directed to remain in the vicinity of Bolivar until further orders, &c.

I have the honor to report my arrival at Bolivar at about 6 p. m. I learned that night that the ferry-boat which Forrest had taken to the mouth of Clover had been moved to Estenaula, some distance below, on the morning of December 24, 1863. I therefore sent two companies, F and M, to destroy a ferry crossing some 7 miles above Bolivar. Sent also A Company, to proceed to mouth of Clover and destroy any means of crossing the rebels might have at that point. I then moved directly to Westville, 12 miles west of Bolivar, thence in the direction of Estenaula, as you will see by the inclosed map.*

On arriving within 4½ miles of Estenaula, we came upon the rebel pickets, and immediately attacked three rebel regiments under command of General Richardson. We succeeded in driving these regiments to the Slough Bridge, 1½ miles this side of Estenaula, at which point we were unable to drive them farther. We were, however, able to hold our ground without difficulty, and did so till about 8 p. m., when, to avoid being flanked, I retired my command in good order, not under fire.

About 10 p. m. the enemy sent about 300 mounted men toward Westville, and attacked, with double the strength of my regiment, the line I had formed, but were repulsed; when, finding that the rebels were sending a heavy column to our left, I found it necessary to again retire, which was done in good order. The main force I sent into Somerville, and held the forks of the road 4½ miles north of Somerville. The command arrived in Somerville about 5 a. m., having fought over four hours the preceding twenty-four hours, and having marched over rough roads a distance of 40 or more miles.

It is to be remarked that Company C, detachments A, F, and M, were only able to join me after the fight. C detachment came in about 11 p. m., having carried dispatches to the general commanding division at La Grange. I remained in Somerville December 25, fed, rested, inspected, and cleaned arms, scouted west, north, and east to New Castle, and received orders about 12.30 a. m., December 26, to immediately move east to New Castle; that Major Burgh was at that point with 300 men and four 12-pounder howitzers. I received, also, word from Major Burgh that he was at that point. I immediately dispatched Major Burgh to remain at New Castle, unless he was forced back, and informed him that I would move east and join him; further directing him to send a scouting party toward Whiteville. At 4.30 a. m. I marched from Somerville, taking the New Castle road, and met the enemy about 4 miles from New Castle. We immediately formed, and pushed by hard fighting, both on foot and mounted, to about 1½ miles from where Major Burgh was resting in line of battle.

I then dispatched messages, two in writing, to General Grierson, stating that I was fighting the enemy and where, and further stating that Major Burgh was not co-operating, and hence had probably been forced to retire. I have since learned that no written messages had come through.

The fight commenced about 9 a. m. and lasted till 12.30, when, the

---

* Not found.

enemy having gained our rear, we were compelled to retire, and owing to the broken character of the ground, in considerable dis order.

The loss the enemy sustained, however, in killed and wounded must have exceeded our entire loss, which will not exceed 40 killed wounded, and missing. I collected all the men I could and flanked the enemy's left, sent word to New Castle, and ascertained that Ma jor Burgh had been some time gone from New Castle. I overtook his rear guard about 3 miles from New Castle, and the major him self about 7 miles from that place (New Castle). The major states that he held a consultation among his officers, and did send out two companies, who had a little skirmish with the enemy.

There can be no question but that, if Major Burgh had made any show on the rear of his foe, or had even discharged a how itzer in his own camp, the fight would have ended in a complete rout of the enemy and the capture of several hundred prisoners As it is, I have only to report Major Burgh for incompetency and violation of orders. I desire also to report that the force fough yesterday consisted of about 300 of Forrest's command, commanded by General F[orrest] in person, General Richardson and Colone Neely, in command of about 1,300 men; that it is my opinion tha at the time of the fight yesterday Forrest's artillery and train wer on the move for Somerville from Fayette Corners, and that it ar rved at that place last night.

Respectfully,

EDWARD PRINCE,
Colonel Seventh Illinois Volunteer Cavalry.

Lieutenant BELDEN, *Acting Assistant Adjutant-General.*

No. 5.

Report of Lieut. Col. Jefferson Brumback, Ninety-fifth Ohio In fantry, of skirmishes at La Fayette and Collierville, Tenn. (27th).

HDQRS. NINETY-FIFTH REGT. OHIO INFANTRY VOLS.,
Camp at Collierville, Tenn., December 28, 1863.

SIR: I have the honor to report that yesterday the enemy, unde command of Forrest, having crossed the Wolf Creek at La Fayett approached this place, driving before them a few cavalry that ha been sent out to oppose their advance and watch their movement About dark they engaged and drove in my pickets, after a shar skirmish. A few shots were fired by the guns in the fort. Durin the night the enemy attacked one of my picket posts, when a fe shots were exchanged between the parties. Beyond this, all remaine quiet during the night, which was very dark, and in the mornin the enemy had disappeared.

The casualties in my regiment are, 2 men missing, Corpl. Georg W. Corbin, and Private Barton Durant. Both were probably ca tured by mistaking, while falling back from the picket post in th darkness, rebel cavalry for our own.

I am, sir, respectfully, your obedient servant,

J. BRUMBACK,
Lieutenant-Colonel, Commanding Regiment.

Lieut. E. A. RAWSON, *Actg. Asst. Adjt. Gen.*

No. 6.

Report of Col. William H. Morgan, Twenty-fifth Indiana Infantry,
commanding Third Brigade.

HEADQUARTERS THIRD BRIGADE, CAVALRY DIVISION,
Grand Junction, Tenn., January 11, 1864.

GENERAL: Compelled by false and slanderous reports, put in circulation in reference to me and the troops which I have the honor to command, to prepare an official report of my and their operations of late, a copy is respectfully submitted for your perusal.

Feeling confident, in fact knowing, that no other motive than a desire to do justice to all within your jurisdiction prompts you or our decisions when estimating their abilities, and believing that an effort has been made to prejudice your mind against us, and this, too, by false representations, we feel it a duty incumbent on us to present the facts clearly, distinctly, and fairly to your mind.

Our case is, therefore, respectfully submitted for your decision. That we are not responsible for the errors committed in the recent operations in this quarter is our opinion, and that we are not willing to shoulder the military blunders of our superiors we boldly assert.

In the highest respect, I have the honor to be, general, your obedient servant,

WILLIAM H. MORGAN,
Colonel Twenty-fifth Indiana Volunteer Infantry, Comdg.

Maj. Gen. STEPHEN A. HURLBUT,
Commanding Sixteenth Corps, Memphis.

[Inclosure.]

HEADQUARTERS THIRD BRIGADE, CAVALRY DIVISION,
Grand Junction, January 4, 1864.

CAPTAIN: We propose herein to furnish in detail, though as briefly as possible, a sketch of the operations of this brigade from the 27th to the 31st day of December, 1863.

In order that its object may be fully understood, or that the facts may be clearly, distinctly, fairly, and correctly presented to the mind of the general commanding, it is thought best that we should particularize a little, or, as stated in the beginning, to conduct our report in detail. The following is, therefore, volunteered and respectfully submitted:

At 2 o'clock in the afternoon of the 27th of December last, we received at brigade headquarters, in Grand Junction, Tenn., a telegram from Brigadier-General Grierson, at La Grange, directing this command to move by rail, and as quickly as possible, west to La Fayette, the object being to intercept the rebel General Forrest, who, with his command, was said to be crossing Wolf River and the railroad at that point from the north.

This order was communicated verbally, and without a moment's hesitation, to each regimental and the artillery commander, and by them in the same manner to their respective commands. We think it would approach very near a correct statement to say that from the time this order was received and issued from these headquarters to that of its reception by the troops near five minutes had elapsed.

At the expiration of this time, however, every officer and man was actively engaged in making such preparations, and such only, as were absolutely necessary for the work we were expecting to per form. This preparation, unnecessary to detail, but familiar to every officer of the infantry arm of the service, added to the time require to form companies and regiments and to march from camp (a dis tance of at least one-fourth of a mile) to the railway train intende to convey us, did not require a less period than twenty or thirt minutes.

If it is possible for this movement to be considered tardy, we thin an apology can be offered which will, or ought to in our opinion dispel any thought of this kind, particularly if entertained by a unprejudiced or impartial mind, when we state that it was and ha been raining very hard for at least one hour. Owing to this, we ex perienced considerable inconvenience and delay on the arrival of th command at the train, so that it was some minutes before the infan try was on board and ready to be moved. It was with the artillery however, that we experienced the most difficulty, and with which greater length of time was occupied. Each gun and caisson had t be unlimbered, and the two parts of each taken by hand and place on the platform cars intended to convey them. This, necessarily slow process at best, was now rendered doubly tedious on account o the rain and mud.

We had succeeded in getting two guns and two caissons with thei limbers, and the remaining guns of the battery without limbers and probably 8 or 10 horses, on and in the cars, when we received dispatch directing us to leave the battery if not loaded. The re maining caissons were immediately ordered to be and were returne to camp; but as the men were engaged in placing on the cars th limbers of the two guns already on board, and at the same time th horses for so much of the battery as was then loaded, we conclude that, as the battery would not probably be of much service to u without the horses, to continue the loading, particularly as it wa asserted that but a moment would be required to accomplish all tha we desired. Up to this time near one hour had been consumed. Now, this may appear to those who have had no experience of thi kind, and under similar circumstances, as an unusual length of time. We, however, think differently, and, as we can truthfully and sin cerely, we will bear testimony to the energy and will displayed by the officers and men of this command, and to the great desire exhib ited by all to reach at the earliest possible moment the place desig nated in the first order received from division headquarters.

Our own preparations being completed, it was reported that the locomotive had not a sufficient supply of wood. It was necessary therefore, to supply this deficiency, and in order to do so the entire train, loaded, had to be backed up some distance. It was now near 3.30 p. m. before we were ready to and did start.

The distance from Grand Junction to La Fayette is by rail near 20 miles, we believe. At the rate of travel over this road, say 20 miles per hour—and this was the best time made by the train that day—it will be seen that had we been able to have proceeded un interruptedly we would have arrived at our destination at 4.30 p. m., just nine minutes before sunset on that day.

But on our arrival at La Grange our progress was cut short for a moment in order that we might communicate with our commanding officer, who, we had learned by telegram, desired an interview with us on our arrival at that place. We here received orders to press the enemy, &c., and a re-enforcement in the person of Maj. M. H.

Starr, acting assistant inspector-general on the staff of the division commander.

To accommodate the major, the train was again stopped at Moscow, a village about 9 miles farther west. We were here detained near five minutes before again proceeding westward. What the object of this detention was has never yet been made clear to our minds, unless it was to report our arrival to his commanding officer, and, in obedience to the orders received from him, as was stated by the major, to report progress every ten minutes, if possible.

Arriving at Grisson's Bridge, distant from Moscow about 6 miles, and finding there detachments of the Eighty-ninth Indiana and One hundred and seventeenth Illinois Volunteer Infantry, under the command of Major Henry, of the first-named regiment, and this location not being far distant from the proposed field of action, we ordered a halt to learn, if possible, the situation of affairs.

The major informed us that he had sent two companies of his command along the road toward La Fayette, and that they had been skirmishing some minutes with the enemy, who was reported in strong force in their front.

It was still raining very hard, and from our position on the locomotive it was barely possible to see distinctly anything at a distance beyond 200 or 300 yards. We concluded, therefore, that if this report of the strength of the enemy was correct, it would be, to say the least, imprudent to rush blindly forward, or to move at any other than a reduced rate of speed. This conclusion became at once an imperative duty, when we took into consideration the probable condition of the arms on account of the rain, and particularly those in the hands of the men who had been compelled to be transported on the roofs of the cars. Added to this was the cramped condition of the men within the cars. There was therefore but little hesitancy in determining the proper course to pursue. We directed Major Henry to leave two companies of his command at the bridge, and with the remainder to proceed in advance of the train, prepared to resist and to give us timely warning of any attempt on the part of the enemy to draw us into an ambush. This order was promptly responded to by the major and his men, who in a moment were marching as rapidly as possible along the railroad toward La Fayette. The train was kept well up, and every man in readiness to quit the cars at any moment the necessity required or the nature of the ground would permit.

Any one familiar with the country along the railroad extending from Grisson's Bridge to La Fayette knows that it is very low, flat, and swampy, and that as a route for infantry is, at almost any season of the year, impracticable; and any officer with the least degree of military talent or common sense will, we think, agree with us that to have ordered the train, loaded as it was, rapidly forward, and this, too, in the face of an enemy reported largely superior to his own force, would have merited the severest censure to say the least. We, therefore, moved cautiously, yet as rapidly as was in our opinion proper under the circumstances, and had reached a distance from La Fayette not to exceed one-half mile when the men were ordered off and out of the cars and into line of battle. We were induced to do this from another report received, that the enemy was in force in front of us, which report was confirmed by the increased and rapid firing of Major Henry's command, deployed a short distance in advance. Our line being formed, we advanced or attempted to ad-

vance in this order, but found it wholly impossible on account of th
swamps, underbrush, and down timber, and were therefore com
pelled to advance by the flank.

It should be borne in mind that it was now quite dark, and suc
being the fact, it is probable that it will be conceded as another an
very serious obstacle to a rapid advance.

Having marched a short distance in the order indicated, we wer
met by Captain Blackburn, of the Ninth Illinois Cavalry, with th
information that the enemy was still in very strong force immed:
ately in advance of us. If this was correct, he was of course pre
pared to resist us.

The command passed again into the order of battle and advanced
with the expectation that the enemy would open on us every mo
ment. We felt the importance of keeping the men well in hand i
case of an engagement at that hour of the night, and exerted ou
selves accordingly. We discovered in a little while, however, that ou
reporters had either been very greatly deceived or that the enem
had retreated precipitately. We continued on the march until w
had reached an elevated position about one-fourth of a mile to th
east of the village, and then bivouacked.

As my command was much fatigued, and all of us without horse
we did not think that much, if anything, could be accomplished b
pursuing with infantry a well-mounted force of the enemy, and no
tified the division commander accordingly.

It affords me pleasure to be able to state that we here parted con
pany with the distinguished (?) acting assistant inspector-general c
the Cavalry Division. Taking the train upon which was the batter
attached to this brigade, he returned, we believe, to La Grange th
same night, there to regale his commanding and superior office
with his exploits, and to assure them of his superior military tale:
by criticising the operations of this brigade and by speaking di
paragingly of it and its commander.

Major Burgh, with the Ninth Illinois Cavalry, arriving shortl
after, continued on the road toward Collierville. At 12 o'clock tha
night we received a message from him to the effect that Forres
with his force, 4,500 strong, was near Collierville, and that he de
signed attacking that place at daylight.

Orders were issued at once, and at 3 a. m. this brigade was on th
march for that place, at which, or the enemy's rear, we expected t
arrive at early dawn, and in time to render assistance to the garr
son.

We selected the railroad as the best route, and the one upon whic
the enemy would be less liable to expect us, and had reached a poir
nearly opposite the ground upon which the command of Majc
Burgh had halted, and about 4 miles distant from La Fayette, whe
we were met by a courier from him, who stated to us that it woul
be impossible for us to continue much farther on this route, as th
enemy's force occupied an extent of country bordering on the rai
road of near 2½ miles, his advance extending to within 1 mile of Co
lierville.

It was now about 5 o'clock in the morning, and of course still dar
Crediting our opponent with a reasonable degree of intelligence an
caution, we did not think it advisable to continue on the railroa
farther. To surprise him in his camp we did not think it possibl
and that he would avail himself of the advantages offered we thoug
very probable. To meet him, therefore, upon an equal footing, w

determined to continue the march on the wagon road. This we found in a most miserable condition, so muddy, in fact, that it was with the utmost difficulty, and at a very slow pace, that we were able to move at all. The consequence was that instead of reaching the enemy's force or Collierville at daylight, it was near 8 o'clock in the morning before we came to a halt in the vicinity of that place. The enemy was reported to have marched a little before daylight in a southerly direction.

Shortly after our arrival at Collierville, not being able to get telegraphic communication with the division commander, we telegraphed to Major-General Hurlbut, at Memphis, informing him of our whereabouts, &c., expecting directions from him before proceeding farther on our own responsibility. We received a telegram from him at 11 a. m., directing us to march at 12 m. with our infantry and artillery in pursuit of the enemy.

Being informed of the absence of our battery, we were then directed to communicate with the division commander by courier, have the battery sent forward at once, and to wait its arrival. At 9 p. m. of the same day, however, we received an order from Brigadier-General Grierson directing us to follow in the trace of the enemy. As no particular route was specified, we concluded to march by the way of Mount Pleasant for the Coldwater crossing on the La Grange and Holly Springs road, and telegraphed the general that we would march as soon as the moon was up, or at 11 p. m. But few, if any, of the men had had any sleep since the night of the 26th, which, added to the fatigue of the marches and the cold weather, had well nigh disabled the command for any further service, so that it was near 2 o'clock in the morning before we were on the way.

We reached Mount Pleasant at 6.30 a. m. and Coldwater at 3 p. m., where we halted, in obedience to instructions received by courier from the division commander when near Hudsonville.

We were joined here by the mounted infantry of this brigade, numbering 250 men of the Thirty-second Wisconsin Volunteers and Cooper's battery. We had with us the command of Major Henry, which it was our intention to have sent back from Collierville to La Fayette or Moscow, on the morning of the 29th, and would have done so but for information received from the major to the effect that he had been ordered by General Tuttle to join us on our arrival at Grisson's Bridge on the 27th.

As the indications were that we would move forward that night or early the next morning, Major Henry and his command were ordered to return to La Grange, and accordingly marched at daylight of the 30th. His route was afterward changed to Moscow instead of the place mentioned, by direction of the division commander, who had arrived about 12 o'clock the night before.

Preparations were being made to move southward in the morning, but at or near 7.30 a. m. the pursuit was abandoned and a retrograde movement ordered. We arrived at Mount Pleasant about 3 p. m. the same day, and bivouacked there that night.

At 10 a. m. the next day, or the 31st, we received orders to march to Collierville and there wait further orders. At 3 p. m., in the midst of a most terrible rain, sleet, and snow storm, without any tents or other shelter, and without axes with which to provide wood for fires, this brigade arrived. It was with the utmost difficulty that our men were kept from perishing that night.

We will bring our sketch to a conclusion by saying that, in our opinion, no troops ever more willingly or cheerfully entered upon the discharge of any duty or met any requisition upon their courage and endurance with a better determination to faithfully discharge all its requirements, or exhibited a greater degree of real genuine heroism and fortitude in the midst of the most trying vicissitudes of wintry weather than did the Indiana, Wisconsin, and Illinois men composing this brigade, and as a reward for sleepless nights, hard marches, wearied limbs, and swollen feet, these men did not expect the ingratitude of their superiors.

We have the honor to be, captain,

WILLIAM H. MORGAN,
Colonel Twenty-fifth Indiana Volunteer Infantry, Comdg.

Capt. SAMUEL L. WOODWARD,
Assistant Adjutant-General.

No. 7.

Reports of Maj. Gen. Nathan B. Forrest, C. S. Army.

HEADQUARTERS DEPARTMENT OF WEST TENNESSEE,
Holly Springs, December 29, 1863.

GENERAL: I arrived with the greater portion of my troops in this vicinity this morning, regretting very much that I had to leave West Tennessee so early. The concentration of a heavy force compelled me to move on the 24th from Jackson. The Corinth force of the enemy reached Jack's Creek, within 25 miles of Jackson, on the 23d. I sent out a force to meet and develop their strength and retard their progress. They were found to consist of three regiments of cavalry, a brigade of infantry, and four pieces of artillery. We drove the cavalry back to the infantry and then retired. I moved my forces to Estenaula, on the Hatchie, crossing it by the night of 25th. Met a cavalry regiment and routed them. Fought the enemy again on the 26th, at Somerville, killing and wounding 8 or 10 and capturing about 35 prisoners. I then moved a part of my force, under Colonel Faulkner, to Raleigh, and with the balance moved square to the left to La Fayette Bridge, on Wolf River.

On the morning of the 27th, my advance reached the bridge and attacked the bridge guard; drove them back and put to flight the force at La Fayette Station, killing several and capturing 4 or 5 prisoners. Cavalry advanced on me from Collierville, which we met and drove back. The enemy also sent re-enforcements by trains from Moscow, which we held in check until all my wagon train was safely across the river and on the road in the rear of my advance on Collierville. We closed the fight at Collierville about 8 o'clock at night, driving the enemy into their fortifications.

Not being able to hear anything of General Chalmers, and my men being worn out, I felt it to be prudent to retire, which I did, and my command is encamped about 7 miles west of this place. Another difficulty in the matter was that all my men armed with Austrian rifles were out of ammunition, having had the misfortune to lose my Austrian ammunition by the upsetting of a wagon at Forked Deer River.

I have brought out about 2,500 men. Colonel Faulkner, who is to cross at Raleigh, has with him about 800 more. I hope to hear that they have gotten out safely by to-morrow. If I could have staid there 10 days longer, could have almost doubled that number. I brought out my wagon train and artillery safely, although I have never experienced such weather and roads. My stock, however, is much jaded and requires rest.

I have a lot of prisoners, and General Tuttle has signified his willingness to exchange man for man. Would I be justified in doing so?

I think of moving my headquarters to Oxford, and will encamp my command in Panola in order to organize it, and arm and equip it. The locality is a good one for forage, unless my command can be supplied with forage from the railroad. If so, I would prefer to be south of the Tallahatchie to organize. I will advise you positively of my location as soon as made.

I am, general, very respectfully, your obedient servant,

N. B. FORREST,
Major-General, Commanding.

Maj. Gen. STEPHEN D. LEE,
Commanding Cavalry in Mississippi.

—

HOLLY SPRINGS, *December* 29, 1863.

GENERAL: I have succeeded in getting out with about 2,500 men. Fought the enemy in heavy force at Jack's Creek, 25 miles east of Jackson, and drove them back. Commenced moving from Jackson on the next day (24th). Fought them on 25th at Estenaula, putting them to flight. Met Seventh Illinois Regiment at Somerville. Succeeded in getting in their rear and cut them up badly, capturing their wagons, a good many arms and horses, and 45 prisoners, and killed and wounded quite a number. We moved by La Fayette Bridge, on Wolf River. Found a heavy guard at the bridge, which my advance drove off; also scattered the force at La Fayette Station, and succeeded in crossing all my unarmed men, wagons, artillery, and beef cattle. The enemy advanced on me from Collierville and Moscow. We held the Moscow force in check and drove the troops from Collierville back to that place and into their fortifications. Fighting ceased at 8 o'clock at night. I then withdrew to this place.

I will move into Panola County, or to Oxford, for the purpose of organizing the men I brought out. Owing to my having to leave Jackson so soon there are about 3,000 men left that I could not get together in time. If arrangements can be made to go back again, can bring out at least 3,000 men.

I am, in haste, general, your obedient servant,

N. B. FORREST,
Major-General, Commanding.

Lieutenant-General POLK.

———

DECEMBER 21–23, 1863.—Scout from Rossville to La Fayette, Ga.

Report of Col. Louis D. Watkins, commanding Third Brigade, First Cavalry Division.

HDQRS. THIRD BRIGADE, FIRST DIVISION CAVALRY,
Rossville, Ga., December 23, 1863.

GENERAL: I have the honor to report that a scouting party of 150 men, from the Fourth and Sixth Kentucky Cavalry, left this post, under command of Major Welling, of the Fourth Kentucky Cavalry, with orders to scout through McLemore's Cove, cross at Bluebird Gap, and enter La Fayette from the west, and then return to camp on the morning of the 21st instant.

These instructions were obeyed, and the command returned at 9 this morning, bringing with them 1 commissioned, 4 non-commissioned officers, and 12 privates, prisoners of war, 10 citizens, said to be violent rebels, and 38 horses and mules.

The command report forage in abundance on the other side of Bluebird Gap.

Lieutenant Edwards, of the Eighth Georgia Battalion, while attempting to escape, was shot by Major Welling, inflicting a severe flesh wound in the thigh.

One of the prisoners, Corpl. J. J. Cutler, was captured in a Federal uniform, and, although he claims to be a courier, doubtless is a rebel scout. I transmit, for your inspection, papers * found upon his person.

I have the honor to be, general, very respectfully, your obedient servant,

> LOUIS D. WATKINS,
> *Colonel, Commanding Brigade.*

Brigadier-General WHIPPLE,
    Chief of Staff.

P. S.—The scout, Lawton, has the papers above referred to.

> L. D. W.

DECEMBER 22, 1863.—Skirmish at Cleveland, Tenn.

Report of Lieut. Jacob Bedtelyon, Fourth Michigan Cavalry.

> CLEVELAND, TENN.,
> *December 23, 1863.*

COLONEL : I was attacked yesterday at 3 p. m. by 60 rebel cavalry. They charged on my picket and drove him in, and followed him within a few rods where I am stationed ; there we held them in check fifteen or twenty minutes until they flanked us and I was compelled to fall back ; they held the place only half an hour. My loss is 1 man mortally wounded and myself somewhat bruised, being struck on the breast by a spent ball. Lost 5 horses, 10 saddles, 7 rifles, 7 revolvers and sabers, and nearly all our overcoats and blankets.

Rebel loss 2 men left wounded ; the rest they have taken with them. From the best information I can get they left their lines yesterday morning and returned last evening. Colonel, this post cannot be held with less than 75 men. It is impossible to keep out a sufficient number of vedettes with the force that I have. I have only 26 men, and they are destitute of all kinds of clothing, even blankets.

With the Seventeenth, which is now here, we could hold the post with more safety.

> J. BEDTELYON,
> *Lieutenant, Fourth Michigan Cavalry.*

Colonel LONG.

---

* Not found.

DECEMBER 23, 1863.—Skirmish near Corinth, Miss.

Report of Brig. Gen. John D. Stevenson, U. S. Army.

CORINTH,
December 23, 1863.

Lieutenant Horton, Third Illinois Cavalry, with 28 men, bearing dispatches to General Mower, was ambushed about 10 miles rom here by 200 rebels and driven back to this post with loss of 2 nen, rebels pursuing to outer line of works. The citizens report arge force of rebels between this and Purdy, but I have no information confirming report. I shall make another effort to communicate vith General Mower.

JOHN D. STEVENSON,
Brigadier-General.

Major-General HURLBUT and
Brigadier-General TUTTLE.

DECEMBER 23, 1863.—Skirmish at Mulberry Village, Tenn.

Report of Col. Silas Colgrove, Twenty-seventh Indiana Infantry.

HEADQUARTERS POST,
Tullahoma, December 26, 1863.

CAPTAIN: I have the honor to report that, on the 23d instant, I ent a forage train out into the neighborhood of Mulberry Village, Lincoln County. The train was accompanied by a guard of 70 men, under the command of First Lieutenant Porter, Company A, Twenty-seventh Indiana Volunteers. Lieutenant Porter was furnished vith copies of General Orders, No. 17, November 17, 1862, and General Orders, No. 30, December 30, 1862, Department of the Cumberand, and also Special Orders, No. —, of these headquarters, for intructions. At or near Mulberry Village, I am informed by Lieutenant Porter, he divided his train into four detachments and sent he several detachments upon different plantations, sending an equal uard with each detachment. This, I understand, was done for the urpose of facilitating the loading of the train. It was about 7 'clock in the evening when that portion of the train which Lieutenant Porter was with finished loading and started to camp.

The lieutenant reports that while he was in the house receipting or the forage a part of the train went ahead and went into camp, eaving three wagons in the rear. He started to camp with these hree wagons, distance about 2 miles. He had with him 15 men as uard. When within one-half mile of camp he discovered that the oremost wagon had got about 300 yards ahead of the other two. He went forward for the purpose of halting it. When he rode up he found the wagon stopped. Two men immediately rode up to him and presented pistols at his head and demanded his surrender. With this wagon was the teamster and wagon-master of the Ninth Ohio Battery, and 2 men who had helped to load the wagons, all unarmed except Lieutenant Porter. The guerrillas numbered but 4, and were armed. Lieutenant Porter, the wagon-master, and 3 men were immediately mounted and taken through a gate, passing about 200 yards up a creek and then into a corn-field; from there they were hurried forward, avoiding roads, &c., until about 1 o'clock in the morning. They were halted on the bank of Elk River, about 1 mile below where the Mulberry empties into it. A fire was built and their captors informed them that they were going to camp for the night.

Their hands were tied behind them; everything of value was taken from them. They were then drawn up in line 4 or 5 steps in front of their captors; one of them, who acted as leader, commanded "Ready", the whole party immediately fired. One of the men was shot through the head and killed, as supposed, instantly; 3 were wounded. Lieutenant Porter was not hit, and immediately broke and ran. He was followed and fired at by one of the party three times. He reports that he saw that he would be overtaken, and changed his course and ran to the river and threw himself over a precipice into the water. Having succeeded in getting his hands loose, he swam to the opposite shore; was fired at five or six times while he was in the water. He secreted himself under the bank of the river. His captors swam their horses across the river and made search for him, but failed to find him. He afterward made his way up the river about three-fourths of a mile and swam back again. He lay in the woods the remainder of the night and the next day. On the night of the 24th, he traveled about a mile and got to a house. The party sent out by me on yesterday brought him in. He is now lying in a critical condition owing to the exposure, cold, fatigue, &c.

He reports that he would know his captors should he see them again, one of whom is believed to be a man by the name of Tulley living near Lynchburg; another a Bowne, who is a deserter from the rebel army and has been during the fall and winter with guerrillas. A third man rode a bay stallion and is known to the citizens of Mulberry; his name I have not yet learned.

The men who were shot were immediately thrown into the river, one of whom was supposed to have been killed, and one, from the nature of the wounds and his appearance after the body was recovered, is supposed to have been drowned. The hands of these two men were found tied behind them when taken out of the river; the other two men succeeded in loosing their hands and got out of the river, one of whom has died since; the other is now in the hospital at this place; wound not considered necessarily mortal.

The names of the murdered men are as follows: John W. Drough and George W. Jacobs, Twenty-second Wisconsin Volunteers (these men were temporarily attached to the Ninth Ohio Battery); Theove E. Orcutt, Ninth Ohio Battery, wounded and since died; James W Foley, Ninth Ohio Battery, wounded and now in the hospital at this place. The three first named are men of families in destitute circumstances. The latter has an aged mother destitute, depending upon him for support.

Respectfully,

S. COLGROVE,
Colonel, Commanding Post.

Capt. WM. RUGER,
Assistant Adjutant-General.

DECEMBER 24-28, 1863.—Operations near Mossy Creek and Dandridge, Tenn.

SUMMARY OF THE PRINCIPAL EVENTS.

Dec. 24, 1863.—Skirmishes at Peck's House, near New Market, and at Mossy Creek Station, Tenn.

            Action at Hays' Ferry, near Dandridge, Tenn.

  26, 1863.—Skirmish at Mossy Creek, Tenn.

  27, 1863.—Skirmish at Talbott's Station, Tenn.

REPORTS.*

No. 1.—Maj. Gen. John G. Foster. U. S. Army, commanding Department of the Ohio.

No. 2.—Brig. Gen. Samuel D. Sturgis, U. S. Army, commanding Cavalry Corps, Department of the Ohio.

No. 3.—Brig. Gen. Washington L. Elliott, U. S. Army, commanding Cavalry Corps, Department of the Cumberland.

No. 4.—Col. Edward M. McCook, Second Indiana Cavalry, commanding First Division.

No. 5.—Col. Archibald P. Campbell, Second Michigan Cavalry, commanding First Brigade.

No. 6.—Col. Oscar H. La Grange, First Wisconsin Cavalry, commanding Second Brigade.

No. 7.—Col. William J. Palmer, Fifteenth Pennsylvania Cavalry, of operations December 24.

No. 8.—Lieut. Samuel E. Miller, Ninth Tennessee Cavalry, of action at Hays' Ferry.

No. 1.

Reports of Maj. Gen. John G. Foster, U. S. Army, commanding Department of the Ohio.

KNOXVILLE, *December* 25, 1863.

Yesterday the cavalry was mainly engaged with the enemy's cavalry beyond New Market. General Sturgis reports that on he Dandridge road Colonel Campbell's brigade met a superior orce of the enemy, and had a severe fight. They at once charged n his rear and captured two guns, but he recaptured them by a ounter charge. The enemy lost 80 killed and wounded. Colonel Campbell, Colonel Garrard's brigade, was also on the Dandridge nd Morristown road, while Sturgis, with the main body, drove he enemy beyond Mossy Creek. Sixty-one prisoners have been rought in.

                        J. G. FOSTER,
                             Major-General.

Major-General GRANT.

—

KNOXVILLE, *December* 28, 1863.

General Sturgis, with his own and Elliott's cavalry, has been lmost constantly engaged with the enemy's cavalry for the past few ays. He has gallantly driven them from every position, and is now

---

* See also Martin's report, p 547.

in the country between Mossy Creek and Morristown.   One of his brigades made a dash into Waiteu's [Witcher's?] camp last night, and put to flight three rebel brigades and captured their camp, with provisions and cooking utensils.   Longstreet is unhappy about his communications.

J. G. FOSTER,
Major-General.

Major-General GRANT.

No. 2.

Reports of Brig. Gen. Samuel D. Sturgis, U. S. Army, command ing Cavalry Corps, Department of the Ohio.

HEADQUARTERS CAVALRY CORPS,
New Market, Tenn., December 24, 1863—2 a. m.

GENERAL : My whole command reached this place this evening From all the information I can gather, I have little doubt but the whole, or nearly so, of the enemy's cavalry are on this side of the Holston.

Colonel Palmer has arrived from Dandridge with his command He captured 4 prisoners of Morgan's division, who were a part of an advanced guard to Dandridge.   From these and from citizens we learn that one brigade, and perhaps a division, is now at Dandridge Armstrong, unless he moves to-night, is in the vicinity of Morris town, and a large force somewhere in the vicinity of Cheek's Cross Roads.   I propose to attempt the separation of the force at Dan dridge from the remainder.   I will move a brigade by Mount Horeb to intercept their retreat, and a brigade with four pieces of artillery on the direct road to Dandridge.   These forces can reach their des tination by daylight, I hope.

The brigade, or division, supposed to be at Dandridge has six pieces artillery, five rifled and one brass.

The prisoners say that the cavalry came over to intercept us, be cause it was understood that we contemplated a raid on Longstreet' rear.

I talked with one—an Alabamian and a straightforward kind of fellow—who says that last Friday Longstreet was joined by A. P Hill's corps, and that what the men say through their camps is that Longstreet has now 50,000.   I give you this for what it is worth.

I think it would be well to send the dismounted men left by Col onel Wolford down to Strawberry Plains, taking their wagons with them, and they would serve as a guard for that place.

Respectfully,

S. D. STURGIS,
Brigadier-General, Commanding Cavalry Corps.

Maj. Gen. JOHN G. FOSTER.

P. S.—If the brigade of Colonel Wolford which went to Tazewell can be reached, I hope you will send it on at once.   The colonel' whole division now here is only some 800 or 900 strong.

[Indorsement.]

DECEMBER 24, 1863—6.30 a. m.

General PARKE :

I send you a dispatch just received from General Sturgis. Send over as soon as you can the first brigade that you can get hold of ; also comply with his request to have Wolford's dismounted men sent, with his wagons, to Strawberry Plains.

J. G. FOSTER,
Major-General, Commanding.

—

HEADQUARTERS CAVALRY CORPS,
New Market, December 24, 1863—11.30 a. m.

GENERAL : The division of Colonel McCook, General Elliott's corps, has been engaging the enemy more or less since early this morning on the Morristown road. The Second Indiana has just made a very handsome charge on the enemy's left and driven him back. There is a rumor to the effect that the force I sent to Dandridge has captured the enemy's battery; nothing official in regard to it, however.

I am anxious to hear from Colonel Garrard, who commands that force, as I do not wish to separate my forces any more by pushing the enemy until Garrard returns, or at least until I can hear of him.

I trust you can spare the brigade now with you and send it as rapidly as possible to join me.

Respectfully,

S. D. STURGIS,
Brigadier-General, Commanding Cavalry Corps.

Major-General FOSTER.

P. S.—This moment I hear firing in the direction of the mouth of Chucky, 8 miles from here. I am apprehensive that Garrard has followed up the enemy's force that way. I have been endeavoring to hear from him all the morning, but so far without success. I expect to hear from him in an hour at the outside, however. I have sent him two couriers, directing him to come to this place on the direct roads.

—

HEADQUARTERS CAVALRY CORPS,
New Market, December 24, 1863—8.30 p. m.

GENERAL : Of the two brigades I sent to Dandridge last night, one (under Colonel Campbell, Second Michigan Cavalry) has returned, and the other (Colonel Garrard) is within supporting distance.

Colonel Campbell had a severe engagement near Dandridge, killing some 80 or 100 of the enemy, and wounding, he thinks, a very large number. Our loss will probably not reach over some 20 or 30 in killed and wounded, among whom are several fine officers. The enemy surrounded him with a very large force, and while defending himself on one side, the enemy charged his battery from the other side, capturing two of his pieces. In this charge the enemy's loss was very severe, and the major who led the charge was killed. Colonel Campbell then handsomely charged the enemy and recovered his guns.

Colonel Campbell informs me that he saw 15 of the enemy's dead in one spot, and says they were strewn around in great profusion. The colonel deserves great credit for the masterly manner in which he extricated his command.

On the Morristown road the fighting was stubborn, but the enemy was driven beyond Mossy Creek.

The brigade of Colonel Garrard was engaged also near Cheek's Cross-Roads, but I have no report as yet of his operations. The whole number of prisoners brought in thus far is about 45 ; several officers among them. The enemy is evidently in great force.

Please accept my thanks for the promptness with which my requests have been granted, and believe me, yours, respectfully,

S. D. STURGIS,
Brigadier-General, Commanding Cavalry Corps.

Major-General PARKE.

P. S.—A copy of this has been sent to the telegraph operator at Strawberry Plains for General Foster.

—

HEADQUARTERS CAVALRY CORPS,
New Market, Tenn., December 25, 1863—2.15 p. m.

GENERAL : The brigade of Colonel Garrard returned last night to this place, having lost some 12 or 15 of his men in killed and wounded. The colonel is of opinion that the enemy's loss was about the same.

Hearing no firing at Dandridge yesterday morning, I feared the enemy had received information of the movement I had ordered and had gotten away, and that a force might be sent from Mossy Creek to intercept our force. I accordingly sent orders to return at once. The enemy had the information, and did march with the intention of cutting them off. Colonel Garrard, however, apprehending the same movement, fell back just in time to secure the intersection of the road from this place with that from Mossy Creek to Dandridge, and thus secured the withdrawal of both brigades. In this move the colonel sustained well the favorable opinion we had formed of his coolness and skill. It is due to Colonel Palmer, of the Fifteenth Pennsylvania Cavalry (commonly called the Anderson Cavalry), to say that he accompanied this expedition with the few troops he had as a volunteer, and rendered valuable aid. His loss was some wounded, and Capt. W. Airey, whose horse was killed, taken prisoner.

I am, general, very respectfully, your obedient servant,

S. D. STURGIS,
Brigadier-General, Commanding Cavalry Corps.

Brig. Gen. E. E. POTTER.

—

HEADQUARTERS CAVALRY CORPS,
December 26, 1863.

GENERAL : This morning my line occupied a fine position about half a mile beyond Mossy Creek, and it was my intention to attack the enemy, whose line was about three-fourths of a mile beyond, and drive him back on his main force. The rain coming on, however, and threatening to raise the river in my rear, I was deterred from undertaking a general action; all of which I reported to you, and was happy to learn that you acquiesced in my action. The weather becoming more favorable, however, about 11 a. m. our line of skirmishers was pushed forward a little and engaged the enemy ; but little injury was done on either side, I presume. Our artillery opened for a little while and was briskly replied to by the enemy's battery, but this latter was soon driven from its position and retired.

The ease with which the enemy was driven back, taken in connection with the cavalry on our right flank, led me to apprehend that he desired to draw us as far as possible toward Morristown with his infantry, and I did not pursue. The position I occupied, though a fine one for defense against an enemy in front, was in advance of the roads coming in from Dyer's Ford, from Chucky Bend, and from Dandridge ; so I withdrew to this side Mossy Creek, so as to command these roads.

While withdrawing, the enemy attempted to regain a wood on Morristown road from which he had been driven, when the Fourth Indiana charged upon and drove him back, killing several of the enemy, [who] thereupon shelled the road, and wounded 1 man.

I learn that the enemy is picketing at Dyer's Ford. The weather is still unsettled, and it is raining. From a citizen just in I learn that rebel soldiers stated, in answer to the question what brought them to Dandridge, that they had intended making a dash on Strawberry Plains and destroying it by a surprise, but were themselves surprised on reaching Dandridge.

I am, general, respectfully, &c.,

S. D. STURGIS,
Commanding Cavalry Corps.

Brig. Gen. E. E. POTTER.

—

HEADQUARTERS CAVALRY CORPS,
Brenner's House, Mossy Creek, December 27, 1863.

Brigadier-General ELLIOTT :

GENERAL : Your welcome dispatch is received. I got up in time to see a part and hear the balance. I congratulate you on having troops to charge with such a vim. Remain where you are, and I will see to the roads. Advance against them in the morning, and let me know what assistance is necessary. You have done exceedingly well, and I will telegraph so to General Foster.

Yours, &c.,

S. D. STURGIS,
Brigadier-General.

If you do not come down to-night, I will go up and see you in the morning.

[Indorsement.]

HDQRS. CHIEF OF CAV., DEPT. OF THE CUMBERLAND,
December 27, 1863.

Col. E. M. McCOOK :

COLONEL : I send you General Sturgis' note. I await your report and those from brigade commanders to send particulars. Return this with report of particulars.

W. L. ELLIOTT,
Brigadier-General.

—

HEADQUARTERS CAVALRY CORPS,
Near Mossy Creek, December 27, 1863—7.30 p. m.

We attacked the enemy this afternoon at this place, and drove him from every position back to within a short distance of Talbott's

Station, when, night coming on, we had to desist. Our troops went forward through the rain and mud in fine spirits. I have no particulars to communicate as yet. Martin's and Armstrong's divisions are both in our front. So far as I can learn, the telegraph wire is undisturbed between this and Strawberry Plains, and I would suggest that it be repaired at the river and an operator sent to me. That would save a great deal in time and horseflesh.

Respectfully,

S. D. STURGIS,
Brigadier-General, Commanding Cavalry Corps.

Major-General FOSTER.

HEADQUARTERS CAVALRY CORPS,
Mossy Creek, Tenn., December 28, 1863—9 a. m.

GENERAL: The enemy is not in sight this morning. Reconnaissances are being made to find his position. About dark last evening the First Brigade, First Division, of General Elliott, drove the enemy from his camp, capturing a few arms and their provisions, then cooking. Generals Martin and Armstrong were both present last evening, with Harrison's, Holmes' [?], and McLemore's brigades. The roads, and especially the fields, are very heavy this morning. I am not sure that I will move in the direction of Morristown. If we can obtain a good foothold between this and mouth of Chucky, their subsistence would be so completely cut off that I do not think they could occupy Morristown in force. Breaking the enemy's backbone is well enough, but I think it will do him equal injury to break his belly.

Respectfully,

S. D. STURGIS,
Brigadier-General, Commanding Cavalry Corps.

Maj. Gen. J. G. PARKE.

HEADQUARTERS CAVALRY CORPS, ARMY OF THE OHIO,
Mossy Creek, December 28, 1863—7 p. m.

GENERAL: I have just received the official report of the operations of the Second Brigade, Colonel McCook's division, of General Elliott's command. In addition to the casualties already reported, Colonel La Grange reports 17 of the enemy, including 1 lieutenant, left dead on the field, in the severe skirmish which took place near this village on the 24th instant. Our loss has already been reported. In the advance upon Talbott's Station yesterday, Major Torrey, commanding the First Wisconsin Cavalry, captured 1 horse and a number of muskets, which his men destroyed. Our loss was 3 slightly wounded, and 2 horses killed by a shell. Colonel La Grange reports the artillery practice of the Eighteenth Indiana Battery in the several engagements as admirable.

Colonel La Grange is an exceedingly energetic, valuable officer, and I take pleasure in asking your attention to the indorsement of General Elliott upon his reports, as follows:

Respectfully forwarded.
Colonel La Grange deserves special mention for the skill with which he managed his brigade in the several skirmishes since the 24th instant.

W. L. ELLIOTT,
Brigadier-General, and Chief of Cavalry.

A deserter came in to-day from the enemy, and reports the main portion of Longstreet's army near Morristown. He says he heard a conversation between two officers on the subject of their wagons which were left in Georgia, and that one of them remarked that they would not miss them long, as they, the troops, would not be here more than a couple of weeks longer. I will forward this prisoner to General Parke in the morning.

Since writing I have received the report of a reconnaissance I sent to Talbott's Station. The reconnaissance was directed by Colonel La Grange with First Wisconsin Cavalry, Major Torrey. The command reached Talbott's Station with but slight skirmishing. General Armstrong's negro boy has just come in. He ran away when the rebels fell back from Talbott's Station. The information I received from him is confirmatory of that from other sources and already reported. The boy says that he heard General Armstrong say that if they should be defeated at Morristown and at Bull's Gap, they would all be taken prisoners.

I am, general, respectfully,

S. D. STURGIS,
Brigadier-General, Commanding Cavalry Corps.

Brigadier-General POTTER,
Chief of Staff.

No. 3.

Reports of Brig. Gen. Washington L. Elliott, U. S. Army, commanding Cavalry Corps, Department of the Cumberland.

HDQRS. CHIEF OF CAV., DEPT. OF THE CUMBERLAND,
Camp near Mossy Creek, Tenn., January 1, 1864.

GENERAL : In compliance with instructions from the major-general commanding the department, and those from Major-General Foster, commanding the Department of the Ohio, I marched from Kingston, Tenn., December 15, 1863, with First and Second Brigades, and Seventh Kentucky Volunteer Cavalry, of Third Brigade, First Division of Cavalry, and Lilly's battery, Eighteenth Indiana, Col. E. M. McCook, Second Indiana Cavalry, commanding, reported in person to Major-General Foster December 15, and received from him verbal instructions to cross Holston River and attack the cavalry of the enemy at or near Morristown, Tenn. The First Brigade crossed the Holston, barely fordable and rising, on the 16th, at Armstrong's Ford.

On the 17th, that brigade marched up the left bank of the Holston, the remainder of the troops marching up the right bank to Strawberry Plains, according to instructions from General Foster. I reported by letter from Strawberry Plains to Brigadier-General Sturgis, chief of cavalry, Army of the Ohio. From him and Major-General Parke I received orders, and on the 18th proceeded with my command to Nancy's Ford, on the Holston, found, upon examination, not to be fordable. The First Brigade recrossed the river at McKinney's Ford, above Strawberry Plains. The orders received by me not explaining that my command was ordered to Nancy's Ford for the purpose of crossing the river, I was led to believe that I was required for service on the right flank of General Parke's command, and on the same side of Holston River. This was admitted to me verbally by General Foster. After I had learned from him that the object of ordering my command to Nancy's Ford was to have me cross the river, I at once returned to McKinney's Ford and recrossed the First Brigade; the river then rising became too deep to ford, and by morning had risen from 3½ to 4 feet.

Brigadier-General Sturgis arrived at McKinney's Ford the night of the 18th. On the 19th, by order of General Sturgis, the First Brigade marched down the left bank of the Holston, and remainder of the command down right bank to Strawberry Plains.

The river did not fall sufficiently to enable the command to ford until the 23d ultimo. The artillery was ferried, and the command marched same day to New Market.

On the 24th ultimo, the First Brigade, with four pieces of Lilly's battery, was ordered to Dandridge, Tenn., to co-operate with a brigade of cavalry from Army of the Ohio in an attack upon a brigade of rebel cavalry at or near Dandridge. The attack was made; the enemy was re-enforced. The commander of the First Brigade reports that support was not given him by the cavalry from the Army of the Ohio, and that he was compelled to retreat. Two pieces of his artillery were captured and recaptured, one piece disabled by the breaking of an axletree, spiked and abandoned. The enemy was repulsed—admitted by them—with severe loss; our loss small.

The same day the enemy, with two brigades, attacked the Second Brigade, First Division, and two pieces, near New Market, but was repulsed with the loss of 17 killed, including 2 officers (our loss slight), and driven beyond Mossy Creek 2 miles.

On the 26th, the enemy was felt, his superior force displayed, but we were prevented by heavy rain from further operations.

On the 27th, we again advanced, driving the enemy from every position to Talbott's Station, 3 to 4 miles.*

On the 29th, the Second Brigade, with one section of Lilly's battery, was, by order of General Sturgis, detached to support, if necessary, two divisions of cavalry, Army of the Ohio, ordered toward Dandridge. The First Brigade was ordered to cover the front of the division, and, if attacked, to fall back to Mossy Creek without much resistance. The entire cavalry force of the enemy, Brigadier-Generals Armstrong's and J. T. Morgan's divisions, each of three brigades and two batteries, the whole commanded by Major-General Martin, attacked the First Brigade and Lilly's three pieces. It stubbornly fell back to Mossy Creek, and for three hours held its ground, supported by the One hundred and eighteenth Ohio Volunteer Infantry. A section of the Elgin (Fifth Illinois) battery, badly served, supported by the Sixteenth Kentucky Infantry, was sent by General Sturgis to strengthen our right. The enemy was repulsed in every attack on right, center, and left. The Second Brigade rejoined about 2.30 p. m. We advanced, driving the enemy beyond our camp of the previous day, with heavy loss to them. The conduct of the cavalry and artillery of the Army of the Cumberland was splendid. It has thus far been kept to the front. Its list of killed and wounded sadly shows by whom the fighting has been done.

Detailed reports have been made through Brigadier-General

---

* For report of Action at Mossy Creek, see pp. 652, 653.

Sturgis. The foregoing summary is furnished for the information of the department commander.

Copies of reports of the several commanders will be furnished as soon as they can be prepared.

I am, general, very respectfully, your obedient servant,

W. L. ELLIOTT,
Brigadier-General, U. S. Vols., and Chief of Cavalry.

Brig. Gen. WILLIAM D. WHIPPLE,
Assistant Adjutant-General, Chattanooga, Tenn.

—

HDQRS. CHIEF OF CAV., DEPT. OF THE CUMBERLAND,
Camp near Mossy Creek, Tenn., January 2, 1864.

CAPTAIN: I have the honor to transmit report of Col. E. M. McCook, Second Indiana Cavalry, commanding First Division, of the operations of his division from 24th to 28th ultimo; also copy of report of Col. A. P. Campbell, Second Michigan Cavalry, commanding First Brigade, First Division, for the same time.

The report of Col. O. H. La Grange, First Wisconsin Cavalry, commanding Second Brigade, First Division, for the same time, I had the honor to forward on the 28th and list of casualties on the 31st ultimo.

The reports of the brigade and division commanders are so complete I have nothing to add to them beyond an expression of my admiration for the gallantry displayed by officers and men of my command in the several affairs with the enemy from the 24th to 28th ultimo, inclusive.

I am, captain, very respectfully, your obedient servant,

W. L. ELLIOTT,
Brigadier-General, U. S. Vols., and Chief of Cavalry.

Capt. W. C. RAWOLLE,
Acting Assistant Adjutant-General.

—

Casualties in the Cavalry command, Army of the Cumberland, in East Tennessee, December 24–29, 1863, inclusive.

Command.	Date.	Officers.			Enlisted men.		
		Killed.	Wounded.	Missing.	Killed.	Wounded.	Missing.
First Brigade, First Division	December 24–27, near Dandridge, Tenn.	1	4	......	4	22	13
Second Brigade, First Division	December 24–27, near Mossy Creek, Tenn.	......	2	......	2	7	......
First Brigade, First Division	December 29, at Mossy Creek, Tenn.	......	a2	......	7	22	5
Second Brigade, First Division	...do	......	1	......	3	10	......
Lilly's Battery, with First Division......	...do	......	1	......	2	7	......
15th Pennsylvania Cavalry	...do	1	......	......	......	5	......
10th Ohio Cavalry	...do	......	......	......	......	4	b1
1st Tennessee Mounted Infantry..........	...do	......	......	......	......	1	......
		2	10	......	18	78	19

a Mortally wounded.   *b* Missing, wounded.

W. L. ELLIOTT,
Brigadier-General, U. S. Vols., and Chief of Cavalry.

HEADQUARTERS CHIEF OF CAV. DEPARTMENT OF THE CUMBERLAND,
Mossy Creek, Tenn,, January 5, 1864.

No. 4.

Reports of Col. Edward M. McCook, Second Indiana Cavalry, commanding First Division.

HEADQUARTERS FIRST DIVISION,
December 25, 1863.

The rebs can't drive us ; we have driven them back.   The Second Indiana charged their right, and had 3 men killed.   The position we have is our real ground.   The woods farther on are thick, and their guns are longer range.

EDWARD M. McCOOK,
Colonel, Commanding.

General ELLIOTT,
Commanding Corps.

I wish you would send me orders whether you want me to advance or merely hold my position and skirmish.

—

HEADQUARTERS FIRST DIVISION CAVALRY,
Peck's House, December 25, 1863.

I have just come from our lines ; our pickets are within 200 yards of the enemy.   They informed the citizens, while falling back, that they would have re-enforcements by daylight and whip us out.   I have ordered Colonel La Grange to hold his position and act on the defensive unless otherwise ordered.   I suppose probably they will attack in the morning.   They sent in a flag of truce while I was down at headquarters for the bodies of 2 of their officers killed to-day. Our position is good, and I will await your orders in the morning. The ammunition in two regiments is a little short.   I would like to have Campbell's brigade up in the morning if you can spare it.

Very respectfully, your obedient servant,
EDWARD M. McCOOK,
Colonel, Commanding.

Lieut. W. L. SHAW,
Acting Assistant Adjutant-General.

—

DANIEL'S HOUSE, 2½ MILES FROM MOSSY CREEK,
December 27, 1863.

SIR: I have the honor to make the following report of the affair of to-day:

In accordance with the order of the general commanding, I advanced my division at 2.30 p. m.   The First Brigade, Colonel Campbell, on the left, and the Second Brigade, Colonel La Grange, on the right of the Morristown road.

The advance was but feebly opposed by the enemy, who made their greatest resistance upon the right.   They did not open with artillery until our arrival at this place, and then with but two pieces slowly served.   From the feeble manner in which our advance was opposed, I am satisfied that it was no part of the enemy's plan to fight us at this point.

I have learned that General Martin, the rebel chief of cavalry, and General Armstrong, were there in person.

So far as heard from the casualties are : Second Brigade, First Wisconsin Cavalry, 2 enlisted men slightly wounded and 2 horses killed.

The lateness of the hour and the darkness prevent the procuring of more detailed reports from brigade commanders. I am induced to believe from my observation of the operations of the enemy, both to-day and yesterday, they desire and design to draw us into an advance upon this road.

I am, very respectfully, your most obedient servant,

EDWARD M. McCOOK,
Colonel, Commanding Division,
Per J. A. S. MITCHELL,
Captain, and A. A. D. C., in Absence of Colonel McCook.

Lieut. W. L. SHAW,
Acting Assistant Adjutant-General.

HEADQUARTERS FIRST CAVALRY DIVISION,
Daniel's House, 2½ *M. from Mossy Creek, Tenn., Dec.* 28, 1863.

LIEUTENANT : I have the honor to make report of the operations of his division from the 24th to the 28th instant, inclusive of both dates :

On the morning of the 24th, the First Brigade (Colonel Campbell, Second Michigan Cavalry, commanding), with two sections of the Eighteenth Indiana Battery, was, under orders from the general commanding, sent from New Market before daybreak toward Dandridge, with orders to reach that place by daylight, co-operating with Colonel Garrard's brigade, of Colonel Foster's division.

Colonel Campbell found no enemy at Dandridge, but receiving notice from Colonel Garrard that the latter was engaging the enemy on the Bull's Gap road, he advanced to his support, the advance First East Tennessee Cavalry, Lieut. Col. James P. Brownlow) soon striking the enemy.

At Hays' Ferry, 4 miles from Dandridge, Colonel Campbell's line was formed with an artillery section in position, and the enemy driven from their line.

Under orders from Colonel Garrard, Colonel Campbell again advanced about half a mile, when, receiving joint orders with Colonel Garrard to that effect from General Sturgis, he recalled his regiments to return to New Market. At this time his brigade was attacked in the rear, three regiments of the enemy charging and for the moment taking a section of artillery not in position, but the Ninth Pennsylvania Cavalry and Second Michigan Cavalry, charging, repulsed the enemy, killing many and recapturing the guns.

Colonel Campbell being unable to get support from Colonel Garrard, and being engaged in front and rear by superior numbers of the enemy, was obliged, after repulsing the attack upon his rear, to retire by the left flank through a by-road, the enemy still pressing upon the rear of his column, but, being driven back in all their efforts to strike his main column, the Second Michigan Cavalry, keeping up a vigorous and well-directed fire, and the Ninth Pennsylvania Cavalry, by dashing saber charges, inflicted severe punishment upon the enemy.

Colonel Campbell returned to New Market that night.   One caisson was disabled at the time of its capture by the enemy, and the axle-tree of one of the gun limbers breaking, while passing through the timber, forced the abandonment of both, the gun being spiked.

Colonel Campbell's casualties were : Commissioned officers, 1 killed, 4 wounded ; enlisted men, 6 killed, 23 wounded, and 27 missing. Total, 61. Six of the missing have since returned. Colonel Campbell took 29 prisoners from the enemy, and estimates their loss in killed and wounded at 150, including 1 major and 3 other officers.

On the same day (the 24th instant) the enemy advanced about 8 a. m. with two brigades to the position occupied by Colonel La Grange, Second Brigade, in front of New Market, and attacked them. Colonel La Grange advanced with his brigade, driving the enemy before him, killing 17, including 2 officers, and advancing to Mossy Creek. His casualties for the day were 2 killed, 4 severely and 5 slightly wounded, all enlisted men.

No movement was made on the 25th instant. On the 26th instant my division was advanced to and a slight distance beyond the line of Mossy Creek, driving the enemy's pickets, but not advancing farther. By order of the general commanding we returned to our encampment at 5 p. m. The Fourth Indiana Cavalry camping ground had been occupied by the enemy, but this regiment drove them out, killing 5 and wounding 2. In the skirmishing of the day 3 men were slightly wounded.

On the 27th instant, at 2.30 p. m., the division advanced to this point, driving the enemy steadily before them to Talbott's Station. Report of this day's affair has been previously forwarded.

A reconnaissance made by a detachment of the Second Brigade to Talbott's Station captured 5 of the enemy.

I am, lieutenant, your obedient servant,

EDWARD M. McCOOK,
Colonel, Commanding First Cavalry Division,
Per J. A. S. MITCHELL,
Captain, and A. A. D. C., in Absence of Colonel McCook.

Lieut. W. L. SHAW,
Acting Assistant Adjutant-General.

No. 5.

Reports of Col. Archibald P. Campbell, Second Michigan Cavalry, commanding First Brigade.

HDQRS. FIRST BRIGADE, FIRST DIVISION CAVALRY,
Two Miles from Mossy Creek, December 28, 1863.

SIR : I have the honor to report that, in obedience to orders from the colonel commanding First Division Cavalry, I marched from New Market, Tenn., at 3 a. m. December 24, with First Brigade, First Division Cavalry, toward Dandridge. At 1 mile distant from New Market my brigade was halted while Colonel Garrard's brigade passed. I marched through Flat Gap, arriving at Dandridge, 10 miles, at 9 a. m., and found no enemy ; halted one hour, when I received a dispatch from Colonel Garrard to advance on Bull's Gap road to his support, as the enemy were advancing on his command. Col. James P. Brownlow, First Tennessee Cavalry, advanced and soon commenced skirmishing with the enemy.

Captain Lilly's (Eighteenth Indiana) battery of four guns, in command of Lieutenant Scott, was immediately placed in position, and the Second Michigan Cavalry ordered to its support.   The Ninth Pennsylvania Cavalry was ordered forward on the trot to support the First Tennessee Cavalry.   A part of First Tennessee Cavalry charged the enemy's dismounted skirmishers, killing 3 and capturing 15 prisoners, whereupon the enemy opened an artillery fire with three guns, which were fired with great precision, but fortunately very few of our men were injured.

Two guns of the battery were immediately ordered forward and placed on the hill near Hays' Ferry, 4 miles from Dandridge, skirmishers were thrown out to the front, and the two guns opened upon the enemy half a mile distant, scattering their line and starting them back.

At this time an order came from Colonel Garrard, on my left, to move forward on the same road, and saying that his brigade "would move on a side road to my left, and be not more than 2 miles distant at any time."

I immediately advanced the Ninth Pennsylvania Cavalry in column along the road, and the First Tennessee Cavalry in line on the right of the road and resting on French Broad River.   The Second Michigan Cavalry was placed in line dismounted, to support the battery.   After the Ninth Pennsylvania and First Tennessee Cavalry had advanced half a mile, I received an order from General Elliott* to return to New Market immediately, which order I forwarded to Colonel Garrard, recalling my regiments in front.   The enemy soon commenced firing in my rear, charged with three regiments, and captured two pieces of my artillery not in position.   I at once ordered Second Michigan and Ninth Pennsylvania Cavalry to charge and recapture the guns, which was executed with great promptness and gallantry, the guns recaptured and the enemy driven nearly 1 mile, with heavy loss in killed and wounded on the field and 14 prisoners in our hands.   Being now surrounded by the enemy, one brigade in front and one in my rear, I sent to Colonel Garrard for support, which he did not send.   I then ordered my artillery, ambulances, and led horses into the woods to the left of the original front, and marched them by a path as rapidly as possible toward the New Market road.   Also the Ninth Pennsylvania and First Tennessee Cavalry to follow, keeping the Second Michigan Regiment dismounted and fighting the enemy as they fell back, covering the rear of my column.

After marching 1 mile through a rough country, the enemy pressing hard my rear and left flank, I formed the Ninth Pennsylvania Cavalry on that flank and fought them until checked, and at the same time placed the battery in position 1 mile beyond, with the First Tennessee Cavalry in line for a support.   The enemy still pressed my rear, the Ninth Pennsylvania Cavalry falling back to the artillery, the Second Michigan Cavalry falling back slowly, keeping up a vigorous fire.   I then opened a withering fire with my artillery, four guns firing rapidly, which checked the enemy for a few minutes, but soon they pressed on.   I then ordered the First Tennessee Cavalry to charge with sabers, which they executed most nobly, driving the enemy's line over a fence, with severe loss to their ranks; the loss of the regiment in this charge was 3 killed, 2 officers and 7 men wounded,

---

* This order was received from General Sturgis, instead of General Elliott, as stated.—A. P. C.

and 7 men missing, and 32 horses killed and wounded. Accompanying this charge the Second Michigan and Ninth Pennsylvania Cavalry opened a galling fire, which closed the fight. The enemy seeming to be satisfied with what they had received, fell back, and I marched to New Market at dark. An enemy appeared upon my right before my brigade left, but too late to do me any injury. The enemy's los is not less than 150 killed and wounded, including 1 major, who led the charge against the artillery, killed. I captured 29 prisoners My loss in killed, wounded, and missing is 61; 6 missing have since returned. One caisson was disabled on the field by the enemy' hurry to get it away at the first charge by them. One piece of ar tillery disabled by the breaking of an axle-tree, which was spiked and abandoned.

Great credit is due to both officers and men of my command for thei gallantry and courage during the whole fight. The officers of my staff deserve much praise for their valuable assistance throughou the whole engagement.

December 26, marched from New Market to Mossy Creek, 4 miles and formed in line of battle, and exchanged shots with the enemy during the day until 5 p. m. One man, Second Michigan Cavalry slightly wounded with a shell from the enemy's battery.

December 27, formed line in front of the enemy at 1 p. m., and skirmished 3 miles, driving them without loss.

Very respectfully submitted.

Your most obedient servant,

A. P. CAMPBELL,
Colonel, Commanding.

Capt. JOHN PRATT, Assistant Adjutant-General.

P. S.—The order received from General Elliott to return to New Market was a joint order to myself and Colonel Garrard, and was sent to Colonel Garrard at once.

—

HDQRS. FIRST BRIGADE, FIRST DIVISION CAVALRY,
New Market, Tenn., December 25, 1863.

SIR: I have the honor to report the following as the casualties in the First Brigade in the fight of yesterday at Hays' Ferry, 4 miles from Dandridge, on Bull's Gap road, viz:

Command.	Killed.	Wounded.	Missing.	Total.
2d Michigan Cavalry:				
Enlisted men	1	7	15	2
Commissioned officers (Capt. T. W. Johnson and First Lieut. J. H. Smith).	......	2	......	
9th Pennsylvania Cavalry:				
Enlisted men	2	8	5	1
Commissioned officer (First Lieut. T. J. Mountz)	1			
1st Tennessee Cavalry:				
Enlisted men	3	7	7	1
Commissioned officers (Major Thornburgh and Second Lieut. Paul Sturm).	......	2	.....	
Section 18th Indiana Battery	......	1	.....	
Total enlisted men	6	23	27	5
Total commissioned officers	1	4	......	
Grand total	7	27	27	61

I have captured 29 prisoners.   One cannon of section of Eighteenth Indiana Battery was disabled on the field, an axle-tree broken, and the piece abandoned ; also, one caisson abandoned.   Several men are slightly wounded, but are doing duty.

Very respectfully submitted.

Your most obedient servant,

A. P. CAMPBELL,
Colonel, Commanding.

Capt. J. E. JACOBS, *Assistant Adjutant-General.*

No. 6.

Report of Col. Oscar H. La Grange, First Wisconsin Cavalry, commanding Second Brigade.

HDQRS. SECOND BRIGADE, FIRST CAVALRY DIVISION,
DEPARTMENT OF THE CUMBERLAND,
Talbott's House, near Mossy Creek, East Tenn., Dec. 27, 1863.

CAPTAIN : I have the honor to report that, at 8 a. m. on the 24th instant, two small brigades of the enemy, under General Armstrong, advanced on the position occupied by this brigade near Dr. Peck's house, 2½ miles west of Mossy Creek Station.   Our picket on the Morristown road was re-enforced, and an important position on the right occupied.   About half of our force was gradually drawn into the engagement.   The enemy was driven back 3½ miles, leaving several dead, including 1 lieutenant, on the field.   We camped for the night at Mossy Creek Station.   Our loss was 2 killed and 9 wounded.   Had we been permitted to assume the offensive, it is thought the enemy might have been severely punished.

Captain Hackleman, and Lieutenants Stover and Thomas, Second Indiana, deserve special mention for the gallant manner in which they held an important position, with only two companies, against a greatly superior force.

On the 26th, drove back the enemy's pickets and made a demonstration to the front, but did not advance.   On returning to camp, the Fourth Indiana found its ground occupied by the enemy, and, after a brisk skirmish, compelled him to retire, leaving 5 dead and 2 wounded on the field.   Our loss during the day was only 2 slightly wounded.

On the 27th, advanced, by order, to the ground occupied on the previous day, and drove the enemy 3 miles on the right of the Morristown road, our advance occupying his camp and capturing arms, cooking utensils, &c.   Darkness put an end to the engagement.   We had 2 men killed by a shell, and 4 others slightly wounded.   Enemy's loss unknown.

On the 28th, Major Torrey, First Wisconsin Cavalry, made a movement on the enemy's left flank, and after a brisk skirmish occupied Talbott's Station, capturing 5 of the enemy with horses, arms, and equipments, without loss.*

Very respectfully,

O. H. LA GRANGE,
Colonel, Commanding.

Capt. JOHN PRATT,
A. A. G., First Cav. Div., Dept. of the Cumberland.

---

* Nominal list of casualties (omitted) from 24th to 29th of December, shows 3 killed and 18 wounded.

No. 7.

Report of Col. William J. Palmer, Fifteenth Pennsylvania Cavalry, of operations December 24.

HEADQUARTERS ANDERSON CAVALRY,
At Jim Brazelton's, December 24, 1863—8 p. m.

GENERAL: Our movement to-day proved a failure. The brigade was there; not exactly at Dandridge, but 6 miles above. If we had got in its rear and fallen upon it at daybreak, I think it would have been ours, but at 8 o'clock in the morning we found it entirely on the alert and moving upon us.

The force that got in the rear of Colonel Campbell's brigade, I am inclined to think, was Armstrong's division. One of the prisoners belonging to it says so, and a loyal citizen living on the Morristown and Dandridge road informed me that 2,000 or 3,000 rebel cavalry passed down that road this afternoon.

It was not until we had acted in accordance with your order and got well out toward the intersection of the road running from Dandridge to Mossy Creek, 3 miles from Dandridge, that we learned of Colonel Campbell's condition. We then headed toward Dandridge and were about to march there to relieve him by attacking the rear of the rebels, when a dispatch came from him stating that he had swung over into the by-road on which we were marching, and was immediately in our rear. He saved all his cannon except one piece.

I am encamped at James Brazelton's, 3 miles from New Market, on the Rocky Valley road, and am picketing this road and Hodge's Gap. Please inform me what there is in front, and what is on the move for to-morrow.

My camp was here last night, and I came here because my ambulances, wagons, dismounted men, &c., were already here.

I am, general, yours, respectfully,

WM. J. PALMER,
Colonel, Commanding.

Brigadier-General ELLIOTT,
Commanding Cavalry.

———

No. 8.

Report of Lieut. Samuel E. Miller, Ninth Tennessee Cavalry, of action at Hays' Ferry.

HEADQUARTERS FIFTEENTH PENNSYLVANIA CAVALRY,
Near Mossy Creek, January 1, 1864.

GENERAL: In accordance with instructions received this a. m., through Captain Sharp, Ninth Tennessee Cavalry, I have the honor to report that I was captured during the engagement near Dandridge on the 24th ultimo, and was taken to the rear beyond Holt's house, on Dandridge and Bend of Chucky road, 7 miles from Dandridge. I was detained there till evening of 25th, and was then moved to Kimbro's Cross-Roads, and to Morristown on Saturday, 26th.

I escaped on the night of the 26th from the guard, and reached our lines at Mossy Creek on the morning of 31st December.

From the best information I could obtain there was but one bri-

ade of infantry at Morristown. Longstreet, with the greater por-
ion of the remainder of the infantry, was at Russellville, with head-
uarters at that place. There were no fortifications at Morristown.
Armstrong's and Martin's cavalry commands were in the vicinity of
Panther Springs and Widow Kimbrough's. I could not learn where
Jones' cavalry was. There was no infantry on the Bend of Chucky
oad between Morristown and Cheek's Cross-Roads.

The rebels have taken all the axes from the citizens about Kim-
rough's Cross-Roads, and reliable citizens informed me that the
nemy were blockading the road between Morristown and Dandridge.
heard a great deal of chopping in the direction of that road on last
Wednesday, December 30, the day after the fight at Mossy Creek.
was then on Bay's Mountain, within 2 miles of Widow Kimbrough's.
At least one-third of the infantry that I saw were without shoes,
nd poorly clothed.

One pound of flour and three-quarters pound meat was the ration
ssued to the prisoners. There were about 30 Federal prisoners at
Morristown when I left. I could learn nothing of any movement
oward Paint Rock. Longstreet's forces are estimated at from 25,000
o 30,000. My guards knew nothing of any re-enforcements hav-
ng arrived lately.

I am, general, very respectfully, your obedient servant,

SAMUEL E. MILLER,
Second Lieutenant, Ninth Tennessee Cavalry.

Major-General PARKE.
I have reported to Brigadier-General Elliott.

DECEMBER 28, 1863.—Action at Calhoun and Skirmish at Charleston, Tenn.

REPORTS.

No. 1.—Maj. Gen. George H. Thomas, U. S. Army, commanding Department of the Cumberland, with complimentary letter to Col. Eli Long.
No. 2.—Col. Eli Long, Fourth Ohio Cavalry, commanding Second Cavalry Brigade.
No. 3.—Col. Bernard Laiboldt, Second Missouri Infantry.

No. 1.

Report of Maj. Gen. George H. Thomas, U. S. Army, commanding Department of the Cumberland, with complimentary letter to Col. Eli Long.

CHATTANOOGA, TENN., *December* 29, 1863.
(Received 1.45 p. m., 30th.)

SIR: Col. Eli Long, Fourth Ohio Cavalry, commanding Second Division of Cavalry, reports from Calhoun, Tenn., December 28, that
he rebel General Wheeler, with 1,200 or 1,500 cavalry and mounted
nfantry, attacked Colonel Laiboldt, escorting a supply train from
Chattanooga to Knoxville, about 10 this a. m., at Charleston, on
south bank of the Hiwassee. The train and escort had reached and
ncamped at Charleston last night, and Colonel Laiboldt's skirmishers
vere hotly engaged with the enemy this a. m., before Colonel Long
vas apprised of their approach. He immediately mounted the small

force for duty in his camp at the time (150 men) and crossed th
river to Colonel Laiboldt's support. The rebels shortly afterwar
gave way, Long pursuing them closely.

Discovering a portion of their force cut off on the right, he charge
them with sabers, completely demoralizing and scattering them i
great confusion in every direction. Several of the enemy (numbe
not known) were killed and wounded. One hundred and twenty
one prisoners, including 5 commissioned officers, were captured
The main rebel column fled, and was pursued for 5 miles, on the Dal
ton road, and, when last seen, was fleeing precipitately. Long's los
was 1 man slightly wounded. For this and many other gallant act
of Colonel Long, since serving in this department, I earnestly recom
mend him for promotion to brigadier-general of volunteers.

The officer in command of the courier station at Cleveland als
reports that he was attacked early this morning, December 28, b
a force of about 100 rebels. He drove them off.

GEO. H. THOMAS,
Major-General.

Maj. Gen. H. W. HALLECK,
General-in-Chief.

—

HEADQUARTERS DEPARTMENT OF THE CUMBERLAND,
Chattanooga, January 1, 1864.
Col. ELI LONG,
Commanding Brigade, Calhoun:

COLONEL: Your report of your engagement with the enemy o
the morning of the 28th was duly received. It was a very prett
affair indeed.

I have the honor to inform you that there are now *en route* t
your station four pieces of artillery, escorted by two regiments o
infantry. This artillery is intended as a re-enforcement to you
post. The infantry will return to this place.

The battery was ordered to Calhoun before we heard of you
defeating Wheeler.

I am, colonel, very respectfully,

WM. D. WHIPPLE,
Assistant Adjutant-General.

P. S.—The command will probably move from Harrison to-mor
row morning. It is reported that Wheeler is at Georgetown pre
paring for an attack on Harrison.

———

No. 2.

*Report of Col. Eli Long, Fourth Ohio Cavalry, commanding Sec
ond Cavalry Brigade.*

HDQRS. SECOND BRIGADE, SECOND DIVISION CAVALRY,
Calhoun, Tenn., December 28, 1863.
GENERAL: I have the honor to forward, for the information o
the major-general commanding the department, report of attac
made this a. m. upon this place by the rebel General Wheeler. Th

tack was made at about 10 o'clock by a force of from 1,200 to 1,500 valry and mounted infantry, led by General Wheeler in person. rigadier-General Kelly, with his brigade, formed part of this rce. Their object was evidently the capture of the supply train hich arrived here last evening under charge of forces commanded Colonel Laiboldt.

Colonel L[aiboldt] encamped on the Charleston side of the river, d his skirmishers were at work with the enemy before I was prised of their approach. I immediately mounted the small com- and which remained in camp not on duty (about 150 men), moved ross the bridge, and found the infantry pretty sharply engaged, e enemy occupying position in the woods. The latter shortly after- ard gave way, and I then started rapidly after them. Discovering small portion of their force now cut off on the right, I ordered a ber charge, and followed a retreating column of several hundred hich had taken out the Chatata road, running up the Hiwassee. Our rapid pursuit and vigorous use of the saber completely de- oralized this force, which was thrown into great confusion, and attered in every direction, their men throwing away large num- rs of arms, accouterments, &c. Several of the enemy (number t known) were killed and wounded, and we captured 121 prisoners, cluding 5 commissioned officers. Drove the remainder till I had rived at a creek, which was scarcely fordable, and deemed it pru- nt to follow no farther. The main rebel column had fled out the alton road. I sent a small force out that road, who followed some miles, and the enemy is still retreating toward Cleveland. My vn loss is 1 man seriously wounded.

Since returning to my headquarters, I have received a dispatch om the officer commanding couriers at Cleveland. He was attacked rly this morning by a force of about 100 men, and drove them off.

Very respectfully, your obedient servant,

ELI LONG,
Colonel, Commanding Second Cavalry Brigade.

Brig. Gen. W. D. WHIPPLE,
Chief of Staff, Army of the Cumberland.

No. 3.

Report of Col. Bernard Laiboldt, Second Missouri Infantry.

CAMP NEAR CALHOUN,
December 28, 1863.

SIR : It affords me great pleasure to report to you that I have iven the rebel General Wheeler a sound thrashing this morning. had succeeded, in spite of the most abominable roads, to reach harleston on the night of the 27th ; and this morning shortly after aylight I was moving my train across Hiwassee River Bridge hen Wheeler's cavalry, reported 1,500 strong, with four guns vhich, however, they had no time to bring into action), appeared in y rear. I placed the infantry in line of battle, then got my train ver the bridge safely, and next asked Colonel Long to place a regi- ent of cavalry at my disposal. These arrangements made, I harged with the infantry in double-quick on the astonished rebels nd routed them completely, when I ordered a cavalry charge to give them the finishing touch.   The charge was made in good style but the number of our cavalry was insufficient for an effectual pur suit, and so the enemy got away, and was even able to take his gun along, which, with innumerable prisoners, must have fallen into m hands could I have made a hot pursuit.

I have now with me, as prisoners, 5 commissioned officers, amon them the inspector-general of General Kelly's division, and a sur geon, and 126 men of different regiments.   Wheeler commanded i person, and it was reported to him, as the prisoners state, that I ha 600 wagons in my train, which he expected to take without grea trouble.

The casualties on my side are as follows : Third Division, 2 com missioned officers wounded, 2 men killed, 8 men wounded, 1 ma missing; Second Division, 4 men wounded.

The rebels lost, besides the number stated, several severel wounded, which I am obliged to leave behind, and probably severa killed.   The number of small-arms thrown away by them is rathe large, and they will undoubtedly be gathered up by Colonel Long I shall pursue my march at daybreak to-morrow.

Very respectfully, your obedient servant,
BERNARD LAIBOLDT,
Colonel Second Infantry Missouri Volunteers.

Brig. Gen. W. D. WHIPPLE,
Assistant Adjutant-General, Dept. of the Cumberland.

P. S.—Our infantry numbered between 2,000 and 3,000 convales cent men returning from furlough, and others, who had been absen and belonged to the two divisions of the Fourth Army Corps Long's cavalry, with which he charged the rebels, 150.

DECEMBER 28, 1863–JANUARY 4, 1864.—Expedition from Nashville Tenn., to Creelsborough, Ky.

Report of Lieut. Col. Andrew J. Cropsey, One hundred an twenty-ninth Illinois Infantry.

HEADQUARTERS 129TH ILLINOIS VOLUNTEER INFANTRY,
Nashville, Tenn., January 4, 1864.

COLONEL : In obedience to orders from you and General Grant with 140 sharpshooters and 3 commissioned officers, on the mornin of the 28th of December, I proceeded up the Cumberland River with two gunboats and three transports.   The transports with 100 of th sharpshooters were left at Carthage.   We then continued up the rive until we arrived, on the evening of the 31st December, 1863, at Creels borough, Ky.   This place is 325 miles from Nashville, and 75 mile below the mouth of Big South Fork, the head of navigation.

On the way up we were fired upon by guerrillas five differen times.   The bands seemed to vary in number from 10 to 15 up to 7 or 100, but they were so high up on the bluffs, and concealed so wel in the thick timber, behind rocks and trees, that their number couldn' to a certainty be ascertained, neither could the 40 sharpshooters hav much effect upon them, though they manifested much zeal and skill but the gunboats with shell and shrapnel quickly dislodged them

d this was done in fine style under the supervision of Captain Glass-
rd, the commanding officer.   Some of them were seen to fall, but
e did not ascertain that any were killed; they did no damage, though
o on the boat were hit with spent balls.   As the bluffs were so
gh and steep, and they could overlook our movements, I did not
ink anything could be effected by making pursuit, and did not land
e sharpshooters.

The only county on the river now under the control of the guer-
las is Jackson, or that part of it south of the Cumberland, and
verton, as far east as the Obey's River; beyond that the country
as reported loyal, and the people from the banks greeted us with
mistakable demonstrations of joy.

From various sources we ascertained that there were no coal-barges
aded with coal below the rapids at the mouth of the Big South
ork, and that barges could not come over them with safety except
 very high water.   Some is being mined and loaded above to come
wn on the spring floods, but as we could not see the coal men,
ore definite information can be obtained by a correspondence with
em through Governor Bramlette, of Kentucky, who is said to be
ell acquainted in that region.   There is also a large coal mine on
bey's River, some 50 miles from its mouth, that is at least 150
iles nearer Nashville and much more accessible than that on the
pper Cumberland, as it frequently can be brought out of the Obey's
 barges when they cannot come over the rapids at the mouth of
g South Fork.   The rebel authorities began working this mine
st before their sudden departure from Nashville.   That region is
w in the possession of the guerrillas, and of course no preparation
ing made for shipping coal.   If the general desires any more defi-
te information concerning this coal mine, it can be had through
aj. Abram E. Ganet, First Tennessee (Union) Guards.   He is now
ationed at Carthage, and is engaged in raising a battalion for
ecial service in that locality.   He lived, before being driven from
ome, within 3 miles of the coal mine, and he is especially anxious
r permission to move his present command, something over 200
en, into that region, being sanguine that he could make the navi-
ation of the Cumberland perfectly safe in a few weeks.   The guer-
lla bands under Hamilton, Hughs, Ferguson, and Richardson
umber some 200 fighting men, and about twice that number for
bbing raids.

As the river was falling rapidly we were compelled to turn back
 Creelsborough.   At Carthage I left 40 of the sharpshooters as
ard for the unloaded boats; with the other 100, on the transport
mma Boyd, we started for this city on the morning of the 2d
stant, but had come only 3 miles from Carthage when, by the
ursting of her pumps, the Emma Boyd was compelled to stop, and
ill have to be towed down by the other boats when unloaded.   As
is might detain them several days, and the general seems anxious
 get information about affairs up the Cumberland, I deemed it
ost conducive to his wishes and the service to come on here at
ace, which I did in the gunboat Reindeer.

All of which is most respectfully submitted.

                                   A. J. CROPSEY,
                    Lieutenant-Colonel 129th Illinois Volunteers.

Lieut. Col. T. S. BOWERS,
        Assistant Adjutant-General.

DECEMBER 29, 1863.—Action at Mossy Creek, Tenn.

REPORTS.*

No. 1.—Maj. Gen. John G. Foster, U. S. Army, commanding Department of
Ohio.

No. 2.—Brig. Gen. Samuel D. Sturgis, U. S. Army, commanding Cavalry Cor
Department of the Ohio, with complimentary orders.

No. 3.—Brig. Gen. Washington L. Elliott, U. S. Army, commanding Cava
Corps, Department of the Cumberland.

No. 4.—Col. Edward M. McCook, Second Indiana Cavalry, commanding Fi
Cavalry Division.

No. 5.—Col. Archibald P. Campbell, Second Michigan Cavalry, commanding Fi
Brigade.

No. 6.—Col. Thomas J. Jordan, Ninth Pennsylvania Cavalry.

No. 7.—Col. Oscar H. La Grange, First Wisconsin Cavalry, commanding Seco
Brigade.

No. 8.—Col. William J. Palmer, Fifteenth Pennsylvania Cavalry.

No. 9.—Capt. Eli Lilly, Eighteenth Indiana Battery.

No. 10.—Col. Samuel R. Mott, One hundred and eighteenth Ohio Infantry, co
manding First Brigade, Second Division, Twenty-third Corps.

No. 11.—Lieut. Col. Thomas L. Young, One hundred and eighteenth Ohio Infant

No. 1.

Report of Maj. Gen. John G. Foster, U. S. Army, commandi
Department of the Ohio.

KNOXVILLE, *December* 29, 1863.

At 11 a. m. to-day the whole of the enemy's cavalry, support
by a division of infantry and two batteries of artillery, attack
General Sturgis near Mossy Creek. The fight was severe and ge
eral, and lasted until 5 p. m. Sturgis held his ground, and end
by driving the enemy entirely off the field, achieving a comple
victory.

J. G. FOSTER,
Major-General.

Major-General GRANT.

No. 2.

Reports of Brig. Gen. Samuel D. Sturgis, U. S. Army, commandi
Cavalry Corps, Department of the Ohio, with complimenta
orders.

STRAWBERRY PLAINS, *December* 29, 1863.

Brig. Gen. E. E. POTTER :

The following dispatches have been received from General Sturg

HEADQUARTERS,
Mossy Creek, [*December*] 29, 1863—3.15 p. m
The enemy advanced this morning, about 11 o'clock, with the mass of his cava

---

*See also Martin's report, p. 547.

nd a division of infantry and two batteries of artillery. We have checked him
ompletely, I trust, but our loss is very severe. I think he is giving way now, and
hope to drive him before night. The engagement is general along the whole line,
nd the troops have behaved with great credit to themselves and their country.
olonels Wolford and Foster have not yet gotten up with their command. Will
eport particulars as soon as I can.

    Yours, &c.,

S. D. STURGIS,
Brigadier-General.

HEADQUARTERS,
Mossy Creek, [*December*] 29, 1863—3.45 p. m.

eneral PARKE:

    My whole line is advancing handsomely and driving the enemy before it. Col-
nels Wolford and Foster have just returned from the reconnaissance to Dandridge,
vhere they found no enemy. His whole force moved to our front last night, and
o-day got damned badly whipped.

    Yours, respectfully,

S. D. STURGIS,
Brigadier-General.

P. S.—All right.

JNO. G. PARKE,
Major-General.

—

HEADQUARTERS CAVALRY CORPS,
Mossy Creek, December 29, 1863—6 p. m.
(Received—12.15 a. m., 30th.)

    The enemy was driven back about 4 miles in great confusion,
and our advance line is near Talbott's Station again. I did not deem
it prudent to pursue farther than was necessary to inflict as great
immediate injury as possible. Neither our own loss nor that of
the enemy can be known yet. We have now in the hospital between
70 and 100 wounded. The brass guns with Colonel Mott's brigade
are not suited to our present situation, either in character or otherwise, and I would ask that a battery of 3-inch rifled guns or 10-
pounder Parrotts be sent to replace them. As infantry could as well
be supplied at Dandridge as at Strawberry Plains, I would suggest
that that place be occupied by a brigade or more of infantry. It
would be a great saving of horses to us, whose horses are pretty well
worn down, watching so large an extent of country, with a wily
enemy ready at all times to take advantage of any division of our
forces. I cannot think there is any of the rebel cavalry on the
north side of the Holston, and would like to have Colonel Pennebaker's brigade here, if you think it can be spared from its present
location.

    Respectfully,

S. D. STURGIS,
Brigadier-General.

General FOSTER.

    P. S.—So far as heard from we have about 50 prisoners. There
may have been more taken, and probably are, but no more have
been reported as yet.

HEADQUARTERS DEPARTMENT OF THE OHIO,
Knoxville, January 21, 1864.

Maj. Gen. H. W. HALLECK,
  General-in-Chief:

GENERAL: I have the honor to transmit herewith a copy of the report of Brig. Gen. S. D. Sturgis, commanding Cavalry Corps, concerning the engagement near Mossy Creek, December 29, 1863.

I am, general, very respectfully, your obedient servant,

J. G. FOSTER,
Major-General.

HEADQUARTERS CAVALRY CORPS,
Mossy Creek, Tenn., January 8, 1864.

GENERAL: I have the honor to submit the following report of the action of Mossy Creek, December 29, 1863:

Having received information during the night of the 28th that a brigade of the enemy's cavalry had moved to Dandridge during the afternoon of that day and had gone into camp there, I determined to take advantage of this division of the enemy's forces and endeavor to surprise and destroy that portion of it.

Accordingly I ordered Colonel Foster's division, with four regiments of Colonel Wolford's division and four mountain howitzers, to move toward Dandridge by the Mossy Creek road, and the remaining regiments of Colonel Wolford's division (picketing the gaps in Bay's Mountain) to move toward Dandridge by the road leading from New Market, so as to reach Dandridge by daylight on the 29th. Colonel La Grange's brigade and two 3-inch rifled guns moved at the dawn of day to the point where the Mossy Creek road to Dandridge crosses Bay's Mountain, for the purpose of watching the roads in the Dumpling Valley, and to be within easy supporting distance of the force remaining at Mossy Creek, or to go toward Dandridge should the enemy have massed his cavalry at either point during the night.

While these troops were being withdrawn from our front (then advanced as far as Talbott's Station), Colonel Campbell, with the only remaining brigade of cavalry, was directed to occupy the entire line and fill up the gaps thus occasioned, and if attacked to fall back without much resistance to the line of Mossy Creek. Colonel Palmer's command (Fifteenth Pennsylvania Cavalry and one company of Tennessee mounted infantry), then guarding the right flank on the Chucky road, was also ordered back and posted on the right of the line selected for battle.

About 9 a. m. on the 29th, the entire cavalry force of the enemy, about 6,000 strong, under Generals Martin, Armstrong, and Morgan, and which had formed a junction during the night at Panther Springs, advanced in line of battle, concentrating their efforts mainly against our left.

As soon as I ascertained the strength of the enemy I ordered the return of Colonel La Grange, and of Foster and Wolford also, should they find no enemy at Dandridge.

The enemy advanced steadily and handsomely over the open country beyond the creek, and Colonel Campbell as handsomely contested the ground while falling back to the position selected for the engagement.

In the meantime, I sent the One hundred and eighteenth Ohio Infantry (Colonel Mott's brigade) unperceived by the enemy into the woods on the left of the Morristown road, and placed a section of 12-pounder guns in position on the right of the road, with the Sixteenth Kentucky Infantry as a support. The Twenty-fifth Michigan Infantry was placed on the road as a reserve, and one battalion of the Eightieth Indiana Infantry was sent to guard the Dyer's Ferry road.

The enemy now made a desperate charge on our left and left center for the purpose of securing a position which would enable him to command the crossing of the creek, but in this attempt signally failed, Colonel Campbell's brigade and three 3-inch rifled guns making sad havoc in his lines as they advanced over the open ground.

The infantry reserved its fire until the enemy came up within easy range, then delivered a deadly volley into his ranks, and, charging with the bayonet, drove him in confusion. While this was being accomplished the First Tennessee Cavalry, Colonel Brownlow, on the extreme left of the line, charged with the saber, breaking the enemy's line and throwing him into disorder.

Meeting with nothing but disaster on our left, the enemy made but little effort against our right, and soon began to fall back.

About this time Colonel La Grange arrived on the field, and was sent forward on the right to harass the retreat. Colonel Campbell advanced on the Morristown road and through the fields on the left. The enemy, finding himself thus hotly pressed, formed in two columns and fell back rapidly to his re-enforcements at Panther Springs; but, darkness coming on, the pursuit was not pushed beyond Talbott's Station. The action lasted from 9 a. m. until dark; for several hours it was general, and at times the fighting was very severe.

For a more detailed account, and for the part taken by individuals, I respectfully refer you to the reports of Brig. Gen. W. L. Elliott, of Colonel McCook, commanding division, and to the reports of brigade commanders.

I may be permitted to say here that much of the success of the day is due to the zeal and energy of Brig. Gen. W. L. Elliott.

I had the honor to forward to your office a day or two after the action a list of the names of the killed and wounded, and will therefore only give the numbers here: Killed, 18 soldiers; wounded, 7 officers and 70 soldiers; total, 77. Missing, 5. Total killed, wounded, and missing, 100.*

The enemy's loss is variously estimated. General Elliott reckons it at 400 killed and wounded; others at from 250 to 300. The enemy admits the latter figure, and the citizens living on the road confirm this estimate. His loss, beyond question, was very large, as his men were much more exposed than ours throughout the whole day.

We took 44 prisoners, and gathered up 22 of his dead and buried them.

I am, general, very respectfully, your obedient servant,
                            S. D. STURGIS,
                    Brigadier-General, Commanding.

Maj. Gen. J. G. FOSTER:

---

* But see revised statement, p. 651.

HEADQUARTERS CAVALRY CORPS,
Mossy Creek, January 1, 1864.

GENERAL: I have the honor to report our casualties in the engage
ment of the 29th ultimo, as follows:

Officers wounded, 7; enlisted men wounded, 66; enlisted mer
killed, 18; enlisted men missing, 5. Total, 96.*

The loss of the enemy, from carefully collected data from rebe
citizens, deserters, and our own officers, was between 300 and 40C
and this disparity in casualties is easily accounted for, since th
enemy advanced over open ground, where he was literally mowe«
down, while our troops were, in a great measure, sheltered. Th
citizens living on the road—rebels, too—report that twenty wagon
and ambulances were constantly running to and from the field, an«
(to use their own expression) the killed and wounded were piled i:
like hogs. We have buried some 20 of their dead ourselves, and hav
some of their wounded in hospital.

In the engagement at Dandridge on the 27th ultimo, our loss wa
as follows:

Officers wounded, 6; officer killed, 1; enlisted men wounded, 29
enlisted men killed, 6; enlisted men missing, 13. Total, 55.

Deserters report that the officers of the enemy estimate their los
in that engagement at 200.

I will send list of names of killed and wounded as soon as it ca
be made up.

Respectfully,

S. D. STURGIS,
Brigadier-General, Commanding.

Brig. Gen. E. E. POTTER,
Chief of Staff.

—

ORDERS.] HDQRS. CAVALRY CORPS, ARMY OF THE OHIO,
Mossy Creek, Tenn., December 29, 1863.

The commanding general takes pleasure in congratulating th
troops of this command upon the eminent and complete victory the
have thus achieved against the combined forces of Generals Martir
Armstrong, and Wheeler.

We must not forget, however, that our success was achieve
through the loss of many of our brave comrades in arms, who:
names will occupy for all coming time a bright and enviable plac
in the history of our country. At the proper time it will be th
pleasant duty of the commanding general to call the attention of th
commander of the department to individual cases of meritoriot
conduct.

By order of Brigadier-General Sturgis:

W. C. RAWOLLE,
Captain, A. D. C., and A. A. A. G.

---

*But see revised statement, p. 651.

ADDENDA.

Return of Casualties in the Union forces commanded by Brig. Gen. Samuel D. Sturgis, engaged at Mossy Creek, Tenn., December 29, 1863.

[Compiled from nominal lists of casualties, returns, &c.]

Command.	Killed.		Wounded.		Captured or missing.		Aggregate.
	Officers.	Enlisted men.	Officers.	Enlisted men.	Officers.	Enlisted men.	
CAVALRY (ARMY OF THE CUMBERLAND).							
Brig. Gen. Washington L. Elliott.							
FIRST DIVISION.							
Col. Edward M. McCook.							
First Brigade.							
Col. Archibald P. Campbell.							
2d Michigan		1	2	6		3	12
9th Pennsylvania		1		5		2	8
1st Tennessee		6	2	9			17
Total First Brigade		8	4	20		5	37
Second Brigade.							
Col. Oscar H. La Grange.							
2d Indiana		1					1
4th Indiana				6			6
7th Kentucky		1	1				2
1st Wisconsin				4			4
Total Second Brigade		2	1	10			13
Unattached.							
Col. William J. Palmer.							
10th Ohio Cavalry (detachment)				4			4
15th Pennsylvania Cavalry (detachment)	1			5			6
1st Tennessee Mounted Infantry (detachment)				2			2
Total unattached	1			11			12
Artillery.							
Indiana Light, 18th Battery		2	1	7			10
Total detachment Army of the Cumberland		12	7	48		5	72
DETACHMENT ARMY OF THE OHIO.							
Infantry.							
16th Kentucky			1				1
118th Ohio		5	1	30			36
Artillery.							
Illinois Light, 5th Battery							
Total detachment Army of the Ohio		5	2	30			37
Grand total		17	9	78		5	109

OFFICERS KILLED OR MORTALLY WOUNDED.

PENNSYLVANIA.

Lieut. Harvey S. Lingle, 15th Cavalry.

TENNESSEE.

Capt. Elbert J. Cannon, 1st Cavalry.
Lieut. George W. Cox, 1st Cavalry.

No. 3.

Report of Brig. Gen. Washington L. Elliott, U. S. Army, commanding Cavalry Corps, Department of the Cumberland.

HDQRS. CHIEF OF CAV., DEPT. OF THE CUMBERLAND,
Camp near Talbott's Station, Tenn., December 31, 1863.

CAPTAIN : I have the honor to make the following report of the action of the 29th near Mossy Creek :

According to instructions the Second Brigade, Colonel La Grange commanding, was detached before daylight, leaving the front of the camp covered by the First Brigade, Col. A. P. Campbell, Second Michigan Cavalry, commanding, of First Division, Col. E. M. Mc-Cook, Second Indiana Cavalry, commanding, with orders to fall back without much resistance from the vicinity of Talbott's Station, skirmishing with the superior force of the enemy, consisting of two divisions of cavalry, three brigades each, commanded by Brigadier-Generals Armstrong and J. T. Morgan, with two batteries of artillery, twelve pieces, the whole commanded by Major-General Martin. This information I received from a rebel officer taken prisoner during the action.

Three pieces of Lilly's (Eighteenth Indiana) battery were posted on a hill on the south side of the Morristown road, supported by the First Brigade, First Division of Cavalry.

Col. W. J. Palmer, Fifteenth Pennsylvania Cavalry, with detachments from Tenth Ohio Cavalry and First Tennessee Mounted Infantry, in all, about 250 men, was directed to fall back from his camp on mouth of Chucky road to Mossy Creek. About 11 a. m. the enemy advanced in line of battle dismounted, his line extending from mouth of Chucky road, crossing Morristown road, to a road leading from east side of Mossy Creek to Dyer's Ferry. The length of this line I estimated at 2 miles. A section of the Elgin (Fifth Illinois) battery and the One hundred and eighteenth Ohio Volunteer Infantry, from Mott's brigade, were placed under my orders by General Sturgis ; the former was posted on the mouth of Chucky road, the latter as support for the three pieces of Lilly's battery, and on its left covered by dense timber. I was instructed to hold my position and informed that the Second Brigade, First Division, with a section of Lilly's battery, Colonel La Grange, First Wisconsin Cavalry, commanding, detached to support the cavalry of the Army of the Ohio, ordered to the vicinity of the Dandridge and Bend of Chucky road, had been ordered and would soon return to Mossy Creek.

The enemy massed troops on his left (my right), evidently with the intention of charging the section of the Elgin battery posted on the right. Finding the section so badly served I directed part of the Ninth Pennsylvania Cavalry, not to exceed 100 men, to take post on the right and front of this section for its support, in addition to the detachments of Colonel Palmer's already posted there ; at the same time sent to inform General Sturgis of the condition of the right, and requested another regiment of infantry. The Sixteenth Kentucky Infantry was sent me, and placed under cover on the right flank to support the section of the Elgin battery.

The enemy was repulsed in his attack upon our right, and in his attack upon Lilly's battery in the center, his batteries at the same time showering upon both of our batteries shot and shell. He then attacked our left, and was there also repulsed. The Second Brigade,

First Division, Colonel La Grange commanding, arrived about 2 p. m. and was sent under cover to the right. About 3 p. m. the enemy was seen to be falling back. As soon as I discovered this, and that the lull in the firing was not caused by a movement of the enemy toward our left, as was reported, I ordered an advance, the section of Lilly's battery, which had joined with the Second Brigade, throwing shot and shell into his retreating lines and columns. The pursuit was rapid and continued until dark, driving the enemy about 4 miles, and beyond the ground occupied in the morning, but on account of scarcity of water the troops occupied their same camps, leaving our picket line on the ground from which the enemy was driven. According to instructions from General Sturgis the infantry and section of the Elgin battery from Colonel Mott's brigade was ordered to return to Mossy Creek.

For the details of the operations of the First Division of Cavalry, and the casualties in same, I refer to the reports of its commander and of his subordinates, and to the report of Colonel Palmer for the operations of his detachments, all herewith inclosed. The losses of the enemy must have greatly exceeded that of ours, his lines and columns being exposed to our fire from small-arms and Lilly's battery, so admirably served. Both in his advance and retreat many of his dead and wounded were left in the field. I do not think that 100 killed and 400 wounded would be an exaggerated estimate of his loss.

In closing this report I desire to refer to the services of Col. E. M. McCook, Second Indiana Cavalry, commanding First Division. The skill with which he disposed of his division on the field, on this as on other occasions, and energy in the pursuit of the enemy, shows him to be capable of exercising the command with which he is intrusted. Brigades, regiments, and the battery of Lilly—officers and men, without exception—performed their duty nobly.

The officers of my personal staff, First Lieuts. C. F. Mardon, Second Iowa Cavalry, and W. L. Shaw, One hundred and tenth Ohio Volunteer Infantry, aides-de-camp; and of the corps staff, Captain McCormick, acting inspector-general; Captain Schuyler, provost-marshal; First Lieut. W. C. Arthur, assistant commissary of subsistence, and Captain Warner, commanding escort, rendered me great assistance, conveying my orders on the field, as did also my orderlies from Company D, Fourth Ohio Cavalry. Surg. L. A. James, Fourth Ohio Cavalry, medical director, faithfully provided for the comfort of the sick and wounded.

I am, captain, very respectfully, your obedient servant,

W. L. ELLIOTT,
Brigadier-General, U. S. Vols., and Chief of Cavalry.

Capt. W. C. RAWOLLE,
A. A. A. G., Hdqrs. Chief of Cav., Army of the Ohio.

———

No. 4.

Report of Col. Edward M. McCook, Second Indiana Cavalry, commanding First Cavalry Division.

HEADQUARTERS FIRST CAVALRY DIVISION,
Daniel's House, 2½ M. from Mossy Creek, Tenn., Dec. 30, 1863.

SIR: Without reports of brigade commanders, I am unable at this time to present as full and detailed a report of the action of yesterday as may be desired.

Nearly all of the operations of the day, however, came under my personal observation, and from such observations and partial returns as have been forwarded by brigade commanders, I have the honor to present the following report:

The Second Brigade, Colonel La Grange commanding, with one section of the Eighteenth Indiana Battery, having been, in accordance with orders of the general commanding, removed from our front on the morning of the 29th instant, before daybreak, and sent toward Dandridge, the remaining three pieces of the Eighteenth Indiana Battery, with one regiment (Ninth Pennsylvania Cavalry) of the First Brigade, were placed in position immediately east of Mossy Creek, and Colonel Campbell was ordered to cover our entire division line near Talbott's Station with his remaining force, only two regiments, Second Michigan and First East Tennessee Cavalry. The wagon train had been sent to the rear before daylight, and I moved my headquarters to Mossy Creek. About 9 a. m. I received a message from Colonel Campbell informing me that the enemy were advancing in line of battle and in force.

In accordance with orders he had previously received, he fell back slowly, his command stubbornly resisting the overwhelmingly superior numbers of the enemy till he reached a position in the timber, on the left of the Morristown road, east of Mossy Creek.

At this time the Eighteenth Indiana Battery, Captain Lilly commanding, opened upon the advancing columns of the enemy, checking them for some time, but drawing upon his battery of three pieces the fire of eight guns of the enemy, placed in commanding positions, and served with great rapidity and terrible precision. Captain Lilly, for over two and one-half hours, kept up his fire on the rebel guns, and poured canister into the enemy's charging columns till the killing of many of his horses, the killing and disabling of some of his gunners, and the exhaustion of his men compelled him to retire. In so doing, by the unmanageableness of some of his horses, one piece was left upon the ground, the enemy obtaining temporary possession of it, but by a gallant saber charge, made by Lieutenant Miller's detachment of scouts, the gun was recaptured and brought off. Upon the withdrawal of the battery, the enemy charged in heavy columns and with great determination upon the force in the woods on the left, which was occupied by Colonel Campbell with two regiments of his brigade and the One hundred and eighteenth Ohio Volunteer Infantry, which had been sent across the creek by General Sturgis as a support to Lilly's battery. The enemy were repulsed with great loss, and upon making a demonstration of preparing for another charge, the First East Tennessee (Colonel Brownlow commanding), by a dashing saber charge, threw their columns into confusion and drove them back, capturing a lieutenant and 25 other prisoners. The enemy having been driven from the timber, the entire line upon the left was retired to the hill on the left of Mossy Creek, and Captain Lilly's battery was also placed in position there.

The Chucky Bend road on the right, upon which a large force of the enemy appeared, being only partially covered by the Fifteenth Pennsylvania Cavalry (Colonel Palmer commanding) in small force, the Ninth Pennsylvania Cavalry (Colonel Jordan) had been, by the orders of General Elliott, withdrawn from the battery and placed in position on the right of that road, and by close pistol fighting held the large columns of the enemy in check. A regiment of infantry subsequently took position on the right, but was not at any time

ngaged. At this time the enemy were before us in force far ex-
eeding our own, and by reason of their superior force had pressed
s at every point. In our center was an uncovered space of a quar-
r of a mile, when the arrival of my Second Brigade, which had
narched 4½ miles in less than three-quarters of an hour, enabled us
o take the offensive, and, immediately advancing my entire line,
ne enemy were driven steadily and rapidly before us, with great
oss, until we reached our position of the 28th instant, near Talbott's
tation, the Second Brigade advancing on the right of the Morris-
own road, and the First Brigade on the left. The advance of the
atter was impeded by the difficult nature of the ground, and many
f the enemy escaped capture from this circumstance.

The enemy stubbornly resisted our advance, and attempted, with
is greater numbers, to hold the several wooded positions from
rhich they were successively driven by the continual steady press-
ng forward of Colonel La Grange's column. Darkness prevented
arther pursuit, and the division occupied its encampment of the
8th instant.

Our casualties are as follows :

Command.	Killed.	Wounded.	Missing.	Total.
rst Brigade, Colonel Campbell commanding :				
Commissioned officers............		3	......	......
Enlisted men............................	6	23	8	40
cond Brigade, Colonel La Grange commanding :				
Commissioned officers........................		1	......	......
Enlisted men........	3	11	......	15
h Indiana Battery, Captain Lilly commanding :				
Commissioned officers		1	......	......
Enlisted men........	2	7	.....	10
Total commissioned officers	....	5	......	......
Total enlisted men	11	41	8	65

Seven horses were killed in Lilly's battery, and a large number in
ne regiments, but not reported.

We captured 38 prisoners, including 2 officers. Several of the
nemy's dead were found on the field, and citizens report that more
nan twenty wagon-loads of the enemy's dead and wounded were
arried to the rear. I do not believe that their loss in killed, wounded,
nd captured can be less than 250.

In this engagement all the officers and men of my command did all
heir duty, and did it nobly, but I cannot refrain from calling the at-
ention of the general commanding to the ability and gallantry with
rhich Captain Lilly's (Eighteenth Indiana) battery was served upon
his occasion. For nearly three hours, exposed to a murderous fire,
e fought the rebel batteries and repelled the successive charges
nade upon him. To his skill and firm courage, and to that of his
nen, much of the final success of the day is due.

To Colonel Campbell, Second Michigan Cavalry, commanding
First Brigade, great credit is due for the able manner with which he
ought his brigade. Though falling back in obedience to orders,
rom vastly superior numbers, his brigade repeatedly and severely
unished a too venturesome foe.

Colonel La Grange, First Wisconsin Cavalry, commanding Second
Brigade, whose timely arrival and spirited advance turned the tide

of battle, and enabled us to pursue a foe still outnumbering us, has with the officers and men of his brigade my especial thanks.

The One hundred and eighteenth Ohio Volunteer Infantry, upon my left, materially aided in repulsing the charges made by the enemy and behaved with great gallantry.

The gallant First East Tennessee cavalry and their brave young commander, Lieutenant-Colonel Brownlow, added new laurels to their brilliant reputation by the splendid saber charge they made The Seventh Kentucky and Fourth Indiana Cavalry, on the extreme right, fought with the steadiness of veterans, driving superior numbers of the enemy from every position they attempted to hold. The First Wisconsin, Second Michigan, Second Indiana, and Ninth Pennsylvania Cavalry Regiments nobly sustained their old reputation The fact that so small a force drove two divisions of the enemy from the field makes me feel renewed pride and confidence in the efficiency and gallantry of my division.

Among the other brave men, whose loss we are called upon to mourn, are Captain Cannon and Lieutenant Cox, First East Tennessee Cavalry, who fell leading a charge at the head of their soldiers

To Captain Pratt, assistant adjutant-general; Captain Porter, Ninth Pennsylvania Cavalry, acting assistant inspector-general; Captain Hancock, Ninth Pennsylvania Cavalry, provost-marshal; Captain Mitchell, Second Indiana Cavalry, acting aide-de-camp; Lieutenant Gannett, Seventh Kansas Cavalry, ordnance officer; Lieutenant Miller, Third Ohio Cavalry, assistant commissary of musters; Lieutenant Cunningham, Fourth Indiana Cavalry, commanding escort members of the division staff, I am much indebted for the assistance rendered me on the field.

I desire to mention the services rendered by Surgeon Robins, Ninth Pennsylvania Cavalry, and division medical director, who was indefatigable in his efforts to care for our wounded, and those of the enemy remaining in our hands.

I inclose herewith copies of reports of brigade and battery commanders received since making this report.

Very respectfully, your obedient servant,

EDWARD M. McCOOK,
Colonel, Commanding.

Lieut. W. L. SHAW,
Acting Assistant Adjutant-General.

No. 5.

Report of Col. Archibald P. Campbell, Second Michigan Cavalry, commanding First Brigade.

HDQRS. FIRST BRIGADE, FIRST DIVISION CAVALRY,
Two Miles from Mossy Creek, December 30, 1863.

SIR: I have the honor to submit the following report of the engagement of the First Brigade, First Division Cavalry, near Mossy Creek yesterday, December 29:

My two regiments, the Second Michigan Cavalry and First Tennessee Cavalry, were encamped, one on each side of the Morristown oad, 3 miles from Mossy Creek. The Ninth Pennsylvania Cavalry was ordered 2 miles back to support Eighteenth Indiana Battery on same road; at 10 a. m. the enemy advanced in line along my whole front rapidly, and in obedience to orders previously received to fall back if attacked, I formed my two regiments in line with two battalions Second Michigan, dismounted, and retired slowly. The enemy pressed forward, showing several lines of battle formed and advancing, and he attempted to flank my command both to the right and left. My skirmishers kept up a brisk fire, as also did the enemy's artillery, at easy range on my line, at one time firing four guns rapidly.

Arriving at the large brick house 1 mile from Mossy Creek I was compelled to fight, and ordered the Second Michigan dismounted men under cover until the enemy's line advanced to within 20 yards, firing as they came, my flanks both giving ground before them. At this time the two battalions under cover opened upon the enemy a withering fire at within short range and checked his advance, with severe loss on both sides.

I then ordered the First Tennessee Cavalry to charge the enemy on the right of the brick house, and drove their center back and halted their whole line. I then ordered First Tennessee and Second Michigan Cavalry into the woods to the left of the road, while the artillery opened fire.

The enemy now marched around to my left, and I placed the First Tennessee Cavalry on the hill to the left of Mossy Creek, and the Second Michigan, dismounted, to the left of One hundredth and Eighteenth Ohio Infantry (the colonel of which regiment reporting to me for orders), formed in the woods in line, and awaited the enemy's attack. Severe firing soon commenced along the front, and the enemy trying to turn the left of the dismounted men, I held the enemy's line in check and ordered the Second Michigan, dismounted, and First Tennessee, mounted, to charge through the woods, which they did with a yell, repulsing and driving the enemy from the woods with heavy loss in killed and wounded and 25 prisoners in our hands. Several of my command were killed and wounded, including 2 officers of First Tennessee Cavalry mortally wounded. I ordered two guns of Eighteenth Indiana Battery to open fire after the men were rallied from the charge and shelled the woods, and no further demonstrations were made.

Seeing the battery on the Morristown road and the troops on the right of the road moving forward, I ordered my command forward on the left of the road, and soon received orders from General Elliott to move forward rapidly, which I did without resistance from any force.

The Ninth Pennsylvania Cavalry supported the battery, and repulsed a charge from the enemy. My loss in killed, wounded, and missing is 40. A list has been forwarded. I have captured 35 prisoners, including 2 officers.

Very respectfully submitted.

Your most obedient servant,

A. P. CAMPBELL,
Colonel, Commanding.

Capt. JOHN PRATT,
Assistant Adjutant-General.

No. 6.

Report of Col. Thomas J. Jordan, Ninth Pennsylvania Cavalry.

HEADQUARTERS NINTH PENNSYLVANIA CAVALRY,
Camp near Mossy Creek, Tenn., December 30, 1863.

SIR : I report that the Ninth Pennsylvania Cavalry, yesterday, took part in the battle of Mossy Creek Station, Tenn. First Brigade, First Division, Army of the Cumberland, under the command of Col. A. P. Campbell, was attacked about 10 a. m., and, after skirmishing with the enemy, gradually fell back toward the station. About 9 a. m., by order of Colonel Campbell, my regiment, with the exception of one battalion, which was on picket, left camp to support the artillery, stationed in the rear, and had scarcely taken position when the artillery, on the part of the enemy, appeared. The force of the enemy largely outnumbered those on our side, and, as we fell back, occupied the position we had left.

The battery of Captain Lilly opened upon the enemy with such effect that their advance was checked for a time. But soon a heavy line appeared upon our right, and by order of Colonel McCook, commanding division, my command was moved from near the Lilly battery to the right and rear, to support a section of the Elgin battery, and repel the enemy from that quarter.

By this time my command had been reduced from seven to five companies by sending detachments to the extreme right and left to cover roads upon our flanks. Soon after taking my new position the enemy made a charge upon the right, and, having no other troops to employ, I left my position near the guns and charged the enemy, driving him back. At this moment the Fifteenth Pennsylvania Cavalry came to my assistance, and the enemy was held in check till the arrival of re-enforcements, about 4 p. m., when I was again ordered to support the Elgin battery, and at once reported to Col. A. P. Campbell, when my regiment was ordered into camp.

My loss was 1 private killed, 6 wounded, and 2 missing. I also had 12 horses killed during the action.

I am, very truly,

THOS. J. JORDAN,
Colonel Ninth Pennsylvania Cavalry.

Lieut. E. HOYT, Jr.,
Acting Assistant Adjutant-General

No. 7.

Report of Col. Oscar H. La Grange, First Wisconsin Cavalry, commanding Second Brigade.

HDQRS. SECOND BRIGADE, FIRST CAVALRY DIVISION,
Talbott's House, Tenn., December 30, 1863.

SIR : I have the honor to report that, in obedience to orders from division headquarters, the Second Brigade moved at 5 a. m. on the 29th to Mossy Creek, reporting to General Sturgis, and receiving an order for two pieces of the Eighteenth Indiana Battery to accompany the brigade to a suitable position near the gap in Bay's Mountain and support a movement on the Dandridge road. A suitable position was taken near Lockhart's house, 5 miles from Mossy Creek, where the brigade remained until 1.30 p. m., when an order was received from General Sturgis to move rapidly to Mossy Creek. At 2.05 the brigade reported, and engaged the enemy on the right of the Morristown road.

A third of the command was dismounted and deployed in the woods on the extreme right of our line and the remainder moved forward in column or line, as the ground demanded, near our left center. The enemy was driven to Talbott's Station, 4 miles from Mossy Creek, when the brigade was halted and encamped in obedience to orders from the general commanding. The Fourth Indiana Cavalry captured 4 prisoners. A considerable number of arms were picked up and destroyed.

Owing to the great exertions made by the enemy to carry off his dead and wounded, no estimate of his loss can be made. Four of his dead have been found and buried, and 8 wounded are reported in houses near. Our loss was as follows:*

All the officers and men of the brigade did their duty. To mention particular actions would appear invidious.

Most respectfully,

> O. H. LA GRANGE,
> *Colonel, Commanding Brigade.*

Capt. JOHN PRATT, *Assistant Adjutant-General.*

No. 8.

Report of Col. William J. Palmer, Fifteenth Pennsylvania Cavalry.

HDQRS. 15TH PENN. CAV., DEPT. OF THE CUMBERLAND,
Stokely Williams', near Mossy Creek, December 30, 1863.

SIR : I have the honor to report that on yesterday morning my command, composed of detachments of the Fifteenth Pennsylvania Cavalry, the Tenth Ohio Cavalry, and the First East Tennessee Mounted Infantry, numbering in all about 250 men, was encamped at Montcastle's, 3 miles from Mossy Creek, on the road to mouth of Chucky. Being able to detect from a point of observation on a high hill near Montcastle's that our forces were falling back from Talbott's, on the Morristown road, and it being apparent that the enemy's cavalry would soon reach the mouth of Chucky road, between my camp and Mossy Creek, I moved my command, at about 11 a. m., in accordance with orders from Brigadier-General Elliott, which provided for this contingency, back toward Mossy Creek. Lieutenant Rogers' company, of the First East Tennessee Mounted Infantry, whom I detached for the purpose and sent into a woods on my flank, immediately became engaged, and held the road until the rest of the command reached Benjamin Branner's and was got into position, immediately in rear of the houses and out-buildings of Benjamin Branner and William Mann, on both sides of the mouth of Chucky road.

My command was ordered to hold this position and to support a battery placed on the hill in rear of it, near Widow Mendenhall's barn, which, I am happy to state, they successfully did (in connection with a squadron of the Ninth Pennsylvania Cavalry) in face of a greatly superior force of the enemy's cavalry, alternately mounted and dismounted, which assailed the position. We captured here 1 prisoner belonging to the Third Alabama Cavalry.

---

* Nominal list (omitted) shows 3 men killed and 1 officer and 11 men wounded.

This position was on the extreme right of our line, and was one o
great importance, as it commanded the single bridge and ford ove:
Mossy Creek and the ground on the west side of the creek for a long
distance. In its defense I lost my acting adjutant, Lieut. Harvey
S. Lingle, who was mortally wounded by a shot through the lungs
and 11 enlisted men who were wounded, most of them severely, bu
none fatally. Of these 1 officer and 5 enlisted men belonged to the
Fifteenth Pennsylvania Cavalry, 4 enlisted men to the Tenth Ohio
Cavalry, and 2 enlisted men to the First Tennessee.

The enemy retired on seeing our re-enforcements come in on the
Dandridge and Mossy Creek road, when I moved my command for
ward on the right of Colonel La Grange's mounted force and behind
his skirmishers, and pursued the enemy to Talbott's Station, when
darkness came on and the pursuit was stopped by order. If we had
had two hours more daylight I think the rebels would have suffered
severely in this pursuit.

I am, lieutenant, very respectfully,

WM. J. PALMER,
Colonel, Commanding.

Lieut. W. L. SHAW,
Aide-de-Camp, and Actg. Asst. Adjt. Gen.

[Inclosure.]

List of Casualties in Col. William J. Palmer's command, composed of detachment
of Fifteenth Pennsylvania Cavalry, Tenth Ohio Cavalry, and First East Tennes
see Mounted Infantry.

Command.	Killed.		Wounded.	Missing.	Total.
	Officers.	Men.			
15th Pennsylvania Cavalry	a1		5		
10th Ohio Cavalry			4	1	
1st East Tennessee Mounted Infantry			1		
Total	1		10	1	1

a Lieut. H. S. Lingle, 15th Pennsylvania Cavalry.

No. 9.

Report of Capt. Eli Lilly, Eighteenth Indiana Battery.

HDQRS. 18TH INDIANA BATTY., ARMY OF THE CUMBERLAND,
Near Talbott's Station, Tenn., December 30, 1863.

CAPTAIN : I have the honor herewith to submit report of the par
taken by my battery in the action at Mossy Creek and the advance
to this place on yesterday, December 29, 1863 :

At 2 a. m. I received orders to take position at daybreak on a sligh
eminence half a mile east of the bridge at Mossy Creek Station wit
my entire battery of five 3-inch rifled guns, covering the open groun
in front. Subsequently a section was detached and ordered to repor
to Colonel La Grange, commanding Second Brigade Cavalry, for
movement toward Dandridge, and the position was taken with bu
three guns. The enemy moved in very heavy force on our fron
few moments before 11 a. m., and opened a severe artillery fire o

is from four pieces, not, however, till I had developed my position
by shelling their advancing lines. I immediately replied, and after a
sharp duel of an hour they brought three more pieces to bear upon
me, at the same time pressing forward their lines. I now refused to
reply to their artillery, save with an occasional shot, but worked with
energy on their lines of dismounted cavalry and infantry, which
were in good canister range. They were held in check nearly an
hour, when, by a vigorous movement, they placed me under a strong
fire of small-arms by advancing to a hill, covered with standing corn,
on my right. From here they were twice driven with canister, when,
simultaneous to gaining it the third time, a strong line was observed
moving directly on my front not more than 150 yards distant.

By this time my cannoneers were almost completely exhausted by
constant labor at the guns on very miry ground, for nearly three
hours, my loss being 20 per cent. of my force, and consequently
having to work the pieces with greatly diminished numbers. By a
desperate effort, however, the guns were once more advanced to the
crest and discharged in the face of the enemy, now nearly on us; but
from the recoil of this fire my men had not the strength to advance
their pieces, though every effort was made to do so, and I ordered the
battery to retire, intending to take position on the only rise between
this and the creek, but received orders to occupy the high hill north
of Mossy Creek, from which point we threw a few shell as occasion
required. On the final advance, later in the day, this part of my
command moved with the First Brigade Cavalry, though not further
engaged.

The section which had reported to Colonel La Grange in the morning now returned, and was put to work on the right of the Chucky
Bend road, covering the advance of the Second Brigade Cavalry,
from which place it was moved forward as the brigade advanced,
firing from eight positions, the last being half a mile from Talbott's
Station, when, night coming on, operations were suspended.

It is impossible to make special mention of any one where all did
their whole duty.*

All of which is respectfully submitted.

I am, captain, your most obedient servant,

ELI LILLY,
Captain, Commanding.

Capt. JOHN PRATT, Assistant Adjutant-General.

No. 10.

Report of Col. Samuel R. Mott, One hundred and eighteenth Ohio
Infantry, commanding First Brigade, Second Division, Twenty-
third Corps.

HDQRS. FIRST BRIG., SECOND DIV., 23D ARMY CORPS,
Mossy Creek, Tenn., December 31, 1863.

CAPTAIN: I have the honor to submit the following report of the
part taken by my command in the battle near this place on the 29th
instant:

The regiments composing my brigade were, by your command, sta-

---

* Nominal list (omitted) shows 2 enlisted men killed; and 1 officer and 7 enlisted
men wounded. Seven horses were killed and 512 rounds of ammunition were
expended.

tioned as follows: The One hundred and eighteenth Ohio Voluntee
Infantry on the road leading to Talbott's Station on the left; th
Sixteenth Kentucky Volunteer Infantry on the right, to support tw
guns of the Elgin battery; the Twenty-fifth Michigan Infantry o:
the road, and the Eightieth Indiana Volunteer Infantry on the Dan
dridge and Dyer's Ferry roads.

The positions occupied by the One hundred and eighteenth Ohi
and Sixteenth Kentucky proved to be very important ones. The:
were exposed to the fire of the enemy for two and one-half hours
and gallantly maintained their position. The One hundred an
eighteenth charged the enemy with the bayonet, and drove then
from the field. The conduct of both officers and men was never sur
passed, I think, on any battle-field.

The casualties were as follows: Killed, One hundred and eight
eenth Ohio 5, and Sixteenth Kentucky 1; wounded, One hundre
and eighteenth Ohio 2 mortally and 32 slightly, and Sixteenth Ken
tucky 2 slightly.

I have the honor to be, your obedient servant,

S. R. MOTT,
Colonel, Commanding First Brigade. Second Division.

Capt. W. C. RAWOLLE,
Assistant Adjutant-General.

No. 11.

*Report of Lieut. Col. Thomas L. Young, One hundred and eight
eenth Ohio Infantry.*

HEADQUARTERS 118TH OHIO VOLUNTEER INFANTRY,
Mossy Creek, Tenn., December 30, 1863.

SIR: In accordance with your request, I have the honor to mak
the following statement of the part taken by this regiment in th
battle of Mossy Creek, fought on yesterday, the 29th instant:

At about 11.30 a. m. I was ordered to take my regiment to a stri
of woods to the left of, and flanking, the dirt and rail roads about
mile in front of our rifle-pits. We took our position in a very shor
time, having marched at a double-quick nearly all day. As soon a
we reached the corn-field in rear of our position the enemy opened
fire of shell and iron slugs upon us, wounding 1 man of Company H

This fire was kept up incessantly during the whole engagemen
About ten minutes after getting to our position (about 20 feet in rea
of the front edge of the woods) we engaged a rebel brigade of dis
mounted cavalry, which had gained a good position in our front
on our right covered by the brow of a hill, on our center covered b
a bluff bank and fence running along the edge of the corn-field, o
our left covered by a hill running through the corn-field in genera
direction with the dirt road, all points from 100 to 250 yards distan

In this way we fought about one hour, doing considerable execu
tion, especially on our left, where the enemy was more exposed
The enemy then changed position by massing on our left, which h
did in the best order I ever witnessed, considering the steady fir
we were pouring in upon him.

The enemy then charged our left with great spirit, driving us back
10 feet; but I strengthened the left, and we rallied and repulsed him,
regaining our ground and driving him back out of the woods with
great loss. The enemy then reformed, and was re-enforced by a
regiment from his left. The distance between us at this time was
about 150 yards. The advantage of position was about equal, except
that the rebel battery on our right continued to throw shells into
the woods, generally overshooting us, while the rebel battery on our
left and front, which seemed to pay particular attention to Lilly's
guns on the road, would drop a shell in front of or over our right
wing occasionally. In this position we fought about half an hour.
In the meantime, I sent Sergeant-Major Thompson to ask General
Elliott (under whose immediate command I was placed early in the
fight) to send a regiment to support my position, as I wanted to
charge the rebel battery on our left, and he replied that he could
send me no assistance.

When I learned this the enemy was pressing us very closely and
was forming in line of battle diagonally to our right and front, as I
thought, to charge us on the right, for the double purpose of flanking us on the right and taking Lilly's battery.

I knew if this movement of the enemy succeeded we, as a regiment, would be lost, because we had suffered severely in killed and
wounded, and the men thought they had no support to fall back
upon. So I determined to forestall the enemy and try his pluck
with cold steel. For this purpose I ordered the regiment to cease
firing, fix bayonets, and shoulder arms. I then told the boys what
I wanted them to do to crown the victory already so gallantly won.
We then charged out of the woods, and charged bayonets at double-
quick up the hill. The enemy preserved his line well until we got
within about 100 yards of him; he then gave us a parting volley
(by which I only lost 3 men), broke, and fled in great disorder to the
left, through the corn-field, and along the road into the woods, and
everywhere out of sight, so much faster than we could run that
when we reached the top of the hill in our front I ordered the men
to halt and lie down; it was vain to pursue any farther, as the rebel
artillery on our left had ceased firing as soon as they saw our bayonets, and limbered up and were in full gallop along the road when
we reached the top of the hill. Besides, I was afraid to venture too far
from my position without orders, lest some unforeseen maneuver of
the enemy should put it out of my power to regain it.

We therefore fell back after a few moments to our old position in
the edge of the woods. During the whole fight a regiment of sharpshooters were hidden, or rather covered, by the bank of the railroad,
about 300 yards to our right, and to them we attributed the most of
our loss on the right wing. After returning to the edge of the woods
we continued to fight the sharpshooters on the railroad on our right
and the skirmishers still in the woods on our left until we were ordered
to fall back by General Elliott, to support Lilly's battery on the hill
in our rear. We fell back in splendid order, and here it gives me
pleasure to speak of the uniform steadiness of every company, and
of the regiment, as a whole, in all the movements performed during
the trying hours we were under fire. After the regiment fell back to
the hill we replenished our ammunition, and when the battery moved
out to the chase we marched in support about 2 miles. Night closed
in. The enemy had been completely routed by our brave comrades
of other regiments; the field and day were ours. Victory perched

securely upon our banners, and the regiment marched, wearied but triumphant, back to camp, where we arrived at 9.30 p. m.

We had present in the fight 24 commissioned officers and 415 enlisted men. Of our conduct as a regiment it would not become me to speak, except to say that I will cheerfully risk my life with it as long as I shall have the honor to fight with it in our glorious cause. Of acts of individual heroism displayed by officers and men I dare not speak, as it would include two-thirds of the whole regiment; but it will not be considered invidious to the rest to mention especially the gallantry of Second Lieut. Josephus S. Parker, upon whom devolved the command of Company B after the gallant Captain Krane fell; also Sergt. Maj. George M. Thompson and Adjt. James M. Russell.

During the fight we fired over 5,000 rounds of cartridges. The enemy's loss in our front I would estimate at 350 killed, wounded and prisoners, including 1 captain (shot dead by Sergeant Roberts, Company B), and 1 lieutenant.

I have the honor to be, very respectfully, your obedient servant,

THOS. L. YOUNG,
Lieutenant-Colonel, Commanding.

Lieut. GEORGE H. TAYLOR,
Acting Assistant Adjutant-General.

DECEMBER 29–30, 1863.—Scout to Bean's Station, Tenn.

REPORTS.

No. 1.—Maj. Gen. John G. Parke, U. S. Army.
No. 2.—Capt. John R. Robinson, Twenty-seventh Kentucky Infantry.

No. 1.

Report of Maj. Gen. John G. Parke, U. S. Army.

STRAWBERRY PLAINS, TENN.,
December 31, 1863.

GENERAL: I have just received reports of reconnaissance up the Rutledge road. The party went 4½ miles beyond Bean's Station. Here they found a rebel hospital with a number of wounded, too badly hurt to be moved. They took 4 prisoners—part of the hospital attendants. They learned that Jones' command was at Moores burg, and Vaughn's, 2 miles in the rear of Mooresburg. The enemy's pickets were about a mile beyond, as reported by citizens. Citizens reported that the main body of the enemy was at Rogersville and Morristown, but could not specify what troops were at these points. The party that went up the river road met a small party of rebels at Turley's Mill, and were fired upon by parties from the south side of the Holston, all important points of which are guarded from Turley's Mill up to Noe's, or Marshall Ferry, where, it is reported, the enemy has one regiment, with artillery, and rifle-pits. Such is the report of the officers in charge of reconnaissance. On the other flank it is reported that the enemy has again sent cavalry to Dandridge, and are foraging on south side of French Broad

Two regiments of infantry and 50 wagons reported as having crossed at mouth of Chucky.

No reports received from General Sturgis of any movements of enemy to-day. I have not yet started the troops to Dandridge.

JNO. G. PARKE,
Major-General.

General E. E. POTTER.

No. 2.

Report of Capt. John R. Robinson, Twenty-seventh Kentucky Infantry.

MASSENGALE'S HOUSE,
December 30, 1863.

Major-General PARKE:

GENERAL: All is quiet in my immediate front. I have the honor to send you the following copy of report to Colonel Love, commanding Mounted Infantry Brigade, from Captain Robinson, who has just returned from a scout up the river. The report is as follows:

I have the honor to report that the detachment of 100 men, 50 from Eleventh Kentucky and 50 from Twenty-seventh Kentucky, with Captain Elms and Lieutenant Morris, of Eleventh Kentucky, and Lieutenants Norris and Fisher, Twenty-seventh Kentucky, left the camp at 1 p. m. yesterday; pushed forward to Turley's Mill, north of the Holston. While near that place the advance guard, under command of Lieutenant Norris, came up with a small squad of the enemy, and pressed them so close as to recapture 2 Union citizens of Greene County and 2 (Union) Fourth East Tennessee soldiers, who the rebels were marching to Morristown. The advance was fired upon by the rebel pickets from the south side of the Holston, at said Turley's Mill, where they are in force, variously estimated at from 3,000 down to two companies. The south bank of the Holston is guarded at all important points from Turley's Mill up to Noe's Ferry, where there is a rebel regiment on the south side the Holston. As the road from Turley's (or May's) Ford to Noe's Ford lies along the north bank of the Holston, at the foot of a cliff of from one-half to three-fourths mile in length, where troops would be exposed to sharpshooters and a piece of artillery from the enemy, it was deemed prudent not to march up the river road, so the detachment marched out the Richland Valley road 2½ miles, to McAllister's, and camped. During the night it was reported by citizens that a large rebel force crossed at Noe's Ford yesterday. This morning a scout, under Captain Elms, returned to near Turley's Mill and found all quiet. The detachment marched early this morning to Richland Valley, thence up to Bean's Station, and from thence, on the Morristown road, to Noe's Ford, where it was ascertained that the rebels have a regiment and one piece of artillery, with rifle-pits on the south side of the ford. The advance guard, under Lieutenant Fisher, proceeded a short distance above the ford, but only saw additional pickets on the south side of the river. This detachment also met a detachment of the Sixth Indiana Cavalry, under command of Captain Stephens, who had been ordered to Mooresburg, but after moving 3 miles above Bean's Station, and finding a rebel hospital of 21 badly wounded, a surgeon, and 16 sick and nurses, &c., and hearing that a rebel cavalry force visited the hospital daily, and that from 30 to 40 rebels were at Bean's Station night before last, that Moore's [?] rebel brigade was at Mooresburg and Vaughn's brigade at Rogersville, he deemed it prudent to return at once.

There is no rebel force, except small squads, north of the Holston below Bean's Station and Noe's Ford, but above these points the enemy have the forces indicated, with picket or scout lines from the Holston to the Valley road, a few miles above and parallel with the Bean's Station and Morristown road.

J. R. ROBINSON,
Captain Twenty-Seventh Kentucky, &c., Commanding Scouts.

I am, general, very respectfully, your obedient servant,

JAMES G. SPEARS,
Brigadier-General, Commanding, &c.

CORRESPONDENCE, ORDERS, AND RETURNS RELATING TO OPERATIONS IN KENTUCKY, SOUTHWEST VIRGINIA, TENNESSEE, MISSISSIPPI, NORTH ALABAMA, AND NORTH GEORGIA, FROM OCTOBER 20, 1863, TO OCTOBER 31, 1863.*

UNION CORRESPONDENCE, ETC.

WAR DEPARTMENT,
Washington, October 20, 1863—10.20 a. m.

Brig. Gen. R. ALLEN,
Saint Louis, Mo.:

Admiral Porter telegraphs from Cairo that gunboats are ready to convoy steamers up the Cumberland and Tennessee Rivers. Cannot you send supplies to Sherman, at Eastport, by water?

H. W. HALLECK,
General-in-Chief.

WASHINGTON,
October 20, 1863—10.20 a. m.

Major-General ROSECRANS:

Burnside telegraphs on the 17th that he had a cavalry brigade at Post Oak Springs and pickets extending to your left, and another brigade on south side of the river picketing down to the Hiwassee. Your wings are, therefore, in communication and should be able to co-operate at any moment against the enemy.

H. W. HALLECK,
General-in-Chief.

LOUISVILLE, KY., *October* 20, 1863—3 p. m.
(Received 6.10 p. m.)

Maj. Gen. H. W. HALLECK,
General-in-Chief:

Sunday night General Grant issued his orders taking command. Generals Burnside, Rosecrans, and Thomas reported last night. General Grant has gone forward with General Meigs, and will reach Chattanooga to-night or to-morrow. Thomas says if the supply wagons now on the road arrive safely they will be all right till November 1, at least. General Grant ordered him to hold Chattanooga at all hazards. He replied: "I will hold the town till we starve." General Meigs has taken with him a large supply of tools, for blasting and opening the road across the mountains, and everything possible has been done for railroad transportation.

EDWIN M. STANTON,
Secretary of War.

---

* The Union Correspondence, etc., from November 1, 1863, to December 31, 1863, and the Confederate Correspondence, etc., from October 20, 1863, to December 31, 1863, to appear in Part III.

HEADQUARTERS OF THE ARMY,
Washington, October 20, 1863.

Major-General GRANT,
          Louisville:

GENERAL : In compliance with my promise, I now proceed to give you a brief statement of the objects aimed at by General Rosecrans' and General Burnside's movement into East Tennessee, and of the measures directed to be taken to attain these objects. It has been the constant desire of the Government from the beginning of the war to secure the loyal inhabitants of East Tennessee from the hands of the rebels, who fully appreciated the importance of continuing their hold upon that country. In addition to the large amount of agricultural products drawn from the upper valley of the Tennessee, they also obtained iron and other military materials from the vicinity of Chattanooga. The possession of East Tennessee would cut off one of their most important railroad communications, and threaten their manufactories at Rome, Atlanta, &c. When General Buell was ordered into East Tennessee in the summer of 1862, Chattanooga was comparatively unprotected; but Bragg reached there before Buell, and, by threatening his communications, forced him to retreat on Nashville and Louisville. Again, after the battle of Perryville, General Buell was urged to pursue Bragg's defeated army and drive it from East Tennessee. The same was urged upon his successor; but the lateness of the season or other causes prevented further operations after the battle of Stone's River. Last spring, when your movements on the Mississippi River had drawn out of Tennessee a large force of the enemy, I again urged upon General Rosecrans to take advantage of that opportunity to carry out his projected plan of campaign, General Burnside being ready to co-operate with a diminished but still effective force. But he could not be persuaded to act in time, preferring to lie still till your campaign should be terminated. I represented to him, but without avail, that by this delay Johnston might be able to re-enforce Bragg with the troops then operating against you. When General Rosecrans finally determined to advance, he was allowed to select his own lines and plans for the carrying out the objects of the expedition. He was directed, however, to report his movements daily till he crossed the Tennessee, and to connect his left, so far as possible, with General Burnside's right. General Burnside was directed to move simultaneously, connecting his right, as far as possible, with General Rosecrans' left, so that, if the enemy concentrated upon either army, the other could move to its assistance. When General Burnside reached Kingston and Knoxville, and found no considerable number of enemy in East Tennessee, he was instructed to move down to the river and co-operate with General Rosecrans. These instructions were repeated some fifteen times, but were not carried out, General Burnside alleging, as an excuse, that he believed Bragg was in retreat, and that General Rosecrans needed no re-enforcements. When the latter had gained possession of Chattanooga, he was directed not to move on Rome, as he proposed, but simply to hold the mountain passes, so as to prevent the ingress of the rebels into East Tennessee. That object accomplished, I considered the campaign as ended, at least for the present. Future operations would depend upon the ascertained strength and movements of the enemy. In other words, the main objects of the campaign were the restoration of East Tennessee to the Union, and by holding the two extremities of the valley to secure it from rebel invasion. The moment I received reliable information of the departure of Longstreet's Corps from the Army of the Potomac I ordered forward to General Rosecrans every available man in the Department of the Ohio, and again urged General Burnside to move to his assistance. I also telegraphed to Generals Hurlbut, and Sherman and yourself to send forward all available troops in your department. If these forces had been sent to General Rosecrans by Nashville they could not have been supplied. I therefore directed them to move by Corinth and the Tennessee River. The necessity of this has been proved by the fact that the re-enforcements sent to him from the Army of the Potomac have not been able, for the want of railroad transportation, to reach General Rosecrans' army in the field. In regard to the relative strength of the opposing armies, it is believed that General Rosecrans, when he first moved against Bragg, had double if not treble his force. General Burnside also had more than double the force of Buckner, and even when Bragg and Buckner united Rosecrans' army was very greatly their superior in numbers. Even the 18,000 men sent from Virginia under Longstreet would not have given the enemy the superiority. It is now ascertained that the greater part of the prisoners paroled by you at Vicksburg and by General Banks at Port Hudson were illegally and improperly declared exchanged, and forced into the ranks to swell the rebel number at Chickamauga. This outrageous act, in violation of the laws of war, of the cartel entered into by the rebel authorities, and of all sense of honor, gives us a useful lesson in regard to the character of the enemy with whom we are contending. He neither regards the rules of civilized warfare nor even his most solemn engagements. You may therefore expect to meet in arms thousands of unexchanged prisoners, released by you and others on parole not to serve again until duly exchanged. Although the enemy by this disgraceful means have been able to concentrate in Georgia and Alabama a much larger force than we anticipated, your armies will be abundantly able to defeat him. Your difficulty will not be in the want of men, but in the means of supplying them at this season of the year. A single-track railroad can supply an army of 60,000 or 70,000 men, with the usual number of cavalry and artillery, but beyond that number or with a large mounted force the difficulty of supply is very great. I do not know the present condition of the road from Nashville to Decatur, but, if practicable to repair it, the use of that triangle will be of great assistance to you. I hope, also, that the recent rise of water in the Cumberland and Tennessee Rivers will enable you to employ water transportation to Nashville and Eastport or Florence. If you re-occupy the passes of Lookout Mountain, which should never have been given up, you will be able to use the railroad and river from Bridgeport to Chattanooga. This seems to me a matter of vital importance, and should receive your early attention. I submit this summary in the hope that it will assist you in fully understanding the object of the campaign and the means of attaining these objects. Probably the Secretary of War in his interviews with you at Louisville has gone over the same ground.

Whatever measures you may deem proper to adopt under existing circumstances you will receive all possible assistance from the authorities at Washington. You have never heretofore complained that such assistance has not been afforded you in your operations, and I think you will have no cause of complaint in your present campaign.

Very respectfully, your obedient servant,

H. W. HALLECK,
General-in-Chief.

CHATTANOOGA, TENN.,
October 20, 1863—1 a. m.

Major-General GRANT:

If the wagons now on the road arrive safe we are all right till November 1, at least.

GEO. H. THOMAS,
Major-General.

SPECIAL ORDERS, }   HDQRS. DIVISION OF THE MISSISSIPPI,
   No. 1.   }   *Louisville, October* 20, 1863.

Major-General ROSECRANS, and
Major-General THOMAS,
      Chattanooga:

Maj. Gen. W. S. Rosecrans having been relieved from the command of the Department of the Cumberland, by direction of the President of the United States, per General Orders, No. 337, of October 16, 1863, Major-General Thomas is hereby assigned to the command, and will at once assume its duties. General Rosecrans will turn over all books, papers, maps, and other property pertaining to the command to Major-General Thomas. All staff officers, except the aides-de-camp authorized by law, now on duty with General Rosecrans, will report to General Thomas for assignment as soon as relieved. General Rosecrans will proceed to Cincinnati, Ohio, and report to the Adjutant-General of the Army, by letter, for orders.

By order of Major-General Grant:

ELY S. PARKER,
Assistant Adjutant-General.

GENERAL ORDERS, }   HDQRS. DEPT. OF THE CUMBERLAND,
   No. 243.   }   *Chattanooga, Tenn., October* 20, 1863.

In obedience to the orders of the President of the United States, the undersigned hereby assumes command of the Department and Army of the Cumberland.

In assuming the control of this army, so long and ably commanded by Major-General Rosecrans, the undersigned confidently relies upon the hearty co-operation of every officer and soldier of the Army of the Cumberland to enable him to perform the arduous duties devolved upon him.

The officers on duty in the various departments of the staff at these headquarters will continue in their respective places.

All orders heretofore published for the government of this army will remain in force until further orders.

GEO. H. THOMAS,
Major-General, U. S. Volunteers.

CHATTANOOGA, TENN., *October* 20, 1863.
(Received 10.30 a. m., 25th.)

Major-General HALLECK,
    General-in-Chief :

To man the defenses of Chattanooga properly will require an entire regiment of artillery. Can authority be given to recruit a regiment of veteran volunteer artillery ? If so, I ask that Major Mendenhall, Fourth Artillery, be authorized to recruit such a regiment.

GEO. H. THOMAS,
Major-General.

NASHVILLE, TENN.,
October 20, 1863.

Maj. Gen. GEORGE H. THOMAS, *Chattanooga :*

I will leave here in the morning, and push through to Chattanooga as soon as possible. Should not large working parties be put upon the road between Bridgeport and Chattanooga at once ? General Meigs suggests this, and also that depots of forage be established on each side of the mountain.

U. S. GRANT,
Major-General.

HEADQUARTERS DEPARTMENT OF THE CUMBERLAND,
Chattanooga, October 20, 1863.

Major-General BURNSIDE,
    Commanding Department of the Ohio :

GENERAL: I regret to have to inform you that General Rosecrans was relieved from duty with this army yesterday, and that I have been placed in command.

The Departments of the Ohio, Cumberland, and Tennessee, have been thrown into one grand division, to be called the Division of the Mississippi, and placed under the command of General Grant, we commanding our armies under him. General Grant will be here in a few days. Cannot you come down to meet him ?

Colonel Clift will explain to you my situation and prospects, and thanking you for sending him down, I hope you will send him again until we can get more rapid communication by telegraph. If not molested within a week I will try to have a telegraph line put up to Kingston.

Our cavalry have gained considerable advantage over the enemy's cavalry during their late raids against the railroads.

The enemy's loss, five pieces artillery, over 2,000 killed, wounded, and prisoners.

Yours, truly,

GEO. H. THOMAS,
Major-General, Commanding.

HEADQUARTERS DEPARTMENT OF THE CUMBERLAND,
Chattanooga, October 20, 1863.

Brigadier-General MITCHELL, *Decherd :*

Information received from Columbia says 2 deserters from Lee's command came in there to-day. Say that Lee, with two brigades cavalry, joined Wheeler at Courtland on Sunday, and were busy cooking rations, intending to cross Tennessee. Colonel Mizner adds, he supposes for Shelbyville or near there. At any rate to trouble our communications. Look out for them. Get all the information you can and keep us advised.

By order of General Thomas :

C. GODDARD,
Assistant Adjutant-General.

HEADQUARTERS RECONNAISSANCE,
16 *Miles of Huntsville, October* 20, 1863.

Colonel LOWE,
Commanding First Brigade, Second Division :

I have the honor to report that Roddey and command swam the Elk River on last Sunday morning, going to Florence, there to cross the Tennessee. Elk River is still impassable. The majority of information says that Roddey is across the Tennessee River. His artillery crossed certainly by ferry. Wheeler and command are patroling the opposite side of the Tennessee River.

Very respectfully, your most obedient,

M. T. PATRICK,
Lieutenant-Colonel, Commanding Expedition.

[Indorsement.]

Received 9.22 p. m., and respectfully forwarded, for information of the general commanding.

W. W. LOWE,
Colonel, Commanding First Brigade.

STEVENSON,
October 20, 1863—9 p. m.

Major-General REYNOLDS :

Advices from General Crook, dated Brownsborough, October 19, inform me that General Lee, from below, has just joined Wheeler, with about 4,000 cavalry, at Courtland, and that the whole force now there is near 8,000. He says that there is plenty of corn about Brownsborough.

From the best information I can gather we have nothing to apprehend from the fords on the Tennessee below Bridgeport before spring.

JOSEPH HOOKER,
Major-General, Commanding.

HEADQUARTERS ELEVENTH AND TWELFTH CORPS,
Stevenson, Ala., October 20, 1863.

Brig. Gen. GEORGE CROOK,
Commanding Second Cavalry Division :

I am directed by the major-general commanding to acknowledge the receipt of your communication of the 9th instant, and to state in answer that he has this day represented to the major-general commanding the condition of the railroad bridges over Paint Rock and Flint Rivers, and suggested to him that a detachment from the regiment of Michigan Engineers be at once sent to put them in proper repair.   The geneual thanks you for the willingness you evince to perform this service, but if possible, he desires that it may be executed by that arm of the service to which it more appropriately belongs.   The general does not consider you as having been assigned to his command, except in the special cases in which he has acted, but you may be assured that it will afford him great pleasure to promote your interest and that of your command whenever it is in his power to do so.   You shall have your share of the remounts, if the distribution is in any way referred to him.   The news of General Lee's whereabouts is very important at this time.   Roddey crossed the river by boats, and from this until spring, from the best information, we have nothing to apprehend from the fords on the river below Bridgeport.   The river is now several feet higher than before the rain.

Very respectfully, &c.,

H. W. PERKINS,
Lieut., Aide-de-Camp, and Actg. Asst. Adjt. Gen.

HDQRS. FIRST DIVISION, TWELFTH ARMY CORPS,
Tullahoma, October 20, 1863.

Lieutenant-Colonel RODGERS,
Assistant Adjutant-General:

COLONEL : I inclose for the information of the major-general commanding corps a communication* from Colonel Coburn, commanding Third Brigade, First Division, Reserve Corps. Colonel Coburn's headquarters are at this post.   It will be seen that his own regiment (Thirty-third Indiana) is greatly scattered.   I beg to suggest that it would be better to concentrate this regiment at Christiana and thus relieve a regiment of Ruger's brigade for duty this way.

I don't see how I can spare a company of Fifth Connecticut (now at Cowan and Cumberland Tunnel) to relieve the company at Tracy City.   The five companies of One hundred and second Ohio which were at Cowan have been relieved and are now on the march for Nashville.   I have ordered four companies of Forty-sixth Pennsylvania to relieve the other five companies of this regiment at Elk River.   This leaves a very inadequate force at Decherd and at Cowan and the Tunnel.   If Ruger can get two regiments toward Murfreesborough relieved so as to occupy Elk River with one I could strengthen the two posts at Decherd and Cowan, and relieve the company of Thirty-third Indiana at Tracy City.   There are two sections of artillery here, claimed by Colonel Coburn as part of his brigade.   They should by all means be kept here, and there should be a section at Decherd.

I don't see how the regiment of Coburn's brigade at Duck River can be safely sent away, unless it be to relieve a regiment of Ruger's brigade on the northern end of the line, and thus enable him to replace the guard at Duck River.   I think it far better to put the regiments of same brigade at consecutive posts, and therefore beg to suggest that Coburn's two regiments—Thirty-third Indiana and the one now at Duck River—be sent to South Fork, Christiana, Foster-

---

* Not found.

ville, and Bell Buckle, and that Ruger's be brought this way to occupy contiguous posts. This would put Coburn's brigade at Murfreesborough, Christiana, and Bell Buckle with one regiment at McMinnville.

The line in this way would be relieved of mixed commands at the same post and of foreign regiments interposed between regiments of one of my brigades. As Coburn's command is ordered to Murfreesborough, I suppose it comes within your authority.

I beg leave also to call the attention of General Slocum to Colonel Coburn's report* on the condition of the McMinnville railroad. It seems in contemplation to open this road, as the telegraph line is being repaired and the burned bridge rebuilt. There are several important bridges on the road without guards. I cannot possibly furnish guards without a most injudicious weakening of my own posts. As Colonel Coburn has already a regiment at McMinnville, would it not be better that one other of his four regiments be sent to the other bridges of that road?

I am, colonel, very respectfully, your obedient servant,

> A. S. WILLIAMS,
> *Brigadier-General, Commanding Division.*

MEMPHIS, TENN., *October* 20, 1863—3 p. m.
(Received 9 p. m., 22d.)

Maj. Gen. H. W. HALLECK,
    General-in-Chief:

General Sherman will have two divisions at or near Tuscumbia to-day. The Tennessee is rising; fords are bad, and growing worse. I have telegraphed General Allen to-day for a steam ferry-boat to go up the Tennessee. There are 3 feet of water. Chalmers and Richardson are said to be re-enforced, but it is doubtful. My cavalry is well out to the front. The danger to this line will be from Forrest and Lee, when driven out of Middle Tennessee. Their attack may be serious with my thin lines.

> S. A. HURLBUT,
> *Major-General.*

MEMPHIS, TENN.,
October 20, 1863.

Brig. Gen. JOHN A. RAWLINS,
    A. A. G., Dept. of the Tenn., Vicksburg, Miss.:

GENERAL: I have this moment learned that Loring is up at Okolona with his division. The cavalry from below are uniting with Chalmers and Richardson. They aim for our railroad and to prevent re-enforcements. We are ready, but if attacked will lose some small posts. There are not less than 15,000, all told and of all arms threatening the road.

Your obedient servant,

> S. A. HURLBUT,
> *Major-General.*

---

* Not found.

MEMPHIS, TENN.,
October 20, 1863.

Maj. Gen. WILLIAM T. SHERMAN,
Fifteenth Army Corps:

I inclose you copy of General Grant's letter to me.* I have n
doubt the order to Louisville foreshadows the assumption of com
mand on the line of the Tennessee River.

I forward to-day, by telegraph, your requisition for a steam ferry
boat. I am informed that Admiral Porter is pushing one or mor
light-draught boats into the Tennessee River. From 30 inches to
feet may, I think, be counted on in that river, and as soon as th
Ohio rises it will be accessible.

Your obedient servant,

S. A. HURLBUT,
Major-General.

MEMPHIS, TENN.,
October 20, 1863.

Maj. Gen. WILLIAM T. SHERMAN:

I know nothing further than in papers of 17th. Meade has falle
back north of Rappahannock. No serious engagement. Five gun
and 300 prisoners captured by us. I do not believe any battle to b
imminent there.

Grant has gone to Louisville; says there is no change in orders a
to this line or your movements. Directs me to cover all the roa
practicable. I have sent to Steele for a brigade; hope it will com
soon. Chalmers and Richardson are reported re-enforced from Oko
lona. This is doubtful, but I shall know to-night.

Letters will come to you. Where shall they be forwarded?

Your obedient servant,

S. A. HURLBUT,
Major-General.

CORINTH, *October* 20, 1863.

Major-General SHERMAN:

All commissary stores that we have are loaded ready to go to you
There are 30 cars on the track now; 7 loaded with hard bread. On
train of commissary stores will be in to-night for us. We will tak
off little salt, and send the rest of the train through to you.

G. M. DODGE,
Brigadier-General.

CORINTH, *October* 20, 1863.

Major-General SHERMAN:

I know of no bad news; papers of 16th give none. We had sma
fight there with Warren's corps, but it was in our favor. Meade i
evidently falling back and preparing for a fight. Warren took tw
batteries and 500 prisoners.

G. M. DODGE,
Brigadier-General.

----

*See Series I, Vol. XXX, Part III, p. —.

HDQRS. FIRST DIVISION, FIFTEENTH ARMY CORPS,
Cherokee, Ala., October 20, 1863.

Maj. Gen. FRANK P. BLAIR, Jr.:

GENERAL: I received reliable information that no force of any consequence is at Tuscumbia. Wheeler's and Lee's cavalry, said to be 10,000, are between Town Creek and Decatur. I will therefore push on to make Tuscumbia before these troops can be brought up. Tennessee River rose 8 feet within the last two days. There are at least 9 to 10 feet water on the shoals at Florence; of course no fording. From Barton's east the railroad is very effectually destroyed. At least one-third of all the rails and ties are burnt, and heavy columns of smoke beyond Cane Creek show that the work of destruction is still going on.

Very respectfully, &c.,

P. JOS. OSTERHAUS,
Brigadier-General of Volunteers.

HEADQUARTERS FIFTEENTH ARMY CORPS,
Iuka, October 20, 1863.

Maj. Gen. FRANK P. BLAIR, Jr.,
In the Advance:

DEAR GENERAL: I am informed through a confidential person from the front that all of Wheeler's, Lee's, and Forrest's cavalry have come out of Tennessee, and are now between Tuscumbia and Decatur, with their advance at Cane Creek. If this is so, we have already drawn from Rosecrans' communications this disturbance of his game. Their aggregate force might trouble you, if you are not well in hand, and if you see signs to confirm this report, you will keep your command well massed, and not pass Cane Creek till I come up.

John E. Smith will come to Bear Creek to-morrow, and will send forward to communicate with you. The telegraph should also be pushed up to Dickson's. With so heavy a force of cavalry to swing round on our flank, I don't want to stretch out too long at present. Thereupon I modify my former order, for you to make a strong position near Cherokee, and keep your cavalry posted well up toward Barton's and Cane Creek, with a watchful eye to your right flank. Corse has gone down to Eastport and Chickasaw, and I believe Admiral Porter will send boats up the Tennessee River when we directly come from the railroad. In time we will disturb the rear of that cavalry, but now I don't want them to catch us too much divided and unprepared.

I am, &c.,

W. T. SHERMAN,
Major-General, Commanding.

DEPARTMENT OF THE TENNESSEE,
Iuka, October 20, 1863.

Major-General HURLBUT, *Memphis:*

I have all my ammunition here. All my troops are up, and I have stores enough for fifteen days. One regiment is at Eastport examining ford and collecting boats. Two divisions, under Blair, crossed

Bear Creek to-day, and will be near Tuscumbia to-morrow. I hold one division beyond Bear Creek and one here till I can finish up the railroad, which is very badly broken at Bear Creek and beyond. As soon as Fuller's brigade is near I will move on with my whole force. I have laid out a fort, and will work a brigade on it for a day or so, leaving Fuller to finish. I attach importance to this point, and will leave my sick and incumbrances here. I was down to Bear Creek to-day, and the break is a very bad one, and will take five days to repair. Send my letters by this route until further notice. Telegraph the substance of this to Generals Grant and Halleck.

                                  W. T. SHERMAN,
                                       Major-General.

                                  CORINTH, *October* 20.

Major-General HURLBUT,
           Memphis:

Scout in from Waynesborough, Tenn. Wheeler, Forrest, Roddey, and Kirk [?] left Pulaski last week, going toward Bainbridge Ferry and Florence. Part of Roddey's force going to the crossings below Florence. Wheeler moved his forces above Florence, and claims to have 8,000 men. Lee had not then arrived.

                                  G. M. DODGE,
                                       Brigadier-General.

                                  OCTOBER 20, 1863.

General DODGE, *Corinth,* and
General HURLBUT, *Memphis:*

I have a message from Mr. Goodloe that all of Wheeler's, Lee's, and Forrest's cavalry have come out of Tennessee, and are now between Tuscumbia and Decatur. I have been to Bear Creek, and the break there is very bad. I want to know about Fuller's brigade where it is, and when expected. The Tennessee is quite full, and the fords are impracticable up to the shoals above Tuscumbia.

                                  W. T. SHERMAN,
                                       Major-General.

                                  CORINTH, *October* 20.

Major-General SHERMAN,
           Iuka:

Your information checks with that from north side of river. They probably crossed at Bainbridge. Scout in from south. No force at Mobile, Meridian, Okolona, or Tupelo. All gone to Bragg. Seven hundred men left Fulton on Thursday last going to Chalmers and same number went to Lee via Russellville. Southern papers of 10th say Bragg draws rations for 180,000 men. This is quoted in all papers, and is evidently put out for effect. Jeff. Davis passed through Atlanta ten days ago on way to Bragg's army. Papers also say Ewell's corps is on way to Bragg. Fuller was at Collierville yesterday on way up. I will occupy road by time you want to leave.

                                  G. M. DODGE,
                                       Brigadier-General.

CORINTH, *October* 20.

Major-General SHERMAN, *Iuka:*

Scout came in from Waynesborough, Tenn. Wheeler, Forrest, Roddey, and Kirk [?] left Pulaski last week, going toward Bainbridge Ferry and Florence. Part of Roddey's force went to ferries below Florence. Rest of force went above. Wheeler claimed to have 8,000 men. Lee was not with him.

G. M. DODGE,
Brigadier-General.

(Same to Hurlbut.)

———

CORINTH, *October* 20.

Major-General SHERMAN, *Iuka:*

Scout sends in word from east side of river that Wheeler is at Bainbridge Ferry with Bragg's cavalry. Reported to have 8,000 men. Scout has gone up there and sends this back as the common report on that side; says that there is a considerable cavalry force watching all the Tennessee roads and ferries.

G. M. DODGE,
Brigadier-General.

———

HEADQUARTERS SIXTEENTH ARMY CORPS,
Memphis, Tenn., October 20, 1863.

Brig. Gen. GRENVILLE M. DODGE,
Corinth, Miss. :

I think Chalmers has been re-enforced somewhat and very probably may feel strong enough to try Collierville, La Fayette, or some minor station. Moscow, La Grange, Pocahontas, and Corinth should be points of concentration. If Collierville is attacked in heavy force the garrison should drop back to Germantown and thence to Memphis, if absolutely necessary. In case of an attack, infantry should move immediately from La Grange to Mount Pleasant. I have no force here to spare. Trains, &c., should be kept at Corinth and La Grange.

Chalmers is reported in camp 5 miles north of Wyatt. Fuller must move on to-morrow and come under your orders beyond Corinth.

Loring has either joined Bragg or will be found by Sherman before he gets to Decatur.

It would be a splendid time for Moyers to take 1,000 men and go to Okolona were it not for Chalmers below us.

Send some man to Holly Springs to his camp and learn the facts.

S. A. HURLBUT,
Major-General.

———

CORINTH, *October* 20, 1863.

Major-General HURLBUT,
Memphis:

I have news from south direct. No troops have left line of Mobile and Ohio Railroad to re-enforce Chalmers. All the troops at Mobile, except provost guard, have gone to Bragg. There are no troops at Okolona; have all gone to Roddey, at Chickasaw. Most of Lee's army are with Bragg; rest of Longstreet's corps have gone up.

Southern papers of October 10 state that Bragg draws rations for 180,000 men; the way it is stated shows it is put out for some purpose. Ferguson's and Ross' brigades went with Lee when he went to Tennessee. Seven hundred men left Fulton on Thursday to go to Salem, and an equal number went to Roddey. Jeff. Davis passed through Atlanta, Ga., ten days ago on way to Bragg's army.

G. M. DODGE,
Brigadier-General.

HDQRS. CAVALRY DIVISION, SIXTEENTH ARMY CORPS,
Memphis, Tenn., October 20. 1863.

Col. L. F. McCRILLIS,
    Commanding Second Cavalry Brigade:

COLONEL : You will immediately throw out from your command as outposts a battalion at Lamar and another at the intersection of the La Grange and Ripley and Saulsbury and Holly Springs roads, at Hardaway's. They will forage on the country, giving receipts for the same, and will be relieved every two days, in accordance with former instructions. A battalion of the Seventh Illinois is stationed at Quinn and Jackson's Mill, and a battalion of the Sixth Illinois at Olive Branch.

By order of Edward Hatch, colonel, commanding division :

S. L. WOODWARD,
Assistant Adjutant-General.

LA GRANGE,
October 20, 1863—9 p. m.

COMMANDING OFFICER :

You will scour the country in your front thoroughly and communicate with me. I have just learned that Chalmers has been reenforced with 4,000 fresh troops from Okolona, and that his scouts are on Coldwater to-night.

T. W. SWEENY,
Brigadier-General Commanding.

FLAG-SHIP BLACK HAWK, *Cairo, Ill., October* 20, 1863.
(Received 1.45 a. m., 21st.)

Hon. GIDEON WELLES,
    Secretary of the Navy:

Water risen 2 feet in the Ohio and still rising in the Tennessee. As it is raining, I am told, heavily in Virginia the rise may be a permanent one. Three gunboats are ordered to go up as high as Florence, if possible, and form a junction with General Sherman, from whom I received a letter on the 4th from Corinth. I have telegraphed to General Meigs that the gunboats were ready to convoy up both rivers, and I have ordered the gunboats to come below the falls at Louisville. Everything seems to work well for us.

DAVID D. PORTER,
Acting Rear-Admiral.

SPECIAL ORDERS, } HEADQUARTERS FIFTEENTH ARMY CORPS,
     No. 198.   }   *Iuka, October* 20, 1863.

I. General Ewing, commanding Fourth Division, will take command of all matters in and near Iuka. He will keep one regiment constantly on duty at the depot, maintaining order, loading and unloading cars with the utmost promptitude, and will impress the labor of every straggler and idler about the depot, and convalescents, where labor more or less will do them no harm. In concert with the chief quartermaster, commissary, and railroad agents, he will see that the utmost dispatch is used in expediting the work of the cars.

He will dispatch General Corse with one regiment and three days' rations, in wagons, to Eastport to reconnoiter, and with instructions to collect forage and meat; to find and collect at Eastport all boats in and near the mouth of Bear Creek, and secure them for our future use. At or before the end of three days General Corse will report back to these headquarters the result of his observations.

*   *   *   *   *   *   *

IV. As a general policy, citizens should go away and stay. The provost-marshal-general will register all who cannot leave Iuka, and explain to them that they must keep close or suffer the penalty of expulsion. Those living in the country must stay at home. Any citizen found lurking about the town or railroad will be sent to Memphis or put in the work-gang.

*   *   *   *   *   *   *

By order of Maj. Gen. W. T. Sherman:

                         R. M. SAWYER,
                         Assistant Adjutant-General.

HDQRS. 17TH ARMY CORPS, DEPT. OF THE TENNESSEE,
                    Vicksburg, October 20, 1863.

Major-General GRANT,
          Commanding, &c.:

GENERAL: I returned yesterday from the reconnaissance in the direction of Canton, the particulars of which will be found in the report* sent this day to Brigadier-General Rawlins. After reaching Robinson's Mills, near Livingston, I was satisfied that the enemy would have a force of infantry superior to mine, besides their cavalry, and under the circumstances, considering the defenseless state of Vicksburg, I deemed it best to return, which I did, via Clinton and Big Black Bridge. On returning, I found General Hawkins, at Goodrich's Landing, had reported that 4,000 men had assembled in the vicinity of Delhi, and were coming across Bayou Macon to attack him, and had called for re-enforcements, 2,000 infantry and a battery of artillery. The main brigade was sent up to his support, and the commander of the gunboat at Lake Providence notified and requested to render him assistance, if required. This was four days ago. Since then, I have heard nothing from him in regard to the movements of the enemy, and am decidedly of the opinion that the enemy's force was greatly exaggerated, and that it consisted of a

_____

*See Series I, Vol. XXX, Part II, p. 802.

regiment of cavalry which has infested that country ever since we came down the river. A boat came down last night. Everything was all right then.

Very respectfully, your obedient servant,

JAS. B. McPHERSON,
Major-General, Commanding.

KNOXVILLE, *October* 20, 1863—12.30 a. m.

Major-General GRANT:

The following is the disposition of the forces in this department : Three thousand cavalry, 1,000 infantry, and 10 pieces artillery at Jonesborough, with advance posts at the ford of the Holston, scouting well out on the north side of the Holston. One thousand cavalry and 4 pieces artillery at Rogersville, scouting in the direction of Kingsport. Four new Indiana regiments, with about 3,000 men for duty and 10 pieces of artillery, at Greeneville. One regiment of infantry, 400 strong, and a six-gun battery and 250 cavalry at Morristown. Two regiments new Ohio troops and one six-gun battery and a battalion of cavalry, 300 strong, at Cumberland Gap, with 13 captured pieces in position. Twelve hundred infantry, three batteries of artillery, and 1,000 cavalry at Knoxville. Nine hundred infantry at Concord. Twenty-seven hundred infantry and three batteries of artillery at Loudon. Twelve hundred cavalry and 4 mountain howitzers, under Colonel Wolford, with headquarters at Philadelphia, and outposts and scouting parties extending out to the Hiwassee River. Fifteen hundred cavalry and one battery of artillery, with headquarters at Post Oak Springs, 9 miles below Kingston, on the north side of the river, picketing down to Blythe's Ferry, connecting with General Rosecrans. Besides these, we have a column of 4,500 infantry, 18 pieces of artillery, and 350 cavalry of the Ninth Corps near this place under orders for Kingston.

These estimates are given in round numbers rather than regiments, as it will give you a better idea of our real strength. Some 2,000 or 3,000 home guards have been armed in different parts of the State, and we have over 2,000 recruits for the three-years' service, all of whom are armed, but not clad.

We have on hand twelve days' half rations of small stores and a good supply of beef-cattle and salt, with an abundance of breadstuffs in the country for present use. We have over 100 rounds of ammunition per man and 150 rounds per gun. Our horses are in fair condition, considering the amount of work they have done.

We are suffering for want of clothing for recruits as well as for old troops, and also for want of horseshoes and nails, but we have commenced to manufacture the latter here.

We find great difficulty in transporting supplies over the long line between here and Camp Nelson, and unless there is a fair prospect for driving the enemy below Dalton, so that the railroad can be opened, I think it would be well to establish communication by wagon train between Kingston and McMinnville.

I have already taken steps to repair the road from Clinton to the mouth of the Big South Fork of the Cumberland, to which point stores can be transported by water as soon as that river becomes navigable, which may not be till January.

A. E. BURNSIDE,
Major-General, Commanding.

(Copy same date to Halleck.)

KNOXVILLE, TENN., *October* 20, 1863.
(Received 11.45 p. m.)

Major-General HALLECK,
          General-in-Chief:

The indications from the front confirm me in the belief, expressed in my dispatch of last night, that the enemy are falling back from in front of Rosecrans.

                              A. E. BURNSIDE,
                                   Major-General.

KNOXVILLE, *October* 20, 1863.
(Received 11.50 p. m.)

His Excellency ABRAHAM LINCOLN,
          President:

Your dispatch of this date received.* We have armed some 2,500 guards and have recruited nearly 3,000 men for three-years' service. We have not been able to clothe them yet, and a large majority of them are in a very destitute condition; but they are armed and fed, and seem to be anxious to make any sacrifice required of them. I think that 10,000 three years' troops can be raised in East Tennessee and Western North Carolina, particularly if we can drive the enemy south of Dalton.

All our information tends to show that the enemy in front of Rosecrans has been decreased. It is said that the Mobile force has gone from Bragg; also forces under Johnston of 8,000 men. The enemy has left our front as far down as the Hiwassee, and his pickets are reported withdrawn from Tennessee River as far down as the mouth of Sale Creek.

I have just sent to General Grant a dispatch giving details of the position of forces, a copy of which I have requested should be sent to General Halleck.

                              A. E. BURNSIDE,
                                   Major-General.

NASHVILLE, *October* 20, 1863.
(Received 11.30 p. m., 21st.)

Major-General BURNSIDE:

Telegraph me the quantity of clothing you want, and what point you will have it shipped to; there is enough here to supply you. Repairing the road to McMinnville. All roads that can be used to get to supplies should be put in order as fast as possible. Can you not lay in large stores of forage, bacon, and supplies by purchasing? If so, do it. Have you tools for fortifying? Important points in East Tennessee should be put in condition to be held by the smallest number of men as soon as possible. Please inform me what you regard as the key-stone position in your department. I count Kingston to be the most important, but do not know now.

Will be in Stevenson to-morrow night and Chattanooga next night.

                              U. S. GRANT,
                                   Major-General.

---

* Probably refers to dispatch of October 17. See Series I, Vol. XXX, Part III, p. —.

LOUDON, *October* 20, 1863.

General BURNSIDE:

My men are most entirely out of ammunition.   Can you send some down to-night?   We need ammunition for 200 Sharps rifles, caliber .56, and the balance for Burnside and Smith carbines and Enfield rifles.   The battery is lost.

WOLFORD,
Colonel.

———

JONESBOROUGH,
October 20, 1863.

Major-General BURNSIDE:

Your dispatch received.   I thank you for your confidence.   We have about 6,000 pounds of hard bread, and not so much sugar and coffee.   Colonel Hoskins' command is about out.   We will issue to him to-day.

I sent two regiments, as you directed, to Rogersville—the Second Tennessee Mounted Infantry and Seventh Ohio Cavalry, with Phillips' battery.

We will get all the flour we can.   Must have wagon train at Bull's Gap brought up.   I have no apprehension but that we can hold the enemy with our present force.

J. M. SHACKELFORD,
Brigadier-General.

———

OCTOBER 20, 1863.

General BURNSIDE:

The infantry and battery I sent out proceeded about 2 miles, and met a part of Colonel Wolford's command.   The enemy is immediately in front on the right flank.   Their numbers are known only from Colonel Wolford's report.

My men are well in hand, and I think if they attack here I can at least hold out until supported by the force you speak of.   I am by no means certain they will give battle here, and I don't choose to fight outside of my proper defensive line.

JULIUS WHITE.

———

HDQRS. FIRST BRIG., FOURTH DIV., 23D ARMY CORPS,
Post Oak Springs, Tenn., October 20, 1863—8 p. m.

Lieutenant WELSH,
Acting Assistant Adjutant-General:

The firing heard to-day was probably at Philadelphia, where Colonel Wolford, with a brigade, is stationed.   A citizen who saw a rebel force on the south side of the Tennessee River reports that they said they were Welcker's [Wheeler's?] force and the advance of Bragg's army.   They were within 3 or 4 miles of Kingston.   The enemy in small force appeared at Kingston to-day and fired on the pickets.

Can it be possible that they have turned on us now, thinking that Rosecrans is too strong for them? The withdrawal of the pickets from the river seems to indicate this movement.

Nothing is known yet of the fight at Philadelphia, except heavy cannonading all the afternoon.

Respectfully, &c.,

EMERY S. BOND,
Lieutenant-Colonel, Commanding.

MUNFORDVILLE,
October 20, 1863.

Capt. A. C. SEMPLE:

Dispatch from Lebanon reports 600 rebels on Greensburg road, moving in direction of railroad near Lebanon. I am not apprised of Federal strength at Glasgow. My cavalry are all at Glasgow; have about 300. Has Colonel Weatherford been mounted?

E. H. HOBSON,
Brigadier-General.

MUNFORDVILLE,
October 20, 1863.

Col. S. A. STRICKLAND,
            Glasgow:

Make requisition for the number of wagons you want. Captain Huntington will fill it. Send over the transportation he furnished you. The wagons can return with commissary stores after your quartermaster settles with him for them. Captain Stone left Columbia this morning. If you can by any means furnish mounted men to pursue rebels, do so. It would be well to send information to Captain Stone and let him get on track of rebels with his forces.

E. H. HOBSON,
Brigadier-General.

MUNFORDVILLE,
October 20, 1863.

Capt. A. C. SEMPLE,
        Assistant Adjutant-General, Louisville:

Fifty rebels passed between Glasgow and Columbia to-day, going north. I have instructed all the available mounted force of my command. It would be well to direct Colonel Weatherford to send 50 mounted men from Lebanon, via Greensburg, and get on their track. This should be done immediately.

E. H. HOBSON,
Brigadier-General.

Abstract from tri-monthly return of the Department of the Cumberland, Maj. Gen. George H. Thomas, U. S. Army, commanding, October 20, 1863; headquarters Chattanooga.

Command.	Present for duty, equipped.*a*			Aggregate present for duty.	Aggregate present.	Aggregate present and absent.	Pieces of field artillery.
	Officers.	Men.	Aggregate.				
Fourth Army Corps (Granger)	1,270	18,511	19,781	20,260	24,278	43,868	53
Eleventh Army Corps (Howard) *b*	313	5,839	6,152	6,101	7,239	11,827	26
Twelfth Army Corps (Slocum) *b*	480	8,671	9,151	9,211	9,966	15,513	20
Fourteenth Army Corps (Thomas)	1,011	18,210	19,221	20,057	24,412	39,920	46
Cavalry Corps (Mitchell)	406	7,458	7,864	9,185	10,081	16,380	9
Artillery Reserve (Brannan)	39	1,180	1,219	1,227	1,284	1,987	50
Coburn's brigade	88	1,555	1,643	1,691	2,043	3,003	6
Miller's brigade	128	1,930	2,058	2,162	2,573	3,405	6
Pioneer Brigade *c*	19	412	431	440	.....	.....	.....
Signal corps *c*	.....	.....	.....	149	.....	.....	.....
Chattanooga	30	405	435	435	715	856	.....
Clarksville	11	243	254	263	452	481	6
Gallatin	34	631	665	906	1,090	1,401	6
Fort Donelson	14	258	272	272	438	470	4
Nashville (R. S. Granger)	151	2,727	2,878	2,885	3,346	3,848	19
Unattached infantry	214	5,209	5,423	5,319	6,181	8,224	.....
Unattached artillery	19	429	448	442	469	525	25
Unattached cavalry	26	397	423	406	459	674	.....
1st Michigan Engineers	21	538	559	557	686	904	.....
Total	4,274	74,603	78,877	81,968	95,712	153,286	276

a Or "actually available for the line of battle on the date of the regimental reports."
b Major-General Hooker commanding both corps.
c Officers and men detailed from other organizations, and elsewhere accounted for in the columns "Aggregate present" and "Aggregate present and absent."

LOUISVILLE, KY., *October* 21, 1863—11 a. m.
(Received 2.40 p. m.)

Hon. P. H. WATSON, *Assistant Secretary of War:*

General Grant reached Nashville safely yesterday. I have dispatch from him stating that he will go on to Stevenson to-day, and thence to Chattanooga, fast as possible. He is in communication with General Burnside.

Generals Garfield and Steedman are here on their way home. Their representations of the incidents of the battle of Chickamauga more than confirm the worst that has reached us from other sources as to the conduct of the commanding general and the great credit that is due to General Thomas.

I expect to leave for home to-morrow, having completed all the arrangements in regard to railroad management and transportation. I will not make as quick time returning as I did coming here.

EDWIN M. STANTON,
Secretary of War.

HEADQUARTERS DEPARTMENT OF THE CUMBERLAND,
Chattanooga, October 21, 1863.

Major-General HOOKER, *Stevenson:*

The general understands from your report that a steam-boat will be ready for use at Bridgeport by Sunday next, the 25th instant.

Do you think it will be done certainly? Can you concentrate your force at Bridgeport by that time, or how much of it can you so concentrate? Is the pontoon bridge at Battle Creek in good order and in readiness for use? Any additional information regarding enemy at Courtland? Any news from Sherman yet?

> J. J. REYNOLDS,
> *Major-General and Chief of Staff.*

> NASHVILLE,
> *October* 21, 1863—6.15 p. m.

Major-General THOMAS:

The following telegram just received by telegraph from Columbia, Tenn., October 21, 1863:

Capt. W. NEVIN,
  Assistant Adjutant-General:

Captain Blake, Thirteenth Wisconsin Volunteers, left Columbia Monday morning, and I learn is at Carter's Creek Station, unable to get farther, no cars having been out for the last two days. Rebel cavalry at Tuscumbia, Courtland, and Florence consists of Wheeler (6,000, with artillery), Roddey (2,000, with artillery), Lee (4,000, no artillery, just ordered from Mississippi to re-enforce Wheeler). If they cross the Tennessee, which is now very high, it will take them some time. I learn they have boats. They will strike the railroad south of Murfreesborough, at Wartrace, Shelbyville, or McMinnville. I have no idea they will come here; at least, only a portion of their force. I can hold my position against five times my number, at least. Why are the Tennesseeans detained? They ought to be here. They can be mounted in this country. They can be sent to Carter's Creek Station by rail; march the rest of the way. They must be armed by this time. Can they be sent at once? The proposed raid by rebel cavalry is surmised from the fact they were cooking five days' rations.

> HENRY R. MIZNER,
> *Colonel, Commanding.*

> R. S. GRANGER,
> *Brigadier-General.*

> HEADQUARTERS CHIEF OF CAVALRY,
> *Decherd, October* 21, 1863.

Lieutenant-Colonel GODDARD:

I received your dispatch of last evening relating to Wheeler. The cavalry is in bad condition to receive Wheeler at this time. We are sadly in need of horses and horse equipments, and cannot be effective until we receive at least 3,000 of each. If Wheeler crosses the river near the shoals, our cavalry should be moved—one division to Shelbyville, and the other near Tullahoma. As they are now situated, taking into consideration the condition of our horses, it would be very hard matter to intercept General Crook's division with the mounted infantry now in camp at Flint River, on the Memphis and Charleston Railroad. I am making every exertion possible to fit up the cavalry, but find there are but few horses and no horse equipments at Nashville. I will await instructions as to the change proposed.

> ROBT. B. MITCHELL,
> *Brigadier-General, Commanding.*

HDQRS. FIRST BRIG., SECOND DIV., 14TH ARMY CORPS,
Dallas, Tenn., October 21, 1863.
Lieut. Col. C. GODDARD,
Assistant Adjutant-General, Dept. of the Cumberland:

COLONEL : I have the honor to report that, in compliance with
orders from Major-General Rosecrans, I moved from Anderson's
Cross-Roads on the 18th instant to this point by way of Poe's road.
I found the road over the mountain nearly impassable. I had to
assign a company of infantry to each gun, and then found great difficulty in moving my artillery.

I arrived here this morning about 9 o'clock, and have stationed my
force (the Sixtieth Illinois, Tenth Michigan, and Beebe's battery) at
Dallas.

I will immediately, in compliance with the order referred to, confer with Colonel Harrison and Brigadier-General Spears, the nearest
commanding officers.

I am, colonel, very respectfully, your obedient servant,
R. F. SMITH,
Colonel, Commanding Brigade.

IUKA, *October* 21, 1863.
Major-General HURLBUT,
Memphis:

The enemy's cavalry is doubtless south of the Tennessee between
me and Decatur. The river has risen so they cannot get back, for
there is 8 feet of water on the Muscle Shoals. I must have a boat
at Eastport or Florence to pass to the point of my destination. I
think Wheeler will rest after his Tennessee raid, and move to Rome
and Chattanooga to rejoin Bragg ; but Forrest and Lee will hang
around our road to devil us.

W. T. SHERMAN,
Major-General.

HEADQUARTERS SIXTEENTH ARMY CORPS,
Memphis, Tenn., October 21, 1863.
Major-General SHERMAN,
Iuka, Miss. :

I have sent forward your dispatches for a ferry-boat and in relation to movements. It is, I think, certain that all the cavalry of the
left of Bragg's army will be found north of the river at Florence.
They are said to be 8,000. This has been sent forward also. I think
unless attacked and driven off by cavalry from Rosecrans they will
be apt to block the river against light gunboats.

S. A. HURLBUT,
Major-General.

HEADQUARTERS SIXTEENTH ARMY CORPS,
Memphis, Tenn., October 21, 1863.
Rear-Admiral DAVID D. PORTER,
Commanding Mississippi Squadron, Cairo, Ill. :

Major-General Sherman telegraphs me that there is 8 feet water
on the shoals, and desires me to inform you. He leaves a regiment

t Eastport. His advance will be in Tuscumbia to-morrow. Wheel-r's cavalry (8,000) is in force from Florence to Decatur on the north side of the river.

Your obedient servant,

S. A. HURLBUT,
Major-General.

LOUISVILLE, *October* 21, 1863.
(Received 22d.)

General BURNSIDE:

The appointment of Col. W. P. Sanders to the rank of brigadier has been ordered, and you may assign him to command according to that rank. The commission will be forwarded immediately after my return to Washington, whither I start to-morrow.

A dispatch from General Meade states that Lee's forces have been withdrawn across the Rappahannock, with a view to operations else-where. Congratulate you upon the brilliant success that has at-ended your operations in East Tennessee. I hope the same good fortune will attend you in the future.

EDWIN M. STANTON,
Secretary of War.

WASHINGTON, *October* 21, 1863—1.30 p. m.

Major-General BURNSIDE,
Knoxville, Tenn.:

Having by a demonstration forced General Meade to retreat, and having destroyed all his line of supply, General Lee will probably send a part of his army to the Southwest. Whether to Bragg or by Abingdon is uncertain. I think your available forces at Kingston and above should be held in readiness to move up the valley, should the enemy appear in force in Southwestern Virginia. A copy of this is sent to General Grant. Communicate with him.

H. W. HALLECK,
General-in-Chief.

JONESBOROUGH, *October* 21, 1863.

General BURNSIDE:

The enemy is between the two rivers, whether in force or not I am unable to determine. If it will meet your approbation, I pro-pose, before sending the expedition to North Carolina, to start to-morrow evening with a sufficient part of the command to give him battle if he is there in force, and if possible drive him again beyond the Holston. If he has nothing but scouting parties between the rivers, we will stand a good chance to capture them.

We have a large number of dismounted men, and as two of the regiments are at Rogersville, I propose taking Colonel Hoskins, with the Twelfth Kentucky and One hundred and third Ohio, leav-ing the Eighth Tennessee and dismounted men here.

A flag of truce came to our outpost this evening, asking permission to come through the lines for Mrs. Colonel Bottles, whose husband they reported dying from his wounds received in the skirmish
day before yesterday. We sent for Mrs. Bottles and sent her over.

                                J. M. SHACKELFORD,
                                        Brigadier-General.

                                LOUDON, *October* 21, 1863.
General BURNSIDE:

I have deferred this dispatch hoping to be more definite than I am
able to be. I have withdrawn the cavalry within my lines, as there
is no object in keeping it at Philadelphia. The enemy is near there.
I am not confident there is any infantry or artillery with them, but
Colonel Wolford says they used both on him yesterday. He is confident they will yet attack this place, and that the stubbornness of
their resistance to-day is evidence that they intend to hold all they
have till the material for a suitable attack can be brought up. I
don't feel authorized to move out from here with a small force to
any great distance, and my entire division numbers but little over
3,000. I am convinced they have a large force between this and
Cleveland, but can't say they will come here with it. The boldness
of their mounted force convinces me it is backed by all arms.

                                JULIUS WHITE,
                                        Brigadier-General.

                                LOUDON, *October* 21, 1863.
Major-General BURNSIDE:

SIR: The Twelfth Kentucky Cavalry of my command is out of
ammunition for the Union rifle carbine, and there is none here. Also
out of ammunition for the Henry rifle, and none to be had. Can it
be procured there? If so, I need 21,000 rounds Union rifle carbine
cartridges and 2,640 Henry rifles. Answer.

                                FRANK WOLFORD,
                        Colonel, Commanding Independent Cavalry Brigade.

                        SAINT LOUIS, MO., *October* 21, 1863.
                                        (Received 5 p. m.)
Maj. Gen. H. W. HALLECK,
                General-in-Chief:

Supplies can now be sent up the Tennessee to Eastport. We are
loading tow-boats for that place to-day. Is General Sherman ready
to receive supplies at that point? Colonel Haines telegraphed him
on the 7th instant, but no answer. Six feet water at Eastport, 3
feet on lower and 2 feet on upper shoals. Will send a tow of hay
from Cairo to Nashville to-morrow.

                                ROBT. ALLEN,
                                        Chief Quartermaster.

SAINT LOUIS, MO., *October* 21, 1863.
(Received 7.15 p. m.)

Major-General HALLECK,
General-in-Chief:

Colonel Haines has this moment received a dispatch from General Sherman. He requests that stores be sent to Eastport, and will be so prepared to receive them. We will ship as fast as possible

ROBT. ALLEN,
Chief Quartermaster.

OCTOBER 21, 1863.

Major-General GRANT:

Gunboats are now on their way up the Tennessee and for up the Cumberland. My intention is to send every gunboat I can spare up the Tennessee. I have also sent below for light-draughts to come up. Am sorry to say the river is at a stand.

PORTER.

MEMPHIS, TENN., *October* 21, 1863—11.30 a. m.
(Received 8.20 p. m., 23d.)

Maj. Gen. H. W. HALLECK,
General-in-Chief:

The following received from Corinth: All troops at Mobile except provost guards have gone to Bragg. No troops at Okolona; have gone to Roddey, at Chickasaw. Much of Lee's army is with Bragg. The rest of Longstreet's corps has arrived. Southern papers of 10th state Bragg draws 180,000 rations. This is published for effect, evidently. Wheeler is reported to be concentrating his whole cavalry, claiming 8,000, at the Tennessee, above and below Florence. General Sherman will make his hospital depot at Iuka. Blair crossed Bear Creek with two divisions yesterday, and will be near Tuscumbia to-day. One other division of Sherman's is beyond Bear Creek, and one will be kept on this side until a brigade sent from Memphis can relieve it. It will take five days longer to repair bridge at Bear Creek for trains. The Tennessee River must be his main dependence. It is now rising. I need 2,000 horse equipments to mount infantry. They were promised some weeks since, but have not arrived. As soon as the force comes from Steele I shall strike for Columbus, Miss. At present I have no disposable infantry.

S. A. HURLBUT,
Major-General.

(Same to General Grant.)

MEMPHIS, TENN., *October* 21, 1863.

Col. L. F. MCCRILLIS,
La Grange, Tenn.:

Send battalion this afternoon to La Fayette to meet horses for your command. They will be at La Fayette in the morning.

EDWARD HATCH,
Colonel, Commanding Division.

MEMPHIS, TENN., *October* 21, 1863.

Colonel WILCOX,
        Commanding Post, Germantown:

COLONEL: The whole force of the Sixth Illinois Cavalry and four guns are ordered to go south in the morning.

EDWARD HATCH,
Colonel, Commanding Division.

MEMPHIS, TENN., *October* 21, 1863.

Lieutenant-Colonel LOOMIS,
        Comdg. Sixth Illinois Cavalry, Germantown:

Furnish two companies as escort for horses for La Grange. Horses will be at Germantown this afternoon. Escort will go to Collierville and return. Prepare your regiment for expedition in the morning.

EDWARD HATCH,
Colonel, Commanding Division.

MEMPHIS, *October* 21, 1863.

Lieut. Col. R. LOOMIS,
        Commanding Sixth Illinois Cavalry:

COLONEL: You will proceed, with the effective force of your command and 4 guns of the battery, taking with you the best battalion now on outpost duty at Olive Branch, on a reconnaissance southward, for the purpose of ascertaining the truth of the report that Chalmers is encamped 5 miles north of Wyatt. You will start immediately upon the receipt of this communication, and use every precaution against surprises. You will gather all possible information concerning the whereabouts and force of the enemy, but avoid a general engagement. It will not be necessary to go all the way to Wyatt, if you can gather reliable and satisfactory information before reaching that point. Should you meet no force of consequence, you can scout the country for a few days, and feed your horses well, always giving receipts for the same. Communicate promptly with these headquarters should you obtain any important information, and immediately upon your arrival telegraph, and make full written report by mail.

By order of Col. Edward Hatch:

S. L. WOODWARD,
Assistant Adjutant-General.

HDQRS. SECOND DIVISION, SIXTEENTH ARMY CORPS,
La Grange, Tenn., October 21, 1863.

Col. L. F. McCRILLIS,
        Commanding Second Brigade Cavalry:

You will send out a force of cavalry from this place, Grand Junction, and Saulsbury. These forces must cross the Coldwater to-morrow, going as far as the Tallahatchie, if no force of the enemy interposes to prevent.

By order of Brig. Gen. T. W. Sweeny:

L. H. EVERTS,
Assistant Adjutant-General.

HDQRS. SECOND DIVISION, SIXTEENTH ARMY CORPS,
La Grange, Tenn., October 21, 1863.

Col. FRANK A. KENDRICK,
  West Tennessee Infantry, A. D., Comdg. Moscow, Tenn.:

COLONEL: A serious complaint from citizens living in your vicinity and the vicinity of La Fayette is referred to these headquarters by General Hurlbut in reference to midnight robberies and raids by your men, who in several cases have deliberately fired upon peaceable citizens in their own houses, and committed thefts and outrages that are a disgrace to the service. Some one is severely to blame in this matter, and you will use every exertion to ascertain who the guilty and responsible parties are, and see that acts of this kind do not occur again. There must be gross carelessness and neglect on the part of some of your officers, and such should be hunted out and means taken to have them dismissed the service, as they are an injury to it and a disgrace to your command. Officers will be held responsible for the conduct of their men, and you will thoroughly investigate the matter, and report to these headquarters all the facts connected with these complaints.

By order of Brig. Gen. T. W. Sweeny:

L. H. EVERTS,
Captain, and Assistant Adjutant-General.

HDQRS. LEFT WING, SIXTEENTH ARMY CORPS,
Corinth, Miss., October 21, 1863.

Capt. T. H. HARRIS,
  Asst. Adj. Gen., 16th Army Corps, Memphis, Tenn.:

CAPTAIN: I have sent General Sweeny written instructions in relation to movements of troops, &c., in time of attack. I shall endeavor to catch them before they reach the railroad. I have considerable reliable information in relation to the orders of Johnston the first of this month. It seems that about the 6th of October he ordered Loring, Lee, Chalmers, Ferguson, Gholson, and Ruggles to concentrate at New Albany, for the purpose of breaking up this railroad, and they claim that their available force to do it would be 25,000 men. And it also appears that Johnston was not then aware of Sherman's movement. As soon as he ascertained this fact, an entire change was made. Loring, Lee, Ferguson, &c., went to Bragg and the Tennessee Valley, Chalmers was allowed to make the attempt alone, by scraping up what men he could. Where Johnston is now I do not know, but I believe Chalmers took all the available force that is in Northern Mississippi with him in his late attack.

The leaders all seem to think that Davis has cast his all on a fight between Chattanooga and Atlanta, and they say that Lee and Davis will be at the fight. They do not believe that Sherman is going to Rosecrans, but think he is going toward Montgomery and Atlanta. The disposition of their forces show this, and they openly say so. There are no troops at Montgomery, Selma, Tuscaloosa, Elyton, or Jasper except provost guards. At Elyton, above and below, are large iron mills, which they are working to get out railroad iron to finish the Selma road to Rome. They are also building a branch railroad from Line Station, near Columbiana, on Selma and Rome railroad, to Elyton. A large force is at work on it, and they say they will finish it by Christmas. This road is being built for the sole purpose of getting out the railroad iron now being manufactured at these mills. No works are being built at Selma, but below Selma fortifications are going up to stop our boats running to Selma.

All Government works are now in full operation at Selma. I expect Spencer to destroy these works and the road. There is some infantry at Columbus, a part of the Forty-third Mississippi or Alabama Infantry, and a battery. Ruggles is also there. Davenport is at Fulton, not armed, and only partly mounted. He has one company at Bay Springs, Captain Pardue's. The runaway conscripts that they pick up they now send to garrison forts; do not send them to Bragg.

The men in the mountains report that large numbers of deserters are beginning to come in again from Bragg's army, and I see several letters that the boys bring in from officers say that Mobile will not be defended. Selma paper of the 10th says Loring's division is on the way to Bragg.

I am, very respectfully, your obedient servant,

G. M. DODGE,
Brigadier-General.

MUNFORDVILLE, *October* 21, 1863.

Captain SEMPLE, *Assistant Adjutant-General:*

One hundred and ten cavalry will move from Glasgow to Sumerville. One hundred and ninety will move from this place, north side of Green River, and unite with force from Glasgow. If rebels have crossed toward New Haven my force will find it out and follow them. If they have moved south, after stealing and plundering, they can be pursued.

E. H. HOBSON,
Brigadier-General.

FORT PILLOW, TENN.,
October 21, 1863.

Capt. J. HOUGH, *Assistant Adjutant-General, Memphis:*

CAPTAIN: A gentleman just arrived from the interior informs me that Captain Hayes, who for some time has been engaged in recruiting and organizing a company of Tennessee militia, was captured on Monday, the 13th instant, and brutally murdered on the 14th instant, by a portion of Faulkner's command. He was shot down and entirely stripped of his clothing, and thrown into the Middle fork of the Forked Deer River, near Lee's Mill, in Gibson County. His body was found in that stream on Monday last, and my informant, together with the Masonic fraternity, buried him on that day.

Captain Hayes was commissioned as first lieutenant by Governor Johnson, to raise a company for the First Regiment Tennessee Cavalry, and as soon as his company was full was to have been commissioned as captain. Captain Hayes, by his personal bravery and daring, and by his indefatigable zeal in hunting down guerrillas, has made himself, together with his little command, a terror to that class of lawless men.

Trusting that prompt and decisive steps will be taken to avenge this inhuman and barbarous outrage, I have the honor to be, captain, your obedient servant,

E. H. WOLFE,
Colonel Fifty-second Indiana Infantry.

SPECIAL ORDERS, } 　　HEADQUARTERS OF THE ARMY,
　　　　　　　　　　　　　ADJUTANT-GENERAL'S OFFICE,
No. 472. 　　　　　　　　　*Washington, October 21, 1863.*

*　　　*　　　*　　　*　　　*　　　*　　　*

III. Brig. Gen. Washington L. Elliott, U. S. Volunteers, will report in person immediately to Major-General Rosecrans.

By command of Major-General Halleck :

　　　　　　　　　　　E. D. TOWNSEND,
　　　　　　　　　　　Assistant Adjutant-General.

GENERAL ORDERS, } 　　HDQRS. FIRST DIV., 12TH CORPS,
　　　　　　　　　　　　　ARMY OF THE CUMBERLAND,
No. 56. 　　　　　　　　　*Decherd, Tenn., October 21, 1863.*

The brigadier-general commanding the division has discovered, very much to his regret, a decided lack of harmony between the detachments from other commands that he found stationed on the line of railroad now under his command and the troops of his division. Upon several occasions this feeling has nearly resulted in a collision between small parties of the respective commands. It is earnestly hoped that the present state of feeling may immediately give place to a spirit of at least apparent harmony. There is really no reason why any disagreement should exist between the soldiers of the commands referred to, and nothing is more likely to produce disagreement than little banterings and reflections which oftentimes are playfully commenced, and it is enjoined upon all officers and men of this division, as well as upon those of the detachments serving with it, to abstain from all assertions or demonstrations tending to create ill-will, and hereafter any officer or enlisted man indulging in such will be arrested and punished.

The Army of the Cumberland and the Army of the Potomac have both performed their duty well, and they should come together as fellow-soldiers engaged in a common and holy cause.

The troops of the Army of the Potomac come here by order of the Chief Magistrate to re-enforce the Army of the Cumberland, by which their respective fortunes are linked together, and it is believed by the division commander that his desire is their desire, viz, that still further brilliant victories may crown the efforts of all the troops serving in the Army of the Cumberland.

This order will be promulgated to all the troops within the limits of this command.

By command of Brig. Gen. A. S. Williams :

　　　　　　　　　　　S. E. PITTMAN,
　　　　　　　Captain, and Assistant Adjutant-General.

　　　　　　　　　　　BRIDGEPORT, TENN.,
　　　　　　　　　　　　October 22, 1863.

Hon. E. M. STANTON :

Arrived here last night. Party all safe. Rained yesterday. Roads worse than ever. General Grant leaves for Chattanooga this morning, and will arrive to-morrow night.

　　　　　　　　　　　[C. A. DANA.]

BRIDGEPORT, TENN.,
October 22, 1863.

Hon. E. M. STANTON:

No news here from Chattanooga. I am just starting for there with Grant. Will report fully on arriving.

[C. A. DANA.]

———

STEVENSON, *October* 22, 1863.

Major-General REYNOLDS:

General Slocum just telegraphs that a force of 600 rebel cavalry guerrillas, under Ferguson, congregated at Rock Island, 14 miles from McMinnville. He has scouts watching them. General Rosecrans advised me some days since that a regiment was ordered to McMinnville from his headquarters. I have telegraphed instructions to the commanding officer at that point, but I am unadvised as to their arrival.

JOSEPH HOOKER,
Major-General.

———

STEVENSON, *October* 22, 1863—10 a. m.

Major-General REYNOLDS,
Chief of Staff:

I desire the general to be correctly advised of the movements of the Twelfth Corps. It is ordered to concentrate at Bridgeport. The wagons for one division of it left Nashville yesterday, and the balance will be put on the road in the course of the week, as the cars are under orders from headquarters. I am instructed to bring nothing but supplies. I cannot move the troops before the wagons come up without leaving all baggage behind. As this may cripple my future movements, I desire that orders may be given to the officers in charge of the railroad to receive the baggage of this corps and deliver it at Bridgeport.

JOSEPH HOOKER,
Major-General.

———

STEVENSON, *October* 22, 1863—10 a. m.

Major-General SLOCUM:

On the receipt of this order you will, with the least possible delay, concentrate your command at Bridgeport; the movement to be made in such way as will soonest effect this object. A train of wagons for one division of your corps left Nashville yesterday morning, and it is required that as soon as it reaches Murfreesborough you make use of it to move General Geary's division, unless cars can be obtained for that purpose. Application has been made for them, but the movement must not be delayed in the absence of this authority.

Station the troops along the line of communication in your district, and not of your corps, at the points most needed for the protection of the line.

HOOKER,
Major-General.

WARTRACE, *October* 22, 1863.
(Received 7.30 p. m.)

Brig. Gen. ALPHEUS S. WILLIAMS:

The major-general commanding directs that you move your entire division and the artillery of the corps that is with you to Bridgeport with least possible delay. Leave baggage in charge of some competent officer until your wagons come; or, if you prefer and can obtain cars, send it by rail. You will give necessary directions to have your wagon train follow you. You will distribute the troops under your command not belonging to this corps so as to guard the most important points, bridges, &c. The movement should begin to-morrow. Please acknowledge.

H. C. RODGERS,
Assistant Adjutant-General.

STEVENSON, *October* 22, 1863—12 m.

Brigadier-General GRANGER:
Nashville:

Wheeler's force numbers 4,000, with artillery, and Lee's force 2,500. These are at Courtland. Roddey's force, numbering about 1,000 men, have not returned to the south side of the Tennessee, but are dispersed in small bands in the vicinity of Huntsville. This is reliable. Sherman should be in the vicinity of Courtland, and should not only disperse the cavalry force there, but cover the country to the north.

JOSEPH HOOKER,
Major-General, Commanding.

HEADQUARTERS DEPARTMENT OF THE CUMBERLAND,
Chattanooga, October 22, 1863.

Brigadier-General MITCHELL, *Decherd,* and
Brigadier-General CROOK, *Flint River:*

There is no doubt that Lee, with 2,500 men, has joined Wheeler at Courtland. A dispatch from Wheeler to Bragg, captured at Trenton, states that Lee had arrived at Florence. Captured rebel dispatches all show that cavalry expect to make another raid into Middle Tennessee.

C. GODDARD,
Assistant Adjutant-General.

MURFREESBOROUGH,
October 22, 1863—6.45 p. m.

Lieut. Col. H. C. RODGERS,
Assistant Adjutant-General, Twelfth Corps:

Orders received. Will send Michigan regiment as ordered, and will make best possible arrangement of the troops here for defense of the bridges on the [railroad], but all I can do will be inadequate to their protection.

JNO. W. GEARY,
Brigadier-General, Commanding.

STEVENSON,
October 22, 1863—1.10 p. m.

Brig. Gen. R. S. GRANGER,
  Nashville:

I am ordered to concentrate my command at Bridgeport. I shall have to turn over this line to you as fast as my troops are able to move from the positions they at present occupy. They are now under orders for the movement.

JOSEPH HOOKER,
Major-General.

HEADQUARTERS FIRST DIVISION, TWELFTH CORPS,
Decherd, Tenn., October 22, 1863.

Brig. Gen. J. F. KNIPE,
  Commanding First Brigade:

GENERAL: I am directed by the brigadier-general commanding the division to say that this division is ordered to Bridgeport without delay, and he desires you to march your command at the earliest hour practicable. You will leave the important points on your line guarded by troops not of your brigade. If you can get cars, you may send your baggage by rail; but if not able to do so, it will be left until wagons come up, and then loaded and brought forward to Bridgeport. You will please report at these headquarters for further instructions.

I am, general, your obedient servant,

S. E. PITTMAN,
Captain, and Assistant Adjutant-General.

HDQRS. FIRST BRIG., SECOND DIV., 14TH ARMY CORPS,
Dallas, Tenn, October 22, 1863.

Lieut. Col. C. GODDARD,
  Asst. Adjt. Gen., Department of the Cumberland:

COLONEL: I have the honor to report that I conferred to-day with Colonels Harrison, Thirty-ninth Indiana, and Atkins, Ninety-second Illinois, whose commands are guarding the river in this vicinity. I also made a partial examination of the river from Harrison's to Igou's Ferry, 8 miles above.

I found two companies of the Ninety-second Illinois (mounted infantry) at Harrison's Landing, with a hastily constructed and imperfect line of rifle-pits. Igou's Ferry is guarded by one company of the Thirty-ninth Indiana (mounted infantry), with posts 1 mile above and a like distance below the ferry, connected by patrols. Penny's Ford, 2 miles above Igou's, is guarded by a force of infantry from General Spears' command, who report to Colonel Harrison, Thirty-ninth Indiana. I will relieve the force at Harrison's and Igou's to-morrow morning with five companies of infantry from my command at each place, and use the mounted force in this vicinity for patrol duty exclusively.

There is no forage in this vicinity, and the stock of the mounted commands referred to is suffering much. One of the regiments has no transportion, and the other but 13 wagons. Unless something an be speedily done to procure forage for them, their horses must perish. I think a few companies of mounted men for patrol duty re all that are absolutely needed here at present.

I am convinced that Igou's Ferry is the most feasible point in this vicinity for laying a pontoon, if the enemy were so disposed. There is an eddy and but very slow current at that point. The water is low about 20 feet deep. The shore on this side, for some distance above and below, is perfectly commanded by high positions; on the other side, both above, below, and directly in front. The height below was fortified by Bragg when he first fell back, but the work has never been used. There are rifle-pits on the opposite bank immediately at the landing. A determined enemy could lay a pontoon here unless opposed vigorously.

The road on each side leading to the ferry is practicable for artillery. The guard at that point report the enemy constantly running trains for forage, up the river day and night, generally returning in about eight or ten hours.

The roads on the other side run near the river, and there is no means of reaching the back country, except by the road running directly back from the ferry. A party of determined men sent secretly across in that vicinity might easily capture and destroy a train, as they are reported to be but lightly guarded.

I can hear of no large force in my immediate front or anything of interest other than I have reported.

I am, colonel, very respectfully, your obedient servant,

R. F. SMITH,
Colonel Commanding Brigade.

OCTOBER 22, 1863—7.40 p. m.

Captain MERRILL,
Chief Signal Officer, Department of the Cumberland:

The enemy has extended his line to a point opposite Williams' Island. Sharpshooters have annoyed our troops passing on the road from foot of Walden's Ridge through the bottom between here and Chattanooga to-day. The road is within easy range of their sharpshooters.

Respectfully,

J. L. JONES,
Lieutenant, and Acting Signal Officer.

HDQRS. SIGNAL DETACHMENT, FOURTH ARMY CORPS,
Chattanooga, October 22, 1863.

Captain MERRILL,
Chief Signal Officer:

The following report has just been received from signal officer at Fort Wood:

Captain LEONARD:

To our left of old stone fence, where abandoned works are, the enemy have constructed two additional redoubts, making four at that point. Farther to our left, on a knoll east of white house near our picket line, they have also constructed four log redoubts, in one of which, I think, is a brass gun. There are two limbers in rear of the redoubt. They must have built these works last night. I saw them at work to our left of the fence where abandoned works are, but not at the other point, on yesterday. I saw one regiment have inspection, another drilling this morning, and at noon a large body of men, without arms, collected at what appears to be headquarters on our left, where, from the display of a different flag from any that I have before seen, and the manner in which it was exhibited, I think some regiment was being presented with a flag.

This evening about a regiment moved from crest of ridge on road at the head quarters in direction of our left. I could not see where they went to for the timber. About a regiment also were at the headquarters on the crest of the ridge. Part of them moved toward our right and the remainder to the left.

Respectfully,

L. M. DE MOTTE,
Lieutenant, and Acting Signal Officer.

Respectfully,

WM. LEONARD,
Captain, and Acting Signal Officer.

WAR DEPARTMENT,
Washington, October 22, 1863—1.10 p. m.

Major-General GRANT,
Chattanooga, Tenn.:

I would suggest that General Sheridan is one of the best men in the army to organize and regulate transportation and supplies. He fully supplied General Curtis' army in midwinter over the most horrible roads. Should not all animals not absolutely required at Chattanooga be sent to the rear? Cannot a part of the troops be sent nearer the depots of provisions? As at Pittsburg, short forage can be sent forward on the backs of artillery and cavalry horses. Men can be successively detailed to carry forward provisions on their backs. Beef on the hoof can be driven over the mountains, and the ration of bread reduced. The issue of small rations can be temporarily suspended.

H. W. HALLECK,
General-in-Chief.

OCTOBER 22, 1863.

General HURLBUT, *Memphis:*

It is universally believed here that Wheeler, Roddey, and Forrest are on this side the Tennessee, between Tuscumbia and Decatur.

A pretty heavy force is directly ahead of my advance. Osterhaus yesterday had a pretty severe fight, losing 8 men and 20-odd wounded. Colonel Torrence, Thirtieth Iowa, is killed.

W. T. SHERMAN,
Major-General.

HEADQUARTERS FIFTEENTH ARMY CORPS,
Iuka, October 22, 1863.

Maj. Gen. S. A. HURLBUT,
Comdg. Sixteenth Army Corps, Memphis, Tenn.:

DEAR GENERAL: I have received yours of 20th, with copy of General Grant's of the 17th, at Cairo. Of course I know that General Grant will not stop at Louisville, but will go to Nashville. I have every reason to know that there is a heavy force of cavalry to my front. I don't suppose it is there by Bragg's order, but the result of an accident, they all having come south across Muscle Shoals. I have had the river examined at Eastport, and an old pilot at Waterloo reports all fords now impracticable and navigation good for 4 feet up to Eastport. I have had a regiment there for three days, but it came in this evening. But I will send another down and keep it there till I hear something positive about a boat. I must have one to cross, for there are no boats in the Tennessee, and to build flats to cross an army would be a big job. But I feel that I am already ful- filling General Halleck's plan in occupying the attention of a mate- rial part of Bragg's men—all his cavalry. The break in the railroad at Bear Creek is very bad—the bridge itself and a great many small trestles for 3 miles out to Buzzard Roost—but Colonel Flad is very active and promises me the road across Bear Creek by Sunday. I was down, but mistrust his ability. Still, Fuller's brigade cannot be up by that time, and I cannot well leave till he is here to cover this point.

I will go to Tuscumbia to attack this cavalry, and may cross at Eastport, according to whether I can get my boats up to Florence or not. Osterhaus, in the advance, has had some hard skirmishing, as he says, with Stephen D. Lee's cavalry, but he drove the enemy in every instance, only at some cost. I will send all my reports through you, and will be obliged if you will forward them to General Grant's headquarters and telegraph such parts to Halleck as you may deem proper.

Yours, truly,

W. T. SHERMAN,
Major-General, Commanding.

HEADQUARTERS FIFTEENTH ARMY CORPS,
Iuka, Miss., October 22, 1863.

Brig. Gen. GRENVILLE M. DODGE,
Corinth:

DEAR GENERAL: I thank you for the budget of news, which is most serviceable, as we can approximate the truth. Of course, here I am balked by Bear Creek, which is a worse break than was repre- sented to me. I have my three leading divisions across Bear Creek, and all hands are busy at the bridge and trestles. The enemy skir- mished briskly the day before yesterday and yesterday. We have lost 8 killed and about 35 wounded in all. Among the dead is Colonel Torrence, Thirtieth Iowa.

I think it well established that both Lee, who came from Jack- son, Clinton, and Canton, with about 4,000 good cavalry, is to my front with Roddey's brigade, and I think also that Wheeler's cav- alry has been driven out of Tennessee, and is now resting between here and Decatur. If all this cavalry turns on me I will have a nice time, but can't help it, and if Porter gets me up some boats to East- port I will checkmate them. The Tennessee is in very fine boating order for 4 feet, and I expect daily a boat up from Cairo; also a ferry boat.

I have had the river examined well, and am more than satisfied we cannot ford even on the shoals. Of course, I don't believe the report you sent of the capture of Banks and fifteen regiments. Dick Taylor was somewhere west of the river, between Alexandria and Shreveport. That is ground familiar to me, and I know Dick Tay- lor cannot get to the east side of the Mississippi with anything like an army. After the capture of Vicksburg we relaxed our efforts and subsided. The secesh, on the contrary, increased theirs amazingly.

The rascals displayed an energy worthy a better cause ; but so it is
But when they come to the pinch they don't fight equal to th
numbers. Chalmers' dispatch is a sample. He captured the cam]
of the Seventh Illinois, off on Hatch's expedition. Nothing els
of moment, but he may again attempt the road; but Hurlbut ha
plenty to checkmate him, if he don't attempt to follow, but antici
pate him and interpose between the railroad and Tallahatchie.
propose to finish the bridge and prepare to move on to Tuscum
bia, but in the end may actually cross at Eastport. My orders ar
fully comprehended in thus drawing from Rosecrans the cavalry
that have heretofore bothered him. I had a regiment at Eastport
A party crossed over who saw no one, but heard the river was pa
troled so as to report all our movements.

I will fortify this place somewhat, so that if the enemy's cavalry
attempts to operate against it they will catch more than they bar
gain for. Corinth is too formidable a place for them to dream o
an attack, but you should keep a couple of regiments disposable t
take the offensive.

I am much obliged for all information, and will impart all posi
tive information to you. Keep me well advised from day to day o1
Fuller's approach.

I have one brigade at Barnesville, two here, and three divisions
front of Bear Creek.

I am, &c.,

W. T. SHERMAN,
Major-General, Commanding.

CHATTANOOGA, TENN., *October* 22, 1863—12 noon.
(Received 6 p. m., 23d.)

Major-General HALLECK, *General-in-Chief:*

By courier I learn that Burnside had a fight yesterday with the
enemy at Philadelphia. Result unknown. He is concentrating at
Kingston. Has withdrawn his cavalry from Post Oak Springs.
River only observed by courier from mouth of Sale Creek up. I
have it guarded as well as I can from Sale Creek down. Scouts
report that a considerable force marched toward Knoxville day
before yesterday. Deserters report that their heavy guns were removed five or six days since. Their force in our front does not
diminish in appearance. We are getting supplies enough, notwithstanding the loss of wagons by Wheeler's raid and the bad condition
of the roads hence to Bridgeport. Hope to move Hooker in a few
days, to open the wagon road and railroad from here to Bridgeport.

GEO. H. THOMAS,
Major-General.

CHATTANOOGA, *October* 22, 1863.

Major-General BURNSIDE :

Our advices indicate activity on the part of the enemy and a
movement of troops toward Loudon. We will guard the river as
far up as Smith's Ferry, but can go no higher. Let us hear from
you.

Very respectfully, your obedient servant,

GEO. H. THOMAS,
Major-General, Commanding.

CHATTANOOGA, *October* 22, 1863.
(Received 26th.)

Major-General BURNSIDE:

Every effort should be made to increase your small-arm ammunition to 500 rounds and artillery to 300 rounds.

U. S. GRANT,
Major-General.

LOUDON, *October* 22, 1863—6 p. m.

General BURNSIDE:

The cavalry have returned to camp. The enemy occupy Philadelphia. It is the half-way ground between this place and Sweet Water.

Our line of battle to-day was formed within half a mile of that place. Beyond our line the road winds through a defile; they had troops on either flank, and doubtless designed to entrap us. The skirmishing to-day was without material results.

JULIUS WHITE,
Brigadier-General.

LOUDON, *October* 22, 1863.

General BURNSIDE:

On the morning of Tuesday, the 20th, I reached Sweet Water about 11 a. m. I met at that point the advance of General Vaughn's, formerly Forrest's, division of cavalry. He violated my flag and kept me a prisoner until this morning.

There is at Sweet Water the division of General Stevenson, numbering about 8,000 infantry, with artillery. They are exchanged Vicksburg prisoners. Have you a locomotive or train you can send me? I would like to come up immediately, unless you are coming down here.

DUNCAN A. PELL,
Captain, and Aide-de-Camp.

KNOXVILLE, *October* 22, 1863—1.30 a. m.
(Received 3.50 p. m.)

His Excellency ABRAHAM LINCOLN,
President:

Your dispatch received. We have already over 3,000 in the three-years' service and half armed; about 2,500 home guards. Many more recruits could have been had for the three-years' service but for the want of clothing and camp equipage; we have not means of bringing those things with us, and since our arrival we have not been able to accumulate them by transportation from Kentucky.

Our command is now and has been ever since our arrival on half rations of everything, except fresh beef. We have no rations of beans, rice, pickles, &c., in fact no small stores but sugar, coffee, and salt; but the command is remarkably happy, cheerful, and willing, and I hope we are all ready for any ordinary emergency. The country thus far has supplied an abundance of forage. We are suffering considerably for want of shoes and clothing, and horseshoes. I have told General Halleck fully as to our position. A road has been surveyed, from Clinton to the mouth of Big South Fork on the Cumberland, from which point are transported supplies. After the Cumberland River becomes navigable to that place we will commence work on it at once with a view to making a good winter road. It runs along the line of the projected railroad and will be of material assistance in building the railroad. The railroad is already built from this place to within 8 miles of Clinton and is graded that 8 miles. I hope to take iron enough from the track above. I have to finish this grade to Clinton, and I have already made arrangements to build the railroad bridge at that place. The abutments are already built. After the wagon road is repaired, the entire force will be put to work grading the railroad from Clinton to the Cumberland to meet the road we are building in Kentucky. I have understood that some obstacles have been thrown in the way of this work by persons declaring that the expenditures would not be authorized. If such is the case, I should have been notified of it, and thereby save myself and others connected with the work, very serious embarrassment. I am daily becoming more satisfied of wisdom, necessity, and efficiency of the work.

A. E. BURNSIDE,
Major-General.

KNOXVILLE, October 22, 1863—3 a. m.

Major-General GRANT:

Your dispatch received. It is owing altogether to the circumstances as to which is the key point in East Tennessee. If we are here with a view to co-operate with the Army of the Cumberland alone, and uniting with that army in case of any reverse to either, a point opposite Kingston on the north side of the Tennessee River is certainly the key point; if we are expected to hold the line between Southwest Kentucky and Chattanooga with a view to creating a diversion in favor of, or rendering assistance to, either army in Kentucky or the Army of the Cumberland, then it is [plain] to me that Loudon, Knoxville, and some point as far up the road as possible should be strongly held.

A dispatch from Halleck to-day, a copy of which he sent to you, would indicate that he now regards the latter place as the proper one, which I did not understand to be his position before. If Kingston is regarded as the key-point, the line of railroad from Bristol to Loudon should be held, I think, by just force enough to completely destroy it upon the approach of the enemy, and fall back upon Kingston, evacuating the entire country east of it, except such portions of it as could be held by small bodies of cavalry.

I have already taken steps for the improvement of the road from Clinton to the mouth of the Big South Fork.

Steps taken by me toward building a railroad from the Cumberland to this. I will have working parties put on the road at once from Kingston to McMinnville, by way of Crossville and Sparta. Cannot working parties be sent out from McMinnville to meet ours ?

We need about 25,000 suits of clothing. We have been on half rations ever since our arrival of everything except fresh beef and bread ; in fact we have had no small rations except sugar, coffee, and salt, but the command is in good condition and ready for any ordered emergency.

A. E. BURNSIDE,
Major-General.

KNOXVILLE, *October* 22, 1863.
(Received 24th.)

Major-General GRANT:

The following dispatch was sent to General Halleck last night:

Your dispatch (21st) received. All portions of this command have been kept in readiness to move at a moment's notice ever since our arrival, and in fact have kept a moving nearly all the time. Our last move up the country was made with a view to discovering the enemy above the Virginia line and showing him that we were ready to meet any force that he might send against us in that direction, and possibly creating a diversion in favor of Meade's army. Had I felt that Rosecrans' army was perfectly secured, I should have pushed the movement farther with a view to the destruction of the salt-works, but my instructions and Rosecrans' call for assistance forbid. I will communicate fully with General Grant and hope to be able to successfully meet any emergency that may arise. The enemy attacked our cavalry under Colonel Wolford yesterday at Philadelphia, driving them back upon Loudon, capturing six mountain howitzers and a portion of the wagon train and camp equipage. To-day we have driven them back beyond Philadelphia. It is reported that the attacking column is composed of infantry, artillery, and cavalry, under command of Buckner, but I am disinclined to believe it. We are ready, however, to make a good defense.

Loudon has been pretty well fortified and has been considerably re-enforced. I hope to report more definitely to-morrow the nature of the attacking force. The indications now are that the enemy is advancing in considerable force on to Loudon, and it is also reported that they are crossing between Post Oak Springs and Cotton-port. This last report is not well defined.

A. E. BURNSIDE,
Major-General.

HEADQUARTERS SIXTEENTH ARMY CORPS,
Memphis, Tenn., October 22, 1863.

Brig. Gen. ROBERT ALLEN,
Saint Louis, Mo.:

Sherman has just telegraphed that there is 8 feet of water on shoals in Tennessee River. Send him a good ferry-boat as soon as possible. Wheeler's cavalry are at Decatur and Florence, 8,000 strong.

S. A. HURLBUT,
Major-General.

MEMPHIS, TENN., *October* 22, 1863.
(Received 12.45 p. m., 27th.)

Major-General HALLECK,
General-in-Chief:

General Sherman telegraphs that Wheeler's cavalry is on the south side of the Tennessee, and cut off by high water from Bragg. He urgently asks for a steam ferry-boat. A pretty heavy force is opposing his advance. Osterhaus had a pretty severe fight yesterday, losing 8 killed and 20 wounded. Colonel Torrence, Thirtieth Iowa, is killed. Dodge telegraphs from Corinth that Pickett went to Grenada to check McPherson's movement from Vicksburg. Few troops on Mobile and Ohio Railroad. Davis reviewed Bragg's troops on the 11th and 12th, and has gone back to Richmond. Chalmers is south of Tallahatchie, recruiting for another move on railroad.

S. A. HURLBUT,
Major-General.

(Same to Grant.)

CORINTH, *October* 22, 1863.

Major-General HURLBUT,
          Memphis:

Southern dates to 18th. On 15th Johnston left Meridian fc
Mobile.

Chalmers sends following dispatch, dated Byhalia, October 12:

We have torn up the railroad in four places and attacked Collierville yesterda
morning. Sherman, with part of Smith's brigade, *en route* for Corinth, arrived a
we did. We drove the enemy into their intrenchments and burned his camp, wit
considerable stores, also 30 wagons, and brought off 20. We took 5 colors and 1(
prisoners. Our loss was 50 killed and wounded. The enemy's loss very heav
General Smith and Colonel Anthony were killed. Re-enforcements coming fro
Germantown and La Fayette. We retreated.

Chalmers' Jackson dispatch of 15th, pretending to be taken fron
New Orleans papers, says Dick Taylor has captured Banks an
fifteen regiments ; that 1,300 paroled prisoners arrived at Ne
Orleans. Charleston dates say that both sides are firing withou
much effect ; that Gilmer was still at work. Richmond dates clair
that Lee took 700 prisoners at Warrenton. Davis has returned t
Richmond. An able editorial in relation to his visit says Davis i
determined to repossess Tennessee ; that it has fed his armies an
we must have it ; that Bragg, in the center, will press Rosecrans
that Lee will sweep down on East Tennessee, while the Mississipj
army comes up on the left ; that the big battle will be fought som
distance from Chattanooga, and that soon.

Accounts from Northern Louisiana give doleful accounts of th
spirits of the citizens. Hopes late victories will cheer them up
Papers are full of orders for paroled Vicksburg troops to rendezvou
at Enterprise, Miss.

G. M. DODGE,
Brigadier-General.

HDQRS. FIRST DIVISION, FIFTEENTH ARMY CORPS,
          Cherokee, Ala., October 22, 1863.

Capt. R. M. SAWYER,
          Asst. Adjt. Gen., Hdqrs. Fifteenth Army Corps:

CAPTAIN : I had an engagement with the enemy yesterday, th
official report of which was forwarded through Maj. Gen. F. P. Blail
jr. To-day I ordered my wounded to be brought to the rear. Pleas
send a train to Clear Creek Station, if you think proper, to meet th
ambulances.

I am, captain, very respectfully, your obedient servant,

P. JOS. OSTERHAUS,
Brigadier-General, Commanding.

P. S.—I ascertained this morning that General Lee, with tw
brigades, was in my front yesterday.

COLUMBUS, KY., *October* 22, 1863.

Col. J. K. MILLS,
          Commanding, Union City:

Colonel Black just informs me from Paducah that Faulkner an
Newsom were at McLemoresville at 10 a m. on the 20th, intendin

to move on Mayfield, to gobble up the company at that point. Keep a sharp watch out in the direction of Boydsville, and move a sufficient cavalry force in that direction. If you ascertain the report to be true, follow them up and cut off their retreat. They are reported to be 700 strong.

> A. J. SMITH,
> *Brigadier-General.*

HEADQUARTERS SIXTEENTH ARMY CORPS,
Memphis, Tenn., October 22, 1863.
Brig. Gen. GRENVILLE M. DODGE,
Corinth, Miss. :

Faulkner has crossed the Tennessee to break up the repairs of the railroad. Ascertain his strength and send word to our force in or north of Jackson. Lee's 500 are to replace the troops gone south. It will be necessary to be very watchful over Wheeler and others, as they may avoid Sherman's infantry and come around upon our line.

Chalmers is at Water Valley, repairing railroad and getting supplies. I have heard nothing of Harrison until now. These disorderly recruiters cost more than they come to. Anything heard from Spencer yet?

> S. A. HURLBUT,
> *Major-General.*

CORINTH, *October 22, 1863.*
Major-General HURLBUT,
Memphis :

Scout in from Decatur. Wheeler's division, Lee's division, two brigades of General Walker's, Roddey's brigade all below Decatur and Tuscumbia on south side of river. Colonel Forrest, with 350 men, near Cane Creek ; they say they are going to make a raid into rear of Sherman on Memphis and Charleston Railroad. There is no doubt that they are there. Don't think they will come this way very soon.

> G. M. DODGE,
> *Brigadier-General.*

CORINTH, *October 22,* [1863.]
Maj. Gen. STEPHEN A. HURLBUT,
Memphis :

Scout left Okolona yesterday morning. One week ago last Monday, Loring went round to Grenada with his forces to check a move of our forces from Vicksburg. Adams' troops are scattered on Mobile and Ohio, and Meridian and Jackson Railroad. Two regiments of Loring's went to Selma, and one, the Twenty-sixth Mississippi, went to Eutaw, Greene County, Ala. Hare went to New Albany on Monday. No troops at Okolona. Report is current that Grant and his army are moving this way to Rosecrans. Jeff. Davis reviewed Bragg's troops on the 11th and 12th. Chalmers is south of Wyatt fixing for another raid. I will send newspaper extracts. Could hear nothing of McPherson.

> G. M. DODGE,
> *Brigadier-General.*

MUNFORDVILLE, *October* 22, 1863.

Capt. A. C. SEMPLE,
          Louisville:

Your dispatch received.   Messenger just in from Greensburg. Rebels left there last night ; at 12 o'clock returned south ; they are by this time on the Cumberland.   Robbed bank, stores, &c.; they made no distinction.   Part of the force went in direction of New Haven.   It is supposed that only 50 or 100 left in that direction. The force sent from this place last night will pursue them.   It embraces part of Thirty-third Kentucky, Captain Baker's company, Thirty-fifth Kentucky, and all the available mounted force at Glasgow.   I have instructed Colonel Strickland to mount all the force he could at Glasgow, and look out for the party in every direction.   I have used every saddle at this post to mount men last night.   No horses here, no saddles at Glasgow.   Is it necessary to pursue on foot?   If you wish, as soon as I can get detachment will go to Greensburg and arrest all persons giving aid and comfort.   Answer.

E. H. HOBSON,
Brigadier-General.

MUNFORDVILLE, *October* 22, 1863.

Captain SEMPLE, *Louisville:*

Say to Colonel Weatherford that all my force is out.   They are either in pursuit of rebels going south from Greensburg or followed those going toward New Haven.   Special messenger left with instructions for Captain Hare to move his mounted force in direction of Lebanon Branch.   The remaining force left at Glasgow are without horses or equipments.   If they will mount 100 men at Lebanon there will be no difficulty in driving the rebels from the road.

E. H. HOBSON,
Brigadier-General.

MUNFORDVILLE, *October* 22, 1863.

Captain SEMPLE,
          Assistant Adjutant-General:

My cavalry and mounted infantry, 200 strong, left here last night, with instructions to get on track of rebels and follow them.   I have sent special messenger to Captain Hare, at Nolin, to intercept them, if possible.

E. H. HOBSON,
Brigadier-General.

CHATTANOOGA, TENN., *October* 23, 1863—9.30 p. m.
(Received 10 p. m., 25th.)

Maj. Gen. H. W. HALLECK,
          General-in-Chief:

Have just arrived.   I will write to-morrow.   Please approve order placing General Sherman in command of Department and Army of the Tennessee, with headquarters in the field.   I think it much preferable to leave departments as they are to consolidating the three into one.

U. S. GRANT,
Major-General, Commanding.

HEADQUARTERS CHIEF OF CAVALRY,
Decherd, October 23, 1863.

General GEORGE CROOK,
 Commanding Cavalry, Maysville:

We have rumors that Generals Wheeler and Lee are preparing to cross the river and make another raid on our communications. From captured dispatches of General Wheeler we learn that General Lee's cavalry, said to be 2,500, had arrived at Florence. What do you hear of the movements of Wheeler, Lee, and Roddey? General Mitchell directs me to inquire.

WM. H. SINCLAIR,
Assistant Adjutant-General.

STEVENSON, *October* 23, 1863.

Major-General REYNOLDS,
 Chief of Staff:

I am informed that railroad transportation will now be furnished to concentrate my command at Bridgeport. General Crook, under date of 21st, advises me that Roddey swam Elk River Sunday, and has now crossed the Tennessee. The river still impassable. Wheeler across the river patrolling the banks. Crook will try and get news of Sherman. Sent scouting party down river in boats on 19th for that purpose, to go as far as shoals. Captain Gurley and his brother, a lieutenant, have been captured. Gurley was the murderer of McCook. Heavy rains last night and now.

JOSEPH HOOKER,
Major-General.

BROWNSBOROUGH,
October 23, 1863.

Brigadier-General GARFIELD,
 Chief of Staff:

My scouts have returned from the other side of Athens, and report that General Roddey with his force only went to Mooresville, where he remained until Sunday morning, when he swam Elk River, and it is said by all the citizens that he has crossed the Tennessee. The Elk River is still impassable. I arrived here Saturday evening. I sent a scouting party down Flint River in a boat to navigate the Tennessee down to the shoals. They will find out all the particulars. Captain Kilburn, with a scouting party, last night caught the notorious Captain Gurley and his brother, a lieutenant, who murdered General McCook. I have caught several of their men since I have been here. If I remain here I hope to clear this country of guerrillas before long.

Yours, respectfully,

GEORGE CROOK,
Brigadier-General.

NEAR MAYSVILLE,
October 23, 1863—11 a. m.

Lieut. Col. C. GODDARD :

General Lee arrived on the opposite side of the river the day Wheeler recrossed. I had reported this fact to General Mitchell at

Decherd.   My scouting parties report that they are not crossing to this side.   The Tennessee River cannot be forded, and with facilities they have for crossing the river it would be a very difficult matter for them to cross.   I will know positively, however, in very short time whether they are crossing or not.   My horses are so badly used up for want of shoes and the hard service they have done the last month, that I could not get on more than half my command, and they with only poor horses.   I wanted to remain at Decherd and get my command in good condition, but I was peremptorily ordered here. Thus far, owing to the high waters, I have been unable to get horses, stores, or clothing for my men, but I expect to get some to-day.

> GEORGE CROOK,
> *Brigadier-General.*

> STEVENSON,
> *October* 23, 1863—2.20 p. m.

Brig. Gen. R. S. GRANGER,
Nashville:

A cavalry guerrilla force of 800, not well armed or well organized, are now at Milton.   A scout of General Slocum's was in their camp yesterday.   Their intention is to cut our communications.   General Hooker expects you to look after them and disperse them.   Acknowledge.

> DANL. BUTTERFIELD,
> *Major-General, Chief of Staff.*

> WAR DEPARTMENT,
> *Washington, October* 23, 1863—4 p. m.

Major-General BURNSIDE,
Knoxville, Tenn.:

I can learn nothing further of Lee's movements.   Would it not be well for your cavalry to destroy the railroad north of Holston River as far as possible, and also to remove all supplies from the upper part of the valley, so that the enemy can find no subsistence?   Some time ago I ordered an expedition from West Virginia to cut the railroad above Wytheville, but have heard nothing of it.   Could you subsist any additional troops, if sent to you?

> H. W. HALLECK,
> *General-in-Chief.*

> HEADQUARTERS SIXTEENTH ARMY CORPS,
> *Memphis, Tenn., October* 23, 1863.

Major-General SHERMAN,
In the Field:

Rosecrans telegraphs to Halleck that on the 10th General Crook defeated Wheeler and drove him over the Tennessee and captured 4 pieces of artillery, 1,000 stand of arms, and 740 prisoners besides wounded.   Total loss estimated, 2,000.

These troops now on this side will probably annoy you and send a force round to operate on this road or will be recalled to Rome.

I have again urgently sent for a steam ferry-boat and have reported to Admiral Porter.

> S. A. HURLBUT,
> *Major-General.*

IUKA, *October 23, 1863.*

Major-General HURLBUT,
          Memphis:

One of my aides is just back from the front. All well to-day. Plenty of forage at the front. The forces encountered yesterday were Lee's cavalry, two brigades, and the only reason why we lost some officers and men was that one of our advance regiments mistook the enemy for our own people on account of their having some of our blue overcoats. Railroad beyond Cane Creek doubtless badly destroyed. I can use it up to Eastport and now need only a steamer. I keep a regiment at Eastport to advise me of an arrival. I send one of my aides to the bridge this afternoon to report progress, but I calculate the bridge being done by Sunday night.

W. T. SHERMAN,
                    Major-General.

(Same to Dodge.)

CORINTH, *October 23, 1863.*

Major-General HURLBUT,
          Memphis:

I heard from Spencer three days out. All right. I hope Sherman's advance will draw their attention from him. Sherman has lost about 40 killed and wounded skirmishing. Colonel Torrence, Thirtieth Iowa, killed. Have sent a man to Jackson. Did not know we had troops there. Where is McPherson?

G. M. DODGE,
                    Brigadier-General.

CORINTH, *October 23, 1863.*

Major-General SHERMAN:

Falkner, who went with Lee, has crossed Tennessee at Tuscumbia and at Swallow Bluff, and is now between here and Jackson, no doubt to break up the railroad to Columbus and stop the repairs. Five hundred of Lee's cavalry passed down the Tuscumbia and Cotton-gin road three nights ago. No doubt were going to replace the force that left Okolona.

Chalmers is at Water Valley, repairing damages, building railroad, &c. Do not hear of McPherson. Fuller will be at Chewalla to-night.

G. M. DODGE,
                    Brigadier-General.

HEADQUARTERS SIXTEENTH ARMY CORPS,
          Memphis, Tenn., October 23, 1863.

Maj. Gen. J. B. McPHERSON,
          Commanding Seventeenth Corps, Vicksburg:

I inclose you letter from Dodge. * Wheeler's entire cavalry has been driven south of the Tennessee, say 8,000, and are now cut off by the rise of the river from Middle Tennessee. They are annoying

---

* See Dodge to Harris, October 21, p. 691.

Sherman considerably, and will be around on my line soon, if they do not start back for Rome.

Colonel Spencer, with his Alabama cavalry, has started four days since for Selma, to destroy the road. Grant is at Louisville. No other news of consequence.

Yours,

S. A. HURLBUT,
Major-General.

HEADQUARTERS FIFTEENTH ARMY CORPS,
Iuka, October 23, 1863.

Major-General HURLBUT,
    Commanding, Memphis:

DEAR GENERAL: I have this moment received the notice * by telegraph that General Grant is to command the Armies of the Ohio, the Cumberland, and the Tennessee, and that I am to command the latter.

I have striven hard to avoid large and independent commands, but am so impressed with the wisdom and importance of this change that I will undertake anything. I think my position here at the shoulder of the Tennessee is a great point for offense or defense, and I must make it tell.

Before sending ammunition for the Burnside carbines wait for the requisition, which goes in to-morrow.

W. T. SHERMAN,
Major-General.

HEADQUARTERS SEVENTEENTH ARMY CORPS,
Vicksburg, Miss., October 23, 1863.

Brig. Gen. JOHN P. HAWKINS,
    Commanding Goodrich's Landing:

GENERAL: Your letter in relation to the employment of a portion of your command in repairing the levees at and in the vicinity of Lake Providence duly received, and forwarded to the major-general commanding the department.

As far as my observation goes, I do not think the present scheme of leasing and working plantations will be of much benefit to the General Government, and I have no doubt that the plan suggested by you of dividing up the plantations into half and quarter sections, and letting them out to industrious laborers of the Northwest would, if carried out, be far more remunerative to the United States, and would eventually result in getting a loyal population along the river sufficiently numerous to protect itself against guerrilla raids, but I doubt whether there is any law for confiscating and dividing up plantations in this manner; and, furthermore, what we want now is soldiers to crush out the rebellion, and, in order that so many may not be required for defensive purposes, simply to hold the country passed over by our troops, we want some strongly fortified places, which comparatively small garrisons can hold, thereby rendering a large portion of the army available for offensive warfare. Therefore, I consider that

---

* Telegraphed by Hurlbut.

your force can be better employed, for the present at least, drilling and erecting fortifications, than in repairing levees; besides, I want as many men here as I can possibly get, to construct the new line of defenses.

Very respectfully, your obedient servant,

JAS. B. McPHERSON,
Major-General.

HEADQUARTERS SOUTHERN CENTRAL KENTUCKY,
Munfordville, October 23, 1863.

Capt. A. C. SEMPLE,
Assistant Adjutant-General:

This post can be held with the force now here belonging to the Second Ohio Volunteer Heavy Artillery. Would it not be a good idea to mount the battalion of the Thirty-third Kentucky Volunteer Infantry, if it can be done? They can be made very effective for scouting purposes. The present mounted force is inefficient, and it is perfect nonsense to think of hunting down rebels with infantry. If we do not get a mounted force, and that speedily, the southern central portion of Kentucky will be subjected to constant raids. In addition the mounted force can move quickly, more thoroughly protect the railroad by using them on the border counties. I have no saddles and but few bridles, and indifferent horses. Requisitions have been made for horses and equipments. Please give my suggestion your earnest attention, and, if favored, assist me in carrying it out.

Very respectfully,

HOBSON,
Brigadier-General.

MUNFORDVILLE, *October 23, 1863.*

Colonel STRICKLAND, *Glasgow:*

Richardson plundered Bardstown this morning. Wires cut on Lebanon branch. Send your 45 men up Bardstown pike toward New Haven. If they require fresh horses, let them get them on road; deliver them to owners when they return. If they meet with any of Major Martin's force on the way, let them go with them. Captain Hare's men were ordered from Nolin last night, going in same direction.

E. H. HOBSON,
Brigadier-General.

MUNFORDVILLE, *October* 23, 1863—11 a. m.

Captain SEMPLE,
Assistant Adjutant-General, Louisville:

Forty-five men have been mounted at Glasgow, and will move toward New Haven. Captain Hare was ordered last night from Nolin to move toward Lebanon branch road. Have not heard from Major Martin. Suppose he is in pursuit of rebels going south from Greensburg. All means for mounting men at this place and Glasgow have been exhausted.

E. H. HOBSON,
Brigadier-General.

MUNFORDVILLE,
October 23, 1863—6.35 p. m.

Captain SEMPLE,
Assistant Adjutant-General, Louisville:

Sixty-five rebels went north from Greensburg. All the roads are guarded. Hope they may be intercepted on their return.

E. H. HOBSON,
Brigadier-General.

WAR DEPARTMENT,
Washington, October 24, 1863—11.40 a. m.

Major-General GRANT,
Chattanooga, Tenn.:

From advices received last night it is pretty certain that Ewell's corps, from 20,000 to 25,000 men, has left Lee's army and gone to Tennessee, probably by way of Abingdon. As Burnside will be obliged to move all his forces up the valley, you must guard against Bragg's entrance into East Tennessee, above Chattanooga.

H. W. HALLECK,
General-in-Chief.

CHATTANOOGA, TENN., *October* 24, 1863—8. p. m.
(Received 5.25, 25th.)

Maj. Gen. H. W. HALLECK,
General-in-Chief:

All animals that can be spared will go back to-morrow to forage. One division of troops started this evening to Dave Rankin's Ferry, to seize that place, to enable Hooker to possess the roads to Mountain Creek. Once there we will have water communications to within 4 miles of here, and can supply this place with beef cattle, or have them driven here as required. Rations have been reduced. The enemy is closely watched, but if he should move against Burnside, or break through our lines between here and Burnside, it would be difficult in the present condition of the roads to follow. I will, however, do the best possible.

U. S. GRANT,
Major-General.

GENERAL ORDERS, } HDQRS. DEPT. AND ARMY OF THE TENN.,
No. 1.   }   *Iuka, Miss., October* 24, 1863.

I. Pursuant to General Orders, No. 2, from headquarters Military Division of the Mississippi, Louisville, Ky., of date October 19, 1863, the undersigned hereby assumes command of the Department and Army of the Tennessee.

II. Maj. R. M. Sawyer, assistant adjutant-general, is announced as chief of staff.

W. T. SHERMAN,
Major-General.

CHATTANOOGA, *October* 24, 1863.

Iaj. Gen. WILLIAM T. SHERMAN,
        Corinth, Miss.:

Drop everything east of Bear Creek and move with your entire
orce toward Stevenson until you receive further orders. The enemy
re evidently moving a large force toward Cleveland, and may break
1rough our lines and move on Nashville, in which event your troops
re the only forces at command that could beat them there. With
our forces here before the enemy cross the Tennessee we could turn
1eir position so as to force them back and save the possibility of a
1ove northward this winter.

                              U. S. GRANT,
                                   Major-General.

NOTE.—Sent in care of General Crook, Brownsborough, to be for-
arded with all haste.

HDQRS. DEPARTMENT AND ARMY OF THE TENNESSEE,
                Iuka, Miss., October 24, 1863.

rig. Gen. JOHN A. RAWLINS,
        Chief of Staff, &c.:

GENERAL: I have this moment received at the hands of Lieuten-
1t Dunn, aide-de-camp, copies of your General Orders, Nos. 1 and
  and your communication of October 19,* which shall have my
1mediate and undivided attention.

Two gunboats, under Lieutenant-Commander Phelps, arrived at
astport, and that officer is now with me, and I will proceed at once
» pass a division over the Tennessee to move to Florence, and I
1ve three divisions in front of Bear Creek, that have had several
1arp encounters with the enemy's cavalry. I have ordered them,
1-morrow, to drive them beyond Tuscumbia. The railroad is now
. fine order from Memphis to Bear Creek, but the break in the
1ad beyond is serious and repairs proceed too slow, but I hope to
1ve the head of my column so advanced that it will influence
1ur enemy in front of Chattanooga. I will persevere to reach
1e neighborhood of Athens, the point designated in General Hal-
ck's orders. I see no reason for a large regiment at Paducah,
1d will order it up in boats to Eastport and Waterloo.

I will order General Smith, at Columbus, to take a force of
1valry or mounted infantry to sweep down from Columbus to
rand Junction, taking all the available horses in the country.
. is useless to be too delicate on this score. Either the United
1ates or guerrillas must have all the horses in that region, and we
1ight as well act on that supposition. I will also instruct General
. J. Smith to instruct the officer in command to notify the Union
1ople that they must now take sides and expel the guerrillas, else
1eir country will be constantly liable to the destruction of pur-
1ing parties of cavalry.

The Tennessee River is now available to us for supplies, and, if
1ecessary, we could absolutely abandon the railroad, but as Corinth,
1 Grange, and other points have formed so effectual a barrier in
1e past, I would like General Grant to order in the case. If infor-
1ation from Chattanooga indicated any danger to your army I

---

*See Series I, Vol. XXX, Part III, p. —.

would drop everything and hasten forward, but General Halleck'
orders were positive, to mend road and look to supplies as I pro
gressed, and this has delayed me.

I wish, if you have not already done so, that you would open com
munication with me at Florence.

I will write to General Steele, and will do all that is pointed ou
in your letter.

I am, &c.,

W. T. SHERMAN,
Major-General, Commanding.

HEADQUARTERS FIFTEENTH ARMY CORPS,
Iuka, October 24, 1863.

Maj. Gen. FRANK P. BLAIR, Jr.,
    Comdg. Advance Fifteenth Army Corps, Cherokee:

GENERAL : I take great pleasure in telling you that two gunboat
have come up to Eastport. Lieutenant-Commander Phelps write
that four more are coming. He found good water all the way up
but says it is now impossible to reach Florence on account of Colber
Shoals. He speaks of a good place to cross 3 miles above Eastpor
which must be on Colbert Shoals.

Please order a small party to reconnoiter down to the river from
Dickson's Station, i. e., John E. Smith's position. .

But my mind is almost concluded that Eastport is our chief poin
and that we can pass men rapidly, but horses and mules slowly, un
less about the foot of Colbert Shoals we can work with a raft fo
wagons, boats for the men, and swim our animals. I expect up soc
a good ferry-boat, but we can't wait for it ; I am behind time now
but first the cavalry to your front must be furnished.

You may send your wagons to the rear of John E. Smith, and
with the handy force of two divisions, push across Cane Creek, ge
ting a moonlight start, if possible, and get a good shot at the ca
alry, then resume your present ground, and I can commence crossin
the rear division first at Eastport.

I have telegraphic notice that Grant has command of the Armie
of the Ohio, the Cumberland, and the Tennessee, and I am to comman
the latter. This gives you the command of my corps; so you see
was right.

To attack cavalry with infantry is always a hard job, but yo
should strip as light of baggage as possible, get your field artillen
near the head of column, break through their picket line before da
light, and be among their camps and bivouacs as quick as possibl
Don't be drawn beyond Tuscumbia. Take what corn you need an
all serviceable horses, giving receipts. Tell Mr. Goodloe, if he sati
fies me further in the campaign that he is as good a Union man a
he ought to be, I will see that his receipts are taken up with cas
but at the outset he must take the same fare as others.

You may make this attack your own way, reporting to John I
Smith that his front is uncovered, that he may be on his guard.

I will draw forward my troops and prepare for the real move.

I expect Captain Phelps up in two hours, and will discuss th
whole subject of passing the Tennessee.

Your friend;

W. T. SHERMAN,
Major-General.

NASHVILLE, *October* 24, 1863.
(Received Wartrace, 24th.)

Iajor-General SLOCUM:

I received a letter from the President, earnestly requesting, if
ossible, that it should be done. I showed it to General Thomas.
Ie considered it a very difficult thing; impracticable at the time.
)ur troops were suffering the shock of consolidation of the Twentieth
nd Twenty-first Corps. It would be easier at a later period, or to
ive Hooker another corps. Sorry I did not see you.

W. S. ROSECRANS,
Major-General.

STEVENSON,
October 24, 1863—9.30 a. m.

Iajor-General REYNOLDS:

The following dispatch just received:

ELK RIVER, [*October*] 24.

The line was cut about 5 miles north of here last night between 5 and 6 o'clock.
. train was thrown off track by rebel guerrillas taking two or three rails out;
ome five or seven cars smashed up; engine turned over on her side. The train
as fired into by guerrillas, numbering from 75 to 100. Several men on train
ounded; none killed as far as known. Captain Sligh, of First Michigan Engi-
ers, had both legs badly smashed. Colonel Hunton is there, or was to be there
om Nashville this a. m. about 4 o'clock. Think track will be cleared sufficient to
t trains pass by 4 or 5 o'clock. Three box-cars and three or four flats, loaded with
erchandise and lumber, are all in a heap. I left there at 2 o'clock this a. m. Men
ad already commenced moving the wreck. Edwards, with men, will leave here
ith tools to help in a few minutes. Three trains now at Estill Springs.

WILLIAMS,
Operator.

JOSEPH HOOKER,
Major-General.

(Same to Goddard.)

HEADQUARTERS CHIEF OF CAVALRY,
Decherd, October 24, 1863.

rigadier-General CROOK,
Maysville:

We have information from Shelbyville that Wheeler is or was on
'hursday crossing the river at Lamb's Ferry. Have you heard any-
hing of it? Answer. The general commanding directs that you
old your command in readiness for any sudden movement.

WM. H. SINCLAIR,
Assistant Adjutant-General.

DECHERD, *October* 24, 1863.

Iajor-General THOMAS:

I have information from Colonel Galbraith, at Shelbyville, which
e considers reliable, that Wheeler was crossing, and had about half
f his command on this side of the Tennessee River on Thursday.

I think the whole command, including Crook's and the mounted infantry, should move at once to Fayetteville and meet him there. I have notified Crook of the information, and directed him to be ready to move at short notice. Send me orders what to do and what dispositions to make of the command at once.

R. B. MITCHELL,
Brigadier-General.

———

DECHERD,
October 24, 1863—10.30 p. m.

Major-General THOMAS:

Later information from Colonel Galbraith says he has reliable information to the effect that General Sherman's cavalry drove Wheeler across the river on Wednesday last. He has heard of only half of his force crossing. However, he has scouts out watching, and will report everything he learns.

R. B. MITCHELL,
Brigadier-General, Cammanding.

———

HEADQUARTERS DEPARTMENT OF THE CUMBERLAND,
Chattanooga, October 24, 1863.

Maj. Gen. JOSEPH HOOKER, *Stevenson:*

A dispatch just received from General R. S. Granger says you are turning over the Nashville and Chattanooga Railroad to him and withdrawing your troops. For fear you may not have received former orders, the general commanding directs me to repeat the order for you to leave one division of the Twelfth Corps to guard from Murfreesborough to and including Bridgeport. Acknowledge receipt of this order.

By order of Major-General Thomas:

C. GODDARD,
Assistant Adjutant-General.

———

HEADQUARTERS DEPARTMENT OF THE CUMBERLAND,
Chattanooga, October 24, 1863.

Maj. Gen. JOSEPH HOOKER, *Stevenson:*

The general commanding directs that the One hundred and second Ohio, now on the line of the railroad, probably at Tullahoma, be sent at once to Nashville. That as soon as the change can be effected Colonel Coburn's brigade, except the regiment at McMinnville, be concentrated at Murfreesborough, relieving the troops of the Twelfth Corps now there, and that Colonel Coburn's present guard duty be performed by the division of the Twelfth Corps, which previous orders directed you to leave to guard the railroad. That division will be held responsible for the road from Murfreesborough to Bridgeport, including that post, while Murfreesborough and the railroad north of there will be provided for from other troops. The change of troops from one station to another can be effected gradually, so as not to leave the road exposed.

By order of Major-General Thomas:

C. GODDARD,
Assistant Adjutant-General.

HEADQUARTERS DEPARTMENT OF THE CUMBERLAND,
Chattanooga, October 24, 1863—7 p. m.

General R. B. MITCHELL,
Decherd:

General Crook will probably ascertain whether Wheeler has crossed; if he has, concentrate and meet him as you may direct, say about Fayetteville. General Williams' troops will be replaced by others.

By order:

J. J. REYNOLDS,
Major-General.

CHATTANOOGA, *October 24, 1863.*

Brigadier-General MITCHELL:

In compliance with your request the general commanding has relieved you from duty with the cavalry and has assigned Brig. Gen. W. L. Elliott to your division. You are ordered to proceed to Nashville and await further orders. This will give you a chance to rest and recruit. You will retain command until the arrival of General Elliott, who will leave here to-morrow for Decherd.

By order of Major-General Thomas:

C. GODDARD,
Assistant Adjutant-General.

HEADQUARTERS CHIEF OF CAVALRY,
Decherd, October 24, 1863.

Col. E. M. McCOOK,
Commanding First Division Cavalry:

COLONEL: The general commanding directs me to inform you that we have information that Wheeler was crossing the river at Lamb's Ferry on Thursday. We are waiting orders from department headquarters, and shall probably move early in the morning. Hold your command in readiness.

I am, your obedient servant,

WM. H. SINCLAIR,
Assistant Adjutant-General.

GENERAL ORDERS, } HEADQUARTERS CHIEF OF ARTILLERY,
                     DEPARTMENT OF THE CUMBERLAND,
No. 7.   }   *Chattanooga, Tenn., October 24, 1863.*

1. Chiefs of artillery of divisions will select 100 of their best horses in the batteries of their divisions to be retained for service, the surplus above that number to be sent as soon as practicable to-morrow (October 25, 1863) to Stevenson, Ala., in charge of a commissioned officer from each division and enlisted men sufficient to allow one to each 4 horses. The officers in charge of these horses will report at Stevenson to Capt. George Estep, Eighth Indiana Battery, and with their men will remain in charge of the horses under his direction.

By command of Brigadier-General Brannan:

LOUIS J. LAMBERT,
Captain, Assistant Adjutant-General, Artillery.

WASHINGTON,
October 24, 1863—11.30 a. m.

Major-General BURNSIDE,
        Knoxville, Tenn.:

It now appears pretty certain that Ewell's corps has gone to Tennessee, and it is probable by Abingdon.   His force is estimated at from 20,000 to 25,000.   It is reported that he left Lee's army on Monday last, and did not pass through to Richmond.   It is therefore most probable that he passed through Lynchburg, taking the road to Abingdon.

H. W. HALLECK,
General-in-Chief.

LOUDON, TENN.,
October 24, 1863—4.30 a. m.

Major-General THOMAS, *Chattanooga:*

I arrived at this place last evening, and am convinced that a large force of the enemy is near this place with a cavalry advance at Philadelphia.   It is reported that Longstreet is in command, but the report is not well authenticated.   Under our orders to hold East Tennessee as high up as possible, we have necessarily to use a considerable portion of our cavalry in the eastern portion of the line, and the attack upon the brigade south of this place on the 20th resulted in the capture of all their camp equipage, clothing, and transportation, so that they are not in the best condition but can be used.   They have been re-enforced by about 800 mounted men from Knoxville.   We cannot do much more than picket river as far down as Blythe's Ferry, particularly while the enemy in our front threatens. We have infantry and artillery enough to make good defense here, unless we are greatly outnumbered, in which case the strength of enemy in your front will be diminished.

A. E. BURNSIDE.

HEADQUARTERS DEPARTMENT OF THE OHIO,
Loudon, Tenn., October 24, 1863—4 a. m.
(Received 10.20 p. m.)

Major-General HALLECK:

The following dispatch has just gone to General Thomas in answer to one from him informing me of a movement of troops in that direction :

We do not need any re-enforcements, as we have as many men as we can feed possibly more.   Much obliged for the offer of assistance.   We have been pursuing the course advised by you in regard to the railroads and the supplies.

A. E. BURNSIDE.

HEADQUARTERS DEPARTMENT OF THE TENNESSEE,
Iuka, October 24, 1863.

Major-General HURLBUT,
        Memphis:

I have now General Grant's Orders, 1 and 2; also a long letter which I will have copied and sent you, that you may see wherein are modified the previous orders.

First, I cannot change the current of events in the Mississippi proper, but will leave McPherson to control in the State of Mississippi and you in Tennessee. As McPherson must act offensively in two cases likely to occur, I do not propose to draw from him at all. I have written to Steele that General Grant expects him to send back Kimball's division of your corps, and the moment I have reason to believe he will do so, I must draw for them on your corps to make my movable force as strong as possible. I wish you to make orders that the regiment at Paducah, the One hundred and eleventh Illinois, proceed up the Tennessee to Waterloo, and march to Florence to report to me; the quartermaster to furnish transportation.

Notify the people of Paducah if any enemy of good government or manners insult or offend any of the Union people, the whole town will be held responsible, and the chief men banished and their property destroyed. It is time for Paducah to stop all nonsense. A garrison is no more needed there than at Saint Louis.

Order General Smith to organize as strong a mounted force as he can, to sweep down the country between the Tennessee and the Mississippi, moving so as to intimidate and destroy the small band that are engaged in enforcing the conscript law. The Tennessee being now patrolled by gunboats, there cannot be any considerable body in there, and the party so ordered can rendezvous at Pillow, Memphis, or Grand Junction. They will help themselves to corn, meat, and what they need, and take all good horses, giving simple receipts, to be settled for at the end of the war or according to circumstances. The officer commanding this party should be instructed to convey to the inhabitants this advice: They must organize and put down robbers and guerrillas. If they cannot, then they will be liable to be overrun and plundered by both sides. They must manifest not only Union sentiment, but must unite in self-defense, and in such a way as to assist the National Government.

Two gunboats have arrived, and Captain Phelps reports there are feet of water; enough for the Continental. There is no need of anything coming to me over the railroad. Please notify the quartermaster and commissary at Saint Louis that the Tennessee is in good boating order up to Eastport, and that I will receive goods at that point. I renew my demand for a ferry-boat.

I have not had time to mature my plans further than independent of the railroad. I shall proceed forthwith to push on or move divisions to Florence, so as to open communications ahead.

I may have to take some of your cavalry and more troops, but will wait for a return from you.

With much respect,

W. T. SHERMAN,
Major-General, Commanding.

IUKA, *October* 24, 1863.

Major-General HURLBUT,
          Memphis:

Gunboats Key West and Holly Springs arrived at Eastport all right. Notify Admiral Porter.

W. T. SHERMAN,
Major-General.

IUKA, *October* 24, 1863.

General HURLBUT:

Send me a field report of your corps, stations, strength for duty—especially at Columbus. Could we raise 1,000 men at Columbus to sweep down the country to Grand Junction, living on the country, gathering horses, mules, &c.? Gunboats will now make the Tennessee impassable to anybody from the east.

W. T. SHERMAN,
Major-General.

HEADQUARTERS SIXTEENTH ARMY CORPS,
Memphis, Tenn., October 24, 1863.

Maj. Gen. WILLIAM T. SHERMAN,
Iuka, Miss.:

The corps field report for October 20 will be sent you on Monday.

I propose to send Hurst's (Sixth Tennessee) cavalry to Jackson and thereabouts, Hawkins' (Seventh Tennessee) to Union City to recruit, and then move down from Columbus with about 750 good cavalry—Fourth Missouri and Second Illinois—and clear that country.

Smith's force at Columbus is small; not more than enough to reach to Trenton.

S. A. HURLBUT,
Major-General.

HEADQUARTERS ARMY OF THE TENNESSEE,
Iuka, October 24, 1863.

Maj. Gen. J. B. McPHERSON,
Commanding Seventeenth Army Corps, Vicksburg:

DEAR GENERAL: Young Dunn has just come out from Memphis with dispatches from Grant, announcing all the changes. These catch us, as we had reason to anticipate, short-handed, but we must do our best. I shall leave you undisturbed. I regard the Yazoo as a kind of shield against the main river, and therefore Vicksburg should be held with the tenacity of life; also Haynes' Bluff. But as the enemy cannot bring artillery against you, make the earth-works as small and perfect as possible. The high point north of Vicksburg is a Gibraltar—one similar south, and a citadel at the old tower. I don't see the use of a force at Natchez; the enemy has drawn from the place every man that is worth a cent to them as a soldier, and the buildings and property of the place is security for the good behavior of the people; that is, a threat to destroy Natchez and valuable plantations there will prevent any molestation of the river, which is the grand desideratum.

I would not advise that a division should be kept at Natchez, but a white regiment, and, say, two negro regiments well intrenched, commanding with heavy guns the water and city. A similar garrison for Haynes' Bluff. The balance of your corps could be held well in hand, ready to embark in whole or part whenever an enemy threatens to interfere with the river.

The general impression here is that all the infantry, except Loring's division, is gone out of Mississippi, and that Stephen D. Lee's cavalry is here to my front is well attested by many who have seen him. Either the Southern leaders are making a strong effort to retake Tennessee, or resist Grant's supposed intention to push to Atlanta, and have pushed all or nearly all their forces to Georgia and Northeast Alabama. Your late trip to Canton will have developed that, but, looking to future combinations, the time is most opportune for executing one of two, or it may be both, projects which I will merely sketch:

1. The destruction *in toto* of a large section of the railroad at Meridian, the larger and more perfect the better.

2. A trip up Yazoo to about Tchula, and strike from there to the railroad between Canton and Grenada, and break a large section of it, making its repair impracticable. The former is of vital importance, the latter of minor; but either would be rich in result at some future time.

All of General Grant's orders remain in force, of course, and will be respected, and I will be able to give little personal direction to events or policing on the river; but I wish you to maintain the security of the river along the west boundary of the State of Mississippi in co-operation with the gunboats, and to strike inland whenever an opportunity offers and your judgment sanctions.

I am satisfied petty trade along the river is wrong, but large trade, such as gives employment to large boats, carrying a crew of 25 men or over, will not only keep open communications, but will be an interest that will aid in the maintenance of the military control of the river.

I throw out these ideas, and leave you to do what is right. I must conduct all the force I can collect east of Florence and leave you and Hurlbut to manage the valley.

I am, &c.,

W. T. SHERMAN,
Major-General.

HEADQUARTERS SEVENTEENTH ARMY CORPS,
Vicksburg, Miss., October 24, 1863.

Maj. Gen. U. S. GRANT,
Commanding Department of the Tennessee:

GENERAL: I inclose herewith a letter just received from Brigadier-General Tuttle, commanding on line of Big Black, giving the report brought in by one of his scouts. From this you will see that there is some talk, and even probability, of the enemy trying to retake this place.

I think their number is greatly exaggerated, but from what I learned during the recent reconnaissance the force they can concentrate is quite formidable. President Davis has been with General Johnston at Meridian, and whether he came any farther west or not I have not learned.

I am pushing the new line of defenses forward as rapidly as possible, but it will require a vast amount of work to complete it.

I have some scouts out, and will endeavor to keep you advised of any decided movement of the enemy.

Very respectfully, your obedient servant,

JAS. B. McPHERSON,
Major-General.

[Inclosure.]

CAMP ON CLEAR CREEK, MISS.,
Hebron, October 24, 1863.

Maj. Gen. J. B. McPHERSON,
　　　　　Vicksburg:

DEAR GENERAL : I have encamped my command as near the places determined on as possible. McMillen found no water either at Albertson's or Templeton's, and has made his camp at the cross-roads in rear of Templeton's. He has a good defensive position, but is not as far forward as is desirable, but after a careful reconnaissance, I think we can do no better for the present and until water is more plentiful.

One of my scouts came in day before yesterday. He has been to Canton, Jackson, Brandon, and Meridian, and reports Johnston's force, that was at Jackson when Sherman was after him, is now at those four places, and talks of retaking Vicksburg. He says there were about 15,000 infantry came in from Brandon and Meridian to re-enforce the cavalry the other day when you were out. They expressed great mortification that you returned, as they thought they had a sure thing on you. He also reports that the conscripting parties are bringing in large numbers of recruits. The officers report that they have increased their army 20,000 in the last sixty days, and that soldiers and citizens express the greatest confidence that Vicksburg will be in their hands in a short time. I have sent him and another one back, with instructions to stay with them until they commence some movement, then to let me know as soon as possible. His statement, so far as he is concerned, is undoubtedly correct, but I think everything is overrated, as they are liable always to be outside of official circles. He was with them at Jackson, and was just starting to give us what information he had, when he heard we were on the return. He says you would have met 15,000 or 18,000 at either Canton or Jackson. They thought you had started to Rosecrans via Canton. Whether that was the opinion among officers is doubtful. I will be down in a few days. When will you be out?

Very truly, your obedient servant,

J. M. TUTTLE,
Brigadier-General.

HDQRS. CAVALRY DIVISION, SIXTEENTH ARMY CORPS,
Memphis, Tenn., October 24, 1863.

Capt. T. H. HARRIS,
　　　Assistant Adjutant-General:

CAPTAIN : One of my scouts, just returned, reports that Chalmers will occupy the Mobile and Ohio Railroad about Okolona. Chalmers' advance was to move on the 24th for Okolona. They will leave small scouting parties, to attract attention, on the Tallahatchie. Chalmers talks of attacking the railroad between Memphis and Moscow, merely as a ruse to cover his movements east.

Respectfully, your obedient servant,

EDWARD HATCH,
Colonel, Commanding Division.

COLUMBUS, KY., *October* 24, 1863.

Col. J. K. MILLS,
    Commanding, Union City:

You will send out all the cavalry you have, except the pickets now
on outpost, under a judicious officer, in the direction of Boydsville,
to get in the rear of the rebels, and follow them up if they have
passed into Kentucky or are lurking near the line. I send you
to-day two companies of cavalry to do picket duty at Union City
during the absence of your cavalry. Send out with the command
several good scouts to keep you constantly advised of the movements of your cavalry, as well as that of the rebels. You will give
the necessary instructions for carrying out the above order if you
regard your information as reliable. Colonel Waring goes out
to-day.

                          A. J. SMITH,
                              Brigadier-General.

CAMP NELSON, *October* 24, 1863.

Major-General BURNSIDE:

When you left Kentucky there seemed to be some objections to
the proposition to introduce contraband negroes from the South into
the State to labor on military roads. Since that time the subject
has been thoroughly canvassed, the advantages and disadvantages
have all been fully weighed, and, as far as I can now learn, it is
almost the unanimous feeling and opinion with slave owners in this
region that no serious difficulty will arise from using them. I have
before me a petition from a large number of slave owners in the
counties of Lincoln, Boyle, and Mercer, praying that slaves be immediately taken to improve the State; a sufficient number of them
to prosecute the work and military road, and completing at the least
possible period.

The great difficulty presented by the opposers of the movement
was that slaves in Kentucky would become demoralized and worthless by coming in contact with the contrabands. To prevent this, it
is now proposed that the contrabands be placed upon the road south
of Danville, and the impressed negroes upon the road between Nicholasville and Danville, thus keeping them entirely separate. I am
satisfied that unless something of this sort is done, the work will not
progress as rapidly as you and its friends desire. The impressed
hands will not amount to more than 2,500; to divide them between
the two roads now in process of construction, will not give to each
sufficient force to complete the work in any reasonable time, and to
impress slaves from the counties upon which the call has been made,
would be doing great injustice to the farming interests of the
country.

I have consulted with Major Simpson upon the subject, and he
gives it as his opinion that it is the only way by which the work can
be successfully prosecuted.

Colonel Bowles was here a short time since, and said if this arrangement could be effected, there would be no difficulty in completing
the Central Kentucky road between Nicholasville and Danville. Besides all this, there is a great deal of work to be done at a depot, and
in the fortifications at this place, and I shall be compelled to keep
a portion of the impressed negroes here for a time to complete that

work.   Had it not been for the impressed hands, the depots and fortifications would have been very far short of completion.

Owing to the scarcity of hands in the country, this difficulty, and
in getting teamsters, I have been compelled to give up all the free
negroes impressed to work the railroad to Captain Hall to drive
teams to East Tennessee.   He is yet in need of more, and where we
are to get them I cannot tell.   The greatest and most important consideration with us all is, to feed and clothe your army; and this
cannot be done without teamsters.

If the railroad is to be pushed forward, we must be supplied with
hands from some other quarter to do the work here yet unfinished,
and to drive teams; they can be obtained from no other quarter
than the South.   I have strained every point and used every means
in my power to secure laborers and teamsters enough without en-
croaching upon impressed slaves, and I now, in the name of the
people of this region of the country, who have cheerfully given us
all the aid in their power, appeal to you.   If you can do so consistently with propriety, ask the privilege from War Department to
send to Nashville, Memphis, and other points for as many contrabands
as may be necessary to carry on the work at this post, and on the
railroad.   Rest assured it will meet with the hearty approbation of
the people in this portion of the country.

                                SPEED S. FRY,
                                    Brigadier-General.

              HEADQUARTERS ELEVENTH AND TWELFTH CORPS,
                        Stevenson, Ala., October 25, 1863.
Major-General SLOCUM,
        Commanding Twelfth Corps:

The major-general commanding has directed me to forward you
the following statement of the posts and garrisons as established by
Major-General Howard, commanding the Eleventh Corps: Along
the line of the railroad from Tantalon to and including Bridgeport,
Tantalon, three companies infantry; Anderson, four companies infantry; between Anderson and Stevenson, two companies infantry;
Stevenson, two regiments and nine companies; Widow Creek, one
company; Long Island, in Tennessee River, one regiment; south
side Tennessee River, one regiment; the balance of his corps at
Bridgeport.

                Very respectfully,

                                H. W. PERKINS,
                Lieut., Aide-de-Camp, and Actg. Asst. Adjt. Gen.

                                STEVENSON, *October 25, 1863.*
Major-General SLOCUM:

If you have ordered Geary's division to Bridgeport in place of that
of Williams, you will send one brigade of the latter to this point
without delay to relieve the one of the former now here.   One of the
regiments is between here and Tantalon and must be relieved as the
brigade marches down.

                                JOSEPH HOOKER,
                                    Major-General.

NASHVILLE, *October* 25, 1863.

Maj. Gen. H. W. SLOCUM:

GENERAL: As soon as the road is open I have made arrangements to have one train report to you at Wartrace, another to stop at Murfreesborough for troops. We have only two flats here and no engine. The accident south of Tullahoma has brought railroad matters to a standstill. If the guerrillas will leave us alone we will be able to fill our orders to-morrow.

Arrangements have been made in pursuance to your orders. Did you get the two box cars, and will you please inform me when you will wish them sent forward? They were ordered to be taken by this a. m. passenger train if ready. Road will probably not be open till late this p. m.

Respectfully,

WM. P. INNES,
Colonel, and Military Superintendent.

MURFREESBOROUGH, *October* 25, 1863.

COMMANDING OFFICER:

If the East Tennessee cavalry is at Wartrace, order them to this place immediately, and all of their force along the road if they can be spared. Inform them to be vigilant in coming.

WM. L. UTLEY,
Colonel, Commanding Post.

MURFREESBOROUGH, *October* 25, 1863.

Lieut. Col. H. C. RODGERS,
Assistant Adjutant-General:

I have no troops quartered in town, and never have had, except the provost guard. The Tennessee cavalry quarters about one-half mile from fortifications; Thirty-first Wisconsin quarters near the depot; Twenty-second Wisconsin in fortifications. We can get to fortifications early, if necessary. There are several hundred sick and wounded that we can't get in fortifications. We think we can lick anything that can come. Is there any immediate necessity? Is the order imperative?

WM. L. UTLEY,
Colonel, Commanding Post.

MURFREESBOROUGH, *October* 25, 1863.

Major-General THOMAS:

I have just received an indirect order, purporting to come from you, to move all my forces to the fortress. My troops are now in the city. I have the Thirty-first Wisconsin near the depot on the heights ready to fall to the fortress in case of necessity. I also have one battalion of the Fourth East Tennessee Cavalry encamped just at General Crittenden's former headquarters, on Liberty pike. I have Twenty-second Wisconsin in fortress, with all the scattering troops. I think my troops are best disposed to defend the place that can be with the force I have. I think of no cause here for alarm. It is reported that 6,000 men are at Milton, but I can hold the position against 10,000 men. I could accommodate the sick should I go to the fort; also stores, commissary subsistence and quartermaster. There are large quantities of stores in hands Quartermaster Williams, and can be properly cared for in the fort. If you know of any cause why I should fall back to the fort please inform me.

WM. L. UTLEY,
Colonel, Commanding Post.

SHELBYVILLE, October 25, 1863.

Major-General SLOCUM :

I have had scouts in every direction, and west as far as Cornersville, and can hear nothing except that the rebels are on this side of the river.

ROBT. GALBRAITH,
Colonel, Commanding Post.

STEVENSON, October 25, 1863—5.30 p. m.

Major-General SLOCUM :

The general directs me to say that there is not a ford south of Knoxville, in present stage of river, where cavalry can cross. Wheeler is reported to have forded. Unless you have information which the general knows nothing of, he thinks you should direct the trains to come on where they are wanted,

DANL. BUTTERFIELD,
Major-General, and Chief of Staff.

DECHERD, October 25, 1863.

Col. H. C. RODGERS :

We have sent a regiment to scour the country in the vicinity of the last raid on the railroad and drive out all rebels. They will go north as far as Tullahoma.

Have you not some of the Tenth Ohio Cavalry at your disposal

WILLIAM H. SINCLAIR,
Assistant Adjutant-General.

NASHVILLE, October 25, 1863.

Maj. Gen. H. W. SLOCUM :

Dispatch received. We are moving General Geary's command a fast as possible under his directions from the different points.

WM. P. INNES,
Colonel, and Military Superintendent.

ANDERSON, October 25, 1863—1 p. m.

Lieut. Col. H. C. RODGERS,
Assistant Adjutant-General :

I ordered the wagon train halted at Tullahoma. Please send on. The roads over the mountain are almost impassable. There a good road from near Cumberland Tunnel, via University Place, by which the wagons should be sent. People at Cowan can guide. Ruger's brigade is here, three of Knipe's ahead, and three coming up from Tantalon. One regiment ordered by General Hooker to relieve posts from Tantalon to Stevenson.

A. S. WILLIAMS,
Brigadier-General.

HEADQUARTERS CHIEF OF CAVALRY,
Decherd, October 25, 1863.

Col. HENRY R. MIZNER,
    Columbia:

We have information via Shelbyville that Sherman's advance whipped the rebs and drove part of them across the river. Send out scouts and get all the information you can in regard to the enemy's cavalry. We are ready to move at a moment's notice. General Mitchell desires you to furnish him all the information you get promptly.

WILLIAM H. SINCLAIR,
Assistant Adjutant-General.

WARTRACE, *October* 25, 1863.

General MITCHELL:

There has been from 600 to 800 of the enemy's cavalry near Liberty and McMinnville for the last four days.

Citizens report this morning 10,000 of them within 4 miles of the railroad, near Fairfield. I think their cavalry are near us, but can't tell in what force. Have sent out infantry scouts, but they have not returned.

We have no mounted men here.

H. C. RODGERS,
Assistant Adjutant-General.

MAYSVILLE, *October* 25, 1863—7 a. m.

Maj. W. H. SINCLAIR,
    Assistant Adjutant-General:

I sent out an expedition day before yesterday toward the fords on the river with orders to let me know at once if the enemy were crossing. I have heard nothing from them yet, but as soon as I do will let you know. It is impossible to make out any reports until I get some desks here with paper and material. I have not been able to get any of my horses shod yet. The streams have all been so high between here and Stevenson that I have been unable to get anything out except rations. I will have a few horses to-day, but they will be in the rough, and as I have no forges or anything for shoeing, it will be a slow process. I could not get out over 1,000 effective men, and if we were to move the whole command from here, we would have to abandon some 700 horses.

GEORGE CROOK,
Brigadier-General.

DECHERD, *October 25, 1863.*

Lieut. Col. C. GODDARD,
    Assistant Adjutant-General:

Report from General Crook at Maysville (7 a. m.) says, he sent out expedition day before yesterday toward enemy's forces on the river. Has not yet heard from them, though he directed them to let him know at once if they found the enemy crossing. He finds it very difficult to get supplies for his command, the streams are so high, and has no horseshoes. I supposed the railroad was in operation; says he has not over 1,000 effective men, and if ordered to leave there would have to abandon 700 horses. General Mitchell is asleep. Have you heard anything from General Stanley?

WILLIAM H. SINCLAIR,
    Assistant Adjutant-General.

STEVENSON,
October 25, 1863—9 a. m.

Major-General REYNOLDS:

Dispatch received. Rifle battery will be furnished.
Colonel Coburn reports 70 to 100 rebels attacked McMinnville last night and were repulsed.

JOSEPH HOOKER.

COLUMBIA, *October 25, 1863.*

W. H. SINCLAIR,
    Assistant Adjutant-General:

On Tuesday last 2 men reached this place from Courtland, took the oath, and went north. They had come direct from Lee's command on Sunday, at which time they were cooking five days' rations as if contemplating a raid in some direction.

Wheeler has 6,000, with artillery; Roddey 2,000 with artillery; Lee from 3,000 to 4,000, no artillery. Lee had just come from Mississippi. They were occupying Courtland, Decatur, and Tuscumbia.

HENRY R. MIZNER,
    Colonel, Commanding.

SHELBYVILLE, *October 25, 1863.*

Brigadier-General MITCHELL:

I learn just now from a very reliable source that Wheeler was recrossing at or near Lamb's Ferry on Wednesday and Thursday last and had crossed about half his command. A man by the name of Neeley had started south with his stock and met them on Wednesday, and as they were taking everything in the way of stock he returned home. I have confidence in the report.

ROBT. GALBRAITH.

NASHVILLE, *October 25, 1863.*

Maj. Gen. GEORGE H. THOMAS:

I have returned from Louisville, where I had an interview with the Secretary of War in reference to the immediate completion of the Northwestern Railroad. He has authorized and instructed me to proceed with it as rapidly as possible. Colonel Innes, of the

Engineer Corps, as you are aware, was selected by me while acting as military superintendent of railroads to take charge of the general direction of the work ; he has since been superseded by the appointment of J. B. Anderson as military superintendent. I doubt this change. Colonel Innes was making a good, efficient officer, and was not under an influence at Louisville operating to our injury. I desire Colonel Innes and as many of his companions as may be needed continued on the road. The work is under way and progressing very well. We are defending it. With the little force we have driven guerrillas off and some of them out of the country. We have a large number of hands at work and could employ a great many more if we had a small force to send to the other end of the road, which would exert a good influence in driving the guerrillas from that section, and cut off an intercourse carried on by the rebels through that region. I am succeeding very well in organizing many companies to be employed in scouring the country to expel and drive beyond our lines rebels and guerrillas. General Gillem will visit you in a few days for the purpose of communicating with you on this and other subjects connected with the State. Permit me to congratulate you upon your new position. It is the one, as you know, I have long desired you should occupy. I trust and hope most sincerely that your efforts in the future will be crowned with brilliant success.

ANDREW JOHNSON,
Military Governor.

CHATTANOOGA, TENN.,
October 25, 1863—4 p. m.

THOMAS A. SCOTT :

The animals with this army will now nearly all need three months' rest to become serviceable. They should be returned to Louisville for this purpose. Hard work, exposure, short grain, and no long fodder have almost destroyed them. No more ambulances or ambulance horses should be sent forward at present. Upon the present rise of water (in cipher), hay, mules, cavalry, and artillery horses, in good condition, should be pressed forward by Cumberland River to Nashville, ready to come to the army the moment it is prepared to advance, which I trust will be soon. I have cavalry and artillery horses at Indianapolis, which should remain there until the stables at Louisville are cleared. All animals coming to Louisville should have several days' careful feed and grooming before being forwarded to Nashville.

M. C. MEIGS,
Quartermaster-General.

HEADQUARTERS DEPARTMENT OF THE OHIO,
Loudon, Tenn., October 25, 1863—11.30 p. m.
(Received 8.40 p. m., 26th.)

Maj. Gen. H. W. HALLECK,
General-in-Chief :

Evidence still seems to indicate that the enemy are concentrated in considerable force on the south side of the river. We can easily give up this place and take up the bridge, but it seems advisable to hold it, and not release the enemy's force to join the army in front of Thomas. Information from General Shackelford on our left seems to corroborate the report of considerable concentration by the enemy in the neighborhood of Abingdon.

A. E. BURNSIDE,
Major-General.

JONESBOROUGH, *October 25, 1863.*

Major-General BURNSIDE :

Your dispatch embracing telegrams from General Halleck [received]. Two Union men who left Abingdon last Tuesday, having come from New River to Abingdon, report a large force of the enemy at Glade Springs, and a larger force at Abingdon ; that one brigade from Lee's army had reached Abingdon ; that they saw and conversed with some of the soldiers. They also report the cars running to within 6 miles of Bristol, the point the farthest bridge east was burned, and that the enemy was rebuilding the bridge above Bristol. I would have attached but little importance to their statements had not General Halleck given you the information contained in his telegram. I have two regiments at Duvall's Ford, on the Watauga, and guards for 8 miles down the river from that point, and since receiving your dispatch I have ordered scouts of 125 men up to Elizabethtown and Taylor's Ford. The detachment of my command is now encamped around this town. The utmost vigilance shall be exercised, and you shall be promptly informed of any and all information I can obtain. I would suggest that the enemy might move from Abingdon, via Estillville, to the Cumberland Gap.

J. M. SHACKELFORD,
Brigadier-General.

SPECIAL ORDERS,) HDQRS. DEPT. AND ARMY OF THE TENN.,
No. 1.   )   *Iuka, Miss., October 25, 1863.*

*   *   *   *   *   *   *

II. The entire Fourth Division, Fifteenth Army Corps, will be prepared to start to-morrow for Eastport, to cross the river and advance to Florence, with ten days' rations in their wagons.

III. Fuller's brigade, of the Sixteenth Corps, will relieve, with one regiment, the brigade now at Burnsville, and with the rest take post at Iuka till further orders.

*   *   *   *   *   *   *

By order of Maj. Gen. W. T. Sherman :

R. M. SAWYER,
Assistant Adjutant-General.

GENERAL ORDERS,) HDQRS. DEPT. AND ARMY OF THE TENN.,
No. 2.   )   *Iuka, Miss., October 25, 1863.*

I. The general commanding the Department and Army of the Tennessee hereby announces the following subdivisions of his command :

1. The Fifteenth Army Corps, Maj. Gen. F. P. Blair, jr., headquarters in the field.

2. The Sixteenth Army Corps, Maj. Gen. S. A. Hurlbut, composed, as at present, of all the troops now at Memphis, Columbus, Corinth, and along the railroad, and of Kimball's division, temporarily detached, headquarters for the present at Memphis.

3. The Seventeenth Army Corps, Maj. Gen. J. B. McPherson, composed, as at present, of all the troops now serving at Natchez, Vicksburg, and in the State of Mississippi south of Tallahatchie, headquarters Vicksburg.

II. The corps commanders will forthwith arrange garrisons for the fortified points in their respective districts, and will organize into proper brigades and divisions all other troops ready for offensive operations.

III. All officers in command of corps and of fixed military posts will assume the very highest powers allowed by the laws of war and Congress. They must maintain the best possible discipline, and repress all disorders, alarms, and dangers in their reach. Citizens who fail to support their Government have no right to ask favor and protection, but if they actively assist us in vindicating the national authority, all commanders will assist them and their families in every possible way. Officers need not meddle with matters of trade and commerce, which by law devolve on the officers of the Treasury Department, but, whenever they discover goods (contraband of war) being conveyed toward the public enemy, they will seize all the goods tainted by the transaction and imprison the parties implicated in the matter, but care must be taken to make a full record and report of each case.

When a district is infested by guerrillas or held by the enemy, horses, mules, wagons, corn, forage, &c., are all means of war, and can be freely taken, but must be accounted for as public property. If the people do not want their horses, corn, &c., taken, they must organize and repress all guerrilla or hostile bands in their neighborhood.

IV. It is represented that officers, provost-marshals, and others in the military service are engaged in business or speculation on their own account, and that they charge fees for passes, permits, &c. All this is a breach of honor and of law. Every salaried officer of the military service owes every hour of his time, every thought of his mind, to his Government, and if he makes one cent of profit beyond his pay he is corrupt and criminal. All officers and soldiers in this department are hereby commanded to engage in no business whatever save their sworn duty to their Government.

V. Every man should be with his proper corps, division, brigade, and regiment, unless absent sick or wounded, or detached by written order of a competent commander. Soldiers when so absent must have their descriptive rolls, and when not provided with them the presumption is they are improperly absent. Mustering officers will see that all absentees, not away by the written order of their proper commander, are reported on the muster-rolls as deserters, that they may lose their pay, bounty, and pensions, which a generous Government and people have provided for the soldiers and officers who have done their whole duty. The best hospitals in the world are provided for the wounded and sick, but these must not be made the receptacle for absentees, who seek to escape the necessary exposure and dangers of a soldier's life. Whenever it is possible, citizens must be employed as nurses, cooks, attendants, stewards, &c., to hospitals, in order that the enlisted men may be, where they

belong, with their regiments. Medical inspectors will attend to this
at once. The general commanding announces that he expects the
wounded and sick to have every care possible, but this feeling must
not be abused to the injury of the only useful part of the army—
"the soldier in the field."

VI. In time of war and rebellion districts of country occupied by
our troops are subject to the laws of war. The inhabitants, be they
friendly or unfriendly, must submit to the controling power. If
any person in an insurgent district corresponds or trades with an
enemy outside, he or she becomes a spy. And all the inhabitants,
moreover, must not only abstain from hostile or unfriendly acts, but
must aid and assist the power that protects them and affords them
trade and commerce. The people who occupy this department had
better make a note of this and conduct themselves accordingly.

By order of Maj. Gen. W. T. Sherman :

R. M. SAWYER,
Assistant Adjutant-General.

SPECIAL ORDERS, }   HDQRS. DEPT. AND ARMY OF THE TENN.,
   No. 1.   }   *Iuka, Miss., October* 25, 1863.

I. First. Col. S. G. Hicks, Fortieth Illinois, will proceed with dispatch to Paducah, Ky., and assume command of that post. He will
take with him Lieut. A. F. Taylor, regimental quartermaster of the
same regiment.

Second. Colonel Hicks, on arrival, will dispatch to Florence,
Tenn., the One hundred and eleventh Illinois, now at Paducah,
if it has not already gone, and will call on the commanding officer
at Columbus or Cairo for three companies, to garrison and hold the
fort at Paducah.

Third. Colonel Hicks will give personal attention to the boats
passing up and down the Tennessee, to see that dispatch is used, and
that no contraband trade is carried on from that quarter.

Fourth. Any citizen in or near Paducah who attempts to create
disorder, alarm, or danger to the peace and quiet of the neighborhood will be promptly imprisoned and reduced to subjection.

II. The entire Fourth Division, Fifteenth Army Corps, will be prepared to start to-morrow for Eastport, to cross the river and advance
to Florence, with ten days' rations in their wagons.

III. Fuller's brigade, of the Sixteenth Corps, will relieve, with one
regiment, the brigade now at Burnsville, and with the rest take post
at Iuka till further orders.

            *   *   *   *   *   *   *

VI. Maj. Gen. F. P. Blair, jr., will assume command of the Fifteenth Army Corps.

By order of Maj. Gen. W. T. Sherman:

R. M. SAWYER,
Assistant Adjutant-General.

IUKA, *October* 25, 1863.

General HURLBUT,
      Memphis :

DEAR GENERAL : I have got up before daylight to write you on
some points. It is now manifest that all the "powers that be"

want the mass of available troops over toward Huntsville, and the only question is how to get them there, and feed them when there.

The Tennessee is now in good stage, and Phelps says there is no danger till next summer as far as Eastport, and any day may make it available to Florence. Thence we must haul. I won't waste much more labor on Bear Creek Bridge. I will push up to the station on the hill at Cherokee, and use that as a picket station for a time, but I will take immediate steps to cross a body of troops to Florence and Huntsville, and I want you now to dispose things so we can draw to this end everything of strength. Order every officer and man to his regiment. Any one absent from his military post on any pretext must be made to go to his regiment or make up some work gang. The civil authorities must relieve the military of police duty. The fort must be made impregnable. The railroad must gradually take care of itself, for it is manifest every soldier on our rolls will be needed till the draft comes.

Write to the invalid commander at Saint Louis that I ask a good guard of 150 men at Paducah, another of 150 at Cairo. I want a good assailing force at Columbus, say 2,500 men, all told, to operate back to Paris, Trenton, Jackson, &c., striking eccentrically.

It will take some time to make these changes, and I want you to help me. I like Memphis and the old Mississippi. It is my hobby, but we must needs leave it for a time.

Notify me at once all changes you think should be made to accomplish the end. The corps remain as hitherto (Fifteenth, Sixteenth, and Seventeenth), commanders the same, and we only point east now instead of south, neglecting for a time the river, and exaggerating the valley of the Tennessee from Huntsville up.

I shall favor the free navigation of the Mississippi to all boats of large size capable of carrying a crew capable of self-defense and carrying large through cargoes—to all commerce on a scale that cannot be corrupted by small interests. All chicken-thieving expeditions or cotton-stealing parties to be prosecuted. As to officers, my rule is, if any officer in the service of the United States, while enjoying a salary, makes one cent by way of profit in any manner traceable to his office, he is guilty of a high crime, and should be punished as a criminal. You may mention this incidentally.

Another notion I have : the United States can claim the military service of every able-bodied man in Memphis, and may organize and use them for local defense, and also, in case of necessity, for offense. I shall make no hasty change, but these ideas will gradually unfold.

    Yours,

                                     SHERMAN,
                                     Major-General.

HEADQUARTERS SIXTEENTH ARMY CORPS,
                Memphis, Tenn., October 25, 1863.

Brigadier-General DODGE,
        Corinth, Miss.:

Ask General Sherman's permission to send force down to Saltillo. If he agrees, send; but telegraph to Hatch what force you send.

                       S. A. HURLBUT,
                           Major-General.

IUKA, *October 25, 1863.*

Major-General HURLBUT:

I approve your order in the matter of your telegraph this morn-ing. Now is a good time to clear out that country. Let it be done without gloves.

W. T. SHERMAN.

CORINTH, *October 25, 1863.*

Major-General SHERMAN,
    Iuka:

Flag of truce sent to Okolona has returned. Met Major-General Gholson, with about 1,300 State militia, on Yocona, for Birmingham. Inge and company are at Marietta. Chalmers down to Grenada and north on railroad. It seems that the State troops are being turned over to Confederate Government for temporary service, and they arrived there within four days.

Lee, who commands North Mississippi, was expected back in a few days. All those troops with Gholson were poorly and only partly armed, their only business appearing to be to collect together all the provisions in the country; were running all the mills and picketing closely all the roads. If Lee goes back, he will go down the Tuscumbia and Cotton-gin roads.

G. M. DODGE,
    Brigadier-General.

CORINTH, *October 25, 1863.*

Major-General HURLBUT,
    Memphis:

Flag of truce returned. Met the enemy on Yocona, stretching from Ellistown to Saltillo, Major-General Gholson in command. They are State militia come in there few days ago, some 1,300 strong. Are only half armed, and are collecting provisions, running mules, &c. Inge, Davenport, and Weatherston [?] are at Marietta, picketing all the roads. Chalmers reported a good deal scattered. Gholson said he would send dispatch to S. D. Lee, who commands North Mississippi. Citizens said Lee was expected back in two or three days. Gholson has two pieces artillery.

It appears that this militia is all being turned over to the Confederate Government, and they were up there to recruit, conscript, and gather provisions. I believe two regiments of cavalry and one of mounted infantry from here would clean them all out.

G. M. DODGE,
    Brigadier-General.

CORINTH, *October 25, 1863.*

Lieutenant-Colonel SAWYER,
    Assistant Adjutant-General:

I am ordered by General Dodge to send a regiment to Burnsville by cars, and to march to Iuka with balance of command by to-morrow night. My artillery horses are so sore and infantry so weary that it will be very difficult to get through, as the guides say

he only way a train can go is via Davenport's. within a mile of
Jacinto. I can reach Barnett, within 8 miles of Iuka, to-morrow
night, and next morning early report in good condition at Iuka. I
had to countermarch yesterday and made 29 miles, getting here at
0.30 p. m. Please answer whether I can be permitted to report
Tuesday morning at Iuka.

JOHN W. FULLER,
Commanding Brigade.

HEADQUARTERS DEPARTMENT OF THE TENNESSEE,
Iuka, October 25, 1863.

General HURLBUT,
      Memphis:

Write an urgent letter to Steele asking for Kimball's division.
General Grant suggests it, and I write fully by the cars to-day.

Write me fully the reasons, if any, why we should not abandon
the railroad and use the Tennessee exclusively. The Tennessee has
now 8 feet of water and has better navigation than the Mississippi,
and will be good for six months, certain.

W. T. SHERMAN,
Major-General.

HEADQUARTERS SIXTEENTH ARMY CORPS,
Memphis, Tenn., October 25, 1863.

Major-General SHERMAN,
      Iuka, Miss.:

I have ordered Bingham, Macfeely, and Parker to report to you
in person.

Steele has orders from Washington to send to me all the infantry
he can spare.

The Tennessee River is far the best channel for supplies for Corinth and points beyond in cheapness and expedition, and everything
for the Fifteenth Corps, at least, should be sent that way. The railroad from here to Corinth is a curse upon military movements. It
takes more troops to hold it than would conquer Mississippi.

S. A. HURLBUT,
Major-General.

HEADQUARTERS ARMY OF THE TENNESSEE,
Iuka, Miss., October 25, 1863.

Hon. SALMON P. CHASE,
      Secretary U. S. Treasury, Washington, D. C.;

DEAR SIR: By the vicissitude of war, I am again forced into the
command of a department. I almost shrink from a command that
involves me with civil matters which I do not understand. Politics
or the means to influence a civil people are mysteries I do not com-
prehend, but am forced to act. Matters involving the navigation of
our great rivers must necessarily fall somewhat under my jurisdiction, but I assure you I have no inclination to influence the officers
of your Department.

I extract parts of a letter I have just written to Admiral Porter at Cairo, which express my general opinion on the main points.

My notions about the Mississippi are these : We must never again allow the enemy to make a lodgment on its banks with artillery, and, therefore, Columbus, Memphis, Vicksburg, and mouth of Yazoo must be held with troops. All else may be trusted to your gunboats, and a surplus force kept at Memphis and Vicksburg available to float to any threatened point to prevent a lodgment. Through traffic on large steam-boats, manned and properly officered, should be encouraged by all means. Each boat might be required to carry a gun, 25 muskets and men, and a musket-proof barricade at each bow and quarter, from which to fire. Also, the boilers might be better sheltered.

Regular packets should be encouraged to keep up daily and rapid communication, which increases a feeling of security. It brings private enterprise to aid the general purpose, viz, uninterrupted navigation of the river.

Trading boats will, of course, be regulated by the Treasury Department. I don't see as we have any right to interfere further than as to contraband of war, and, to make this more clear, you and I ought to say what is "contraband of war." The term is very indefinite, but I am clearly of opinion that the laws of war give the rrmy and navy a legal right to protect themselves against contraband traffic and its agents.

Merchants as a class are governed by the law of self-interest, and the temptation to import and sell contraband goods is so great, that many will engage in it, but this is confined to a class of men that you and I know well. The real merchant— the man who loves his country as we do—would not ask to send down the river arms and ammunition, or anything that would endanger our lives or the lives of our command.

There are some things, such as salt for curing meats, medicines for curing wounds and sickness, that I am not so clear about and care less. If you will prepare a list of contraband and send it to Secretary Chase, I know he will make it public and save us a world of trouble.

I have announced in orders that any officer of my command who makes a cent of profit by selling permits, passes, &c., or by any species of trade and speculation, is corrupt and criminal. I hear of such things, but really find few or no real cases, but I must stop scandal. Also, I contend I have a right to impress for military service any men who have run from the North and come here to make a living and avoid the draft. I will pick up a few such, and this will stop that class of meddlers and unauthorized hangers-on, that have given me so much trouble.

I beg to convey to you direct these ideas, with the assurance that I wish to make all my acts conform to the law and policy of the Government, whatever it may be, only, like many other people, having my own notions, I find it easier to execute them.

With great respect, &c.,

W. T. SHERMAN,
Major-General of Volunteers.

HEADQUARTERS DEPARTMENT OF THE TENNESSEE,
Iuka, October 25, 1863.

Admiral DAVID D. PORTER,
Cairo:

DEAR ADMIRAL : I was much gratified to hear from you yesterday and to see the prompt arrival of Captain Phelps with two gunboats. The moment I learned of the arrival I sent down an officer and escort to Eastport, where I had a regiment to watch for the boats, and brought the captain up. He spent the night with me, and we talked over matters generally. Of course we will get along together elegantly. All I have he can command, and I know the same feeling pervades every sailor's and soldier's heart. We are as one. Now I want to cross the Tennessee to reach a point where I can communicate with General Grant.

Captain Phelps instantly offered to ferry over my men, horses, wagons, &c., but to facilitate the matter, I have sent down to Eastport plenty of carpenters, tools, and materials, to deck over one of your coal-barges to make a float on which to carry wagons and mules. The gunboats can handle my men fast enough, but it is these cursed wagons and mules that bother us. If soldiers and mules could flourish without eating, "I myself would be a soldier." It is not "villainous saltpeter" that makes one's life so hard, but grub and mules; still we will make it all right. Boats cannot yet pass Colbert Shoals, so for the time we must foot it for Eastport and Waterloo; but I will occupy both banks up to Florence and Tuscumbia, trusting in a short time to get a ferry-boat up to Florence.

We are much obliged to the Tennessee, which has favored us most opportunely, for I am never easy with a railroad, which takes a whole army to guard, each foot of rail being essential to the whole, whereas they cannot stop the Tennessee, and each boat can make its own game. I think, also, we can clean out anything, except occasional shots at passing boats.

My notions about the Mississippi are these: We must never again allow the enemy to make a lodgment on its banks with artillery, and, therefore, Columbus, Memphis, Vicksburg, and mouth of Yazoo must be held with troops. All else may be trusted to your gunboats and a force at Memphis and Vicksburg, surplus and available at all times, to float to the threatened point to prevent a lodgment. Through traffic, on large steam-boats, manned and properly officered, should be encouraged by all means. Each boat might be required to carry a gun, 25 muskets and men, and a musket-proof barricade at each bow and quarter, from which to fire. Also, boilers might be sheltered somewhat.

Regular packets should be encouraged to keep up daily and rapid communication, which increases a feeling of security. It brings private enterprise to the aid of the general purpose, viz, uninterrupted navigation of the river.

Trading boats will, of course, be regulated by the Treasury Department. I don't see as we have any right to interfere further than as to "contraband of war," and, to make this more clear, you and I ought to say what is contraband of war. The term is very indefinite, but I am clearly of opinion that the laws of war give the army and navy a legal right to protect themselves against contraband traffic and its agents.

Merchants as a class are governed by the law of self-interest, and the temptation to import and sell goods contraband is so great that many will engage in it, but this is confined to a class of men that you and I know well. The real merchant—the man who loves his country as we do—would not ask to send down the river arms and ammunition, or anything that would endanger our lives or the lives of our command.

There are some things, such as salt for curing meats, medicines to cure wounds and sickness, that I am not so clear about and care less. If you will prepare a list of contraband and send it to Secretary Chase, I know he will make it public and save us a world of trouble.

I have announced in orders that any officer of my command who makes a cent of profit by selling permits, passes, &c., or by any species of trade and speculation, is corrupt and criminal. I hear of such things, but really find few or no real cases, but I must stop scandal. Also, I contend I have a right to impress for military serv-

ice any men who have run from the North and come here to make
a living and avoid draft. I will pick up a few such, and this will
stop that class of meddlers and unauthorized hangers-on, who have
given us so much trouble.

As ever, your friend,

W. T. SHERMAN.

HDQRS. SECOND DIVISION, SIXTEENTH ARMY CORPS,
La Grange, Tenn., October 25, 1863.
COMDG. OFFICER SECOND CAVALRY BRIGADE,
La Grange:

COLONEL: You will send three of your squadrons of the Sixth
Tennessee Cavalry on a reconnaissance in the direction of Brownsville, Tenn., to start early to-morrow morning. The commanding
officer of said force will report to these headquarters in person this
evening for instructions.

By order of Brig. Gen. T. W. Sweeny:

L. H. EVERTS,
Captain, and Assistant Adjutant-General.

CIRCULAR.]   HEADQUARTERS CHIEF OF ARTILLERY,
DEPARTMENT OF THE CUMBERLAND,
Chattanooga, Tenn., October 25, 1863.

The general commanding the department directs that all the artillery in the divisions of your command be placed in position before
to-morrow morning (October 26) to resist an attack of the enemy.

J. M. BRANNAN,
Brigadier-General, Chief of Artillery.

CHATTANOOGA, TENN., *October 26, 1863—2 p. m.*
(Received 9 p. m.)
Maj. Gen. H. W. HALLECK,
General-in-Chief:

I have sent orders to General Sherman to move east toward Stevenson, leaving everything unguarded, except by the way of the
Army of the Cumberland, east of Bear Creek. The possibility of
the enemy breaking through our lines east of this, and present ina-
bility to follow him from there, if he should, is the cause of this
order. Sherman's forces are the only troops I could throw in to
head such a move.

U. S. GRANT,
Major-General.

WAR DEPARTMENT,
Washington, October 26, 1863—2.30 p. m.
Major-General GRANT,
Chattanooga, Tenn.:

Orders will be issued placing General Sherman in command of the
Army and Department of the Tennessee.

H. W. HALLECK,
General-in-Chief.

CHATTANOOGA, TENN., *October* 26, 1863.
(Received 1.25 a. m., 27th.)

Maj. Gen. H. W. HALLECK,
General-in-Chief:

I would respectfully recommend Maj. Gen. John A. Logan as a suitable commander for Sherman's corps.

U. S. GRANT,
Major-General.

HDQRS. MILITARY DIVISION OF THE MISSISSIPPI,
Chattanooga, Tenn., October 26, 1863.

Maj. Gen. H. W. HALLECK,
General-in-Chief, Washington :

I arrived here on the night of the 23d, after a ride on horseback of 50 miles from Bridgeport, over the worst roads it is possible to conceive of, and through a continuous drenching rain. It is now clear, and so long as it continues so it is barely possible to supply this army from its present base, but when winter rains set in it will be impossible. To guard against the possible contingency of having to abandon Chattanooga for want of supplies every precaution is being taken. The fortifications are being pushed to completion, and when done a large part of the troops could be removed back near to their supplies. The troops at Bridgeport are engaged on the railroad to Jasper, and can finish it in about two weeks. Rails are being taken from one of the branch roads, which we do not use. This shortens the distance to supplies 12 miles, and avoids the worst part of the roads in wet weather. General Thomas has also set on foot before my arrival a plan for getting possession of the river from a point below Lookout Mountain to Bridgeport. If successful, and I think it will be, the question of supplies will be fully settled.

The greatest apprehension I now have is that the enemy will move a large force up the river and force a passage through our lines between Blythe's Ferry and Cotton Port. Should he do this, our artillery horses are not in a condition to enable us to follow, and neither is our larder. This part of the line is well watched, but I can not say guarded. To guard against this, in addition to the troops now on that part of the river, I have directed General Thomas to increase the force at McMinnville immediately by one regiment of cavalry, with instructions to collect all the provisions and forage which the enemy would have to depend on for his subsistence, giving vouchers, payable at once, where taken from loyal citizens, and payable at the end of the war, on proof of good conduct, where disloyal. As soon as the fortifications are sufficiently defensible, a division will be sent there. I have also ordered Sherman to move eastward toward Stevenson until he received further orders, guarding nothing this side of Bear Creek, with a view of having his forces in a position to use if the enemy should attempt this move. Should this not be attempted when Sherman gets well up, there will be force enough to insure a line for our supplies, and enable me to move Thomas to the left, thus securing Burnside's position and give a strong hold upon that part of the line, from which I suppose a move will finally have to be made to turn Bragg. I think this will have to be done from the northeast. This leaves a gap to the west for the enemy to get into Middle Tennessee by, but he has no force to avail himself of this opportunity with except cavalry, and our cavalry can be held ready to oppose this.   I will endeavor to study up my position well, and post the troops to the best of my judgment, to meet all contingencies.   I will also endeavor to get the troops in a state of readiness for a forward movement at the earliest possible day.   What force the enemy have to my front, I have no means of judging accurately.   Deserters come in every day, but their information is limited to their own brigades, or divisions at furthest.   The camps of the enemy are in sight, and for the last few days there seems to have been some moving of troops; but where to I cannot tell.   Some seem to have gone toward Cleveland, whilst others moved in exactly an opposite direction.

I am, general, &c.,

U. S. GRANT,
Major-General.

HDQRS. MILITARY DIVISION OF THE MISSISSIPPI,
Chattanooga, October 26, 1863.

Indorsement on letter from Maj. Gen. H. W. Slocum, Twelfth Corps, asking to be relieved from duty under General Hooker:

Respectfully forwarded to headquarters of the army, Washington, D. C.

On taking command of the Military Division of the Mississippi, I found Major-General Hooker in command of the Eleventh and Twelfth Army Corps.   His position is one that rather embarrasses the service than benefits it, inasmuch as detaching one of these corps would leave two commanders for one small army corps.   As General Slocum objects to serving under General Hooker, who has been assigned to his present command by the President, I would respectfully recommend that General Hooker be assigned to the command of the Twelfth Army Corps and General Slocum relieved from further duty.

[U. S. GRANT,]
Major-General.

ST. LOUIS, MO., *October* 26, 1863.

Major-General GRANT:

I have sent a commissary to Eastport with 250,000 rations.   Five hundred thousand more and 250 head of cattle will follow this week. These will, I presume, be sufficient for Sherman's force, unless you desire a permanent depot of supplies forwarded thence in the direction of Chattanooga.   Shall a depot at Eastport be established?

T. J. HAINES,
Colonel, and Commissary of Subsistence.

DECHERD, *October* 26, [1863]—1 a. m.

Colonel McCOOK:

COLONEL: Keep your command saddled all night, and stand to horse at daylight in the morning.   Keep a good lookout and camp guards wide awake.   The explosion was at the mountain.   Rumored a torpedo blew up a locomotive.

By order:

WILLIAM H. SINCLAIR,
Assistant Adjutant-General.

[Indorsement.]

Colonel CAMPBELL :

I send this order for your information.   Comply with it.   Return his by the orderly.

EDWARD M. McCOOK,
Colonel, Commanding Division.

HEADQUARTERS DEPARTMENT OF THE CUMBERLAND,
Chattanooga, October 26, 1863—9 a. m.

Maj. Gen. H. W. SLOCUM, *Wartrace:*

You are to command all troops stationed on the railroad from Murfreesborough to Bridgeport, both inclusive.   You will pass over he line and make such disposition as you deem best, and report to hese headquarters where you think it advisable to establish your headquarters.   The message sent you in cipher referred to your communication marked personal, which has been referred to General Grant.

By order General Thomas :

J. J. REYNOLDS,
Major-General, Chief of Staff.

STEVENSON, *October 26,* 1863.

General SLOCUM :

Was requested to give you the following message :

STEVENSON, *October 25,* 1863—11 p. m.

General WILLIAMS, *Anderson:*

Yours of 9 p. m. just received.   General Slocum, with one division (yours, I believe), is responsible for the line south of Murfreesborough to Bridgeport, including Bridgeport.   No other directions have been given, save that he has been advised of how General Howard posted his troops.   General Slocum will advise you, but I should think not intended, to send Ruger's brigade to Bridgeport.

DANL. BUTTERFIELD,
Major-General, Chief of Staff.

OPERATOR.

CHATTANOOGA, *October 26,* 1863.

Maj. Gen. GEORGE H. THOMAS :

The Quartermaster-General suggests that Colonel Buell be detailed to take general supervision of all the troops between here and Bridgeport and Stevenson, and direct the repairs on the roads over which supplies are now brought.*   Colonel Buell is an engineer, and even with the small force on the road, could repair the worst places so as to materially facilitate the transportation of supplies.   I would also suggest that a call be made for ship carpenters and such mechanics as can work on the building of a steam-boat, and that 30, if that number can be got, be detailed on extra duty, and ordered to report to Capt. A. Edwards, acting quartermaster, Bridgeport, Ala.

U. S. GRANT,
Major-General.

---

* Colonel Buell so detailed by Special Field Orders, No. 286, headquarters Department of the Cumberland, same date.

ANDERSON, *October* 26, 1863.

Major-General BUTTERFIELD,
      Chief of Staff, Stevenson:

All of Howard's infantry has been relieved, and all of Geary's, except some near Murfreesborough. My troops are now on the way to relieve them. One of Geary's batteries is behind, but I understand on railroad train. One, or part of one, of Howard's batteries, I learn, is at Tantalon, or near it, without horses; horses at Bridgeport. It has been there, I am told, for some time, waiting railroad transportation. I will send the train up for it if possible.

Your dispatch ordered the batteries at Tantalon to be sent forward. I knew of none but my two batteries being there, and, of course, sent them forward. I reported to you at 12.30 o'clock yesterday that my batteries were at Tantalon.

A. S. WILLIAMS,
Brigadier-General.

BRIDGEPORT, *October* 26, 1863.

Major-General SLOCUM:

The general directs me to say under no circumstances make an order for any cars or trains to move General Williams' troops or batteries. Hereafter your troops will have to march to positions you assign them; the road is needed for supplies.

Acknowledge the receipt of this. Answer immediately.

DANL. BUTTERFIELD,
Major-General, Chief of Staff.

SPECIAL ORDERS,) HDQRS. DEPT. AND ARMY OF THE TENN.,
      No. 2.   (*Iuka, Miss., October* 26, 1863.

*   *   *   *   *   *   *

II. Capt. O. H. Howard, chief signal officer, Department of the Tennessee, having reported for duty, will distribute his officers equally among the Fifteenth, Sixteenth, and Seventeenth Corps, and will himself, with an assistant and two field signal apparatus, report at headquarters of the department in the field.

By order of Maj. Gen. W. T. Sherman:

R. M. SAWYER,
Assistant Adjutant-General.

ANDERSON, *October* 26, 1863.

Lieut. Col. H. C. RODGERS,
      Assistant Adjutant-General:

Ruger's brigade will be at Cowan this evening. It is ordered to guard from Elk River to Murfreesborough. I will telegraph him to send a regiment by first train to Christiana. The road has been interrupted to-day. Knipe's brigade is taking the posts from Bridgeport to Elk River, and is in possession as far up as Cowan. Have received no instructions from corps headquarters, except, generally, that I was to guard road from Bridgeport to Murfreesborough. Ruger will take first cars for all posts above; he is marching to-day.

A. S. WILLIAMS,
Brigadier-General.

ANDERSON, *October* 26, 1863—6 p. m.

Major-General BUTTERFIELD,
   Chief of Staff:

The train is here with the two batteries of my division. It has been detained by getting off track. Shall these batteries be taken up to Cowan and Eleventh Corps battery brought back on return, or shall my two batteries go on to Stevenson? I ordered my battery horses back, but messenger has not returned. They may be in Bridgeport.

        A. S. WILLIAMS,
         Brigadier-General.

STEVENSON, *October* 26, 1863—11.30 a. m.
     (Received 11.45 a. m., 26th.)

General ALPHEUS S. WILLIAMS:

No batteries of yours have been ordered to Bridgeport; it was the batteries of General Geary's division and General Howard's corps, that you were relieving, that were ordered forward. If you have started horses from your batteries you had better send and have them return at once. If you have not relieved Howard's and Geary's troops, do so at once, and send them to Bridgeport, short route. General Slocum will give all orders for your division.

        DANL. BUTTERFIELD.

BRIDGEPORT, *October* 26, 1863—6.30 p. m.
     (Received 6.45 p. m.)

ALPHEUS S. WILLIAMS:

Your dispatch of 3 p. m.* just received. The general directs me to repeat that orders for your batteries will only come from General Slocum. Make every possible exertion to send the batteries of the Eleventh Corps and of General Geary here without delay.

        DANL. BUTTERFIELD,
         Major-General.

MURFREESBOROUGH, *October* 26, 1863.

Major-General SLOCUM:

Wagon train of the Twelfth Corps left at 8 this morning. Information has been received here that Wheeler's cavalry are approaching Shelbyville and are within 8 miles of there.

Have you any cavalry?

        WM. L. UTLEY,
        Colonel, Commanding Post.

MURFREESBOROUGH, *October* 26, 1863.

Lieut. Col. H. C. RODGERS,
  Assistant Adjutant-General:

I have but two small regiments, numbering about 500. I have therefore sent five companies, under a competent officer; two com-

---

*Probably 6 p. m.

panies of the Twenty-second Wisconsin and three of the Thirty-first Wisconsin, leaving the remainder of the Thirty-first to guard water-tank and depot buildings.

WM. L. UTLEY,
Colonel, Commanding Post.

CHATTANOOGA, *October* 26, 1863—11.30 a. m.
Brig. Gen. R. B. MITCHELL:

The general commanding directs you to send two regiments of cavalry from your command, to relieve mounted troops now on duty, from here to Blythe's Ferry. One regiment will go to Blythe's Ferry, and relieve the battalion of Fourth Ohio Cavalry, under Lieutenant-Colonel Robie ; the other to relieve Colonel Harrison, Thirty-ninth Indiana. Send their transportation with them, and direct them to have their wagons loaded and follow along the line of railroad as soon as possible, while the regiments push on in advance.

The detachment guarding the river below this will be relieved as soon as possible.

C. GODDARD,
Assistant Adjutant-General.

MURFREESBOROUGH,
October 26, 1863—2.30 p. m.
Major-General SLOCUM:

My forces all inside the fortifications, except the Fourth Tennessee Cavalry and Thirty-first Wisconsin and one section Ninth Ohio Battery. The Thirty-first Wisconsin is situated on a hill about 400 yards from the fort, with a good redoubt and the section of Ninth Ohio Battery. They can easily fall into the fort, if necessary.

WM. L. UTLEY,
Colonel, Commanding Post.

HEADQUARTERS DEPARTMENT OF THE CUMBERLAND,
Chattanooga, October 26, 1863—1 p. m.
Governor ANDREW JOHNSON,
Nashville, Tenn.:

Dispatch of yesterday received. I deem it of vital importance that the Northwestern Railroad be finished as soon as possible, and will therefore cheerfully give you as many companies from the Michigan Engineers as can be spared. General Grant informed me that J. B. Anderson had been appointed by the War Department. I sincerely hope the new arrangement will work. Colonel Innes is an energetic and intelligent officer. I shall be glad to see General Gillem and confer with him on the matters you mention in your dispatch. Nothing will give me more pleasure than to aid all in my power to restore Tennessee to the Union.

GEO. H. THOMAS,
Major-General, Commanding.

NASHVILLE, *October* 26, 1863—8.10 p. m.
Lieutenant-Colonel GODDARD,
    Assistant Adjutant-General:

Dispatch of 22d just received. Answered yesterday. In answer to dispatch of 24th, effective force Seventh Kentucky, 342; Third East Tennessee, 189. Every available man now out after Hawkins, with orders to follow as long as a trace of him can be found.
R. S. GRANGER,
Brigadier-General, Commanding.

CHATTANOOGA, *October* 26, 1863—2 p. m.
(Received 27th.)
General BURNSIDE :

Have you indications of a force coming from Lee's army by way of Abingdon toward you? Do you hear of any of Bragg's troops threatening you from the southwest? Thomas' command is in bad condition to move, for want of animals of sufficient strength to move his artillery, and for want of subsistence. If you are threatened with a force beyond what you can compete with, efforts must be made to assist you. Answer.
U. S. GRANT,
Major-General, Commanding.

LOUDON, *October* 26, 1863.
General A. E. BURNSIDE,
    Commanding Army of the Ohio, Loudon, Tenn.:

GENERAL : The command, owing to broken-down horses and sick men, will not be as large as I expected. The Second Brigade can only start about 450, and report that it is every effective man. This brigade has about 1,300 men for duty, but has a line of pickets down the river and also couriers. I think, therefore, it will not be advisable to divide the command to send a large party to the rear.
Very respectfully, your obedient servant,
W. P. SANDERS,
Brigadier-General of Volunteers, Commanding Cavalry.

JONESBOROUGH, *October* 26, 1863.
Major-General BURNSIDE :

My advance and scouts on the river report all quiet during the night.

I give you below the statement of a discharged soldier, who was arrested by rebels in their retreat, and taken to Abingdon and released, and captured by our forces. He says he left Abingdon on the 16th instant, the day we were engaged in destroying the road above Bristol; that re-enforcements from the Tenth and Eleventh Corps had reached Abingdon; that the force at Abingdon on that day was 16,000; that they had sixty-odd pieces of artillery; that these re-enforcements were to have come down to Bull's Gap, but that we whipped the enemy back before they could get farther than

Abingdon. He also states that he has an uncle on General Williams' staff; that his uncle told him that General Ransom had started an infantry force, via Morrison Gap, to join Wheeler, Pegram, &c., at Cumberland Gap, and when that junction was effected there the force at Abingdon under Maj. Gen. William E. Jones and Hampton were to move down in this direction. I give you this for what it is worth. He says General William E. Jones and Hampton came with the re-enforcements. I think I will be able by night to give you some definite information in relation to the enemy.

J. M. SHACKELFORD,
Brigadier-General.

HEADQUARTERS DEPARTMENT OF THE TENNESSEE,
Iuka, October 26, 1863.

Major-General HURLBUT,
    Memphis:
Your corps report is received. I am forced to draw from your corps every man that can possibly be spared. Three hundred men at Paducah, 2,000 at Columbus, 3,500 at Memphis, 3,000 at Corinth, and 2,000 at intermediate points of the railroad must suffice for the present. This makes 10,000. Your report shows 23,000, besides the troops in Arkansas, some of which may be reasonably expected.

I want you to organize a strong division under General Dodge, of at least 8,000 effectives, and put them as quick as possible at East-port or Florence, to follow the Fifteenth Army Corps. You can use the railroad now exclusively, as I will trust to the river. Do you want to remain at Memphis or to take the field? Telegraph and write me fully your wishes. I send you to-morrow General Grant's letter, which makes the foregoing a necessity.

W. T. SHERMAN,
Major-General.

HEADQUARTERS SIXTEENTH ARMY CORPS,
Memphis, Tenn., October 26, 1863.

Brig. Gen. ROBERT ALLEN,
    Saint Louis, Mo.:
General Sherman directs that all stores and supplies for the Fifteenth Corps be sent by the Tennessee River.

S. A. HURLBUT,
Major-General.

HEADQUARTERS SIXTEENTH ARMY CORPS,
Memphis, Tenn., October 26, 1863.

Brig. Gen. G. M. DODGE,
    Corinth, Miss.:
GENERAL: I send General Stevenson to you for assignment to command. It will probably be well for you to break your force into two divisions, and give him the eastern one. Any arrangement you may make of this kind will be approved by me.
    Your obedient servant,

S. A. HURLBUT,
Major-General.

HEADQUARTERS FIFTEENTH ARMY CORPS,
Iuka, October 26, 1863.

General G. M. DODGE,
    Corinth, and
General S. A. HURLBUT,
    Memphis:

It will exactly suit us if Joe Johnston will assemble a force at Okolona. Don't disturb them now, but keep a spy there to report their object. I expect the Tennessee River will supply me in future, and I will look to the railroad only as auxiliary. I will gradually draw this way all the troops but a small command at Memphis, and from Tuscumbia or Iuka or Corinth we could strike any force the enemy may assemble on the Mobile and Ohio Railroad about Okolona or Columbus.

We want the enemy to divide, and not pile on too heavy at Chattanooga, where it is so hard to feed and supply our troops.

W. T. SHERMAN,
Major-General.

HEADQUARTERS SIXTEENTH ARMY CORPS,
Memphis, Tenn., October 26, 1863.

Brig. Gen. G. M. DODGE, *Corinth, Miss.:*

Make no movement on Okolona now. General Sherman wishes them to mass at that point. Keep close watch on their movement at and about Okolona, and report to him, as well as here, whatever you learn.

S. A. HURLBUT,
Major-General.

HEADQUARTERS SIXTEENTH ARMY CORPS,
Memphis, Tenn., October 26, 1863.

Brig. Gen. A. J. SMITH,
    Commanding Sixth Division, Columbus, Ky.:

GENERAL: I send you a copy of General Sherman's orders in letter form.[*]

I have ordered the Sixth Tennessee Cavalry to occupy the country about Jackson, and thence to Trenton, east of the Memphis and Ohio Railroad.

The Seventh Tennessee is ordered to move up to Union City to report to you as the nucleus of recruiting. Lieutenant-Colonel Hawkins is a very inferior officer, and should be got rid of.

With the Sixth established about Jackson, you will keep a considerable force in motion above and follow General Sherman's instructions.

Your obedient servant,

S. A. HURLBUT,
Major-General.

IUKA, *October 26, 1863.*

General HURLBUT:

Caution the newspapers of Memphis; they publish too much nonsense. No anonymous letters, no praise or censure of officers, no

---

* See p. 732.

discussion of the policy and measures of Government without the article is reviewed by the commanding officer at Memphis, and editor responsible for the general tenor of extracts of other papers. The manifold publications about the Collierville affair are ridiculous. My orders must not be published unless sent direct to the editor with an order of publication indorsed thereon.

W. T. SHERMAN,
Major-General.

CORINTH, *October* 26, 1863.

Col. AUGUST MERSY:

General Dodge wishes to know from what direction Richardson is moving or in what locality the scouts understand him to be.

Respectfully,

J. W. BARNES,
Assistant Adjutant-General.

HDQRS. DEPARTMENT AND ARMY OF THE TENNESSEE,
Iuka, Miss., October 26, 1863.

Maj. Gen. S. A. HURLBUT,
Comdg. Sixteenth Army Corps, Memphis, Tenn.:

GENERAL: By direction of the general commanding, I have the honor herewith to inclose for your perusal a copy of General Grant's letter* of date 19th instant; also a copy of telegram sent to you this evening.

Very respectfully, your obedient servant,

R. M. SAWYER,
Assistant Adjutant-General.

HEADQUARTERS SEVENTEENTH ARMY CORPS,
Vicksburg, Miss., October 26, 1863.

Maj. Gen. U. S. GRANT,
Commanding Department of the Tennessee:

DEAR GENERAL: I am just in receipt of your letter of the 17th instant, and am gratified to learn of your safe arrival in Cairo. I presume ere this you have received a full account of the reconnaissance toward Canton, as I sent you a full report the day I returned. I am satisfied the rebels have a much larger force of mounted men in this State than we have given them credit for.

If Chalmers had from 3,000 to 4,000 at Collierville and Lee 4,000 at Tuscumbia, they have not less than 10,000, as I know there were fully 2,500, with six pieces of artillery, in front of me when I was near Livingston, all cavalry and well armed. We got some few of their arms, short Enfield rifles, with sword bayonets, an excellent weapon for fighting on foot or on horseback.

I started the cavalry off several times on side roads to make a

---

* See Series I, Vol. XXX, Part III, p. —.

détour and come in on the rear flank of the enemy, but they invariably got stopped, and sent back for infantry and artillery to assist in dislodging the enemy. It is well they did not strike off for the Mobile and Ohio road; if they had they would have stood nine chances out of ten of being cut off.

There is no disguising the fact the cavalry of Cosby's and Whitfield's brigades is far superior to ours under Winslow. Winslow himself is a very good officer, though somewhat lacking in spirit and dash, but many of his subordinate officers are of no account whatever; even the horses have caught the timidity of the men, and turn around involuntarily and break for the rear as soon as a cannon shot is fired. This occurred twice on the expedition, and before any one was hurt. Winslow is doing his best to get the cavalry in shape, and make up a proper spirit. I am going to give him two rifled guns and two 12-pounder howitzers, in the place of his mountain howitzers, and I hope to see some signs of improvement.

All the information I can get confirms the report sent to you by Captain Gile, aide-de-camp, that the rebels have a very respectable force of infantry at Canton, Brandon, and other points toward Meridian.

Davis was as far west as Jackson with Joe Johnston. If they attempt to retake this place, I don't think they will find us unprepared, and they may expect to fight and fight hard and long before they get it. I have not had anything alarming from Hawkins for several days.

I learned to-day that an expedition of about 2,500 mounted men, with a battery of artillery, was organizing at some point northwest of Monroe, with a view of making a raid on the river, though I do not place much reliance on the information. It would be, however, in accordance with the instructions of the rebel Secretary of War, as contained in the letter which was captured. The fact is, general, I believe the rebels have more men in the field east of the Mississippi River to-day than we have, and they are able to concentrate them more rapidly than we can possibly do.

What shall I do with the Confederate prisoners who were left here in hospitals? There are 113 and 3 surgeons. All of them are convalescent, and can be moved, except 12. They ought to be disposed of in some way, and I do not feel like sending them out of the lines here until I hear from you.

I have presented your regards to all, and they all unite in sending their best wishes for your success. I assure you, general, nothing would give me more pleasure than to be near you, and to assist, to the best of my ability, in rendering your operations successful.

My kindest regards to all the staff, and believe me, truly, your friend,

JAS. B. McPHERSON,
Major-General.

HEADQUARTERS SEVENTEENTH ARMY CORPS,
Vicksburg, Miss., October 26, 1863.

Brig. Gen. JOHN P. HAWKINS,
Commanding Goodrich's Landing:

GENERAL: I have decided to retain the two negro regiments which you sent down here for the present, and have sent up for their camp and garrison equipage.   There is a vast amount of work required to complete the new line of defense for this place, and I am working all the men I can from Logan's and McArthur's divisions, as well as the negro brigade.   When this work is done I will order them back to you unless there are good reasons for detaining them here.   Do you hear anything more of the movements of the rebels west of Bayou Macon? It is reported that an expedition of about 2,000 is organizing at some point northwest of Monroe to make a raid on the river.   You will keep on the alert, and, if possible, get information of their movements in time for us to anticipate them.

Very respectfully, your obedient servant,

JAS. B. McPHERSON,
Major-General.

FRANKFORT, *October 26, 1863.*

Captain ANDERSON:

The guerrillas overrun the border and rob banks, sack towns, and pillage the people; all for want of horses, horse equipments, and arms. We have more than 3,000, and can clear the country if the men be mounted and equipped.   Can you have horses, &c., furnished?   Go to Camp Nelson now.

J. T. BOYLE,
Brigadier-General.

MUNFORDVILLE, *October 26, 1863—10 a. m.*

Colonel STRICKLAND,
Glasgow :

Send 100 mounted men toward and to Burkesville.   It is possible they may intercept Richardson.   Let them move immediately under some discreet officer.

E. H. HOBSON,
Brigadier-General.

SPECIAL ORDERS, }   HDQRS. SIXTEENTH ARMY CORPS,
No. 264.   }   *Memphis, Tenn., October 26, 1863.*

I. Pursuant to orders received from Maj. Gen. W. T. Sherman, commanding Department of the Tennessee, Brig. Gen. A. J. Smith, commanding District of Columbus, will cause the One hundred and eleventh Illinois Infantry to be embarked at Paducah and be transported by steamer to Waterloo, Tenn.; thence to march by land to Florence, Ala., reporting to Major-General Sherman.   All public military stores will be withdrawn from Paducah and the place abandoned as a military post.   The people of Paducah will be held responsible in person and in property for the maintenance of good order and peace within its limits, and will be notified that any insult or injury offered to any Union man will be visited upon the city in the banishment of its principal men and the destruction of property.

II. The Sixth Tennessee Cavalry, Colonel Hurst, will move upon

Bolivar and Jackson, covering the country east of the Memphis and Ohio Railroad, and suppressing with all necessary severity the guerrilla and conscripting parties south of Trenton. They will draw supplies from the country, giving receipts, to be settled at the close of the war. No plundering or pillaging by men or officers will be allowed. Colonel Hurst will report weekly, through the commanding officer at La Grange, to the chief of cavalry. The men of this regiment will not be permitted to scatter, but will move actively in organized force. All horses fit for Government service will be taken by the quartermaster of the regiment and turned over at once to the quartermaster at La Grange, and receipts given as above. The people of the country will be informed that they must organize to put down robbers and guerrillas or be subject to the continual presence of a force that will; they must co-operate with the National forces.*

*   *   *   *   *   *   *

IV. Brig. Gen. A. J. Smith will assemble all the mounted force he can spare at and near Union City and move down, sweeping the country between the Tennessee and Mississippi Rivers, in accordance with letter from General Sherman, a copy of which accompanies this order.†

*   *   *   *   *   *   *

V. Brig. Gen. J. D. Stevenson, having been assigned to this corps, will report to Brig. Gen. G. M. Dodge, at Corinth, commanding Left Wing, for duty.

*   *   *   *   *   *   *

VI. By direction of Major-General Sherman, commanding department, the several newspapers published in Memphis are warned that they must cease publication of reports, anonymous or otherwise, of action or movement of troops within this department. No discussion of the policy or measures of the Government will be tolerated, and the editors and publishers of newspapers will be held accountable for the character of extracts published by them from Northern papers. Neither officers nor troops within this command will be the subject of either praise or censure through these newspapers, as neither the editors nor the correspondents have the right or the ability to give praise where deserved or to withhold it when undeserved. No order of the major-general commanding department will be published unless accompanied with an order for publication from headquarters of the department.

By order of Maj. Gen. S. A. Hurlbut:

T. H. HARRIS,
Assistant Adjutant-General.

WASHINGTON, D. C.,
October 27, 1863—2.15 p. m.

Major-General GRANT,
      Chattanooga, Tenn.:

General John A. Logan has been placed in command of Sherman's corps. General G. H. Thomas has been appointed a brigadier-general, U. S. Army, in place of General R. Anderson, retired. Three Western batteries from here and a heavy battery from Wis-

---

*See p. 731.   †See p. 732.

consin have been ordered to Chattanooga. They can be used as garrison artillery, if required. I fear General Thomas' plan of raising a veteran regiment of artillery is impracticable, as the men would be drawn from different States, and, therefore, in violation of law and General Orders. An infantry regiment or several batteries from the same State can be organized as a regiment of heavy artillery. Had not any additional troops we can obtain better be sent to Corinth and Eastport, to secure General Sherman's rear?

H. W. HALLECK,
General-in-Chief.

CHATTANOOGA, TENN., *October* 27, 1863—9 p. m.
(Received 3.05 a. m., 28th.)
Maj. Gen. H. W. HALLECK,
General-in-Chief:

I have ordered McPherson to send one division of troops to Sherman. This will leave him a present effective force of at least 13,000 white troops. These will go by way of Corinth. I think it advisable to send all troops intended to join Sherman from the north up Tennessee River to Eastport.

U. S. GRANT,
Major-General.

CHATTANOOGA, TENN., *October* 27, 1863.
(Received 11.25 p. m.)
Major-General HALLECK,
General-in-Chief:

Four thousand sets horse equipments are required for the Department of the Cumberland as soon as they can be had. They should be sent to Nashville.

U. S. GRANT,
Major-General.

CHATTANOOGA, TENN., *October* 27, 1863—7 p. m.
(Received 3.10 a. m., 28th.)
Maj. Gen. H. W. HALLECK,
General-in-Chief:

Thomas Crutchfield is here, and reported to be a strong Union man. Thompson I do not know. I have ordered the immediate arrest of both, and will send them under guard to Louisville for trial.

U. S. GRANT,
Major-General.

HEADQUARTERS CHIEF OF ARTILLERY,
Decherd, Tenn., October 27, 1863.
Col. E. M. McCOOK,
Commanding First Division Cavalry:

COLONEL: Having been relieved from duty with the cavalry command, and from the First Cavalry Division of this department, I desire, through you, to convey to the officers and men of that division my thanks for the manner in which they have, with few exceptions, performed their whole duty, thereby greatly aiding me in the exercise of the command of such division. To you and to them I tender my acknowledgments of their gallantry and their soldierly conduct on all occasions, both on the field and in camp.

For your own services in the command of my division I have to thank you, and to assure you of my appreciation of your labors in the camp and your gallantry and skill in the field.

I remain, very respectfully, your obedient servant,

ROBT. B. MITCHELL,
Brigadier-General.

DECHERD, *October* 27, 1863.

Lieut. Col. C. GODDARD,
Assistant Adjutant-General:

The following dispatch is just received:

COLUMBIA, *October* 27, 1863.

Maj. W. H. SINCLAIR,
Assistant Adjutant-General, Decherd:

My scouts have returned from Pulaski. They learn from deserters that rebel cavalry have not crossed the Tennessee; that Wheeler had stated his intention to cross as soon as organized. The deserters left the river Saturday morning. Scouts from Shelbyville have been to Pulaski. I shall send scouts to penetrate as far as the river, if possible, and will keep you advised.

H. R. MIZNER,
Colonel, Commanding.

WILLIAM H. SINCLAIR,
Assistant Adjutant-General.

TULLAHOMA, *October* 27, 1863.

Lieutenant-Colonel RODGERS,
Assistant Adjutant-General:

Have just arrived. My headquarters will be here for the present. Will report position of troops to-morrow. Please send division mail here.

A. S. WILLIAMS,
Brigadier-General, Commanding Division.

TULLAHOMA, *October* 27, 1863—6 p. m.

Lieutenant-Colonel RODGERS,
Assistant Adjutant-General:

Have the kindness to inform me whether my orders, sending the Second Massachusetts to Christiana and the Third Wisconsin to Wartrace, were changed upon their reporting at corps headquarters, and, if so, what are their present positions?

THOS. H. RUGER,
Brigadier-General.

TULLAHOMA, *October 27, 1863.*

Lieutenant-Colonel RODGERS,
        Assistant Adjutant-General:

Have arrived here. Received dispatch to leave two regiments here. Will leave Twenty-seventh Indiana and One hundred and fiftieth New York. Will have Thirteenth New Jersey and One hundred and seventh New York as far as Wartrace to-morrow.

THOS. H. RUGER,
        Brigadier-General.

COWAN, *October 27, 1863.*

Lieutenant-Colonel RODGERS,
        Assistant Adjutant-General:

Muhlenberg's and Woodbury's batteries were loaded on cars to go to Bridgeport, under General Butterfield's orders, and it was afterward found he intended one battery of the Eleventh Corps and one of Geary's instead. I held them at Anderson until 2 o'clock this morning awaiting Moseley's arrival with the instructions, but Moseley did not reach me, and an engine having been sent from Stevenson to haul our batteries, I have brought them here. I find here the orders Moseley brought, which direct that these batteries shall go to Stevenson and Bridgeport. I cannot control the train only to Decherd. Shall I ask Innes for an engine to haul the batteries to Stevenson, or shall I unload here and send them by land? I do not think the horses can draw them over the mountain, and besides some of the wheels cannot stand it. Will give further particulars hereafter.

A. S. WILLIAMS,
        Brigadier-General.

COLUMBIA, *October 27, 1863.*

W. H. SINCLAIR,
        Assistant Adjutant-General:

Daily information confirms the belief that there are no rebels this side of Tennessee River, except scouting and foraging parties and bands of stragglers and deserters. I captured 12 guerrillas last night.

H. R. MIZNER,
        Colonel, Commanding.

NASHVILLE, *October 27, 1863.*

Col. C. GODDARD,
        Assistant Adjutant-General:

The garrison at this post is as follows: Seventy-ninth Ohio Volunteer Infantry, Seventieth Indiana, One hundred and fifth Illinois, One hundred and twenty-ninth Illinois, and Eighteenth Michigan; total infantry, 2,882; Seventh Kentucky and Third East Tennessee Cavalry; total cavalry, 531; total artillery, 182. On railroad between this and Murfreesborough—One hundred and second Illinois, 476 strong, disposed as follows: One company at Overall's Creek one company at Stewart's Creek, one company at stockades Nos. 1, 2, and 3 each, five companies at La Vergne, one battery of artillery, one piece at stockade No. 1, one piece at stockade No. 2, two at La Vergne, and one at Stewart's Creek.

Thirteenth Wisconsin, about 600 strong, arrived this evening. This, with the infantry at this post, is the least possible infantry force with which the duty at this post can be performed. The cavalry should be increased to 1,000 effective men to patrol the road, to escort trains, droves of cattle, droves of horses, for vedettes on the numerous pikes out of this post, and to leave a reasonable force to look after the large force of guerrillas to the west and east of this post. Hawkins and other guerrilla chiefs have not less than 1,000, and more, probably 800 men, along the Harpeth and west of it. Fifty men are reported to-night within 6 miles of La Vergne. General Hooker and commanding officer at Murfreesborough report 800 at Milton. There are in addition small bands in Wilson County, which would increase the force 50 more, making a total of 1,700. If the force at Milton is not exaggerated, I am certain the number (1,700) is a low estimate of the enemy's mounted force which this force would have to look after. Hawkins and two other chiefs to the west have been reported to me from Clarksville and other forces [places?] as high as 1,000. No reports have recently been received from my division occupying my station south of Murfreesborough. Franklin and Columbia are occupied by the Fourteenth Michigan. Two companies arrived at Franklin and eight at Columbia. If guns on fortifications are to be manned 200 artillerists will be required. I strengthened the posts between this and Gallatin with troops sent by General Boyle, now under command of General Paine, and which are to be relieved as soon as possible and returned to Kentucky.

R. S. GRANGER,
Brigadier-General.

NASHVILLE, *October 27.* 1863—3.30 p. m.
Maj. Gén. JOSEPH J. REYNOLDS,
Chief of Staff:

I have the honor to report another accident upon the road last night. The rebels placed a torpedo upon the track just south of the tunnel, and as soon as the engine struck it, it blew her up, throwing her across the track and making a complete wreck of her. I have a large force hard at work getting things righted again.

W. P. INNES,
Colonel, and Military Superintendent.

CHATTANOOGA, *October 27,* 1863—1.30 p. m.
Maj. Gen. A. E. BURNSIDE,
Knoxville, Tenn.:

Relieve General Boyle from duty at Louisville and order him to the field. In choosing a successor, we want a man of firmness and free from all politics and isms, one who will do his duty without fear and with good judgment.

U. S. GRANT,
Major-General.

LOUDON, TENN., *October* 27, 1863—7 p. m.
(Received 11.45 a. m., 28th.)

Maj. Gen. U. S. GRANT,
Chattanooga, Tenn., and
Maj. Gen. H. W. HALLECK,
General-in-Chief:

We have had many reports here with reference to Ewell's corps coming from Lee's army against us by way of Abingdon, but the indications are that no such force has yet made its appearance at Abingdon, and I am inclined to believe the reports to be incorrect. But there is a considerable force from Bragg's army on this side of the Hiwassee; one division at Sweet Water and two others said to be approaching there. We have had constant cavalry skirmishing for several days, the first day resulting in a loss to us of over 400 prisoners from Wolford's brigade, but since that day the results have been in our favor. The morning I came here I determined that the position held by our troops on the railroad side of the river was not a good position for defense, except for a larger force than can possibly be spared. For this place I ordered what I considered to be sufficient re-enforcements to make a move toward the Hiwassee, but I am now satisfied that no decisive result will follow a movement of that kind, particularly as this army is not ready for a movement. We might drive the enemy to the Hiwassee River, but as their cars run up to the crossing a sufficient force could be concentrated against us by them, no doubt, to drive us back, and no good would result from the movement. I have been warned by General Halleck not to be caught on the south side of the river, and nothing but a strong desire to attack a force from the front of the Army of the Cumberland ever kept me on that side, because I am not strong enough to attack them in the flank, although I was at one time favorable to passing their flank and attacking their communications. I have, therefore, thought it best to withdraw the force from the south side of the river, and only attempt to hold that part of the country south of the Holston and east of Little Tennessee River, and all of that part of the State north of the Big Tennessee. Neither the Little Tennessee nor the Holston are now fordable, and I shall now move the pontoon-bridge to some point above the junction of these rivers, and hold Kingston and Knoxville as strongly as possible. We are building pontoon-boats as rapidly as possible at Kingston for a bridge across the Tennessee just below the mouth of the Clinch River, which, with a flank movement in case they attempt to move up the railroad to Loudon in force, [*sic*]

I telegraphed you several days ago in reference to the construction of a road which we propose to draw our supplies on. If the railroad to McMinnville is in operation, it is possible that supplies might be drawn from there; but it is reported as almost impracticable, particularly at the crossing of the Caney Fork River. I am satisfied that if the enemy hold the country about Chattanooga so that we cannot command the railroad, we shall have to draw our supplies from the head of navigation on the Cumberland, near the mouth of the Big South Fork. Steps have been taken to put the road in condition for winter travel from that place. The only Indiana regiments we have are in the extreme front. Details will be sent as soon as possible. Our necessities for subsistence and clothing will prevent us from accumulating a supply of ammunition as rapidly as you order.   Unless Captain Irvin can furnish wagon transportation from McMinnville for the clothing which he proposes to send up from Nashville, we can probably get it sooner from Camp Nelson. If he could possibly send the amount you ordered to Kingston, it would be a very great service to us.   If the disposition of my forces is not satisfactory to you, I shall be very glad to receive from you specific instructions.   If it becomes necessary to evacuate this country in order to re-enforce Thomas, we hold ourselves ready to do it, though it would be a sad thing for this country.   While I do not believe that Ewell's corps is at Abingdon, I am satisfied that all the rebel forces of West Virginia are concentrated in that neighborhood, and will probably amount to 15,000.

A. E. BURNSIDE,
Major-General.

LOUDON, TENN., October 27, 1863—2 p. m.
(Received 11.10 p. m.)

His Excellency ABRAHAM LINCOLN,
President United States:

I deem it my duty to say to you that the state of my health is such that I may at any moment become unfit for duty in the field.   I have been suffering more or less ever since the Mexican war with chronic diarrhea, but having a remarkable constitution the effects of disease have not been apparent to any save those intimately connected with me.   This is one of the reasons why I have been so anxious to quit the field, and I am now suffering very much from it, and therefore deem it my duty to let you know this that you may think of the possibility of making other arrangements for the command of the department.   I do not ask to be relieved during the present emergency, and shall continue at my post as long as it is possible and desirable for the interests of the public service.

A. E. BURNSIDE,
Major-General.

HEADQUARTERS ARMY OF THE OHIO,
October 27, 1863.

Brigadier-General WHITE,
Comdg. Second Division, Twenty-third Army Corps:

GENERAL: By direction of the commanding general, I have the honor to give you the following as the arrangement for withdrawing the troops from the south side of the river to-morrow.   General Potter has been ordered to be on this side of the river before daylight with the main body of his troops and his baggage, but will leave his line of pickets till the main body of your troops have crossed.   Your pickets as well as those of General Potter will maintain their position till the return of a body of cavalry, which will go out before daylight; when that returns the pickets will be withdrawn and will cross together with the cavalry.   The citizens can cross at any time you may find most convenient.   It will be necessary to instruct the pickets to allow no one with any pass whatever to go out of the lines, though they can permit persons to enter.   The commanding general directs that the locomotive and cars be thrown into the river and pontoon bridge be swung to the north side entire, if it is possible to do so.

I have the honor to be, general, very respectfully, your obedient servant,

LEWIS RICHMOND,
Assistant Adjutant-General.

HEADQUARTERS NINTH ARMY CORPS,
Camp opposite Loudon, October 27, 1863.

Brigadier-General FERRERO,
Commanding First Division, Ninth Army Corps:

GENERAL : You will have your entire command in readiness, and recross the river to-morrow morning (28th) punctually at 5 a. m. (not earlier), sending your train and batteries in advance. You will have everything over the river by 6 a. m., punctuality and celerity of movement being particularly enjoined. Your pickets will be withdrawn at the same time with those of General White's command.

On receipt of this order you will instruct your pickets to allow no one at all to pass out of the lines. Make your preparations and conduct the movement as rapidly and quietly as possible. On reaching this side of the river you will move out on the road leading to Lenoir's, halting at 1½ miles.

By command of Brigadier-General Potter :
SAM'L WRIGHT,
Assistant Adjutant-General.

JONESBOROUGH, *October 27, 1863.*

General BURNSIDE:

One of my scouts is just in. From the information he brings, on which I rely, I am satisfied that it is a mistake about Ewell's corps, or any part of it, having come to Abingdon. They have received some re-enforcements, probably 2,000, I think not more. I have arrangements by which I think I can get information of any movement they may make.

Can I now send expedition to North Carolina for horses? I now have plenty horseshoe iron, and if we had sufficient number of horses the command, excepting clothing, could soon be in good condition.

You will please answer.

J. M. SHACKELFORD,
Brigadier-General.

JONESBOROUGH, *October 27, 1863.*

Colonel RICHMOND :

Since my telegram of this morning I have also received information that the rebel cavalry had made its appearance at Kingsport and that about 100 had crossed the river. The statements of Burk are directly at variance with the information obtained by my scouts, except as to re-enforcements, which the scouts estimate at 2,000. I have also seen two from North Carolina, from above Abingdon. On the 17th they were moving to Indiana, and state that on that day they saw those trains pass with troops for Abingdon. The trains had from 9 to 14 coaches, and filled inside and on top. The rebels claimed 10,000 re-enforcements. I cannot think their force as large as represented. I will send you soon official report of my command, as requested by the general. I have a large number of dismounted men, reaching nearly to, if not entirely, one-fourth. We have plenty of flour and beef. I have telegraphed Colonel Garrard, at Rogersville, to keep on the alert, and learn all he can of the movements of the enemy. You may rest assured I will leave nothing undone that I could possibly do to ascertain the facts, and will soon advise you and the general.

J. M. SHACKELFORD,
Brigadier-General.

JONESBOROUGH, October 27, 1863.
(Received 9.30 p. m.)

General BURNSIDE:

An Irishman just in from between rivers reports that a lady who lives in this town, who had been up into Virginia, came into his neighborhood late this evening, and that she reported four brigades of the enemy on this side of Zollicoffer, and also troops marching between Bristol and Zollicoffer; all moving for Carter's Station. The Irishman is entirely honest in his statements, and the approach of rebel cavalry at Kingsport to-day and the woman's statements seem to corroborate the statements of Burke.

J. M. SHACKELFORD,
Brigadier-General.

GENERAL ORDERS, }   WAR DEPT., ADJT. GENERAL'S OFFICE,
No. 349.   }   Washington, October 27, 1863.

By direction of the President, Maj. Gen. William T. Sherman is appointed to the command of the Department and Army of the Tennessee, headquarters in the field, and Maj. Gen. John A. Logan to the command of the Fifteenth Army Corps.

By order of the Secretary of War:

E. D. TOWNSEND,
Assistant Adjutant-General.

CHATTANOOGA, October 27, 1863—2 p. m.

Maj. Gen. WILLIAM T. SHERMAN
    (Care General Crook, Maysville, Ala.):

I have ordered McPherson* to send forward Tuttle's division to report to you. Repeat the order, stating how you wish it to come. The order placing you in command of the Department and Army of the Tennessee has been made in Washington.

U. S. GRANT,
Major-General.

---

* By dispatch of same date.

IUKA, *October 27, 1863.*

Major-General HURLBUT:

General Dodge was here last night, and spoke of his division as the Second Division of your corps. Its aggregate, he said, would be about 8,000 men, leaving out Sweeny's command at La Grange. General Dodge wrote you last night a letter, which you will get this evening, giving the regiments composing his old division.

W. T. SHERMAN,
Major-General.

HEADQUARTERS DEPARTMENT OF THE TENNESSEE,
Iuka, October 27, 1863.

General HURLBUT,
Memphis:

I made up my figures from the field report made by you. Dodge proposes to take two regiments of cavalry, two batteries of artillery, and certain regiments of infantry, which he enumerated and wrote to you. After I cut loose, if our road be found to be an element of weakness, we will drop it for a time. With our present force we cannot attempt to reopen the northern road. It will be time for us to replace our roads when the new levies come to us next spring. This present pressure is a crisis, and we must strip for it. General Dodge's letter will explain all when received by you.

W. T. SHERMAN,
Major-General.

MEMPHIS, *October 27, 1863.*

Major-General SHERMAN:

I have at Memphis, infantry and artillery, 4,793; in Dodge's command, 8,978; at Columbus, 2,777; deduct from Columbus the One hundred and eleventh Illinois, ordered to Florence, and the One hundred and thirty-first, gone to Vicksburg, by Grant's order, and Columbus is within your margin. I have in the Cavalry Division 5,653. I will organize at once the division you speak of, but wish to know in what proportions of infantry and cavalry you want, as that number (8,000) cannot be made of infantry, without stripping every post of infantry, and leaving less on the line by far than you propose. My effective infantry and artillery this side the Mississippi is 16,548 to be retained, and your order, 10,000, leaving available 6,548. Do you still want the Columbus and Corinth Railroad opened, as formerly directed? It appears to me a useless expense, as it certainly cannot be kept.

S. A. HURLBUT,
Major General.

HEADQUARTERS SIXTEENTH ARMY CORPS,
Memphis, Tenn., October 27, 1863.

Brig. Gen. G. M. DODGE,
Corinth, Miss.:

Letters received. You will take your old division unbroken. Supply the points mentioned in your letter as you indicate. It seems the best thing that can be done until troops come from Arkansas.

Make requisitions by telegraph for what you want and let it be pushed to you while the road stands, which will not be long. I will see you to-morrow.

S. A. HURLBUT,
Major-General.

CORINTH, *October 27, 1863.*

Major-General SHERMAN :

Scouts from Savannah and east side of river say scouts are all preparing to leave east side of river. Lieutenant-Colonel Cooper is at or near Clifton with two companies. Captains Harden and Russell are on Indian Creek; Newsom west of river, crossed at Clifton. They have a ferry-boat at that place. General Wheeler crossed at Lamb's Ferry south of Tennessee some time ago. He reports the loss of 2,000 in his raid.

G. M. DODGE,
Brigadier-General.

HEADQUARTERS SIXTEENTH ARMY CORPS,
Memphis, Tenn., October 27, 1863.

Brig. Gen. G. M. DODGE,
Corinth, Miss.:

Repeat your dispatch to General Sherman; I think it exaggerated. I shall come out to Iuka in the morning.

S. A. HURLBUT,
Major-General.

CORINTH, *October 27, 1863.*

Major-General SHERMAN :

General Sweeny sends the following dispatch :

An escaped conscript reports to commanding officer at White's Station that Chalmers and Ruggles are building bridges across Tallahatchie near Wyatt; have seventeen pieces of artillery and about 8,000 troops, Tennessee, Mississippi, Missouri, and Texas troops.

G. M. DODGE,
Brigadier-General.

HEADQUARTERS SIXTEENTH ARMY CORPS,
Memphis, Tenn., October 27, 1863.

Brigadier-General DODGE,
Corinth, Miss.:

Cavalry will move from this line to Tallahatchie. I do not believe the story.

S. A. HURLBUT,
Major-General.

HEADQUARTERS SIXTEENTH ARMY CORPS,
Memphis, Tenn., October 27, 1863.

Captain HOPKINS,
  Depot Commissary, Memphis, Tenn.:

It is necessary that all the stores possible should be collected at Corinth as soon as practicable. We should have on hand there 500,000 rations. The road cannot be secure long, and they should be pushed out as speedily as possible.

  Your obedient servant,

S. A. HURLBUT,
Major-General.

U. S. GUNBOAT HASTINGS,
Eastport, October 27, 1863.

Maj. Gen. WILLIAM T. SHERMAN, U. S. Army,
  Commanding Department of the Tennessee:

GENERAL: The river has been rising for two days, but is again on a stand, with scant 3 feet on the shoals. It would be a risk to send the Key West up to Cane Creek, and she could not remain there to cross the divisions with the river in its present condition. A light-draught steamer could take the barge up—always provided the sunken coal barges will not prevent—and cross the troops. No such boat has arrived, and we do not know when one will come. The remaining transportation of this division will be across during the night. I judge from what we have so far experienced that it will take thirty-six hours of good weather to cross the division. I propose to go down the river this evening to hurry up transports to assist in the crossing, and, if no boat is met, at all events to bring up a flat, with which we can reduce the time of crossing a division to twenty hours. I can reach Fort Henry to-morrow morning, and turn back, so as to be here day after to-morrow evening. I think I shall in this way do the best to the end of getting your forces over. Meanwhile, this vessel will remain here, and will cross transportation and troops as well as has been so far done. In the morning there will be no people to cross, and if the 4 or 5 inch rope (three coils of that circumference) could be got here—and I am told an officer of the pioneers has gone for it—it could be got across, the barge established as a ferry, and the Hastings then could take troops over, thus expediting matters. Your men will have a march of 15 miles to make, which will delay arrival at Chickasaw till day after to-morrow. The next division might not leave the present position till a day later, when, perhaps, the arrival of a suitable boat may enable you to cross it at Cane Creek.

  I am, respectfully, your obedient servant,

S. L. PHELPS,
Lieutenant-Commander.

HDQRS. DEPARTMENT AND ARMY OF THE TENNESSEE,
Iuka, October 27, 1863.

Maj. Gen. FRANK P. BLAIR, Jr.,
  Commanding Fifteenth Army Corps:

DEAR GENERAL: General Ewing is marching to-day for Eastport; will cross and march to Florence. I was down to Eastport yesterday, and we went up to the Colbert Shoals and grounded in less than 4 feet. No boat yet at hand can reach Florence. I expect one or more daily, and should it come before you are ready to move, I will want you to send back to load up and march to Tuscumbia and cross with the whole corps—Fifteenth. But if boats should not arrive in time, I want you to send back all ambulances and light wagons, to load up and move to Eastport, there to cross over and proceed to Florence. The troops, however, and loaded wagons should march direct to Chickasaw, from which point (1 mile above) you can be crossed directly to Waterloo, saving 3 miles on the other side, and more than 10 on this.

As soon as I hear the result of your operations at the front, I will give you the orders to start, and point out these facts now that you may prepare.

We will need a good many of the wagons now with the First, Second, and Third Divisions to move ammunition, provisions, and forage to the river, but hereafter I hope all stores will come to us up the Tennessee.

Fuller's command is arrived, and Dodge's strong command will be ready to follow us close.

Ewing will be in Florence 29th. I want the whole corps there as soon as possible, and only await your return and the arrival of boats. We have a magnificent coal-barge decked over, and two gunboats, which can cross men and wagons at Eastport or Waterloo, but before you get over I hope to have some more flats and a steam ferry-boat. The moment you return, send me a courier with all news. Nothing new since my last. The enemy's cavalry attacked an Alabama (Union) regiment of cavalry 25 miles south of this last evening, the full details of which are not yet received.

It is reported at Okolona that Lee is expected back there with the cavalry that was to your front, and it may be he was on his way to Okolona when he caught this erratic Alabama regiment of ours, which had gone off on some recruiting or other errand.

Truly, yours,

W. T. SHERMAN,
Major-General, Commanding.

HEADQUARTERS,
Tuscumbia, Ala., October 27, 1863.

Maj. Gen. WILLIAM T. SHERMAN,
Commanding Department and Army of the Tennessee:

GENERAL : We left camp at Cherokee yesterday morning at daybreak, and found the enemy wide awake. They first resisted us at Little Cane Creek, then at Cane Creek, 1 mile beyond. They showed fight at another small creek or defile 3 miles this side of Cane, and finally at Little Bear Creek, where they had a very strong position, and as it had grown late I thought it best to encamp. This morning the Second Division made a *détour* to the right and crossed a mile above the railroad crossing after a pretty sharp skirmish. At the same moment, De Gress' battery went into position and opened with the 20-pounder Parrotts on them, and they left in a very great hurry, after which we entered Tuscumbia without any further opposition.

The enemy, I understand, have fallen back beyond Town Creek,

14 miles from here, where Wheeler is reported with some force. His force is estimated by some very large, say 14,000, of course grossly exaggerated. Lee was in command of the force which opposed us. His force at the very largest estimate did not exceed 3,000 men, with six pieces of artillery. It is said that Ferguson left them the day before and we marched, with a small force, intending to operate against the railroad. Our losses are inconsiderable, say 3 men killed and 10 wounded. The enemy must have suffered much more severely. Lightburn, in flanking them this morning, saw 4 of their dead. I have heard from several sources of many of them being killed and wounded, and find in this town Colonel Forrest and a captain and 6 privates, rebel wounded; severely wounded all of them. Dr. Bailey thinks that Forrest can be removed, and I propose to bring him in because of the conduct of the rebels in declaring their men and officers exchanged in violation of the cartel.

We shall return to-morrow morning, and probably reach our camp to-morrow night.

I forgot to say that we lost some doctors and a medicine wagon at Little Cane, in consequence of a positive disobedience of orders. They were too anxious to be in the rear. The wagon I understand was burned, and I don't care if the doctors were in it.

The country is pretty well cleaned out of everything, and these people I think are losing faith in the rebel leaders, who have promised to clean us out every step of the way. I hope you have not been molested in your operations. I will be back in time, I hope, to prevent any delay in the move.

The river is said to be falling here. It is reported here from various sources that Bragg is falling back to Atlanta.

Very respectfully, your obedient servant,

FRANK P. BLAIR, Jr.,
Major-General, Commanding.

HEADQUARTERS DEPARTMENT OF THE TENNESSEE,
Iuka, October 27, 1863.

Col. D. C. ANTHONY,
Sixty-sixth Indiana, Collierville:

DEAR COLONEL: Captain Fitch has just shown me your letter. The accounts published in the newspapers of that affair at Collierville are generally ridiculous and nonsensical, and I shall stop all such trash hereafter from originating in Memphis.

Your command, of course, did all any person could expect, and is entitled to credit equally with the regulars. You will remember on leaving you I told you to make the official report, and I hope you have done so. It was your fight, not mine. I happened to drop in accidentally, and the regulars, as usual, were welcome guests, but the moment Chalmers drew off I came along on my journey. I assure you of my personal respect, and you may convey to your officers and men my personal thanks for defending their posts manfully.

Yours, truly,

W. T. SHERMAN,
Major-General, Commanding.

HDQRS. DEPARTMENT AND ARMY OF THE TENNESSEE,
Iuka, October 27, 1863.

Brig. Gen. J. E. SMITH,
Commanding Division, Dickson's:

DEAR GENERAL : That you may act understandingly, I now advise you that at this moment General Ewing's command is moving, via Eastport, Waterloo, and Gravelly Spring, to Florence. There are two gunboats now at Eastport and more coming with transports, &c. I tried to go over the Colbert Shoals yesterday, but the boat Hastings, drawing fully 4 feet, could not pass, but I expect every hour boats of lighter draught, in which case I will get one or more to Florence, in which event I will have the three divisions now in front of Bear Creek move on to Tuscumbia, &c. Otherwise, I will move you all by the left flank to Chickasaw and cross you to Waterloo, Florence, &c.

General Blair's command will be at Cherokee, I expect, to-morrow. Will take the command of the Fifteenth Corps, of which your division must, of necessity, supply the place of the Third till some future chance enables us to make the change without too much cost to the Government.

When the time comes for you to move either way, if we do not have the railroad up to you, you will be able to send back all empty or light wagons to this point, to load up and join you at Waterloo. The road hence to Eastport is elegant, and I suppose that from Dickson to Chickasaw is also very good, though hilly.

I am, &c.,

W. T. SHERMAN,
Major-General, Commanding.

HEADQUARTERS DEPARTMENT OF THE TENNESSEE,
Iuka, Miss., October 27, 1863.

Editors of Memphis Bulletin :

I don't think you can conceive the mortification a soldier feels at the nauseating accounts given to the public as history. That affair at Collierville should have been described in these words : "Chalmers tried to take Collierville, and did not ;" but ridiculous, nonsensical descriptions have followed each other so fast that you ought to be ashamed to print Collierville. Now I am again in authority over you, and you must heed my advice. Freedom of speech and freedom of the press, precious relics of former history, must not be construed too largely. You must print nothing that prejudices government or excites envy, hatred, and malice in a community. Persons in office or out of office must not be flattered or abused. Don't publish an account of any skirmish, battle, or movement of an army unless the name of the writer is given in full and printed. I wish you success, but my first duty is to maintain "order and harmony."

Yours,

W. T. SHERMAN,
Major-General, Commanding.

SPECIAL ORDERS, }   HDQRS. DEPT. AND ARMY OF THE TENN.,
No. 3.   }   *Iuka, October 27, 1863.*

I. General Dodge's division and Fuller's brigade, of the Sixteenth Army Corps, will be forthwith fitted out for field service, and will move east of Corinth, hold for the time being Iuka and Bear Creek, and the moment the command is fitted for the field will move forward and report to headquarters, wherever they may be. Major-General Hurlbut will make all necessary orders and dispositions to carry this into effect.

*   *   *   *   *   *   *

By order of Maj. Gen. W. T. Sherman :

R. M. SAWYER,
Assistant Adjutant-General.

GENERAL ORDERS, }   HDQRS. SIXTEENTH ARMY CORPS,
No. 148.   }   *Memphis, Tenn., October 27, 1863.*

I. In conformity with the spirit and tenor of General Orders, No. 2, current series, from headquarters Department and Army of the Tennessee, October 25, 1863, commandants of posts and military districts, and local provost-marshals hitherto acting under General Orders, No. 57, dated headquarters Department of the Tennessee, September 22, 1863, are relieved from the duty prescribed by that order.

Henceforward the authorized agents of the Treasury Department will alone issue permits for the purchase and sale of cotton and other products of the soil, and for the other matters incident to trade and commerce.

II. Permits hitherto granted under the above General Orders, No. 57, will be reported, on arrival at Memphis, to the Treasury agents, who are authorized and requested to examine the same rigorously, with a view to the detection and punishment of fraud.

III. Military officers will in all cases promptly notify Mr. Thomas H. Yeatman, special agent at Memphis, of any parties of rebel force or guerrillas in their respective limits, which may render the shipment of supplies dangerous or improper.

By order of Maj. Gen. S. A. Hurlbut :

T. H. HARRIS,
Assistant Adjutant-General.

HEADQUARTERS DEPARTMENT OF THE TENNESSEE,
Iuka, Miss., October 28, 1863.
(Received 12 p. m., 30th.)

Maj. Gen. H. W. HALLECK, *General-in-Chief :*

General Blair entered Tuscumbia yesterday, and General Ewing will be in Florence to-morrow, having crossed at Eastport. I tried to get a boat over Colbert Shoals, to enable Blair to cross over, but failed. Water good up to Eastport, but not above. I will push the whole of the Fifteenth Army Corps at Eastport, and occupy Florence at once. Parish's [?], Lee's, Wheeler's, and Ferguson's cavalry are on my front and right flank. Blair drove them beyond Town Creek. Ferguson's (rebel) encountered the First Alabama (Union) Regiment, on its return from a raid, and worsted it. Details not yet received in full. At all other points we got decidedly the advantage. Railroad across Bear Creek is done, but unless I can get boats to Tuscumbia, so as to cross over, we gain nothing by repairing any more of it. Tennessee River is in fine stage up to Colbert Shoals.

W. T. SHERMAN,
Major-General, Commanding.

(Same to Grant.)

GENERAL ORDERS, }   HDQRS. DEPT. AND ARMY OF THE TENN.,
     No. 4.   }   *Iuka, Miss., October* 28, 1863.

I. This department being an insurrectionary district, and the execution of the laws of the United States being resisted by armed rebels, every citizen is liable to be called on for military service; and, if so called on, must render it.

II. Every commanding officer of a fixed military post, or of an organized brigade or division of the army in the field, may impress any citizen whatever, and may compel his services in any of the old organized regiments or companies. If the party so impressed be a conscript, according to the laws of Congress, his name will be properly enrolled by the provost-marshal-general, and he will be entitled to all the pay, bounty, and allowances provided by law; but if the individual is not enrolled on the proper lists his services will be compelled till such time as he is no longer needed, when he will be dismissed. During the period of such forced service the individual will be entitled to rations and clothing, but no compensation, in the nature of a *posse comitatus* called out by a United States marshal.*

III. Every officer making such forced levies will report the same, with lists, to the provost-marshal-general of this department, to be filed with the Provost-Marshal-General at Washington, D. C., and will assign them by Special Orders to old regiments and companies. Their names will be borne on the muster-rolls of the companies to which they are attached, with a remark explanatory of the nature of the service, its beginning and ending.

By order of Maj. Gen. W. T. Sherman:

                              R. M. SAWYER,
                                   Assistant Adjutant-General.

HDQRS. FOURTH DIVISION, FIFTEENTH ARMY CORPS,
     DEPARTMENT AND ARMY OF THE TENNESSEE,
          Waterloo, Ala., October 28, 1863—11 a. m.

Major-General SHERMAN,
     Commanding Department and Army of the Tennessee:

GENERAL: I camped here last night with Cockerill's brigade. I move with it immediately to Gravelly Spring, where Corse promises to close on us this evening. To-morrow at daylight I will move with the two brigades to Florence, and at dark start a messenger to General Grant. Loomis, with the division train, will stretch out to-night, and camp to-morrow night beyond Gravelly Spring. The passage of the Tennessee proves more tedious than anticipated. I hear of no considerable force north of the river.

I have the honor to be, general, very respectfully, your obedient servant,

                              HUGH EWING,
                    Brigadier-General, Commanding Division.

CHATTANOOGA, TENN., *October* 28, 1863—11.30 p. m.
                         (Received 11.50 a. m., 29th.)

Maj. Gen. H. W. HALLECK, *General-in-Chief:*

General Burnside thinks troops from West Virginia are concentrating about Abingdon to the number of 15,000 men; also toward

----

* See Hurlbut to Bowers, December 28, Part III, p. 522.

Loudon, from Bragg's army. Present lack of supplies and poverty of stock will prevent effective assistance being given from here for a few days. Can General Kelley do anything toward Abingdon from his position? I want to hold all the ground Burnside now has, but if any must be given up, think it should not be that between him and Thomas.

> U. S. GRANT,
> *Major-General.*

SPECIAL FIELD ORDERS, }   HDQRS. MIL. DIV. OF THE MISSISSIPPI,
No. 4.   }   *Chattanooga, Tenn., October 28, 1863.*

I. Maj. Gen. John A. Logan, having been appointed by the President to the command of the Fifteenth Army Corps, is hereby relieved from duty in the Seventeenth Army Corps, and will report in person without delay to Maj. Gen. W. T. Sherman, commanding Department of the Tennessee, to assume command of the Fifteenth Army Corps in accordance with said appointment.

II. Maj. Gen. W. T. Sherman having been appointed to the command of the Army of the Tennessee, the chiefs of the several staff departments of that army, with the exception of the assistant adjutant-general and assistant inspector-general, will report to him for orders.

By order of Maj. Gen. U. S. Grant:

> ELY S. PARKER,
> *Assistant Adjutant-General.*

HDQRS. SECOND DIVISION, TWELFTH ARMY CORPS,
October 28, 1863.

Brig. Gen. GEORGE S. GREENE,
Commanding Third Brigade:

GENERAL: The general commanding directs that when your command reaches Whiteside's, you detach the Sixtieth New York Volunteers to hold the branch road leading to Trenton, and direct the officer in command to examine the pass and elect that position that will enable him to hold it against any force that may be sent against him. This to continue until further orders.

Very respectfully, your obedient servant,

> THOMAS H. ELLIOTT,
> *Captain, and Assistant Adjutant-General.*

BRIDGEPORT, *October 28, 1863—2 p. m.*

Lieut. Col. C. GODDARD,
Assistant Adjutant-General:

Two deserters from Twentieth Tennessee Infantry have just come in. They have been eight days in the mountains. They report that General Wheeler's whole command passed down the river on Sunday, the 25th, for another raid in Middle Tennessee. They were to cross at Guntersville, which point they expected to reach on Monday. The two cavalry regiments at Trenton left on Sunday to join Wheeler at Guntersville. This information seems reliable. They also report that a portion of Longstreet's corps was moving into Will's Valley, between Lookout and Pigeon Mountains on Sunday. These deserters live near Nashville; they wish to take the oath and go home. They also report that before deserting they were at work on rafts, with which Bragg intended to destroy the pontoons at Chattanooga.

JAS. C. ROGERS,
Lieutenant-Colonel 123d New York Vols., Comdg. Post.

HDQRS. FIRST BRIG., SECOND DIV., 14TH ARMY CORPS,
Near Dallas, Tenn., October 28, 1863—7 p. m.

Lieut. Col. C. GODDARD,
   Asst. Adjt. Gen., Department of the Cumberland:

COLONEL: I have the honor to report nothing of special interest in this locality. Col. John Tillson, commanding Tenth Illinois Infantry, stationed at Igou's Ferry, succeeded in capturing a squad of rebels opposite his camp this afternoon. I regret that this creditable action on his part could not have been rendered still more so by larger facilities for crossing the river. The men captured consist of a quartermaster-sergeant and 4 privates of the First Arkansas Battery, light artillery. I will send them to Chattanooga early in the morning. I send inclosed copy* of Colonel Tillson's report.

My assistant adjutant-general has just returned from an examination of the roads over Walden's Ridge above Poe road. He finds a comparatively good road going up from the Sequatchie Valley, near Colonel Hickman's, and coming down on this side near Sale Creek. It is called the Hamilton trace. While the Poe road remains in its present wretched condition, I think I will send some of my teams that way.

Colonel Tillson reports that he has learned from sources over the river that a conflict has taken place at Lenoir's, and that the rebels have fallen back to the Hiwassee; also that Cheatham's division is moving up the valley.

I am, colonel, very respectfully, your obedient servant,

R. F. SMITH,
Colonel, Commanding Brigade.

DECHERD, *October 28, 1863.*

Brigadier-General WILLIAMS,
   Tullahoma:

General Elliott has no information of any such movements on the part of Wheeler; thinks he would be advised by Crook or Galbraith, who are in a position to know, of Wheeler crossing the river. I will order the five companies of One hundred and second Ohio to move at daylight in the morning. I have directed Colonel Rogers to telegraph his information to General Granger.

JOS. F. KNIPE,
Brigadier-General, Commanding.

---

* Not found.

TULLAHOMA, *October* 28, 1863.

Lieut. Col. H. C. RODGERS,
        Assistant Adjutant-General:

Dispatch ordering me to send one regiment to Normandy to relieve troops at tank south of there received. The One hundred and fiftieth New York will be sent at once. The One hundred and seventh New York and Thirteenth New Jersey left here at half past 6 o'clock this morning, with orders to report at corps headquarters.

THOS. H. RUGER,
        Brigadier-General.

MURFREESBOROUGH, *October* 28, 1863.

Lieut. Col. H. C. RODGERS,
        Assistant Adjutant-General:

The troops at Bell Buckle have been six days on three days' rations. Will they be relieved, or shall I forward their rations? Acknowledge.

WM. L. UTLEY,
        Colonel, Commanding.

MAYSVILLE, *October* 28, 1863.

Maj. W. H. SINCLAIR,
        Assistant Adjutant-General:

Gurley is captured, and a good many of his men, some thirty-odd in all, and some killed, and they were all forwarded to Stevenson. They are now all regular soldiers of the rebel army.

The date of my commission is September 7, 1862.

GEORGE CROOK,
        Brigadier-General, Commanding.

CHATTANOOGA, *October* 28, 1863—11.30 p. m.

Maj. Gen. AMBROSE E. BURNSIDE,
        Knoxville, Tenn.:

The positions taken by you are, I suppose, the best that could be taken under the circumstances. I would like, however, if you could hold the line of the Hiwassee. It is particularly desirable that all the territory you now have should be held, but if any portion must be given up, let it be to the east, and keep your army so that it and Thomas' army can support each other. It is better that you should be forced from the eastern end of the valley than from the west.

Thomas is in no condition to move from his present position. He has succeeded, however, in getting possession of the river and roads south of it from Brown's Ferry to Bridgeport. It is to be hoped with this line open and Sherman up here, as he may be expected to be in a few days, Thomas will be able to place one division at Mc-Minnville and the remainder of the corps between here and you.

I have telegraphed General Halleck to know if General Kelley cannot move out from Western Virginia to threaten any force collecting about Abingdon.

U. S. GRANT,
        Major-General.

CHATTANOOGA, *October* 28, 1863.

Maj. Gen. AMBROSE E. BURNSIDE,
　　Knoxville, Tenn.:

If you have not designated an officer to take command at Louisville, I would like to send Major-General Rousseau.

　　　　　　　　　　　U. S. GRANT,
　　　　　　　　　　　　　Major-General.

JONESBOROUGH, *October* 28, 1863.

General BURNSIDE:

My scouts all bring in reports corroborating statements of Burke to General Willcox. There is no question but the enemy is advancing in large force. I will fall back to Greeneville to-day. I have sent orders to Colonel Garrard, at Rogersville, to send his train to Bull's Gap, and, if the enemy advanced in overwhelming numbers, to fall back to Bull's Gap with his command.

　　　　　　　　　　　J. M. SHACKELFORD,
　　　　　　　　　　　　　Brigadier-General.

GREENEVILLE, *October* 28, 1863.

Major-General BURNSIDE:

The operator at Loudon sends me word my cipher dispatch of yesterday p. m. was incorrect. The blunder is not in the cipher, but the purport of it is this: Burke says the plan is for a heavy cavalry force to move rapidly down through Kingsport, Rogersville, and try and take us in rear, striking at Knoxville. Perhaps their infantry move by Carter's Station, Jonesborough, &c.

　　　　　　　　　　　O. B. WILLCOX,
　　　　　　　　　　　　　Brigadier-General.

IUKA, *October* 28, 1863.

General DODGE, *Corinth:*

A messenger just arrived from Chattanooga, with dates of 24th, makes it necessary for me to drop everything, and with my old corps (Fifteenth) push for Stevenson. Push your preparations to follow with all possible speed, working night and day. Cross at Eastport and follow, via Florence, Athens, Huntsville, to Stevenson.

　　　　　　　　　　　W. T. SHERMAN,
　　　　　　　　　　　　　Major-General.

U. S. MISSISSIPPI SQUADRON, FLAG-SHIP BLACK HAWK,
　　　　　　　　　　　Cairo, October 28, 1863.

Maj. Gen. WILLIAM T. SHERMAN,
　　Eastport, Tenn.:

DEAR GENERAL: I have only time to write a few lines, but now that communication is open between us, you shall hear from me often. I am glad you have the gunboats with you, for though, as the reporters say, "they do nothing," yet I know you don't object to having them on certain occasions. I intend to line the Tennessee with gunboats, and promise you that your communication shall never be interrupted if there is water in the river.

　　　Very truly and sincerely,

　　　　　　　　　　　DAVID D. PORTER,
　　　　　　　　　　　　　Rear-Admiral.

HEADQUARTERS SIXTEENTH ARMY CORPS,
Memphis, Tenn., October 28, 1863.
Brig. Gen. A. J. SMITH,
Commanding District of Columbus, Columbus, Ky.:

GENERAL: I am directed by the general commanding corps to inform you of the decision of the general commanding department, that "with our present force we cannot attempt to re-open the northern road;" the general therefore directs that all operations upon the Mobile and Ohio Railroad be dropped. The general also directs that when you send your cavalry to Jackson, to order them, on their return, to clear the country of rebels.

I have the honor to be, general, very respectfully, your obedient servant,

T. H. HARRIS,
Assistant Adjutant-General.

HEADQUARTERS SEVENTEENTH ARMY CORPS,
Vicksburg, Miss., October 28, 1863.
Brig. Gen. JOHN P. HAWKINS,
Commanding Goodrich's Landing:

GENERAL: Numerous representations having been made to Major-General Grant, a short time before he left, that raids were being made from the Mississippi River, within your jurisdiction, across Bayou Macon, for the purpose of bringing in cotton, and in consequence of which orders were about being issued by the Confederate authorities to have every bale of cotton burned between the Washita and Bayou Macon, thereby causing the destruction of vast amounts of property to persons who are truly loyal at heart, the general directed me to say to you that you would prevent any more raids of this kind for the present. Of course if private individuals bring their cotton in from there you can permit them to do so, unless some military reasons exist at the time which render it inexpedient.

Very respectfully, your obedient servant,

JAS. B. McPHERSON,
Major-General.

HEADQUARTERS,
Saint Louis, Mo., October 28, 1863—11 a. m.
(Received 2 p. m.)
Major-General HALLECK, *General-in-Chief:*

The following dispatch was sent by Colonel Parsons on the 24th to the quartermaster at Paducah:

General Allen directs that the ferry-boat Blue Beard be ordered up the Tennessee by the first convoy, to report to General Sherman. Convoy will probably leave Cairo to-day.

I have no doubt that the boat has gone from Paducah, although the fact has not yet been reported. Captain Woolfolk, at Cairo, was instructed immediately after the receipt of your dispatch to send the first ferry-boat he could possibly procure to Eastport, and to direct that the first freight boats that went up to Eastport should be used for ferrying in the meantime, if required. I will hear more on the subject to-day. There was no ferry-boat here.

ROBT. ALLEN,
Chief Quartermaster.

HDQRS. U. S. FORCES, SOUTHWESTERN KENTUCKY,
Bowling Green, Ky., October 28, 1863.

Maj. Gen. U. S. GRANT,
Commanding Division of the Mississippi:

GENERAL: The nature and importance of the subject on which I write will, I hope, be deemed a sufficient apology for addressing you directly and personally. I wish respectfully to call your attention to the unfinished railroad between Henderson, Ky., and Nashville. The route has long since been surveyed and located, the road is graded nearly all the way, and about one-third of the distance entirely completed. It passes from Henderson, Ky., through Madisonville, Hopkins County, Ky.; Hopkinsville, Christian County, Ky.; Trenton, Todd County, Ky.; intersects the Memphis branch of the Louisville and Nashville Railroad 14 miles from Clarksville, and, passing through Springfield, Robertson County, Tenn., intersects the Louisville and Nashville Railroad at Edgefield Junction, about 12 miles from Nashville, the entire distance from Henderson to Nashville being about 140 miles. From Henderson to Madisonville, 40 miles, the road is graded and several miles of track laid; from Madisonville to Hopkinsville, 34 miles, but little grading has been done, though some; from Hopkinsville to the State line, 26 miles, the road is graded, and from the State line to Nashville, 40 miles, it is completed and in running order, excepting across Red River, where the trestle-work and bridge have been burned, but which can soon be repaired.

It will be observed that the distance by this route from Nashville to the Ohio River is about 45 miles less than by the Louisville and Nashville Railroad. There is no tunnel on the route. It crosses no considerable stream, excepting the Cumberland, at Nashville. It passes a considerable portion of the way through loyal communities, and is well protected on the west by the Cumberland and Tennessee Rivers, and for a considerable distance on the northeast by Green River. It passes through the richest portion of Southern Kentucky, where there are great quantities of wheat, corn, oats, and hay that the farmers are unable to get to market with the present means of transportation. I am told that many of them now have two crops on hand, particularly of wheat. Some of the finest coal in Kentucky is in Hopkins County, and by completing 45 miles more of the road, a great portion of which distance is already graded, Nashville will be in communication by railroad with inexhaustible coal-fields, and distant only about 85 miles. The coal is said to be very accessible, and will require but little labor in mining. They are now paying in Nashville, as I am informed, 60 and 70 cents per bushel for coal; but, complete this railroad to the coal-fields of Hopkins County, and any quantities of the finest coal can readily be obtained for 12 or 15 cents per bushel. Henderson is only 12 miles from Evansville, and from which place great quantities of the forage of the Army of the Cumberland are being shipped up Green River and through this place over the Louisville and Nashville Railroad to Nashville. The distance from Evansville to this place by the way of Green River is 180 miles, and from here to Nashville by railroad is about 70 miles.

The slaves in Southern Kentucky are running away in great numbers, and are seized by the military authorities in Tennessee and placed at work on the Northwestern Railroad. The citizens of that section are not only willing, but, as I am informed, exceedingly anxious that their negroes should be put to work on this unfinished railroad in their own State, and intelligent men from there say that if notice were given that hands were wanted to complete the road, the owners of the negroes in several counties, the disloyal as well as the loyal, would in a week's time cheerfully furnish negroes enough to complete the road in a month from the State line to Henderson, and without any more cost to the Government than the rations and clothes of the negroes while at work. It is said they would gladly have their negroes taken for this purpose. Many of the citizens of Southern Kentucky regard slavery as done for, and they say if their negroes could be used to complete a work of such importance to them, as well as the Government, they care but little if they then go. General, I hope that in consideration of the importance of the subject you will pardon any impropriety in this lengthy communication.

Very respectfully, your obedient servant,

CICERO MAXWELL,
Colonel Twenty-sixth Kentucky Vols., Comdg. S. W. Ky.

WAR DEPARTMENT,
Washington, October 29, 1863—11.30 a. m.

Major-General GRANT,
Chattanooga, Tenn.:

Lieutenant Meigs is the only engineer officer in General Kelley's department, and cannot possibly be spared. Captain Comstock will soon be able to report to you. I have received General Burnside's dispatch of the 27th. I fear the road from Nashville cannot supply both your armies. Cannot supplies for Burnside be sent up the Cumberland to Burkesville, or above, on flats, towed by light steamers? Burkesville is only 100 miles from Kingston, with a hard mountain road—so reported. I do not think that Ewell's corps has left Lee's army. Can you not, by a flank movement from Chattanooga on Cleveland, cut off Bragg's railroad communications to East Tennessee? If this could be done it would prevent a concentration on Burnside.

H. W. HALLECK,
General-in-Chief.

CHATTANOOGA, *October* 29, 1863.
(Received 6.30 a. m., November 1.)

E. M. STANTON,
Secretary of War:

Last night the Eleventh Corps hotly entered on this central campaign. General Geary, some 4 miles up the Lookout Valley, being attacked by Longstreet, the Eleventh Corps about 1 o'clock marched to his aid. Passing two steep wooded hills, about 150 feet in height, they received a volley from a rebel force, which had occupied and intrenched their summits. After dark four regiments assaulted the east hill, and without firing a shot steadily advanced by the light of the moon, and drove the rebels out of their rifle-pits and down the other slope of the hills. Thirty-one dead soldiers attest the difficulty of the assault and valor and steadiness of the troops, which in a night attack accomplished one of the most brilliant feats of the campaign. Only after walking over the ground to-day do I fully appreciate the exploit. When these hills were taken they marched to the assistance of General Geary, who had held his position, and Longstreet was driven back with slaughter. As prisoners from two divisions attest that his whole disposable force was engaged, the whole affair is most creditable to those corps from the Army of the Potomac.

M. C. MEIGS,
Quartermaster-General.

SPECIAL FIELD ORDERS, ⎰ HDQRS. MIL. DIV. OF THE MISS.,
     No. 5.   ⎱   *Chattanooga, Tenn., October* 29, 1863.

I. Lieut. Col. J. H. Wilson, assistant inspector-general, and captain of Engineers, will report without delay to Maj. Gen. G. H. Thomas, commanding Army of the Cumberland, to take charge of the laying out and construction of the defenses of the passes on the south side of the Tennessee River through which the enemy might reach it. Major-General Thomas will direct the commanding officers of troops defending such passes to furnish him such details of men for the prosecution of said work as he may require.

*   *   *   *   *   *   *

By order of Maj. Gen. U. S. Grant:

ELY S. PARKER,
Assistant Adjutant-General.

HEADQUARTERS DEPARTMENT OF THE CUMBERLAND,
Chattanooga, October 29, 1863—6 p m.

Brigadier-General MORTON,
     Shellmound, via Bridgeport:

Your pontoon bridge will remain in place at Shellmound for the present. In a few days, as soon as the steamer can be spared, she will transport your bridge to Kelley's Ferry.

By command of Major-General Thomas:

J. J. REYNOLDS,
Major-General, and Chief of Staff.

HEADQUARTERS DEPARTMENT OF THE CUMBERLAND,
Chattanooga, October 29, 1863—9.30 a. m.

Brig. Gen. GEORGE CROOK, *Maysville:*

It is reported here from several sources that Wheeler is about to cross to the north bank of the river some place in your vicinity.

J. J. REYNOLDS,
Major-General, and Chief of Staff.

HDQRS. FIRST BRIGADE, SECOND CAVALRY DIVISION,
October 29, 1863.

[General CROOK:]

GENERAL: From two young men now here, who came in voluntarily, I have obtained some statements that may be of use to you.

I am disposed to credit them. Sunday evening, the 11th instant, they left the rebel force at Courtland. Before leaving they were told of Wheeler being re-enforced by Lee's command, reported at 5,000. General Martin told his artillery officers to "fix up the artillery—to lose no time," saying "the raid is only about half over." They heard their brigade surgeon say in effect the same thing. The rebels were collecting all the boats from above at Lamb's Ferry. From the estimate of these boys they could collect about ten boats, the capacity of each about a dozen men and horses. Steele, a rebel conscript officer, stated that on the 21st instant all the boats had disappeared from points above Lamb's. Wheeler got across to west side with eight pieces, two of them Napoleon guns. They had some surplus mules, but no horses; but few horses could be procured in the valley about Courtland. It would take "about four weeks to recruit the horses so that they would be fit to go on another raid." Plenty of corn in the valley. They had mules enough to mount all the dismounted men. Roddey was still on this side of the river when the young men left.

I am, general, your obedient servant,

W. W. LOWE,
Colonel, Commanding.

HEADQUARTERS SECOND CAVALRY DIVISION,
Maysville. October 29, 1863—8 p. m.

Col. ELI LONG,
Second Brigade:

COLONEL: It is reported that General Wheeler is about crossing to this side of the river, in your vicinity. Keep patrols going so as to keep you informed of any movement; also ascertain whether the river is fordable at any point.

Have your dismounted men sent from Stevenson to Nashville to report to Major Baird, Fifth Iowa Cavalry, who will be there in a few days. He started yesterday with old horses.

By command of Brigadier-General Crook:

B. H. MOON,
Aide-de-Camp.

HEADQUARTERS DEPARTMENT OF THE CUMBERLAND,
Chattanooga, October 29, 1863—9 p. m.

Brigadier-General GRANGER, *Nashville:*

The guerrilla, Captain Gurley, who killed McCook,* was captured by Crook. A dispatch from Stevenson to-day says he was sent, with other prisoners, to Nashville to-day. Keep him securely; we may be able to convict him of murder. Report his arrival.

By order:

C. GODDARD,
Assistant Adjutant-General.

----

* See Series I, Vol. XVI, Part I, pp. 838–841.

HEADQUARTERS FIRST DIVISION, TWELFTH CORPS,
Tullahoma, Tenn., October 29, 1863.

Lieut. Col. H. C. RODGERS,
  Assistant Adjutant-General, Wartrace:

COLONEL : I have the honor to submit, for the information of the major-general commanding the corps, the following memorandum report of the position of my troops on the railroad from Bridgeport to Elk River Bridge, both posts included, a report of the remaining portion of our line having already been made :

1. At Bridgeport and toward Stevenson, One hundred and twenty-third New York Volunteers and Battery M, First New York Artillery. The battery will be posted at Bridgeport as soon as it can be transported by rail from Decherd. The horses have gone on by mountain path from Anderson. Lieutenant-Colonel Rogers, One hundred and twenty-third New York Volunteers, commanding post at Bridgeport.

2. At Stevenson and vicinity, Twentieth Regiment Connecticut Volunteers and Battery F, Fourth U. S. Artillery. The battery will be posted at Stevenson as soon as it can be transported by rail from Decherd. The horses have gone on by wagon road from Anderson. Col. Samuel Ross, Twentieth Connecticut Volunteers, commanding post at Stevenson.

3. At bridges from Stevenson to Anderson and at Anderson, Third Regiment Maryland Volunteers. Each bridge is guarded by one company of this regiment. Col. J. M. Sudsburg, Third Maryland Volunteers, commanding post at Anderson.

4. At bridges from Anderson to Tantalon and at Tantalon, One hundred and forty-fifth Regiment New York Volunteers. Each bridge is guarded by one company of this regiment. Capt. S. T. Allen, commanding One hundred and forty-fifth New York, commanding post at Tantalon.

5. At Cumberland Tunnel and Cowan, Fifth Regiment Connecticut Volunteers, eight companies. Col. W. W. Packer, Fifth Connecticut Volunteers, commanding post at Cowan.

6. At Decherd and vicinity, six companies Forty-sixth Regiment Pennsylvania Volunteers, Lieutenant-Colonel Foulk commanding, Colonel Selfridge being president of general court-martial to meet to-day at Tullahoma. Brig. Gen. J. F. Knipe, First Brigade, commanding post at Decherd.

7. At Elk River Bridge, four companies Forty-sixth Pennsylvania Volunteers. This detachment is under orders to remain here temporarily only. A map of defenses and more precise details of strength at each post will be forwarded as soon as they can be prepared.

I have the honor to be, colonel, your obedient servant,
A. S. WILLIAMS,
Brigadier-General, Commanding Division.

BRIDGEPORT, *October* 29, 1863—5 p. m.

Lieut. Col. C. GODDARD,
  Assistant Adjutant-General:

W. L. Riley has just come in from the enemy's lines. He is a Kentucky man, and represents that he has passed through the entire rebel army within the last four days. He says Cheatham's division was sent to Charleston, Tenn., on Saturday. Two divisions of Pemberton's old corps were at Dalton at the same time *en route* for same place. He also heard it said that Breckinridge's corps had been ordered there yesterday. Bragg moved fifty-eight pieces of artillery over Missionary Ridge toward Chickamauga Station. Hood's division was the only rebel force on Lookout Mountain. They were throwing up rifle-pits last night. There were three regiments rebel cavalry yesterday near Summerville—Seventh Alabama, Eighth Confederate, and Ninth Kentucky. Heard at commissary department that rations were issued daily for 82,000 infantry. He wishes to be employed as a spy at headquarters.

JAMES C. ROGERS,
Lieutenant-Colonel 123d New York Volunteers.

LENOIR'S, TENN., *October* 29, 1863.
(Received 10.10 p. m., 31st.)

Maj. Gen. H. W. HALLECK, *Washington,*
Major-General GRANT, *Chattanooga:*

The following dispatch has just been received from Colonel Byrd, commanding at Kingston, which is forwarded for your information:

KINGSTON, TENN., *October* 29, 1863.

Major-General BURNSIDE:

I have just received this report from Louis Patterson, a private in the Sixty-fifth Indiana, who lives in Meigs County, on south side of river, who left your headquarters on last Monday, the 26th. He says:

"The forces that attacked Wolford were 5,000 of cavalry and three regiments of infantry, commanded by Brigadier-General [Colonel] Morrison. Stevenson's division, 5,000 strong, were at Sweet Water on the 28th. Cheatham's division, numbering 15,000, were at Athens, or above there. These were all the forces above the Hiwassee on 27th. Breckinridge, with 15,000 or 20,000 men, is expected to cross the Hiwassee. The rebels are at work on the bridge at Calhoun, and are destitute of salt, or nearly so. One regiment of cavalry is 3 miles from Tennessee River, up the creek, 3 miles from the mouth of Seewee. Four hundred others are 5 miles from the river, 8 miles above the mouth of Seewee. This information was obtained within 8 and 15 miles from Athens, in McMinn and Meigs Counties, yesterday and last night. I received it through my father, from W. G. Laff, a major in McKenzie's regiment of rebels. He is my brother-in-law, and his family are at father's. He knew nothing of me being in that county when he gave the information to my father; also, substantially the same facts were received from David Hutzell, an intelligent, reliable Union man."

I am well acquainted with Mr. L. Patterson, who made the above statement, and know him to be reliable. He adds, he heard distinctly heavy firing in direction of Chattanooga at 2 a. m. and daylight this morning.

R. K. BYRD,
Colonel, Commanding.

I cannot vouch for the truth of these statements, but they agree substantially with the reports I have been getting for some days. That there is a considerable force moving in this direction there can be no question. If such is the case the force in front of Thomas must be materially weakened. I have removed the forces at Loudon to this side of the river, holding the heights commanding the town. If the enemy were to succeed in crossing the river below, it would be impossible for me to concentrate the forces that are now in the eastern part of the State to join Thomas, but unless they have pontoon trains with them I can probably prevent them from crossing. I am drawing the forces back from the eastern part of the State gradually, and the enemy's cavalry follows on after them. A rapid retreat of our forces in the eastern part of the State would probably cause us to lose our communication with Cumberland Gap, and also many trains now on that route, and no other route is now practicable without troops to assist over the bad parts. If you should think it desirable at any time for me to order all the trains back that have not yet arrived at Cumberland Gap, and make a rapid concentration at Kingston, I think it can be done if the enemy's movements are not too far advanced, and even should he be he could not well prevent us from getting there unless he had a very large force; or we can concentrate and fight him at a part where we can meet him under the most favorable circumstances, and do our best to hold him in check until Thomas can attack Bragg and probably defeat him; but in case of disaster we could try to make our way to some of the mountain passes which we could hold until supplies could come to us. The concentration would probably be at Knoxville. Our great trouble lies in the shortness of supplies; but we have nearly ten days' salt on hand, and probably as many days of beef cattle, and will probably receive more before an attack can be made. Our cavalry has suffered a great deal from constant service along so extended a line; but I have held this long line in accordance with what I considered to be the spirit of the instructions from Washington, as well as their wishes, and it would be a sad thing indeed to have to give up this country. I had already designated General Willcox for the command in Kentucky, but if you direct it General Rousseau can be ordered to the command. I beg to say that I very much regret the ordering of General Boyle from his present work, as he seems to me almost essential to its prosecution, as he is so intimately identified with the work now being carried on under previous orders in Kentucky. I have always regarded him as a most faithful, fearless, and efficient officer, and in all my intercourse with him I have never discovered any disposition in him to meddle with politics, except that he ran for Congress.

A. E. BURNSIDE,
Major-General.

HDQRS. SECOND DIVISION, TWENTY-THIRD ARMY CORPS,

Near Loudon, October 29, 1863.

Lieutenant-Colonel RICHMOND,
Assistant Adjutant-General:

COLONEL: The enemy are about to occupy Loudon, from appearances. I respectfully suggest that the train intended to carry away the balance of the bridge be sent down as speedily as possible, as the loading will be attended with some trouble, under fire, should the enemy open.

Very respectfully, your obedient servant,

JULIUS WHITE,
Brigadier-General.

WAR DEPARTMENT,
Washington, October 29, 1863—1 p. m.

Maj. Gen. S. A. HURLBUT, *Memphis, Tenn.:*

It is of great importance that the telegraph line between Corinth and Columbus be put in working order. General Dodge says he has no troops at Corinth to open the line. You must help him and see that the line is kept open.

H. W. HALLECK,
General-in-Chief.

FLAG-SHIP BLACK HAWK, *Cairo, October* 29, 1863.

Maj. Gen. WILLIAM T. SHERMAN:

DEAR GENERAL: I have just received yours of October 25, and am glad to have the Army and Navy in conjunction once more. You don't know how I miss my old occupation. It has been very dry work since Vicksburg fell, for then we had something in anticipation, while lately I have thought the whole affair was getting to be very stupid.

I congratulate you on your accession of honors in having the command of the Department of the Tennessee transferred to you. I am sure you will do justice to the position. It is one requiring considerable address just now, for our Secretary of the Treasury has started two or three systems of trade, all as various as the hues of the chamelion. General Grant and myself recommended a very simple plan by which all parties would have been satisfied, and Mr. Mellen, the Treasury agent, was sent out here to set the ball in motion. The plan was to make everything subordinate to military necessity in those States that are not actually in the Union, and the general commanding was to decide when the line of trade should commence, and when it was to end. I was to see that the regulations were carried out on the water. A big circular was issued by the Treasury Department, and an army of Treasury aids appointed to carry out the regulations. A greater pack of knaves never went unhung. Human nature is very weak, and the poor aids, with their small pay, could easily be bribed to allow a man to land 100 barrels of salt when he only had permit for 2. And so on with everything else. The thing is done now so openly that the guerrillas come down to the bank and purchase what they want. Sometimes they take what is necessary for them and then burn the boat, as they did last week with the steamer Mist, that landed without the cover of a gunboat.

I think there should be but one rule of trade. Steamers should not be allowed to land anywhere but at a military post, or a place guarded by a gunboat; this gives them fifty landing places on the River Mississippi.

Wood-piles should be guarded by gunboats, and by troops near posts. All through trade to New Orleans and back should be protected, the people made to feel that the navigation is uninterrupted, and such through vessels should not be allowed to land anywhere except under cover of a gunboat for wood, except at military posts.

It would be very difficult to discriminate just now as to what constitutes contraband of war. The inclosed paper* shows what the President considered contraband just after the war commenced, and I do not see why the rebels should have any more favors shown them now than then. One thing is certain, if trade is permitted along the river indiscriminately, the rebel armies will be much better fed and clothed than they have been. I have endeavored to shift around with the orders from the Treasury Department, and the orders that have heretofore come from General Grant, or indorsements made by him on permits. There has been a great system of speculation carried on by persons who have taken advantage of permits and by Treasury aids, I am told, but that is no business of mine; and as I don't want the gunboats to perform the part of excise vessels, I have confined them to looking out for powder and ball, military clothing, or what might be used as such—medicines, gold and silver, Confederate money, and such provisions as could be used in an army.

---

* Not found.

It requires a nice distinction on the part of an officer to discriminate in these matters and not run against the regulations of the Treasury Department, and I am sorry to say that some of my command commit blunders enough. I can give them all orders, but I cannot furnish them with brains.

I inclose you all the General Orders * I have issued in regard to trade, and you will see that my plan has been to touch it as lightly as possible, and not go counter to the wishes of the Government. I have also been waiting to see General F. P. Blair, jr., come out with a book on trade generally in these waters, telling how the matter is to be arranged. He says the trade should be free and unrestricted, but he does not say how much of it will go to the rebels and how much to the plantations. I think the whole matter is contained in a nut-shell. The military status must determine the direction of trade. The navy must see the rules enforced along the river. The military commander of posts should examine and indorse all manifests and permits. All towns should be so guarded that neither goods nor provisions should get into the hands of the enemy, and as much through trade to New Orleans allowed as the boats can convoy, the general commanding the department to say when and where traffic is to cease.

I think commerce should be a secondary consideration now ; the Government do not get repaid for the army of Treasury aids they have appointed. It is very much like setting a rat to watch the cheese to see that the mice don't get at it.

I am more interested in war matters myself, and in holding on to this river, which I know we can do. The rebels are now reduced to their two big armies at Chattanooga and Richmond, and the small squads they have at other places, supplying their armies as rivulets supply the Mississippi. The rivulets are nearly run out, and the rebels cannot, I think, raise 20,000 men with which to trouble the banks of the Mississippi.

These would be scattered about if they attempted it, and in such small parties that the home guards, if once established, could keep them down. Indiscriminate trade will aid these rebel parties very much if once established. There is one place I am a little afraid of, and that is Port Hudson. It is kept so poorly guarded, and the guns on the water line are all kept mounted, when there is no use for them there. Port Hudson is only 40 miles from the great northern railroad, and you know that it don't take rebels long to travel 40 miles, especially as half the way is railroad—from Clinton to Port Hudson. Some party of 4,000 or 5,000 men could go into Port Hudson any night and take it. It is a trifling affair altogether; I went all through the works, and there were twenty places where a determined set of men would walk in without trouble. It is manned entirely by negroes, who are not, in my opinion, equal to the old Napoleon Guard, or to the French zouaves I saw in the Crimea.

You would have laughed, I know, had you seen the fortifications about which Banks' army made so much ado. The Army of the Tennessee would not have stopped to dig a ditch before such a place, and yet when General Grant was in New Orleans, the newspaper organ of General Banks was guilty of the bad taste of trying to prove in some very lame articles that Banks was the hero of the Mississippi.

We all know that when Vicksburg fell that Port Hudson fell in

---

* Not found.

consequence, and I really think the latter never would have fallen had not the former "caved in."

I write now confidentially to you, and say what I would to no one else. I don't profess to be a soldier, but I know how to play a good game of chess and can see the moves on the board as well as any one. The whole campaign of Banks has been a failure in Louisiana, and his disasters have been terrible, though kindly covered up by his reporters. He is, I am told, one of the best of the militia generals, and is a pleasant, agreeable gentleman, but I do not think he has the proper appreciation of what is required at certain points nor is he posted in the topography or hydrography of the country in which he is operating. He is entering Texas by three lines, when neither corps was able to meet separately the force in front of them, and were without means of making a junction. The First Corps, under General Dana, was defeated, and had to fall back on the gunboats at Morganza, which kept the rebels from cutting them off; the Second at Sabine Pass witnessed the demolition of wooden gunboats, and, like the French King, "marched back again;" and the Third is wandering around Grand Lake, in Louisiana, wondering why I don't send them tin-clads.

I would be glad to do so if any one could tell me how to get into the Atchafalaya, or through Bayou La Fourche into Plaquemine.

The bar at the mouth of the former is dry, and there is 2 feet of water only at the mouth of Bayou La Fourche. Now, I am coming to the gist of the matter, though you will think I have taken a round-about way to do it. The rebels are making use of Red River, Black, and Washita, to supply themselves with provisions, ammunition, &c., in Louisiana, and they have by these rivers been enabled to interrupt General Banks' communications. The smallest of our gunboats have not been able to get into Red River to stop this, but one of the gunboats sent a party of 20 men overland at Union Point, on the Mississippi, 25 miles above the mouth of Red River. At this point the Red River and Mississippi come within 3 miles of each other, as you will see by the sketch* I send you. At Point A the party of sailors found a steamer lying in the river. They drove the men below with musketry, and 12 of the sailors swam to her and captured her. A few minutes after another large boat came around the bend; the sailors concealed themselves and signaled the steamer to come alongside, when she was also captured. On these two steamers General Dick Taylor depended to transport his men in and about the Atchafalaya and bayous. Our men burned the steamers because they could not get them out of the river, but brought over 16 prisoners, one of whom was an aide of General Dick Taylor and a very communicative gentleman.

Now, this affair suggested to me the idea of fortifying Point A on the sketch and holding it with troops. It effectually blocks up Red River, which is almost, if not quite, within reach of our guns on the gunboats in the Mississippi. Three hundred men can hold the point against any number the rebels will be able to send there. Dick Taylor will be cut off, and have to march all the way back to Alexandria. You will see the importance of this by examining the maps; it will be a great relief and assistance to General Banks. I took the liberty of writing to General Crocker at Natchez, and General McPherson at Natchez, about this. I don't know whether they will agree with me.

I have written you rather a long letter, which, to a general in

* Not found.

command of a large department, and with so much to do just now, may seem longer than necessary, but sailors will spin long yarns—it is part of their nature.

I inclose you certain general orders* that I have issued at various times, showing you my desire to act in accord with the army. I hope if any of my "Bashi Bazouks" run counter to them, that you will do me the favor to attach no blame to me. I sent you a large barge or two to make flying bridges with, but am sorry to say the boat Lexington had to drop them. I will still get them up to you.

With best wishes, I remain, very truly and respectfully, yours,

DAVID D. PORTER,
Rear-Admiral.

P. S.—I have just received a notice from the Secretary of the Navy that the Marine Brigade and ram fleet was turned over to General Grant, and, of course, it is in your department. The general and myself came to one conclusion long since, that the brigade should be broken up, the vessels used as transports, and the officers and men put on shore. I cannot tell you of all the reports made to me against the brigade. Its robberies and house-burning are shameful; and though I felt it to be my duty to report all the matters that came to my notice, yet a feeling of delicacy toward a branch of another corps prevented my so doing. Moreover, the Ellets have been guilty of some very dirty, underhand work toward myself, in publishing contemptible articles in the papers, which I never noticed beyond exposing the parties to General Hurlbut, and having the progress of the editor suddenly arrested. In these transactions the Ellets were guilty of gross falsehoods in making malicious statements, and lied deliberately in afterward denying them. I made the editor show them up, as they deserved to be. Still I never took any notice to them of the matter, but lost my respect for the whole party, and was glad to get rid of the command. They are here now doing nothing. The quartermasters can scarcely raise vessels to transport provisions, while these brigade vessels are idling away time at great expense. I do hope you will break up the whole concern as General Grant intended to do. The country will be served by so doing. These are the very vessels wanted in the Tennessee as transports. With a guard of 10 men and their wooden protections against riflemen they can go and come as they like.

HDQRS. SECOND DIVISION, SIXTEENTH ARMY CORPS,
La Grange, Tenn., October 29, 1863.

Lieutenant HILLIER,
Comdg. Detachment of Ninth Illinois Cavalry:

You will proceed immediately to La Fayette, Tenn., and, if you find the railroad bridge destroyed and cannot find the men who did it, you will promptly arrest every man and lad in that neighborhood and send them here. You will then burn down every house in that vicinity.

By order of Brig. Gen. Thos. W. Sweeny:

THOS. G. MORRISON,
Major, and Chief of Outposts, Second Div., 16th Army Corps.

---

* Not found.

CHATTANOOGA, TENN., *October* 30, 1863—10 a. m.
(Received 6.40 a. m., November 1.)
Maj. Gen. H. W. HALLECK,
General-in-Chief:

Carthage will probably be the best point on the Cumberland River from which to get supplies to Kingston. Burnside has been directed to collect all the supplies he can from the country, and ought to be able to get the bulk of what he will use for the winter. The Nashville and Kingston Railroad will be used, if too much repairing is not required. Soon as supplies reach us I will turn my attention to destroying all chance of the enemy's attacking Burnside from the southwest.

U. S. GRANT,
Major-General, Commanding.

HEADQUARTERS DEPARTMENT OF THE CUMBERLAND,
Chattanooga, October 30, 1863.
Major-General GRANT,
Comdg. Military Division of the Mississippi:

GENERAL: The best wagon route for General Burnside to supply his army at Kingston will be from a depot at Carthage. The road from that place to Kingston runs along the eastern bank of Caney Fork, through a fine forage region, from Carthage to Sparta. A depot of forage can be made there to supply trains on their way to Kingston and back to Carthage. The road from Carthage to Kingston is graded, and runs over a barren region, generally hard gravel and firm. The Caney Fork is also navigable as far as Sligo Ferry in the winter, which will decrease the land transportation to about 60 miles.

Very respectfully, your obedient servant,
GEO. H. THOMAS,
Major-General.

HDQRS. SECOND DIVISION, TWELFTH ARMY CORPS,
October 30, 1863.
Maj. Gen. D. BUTTERFIELD,
Chief of Staff, Eleventh and Twelfth Army Corps:

GENERAL: I have just received information from parties here whom I deem reliable, that in a few days we shall be sorely pressed. My informants state that a force of 10,000 of the enemy, with 12-pounder artillery, is on Lookout Mountain, preparing to descend to attack our right flank, and that a like force will attack your left. I send you the information and would like to see you and Major-General Hooker, if convenient. I would call upon you early, but there being no other general officer here, I deem it not proper to leave. I desire to consult with you upon matters of utmost importance. I send you a man named J. W. People, who gave himself up, and who can furnish you valuable information.

Very respectfully, your obedient servant,
JNO. W. GEARY,
Brigadier-General, U. S. Volunteers, Commanding.

HEADQUARTERS ELEVENTH AND TWELFTH CORPS,
Lookout Valley, Tenn., October 30, 1863—6.15 p. m.

Major-General REYNOLDS,
    Chief of Staff, Chattanooga:

I would like to have General Cruft instructed to relieve the regiment of General Geary's command at Shellmound (in the pass) and direct the commanding officer to join General Geary, via Whiteside's, as soon as Crook's cavalry are in advance sufficiently to communicate timely information to make it safe for the regiment to move by the same route we came. I would also request that from the brigade of General Cruft at Bridgeport or Shellmound the regiment of General Howard's corps at Battle Creek be relieved and ordered to join him, via the bridge at Shellmound. If these orders are given please advise me. I presume you can reach General Cruft via telegraph to Jasper or Bridgeport. Also to relieve the detachment at Whiteside's (a regiment of General Geary's) by at least 500 men, proper instructions to be given to the troops posted at the passes this side of the river to intrench in strong position. The troops relieved to be instructed to draw and march with three days' rations from the depots where they are when they move to join. Without knowing the views of the engineers on the subject, from a personal examination of the line necessary to guard effectually the entrance to the gap into this (Lookout) valley, in my opinion it will not be less than 3 miles in length, requiring an unusual amount of labor to make necessary slashings and throwing up the earth-works.

I would, therefore, like to have the assistance of my whole command for these services. I would like to have the engineer officer, who is to point out the line, report early to-morrow morning.

    Very respectfully,

                                JOSEPH HOOKER,
                            Major-General, Commanding.

HEADQUARTERS DEPARTMENT OF THE CUMBERLAND,
Chattanooga, October 30, 1863—11 a. m.

Brigadier-General CRUFT,
        Shellmound:

Send the brigade at Shellmound to Bridgeport. A wagon train is expected to pass from Bridgeport to-day. Escort it through to General Geary with a portion of the brigade that goes to Whiteside's.

By command of Major-General Thomas:
                                J. J. REYNOLDS,
                                    Major-General.

HEADQUARTERS DEPARTMENT OF THE CUMBERLAND,
Chattanooga, October 30, 1863.

COMMANDING OFFICER,
        Bridgeport:

If Crook's cavalry has not passed Bridgeport to join General Hooker, give the commanding officer this order: Make a reconnaissance toward Trenton, and then report to General Hooker.

By command of Major-General Thomas:
                                J. J. REYNOLDS,
                                Major-General Chief of Staff.

MAYSVILLE, *October* 30, 1863.

Major-General REYNOLDS:

Had a party down to Claysville yesterday. They reported Wheeler on the opposite side, but not crossing. I will keep a close watch on him.

GEORGE CROOK,
Brigadier-General.

HDQRS. THIRD BRIG., FIRST DIV., RESERVE CORPS,
Tullahoma, Tenn., October 30, 1863.

Brigadier-General WILLIAMS,
First Division, Twelfth Corps:

GENERAL: In accordance with your request, I make a statement as to the McMinnville railroad:

The whole distance is 35 miles from Tullahoma. About 4 miles from Tullahoma there is a trestle-work bridge some 50 feet long. At Manchester, 12 miles from here, there are two bridges, a small one some 70 feet long, just this side, and a large one, just beyond the town, some 300 feet long and 50 feet high. There are two small bridges some 7 to 9 miles farther along toward McMinnville. Three miles this side of McMinnville there is a bridge some 100 feet long, now destroyed. Beyond this bridge is the only locomotive on the road, somewhat damaged. McMinnville is at this end of a mountain pass, and, if held, strongly commands quite a range of country, the extent I do not know. At McMinnville are stationed part of two cavalry regiments, I am informed. Report says that they have gone, for what time and where I do not know. The Nineteenth Michigan Infantry is also there. I am informed there is no artillery there. The telegraph line is repaired and an operator expected to-day. There are no good fortifications at any point.

Yours, very respectfully,

JOHN COBURN,
Colonel, &c.

[Indorsement.]

HDQRS. FIRST DIVISION, TWELFTH ARMY CORPS,
October 31, 1863.

Respectfully forwarded, with the suggestion that as one of Colonel Coburn's regiments is at McMinnville, another be sent to guard the other bridges of that railroad.

A. S. WILLIAMS,
Brigadier-General, Commanding Division.

HEADQUARTERS SIXTEENTH ARMY CORPS,
Memphis, Tenn., October 30, 1863—noon.
(Received 11.55 p. m., November 1.)

Maj. Gen. H. W. HALLECK,
General-in-Chief:

I left Iuka yesterday morning. Sherman moved yesterday across the Tennessee at Eastport. Ewing's division was in Florence yesterday. John E. Smith was to cross yesterday. Blair, with Osterhaus and Morgan L. Smith. having penetrated to Tuscumbia and driven the enemy with loss, are marching by left flank to Chickasaw to cross. Sherman received your orders by messenger. I have given Sherman eighteen regiments of infantry, my best artillery, and a regiment of cavalry, in all 11,000 men. This strips me to a position of positive weakness. I have at and near Memphis 3,500 infantry. Beyond Memphis two white and three colored regiments and 4,500 cavalry; one colored regiment at Moscow, two white and two colored at Corinth. I shall try to hold the railroad with cavalry, but know it cannot be done if seriously attacked. I sent, ten days since, a request to Steele to send me some regiments. From this I have just heard. He declines doing it, except under orders from Schofield. Those orders have gone, but it will be two weeks before the troops arrive. If I am seriously threatened I shall bring everything to Moscow and abandon the railroad beyond. Dodge will cross at Eastport as soon as Sherman gets out of his way. Provisions for 30,000 men should be at Stevenson for them within ten days. I will do my best on the line, but must not be blamed if it is broken. Lee's cavalry is very bold, and will follow our troops down to Iuka.

S. A. HURLBUT,
Major-General, Commanding.

(Same to Grant, received at Chattanooga November 2.)

HEADQUARTERS SIXTEENTH ARMY CORPS,
Memphis, Tenn., October 30, 1863.

Col. J. C. KELTON,
    Asst. Adjt. Gen., Hdqrs. Army, Washington, D. C.:

SIR : General William T. Sherman having received pressing orders from Maj. Gen. U. S. Grant directing a rapid advance with all disposable force on the north side of the Tennessee to Stevenson, I have detached from this corps to accompany him eighteen of my best regiments of infantry with a full proportion of artillery. I had previously permanently transferred the Fifth Ohio Volunteer Cavalry and one battery of artillery from the Sixteenth Corps. In all, the draft from this corps within ten days will amount to 11,000 men. These troops thus sent are, as they should be, the best that I have, and in capital order for active duty. I desire in stating these facts simply to call your attention in advance to the fact that these drafts have so weakened my force on the line of the Charleston and Memphis Railroad as to render its possession and security very problematical.

I have no force in the city of Memphis which can well be moved without endangering our heavy depot of ordnance and other supplies. East of Memphis, and including Corinth, I shall have six regiments of infantry and about 4,500 cavalry; force enough, if together, to repel and punish any probable attack, but liable to be struck in detail and cut off from communications. Corinth has heavy stores and strong works, and even with its light garrison of four regiments, two white and two colored, can hold out within its fortifications, but scarcely save the stores and track. The cavalry is kept actively at work and well to the front, and is fully able to hold its own with the force from Mississippi. My apprehension, however, is that as soon as my detached force is thrown across the Tennessee, Stephen D. Lee, who has 4,000 mounted men, with good artillery, will pass into West Tennessee, and, being joined by the many guerrilla bands there, will move rapidly on Paducah and Fort Henry. I do not think he will try Columbus. In view of this state of affairs, with the railroad threatened in front and rear and on the left flank, I should not hesitate to abandon it as far as Moscow or La Grange, were it not that General Grant has ordered Tuttle's division to move instantly from Vicksburg, via Corinth, to Stevenson.

This compels the holding of Corinth as a depot of provisions and supplies for their movement. I had hoped to have received troops from Steele before this, and addressed him a request ten days since. I have just heard from him, and he declines moving them without an order from General Schofield. That order passed through this place five days since, and I may hope for a brigade in about ten days from this date.

I send these details that the general-in-chief may fully understand my position here and my belief that before the troops from Arkansas shall reach me the railroad communication will be broken. Every effort on my part will be made to prevent this result, but it may reasonably be expected.

I have the honor to be, sir, very respectfully, your obedient servant,

S. A. HURLBUT,
Major-General.

WATERLOO, ALA., *October* 30, [1863.]

Brig. Gen. G. M. DODGE, *Corinth:*

The rains make the passage of boats very bad. One gunboat has gone back to see what delays the ferry and other boats expected. I am now at Waterloo. Ewing's division is at Florence, and John E. Smith has the boat, but the pouring rain makes it terrible to handle the wagons. All are impressed with the necessity of haste, but we can do no better. I want to hear how you are getting along. I am now satisfied that Eastport and the shore opposite are the best places for us to hold. Eastport, with a gunboat in the river and a regiment intrenched on the hill, will be impregnable. I have made an order for you to leave a regiment there and two guns, which you had better bring out from Corinth.

W. T. SHERMAN,
Major-General.

CHATTANOOGA, *October* 30, 1863—10 a. m.
(Received November 1.)

Major-General BURNSIDE:

Can you get supplies from Carthage if sent there by boat? They can be sent from Nashville to any point on the Cumberland you designate, where boats can go. I will order your clothing to McMinnville, if you have not already designated another route, and order the commanding officer there to send them by wagon to river or cross valley to meet trains sent out by you. If they take this route I will inform you of the exact day they will leave McMinnville, so that you can arrange to meet them.

U. S. GRANT,
Major-General.

HEADQUARTERS DEPARTMENT OF THE TENNESSEE,
Waterloo, Ala., October 30, 1863.

Major-General GRANT,
Chattanooga:

The Tennessee is impassable, except by ferrying. Anticipating this, I ordered a ferry-boat before I left Corinth, and I am officially informed that one was ordered out from Paducah on the 24th instant, but it has not yet come. There is plenty of water in the Tennessee. Two gunboats have come up, and one has returned to see what causes delay to the others. I have but one gunboat and one coal barge to pass my troops, and, heavy rains having set in, our progress is slow. We work day and night. One division is forward at Florence, another is crossing, and I will do all that man can to hasten forward. I have received your dispatch by way of Cairo and through General Crook.

W. T. SHERMAN,
Major-General.

HEADQUARTERS DEPARTMENT OF THE TENNESSEE,
Eastport, Miss., October 30, 1863.

Major-General GRANT,
Chattanooga:

I have your dispatch of the 24th, sent through General Crook. I had two divisions at Tuscumbia driving out all the cavalry, and, finding Muscle Shoals impracticable, I had to fall back to Eastport and Chickasaw, where I had crossed one division, which is now at Florence. Another is nearly over and will go forward at once, and I will start with these two divisions for Athens, the effect of which will be to make the enemy believe all my army is there. I have been working in foul weather; had one gunboat and a coal barge decked over, which, with the muddy, slippery banks, made very slow and awkward work, but this moment have arrived three transports, one small ferry-boat, and two more gunboats, so that our progress will be better. I think I can have all the Fifteenth Army Corps over to-morrow. I can only carry ten days' rations, and will draw liberally of meats and corn of the country. The country is full of cavalry and guerrillas. We have had numerous skirmishes, but thus far we have the advantage.

W. T. SHERMAN,
Major-General.

IUKA, MISS., *October* 30, 1863—2.15 p. m.

Major-General SHERMAN,
Chickasaw:

GENERAL: The rebels came close up to our pickets, apparently following the wagon train of engineer regiment, and then went back. They have torn up the railroad ties and set fire to them in several places 5 miles east of us, and the cavalry officer feels satisfied that they burned the railroad bridge over Bear Creek, though he did not get near enough to see that himself. The captain commanding our cavalry thinks that the rebels crossed the creek at some ferry higher up and passed around near us, when they made for the railroad. His lieutenant thinks they came directly from the east, and then went back by same route. Both officers agree that Roddey was in command, and they think the force was not less than 1,000. The rebels were at the creek an hour ago, too strong for the force I sent out.

General Dodge's instructions, just received by telegraph, forbid my sending a regiment or two with section of artillery to the creek.

Your obedient servant,

JOHN W. FULLER,
Colonel, Commanding.

The engineer train is here, so we are not hurt by damages to railroad. Two regiments came in by train from the west. General Dodge has just told me to say, "Let Blair destroy the bridge over Bear Creek before he leaves." Probably the rebels have done it already.

CORINTH, *October* 30, 1863—10.15 p. m.

Col. J. W. FULLER:

Early in morning send following dispatch to General Sherman, at Waterloo:

I am getting along as well as can be expected. Will have most if not all of my troops in Eastport and Iuka by Sunday night. I may be delayed at those points by my trains and want of commissary stores, but hope not. Will be prepared to carry out orders in relation to force at Eastport, but please leave such orders that it will never be without protection of gunboat, and if you have any spare intrenching tools leave a few for me. Also, inform me by return messenger whether I can depend upon any commissary stores at Eastport. I think it will be well to have one of the companies of the regiment left. Mounted scouts in from all parts of south show that no force of any account is north of Okolona.

Chalmers is south of Oxford, and it is pretty quiet north of us toward Jackson, and will push with all my power and get across as soon as possible. Wet weather delays me; also the railroad. Enemy have fallen back east of Buzzard Roost to-night.

G. M. DODGE,
Brigadier-General.

HEADQUARTERS SIXTEENTH ARMY CORPS,
Memphis, Tenn., October 30, 1863.

Maj. Gen. J. B. McPHERSON,
Comdg. Seventeenth Army Corps, Vicksburg, Miss.:

GENERAL: I send you important dispatches from Grant. I am reduced to the minimum of force. I have barely 6,000 infantry and artillery. Everything tends to Chattanooga now. Relieve me if you can by a demonstration on Meridian and Selma. My railroad will be broken within ten days.

S. A. HURLBUT,
Major-General.

HDQRS. FOURTH DIVISION, FIFTEENTH ARMY CORPS,
Florence, Ala., October 30, 1863.

Major-General GRANT:

My division, the head of Sherman's column, is here. Your dispatch, via Huntsville, will reach him to-night. Courier reports but few rebels between this and Huntsville.

[HUGH EWING,]
Brigadier-General, Commanding Fourth Division.

WAR DEPARTMENT,
Washington, October 30, 1863—7.15 p. m.

JOHN W. GARRETT,
Baltimore, Md.:

General Augur will have two regiments ready at Washington depot to-morrow morning for transportation to Cincinnati, and thence to Eastport, Miss. The third regiment will be ready as soon as these two are disposed of.

H. W. HALLECK,
General-in-Chief.

OFFICE CHIEF Q. M., DEPOT OF WASHINGTON,
Washington, D. C., October 30, 1863.

Col. THOMAS SWORDS,
Assistant Quartermaster-General, Cincinnati, Ohio:

I am directed by the General-in-Chief to inform you that to-morrow, or the next day thereafter, a body of troops, numbering about 2,200, will leave this point by rail, via Cincinnati, to Eastport, Miss. If the Tennessee River is sufficiently high they are to be sent to the point of their destination by water, and if not, they will be landed at Cairo, and proceed thence by rail. Please have the boats in readiness, and make such other arrangements as you may deem to be necessary. Please answer.

D. H. RUCKER,
Brigadier-General, and Quartermaster.

WAR DEPARTMENT,
Washington, October 30, 1863—3 p. m.

CHIEF QUARTERMASTER,
Louisville, Ky.:

Three regiments will soon leave here for General Sherman's army. Arrangements have been made for the transportation to Cincinnati. You will arrange for their transportation from Cincinnati to Eastport or Florence, on the Tennessee River. If that river is not navigable they will be sent to Columbus, and thence by rail to Tuscumbia. They will number in all about 2,200. They have no supply trains. General Rucker will notify you of their movements.

H. W. HALLECK,
General-in-Chief.

MUNFORDVILLE, *October* 30, 1863.

Colonel STRICKLAND, *Glasgow:*

Keep scouts out to ascertain if rebels are concentrating. If they attempt to move into the State, be ready to send every available man in pursuit, and not stop until they are captured or whipped. If necessary, they can press horses and saddles, returning them when done with.

Keep me advised of every movement.

E. H. HOBSON,
Brigadier-General.

SPECIAL ORDERS, } HDQRS. DEPT. AND ARMY OF THE TENN.,
No. 5.   }   *Waterloo, Ala., October* 30, 1863.

I. Pursuant to instructions of the general commanding the Division of the Mississippi, the Fifteenth Army Corps, and the command of General Dodge will cross the Tennessee with as much expedition as possible, and move east, via Florence, Huntsville, &c., to meet further orders.

II. Eastport will be considered the head of navigation of the Tennessee for the present, and all transports will be discharged there, or held subject to orders. The marching columns will leave their sick and all incumbrances at Eastport or Waterloo, subject to further orders.

III. General Dodge will designate a regiment to hold Eastport, and will instruct the commanding officer to intrench the position on the hill over the town. He will detach two guns with ammunition for the use of the garrison at Eastport.

IV. The senior officer of each of the ordnance, quartermaster's, and commissary departments, now present with the army, will designate an officer of his department to remain at Eastport and take charge of the stores of their departments that may be left there or that may arrive by the river.

V. Colonel Siber will collect all invalids or sick men left behind, and organize them at Eastport, and the ordnance officer will issue to them arms and ammunition, on the requisition of Colonel Siber, or whomsoever may have charge of them. The medical officer will also designate one or more medical officers to remain with the sick, with the necessary medical supplies.

By order of Maj. Gen. W. T. Sherman :

R. M. SAWYER,
Assistant Adjutant-General.

SPECIAL ORDERS, } HDQRS. TWENTY-THIRD ARMY CORPS,
No. 102.   }   *Knoxville, Tenn., October* 30, 1863.

*   *   *   *   *   *   *

II. Col. Frank Wolford, commanding First Brigade, Fourth Division, will move at once with all the effective cavalry of his command and one section of artillery to Maryville, Tenn., where he will take position and scout to the front as far as Little Tennessee River. The ineffective force will be left in Knoxville to be refitted.

By command of Brigadier-General Manson :

R. C. KISE,
Captain, and Assistant Adjutant-General.

HEADQUARTERS ELEVENTH AND TWELFTH CORPS,
Lookout Valley, Tenn., October 31, 1863—1.10 p. m.

Brigadier-General CRUFT:

Your dispatch of to-day just received, and I am directed by the major-general commanding to reply that you will remain in position at Whiteside's until further orders. You will select such point as will enable you with your command to defend the passage through the mountain against any force that the enemy can send against it. The general is informed that an engineer will soon lay out the works deemed necessary for its perfect defense, and when this is done it is expected that your command will do the work that will be necessary to complete them. The general desires that you will make a thorough examination of all roads and by-roads in your vicinity leading from Newton to the river, and put out pickets sufficient to prevent them being made use of by the rebels. If you have any cavalry he desires that you will dispatch it in the direction of Newton to collect all information relating to movements of the enemy, his numbers, position, and intentions, and, if of value, to report all such information; that you will look for corn and forage, and procure as much for your animals as practicable. Your rations you will be required to draw from Bridgeport, unless landed at some nearer point. The general desires that all detachments, batteries, and transportation belonging to the Eleventh and Twelfth Corps may be sent forward without delay whenever you deem it safe for them to pass over the road. He suggests that no trains be allowed to pass without at least a regiment to guard them. You will make requisition at Bridgeport for one hundred axes, twelve picks, and twelve spades. Further instructions will be sent you hereafter.

Very respectfully, &c.,

H. W. PERKINS,
Lieutenant, Aide-de-Camp, and Actg. Asst. Adjt. Gen.

HEADQUARTERS ELEVENTH AND TWELFTH CORPS,
Lookout Valley, Tenn., October 31, 1863.

Brigadier-General GEARY,
Commanding Second Division, Twelfth Corps:

The general commanding directs me to say that you will leave one of your regiments in your present position, and post the balance of your command on the line now being established. Rations have arrived at Kelley's Ferry. You had better send your wagons there for them and for forage. Select suitable shelters within your new line for your depot. Send a staff officer to report to General Butterfield, who is now with the engineer establishing the new line. They will be found on the right of it.

Very respectfully,

H. W. PERKINS,
Lieutenant, Aide-de-Camp, and Actg. Asst. Adjt. Gen.

CHATTANOOGA, *October* 31, 1863—3 p. m.

Major-General SLOCUM:

General Hooker desires a report how and where you have posted your troops, and acknowledgment of the receipt of printed copies of instructions. A brigade will probably be sent from here to bridge-head at Bridgeport. If so, you will be notified.

DANL. BUTTERFIELD,
Major-General, Chief of Staff.

HQDRS. SECOND DIVISION, TWELFTH ARMY CORPS,
October 31, 1863.

Major-General HOWARD,
Commanding Eleventh Army Corps:

GENERAL: Yours of this [morning] has been received. With re-gard to your troops forming in junction with mine, I verbally mentioned to General Hooker 8 o'clock as the time. Upon consulting my records, I find in my written communications to the general that I reported one brigade as having reported at half past 5 o'clock and the other at 7 o'clock. My verbal statement was a mistake.

I have the honor to be, general, very respectfully, your obedient servant,

JNO. W. GEARY,
Brigadier-General of Volunteers.

HEADQUARTERS ELEVENTH AND TWELFTH CORPS,
Lookout Valley, Tenn., October 31, 1863.

Brigadier-General GEARY:

General Hooker directs that not a tree or a limb be disturbed inside our new line. All the woods and brush must be preserved to conceal our troops and the movement of trains.

Very respectfully, &c.,

DANL. BUTTERFIELD,
Major-General, Chief of Staff.

OCTOBER 31, 1863—11.10 p. m.

General REYNOLDS:

Tents of the enemy in and on Lookout moved before dark. No lights in Lookout Valley at this hour.

WHITAKER,
Brigadier-General.

MAYSVILLE, *October* 31, 1863.

Maj. W. H. SINCLAIR,
Assistant Adjutant-General:

Have just captured Lieutenant Manohen [?], of General Wheeler's staff, with 3 of his men. I got back the horses taken from my men

GEORGE CROOK,
Brigadier-General.

HEADQUARTERS DEPARTMENT OF THE CUMBERLAND,
Chattanooga, October 31, 1863.
Brigadier-General CROOK,
Commanding, Maysville, Ala.:

It is of the utmost importance that the cavalry you were ordered to send General Hooker should reach him as soon as possible. Have you sent it?

GEO. H. THOMAS,
Major-General, U. S. Volunteers, Commanding.

HEADQUARTERS DEPARTMENT OF THE CUMBERLAND,
Chattanooga, October 31, 1863.
Brigadier-General CRUFT,
Comdg. First Division, Fourth Army Corps:

The brigades of your division at Bridgeport will be stationed on the hill near the bridge-head, a detail being warned to be at all times [ready] to occupy and defend the bridge-head. You will effectually destroy the Moore's Gap road somewhere on the mountain side; also the road near Island Creek. Brigadier-General Whitaker, with his brigade, is ordered to report to you, which will put the whole division on the south side of the river. You will establish your headquarters at Shellmound. Whitaker's brigade will relieve, by two regiments, the regiment now occupying a pass near Shellmound on the road toward Trenton. The latter regiment will rejoin its division. The headquarters of Whitaker's brigade will be at Shellmound. You will picket well to the front toward Trenton. Avail yourself of every means to procure information, which will be promptly reported to these headquarters. Draw your supplies from Bridgeport.

By command of Major-General Thomas:
J. J. REYNOLDS,
Major-General, Chief of Staff.

DECHERD, TENN., *October* 31, 1863.
Col. A. P. CAMPBELL,
Commanding First Brigade:

The general commanding directs that you march with your brigade immediately to Winchester, Tenn., and encamp in the locality selected by Captain Porter, acting assistant inspector-general, First Cavalry Division, who will accompany you.

I am, colonel, your very obedient servant,
J. E. JACOBS,
Captain, and Assistant Adjutant-General.

HDQRS. FIRST BRIG., SECOND DIV., 14TH ARMY CORPS,
Near Dallas, Tenn., October 31, 1863.
Lieut. Col. C. GODDARD,
Assistant Adjutant-General, Dept. of the Cumberland:

COLONEL: I have the honor to report that Mrs. Whiteburg has returned from the other side of the river, and reports that the rebels are sending a heavy force, supposed to be about 45,000, to meet

Burnside. Their convalescents and trains are following up. The general impression among the citizens is that Bragg will not fight in front of Chattanooga. This report of Mrs. Whiteburg is taken from a written statement of Maj. Robert S. McNabb, a Union man, who lives over the river and has opportunities for learning the movements and intentions of the rebels.

I am, colonel, very respectfully, your obedient servant,

R. F. SMITH,
Colonel, Commanding Brigade.

CHATTANOOGA, *October* 31, 1863—3 p. m.

Major-General BURNSIDE:

It is reported on [reliable] authority large force of Bragg's army is moving toward you. Do you hear anything of such a move?

U. S. GRANT,
Major-General, Commanding.

KNOXVILLE, *October* 31, 1863—2.30 p. m.

Major-General GRANT:

There are indications that a heavy cavalry force of the enemy is crossing the Little Tennessee, and advancing up the south side of the Holston, with a view of breaking through our lines or passing by our left flank, and in too great force to be resisted by our cavalry as at present disposed. I am sending a force to resist the advance, and may be able to check them. If it were possible for Thomas to make a demonstration with his cavalry against Bragg's left it would probably cause the withdrawal of this force. The disposition of affairs, with this exception, remains as I advised you in my last dispatch.

A. E. BURNSIDE,
Major-General.

LENOIR'S, *October* 31, 1863.

General BURNSIDE:

All quiet at Leiper's Ferry. Pennebaker has moved off; has some 30 or 40 missing, and lost more horses. The enemy active, driving in stock and arresting citizens. They were scouting all along the other bank of the river last evening.

ROBERT B. POTTER,
Brigadier-General.

GREENEVILLE, *October* 31, 1863.

Major-General BURNSIDE:

Following just received from Colonel Garrard:

CAMP 8 MILES FROM KINGSPORT,
October 30, [1863.]

Brigadier-General SHACKELFORD,
Greeneville:

I moved my force up to Kingsport yesterday. A part of it was sent to Moccasin Gap and Estaville, and a part across the north fork of Holston, 3 miles out on the Reedy Creek road. There was no enemy within reach, nor did we hear of any.

The force that had been in camp on Reedy Creek had left two days before for Blountsville. On returning [to] camp I was informed of the movement of the forces at Jonesborough to Greeneville, and have moved my camp back to Lyons' farm, on the west side of Big Creek, 3½ miles east of Rogersville. My command is now on the road to that camp.

Very respectfully, yours,

ISRAEL GARRARD,
Commanding Seventh Ohio Volunteer Cavalry.

O. B. WILLCOX,
Brigadier-General.

EASTPORT, MISS., *October* 31, [1863.]
(Received 12.40 a. m., November 3.)

Major-General GRANT :

I have your dispatch of the 24th, through General Crook. I had three divisions in Tuscumbia, and drove Lee's cavalry beyond Town Creek, but the Muscle Shoals had too much water for us and I had to fall back to Eastport and Chickasaw, where I had crossed one division (Ewing's), which is now at Florence. Another (John E. Smith's) is nearly over, and it will go forward at once. I will start to-morrow with these two divisions rapidly for Athens, the effect of which will be to make the enemy believe all my army is there. I have heretofore been working in foul weather, with a single coal-barge, decked over ; but this moment have arrived a ferry-boat, three transports, and two more gunboats, so that my progress will be more rapid. I think I can have all the Fifteenth Army Corps over to-morrow, and Dodge ought to follow with his division the day after. I can carry ten days' rations, and will draw liberally of meats and corn on the country. The country is full of cavalry and guerrillas. We have had numerous skirmishes, and thus far have had the advantage.

W. T. SHERMAN,
Major-General.

(Same to Halleck, received November 2.)

HEADQUARTERS ARMY OF THE TENNESSEE,
Waterloo, Lauderdale County, Ala., October 31, 1863.

Brig. Gen. GEORGE CROOK,
Commanding Second Cavalry Division, Georgetown :

SIR : Corporal Pike came through safe, also a private, to-day. Lieutenant Fitzgerald came through with your letter of the 27th. One of my divisions is nearly over the Tennessee, and will be at Florence to-morrow night. Two more divisions are on the other side of the Tennessee, and will cross as fast as possible. At first I only had a coal-barge to cross the command, but to-day a ferry-boat arrived and three transports, and the work moves faster. We have also had some villainous weather, but this is also over, and now I hope to be in Athens in four days.

I have sent message to Cairo to be telegraphed to General Grant, but I wish you would cause the substance of this to go to him. We drove the enemy's cavalry below the Tennessee beyond Town Creek, but Roddey's cavalry returned and is hanging round Iuka. I think Wheeler has gone back to Bragg, and that Lee has gone back to Okolona.

There are small bands of guerillas in every direction, but they give us a wide berth. As soon as the head of my column reaches Athens I will send forward to advise you, and would be pleased if you would advise me in the meantime of your whereabouts ; also, what is the best road from Athens to the Stevenson road. That from Huntsville, via Bellefonte, to Stevenson used to be very bad.

I have received General Grant's dispatch of October 24, inclosed in yours.

I am, &c.,

W. T. SHERMAN,
Major-General.

U. S. Gunboat Key West,
October 31, 1863.

Maj. Gen. William T. Sherman, U. S. Army,
Comdg. Department of the Tennessee, Iuka, Miss.:

General : We will be due at Eastport at 4 a. m. with the transport Anglo-Saxon. The Nashville and a small ferry-boat should arrive by 8 or 9 o'clock this morning. I am writing, as well as this shaking vessel will permit, to advise you of this arrival, and to get my letter off as soon as we arrive. Either of the transports will require about 2 feet water when light, and the ferry-boat some 12 inches, I suppose. If sufficient detail of men is made, the cargo of the two steamers can be landed in a few hours, when they can cross men and horses very rapidly, but not wagons. The ferry-boat can take on eight wagons without teams, and some 50 horses. These boats, with the barge, can cross a division in twelve to fifteen hours. Fuel will be an immediate necessity. I have had to lend them all we could spare to get the boats up. The fences about may answer for a little while, but you will need to have wood cut immediately. I am told pine knots can be easily obtained about here. A steamer came up from Paducah, which I suppose was one of the convoy. I missed her at Duck River, and was informed by the gunboat astern that she was on a private trading voyage, and had landed below us. I was in a hurry to get these vessels up, or I should have gone down and brought the steamer up here. The river is everywhere thronged with guerrillas, and it is useless for us to patrol it and destroy skiffs, flats, &c., to prevent crossing the stream, when a steamer is permitted by the custom-house authorities to be on trading voyages. The permits are given by the Paducah custom-house officers. Would it not, as a military measure, be proper for you to order that no vessel shall be permitted to come up the Tennessee, except in convoy of a gunboat, and not to land except when the naval commander shall deem it safe and otherwise proper to do so ? Your order to the custom-house officers they have to observe, and must give permits subject to them. The restrictions will enable gunboat officers to prevent detention to transports arising from the presence of trading vessels. In short, such an order will enable us to control the trade to the desirable point, permitting loyal people to get their products

o market and to procure family supplies, while we can shut down
on smuggling and make all conform to the public interests of a mili-
ary character. If you give such an order please send it to me as
soon as you can, and I will notify the Paducah authorities.

I shall send a gunboat down this morning, but will detain her till
I can hear from you, and get what mail you may wish to send. She
will reach Paducah in twenty hours, and, if you desire it, I will send
her through to Cairo with your dispatches.

We captured some men, horses, arms, and saddles.

I am, respectfully, your obedient servant,

S. L. PHELPS,
Commander Sixth and Seventh Divisions, Miss. Squadron.

HEADQUARTERS SEVENTH ILLINOIS CAVALRY,
Collierville, Tenn., October 31, 1863.

Col. EDWARD HATCH,
Comdg. Cavalry Division, Sixteenth Army Corps:

SIR: Your order to send a company to La Fayette is received and
complied with. The battalion at Quinn and Jackson's Mill we still
continue, but I learn from good authority that Chalmers is preparing an expedition expressly to capture them. We have no force at
Mount Pleasant, as it is impossible to keep one there and furnish
pickets to this place. We have now, including the force at Quinn's
Mill, over six companies on duty every day. We have all the guard
duty and picketing for this post, which, from the nature of the
country, requires a large force. I wish to inquire if it will not be
policy to relieve the force at Quinn's Mill, as the enemy can cross
either above or below and cut them off effectually.

I am, colonel, your most obedient servant,

G. W. TRAFTON,
Lieutenant-Colonel Seventh Illinois Cavalry, Comdg. Post.

MEMPHIS, TENN., *October 31, 1863.*

Lieutenant-Colonel TRAFTON,
Collierville, Tenn.:

Keep a sharp lookout. Notify the battalion at Quinn and Jackson's Mill that they are in danger. They must not occupy the same
ground more than twenty-four hours at a time.

EDWARD HATCH,
Colonel, Commanding Division.

MEMPHIS, TENN., *October 31, 1863.*

COMMANDING OFFICER CAVALRY BRIGADE,
Corinth, Miss.:

You will immediately, on the receipt of this, move with your entire
available force to La Grange, taking with you a full supply of ammunition and two days' rations and blankets. Upon arriving at La
Grange, bivouac your command and report to me by telegraph. Make

your arrangements to draw rations and forage at La Grange for five days. There is information that an attack may be made in a few days, and in our present condition great vigilance is necessary. Look especially to your left flank while on the march, and instructions will be forwarded to you when you arrive at La Grange.

By order of Edward Hatch, colonel commanding division :
                                    S. L. WOODWARD,
                                    Assistant Adjutant-General.

                                    COLUMBUS, KY., *October 31, 1863.*
Brigadier-General REID :

A large force is approaching Paducah. Please ask Admiral Porter to send a gunboat there at once, if practicable.
                                    A. J. SMITH,
                                    Brigadier-General.

SPECIAL ORDERS,) HDQRS. DEPT. AND ARMY OF THE TENN.,
    No. 6.   )   *Waterloo, Ala., October 31, 1863.*

I. Pursuant to instructions from the general commanding the Military Division of the Mississippi, the Third Division of the Fifteenth Army Corps, Brigadier-General Tuttle commanding, will move at once by boats, via Cairo and up the Tennessee River, landing opposite Eastport, and push forward, via Florence, to join its proper corps.

*   *   *   *   *   *   *

By order of Maj. Gen. W. T. Sherman :
                                    R. M. SAWYER,
                                    Assistant Adjutant-General.

Abstract from returns of the Military Division of the Mississippi, Maj. Gen. Ulysses S. Grant, U. S. Army, commanding, for the month of October, 1863.*

Command.	Present for duty.		Aggregate present.	Aggregate present and absent.	Pieces of artillery.	
	Officers.	Men.			Heavy.	Field.
General headquarters...........................	14	....	14	14	....	....
Department of the Cumberland...................	4,628	78,202	97,018	154,289	22	252
Department of the Ohio.........................	2,047	39,907	49,367	67,016	8	196
Department of the Tennessee....................	3,747	64,207	84,159	123,084	88	235
Total.......................................	10,436	182,316	230,558	344,403	118	683
Total according to General Grant's return...	11,029	191,972	244,731	348,058	130	633

* Compiled from the subordinate, as the most accurate, returns.

Abstract from returns of the Department of the Cumberland, Maj. Gen. George H. Thomas, U. S. Army, commanding, October 31, 1863.

Command.	Present for duty. Officers.	Present for duty. Men.	Aggregate present.	Aggregate present and absent.	Aggregate last return.	Pieces of artillery. Heavy.	Pieces of artillery. Field.	Headquarters.
General headquarters.............	47	518	721	889	904	....	......	
Fourth Army Corps:								
Headquarters...................	6	....	6	6	6	....	......	Shellmound.
First Division.................	439	6,142	7,546	13,880	14,149	....	18	Shellmound.
Second Division................	486	6,540	8,428	15,109	14,966	....	18	Chattanooga.
Third Division.................	441	7,029	8,785	15,392	12,614	....	19	Do.
Total Fourth Army Corps...	1,372	19,711	24,765	44,387	41,735	....	55	
Hooker's command:								
Headquarters...................	7	....	7	9	8	....	......	Lookout Valley.
Eleventh Army Corps:								
Headquarters...................	11	42	63	77	77	....	......	Lookout Valley.
Second Division...............	150	2,614	3,187	5,318	5,838	....	......	Do.
Third Division.................	181	3,145	3,855	6,651	7,343	....	......	Do.
Artillery.....................	16	530	588	796	795	....	26	
Total Eleventh Army Corps.	358	6,331	7,593	12,842	14,053	....	26	
Twelfth Army Corps:								
Headquarters...................	14	145	191	237	247	....	......	Wartrace.
First Division.................	255	4,310	4,884	7,417	7,449	....	......	Tullahoma.
Second Division................	219	3,904	4,455	7,248	7,348	....	......	Wauhatchie.
Artillery.....................	11	343	376	469	474	....	20	
Total Twelfth Army Corps..	499	8,702	9,906	15,371	15,518	....	20	
Total Hooker's command...	864	15,033	17,606	28,222	29,579	....	46	
Fourteenth Army Corps:								
Headquarters...................	22	239	372	479	484	....	......	Chattanooga.
First Division.................	329	5,914	7,604	14,327	7,653	....	16	Do.
Second Division................	378	7,114	8,553	11,406	11,542	....	18	Near Rossville.
Third Division.................	335	6,008	7,779	13,199	13,366	....	18	Chattanooga.
Fourth Division................	....	....	....	....	9,375	....	......	
Total Fourteenth Army Corps.	1,064	19,275	24,308	39,411	42,420	....	52	
Cavalry Corps:								
Headquarters...................	4	....	4	5	5	....	......	Chattanooga.
First Division.................	253	4,099	5,360	8,246	8,307	....	2	Winchester.
Second Division................	172	2,964	3,643	6,689	6,697	....	7	Maysville.
Wilder's brigade	130	2,110	2,644	3,414	3,450	....	......	Do.
Total Cavalry Corps	559	9,173	11,651	18,354	18,459	....	9	
Artillery Reserve	33	1,136	1,235	1,973	2,052	....	51	Chattanooga.
Pioneer Brigade................	50	849	1,215	2,617	2,643	....	......	Do.
Coburn's brigade...............	105	1,980	2,403	2,992	3,002	....	6	Tullahoma.
Clarksville	12	254	454	481	481	....	......	
Fort Donelson	14	256	436	468	469	....	4	
Gallatin.......................	50	784	1,003	1,139	1,133	....	6	
Nashville......................	203	3,899	4,796	5,393	4,877	22	10	
Unassigned:								
Artillery*a*	18	422	468	526	526	....	13	
Cavalry (15th Pennsylvania)	25	388	465	667	688	....	......	Sequatchie Valley.
Engineer troops (1st Michigan)	25	608	771	965	896	....	......	Big Harpeth, Tenn.
Infantry *b*	187	3,916	4,721	5,805	4,900	....	......	
Grand total	4,628	78,202	97,018	154,289	154,764	22	252	

a Murfreesborough, Elk River, Dallas, Anderson's Cross-Roads.
b Tullahoma, Stevenson, Ala., Chattanooga, Murfreesborough, Anderson's Cross-Roads, Big Harpeth, Walden's Ridge, and Sullivan's Branch.

51 R R—VOL XXXI, PT I

Organization of troops in the Department of the Cumberland, Maj. Gen. George H. Thomas, U. S. Army, commanding, October 31, 1863.

GENERAL HEADQUARTERS.

10th Ohio, Lieut. Col. William M. Ward.
1st Battalion Ohio Sharpshooters, Capt. Gershom M. Barber.
Pioneer Brigade, Brig. Gen. J. St. Clair Morton.
1st Michigan Engineers, Col. William P. Innes.
Signal Corps, Capt. Jesse Merrill.

FOURTH ARMY CORPS.

Maj. Gen. GORDON GRANGER.

SIGNAL CORPS.

Capt. WILLIAM LEONARD.

FIRST DIVISION.

Brig. Gen. CHARLES CRUFT.

First Brigade.

Col. THOMAS D. SEDGEWICK.

21st Illinois, Capt. Chester K. Knight.
38th Illinois, Capt. William C. Harris.
29th Indiana, Lieut. Col. David M. Dunn.
31st Indiana, Col. John T. Smith.
81st Indiana, Lieut. Col. William C. Wheeler.
1st Kentucky, Lieut. Col. Alva R. Hadlock.
2d Kentucky, Lieut. Col. John R. Hurd.
90th Ohio, Lieut. Col. Samuel N. Yeoman.
101st Ohio, Col. Isaac M. Kirby.

Second Brigade.

Brig. Gen. WALTER C. WHITAKER.

96th Illinois, Col. Thomas E. Champion.
115th Illinois, Col. Jesse H. Moore.
35th Indiana, Col. Bernard F. Mullen.
84th Indiana, Maj. Andrew J. Neff.
8th Kentucky, Col. Sidney M. Barnes.
40th Ohio, Col. Jacob E. Taylor.
51st Ohio, Lieut. Col. Charles H. Wood.
99th Ohio, Lieut. Col. John E. Cummins.

Third Brigade.

Col. WILLIAM GROSE.

59th Illinois, Lieut. Col. Joshua C. Winters.
75th Illinois, Lieut. Col. William M. Kilgour.
84th Illinois, Lieut. Col. Louis H. Waters.
9th Indiana, Col. Isaac C. B. Suman.
30th Indiana, Lieut. Col. Orrin D. Hurd.
36th Indiana, Maj. Gilbert Trusler.
24th Ohio, Capt. George M. Bacon.
77th Pennsylvania, Capt. Joseph J. Lawson.

Artillery.

Capt. PETER SIMONSON.

Indiana Light, 5th Battery, Capt. Peter Simonson.
4th United States, Battery H, Lieut. Harry C. Cushing.
4th United States, Battery M, Lieut. Francis L. D. Russell.

SECOND DIVISION.

Maj. Gen. PHILIP H. SHERIDAN.

First Brigade.	*Second Brigade.*
Col. FRANCIS T. SHERMAN.	Brig. Gen. GEORGE D. WAGNER.

36th Illinois, Col. Silas Miller.	100th Illinois, Col. Frederick A. Bartleson.
44th Illinois, Col. Wallace W. Barrett.	
73d Illinois, Lieut. Col. James I. Davidson.	15th Indiana, Col. Gustavus A. Wood.
	40th Indiana, Col. John W. Blake.
74th Illinois, Col. Jason Marsh.	57th Indiana, Lieut. Col. George W. Lennard.
88th Illinois, Maj. George W. Chandler.	
22d Indiana, Col. Michael Gooding.	58th Indiana, Col. George P. Buell.
21st Michigan, Capt. Loomis K. Bishop.	13th Michigan, Col. Joshua B. Culver.
2d Missouri, Lieut. Col. Arnold Beck.	26th Ohio, Col. Edward P. Fyffe.
15th Missouri, Col. Joseph Conrad.	97th Ohio, Col. John Q. Lane.
24th Wisconsin, Maj. Carl von Baumbach.	

Third Brigade.

Col. CHARLES G. HARKER.

22d Illinois, Lieut. Col. Francis Swanwick.
27th Illinois, Col. Jonathan R. Miles.
42d Illinois, Lieut. Col. Nathan H. Walworth.
51st Illinois, Maj. Charles W. Davis.
79th Illinois, Col. Allen Buckner.
3d Kentucky, Maj. John Brennan.
64th Ohio, Col. Alexander McIlvain.
65th Ohio, Lieut. Col. William A. Bullitt.
125th Ohio, Col. Emerson Opdycke.

Artillery.

Capt. WILLIAM A. NAYLOR.

1st Illinois Light, Battery M, Capt. George W. Spencer.
Indiana Light, 10th Battery, Capt. William A. Naylor.
1st Missouri Light, Battery G, Lieut. Gustavus Schueler.

THIRD DIVISION.

Brig. Gen. THOMAS J. WOOD.

First Brigade.	*Second Brigade.*
Brig. Gen. AUGUST WILLICH.	Brig. Gen. WILLIAM B. HAZEN.

25th Illinois, Capt. Wesford Taggart.	6th Indiana, Maj. Calvin D. Campbell.
35th Illinois, Lieut. Col. William P. Chandler.	5th Kentucky, Lieut. Col. John L. Treanor.
89th Illinois, Lieut. Col. William D. Williams.	6th Kentucky, Maj. Richard T. Whitaker.
32d Indiana, Lieut. Col. Frank Erdelmeyer.	23d Kentucky, Lieut. Col. James C. Foy.
68th Indiana, Lieut. Col. John S. Scobey.	1st Ohio, Lieut. Col. Bassett Langdon.
8th Kansas, Col. John A. Martin.	6th Ohio, Lieut. Col. Alexander C. Christopher.
15th Ohio, Lieut. Col. Frank Askew.	
49th Ohio, Maj. Samuel F. Gray.	41st Ohio, Col. Aquila Wiley.
15th Wisconsin, Capt. Mons Grinager.	93d Ohio, Maj. William Birch.
	124th Ohio, Lieut. Col. James Pickands.

Third Brigade.

Brig. Gen. SAMUEL BEATTY.

44th Indiana, Lieut. Col. Simeon C. Aldrich.
79th Indiana, Col. Frederick Knefler.
86th Indiana, Col. George F. Dick.
9th Kentucky, Col. George H. Cram.
17th Kentucky, Col. Alexander M. Stout.
13th Ohio, Col. Dwight Jarvis, jr.
19th Ohio, Col. Charles F. Manderson.
59th Ohio, Maj. Robert J. Vanosdol.

Artillery.

Capt. CULLEN BRADLEY.

Bridges' (Illinois) Battery, Capt. Lyman Bridges.
Ohio Light, 6th Battery, Lieut. Oliver H. P. Ayres.
Pennsylvania Light, Battery B, Lieut. Samuel M. McDowell.

ELEVENTH AND TWELFTH ARMY CORPS.

Maj. Gen. JOSEPH HOOKER.

PROVOST GUARD.

10th Maine, 1st Battalion, Capt. John D. Beardsley.

ELEVENTH ARMY CORPS.

Maj. Gen. OLIVER O. HOWARD.

HEADQUARTERS.

Independent Company, 8th New York Infantry, Capt. Anton Bruhn.

SECOND DIVISION.

Brig. Gen. ADOLPH VON STEINWEHR.

First Brigade.

Col. ADOLPHUS BUSCHBECK.

33d New Jersey, Col. George W. Mindil.
134th New York, Lieut. Col. Allan H. Jackson.
154th New York, Maj. Lewis D. Warner.
27th Pennsylvania, Maj. Peter A. McAloon.
73d Pennsylvania, Col. William Moore.

Second Brigade.

Col. ORLAND SMITH.

33d Massachusetts, Lieut. Col. Godfrey Rider, jr.
136th New York, Col. James Wood, jr.
168th New York, Col. William R. Brown.
55th Ohio, Col. Charles B. Gambee.
73d Ohio, Maj. Samuel H. Hurst.

THIRD DIVISION.

Maj. Gen. CARL SCHURZ.

First Brigade.

Brig. Gen. HECTOR TYNDALE.

101st Illinois, Col. Charles H. Fox.
45th New York, Col. George von Amsberg.
143d New York, Col. Horace Boughton.
61st Ohio, Col. Stephen J. McGroarty.
82d Ohio, Col. James S. Robinson.

Second Brigade.

Col. WLADIMIR KRZYZANOWSKI.

58th New York, Capt. Michael Esembaux.
119th New York, Col. John T. Lockman.
141st New York, Col. William K. Logie.
26th Wisconsin, Col. William H. Jacobs.

Third Brigade.

Col. FREDERICK HECKER.

80th Illinois, Capt. James Neville.
82d Illinois, Lieut. Col. Edward S. Salomon.
68th New York, Lieut. Col. Albert von Steinhausen.
75th Pennsylvania, Maj. August Ledig.

ARTILLERY.

Maj. THOMAS W. OSBORN.

1st New York Light, Battery I, Capt. Michael Wiedrich.
New York Light, 13th Battery, Capt. William Wheeler.
1st Ohio Light, Battery I, Capt. Hubert Dilger.
1st Ohio Light, Battery K, Lieut. Nicholas Sahm.
4th United States, Battery G, Lieut. Eugene A. Bancroft.

TWELFTH ARMY CORPS.

Maj. Gen. HENRY W. SLOCUM.

FIRST DIVISION.

Brig. Gen. ALPHEUS S. WILLIAMS.

First Brigade.

Brig. Gen. JOSEPH F. KNIPE.

5th Connecticut, Col. Warren W. Packer.
20th Connecticut, Col. Samuel Ross.
3d Maryland, Col. Joseph M. Sudsburg.
123d New York, Lieut. Col. James C. Rogers.
145th New York, Capt. Samuel T. Allen.
46th Pennsylvania, Lieut. Col. William L. Foulk.

Third Brigade.

Brig. Gen. THOMAS H. RUGER.

27th Indiana, Col. Silas Colgrove.
2d Massachusetts, Col. William Cogswell.
13th New Jersey, Col. Ezra A. Carman.
107th New York, Col. Nirom M. Crane.
150th New York, Col. John H. Ketcham.
3d Wisconsin, Col. William Hawley.

SECOND DIVISION.

Brig. Gen. JOHN W. GEARY.

First Brigade.

Col. CHARLES CANDY.

5th Ohio, Col. John H. Patrick.
7th Ohio, Col. William R. Creighton.
29th Ohio, Col. William T. Fitch.
66th Ohio, Lieut. Col. Eugene Powell.
28th Pennsylvania, Capt. John Flynn.
147th Pennsylvania, Lieut. Col. Ario Pardee, jr.

Second Brigade.

Col. GEORGE A. COBHAM, Jr.

29th Pennsylvania, Col. William Rickards, jr.
109th Pennsylvania, Capt. Frederick L. Gimber.
111th Pennsylvania, Lieut. Col. Thomas M. Walker.

Third Brigade.

Col. DAVID IRELAND.

60th New York, Col. Abel Godard.
78th New York, Lieut. Col. Herbert von Hammerstein.
102d New York, Col. James C. Lane.
137th New York, Capt. Milo B. Eldredge.
149th New York, Lieut. Col. Charles B. Randall.

ARTILLERY.

Maj. John A. Reynolds.

1st New York Light, Battery M, Capt. John D. Woodbury.
Pennsylvania Light, Battery E, Lieut. James A. Dunlevy.
4th United States, Battery F, Lieut. Edward D. Muhlenberg.
5th United States, Battery K, Capt. Edmund C. Bainbridge.

FOURTEENTH ARMY CORPS.

Maj. Gen. John M. Palmer.

PROVOST GUARD.

9th Michigan, Col. John G. Parkhurst.

FIRST DIVISION.

Máj. Gen. Lovell H. Rousseau.

First Brigade.	*Second Brigade.*
Brig. Gen. William P. Carlin.	Col. Marshall F. Moore.
104th Illinois, Maj. John H. Widmer.	19th Illinois, Lieut. Col. Alexander W. Raffen.
38th Indiana, Lieut. Col. Daniel F. Griffin.	11th Michigan, Capt. Patrick H. Keegan.
42d Indiana, Lieut. Col. William T. B. McIntire.	18th Ohio, Col. Timothy R. Stanley.
88th Indiana, Capt. Joseph R. Webster.	69th Ohio, Capt. Ross J. Hazletine.
15th Kentucky, Maj. William G. Halpin.	15th United States, 1st Battalion, Capt. Henry Keteltas.
2d Ohio, Col. Anson G. McCook.	15th United States, 2d Battalion, Maj. John R. Edie.
33d Ohio, Col. Oscar F. Moore.	16th United States, 1st Battalion, Capt. Robert E. A. Crofton.
94th Ohio, Maj. Rue P. Hutchins.	18th United States, 1st Battalion, Capt. George W. Smith.
10th Wisconsin, Capt. Jacob W. Roby.	18th United States, 2d Battalion, Capt. Henry Haymond.
	19th United States, 1st Battalion, Capt. Henry S. Welton.

Third Brigade.

Col. William Sirwell.

24th Illinois, Capt. August Mauff.
37th Indiana, Col. James S. Hull.
21st Ohio, Capt. Charles H. Vantine.
74th Ohio, Maj. Joseph Fisher.
78th Pennsylvania, Maj. Augustus B. Bonnaffon.
79th Pennsylvania, Capt. William G. Kendrick.
1st Wisconsin, Capt. John C. Goodrich.
21st Wisconsin, Capt. Charles H. Walker.

Artillery.

Capt. Mark H. Prescott.

1st Illinois Light, Battery C, Capt. Mark H. Prescott.
1st Michigan Light, Battery A, Lieut. Francis E. Hale.
5th United States, Battery H, Lieut. Edmund D. Spooner.

SECOND DIVISION.

Brig. Gen. JEFFERSON C. DAVIS.

First Brigade.	*Second Brigade.**
Col. ROBERT F. SMITH.	Brig. Gen. JAMES G. SPEARS.
10th Illinois, Col. John Tillson.	78th Illinois, Lieut. George Green.
16th Illinois, Lieut. Col. James B. Cahill.	98th Ohio, Maj. James M. Shane.
60th Illinois, Col. William B. Anderson.	113th Ohio, Maj. Lyne S. Sullivant.
10th Michigan, Lieut. Col. Christopher J. Dickerson.	121st Ohio, Maj. John Yager.
14th Michigan, Col. Henry R. Mizner.	3d Tennessee, Col. William Cross.
	5th Tennessee, Col. James T. Shelley.
	6th Tennessee, Col. Joseph A. Cooper.

Third Brigade.

Col. DANIEL McCOOK.

85th Illinois, Col. Caleb J. Dilworth.
86th Illinois, Lieut. Col. David W. Magee.
110th Illinois, Lieut. Col. E. Hibbard Topping.
125th Illinois, Col. Oscar F. Harmon.
22d Michigan, Maj. Henry S. Dean.
52d Ohio, Maj. James T. Holmes.

Artillery.

Capt. WILLIAM A. HOTCHKISS.

2d Illinois Light, Battery I, Capt. Charles M. Barnett.
Minnesota Light, 2d Battery, Lieut. Richard L. Dawley.
Wisconsin Light, 5th Battery, Lieut. Joseph McKnight.

THIRD DIVISION.

Brig. Gen. ABSALOM BAIRD.

First Brigade.	*Second Brigade.*
Brig. Gen. JOHN B. TURCHIN.	Col. JAMES GEORGE.
82d Indiana, Col. Morton C. Hunter.	75th Indiana, Col. Milton S. Robinson.
11th Ohio, Col. Philander P. Lane.	87th Indiana, Col. Newell Gleason.
17th Ohio, Col. John M. Connell.	101st Indiana, Lieut. Col. Thomas Doan.
31st Ohio, Lieut. Col. Frederick W. Lister.	2d Minnesota, Lieut. Col. Judson W. Bishop.
36th Ohio, Lieut. Col. Hiram F. Devol.	9th Ohio, Col. Gustave Kammerling.
89th Ohio, Capt. Edward P. Henry.	35th Ohio, Maj. Joseph L. Budd.
92d Ohio, Lieut. Col. Douglas Putnam, jr.	105th Ohio, Capt. Charles G. Edwards.

Third Brigade.

Col. EDWARD H. PHELPS.

10th Indiana, Lieut. Col. Marsh B. Taylor.
74th Indiana, Col. Charles W. Chapman.
4th Kentucky, Maj. Robert M. Kelly.
10th Kentucky, Col. William H. Hays.
18th Kentucky, Lieut. Col. Hubbard K. Milward.
14th Ohio, Lieut. Col. Henry D. Kingsbury.
38th Ohio, Maj. Charles Greenwood.

---

* The 78th Illinois, 98th, 113th, and 121st Ohio Regiments on detached duty under Col. John G. Mitchell.

Artillery.

Capt. GEORGE R. SWALLOW.

Indiana Light, 7th Battery, Lieut. Otho H. Morgan.
Indiana Light, 19th Battery, Capt. Samuel J. Harris.
4th United States, Battery I, Lieut. Frank G. Smith.

UNATTACHED.

Coburn's Brigade.

Col. JOHN COBURN.

33d Indiana, Lieut. Col. James M. Henderson.
85th Indiana, Col. John P. Baird.
19th Michigan, Col. Henry C. Gilbert.
22d Wisconsin, Col. William L. Utley.
9th Ohio Battery, Capt. Harrison B. York.

ARTILLERY RESERVE.

Brig. Gen. JOHN M. BRANNAN.

FIRST DIVISION.

Col. JAMES BARNETT.

First Brigade. *

1st Ohio Light, Battery A, Capt. Wilbur
F. Goodspeed.
1st Ohio Light, Battery B, Lieut. Norman A. Baldwin.
1st Ohio Light, Battery C, Lieut. Marco B. Gary.
1st Ohio Light, Battery F, Lieut. Giles J. Cockerill.

Second Brigade. *

1st Ohio Light, Battery G, Capt. Alexander Marshall.
1st Ohio Light, Battery M, Capt. Frederick Schultz.
Ohio Light, 18th Battery, Capt. Charles C. Aleshire.
Ohio Light, 20th Battery, Lieut. John Otto.

SECOND DIVISION. *

First Brigade.

Capt. JOSIAH W. CHURCH.

1st Michigan Light, Battery D, Capt. Josiah W. Church.
1st Tennessee Light, Battery A, Capt. Ephraim P. Abbott.
Wisconsin Light, 3d Battery, Lieut. Hiram F. Hubbard.
Wisconsin Light, 8th Battery, Lieut. John D. McLean.

Second Brigade.

Capt. ARNOLD SUTERMEISTER.

Indiana Light, 4th Battery, Lieut. Willis H. Pettit.
Indiana Light, 8th Battery, Lieut. Jeremiah Voris.
Indiana Light, 11th Battery, Capt. Arnold Sutermeister.
Indiana Light, 21st Battery, Lieut. William E. Chess.

* Commander not of record.

CAVALRY CORPS.

Maj. Gen. DAVID S. STANLEY.

Brig. Gen. WASHINGTON L. ELLIOTT.

First Brigade.

Col. ARCHIBALD P. CAMPBELL.

2d Michigan, Maj. Leonidas S. Scranton.
9th Pennsylvania, Lieut. Col. Roswell M. Russell.
1st Tennessee, Lieut. Col. James P. Brownlow.

Second Brigade.

Col. EDWARD M. McCOOK.

2d Indiana, Maj. Joseph B. Presdee.
4th Indiana, Lieut. Col. John T. Deweese.
2d Tennessee, Col. Daniel M. Ray.
3d Tennessee, Col. William C. Pickens.
1st Wisconsin, Col. Oscar H. La Grange.
1st Ohio Light Artillery, Battery D (section of), Lieut. Nathaniel M. Newell.

Third Brigade.

Col. LOUIS D. WATKINS.

4th Kentucky, Col. Wickliffe Cooper.
5th Kentucky, Lieut. Col. William T. Hoblitzell.
6th Kentucky, Lieut. Col. William P. Roper.
7th Kentucky, Col. John K. Faulkner.

Brig. Gen. GEORGE CROOK.

First Brigade.

Col. ROBERT H. G. MINTY.

3d Indiana, Lieut. Col. Robert Klein.
4th Michigan, Maj. Horace Gray.
7th Pennsylvania, Col. William B. Sipes.
4th United States, Capt. James B. McIntyre.

Second Brigade.

Col. ELI LONG.

2d Kentucky, Col. Thomas P. Nicholas.
1st Ohio, Maj. Thomas J. Patten.
3d Ohio, Lieut. Col. Charles B. Seidel.
4th Ohio, Lieut. Col. Oliver P. Robie.

Third Brigade.

Col. WILLIAM W. LOWE.

5th Iowa, Lieut. Col. Matthewson T. Patrick.
10th Ohio, Col. Charles C. Smith.
5th Tennessee, Col. William B. Stokes.

ARTILLERY.

Chicago (Illinois) Board of Trade Battery, Lieut. George J. Robinson.

MOUNTED INFANTRY BRIGADE.

Col. JOHN T. WILDER.

92d Illinois, Col. Smith D. Atkins.
98th Illinois, Lieut. Col. Edward Kitchell.
123d Illinois, Lieut. Col. Jonathan Biggs.
17th Indiana, Maj. William T. Jones.
72d Indiana, Lieut. Col. Samuel C. Kirkpatrick.
18th Indiana Battery, Capt. Eli Lilly.

MISCELLANEOUS.

CLARKSVILLE, TENN.

Col. ARTHUR A. SMITH.

83d Illinois (detachment), Col. Arthur A. Smith.
2d Illinois Light Artillery, Battery H, Capt. Henry C. Whittemore.

FORT DONELSON, TENN.

Lieut. Col. ELIJAH C. BROTT.

83d Illinois (detachment), Lieut. Col. Elijah C. Brott.
2d Illinois Light Artillery, Battery C, Capt. James P. Flood.

GALLATIN, TENN.

Brig. Gen. ELEAZER A. PAINE.

50th Ohio, Maj. Hamilton S. Gillespie.
71st Ohio, Col. Henry K. McConnell.
106th Ohio, Lieut. Col. Gustavus Tafel.
13th Indiana Battery, Capt. Benjamin S. Nicklin.
5th Michigan Battery (section), Lieut. Charles M. Durand.

NASHVILLE, TENN.

Brig. Gen. ROBERT S. GRANGER.

Ward's Brigade.

Brig. Gen. WILLIAM T. WARD.

102d Illinois, Col. Franklin C. Smith.
105th Illinois, Col. Daniel Dustin.
129th Illinois, Col. Henry Case.
70th Indiana, Col. Benjamin Harrison.
79th Ohio, Col. Henry G. Kennett.
5th Michigan Battery, Capt. John J. Ely.

Unattached.

73d Indiana, Capt. Emanuel M. Williamson.
18th Michigan, Col. Charles C. Doolittle.
13th Wisconsin, Col. William P. Lyon.
Convalescents, Capt. Ralph Hunt.
12th Indiana Battery, Capt. James E. White.

UNASSIGNED. *

34th Illinois, Lieut. Col. Oscar Van Tassell.
39th Indiana, Col. Thomas J. Harrison.
21st Kentucky, Col. Samuel W. Price.
28th Kentucky, Col. William P. Boone.
3d Ohio, Capt. Leroy S. Bell.
102d Ohio, Col. George H. Bowman.
108th Ohio, Lieut. Col. Carlo Piepho.
10th Tennessee, Lieut. Col. James W. Scully.
31st Wisconsin, Lieut. Col. Francis H. West.
15th Pennsylvania Cavalry, Col. William J. Palmer.
20th Indiana Battery, Capt. Milton A. Osborne.
1st Kentucky Battery, Capt. Theodore S. Thomasson.
2d Kentucky Battery, Capt. John M. Hewett.
1st Ohio Light Artillery, Battery E, Capt. Warren P. Edgarton.
10th Wisconsin Battery, Capt. Yates V. Beebe.

---

*At Anderson's Cross-Roads, Chattanooga, Dallas, Elk River, Murfreesborough, Stevenson, Sullivan's Branch, Tullahoma, and Walden's Ridge.

Abstract from returns of the Department of the Ohio, Maj. Gen. Ambrose E. Burnside, U. S. Army, commanding, for the month of October, 1863.

Command.	Present for duty.		Aggregate present.	Aggregate present and absent.	Aggregate last monthly return.	Pieces of artillery.		Headquarters.
	Officers.	Men.				Heavy.	Field.	
General headquarters............	79	....	80	82	82	....	..	In the field.
Ninth Army Corps (Potter):								Lenoir's Station.
Staff..........................	14	....	14	18	16	....	....	Do.
Troops unassigned............	31	551	627	981	142	....	4	Do.
First Division................	177	2,683	3,445	6,581	6,988	....	10	Do.
Second Division..............	150	2,746	3,563	5,327	4,900	....	17	Do.
Total Ninth Army Corps..	372	5,980	7,649	12,907	12,046	....	31	
Twenty-third Army Corps (Manson):								
Staff and escort..............	14	95	110	180	181	....	....	Knoxville, Tenn.
First Division................	450	9,659	11,957	14,786	9,827	8	88	Kentucky.
Second Division..............	191	3,308	4,060	5,654	5,741	....	12	Loudon, Tenn.
Third Division................	168	3,646	4,480	5,941	5,809	....	16	Knoxville, Tenn.
Fourth (cavalry) Division	345	7,113	8,552	12,004	12,020	....	20	In the field, East Tennessee.
Reserve Artillery (Konkle)....	12	290	316	363	370	....	12	Knoxville, Tenn.
Engineer troops..............	3	185	225	262	319	....	....	Do.
Total Twenty-third Army Corps.	1,183	24,296	29,700	39,190	34,267	8	148	
Left Wing forces in East Tennessee (Willcox).	178	4,213	4,994	6,419	6,473	....	16	Greeneville, Tenn.
District of Ohio (Cox).............	115	3,028	3,675	4,499	6,497	....	....	
District of Illinois (Ammen)......	55	979	1,377	1,660	2,167	....	1	
District of Indiana and Michigan (Simonson).	49	1,103	1,444	1,749	3,020	....	....	
Newport Barracks, Ky. (Eastman)	4	77	107	111	104	....	....	
Sandusky, Ohio (Pierson)	12	231	341	399	397	....	....	
Grand total	2,047	39,907	49,367	67,016	65,053	8	196	

Abstract from returns of the First Division, Twenty-third Army Corps, Brig. Gen. Jeremiah T. Boyle, U. S. Army, commanding, for the month of October, 1863.

Command.	Present for duty.		Aggregate present.	Aggregate present and absent.	Aggregate last monthly return.	Pieces of artillery.		Headquarters.
	Officers.	Men.				Heavy.	Field.	
Headquarters......................	11	7	18	19	19	....	....	Louisville, Ky.
Louisville, Ky....................	26	411	555	723	712	....	4	
Eastern Kentucky.................	53	1,310	1,595	1,863	1,835	....	8	Louisa.
Northern Central Kentucky.......	151	3,125	3,942	5,491	3,566	5	30	Camp Nelson.
Somerset, Ky.....................	33	964	1,131	1,320	489	....	2	
Southern Central Kentucky.......	110	2,199	2,758	3,160	1,435	2	25	Munfordville.
Southwestern Kentucky	66	1,643	1,958	2,210	1,771	1	19	Bowling Green.
Total........:..	450	9,659	11,957	14,786	9,827	8	88	

Troops in the Department of the Ohio, Maj. Gen. Ambrose E. Burnside, U. S. Army, commanding, October 31, 1863.

NINTH ARMY CORPS.

Brig. Gen. ROBERT B. POTTER.

HEADQUARTERS.

6th Indiana Cavalry (four companies), Col. James Biddle.
79th New York, Capt. William S. Montgomery.
2d U. S. Artillery, Battery E, Lieut. Samuel N. Benjamin.

FIRST DIVISION.

Brig. Gen. EDWARD FERRERO.

First Brigade.	*Second Brigade.*
Col. DAVID MORRISON.	Col. BENJAMIN C. CHRIST.
36th Massachusetts, Maj. William F. Draper.	29th Massachusetts, Col. Ebenezer W. Peirce.
8th Michigan, Lieut. Col. Ralph Ely.	27th Michigan (eight companies), Maj. William B. Wright.
45th Pennsylvania, Lieut. Col. Francis M. Hills.	46th New York, Capt. Alphons Serviere.
	50th Pennsylvania, Maj. Edward Overton, jr.

Third Brigade.

Col. DANIEL LEASURE.

2d Michigan, Col. William Humphrey.
17th Michigan, Lieut. Col. Lorin L. Comstock.
20th Michigan, Lieut. Col. W. Huntington Smith.
100th Pennsylvania, Lieut. Col. Mathew M. Dawson.

Artillery.

2d New York Light, Battery L, Capt. Jacob Roemer.
1st Rhode Island Light, Battery D, Capt. William W. Buckley.

SECOND DIVISION.*

Col. JOSHUA K. SIGFRIED.

First Brigade.	*Second Brigade.*
Col. THOMAS B. ALLARD.	Lieut. Col. EDWIN SCHALL.
2d Maryland, Maj. John M. Santmyer.	35th Massachusetts, Maj. Nathaniel Wales.
21st Massachusetts, Lieut. Col. George P. Hawkes.	11th New Hampshire, Capt. Leander W. Cogswell.
48th Pennsylvania, Capt. Daniel B. Kaufman.	51st Pennsylvania, Maj. William J. Bolton.

---

*At Lenoir's Station, except the Third Brigade, the artillery, and cavalry of Second Division, which are reported as at Cumberland Gap.

Third Brigade.

Col. WILSON C. LEMERT.

86th Ohio (nine companies), Maj. William Kraus.
129th Ohio (nine companies), Col. Howard D. John.

Artillery.

Capt. HENRY M. NEIL.

22d Ohio Battery, Lieut. Amos B. Alger.
86th Ohio Infantry, Company K, Capt. James W. Owens.
129th Ohio Infantry, Company K, Capt. Allen D. S. McArthur.

Cavalry.

4th Ohio Battalion, Maj. Joseph T. Wheeler.

TWENTY-THIRD ARMY CORPS.

Brig. Gen. MAHLON D. MANSON.*

HEADQUARTERS.

McLaughlin's (Ohio) Squadron, Maj. Richard Rice.
Engineer Battalion, Capt. Oliver S. McClure.

FIRST DIVISION.

Brig. Gen. JEREMIAH T. BOYLE.

Louisville.

20th Kentucky, Maj. Thomas B. Waller.
1st Kentucky Artillery, Battery C, Capt. John W. Neville.

District of Eastern Kentucky.†

Col. GEORGE W. GALLUP.

14th Kentucky, Lieut. Col. Orlando Brown, jr.
39th Kentucky, Lieut. Col. David A. Mims.

District of Northern Central Kentucky.‡

Brig. Gen. SPEED S. FRY.

6th Indiana Cavalry, Company H, Capt. Elijah W. Peck.
1st Kentucky Artillery, Battery E, Lieut. John J. Hawes.
14th Kentucky Cavalry (eight companies), Col. Henry C. Lilly.
40th Kentucky, Col. Clinton J. True.
47th Kentucky (nine companies), Lieut. Col. Andrew H. Clark.
6th New Hampshire, Lieut. Col. Henry H. Pearson.

9th New Hampshire, Col. Herbert B. Titus.
51st New York, Col. Charles W. Le Gendre.
1st Ohio Heavy Artillery (two companies), Capt. Amos B. Cole.
2d Ohio Heavy Artillery, Company L, Capt. Lemon S. Powell.
5th Ohio Cavalry Battalion, Maj. John F. Ijams.
7th Rhode Island, Maj. Thomas F. Tobey.

---

* Since September 24, in temporary absence of Major-General Hartsuff.
† Troops at Louisa.
‡ Troops at Camp Nelson, Flemingsburg, Frankfort, Lexington, Mount Sterling, and Paris.

Somerset.

Brig. Gen. Theophilus T. Garrard.

6th Indiana Cavalry (five companies), Lieut. Col. Courtland C. Matson.
49th Kentucky, Lieut. Col. John G. Eve.

District of Southern Central Kentucky.*

Brig. Gen. Edward H. Hobson.

63d Indiana (six companies), Col. James McManomy.
33d Kentucky (four companies), Lieut. Col. James F. Lauck.
34th Kentucky, Company G, Capt. Christopher C. Hare.
35th Kentucky, Company B, Capt. Hendrick D. Baker.
37th Kentucky (seven companies), Lieut. Col. Benjamin J. Spaulding.

6th Michigan Battery, Capt. Luther F. Hale.
2d Ohio Heavy Artillery (seven companies), Col. Horatio G. Gibson.
50th Ohio (six companies), Lieut. Col. George R. Elstner.
1st Wisconsin Heavy Artillery, Company B, Capt. Walter S. Babcock.

District of Southwestern Kentucky.†

Col. Cicero Maxwell.

91st Indiana, Company C, Capt. Zimry V. Garten.
91st Indiana, Company G, Capt. William P. Hargrave.
3d Kentucky Cavalry, Maj. George F. White.
26th Kentucky (seven companies), Maj. Ignatius E. Mattingly.

35th Kentucky (six companies), Col. Edmund A. Starling.
2d Ohio Heavy Artillery, Companies B, C, F, and G, Lieut. Col. Martin B. Ewing.
22d Indiana Battery, Capt. Benjamin F. Denning.

SECOND DIVISION.‡

Brig. Gen. Julius White.

First Brigade.

Col. Samuel R. Mott.

80th Indiana, Col. James L. Culbertson.
16th Kentucky, Col. James W. Gault.
25th Michigan, Capt. Samuel L. Demarest.
118th Ohio, Lieut. Col. Thomas L. Young.
Elgin (Illinois) Battery, Capt. Andrew M. Wood.

Second Brigade.

Col. Marshal W. Chapin.

107th Illinois, Col. Joseph J. Kelly.
13th Kentucky, Col. William E. Hobson.
23d Michigan, Maj. William W. Wheeler.
111th Ohio, Maj. Isaac R. Sherwood.
Illinois Battery, Capt. Edward C. Henshaw.

Cavalry.

11th Kentucky (mounted) Infantry, Companies F and G, Capt. David Poole.

---

* Troops at Cave City, Glasgow, Muldraugh's Hill, Munfordville, New Haven, and Nolin.
† Troops at Bowling Green, Elk Fork Bridge, Henderson, Hopkinsville, Russellville, and Smithland.
‡ Near Loudon, Tenn.

THIRD DIVISION.*

Brig. Gen. MILO S. HASCALL.

First Brigade.

Col. JAMES W. REILLY.

12th Kentucky, Col. William A. Hoskins.
44th Ohio, Maj. Alpheus S. Moore.
100th Ohio, Col. Patrick S. Slevin.
104th Ohio, Lieut. Col. Oscar W. Sterl.
1st Ohio Artillery, Battery D, Lieut. William H. Pease.

Second Brigade.

Col. DANIEL CAMERON.

65th Illinois, Lieut. Col. William S. Stewart.
24th Kentucky, Col. John S. Hurt.
103d Ohio, Col. John S. Casement.
8th Tennessee, Col. Felix A. Reeve.
Wilder Indiana Battery, Capt. Hubbard T. Thomas.

FOURTH (CAVALRY) DIVISION.

Brig. Gen. JAMES M. SHACKELFORD.†

First Brigade.‡

Col. CHARLES D. PENNEBAKER.

11th Kentucky Infantry,§ Col. S. Palace Love.
27th Kentucky Infantry,§ Lieut. Col. John H. Ward.

Second Brigade.

Lieut. Col. EMERY S. BOND.

112th Illinois Infantry,§ Maj. Tristram T. Dow.
8th Michigan Cavalry, Maj. Henry C. Edgerly.
45th Ohio Infantry, Lieut. Col. George E. Ross.
1st Tennessee Infantry,§ Maj. John Ellis.
15th Indiana Battery, Capt. John C. H. von Sehlen.

Third Brigade.

Col. JAMES P. T. CARTER.

9th Michigan Cavalry, Col. James I. David.
2d Ohio Cavalry, Lieut. Col. George A. Purington.
7th Ohio Cavalry, Col. Israel Garrard.
2d Tennessee Infantry,§ Lieut. Col. James M. Melton.
2d Illinois Light Artillery, Battery M, Capt. John C. Phillips.
1st Tennessee Battery, Capt. James A. Childress.

Fourth Brigade.

Col. JOHN W. FOSTER.

14th Illinois Cavalry, Col. Horace Capron.
5th Indiana Cavalry, Col. Felix W. Graham.
65th Indiana Infantry,§ Maj. Thomas G. Brown.
9th Ohio Cavalry (four companies), Maj. William D. Hamilton.
8th Tennessee Cavalry, Maj. John M. Sawyers.
Illinois Light Battery, Capt. John H. Colvin.

---

* At and about Knoxville.
† Since September 10, *vice* Carter, appointed provost-marshal of East Tennessee.
‡ Detached from division.
§ Mounted.

RESERVE ARTILLERY.

Capt. ANDREW J. KONKLE.

Indiana Light, 24th Battery, Lieut. Henry W. Shafer.
Ohio Light, 19th Battery, Capt. Joseph C. Shields.

LEFT WING FORCES IN EAST TENNESSEE.*

Brig. Gen. ORLANDO B. WILLCOX.

First Brigade.

Col. JOHN R. MAHAN.

115th Indiana, Lieut. Col. Alfred J. Hawn.
116th Indiana, Col. William C. Kise.
117th Indiana, Col. Thomas J. Brady.
118th Indiana, Col. George W. Jackson.

Second Brigade.†

Col. WILLIAM A. HOSKINS.

12th Kentucky, Maj. Joseph M. Owens.
103d Ohio, Col. John S. Casement.
8th Tennessee, Col. Felix A. Reeve.

Not Brigaded.

3d Indiana Cavalry, Company L, Capt. Oliver M. Powers.
3d Indiana Cavalry, Company M, Capt. Charles U. Patton.
23d Indiana Battery, Capt. James H. Myers.
12th Michigan Battery, Capt. Edward G. Hillier.
21st Ohio Battery, Capt. James W. Patterson.

DISTRICT OF OHIO.

Brig. Gen. JACOB D. COX.

Mason's Command.‡

Brig. Gen. JOHN S. MASON.

74th Ohio (detachment), Lieut. William
J. Holmes.
18th United States (detachment), Capt.
Nathaniel C. Kinney.
U. S. Veteran Reserve Corps (eleven
companies), Col. Andrew J. Johnson.
Exchanged Prisoners, Capt. Waldo T.
Davis.
Provost Guard, Maj. John W. Skiles.

Camp Dennison.

Brig. Gen. MASON BRAYMAN.

9th Ohio Cavalry (three companies),
Capt. Henry Plessner.
24th Ohio Battery, Capt. John L. Hill.

Cincinnati.

Lieut. Col. SETH EASTMAN.

88th Ohio (eight companies), Col. George
W. Neff.
Ohio Sharpshooters, 8th Company, Capt.
Charles A. Barton.

Covington, Ky.

1st Ohio Heavy Artillery (six companies), Col. Chauncey G. Hawley.

---

* Near Greeneville, Tenn.
† Regiments also borne on return of Third Division, Twenty-third Army Corps.
See p. 815.
‡ Headquarters at Columbus. Troops at Camp Chase, Camp Thomas, and Columbus.

DISTRICT OF ILLINOIS.

Brig. Gen. JACOB AMMEN.

39th Illinois (detachment), Capt. Oscar F. Rudd.
113th Illinois (five companies), Capt. George W. Lyman.
16th Illinois Cavalry (seven companies), Col. Christian Thielemann.*
1st Michigan Sharpshooters, Maj. John Piper.
U. S. Veteran Reserve Corps (six companies), Lieut. Col. Carlisle Boyd.
9th Vermont, Company G, Lieut. William C. Holman.

DISTRICT OF INDIANA AND MICHIGAN.

Col. JOHN S. SIMONSON.

63d Indiana (four companies), Maj. Henry Tindall.
7th Indiana Cavalry, Col. John P. C. Shanks.
5th U. S. Veteran Reserve Corps, Company G, Lieut. Samuel Dickson.

Abstract from returns of the Department of the Tennessee, Maj. Gen. William T. Sherman, U. S. Army, commanding, October 31, 1863.

Command.	Present for duty.		Aggregate present.	Aggregate present and absent.	Aggregate last return.	Pieces of artillery.		Headquarters.
	Officers.	Men.				Heavy.	Field.	
General headquarters	12	......	12	12	....	......	......	Florence, Ala.
Fifteeenth Army Corps:								
Headquarters	6	......	6	7	7	......	......	
First Division	291	3,353	4,901	7,861	8,166	......	14	Chickasaw, Ala.
Second Division	259	3,817	4,891	7,387	7,565	......	16	Do.
Third Division	323	5,463	7,233	10,227	10,353	......	18	Hebron Plantation, Miss.
Fourth Division	310	5,211	6,411	8,280	8,391	......	14	Florence, Ala.
Total Fifteenth Army Corps.	1,189	17,844	23,442	33,762	34,482	......	62	
Sixteenth Army Corps:								
Headquarters	17	......	17	18	14	......	......	Memphis, Tenn.
Engineer troops	......	......	437	477	485	......	......	Pocahontas, Tenn.
Left Wing	486	9,121	11,589	13,506	14,784	25	36	Corinth, Miss.
District of Columbus	154	3,142	4,302	5,016	6,258	......	4	Columbus, Ky.
District of Memphis	280	6,596	8,310	9,792	10,121	61	22	Memphis, Tenn.
Cavalry Division	257	4,934	6,496	7,525	7,776	......	24	Do.
Troops in Arkansas *a*	......	......	......	13,854	21,304	......	19	
Total Sixteenth Army Corps.	1,194	23,793	31,151	50,188	60,742	86	105	
Seventeenth Army Corps:								
Headquarters	14	30	96	105	536	......	......	Vicksburg, Miss.
First Division	258	4,000	5,347	7,268	7,994	2	16	Do.
Second Division	262	3,780	4,817	7,416	7,488	......	14	Chickasaw, Ala.
Third Division	304	4,697	6,229	9,184	9,101	......	22	Vicksburg, Miss.
Fourth Division	225	4,377	5,548	7,306	7,255	......	16	Natchez, Miss.
Total Seventeenth Army Corps.	1,063	16,884	22,037	31,279	32,374	2	68	
United States Colored Troops.	289	5,686	7,517	7,843	7,843	......	......	Goodrich's Landing, La.
Grand total *b*	3,747	64,207	84,159	123,084	135,441	88	235	

a But see Series I, Vol. XXII, Part II, p. 687.   *b* The Mississippi Marine Brigade not accounted for.

---

* At Camp Nelson, Ky.

Organization of troops in the Department and Army of the Tennessee, Maj. Gen. William T. Sherman, U. S. Army, commanding, October 31, 1863.

FIFTEENTH ARMY CORPS.

Maj. Gen. FRANK P. BLAIR, Jr.

ESCORT.

16th Illinois Cavalry, Companies A and B, Lieut. Solomon W. Kelly.

FIRST DIVISION.

Brig. Gen. PETER J. OSTERHAUS.

First Brigade.

Brig. Gen. CHARLES R. WOODS.

13th Illinois, Col. Adam B. Gorgas.
3d   Missouri, Lieut. Col. Theodore Meumann.
12th Missouri, Col. Hugo Wangelin.
17th Missouri, Col John F. Cramer.
27th Missouri, Col. Thomas Curly.
29th Missouri, Col. James Peckham.
31st Missouri, Col. Thomas C. Fletcher.
32d   Missouri, Lieut. Col. Henry C. Warmoth.
76th Ohio, Maj. Willard Warner.

Second Brigade.

Col. JAMES A. WILLIAMSON.

4th Iowa, Lieut. Col. George Burton.
9th Iowa, Col. David Carskaddon.
25th Iowa, Col. George A. Stone.
26th Iowa, Col. Milo Smith,
30th Iowa, Lieut. Col. Aurelius Roberts.
31st Iowa, Lieut. Col. Jeremiah W. Jenkins.

Artillery.

Capt. HENRY H. GRIFFITHS.

Iowa Light, 1st Battery, Lieut. James M. Williams.
1st Missouri Horse Artillery, Capt. Clemens Landgraeber.
Ohio Light, 4th Battery, Capt. George Froehlich.

SECOND DIVISION.

Brig. Gen. MORGAN L. SMITH.

First Brigade.

Brig. Gen. GILES A. SMITH.

55th Illinois, Col. Oscar Malmborg.
116th Illinois, Col. Nathan W. Tupper.
127th Illinois, Lieut. Col. Frank S. Curtiss.
6th Missouri, Lieut. Col. Ira Boutell.
8th Missouri, Lieut. Col. David C. Coleman.
57th Ohio, Lieut. Col. Samuel R. Mott.
13th United States, 1st Battalion, Capt. Charles C. Smith.

Second Brigade.

Brig. Gen. JOSEPH A. J. LIGHTBURN.

83d Indiana, Col. Benjamin J. Spooner.
30th Ohio, Col. Theodore Jones.
37th Ohio, Lieut. Col. Louis von Blessingh.
47th Ohio, Col. Augustus C. Parry.
54th Ohio, Maj. Robert Williams, jr.
4th West Virginia, Col. James H. Dayton.

Artillery.

1st Illinois Light, Battery A, Capt. Peter P. Wood.
1st Illinois Light, Battery B, Capt. Israel P. Rumsey.
1st Illinois Light, Battery H, Lieut. Francis De Gress.

THIRD DIVISION.

Brig. Gen. JAMES M. TUTTLE.

First Brigade.

Col. WILLIAM L. McMILLEN.

114th Illinois, Lieut. Col. John F. King.
93d Indiana, Col. De Witt C. Thomas.
72d Ohio, Capt. Le Roy Moore.
95th Ohio, Lieut. Col. Jefferson Brumback.

Second Brigade.

Brig. Gen. JOSEPH A. MOWER.

47th Illinois, Col. John D. McClure.
5th Minnesota, Col. Lucius F. Hubbard.
11th Missouri, Lieut. Col. William L. Barnum.
8th Wisconsin, Maj. William B. Britton.

Third Brigade.

Col. James L. Geddes.

8th Iowa, Lieut. Col. William B. Bell.
12th Iowa, Lieut. Col. John H. Stibbs.
35th Iowa, Col. Sylvester G. Hill.

Cavalry Brigade.

Col. Edward F. Winslow.

4th Illinois, Lieut. Col. Martin R. M. Wallace.
5th Illinois, Maj. Abel H. Seley.
11th Illinois, Lieut. Col. Lucien H. Kerr.
4th Iowa, Maj. Cornelius F. Spearman.
10th Missouri, Maj. William H. Lusk.

Artillery.

Capt. Nelson T. Spoor.

1st Illinois Light, Battery E, Lieut. John A. Fitch.
Indiana Light, 6th Battery, Capt. Michael Mueller.
Iowa Light, 2d Battery, Lieut. Joseph R. Reed.

FOURTH DIVISION.

Brig. Gen. Hugh Ewing.

First Brigade.

Col. John M. Loomis.

26th Illinois, Lieut. Col. Robert A. Gillmore.
90th Illinois, Col. Timothy O'Meara.
12th Indiana, Col. Reuben Williams.
100th Indiana, Lieut. Col. Albert Heath.

Second Brigade.

Brig. Gen. John M. Corse.

40th Illinois, Maj. Hiram W. Hall.
103d Illinois, Col. Willard A. Dickerman.
6th Iowa, Lieut. Col. Alexander J. Miller.
15th Michigan, Col. John M. Oliver.
46th Ohio, Col. Charles C. Walcutt.

Third Brigade.

Col. Joseph R. Cockerill.

48th Illinois, Lieut. Col. Lucien Greathouse.
97th Indiana, Col. Robert F. Catterson.
99th Indiana, Maj. John M. Berkey.
53d Ohio, Lieut. Col. Robert A. Fulton.
70th Ohio, Maj. William B. Brown.

Artillery.

Capt. Henry Richardson.

1st Illinois Light, Battery F, Capt. John T. Cheney.
1st Illinois Light, Battery I, Capt. Albert Cudney.
1st Missouri Light, Battery D, Lieut. Byron M. Callender.

SIXTEENTH ARMY CORPS.

Maj. Gen. STEPHEN A. HURLBUT.

ENGINEER REGIMENT.

Lieut. Col. HENRY FLAD.

DISTRICT OF MEMPHIS—FIFTH DIVISION.

Brig. Gen. JAMES C. VEATCH.

First Brigade.

Col. CHARLES D. MURRAY.

117th Illinois, Col. Risdon M. Moore.
89th Indiana, Maj. Samuel Henry.

Fuller's Brigade.

Col. JOHN W. FULLER.

27th Ohio, Lieut. Col. Zeph. S. Spaulding.
39th Ohio, Col. Edward F. Noyes.
43d Ohio, Col. Wager Swayne.
63d Ohio, Col. John W. Sprague.
3d Michigan Battery, Capt. George
    Robinson.
2d United States, Battery F, Lieut. Albert M. Murray.

Second Brigade.

Col. WILLIAM H. MORGAN.

25th Indiana, Lieut. Col. John Rheinlander.
32d Wisconsin, Col. James H. Howe.
2d Illinois Light Artillery, Battery D,
    Capt. Charles S. Cooper.

Fourth Brigade.

Col. DAVID MOORE.

119th Illinois, Lieut. Col. Samuel E. Taylor.
21st Missouri, Lieut. Col. Humphrey
    M. Woodyard.
7th Wisconsin Battery, Capt. Henry S.
    Lee.

Fort Pickering.

Col. IGNATZ G. KAPPNER.

1st Tennessee Heavy Artillery (A. D.), Maj. Emil Smith.
U. S. Colored Light Artillery, Battery F, Capt. Carl A. Lamberg.

DISTRICT OF COLUMBUS—SIXTH DIVISION.

Brig. Gen. ANDREW J. SMITH.

First Brigade (near Union City, Tenn.).

Col. GEORGE E. WARING, Jr.

32d Iowa, Company C, Capt. Hubert F.
    Peebles.
24th Missouri, Col. James K. Mills.
2d Illinois Cavalry, 1st Battalion, Maj.
    Thomas J. Larison.
4th Missouri Cavalry, Maj. Gustav
    Heinrichs.
7th Tennessee Cavalry (detachment of),
    Capt. Jacob H. Hays.
9th Indiana Battery, Capt. George R.
    Brown.
2d Tennessee Heavy Artillery (A. D.)
    (eight companies), Lieut. Abraham T. Dearborn.

Island No. 10, Tenn.

32d Iowa (detachment of), Capt. Rufus
    S. Benson.

Columbus, Ky.

Col. JOHN SCOTT.

14th Iowa, Lieut. Col. Joseph H. Newbold.
32d Iowa (six companies), Capt. Jonathan Hutchison.
4th Missouri Cavalry (nine companies),
    Maj. Edward Langen.
16th United States, Company A, 2d Battalion, Capt. Solomon S. Robinson.
Tennessee Heavy Artillery (A. D.) (eight
    companies), Col. Charles H.
    Adams.

Cairo, Ill.

Brig. Gen. HUGH T. REID.

58th Illinois (seven companies), Lieut.
    Col. Isaac Rutishauser.
1st Kansas Battery (one section), Lieut.
    John B. Cook.

Fort Pillow, Tenn.

Col. EDWARD H. WOLFE.

52d Indiana, Lieut. Col. Zalmon S. Main.
2d Illinois Cavalry, Company B, Lieut. Curtin Dement.

Paducah, Ky.

Col. STEPHEN G. HICKS.

58th Illinois Infantry, Companies A, B, and C, Capt. George W. Kittell.
111th Illinois, Col. James S. Martin.
15th Kentucky Cavalry, Company C, Capt. Jonathan Belt.

LEFT WING.

Brig. Gen. GRENVILLE M. DODGE.

*First Brigade.**	*Second Brigade.†*
Col. ELLIOTT W. RICE.	**Col. AUGUST MERSY.**
52d Illinois, Col. John S. Wilcox.	9th Illinois, Lieut. Col. Jesse J. Phillips.
108th Illinois, Col. Charles Turner.	12th Illinois, Maj. James R. Hugunin.
66th Indiana, Col. De Witt C. Anthony.	122d Illinois, Col. John I. Rinaker.
2d Iowa, Col. James B. Weaver.	81st Ohio, Lieut. Col. Robert N. Adams.
7th Iowa, Lieut. Col. James C. Parrott.	
2d Tennessee (A. D.), Col. Frank A. Kendrick.	

Third Brigade.‡

Col. MOSES M. BANE.

7th Illinois, Col. Richard Rowett.
50th Illinois, Lieut. Col. Thomas W. Gaines.
57th Illinois, Lieut. Col. Frederick J. Hurlbut.
113th Illinois, Capt. Bliss Sutherland.
120th Illinois, Capt. Parker B. Pillow.
39th Iowa, Col. Henry J. B. Cummings.
18th Missouri, Col. Madison Miller.

Heavy Artillery.§

Maj. GEORGE H. STONE.

1st Alabama, Company A (A. D.), Capt. Henry Simmons.
1st Alabama, Company B (A. D.), Capt. Frank M. Ewing.
1st Illinois, Battery G, Lieut. Gustave Dachsel.
2d Illinois Light, Battery B, Capt. Fletcher H. Chapman.
12th Illinois Infantry, Company G, Capt. James N. McArthur.

Light Artillery.‖	*Unattached.¶*
Capt. FREDERICK WELKER.	1st Alabama (A. D.), Col. James M. Alexander.
1st Michigan, Battery B, Capt. Albert F. R. Arndt.	64th Illinois, Maj. Samuel T. Thomson.
1st Missouri, Battery H, Lieut. John H. Conant.	66th Illinois, Col. Patrick E. Burke.
1st Missouri, Battery I, Capt. Benjamin Tannrath.	1st Tennessee (A. D.), Lieut. Col. Robert E. Phillips.
14th Ohio Battery, Lieut. Hamilton H. Burrows.	

---

* At Iuka; the 108th Illinois ordered to Pocahontas, where it arrived October 29, and the 2d Tennessee (detached) at Moscow.
† At Pocahontas, Pulaski, and Saulsbury.
‡ At Burnsville, Chewalla, Corinth, Iuka, and La Grange.
§ At Corinth.
‖ Corinth and Iuka.
¶ At Camp Davies, Corinth, and Glendale.

CAVALRY DIVISION.

Brig. Gen. BENJAMIN H. GRIERSON.

First Brigade.

Col. JOHN K. MIZNER.

1st Alabama, Lieut. Col. Ozro J. Dodds.
7th Kansas, Col. Thomas P. Herrick.
3d Michigan, Lieut. Col. Gilbert Moyers.

Second Brigade.

Col. LA FAYETTE MCCRILLIS.

3d Illinois, Lieut. Col. James M. Ruggles.
9th Illinois, Maj. Ira R. Gifford.
6th Tennessee, Col. Fielding Hurst.

Third Brigade.

Col. EDWARD HATCH.

6th Illinois, Maj. Charles W. Whitsit.
7th Illinois, Lieut. Col. George W. Trafton.
2d Iowa, Lieut. Col. William P. Hepburn.
1st Illinois Light Artillery, Battery K, Capt. Jason B. Smith.

Detached.

15th Illinois (seven companies), Col. George A. Bacon.
15th Kentucky (six companies), Maj. Wiley Waller.
7th Tennessee (nine companies), Col. Isaac R. Hawkins.

SEVENTEENTH ARMY CORPS.

Maj. Gen. JAMES B. MCPHERSON.

ESCORT.

4th Independent Company Ohio Cavalry, Capt. John S. Foster.

FIRST DIVISION.

Brig. Gen. ELIAS S. DENNIS.

Escort.

2d Wisconsin Cavalry, Maj. Harry E. Eastman.

First Brigade.

Col. FREDERICK A. STARRING.

72d Illinois, Lieut. Col. Joseph Stockton.
58th Ohio, Lieut. Col. Ezra P. Jackson.
16th Wisconsin, Maj. Thomas Reynolds.
1st Kansas Mounted Infantry, Maj. James Ketner.

Second Brigade.

Col. THOMAS W. HUMPHREY.

11th Illinois, Col. James H. Coates.
95th Illinois, Lieut. Col. Leander Blanden.
14th Wisconsin, Capt. Calvin R. Johnson.
17th Wisconsin, Lieut. Col. Thomas McMahon.

Third Brigade

Brig. Gen. ALEXANDER CHAMBERS.

11th Iowa, Lieut. Col. John C. Abercrombie.
13th Iowa, Col. John Shane.
15th Iowa, Col. William W. Belknap.
16th Iowa, Maj. William Purcell.

Artillery.

Maj. THOMAS D. MAURICE.

Minnesota Light, 1st Battery, Capt. William Z. Clayton.
1st Missouri Light, Battery C, Capt. Charles Mann.
1st Missouri Light, Battery M, Lieut. John H. Tiemeyer.
Ohio Light, 8th Battery, Capt. James F. Putnam.
Ohio Light, 10th Battery, Capt. Hamilton B. White.

SECOND DIVISION.

Brig. Gen. JOHN E. SMITH.

Escort.

4th Missouri Cavalry, Company F, Lieut. Alexander Mueller.

First Brigade.	*Second Brigade.*
Col. JESSE I. ALEXANDER.	Col. GREEN B. RAUM.
63d Illinois, Col. Joseph B. McCown.	56th Illinois, Maj. Pinckney J. Welsh.
48th Indiana, Lieut. Col. Edward J. Wood.	17th Iowa, Col. Clark R. Wever.
59th Indiana, Capt. Wilford H. Welman.	10th Missouri, Col. Francis C. Deimling.
4th Minnesota, Lieut. Col. John E. Tourtellotte.	24th Missouri (Company E), Lieut. Daniel Driscoll.
18th Wisconsin, Col. Gabriel Bouck.	80th Ohio, Lieut. Col. Pren Metham.

Third Brigade.

Brig. Gen. CHARLES L. MATTHIES.

93d Illinois, Col. Holden Putnam.
5th Iowa, Col. Jabez Banbury.
10th Iowa, Lieut. Col. Paris P. Henderson.
26th Missouri, Col. Benjamin D. Dean.

Artillery.

Capt. HENRY DILLON.

Cogswell's (Illinois) Battery, Capt. William Cogswell.
Wisconsin Light, 6th Battery, Lieut. Samuel F. Clark.
Wisconsin Light, 12th Battery, Capt. William Zickerick.

THIRD DIVISION.

Maj. Gen. JOHN A. LOGAN.

Escort.

2d Wisconsin Cavalry, Company H, Capt. Ernest J. Meyers.

First Brigade.	*Second Brigade.*
Brig. Gen. MORTIMER D. LEGGETT.	Brig. Gen. MANNING F. FORCE.
20th Illinois, Maj. George W. Kennard.	30th Illinois, Col. Warren Shedd.
29th Illinois, Maj. John A. Callicott.	20th Ohio, Capt. Edward C. Downs.
31st Illinois, Lieut. Col. Robert N. Pearson.	68th Ohio, Capt. Patrick H. Mooney.
45th Illinois, Lieut. Col. Robert P. Sealy.	78th Ohio, Col. Greenberry F. Wiles.
124th Illinois, Col. Thomas J. Sloan.	
131st Illinois, Lieut. Col. Richard A. Peter.	
23d Indiana, Lieut. Col. William P. Davis.	

Third Brigade.

Brig. Gen. JASPER A. MALTBY.

8th Illinois, Lieut. Col. Josiah A. Sheetz.
17th Illinois, Maj. Frank F. Peats.
81st Illinois, Col. Franklin Campbell.
7th Missouri, Col. William S. Oliver.
32d Ohio, Col. Benjamin F. Potts.

Artillery.

Maj. CHARLES J. STOLBRAND.

1st Illinois Light, Battery D, Lieut. Thobald D. Yost.
2d Illinois Light, Battery G, Lieut. John W. Lowell.
2d Illinois Light, Battery L, Capt. William H. Bolton.
Michigan Light, 8th Battery (H), Lieut. Marcus D. Elliott.
Ohio Light, 3d Battery, Lieut. John Sullivan.

FOURTH DIVISION.

Brig. Gen. MARCELLUS M. CROCKER.

Escort.

11th Illinois Cavalry, Company G, Capt. Stephen S. Tripp.

First Brigade.

Brig. Gen. THOMAS K. SMITH.

41st Illinois, Maj. Robert H. McFadden.
53d Illinois, Lieut. Col. John W. Mc-
Clanahan.
3d Iowa, Maj. George W. Crosley.
33d Wisconsin, Col. Jonathan B. Moore.

Second Brigade.

Col. CYRUS HALL.

14th Illinois, Maj. John F. Nolte.
15th Illinois, Col. George C. Rogers.
46th Illinois, Col. Benjamin Dornblaser.
76th Illinois, Lieut. Col. Charles C.
Jones.

Third Brigade.

Brig. Gen. WALTER Q. GRESHAM.

28th Illinois, Lieut. Col. Richard Ritter.
32d Illinois, Col. John Logan.
53d Indiana, Lieut. Col. William Jones.
12th Wisconsin, Col. George E. Bryant.

Artillery.

Capt. BENJAMIN F. RODGERS.

2d Illinois Light, Battery F, Lieut. Walter H. Powell.
2d Illinois Light, Battery K, Lieut. Francis M. Ross.
Ohio Light, 7th Battery, Lieut. Ellis Conant.
Ohio Light, 15th Battery, Lieut. Edwin F. Reeve.

DISTRICT OF NORTHEAST LOUISIANA.

Brig. Gen. JOHN P. HAWKINS.

1st Arkansas (A. D.), Col. William F. Wood.
10th Louisiana (A. D.), Col. Frederick M. Crandal.
11th Louisiana (A. D.), Col. Van E. Young.
3d Mississippi (A. D.), Col. Richard H. Ballinger.

MISSISSIPPI MARINE BRIGADE.*

Brig. Gen. ALFRED W. ELLET.

1st Infantry, Maj. David S. Tallerday.
1st Battalion Cavalry, Capt. Oscar F. Brown.
Pennsylvania Artillery, Battery C (Segebarth's), Capt. Daniel P. Walling.
Ram Fleet, Lieut. Col. John A. Ellet.

---

* At Cairo.

APPENDIX.

NASHVILLE, TENN.,
October 20, 1863.

Hon. E. M. STANTON,
Louisville, Ky.:

Just arrived. I will leave here early in the morning, and get through to Chattanooga as soon as possible. I presume you saw General Thomas' dispatch to me on the subject of rations.

U. S. GRANT,
Major-General.

NASHVILLE, TENN.,
October 20, 1863.

Admiral D. D. PORTER,
Cairo, Ill.:

General Sherman's advance was at Eastport on the 15th. The sooner a gun-boat can be got to him the better. Boats must now be on the way from Saint Louis with supplies to go up the Tennessee for Sherman.

U. S. GRANT,
Major-General.

HEADQUARTERS DEPARTMENT OF THE CUMBERLAND,
Chattanooga, October 20, 1863.

Maj. Gen. U. S. GRANT,
Nashville:

No change to report. Five days' rations issued to troops to-day. Three hundred wagons between here and Stevenson with provisions. General Rosecrans left this morning. Communicate with Burnside to-day. He is moving toward Kingston. His couriers connect with mine near Washington.

G. H. THOMAS,
Major-General.

HEADQUARTERS PIONEER BRIGADE,
Chattanooga, October 20, 1863.

Brigadier-General SMITH,
Chief Engineer, Department of the Cumberland:

I have the honor to report the flying bridge completed, and that one trip has been made across the river with it.

I am, very respectfully, your obedient servant,
J. ST. C. MORTON,
Brigadier-General of Volunteers.

(825)

Hdqrs. Second Brig., First Div., 4th Army Corps,
Camp Clark, October 20, 1863.

Major Fullerton,
Assistant Adjutant-General:

Dear Sir: The fog this morning has been so dense that I have
delayed reporting until it cleared. The enemy had forces upon the
island yesterday. If I had transportation for men to [do] it, I would
throw a force on the island that would hold it at all hazards. I
should like to be supplied immediately either with boats or boards
and tools to make them. Since last report wagons, supposed to
number 300 or 400, were heard moving over the mountain, and yesterday evening a large number of pack-mules were seen being driven
over Lookout, in the direction of Bridgeport.

Very respectfully, your obedient servant,
W. C. WHITAKER,
Brigadier-General, Commanding.

[Indorsement.]

HEADQUARTERS FOURTH ARMY CORPS,
Chattanooga, Tenn., October 20, 1863—2.45 p. m.

Just received.

Respectfully forwarded for the information of Major-General
Thomas.

G. GRANGER,
Major-General, Commanding.

———

STEVENSON, *October* 20, 1863—1 p. m.

Major-General REYNOLDS:

No tidings from Sherman's command. Had the Huntsville railroad examined yesterday. Find that the bridges over the Flint
and Paint Rock Rivers can be repaired by a company of engineers
in about one week and not four, as I was previously advised. Have
asked Colonel Innes if the engineers can be spared for the purpose,
not knowing but that the road might be of great use in the event of
Sherman's advance in that direction. I am informed that the steamer
at Bridgeport cannot be completed before Sunday next. The transportation for the Twelfth Corps commenced leaving Nashville this
morning. As I am not permitted to make use of the railroad, I cannot move any considerable portion of it without wagons, except the
necessity is pressing.

JOSEPH HOOKER,
Major-General, Commanding.

———

WAR DEPARTMENT,
October 20, 1863—8.05 a. m.

Major-General BURNSIDE,
Knoxville:

The juxtaposition of the sentence in your dispatch * relating to
Colonel De Courcy and that reporting the march of the regiment

———

* See Series I, Vol. XXX, Part III, p. 501.

of infantry of 52 miles in sixty hours caused the impression that that officer was in command of those regiments. Please return the letter of thanks, which will be submitted to the Secretary of War, and his instructions asked as to the necessary corrections. The Secretary of War deemed the rapid march of the troops in question worthy of notice.

JAS. A. HARDIE,
Assistant Adjutant-General.

FORT WHITAKER, OPPOSITE LOOKOUT,
Near Chattanooga, October 21, 1863.

Major FULLERTON,
 Assistant Adjutant-General:

The sentinel on duty at one of the batteries in the fort reports having seen a brigade of the enemy with wagons and ambulances passing up Lookout, westward, this evening late. They can pass to a certain point and then over and out of range of shell as far as we observe. A great number of mules with packs and panniers or baskets also passed this evening. It all took place late. This is the information detailed me by my adjutant on my arrival from head-quarters. The sharpshooters wounded one of Aleshire's men se-verely, not seriously, from the mountain this evening. The force, if any, on the island is reported very small this evening; thought to be foragers. The boats were so heavy that Captain Fox could not get them loaded to-day. Would be very hazardous to attempt to haul one of those boats with the roads so slippery.

 Respectfully,

W. C. WHITAKER,
Brigadier-General.

[Indorsement.]

HEADQUARTERS FOURTH ARMY CORPS,
Chattanooga, Tenn., October 21, 1863—8.40 p. m.

Respectfully forwarded for the information of Major-General Thomas.

G. GRANGER,
Major-General, Commanding.

HEADQUARTERS DEPARTMENT OF THE CUMBERLAND,
Chattanooga, October 22, 1863—10 a. m.

Brigadier-General SPEARS:

It is reported that the enemy threaten to cross at Cotton Port Ferry. The general commanding desires to know what information you have on this point and how your forces are disposed. Give a full report as soon as possible.

 Very respectfully,

J. J. REYNOLDS,
Major-General and Chief of Staff.

HEADQUARTERS DEPARTMENT OF THE CUMBERLAND,
Chattanooga, October 22, 1863.

Col. WILLIAM P. INNES,
      Nashville :

General Hooker reports that the railroad to Jasper is ready for the tracklayers to commence work, and that he shall need, in addition to track, materials for three switches and one water-tank. Push the work as much as possible.

By order of Major-General Thomas:

C. GODDARD,
Assistant Adjutant-General.

HDQRS. SECOND BRIG., SECOND DIV., 14TH ARMY CORPS,
Sale Creek, Tenn., October 22, 1863.

Lieut. Col. C. GODDARD,
      Assistant Adjutant-General :

SIR : The enemy are reported crossing at Muddy Creek, 6 miles below Cotton Port, and that one regiment of infantry are already across. The dispatch is from Lieutenant Carr at Washington. The general, with remainder of Fifth Tennessee Infantry and two sections of artillery, has gone to that point, and ordered Colonel Cooper to leave a guard sufficient to picket at Blythe's Ferry, and proceed to re-enforce. I am directed to remain here and forward information rapidly to you and other points of ours. We need forces above which is contained in the account of last night and to-day.

Yours, &c.,

JOHN B. WELSH,
First Lieutenant and Acting Assistant Adjutant-General.

HDQRS. SECOND BRIG., SECOND DIV., 14TH ARMY CORPS,
Sale Creek, Tenn., October 22, 1863—8 p. m.

Lieut. Col. C. GODDARD,
      Assistant Adjutant-General :

SIR : I have no news from the general up to this hour. As far as the report of Lieutenant Carr is concerned, I cannot think it possible for his statement to be correct about the enemy crossing below Cotton Port. Lieutenant-Colonel Klein dispatched this noon that he was at Spence's farm, 2 miles from cross-roads (Smith's), and would be there until rations reached him. Since noon I have had no news from him at all. He is much nearer to Muddy Creek than Lieutenant Carr, and would certainly have reported any indications of the enemy's attempting to cross. One of our clerks, Mr. Morgan, who is acquainted with the locality, informs me that there is no ford at Muddy Creek ; and without they have used pontoons or boats, they could not have crossed, as stated by Lieutenant Carr. In either of these last events our river patrols certainly would have had information to that effect. No such information is received from them, for their reports are all to the contrary, giving everything as quiet from Cotton Port to Blythe's Ferry. I here give you an exact copy of the dispatch from Lieutenant Carr :

WASHINGTON, *October 22, 1863.*

General SPEARS,
　　Commanding Brigade :

GENERAL : The rebels are crossing the river at Muddy Creek, 6 miles below Cotton Port. They are infantry. One regiment over now.
　　Yours, most respectfully,

JOHN CARR,
Lieutenant, Commanding Courier-Line.

Seven men of Lieutenant-Colonel Klein's command are here in camp (left there by him when he left here), and I have started 3 of them to join him at Spence's farm (where I still believe him to be), and to ascertain the truth of the affair. The locality of Spence's farm is in near proximity to the river where Muddy Creek empties in, and is about 10 miles from this place. All is reported quiet along the whole line from Cotton Port to Penny's Ford up to the arrival of Lieutenant Carr's dispatch, which reached here at 7 p. m. I will send dispatches hourly.
　　Yours, respectfully, &c.,

JOHN B. WELSH,
First Lieutenant and Acting Assistant Adjutant-General.

HDQRS. NINETY-SECOND ILLINOIS VOLS., WILDER'S BRIG.,
Harrison's Landing, Tenn., October 22, 1863—9 p. m.

Col. C. GODDARD,
　　A. A. G., Dept. of the Cumberland, Chattanooga, Tenn. :

COLONEL : Mrs. Puckett, a good Union lady living opposite here, came to the bank of the river this evening and reports that the rebels say that they have re-enforcements from Charleston and Virginia, and are throwing them against Burnside, and that if they cannot whip him, they cannot hold East Tennessee, and without it they are " gone up." I can vouch that Mrs. Puckett is a good Union lady, and she obtains her information from other Union ladies over the river. She says cavalry and infantry passed up toward Cleveland this afternoon.
　　I am, colonel, very respectfully, your obedient servant,

SMITH D. ATKINS,
Colonel Ninety-second Illinois Volunteers.

OFFICE OF PROVOST-MARSHAL-GENERAL OF EAST TENN.,
Knoxville, Tenn., October 22, 1863.

Lieut. Col. L. RICHMOND,
　　Assistant Adjutant-General, Army of the Ohio :

COLONEL : I have the honor to call the attention of the commanding general to the lawlessness of troops in the vicinity of Strawberry Plains and Mossy Creek. Representations are made to this office that outrages are frequently committed by the soldiers of that vicinity upon the persons and property of unoffending citizens for the alleged reason that they have heretofore manifested sympathy with the rebellion. The frequent recurrence of these outrages calls for some stringent measures to repress the growing evil, which threatens to work serious injury to our cause.

On Thursday, the 8th instant, 4 soldiers, professing to be from Strawberry Plains, and one, calling himself Jeff. Bull, and understood to belong to the Eighth Regiment Tennessee Volunteer Cavalry, visited the house of John Nance, a citizen of Grainger County, Tenn., on the pretense of searching for arms. They told Mr. Nance that they understood he had money, and demanded $10 apiece, which being refused them, they procured an ax and split open his bureau, but were disappointed in not finding any money. They then demanded Mr. Nance's only horse, which he refused to surrender, whereupon they threatened to hang him, but were finally dissuaded, and went away. On the 16th instant an armed force of 7 men again visited his house during his absence, abused his wife, demanded to know where her husband's money was, and threatened to burn the house over her head. They then helped themselves to wearing apparel and other articles and went away. Mr. Nance states that such things are common in his neighborhood, and cites numerous examples.

Respectfully, &c.,

S. P. CARTER,
Brigadier-General, and Provost-Marshal, East Tennessee.

HEADQUARTERS U. S. FORCES,
Anderson's Cross-Roads, Tenn., October 23, 1863.

Major-General REYNOLDS,
Chief of Staff, Department of the Cumberland:

GENERAL : Excessive rains during the day have rendered the passage of the mountain at this place exceedingly difficult and tedious, and the number of wagons are in consequence accumulating. All the assistance possible is being rendered by the force here under my command. It will take several days' good weather to put the road in anything like passable condition.

I forwarded by courier this morning copy of report from Lieutenant-Colonel Cahill, commanding Sixteenth Illinois, at Bob White's, stating that the road had been cut out to Burnett's. I have issued no order as to the movement of trains, for fear of confusion, expecting that general orders for their movement are issued from department headquarters. The Sequatchie was fordable at 4 p. m., but rising rapidly.

I am, general, very respectfully, your obedient servant,

JAMES D. MORGAN,
Brigadier-General.

HDQRS. EIGHTEENTH KENTUCKY VOLUNTEER INFANTRY,
Camp near Williams' Island, October 23, 1863.

Maj. WILLIAM MCMICHAEL,
Asst. Adjt. Gen., Department of the Cumberland :

MAJOR : I have the honor to report considerable firing by the sharpshooters of the enemy on yesterday. Their firing was principally directed to the small extent of exposed road from the point where he new road begins to ascend the hill, and the courier post at Williams' house, and was well directed ; they reach the road with their pullets easily. If the firing to-day is as heavy as yesterday I shall be forced to again move camp. The enemy seems to be in small squads along the entire length of the river to Big Suck Creek, though they manifest no disposition to cross the river.

I am, very respectfully,

H. K. MILWARD,
Lieutenant-Colonel, Commanding.

HDQRS. ANDERSON CAVALRY, ROBERSON'S PLANTATION,
Sequatchie Valley, October 23, 1863.

Lieut. Col. C. GODDARD,
Asst. Adjt. Gen., Hdqrs. Department of the Cumberland:

COLONEL : Having returned last evening from a scout with a small detachment of my regiment through the upper part of the Sequatchie Valley and the coves in the mountains dividing this valley from the Tennessee Valley at Post Oak Springs, near Kingston, I deem it proper to report that I consider it practicable to obtain, with proper energy, a sufficient number of cattle and sheep in that belt of the country to feed the army at Chattanooga for several weeks. And I would suggest that in case the wants of the army render it necessary, a small mounted force be sent there, with directions to seize and receipt for all sheep and cattle fit for meat, excepting yoke cattle and milch cows. If necessary I can furnish from my regiment the mounted force necessary to do this. I also think that a considerable amount of wheat might be seized in the same region and ground at the numerous mills in this valley into flour for the use of the army; and if the corn is more necessary for subsistence than forage, it might be made into meal. Country ox-teams could be used to haul the wheat to mill.

Lieutenant Window, of the Seventy-third Illinois Regiment, Sheridan's division, has in four days collected in this valley in a few miles above and below Pikeville (a country which had already been foraged over) 350 head of cattle and over 100 head of sheep, with a force of but 15 men. He has exhibited so much energy, and has been so successful, that in case the scarcity of meat still exists at Chattanooga, he should be detailed to obtain fresh beef for the army from this country. If the several division commanders send out their detachments for this purpose, the distribution will not be as equal throughout the army as it should be. I have ventured to make these suggestions, without being aware that such an urgency exists as to render it necessary to adopt them, resulting, as such adoption would, in nearly stripping this country of the means of subsistence for the citizens.

I am, colonel, your obedient servant,

WM. J. PALMER,
Colonel, Commanding.

OCTOBER 23, 1863.

Major-General BURNSIDE,
Commanding Department of the Ohio, Knoxville:

Your telegram of 22d received. Have telegraphed to know if pontoon train now on hand, and ordered before the battle of Chick-

amauga by General Rosecrans, is needed. If not I shall send it t
the point you have indicated. I have been told there are some rough
pontoons near Nicholasville and at Stanford. If so, these are avail
able for your purpose and will be forwarded. Am pushing on th
railroad all I can. The great difficulty is in providing the necessar
labor. I have already written you several letters by mail on thi
subject. If the citizens of Kentucky do not object, could not con
traband laborers be ordered to the road by the Government ? Gen
eral Fry has already necessarily crippled railroad operations by tak
ing off a large number for common road purposes, ordered by you
To-night I hope to go to Louisville to see General Boyle as you
direct. Has the Government yet authorized the purchase of railroac
iron ?

J. H. SIMPSON,
Major and Chief Engineer.

HEADQUARTERS THIRD DIVISION, FOURTH ARMY CORPS,
Chattanooga, October 24, 1863.

Maj. Gen. J. J. REYNOLDS,
    Chief of Staff:

SIR : In accordance with the request of the commanding general
of this army made to me this a. m., I have the honor to submit the
following information and suggestions:

First. The dirt road from Shellmound via Whiteside's to Look
out Mountain Valley is a single track, just wide enough for one
wagon. It is a bad road in good weather, but practicable. In in
clement weather it will, of course, become much worse, but I am
not prepared to say it will become entirely impracticable, though I
incline to that opinion.

Second. I think it will be necessary to have a force at Wauhatchie,
to guard the river and prevent the enemy from striking it by the
roads which lead down Lookout Mountain Valley to the ferries
below. These roads are practicable for the movement of troops of
all arms. A brigade taking advantage of the strong ground in the
vicinity of Wauhatchie and intrenching itself at once, would prob
ably answer this purpose, if there were troops in supporting distance.

Third. There is strong ground for defensive purposes at Parrish's
(it is where the dirt road from Shellmound via Whiteside's falls into
Lookout Mountain Valley), where a strong division ought to be posted.
It should intrench itself. This position is 1½ miles from Wau
hatchie. A sufficient force holding it would in a great measure com
mand Lookout Mountain Valley, and check any force coming from
the direction of Trenton. It should post itself with its rear toward
Whiteside's and secure its flanks against the spurs of the mountains
in rear of it—spurs of Raccoon Mountain.

Fourth. It would be necessary to have a force at Whiteside's, to
prevent a movement of the enemy down Murphy's Valley to get in
rear of the force at Parrish's. A brigade, well intrenched, ought to
answer this purpose.

Fifth. Of course it would be necessary to guard Shellmound
securely against an attack from the direction of Trenton.

I am, sir, very respectfully, your obedient servant,

TH. J. WOOD,
Brigadier-General, Commanding.

HDQRS. SECOND BRIG., SECOND DIV., 14TH ARMY CORPS,
Sale Creek, Tenn., October 24, 1863.

Lieut. Col. C. GODDARD,
Assistant Adjutant-General:

SIR : I have the honor to render the following report, with all the information learned since making report of yesterday :

From dispatches received from all of the points at which we have guards and pickets, everything is quiet. Major Gamble, Sixth Tennessee Infantry, in command of forces at Cotton Port, reports that the rebels have been crossing the river in small squads of 2 and 3, and have interfered with our courier-line. It was by this means that Colonel Clift and 1 courier were captured and carried across the river. This crossing has been done above Cotton Port, some 6 miles.

Four deserters came into our lines at Blythe's Ferry, and were sent into headquarters here to-day. They report that the rebels, 20,000 cavalry and 6,000 infantry, have gone up the river in the direction of Loudon, and that they left Chattanooga front on Monday last. Three of the four are known here, and are said to be Union men, having been pressed into the rebel service only eight weeks since. They appear to be honest in what they relate concerning the movements of the enemy. Lieutenant-Colonel Dickerson, commanding, passed here this evening with Tenth Michigan Infantry and one section [Fifth] Wisconsin Battery, en route for Smith's Ferry. The lieutenant-colonel reported for information concerning the locality to which he was ordered, and by reference to a sketch of that section he was thoroughly informed. His camp to-night is 2 miles beyond Sale Creek, at what is called the "Camp-ground." Rations in part and forage were furnished him here. He moves forward to-morrow morning. The distance from this point to Smith's Ferry is 21 miles. I regret exceedingly to announce the appearance of one new case of small-pox in quarantine this morning. The case first occasioning this establishing of quarantine is fast recovering. Statement forwarded last evening gives the number of men in quarantine 110. The rain that has fallen in the last two days will place the river beyond all possibility of fording, and is even now too deep to be safe.

I am, colonel, very respectfully, your obedient servant,

JOHN B. WELSH,
First Lieutenant and Acting Assistant Adjutant-General.

DECHERD, *October 24, 1863—5.30 p. m.*

Major-General BUTTERFIELD,
Chief of Staff, Stevenson :

General Mitchell has reliable information that Wheeler has crossed at Lamb's Ferry and that Lee has joined him. Shall I stop march of my division ? Ruger's brigade will be at Tantalon to-night.

A. S. WILLIAMS,
Brigadier-General.

DECHERD, *October* 24, 1863.

General WILLIAMS,
    On Passenger Train, Cowan:

The order for your division to move is countermanded. Remain where you are for the present, and take measures to stop your wagon train. Make the best disposition to guard the railroad temporarily. Detailed instructions will be sent you to-morrow. Please acknowledge.

By command of Major-General Slocum :

H. C. RODGERS,
Assistant Adjutant-General.

———

TULLAHOMA, TENN.,
October 24, 1863.

Maj. J. S. FULLERTON,
    Assistant Adjutant-General :

MAJOR : Your order of the 17th instant, to send a regiment to McMinnville, came here on the 22d instant, and was immediately forwarded to Colonel Gilbert, Nineteenth Michigan, who will reach McMinnville to-day. The railroad is not completed to that place, and supplies may have to be drawn from Murfreesborough. There is also now at McMinnville a force of some 300 Tennessee cavalry. The force at Murfreesborough now is weaker than ever before, the Nineteenth Michigan being withdrawn. There are seven companies of the Twenty-second Wisconsin there, three being at Normandy. The Eighty-fifth Indiana has been ordered to Duck River bridge by General Slocum, so that if to-day the Twelfth Corps moves south there will be no guards from Duck River to Stone's River. There is no cavalry force to patrol the road. Last night, about 5 miles south of this place, the rebel cavalry, 70 in number, tore up the track, which caused a train with eight cars to run off; Captain Sligh, of the Michigan Engineers and Mechanics, lost both his legs ; the cars all badly smashed. Ferguson threatens with 600 mounted men on the east near McMinnville. I fear much interruption and damage unless cavalry is supplied to chase these fellows away. A rail torn at any point throws off a train. A negro, captured by the rebels last night, and who escaped this morning, says they say they intend to stop the running of cars on the railroad. He says they told him General Roddey was some miles west of this place toward Fayetteville.

Yours, very truly,

JOHN COBURN,
Colonel, &c.

[Indorsement.]

HEADQUARTERS FOURTH ARMY CORPS,
October 27, 1863.

Respectfully referred to department headquarters.

G. GRANGER,
Major-General, Commanding.

IUKA, MISS.,
October 24, 1863.

General DODGE,
    Corinth :

Two gun-boats arrived at Eastport this morning. I telegraphed the fact to Hurlbut, but omitted doing so to you. I sent one of my staff with an escort to bring up Commodore Phelps. You have doubtless heard that Grant is to command the Armies of the Ohio, Cumberland, and Tennessee united into one. He will devolve his present army on me, and I will want a most minute account of your troops for actual duty, arms, ammunition, &c.

                        W. T. SHERMAN,
                              Major-General.

HEADQUARTERS CHIEF OF CAVALRY,
Decherd, Tenn., October 25, 1863.

Major-General REYNOLDS,
    Chief of Staff :

GENERAL : The necessity of prompt and immediate measures being taken to secure for the cavalry command of this department a new supply of horses and horse equipments, for almost the entire command, is very great. General Crook telegraphed me to-day that out of his whole command, which includes Wilder's brigade of mounted infantry, he has only 1,000 effective men, and that were he ordered to leave his present encampment to-day he should be obliged to abandon at least 700 horses.

In the whole of the First Division of Cavalry there is only about 1,400 men effective, simply because we have no horses fit for service. The pursuit of Wheeler and Roddey ruined so many, the effective force of cavalry is thus sadly reduced.

The saddles issued to us simply murder horses ; it is sure ruin to a horse to put one on his back. It was not the hard marching that ruined our stock, but the worthless, murderous saddles, that dig holes into the backs the first day and break them down. New saddles are worse than old ; the hides on them are green, and the first rain they are in pulls it all off. The trees are made of green wood and also helps ; the iron holding the tree is too weak, and the saddle spreads and settles upon the horse's back, making it set in the worst possible shape, which no ingenuity on the part of the trooper, in folding his saddle-blanket, can obviate. Why the Government will purchase such horse equipments and why they will keep employed inspectors who pass such saddles and receive them as fit for use, I cannot see. This blind, short-sighted manner of supplying us is ruining us much more effectually than the enemy could ever hope to do. They need only to keep us engaged in pursuing them and they would use us up as often as we could get refitted, if more attention is not paid by the ordnance department in the quality of equipments furnished us.

Many saddles that were drawn just before the pursuit of Wheeler began are now being condemned by the inspector, and have, the most of them, ruined the horses they were put upon.

I write thus lengthy, feeling that the importance of the subject demands it. Something must be done to give us at least 3,000 horses and 3,000 or 4,000 horse equipments immediately, for we are now completely crippled for the want of them, and some measures ought to be taken at once to improve the quality of both. It is certainly economy to the Government in a pecuniary point of view, saying nothing of the benefits which would arise from our being then always in good condition, which is in reality of much greater importance.

I respectfully submit the subject for your action.

ROBERT B. MITCHELL,
Brigadier-General, Commanding.

MAYSVILLE, *October* 25, 1863.
(Via Stevenson, 26th.)

Maj. Gen. U. S. GRANT:

I have sent your communication* by a courier with instructions not to sleep until he finds General Sherman. My expedition to the Tennessee report no rebel cavalry on this side. The citizens here report that General Wheeler has been skirmishing with Sherman at or near Bear Creek on Tuesday, Wednesday, and Thursday. I have the honor to report that my cavalry have been on a constant go, and the cold drenching rains we have had since this last raid have so completely used up my horses that there are scarcely any of them fit for service. I would like them sent to me by way of Decherd; also have shoes that are set sent me. Have no forge to work. Rough shoes here. I have been trying to get these things ever since I arrived here.

GEORGE CROOK,
Brigadier-General.

COLUMBIA, *October* 25, 1863.

Maj. WILLIAM H. SINCLAIR,
Assistant Adjutant-General:

I have had flying rumors of Wheeler, Lee, and Roddey crossing the Tennessee this way; that Roddey had crossed; that river was high and crossing difficult. I do not know how reliable this may be, though I am inclined to credit in part. I have sent scouts to investigate and will report all information promptly. They may try to pick me up as I have only 300 men, but I am intrenched on hill with two pieces of artillery.

H. R. MIZNER,
Colonel, Commanding.

HEADQUARTERS CAVALRY DETACHMENT,
Rankin's Ferry, October 25, 1863.

Lieutenant-Colonel GODDARD,
Assistant Adjutant-General, Army of the Cumberland:

SIR: I have just received information that the rebels are hauling boats up the river opposite Williams' Island and intend crossing behind the island. The information is reliable and can be depended upon.

By order of B. P. Wells, captain commanding:

P. S. SCHUYLER,
Captain and Acting Adjutant.

---

* See p. 713.

WARTRACE, *October* 25, 1863.

General WILLIAMS:

The major-general commanding directs that you continue the march in the advance regardless of all orders countermanding.

He has telegraphed to General Hooker for instructions.

H. C. RODGERS,
Assistant Adjutant-General.

WARTRACE, *October* 25, 1863.

General A. S. WILLIAMS:

The major-general commanding directs that you send one regiment and a battery to Bridgeport and one regiment and a battery to Stevenson at once. This arrangement will be permanent. Knap's battery only goes with General Geary.

H. C. RODGERS,
Assistant Adjutant-General.

WARTRACE, *October* 25, 1863.

General WILLIAMS:

Your division will occupy the road from Bridgeport to Murfreesborough. Do you want all your train sent forward? If so, to what point? I should think it better to have part of it at Tullahoma, as it will have to come back this way.

H. C. RODGERS,
Assistant Adjutant-General.

ANDERSON, *October* 25, 1863—12.15 p. m.

Major-General BUTTERFIELD,
Chief of Staff:

Your dispatch received. I understand that all troops of Eleventh Corps and Geary's are to be relieved at Tantalon and Anderson and at the bridges between and in this vicinity.

I will have it done as soon as I can get an order to my troops now at Tantalon. There is no telegraph station there. The troops here and vicinity I can relieve at once. The batteries are at Tantalon. Roads extremely bad and artillery moves with difficulty.

A. S. WILLIAMS,
Brigadier-General.

ANDERSON, *October* 25, 1863—12 m.

Col. W. W. PACKER,
Commanding at Tantalon:

COLONEL: Pursuant to orders General Williams desires you to relieve all the guards of the Eleventh Corps and General Geary's division you find at Tantalon and Anderson and between those point. From the best he can ascertain the present position of the troops to be relieved by you is as follows:

Tantalon, three companies One hundred and eleventh Pennsylvania; three bridges between Tantalon and here, three companies, One hundred and thirty-sixth New York.

Anderson, three companies One hundred and thirty-sixth New York ; first bridge below Anderson, one company One hundred and thirty-sixth New York.

This will take one entire regiment and it should be a good one.

You will move the other two regiments and the batteries to this point at once, and report to General Williams at this post for further orders. You can relieve the troops referred to as you come along, as the railroad track is the best way for the troops to come, keeping a guard with the batteries, which will not have to leave the track a great distance.

I am, colonel, your obedient servant,

S. E. PITTMAN,
Captain and Assistant Adjutant-General.

P. S.—General Hooker's orders are that as fast as these troops are relieved they shall march to Bridgeport.

S. E. PITTMAN,
Assistant Adjutant-General.

STEVENSON, *October* 25, 1863.

Brig. Gen. A. S. WILLIAMS:

GENERAL : I am directed by Major-General Hooker to send the Third Maryland and One hundred and twenty-fifth New York to Bridgeport. Have done so. Also to relieve one of Geary's regiments by the Twentieth Connecticut, which I am about doing. The advance of the Twentieth is just arrived. Any orders for me will find me at the Alabama House.

J. F. KNIPE,
Brigadier-General, First Brigade.

ANDERSON, *October* 25, 1863—1 p. m.

Brigadier-General KNIPE,
Alabama House, Stevenson:

General Butterfield orders troops of Geary and Eleventh Corps to be relieved from Tantalon to this place, including bridges below this. I have directed Packer to make the details and march the rest this way. Where have you sent Twentieth Connecticut ? This side or below Stevenson ?

General B. also orders three regiments and a battery to Stevenson for duty. Are these wanted besides Twentieth Connecticut ?

A. S. WILLIAMS,
Brigadier-General.

HEADQUARTERS DEPARTMENT OF THE TENNESSEE.
October 25, 1863.

Colonel LOOMIS,
Burnsville:

I have ordered forward one regiment of Fuller's brigade to Burnsville. On its arrival move to this place with your whole brigade, marching by land. I want you to arrive to-morrow certain.

W. T. SHERMAN,
Major-General.

CORINTH, *October* 25, 1863—4 p. m.

Major-General HURLBUT:

Scout returned from Union City. Met Faulkner's command, consisting of Wilson, Newsom, Greer, Bell, and Franklin near Huntingdon. They were 1,000 strong and going north rapidly to attack Murray, Mayfield, and other points in that part of Kentucky and Tennessee, intending to obtain stores and commissaries. Major Kizer, with one battalion of rebels, is at Lexington. Faulkner's stragglers left White Oak yesterday following him up.

G. M. DODGE,
Brigadier-General.

(Copy to Brig. Gen. A. J. Smith, Columbus, Ky., by steamer Anderson, October 25, 1863.)

MAYSVILLE, *October* 26, 1863.

Maj. Gen. J. J. REYNOLDS,
Chief of Staff:

I will send men as directed. They will have to go 35 miles out of the way in order to get over the Paint Rock River. I would like to retain this mounted infantry in my division, and if possible retain my division, together with the present organization of my division. Altogether I would have about 4,000 men, with which I could hold my own against all the rebel cavalry they could bring against me in this department.

GEORGE CROOK,
Brigadier-General.

MAYSVILLE, ALA., *October* 26, 1863.

Maj. Gen. U. S. GRANT:

A wounded prisoner captured yesterday and brought in to-day states he was wounded at Bear Creek, and reports General Sherman had completed the bridge across the Bear Creek and part of his force had crossed. I expect to hear very soon from him, as I sent escort to find him some days ago.

GEORGE CROOK,
Brigadier-General.

HDQRS. SECOND BRIG., FIRST DIV., 4TH ARMY CORPS,
October 26, 1863.

Major FULLERTON,
Assistant Adjutant-General:

I had occasion to fire a couple of shell from Naylor's battery yesterday afternoon about 3 o'clock at a detachment of the enemy engaged in throwing up an earth-work on the east slope of Lookout Mountain, to the right of the huge rock projecting over or near the road running up the mountain, and directly opposite the point on which is posted Naylor's battery and which is used also by a signal officer. The shots had the effect to cause a desertion of the work forthwith by the party. On the south side of Williams' Island the enemy gave some evidence of activity and employed sharpshooters on my pickets on the island during the afternoon. About 7.30 o'clock I was notified from department headquarters of an intention on the part of the enemy to effect a crossing "behind the island." To defeat any such attempt I ordered one regiment to re-enforce my pickets on the island, and planted a section of battery on the hill back of island, having transported the section to that point by mules, as the horses of the battery have been sent to Stevenson.

To support this battery I placed the Eighth Kentucky Infantry in its rear. My picket-line was doubled throughout and orders were given that no enemy of whatever force must be permitted to mount this bank of the river.

Two efforts were made to lodge troops on the island, but were defeated and driven off both times. This morning finds me in possession of the crossings and of the island, and all of them cannot drive me off. I caused the range of the enemy's camps to be taken yesterday, and in the night opened fire and caused every light to be quickly extinguished, having planted the shell in and over their camps. The force that attempted a lodgment on the island I cannot determine. It was night, but the two efforts and sharpshooters show to my mind that it was strong.

Respectfully,

W. C. WHITAKER,
Brigadier-General, Commanding.

HEADQUARTERS DEPARTMENT OF THE CUMBERLAND,
Chattanooga, October 26, 1863—8 p. m.

Brigadier-General CRUFT:

You will assume command of the First Division, Fourth Corps, Major-General Palmer's wound obliging him to leave the field, and move with it to Rankin's Ferry, and co-operate with General Hooker, who proceeds to the same point via the south side of the river. If your battery cannot make the ferry to-morrow, you will move on with your infantry. A battery has already been ordered from Bridgeport to join you at Rankin's Ferry to provide against the possibility of the battery of the First Division not succeeding in getting through. A pontoon bridge is also on the way to the ferry.

By command of Major-General Thomas:

J. J. REYNOLDS,
Major-General, Chief of Staff.

HEADQUARTERS DEPARTMENT OF THE CUMBERLAND,
Chattanooga, October 26, 1863—6.15 p. m.

Col. D. McCOOK,
Comdg. Third Brig., Second Div., 14th Army Corps:

Send your battery (Barnett's) down to Brown's Ferry, to report to General W. F. Smith, by 5 o'clock to-morrow morning, and hold your brigade in readiness to march at any moment, taking three lays' rations in haversacks. Designate two regiments to remain with General Davis' two batteries to guard the river, should you receive orders to move.

Respectfully,

GEO. H. THOMAS,
Major-General, Commanding.

WARTRACE, *October* 26, 1863.

General A. S. WILLIAMS:

Captain Moseley left here yesterday with orders for you. It is of the utmost importance that some of your troops should be at this end of the line. One regiment must be sent to Christiana to-day, and if possible one to this place to-morrow, and the others that are ordered this way, as soon as possible.

By command, &c.:

H. C. RODGERS,
Assistant Adjutant-General.

GENERAL ORDERS, }   HEADQUARTERS TWELFTH CORPS,
    No. 27.   }   *Wartrace, Tenn., October* 26, 1863.

Pursuant to orders from headquarters Department of the Cumberland, the undersigned hereby assumes command of all the troops for the defense of the railroad from Murfreesborough to Bridgeport, including those at both the above-named points.

All reports required by existing orders will be promptly forwarded to these headquarters.

H. W. SLOCUM,
Major-General of Volunteers, Commanding.

IUKA, *October* 26, 1863.

Colonel MACFEELY:

I want preparations made at once to supply 25,000 men with rations at Florence and beyond. Tennessee River is good up to Eastport and rising. Railroad is of no account, but we have stores enough for about twenty days. You may join me at Florence by the way of Saint Louis, using dispatch and making all proper arrangements.

W. T. SHERMAN,
Major-General.

IUKA, *October* 26, 1863.

Colonel BINGHAM,
        Memphis:

I suppose you are the department quartermaster. If so, I want you to proceed to Saint Louis and see that a ferry-boat, not drawing over 3 feet, has gone up the Tennessee. Then estimate for forage for 25,000 men, and a due proportion of horses, and either bring it up or contract for it along the Tennessee. Make all arrangements for

supplies by the Tennessee and overtake me at Florence. The rail
road is a nuisance, and I find the Tennessee in fine order, good for
feet up to Eastport, Chickasaw, and Waterloo. I tried Colbert Shoal
to-day with a gun-boat of 4 feet, but we could not pass. We mus
haul from Waterloo till I can get a boat to Florence.

> W. T. SHERMAN,
> *Major-General.*

HEADQUARTERS DEPARTMENT OF THE CUMBERLAND,
Chattanooga, October 27, 1863. (Received 11.25 p. m.)
Major-General HALLECK,
Washington, D. C.:

General Grant has placed General Palmer in command of the
Fourteenth Army Corps, subject to the approval of the President

> GEO. H. THOMAS,
> *Major-General, U. S. Volunteers, Commanding.*

BRIDGEPORT, *October 27, 1863*—6.30 p. m.
Major-General REYNOLDS:

Troops just moving out. Schurz leads, followed by Steinwehr
and Geary. They fear the pontoon train will be in their way. There
has been much difficulty in getting this train across the island and
up the southern shore of the river.

> C. A. DANA.

MAYSVILLE, *October 27, 1863.*
Lieut. Col. C. GODDARD,
Assistant Adjutant-General:

My cavalry is in such a bad condition that I could not possibly
spare men to go up the river above you.

> GEORGE CROOK,
> *Brigadier-General.*

HEADQUARTERS FOURTH ARMY CORPS,
Chattanooga, Tenn., October 27, 1863.
[General J. J. REYNOLDS:]

GENERAL: A deserter who came in a short time ago, late this
evening, says:

First. He has been up from Atlanta but about one week; was
quartermaster's clerk for a while there.

Second. The rebels have been in line of battle the greater part of
to-day.

Third. Longstreet's men crossed the mountain to-day (Lookout).

Fourth. That we are to be attacked in the morning.

He can give no substantial reasons for the last report, only that it
is the talk and belief in camp.

> Truly,
> FULLERTON.

HDQRS. SECOND DIVISION, FOURTH ARMY CORPS,
Chattanooga, October 27, 1863.

Maj. J. S. FULLERTON,
Assistant Adjutant-General, Fourth Army Corps:

MAJOR: The enemy have moved one of their camps on Missionary Ridge directly in my front. The troops passed over the ridge. The size of the camp was about one brigade. They are now moving artillery over the ridge on the same road. There are, also, wagons moving very rapidly along the crest of the ridge from our right to left.

I am, very respectfully, your obedient servant,

P. H. SHERIDAN,
Major-General, Commanding.

[Indorsement.]

OCTOBER 27, 1863—2.45 p. m.

Respectfully forwarded.

G. GRANGER,
Major-General.

———

HEADQUARTERS U. S. FORCES,
Anderson's Cross-Roads, Tenn., October 27, 1863.

Major-General REYNOLDS,
Chief of Staff:

GENERAL: Yesterday 51 wagons passed over the mountain and 81 to-day. There are remaining at this place 140 wagons. The general supply trains are more trouble than all others. Mr. Lettler is here with one of 32 wagons; he has been 8 days coming from Stevenson. He has 9 wagons loaded with ammunition, the balance with salt and bacon. More than half of his teams are broken down and worthless. The ammunition will cross in the morning. Sequatchie fordable at this point. Forage getting very scarce and difficult to obtain. One company of Tenth Ohio Cavalry, returned from scout up the valley, report guerrillas in the vicinity of Pikeville. Lieutenant-Colonel Cahill, in command of Sixteenth Illinois Infantry, reports that on south side of Tennessee, opposite Kelley's Ferry, a rebel picket station, and that from information received he thinks that three regiments of rebels are at or near Lookout Station. I am doing all I can with my small force to assist trains over the mountains and repair the road.

I am, general, very respectfully, your obedient servant,

JAMES D. MORGAN,
Brigadier-General.

———

HEADQUARTERS DEPARTMENT OF THE CUMBERLAND,
Chattanooga, October 28, 1863—11 a. m.

Brigadier-General MORTON,
Shellmound, via Bridgeport:

Your telegram to General W. F. Smith received. Communicate with General Hooker, and, if he deems it safe, move the pontoon bridge to Rankin's Ferry to-morrow. If General Hooker should want the co-operation of the force at Rankin's Ferry now under General Cruft, they must join him via Shellmound. Notify General Cruft that the bridge is finished at Shellmound.

By order of General Thomas:

J. J. REYNOLDS,
Major-General, Chief of Staff.

BRIDGEPORT, *October* 28, 1863—10 p. m.

Major-General REYNOLDS,
Chief of Staff:

GENERAL: The steam-boat moves off very well—slow, but will improve as her machinery wears smooth. Thirty-four thousand rations are shipped in barges alongside her. A slight alteration in a rod and a steam gasket, and she will try her first trip. The machinist promises she shall be off at or before 1 o'clock, unless detained by fog. I think she will make Rankin's Landing by daylight. If very foggy, and there is every indication of it, she will be compelled to lie by until sunrise. I will have other barges loaded, ready for her on her return. No forage on hand to-night to ship. Will send some to-morrow if possible.

W. G. LE DUC,
Lieutenant-Colonel and Chief Quartermaster.

MURFREESBOROUGH, TENN.,
October 28, 1863.

ASSISTANT ADJUTANT-GENERAL,
Department of the Cumberland:

SIR: On the 7th instant, at Farmington, Middle Tenn., Brigadier-General Crook, commanding Second Cavalry Division, charged me with endeavoring to thwart his plans, and placed me under arrest; the next morning he ordered me back to this place, and directed me to wait here for further orders. I have now been here for three weeks, but have received no orders of any kind. I have had command of a brigade since before the advance from Nashville in December last, and during that time have captured three pieces of artillery and twice as many prisoners as I have had effective men in my brigade, and have been three times recommended for promotion by Major-General Rosecrans. During my two years' service I have been engaged in eighty-four battles or skirmishes, in which blood has been drawn, and I do think that I have performed my duties as a soldier too zealously and faithfully to be now cast aside like a piece of useless furniture. I declare the charge against me to be entirely false and without foundation, and most respectfully ask the major-general commanding to grant me an immediate court-martial or court of inquiry.*

I am, respectfully, your obedient servant,

ROBT. H. G. MINTY,
Col. Fourth Mich. Cav., late Comdg. First Brig., Second Cav. Div.

---

* See foot-note, Series I, Vol. XXX, Part II, p. 668.

[Indorsement.]

HEADQUARTERS U. S. FORCES,
Murfreesborough, Tenn., October 28, 1863.

Approved and respectfully forwarded.

WM. L. UTLEY,
Colonel, Commanding Post.

———

HDQRS. FIRST DIVISION, FOURTH ARMY CORPS,
Rankin's Ferry, Tennessee River, October 28, 1863—6 p. m.

Major-General REYNOLDS,
Chief of Staff, Army of the Cumberland:

Your dispatch of 26th instant, ordering me to assume command of the First Division, Fourth Corps, was received through division headquarters at 6.30 p. m. on yesterday at Prigmore's house, foot of the mountains. General Palmer immediately placed me in command. According to orders I marched at 5.30 a. m. to-day and reached here with head of column at 10 a. m. The artillery and train (except the ammunition train) have arrived this afternoon. The dispatch of Colonel Goddard, dated 26th instant (by signal to Bob White's), directed to Major-General Palmer, was handed me by him. On arriving at this point the detachment of cavalry, Captain Wells (Second Michigan), was promptly relieved as ordered at 10 a. m. A detachment of 100 men was sent also promptly to Love's Ferry, opposite Shellmound. Soon after starting the command in the morning dispatches were received from Brigadier-General Morton that he had a pontoon in process of building, and later that it could be crossed. My orders were imperative to go to Rankin's and report from thence to Major-General Hooker. General Morton, in addition to his written communications, sent me a verbal statement that the enemy were making some demonstration in the Nickajack Valley from the direction of Trenton ; that there was a large force at Trenton, and that he deemed the pontoon guard insufficient. At 2.30 I sent to report to him four regiments, and will send a section or half battery from the artillery here during the night, if he deems it necessary from any threatening demonstrations. It is, say, 4 miles from here to Shellmound. The rations of this command expired this evening. According to orders from Major-General Palmer I took from a passing train under charge of Lieutenant Ferguson (Pioneer Brigade) partial rations for two days, receipting for same and giving him an order on the commissary of subsistence of the division at Chattanooga for a like quantity out of stores he has. On arrival here I reported to Major-General Hooker by dispatch, sending via Shellmound, and (in duplicate) by crossing an orderly at this point on raft. It is probable that his orders will reach me very soon. He passed this point on yesterday and is reported to be at Whiteside's.

I am, general, very respectfully, &c.,

CHARLES CRUFT,
Brigadier-General.

———

HEADQUARTERS SECOND BRIGADE, FIRST DIVISION,
Fort Whitaker, October 28, 1863.

Major FULLERTON, *Asst. Adjt. Gen., Fourth Army Corps:*

The batteries from Fort Whitaker effectually prevented the enemy from using the main road over Lookout and the railroad. They attempted it several times. They passed by a road diverging from the main road at the two large rocks, passing southeast toward the white house, going around and between it and the summit of Lookout at the upper edge of the clearing. Not less than a division passed there. They were mixed troops. The space over which they had to pass in view was short, but the range of the batteries was so good that they did not attempt it but once in column; the balance passed in groups of 3 or 4, and on a run generally.

Over 150 men assembled at the water-tank, mouth of Chickamauga, for the purpose as we supposed of taking the railroad or preventing our troops from taking Lookout (which might have been done) by that route. They were driven off by the batteries. The entire range of hills skirting on the river above Brown's Ferry should be held by our forces, otherwise eligible positions can be obtained for the enemy's guns to operate on the pontoon bridge. It is true these positions are quasi under range of Fort Whitaker, but heavy embankments thrown up in the night would, in a great measure, if not entirely, protect them. The sharpshooters of the enemy at the Narrows did not retire till late last evening and then only partially. They went down the river around the point of Raccoon. Over the top of Raccoon north to the right (as you face it) from Pass Gap (the gap opposite the pontoon bridge), it is 5 miles across to the river; a good fair road leads to the summit of the mountain. A citizen informed one of my front skirmishers that it could be made available for wagons. He was sent to General Smith. Immediate steps being taken, the river could be secured across the mountain. My men who were on top of Raccoon report fires and the presence of troops (whether friend or foe they did not know) on the opposite side of Raccoon, next the river. I have sent to have the boat at the Narrows raised. Have not heard from there since 9 o'clock. Shall I move the picket from the island? I think it should be guarded, and that the Narrows should also, to keep them from crossing from around Raccoon to this side. Since beginning the above the enemy have opened fire on Fort Whitaker with three heavy guns. They have works casemated, and have the range tolerably well. I think they will endeavor to pass troops over the lower road and the railroad, but I think we can keep them off.

Most respectfully,

W. C. WHITAKER,
Brigadier-General, Commanding.

HEADQUARTERS U. S. FORCES,
Anderson's Cross-Roads, Tenn., October 28, 1863.

Capt. T. W. MORRISON,
Asst. Adjt. Gen., Second Div., Fourteenth Army Corps:

CAPTAIN: A few days since I had the honor of reporting the whereabouts of First Brigade, Second Division, Fourteenth Army Corps. Since then the following change has been made: The Tenth Michigan Infantry has been moved to Smith's Ferry, some 30 miles up the Tennessee from Dallas; the Sixteenth Illinois Infantry to the vicinity of Kelley's Ferry, some 5 miles below Lookout Station; Colonel Smith still in command of the brigade, with headquarters at Dallas. To facilitate the forwarding of supplies, I have ordered part of the brigade train to this point to be used in getting commissary stores from Stevenson to this place and establish a depot here. The roads are perfectly horrible; no one but those passing over them can form any idea of their condition. I am working away here with half of my small force daily on duty assisting trains over the mountain and repairing road.

Very respectfully, your obedient servant,

JAMES D. MORGAN,
Brigadier-General.

GENERAL ORDERS, } WAR DEPT., ADJT. GENERAL'S OFFICE,
No. 350.   }   *Washington, October 28, 1863.*

*   *   *   *   *   *   *

II. Maj. Gen. John M. Palmer, U. S. Volunteers, is assigned to the command of the Fourteenth Army Corps.

By order of the Secretary of War:

E. D. TOWNSEND,
Assistant Adjutant-General.

HDQRS. THIRD BRIG., SECOND DIV., 14TH ARMY CORPS,
October 28, 1863—6.45 p. m.

Major-General REYNOLDS,
        Chief of Staff:

Your order upon communication of Colonel Stanley just came to hand. It is so dark that you can't see your hand. A fire would do no good at this point. The river is so wide it would require a Drummond light of huge capacity. I have only three small canoes here. Colonel Hazen below has none. To-morrow I will send for the boats and do the best I can. They construct their rafts up South Chickamauga Creek, for the banks are so closely patrolled between this point and Hazen's that they cannot make any; moreover, the river bank is almost clear of timber that would afford cover for such work; again the current of the river is so that they would lodge against a point this side of Hazen and the one below him. Citico Creek may also afford them facilities for bridge building.

I am, very respectfully, your obedient servant,

DANIEL McCOOK,
Colonel, Commanding Brigade.

HEADQUARTERS NINETEENTH MICHIGAN REGIMENT,
McMinnville, Tenn., October 28, 1863.

Col. JOHN COBURN,
        Commanding Third Brigade, &c., Tullahoma:

COLONEL: I arrived here with my regiment on Sunday last at 12 m. I found the town in a most deplorable condition. The rebels robbed the citizens of pretty much all they had. And after they left the First East Tennessee Cavalry were sent here, and from what I learn were a nuisance hardly inferior to the rebels. They stabled their horses in public buildings and quartered in the houses. The town is filthy beyond description. I have got soldiers and contrabands at work cleaning up. I have posted a company on each of the main roads leading into town, and am throwing up breast-works for their protection. The place is very defensible, and I think we can hold it against any force that will be likely to attack it. It is commanded, however, by mountains about it, and artillery might after awhile do us much damage. The cavalry all left yesterday. There is a small company of home guards that are worth but little, and about 70 or 80 men in hospital. Supplies are needed for them immediately. We ought to draw our rations in bulk and have a post commissary. I shall want a small supply for contrabands that I have set to work and for some families that I find literally starving. How are we to get rations? Having had no instructions on the subject, I sent a small train to Murfreesborough this morning. We shall be out before they get back.

> Your obedient servant,
>
> H. C. GILBERT,
> *Colonel, Commanding.*

OCTOBER 28, 1863.

General G. M. DODGE, *Corinth:*

I will probably go to-morrow leaving Fuller here, and the divisions at Cherokee and Dickson's will move down to Chickasaw and cross there. Captain Phelps has gone down the Tennessee to hurry up the boats that should have been up some days since.

> W. T. SHERMAN,
> *Major-General.*

IUKA, *October* 28, 1863.

J. B. BINGHAM, *Memphis:*

Bulletin can publish articles of editorial, or when contributed, signed by the writer, favorable or unfavorable to the general policy of the Government, if in proper spirit and designed to do good. Also questions calculated to interest the people of West Tennessee and Arkansas may be discussed pretty freely, but the paper must be held responsible for the truth of every statement of facts, and that the article is calculated to do good and not excite resentment. Try and stop this universal spirit of fault-finding and personality that has brought the press down beneath the contempt of every decent man. Encourage business advertisements, improvements in the arts, narrations of events abroad in the past or, when well authenticated, of the present. In other words, let the Government and its agents do their business in their own way.

> W. T. SHERMAN,
> *Major-General.*

HEADQUARTERS PIONEER BRIGADE,
Shellmound, October 29, 1863—3.15 p. m.

Maj. Gen. J. J. REYNOLDS,
Chief of Staff:

General Cruft was apprised by me of the bridge being constructed while on his march. I have communicated with General Hooker,

who states that he requires General Cruft's force. I have also sent
orders in your name to General Cruft to join General Hooker, crossing the bridge at this place. As soon as he has crossed I will move
the bridge to Rankin's Ferry as ordered, unless you see fit to change
its location to Kelley's Ferry, which General Hooker states he would
prefer if it was left to his choice. It would not be much harder to
move the bridge by water to Kelley's Ferry, provided I had the use
of the steam-boat. It would take about forty-eight hours with the
aid of the steam-boat; without such aid the bridge cannot be moved
in any reasonable time beyond Rankin's Ferry. We cannot now
move [more] than ten boats at a time for want of oars, and the progress against the current is very slow. It is too deep to pole up.
The pontoon teams were so jaded in transporting the bridge to this
place that it will be impracticable, in my opinion, to move the
bridge by land to Rankin's Ferry. I respectfully request that the
steam-boat be ordered to report to me at once.

J. ST. C. MORTON,
Brigadier-General.

BRIDGEPORT, *October* 29, 1863.

Major-General REYNOLDS, *Chief of Staff:*

GENERAL : The steam-boat has now returned, having landed her
rations at Rankin's Ferry, north side, as instructed. The trip is
very fair for the trial trip. Where shall the next cargo be landed?
I have not heard from General Hooker since yesterday morning. He
started with three days' rations, and I sent him 10,000 rations and
6,000 pounds forage by teams yesterday. No forage here to send.
Gardenhire's Ferry, 2 miles above Rankin's, is said to cut off all bad
roads to Chattanooga.

Awaiting instructions,

W. G. LE DUC,
Quartermaster, Eleventh Army Corps.

HEADQUARTERS DEPARTMENT OF THE CUMBERLAND,
Chattanooga, October 29, 1863.

Lieutenant-Colonel LE DUC,
Assistant Quartermaster, Bridgeport:

Transport rations and forage to Kelley's Ferry as fast as you can
with the steamer, and deposit them on the south bank. A commissary of subsistence will be ordered there to receive them.

By command of Major-General Thomas :

J. J. REYNOLDS,
Major-General and Chief of Staff.

HDQRS. FIRST DIVISION, FOURTH ARMY CORPS,
Rankin's Ferry, Tennessee River, Oct. 29, 1863—1.15 p. m.

Major-General REYNOLDS,
Chief of Staff:

GENERAL : Yours of 4 a. m. this date just received. A steamer
has arrived here at, say, 10 a. m. with two barges of rations for General Hooker. I have again dispatched to the general notifying him

of this. There are four communications from myself to General Hooker on way to him, none of which are as yet heard from; I must, however, hear very soon, I think. There has been some cannonading heard in direction of Whiteside's and Raccoon range at intervals since 1 a. m., but not heavy or indicative of any severe engagement, and has now ceased. The officers of the steamer brought me verbal intelligence that General Morton was moving the pontoon to this point. I have sent to General Morton to know if the bridge has been taken up. If it has not, I will move in next hour, and am getting in shape to do this, leaving small guard here to protect the barges, which are on north side of the river at present. I inclose copy of my notes to General Hooker.

Very truly, your obedient servant,

CHARLES CRUFT,
Brigadier-General, Commanding.

[Inclosure No. 1.]

HEADQUARTERS FIRST DIVISION, FOURTH ARMY CORPS,
Rankin's Ferry, Tennessee River, Oct. 28, 1863—10 a. m.

Major-General HOOKER,
Commanding Corps:

GENERAL : Two brigades of this division have arrived at Rankin's Ferry with Simonson's battery, say 3,600 infantry and the battery of six pieces, 12-pounder Parrotts. My orders from Major-General Thomas, commanding Department of the Cumberland, are to "cooperate with Major-General Hooker, who proceeds to the same point via south side of the river." I, therefore, report to you and await any orders.

I am, general, very respectfully, yours,

CHARLES CRUFT,
Brigadier-General, Commanding.

(Original sent via Shellmound at 10 a. m., 28th. Duplicate sent from Rankin's Ferry at 11.30 a. m. Triplicate sent from Rankin's Ferry at 7 a. m. on 29th.)

[Inclosure No. 2.]

HEADQUARTERS FIRST DIVISION, FOURTH ARMY CORPS,
Rankin's Ferry, Tennessee River, Oct. 29, 1863—10 a. m.

Major-General HOOKER :

I have (some hours ago) to-day forwarded you triplicate of my report to you of yesterday. I now have the honor to inform you that I have placed four regiments of my command at Love's Ferry, opposite Shellmound, to strengthen the guard of the pontoon bridge at that point ; that a steam-tug has arrived here with two barges loaded with rations for your command, and that she returns immediately to bring up others. The barges can be placed on the opposite side of the river by time your wagon train reaches here for contents. There is no way to cross river here, however, except by the towage of the steamer. Any details wanted or guards can be furnished from this command. Please be kind enough to send me your orders in the premises.

Very respectfully, yours,

CHARLES CRUFT,
Brigadier-General, Commanding.

HEADQUARTERS FIRST DIVISION, FOURTH CORPS,
Shellmound, Tenn., October 29, 1863—5.30 p. m.

Maj. Gen. J. J. REYNOLDS,
Chief of Staff, Army of the Cumberland :

GENERAL : The head of my column is at Shellmound. I left one regiment (One hundred and first Ohio, Colonel Kirby), at Rankin's Ferry, with one company Sixteenth Illinois and two companies Second Michigan Cavalry, and the four-gun battery (Lieutenant Sahm) to protect the barges of rations and to cover the laying of the pontoon in case of removal. Rankin's Ferry seems to be best point for the bridge, all things considered, and it seems to have been unfortunate that it was not placed there originally. A much smaller force can protect it there than here. My troops are passing to south side of river, as ordered, and General Hooker advised of their position. I am in communication with General Hooker, who was at Brown's Ferry this a. m. My aide-de-camp advises me at 12 m. to-day, from Whiteside's, that General Hooker is at Lookout Mountain and that all is quiet in front. I will await General Hooker's orders or further orders from General Thomas.

I am, very truly, yours,

CHARLES CRUFT,
Brigadier-General, Commanding.

HEADQUARTERS DEPARTMENT OF THE CUMBERLAND,
Chattanooga, October 29, 1863.

Brigadier-General CRUFT,
Rankin's Ferry, via Jasper:

Cross your division on the bridge at Shellmound and join General Hooker's command near Wauhatchie.

By order of Major-General Thomas:

C. GODDARD,
Lieutenant-Colonel and Assistant Adjutant-General.

HEADQUARTERS DEPARTMENT OF THE CUMBERLAND,
Chattanooga, October 29, 1863—5.15 a. m.

Major-General HOOKER:

Have ordered signal party to report to you at once. Have also ordered two additional regiments from Col. Daniel McCook's brigade to move to the bridge and be in readiness if you call upon them.

J. J. REYNOLDS,
Major-General, Chief of Staff.

CORINTH, *October* 30, 1863.

Major-General HURLBUT:

Colonel Fuller reports that rebels followed Engineer regiment to Iuka, burning railroad up to that point. A considerable force is this side of Bear Creek.

G. M. DODGE,
Brigadier-General.

COLLIERVILLE, *October* 30, 1863.

Major-General HURLBUT:

I have just returned. Will be in Memphis to-morrow. Chalmers is at Oxford. His force is scattered from Belmont to Birmingham. He will concentrate and cross the Tallahatchie within five days. He is jerking beef and baking bread for the movement. No force west of the Mobile and Ohio Railroad except Richardson, who is on Cherry Creek, 8 miles north of Pontotoc.

Yours,

BELL.

HEADQUARTERS DEPARTMENT OF THE CUMBERLAND,
Chattanooga, October 31, 1863.

Brigadier-General WHITAKER,
Comdg. Second Brigade, First Division, Fourth Corps:

You will move with your entire brigade to the south side of the river and establish your headquarters at Shellmound, on the road to Trenton, and relieve the forces now there. The latter belong to General Geary's command, and on being relieved by your regiments will rejoin its division. You will take your camp and garrison equipage and sufficient supplies to serve you until you can be resupplied from Bridgeport. You will report at Shellmound to Brig. Gen. Charles Cruft, commanding First Division, Fourth Army Corps.

By command of Major-General Thomas:

J. J. REYNOLDS,
Major-General, Chief of Staff.

CORINTH, *October* 31, 1863.

General HURLBUT:

General Sherman will be all over on Monday, and I shall commence crossing on that day.

G. M. DODGE,
Brigadier-General.

ALTERNATE DESIGNATIONS

OF

ORGANIZATIONS MENTIONED IN THIS VOLUME.*

Abbott's (Ephraim P.) **Artillery.** See *Tennessee Troops, Union, 1st Battalion, Battery A.*

Abercrombie's (John C.) **Infantry.** See *Iowa Troops, 11th Regiment.*

Adams' (Charles H.) **Heavy Artillery.** See *Tennessee Troops, Union, 2d Regiment, Colored.*

Adams' (Robert N.) **Infantry.** See *Ohio Troops, 81st Regiment.*

Adams' (Silas) **Cavalry.** See *Kentucky Troops, Union, 1st Regiment.*

Adams' (Wirt) **Cavalry.** See *Mississippi Troops, Confederate.*

Aiken's (D. Wyatt) **Infantry.** See *South Carolina Troops, 7th Regiment.*

Aiken's (John A.) **Infantry.** See *Tennessee Troops, Confederate, 63d Regiment.*

Aldrich's (Simeon C.) **Infantry.** See *Indiana Troops, 44th Regiment.*

Aleshire's (Charles C.) **Artillery.** See *Ohio Troops, 18th Battery.*

Alexander's (James M.) **Infantry.** See *Alabama Troops, Union, 1st Regiment, Colored.*

Alger's (Amos B.) **Artillery.** See *Ohio Troops, 22d Battery.*

Allen's (Samuel T.) **Infantry.** See *New York Troops, 145th Regiment.*

Amsberg's (George von) **Infantry.** See *New York Troops, 45th Regiment.*

Anderson Cavalry. See *Pennsylvania Troops, 15th Regiment.*

Anderson's (Paul F.) **Cavalry.** See *Baxter Smith's Cavalry, post.*

Anderson's (William B.) **Infantry.** See *Illinois Troops, 60th Regiment.*

Anthony's (De Witt C.) **Infantry.** See *Indiana Troops, 66th Regiment.*

Armstrong's (Robert H.) **Infantry.** See *Kentucky Troops, Union, 6th Regiment.*

Arndt's (Albert F. R.) **Artillery.** See *Michigan Troops, 1st Regiment, Battery B.*

Ashby's (H. M.) **Cavalry.** See *Tennessee Troops, Confederate.*

Ashland Artillery. See *Virginia Troops.*

Askew's (Frank) **Infantry.** See *Ohio Troops, 15th Regiment.*

Atkins' (Smith D.) **Infantry.** See *Illinois Troops, 92d Regiment.*

Atwell's (Charles A.) **Artillery.** See *Pennsylvania Troops, Battery E.*

Avery's (Isaac W.) **Cavalry.** See *Georgia Troops, 4th Regiment (Avery's).*

Ayres' (Oliver H. P.) **Artillery.** See *Ohio Troops, 6th Battery.*

Babcock's (Walter S.) **Heavy Artillery.** See *Wisconsin Troops, 1st Regiment, Battery B.*

Bacon's (George A.) **Cavalry.** See *Illinois Troops, 15th Regiment.*

Bacon's (George M.) **Infantry.** See *Ohio Troops, 24th Regiment.*

Bainbridge's (Edmund C.) **Artillery.** See *Union Troops, Regulars, 5th Regiment, Battery K.*

Baird's (John P.) **Infantry.** See *Indiana Troops, 85th Regiment.*

Baker's (Volney) **Infantry.** See *Kentucky Troops, Union, 35th Regiment.*

Baldwin's (Norman A.) **Artillery.** See *Ohio Troops, 1st Regiment, Battery B.*

Ball's (Edward) **Infantry.** See *Georgia Troops, 51st Regiment.*

Ballinger's (Richard H.) **Infantry.** See *Mississippi Troops, Union, 3d Regiment.*

Banbury's (Jabez) **Infantry.** See *Iowa Troops,* 5th *Regiment.*

Bancroft's (Eugene A.) **Artillery.** See *Union Troops, Regulars,* 4th *Regiment, Battery G.*

Barber's (Gershom M.) **Sharpshooters.** See *Ohio Troops,* 5th *Company.*

Barclay's (E. S.) **Infantry.** See *Phillips Legion, post.*

Barksdale's (James A.) **Cavalry.** See *Mississippi Troops, Confederate,* 5th *Regiment.*

Barnes' (Sidney M.) **Infantry.** See *Kentucky Troops, Union,* 8th *Regiment.*

Barnett's (Charles M.) **Artillery.** See *Illinois Troops,* 2d *Regiment, Battery I.*

Barnum's (William L.) **Infantry.** See *Missouri Troops, Union,* 11th *Regiment.*

Barret's (Overton W.) **Artillery.** See *Missouri Troops, Confederate.*

Barrett's (Wallace W.) **Infantry.** See *Illinois Troops,* 44th *Regiment.*

Bart's Cavalry. Official designation r ot of record. See ―――― *Bart.*

Bartleson's (Frederick A.) **Infantry.** See *Illinois Troops,* 100th *Regiment.*

Barton's (Charles A.) **Sharpshooters.** See *Ohio Troops,* 8th *Company.*

Baumbach's (Carl von) **Infantry.** See *Wisconsin Troops,* 24th *Regiment.*

Bean's (Onslow) **Cavalry.** See *James E. Carter's Cavalry, post.*

Beardsley's (John D.) **Infantry.** See *Maine Troops,* 10th *Regiment.*

Beck's (Arnold) **Infantry.** See *Missouri Troops, Union,* 2d *Regiment.*

Beck's (Benjamin) **Infantry.** See *Georgia Troops,* 9th *Regiment.*

Bedford Artillery. See *Virginia Troops.*

Bedtelyon's (Jacob) **Cavalry.** See *Michigan Troops,* 4th *Regiment.*

Beebe's (Yates V.) **Artillery.** See *Wisconsin Troops,* 10th *Battery.*

Belknap's (William W.) **Infantry.** See *Iowa Troops,* 15th *Regiment.*

Bell's (Leroy S.) **Infantry.** See *Ohio Troops,* 3d *Regiment.*

Bell's (William B.) **Infantry.** See *Iowa Troops,* 8th *Regiment.*

Belt's (Jonathan) **Cavalry.** See *Kentucky Troops, Union,* 15th *Regiment.*

Benjamin's (Samuel N.) **Artillery.** See *Union Troops, Regulars,* 2d *Regiment, Battery E.*

Benson's (Rufus S.) **Infantry.** See *Iowa Troops,* 32d *Regiment.*

Berkey's (John M.) **Infantry.** See *Indiana Troops,* 99th *Regiment.*

Biddle's (James) **Cavalry.** See *Indiana Troops,* 6th *Regiment.*

Biffle's (Jacob B.) **Cavalry.** See *Tennessee Troops, Confederate.*

Biggs' (Jonathan) **Infantry.** See *Illinois Troops,* 123d *Regiment.*

Birch's (William) **Infantry.** See *Ohio Troops,* 93d *Regiment.*

Bishop's (Judson W.) **Infantry.** See *Minnesota Troops,* 2d *Regiment.*

Bishop's (Loomis K.) **Infantry.** See *Michigan Troops,* 21st *Regiment.*

Bissell's (Josiah W.) **Engineers.** See *Missouri Troops, Union.*

Blake's (John W.) **Infantry.** See *Indiana Troops,* 40th *Regiment.*

Blakey's (D. T.) **Cavalry.** See *Alabama Troops, Confederate,* 1st *Regiment.*

Blanden's (Leander) **Infantry.** See *Illinois Troops,* 95th *Regiment.*

Blessingh's (Louis von) **Infantry.** See *Ohio Troops,* 37th *Regiment.*

Bolton's (William H.) **Artillery.** See *Illinois Troops,* 2d *Regiment, Battery L.*

Bolton's (William J.) **Infantry.** See *Pennsylvania Troops,* 51st *Regiment.*

Bonnaffon's (Augustus B.) **Infantry.** See *Pennsylvania Troops,* 78th *Regiment.*

Boone's (William P.) **Infantry.** See *Kentucky Troops, Union,* 28th *Regiment.*

Bouck's (Gabriel) **Infantry.** See *Wisconsin Troops,* 18th *Regiment.*

Boughton's (Horace) **Infantry.** See *New York Troops,* 143d *Regiment.*

Bounds' (J. M.) **Cavalry.** See *Texas Troops,* 11th *Regiment.*

Boutell's (Ira) **Infantry.** See *Missouri Troops, Union,* 6th *Regiment.*

Bowles' (Pinckney D.) **Infantry.** See *Alabama Troops, Confederate,* 4th *Regiment.*

Bowman's (Daniel) **Infantry.** See *Ohio Troops,* 93d *Regiment.*

Bowman's (George H.) **Infantry.** See *Ohio Troops,* 102d *Regiment.*

Boyd's (Carlisle) **Infantry.** See *Union Troops, Veteran Reserve Corps.*

Brady's (Thomas J.) **Infantry.** See *Indiana Troops,* 117th *Regiment.*

Brandon's (William L.) **Infantry.** See *Mississippi Troops, Confederate,* 21st *Regiment.*

Bratton's (John) **Infantry.** See *South Carolina Troops,* 6th *Regiment.*
Brennan's (John) **Infantry.** See *Kentucky Troops, Union,* 3d *Regiment.*
Bridges' (Lyman) **Artillery.** See *Illinois Troops.*
Britton's (William B.) **Infantry.** See *Wisconsin Troops,* 8th *Regiment.*
Brooks Artillery. See *South Carolina Troops.*
Brott's (Elijah C.) **Infantry.** See *Illinois Troops,* 83d *Regiment.*
Brown's (George R.) **Artillery.** See *Indiana Troops,* 9th *Battery.*
Brown's (Jack) **Infantry.** See *Georgia Troops,* 59th *Regiment.*
Brown's (Orlando, jr.) **Infantry.** See *Kentucky Troops, Union,* 14th *Regiment.*
Brown's (Oscar F.) **Cavalry.** See *Missouri Troops, Union (Mississippi Marine Brigade),* 1st *Battalion.*
Brown's (Thomas G.) **Infantry.** See *Indiana Troops,* 65th *Regiment.*
Brown's (William B.) **Infantry.** See *Ohio Troops,* 70th *Regiment.*
Brown's (William R.) **Infantry.** See *New York Troops,* 168th *Regiment.*
Browne's (William H.) **Infantry.** See *Virginia Troops,* 45th *Regiment.*
Brownlow's (James P.) **Cavalry.** See *Tennessee Troops, Union,* 1st *Regiment.*
Bruhn's (Anton) **Infantry.** See *New York Troops,* 8th *Regiment.*
Brumback's (Jefferson) **Infantry.** See *Ohio Troops,* 95th *Regiment.*
Bryant's (George E.) **Infantry.** See *Wisconsin Troops,* 12th *Regiment.*
Bryson's (Goldman) **Cavalry.** See *Tennessee Troops, Union.*
Buckley's (William W.) **Artillery.** See *Rhode Island Troops,* 1st *Regiment, Battery D.*
Buckner's (Allen) **Infantry.** See *Illinois Troops,* 79th *Regiment.*
Budd's (Joseph L.) **Infantry.** See *Ohio Troops,* 35th *Regiment.*
Buell's (George P.) **Infantry.** See *Indiana Troops,* 58th *Regiment.*
Bulger's (M. J.) **Infantry.** See *Alabama Troops, Confederate,* 47th *Regiment.*
Bullitt's (William A.) **Infantry.*** See *Ohio Troops,* 65th *Regiment.*
Burgh's (Henry B.) **Cavalry.** See *Illinois Troops,* 9th *Regiment.*
Burke's (Patrick E.) **Infantry.** See *Illinois Troops,* 66th *Regiment.*
Burroughs' (William H.) **Artillery.** See *Rhett Artillery, post.*
Burrows' (Hamilton H.) **Artillery.** See *Ohio Troops,* 14th *Battery.*
Burton's (George) **Infantry.** See *Iowa Troops,* 4th *Regiment.*
Butler's (Thomas H.) **Cavalry.** See *Indiana Troops,* 5th *Regiment.*
Butt's (Edgar M.) **Infantry.** See *Georgia Troops,* 2d *Regiment.*
Byington's (Cornelius) **Infantry.** See *Michigan Troops,* 2d *Regiment.*
Byrd's (Robert K) **Infantry.** See *Tennessee Troops, Union,* 1st *Regiment.*
Cahill's (James B.) **Infantry.** See *Illinois Troops,* 16th *Regiment.*
Call's (Charles H.) **Infantry.** See *Illinois Troops,* 29th *Regiment.*
Callender's (Byron M.) **Artillery.** See *Missouri Troops, Union,* 1st *Regiment, Battery D.*
Callicott's (John A.) **Infantry.** See *Illinois Troops,* 29th *Regiment.*
Campbell's (Calvin D.) **Infantry.** See *Indiana Troops,* 6th *Regiment.*
Campbell's (Franklin) **Infantry.** See *Illinois Troops,* 81st *Regiment.*
Capron's (Horace) **Cavalry.** See *Illinois Troops,* 14th *Regiment.*
Carman's (Ezra A.) **Infantry.** See *New Jersey Troops,* 13th *Regiment.*
Carpenter's (Daniel A.) **Infantry.** See *Tennessee Troops, Union,* 2d *Regiment.*
Carskaddon's (David) **Infantry.** See *Iowa Troops,* 9th *Regiment.*
Carter's (James E.) **Cavalry.** See *Tennessee Troops, Confederate.*
Case's (Henry) **Infantry.** See *Illinois Troops,* 129th *Regiment.*
Casement's (John S.) **Infantry.** See *Ohio Troops,* 103d *Regiment.*
Catterson's (Robert F.) **Infantry.** See *Indiana Troops,* 97th *Regiment.*
Chalmers' (A. H.) **Cavalry.** See *Mississippi Troops, Confederate,* 18th *Battalion.*
Champion's (Thomas E.) **Infantry.** See *Illinois Troops,* 96th *Regiment.*
Chandler's (George W.) **Infantry.** See *Illinois Troops,* 88th *Regiment.*
Chandler's (William P.) **Infantry.** See *Illinois Troops,* 35th *Regiment.*

---

* Temporarily commanding.

Chapman's (Charles W.) Infantry. See *Indiana Troops, 74th Regiment.*
Chapman's (Fletcher H.) Artillery. See *Illinois Troops, 2d Regiment, Battery B.*
Cheney's (John T.) Artillery. See *Illinois Troops, 1st Regiment, Battery F.*
Chess' (William E.) Artillery. See *Indiana Troops, 21st Battery.*
Chew's (Robert S.) Infantry. See *Virginia Troops, 30th Regiment.*
Chicago Board of Trade Artillery. See *Illinois Troops.*
Childress' (James A.) Artillery. See *Tennessee Troops, Union, 1st Battalion, Battery B.*
Christopher's (Alexander C.) Infantry. See *Ohio Troops, 6th Regiment.*
Church's (Josiah W.) Artillery. See *Michigan Troops, 1st Regiment, Battery D.*
Claiborne's (James R.) Cavalry. See *Virginia Troops, 37th Battalion.*
Clark's (Andrew H.) Infantry. See *Kentucky Troops, Union, 47th Regiment.*
Clark's (Samuel F.) Artillery. See *Wisconsin Troops, 6th Battery.*
Clarke's (Edward Y.) Cavalry. See *Georgia Troops, 16th Battalion.*
Clarke's (J. Lyle) Infantry. See *Virginia Troops, 30th Battalion.*
Clay's (Ezekiel F.) Cavalry. See *Kentucky Troops, Confederate, 3d. Battalion Rifles.*
Clayton's (William Z.) Artillery. See *Minnesota Troops, 1st Battery.*
Coates' (James H.) Infantry. See *Illinois Troops, 11th Regiment.*
Cobb's Legion. See *Georgia Troops.*
Coburn's (John) Infantry. See *Indiana Troops, 33d Regiment.*
Cochran's (James) Cavalry. See *Virginia Troops, 14th Regiment.*
Cockerill's (Giles J.) Artillery. See *Ohio Troops, 1st Regiment, Battery F.*
Cogswell's (Leander W.) Infantry. See *New Hampshire Troops, 11th Regiment.*
Cogswell's (William) Artillery. See *Illinois Troops.*
Cogswell's (William) Infantry. See *Massachusetts Troops, 2d Regiment.*
Cole's (Amos B.) Heavy Artillery. See *Ohio Troops, 1st Regiment.*
Coleman's (David C.) Infantry. See *Missouri Troops, Union, 8th Regiment.*
Colgrove's (Silas) Infantry. See *Indiana Troops, 27th Regiment.*
Colvin's (John H.) Artillery. See *Illinois Troops.*
Comstock's (Lorin L.) Infantry. See *Michigan Troops, 17th Regiment.*
Conant's (Ellis) Artillery. See *Ohio Troops, 7th Battery.*
Conant's (John H.) Artillery. See *Missouri Troops, Union, 1st Regiment, Battery H.*
Connell's (John M.) Infantry. See *Ohio Troops, 17th Regiment.*
Conrad's (Joseph) Infantry. See *Missouri Troops, Union, 15th Regiment.*
Conyers' (William D.) Infantry. See *Cobb's Legion, ante.*
Cook's (Gustave) Cavalry. See *Texas Troops, 8th Regiment.*
Cook's (John B.) Artillery. See *Kansas Troops, 1st Battery.*
Cooper's (Charles S.) Artillery. See *Illinois Troops, 2d Regiment, Battery D.*
Cooper's (Joseph A.) Infantry. See *Tennessee Troops, Union, 6th Regiment.*
Cooper's (Wickliffe) Cavalry. See *Kentucky Troops, Union, 4th Regiment.*
Corns' (James M.) Cavalry. See *Virginia Troops, 8th Regiment.*
Coward's (A.) Infantry. See *South Carolina Troops, 5th Regiment.*
Cox's (Nicholas N.) Cavalry. See *Tennessee Troops, Confederate.*
Cram's (George H.) Infantry. See *Kentucky Troops, Union, 9th Regiment.*
Cramer's (John F.) Infantry. See *Missouri Troops, Union, 17th Regiment.*
Crandal's (Frederick M.) Infantry. See *Louisiana Troops, Union, 10th Regiment (Colored).*
Crane's (Nirom M.) Infantry. See *New York Troops, 107th Regiment.*
Crawford's (John A.) Infantry. See *Georgia Troops, 18th Regiment.*
Creighton's (William R.) Infantry. See *Ohio Troops, 7th Regiment.*
Crofton's (Robert E. A.) Infantry. See *Union Troops, Regulars, 16th Regiment, 1st Battalion.*
Crosley's (George W.) Infantry. See *Iowa Troops, 3d Regiment.*
Cross' (William) Infantry. See *Tennessee Troops, Union, 3d Regiment.*
Cudney's (Albert) Artillery. See *Illinois Troops, 1st Regiment, Battery I.*

Culbertson's (James L.) **Infantry.** See *Indiana Troops,* 80th *Regiment.*

Culver's (Joshua B.) **Infantry.** See *Michigan Troops,* 13th *Regiment.*

Cummings' (Henry J. B.) **Infantry.** See *Iowa Troops,* 39th *Regiment.*

Cummins' (John E.) **Infantry.** See *Ohio Troops,* 99th *Regiment.*

Curly's (Thomas) **Infantry.** See *Missouri Troops, Union,* 27th *Regiment.*

Curtis' (Isaac W.) **Artillery.** See *Illinois Troops,* 1st *Regiment, Battery K.*

Curtiss' (Frank S.) **Infantry.** See *Illinois Troops,* 127th *Regiment.*

Cushing's (Harry C.) **Artillery.** See *Union Troops, Regulars,* 4th *Regiment, Battery H.*

Cutcheon's (Byron M.) **Infantry.** See *Michigan Troops,* 20th *Regiment.*

Dachsel's (Gustave) **Artillery.** See *Illinois Troops,* 1st *Regiment, Battery G.*

Daugherty's (Ferdinand H.) **Cavalry.** See *George G. Dibrell's Cavalry, post.*

Davenport's (Stephen) **Cavalry.** See *Mississippi Troops, Confederate.*

David's (James I.) **Cavalry.** See *Michigan Troops,* 9th *Regiment.*

Davidson's (George S.) **Artillery.** See *Virginia Troops.*

Davidson's (James I.) **Infantry.** See *Illinois Troops,* 73d *Regiment.*

Davis' (Charles W.) **Infantry.** See *Illinois Troops,* 51st *Regiment.*

Davis' (William P.) **Infantry.** See *Indiana Troops,* 23d *Regiment.*

Davitte's (S. W.) **Cavalry.** See *Georgia Troops,* 1st *Regiment.*

Dawley's (Richard L.) **Artillery.** See *Minnesota Troops,* 2d *Battery.*

Dawson's (Mathew M.) **Infantry.** See *Pennsylvania Troops,* 100th *Regiment.*

Dayton's (James H.) **Infantry.** See *West Virginia Troops,* 4th *Regiment.*

Dean's (Benjamin D.) **Infantry.** See *Missouri Troops, Union,* 26th *Regiment.*

Dean's (Henry S.) **Infantry.** See *Michigan Troops,* 22d *Regiment.*

Dearborn's (Abraham T.) **Heavy Artillery.** See *Tennessee Troops, Union,* 2d *Regiment (Colored).*

De Gress' (Francis) **Artillery.** See *Illinois Troops,* 1st *Regiment, Battery H.*

Deimling's (Francis C.) **Infantry.** See *Missouri Troops, Union,* 10th *Regiment.*

Demarest's (Samuel L.) **Infantry** See *Michigan Troops,* 25th *Regiment.*

Dement's (Curtin) **Cavalry.** See *Illinois Troops,* 2d *Regiment.*

Denning's (Benjamin F.) **Artillery.** See *Indiana Troops,* 22d *Battery.*

Devol's (Hiram F.) **Infantry.** See *Ohio Troops,* 36th *Regiment.*

Deweese's (John T.) **Cavalry.** See *Indiana Troops,* 4th *Regiment.*

Dibrell's (George G.) **Cavalry.** See *Tennessee Troops, Confederate.*

Dick's (George F.) **Infantry.** See *Indiana Troops,* 86th *Regiment.*

Dickenson's (Crispin) **Artillery.** See *Ringgold Artillery, post.*

Dickerman's (Willard A.) **Infantry.** See *Illinois Troops,* 103d *Regiment.*

Dickerson's (Christopher J.) **Infantry.** See *Michigan Troops,* 10th *Regiment.*

Dickson's (Samuel) **Infantry.** See *Union Troops, Veteran Reserve Corps,* 5th *Regiment.*

Dilger's (Hubert) **Artillery.** See *Ohio Troops,* 1st *Regiment, Battery I.*

Dillard's (John H.) **Infantry.** See *Hilliard's Legion,* 2d *Battalion, post.*

Dilworth's (Caleb J.) **Infantry.** See *Illinois Troops,* 85th *Regiment.*

Doan's (Thomas) **Infantry.** See *Indiana Troops,* 101st *Regiment.*

Dodds' (Ozro J.) **Cavalry.** See *Alabama Troops, Union,* 1st *Regiment.*

Donald's (G. L.) **Infantry.** See *Mississippi Troops, Confederate,* 13th *Regiment.*

Doolittle's (Charles C.) **Infantry.** See *Michigan Troops,* 18th *Regiment.*

Dornblaser's (Benjamin) **Infantry.** See *Illinois Troops,* 46th *Regiment.*

Dow's (Tristram T.) **Infantry.** See *Illinois Troops,* 112th *Regiment.*

Downs' (Edward C.) **Infantry.** See *Ohio Troops,* 20th *Regiment.*

Draper's (William F.) **Infantry.** See *Massachusetts Troops,* 36th *Regiment.*

Driscoll's (Daniel) **Infantry.** See *Missouri Troops, Union,* 24th *Regiment.*

Du Bose's (Dudley M.) **Infantry.** See *Georgia Troops,* 15th *Regiment.*

Duckworth's (W. L.) **Cavalry.** See *Tennessee Troops, Confederate.*

Dunlevy's (James A.) **Artillery.** See *Pennsylvania Troops, Battery E.*

Dunn's (David M.) **Infantry.** See *Indiana Troops,* 29th *Regiment.*

Durand's (Charles M.) **Artillery.** See *Michigan Troops, 1st Regiment, Battery E.*
Dustin's (Daniel) **Infantry.** See *Illinois Troops, 105th Regiment.*
Earl's (R. G.) **Cavalry.** See *Alabama Troops, Confederate, 2d Regiment.*
Eastman's (Harry E.) **Cavalry.** See *Wisconsin Troops, 2d Regiment.*
Edgarton's (Warren P.) **Artillery.** See *Ohio Troops, 1st Regiment, Battery E.*
Edgerly's (Henry C.) **Cavalry.** See *Michigan Troops, 8th Regiment.*
Edie's (John R.) **Infantry.** See *Union Troops, Regulars, 15th Regiment, 2d Battalion.*
Edmundson's (Henry A.) **Cavalry.** See *Virginia Troops, 27th Battalion.*
Edwards' (Charles G.) **Infantry.** See *Ohio Troops, 105th Regiment.*
Edwards' (John, jr.) **Artillery.** See *Union Troops, Regulars, 3d Regiment, Batteries L and M.*
Elgin Artillery. See *Illinois Troops.*
Elliott's (Marcus D.) **Artillery.** See *Michigan Troops, 1st Regiment, Battery H.*
Ellis' (John) **Infantry.** See *Tennessee Troops, Union, 1st Regiment.*
Elstner's (George R.) **Infantry.** See *Ohio Troops, 50th Regiment.*
Ely's (John J.) **Artillery.** See *Michigan Troops, 1st Regiment, Battery E.*
Ely's (Ralph) **Infantry.** See *Michigan Troops, 8th Regiment.*
Engineer Battalion, 23d Army Corps. See *Oliver S. McClure.*
Erdelmeyer's (Frank) **Infantry.** See *Indiana Troops, 32d Regiment.*
Erwin's (Samuel C.) **Infantry.** See *Ohio Troops, 6th Regiment.*
Esembaux's (Michael) **Infantry.** See *New York Troops, 58th Regiment.*
Eve's (John G.) **Infantry.** See *Kentucky Troops, Union, 49th Regiment.*
Ewing's (Frank M.) **Infantry.** See *Alabama Troops, Union, 1st Regiment (Colored).*
Ewing's (Martin B.) **Heavy Artillery.** See *Ohio Troops, 2d Regiment.*
Faulkner's (John K.) **Cavalry.** See *Kentucky Troops, Union, 7th Regiment.*
Ferguson's (Milton J.) **Cavalry.** See *Virginia Troops, 16th Regiment.*
Fickling's (William W.) **Artillery.** See *Brooks Artillery, ante.*
Fiser's (John C.) **Infantry.** See *Mississippi Troops, Confederate, 17th Regiment.*
Fisher's (Joseph) **Infantry.** See *Ohio Troops, 74th Regiment.*
Fitch's (John A.) **Artillery.** See *Illinois Troops, 1st Regiment, Battery E.*
Fitch's (William T.) **Infantry.** See *Ohio Troops, 29th Regiment.*
Fitz Gibbon's (Thomas C.) **Infantry.** See *Michigan Troops, 14th Regiment.*
Flad's (Henry) **Engineers.** See *Josiah W. Bissell's Engineers, ante.*
Fletcher's (Thomas C.) **Infantry.** See *Missouri Troops, Union, 31st Regiment.*
Flood's (James P.) **Artillery.** See *Illinois Troops, 2d Regiment, Battery C.*
Floyd's (Watt W.) **Infantry.** See *Tennessee Troops, Confederate, 17th and 23d Regiments.*
Flynn's (John) **Infantry.** See *Pennsylvania Troops, 28th Regiment.*
Folk's (George N.) **Cavalry.** See *North Carolina Troops, Confederate, 6th Regiment.*
Forsberg's (Augustus) **Infantry.** See *Virginia Troops, 51st Regiment.*
Foster's (John S.) **Cavalry.** See *Ohio Troops, 4th Company.*
Foulk's (William L.) **Infantry.** See *Pennsylvania Troops, 46th Regiment.*
Fox's (Charles H.) **Infantry.** See *Illinois Troops, 101st Regiment.*
Fox's (Perrin V.) **Engineers.** See *Michigan Troops, 1st Regiment.*
Foy's (James C.) **Infantry.** See *Kentucky Troops, Union, 23d Regiment.*
Freeman's (S. L.) **Artillery.** See *A. L. Huggins' Artillery, post.*
Froelich's (George) **Artillery.** See *Ohio Troops, 4th Battery.*
Fulton's (Robert A.) **Infantry.** See *Ohio Troops, 53d Regiment.*
Fyffe's (Edward P.) **Infantry.** See *Ohio Troops, 26th Regiment.*
Gaines' (Thomas W.) **Infantry.** See *Illinois Troops, 50th Regiment.*
Gambee's (Charles B.) **Infantry.** See *Ohio Troops, 55th Regiment.*
Garrard's (Israel) **Cavalry.** See *Ohio Troops, 7th Regiment.*
Garten's (Zimry V.) **Infantry.** See *Indiana Troops, 91st Regiment.*
Gary's (Marco B.) **Artillery.** See *Ohio Troops, 1st Regiment, Battery C.*
Gary's (Martin W.) **Infantry.** See *Hampton Legion, post.*

Gault's (James W.) **Infantry.** See *Kentucky Troops, Union,* 16th *Regiment.*

Geary's (Edward R.) **Artillery.** See *Pennsylvania Troops, Battery E.*

George's (J. Z.) **Cavalry.** See *Mississippi Troops, Confederate,* 5th *Regiment.*

Gibson's (Horatio G.) **Heavy Artillery.** See *Ohio Troops,* 2d *Regiment.*

Gifford's (Ira R.) **Cavalry.** See *Illinois Troops,* 9th *Regiment.*

Gilbert's (Henry C.) **Infantry.** See *Michigan Troops,* 19th *Regiment.*

Giles' (James) **Infantry.** See *Virginia Troops,* 29th *Regiment.*

Gillespie's (Hamilton S.) **Infantry.** See *Ohio Troops,* 50th *Regiment.*

Gillmore's (Robert A.) **Infantry.** See *Illinois Troops,* 26th *Regiment.*

Gimber's (Frederick L.) **Infantry.** See *Pennsylvania Troops,* 109th *Regiment.*

Gist's (Joseph F.) **Infantry.** See *South Carolina Troops,* 15th *Regiment.*

Gist's (William M.) **Infantry.** See *South Carolina Troops,* 15th *Regiment.*

Gittings' (Erskine) **Artillery.** See *Union Troops, Regulars,* 3d *Regiment, Batteries L and M.*

Gleason's (Newell) **Infantry.** See *Indiana Troops,* 87th *Regiment.*

Glenn's (Luther J.) **Infantry.** See *Cobb's Legion, ante.*

Godard's (Abel) **Infantry.** See *New York Troops,* 60th *Regiment.*

Goggans' (E. J.) **Infantry.** See *South Carolina Troops,* 7th *Regiment.*

Gooding's (Michael) **Infantry.** See *Indiana Troops,* 22d *Regiment.*

Goodrich's (John C.) **Infantry.** See *Wisconsin Troops,* 1st *Regiment.*

Goodspeed's (Wilbur F.) **Artillery.** See *Ohio Troops,* 1st *Regiment, Battery A.*

Gorgas' (Adam B.) **Infantry.** See *Illinois Troops,* 13th *Regiment.*

Graham's (Felix W.) **Cavalry.** See *Indiana Troops,* 5th *Regiment.*

Gray's (Horace) **Cavalry.** See *Michigan Troops,* 4th *Regiment.*

Gray's (Samuel F.) **Infantry.** See *Ohio Troops,* 49th *Regiment.*

Greathouse's (Lucien) **Infantry.** See *Illinois Troops,* 48th *Regiment.*

Green's (George) **Infantry.** See *Illinois Troops,* 78th *Regiment.*

Green's (John U.) **Cavalry.** See *Robert V. Richardson's Cavalry, post.*

Greenwood's (Charles) **Infantry.** See *Ohio Troops,* 38th *Regiment.*

Griffin's (Daniel F.) **Infantry.** See *Indiana Troops,* 38th *Regiment.*

Griffin's (Thomas M.) **Infantry.** See *Mississippi Troops, Confederate,* 18th *Regiment.*

Griffiths' (Henry H.) **Artillery.** See *Iowa Troops,* 1st *Battery.*

Grinager's (Mons) **Infantry.** See *Wisconsin Troops,* 15th *Regiment.*

Gwynne's (A. D.) **Infantry.** See *Tennessee Troops, Confederate,* 38th *Regiment.*

Hadlock's (Alva R.) **Infantry.** See *Kentucky Troops, Union,* 1st *Regiment.*

Hale's (Francis E.) **Artillery.** See *Michigan Troops,* 1st *Regiment, Battery A.*

Hale's (Luther F.) **Artillery.** See *Michigan Troops,* 1st *Regiment, Battery F.*

Hall's (Hiram W.) **Infantry.** See *Illinois Troops,* 40th *Regiment.*

Halpin's (William G.) **Infantry.** See *Kentucky Troops, Union,* 15th *Regiment.*

Ham's (T. W.) **Cavalry.** See *Mississippi Troops, Confederate.*

Hambrick's (J. M.) **Cavalry.** See *Alabama Troops, Confederate,* 4th *Regiment.*

Hamilton's (Joseph) **Infantry.** See *Phillips Legion, post.*

Hamilton's (William D.) **Cavalry.** See *Ohio Troops,* 9th *Regiment.*

Hammerstein's (Herbert von) **Infantry.** See *New York Troops,* 78th *Regiment.*

Hampson's (James B.) **Infantry.** See *Ohio Troops,* 124th *Regiment.*

Hampton Legion. See *South Carolina Troops.*

Hardiman's (Thomas W.) **Infantry.** See *Kentucky Troops, Union,* 23d *Regiment.*

Hare's (Christopher C.) **Infantry.** See *Kentucky Troops, Union,* 34th *Regiment.*

Hargrave's (William P.) **Infantry.** See *Indiana Troops,* 91st *Regiment.*

Harmon's (Oscar F.) **Infantry.** See *Illinois Troops,* 125th *Regiment.*

Harney's (Selby) **Infantry.** See *Kentucky Troops, Union,* 34th *Regiment.*

Harris' (Samuel J.) **Artillery.** See *Indiana Troops,* 19th *Battery.*

Harris' (William C.) **Infantry.** See *Illinois Troops,* 38th *Regiment.*

Harris' (William C.) **Infantry.** See *South Carolina Troops,* 3d *Battalion.*

Harrison's (Benjamin) **Infantry.** See *Indiana Troops,* 70th *Regiment.*

Harrison's (Thomas J.) **Infantry.**   See *Indiana Troops, 39th Regiment.*
Hart's (John R.) **Cavalry.**   See *Georgia Troops, 6th Regiment.*
Hawes' (John J.) **Artillery.**   See *Kentucky Troops, Union, Battery E.*
Hawkes' (George P.) **Infantry.**   See *Massachusetts Troops, 21st Regiment.*
Hawkins' (Isaac R.) **Cavalry.**   See *Tennessee Troops, Union, 7th Regiment.*
Hawley's (Chauncey G.) **Heavy Artillery.**   See *Ohio Troops, 1st Regiment.*
Hawley's (William) **Infantry.**   See *Wisconsin Troops, 3d Regiment.*
Hawn's (Alfred J.) **Infantry.**   See *Indiana Troops, 115th Regiment.*
Haymond's (Henry) **Infantry.**   See *Union Troops, Regulars, 18th Regiment, 2d Battalion.*
Hays' (Jacob H.) **Cavalry.**   See *Tennessee Troops, Union, 7th Regiment.*
Hays' (William H.) **Infantry.**   See *Kentucky Troops, Union, 10th Regiment.*
Hazletine's (Ross J.) **Infantry.**   See *Ohio Troops, 69th Regiment.*
Heath's (Albert) **Infantry.**   See *Indiana Troops, 100th Regiment.*
Heath's (Thomas T.) **Cavalry.**   See *Ohio Troops, 5th Regiment.*
Heinrichs' (Gustav) **Cavalry.**   See *Missouri Troops, Union, 4th Regiment.*
Henagan's (John W.) **Infantry.**   See *South Carolina Troops, 8th Regiment.*
Henderson's (James M.) **Infantry.**   See *Indiana Troops, 33d Regiment.*
Henderson's (M. J.) **Cavalry.**   See *Arkansas Troops, Confederate, 3d Regiment.*
Henderson's (Paris P.) **Infantry.**   See *Iowa Troops, 10th Regiment.*
Henry's (Edward P.) **Infantry.**   See *Ohio Troops, 89th Regiment.*
Henry's (Samuel) **Infantry.**   See *Indiana Troops, 89th Regiment.*
Henshaw's (Edward C.) **Artillery.**   See *Illinois Troops.*
Hepburn's (William P.) **Cavalry.**   See *Iowa Troops, 2d Regiment.*
Herrick's (Thomas P.) **Cavalry.**   See *Kansas Troops, 7th Regiment.*
Hewett's (John M.) **Artillery.**   See *Kentucky Troops, Union, Battery B.*
Hill's (John L.) **Artillery.**   See *Ohio Troops, 24th Battery.*
Hill's (Sylvester G.) **Infantry.**   See *Iowa Troops, 35th Regiment.*
Hilliard's Legion.   See *Alabama Troops, Confederate.*
Hillier's (Edward G.) **Artillery.**   See *Michigan Troops, 1st Regiment, Battery M.*
Hills' (Francis M.) **Infantry.**   See *Pennsylvania Troops, 45th Regiment.*
Hoblitzell's (William T.) **Cavalry.**   See *Kentucky Troops, Union, 5th Regiment.*
Hobson's (William E.) **Infantry.**   See *Kentucky Troops, Union, 13th Regiment.*
Hodge's (Walter G.) **Infantry.**   See *Indiana Troops, 65th Regiment.*
Hodges' (Wesley C.) **Infantry.**   See *Georgia Troops, 17th Regiment.*
Holder's (William D.) **Infantry.**   See *Mississippi Troops, Confederate, 17th Regiment.*
Holman's (William C.) **Infantry.**   See *Vermont Troops, 9th Regiment.*
Holmes' (James T.) **Infantry.**   See *Ohio Troops, 52d Regiment.*
Holmes' (William J.) **Infantry.**   See *Ohio Troops, 74th Regiment.*
Holt's (Willis C.) **Infantry.**   See *Georgia Troops, 10th Regiment.*
Horner's (James) **Infantry.**   See *Ohio Troops, 41st Regiment.*
Hoskins' (William A.) **Infantry.**   See *Kentucky Troops, Union, 12th Regiment.*
Hovis' (L. B.) **Cavalry.**   See *Mississippi Troops, Confederate, 1st Regiment, Partisan Rangers.*
Howe's (James H.) **Infantry.**   See *Wisconsin Troops, 32d Regiment,*
Hubbard s (Hiram F.) **Artillery.**   See *Wisconsin Troops, 3d Battery.*
Hubbard's (Lucius F.) **Infantry.**   See *Minnesota Troops, 5th Regiment.*
Huggins' (A. L.) **Artillery.**   See *Tennessee Troops, Confederate.*
Hugunin's (James R.) **Infantry.**   See *Illinois Troops, 12th Regiment.*
Hull's (James S.) **Infantry.**   See *Indiana Troops, 37th Regiment.*
Humphrey's (William) **Infantry.**   See *Michigan Troops, 2d Regiment.*
Hunter's (Morton C.) **Infantry.**   See *Indiana Troops, 82d Regiment.*
Hurd's (John R.) **Infantry.**   See *Kentucky Troops, Union, 2d Regiment.*
Hurd's (Orrin D.) **Infantry.**   See *Indiana Troops, 30th Regiment.*
Hurlbut's (Frederick J.) **Infantry.**   See *Illinois Troops, 57th Regiment.*

Hurst's (Fielding) **Cavalry.** See *Tennessee Troops, Union, 6th Regiment.*
Hurst's (Samuel H.) **Infantry.** See *Ohio Troops, 73d Regiment.*
Hurt's (Harrison M.) **Cavalry.** See *Kentucky Troops, Union, 13th Regiment.*
Hurt's (John S.) **Infantry.** See *Kentucky Troops, Union, 24th Regiment.*
Huston's (John M.) **Infantry.** See *Kentucky Troops, Union, 5th Regiment.*
Hutchins' (N. L., jr.) **Sharpshooters.** See *Georgia Troops, 3d Battalion.*
Hutchins' (Rue P.) **Infantry.** See *Ohio Troops, 94th Regiment.*
Hutchison's (Jonathan) **Infantry.** See *Iowa Troops, 32d Regiment.*
Ijams' (John F.) **Cavalry.** See *Ohio Troops, 5th Battalion.*
Innes' (William P.) **Engineers.** See *Michigan Troops, 1st Regiment.*
Ireland's (David) **Infantry.** See *New York Troops, 137th Regiment.*
Ison's (F. M.) **Cavalry.** See *Georgia Troops, 2d Regiment.*
Jackson's (Allan H.) **Infantry.** See *New York Troops, 134th Regiment.*
Jackson's (Ezra P.) **Infantry.** See *Ohio Troops, 58th Regiment.*
Jackson's (George W.) **Infantry.** See *Indiana Troops, 118th Regiment.*
Jackson's (William H.) **Cavalry.** See *W. L. Duckworth's Cavalry, ante.*
Jacobs' (William H.) **Infantry.** See *Wisconsin Troops, 26th Regiment.*
James' (George S.) **Infantry.** See *South Carolina Troops, 3d Battalion.*
Jarvis' (Dwight, jr.) **Infantry.** See *Ohio Troops, 13th Regiment.*
Jenkins' (Jeremiah W.) **Infantry.** See *Iowa Troops, 31st Regiment.*
Jessee's (George M.) **Rifles.** See *Kentucky Troops, Confederate.*
John's (Howard D.) **Infantry.** See *Ohio Troops, 129th Regiment.*
Johnson's (Andrew J.) **Infantry.** See *Union Troops, Veteran Reserve Corps.*
Johnson's (Calvin R.) **Infantry.** See *Wisconsin Troops, 14th Regiment.*
Johnson's (Thomas) **Cavalry.** See *Kentucky Troops, Confederate, 2d Battalion, Rifles.*
Johnson's (William A.) **Cavalry.** See *Alabama Troops, Confederate, 4th Regiment.*
Jones' (Charles C.) **Infantry.** See *Illinois Troops, 76th Regiment.*
Jones' (Theodore) **Infantry.** See *Ohio Troops, 30th Regiment.*
Jones' (William) **Infantry.** See *Indiana Troops, 53d Regiment.*
Jones' (William T.) **Infantry.** See *Indiana Troops, 17th Regiment.*
Jordan's (Thomas J.) **Cavalry.** See *Pennsylvania Troops, 9th Regiment.*
Jordan's (Tyler C.) **Artillery.** See *Bedford Artillery, ante.*
Kammerling's (Gustave) **Infantry.** See *Ohio Troops, 9th Regiment.*
Kaufman's (Daniel B.) **Infantry.** See *Pennsylvania Troops, 48th Regiment.*
Keegan's (Patrick H.) **Infantry.** See *Michigan Troops, 11th Regiment.*
Kelly's (Joseph J.) **Infantry.** See *Illinois Troops, 107th Regiment.*
Kelly's (Robert M.) **Infantry.** See *Kentucky Troops, Union, 4th Regiment.*
Kelly's (Solomon W.) **Cavalry.** See *Illinois Troops, 16th Regiment.*
Kendrick's (Frank A.) **Infantry.** See *Tennessee Troops, Union, 2d Regiment (Colored).*
Kendrick's (William G.) **Infantry.** See *Pennsylvania Troops, 79th Regiment.*
Kennard's (George W.) **Infantry.** See *Illinois Troops, 20th Regiment.*
Kennedy's (John D.) **Infantry.** See *South Carolina Troops, 2d Regiment.*
Kennett's (Henry G.) **Infantry.** See *Ohio Troops, 79th Regiment.*
Kerr's (Lucien H.) **Cavalry.** See *Illinois Troops, 11th Regiment.*
Ketcham's (John H.) **Infantry.** See *New York Troops, 150th Regiment.*
Keteltas' (Henry) **Infantry.** See *Union Troops, Regulars, 15th Regiment, 1st Battalion.*
Ketner's (James) **Infantry.** See *Kansas Troops, 1st Regiment.*
Key's (J. C. G.) **Infantry.** See *Texas Troops, 4th Regiment.*
Kilgour's (William M.) **Infantry.** See *Illinois Troops, 75th Regiment.*
Kilpatrick's (Franklin W.) **Infantry.** See *South Carolina Troops, 1st Regiment.*
King's (John F.) **Infantry.** See *Illinois Troops, 114th Regiment.*
Kingsbury's (Henry D.) **Infantry.** See *Ohio Troops, 14th Regiment.*
Kinney's (Nathaniel C.) **Infantry.** See *Union Troops, Regulars, 18th Regiment.*
Kirby's (Isaac M.) **Infantry.** See *Ohio Troops, 101st Regiment.*

Kirkpatrick's (M. L.) **Cavalry.** See *Alabama Troops, Confederate*, 51st *Regiment*.
Kirkpatrick's (Samuel C.) **Infantry.** See *Indiana Troops*, 72d *Regiment*.
Kise's (William C.) **Infantry.** See *Indiana Troops*, 116th *Regiment*.
Kitchell's (Edward) **Infantry.** See *Illinois Troops*, 98th *Regiment*.
Kittell's (George W.) **Infantry.** See *Illinois Troops*, 58th *Regiment*.
Klein's (Robert) **Cavalry.** See *Indiana Troops*, 3d *Regiment*.
Knap's (Joseph M.) **Artillery.** See *Pennsylvania Troops, Battery E*.
Knefler's (Frederick) **Infantry.** See *Indiana Troops*, 79th *Regiment*.
Knight's (Chester K.) **Infantry.** See *Illinois Troops*, 21st *Regiment*.
Konkle's (Andrew J.) **Artillery.** See *Ohio Troops*, 1st *Regiment, Battery D*.
Kraus' (William) **Infantry.** See *Ohio Troops*, 86th *Regiment*.
La Grange's (Oscar H.) **Cavalry.** See *Wisconsin Troops*, 1st *Regiment*.
Lake's (Jarvis N.) **Infantry.** See *Ohio Troops*, 93d *Regiment*.
Lamberg's (Carl A.) **Artillery.** See *Union Troops (Colored)*, 2d *Regiment, Battery F*.
Landgraeber's (Clemens) **Artillery.** See *Missouri Troops, Union*, 2d *Regiment, Battery F*.
Lane's (James C.) **Infantry.** See *New York Troops*, 102d *Regiment*.
Lane's (John Q.) **Infantry.** See *Ohio Troops*, 97th *Regiment*.
Lane's (Philander P.) **Infantry.** See *Ohio Troops*, 11th *Regiment*.
Langdon's (Bassett) **Infantry.** See *Ohio Troops*, 1st *Regiment*.
Langen's (Edward) **Cavalry.** See *Missouri Troops, Union*, 4th *Regiment*.
Larison's (Thomas J.) **Cavalry.** See *Illinois Troops*, 2d *Regiment*.
Lauck's (James F.) **Infantry.** See *Kentucky Troops, Union*, 33d *Regiment*.
Law's (Jesse S.) **Artillery.*** See *Jesse S. Law*.
Lawson's (Joseph J.) **Infantry.** See *Pennsylvania Troops*, 77th *Regiment*.
Ledig's (August) **Infantry.** See *Pennsylvania Troops*, 75th *Regiment*.
Lee's (Henry S.) **Artillery.** See *Wisconsin Troops*, 7th *Battery*.
Le Gendre's (Charles W.) **Infantry.** See *New York Troops*, 51st *Regiment*.
Lennard's (George W.) **Infantry.** See *Indiana Troops*, 57th *Regiment*.
Lesslie's (Joseph P.) **Cavalry.** See *Indiana Troops*, 4th *Regiment*.
Lilly's (Eli) **Artillery.** See *Indiana Troops*, 18th *Battery*.
Lilly's (Henry C.) **Cavalry.** See *Kentucky Troops, Union*, 14th *Regiment*.
Lister's (Frederick W.) **Infantry.** See *Ohio Troops*, 31st *Regiment*.
Little's (F. H.) **Infantry.** See *Georgia Troops*, 11th *Regiment*.
Lockman's (John T.) **Infantry.** See *New York Troops*, 119th *Regiment*.
Logan's (John) **Infantry.** See *Illinois Troops*, 32d *Regiment*.
Logie's (William K.) **Infantry.** See *New York Troops*, 141st *Regiment*.
Loomis' (Reuben) **Cavalry.** See *Illinois Troops*, 6th *Regiment*.
Love's (James R.) **Infantry.** See *W. H. Thomas' Legion, post*.
Love's (S. Palace) **Infantry.** See *Kentucky Troops, Union*, 11th *Regiment*.
Lowell's (John W.) **Artillery.** See *Illinois Troops*, 2d *Regiment, Battery G*.
Lowry's (Francis H.) **Infantry.** See *Illinois Troops*, 107th *Regiment*.
Lowry's (William M.) **Artillery.** See *Virginia Troops*.
Lusk's (William H.) **Cavalry.** See *Missouri Troops, Union*, 10th *Regiment*.
Lyman's (George W.) **Infantry.** See *Illinois Troops*, 113th *Regiment*.
Lyon's (William P.) **Infantry.** See *Wisconsin Troops*, 13th *Regiment*.
McAfee's (A. L.) **Cavalry.** See *George M. Jessee's Rifles, ante*.
McAloon's (Peter A.) **Infantry.** See *Pennsylvania Troops*, 27th *Regiment*.
McArthur's (Allen D. S.) **Infantry.** See *Ohio Troops*, 129th *Regiment*.
McArthur's (James N.) **Infantry.** See *Illinois Troops*, 12th *Regiment*.
McBride's (A. J.) **Infantry.** See *Georgia Troops*, 10th *Regiment*.
McClanahan's (John W.) **Infantry.** See *Illinois Troops*, 53d *Regiment*.
McClung's (Hugh L. W.) **Artillery.** See *Tennessee Troops, Confederate*.
McClure's (John D.) **Infantry.** See *Illinois Troops*, 47th *Regiment*.

---

* Improvised.

McConnell's (Henry K.) **Infantry.** See *Ohio Troops, 71st Regiment.*
McConnell's (Sylvester P.) **Cavalry.** See *Virginia Troops, 27th Battalion.*
McCook's (Anson G.) **Infantry.** See *Ohio Troops, 2d Regiment.*
McCown's (Joseph B.) **Infantry.** See *Illinois Troops, 63d Regiment.*
McCulloch's (Robert) **Cavalry.** See *Missouri Troops, Confederate, 2d Regiment.*
McCulloch's (Robert A.) **Cavalry.** See *Missouri Troops, Confederate, 2d Regiment.*
McDowell's (Samuel M.) **Artillery.** See *Pennsylvania Troops, Battery B.*
McElroy's (Kennon) **Infantry.** See *Mississippi Troops, Confederate, 13th Regiment.*
McEwen's (John L., jr.) **Infantry.** See *Tennessee Troops, Confederate, 25th and 44th Regiments.*
McFadden's (Robert H.) **Infantry.** See *Illinois Troops, 41st Regiment.*
McGlashan's (Peter) **Infantry.** See *Georgia Troops, 50th Regiment.*
McGroarty's (Stephen J.) **Infantry.** See *Ohio Troops, 61st Regiment.*
McGuirk's (John) **Cavalry.** See *Mississippi Troops, Confederate, 3d Regiment (State).*
McIlvain's (Alexander) **Infantry.** See *Ohio Troops, 64th Regiment.*
McIntire's (James) **Cavalry.** See *Ohio Troops, 7th Regiment.*
McIntire's (William T. B.) **Infantry.** See *Indiana Troops, 42d Regiment.*
McIntyre's (Duncan) **Infantry.** See *South Carolina Troops, 8th Regiment.*
McIntyre's (James B.) **Cavalry.** See *Union Troops, Regulars, 4th Regiment.*
McKamy's (James A.) **Infantry.** See *W. H. Thomas' Legion, post.*
McKenzie's (George W.) **Cavalry.** See *Tennessee Troops, Confederate.*
McKnight's (Joseph) **Artillery.** See *Wisconsin Troops, 5th Battery.*
McLaughlin's (William) **Cavalry.** See *Ohio Troops.*
McLean's (John D.) **Artillery.** See *Wisconsin Troops, 8th Battery.*
McLennan's (John D.) **Infantry.** See *Hilliard's Legion, ante, 4th Battalion; also 59th Alabama.*
McMahon's (Thomas) **Infantry.** See *Wisconsin Troops, 17th Regiment.*
McManomy's (James) **Infantry.** See *Indiana Troops, 63d Regiment.*
McMillan's (Robert) **Infantry.** See *Georgia Troops, 24th Regiment.*
Madison **Artillery.** See *Louisiana Troops, Confederate.*
Magee's (David W.) **Infantry.** See *Illinois Troops, 86th Regiment.*
Main's (Zalmon S.) **Infantry.** See *Indiana Troops, 52d Regiment.*
Malmborg's (Oscar) **Infantry.** See *Illinois Troops, 55th Regiment.*
Malone's (James C., jr.) **Cavalry.** See *Alabama Troops, Confederate, 7th Regiment.*
Manderson's (Charles F.) **Infantry.** See *Ohio Troops, 19th Regiment.*
Mann's (Charles) **Artillery.** See *Missouri Troops, Union, 1st Regiment, Battery C.*
Manning's (Van H.) **Infantry.** See *Arkansas Troops, Confederate, 3d Regiment.*
Marsh's (Jason) **Infantry.** See *Illinois Troops, 74th Regiment.*
Marshall's (Alexander) **Artillery.** See *Ohio Troops, 1st Regiment, Battery G.*
Martin's (James S.) **Infantry.** See *Illinois Troops, 111th Regiment.*
Martin's (John A.) **Infantry.** See *Kansas Troops, 8th Regiment.*
Matson's (Courtland C.) **Cavalry.** See *Indiana Troops, 6th Regiment.*
Mattingly's (Ignatius E.) **Infantry.** See *Kentucky Troops, Union, 26th Regiment.*
Mauff's (August) **Infantry.** See *Illinois Troops, 24th Regiment.*
Mauldin's (T. H.) **Cavalry.** See *Alabama Troops, Confederate, 3d Regiment.*
May's (A. J.) **Mounted Rifles.** See *Kentucky Troops, Confederate.*
Meline's (James F.) **Infantry.** See *Ohio Troops, 6th Regiment.*
Melton's (James M.) **Infantry.** See *Tennessee Troops, Union, 2d Regiment.*
Metham's (Pren) **Infantry.** See *Ohio Troops, 80th Regiment.*
Meumann's (Theodore) **Infantry.** See *Missouri Troops, Union, 3d Regiment.*
Meyers' (Ernest J.) **Cavalry.** See *Wisconsin Troops, 2d Regiment.*
Miles' (Jonathan R.) **Infantry.** See *Illinois Troops, 27th Regiment.*
Miller's (Alexander J.) **Infantry.** See *Iowa Troops, 6th Regiment.*
Miller's (Madison) **Infantry.** See *Missouri Troops, Union, 18th Regiment.*
Miller's (Silas) **Infantry.** See *Illinois Troops, 36th Regiment.*
Mills' (James K.) **Infantry.** See *Missouri Troops, Union, 24th Regiment.*

Milward's (Hubbard K.) **Infantry.** See *Kentucky Troops, Union,* 18*th Regiment.*
Mims' (David A.) **Infantry.** See *Kentucky Troops, Union,* 39*th Regiment.*
Mindil's (George W.) **Infantry.** See *New Jersey Troops,* 33*d Regiment.*
Mitchell's (W. R.) **Cavalry.** See *Mississippi Troops, Confederate,* 18*th Battalion.*
Mizner's (Henry R.) **Infantry.** See *Michigan Troops,* 14*th Regiment.*
Montgomery's (William S.) **Infantry.** See *New York Troops,* 79*th Regiment.*
Moody's (George V.) **Artillery.** See *Madison Artillery, ante.*
Moody's (Young M.) **Infantry.** See *Alabama Troops, Confederate,* 43*d Regiment.*
Mooney's (Patrick H.) **Infantry.** See *Ohio Troops,* 68*th Regiment.*
Moore's (Alpheus S.) **Infantry.** See *Ohio Troops,* 44*th Regiment.*
Moore's (Jesse H.) **Infantry.** See *Illinois Troops,* 115*th Regiment.*
Moore's (Jonathan B.) **Infantry.** See *Wisconsin Troops,* 33*d Regiment.*
Moore's (Le R'y) **Infantry.** See *Ohio Troops,* 72*d Regiment.*
Moore's (Oscar F.) **Infantry.** See *Ohio Troops,* 33*d Regiment.*
Moore's (Risdon M.) **Infantry.** See *Illinois Troops,* 117*th Regiment.*
Moore's (William) **Infantry.** See *Pennsylvania Troops,* 73*d Regiment.*
Moreland's (M. D.) **Cavalry.** See *Alabama Troops, Confederate.*
Morgan's (Otho H.) **Artillery.** See *Indiana Troops,* 7*th Battery.*
Morrison's (E. M.) **Infantry.** See *Virginia Troops,* 15*th Regiment.*
Morton's (G. H.) **Cavalry.** See *H. M. Ashby's Cavalry, ante.*
Mott's (Samuel R.) **Infantry.** See *Ohio Troops,* 57*th Regiment.*
Moyers' (Gilbert) **Cavalry.** See *Michigan Troops,* 3*d Regiment.*
Mueller's (Alexander) **Cavalry.** See *Missouri Troops, Union,* 4*th Regiment.*
Mueller's (Michael) **Artillery.** See *Indiana Troops,* 6*th Battery.*
Muhlenberg's (Edward D.) **Artillery.** See *Union Troops, Regulars,* 4*th Regiment, Battery F.*
Mullen's (Bernard F.) **Infantry.** See *Indiana Troops,* 35*th Regiment.*
Munn's (W. W.) **Infantry.** See *Ohio Troops,* 41*st Regiment.*
Murray's (Albert M.) **Artillery.** See *Union Troops, Regulars,* 2*d Regimen., Battery F.*
Myers' (James H.) **Artillery.** See *Indiana Troops,* 23*d Battery.*
Nance's (James D.) **Infantry.** See *South Carolina Troops,* 3*d Regiment.*
Naylor's (William A.) **Artillery.** See *Indiana Troops,* 10*th Battery.*
Neely's (James J.) **Cavalry.** See *Tennessee Troops, Confederate.*
Neet's (F. R.) **Cavalry.** See *Missouri Troops, Union,* 10*th Regiment.*
Neff's (Andrew J.) **Infantry.** See *Indiana Troops,* 84*th Regiment.*
Neff's (George W.) **Infantry.** See *Ohio Troops,* 88*th Regiment.*
Neville's (James) **Infantry.** See *Illinois Troops,* 80*th Regiment.*
Neville's (John W.) **Artillery.** See *Kentucky Troops, Union, Battery C.*
Newbold's (Joseph H.) **Infantry.** See *Iowa Troops,* 14*th Regiment.* ·
Newell's (Nathaniel M.) **Artillery.** See *Ohio Troops,* 1*st Regiment, Battery D.*
Nicholas' (Thomas P.) **Cavalry.** See *Kentucky Troops, Union,* 2*d Regiment.*
Nicklin's (Benjamin S.) **Artillery.** See *Indiana Troops,* 13*th Battery.*
Nolte's (John F.) **Infantry.** See *Illinois Troops,* 14*th Regiment.*
Northup's (George W.) **Infantry.** See *Kentucky Troops, Union,* 23*d Regiment.*
Noyes' (Edward F.) **Infantry.** See *Ohio Troops,* 39*th Regiment.*
Oates' (William C.) **Infantry.** See *Alabama Troops, Confederate,* 15*th Regiment.*
Oliver's (John M.) **Infantry.** See *Michigan Troops,* 15*th Regiment.*
Oliver's (William S.) **Infantry.** See *Missouri Troops, Union,* 7*th Regiment.*
O'Meara's (Timothy) **Infantry.** See *Illinois Troops,* 90*th Regiment.*
Opdycke's (Emerson) **Infantry.** See *Ohio Troops,* 125*th Regiment.*
Organ's (Henry A.) **Heavy Artillery.** See *Mississippi Troops, Union,* 2*d Regiment, Colored.*
Osborne's (Milton A.) **Artillery.** See *Indiana Troops,* 20*th Battery.*
Otey Artillery. See *Virginia Troops.*
Otto's (John) **Artillery.** See *Ohio Troops,* 20*th Battery.*
Overton's (Edward, jr.) **Infantry.** See *Pennsylvania Troops,* 50*th Regiment.*

Owens' (James W.) **Infantry.** See *Ohio Troops,* 86th *Regiment.*
Owens' (Joseph M.) **Infantry.** See *Kentucky Troops, Union,* 12th *Regiment.*
Packer's (Warren W.) **Infantry.** See *Connecticut Troops,* 5th *Regiment.*
Palmer's (David J.) **Infantry.** See *Iowa Troops,* 25th *Regiment.*
Palmer's (William J.) **Cavalry.** See *Pennsylvania Troops,* 15th *Regiment.*
Palmetto Sharpshooters. See *South Carolina Troops.*
Pardee's (Ario, jr.) **Infantry.** See *Pennsylvania Troops,* 147th *Regiment.*
Pardue's (W. P.) **Cavalry.** See *Stephen Davenport's Cavalry, ante.*
Parker's (Nathan) **Cavalry.** See *Kentucky Troops, Confederate,* 4th *Regiment.*
Parker's (William W.) **Artillery.** See *Virginia Troops.*
Parkhurst's (John G.) **Infantry.** See *Michigan Troops,* 9th *Regiment.*
Parrott's (James C.) **Infantry.** See *Iowa Troops,* 7th *Regiment.*
Parry's (Augustus C.) **Infantry.** See *Ohio Troops,* 47th *Regiment.*
Patrick's (John H.) **Infantry.** See *Ohio Troops,* 5th *Regiment.*
Patrick's (Matthewson T.) **Cavalry.** See *Iowa Troops,* 5th *Regiment.*
Patten's (Thomas J.) **Cavalry.** See *Ohio Troops,* 1st *Regiment.*
Patterson's (James W.) **Artillery.** See *Ohio Troops,* 21st *Battery.*
Patton's (Charles U.) **Cavalry.** See *Indiana Troops,* 3d *Regiment.*
Pearson's (Henry H.) **Infantry.** See *New Hampshire Troops,* 6th *Regiment.*
Pearson's (Robert N.) **Infantry.** See *Illinois Troops,* 31st *Regiment.*
Pease's (William H.) **Artillery.** See *Ohio Troops,* 1st *Regiment, Battery D.*
Peats' (Frank F.) **Infantry.** · See *Illinois Troops,* 17th *Regiment.*
Peck's (Elijah W.) **Cavalry.** See *Indiana Troops,* 6th *Regiment.*
Peckham's (James) **Infantry.** See *Missouri Troops, Union,* 29th *Regiment.*
Peebles' (Hubert F.) **Infantry.** See *Iowa Troops,* 32d *Regiment.*
Peeples' (Tyler M.) **Artillery.** See *Georgia Troops,* 9th *Battalion, Battery D.*
Peirce's (Ebenezer W.) **Infantry.** See *Massachusetts Troops,* 29th *Regiment.*
Perry's (William F.) **Infantry.** See *Alabama Troops, Confederate,* 44th *Regiment.*
Peter's (Richard A.) **Infantry.** See *Illinois Troops,* 131st *Regiment.*
Peters' (William E.) **Cavalry.** See *Virginia Troops,* 21st *Regiment.*
Pettit's (Willis H.) **Artillery.** See *Indiana Troops,* 4th *Battery.*
Phillips' (Jesse J.) **Infantry.** See *Illinois Troops,* 9th *Regiment.*
Phillips' (John C.) **Artillery.** See *Illinois Troops,* 2d *Regiment, Battery M.*
Phillips Legion. See *Georgia Troops.*
Phillips' (Robert E.) **Infantry.** See *Tennessee Troops, Union,* 1st *Regiment, Colored.*
Pickands' (James) **Infantry.** See *Ohio Troops,* 124th *Regiment.*
Pickens' (William C.) **Cavalry.** See *Tennessee Troops, Union,* 3d *Regiment.*
Piepho's (Carlo) **Infantry.** See *Ohio Troops,* 10·th *Regiment.*
Pillow's (Parker B.) **Infantry.** See *Illinois Troops,* 120th *Regiment.*
Pioneer Brigade. See *James St. Clair Morton.*
Piper's (John) **Sharpshooters.** See *Michigan Troops,* 1st *Regiment.*
Plessner's (Henry) **Cavalry.** See *Ohio Troops,* 9th *Regiment.*
Poole's (David) **Infantry.** See *Kentucky Troops, Union,* 11th *Regiment.*
Potts' (Benjamin F.) **Infantry.** See *Ohio Troops,* 32d *Regiment.*
Powell's (Eugene) **Infantry.** See *Ohio Troops,* 66th *Regiment.*
Powell's (Lemon S.) **Heavy Artillery.** See *Ohio Troops,* 2d *Regiment.*
Powell's (R. M.) **Infantry.** See *Texas Troops,* 5th *Regiment.*
Powell's (Walter H.) **Artillery.** See *Illinois Troops,* 2d *Regiment, Battery F.*
Powers' (Oliver M.) **Cavalry.** See *Indiana Troops,* 3d *Regiment.*
Prather's (Allen W.) **Infantry.** See *Indiana Troops,* 6th *Regiment.*
Prescott's (Mark H.) **Artillery.** See *Illinois Troops,* 1st *Regiment, Battery C.*
Presdee's (Joseph B.) **Cavalry.** See *Indiana Troops,* 2d *Regiment.*
Price's (Samuel W.) **Infantry.** See *Kentucky Troops, Union,* 21st *Regiment.*
Prince's (Edward) **Cavalry.** See *Illinois Troops,* 7th *Regiment.*
Purcell's (William) **Infantry.** See *Iowa Troops,* 16th *Regiment.*

Purington's (George A.) **Cavalry.** See *Ohio Troops, 2d Regiment.*
Putnam's (Azro C.) **Artillery.** See *Edward C. Henshaw's Artillery, ante.*
Putnam's (Douglas, jr.) **Infantry.** See *Ohio Troops, 92d Regiment.*
Putnam's (Holden) **Infantry.** See *Illinois Troops, 93d Regiment.*
Putnam's (James F.) **Artillery.** See *Ohio Troops, 8th Battery.*
Raffen's (Alexander W.) **Infantry.** See *Illinois Troops, 19th Regiment.*
Rainey's (A. T.) **Infantry.** See *Texas Troops, 1st Regiment.*
Randall's (Charles B.) **Infantry.** See *New York Troops, 149th Regiment.*
Ray's (Daniel M.) **Cavalry.** See *Tennessee Troops, Union, 2d Regiment.*
Reed's (Joseph R.) **Artillery.** See *Iowa Troops, 2d Battery.*
Reeve's (Edwin F.) **Artillery.** See *Ohio Troops, 15th Battery.*
Reeve's (Felix A.) **Infantry.** See *Tennessee Troops, Union, 8th Regiment.*
Reynolds' (Thomas) **Infantry.** See *Wisconsin Troops, 16th Regiment.*
Rheinlander's (John) **Infantry.** See *Indiana Troops, 25th Regiment.*
Rhett **Artillery.** See *Tennessee Troops, Confederate.*
Rice's (Richard) **Cavalry.** See *William McLaughlin's Cavalry, ante.*
Rice's (William G.) **Infantry.** See *South Carolina Troops, 3d Battalion.*
Richardson's (Robert V.) **Cavalry.** See *Tennessee Troops, Confederate.*
Rickards' (William, jr.) **Infantry.** See *Pennsylvania Troops, 29th Regiment.*
Rider's (Godfrey, jr.) **Infantry.** See *Massachusetts Troops, 33d Regiment.*
Rinaker's (John I.) **Infantry.** See *Illinois Troops, 122d Regiment.*
Ringgold **Artillery.** See *Virginia Troops.*
Ritter's (Richard) **Infantry.** See *Illinois Troops, 28th Regiment.*
Roberts' (Aurelius) **Infantry.** See *Iowa Troops, 30th Regiment.*
Robie's (Oliver P.) **Cavalry.** See *Ohio Troops, 4th Regiment.*
Robinson's (George) **Artillery.** See *Michigan Troops, 1st Regiment, Battery C.*
Robinson's (George J.) **Artillery.** See *Chicago Board of Trade Artillery, ante.*
Robinson's (James S.) **Infantry.** See *Ohio Troops, 82d Regiment.*
Robinson's (Milton S.) **Infantry.** See *Indiana Troops, 75th Regiment.*
Robinson's (Solomon S.) **Infantry.** See *Union Troops, Regulars, 16th Regiment, 2d Battalion.*
Roby's (Jacob W.) **Infantry.** See *Wisconsin Troops, 10th Regiment.*
Roemer's (Jacob) **Artillery.** See *New York Troops, 2d Regiment, Battery L.*
Rogers' (George C.) **Infantry.** See *Illinois Troops, 15th Regiment.*
Rogers' (James C.) **Infantry.** See *New York Troops, 123d Regiment.*
Roper's (William P.) **Cavalry.** See *Kentucky Troops, Union, 6th Regiment.*
Ross' (Francis M.) **Artillery.** See *Illinois Troops, 2d Regiment, Battery K.*
Ross' (George E.) **Infantry.** See *Ohio Troops, 45th Regiment.*
Ross' (Samuel) **Infantry.** See *Connecticut Troops, 20th Regiment.*
Rowett's (Richard) **Infantry.** See *Illinois Troops, 7th Regiment.*
Rudd's (Oscar F.) **Infantry.** See *Illinois Troops, 39th Regiment.*
Ruehle's (John V.) **Infantry.** See *Michigan Troops, 2d Regiment.*
Ruff's (S. Z.) **Infantry.** See *Georgia Troops, 18th Regiment.*
Ruggles' (James M.) **Cavalry.** See *Illinois Troops, 3d Regiment.*
Rumsey's (Israel P.) **Artillery.** See *Illinois Troops, 1st Regiment, Battery B.*
Russell's (Francis L. D.) **Artillery.** See *Union Troops, Regulars, 4th Regiment, Battery M.*
Russell's (Roswell M.) **Cavalry.** See *Pennsylvania Troops, 9th Regiment.*
Rutishauser's (Isaac) **Infantry.** See *Illinois Troops, 58th Regiment.*
Sahm's (Nicholas) **Artillery.** See *Ohio Troops, 1st Regiment, Battery K.*
Salomon's (Edward S.) **Artillery.** See *Illinois Troops, 82d Regiment.*
Sanford's (John W. A.) **Infantry.** See *Hilliard's Legion, ante, 3d Battalion; also 60th Alabama.*
Santmyer's (John M.) **Infantry.** See *Maryland Troops, Union, 2d Regiment.*
Sawyers' (John M.) **Cavalry.** See *Tennessee Troops, Union, 8th Regiment.*

Schueler's (Gustavus) **Artillery**. See *Missouri Troops, Union, 1st Regiment, Battery G*.
Schultz's (Frederick) **Artillery**. See *Ohio Troops, 1st Regiment, Battery M*.
Scobey's (John S.) **Infantry**. See *Indiana Troops, 68th Regiment*.
Scott's (Joseph A.) **Artillery**. See *Indiana Troops, 18th Battery*.
Scranton's (Leonidas S.) **Cavalry**. See *Michigan Troops, 2d Regiment*.
Scruggs' (L. H.) **Infantry**. See *Alabama Troops, Confederate, 4th Regiment*.
Scully's (James W.) **Infantry**. See *Tennessee Troops, Union, 10th Regiment*.
Sealy's (Robert P.) **Infantry**. See *Illinois Troops, 45th Regiment*.
Segebarth's (Pennsylvania) **Artillery**. See *Daniel P. Walling's Artillery, post*.
Sehlen's (John C. H. von) **Artillery**. See *Indiana Troops, 15th Battery*.
Seidel's (Charles B.) **Cavalry**. See *Ohio Troops, 3d Regiment*.
Seley's (Abel H.) **Cavalry**. See *Illinois Troops, 5th Regiment*.
Serviere's (Alphons) **Infantry**. See *New York Troops, 46th Regiment*.
Shafer's (Henry W.) **Artillery**. See *Indiana Troops, 24th Battery*.
Shane's (James M.) **Infantry**. See *Ohio Troops, 98th Regiment*.
Shane's (John) **Infantry**. See *Iowa Troops, 13th Regiment*.
Shanks' (John P. C.) **Cavalry**. See *Indiana Troops, 7th Regiment*.
Shaw's (Joseph) **Cavalry**. See *Tennessee Troops, Confederate*.
Shedd's (Warren) **Infantry**. See *Illinois Troops, 30th Regiment*.
Sheetz's (Josiah A.) **Infantry**. See *Illinois Troops, 8th Regiment*.
Sheffield's (James L.) **Infantry**. See *Alabama Troops, Confederate, 48th Regiment*.
Sheldon's (Stephen H.) **Infantry**. See *South Carolina Troops, 15th Regiment*.
Shelley's (James T.) **Infantry**. See *Tennessee Troops, Union, 5th Regiment*.
Sherwood's (Isaac R.) **Infantry**. See *Ohio Troops, 111th Regiment*.
Shields' (Joseph C.) **Artillery**. See *Ohio Troops, 19th Battery*.
Simmons' (Henry) **Infantry**. See *Alabama Troops, Union, 1st Regiment (Colored)*.
Simms' (James P.) **Infantry**. See *Georgia Troops, 53d Regiment*.
Simonson's (Peter) **Artillery**. See *Indiana Troops, 5th Battery*.
Simpson's (Samuel P.) **Infantry**. See *Missouri Troops, Union, 17th and 31st Regiments*.
Sims' (Joseph A.) **Artillery**. See *Indiana Troops, 24th Battery*.
Sipes' (William B.) **Cavalry**. See *Pennsylvania Troops, 7th Regiment*.
Skinner's (Lucius B.) **Cavalry**. See *Illinois Troops, 6th Regiment*.
Slemons' (W. F.) **Cavalry**. See *Arkansas Troops, Confederate, 2d Regiment*.
Slemp's (Campbell) **Infantry**. See *Virginia Troops, 64th Regiment*.
Slevin's (Patrick S.) **Infantry**. See *Ohio Troops, 100th Regiment*.
Sloan's (Thomas J.) **Infantry**. See *Illinois Troops, 124th Regiment*.
Smith's (Arthur A.) **Infantry**. See *Illinois Troops, 83d Regiment*.
Smith's (Baxter) **Cavalry**. See *Tennessee Troops, Confederate*.
Smith's (Charles C.) **Cavalry**. See *Ohio Troops, 10th Regiment*.
Smith's (Charles C.) **Infantry**. See *Union Troops, Regulars, 13th Regiment, 1st Battalion*.
Smith's (C. T.) **Cavalry**. See *Virginia Troops, 36th Battalion*.
Smith's (Emil) **Heavy Artillery**. See *Tennessee Troops, Union, 1st Regiment (Colored)*.
Smith's (Frank G.) **Artillery**. See *Union Troops, Regulars, 4th Regiment, Battery I*.
Smith's (Franklin C.) **Infantry**. See *Illinois Troops, 102d Regiment*.
Smith's (Frederick F.) **Cavalry**. See *Virginia Troops, 17th Regiment*.
Smith's (George W.) **Infantry**. See *Union Troops, Regulars, 18th Regiment, 1st Battalion*.
Smith's (Jason B.) **Artillery**. See *Illinois Troops, 1st Regiment, Battery K*.
Smith's (John T.) **Infantry**. See *Indiana Troops, 31st Regiment*.
Smith's (Milo) **Infantry**. See *Iowa Troops, 26th Regiment*.
Smith's (W. Huntington) **Infantry**. See *Michigan Troops, 20th Regiment*.
Spaulding's (Benjamin J.) **Infantry**. See *Kentucky Troops, Union, 37th Regiment*.
Spaulding's (Zeph. S.) **Infantry**. See *Ohio Troops, 27th Regiment*.

Spearman's (Cornelius F.) **Cavalry.** See *Iowa Troops,* 4th *Regiment.*

Spencer's (George W.) **Artillery.** See *Illinois Troops,* 1st *Regiment, Battery M.*

Spicer's (Newell W.) **Infantry.** See *Kansas Troops,* 1st *Regiment.*

Spooner's (Benjamin J.) **Infantry.** See *Indiana Troops,* 83d *Regiment.*

Spooner's (Edmund D.) **Artillery.** See *Union Troops, Regulars,* 5th *Regiment, Battery H.*

Sprague's (John W.) **Infantry.** See *Ohio Troops,* 63d *Regiment.*

Stafford's (Joab A.) **Infantry.** See *Ohio Troops,* 1st *Regiment.*

Stanley's (Timothy R.) **Infantry.** See *Ohio Troops,* 18th *Regiment.*

Starling's (Edmund A.) **Infantry.** See *Kentucky Troops, Union,* 35th *Regiment.*

Steinhausen's (Albert von) **Infantry.** See *New York Troops,* 68th *Regiment.*

Sterl's (Oscar W.) **Infantry.** See *Ohio Troops,* 104th *Regiment.*

Stewart's (William S.) **Infantry.** See *Illinois Troops,* 65th *Regiment.*

Stibbs' (John H.) **Infantry.** See *Iowa Troops,* 12th *Regiment.*

Stockdale's (Thomas R.) **Cavalry.** See *Mississippi Troops, Confederate.*

Stockton's (Joseph) **Infantry.** See *Illinois Troops,* 72d *Regiment.*

Stokes' (William B.) **Cavalry.** See *Tennessee Troops, Union,* 5th *Regiment.*

Stone's (George A.) **Infantry.** See *Iowa Troops,* 25th *Regiment.*

Stout's (Alexander M.) **Infantry.** See *Kentucky Troops, Union,* 17th *Regiment.*

Sudsburg's (Joseph M.) **Infantry.** See *Maryland Troops, Union,* 3d *Regiment.*

Sullivan's (John) **Artillery.** See *Ohio Troops,* 3d *Battery.*

Sullivant's (Lyne S.) **Infantry.** See *Ohio Troops,* 113th *Regiment.*

Suman's (Isaac C. B.) **Infantry.** See *Indiana Troops,* 9th *Regiment.*

Sutermeister's (Arnold) **Artillery.** See *Indiana Troops,* 11th *Battery.*

Sutherland's (Bliss) **Infantry.** See *Illinois Troops,* 113th *Regiment.*

Swanwick's (Francis) **Infantry.** See *Illinois Troops,* 22d *Regiment.*

Swayne's (Wager) **Infantry.** See *Ohio Troops,* 43d *Regiment.*

Tafel's (Gustavus) **Infantry.** See *Ohio Troops,* 106th *Regiment.*

Taggart's (Wesford) **Infantry.** See *Illinois Troops,* 25th *Regiment.*

Tallerday's (David S.) **Infantry.** See *Missouri Troops, Union* (*Mississippi Marine Brigade*), 1st *Regiment.*

Tannrath's (Benjamin) **Artillery.** See *Missouri Troops, Union,* 1st *Regiment, Battery I.*

Taylor's (Jacob E.) **Infantry.** See *Ohio Troops,* 40th *Regiment.*

Taylor's (Marsh B.) **Infantry.** See *Indiana Troops,* 10th *Regiment.*

Taylor's (Osmond B.) **Artillery.** See *Virginia Troops.*

Taylor's (Samuel E.) **Infantry.** See *Illinois Troops,* 119th *Regiment.*

Tennessee (Confederate) **First Cavalry.** See *James E. Carter's Cavalry, ante.*

Tennessee (Confederate) **First [Seventh] Cavalry.** See *W. L. Duckworth's Cavalry, ante.*

Tennessee (Confederate) **Second Cavalry.** See *H. M. Ashby's Cavalry, ante.*

Tennessee (Confederate) **Fourth [Eighth] Cavalry.** See *Baxter Smith's Cavalry, ante.*

Tennessee (Confederate) **Eighth [Thirteenth] Cavalry.** See *George G. Dibrell's Cavalry, ante.*

Tennessee (Confederate) **Ninth [Nineteenth] Cavalry.** See *Jacob B. Biffle's Cavalry, ante.*

Tennessee (Confederate) **Tenth Cavalry.** See *Nicholas N. Cox's Cavalry, ante.*

Tennessee (Confederate) **Twelfth Cavalry.** See *Robert V. Richardson's Cavalry, ante.*

Tennessee (Confederate) **Thirteenth Cavalry.** See *James J. Neely's Cavalry, ante.*

Tenney's (O. S.) **Cavalry.** See *Kentucky Troops, Confederate,* 2d *Battalion, Rifles.*

Thielemann's (Christian) **Cavalry.** See *Illinois Troops,* 16th *Regiment.*

Thomas' (De Witt C.) **Infantry.** See *Indiana Troops,* 93d *Regiment.*

Thomas' (Henry P.) **Infantry.** See *Georgia Troops,* 16th *Regiment.*

Thomas' (Hubbard T.) **Artillery.** See *Wilder Artillery, post.*

Thomas' (W. H.) **Legion.** See *North Carolina Troops, Confederate.*

Thomasson's (Theodore S.) **Artillery.** See *Kentucky Troops, Union, Battery A.*

Thompson's (J. B.) **Cavalry.** See *Virginia Troops,* 27th *Battalion.*

Thompson's (R.) **Cavalry.** See *Georgia Troops, 3d Regiment.*
Thomson's (Samuel T.) **Infantry.** See *Illinois Troops, 64th Regiment.*
Thomson's (Thomas) **Infantry.** See *South Carolina Troops, 2d Regiment, Rifles.*
Thurmond's (J. G.) **Cavalry.** See *James J. Neely's Cavalry, ante.*
Tiemeyer's (John H.) **Artillery.** See *Missouri Troops, Union, 1st Regiment, Battery M.*
Tillson's (John) **Infantry.** See *Illinois Troops, 10th Regiment.*
Tindall's (Henry) **Infantry.** See *Indiana Troops, 63d Regiment.*
Titus' (Herbert B.) **Infantry.** See *New Hampshire Troops, 9th Regiment.*
Tobey's (Thomas F.) **Infantry.** See *Rhode Island Troops, 7th Regiment.*
Topping's (E. Hibbard) **Infantry.** See *Illinois Troops, 110th Regiment.*
Torrey's (William H.) **Cavalry.** See *Wisconsin Troops, 1st Regiment.*
Tourtellotte's (John E.) **Infantry.** See *Minnesota Troops, 4th Regiment.*
Towers' (John R.) **Infantry.** See *Georgia Troops, 8th Regiment.*
Trafton's (George W.) **Cavalry.** See *Illinois Troops, 7th Regiment.*
Trapp's (Nicholas) **Infantry.** See *Ohio Troops, 1st Regiment.*
Treanor's (John L.) **Infantry.** See *Kentucky Troops, Union, 5th Regiment.*
Trimble's (Edwin) **Cavalry.** See *A. J. May's Mounted Rifles, ante.*
Trimmier's (Theodore G.) **Infantry.** See *Alabama Troops, Confederate, 41st Regiment.*
Tripp's (Stephen S.) **Cavalry.** See *Illinois Troops, 11th Regiment.*
Troy's (Daniel S.) **Infantry.** See *Hilliard's Legion, ante, 1st Battalion.*
True's (Clinton J.) **Infantry.** See *Kentucky Troops, Union, 40th Regiment.*
Trusler's (Gilbert) **Infantry.** See *Indiana Troops, 36th Regiment.*
Tupper's (Nathan W.) **Infantry.** See *Illinois Troops, 116th Regiment.*
Turner's (Charles) **Infantry.** See *Illinois Troops, 108th Regiment.*
Utley's (William L.) **Infantry.** See *Wisconsin Troops, 22d Regiment.*
Van Dyke's (R. S.) **Cavalry.** See *James E. Carter's Cavalry, ante.*
Vanosdol's (Robert J.) **Infantry.** See *Ohio Troops, 59th Regiment.*
Van Tassell's (Oscar) **Infantry.** See *Illinois Troops, 34th Regiment.*
Vantine's (Charles H.) **Infantry.** See *Ohio Troops, 21st Regiment.*
Voris' (Jeremiah) **Artillery.** See *Indiana Troops, 8th Battery.*
Waddell's (J. D.) **Infantry.** See *Georgia Troops, 20th Regiment.*
Walcutt's (Charles C.) **Infantry.** See *Ohio Troops, 46th Regiment.*
Wales' (Nathaniel) **Infantry.** See *Massachusetts Troops, 35th Regiment.*
Walker's (Charles H.) **Infantry.** See *Wisconsin Troops, 21st Regiment.*
Walker's (David N.) **Artillery.** See *Otey Artillery, ante.*
Walker's (Joseph) **Infantry.** See *Palmetto Sharpshooters, ante.*
Walker's (Thomas M.) **Infantry.** See *Pennsylvania Troops, 111th Regiment.*
Walker's (W. C.) **Infantry.** See *W. H. Thomas' Legion, ante.*
Wallace's (Martin R. M.) **Cavalry.** See *Illinois Troops, 4th Regiment.*
Wallace's (William) **Infantry.** See *South Carolina Troops, 2d Regiment.*
Waller's (Thomas B.) **Infantry.** See *Kentucky Troops, Union, 20th Regiment.*
Waller's (Wiley) **Cavalry.** See *Kentucky Troops, Union, 15th Regiment.*
Walling's (Daniel P.) **Artillery.** See *Missouri Troops, Union (Mississippi Marine Brigade).*
Walworth's (Nathan H.) **Infantry.** See *Illinois Troops, 42d Regiment.*
Wangelin's (Hugo) **Infantry.** See *Missouri Troops, Union, 12th Regiment.*
Ward's (John H.) **Infantry.** See *Kentucky Troops, Union, 27th Regiment.*
Ward's (William M.) **Infantry.** See *Ohio Troops, 10th Regiment.*
Warmoth's (Henry C.) **Infantry.** See *Missouri Troops, Union, 29th and 32d Regiments.*
Warner's (Lewis D.) **Infantry.** See *New York Troops, 154th Regiment.*
Warner's (Willard) **Infantry.** See *Ohio Troops, 76th Regiment.*
Waters' (Louis H.) **Infantry.** See *Illinois Troops, 84th Regiment.*
Weaver's (James B.) **Infantry.** See *Iowa Troops, 2d Regiment.*
Webster's (Joseph R.) **Infantry.** See *Indiana Troops, 88th Regiment.*
Weems' (John B.) **Infantry.** See *Georgia Troops, 10th Regiment.*
Welman's (Wilford H.) **Infantry.** See *Indiana Troops, 59th Regiment.*

Welsh's (Pinckney J.) **Infantry.** See *Illinois Troops, 56th Regiment.*
Welton's (Henry S.) **Infantry.** See *Union Troops, Regulars, 19th Regiment, 1st Battalion.*
West's (Francis H.) **Infantry.** See *Wisconsin Troops, 31st Regiment.*
Wever's (Clark R.) **Infantry.** See *Iowa Troops, 17th Regiment.*
Wheeler's (Joseph T.) **Cavalry.** See *Ohio Troops, 4th Battalion.*
Wheeler's (William) **Artillery.** See *New York Troops, 13th Battery.*
Wheeler's (William C.) **Infantry.** See *Indiana Troops, 81st Regiment.*
Wheeler's (William W.) **Infantry.** See *Michigan Troops, 23d Regiment.*
Whitaker's (Richard T.) **Infantry.** See *Kentucky Troops, Union, 6th Regiment.*
White's (B. F., jr.) **Artillery.** See *Tennessee Troops, Confederate.*
White's (George F.) **Cavalry.** See *Kentucky Troops, Union, 3d Regiment.*
White's (Hamilton B.) **Artillery.** See *Ohio Troops, 10th Battery.*
White's (James E.) **Artillery.** See *Indiana Troops, 12th Battery.*
White's (John M.) **Infantry.** See *South Carolina Troops, 6th Regiment.*
White's (W. W.) **Infantry.** See *Georgia Troops, 7th Regiment.*
Whitsit's (Charles W.) **Cavalry.** See *Illinois Troops, 6th Regiment.*
Whittemore's (Henry C.) **Artillery.** See *Illinois Troops, 2d Regiment, Battery H.*
Widmer's (John H.) **Infantry.** See *Illinois Troops, 104th Regiment.*
Wiedrich's (Michael) **Artillery.** See *New York Troops, 1st Regiment, Battery I.*
Wiggins' (J. H.) **Artillery.** See *Arkansas Troops, Confederate.*
Wilcox's (John S.) **Infantry.** See *Illinois Troops, 52d Regiment.*
Wilder Artillery. See *Indiana Troops.*
Wiles' (Greenberry F.) **Infantry.** See *Ohio Troops, 78th Regiment.*
Wiley's (Aquila) **Infantry.** See *Ohio Troops, 41st Regiment.*
Wilkinson's (William T.) **Infantry.** See *Missouri Troops, Union, 30th Regiment.*
Williams' (James M.) **Artillery.** See *Iowa Troops, 1st Battery.*
Williams' (Reuben) **Infantry.** See *Indiana Troops, 12th Regiment.*
Williams' (Robert, jr.) **Infantry.** See *Ohio Troops, 54th Regiment.*
Williams' (William D.) **Infantry.** See *Illinois Troops, 89th Regiment.*
Williamson's (Emanuel M.) **Infantry.** See *Indiana Troops, 73d Regiment.*
Winters' (Joshua C.) **Infantry.** See *Illinois Troops, 59th Regiment.*
Witcher's (V. A.) **Cavalry.** See *Virginia Troops, 34th Battalion.*
Wolihin's (Andrew M.) **Artillery.** See *Georgia Troops, 9th Battalion, Battery C.*
Wood's (Andrew M.) **Artillery.** See *Elgin Artillery, ante.*
Wood's (Charles H.) **Infantry.** See *Ohio Troops, 51st Regiment.*
Wood's (Edward J.) **Infantry.** See *Indiana Troops, 48th Regiment.*
Wood's (Gustavus A.) **Infantry.** See *Indiana Troops, 15th Regiment.*
Wood's (James, jr.) **Infantry.** See *New York Troops, 136th Regiment.*
Wood's (Peter P.) **Artillery.** See *Illinois Troops, 1st Regiment, Battery A.*
Wood's (Robert C., jr.) **Cavalry.** See *Wirt Adams' Cavalry, ante.*
Wood's (William F.) **Infantry.** See *Arkansas Troops, Union, 1st Regiment (Colored).*
Woodbury's (John D.) **Artillery.** See *New York Troops, 1st Regiment, Battery M.*
Woodyard's (Humphrey M.) **Infantry.** See *Missouri Troops, Union, 21st Regiment.*
Woolfolk's (Pichegru, jr.) **Artillery.** See *Ashland Artillery, ante.*
Wright's (William B.) **Infantry.** See *Michigan Troops, 27th Regiment.*
Yager's (John) **Infantry.** See *Ohio Troops, 121st Regiment.*
Yeoman's (Samuel N.) **Infantry.** See *Ohio Troops, 90th Regiment.*
York's (Billington W.) **Artillery.** See *Georgia Troops, 9th Battalion, Battery E.*
York's (Harrison B.) **Artillery.** See *Ohio Troops, 9th Battery.*
Yost's (Thobald D.) **Artillery.*** See *Illinois Troops, 1st Regiment, Battery D.*
Young's (Thomas L.) **Infantry.** See *Ohio Troops, 118th Regiment.*
Young's (Van E.) **Infantry.** See *Louisiana Troops, Union, 11th Regiment (Colored).*
Zickerick's (William) **Artillery.** See *Wisconsin Troops, 12th Battery.*

---

* Temporarily commanding.

INDEX.

Brigades, Divisions, Corps, Armies, and improvised organizations are "Mentioned" under name of command-ing officer; State and other organizations under their official designation. (See Alternate Designations, pp. 853-870.)

(871)

---

* Consolidation of 2d and 4th Battalions, Hilliard's Legion.
† Consolidation of 1st and 3d Battalions, Hilliard's Legion.

Page.

---

*No circumstantial reports on file.

---

* No circumstantial reports on file.

* No circumstantial reports on file.

---

* No circumstantial reports on file.

* No circumstantial reports on file.

---

* No circumstantial reports on file.

* No circumstantial reports on file.

Page.

* No circumstantial reports on file.

----

* No circumstantial reports on file.

Page.

---

*No circumstantial reports on file.

Page.

* No circumstantial reports on file.

*No circumstantial reports on file.

---

* No circumstantial reports on file.

* No circumstantial reports on file.

---

* No circumstantial reports on file.

---

* No circumstantial reports on file.

---

* Sometimes called 5th Battery.   † No circumstantial reports on file.

* No circumstantial reports on file.

Page.

* No circumstantial reports on file.   †Also known as 10th Kentucky.

Page.

Knoxville, Tenn., Campaign, Nov. 4–Dec. 23, 1863—Continued.

Communications from

Longstreet, James 454, 466, 467, 482, 484–486, 494, 497, 542–544

McLaws, Lafayette 480, 486, 491, 497, 501

Parke, John G 329, 406, 415

Shackelford, James M 375, 376

Sherman, William T. 278

Willcox, Orlando B 412

Congratulatory Orders. Burnside 280

Dispatches of Charles A. Dana 258–265

Itineraries.

Cameron, Daniel (2d Brigade, 3d Division, 23d Army Corps) 394

Davis, Jefferson C. (2d Division, 14th Army Corps) 433

Elliott, Washington L. (Cavalry command, Army of the Cumberland). 436

Granger, Gordon (2d and 3d Divisions, 4th Army Corps) 432

Hascall, Milo S. (3d Division, 23d Army Corps) 393

Howard, Oliver O. (11th Army Corps) 433

Long, Eli (2d Brigade, 2d Cavalry Division, Army of the Cumberland). 435

Mott, Samuel R. (1st Brigade, 2d Division, 23d Army Corps) 382

Pennebaker, Charles D. (3d Brigade, 1st Division, Cavalry Corps) 422

Potter, Robert B. (9th Army Corps) 339

Reilly, James W. (1st Brigade, 3d Division, 23d Army Corps) 393

Stanley, David S. (Cavalry command, Army of the Cumberland) 436

White, Julius (2d Division, 23d Army Corps) 381

Wolford, Frank (1st Cavalry Division) 421

Reports of

Alexander, E. Porter 477

Ball, Edward 522

Benjamin, Samuel N 341

Buckley, William W 346, 347

Burnside, Ambrose E 268–272, 2-0

Byington, Cornelius 365

Byrd, Robert K 422

Capron, Horace 429

Carter, John C 537

Chapin, Marshal W 382

Christ, Benjamin C 357

Comstock, Lorin L. 367, 369

Cutcheon, Byron M 369, 372

Dawson, Mathew M 373

Ferrero, Edward 349

Foster, John G 281, 284–286

Foster, John W 424

Goggans, E. J 512

Graham, Felix W 424–426

Harris, William C. 517

Harris, William H 324

Hartranft, John F 374

Humphrey, William 361

Humphreys, Benjamin G 520

Hutchins, N. L., jr 518

Jenkins, Micah 524

Johnson, Bushrod R 531

Longstreet, James 455

Page.

---

* No circumstantial reports on file.

* No circumstantial reports on file.

---

* No circumstantial reports on file.

---

* No circumstantial reports on file.

---

* No circumstantial reports on file.

────────────────────────────────

* No circumstantial reports on file.

Page.

Memphis and Charleston Railroad, in West Tennessee. Operations against, Nov. 28–Dec. 10, 1863—Continued.

* Formerly 3d Michigan Battery. ‡ Formerly 5th Michigan Battery. || Formerly 8th Michigan Battery.
† Formerly 4th Michigan Battery. § Formerly 6th Michigan Battery. ¶ Formerly 12th Michigan Battery.

Page.

Mississippi, Military Division of the.
  Orders, Special, series 1863: **No. 1,** 669.
  Orders, Special Field, series 1863: **No. 4,** 768; **No. 5,** 775.
  Union Troops in. Organization, strength, etc., Oct. 31, 1863............... 800
Mississippi River. Destruction of Steamer Mist, on the. See *Mist, Steamer.*
    Destruction of the, on the Mississippi River, Oct. 22, 1863.
Mississippi Troops. Mentioned. (Confederate.)
  Cavalry—*Battalions:* **18th,** 244, 247, 249, 250; **Davenport's** (*State*), 692;
    Ham's (*State*), 253; **Stockdale's,** 600. *Regiments:* **1st Partisan**
    Rangers, 249, 250, 590; **3d** (*State*), 244, 249, 251, 252; **5th,** 244, 249, 251,
    252, 566, 590; **Wirt Adams',** 599.
  Infantry—*Regiments:* **13th,** 299, 309, 319, 451, 496, 521, 522; **17th,** 299, 309,
    319, 359, 451, 496, 501, 521, 522; **18th, 21st,** 451, 521; **26th,** 705; **43d,** 692.
Mississippi Troops. Mentioned. (Union.)
  Artillery, Heavy—*Regiments:* **2d** (*Colored*), 596.
  Cavalry—*Regiments:* **1st** (*Colored*), 566; **3d** (*Colored*), 824.
Missouri Troops. Mentioned. (Confederate.)
  Artillery, Light—*Batteries:* **Barret's,** 224.
  Cavalry—*Regiments:* **2d,** 244, 249, 250.
Missouri Troops. Mentioned. (Union.)
  Artillery, Light—*Batteries:* **Walling's** (*Mississippi Marine Brigade*), 34, 824.
    Regiments: **1st** (*Batteries*), **C,** 823; **D,** 819; **G,** 803; **H,** 821; **I,** 821; **M,**
    823; **2d** (*Batteries*), **F,** * 17–22, 818.
  Cavalry, *Battalions:* **1st** (*Mississippi Marine Brigade*), 824. *Regiments:* **4th,**
    720, 820, 823; **10th,** 596, 819.
  Engineers—*Regiments:* **Bissell's,** 820, 851.
  Infantry—*Regiments:* **1st** (*Mississippi Marine Brigade*), 824; **2d,** 803; **3d,**
    20–23, 818; **6th,** 818; **7th,** 824; **8th,** 818; **10th,** 823; **11th,** 818; **12th,**
    18, 20, 22, 818; **15th,** 803; **17th,** 22, 23, 818; **18th,** 821; **21st,** 820; **24th,**
    820, 823; **26th,** 823; **27th,** 21–23, 818; **29th,** 18, 22, 818; **30th,** 596; **31st,**
    18, 22, 818; **32d,** 22, 818.
Mist, Steamer.
  Destruction of, on the Mississippi River, Oct. 22, 1863. Report of Napoleon
      B. Buford 32
  Mentioned 32, 780
Mitchell, John G.
  Correspondence with
    Hooker, Joseph 61
    Thomas, George H 62
  Mentioned.. 61–63, 118, 807
Mitchell, Joseph A. S. Mentioned 656
      For correspondence as A. A. D. C., see *Edward M. McCook.*
Mitchell, Robert B.
  Correspondence with
    Galbraith, Robert.. 728
    McCook, Edward M.. 752
    Mizner, Henry R... 836
    Slocum, Henry W... 727
    Thomas, George H................................. 670, 685, 695, 715–717, 744, 835
  Mentioned.. 684, 707, 727, 728, 833
Mitchell, W. R. Mentioned.. 247, 250
Mix, James E. Mentioned.. 115, 132

* Sometimes called Missouri Horse Artillery.

* No circumstantial reports on file.

*No circumstantial reports on file.

* No circumstantial reports on file.

---

* No circumstantial reports on file.
† After Nov. 19, 1863, known as 34th New York Battery.

---

* No circumstantial reports on file.

* No circumstantial reports on file.

* No circumstantial reports on file.

---

*No circumstantial reports on file.

* No circumstantial reports on file.

---

* No circumstantial reports on file.

Page.

---

* No circumstantial reports on file.

---

* No circumstantial reports on file.

---

* No circumstantial reports on file.

*No circumstantial reports on file.

---

* No circumstantial reports on file.

---

* No circumstantial reports on file.

---

* No circumstantial reports on file.
  † Formerly Freeman's.
  ‡ Formerly Jackson's.
  § Also called 2d West Tennessee Cavalry.

*No circumstantial reports on file.

---

* Consolidated.

Page.

------

*No circumstantial reports on file.

* No circumstantial reports on file.

* No circumstantial reports on file.